More information about this series at http://www.springer.com/series/7407

Peter Thiemann (Ed.)

Programming Languages and Systems

25th European Symposium on Programming, ESOP 2016
Held as Part of the European Joint Conferences
on Theory and Practice of Software, ETAPS 2016
Eindhoven, The Netherlands, April 2–8, 2016
Proceedings

Springer

Editor
Peter Thiemann
Institut für Informatik
Albert-Ludwigs-Universität Freiburg
Freiburg
Germany

ISSN 0302-9743 ISSN 1611-3349 (electronic)
Lecture Notes in Computer Science
ISBN 978-3-662-49497-4 ISBN 978-3-662-49498-1 (eBook)
DOI 10.1007/978-3-662-49498-1

Library of Congress Control Number: 2015954608

LNCS Sublibrary: SL1 – Theoretical Computer Science and General Issues

Printed on acid-free paper

This Springer imprint is published by SpringerNature
The registered company is Springer-Verlag GmbH Berlin Heidelberg

ETAPS Foreword

Welcome to the proceedings of ETAPS 2016, which was held in Eindhoven, located in "the world's smartest region," also known as the Dutch Silicon Valley. Since ETAPS' second edition held in Amsterdam (1999), ETAPS returned to The Netherlands this year.

ETAPS 2016 was the 19th instance of the European Joint Conferences on Theory and Practice of Software. ETAPS is an annual federated conference established in 1998, consisting of five constituting conferences (ESOP, FASE, FoSSaCS, TACAS, and POST) this year. Each conference has its own Programme Committee and its own Steering Committee. The conferences cover various aspects of software systems, ranging from theoretical computer science to foundations to programming language developments, analysis tools, formal approaches to software engineering, and security. Organizing these conferences in a coherent, highly synchronized conference program, enables attendees to participate in an exciting event, having the possibility to meet many researchers working in different directions in the field, and to easily attend the talks of various conferences. Before and after the main conference, numerous satellite workshops took place and attracted many researchers from all over the globe.

The ETAPS conferences received 474 submissions in total, 143 of which were accepted, yielding an overall acceptance rate of 30.2 %. I thank all authors for their interest in ETAPS, all reviewers for their peer-reviewing efforts, the Program Committee members for their contributions, and in particular the program co-chairs for their hard work in running this intensive process. Last but not least, my congratulations to all the authors of the accepted papers!

ETAPS 2016 was greatly enriched by the unifying invited speakers Andrew Gordon (MSR Cambridge and University of Edinburgh, UK), and Rupak Majumdar (MPI Kaiserslautern, Germany), as well as the conference-specific invited speakers (ESOP) Cristina Lopes (University of California at Irvine, USA), (FASE) Oscar Nierstrasz (University of Bern, Switzerland), and (POST) Vitaly Shmatikov (University of Texas at Austin, USA). Invited tutorials were organised by Lenore Zuck (Chicago) and were provided by Grigore Rosu (University of Illinois at Urbana-Champaign, USA) on software verification and Peter Ryan (University of Luxembourg, Luxembourg) on security. My sincere thanks to all these speakers for their inspiring and interesting talks!

ETAPS 2016 took place in Eindhoven, The Netherlands. It was organized by the Department of Computer Science of the Eindhoven University of Technology. It was further supported by the following associations and societies: ETAPS e.V., EATCS (European Association for Theoretical Computer Science), EAPLS (European Association for Programming Languages and Systems), and EASST (European Association of Software Science and Technology). The local organization team consisted of Mark van den Brand, Jan Friso Groote (general chair), Margje Mommers, Erik Scheffers, Julien Schmaltz, Erik de Vink, Anton Wijs, Tim Willemse, and Hans Zantema.

The overall planning for ETAPS is the main responsibility of the Steering Committee, and in particular of its Executive Board. The ETAPS Steering Committee consists of an Executive Board and representatives of the individual ETAPS conferences, as well as representatives of EATCS, EAPLS, and EASST. The Executive Board consists of Gilles Barthe (Madrid), Holger Hermanns (Saarbrücken), Joost-Pieter Katoen (chair, Aachen and Twente), Gerald Lüttgen (Bamberg), Vladimiro Sassone (Southampton), and Tarmo Uustalu (Tallinn). Other members of the Steering Committee are: Parosh Abdulla (Uppsala), David Basin (Zurich), Giuseppe Castagna (Paris), Marsha Chechik (Toronto), Javier Esparza (Munich), Jan Friso Groote (Eindhoven), Reiko Heckel (Leicester), Marieke Huisman (Twente), Bart Jacobs (Nijmegen), Paul Klint (Amsterdam), Jens Knoop (Vienna), Kim G. Larsen (Aalborg), Axel Legay (Rennes), Christof Löding (Aachen), Matteo Maffei (Saarbrücken), Pasquale Malacaria (London), Tiziana Margaria (Limerick), Andrzej Murawski (Warwick), Catuscia Palamidessi (Palaiseau), Frank Piessens (Leuven), Jean-Francois Raskin (Brussels), Mark Ryan (Birmingham), Julia Rubin (Massachussetts), Don Sannella (Edinburgh), Perdita Stevens (Edinburgh), Gabriele Taentzer (Marburg), Peter Thiemann (Freiburg), Luca Vigano (London), Igor Walukiewicz (Bordeaux), Andrzej Wąsowski (Copenhagen), and Hongseok Yang (Oxford).

I sincerely thank all ETAPS Steering Committee members for all their work in making the 19th edition of ETAPS a success. Moreover, thanks to all speakers, attendees, organizers of the satellite workshops, and Springer for their support. Finally, a big thanks to Jan Friso and his local organization team for all their enormous efforts enabling ETAPS to take place in Eindhoven!

January 2016

Joost-Pieter Katoen
ETAPS SC Chair
ETAPS e.V. President

Preface

This volume contains the papers presented at ESOP 2016, the 25th European Symposium on Programming, held during April 3–7, 2016, in Eindhoven, The Netherlands, as part of the ETAPS confederation. This year's program consisted of 29 papers selected from 89 submissions on topics covering every aspect of programming languages research.

Following the positive experience of the previous year, the reviewing process included a rebuttal phase from December 2 to 4, where authors were sent a first cut of their reviews and were able to respond to these reviews, and the selection process concluded with a two-day physical meeting of the program committee. This meeting took place from December 14 to 15, 2015, and was kindly hosted by the University of Frankfurt. Each submission was reviewed by at least three, and on average 3.5, program committee members. Furthermore, each paper had assigned to it a reporting reviewer, whose responsibility was twofold: to make sure that external reviewers were invited whenever not enough non-conflicted expertise could be found in the committee and to present a summary of the reviews and the author responses at the meeting. All non-conflicted program committee members participated in the discussion of a paper's merits. One paper was desk-rejected before the meeting, as it turned out to be a double submission. Papers authored by members of the program committee were held to a higher standard; no such paper was accepted. Papers for which the program chair had a conflict of interest were kindly handled by Didier Rémy.

My sincere thanks to all who contributed to the success of the conference. First of all, to the authors who chose to submit their work to ESOP. To the external reviewers, who provided timely expert reviews, sometimes on short notice. To the program committee members, who went the extra mile to provide extensive reviews, made well-balanced presentations at the meeting, and added detailed comments to explain the decision taken after the rebuttal and the discussion at the meeting. Luminous Fennell helped with preparing and running the meeting smoothly, as well as with the preparation of the proceedings. Marlis Jost helped with organizing the meeting. At the University of Frankfurt, Christian Reichenbach and Jutta Nadland kindly and generously provided local organization and catering for the meeting. EasyChair's quickly acting support helped manage the online submission and discussion phase as well as the compilation of the proceedings. I really appreciate the effort you all put into ESOP 2016; it would not have been possible without your help.

January 2016 Peter Thiemann

Organization

Program Committee

Andreas Abel	Gothenburg University, Sweden
Elvira Albert	Complutense University of Madrid, Spain
Arthur Charguéraud	Inria, France
Dominique Devriese	KU Leuven, Belgium
Sophia Drossopoulou	Imperial College London, UK
Joshua Dunfield	University of British Columbia, Canada
Matthew Fluet	Rochester Institute of Technology, USA
Christian Hammer	Saarland University, Germany
Atsushi Igarashi	Kyoto University, Japan
Ranjit Jhala	UC San Diego, USA
Ivan Lanese	University of Bologna, Italy and Inria, France
Anders Møller	Aarhus University, Denmark
Keiko Nakata	FireEye Dresden, Germany
James Noble	Victoria University of Wellington, New Zealand
Nate Nystrom	University of Lugano, Switzerland
Klaus Ostermann	University of Tübingen, Germany
Matthew Parkinson	Microsoft Research, UK
Francesco Ranzato	University of Padova, Italy
Didier Rémy	Inria, France
Ilya Sergey	University College London, UK
Jeremy Siek	Indiana University, USA
Wouter Swierstra	Utrecht University, The Netherlands
Peter Thiemann	University of Freiburg, Germany
Vasco Vasconcelos	Universidade de Lisboa, Portugal
Jan Vitek	Northeastern University, USA

Additional Reviewers

Alistarh, Dan
Andrysco, Marc
Arenas, Puri
Askarov, Aslan
Bach Poulsen, Casper
Baldan, Paolo
Barowy, Daniel
Biernacki, Dariusz
Blanchette, Jasmin Christian
Brockschmidt, Marc
Brotherston, James
Cacciari Miraldo, Victor
Carbone, Marco
Cockx, Jesper
Costa Seco, João
Crafa, Silvia
Crespo, Juan Manuel
Cunha, Jácome

Dezani-Ciancaglini, Mariangiola
Din, Crystal Chang
Dolstra, Eelco
Downen, Paul
Enea, Constantin
Fuhs, Carsten
Garcia, Ronald
Genaim, Samir
Giarrusso, Paolo G.
Gotsman, Alexey
Gregoire, Benjamin
Guimarães, Mário Luís
Hayman, Jonathan
Hoenicke, Jochen
Inaba, Kazuhiro
Jacobs, Bart
Koot, Ruud
Krishna, Siddharth
Krishnaswami, Neelakantan
Kunz, César
Levy, Paul Blain
López Juan, Víctor
López, Hugo A.
Martin-Martin, Enrique
Martins, Francisco
Matthes, Ralph
Miculan, Marino
Midtgaard, Jan
Miller, Heather
Montenegro, Manuel
Mostrous, Dimitris
Nakazawa, Koji
Orchard, Dominic
Paskevich, Andrei
Pientka, Brigitte
Podkopaev, Anton
Proença, José
Rainey, Mike
Reynders, Bob
Rosa-Velardo, Fernando
Sangiorgi, Davide
Sankaranarayanan, Sriram
Schlatte, Rudolf
Schöpp, Ulrich
Sezgin, Ali
Sieczkowski, Filip
Simon, Axel
Sjöberg, Vilhelm
Strub, Pierre-Yves
Suenaga, Kohei
Sumii, Eijiro
Svenningsson, Josef
Toninho, Bernardo
Vezzosi, Andrea
Vitousek, Michael
Winant, Thomas
Yanok, Ilya
Yuen, Shoji
Zeilberger, Noam
Ziliani, Beta

Contents

Simulating Cities: A Software Engineering Perspective

Cristina V. Lopes(✉)

University of California, Irvine, CA 92697, USA
lopes@uci.edu
http://www.ics.uci.edu/~lopes/

Abstract. Despite all the reasons why complex simulations are desirable for decision and policy making, and despite advances in computing power, large distributed simulations of urban areas are still rarely used, with most of their adoption in military applications. The reality is that developing distributed simulations is much harder than developing non-distributed, specialized ones, and requires a much higher level of software engineering expertise.

This paper looks at urban simulations from a software engineering and systems design perspective, and puts forward the idea that non-traditional decompositions in simulation load management are not just beneficial for these applications, but are likely the only way to move that field forward.

Keywords: Simulation · Programming · Software architecture · Systems design

1 Introduction

Population, environmental, and technological changes are reshaping the infrastructure of our urban environments, and will be a major focus of attention in the near future [36,45]. Cities have always accommodated new technologies in transportation, such as the invention and widespread use of motorized vehicles, mass transportation, and recently, electric vehicles. Yet every new technology brings with it challenges in policy making. With the advent of alternative energy and the Internet of Things, there is suddenly a plethora of new technologies that will require major restructuring of cities. Some examples are electric and autonomous vehicles, solar energy, unmanned aerial vehicles, and smart homes and buildings. In order to establish sound public policies, all these new technologies can greatly benefit from urban simulations, to measure their impact on the city and on the people before the policies are defined. According to Fujimoto [16], the combination of a severe need for investment in infrastructure redevelopment [44], an increased percentage of the world moving to cities [40], and the need for better disaster resilience to reduce both costs and deaths [10], are reasons why the development of effective platforms for urban environment simulations is one of the greatest challenges in the Modeling and Simulation (M&S) field.

P. Thiemann (Ed.): ESOP 2016, LNCS 9632, pp. 1–14, 2016.
DOI: 10.1007/978-3-662-49498-1_1

Increasing the complexity of simulations requires an increased amount of computation power, which has been made available in the past decade through parallel and distributed computing. Barnes et al. [1] provide a chronological history of the computing capacity using the PHOLD benchmark, a benchmark designed for performance evaluation of parallel and distributed discrete event processing. From 2007 to 2013, there was an improvement from 100 million to 500 billion events per second, a 5000x speedup in 6 years. The speedup was mainly due to an increasing number of cores in supercomputers, with the experiment in 2013 using nearly 2 million cores.

Despite all the reasons why complex simulations are desirable for decision and policy making, and despite advances in computing power, distributed simulations are still rarely used, with most of their adoption in military applications [2–4,37,39]. The reality is that developing distributed simulations is much harder than developing non-distributed ones, and requires a much higher level of software engineering expertise, which usually modeling and simulation experts don't have. The difficulties have been well-known by researchers and engineers, and over the years there have been a few efforts to address them. One of the most important efforts was the development of the High Level Architecture (HLA) standard [19]. HLA specifies a powerful model and an API for distributed simulation components (called *federates*) to interact. The adoption of HLA in practice, however, has been very slow. Boer et al. [2–4] published a three-part survey on the topic of distributed simulation in industry, including the use (or lack thereof) of HLA. In their findings, the major cause of low adoption is cost-benefit: it is technically complex to design and build distributed simulations, even with HLA. The reasons given included semantic interoperability, complexity, and efficiency of implementations. Surveyees suggest that domain-specific adaptors and middleware could help bridge the technical gap in software knowledge. We believe that the use of appropriate software engineering concepts and theories can greatly reduce the technical complexity of developing such middleware, and make distrubuted simulations accessible to a much wider audience, including scientists.

This paper explores the domain of distributed simulations, its historical development, its applications in urban planning, and the challenges and opportunities related to software engineering and systems design. It then presents a design experiment that mixes concepts from Aspect-Oriented Programming (AOP), relational queries and dependent types.

2 Workload Partitions in Simulations

One of the main challenges in doing complex systems simulations, including living organisms and cities, is the fact that they embody many different subsystems, each of them relatively, but not completely, independent from the others.

For example, there are many similarities between the concept of aspect (as given by AOP [21]) and the general concept of *aspect of a city* that urban planning researchers routinely use. Figure 1 shows an informal model of a city; similar models depicting infrastructure interactions are found in urban planning

Fig. 1. Aspects of cities.

literature, such as Xu et al. [45]. All these *aspects* are conceptually distinct, but interact with each other over essentially the same objects (data) of the simulation. Moreover, each of these subsystems tends to fall under different expertises, different groups of people who understand them. Aggregating that knowledge under one large simulation is a daunting task.

A model such as the one in Fig. 1 is ripe for decentralized and distributed simulation: we can envision each of these urban aspects being developed by a different team (because they require completely different expertise) and being simulated by a different machine, and yet cooperate for the global simulation of the city. Distributing a single simulation run where the workload is too large to be computed in a single processor, or worse, a single machine, is a challenging research problem in software architecture and design. In such cases, how does one divide and distribute the workload?

One way is to distribute the data. Simulators partition the workload by simulating different objects at each time frame. While scalable in terms of number of objects, this approach is not scalable in terms of simulation complexity: many different subsystems need to access the same data, so each simulation node needs to simulate all subsystems. Another approach is to divide the load by subsystem: functions such as physics simulation, scripts processing, and client management, are run in distributed simulators, and object attributes are synchronized when updated. This a good solution for synchronizing updates, but has some performance penalties, because data needs to be shared among simulators.

Much more can be done to help tame the complexity of these systems and improve the workflow of collaborating groups. Part of it consists in experimenting with the myriad of interesting concepts that exist in the small world of programming languages. Recently, we have been experimenting with Aspect-Oriented Programming (AOP) concepts, but other concepts can be used.

3 Historical Context

3.1 Distributed Virtual Environments

Distributed Virtual Environments (DVEs) are online multi-user interactive systems that simulate shared 3D spaces. The first successful standard for distributed simulation was SIMNET [29], funded by the DoD and developed by DARPA. With SIMNET, it became possible to link hundreds of simulators to produce a virtual world, used for real-time, man-in-the-loop, coordination and tactic simulations. SIMNET eventually evolved into the Distributed Interactive Simulation (DIS) standard, becoming an IEEE standard (IEEE 1278–1993) [9].

Strassburger et al. [37] conducted a peer study of future trends in DVEs, in which experts saw high potential for training sessions, joining computer resources, and integrating heterogenous resources for distributed simulations. We see the same opportunity to use DVEs for our urban platform, while additionally providing visualization and interaction of the environment for any future simulations purposes. Two foundational papers in DVE are DIVE [8] and Diamond Park [43], which both proposes VEs that scale by partitioning the workload in terms of space. Each process handles an area of the virtual world, achieving optimal scalability in terms of virtual land area, and improved scalability of users and objects. Most DVEs used today utilize the same scalable approach of partitioning the world by space.

There are many widely used DVE implementations, most in games such as World of Warcraft, Second Life, and Minecraft. Second Life is particular in its lack of an end goal. It is meant to be an experience of living a different life, with no particular goal other than experience the VE with other users. OpenSimulator [32] is an open-sourced VE that uses the same protocol from Second Life. Both Second Life and OpenSimulator scale through the same approach from DIVE and Diamond Park: object-based space partitioning: the world is divided in blocks of 256 meters squared, and each region is simulated on a different simulator. Other known VE open-sourced distributed simulator implementations are OpenWonderland [20] and Meru [18], but are far less popular than OpenSimulator and Second Life.

The Distributed Scene Graph (DSG) architecture is a novel approach to partitioning the virtual world simulation by functionality instead of space [23,26,27]. In certain workloads, DSG proved to be a much more effective load balancing technique than the traditional space partitioning method. DSG was highly influential in our aspect-based proposal approach for distributed simulations in general. Our group collaborated with Intel on the DSG architecture, to reintroduce space-partitioning to DSG.

3.2 Distributed Simulations

Concurrently to the effort of developing DVEs, another effort unfolded to generalize the concept of distributed simulations beyond interactive environments. The idea here was that simulations don't always have an interactive component, and even if they do, it is important to generalize the model by which the different simulators work together to produce the collaborative, complex simulation.

For this purpose, another standard was developed with the participation of industry and academia partners: the High Level Architecture (HLA) [19]. The HLA is, as the name implies, higher level when compared to DIS. In DIS, most of the simulation design decisions, such as networking protocols, are fixed. The HLA is flexible, and enforces an API that simulation designers can use to make decisions for their own simulation. The HLA defines two separate entities: the federates and the runtime infrastructure (RTI). The RTI is the communication bus for simulators to share events and updates. It is also used to specify and share the object model template (OMT), a shared specification of what objects are available to be instatiated. New objects can be defined and shared between simulators. The federates are the simulators, and together with the RTI, they form the federation. The API from the HLA defines how federates should share object models, updates, events, and interactions.

The RTI has many commercial implementations, including VT Mak RTI and Pitch pRTI. In our project, we wish to use an open-sourced implementation so we can modify the functionality for better performance and to better fit the aspect-based approach we propose. Two well known open-source implementations are OpenHLA and Portico. For our implementation, we will use Portico, which we believe has more support and use than OpenHLA. Simulators can be adapted to the HLA protocol through what is called an HLA ambassador: a software module that translates events from the RTI to the simulator, and interprets internal events and routes back to RTI. We use ambassadors to leverage existing simulators in our proposal.

Arguably the most important related work to this proposal is NASA's Simulation Exploration Experience (SEE), originally called Smackdown [11]. The SEE was created to encourage education in distributed simulation and the HLA standard. NASA created a scenario, building a moon base, and gave researchers all the tools necessary to start a moon base simulation. The tools include a federate for coordinating the federation and for delivering common data types, documentation, and functionalities, such as reference coordinates from Earth and the moon, a visualization federate, and APIs for the simulation. From there, researchers from many different universities volunteered to help. Many scenarios were proposed and built for the simulation, including communication systems [13], surveillance and defense of base [6] and a lunar mining operation [38]. The success of SEE was presented at several simulation conferences, with researchers from multiple universities presenting positive experience and results [6,13,38], and positive impact for education in distributed simulation [12]. While the simulation was executed successfully, the product was a toy example: the moon base simulation is not in any predictable way useful to real world NASA missions or plans for a moon base. On their analysis of SEE, Essilfie-Conduah et al. [12] say that SEE has potential to tackle real world M&S engineering problems. The experience from researchers participating in SEE also showed that HLA was difficult to implement, and the lack of tutorial examples made the learning curve even steeper. Essilfe-Conduah et al. also notice that while HLA is highly functional, it is also dense in content. We believe that the lack of any domain-specific design in HLA makes it powerful, but places a large burden on simulation designers. HLA should remain powerful, but if simulation designers are to use HLA, a form of middleware that bridges the gap of highly technical software engineering knowledge is required.

3.3 Urban Simulations

Urban simulations model and simulate urban environments and they can be both interactive and non-interactive. Wadell [42] interprets urban simulations as "operational models that attempt to represent dynamic processes and interactions of urban development and transportation". He argues that urban models have grown in complexity, and simulations are becoming a vital part of decision making by stakeholders for urban policies. A comprehensive history of urban modeling can be seen in [41]. In a talk presented at the Winter Simulation Conference 2014, Fujimoto [16] reiterates the importance of urban simulations today and in the near future. The advent of new technologies (e.g. smart power grid, smart homes) and new vehicles (e.g. unmanned aerial vehicles, electric vehicles, autonomous vehicles) will require redevelopment the urban infrastructure. One of the grand M&S challenges proposed by Fujimoto is to handle the complexity of so many different interacting simulations by composing distributed simulations.

Transportation simulation is an important part of urban simulations, and has a large body of previous work in traffic, logistics, and business. For the scope of our proposal, we will focus only in traffic simulations. Pursula [34] provides a comprehensive overview of the different models and approaches to traffic simulation. Mainly, traffic simulation is divided in degree of detail: microscopic, mesoscopic, and macroscopic. The macroscopic models were the first simulation models for traffic, treating traffic as a continuous flows that can be modeled mathematically, for instance, as waves [25]. Microscopic simulations attempt to model and simulate vehicles individually, determining starting and ending points, and calculating routes through roads and intersections. Most traffic simulation applications used nowadays are of microscopic nature. The car-following model [17] and cellular-automaton [31] variations are typically used in microscopic simulations. Mesoscopic simulations are a mix of macroscopic and microscopic models. One example for modeling mesoscopic simulations is the gas-kinectic approach for two-dimensional traffic flow [30]. Another example of a mesoscopic approach is CONTRAM (COntinuous TRaffic Assignment Model) [24], where movement of traffic is modeled by grouping vehicles in"packets". We focus on microscopic simulations for its widespread use and the leveraging of computing power increase from parallel and distributed simulations. There are many distributed and parallel models for large microscopic traffic simulations [15,33,46], that can be scaled independently from our urban simulation platform.

There are multiple microscopic traffic simulator implementations available for use. Some of the more popular ones are SUMO [22], TRANSIMS [35], PARAMICS [7], and VISSIM [14]. Maciejewski [28] provides a comparison between SUMO, TRANSIMS and VISSIM. PARAMICS is focused in parallel and distributed simulations, optimal for use with thousands of cores, tightly coupled and interconnected by network. For our project, we decided to use SUMO for two reasons: it is open-sourced (PARAMICS and VISSIM are not), and has a remote controlling feature, required to integrate it with our urban simulation. Additionally, we are leveraging previous work done to integrate SUMO and a virtual environment simulator, OpenSimulator, on the Mobdat project [5].

4 An AOP Design Experiment

We have been experimenting with partitioning the simulation load using AOP concepts. The architecture we have is guided by the HLA, but provides concrete design choices and a powerful expression mechanism (inspired by relational queries, in general, and dependent types, in particular) to reduce the technical complexity of distributing an urban simulation.

5 Architecture

The canonical HLA is a generic event distribution system. It can be seen in Fig. 2, where federates (i.e. simulators) communicate through the run-time infrastructure, publishing and subscribing to object attributes. The HLA is a powerful architecture for enabling interoperability between many simulations, but to achieve flexibility, major design decisions are left to the designer. Requirements such as message ordering, software patterns, object modeling, and networking protocols are complex technical decisions that may jeopardize the entire simulation if not planned properly. The HLA enables all such options to be configured and agreed upon between federates, but the excessive number of choices essentially leaves simulation designers with most of the architectural work, requiring highly knowledgeable software engineers and M&S experts to achieve the desired performance and behavior. Simulations designers are often knowledgeable of the simulation concerns and desired results, but not necessarily of building and planning distributed simulations for consistency and scalability. If successful, our effort will reduce this entrance barrier to HLA, allowing simulation designers of different fields to exert their full expertise in their own aspect of the simulation.

Architecturally speaking, we introduce a bridge between the flexible HLA abstractions and the aspect simulators, or federates[1]. Figure 3 illustrates what the resulting architecture will be. Our platform handles composing messages within the HLA standard, but with meaningful functional calls from the simulation federates. The intention is to transform HLA configuration into simulation semantic settings that designers understand. For instance, if the simulation is meant to be human-in-the-loop, our platform makes design choices for interactive real-time simulations, and communicates them with other federates. From the federate (aspect) point of view, there are only two components: itself and the rest of the simulation. The urban platform mediates the interaction of the world with each federate, in terms of publications and subscriptions, and manages synchronization of objects with multiple aspects.

[1] We use the terms "aspect simulator" and "federate" interchangeably.

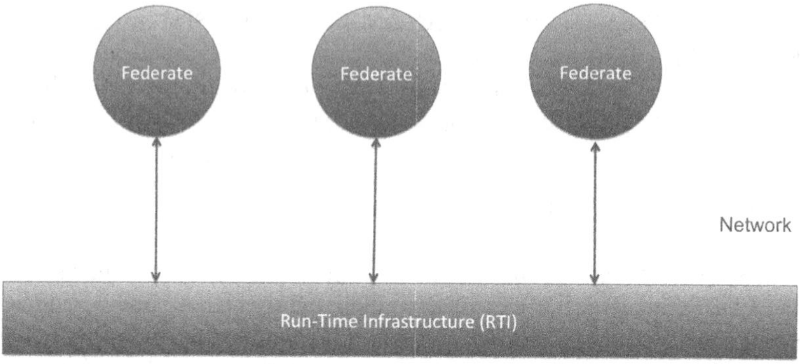

Fig. 2. The High Level Architecture (HLA) representation. Federates are the simulators, that together form the federation. The Run-Time Infrastructure is responsible for handling publish and subscribe events for object attributes.

This urban simulation architecture raises several research questions about building distributed simulations with cross-cutting concerns. How do we represent the same entity in multiple simulations, with each simulation interested in a different aspect of the entity? What kinds of interfaces should the federates expose to the rest of the simulation? In what way will AOP concepts, such as join points and before and after actions, simplify the architecture? How can we specify a universal [base] object model that will scale with new and yet unknown aspects of the urban simulation? Can the RTI, a centralized communication bus, handle real-time simulations at a large scale? Establishing a large-scale urban simulation platform requires addressing such issues, and we hope to reach new insights and knowledge for building distributed real-time simulation models in general.

5.1 Data Specifications

The architecture we are using is essentially one where data is shared among any number of simulators, each one simulating an aspect of the simulation. It is clear that the different aspects have different perspectives on the shared data. For example, a car might have a rich representation in an aspect decicated to simulating cars, but it is reduced to essentially a bounding box and a position in 3D space for purposes of traffic simulation. We see the data space as a collection of data sets, some of which may be subsets, projections or augmentations of existing sets. Every new aspect that is added to the simulation needs to know about the schema of the existing data, but that is all: it does not need to know about any behavior of other aspects; there is no need for functional APIs between the aspects. Depedencies are purely data dependencies.

As such, we are designing an expressive data specification language based on SQL (relational algebra) that is also inspired by the concept of dependent types. The idea is to allow the different aspects to reduce / augment / change the existing data types so that it better fits their own function.

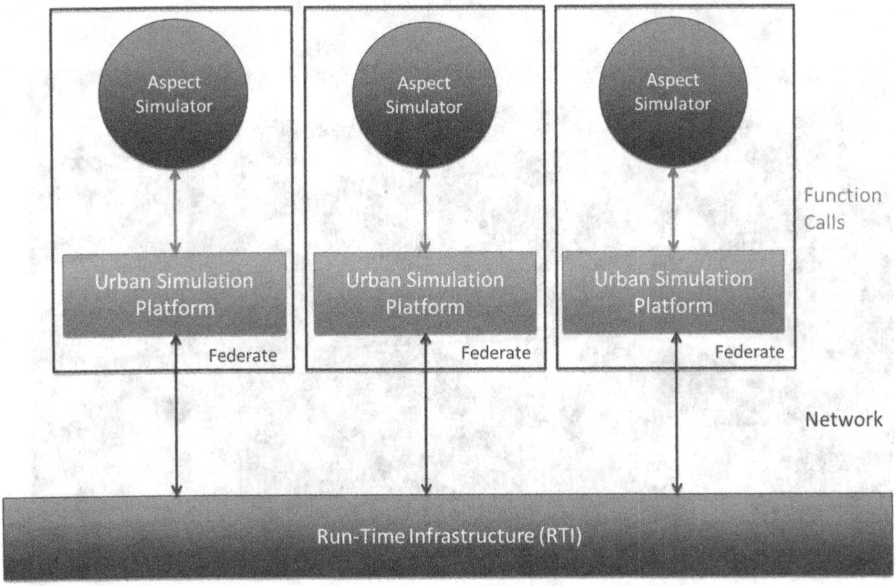

Fig. 3. AOP urban simulation architecture, a concrete realization of the canonical HLA.

Consider, for example, two different, but collaborating, simulations: a pedestrian simulation and a traffic simulation. When they are separated in different processes using our AOP architecture, the pedestrian simulation needs to know something about the cars (their position, at least), so that it prevents pedestrians from crossing streets when cars may hit them. But the representation of cars used by the pedestrian simulation isn't necessarily the same as that of the traffic simulation. Without the language that we are designing, car data would necessarily need to be transferred into the pedestrian simulation. With our language, that isn't necessary; the pedestrian simulation can simply issue a query into the data store that returns information about the pedestrians in danger without any car data having to be transferred. The following pseudo-code explains the idea:

```
[Set]
public class Pedestrian {
    int id;
    Position pos;
}

[Subset(Of = typeof(Pedestrian)]
public class EndangeredPedestrian : Pedestrian {
    Query = SELECT Pedestrian.* FROM Pedestrian JOIN Car ON
                  ABS (Pedestrian.pos - Car.pos) < 10;
}
```

Fig. 4. View of the urban simulation platform prototype. The colored rectangles are vehicles, with each color indicating a different type of vehicle (Color figure online).

We are still in the early stages of prototyping this idea, but the results are encouraging. We have tested a working urban simulation with 3 aspects: socioeconomic, traffic, and virtual environment. Our work is an adaptation of a project called Mobdat, which is available open-sourced[2], and integrates the OpenSimulator VE platform, the SUMO traffic simulator, and its own implementation of socioeconomic factors, including daily routines (e.g. sleep, lunch, dinner, coffee), job, residence, and vehicles. Figure 4 shows a screenshot from an OpenSimulator viewer.

Our work so far is a proof of concept for the urban simulation platform. The ideas here will allow us to support independent teams with different expertise, each one being responsible for their own partial simulation without having to coordinate with the other teams other than on the knowledge of what kind of the data is shared.

6 Final Remarks

If AOP with data-only dependencies proves to be a good fit for distributed simulations, this work can have a tremendouns influence on the accessibility of distributed simulations for a large number of modeling and simulation experts, therefore also having a potential impact on policy making. While the Department of Defense (DoD) has been the primary force behind the development of distributed

[2] https://github.com/cmickeyb/mobdat.

simulations, nowadays, simulations are being used in a much wider spectrum of applications; science, logistics, social behavioral, transportation management, health, and land use are some domains where simulations play an increasingly important role. Parallel and distributed simulations, in particular, are becoming a necessity for complex simulations that don't fit one computer's hardware limits, not only in the military, but in all branches of Science and Engineering. However, as mentioned before, domain experts tend to stay away from distributed simulations, because of their software engineering complexity. Better and easier models and middleware are needed if we are to take advantage of the power of complex simulations.

References

1. Barnes, P.D., Carothers, C.D., Jefferson, D.R., LaPre, J.M.: Warp speed: executing time warp on 1,966,080 cores. In: Proceedings of the 2013 ACM SIGSIM Conference on Principles of Advanced Discrete Simulation - SIGSIM-PADS 2013, New York, USA, p. 327. ACM, New York (2013). http://dl.acm.org/citation.cfm?id=2486134dl.acm.org/citation.cfm?d=2486092.2486134
2. Boer, C., Bruin, A., Verbraeck, A.: Distributed simulation in industry - a survey part 2 - experts on distributed simulation. In: Proceedings of the 2006 Winter Simulation Conference, pp. 1061–1068. IEEE, December 2006. http://dl.acm.org/citation.cfm?id=1218306, http://ieeexplore.ieee.org/lpdocs/epic03/wrapper.htm?arnumber=4117719
3. Boer, C., De Bruin, A., Verbraeck, A.: Distributed simulation in industry - a survey part 1 - the cots vendors. In: Proceedings of the 2006 Winter Simulation Conference, pp. 1053–1060. IEEE, December 2006. http://ieeexplore.ieee.org/xpls/abs_all.jsp?arnumber=4117718, http://ieeexplore.ieee.org/lpdocs/epic03/wrapper.htm?arnumber=4117718
4. Boer, C.A., de Bruin, A., Verbraeck, A.: Distributed simulation in industry - a survey part 3 - the HLA standard in industry. In: Proceedings of the 2008 Winter Simulation Conference, pp. 1094–1102. IEEE, December 2008. http://ieeexplore.ieee.org/xpls/abs_all.jsp?arnumber=4736178, http://ieeexplore.ieee.org/lpdocs/epic03/wrapper.htm?arnumber=4736178
5. Bowman, M.: Mobdat. https://github.com/cmickeyb/mobdat
6. Bruzzone, A.G., Dato, L., Ferrando, A.: Simulation exploration experience: providing effective surveillance and defense for a moon base against threats from outer space. In: 2014 IEEE/ACM 18th International Symposium on Distributed Simulation and Real Time Applications, pp. 121–126, October 2014. http://ieeexplore.ieee.org/lpdocs/epic03/wrapper.htm?arnumber=6957184
7. Cameron, G.D., Duncan, G.I.: Paramicsparallel microscopic simulation of road traffic. J. Supercomput. **10**(1), 25–53 (1996)
8. Carlsson, C., Hagsand, O.: DIVE a multi-user virtual reality system. In: Proceedings of IEEE Virtual Reality Annual International Symposium - VRAIS 1993, pp. 394–400 (1993). http://ieeexplore.ieee.org/xpls/abs_all.jsp?arnumber=380753
9. Committee, D.S.: IEEE Standard for Distributed Interactive Simulation-Application Protocols. IEEE Standard 1995 (1998)
10. Cutter, S.L., Ahearn, J.A., Amadei, B., Crawford, P., Eide, E.A., Galloway, G.E., Goodchild, M.F., Kunreuther, H.C., Li-Vollmer, M., Schoch-Spana, M., et al.: Disaster resilience: a national imperative. Environ. Sci. Policy Sustain. Dev. **55**(2), 25–29 (2013)

11. Elfrey, P.R., Zacharewicz, G., Ni, M.: Smackdown: adventures in simulation standards and interoperability. In: Winter Simulation Conference Proceedings of the Winter Simulation Conference, pp. 3963–3967 (2011)
12. Essilfie-Conduah, N., Grogan, P., Cunio, P.M., McLinko, R., de Weck, O.L.: A university perspective on the nasa/siso smackdown modeling and simulation outreach event (2011)
13. Falcone, A., Garro, A., Longo, F., Spadafora, F.: Simulation exploration experience: a communication system and a 3D real time visualization for a moon base simulated scenario. In: 2014 IEEE/ACM 18th International Symposium on Distributed Simulation and Real Time Applications, pp. 113–120, October 2014. http://ieeexplore.ieee.org/lpdocs/epic03/wrapper.htm?arnumber=6957183
14. Fellendorf, M.: Vissim: a microscopic simulation tool to evaluate actuated signal control including bus priority. In: 64th Institute of Transportation Engineers Annual Meeting, pp. 1–9 (1994)
15. Fernandes, R., Vieira, F., Ferreira, M.: Parallel microscopic simulation of metropolitan-scale traffic. In: Proceedings of the 46th Annual Simulation Symposium, ANSS 2013, pp. 10:1–10:8. Society for Computer Simulation International, San Diego (2013). http://dl.acm.org/citation.cfm?id=2499604.2499614
16. Fujimoto, R.M.: Parallel and distributed simulation. In: Proceedings of the 2014 Winter Simulation Conference, WSC 2014, p. 5. IEEE Press, Piscataway (2014). http://dl.acm.org/citation.cfm?id=2693848.2693854
17. Gipps, P.G.: A behavioural car-following model for computer simulation. Transp. Res. Part B Methodological **15**(2), 105–111 (1981)
18. Horn, D., Cheslack-Postava, E., Mistree, B.F., Azim, T., Terrace, J., Freedman, M.J., Levis, P.: To infinity and not beyond: scaling communication in virtual worlds with Meru. Technical report, Stanford University (2010). http://ewencp.net/papers/to_infinity_and_not_beyond_tr.pdf
19. IEEE Standards Association: 1516–2000 IEEE Standard for Modeling and Simulation (M&S) High Level Architecture (HLA)-Framework and Rules (2000)
20. Kaplan, J., Yankelovich, N.: Open wonderland: an extensible virtual world architecture. IEEE Internet Computing **15**(5), 38–45 (2011). http://ieeexplore.ieee.org/lpdocs/epic03/wrapper.htm?arnumber=5871568
21. Kiczales, G., Lamping, J., Mendhekar, A., Maeda, C., Lopes, C.V., Loingtier, J.-M., Irwin, J.: Aspect-oriented programming. In: Akşit, M., Matsuoka, S. (eds.) ECOOP 1997. LNCS, vol. 1241, pp. 220–242. Springer, Heidelberg (1997). http://dx.org/10.1007/BFb0053381
22. Krajzewicz, D., Erdmann, J., Behrisch, M., Bieker, L.: Recent development and applications of SUMO - simulation of urban mobility. Int. J. Adv. Syst. Meas. **5**(3&4), 128–138 (2012)
23. Lake, D., Bowman, M., Liu, H.: Distributed scene graph to enable thousands of interacting users in a virtual environment. In: Proceedings of the 9th Annual Workshop on Network and Systems Support for Games - NetGames 2010, pp. 1–6. IEEE Computer Society, November 2010. http://ieeexplore.ieee.org/lpdocs/epic03/wrapper.htm?arnumber=5679669
24. Leonard, D., Tough, J., Baguley, P.: Contram: a traffic assignment model for predicting flows and queues during peak periods. Technical report, Transport and Road Research Laboratory (1978)
25. Lighthill, M.J., Whitham, G.B.: On kinematic waves. II. a theory of traffic flow on long crowded roads. Proc. R. Soc. Lond. Ser. A Math. Phys. Sci. **229**(1178), 317–345 (1955)

26. Liu, H., Bowman, M.: Scale virtual worlds through dynamic load balancing. In: 2010 IEEE/ACM 14th International Symposium on Distributed Simulation and Real Time Applications, pp. 43–52, October 2010
27. Liu, H., Bowman, M., Adams, R., Hurliman, J., Lake, D.: Scaling virtual worlds: simulation requirements and challenges. In: Johansson, B., Jain, S., Montoya-Torres, J., Hugan, J., Yücesan, E. (eds.) Proceedings of the 2010 Winter Simulation Conference (WSC), WSC 2010, pp. 778–790. IEEE Computer Society, Baltimore, December 2010. http://ieeexplore.ieee.org/lpdocs/epic03/wrapper.htm?arnumber=5679112
28. Maciejewski, M.: A comparison of microscopic traffic flow simulation systems for an urban area. Probl. Transportu **5**, 27–38 (2010)
29. Miller, D., Thorpe, J.: SIMNET: the advent of simulator networking. Proc. IEEE **83**(8), 1114–1123 (1995)
30. Nagatani, T.: Gas kinetic approach to two-dimensional traffic flow. J. Phys. Soc. Jpn. **65**(10), 3150–3152 (1996)
31. Nagel, K., Schreckenberg, M.: A cellular automaton model for freeway traffic. J. Phys. **2**(12), 2221–2229 (1992)
32. OpenSimulator: OpenSimulator. http://opensimulator.org
33. Potuzak, T.: Distributed-parallel road traffic simulator for clusters of multi-core computers. In: 2012 IEEE/ACM 16th International Symposium on Distributed Simulation and Real Time Applications, pp. 195–201, October 2012. http://ieeexplore.ieee.org/lpdocs/epic03/wrapper.htm?arnumber=6365074
34. Pursula, M.: Simulation of traffic systems-an overview. J. Geogr. Inf. Decis. Anal. **3**(1), 1–8 (1999)
35. Smith, L., Beckman, R., Anson, D., Nagel, K., Williams, M.E.: Transims: transportation analysis and simulation system. In: Fifth National Conference on Transportation Planning Methods Applications-Volume II: A Compendium of Papers Based on a Conference Held in Seattle, Washington (1995)
36. Stafford, S.G., Bartels, D.M., Begay-Campbell, S., Bubier, J.L., Crittenden, J.C., Cutter, S.L., Delaney, J.R., Jordan, T.E., Kay, A.C., Libecap, G.D., et al.: Now is the time for action: transitions and tipping points in complex environmental systems. Environ. Sci. Policy Sustain. Dev. **52**(1), 38–45 (2010)
37. Strassburger, S., Schulze, T., Fujimoto, R.: Future trends in distributed simulation and distributed virtual environments: results of a peer study. In: Proceedings of the 2008 Winter Simulation Conference, pp. 777–785. IEEE, December 2008. http://dl.acm.org/citation.cfm?id=1516887, http://ieeexplore.ieee.org/lpdocs/epic03/wrapper.htm?arnumber=4736140
38. Taylor, S.J., Revagar, N., Chambers, J., Yero, M., Anagnostou, A., Nouman, A., Chaudhry, N.R., Elfrey, P.R.: Simulation exploration experience: a distributed hybrid simulation of a lunar mining operation. In: 2014 IEEE/ACM 18th International Symposium on Distributed Simulation and Real Time Applications, pp. 107–112, October 2014. http://ieeexplore.ieee.org/lpdocs/epic03/wrapper.htm?arnumber=6957182
39. Tolk, A.: Avoiding another Green Elephant - a proposal for the next generation HLA based on the model driven architecture. In: 2002 Fall Simulation Interoperability Workshop, Orlando, Florida, pp. 1–12, November 2010. http://arxiv.org/abs/1011.6671
40. United Nations: World Urbanization Prospects (2014). http://esa.un.org/unpd/wup/Highlights/WUP2014-Highlights.pdf

41. Waddell, P.: UrbanSim: modeling urban development for land use, transportation, and environmental planning. J. Am. Plan. Assoc. **68**(3), 297–314 (2002). http://www.tandfonline.com//abs/10.1080/01944360208976274
42. Waddell, P., Ulfarsson, G.: Introduction to urban simulation: design and developmentof operational models. In: Haynes, K., Stopher, P., Button, K., Hensher, D. (eds.) Handbooks in Transport, vol. 5. Elsevier, Oxford (2004)
43. Waters, R.C., Anderson, D.B., Barrus, J.W., Brogan, D.C., Casey, M.A., McKeown, S.G., Nitta, T., Sterns, I.B., Yerazunis, W.S.: Diamond park and spline: a social virtual reality system with 3D animation, spoken interaction, and runtime modifiability. Presence Teleoperators Virtual Environ. **6**(4), 461–480 (1997). http://citeseerx.ist.psu.edu/viewdoc/summary?=10.1.1.2.9500
44. White, J., Stevens, B., Holden, R.: Strategic Transport Infrastructure Needs to 2030. OECD, Paris (2012). http://trid.trb.org/view.aspx?id=1214312
45. Xu, M., Crittenden, J.C., Chen, Y., Thomas, V.M., Noonan, D.S., DesRoches, R., Brown, M.A., French, S.P.: Gigaton problems need gigaton solutions 1. Environ. Sci. Technol. **44**(11), 4037–4041 (2010)
46. Xu, Y., Tan, G.: An offline road network partitioning solution in distributed transportation simulation. In: 2012 IEEE/ACM 16th International Symposium on Distributed Simulation and Real Time Applications (DS-RT), pp. 210–217. IEEE (2012)

Regular Programming for Quantitative Properties of Data Streams

Rajeev Alur(✉), Dana Fisman(✉), and Mukund Raghothaman(✉)

University of Pennsylvania, Philadelphia, USA
{alur,fisman,rmukund}@cis.upenn.edu

Abstract. We propose *quantitative regular expressions* (QREs) as a high-level programming abstraction for specifying complex numerical queries over data streams in a modular way. Our language allows the arbitrary nesting of orthogonal sets of combinators: (*a*) generalized versions of choice, concatenation, and Kleene-iteration from regular expressions, (*b*) streaming (serial) composition, and (*c*) numerical operators such as min, max, sum, difference, and averaging. Instead of requiring the programmer to figure out the low-level details of what state needs to be maintained and how to update it while processing each data item, the regular constructs facilitate a global view of the entire data stream splitting it into different cases and multiple chunks. The key technical challenge in defining our language is the design of typing rules that can be enforced efficiently and which strike a balance between expressiveness and theoretical guarantees for well-typed programs. We describe how to compile each QRE into an efficient streaming algorithm. The time and space complexity is dependent on the complexity of the data structure for representing terms over the basic numerical operators. In particular, we show that when the set of numerical operations is sum, difference, minimum, maximum, and average, the compiled algorithm uses constant space and processes each symbol in the data stream in constant time outputting the cost of the stream processed so far. Finally, we prove that the expressiveness of QREs coincides with the streaming composition of regular functions, that is, MSO-definable string-to-term transformations, leading to a potentially robust foundation for understanding their expressiveness and the complexity of analysis problems.

1 Introduction

In a diverse range of applications such as financial tickers, data feeds from sensors, network traffic monitoring, and click-streams of web usage, the core computational problem is to map a stream of data items to a numerical value. Prior research on stream processing has focused on designing space-efficient algorithms for specific functions such as computing the average or the median of a sequence of values, and integrating stream processing in traditional data management software such as relational databases and spreadsheets. Our goal is orthogonal,

This research was partially supported by the NSF Expeditions Award CCF 1138996.

P. Thiemann (Ed.): ESOP 2016, LNCS 9632, pp. 15–40, 2016.
DOI: 10.1007/978-3-662-49498-1_2

namely, to provide high-level programming abstractions for the modular specification of complex queries over data streams, with a mix of numerical operators such as sum, difference, min, max, and average, supported by automatic compilation into an efficient low-level stream processing implementation.

To motivate our work, suppose the input data stream consists of transactions at a bank ATM, and consider how the following query f can be expressed in a natural, modular, and high-level manner: "On average, how much money does Alice deposit into her account during a month?" We can express this query naturally as a composition of two queries: the query f_1 that maps the input stream to a stream consisting of only the transactions corresponding to the deposits by Alice, and the query f_2 that computes the average of the sum of deposits during each month. This form of filtering, and cascaded composition of stream processors, is common in many existing stream processing languages (such as ActiveSheets [35]) and systems (such as Apache Storm), and our proposal includes a *streaming composition* operator to express it: $f_1 \gg f_2$.

Now let us turn our attention to expressing the numerical computation f_2. An intuitive decomposition for specifying f_2 is to break up the input stream into a sequence of substreams, each corresponding to the transactions during a single month. We can a write a function f_3 that maps a sequence of transactions during a month to its cumulative sum. The desired function f_2 then splits its input stream into substreams, each matching the input pattern of f_3, applies f_3 to each substream, and combines the results by averaging. In our proposed calculus, f_2 is written as $\mathit{iter\text{-}avg}(f_3)$. This is exactly the "quantitative" generalization of the Kleene-* operation from regular expressions—a declarative language for specifying patterns in strings that is widely used in practical applications and has a strong theoretical foundation. However, we are not aware of any existing language for specifying quantitative properties of sequences that allows such a regular iteration over chunks of inputs.

As in regular expressions, iterators in our language can be nested, and one can use different aggregation operators at different levels. For example, to specify the modified query, "On an average, during a month, what is the maximum money that Alice deposits during a single day?" in the program for the original query f, we can essentially replace the computation f_3 for processing month-substreams by $\mathit{iter\text{-}max}(f_4)$, where the function f_4 maps a sequence of transactions during a *single day* to its sum. Analogous to the iteration, the generalization of the concatenation operation $\mathit{split\text{-}op}(f, g)$, splits the input stream in two parts, applies f to the first part, g to the second part, and combines the results using the arithmetic combinator *op*. If we want to process streams in which no individual withdrawal exceeds a threshold value in a special manner, our program can be f *else* g, where the program f is written to process streams where all withdrawals are below the threshold and g handles streams with some withdrawal above the threshold. These core regular constructs, *else*, *split* and *iter*, are natural as they are the analogs of the fundamental programming constructs of conditionals, sequential composition, and iteration, but also allow the programmer a global view of the entire stream.

We formalize this idea of regular programming by designing the language of *quantitative regular expressions* for processing data streams (Sect. 2). Each quantitative regular expression (QRE) maps a (regular) subset of data streams to cost values. The language constructs themselves are agnostic to the cost types and combinators for combining cost values. The design of the language is influenced by two competing goals: on one hand, we want as much expressiveness as possible, and on the other hand, we want to ensure that every QRE can be automatically compiled into a streaming algorithm with provably small space and time complexity bounds. For the former, the same way as deterministic finite automata and regular languages serve as the measuring yardstick for design choices in formalizing regular expressions, the most suitable class of functions is the recently introduced notion of *regular functions* [7]. Unlike the better known and well-studied formalism of weighted automata, whose definition is inherently limited to costs with two operations that form a commutative semiring [21], this class is parametrized by an arbitrary set of cost types and operations. It has both a machine-based characterization using *streaming string-to-term transducers* [7] and a logic-based characterization using *MSO-definable string-to-term transformations* [16]. While this class is *not* closed under streaming composition, in Sect. 4, we show that QREs define exactly streaming compositions of *regular functions*. This expressiveness result justifies the various design choices we made in defining QREs.

In Sect. 3, we show how to compile a QRE into an efficient streaming algorithm. The implementation consists of a set of interacting machines, one for each sub-expression. To process operators such as *split* and *iter*, the algorithm needs to figure out how to split the input stream. Since the splitting cannot be deterministically computed in a streaming manner, the algorithm needs to keep track of all potential splits. The typing rules are used to ensure that the number of splits under consideration are proportional to the size of the expression rather than the length of the input stream. While the compilation procedure is generic with respect to the set of cost types and operators, the exact time and space complexity of the algorithm is parametrized by the complexity of the data structure for representing cost terms. For example, every term that can be constructed using numerical constants, a single variable x, and operations of min and $+$, is equivalent to a term in the canonical form $\min(x + a, b)$, and can therefore be summarized by two numerical values allowing constant-time updates. When we have both numerical values and sequences of such values, if we know that the only aggregate operator over sequences is averaging, then the sequence can be summarized by the sum of all values and the length (such a succinct representation is not possible if, for instance, we allow mapping of a sequence of values to its median). In particular, we show that when a QRE is constructed using the operations of sum, difference, minimum, maximum, and average, the compiled streaming algorithm has time complexity that is linear in the length of the data stream (that is, constant time for processing each symbol) and constant space complexity (in terms of the size of the QRE itself, both complexities are polynomial). This generalizes the class of queries for which efficient streaming algorithms have been reported in the existing literature.

2 Quantitative Regular Expressions

2.1 Preliminaries

The Data and Cost Types. We first fix a set $\mathcal{T} = \{T_1, T_2, \ldots\}$ of types, each of which is non-empty. Typical examples might include the sets $\mathbb{R}$, $\mathbb{Z}$ and $\mathbb{N}$ of real numbers, integers and natural numbers respectively, the set $\mathbb{B} = \{\mathit{true}, \mathit{false}\}$ of boolean values, and the set $\mathbb{M}$ of multisets of real numbers.

Another example is $D_{bank} = \mathbb{R} \cup \{end_d, end_m\}$, indicating the transactions of a customer with a bank. The symbol end_d indicates the end of a working day, end_m indicates the passage of a calendar month, and each real number $x \in \mathbb{R}$ indicates the deposit (withdrawal if negative) of x dollars into the account.

$f, g, \ldots ::= \varphi ? \lambda$	Basic functions
$\mid \epsilon ? x$	
$\mid op(f_1, f_2, \ldots, f_k)$	Cost operations
$\mid f[x/g]$	
$\mid f \; \mathit{else} \; g$	Regular operators
$\mid \mathit{split}(f \; [x\rangle \; g)$	
$\mid \mathit{split}(f \; \langle x] \; g)$	
$\mid \mathit{iter}[x\rangle(f[g_1, g_2, \ldots, g_k])$	
$\mid \mathit{iter}\langle x](f[g_1, g_2, \ldots, g_k])$	
$\mid f \gg g$	Streaming composition

Fig. 1. List of expression combinators.

Data Predicates. For each $D \in \mathcal{T}$, let Φ_D be a non-empty collection of predicates over D. In the case of D_{bank}, an example choice is $\Phi_{D_{bank}} = \{d = end_d, d = end_m, d \in \mathbb{R}, d \geq 0, d < 0, \ldots\}$. We require the following:

1. Φ_D be closed under Boolean connectives: for each $\varphi_1, \varphi_2 \in \Phi_D$, $\varphi_1 \vee \varphi_2, \varphi_1 \wedge \varphi_2, \neg\varphi_1 \in \Phi_D$,
2. whether a data value d satisfies a predicate φ is decidable, and
3. there is a quantity $time_{\varphi\text{-}sat}$ such that the satisfiability of each predicate φ is mechanically decidable in time $\leq time_{\varphi\text{-}sat}$. Satisfiability of predicates would typically be determined by an SMT solver [20].

We refer to a set of predicates satisfying these properties as an *effective boolean algebra.*

Data Streams, Data Languages, and Symbolic Regular Expressions. For each $D \in \mathcal{T}$, a *data stream* is simply an element $w \in D^*$, and a *data language* L is a subset of D^*.

Symbolic regular expressions provide a way to identify data languages L. Our definitions here are mostly standard, except for the additional requirement of *unambiguous parseability*, which is for uniformity with our later definitions of function combinators. They are *symbolic* because the basic regular expressions are predicates over D. Through the rest of this paper, the unqualified phrase "regular expression" will refer to a "symbolic" regular expression.

Consider two non-empty languages $L_1, L_2 \subseteq D^*$. They are *unambiguously concatenable* if for each stream $w \in L_1 L_2$, there is a unique pair of streams $w_1 \in L_1$ and $w_2 \in L_2$ such that $w = w_1 w_2$. The language L is *unambiguously iterable* if L is non-empty and for each stream $w \in L^*$, there is a unique sequence of streams $w_1, w_2, \ldots, w_k \in L$ such that $w = w_1 w_2 \cdots w_k$.

We write $[\![r]\!] \subseteq D^*$ for the language defined by the symbolic regular expression r. *Symbolic unambiguous regular expressions* are inductively defined as follows:

1. ϵ is a regular expression, and identifies the language $[\![\epsilon]\!] = \{\epsilon\}$.
2. For each predicate $\varphi \in \Phi$, φ is a regular expression, and $[\![\varphi]\!] = \{d \in D \mid \varphi(d) \text{ holds}\}$.
3. For each pair of regular expressions r_1, r_2, if $[\![r_1]\!]$ and $[\![r_2]\!]$ are disjoint, then $r_1 + r_2$ is a regular expression and $[\![r_1 + r_2]\!] = [\![r_1]\!] \cup [\![r_2]\!]$.
4. For each pair of regular expressions r_1, r_2, if $[\![r_1]\!]$ and $[\![r_2]\!]$ are unambiguously concatenable, then $r_1 r_2$ is a regular expression which identifies the language $[\![r_1 r_2]\!] = [\![r_1]\!][\![r_2]\!]$.
5. When r is a regular expression such that $[\![r]\!]$ is unambiguously iterable, then r^* is also a regular expression, and identifies the language $[\![r^*]\!] = [\![r]\!]^*$.

Example 1. In the bank transaction example, the languages $[\![\mathbb{R}^* end_d]\!]$ and D^*_{bank} are unambiguously concatenable: the only way to split a string which matches $\mathbb{R}^* end_d \cdot D^*_{bank}$ is immediately after the first occurrence of end_d. On the other hand, observe that $\mathbb{R}^*$ and $\mathbb{R}^* end_d$ are not unambiguously concatenable: the string $2, end_d \in [\![\mathbb{R}^*]\!] \cdot [\![\mathbb{R}^* end_d]\!]$ can be split as $2, end_d = (\epsilon)(2, end_d)$, where $\epsilon \in [\![\mathbb{R}^*]\!]$ and $2, end_d \in [\![\mathbb{R}^* end_d]\!]$, and can also be split as $2, end_d = (2)(end_d)$, where $2 \in [\![\mathbb{R}^*]\!]$ and $end_d \in [\![\mathbb{R}^* end_d]\!]$.

Similarly, the language $[\![\mathbb{R}^* end_d]\!]$ is unambiguously iterable: the only viable split for any matching string is immediately after each occurrence of end_d. The language $[\![\mathbb{R}]\!]$ is also unambiguously iterable, but observe that $[\![\mathbb{R}^*]\!]$ is not.

Given a regular expression r_1 and r_2, let *min-terms* be the set of distinct character classes formed by predicates from Φ [18]. The first three claims below can be proved by straightforward extensions to the traditional regular expression-to-NFA translation algorithm [12,13,33]. The final claim is proved in [34].

Theorem 1. *Given unambiguous regular expressions r_1 and r_2, the following problems can be decided in time poly $(|r_1|, |r_2|, |min\text{-}terms|)$ $time_{\varphi\text{-}sat}$:*

1. *Are* $[\![r_1]\!]$ *and* $[\![r_2]\!]$ *disjoint?*
2. *Are* $[\![r_1]\!]$ *and* $[\![r_2]\!]$ *unambiguously concatenable?*
3. *Is* $[\![r_1]\!]$ *unambiguously iterable?*
4. *Are* r_1 *and* r_2 *equivalent, i.e. is* $[\![r_1]\!] = [\![r_2]\!]$*?*

Example 2. Consider again the case of the customer and the bank. We picked $D_{bank} = \mathbb{R} \cup \{end_d, end_m\}$ and $\Phi_{D_{bank}} = \{d = end_d, d = end_m, d \in \mathbb{R}, d \geq 0, d < 0\}$. The transactions of a single day may then be described by the regular expression $r_{day} = (d \in \mathbb{R})^* \cdot (d = end_d)$, the transactions of a week, by the regular expression $r_{week} = r_{day}^7$. Months which involve only deposits are given by the regular expression $((d \geq 0) + (d = end_d))^* \cdot (d = end_m)$.

An important restriction for the predicates is that they are only allowed to examine individual data values. The language $w \in \mathbb{R}^*$ of monotonically increasing sequences can therefore not be expressed by a symbolic regular expression. Without this restriction, all problems listed in Theorem 1 are undecidable [17].

Cost Terms. Let $\mathcal{G} = \{op_1, op_2, \ldots\}$ be a collection of operations over values of various types. Each operation is a function of the form $op : T_1 \times T_2 \times \cdots \times T_k \to T$.

Example 3. Over the space of types $\mathcal{T}_s = \{\mathbb{Z}, \mathbb{B}\}$, a simple choice of operators is $\mathcal{G}_s = \{+, \min, \max, x < 7\}$ where $+, \min, \max : \mathbb{Z} \times \mathbb{Z} \to \mathbb{Z}$, are the usual operations of addition, minimum and maximum respectively, and the unary operator $x < 7 : \mathbb{Z} \to \mathbb{B}$ determines whether the input argument is less than 7.

Over the space of types $\mathcal{T}_m = \{\mathbb{R}, \mathbb{M}\}$ where $\mathbb{M}$ is the set of multisets of real numbers, the chosen operations might be $\mathcal{G}_m = \{\mathtt{ins}, \mathtt{avg}, \mathtt{mdn}\}$, where $\mathtt{ins} : \mathbb{M} \times \mathbb{R} \to \mathbb{M}$ is insertion into sets, defined as $\mathtt{ins}(A, x) = A \cup \{x\}$, and $\mathtt{avg}, \mathtt{mdn} : \mathbb{M} \to \mathbb{R}$ return the average and median of a multiset of numbers respectively.

Let $X = \{x_1, x_2, \ldots\}$ be a sequence of parameters, and each parameter x_i be associated with a type $T_i \in \mathcal{T}$. We use $x : T$ when we want to emphasize that the type of x is T. Parameters in X can be combined using cost operations from $\mathcal{G}$ to construct *cost terms*:

$$\tau ::= x \mid t \in T \mid op(\tau_1, \tau_2, \ldots, \tau_k)$$

We will only consider those terms τ that are well-typed and *single-use*, i.e. where each parameter x occurs at most once in τ. For example, $\min(x, y)$ is a well-typed single-use term when both parameters are of type $\mathbb{R}$. On the other hand, the term $\min(x, x + y)$ is not single-use. Each term is associated with the set $Param(\tau) = \{x_{t1}, x_{t2}, \ldots, x_{tk}\}$ of parameters appearing in its description, and naturally encodes a function $[\![\tau]\!] : T_1 \times T_2 \times \cdots \times T_k \to T$ from parameter valuations $\overline{v}$ to costs $[\![\tau]\!](\overline{v})$, where T_i is the type of the parameter x_i.

2.2 Quantitative Regular Expressions and Function Combinators

Informally, for some data and cost domains $D, C \in \mathcal{T}$, QREs map data streams $w \in D^*$ to terms $f(w)$ over the cost domain C. Formally, given the data domain $D \in \mathcal{T}$, cost domain $C \in \mathcal{T}$, and the list of parameters $X = \langle x_1, x_2, \ldots, x_k \rangle$, each QRE f identifies a function $[\![f]\!] : D^* \to (T_1 \times T_2 \times \cdots \times T_k \to C)_\perp$.[1] Observe that whether $[\![f]\!](w, \overline{v})$ is defined depends only on the data stream w, and not on the parameter valuation $\overline{v}$.[2]

In addition to the data domain D, cost domain C, and the parameters of interest $X = \langle x_1, x_2, \ldots \rangle$, each QRE f is therefore also associated with a regular expression r, describing the subset of data streams over which it is defined: $[\![r]\!] = \{w \in D^* \mid [\![f]\!](w) \neq \perp\}$. We will represent this by saying that f is of the form QRE(r, X, C), or even more succinctly as $f :$ QRE(r, X, C).

We will now inductively define quantitative regular expressions. A summary of the syntax can be found in Fig. 1.

Basic Functions. If $\varphi \in \Phi_D$ is a predicate over data values $d \in D$, and $\lambda : D \to C$ is an operation in $\mathcal{G}$, then $\varphi ? \lambda :$ QRE$(\varphi, \emptyset, C)$ defined as follows:

$$[\![\varphi ? \lambda]\!](w, \overline{v}) = \begin{cases} \lambda(w) & \text{if } |w| = 1 \text{ and } \varphi(w) \text{ is true, and} \\ \perp & \text{otherwise.} \end{cases}$$

For each data domain D and parameter x of type C, $\epsilon ? x$ is a QRE$(\epsilon, \{x\}, C)$. If the input stream w is empty, then it produces the output v_x, where v_x is the assignment to x in the parameter valuation $\overline{v}$:

$$[\![\epsilon ? x]\!](w, \overline{v}) = \begin{cases} v_x & \text{if } w = \epsilon, \text{ and} \\ \perp & \text{otherwise.} \end{cases}$$

Example 4. In the bank transaction example, if we wish to count the number of transactions made by the customer in a month, we would be interested in the functions $d \in \mathbb{R} ? 1$ and $d \notin \mathbb{R} ? 0$, where 0 and 1 are the functions returning the constant values 0 and 1 respectively.

Cost Operations. Consider two competing banks, which given the transaction history w of the customer, yield interest amounts of $f_1(w)$ and $f_2(w)$ respectively. The customer wishes to maximize the interest received: given the binary operation max : $\mathbb{R} \times \mathbb{R} \to \mathbb{R}$ from $\mathcal{G}$, we are therefore interested in the QRE max(f_1, f_2).

---

[1] Note our convention of describing partial functions $f : A \to B$ as total functions $f : A \to B_\perp$, where $B_\perp = B \cup \{\perp\}$ and $\perp \notin B$ is the undefined value. The *domain* $Dom f$ of f is given by $Dom f = \{a \in A \mid f(a) \neq \perp\}$.

[2] We will be flexible in our use of function application, and freely use both the uncurried form $[\![f]\!](w, \overline{v})$ and the partial application $[\![f]\!](w)$ which maps parameter valuations to costs.

More generally, pick an operator $op : T_1 \times T_2 \times \cdots \times T_k \to C$ and expressions $f_1 : \text{QRE}(r_1, X_1, T_1)$, $f_2 : \text{QRE}(r_2, X_2, T_2)$, ..., $f_k : \text{QRE}(r_k, X_k, T_k)$. If the domains are equal, $[\![r_1]\!] = [\![r_2]\!] = \cdots = [\![r_k]\!]$, and the parameter lists are pairwise-disjoint, $X_i \cap X_j = \emptyset$, for all $i \neq j$, then $op(f_1, f_2, \ldots, f_k)$ is an expression of the form $\text{QRE}(r_1, \bigcup_i X_i, C)$.

Given an input stream $w \in D^*$, if $[\![f_i]\!](w)$ is defined for each i, then:

$$[\![op(f_1, f_2, \ldots, f_k)]\!](w, \overline{v}) = op(int_1, int_2, \ldots, int_k), \text{ where}$$
$$\text{for each } i, int_i = [\![f_i]\!](w, \overline{v}).$$

Otherwise, $[\![op(f_1, f_2, \ldots, f_k)]\!](w, \overline{v}) = \bot$.

Substitution. Informally, the expression $f[x/g]$ substitutes the result of applying g to the input stream into the parameter x while evaluating f.

Example 5. In the bank transaction example, the bank may determine interest rates by a complicated formula *rate* of the form $\text{QRE}(D^*_{bank}, \emptyset, \mathbb{R})$, which is possibly a function of the entire transaction history of the customer. Given the monthly interest rate $p \in \mathbb{R}$, we can define a formula *earning* of the form $\text{QRE}(D^*_{bank}, \{p\}, \mathbb{R})$ which returns the total earnings of the customer's account. The QREs *rate* and *earnings* thus encode functions $[\![rate]\!] : D^*_{bank} \to \mathbb{R}$ and $[\![earnings]\!] : D^*_{bank} \times \mathbb{R} \to \mathbb{R}$ respectively. The QRE $earnings[p/rate]$ plugs the result of the rate computation into the earning computation, and maps the transaction history to the total interest earned.

Formally, let f and g be of the form $\text{QRE}(r_f, X_f, T_f)$ and $\text{QRE}(r_g, X_g, T_g)$ respectively and with equal domains $[\![r_f]\!] = [\![r_g]\!]$, let $x \in X_f$ be of type T_g, and let $(X_f \setminus \{x\}) \cap X_g = \emptyset$. Then, $f[x/g]$ is of the form $\text{QRE}(r_f, (X_f \setminus \{x\}) \cup X_g, T_f)$. If $[\![f]\!](w)$ and $[\![g]\!](w)$ are both defined, then:

$$[\![f[x/g]]\!](w, \overline{v}) = [\![f]\!](w, \overline{v}[x/[\![g]\!](w, \overline{v})]).$$

where $\overline{v}[x/t]$ replaces the value of x in $\overline{v}$ with t. Otherwise, $[\![f[x/g]]\!](w, \overline{v})$ is undefined.

Conditional Choice. If f and g are QREs with disjoint domains then $f \; else \; g$ is a QRE defined as follows:

$$[\![f \; else \; g]\!](w, \overline{v}) = \begin{cases} int_f & \text{if } int_f \neq \bot, \text{ and} \\ int_g & \text{otherwise,} \end{cases}$$

where $int_f = [\![f]\!](w, \overline{v})$ and $int_g = [\![g]\!](w, \overline{v})$ respectively.

Example 6. The expression $isPositive = d \geq 0 \,?\, true \; else \; d < 0 \,?\, false$ examines a single customer transaction with the bank, and maps it to *true* if it was a deposit, and *false* otherwise.

The bank rewards program may reserve a higher reward rate for each transaction made in a "deposit-only" month, and a lower reward rate for other months. Say we have expressions *hiReward* and *loReward* which compute the total customer rewards in qualifying and non-qualifying months respectively. The expression $reward = hiReward \; else \; loReward$ then maps the transactions of an arbitrary month to the total reward earned.

Observe that the choice of *isPositive* depends only on the next customer transaction. On the other hand, the choice in *reward* depends on the *entire* list of transactions made in that month, and resolving this choice requires a global view of the data stream.

Concatenation. In the bank transaction example, say we have the transactions of two consecutive months, $w \in r^2_{month}$, and that the QRE *count* returns the number of transactions made in a single month.

To express the minimum number of transactions for both months, a natural description is *split-min*(*count*, *count*), where the combinator *split-min* splits the input string w into two parts w_1 and w_2, applies *count* to each part, and combines the results using the min operator. Similarly, the expression *split-plus*(*count*), *count* would total the number of transactions made in both months. One reasonable choice for function concatenation is therefore to have a k-ary combinator *split-op*, for each k-ary operator $op \in G$.

We instead choose to have a pair of uniform *binary, operator-agnostic* combinators *split*: $split(f \; [x\rangle \; g)$ and $split(f \; \langle x] \; g)$. They split the given input stream into two parts, applying f to the prefix and g to the suffix, and use parameter x to pass the result from f to g in the case of $[x\rangle$ and vice-versa in the case of $\langle x]$ (see Fig. 2). Therefore the sub-expressions f and g themselves determine how the intermediate results are combined. The *split-op* combinators are just a special case of this more general construct (see Example 7). We now formalize this intuition.

Let $f : \mathrm{QRE}(r_f, X_f, T_f)$ and $g : \mathrm{QRE}(r_g, X_g, T_g)$ be a pair of QREs whose domains $[\![r_f]\!]$ and $[\![r_g]\!]$ are unambiguously concatenable. Let $x : T_f$ be a parameter in X_g and let $X_f \cap (X_g \setminus \{x\}) = \emptyset$. Then $split(f \; [x\rangle \; g)$ is a QRE of the form $\mathrm{QRE}(r_f \cdot r_g, X, T_g)$ where $X = X_f \cup (X_g \setminus \{x\})$. Given an input stream w, if there exist sub-streams w_f, w_g such that $w = w_f w_g$ and such that both $[\![f]\!](w_f)$ and $[\![g]\!](w_g)$ are defined, then:

$$\begin{aligned} [\![split(f \; [x\rangle \; g)]\!](w, \overline{v}) &= [\![g]\!](w_g, \overline{v}_g), \text{ where} \\ \overline{v}_g &= \overline{v}[x/int_f], \text{ and} \\ int_f &= [\![f]\!](w_f, \overline{v}). \end{aligned}$$

Otherwise, $[\![split(f \; \langle x] \; g)]\!](w, \overline{v}) = \bot$.

Example 7. We promised earlier that for each cost domain operator *op*, the *split-op* combinator was a special case of the more general *split* combinator just defined. We illustrate this in the bank transaction example by constructing

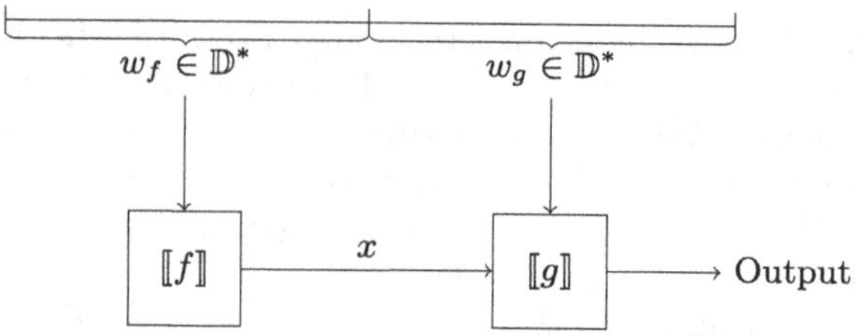

Fig. 2. The split combinator, $split(f\ [x\rangle\ g)$, divides the input data string w into two parts, $w = w_f w_g$, applies f to w_f and g to w_g, and substitutes the result of f into the parameter x of the term generated by g. The expression $split(f\ \langle x]\ g)$ is similar except for the direction of the f-g data flow.

a QRE for $split\text{-}min(count, count)$, where $count$ is the expression counting the number of transactions in a single month.

The desired function may be expressed by the QRE $split(count\ [p\rangle\ minCount)$, where the QRE $minCount(p) = \min(p, count)$.[3] The *split* combinator splits the input data string into a prefix and a suffix, and propagates the output of *count* on the prefix into the parameter p of the QRE $minCount$ on the suffix.

In general, given appropriate QREs f and g, and a binary operator op, the expression $split\text{-}op(f, g)$ can be expressed as $split(f\ [p\rangle\ g')$, where $g' = op(Dom(f)\,?\,p, g)$ and p is a new temporary parameter.

The definition of the left version of the split combinator, $split(f\ \langle x]\ g)$ is similar to the definition of $split(f\ [x\rangle\ g)$, with just the direction of the f-g information flow reversed, and is given in the appendix.

Iteration. Our next combinator is iteration, the analog of Kleene-* from regular expressions. The definition of the combinator is similar to that of *split*, to permit more general forms of iteration than just those offered a hypothetical *iter-op* operator.

Consider an expression f : QRE$(r, \{x\}, T)$, such that $[\![r]\!]$ is unambiguously iterable, and $x : T$. Then $iter[x\rangle(f)$ is an expression of the form QRE$(r^*, \{x\}, T)$. The expression $iter[x\rangle(f)$ divides the input stream w into a sequence of substreams, $w_1, w_2, \ldots, w_k$, such that $[\![f]\!](w_i)$ is defined for each i. $[\![iter[x\rangle(f)]\!](w)$ is defined if this split exists and is unique. In that case, for each $i \in \{0, 1, 2, \ldots, k\}$, define int_i as follows:

1. $int_0 = v_x$, and
2. for each $i \geq 1$, $int_i = [\![f]\!](w_i, \{x \mapsto int_{i-1}\})$.

Finally, $[\![iter[x\rangle(f)]\!](w, \overline{v}) = int_k$.

---

[3] Note that this QRE is pedantically ill-formed, because the first argument to the min operator is a parameter p, and the second argument is a QRE *count*. The parameter p on the left should be read as the QRE $r_{month}\,?\,p$, where $r_{month} = Dom(count)$.

Example 8. In the bank transaction example, consider the query $currBal$ which maps the transaction history w of the customer to her current account balance. We can write $currBal = iter\text{-}plus(tx)$, where the expression $tx = (d \in \mathbb{R}\,?\,d)$ *else* $(d \notin \mathbb{R}\,?\,0)$ records the change in account balance as a result of a single transaction.

To desugar $currBal$ to use the parametrized version of the iteration combinator, we adopt a similar approach as in Example 7. We first write the expression $tx' = plus(p, tx)$. Observe that tx' is a QRE dependent on a single parameter p, the previous account balance, and returns the new balance. Then, we can write: $currBal = iter\text{-}plus(tx) = iter[p\rangle(tx')$.

A similar approach works to desugar $iter\text{-}op(f)$, for any associative cost operator op with the identity element 0. We first write $f' = op(r_f\,?\,p, f)$, for some new parameter p of type T_f. Then, observe that $iter\text{-}op(f) = (iter[p\rangle(f'))[p/0]$.

Remark 1. We have presented here a simplified version of the iteration combinator, which is sufficient for most examples. The full combinator, used in the proof of expressive completeness, allows f to depend on multiple parameters (instead of just a single parameter as above), and multiple values are computed in each substream w_i. This full combinator and the symmetric left-iteration combinator are defined in the full paper.

Streaming Composition. In the bank transaction example, suppose we wish to compute the minimum balance over the entire account history. Recall that the stream w is a sequence of transactions, each data value indicating the deposit / withdrawal of some money from the account. The expression $currBal$ from Example 8 maps the transaction history of the customer to her current balance. It is also simple to express the function $minValue = iter\text{-}min(d \in \mathbb{R}\,?\,d)$ which returns the minimum of a stream of real numbers. We can then express the minimum account balance query using the streaming composition operator: $minBal = currBal \gg minValue$.

Informally, the streaming composition $currBal \gg minValue$ applies the expression $currBal$ to *each prefix* $w_1, w_2, \ldots, w_i$ of the input data stream $w = w_1, w_2, \ldots$, thus producing the account balance after each transaction. It then produces an intermediate data stream w' by concatenating the results of $currBal$. This intermediate stream w' is supplied to the function $minValue$, which then produces the historical minimum account balance.

Formally, let f and g be of the form $\text{QRE}(r, \emptyset, T_f)$ and $\text{QRE}(T_f^*, X, T_g)$ respectively. Note that f produces results independent of any parameter, and that g is defined over all intermediate data streams $w' \in T_f^*$. Then $f \gg g$: $\text{QRE}(D^*, X, T_g)$. Given the input stream $w = w_1, w_2, \ldots, w_k$ and parameter valuation $\overline{v}$, for each i such that $1 \le i \le k$, define int_i as follows:

1. If $[\![f]\!](w_1, w_2, \ldots, w_i, \overline{v}_\emptyset) \ne \bot$, then $int_i = [\![f]\!](w_1, w_2, \ldots, w_i, \overline{v}_\emptyset)$, where $\overline{v}_\emptyset$ is the empty parameter valuation.
2. Otherwise, $int_i = \epsilon$.

Then $[\![f \gg g]\!](w, \overline{v})$ is given by:

$$[\![f \gg g]\!](w, \overline{v}) = [\![g]\!](int_1, int_2, \ldots, int_k, \overline{v}).$$

2.3 Examples

Analyzing a Regional Rail System. Consider the rail network of a small city. There are two lines, the airport line, *al*, between the city and the airport, and the suburban line, *sl*, between the city and the suburbs. The managers of the network want to determine the average time for a traveler in the suburbs to get to the airport.

The data is a sequence of event tuples $(line, station, time)$, where $line \in \{al, sl\}$ indicates the railway line on which the event occurs, $station \in \{air, city, suburb\}$ indicates the station at which the train is stopped, and $time \in \mathbb{R}$ indicates the event time.

We first write the expression t_{sc} which calculates the time needed to travel from the suburbs to the city. Let $\varphi_{ss}(d) = (d.line = sl \wedge d.station = suburb)$ and $\varphi_{sc}(d) = (d.line = sl \wedge d.station = city)$ be the predicates indicating that the suburban line train is at the suburban station and at the city station respectively. Consider the expression:

$$t_{sc-drop} = split\text{-}plus(\neg\varphi_{ss}^* \cdot \varphi_{ss} \cdot \neg\varphi_{sc}^* \,?\, 0, \varphi_{sc} \,?\, time)$$

that maps event streams of the form $\neg\varphi_{ss}^* \cdot \varphi_{ss} \cdot \neg\varphi_{sc}^* \cdot \varphi_{sc}$ to the time at which the train stops at the city station. The expression $t_{sc-pickup}$ that maps event streams to the pickup time from the suburban station can be similarly expressed:

$$t_{sc-pickup} = split\text{-}plus(\neg\varphi_{ss}^* \,?\, 0, \varphi_{ss} \,?\, time, \neg\varphi_{sc}^* \cdot \varphi_{sc} \,?\, 0).$$

Our goal is to express the commute time from the suburbs to the city. This is done by the expression: $t_{sc} = minus(t_{sc-drop}, t_{sc-pickup})$.

The QRE t_{ca} that expresses the commute time from the city to the airport can be similarly constructed. We want to talk about the total travel time from the suburbs to the airport: $t_{sa} = split\text{-}plus(t_{sc}, t_{ca})$. Our ultimate goal is the average travel time from the suburbs to the airport. The following QRE solves our problem: $t_{avg} = iter\text{-}avg(t_{sa})$.

Rolling Data Telephone Plans. Now consider a simple telephone plan, where the customer pays 50 dollars each month for a 5 GB monthly download limit. If the customer uses more than this amount, she pays 30 dollars extra, but otherwise, the unused quota is added to her next month's limit, up to a maximum of 20 GB.

The data domain $D_{tel} = \mathbb{R} \cup \{end_m\}$, where $d \in \mathbb{R}$ indicates a download of d gigabytes and end_m indicates the end of the billing cycle and payment of the telephone bill. Given the entire browsing history of the customer, we wish to compute the download limit for the current month.

First, the QRE $totalDown = iter\text{-}plus(d \in \mathbb{R}\,?\,d)$ takes a sequence of downloads and returns the total data downloaded. The browsing history of a single month is given by the regular expression $r_m = \mathbb{R}^* \cdot end_m$, and the QRE $monthDown = split\text{-}plus(totalDown, end_m\,?\,0)$ maps data streams $w \in [\![r_m]\!]$ to the total quantity of data downloaded.

The following expression gives the unused allowance available at the end of the month, in terms of $initLim$, the download limit at the beginning of the month: $unused(initLim) = (r_m\,?\,initLim) - monthDown$, and the QRE $rollover(initLim) = \min(\max(unused(initLim), 0), 20)$ gives the amount to be added to the next month's limit.

The QRE $nextQuota(initLim) = rollover(initLim) + 5$ provides the download limit for the next month in terms of $initLim$ and the current month's browsing history. Finally, the QRE $quota = iter[initLim\rangle(nextQuota)[initLim/5]$ maps the entire browsing history of the customer to the download limit of the current month.

Aggregating Weather Reports. Our final example deals with a stream of weather reports. Let the data domain $D_{wth} = \mathbb{R} \cup \{autEqx, sprEqx, newYear, \ldots\}$, where the symbols $autEqx$ and $sprEqx$ represent the autumn and spring equinoxes. Here a number $d \in \mathbb{R}$ indicates a temperature reading of d°C. We wish to compute the average winter-time temperature reading. For this query, let winter be defined as the time between an autumn equinox and the subsequent spring equinox.

The regular expression $r_{summ} = \mathbb{R}^* \cdot autEqx$ captures a sequence of temperature readings made before the start of winter, and the expression $summer = r_{summ}\,?\,\emptyset$ maps the summer readings to the empty set. The QRE $collect = iter\text{-}union(d \in \mathbb{R}\,?\,\{d\})$ collects a sequence of temperature readings into a set and so we can write QRE $winter = split\text{-}union(collect, (sprEqx\,?\,\emptyset))$.

The QRE $year = split\text{-}union(summer, winter)$ constructs the set of winter-time temperatures seen in a data stream. The average winter-time temperature over all years is then given by: $avgWinter = \mathbf{avg}(iter\text{-}union(year))$.

3 Compiling QREs into Streaming Evaluation Algorithms

In this section, we show how to compile a QRE f into a streaming algorithm M_f that computes $[\![f]\!](w, \overline{v})$. Recall that the partial application $[\![f]\!](w) : T_1 \times T_2 \times \cdots \times T_k \to T$ is a term which maps parameter valuations $\overline{v}$ to cost values c. Therefore, the complexity of expression evaluation depends on the complexity of performing operations on terms. This in turn depends on the choice of cost types $\mathcal{T}$, cost operations $\mathcal{G}$, and on the number of parameters appearing in f. Let $time_{\varphi\text{-}eval}(f)$ be the maximum time needed to evaluate predicates appearing in f on data values, and let $time_\tau$ (resp. mem_τ) be the maximum time (resp. memory) needed to perform an operation $op \in \mathcal{G}$ on terms $\tau_1, \tau_2, \ldots, \tau_k$. Then we have:

Theorem 2. *Every QRE f can be compiled into a streaming algorithm M_f which processes each data item in time $poly(|f|) time_\mathcal{T} time_{\varphi\text{-}eval}(f)$ and which consumes $poly\,(|f|)\, mem_\mathcal{T}$ memory.*

Since the size of all intermediate terms produced, $|\tau|$, is bounded by $|w|\,poly(|f|)$, this is also an upper bound on $time_\mathcal{T}$ and $mem_\mathcal{T}$. However, depending on the cost types $\mathcal{T}$ and the cost operators $\mathcal{G}$, they might be smaller. For instance, in the case of real-valued terms over $\mathcal{G}\{*, +, \min, \max, \text{ins}, \text{avg}\}$, the term simplification procedure of Subsect. 3.2 guarantees that $time_\mathcal{T} = poly(|f|)$ and $mem_\mathcal{T} = O(|f|)$.

Theorem 3. *1. For every choice of cost types $\mathcal{T}$, and cost operations, $\mathcal{G}$, $time_\mathcal{T} = |w| poly(|f|)$ and $mem_\mathcal{T} = |w| poly(|f|)$.*
2. If $\mathcal{T} = \mathbb{R}, \mathbb{M}$, where $\mathbb{M}$ is the set of multisets of real numbers, and $\mathcal{G}\{*, +, \min, \max, \textbf{\textit{ins}}, \textbf{\textit{avg}}\}$, then $time_\mathcal{T} = poly(|f|)$ and $mem_\mathcal{T} = poly(|f|)$, independent of the length of the data stream stream$|w|$.

3.1 Overview

We construct, by structural induction on the QRE f, an *evaluator* M_f that computes the function $[\![f]\!]$. Let us first assume that each element $w_i \in d$ of the data stream is annotated with its index i, so the input to the streaming evaluator is a sequence of pairs (i, w_i). Now consider the evaluator $M_{split(f\ [x\rangle\ g)}$ when processing the stream w, as shown in Fig. 3. $M_{split(f\ [x\rangle\ g)}$ forwards each element of the stream to both sub-evaluators M_f and M_g. After reading the prefix w_{pre}, M_f reports that $[\![f]\!](w_{pre})$ is defined, and returns the term produced. We are therefore now interested in evaluating g over the suffix beginning at the current position of the stream. Each evaluator therefore also accepts input signals of the form (START, i), which indicates positions of the input stream from which to start processing the function. While evaluating $split(f\ [x\rangle\ g)$, there may be multiple prefixes, such as w_{pre} and w'_{pre}, for which $[\![f]\!]$ is defined. M_g gets a start signal after each of these prefixes is read, and may therefore be simultaneously evaluating g over multiple suffixes of the data stream. We refer to the suffix beginning at each start signal as a *thread* of evaluation.

After reading the data stream, M_g may report a result, i.e. that $[\![g]\!]$ is defined on some thread. Recall the semantics of the split operator: $split(f\ [x\rangle\ g)$ is now defined on the entire data stream, and the result is $\tau_f[x/\tau_g]$, where τ_f and τ_g are respectively the results of evaluating $[\![f]\!]$ and $[\![g]\!]$ on the appropriate substrings. The compound evaluator therefore needs to "remember" the result τ_f reported by M_f after processing w_{pre}—a key part of the complexity analysis involves bounding the amount of auxiliary state that needs to be maintained. Next, since M_g may be processing threads simultaneously, it needs to uniquely identify the thread which is currently returning a result. Result signals are therefore triples of the form (RESULT, i, τ), indicating that the thread beginning at index i is currently returning the result τ. On receiving the result τ_g from M_g at the end of the input stream, the compound evaluator reconciles this with the result τ_f

earlier obtained from T_f, and itself emits the result $\tau_f[x/\tau_g]$. The response time of each evaluator therefore depends on the time $time_\tau$ required to perform basic operations over terms.

Finally, let us consider the auxiliary state that $M_{split(f\ [x\rangle\ g)}$ needs to maintain during processing. It maintains a table of results Th_g reported by M_f (the subscript g indicates that the thread is currently being processed by M_g). Each time M_f reports a result $(\text{RESULT}, i, \tau_f)$, it adds the triple (i, j, τ_f) to Th_g: this indicates that the thread of $M_{split(f\ [x\rangle\ g)}$ beginning at index i received the result τ_f from M_f at index j. $M_{split(f\ [x\rangle\ g)}$ then sends a start signal to M_g. If left unoptimized, the number of entries in Th_g is therefore the number of start signals sent to M_g, which is, in the worst case, $O(|w|)$.

The evaluator M_g therefore emits kill signals of the form (KILL, i), indicating that the thread beginning at index i will not be producing any more results, and that parent evaluators may recycle auxiliary state as necessary. Note that a kill signal (KILL, i) is a strong prediction about the fate of a thread: it is the assertion that for all future inputs, $[\![g]\!]$ is undefined for the suffix of the data stream beginning at index i. Because of the unambiguity requirements on QREs, it follows that each function evaluator M_f will always have at most $O(|f|)$ active threads. Such claims can be immediately lifted to upper bounds on the response times and memory consumption of the evaluator, $poly(|f|)time_\tau$ and $poly(|f|)mem_\tau$.

In summary, the evaluator accepts two types of signals: start signals of the form (START, i) and data signals of the form (SYMBOL, i, d). It emits two types of signals as output: result signals of the form (RESULT, i, τ) and kill signals of the form (KILL, i). The input fed to the evaluator satisfies the guarantee that no two threads ever simultaneously produce a result (input validity). In return, the evaluator is guaranteed to report results correctly, and eagerly kill threads.

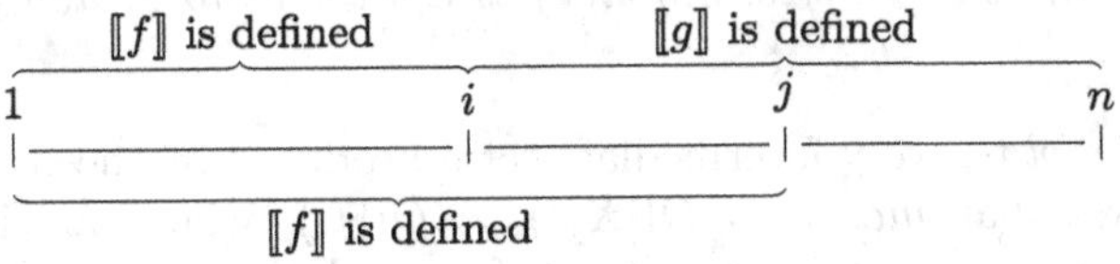

Fig. 3. Processing $split(f\ [x\rangle\ g)$ over an input data stream w. There are two prefixes $w_{pre} = w_1 w_2 \cdots w_i$ and $w'_{pre} = w_1 w_2 \cdots w_j$ of w for which $[\![f]\!]$ is defined. $[\![g]\!]$ is defined for the suffix $w_{suff} = w_{i+1} w_{i+2} \cdots w_n$.

The input-output requirements of function evaluators are formally stated in the full paper. The construction is similar to the streaming evaluation algorithm for DReX [6]. The major differences are the following:

1. QREs map data streams to terms, while DReX maps input strings to output strings. Even if the top-level QRE is parameter-free, sub-expressions might still involve terms, and intermediate results involve storing terms. We thus

pay attention to the computational costs of manipulating terms: this includes the time $time_\tau$ to perform basic operations on them, and the memory mem_τ needed to store terms.

2. The *iter* combinator, as defined in this paper, is conceptually different from both the iteration and the chained sum combinators of DReX.

3.2   Succinct Representation of Terms

Recall that the evaluation time is parametrized by mem_τ and $time_\tau$, the maximum memory and time required to perform operations on terms. It is therefore important to be able to succinctly represent terms. To prove the second part of Theorem 3, we now present a simplification procedure for terms over $\mathcal{G} = \{*, +, min, max, \mathtt{ins}, \mathtt{avg}\}$ so that mem_τ and $time_\tau$ are both bounded by $poly(|f|)$, independent of the length of the input stream. The representation we develop must support the following operations:

1. Construct the term $op(\tau_1, \tau_2, \ldots, \tau_k)$, for each operator $op \in \mathcal{G}$, and appropriately typed terms $\tau_1, \tau_2, \ldots, \tau_k$,
2. given terms τ_1 and τ_2, and an appropriately typed $x \in Param\tau_1$, construct the term $\tau_1[x/\tau_2]$, and
3. given a term τ and a parameter valuation $\overline{v}$, compute $[\![\tau]\!](\overline{v})$.

Intuitively, the simplification procedure *simpl* compiles an arbitrary copyless input term τ into an equivalent term $simpl(\tau)$ of bounded size. Consider, for example, a "large" term such as $\tau(x) = min(min(x, 3) + 2, 9)$. By routine algebraic laws such as distributivity, we have $\tau(x) = min(min(x + 2, 3 + 2), 9) = min(x + 2, 5, 9) = min(x + 2, 5)$.

Proposition 4. *For each input τ, simpl runs in time $O(|\tau|^2)$ and returns an equivalent term of bounded size: $simpl(\tau)$ is equivalent to τ, and $|simpl(\tau)| = O(|Param(\tau)|)$.*

We apply *simpl* to every intermediate term produced by the streaming algorithm. It follows that $mem_\tau = O(|X_f|) = O(|f|)$, where X_f is the set of parameters appearing in the description of f, and $time_\tau = O(poly(|X_f|)) = O(poly(|f|))$, and this establishes Theorem 3.

A first attempt at designing *simpl* might be to repeatedly apply algebraic laws until terms reach a normal form. For example, the term $min(x + 2, 5) + min(y + 8, 7)$ could be mechanically simplified into the equivalent term $min(12, x + 9, y + 13, x + y + 10)$. Notice however, that this simplification potentially involves a constant for each *subset* of parameters, thus producing terms of size $O(2^{|f|})$ (but still independent of the stream length $|w|$).

The simplification routine instead only propagates constants and does not attempt to completely reduce the term to a normal form. The term $min(x + 2, 5) + min(y + 8, 7)$ would therefore be left unchanged.

Consider the set of elements $A = \{3, 4, x, y + 3\}$. The only operation over multisets is insertion and average. A is therefore represented by the pair

$(x + y + 10, 4)$, indicating the sum of the elements in A and the number of elements in A respectively. The average $\mathtt{avg}(A)$ would be represented by the term $(x+y+10)/4 = x/4+y/4+2.5$. The simplified term may therefore also contain division terms of the form x/n and is drawn from the following grammar:

$$\begin{aligned}
\tau_{\mathbb{R}} ::= & \; c \text{ (for } c \in \mathbb{R}) \mid x \mid x/n \text{ (for } n \in \mathbb{N}) \\
\mid & \; \tau_1 * \tau_2 \mid \tau_1 + \tau_2 \mid \tau_1 - \tau_2 \\
\mid & \; \min(\tau_1, \tau_2) \mid \max(\tau_1, \tau_2) \\
\tau_{\mathbb{M}} ::= & \; (\tau_{\mathbb{R}}, n)
\end{aligned}$$

The procedure $simpl(\tau)$ works as follows:

1. If τ is a constant c or a parameter x, then return τ.
2. Otherwise, if $\tau = op(\tau_1, \tau_2)$, then compute $\tau_1' = simpl(\tau_1)$ and $\tau_2' = simpl(\tau_2)$. Output $prop\text{-}const(op(\tau_1', \tau_2'))$.

The procedure $prop\text{-}const(\tau)$ performs constant propagation, and is essentially a large case-analysis with various pre-applied algebraic simplification laws. For example,

$$\begin{aligned}
\text{if } \tau &= \tau_1 + \tau_2, \\
\tau_1 &= c_1, \text{ for some constant } c_1, \text{ and} \\
\tau_2 &= \min(\tau_2', \tau_2''), \\
\text{then } prop\text{-}const(\tau) &= \min(simpl(c_1 + \tau_2', c_1 + \tau_2'')).
\end{aligned}$$

The full case-analysis is described in the full paper.

The key observation is that such constant propagation is sufficient to guarantee small terms: if all non-trivial sub-terms contain at least one parameter, and each parameter appears at most once in each term, then there are at most a bounded number of constants in the simplified term, and thus a bounded number of leaves in the term-tree, and the term is therefore itself of a bounded size. Proposition 4 follows.

3.3 Why the Unambiguity and Single-Use Restrictions?

We first consider the unambiguity rules we used while defining QREs. While defining $op(f_1, f_2)$, we require the sub-expressions to have equal domains. Otherwise, the compound expression is only defined for data streams in the intersection of $Dom(f_1)$ and $Dom(f_2)$. Efficiently determining whether strings match regular expressions with intersection is an open problem (see [32] for the state of the art).

Now consider $split(f \; [x\rangle \; g)$ without the unambiguous concatenability requirement. For a stream w with two splits $w = w_1 w_2 = w_1' w_2'$, such that all of $[\![f]\!](w_1)$, $[\![f]\!](w_1')$, $[\![g]\!](w_2)$ and $[\![g]\!](w_2')$ are defined. Since we are defining functions and not relations, the natural choice is to leave $split(f \; [x\rangle \; g)$ undefined for w. In the compound evaluator, we can no longer assume input validity, as two threads of T_g will report a result after reading w. Furthermore, the compound evaluator has to perform non-trivial bookkeeping and not report *any* result after reading w. Requiring unambiguous concatenability is a convenient way to avoid these issues.

We conjecture that non-regular functions are expressible if the single-use restrictions are relaxed. Furthermore, lifting the single-use restrictions makes the term simplification procedure of Subsect. 3.2 more complicated. Consider the "copyful" term $\tau = \min((x+y), (x+y)+z)$. Observe that terms are now best represented as DAGs, and consider applying constant propagation to the expression $\tau + 3$: this results in the term $\min(x+(y+3), (x+y)+z+3)$, thus causing the shared node $x+y$ of the term DAG to be split. It is not clear that the constant propagation procedure *prop-const* does not cause a large blow-up in the size of the term being represented, because of reduced sharing.

4 The Expressiveness of Quantitative Regular Expressions

We now study the expressive power of QREs. The recently introduced formalism of *regular functions* [7] is parametrized by an arbitrary set of cost types and operations over cost values. Regular functions can be equivalently expressed both by the operational model of *streaming string-to-term transducers (SSTTs)*, and as logical formulas mapping strings to terms in monadic second-order (MSO) logic. In this section, we show that QREs are expressively equivalent to the streaming composition of regular functions. This mirrors similar results from classical language theory, where regular languages can be alternately expressed by finite automata, by regular expressions and as formulas in MSO.

See Fig. 4 for an example of an SSTT. Informally, an SSTT maintains a finite state control, and a finite set of typed registers. Each register holds a term τ of the appropriate type, and register contents are updated during each transition. The main restrictions are: (a) transitions depend only on the current state, and

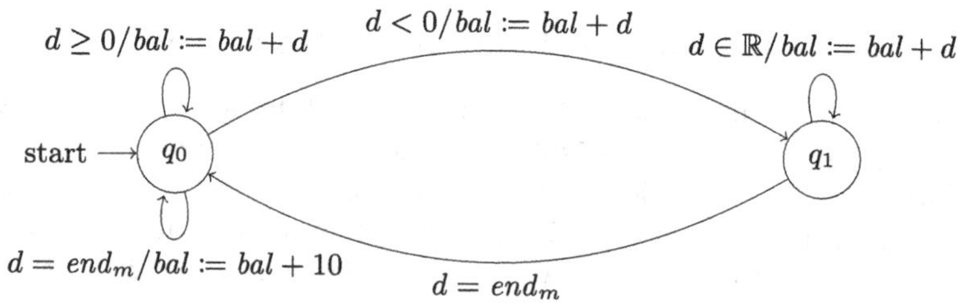

Fig. 4. The bank gives the customer a \$10 reward for each month in which no withdrawal is made. The current account balance is computed by the SSTT $\mathcal{S}_{bal}$. The machine maintains a single register *bal*, the state q_0 indicates that no withdrawal has been made in the current month, and the machine moves to q_1 if at least one withdrawal has been made.

not on the contents of the registers, (*b*) register updates are *copyless*: the update $x := x + y$ is allowed, but not the update $x := y + y$, and (*c*) at each point, the term held by each register is itself single-use.

We first describe the translation from QREs to the streaming composition of SSTTs. The construction proceeds in two steps: we first rewrite the given QRE as a streaming composition of composition-free QREs (Subsect. 4.1), and then we translate each composition-free QRE into an equivalent SSTT (Subsect. 4.2). In Subsect. 4.3, we describe the proof of expressive completeness: each SSTT can also be expressed by an equivalent QRE. For SSTTs with multiple registers, data may flow between the registers in complicated ways. The main part of the SSTT-to-QRE translation procedure is analysis of these data flows, and the imposition of a partial order among data flows so that an inductive construction may be performed. Definitions and omitted proofs may be found in the full paper.

4.1 A Normal Form for QREs

Our main goal is to convert each QRE into the streaming composition of SSTTs. We first rewrite the given QRE as the streaming composition of several QREs, each of which is itself composition-free (Theorem 5). We use the term $\text{QRE}_{\not\gg}$ to highlight that the QRE does not include occurrences of the streaming composition operator. In Subsect. 4.2 we translate each of these intermediate $\text{QRE}_{\not\gg}$-s into a single SSTT.

Theorem 5. *For each QRE e, there exists a k and $QRE_{\not\gg}$-s $f_1, f_2, \ldots, f_k$, such that e is equivalent to $f_1 \gg f_2 \gg \cdots \gg f_k$.*

The proof is by induction on the structure of e. The claim clearly holds if e is a basic expression or itself of the form $f \gg g$. We now handle each of the other cases in turn.

Consider the expression $e = op(f \gg g, h)$. The idea is to produce, after reading each element w_i of the input stream w, the pair $int_i = ([\![f]\!](w_1, w_2, \ldots, w_i), w_i)$. We can now apply g to the first element and h to the second element of each pair in the stream of intermediate values $int = int_1, int_2, \ldots$, and use the cost operator op to produce the final result.

We are therefore interested in the operator *tuple*, which produces the output $(t_1, t_2) \in T_1 \times T_2$ for each pair of input values $t_1 \in T_2$ and $t_2 \in T_2$. Observe that g cannot be directly applied to elements of the intermediate data stream, because they are pairs, and only the first element of this pair is of interest to g. Instead, we write the expression $project_1(g)$, which is identical to g except that each data predicate $\varphi(d)$ is replaced with $\varphi(d.first)$, and each atomic function $\lambda(d)$ is replaced with $\lambda(d.first)$. Similarly, $project_2(h)$ is identical to h except that it looks at the second element in each input data pair.

Now, observe that the original expression $e = op(f \gg g, h)$ is equivalent to the expression $tuple(f, last) \gg op(project_1(g), project_2(h))$, where the expression *last* simply outputs the last element of the input stream: $last = split(D^* \; [x\rangle \; (true \,?\, d))$. The remaining cases are presented in the full paper.

4.2 From QREs to SSTTs

Theorem 6. *Let f be a $QRE_{\gg}$ over a data domain D. There exists an SSTT $\mathcal{S}_f$ such that $[\![f]\!] = [\![\mathcal{S}_f]\!]$.*

The proof proceeds by structural induction on f. The challenging cases are those of *split* and *iter*. Consider the case $f = split(g\ [x\rangle\ h)$. Just as in Fig. 3, it is not possible to determine, before seeing the entire stream w, where to split the stream into $w = w_{pre}w_{suff}$ such that both $[\![g]\!](w_{pre})$ and $[\![g]\!](w_{suff})$ are defined. However, it is known that SSTTs are closed under *regular lookahead*, a powerful primitive operation by which the automaton can make a transition not just based on the next input symbol, but based on a regular property of the entire (as yet unseen) suffix. The detailed proof of Theorem 6, including a formal definition of regular lookahead, may be found in the full paper.

4.3 From SSTTs to QREs

Theorem 7. *Let $\mathcal{S}$ be an SSTT. There exists a $QRE_{\gg}$ f such that $[\![\mathcal{S}]\!] = [\![f]\!]$.*

Proof Outline. The proof follows the idea in [33] for constructing a regular expression from a given DFA. Suppose the DFA has n states $\{q_1, q_2, \ldots, q_n\}$. Let $R^k_{i,j}$ denote the set of input strings w that take the DFA from state q_i to state q_j without going through any intermediate state numbered higher than k (the origin and target states i and j can be of index greater than k).

The regular expressions corresponding to the sets $R^k_{i,j}$ can be defined inductively. The base case when $k = 0$ corresponds to a single transition. For the inductive definition we have $R^k_{i,j} = R^{k-1}_{i,k}(R^{k-1}_{k,k})^* R^{k-1}_{k,j} \cup R^{k-1}_{i,j}$. Given the accepting states are $F = \{f_1, f_2, \ldots, f_\ell\}$ and the initial state is 1 then the regular expression $R^n_{1,f_1} + R^n_{1,f_2} + \ldots + R^n_{1,f_\ell}$ recognizes the same language as the given DFA.

We note that this construction works with unambiguous regular expressions. That is, whenever R and R' above are combined using $\cup$ their domain is disjoint, when they are concatenated they are unambiguously concatenable, and when R is iterated it is unambiguously iterable.

Generalizing the Idea to SSTTs. Let $\mathcal{R}$ be the set of regular expressions used in the construction above. To extend this idea to SSTTs we would like to create for every $R \in \mathcal{R}$ and every variable x of a given SSTT $\mathcal{S}$ a quantitative regular expression $f_{[x,R]}$ such that for $w \in R$ the value of variable x when processing of w by $\mathcal{S}$ terminates is given by $f_{[x,R]}(w)$. If the SSTT has m variables $\{x_1, \ldots, x_m\}$ we can work with vectors of QREs $\mathbf{V}_R = (f_{[1,R]}, \ldots, f_{[m,R]})$ where $f_{[i,R]}$ abbreviates $f_{[x_i,R]}$. In order to use the same inductive steps for building these vectors of QREs, given $\mathbf{V}_R$ and $\mathbf{V}_{R'}$ we need to be able to calculate $\mathbf{V}_{R \cdot R'}$, $\mathbf{V}_{R^*}$ and $\mathbf{V}_{R \cup R'}$ whenever R and R' are combined in a respective manner in the construction above. The major difficulty is calculating $\mathbf{V}_{R^*}$. This is since variables may flow to one another in complicated forms. For instance, on a transition where variable x is updated to $\max(x, y)$ and variable y is updated to $z + 1$, the QRE for iterating this transition, zero, one or two times looks very different. Fortunately, there is a finite number of such variations, i.e. we can define terms that should capture each variation so that repeating the loop more than m times will yield a previously encountered term. The situation, though, is more complicated since there may be several loops on the same state, and in each such loop the variables flow may be different, and we will need to account for all loops consisting of arbitrary long concatenations of these paths. Thus, we will consider regular expressions of the form $R[i, j, k, \theta]$ where θ describes the flow of variables as defined below, and we will need to find some partial order on such regular expressions so that we can always compute $\mathbf{V}_{R''}$ using previously computed $\mathbf{V}_R$ and $\mathbf{V}_{R'}$, and whenever these are combined they do not violate the unambiguity requirements.

Variable Flows. The *variable-flow* (in short *flow*) of a stream $w \in R^k_{i,j}$ is a function $\theta : [1..m] \to [1..m]$ such that $\theta(i) = j$ if x_j depends on x_i. By the copyless restriction there is at most one variable x_j which may depend on x_i and we assume without loss of generality that every variable flows into some other variable. We use Θ to denote the set of all flows. For $\theta_1, \theta_2 \in \Theta$ we use $\theta_1 \cdot \theta_2$ (or simply $\theta_1\theta_2$) to denote the flow function $\theta(i) = \theta_2(\theta_1(i))$. Note that if $w = w_1w_2$ and w_1, w_2 have flows θ_1, θ_2 respectively, then w has flow $\theta_1\theta_2$. We use θ^0 to denote the identity flow, θ^1 to denote θ and for $k > 1$ we use θ^k to denote $\theta \cdot \theta^{k-1}$. We say that a flow θ is *idempotent* if $\theta^k = \theta$ for every $k \in \mathbb{N}$. We use Θ_I to denote the set of all idempotent flows. We say that a flow θ is *normal* if $\theta(i) = j$ implies $i \geq j$ (i.e. the variables flow only upwards). Given an SSTT $\mathcal{S}$ with set of states Q we can transform it to an SSTT $\mathcal{S}_N$ where all updates on the edges are normal by letting the states of $\mathcal{S}_N$ be $Q \times P_n$ where P_n are all the permutations of $[1..n]$. The SSTT $\mathcal{S}_N$ remembers in the state the permutation needed to convert the flow to that of the original $\mathcal{S}$. Let Θ_N be the set of normal flows. It can be shown that concatenations of normal flows is a normal flow. Thus, we consider henceforth only normal flows.

For $\theta \in \Theta_N$ and $i, j, k \in [1..n]$, let $R[i, j, k, \theta]$ denote the set of all streams w such that when $\mathcal{S}$ processes w starting in state i, it reaches state j without passing through any state indexed greater than k and the overall flow is θ. We use $\mathcal{R}^\Theta$ to denote the set of all such regular expressions. We are now ready to define the vectors $\mathbf{V}_R$ corresponding to $R \in \mathcal{R}^\Theta$ for R's that appear in the inductive construction.

5 Related Work

Data Management Systems. Traditional database management systems focus on efficient processing of queries over static data. When data is updated frequently, and queries need to be answered incrementally with each update, ideally without reprocessing the entire data set (due to its large size), the resulting data management problem of *continuous queries* has been studied in the database literature (see [9] for a survey, [1] for an example system, and [8] for CQL, an extension of the standard relational query language SQL for continuous queries). The literature on continuous queries assumes a more general data model compared to ours: there can be multiple data streams that encode relational data and queries involve, in addition to aggregation statistics, classical relational operators such as join. Solutions involve maintaining a window of the stream in memory and answer queries only approximately. A recent project on continuous queries is ActiveSheets [35] that integrates stream processing in spreadsheets and provides many high-level features aimed at helping end-users. In recent years, there is also increased focus on evaluating queries over data streams in a distributed manner, and systems such as Apache Storm (see http://storm.apache.org) and Twitter Heron [27] facilitate the design of distributed algorithms for query evaluation. There is also extensive literature on querying XML data using languages such as XPath and XQuery and their extensions [15,26,28].

Many of these query languages support *filtering* operation that maps an input data stream to an output stream that can be fed as an input to another query. The streaming composition operation in QREs is inspired by this. The novelty in our work lies in the regular constructs for modular specification of numerical queries by exploiting the structure in the sequence.

Streaming Algorithms. Designing efficient streaming algorithms has been an active area of research in theoretical computer science (see [2,29] for illustrative results and [30] for a comprehensive survey). Such algorithms are designed for specific computational problems (for example, finding the k-median) using tools such as approximation and randomization. While we have considered only simple aggregation operators such as sum and averaging which have obvious streaming algorithms for exact computation, the complexity in QRE queries is due to the nesting of regular constructs and aggregation operations. Since our evaluation algorithm is oblivious to the set of cost combinators and the data structure used to summarize terms to be able to compute desired aggregates, our results are orthogonal and complementary to the literature on streaming algorithms.

String Transformations. Domain-specific languages for string manipulation such as sed, AWK, and Perl are widely used to query and reformat text files. However, these languages are Turing complete and thus do not support any algorithmic analysis. In recent years, motivated by applications to verification of string sanitizers and string encoders, there is a renewed interest in designing languages based on automata and transducers [3,17,19,24]. While such languages limit expressiveness, they have appealing theoretical properties such as closure under composition and decidable test for functional equivalence, that have been shown to be useful in practical applications. Symbolic automata and transducers introduced the idea of using unary predicates from a decidable theory, supported by modern SMT solvers [20], to process strings over unbounded or large alphabets [36], and we use the same idea for defining symbolic regular expressions.

Furthermore, checking typing rules regarding the domains of QREs relies on the constructions on symbolic automata.

The work most relevant to this paper is the design of the language DReX, a declarative language that can express all regular string-to-string transformations [6,7]. In DReX, the only cost type is strings and the only operation is string concatenation, and thus, quantitative regular expressions can be viewed as a generalization of DReX. In the design of QREs, the key new insights are: (*a*) the introduction of parameters to pass values across chunks during iteration, (*b*) the clear separation between the regular constructs and cost combinators, and (*c*) the inclusion of the streaming composition operation. The compilation of QREs into a single-pass streaming algorithm generalizes the evaluation algorithm for DReX, and its analysis now needs to be parametrized by the design of efficient data structures for representing terms for different choices of cost combinators.

The single-use restriction is common in theory of transducers to ensure that the output grows only linearly with the input [22,23]. Parameters in QREs are conceptually similar to attribute grammars in which attributes are used to pass information across non-terminals during parsing of programs [31]. Our goal is quite different, namely, specification of space-efficient streaming algorithms resulting in different design choices: rules are regular (and not context-free), there are no tests on attributes, and even though the splitting of the stream using *split* and *iter* imparts a hierarchical structure to the input stream as parse-trees do, in the QRE $op(f, g)$, the computation of f and g can impart *different* hierarchical structures to the same input stream.

Quantitative Analysis. The notion of *regularity* for mapping strings to cost values is introduced in [5] using the model of *cost register automata* and shown to coincide with MSO-definable graph transformations [16] using the theory of tree transducers [4,22]. Section 4 shows that the expressiveness of QREs without the streaming composition operator coincides with this class using the model of streaming string-to-tree transducers. Note that in this model, the control-flow does not involve any tests on the registers, but cost values can be combined by arbitrary operations. In contrast, models such as register machines and data automata allow tests, but analyzability typically limits the set of arithmetic operations allowed on data values (for example, in data languages, only equality over data values is allowed) [10,11,25].

There is a growing literature in formal methods on extending algorithms for verification and synthesis of finite-state systems from temporal correctness requirements to quantitative properties [14,21]. Typically, the system is modeled as a state-transition graph with costs associated with transitions, the cost of an execution is an aggregation of costs of transitions it contains (for example, maximum or limit-average for an infinite execution), and the analysis problem corresponds to checking that the minimum or maximum of the costs of all executions does not exceed a threshold. In contrast, we are analyzing a single execution, but QREs are significantly more expressive than the properties considered in quantitative verification literature.

6 Conclusion

Contributions. In summary, we have argued that suitably generalized versions of the classical regular operators, in conjunction with arithmetic operators for combining costs, and the streaming composition operation, provide an appealing foundation for specifying quantitative properties of data streams in a modular fashion. This paper makes the following contributions:

1. The idea of **regular programming** allows the programmer to specify the processing of a data stream in a modular way by considering different cases and breaking up the stream into substreams using the constructs of *else*, *split*, and *iter*.
2. The language of **quantitative regular expressions** integrates regular constructs and the streaming composition operation, with cost types and combinators in a generic manner, and with a set of typing rules designed to achieve a trade-off between expressiveness and efficiency of evaluation and analysis.
3. The compilation of quantitative regular expressions into an efficient streaming implementation, and in particular, an **incremental, constant-space, linear-time, single pass streaming algorithm** for QREs with the numerical operators of sum, difference, minimum, maximum, and averaging.
4. **Expressiveness results** establishing the relationship between QREs and the class of regular functions defined using the machine model of cost register automata and MSO-definable string-to-tree transformations.

Future Work. We are currently working on an implementation of the proposed language for specifying flow-based routing policies in network switches. We also want to explore applications to the quantitative monitoring of executions of cyber-physical systems, and in particular, for analyzing simulations of hybrid systems models for robustness measures [37]. In terms of design of space-efficient data structures, in this paper we have considered only the operations of sum, difference, minimum, maximum, and averaging, for which each term can be summarized in constant space. In future work, we want to consider more challenging aggregate operators such as medians and frequency moments, for which sub-linear-space streaming algorithms are possible only if answers can be approximate.

References

1. Abadi, D., Carney, D., Çetintemel, U., Cherniack, M., Convey, C., Lee, S., Stonebraker, M., Tatbul, N., Zdonik, S.: Aurora: a new model and architecture for data stream management. VLDB J. **12**(2), 120–139 (2003)
2. Alon, N., Matias, Y., Szegedy, M.: The space complexity of approximating the frequency moments. In: Proceedings of the 28th Annual Symposium on Theory of Computing, STOC 1996, pp. 20–29. ACM (1996)
3. Alur, R., Černý, P.: Streaming transducers for algorithmic verification of single-pass list-processing programs. In: Proceedings of the 38th Annual Symposium on Principles of Programming Languages, POPL 2011, pp. 599–610. ACM (2011)

4. Alur, R., D'Antoni, L.: Streaming tree transducers. In: Czumaj, A., Mehlhorn, K., Pitts, A., Wattenhofer, R. (eds.) ICALP 2012, Part II. LNCS, vol. 7392, pp. 42–53. Springer, Heidelberg (2012)
5. Alur, R., D'Antoni, L., Deshmukh, J., Raghothaman, M., Yuan, Y.: Regular functions and cost register automata. In: 28th Annual Symposium on Logic in Computer Science, pp. 13–22 (2013)
6. Alur, R., D'Antoni, L., Raghothaman, M.: DReX: a declarative language for efficiently evaluating regular string transformations. In: Proceedings of the 42nd Annual Symposium on Principles of Programming Languages, POPL 2015, pp. 125–137. ACM (2015)
7. Alur, R., Freilich, A., Raghothaman, M.: Regular combinators for string transformations. In: The 29th Annual Symposium on Logic in Computer Science of Proceedings of the Joint Meeting of the 23rd Annual Conference on Computer Science Logic, CSL-LICS 2014, pp. 9:1–9:10. ACM (2014)
8. Arasu, A., Babu, S., Widom, J.: CQL: a language for continuous queries over streams and relations. In: Lausen, G., Suciu, D. (eds.) DBPL 2003. LNCS, vol. 2921, pp. 1–19. Springer, Heidelberg (2004)
9. Babu, S., Widom, J.: Continuous queries over data streams. SIGMOD Rec. **30**(3), 109–120 (2001)
10. Björklund, H., Schwentick, T.: On notions of regularity for data languages. Theoret. Comput. Sci. **411**(4–5), 702–715 (2010)
11. Bojańczyk, M., Muscholl, A., Schwentick, T., Segoufin, L.: Two-variable logic on data trees, XML reasoning. J. ACM **56**(3), 13:1–13:48 (2009)
12. Book, R., Even, S., Greibach, S., Ott, G.: Ambiguity in graphs and expressions. IEEE Trans. Comput. **20**(2), 149–153 (1971)
13. Brüggemann-Klein, A.: Regular expressions into finite automata. In: Simon, I. (ed.) LATIN 1992. LNCS, vol. 583, pp. 87–98. Springer, Heidelberg (1992)
14. Chatterjee, K., Doyen, L., Henzinger, T.: Quantitative languages. ACM Trans. Comput. Logic **11**(4), 23:1–23:38 (2010)
15. Chen, Y., Davidson, S., Zheng, Y.: An efficient XPath query processor for XML streams. In: Proceedings of the 22nd International Conference on Data Engineering, ICDE 2006. IEEE Computer Society (2006)
16. Courcelle, B.: Monadic second-order definable graph transductions: a survey. Theoret. Comput. Sci. **126**(1), 53–75 (1994)
17. D'Antoni, L., Veanes, M.: Equivalence of extended symbolic finite transducers. In: Sharygina, N., Veith, H. (eds.) CAV 2013. LNCS, vol. 8044, pp. 624–639. Springer, Heidelberg (2013)
18. D'Antoni, L., Veanes, M.: Minimization of symbolic automata. In: Proceedings of the 41st Symposium on Principles of Programming Languages, POPL 2014, pp. 541–553. ACM (2014)
19. D'Antoni, L., Veanes, M., Livshits, B., Molnar, D.: Fast: a transducer-based language for tree manipulation. In: Proceedings of the 35th Conference on Programming Language Design and Implementation, PLDI 2014, pp. 384–394. ACM (2014)
20. de Moura, L., Bjørner, N.: Satisfiability modulo theories: introduction and applications. Commun. ACM **54**(9), 69–77 (2011)
21. Droste, M., Kuich, W., Vogler, H.: Handbook of Weighted Automata, 1st edn. Springer, Heidelberg (2009)
22. Engelfriet, J., Maneth, S.: Macro tree transducers, attribute grammars, and MSO definable tree translations. Inf. Comput. **154**(1), 34–91 (1999)
23. Engelfriet, J., Vogler, H.: Macro tree transducers. J. Comput. Syst. Sci. **31**(1), 71–146 (1985)

24. Hooimeijer, P., Livshits, B., Molnar, D., Saxena, P., Veanes, M.: Fast and precise sanitizer analysis with BEK. In: Proceedings of the 20th USENIX Conference on Security, SEC 2011. USENIX Association (2011)
25. Kaminski, M., Francez, N.: Finite-memory automata. Theoret. Comput. Sci. **134**(2), 329–363 (1994)
26. Koch, C.: XML stream processing. In: Liu, L., Özsu, M.T. (eds.) Encyclopedia of Database Systems, pp. 3634–3637. Springer, Heidelberg (2009)
27. Kulkarni, S., Bhagat, N., Fu, M., Kedigehalli, V., Kellogg, C., Mittal, S., Patel, J., Ramasamy, K., Taneja, S., Heron, T.: Stream processing at scale. In: Proceedings of the ACM SIGMOD International Conference on Management of Data, SIGMOD 2015, pp. 239–250. ACM (2015)
28. Mozafari, B., Zeng, K., Zaniolo, C.: High-performance complex event processing over XML streams. In: Proceedings of the ACM SIGMOD International Conference on Management of Data, SIGMOD 2012, pp. 253–264. ACM (2012)
29. Munro, I., Paterson, M.: Selection and sorting with limited storage. In: Proceedings of the 19th Annual Symposium on Foundations of Computer Science, SFCS 1978, pp. 253–258. IEEE Computer Society (1978)
30. Muthukrishnan, S.: Data streams: algorithms and applications. Found. Trends Theoret. Comput. Sci. **1**(2), 117–236 (2005)
31. Paakki, J.: Attribute grammar paradigms–a high-level methodology in language implementation. ACM Comput. Surv. **27**(2), 196–255 (1995)
32. Roşu, G.: An effective algorithm for the membership problem for extended regular expressions. In: Seidl, H. (ed.) FOSSACS 2007. LNCS, vol. 4423, pp. 332–345. Springer, Heidelberg (2007)
33. Sipser, M.: Introduction to the Theory of Computation, 3rd edn. Cengage Learning, Boston (2012)
34. Stearns, R., Hunt, H.: On the equivalence and containment problems for unambiguous regular expressions, grammars, and automata. In: Proceedings of the 22nd Annual Symposium on Foundations of Computer Science, pp. 74–81. IEEE Computer Society (1981)
35. Vaziri, M., Tardieu, O., Rabbah, R., Suter, P., Hirzel, M.: Stream processing with a spreadsheet. In: Jones, R. (ed.) ECOOP 2014. LNCS, vol. 8586, pp. 360–384. Springer, Heidelberg (2014)
36. Veanes, M., Hooimeijer, P., Livshits, B., Molnar, D., Bjorner, N.: Symbolic finite state transducers: algorithms and applications. In: Proceedings of the 39th Annual Symposium on Principles of Programming Languages, pp. 137–150. ACM (2012)
37. Zutshi, A., Sankaranarayanan, S., Deshmukh, J., Kapinski, J., Jin, X.: Falsification of safety properties for closed loop control systems. In: Proceedings of the 18th International Conference on Hybrid Systems: Computation and Control, HSCC 2015, pp. 299–300. ACM (2015)

Formalizing Single-Assignment Program Verification: An Adaptation-Complete Approach

Cláudio Belo Lourenço(✉), Maria João Frade, and Jorge Sousa Pinto

HASLab/INESC TEC, Universidade do Minho, Braga, Portugal
{belolourenco,mjf,jsp}@di.uminho.pt

Abstract. Deductive verification tools typically rely on the conversion of code to a single-assignment (SA) form. In this paper we formalize program verification based on the translation of *While* programs annotated with loop invariants into a dynamic single-assignment language with a dedicated iterating construct, and the subsequent generation of compact, indeed linear-size, verification conditions. Soundness and completeness proofs are given for the entire workflow, including the translation of annotated programs to SA form. The formalization is based on a program logic that we show to be *adaptation-complete*. Although this important property has not, as far as we know, been established for any existing program verification tool, we believe that adaptation-completeness is one of the major motivations for the use of SA form as an intermediate language. Our results here show that indeed this allows for the tools to achieve the maximum degree of adaptation when handling subprograms.

1 Introduction

In the last years deductive program verification has reached a stage of a certain maturity, to the point that a number of tools are now available allowing users to prove properties of programs written in real-world languages like C, Java, or SPARK [3,6,10,25]. Deductive techniques attempt to establish the correctness of a software system with respect to a specification, usually given as a set of *contracts* expressed in first-order logic. Their precision depends on information provided by the user in the form of *annotations*, in particular *loop invariants*.

Three trends have characterized the development of modern program verifiers: first, they employ Satisfiability Modulo Theories (SMT) solvers to check the validity of first-order formulas. The nuclear component is a Verification Conditions Generator (VCGen), that takes as input a program and a specification, and produces a set of first-order proof obligations that are sent to a solver. If all the conditions are valid, then the program is correct. The second trend is that deductive verification tools are usually *generic*, based on programming languages tailored for verification. Rather than producing from scratch a dedicated verifier, programs of a particular language are translated into the intermediate language of the tool, together with a background encoding of the relevant aspects of that language. Two widely used generic verifiers are Boogie [4] and Why3 [13].

P. Thiemann (Ed.): ESOP 2016, LNCS 9632, pp. 41–67, 2016.
DOI: 10.1007/978-3-662-49498-1_3

Finally, and this is the subject of the present paper, modern tools employ internally a *Single-Assignment* (SA) representation of the code [11], in which variables may not be assigned after they have been read or written. Not only are SA branching programs easier to encode logically, but its use also solves a fundamental inefficiency issue. Verification conditions generated from standard imperative code may be of *exponential size* in the size of the programs, which destroys any hope of effectively verifying reasonably-sized programs. However, Flanagan and Saxe [14] have shown that conversion of the code to SA form allows for the generation of quadratic size VCs (a technique that achieves conditions of linear-size with respect to the SA program was later proposed [5]). Other advantages have to do with the fact that intermediate values of computations are never lost: when an instruction like $x := x + 1$ is executed, one variable will store the initial value of x, and a new variable will store its new value. Specification languages like ACSL, for ANSI-C [7], often allow the value of a variable at a given program point to be used in assertions. In an SA setting this amounts to simply fetching the adequate "version variable". This also means that *continuous invariants* (that are not relevant for a loop but may be required after it) are transported automatically, and do not have to be explicitly included.

On the theoretical side, the foundations of program verification have traditionally lied in two different frameworks: Dijkstra's predicate transformers for a *guarded commands* language [12] and program logics, like Hoare logic [17] and separation logic [26]. Guarded commands have been used as an intermediate language in tools like ESC/Java [22] and more recently the Boogie generic verifier. Many pragmatic aspects of program verification have been addressed and described in this setting, in particular the generation of efficiently provable Verification Conditions (VCs) and the treatment of unstructured programs [5,14]. The program logic tradition on the other hand, which is based on separate operational and axiomatic semantics of programming languages, has allowed for the study of properties like soundness and (relative) completeness of Hoare logic with respect to the standard semantics of a While language [2], an approach that has been extended with the treatment of pointers and aliasing in separation logic.

An important issue is that of *modular verification* and proof reuse. Ideally, one produces a separate proof of correctness for each occurrence (or call) of a subprogram C inside a program P, and then *adapts* the proved specification of C to different 'local' specifications. A formalism that always allows for this to be done is said to be *adaptation-complete* [20]; in its original formulation Hoare logic is not adaptation-complete. This is a problem in the presence of recursive procedures, since it leads to incompleteness of the program logic itself, but it is also a problem for the implementation of tools where the correctness of each procedure is proved once and for all with respect to a *contract* that must be adapted to the local context of each call to it. Our work shows that adaptation-completeness is a natural property of reasoning in the single-assignment setting.

Contributions. In this paper we formalize a verification technique for *While* programs annotated with invariants, based on their conversion to an intermediate SA form. Verification tools convert programs to single-assignment form internally and profit from this in various ways, in particular to achieve efficiency and to handle subprograms – our technique is a minimal model of such a tool. It relies on (i) a novel notion of single-assignment program that supports loops annotated with invariants; (ii) a notion of translation of *While* programs annotated with loop invariants (resp. Hoare triples containing such programs) into SA programs (resp. Hoare triples containing SA programs); (iii) a Hoare-style logic for these programs; and (iv) a VCGen generating *linear-size* verification conditions for Hoare triples containing SA programs. The entire workflow is proved to be sound and complete – in particular, we show how invariants annotated in the initial *While* program are translated into the intermediate SA form in a way that guarantees the completeness of the approach. This means that if the invariants annotated in the original program are appropriate for showing its correctness, then the verification of the translated SA program will be successful.

An adaptation-complete variant of the logic is also proposed, by adding to the inference system a dedicated consequence rule with a simple side condition. This new consequence rule is restricted to reasoning about triples in which the program does not assign any variable occurring free in the precondition; since the Hoare logic for SA programs propagates preconditions forward in a way that preserves this property, the rule can be applied at any point in a derivation. It provides the highest degree of adaptation, without the need to check any additional complicated conditions or rules, as used to be the case in adaptation-complete presentations of Hoare logic [1,2,20].

As an added bonus, this paper can also be seen as bridging a gap between two different theoretical traditions – the guarded commands/predicate transformers setting, where the use of single-assignment form was first introduced for the sake of proof efficiency, and the Hoare logic tradition, that formalizes reasoning with loop invariants based on a standard interpretation of imperative programs.

The paper is organized as follows: Sect. 2 contains background material. In Sect. 3 we introduce a language of iterating SA programs: loops are annotated with invariants; they have single-assignment bodies; and a *renaming* allows for the values of the initial variables to be updated between iterations. We propose a Hoare-style partial correctness program logic for this language in Sect. 4; its inference system admits only derivations guided by the annotated loop invariants, following a forward-propagation strategy. We also give an algorithm that generates compact conditions (in the sense of Flanagan and Saxe [14]) for a given Hoare triple, and then optimize it to generate *linear-sized* VCs. The next sections contain our main results. We first consider the verification workflow based on the translation of annotated While programs to the SA language. We identify, in Sect. 5, the semantic requirements that are expected from such a translation. The workflow is validated by showing that the generation of VCs from the SA form is sound and complete for the verification of the initial program (a concrete translation is given in the appendix, together with the proof that it meets the requirements). In Sect. 6 we show how the program logic can be extended with a special consequence rule that makes it *adaptation-complete*. Finally Sect. 7 discusses related work and Sect. 8 concludes the paper.

2 Hoare Logic

We briefly review Hoare logic for While programs. The logic deals with the notion of correctness of a program w.r.t. a *specification.*

Syntax. We consider a typical While language whose commands $C \in \mathbf{Comm}$ are defined over a set of variables $x \in \mathbf{Var}$ in the following way:

$$C \ ::= \ \mathbf{skip} \ | \ x := e \ | \ C\,;C \ | \ \mathbf{if}\ b\ \mathbf{then}\ C\ \mathbf{else}\ C \ | \ \mathbf{while}\ b\ \mathbf{do}\ C$$

We will not fix the language of program expressions $e \in \mathbf{Exp}$ and Boolean expressions $b \in \mathbf{Exp^{bool}}$, both constructed over variables from $\mathbf{Var}$ (a standard instantiation is for $\mathbf{Exp}$ to be a language of integer expressions and $\mathbf{Exp^{bool}}$ constructed from comparison operators over $\mathbf{Exp}$, together with Boolean operators). In addition to expressions and commands, we need formulas that express properties of particular states of the program. Program assertions $\phi, \theta, \psi \in \mathbf{Assert}$ (preconditions and postconditions in particular) are formulas of a first-order language obtained as an expansion of $\mathbf{Exp^{bool}}$.

We also require a class of formulas for specifying the behaviour of programs. Specifications are pairs (ϕ, ψ), with $\phi, \psi \in \mathbf{Assert}$ intended as precondition and postcondition for a program. The precondition is an assertion that is assumed to hold when the program is executed, whereas the postcondition is required to hold when its execution stops. A *Hoare triple*, written as $\{\phi\}\,C\,\{\psi\}$, expresses the fact that the program C conforms to the specification (ϕ, ψ).

Semantics. We will consider an *interpretation structure* $\mathcal{M} = (D, I)$ for the vocabulary describing the concrete syntax of program expressions. This structure provides an interpretation domain D as well as a concrete interpretation of constants and operators, given by I. The interpretation of expressions depends on a *state*, which is a function that maps each variable into its value. We will write $\Sigma = \mathbf{Var} \to D$ for the set of states (note that this approach extends to a multi-sorted setting by letting Σ become a *generic function space*). For $s \in \Sigma$, $s[x \mapsto a]$ will denote the state that maps x to a and any other variable y to $s(y)$. The interpretation of $e \in \mathbf{Exp}$ will be given by a function $[\![e]\!]_{\mathcal{M}} : \Sigma \to D$, and the interpretation of $b \in \mathbf{Exp^{bool}}$ will be given by $[\![b]\!]_{\mathcal{M}} : \Sigma \to \{\mathbf{F}, \mathbf{T}\}$. This reflects our assumption that an expression has a value at every state (evaluation always terminates without error) and that expression evaluation never changes the state (the language is free of *side effects*). For the interpretation of assertions we take the usual interpretation of first-order formulas, noting two facts: since assertions build on the language of program expressions their interpretation also depends on $\mathcal{M}$ (possibly extended to account for user-defined predicates and functions), and states from Σ can be used as *variable assignments* in the interpretation of assertions. The interpretation of the assertion $\phi \in \mathbf{Assert}$ is then given by $[\![\phi]\!]_{\mathcal{M}} : \Sigma \to \{\mathbf{F}, \mathbf{T}\}$, and we will write $s \models \phi$ as a shorthand for $[\![\phi]\!]_{\mathcal{M}}(s) = \mathbf{T}$. In the rest of the paper we will omit the $\mathcal{M}$ subscripts for the sake of readability; the interpretation structure will be left implicit.

1. $\langle \mathbf{skip}, s \rangle \rightsquigarrow s$
2. $\langle x := e, s \rangle \rightsquigarrow s[x \mapsto [\![e]\!](s)]$
3. if $\langle C_1, s \rangle \rightsquigarrow s'$ and $\langle C_2, s' \rangle \rightsquigarrow s''$, then $\langle C_1 \,;\, C_2, s \rangle \rightsquigarrow s''$
4. if $[\![b]\!](s) = \mathbf{T}$ and $\langle C_t, s \rangle \rightsquigarrow s'$, then $\langle \mathbf{if}\ b\ \mathbf{then}\ C_t\ \mathbf{else}\ C_f, s \rangle \rightsquigarrow s'$
5. if $[\![b]\!](s) = \mathbf{F}$ and $\langle C_f, s \rangle \rightsquigarrow s'$, then $\langle \mathbf{if}\ b\ \mathbf{then}\ C_t\ \mathbf{else}\ C_f, s \rangle \rightsquigarrow s'$
6. if $[\![b]\!](s) = \mathbf{T}$, $\langle C, s \rangle \rightsquigarrow s'$ and $\langle \mathbf{while}\ b\ \mathbf{do}\ C, s' \rangle \rightsquigarrow s''$, then $\langle \mathbf{while}\ b\ \mathbf{do}\ C, s \rangle \rightsquigarrow s''$
7. if $[\![b]\!](s) = \mathbf{F}$, then $\langle \mathbf{while}\ b\ \mathbf{do}\ C, s \rangle \rightsquigarrow s$

Fig. 1. Evaluation semantics for *While* programs

For commands, we consider a standard operational, natural style semantics, based on a deterministic *evaluation relation* $\rightsquigarrow \subseteq \mathbf{Comm} \times \Sigma \times \Sigma$ (which again depends on an implicit interpretation of program expressions). We will write $\langle C, s \rangle \rightsquigarrow s'$ to denote the fact that if C is executed in the initial state s, then its execution terminates, and the final state is s'. The usual inductive definition of this relation is given in Fig. 1.

The intuitive meaning of the triple $\{\phi\}\, C\, \{\psi\}$ is that if the program C is executed in an initial state in which the precondition ϕ is true, then either execution of C does not terminate or if it does, the postcondition ψ will be true in the final state. Because termination is not guaranteed, this is called a *partial correctness* specification. Let us define formally the validity of a Hoare triple.

Definition 1. *The Hoare triple* $\{\phi\}\, C\, \{\psi\}$ *is said to be* valid, *denoted* $\models \{\phi\}\, C\, \{\psi\}$, *whenever for all* $s, s' \in \Sigma$, *if* $s \models \phi$ *and* $\langle C, s \rangle \rightsquigarrow s'$, *then* $s' \models \psi$.

Hoare Calculus. Hoare [17] introduced an inference system for reasoning about Hoare triples, which we will call system H - see Fig. 2 (left). Note that the system contains one rule (conseq) whose application is guarded by first-order conditions. We will consider that reasoning in this system takes place in the context of the *complete theory* Th($\mathcal{M}$) of the implicit structure $\mathcal{M}$, so that when constructing derivations in H one simply checks, when applying the (conseq) rule, whether the side conditions are elements of Th($\mathcal{M}$). We will write $\vdash_{\mathsf{H}} \{\phi\}\, C\, \{\psi\}$ to denote the fact that the triple is derivable in this system with Th($\mathcal{M}$).

System H is sound w.r.t. the semantics of Hoare triples; it is also complete as long as the assertion language is sufficiently expressive (a result due to Cook [9]). One way to ensure this is to force the existence of a *strongest postcondition* for every command and assertion. Let $C \in \mathbf{Comm}$ and $\phi \in \mathbf{Assert}$, and denote by post(ϕ, C) the set of states $\{s' \in \Sigma \mid \langle C, s \rangle \rightsquigarrow s'$ for some $s \in \Sigma$ such that $[\![\phi]\!](s) = \mathbf{T}\}$. In what follows we will assume that the assertion language **Assert** is *expressive* with respect to the command language **Comm** and interpretation structure $\mathcal{M}$, i.e., for every $\phi \in \mathbf{Assert}$ and $C \in \mathbf{Comm}$ there exists $\psi \in \mathbf{Assert}$ such that $s \models \psi$ iff $s \in \text{post}(\phi, C)$ for any $s \in \Sigma$. The reader is directed to [2] for details.

Proposition 1 (Soundness of System H). *Let* $C \in \mathbf{Comm}$ *and* $\phi, \psi \in \mathbf{Assert}$. *If* $\vdash_{\mathsf{H}} \{\phi\}\, C\, \{\psi\}$, *then* $\models \{\phi\}\, C\, \{\psi\}$.

H		Hg
$\dfrac{}{\{\phi\}\,\mathbf{skip}\,\{\phi\}}$	(skip)	$\dfrac{}{\{\phi\}\,\mathbf{skip}\,\{\psi\}}$ if $\phi \to \psi$
$\dfrac{}{\{\psi[e/x]\}\,x := e\,\{\psi\}}$	(assign)	$\dfrac{}{\{\phi\}\,x := e\,\{\psi\}}$ if $\phi \to \psi[e/x]$
$\dfrac{\{\phi\}\,C_1\,\{\theta\} \quad \{\theta\}\,C_2\,\{\psi\}}{\{\phi\}\,C_1\,;\,C_2\,\{\psi\}}$	(seq)	$\dfrac{\{\phi\}\,C_1\,\{\theta\} \quad \{\theta\}\,C_2\,\{\psi\}}{\{\phi\}\,C_1\,;\,C_2\,\{\psi\}}$
$\dfrac{\{\phi \wedge b\}\,C_t\,\{\psi\} \quad \{\phi \wedge \neg b\}\,C_f\,\{\psi\}}{\{\phi\}\,\mathbf{if}\ b\ \mathbf{then}\ C_t\ \mathbf{else}\ C_f\,\{\psi\}}$	(if)	$\dfrac{\{\phi \wedge b\}\,C_t\,\{\psi\} \quad \{\phi \wedge \neg b\}\,C_f\,\{\psi\}}{\{\phi\}\,\mathbf{if}\ b\ \mathbf{then}\ C_t\ \mathbf{else}\ C_f\,\{\psi\}}$
$\dfrac{\{\theta \wedge b\}\,C\,\{\theta\}}{\{\theta\}\,\mathbf{while}\ b\ \mathbf{do}\ C\,\{\theta \wedge \neg b\}}$	(while)	$\dfrac{\{\theta \wedge b\}\,C\,\{\theta\}}{\{\phi\}\,\mathbf{while}\ b\ \mathbf{do}\,\{\theta\}\,C\,\{\psi\}}$ if $\phi \to \theta$ and $\theta \wedge \neg b \to \psi$
$\dfrac{\{\phi\}\,C\,\{\psi\}}{\{\phi'\}\,C\,\{\psi'\}}$ if $\phi' \to \phi$ and $\psi \to \psi'$	(conseq)	

Fig. 2. Systems H (left) and Hg (right)

Proposition 2 (Completeness of System H). *Let* $C \in$ **Comm** *and* $\phi, \psi \in$ **Assert**. *With* **Assert** *expressive in the above sense, if* $\models \{\phi\}\,C\,\{\psi\}$, *then* $\vdash_{\mathsf{H}} \{\phi\}\,C\,\{\psi\}$.

The sets of *variables occurring* and *assigned* in the program C will be given by $\mathsf{Vars}(C)$ and $\mathsf{Asgn}(C)$ respectively; $\mathsf{FV}(\phi)$ denotes the set of free variables occurring in ϕ (all are defined in the obvious way). We will write $\phi \# C$ to denote $\mathsf{Asgn}(C) \cap \mathsf{FV}(\phi) = \emptyset$, i.e. C does not assign variables occurring free in ϕ.

Lemma 1. *Let* $\phi, \psi \in$ **Assert** *and* $C \in$ **Comm**, *such that* $\phi \# C$. *If* $\vdash_{\mathsf{H}} \{\phi\}\,C\,\{\psi\}$, *then* $\vdash_{\mathsf{H}} \{\phi\}\,C\,\{\phi \wedge \psi\}$.

Goal-directed Logic. We introduce a syntactic class **AComm** of *annotated programs*, which differs from **Comm** only in the case of while commands, which are of the form **while** b **do** $\{\theta\}\,C$ where the assertion θ is a loop invariant annotation (see for instance [15]). Annotations do not affect the operational semantics. Note that for $C \in$ **AComm**, $\mathsf{Vars}(C)$ includes the free variables of the annotations in C. In what follows we will use the auxiliary function $\lfloor \cdot \rfloor$: **AComm** $\to$ **Comm** that erases all annotations from a program (defined in the obvious way).

In Fig. 2 (right) we present system Hg, a *goal-directed* version of Hoare logic for triples containing annotated programs. This system is intended for mechanical construction of derivations: loop invariants are not invented at this point but taken from the annotations, and there is no ambiguity in the choice of rule to apply, since a consequence rule is not present. The possible derivations of the same triple in Hg differ only in the intermediate assertions used. The following can be proved by induction on the derivation of $\vdash_{\mathsf{Hg}} \{\phi\}\,C\,\{\psi\}$.

$\{n \geq 0 \wedge n_{aux} = n\}$ Fact $\{f = n_{aux}!\}$
(seq)
1. $\{n \geq 0 \wedge n_{aux} = n\}\, f := 1; i := 1\, \{n \geq 0 \wedge n_{aux} = n \wedge f = 1 \wedge i = 1\}$
   (seq)
   1. (assign) $\{n \geq 0 \wedge n_{aux} = n\}\, f := 1\, \{n \geq 0 \wedge n_{aux} = n \wedge f = 1\}$
   2. (assign) $\{n \geq 0 \wedge n_{aux} = n \wedge f = 1\}\, i := 1\, \{n \geq 0 \wedge n_{aux} = n \wedge f = 1 \wedge i = 1\}$
2. $\{n \geq 0 \wedge n_{aux} = n \wedge f = 1 \wedge i = 1\}$ **while** $i \leq n$ **do** $\{f = (i-1)! \wedge i \leq n+1 \wedge n_{aux} = n\}\, f := f * i; i := i + 1\, \{f = n_{aux}!\}$
   (while)
   1. $\{f = (i-1)! \wedge i \leq n+1 \wedge n_{aux} = n \wedge i \leq n\}\, f := f * i; i := i+1\, \{f = (i-1)! \wedge i \leq n+1 \wedge n_{aux} = n\}$
      (seq)
      1. (assign) $\{f = (i-1)! \wedge i \leq n+1 \wedge n_{aux} = n \wedge i \leq n\}\, f := f * i\, \{f = (i-1)! * i \wedge i \leq n+1 \wedge n_{aux} = n \wedge i \leq n\}$
      2. (assign) $\{f = (i-1)! * i \wedge i \leq n+1 \wedge n_{aux} = n \wedge i \leq n\}\, i := i+1\, \{f = (i-1)! \wedge i \leq n+1 \wedge n_{aux} = n\}$

Side conditions for application of the (assign) rules:
- $n \geq 0 \wedge n_{aux} = n \implies (n \geq 0 \wedge n_{aux} = n \wedge f = 1)[1/f]$
- $n \geq 0 \wedge n_{aux} = n \wedge f = 1 \implies (n \geq 0 \wedge n_{aux} = n \wedge f = 1 \wedge i = 1)[1/i]$
- $f = (i-1)! \wedge i \leq n+1 \wedge n_{aux} = n \wedge i \leq n \implies (f = (i-1)! * i \wedge i \leq n+1 \wedge n_{aux} = n \wedge i \leq n)[f*i/f]$
- $f = (i-1)! * i \wedge i \leq n+1 \wedge n_{aux} = n \wedge i \leq n \implies (f = (i-1)! \wedge i \leq n+1 \wedge n_{aux} = n)[i+1/i]$

Side conditions for application of the (while) rule:
- $n \geq 0 \wedge n_{aux} = n \wedge f = 1 \wedge i = 1 \implies f = (i-1)! \wedge i \leq n+1 \wedge n_{aux} = n$
- $f = (i-1)! \wedge i \leq n+1 \wedge n_{aux} = n \wedge \neg(i \leq n) \implies f = n_{aux}!$

Fig. 3. Example derivation in system Hg

Proposition 3 (Soundness of Hg). *Let* $C \in$ **AComm** *and* $\phi, \psi \in$ **Assert**. *If* $\vdash_{\mathsf{Hg}} \{\phi\}\, C\, \{\psi\}$ *then* $\vdash_{\mathsf{H}} \{\phi\}\, \lfloor C \rfloor\, \{\psi\}$.

The converse implication does not hold, since the annotated invariants may be inadequate for deriving the triple. Instead we need the following definition:

Definition 2. *Let* $C \in$ **AComm** *and* $\phi, \psi \in$ **Assert**. *We say that* C *is* correctly-annotated *w.r.t.* (ϕ, ψ) *if* $\vdash_{\mathsf{H}} \{\phi\}\, \lfloor C \rfloor\, \{\psi\}$ *implies* $\vdash_{\mathsf{Hg}} \{\phi\}\, C\, \{\psi\}$.

The following lemma states the admissibility of the consequence rule in Hg.

Lemma 2. *Let* $C \in$ **AComm** *and* $\phi, \psi, \phi', \psi' \in$ **Assert** *such that* $\vdash_{\mathsf{Hg}} \{\phi\}\, C\, \{\psi\}$, $\models \phi' \rightarrow \phi$, *and* $\models \psi \rightarrow \psi'$. *Then* $\vdash_{\mathsf{Hg}} \{\phi'\}\, C\, \{\psi'\}$.

Consider the factorial program shown in Fig. 4a. The counter i ranges from 1 to n and the accumulator f contains at each step the factorial of $i-1$. The program is annotated with an appropriate loop invariant; it is easy to show that it is correct with respect to the specification $(n \geq 0 \wedge n_{aux} = n, f = n_{aux}!)$. We show in Fig. 3 a derivation of this triple in system Hg. Note that the axioms $0! = 1$ and $n! = n * (n-1)!$ are required to prove the side conditions.

It is possible to write an algorithm, known as a verification conditions generator, that simply collects the side conditions of a derivation without actually constructing it. Hg is agnostic with respect to a strategy for propagating assertions, but the VCGen necessarily imposes one such strategy [15].

Exponential Explosion. To understand the exponential explosion problem mentioned in Sect. 1, consider a program consisting of a sequence of n conditional statements: since each such statement doubles the number of execution paths, the program has 2^n paths. Consider now the (if) rule of Hoare logic. If one uses a backward propagation strategy, one starts with a given postcondition ψ, which will be propagated through both branches of the last conditional, to produce two assertions ϕ_t, ϕ_f, both of which may contain occurrences of ψ. These will be combined in an assertion ϕ, for instance $(b \to \phi_t) \wedge (\neg b \to \phi_f)$, where ψ may occur twice. The (seq) rule will then use ϕ as postcondition for the prefix of the program, repeating the process and generating the exponential pattern. A similar exponential pattern may be generated by duplicating variables rather than assertions, in a sequence of assignment statements whose right-hand sides contain multiple occurrences of the same variable. For instance propagating backwards an assertion containing a single occurrence of z through the sequence $y := x + x\,;\ z := y + y$ produces a formula containing 4 occurrences of x.

Adaptation Incompleteness. Consider a block of code that has been proved correct with respect to a specification. Take for instance the triple $\{n \geq 0 \wedge n_{aux} = n\}\,\mathsf{Fact}\,\{f = n_{aux}!\}$. The specification makes use of an *auxiliary variable* n_{aux}. These variables do not have a special status; they are simply not used as program variables, and can be safely employed for writing specifications relating the pre-state and post-state. According to the above, the program Fact computes the factorial of the *initial* value of n. Now suppose Fact is part of a bigger program P, and one would like to establish the validity of the triple $\{n = K\}\,\mathsf{Fact}\,\{f = K!\}$, with K a positive constant. *Adaptation-completeness* would mean that one would be able to derive this from the specification of Fact without constructing a dedicated proof – indeed, it should not even be necessary to know the implementation of Fact, since it has already been proved correct. The (conseq) rule of Hoare logic is meant precisely for this, but it cannot be applied here, since both side conditions are clearly *not valid*. This shows that system H is not adaptation-complete:

$$\frac{\{n \geq 0 \wedge n_{aux} = n\}\,\mathsf{Fact}\,\{f = n_{aux}!\}}{\{n = K\}\,\mathsf{Fact}\,\{f = K!\}} \quad \text{if} \quad \begin{array}{l} n = K \to n \geq 0 \wedge n_{aux} = n \quad \text{and} \\ f = n_{aux}! \to f = K! \end{array}$$

3 Single-Assignment Programs

Translation of code into Single-Assignment (SA) form has been part of the standard compilation pipeline for decades now; in such a program each variable is assigned at most once. The fragment $x := 10\,;\ x := x + 10$ could be translated as $x_1 := 10\,;\ x_2 := x_1 + 10$, using a different "version of x" variable for each assignment. In this paper we will use a dynamic notion of single-assignment (DSA) program [27], in which each variable may occur syntactically as the left-hand side of more than one assignment instruction, as long as it is not assigned more than once *in each execution*. For instance the fragment **if** $x > 0$ **then** $x := x + 10$ **else skip** could be translated into DSA form as

```
f := 1;
i := 1;
while i ≤ n do {f = (i − 1)! ∧ i ≤ n + 1
∧n_aux = n}
{
  f := f * i;
  i := i + 1
}
```

(a) Initial annotated program Fact

```
f1 := 1;
i1 := 1;
I
while (ia0 ≤ n) do {fa0 = (ia0 − 1)! ∧ ia0 ≤ n + 1}
{
  fa1 := fa0 * ia0;
  ia1 := ia0 + 1;
  U
}
```

(b) With blocks converted to SA form

```
f1 := 1;
i1 := 1;
for ({ia0 := i1 ; fa0 := f1}, ia0 ≤ n, {ia0 := ia1 ; fa0 := fa1}) do {fa0 = (ia0 − 1)! ∧ ia0 ≤ n + 1}
{
  fa1 := fa0 * ia0;
  ia1 := ia0 + 1
}
```

(c) Annotated single-assignment program Fact^{sa}

Fig. 4. Factorial example

if $x_0 > 0$ **then** $x_1 := x_0 + 10$ **else** $x_1 := x_0$. Note the *else* branch cannot be simply **skip**, since it is necessary to have a single version variable (in this case x_1) representing x when exiting the conditional.

In the context of the guarded commands language, it has been shown [14] that VCs for *passive programs* (essentially DSA programs without loops, where assignments are replaced with assume commands) can be generated avoiding exponential explosion. However, a single-assignment language of programs with loops, tailored for verification, does not exist. In what follows we will introduce precisely such a language, based on dynamic single-assignment form.

Definition 3. *The set* **Rnm** $\subseteq$ **Comm** *of* renamings *consists of all programs of the form* $\{x_1 := y_1 ; \ldots ; x_n := y_n\}$ *such that all* x_i *and* y_i *are distinct. The empty renaming will be written as* **skip**.

A renaming $\mathcal{R} = \{x_1 := y_1 ; \ldots ; x_n := y_n\}$ represents the finite bijection $[x_1 \mapsto y_1, \ldots, x_n \mapsto y_n]$, which we will also denote by $\mathcal{R}$. We will write $\mathsf{dom}(\mathcal{R})$ and $\mathsf{rng}(\mathcal{R})$ to denote the domain and range of $\mathcal{R}$, respectively. Furthermore, $\mathcal{R}(\phi)$ will denote the assertion that results from applying the substitution $[y_1/x_1, \ldots, y_n/x_n]$ to ϕ. Also, for $s \in \Sigma$ we define the state $\mathcal{R}(s)$ as follows: $\mathcal{R}(s)(x) = s(\mathcal{R}(x))$ if $x \in \mathsf{dom}(\mathcal{R})$, and $\mathcal{R}(s)(x) = s(x)$ otherwise.

Lemma 3. *Let* $\mathcal{R} \in$ **Rnm**, $\phi, \psi \in$ **Assert** *and* $s \in \Sigma$.

1. $\langle \mathcal{R}, s\rangle \rightsquigarrow \mathcal{R}(s)$
2. $[\![\mathcal{R}(\phi)]\!](s) = [\![\phi]\!](\mathcal{R}(s))$
3. $\models \{\phi\}\, \mathcal{R}\, \{\psi\}$ *iff* $\models \phi \rightarrow \mathcal{R}(\psi)$.

Proof. 1. By inspection on the evaluation relation. 2. By induction on the interpretation assertions. 3. Follows from 1 and 2. □

In a strict sense it is not possible to write iterating programs in DSA form. So what we propose here is a syntactically controlled violation of the single-assignment constraints that allows for structured reasoning. Loop bodies are still SA blocks, but two renamings, responsible for propagating the values inside, outside and between iterations, are free of single-assignment restrictions.

Definition 4. *Let* $\mathbf{AComm}^{\text{SA}}$ *be the class of* annotated single-assignment programs. *Its abstract syntax is defined by*

$$C \ ::= \ \mathbf{skip} \ | \ x := e \ | \ C\,;C \ | \ \mathbf{if}\ b\ \mathbf{then}\ C\ \mathbf{else}\ C \ | \ \mathbf{for}\ (\mathcal{I}, b, \mathcal{U})\ \mathbf{do}\,\{\theta\}\,C$$

where:

- $\mathbf{skip} \in \mathbf{AComm}^{\text{SA}}$
- $x := e \in \mathbf{AComm}^{\text{SA}}$ *if* $x \notin \mathsf{Vars}(e)$
- $C_1\,; C_2 \in \mathbf{AComm}^{\text{SA}}$ *if* $C_1, C_2 \in \mathbf{AComm}^{\text{SA}}$ *and* $\mathsf{Vars}(C_1) \cap \mathsf{Asgn}(C_2) = \emptyset$
- $\mathbf{if}\ b\ \mathbf{then}\ C_t\ \mathbf{else}\ C_f \in \mathbf{AComm}^{\text{SA}}$ *if* $C_t, C_f \in \mathbf{AComm}^{\text{SA}}$ *and* $\mathsf{Vars}(b) \cap (\mathsf{Asgn}(C_t) \cup \mathsf{Asgn}(C_f)) = \emptyset$
- $\mathbf{for}\ (\mathcal{I}, b, \mathcal{U})\ \mathbf{do}\,\{\theta\}\,C \in \mathbf{AComm}^{\text{SA}}$ *if* $C \in \mathbf{AComm}^{\text{SA}}$, $\mathcal{I}, \mathcal{U} \in \mathbf{Rnm}$, $\mathsf{Asgn}(\mathcal{I}) = \mathsf{Asgn}(\mathcal{U})$, $\mathsf{rng}(\mathcal{U}) \subseteq \mathsf{Asgn}(C)$, *and* $(\mathsf{Vars}(\mathcal{I}) \cup \mathsf{Vars}(b) \cup \mathsf{FV}(\theta)) \cap \mathsf{Asgn}(C) = \emptyset$

and Vars *and* Asgn *are extended to the* **for** *command as follows:*

- $\mathsf{Vars}(\mathbf{for}\ (\mathcal{I}, b, \mathcal{U})\ \mathbf{do}\,\{\theta\}\,C) = \mathsf{Vars}(\mathcal{I}) \cup \mathsf{Vars}(b) \cup \mathsf{FV}(\theta) \cup \mathsf{Vars}(C)$
- $\mathsf{Asgn}(\mathbf{for}\ (\mathcal{I}, b, \mathcal{U})\ \mathbf{do}\,\{\theta\}\,C) = \mathsf{Asgn}(\mathcal{I}) \cup \mathsf{Asgn}(C)$

Definition 4 is straightforward except in the case of loops. The initialization code $\mathcal{I}$ contains a renaming that runs exactly once, even if no iterations take place. On the other hand the code in $\mathcal{U}$ is executed after every iteration. This ensures that the variables in $\mathsf{dom}(\mathcal{U})$ (equal to $\mathsf{dom}(\mathcal{I})$) always contain the appropriate output values at the beginning of each iteration and when the loop terminates. Note that the definition of $\phi\#C$ extends to annotated programs as expected.

In Fig. 4b we show again the factorial program, where we have converted the blocks to SA form (the variables occurring in the loop are signalled with an 'a' subscript for clarity, but any other fresh variables would do). The initial version variables of the loop body f_{a0} and i_{a0} are the ones used in the Boolean expression, which is evaluated at the beginning of each iteration. They are also used in the invariant annotation. We have placed in the code the required renamings $\mathcal{I}$ and $\mathcal{U}$, and it is straightforward to instantiate them. $\mathcal{I}$ should be defined as $i_{a0} := i_1\,; f_{a0} := f_1$, and $\mathcal{U}$ as $i_{a0} := i_{a1}\,; f_{a0} := f_{a1}$. The initial version variables can be used after the loop to access the value of the counter and accumulator; so a specification for this program can be written as $(n \geq 0 \wedge n_{aux} = n, f_{a0} = n_{aux}!)$. It is now immediate to write the program with a *for* command encapsulating the structure of the loop, in accordance with Definition 4. This is shown in Fig. 4c. Incidentally, note that the invariant does not contain the 'continuous' part $n_{aux} = n$ of the initial code, since it becomes unnecessary in the SA version.

The function $\mathcal{W} : \mathbf{AComm}^{\text{SA}} \to \mathbf{AComm}$ translates SA programs back to (annotated) While programs in the obvious way: $\mathcal{W}(\mathbf{for}\ (\mathcal{I}, b, \mathcal{U})\ \mathbf{do}\,\{\theta\}\,C) = \mathcal{I}\,; \mathbf{while}\ b\ \mathbf{do}\,\{\theta\}\,\{\mathcal{W}(C)\,; \mathcal{U}\}$. Otherwise the function is defined as expected.

$$\text{(skip)} \qquad \frac{}{\{\phi\}\,\mathbf{skip}\,\{\phi \wedge \top\}}$$

$$\text{(assign)} \qquad \frac{}{\{\phi\}\,x := e\,\{\phi \wedge x = e\}}$$

$$\text{(seq)} \qquad \frac{\{\phi\}\,C_1\,\{\phi \wedge \psi_1\} \qquad \{\phi \wedge \psi_1\}\,C_2\,\{\phi \wedge \psi_1 \wedge \psi_2\}}{\{\phi\}\,C_1\,;\,C_2\,\{\phi \wedge \psi_1 \wedge \psi_2\}}$$

$$\text{(if)} \qquad \frac{\{\phi \wedge b\}\,C_t\,\{\phi \wedge b \wedge \psi_t\} \qquad \{\phi \wedge \neg b\}\,C_f\,\{\phi \wedge \neg b \wedge \psi_f\}}{\{\phi\}\,\mathbf{if}\ b\ \mathbf{then}\ C_t\ \mathbf{else}\ C_f\,\{\phi \wedge ((b \wedge \psi_t) \vee (\neg b \wedge \psi_f))\}}$$

$$\text{(for)} \quad \frac{\{\theta \wedge b\}\,C\,\{\theta \wedge b \wedge \psi\}}{\{\phi\}\,\mathbf{for}\ (\mathcal{I}, b, \mathcal{U})\ \mathbf{do}\ \{\theta\}\,C\,\{\phi \wedge \theta \wedge \neg b\}} \ \text{if} \ \begin{array}{l}\phi \rightarrow \mathcal{I}(\theta) \ \text{and} \\ \theta \wedge b \wedge \psi \rightarrow \mathcal{U}(\theta)\end{array}$$

Fig. 5. Inference system for annotated SA triples – System Hsa

4 Logic and Verification Conditions for SA Programs

We propose in Fig. 5 an inference system for Hoare triples containing annotated SA programs. Hsa is goal-directed like system Hg but it incorporates a strategy, based on forward propagation (reminiscent of strongest postcondition computations). It is proved sound with respect to system H, and complete with respect to Hg. Note that Hsa derives triples of the form $\{\phi\}\,C\,\{\phi \wedge \psi\}$, where the program does not interfere with the truth of the precondition. For this reason we restrict our results to triples satisfying the $\phi \# C$ condition (SA translations will generate triples of this kind only).

Lemma 4. *Let* $C \in \mathbf{AComm}^{\mathrm{SA}}$ *and* $\phi, \psi \in \mathbf{Assert}$ *such that* $\phi \# C$, $\vdash_{\mathsf{Hsa}} \{\phi\}\,C\,\{\psi\}$. *Then (i)* $\mathsf{FV}(\psi) \subseteq \mathsf{FV}(\phi) \cup \mathsf{Vars}(C)$ *and (ii) all triples* $\{\alpha\}\,C'\,\{\beta\}$ *occurring in this derivation satisfy* $\alpha \# C'$.

Proof. Both are proved by induction on the structure of the derivation of $\vdash_{\mathsf{Hsa}} \{\phi\}\,C\,\{\psi\}$. □

Proposition 4 (Soundness of system Hsa). *Let* $C \in \mathbf{AComm}^{\mathrm{SA}}$ *and* ϕ, $\psi' \in \mathbf{Assert}$ *such that* $\phi \# C$. *If* $\vdash_{\mathsf{Hsa}} \{\phi\}\,C\,\{\phi \wedge \psi'\}$, *then* $\vdash_{\mathsf{H}} \{\phi\}\,\lfloor \mathcal{W}(C) \rfloor\,\{\phi \wedge \psi'\}$.

Proof. By induction on the derivation of $\vdash_{\mathsf{Hsa}} \{\phi\}\,C\,\{\phi \wedge \psi'\}$, using Lemma 4 and induction hypotheses. We show the interesting case, where the last rule applied is (for). Assume the last step is

$$\frac{\{\theta \wedge b\}\,C\,\{\theta \wedge b \wedge \psi\}}{\{\phi\}\,\mathbf{for}\ (\mathcal{I}, b, \mathcal{U})\ \mathbf{do}\ \{\theta\}\,C\,\{\phi \wedge \theta \wedge \neg b\}} \ \text{with} \ \begin{array}{l}\phi \rightarrow \mathcal{I}(\theta) \ \text{and} \\ \theta \wedge b \wedge \psi \rightarrow \mathcal{U}(\theta)\end{array}$$

By Lemma 4, we have that $(\theta \wedge b) \# C$. So, by induction hypothesis, we have $\vdash_{\mathsf{H}} \{\theta \wedge b\}\,\lfloor \mathcal{W}(C) \rfloor\,\{\theta \wedge b \wedge \psi\}$. From the validity of the side conditions, by

Lemma 3 and completeness of H, we have $\vdash_{\mathsf{H}} \{\theta \wedge b \wedge \psi\}\,\mathcal{U}\,\{\theta\}$ and $\vdash_{\mathsf{H}} \{\phi\}\,\mathcal{I}\,\{\theta\}$. Now applying sequentially the rules (seq), (while) and again (seq), we get $\vdash_{\mathsf{H}} \{\phi\}\,\mathcal{I}\,;\,\textbf{while}\ b\ \textbf{do}\ \{\lfloor\mathcal{W}(C)\rfloor\,;\,\mathcal{U}\}\,\{\theta \wedge \neg b\}$. Hence, by definition of $\mathcal{W}$ and Lemma 1, we have $\vdash_{\mathsf{H}} \{\phi\}\,\lfloor\mathcal{W}(\textbf{for}\ (\mathcal{I}, b, \mathcal{U})\ \textbf{do}\,\{\theta\}\,C)\rfloor\,\{\phi \wedge \theta \wedge \neg b\}$. □

Proposition 5 (Completeness of System Hsa). *Let $C \in \mathbf{AComm}^{\mathrm{SA}}$ and ϕ, $\psi \in \mathbf{Assert}$ such that $\phi \# C$ and $\vdash_{\mathsf{Hg}} \{\phi\}\,\mathcal{W}(C)\,\{\psi\}$. Then $\vdash_{\mathsf{Hsa}} \{\phi\}\,C\,\{\phi \wedge \psi'\}$ for some $\psi' \in \mathbf{Assert}$ such that $\models \phi \wedge \psi' \rightarrow \psi$.*

Proof. By induction on the structure of C. Assume $\phi \# C$ and $\vdash_{\mathsf{Hg}} \{\phi\}\,\mathcal{W}(C)\,\{\psi\}$.

- Case $C \equiv x := e$, we must have $\models \phi \rightarrow \psi[e/x]$. Since $x \notin (\mathsf{FV}(e) \cup \mathsf{FV}(\phi))$, it follows that $\models \phi \wedge x = e \rightarrow \psi$. As $\vdash_{\mathsf{Hsa}} \{\phi\}\,x := e\,\{\phi \wedge x = e\}$ we are done.
- Case $C \equiv C_1; C_2$, we must have for some $\gamma \in \mathbf{Assert}$ $\vdash_{\mathsf{Hg}} \{\phi\}\,\mathcal{W}(C_1)\,\{\gamma\}$ and $\vdash_{\mathsf{Hg}} \{\gamma\}\,\mathcal{W}(C_2)\,\{\psi\}$. Since $\phi \# C_1; C_2$ we have $\phi \# C_1$. Hence by induction hypothesis we have $\vdash_{\mathsf{Hsa}} \{\phi\}\,C_1\,\{\phi \wedge \gamma'\}$ for some $\gamma' \in \mathbf{Assert}$ such that $\models \phi \wedge \gamma' \rightarrow \gamma$. Therefore, by Lemma 2, $\vdash_{\mathsf{Hg}} \{\phi \wedge \gamma'\}\,\mathcal{W}(C_2)\,\{\psi\}$. From Lemma 4 we have that $\mathsf{FV}(\phi \wedge \gamma') \subseteq \mathsf{FV}(\phi) \cup \mathsf{Vars}(C_1)$, and thus $(\phi \wedge \gamma') \# C_2$. Hence by induction hypothesis $\vdash_{\mathsf{Hsa}} \{\phi \wedge \gamma'\}\,C_2\,\{\phi \wedge \gamma' \wedge \psi'\}$ for some $\psi' \in \mathbf{Assert}$ such that $\models \phi \wedge \gamma' \wedge \psi' \rightarrow \psi$. Applying rule (seq) we then get $\vdash_{\mathsf{Hsa}} \{\phi\}\,C_1\,;\,C_2\,\{\phi \wedge \gamma' \wedge \psi'\}$.
- Case $C \equiv \textbf{for}\ (\mathcal{I}, b, \mathcal{U})\ \textbf{do}\,\{\theta\}\,C_t$, we must have, for some $\gamma \in \mathbf{Assert}$, that $\vdash_{\mathsf{Hg}} \{\phi\}\,\mathcal{I}\,\{\theta\}$, $\vdash_{\mathsf{Hg}} \{\theta \wedge b\}\,\mathcal{W}(C_t)\,\{\gamma\}$, $\vdash_{\mathsf{Hg}} \{\gamma\}\,\mathcal{U}\,\{\theta\}$, and $\models \theta \wedge \neg b \rightarrow \psi$. We have that $(\theta \wedge b) \# C_t$, so it follows by induction hypothesis that $\vdash_{\mathsf{Hsa}} \{\theta \wedge b\}\,C_t\,\{\theta \wedge b \wedge \gamma'\}$, for some $\gamma' \in \mathbf{Assert}$ and $\models \theta \wedge b \wedge \gamma' \rightarrow \gamma$. Therefore, by Lemma 2, $\vdash_{\mathsf{Hg}} \{\theta \wedge b \wedge \gamma'\}\,\mathcal{U}\,\{\theta\}$. Since Hg is sound, by Lemma 3, it follows that $\models \phi \rightarrow \mathcal{I}(\theta)$ and $\models \theta \wedge b \wedge \gamma' \rightarrow \mathcal{U}(\theta)$, which allow us to apply rule (for) and get the conclusion $\vdash_{\mathsf{Hsa}} \{\phi\}\,\textbf{for}\ (\mathcal{I}, b, \mathcal{U})\ \textbf{do}\,\{\theta\}\,C\,\{\phi \wedge \theta \wedge \neg b\}$.

The remaining cases are routine. □

All the rules of system Hsa propagate the precondition ϕ forward. Note that in the (for) rule this happens even though ϕ is not implied by the annotated loop invariant. Observe also how in this same rule we reason structurally about the body of the loop (an SA piece of code), with the renamings applied to the invariant in the side conditions.

Figure 6 shows an example of a Hsa derivation, where Fact^{sa} is the factorial single-assignment program of Fig. 4c. The assertion $n \geq 0 \wedge n_{aux} = n$ is used as precondition. Note that the application of the (for) rule introduces two side conditions, which are both valid. The derivation generates a unique postcondition for the program, with the given precondition. Other valid triples with the same precondition may be obtained by weakening this postcondition, following Proposition 5. For the triple $\{n \geq 0 \wedge n_{aux} = n\}\,\mathsf{Fact}\,\{f_{a0} = n_{aux}!\}$ we would check the validity of:

$$n \geq 0 \wedge n_{aux} = n \wedge f_1 = 1 \wedge i_1 = 1 \wedge f_{a0} = (i_{a0} - 1)! \wedge i_{a0} \leq n + 1 \wedge \neg(i_{a0} \leq n) \ \rightarrow\ f_{a0} = n_{aux}!$$

A set of verification conditions for a triple $\{\phi\}\,C\,\{\psi\}$ can be obtained from a candidate derivation of a triple of the form $\{\phi\}\,C\,\{\phi \wedge \psi'\}$ in system Hsa. The VCs

$\{n \geq 0 \wedge n_{aux} = n\}$
Fact^{sa}
$\{n \geq 0 \wedge n_{aux} = n \wedge f_1 = 1 \wedge i_1 = 1 \wedge f_{a0} = (i_{a0} - 1)! \wedge i_{a0} \leq n + 1 \wedge \neg(i_{a0} \leq n)\}$
(seq)

1. $\{n \geq 0 \wedge n_{aux} = n\}\, f_1 := 1; i_1 := 1\, \{n \geq 0 \wedge n_{aux} = n \wedge f_1 = 1 \wedge i_1 = 1\}$
   (seq)
   1. (assign) $\{n \geq 0 \wedge n_{aux} = n\}\, f_1 := 1\, \{n \geq 0 \wedge n_{aux} = n \wedge f_1 = 1\}$
   2. (assign) $\{n \geq 0 \wedge n_{aux} = n \wedge f_1 = 1\}\, i_1 := 1\, \{n \geq 0 \wedge n_{aux} = n \wedge f_1 = 1 \wedge i_1 = 1\}$
2. $\{n \geq 0 \wedge n_{aux} = n \wedge f_1 = 1 \wedge i_1 = 1\}$
   for $(\{i_{a0} := i_1; f_{a0} := f_1\}, i_{a0} \leq n, \{i_{a0} := i_{a1}; f_{a0} := f_{a1}\})$ **do** $\{f_{a0} = (i_{a0} - 1)! \wedge i_{a0} \leq n + 1\}\, \{f_{a1} := f_{a0} * i_{a0}; i_{a1} := i_{a0} + 1\}$
   $\{n \geq 0 \wedge n_{aux} = n \wedge f_1 = 1 \wedge i_1 = 1 \wedge f_{a0} = (i_{a0} - 1)! \wedge i_{a0} \leq n + 1 \wedge \neg(i_{a0} \leq n)\}$
   (for)
   1. $\{f_{a0} = (i_{a0} - 1)! \wedge i_{a0} \leq n + 1 \wedge i_{a0} \leq n\}$
      $f_{a1} := f_{a0} * i_{a0}; i_{a1} := i_{a0} + 1$
      $\{f_{a0} = (i_{a0} - 1)! \wedge i_{a0} \leq n + 1 \wedge i_{a0} \leq n \wedge f_{a1} = f_{a0} * i_{a0} \wedge i_{a1} = i_{a0} + 1\}$
      (seq)
      1. (assign) $\{f_{a0} = (i_{a0} - 1)! \wedge i_{a0} \leq n + 1 \wedge i_{a0} \leq n\}\, f_{a1} := f_{a0} * i_{a0}\, \{f_{a0} = (i_{a0} - 1)! \wedge i_{a0} \leq n + 1 \wedge i_{a0} \leq n \wedge f_{a1} = f_{a0} * i_{a0}\}$
      2. (assign) $\{f_{a0} = (i_{a0} - 1)! \wedge i_{a0} \leq n + 1 \wedge i_{a0} \leq n \wedge f_{a1} = f_{a0} * i_{a0}\}\, i_{a1} := i_{a0} + 1\, \{f_{a0} = (i_{a0} - 1)! \wedge i_{a0} \leq n + 1 \wedge i_{a0} \leq n \wedge f_{a1} = f_{a0} * i_{a0} \wedge i_{a1} = i_{a0} + 1\}$

Side conditions for application of the (for) rule:

- $n \geq 0 \wedge n_{aux} = n \wedge f_1 = 1 \wedge i_1 = 1 \rightarrow f_1 = (i_1 - 1)! \wedge i_1 \leq n + 1$
- $f_{a0} = (i_{a0} - 1)! \wedge i_{a0} \leq n + 1 \wedge i_{a0} \leq n \wedge f_{a1} = f_{a0} * i_{a0} \wedge i_{a1} = i_{a0} + 1 \rightarrow f_{a1} = (i_{a1} - 1)! \wedge i_{a1} \leq n + 1$

Fig. 6. Example derivation in system Hsa

are the side conditions introduced by the (for) rule, together with $\phi \wedge \psi' \rightarrow \psi$: the triple is valid if and only if all these VCs are valid. It is possible to calculate the VCs and the formula ψ' without explicitly constructing the derivation. The following function does precisely this.

Definition 5 (Verification Conditions Generator). *The VCGen function* $\mathsf{VC} : \mathbf{Assert} \times \mathbf{AComm}^{SA} \rightarrow \mathbf{Assert} \times \mathcal{P}(\mathbf{Assert})$ *is defined as follows:*

$$\begin{aligned}
\mathsf{VC}(\phi, \mathbf{skip}) &= (\top, \emptyset) \\
\mathsf{VC}(\phi, x := e) &= (x = e, \emptyset) \\
\mathsf{VC}(\phi, C_1 \,;\, C_2) &= (\psi_1 \wedge \psi_2, \Gamma_1 \cup \Gamma_2) \\
&\quad \textit{where } (\psi_1, \Gamma_1) = \mathsf{VC}(\phi, C_1) \textit{ and} \\
&\quad\quad (\psi_2, \Gamma_2) = \mathsf{VC}(\phi \wedge \psi_1, C_2) \\
\mathsf{VC}(\phi, \mathbf{if}\ b\ \mathbf{then}\ C_t\ \mathbf{else}\ C_f) &= ((b \wedge \psi_t) \vee (\neg b \wedge \psi_f), \Gamma_t \cup \Gamma_f) \\
&\quad \textit{where } (\psi_t, \Gamma_t) = \mathsf{VC}(\phi \wedge b, C_t) \textit{ and} \\
&\quad\quad (\psi_f, \Gamma_f) = \mathsf{VC}(\phi \wedge \neg b, C_f) \\
\mathsf{VC}(\phi, \mathbf{for}\ (\mathcal{I}, b, \mathcal{U})\ \mathbf{do}\ \{\theta\}\ C) &= (\theta \wedge \neg b, \Gamma \cup \{\phi \rightarrow \mathcal{I}(\theta), \theta \wedge b \wedge \psi \rightarrow \mathcal{U}(\theta)\}) \\
&\quad \textit{where } (\psi, \Gamma) = \mathsf{VC}(\theta \wedge b, C)
\end{aligned}$$

Let $(\psi', \Gamma) = \mathsf{VC}(\phi, C)$. The verification conditions of C with the precondition ϕ are given by the set Γ, and the formula ψ' approximates (since it relies on loop invariants) a logical encoding of the program; it is clear from the definition that ψ' does not depend on the formula ϕ. The VCs of a Hoare triple $\{\phi\}\, C\, \{\psi\}$ are then given by $\Gamma \cup \{\phi \wedge \psi' \rightarrow \psi\}$.

Proposition 6. *Let* $C \in \mathbf{AComm}^{SA}$, $\phi, \psi', \psi'' \in \mathbf{Assert}$ *and* $\Gamma \subseteq \mathbf{Assert}$, *such that* $(\psi', \Gamma) = \mathsf{VC}(\phi, C)$. *Then:*

1. *If* $\models \Gamma$, *then* $\vdash_{\mathsf{Hsa}} \{\phi\}\, C\, \{\phi \wedge \psi'\}$.
2. *If* $\vdash_{\mathsf{Hsa}} \{\phi\}\, C\, \{\phi \wedge \psi''\}$, *then* $\models \Gamma$ *and* $\psi'' \equiv \psi'$.

Proof. 1. By induction on the structure of C. 2. By induction on the derivation of $\vdash_{\mathsf{Hsa}} \{\phi\}\, C\, \{\phi \wedge \psi''\}$. □

The reader may check that for our factorial example we have $\mathsf{VC}(n \geq 0 \wedge n_{aux} = n, \mathsf{Fact}) = (f_1 = 1 \wedge i_1 = 1 \wedge f_{a0} = (i_{a0}-1)! \wedge i_{a0} \leq n+1 \wedge \neg(i_{a0} \leq n), \{n \geq 0 \wedge n_{aux} = n \wedge f_1 = 1 \wedge i_1 = 1 \rightarrow f_1 = (i_1-1)! \wedge i_1 \leq n+1, f_{a0} = (i_{a0}-1)! \wedge i_{a0} \leq n+1 \wedge i_{a0} \leq n \wedge f_{a1} = f_{a0} * i_{a0} \wedge i_{a1} = i_{a0}+1 \rightarrow f_{a1} = (i_{a1}-1)! \wedge i_{a1} \leq n+1\})$, in accordance with the derivation of Fig. 6.

Consider the calculation of $\mathsf{VC}(\phi, \{\mathbf{if}\ b\ \mathbf{then}\, C_t\, \mathbf{else}\, C_f\}; C_2)$. The recursive call on C_2 will be $\mathsf{VC}(\phi \wedge ((b \wedge \psi_t) \vee (\neg b \wedge \psi_f)), C_2)$, where ψ_t, ψ_f do not depend on ϕ. The resulting VCs avoid the exponential pattern described in Sect. 2, since a single copy of the precondition ϕ is propagated to C_2. In fact the size of the VCs is *quadratic* on the size of the program. It is clear from the $\mathsf{VC}(\phi, C_1\,;\, C_2)$ clause of the definition that the propagated precondition ϕ is duplicated, with one copy used to generate VCs for C_1, and another propagated to C_2 together with the encoding of C_1. Now observe that each loop in the program generates two VCs, one corresponding to the initialization of the invariant $(\phi \rightarrow \mathcal{I}(\theta))$, and another to its preservation. The size of loop preservation VCs depends only on the size of the loop's body, but initialization conditions contain an encoding of the prefix of the program leading to the loop (propagated in the ϕ parameter), so they have size linear in the size of that prefix. The worst case occurs for a program consisting in a sequence of n loops: the ith loop will generate an initialization VC of size $\mathcal{O}(i)$, so the total size of the VCs is $\mathcal{O}(n^2)$.

This VCGen can in fact be simplified, in a way that potentially decreases the size of the VCs. We have seen that the propagation of assertions (using the ϕ parameter) is a potential source of formula duplication, but in fact the ϕ parameter can be eliminated. For this, the algorithm must now return a triple (ψ, γ, Γ) containing, in addition to an encoding ψ of the program and a set Γ of VCs, the VC that is currently being constructed (whereas the conditions in Γ have already been fully generated, inside inner loops of the current block). The simplified VCGen highlights the fundamental fact that VC generation for SA programs is not a matter of directed 'propagation' of assertions, either forward or backward: it suffices to perform a single program traversal collecting pieces of information along the way, and conveniently structuring them:

$$
\begin{aligned}
\mathsf{VC_L}(\mathbf{skip}) &= (\top, \top, \emptyset)\\
\mathsf{VC_L}(x := e) &= (x = e, \top, \emptyset)\\
\mathsf{VC_L}(C_1\,;\, C_2) &= (\psi_1 \wedge \psi_2, \gamma_1 \wedge (\psi_1 \rightarrow \gamma_2), \Gamma_1 \cup \Gamma_2)\\
&\quad \text{where } (\psi_1, \gamma_1, \Gamma_1) = \mathsf{VC_L}(C_1) \text{ and } (\psi_2, \gamma_2, \Gamma_2) = \mathsf{VC_L}(C_2)\\
\mathsf{VC_L}(\mathbf{if}\ b\ \mathbf{then}\ C_t\ \mathbf{else}\ C_f) &= ((b \wedge \psi_t) \vee (\neg b \wedge \psi_f), (b \rightarrow \gamma_t) \wedge (\neg b \rightarrow \gamma_f), \Gamma_t \cup \Gamma_f)\\
&\quad \text{where } (\psi_t, \gamma_t, \Gamma_t) = \mathsf{VC_L}(C_t) \text{ and } (\psi_f, \gamma_f, \Gamma_f) = \mathsf{VC_L}(C_f)\\
\mathsf{VC_L}(\mathbf{for}\ (\mathcal{I}, b, \mathcal{U})\ \mathbf{do}\ \{\theta\}\ C) &= (\theta \wedge \neg b, \mathcal{I}(\theta), \{\theta \wedge b \rightarrow \gamma \wedge (\psi \rightarrow \mathcal{U}(\theta))\} \cup \Gamma)\\
&\quad \text{where } (\psi, \gamma, \Gamma) = \mathsf{VC_L}(C)
\end{aligned}
$$

Let $(\psi_l', \gamma_l, \Gamma_l) = \mathsf{VC_L}(C)$ and $(\psi', \Gamma) = \mathsf{VC}(\phi, C)$. Clearly ψ_l' and ψ' are the same, and it can be proved by induction that $\bigwedge \Gamma \Leftrightarrow \bigwedge \Gamma_l \wedge (\phi \to \gamma_l)$. The VCs of a Hoare triple $\{\phi\}\, C\, \{\psi\}$ are then given by $\Gamma_l \cup \{\phi \to \gamma_l \wedge (\psi_l' \to \psi)\}$.

With respect to VC size, note that this VCGen joins the initialization VCs of all the top-level loops in each sequence in a single condition. Instead of replicating prefixes of the program for each VC, a single formula is generated, that will be valid only when all initialization conditions hold. For left-associative sequences the size of this formula may still be quadratic, since the sequence clause duplicates the program formula ψ_1 of C_1; however, if sequences are represented in a right-associative way (a reasonable assumption for an intermediate language), the size of the resulting VCs is *linear in the size of* C in the worst-case.

5 Program Verification Using Intermediate SA Form

We will now put up a framework for the verification of annotated While programs, based on their translation to single-assignment form and the subsequent generation of compact verification conditions from this intermediate code.

The translation into SA form will operate at the level of Hoare triples, rather than of isolated annotated programs. Such a translation must of course abide by the syntactic restrictions of $\mathbf{AComm}^{\mathrm{SA}}$ (as ilustrated by the factorial example), with additional requirements of a semantic nature. In particular, the translation will annotate the SA program with loop invariants (produced from those contained in the original program), and Hg-derivability guided by these annotations must be preserved. On the other hand, the translation must be sound: it will not translate invalid triples into valid ones. These requirements are expressed by translating back to While programs.

Definition 6 (SA Translation). *A function* $\mathcal{T} : \mathbf{Assert} \times \mathbf{AComm} \times \mathbf{Assert} \to \mathbf{Assert} \times \mathbf{AComm}^{\mathrm{SA}} \times \mathbf{Assert}$ *is said to be a* single-assignment translation *if when* $\mathcal{T}(\phi, C, \psi) = (\phi', C', \psi')$ *we have* $\phi' \# C'$*, and both the following hold:*

1. *If* $\models \{\phi'\}\, \lfloor \mathcal{W}(C') \rfloor\, \{\psi'\}$*, then* $\models \{\phi\}\, \lfloor C \rfloor\, \{\psi\}$*.*
2. *If* $\vdash_{\mathsf{Hg}} \{\phi\}\, C\, \{\psi\}$*, then* $\vdash_{\mathsf{Hg}} \{\phi'\}\, \mathcal{W}(C')\, \{\psi'\}$*.*

The following results establish that translating annotated programs to an intermediate SA form before generating VCs results in a sound and complete technique for deductive verification.

Proposition 7 (Soundness of Verification Technique). *Let* $C \in \mathbf{AComm}$*,* $C' \in \mathbf{AComm}^{\mathrm{SA}}$*,* $\phi, \phi', \psi, \psi', \gamma \in \mathbf{Assert}$ *and* $\Gamma \subseteq \mathbf{Assert}$*, such that* $(\phi', C', \psi') = \mathcal{T}(\phi, C, \psi)$ *for some SA translation* $\mathcal{T}$*, and* $(\gamma, \Gamma) = \mathsf{VC}(\phi', C')$*. If* $\models \Gamma, \phi' \wedge \gamma \to \psi'$ *then* $\models \{\phi\}\, \lfloor C \rfloor\, \{\psi\}$*.*

Proof. From Proposition 6(1) we have $\vdash_{\mathsf{Hsa}} \{\phi'\}\, C'\, \{\phi' \wedge \gamma\}$ and from Definition 6 we have $\phi' \# C'$. Thus Proposition 4 applies yielding $\vdash_{\mathsf{H}} \{\phi'\}\, \lfloor \mathcal{W}(C') \rfloor\, \{\phi' \wedge \gamma\}$. From soundness of H, and because $\models \phi' \wedge \gamma \to \psi'$, it follows that $\models \{\phi'\}\, \lfloor \mathcal{W}(C') \rfloor\, \{\psi'\}$. Finally, by Definition 6, we have $\models \{\phi\}\, \lfloor C \rfloor\, \{\psi\}$. □

Proposition 8 (Completeness of Verification Technique). *Let* $C \in$ **AComm**, $C' \in \mathbf{AComm}^{\mathrm{SA}}$, $\phi, \phi', \psi, \psi', \gamma \in$ **Assert** *and* $\Gamma \subseteq$ **Assert** *such that* $(\phi', C', \psi') = \mathcal{T}(\phi, C, \psi)$ *for some SA translation* $\mathcal{T}$, *and* $(\gamma, \Gamma) = \mathsf{VC}(\phi', C')$. *If* $\models \{\phi\} \lfloor C \rfloor \{\psi\}$ *and* C *is correctly-annotated w.r.t.* (ϕ, ψ), *then* $\models \Gamma$, $\phi' \wedge \gamma \rightarrow \psi'$.

Proof. First note that by completeness of system H we have $\vdash_{\mathsf{H}} \{\phi\} \lfloor C \rfloor \{\psi\}$. By Definitions 2 and 6 it follows that $\vdash_{\mathsf{Hg}} \{\phi\} C \{\psi\}$ and $\vdash_{\mathsf{Hg}} \{\phi'\} \mathcal{W}(C') \{\psi'\}$. The latter definition implies that $\phi' \# C'$, and by Proposition 5 $\vdash_{\mathsf{Hsa}} \{\phi'\} C' \{\phi' \wedge \psi''\}$ for some $\psi'' \in$ **Assert** such that $\models \phi' \wedge \psi'' \rightarrow \psi'$. Proposition 6(2) then gives us $\models \Gamma$ and $\psi'' \equiv \gamma$, which concludes the proof. □

An example of a detailed translation can be found in Appendix A, together with the proof that it complies to Definition 6.

6 Adaptation Completeness of SA Program Logic

Let (ϕ, ψ) and (ϕ', ψ') be specifications, and assume that (ϕ, ψ) is satisfiable (there exists some program that is correct w.r.t. it). Suppose now that C is a program such that if the Hoare triple $\{\phi\} C \{\psi\}$ is valid then so is $\{\phi'\} C \{\psi'\}$. An inference system for Hoare logic is said to be *adaptation-complete* if whenever this happens, then $\{\phi'\} C \{\psi'\}$ is derivable in that system from the triple $\{\phi\} C \{\psi\}$.

Adaptation is closely linked to the existence of a *consequence rule* that dictates when a triple is derivable in one step from another triple containing the same program. Adaptation is by design entirely absent from goal-directed systems like Hg or Hsa, which have no consequence rule. System H is capable of adaptation, but not in a complete way. An example of this was already seen at the end of Sect. 2, involving the use of auxiliary variables. For an even simpler example of how adaptation fails in system H, consider the triple $\{x > 0\} P \{y = x\}$ where x is now a program variable, used outside P, but *not assigned in* P. Again let K be some positive constant. Clearly if the triple is valid then so is $\{x = K\} P \{y = K\}$, since the value of x is preserved. However, attempting to apply the consequence rule would yield the following, where the first side condition is valid, but the second is invalid

$$\frac{\{x > 0\}\, P\, \{y = x\}}{\{x = K\}\, P\, \{y = K\}} \quad \text{if} \quad \begin{array}{l} x = K \rightarrow x > 0 \ \text{ and} \\ y = x \rightarrow y = K \end{array}$$

The problem of adaptation was raised by the study of complete extensions of Hoare logic for reasoning about recursive procedures. The initial proposal by Hoare [18] was to derive a triple concerning a procedure call by assuming that same triple as a hypothesis when reasoning about the procedure's body:

$$\frac{\{\phi\}\, \mathbf{call\, p}\, \{\psi\} \vdash \{\phi\}\, \mathbf{body(p)}\, \{\psi\}}{\{\phi\}\, \mathbf{call\, p}\, \{\psi\}}$$

(assuming that an identity axiom is present, and system H rules are lifted to work with sequents). It was soon discovered that, in the presence of auxiliary variables in the procedure's specification, the resulting system turned out to be incomplete, and the reason for this was the failure to handle the adaptation of the procedure's specification to the local context of the recursive call.

One solution for this problem was to introduce additional structural rules [1], but Kleymann [20] has shown that the adaptation problem is orthogonal to the handling of recursive procedures: if the base system is made adaptation-complete, then Hoare's rule for recursive procedure calls is sufficient to achieve a Cook-complete system, with no need for further structural rules.

Kleymann obtains an adaptation-complete inference system for Hoare logic by proposing the following consequence rule, whose side condition is a meta-level formula with quantification over states/variable assignments:

$$(\text{conseq}_K) \qquad \frac{\{\phi\}\,C\,\{\psi\}}{\{\phi'\}\,C\,\{\psi'\}} \quad \begin{array}{l}\text{if } \forall Z.\forall\sigma.[\![\phi']\!](Z,\sigma) \rightarrow \\ \quad \forall\tau.(\forall Z_1.[\![\phi]\!](Z_1,\sigma) \rightarrow [\![\psi]\!](Z_1,\tau)) \\ \quad \rightarrow [\![\psi']\!](Z,\tau)\end{array}$$

$[\![\phi']\!](Z,\sigma)$ denotes the truth value of ϕ' in the state (Z,σ), partitioned between auxiliary (Z) and program (σ) variables. As it is, (conseq_K) cannot be handled directly by an SMT solver, since the condition is not a first-order formula.

We will show that reasoning with single-assignment programs is advantageous from the point of view of adaptation: our Hsa system will be made adaptation-complete by adding a rule with a simple syntactic side condition. We start with a result showing that the side condition of a consequence rule that always leads to adaptation-completeness, in general terms, turns out to be the result of stripping away the states and quantifiers in the side condition of (conseq_K) above.

Lemma 5. *Let* $\phi, \phi', \psi, \psi' \in$ **Assert**. *If there exists at least one program* $C_0 \in$ **Comm** *such that* $\models \{\phi\}\,C_0\,\{\psi\}$, *and for arbitrary* C *one has that* $\models \{\phi\}\,C\,\{\psi\}$ *implies* $\models \{\phi'\}\,C\,\{\psi'\}$, *then it must be the case that* $\models \phi' \rightarrow (\phi \rightarrow \psi) \rightarrow \psi'$.

Proof. We assume $\not\models \phi' \rightarrow (\phi \rightarrow \psi) \rightarrow \psi'$, i.e. there exists a state s_0 such that $s_0 \models \phi'$, $s_0 \models \phi \rightarrow \psi$, and $s_0 \not\models \psi'$. To show that in this context $\models \{\phi'\}\,C\,\{\psi'\}$ does not follow from $\models \{\phi\}\,C\,\{\psi\}$ for arbitrary C, we construct a particular program C_1 with the following behavior: $\langle C_1, s_0\rangle \leadsto s_0$ and for $s \neq s_0$,$\langle C_1, s\rangle \leadsto s'$ whenever $\langle C_0, s\rangle \leadsto s'$. To see that $\{\phi\}\,C_1\,\{\psi\}$ is a valid triple, observe that if $s_0 \models \phi$ and C_1 is executed in state s_0 we will have $s_0 \models \psi$ since $s_0 \models \phi \rightarrow \psi$, and for other executions we note that $\models \{\phi\}\,C_0\,\{\psi\}$. The triple $\{\phi'\}\,C_1\,\{\psi'\}$ is however not valid, since $s_0 \models \phi'$, but $\langle C_1, s_0\rangle \leadsto s_0$ and $s_0 \not\models \psi'$. □

The problem is that a consequence rule with side condition $\phi' \rightarrow (\phi \rightarrow \psi) \rightarrow \psi'$ would not be sound. But it is sound for triples satisfying the simple syntactic restriction that free variables of the precondition are not assigned in the program.

Lemma 6. *Let* $C \in$ **Comm** *and* $\phi \in$ **Assert**. *If* $\phi \# C$ *and* $\langle C, s\rangle \leadsto s'$, *then* $[\![\phi]\!](s) = [\![\phi]\!](s')$.

Proof. Since $\phi \# C$, $s(x) = s'(x)$ for every $x \in \mathsf{FV}(\phi)$. Hence, $[\![\phi]\!](s) = [\![\phi]\!](s')$. □

Lemma 7. *Let $C \in$* **Comm** *and $\phi, \phi', \psi, \psi' \in$* **Assert**, *such that $\phi \# C$ and $\phi' \# C$. If $\models \{\phi\} C \{\psi\}$ and $\models \phi' \to (\phi \to \psi) \to \psi'$, then $\models \{\phi'\} C \{\psi'\}$.*

Proof. Assume $s \models \phi'$ and $\langle C, s\rangle \rightsquigarrow s'$. Since $\phi' \# C$, by Lemma 6, we get $s' \models \phi'$. We also have $s' \models \phi \to \psi$ because, if $s' \models \phi$, then $s \models \phi$ (by Lemma 6, since $\phi \# C$) so, as $\models \{\phi\} C \{\psi\}$, we get $s' \models \psi$. Now, $s' \models \psi'$ follows directly from $\models \phi' \to (\phi \to \psi) \to \psi'$, $s' \models \phi'$ and $s' \models \phi \to \psi$. □

Recall from Lemma 4 that Hsa derivations consist entirely of triples $\{\phi\} C \{\psi\}$ satisfying the $\phi \# C$ condition, which means that an adaptation rule with the side condition given above can be naturally incorporated in the system. We must however be careful to ensure that the new rule *preserves* Lemma 4; in particular, the postcondition ψ' should not contain free occurrences of variables not occurring either in the program or free in the precondition ϕ'. The following result will allow us to eliminate these free occurrences.

Lemma 8. *Let $C \in$* **Comm**, *$\phi, \psi \in$* **Assert** *and $x \in$* **Var**, *such that $x \notin \mathsf{FV}(\phi) \cup \mathsf{Vars}(C)$. If $\models \{\phi\} C \{\psi\}$ then $\models \{\phi\} C \{\forall x.\, \psi\}$.*

Proof. Assume $s \models \phi$ and $\langle C, s\rangle \rightsquigarrow s'$. As $x \notin \mathsf{FV}(\phi) \cup \mathsf{Vars}(C)$, for every $a \in D$, $s[x \mapsto a] \models \phi$ and $\langle C, s[x \mapsto a]\rangle \rightsquigarrow s'[x \mapsto a]$. Since $\models \{\phi\} C \{\psi\}$, it follows that $s'[x \mapsto a] \models \psi$. Hence, $s' \models \forall x.\, \psi$.

Let Hsa^+ be the inference system consisting of all the rules of system Hsa together with the following rule:

$$(\text{conseq}_a) \quad \frac{\{\phi\} C \{\phi \wedge \psi\}}{\{\phi'\} C \{\phi' \wedge (\forall \boldsymbol{x}.\, \phi \to \psi)\}} \quad \text{if } \phi \# C \text{ and } \boldsymbol{x} = \mathsf{FV}(\phi) \backslash (\mathsf{FV}(\phi') \cup \mathsf{Vars}(C))$$

Recall that Hsa is a forward propagation system, so the rule will be applied when we reach C with the propagated precondition ϕ' (in which case Lemma 4 ensures that $\phi' \# C$ holds). The rule will produce a postcondition not directly by propagating ϕ' through the structure of C, but instead by adapting the triple $\{\phi\} C \{\phi \wedge \psi\}$. The conditions ϕ and ψ may well contain occurrences of variables not occurring either in C or free in ϕ', but the quantification ensures that Lemma 4 remains valid in system Hsa^+. Note that the lemma guarantees that $\mathsf{FV}(\psi) \subseteq \mathsf{FV}(\phi) \cup \mathsf{Vars}(C)$, so $\mathsf{FV}(\psi)$ does not need to be included in $\boldsymbol{x}$.

System Hsa^+ is not goal-directed, but it is still a forward-propagation system (the postcondition is the strongest allowed by Lemma 7).

Proposition 9 (Soundness of Hsa^+). *Let $C \in$* **AComm**^{SA} *and $\phi, \psi' \in$* **Assert** *such that $\phi \# C$ and $\vdash_{\mathsf{Hsa}^+} \{\phi\} C \{\phi \wedge \psi'\}$. Then $\vdash_{\mathsf{H}} \{\phi\} \lfloor \mathcal{W}(C) \rfloor \{\phi \wedge \psi'\}$.*

Proof. The proof, by induction on the structure of the derivation of $\vdash_{\mathsf{Hsa}^+} \{\phi\} C \{\phi \wedge \psi'\}$, extends the proof of Proposition 4 with the (conseq_a) rule case.

Assume the last step is

$$\frac{\{\phi_1\} C \{\phi_1 \wedge \psi_1\}}{\{\phi\} C \{\phi \wedge (\forall \boldsymbol{x}.\, \phi_1 \to \psi_1)\}} \quad \text{with } \phi_1 \# C \text{ and } \boldsymbol{x} = \mathsf{FV}(\phi_1) \backslash (\mathsf{FV}(\phi) \cup \mathsf{Vars}(C))$$

By induction hypothesis we have $\vdash_{\mathsf{H}} \{\phi_1\} \lfloor \mathcal{W}(C) \rfloor \{\phi_1 \wedge \psi_1\}$ and since H is sound it follows that $\models \{\phi_1\} \lfloor \mathcal{W}(C) \rfloor \{\phi_1 \wedge \psi_1\}$. As $\models \phi \rightarrow (\phi_1 \rightarrow \phi_1 \wedge \psi_1) \rightarrow \phi \wedge (\phi_1 \rightarrow \psi_1)$, we get $\models \{\phi\} \lfloor \mathcal{W}(C) \rfloor \{\phi \wedge (\phi_1 \rightarrow \psi_1)\}$ by Lemma 7. Now note that $\boldsymbol{x} \cap (\mathsf{FV}(\phi) \cup \mathsf{Vars}(C)) = \emptyset$, thus Lemma 8 can be applied, and it follows that $\models \{\phi\} \lfloor \mathcal{W}(C) \rfloor \{\phi \wedge (\forall \boldsymbol{x}.\, \phi_1 \rightarrow \psi_1)\}$. Finally, by completeness of H we obtain $\vdash_{\mathsf{H}} \{\phi\} \lfloor \mathcal{W}(C) \rfloor \{\phi \wedge (\forall \boldsymbol{x}.\, \phi_1 \rightarrow \psi_1)\}$. □

The system is obviously complete in the same sense as Hsa, since it extends it. But unlike Hsa it is also adaptation-complete.

Proposition 10 (Adaptation Completeness of Hsa^+). *Let $C \in$* **AComm**^{SA} *and $\phi, \phi', \psi, \psi' \in$* **Assert** *such that $\phi \# C$, (ϕ, ψ) is satisfiable, and $\models \{\phi\} \lfloor \mathcal{W}(C) \rfloor \{\psi\}$ implies $\models \{\phi'\} \lfloor \mathcal{W}(C) \rfloor \{\psi'\}$.*

If $\vdash_{\mathsf{Hsa}^+} \{\phi\}\, C\, \{\phi \wedge \gamma\}$ for some $\gamma \in$ **Assert** *such that $\models \phi \wedge \gamma \rightarrow \psi$, then $\{\phi'\}\, C\, \{\phi' \wedge (\forall \boldsymbol{x}.\, \phi \rightarrow \gamma)\}$ with $\boldsymbol{x} = \mathsf{FV}(\phi) \backslash (\mathsf{FV}(\phi') \cup \mathsf{Vars}(C))$ can be derived from that triple in system Hsa^+, and $\models \phi' \wedge (\forall \boldsymbol{x}.\, \phi \rightarrow \gamma) \rightarrow \psi'$.*

Proof. From $\vdash_{\mathsf{Hsa}^+} \{\phi\}\, C\, \{\phi \wedge \gamma\}$ we can apply the (conseq$_a$) rule to produce $\vdash_{\mathsf{Hsa}^+} \{\phi'\}\, C\, \{\phi' \wedge (\forall \boldsymbol{x}.\, \phi \rightarrow \gamma)\}$ with $\boldsymbol{x} = \mathsf{FV}(\phi) \backslash (\mathsf{FV}(\phi') \cup \mathsf{Vars}(C))$, since $\phi \# C$. So it just remains to prove the validity of the formula $\phi' \wedge (\forall \boldsymbol{x}.\, \phi \rightarrow \gamma) \rightarrow \psi'$.

From $\models \phi \wedge \gamma \rightarrow \psi$ it follows that $\models (\phi \rightarrow \gamma) \rightarrow (\phi \rightarrow \psi)$, and so we also have $\models (\forall \boldsymbol{x}.\, \phi \rightarrow \gamma) \rightarrow (\forall \boldsymbol{x}.\, \phi \rightarrow \psi)$. Consequently $\models \phi' \wedge (\forall \boldsymbol{x}.\, \phi \rightarrow \gamma) \rightarrow \phi' \wedge (\forall \boldsymbol{x}.\, \phi \rightarrow \psi)$, and thus $\phi' \wedge (\forall \boldsymbol{x}.\, \phi \rightarrow \gamma) \models \phi' \wedge (\forall \boldsymbol{x}.\, \phi \rightarrow \psi)$. On the other hand, as $\boldsymbol{x} \cap \mathsf{FV}(\phi') = \emptyset$, we have $\phi' \wedge (\forall \boldsymbol{x}.\, \phi \rightarrow \psi) \models \phi' \wedge (\phi \rightarrow \psi)$. Now, since $\models \{\phi\} \lfloor \mathcal{W}(C) \rfloor \{\psi\}$ implies $\models \{\phi'\} \lfloor \mathcal{W}(C) \rfloor \{\psi'\}$, it follows by Lemma 5 that $\models \phi' \rightarrow (\phi \rightarrow \psi) \rightarrow \psi'$, and hence we get $\phi' \wedge (\forall \boldsymbol{x}.\, \phi \rightarrow \gamma) \models \psi'$. Now we can conclude that $\models \phi' \wedge (\forall \boldsymbol{x}.\, \phi \rightarrow \gamma) \rightarrow \psi'$. □

Consider again the example introduced at the end of Sect. 2. Let K be a positive constant; the Hoare triple $\{n = K\}\, \mathsf{Fact}^{\mathsf{sa}}\, \{f_{a0} = K!\}$ can now be derived from $\{n \geq 0 \wedge n_{aux} = n\}\, \mathsf{Fact}^{\mathsf{sa}}\, \{n \geq 0 \wedge n_{aux} = n \wedge f_{a0} = n_{aux}!\}$:

$$\frac{\{n \geq 0 \wedge n_{aux} = n\}\ \mathsf{Fact}^{\mathsf{sa}}\ \{n \geq 0 \wedge n_{aux} = n \wedge f_{a0} = n_{aux}!\}}{\{n = K\}\ \mathsf{Fact}^{\mathsf{sa}}\ \{n = K \wedge (\forall n_{aux}.\, n \geq 0 \wedge n_{aux} = n \rightarrow f_{a0} = n_{aux}!)\}}$$

since $\models n = K \wedge (\forall n_{aux}.\, n \geq 0 \wedge n_{aux} = n \rightarrow f_{a0} = n_{aux}!) \rightarrow f_{a0} = K!$. As to the example at the beginning of the present section, consider the following derivation (recall that x is not assigned in P):

$$\frac{\{x > 0\}\ P\ \{x > 0 \wedge y = x\}}{\{x = K\}\ P\ \{x = K \wedge (x > 0 \rightarrow y = x)\}}$$

This proves $\{x = K\}\, P\, \{y = K\}$ since $\models x = K \wedge (x > 0 \rightarrow y = x) \rightarrow y = K$.

7 Related Work

The original notion of Static Single-Assignment (SSA) form [11] limits the syntactic occurrence of each variable as L-value of a single assignment instruction. A construct called "Φ-function" is used to synchronize versions of the same variable used in different paths. For instance the fragment **if** $x > 0$ **then** $x := x + 10$ **else** $x := x + 20$ could be translated as $\{$**if** $x_0 > 0$ **then** $x_1 := x_0 + 10$ **else** $x_2 := x_0 + 20\}$; $x_3 := \Phi(x_1, x_2)$. This means that the value assigned to x_3 depends on whether execution has reached this point through the first or the second branch of the conditional. In dynamic single-assignment form [27] variables may occur in multiple assignments in different paths.

Abstracting from the fact that assignments are replaced by assume statements, the original notion of *passive form* of [14] can be seen as a kind of dynamic SA where assignment instructions are replaced by *assume* commands, but similarly to the static notion, variable synchronization is achieved by introducing fresh variables assigned in both branches. Adapting this to standard imperative syntax, the above fragment would be translated as **if** $x_0 > 0$ **then** $x_1 := x_0 + 10$; $x_3 := x_1$ **else** $x_2 := x_0 + 20$; $x_3 := x_2$. Our translation resembles the *passify* function introduced in [14], but there are significant differences: *passify* generates fresh variables abstractly, whereas we provide a concrete mechanism for this purpose; while *passify* only handles loop-free programs, our translation considers programs with loops annotated with invariants; *passify* is proved to be sound in the sense that it preserves the weakest precondition interpretation of programs, while our translation is proved to be sound with respect to the validity of Hoare triples, and moreover it is shown to be complete since it preserves derivability guided by the invariants. This is a crucial issue from the point of view of the completeness of using an intermediate SA form for verification.

Finally, *passify* does not generate version-optimal programs; the notion of *version-optimal* passive form, which uses the minimum number of version variables, is defined for unstructured programs in [16], together with a translation algorithm. In this form the above fragment becomes simply **if** $x_0 > 0$ **then** $x_1 := x_0 + 10$ **else** $x_1 := x_0 + 20$. The algorithm differs from the translation of Appendix A in that it does not contemplate annotated loops, and no proof of soundness is given. However, they are similar in the use of variables: for loop-free programs, the DSA form produced by our translation is version-optimal.

Single-assignment forms have played an important role in two different families of efficient program verification techniques.

(I) In the generation of VCs using weakest precondition computations for programs based on Dijkstra's guarded commands [12]. This setting is used as the basis for verification condition generation in ESC/Java and Boogie. For DSA programs, which appear here disguised as passive programs, weakest preconditions can be computed with quadratic size [14,23]. Note that VCs are here created by *assert* commands instead of loop conditions. The approach was extended to programs with unstructured control flow [5] in an optimized way that produces linear-size VCs. It has also been shown that efficiently provable verification conditions can be generated using instead strongest postcondition computations [16].

There exists a single semantics of guarded commands programs, given by the definition of the predicate transformers, from which a VCGen is directly derived. This stands in contrast to our approach: soundness and relative completeness of the logic and VCGen are established with respect to a standard operational semantics of *While* programs. A second important difference is the treatment of iteration. The fixpoint definition of predicate transformers for iterating commands are of no use in the verification of programs annotated with loop invariants. The approach used in ESC/Java and Boogie has been instead to convert each program into an iteration-free program, such that the verification conditions generated for the latter guarantee the soundness of the initial program (in the approach implemented in Boogie [5] loops are first converted to unstructured code with *goto* statements, but back edges are them eliminated to produce an iteration-free program). As an example consider the program shown below on the left annotated with a pre- and postcondition, and a loop invariant.

```
@requires 100 ≤ x
@ensures x = 0
while (0 < x) {
  @invariant 0 ≤ x
  x := x − 1
}
```

```
// assume precondition
assume 100 ≤ x0;
// check invariant initialization
assert 0 ≤ x0;
// assume invariant and loop condition
assume 0 ≤ x1 ∧ 0 < x1;
assume x2 = x1 − 1;
// check invariant preservation
assert 0 ≤ x2;
// assume invariant and negated condition
assume 0 ≤ x3 ∧ ¬(0 < x3);
// assert postcondition
assert x3 = 0;
```

In simplified terms, this could be converted to the program shown on the right side of the figure. Observe how the fresh version variables x_1 and x_3 isolate the three relevant parts of the program (before, inside, and after the loop).

Our work differs from this in that loops are part of the intermediate SA language; they are translated into this language together with their invariants; and soundness and completeness properties are established based on the standard semantics of iteration. Annotated programs are treated explicitly, and the notion of correctly-annotated program is introduced, which allows us to distinguish between incorrect programs and correct programs containing 'wrong' invariants.

(II) In *software model checking*, where the verification is performed on a model of the system containing only bounded executions (as in *bounded model checking of software* [8]), or on an abstract model containing spurious errors (false positives, as in *predicate abstraction* [19]). In these techniques a model is usually extracted from the code by first converting it to SA form [21].

The interest and power of bounded model checking has been decidedly demonstrated in practice by the success of the CBMC tool [8]. The idea of this technique is that loops are unfolded a given number of times, and the resulting branching code is converted to a static single-assignment form (using C *conditional expressions* to encode Φ-functions). Loops are thus not converted to SA form: they are eliminated by a bounded expansion before conversion. A number of transformations are then performed on the SA form, and the resulting program is easily encoded as a satisfiability problem. The transformations avoid exponential explosion, although they are not based on the observations that led to the definition of efficient predicate transformers. To the best of our knowledge, no proofs of soundness or completeness are available for bounded model checking of software.

8 Conclusion

Based on a Hoare-style logic for single-assignment programs, we have formalized a program verification technique that consists in translating annotated programs and specifications into an intermediate SA language, and generating VCs from these intermediate programs. An adaptation-complete variant of the logic is obtained by adding a dedicated consequence rule with a simple condition.

We have also shown how compact verification conditions can be produced directly from annotated SA programs. Assuming a right-associative representation of command sequences, the resulting VCs have linear size without requiring conversion of programs to unstructured form with *goto* commands as in [5].

Single-assignment intermediate forms are used extensively in software verification, both in model checking and in deductive verification; tools from both of these families eliminate iterating constructs before programs are converted to SA form. This stands in contrast with our work in this paper: we define rigorously a notion of single-assignment iterating program, and use it as the basis for a sound and complete verification technique, which includes the translation of annotated programs to SA form. We remark that the translation of loop invariants is a crucial component of the workflow, that *doesn't trivially lead to completeness.* To the best of our knowledge, this is the first time that completeness is established for a verification technique based on the use of an intermediate SA form for programs annotated with invariants.

Tools based on predicate transformers and bounded model checking incorporate many advanced features that our framework does not cover. For instance, Boogie includes automatic inference of loop invariants based on abstract interpretation, and CBMC, which natively uses a SAT (rather than SMT) solver, incorporates constant propagation and simplification functionality that is essential for making bounded verification work in practice. Still, our work here proposes a common theoretical foundation for program verification based on intermediate single-assignment form, unifying ideas from predicate transformers and program logic, while at the same time presenting adaptation-completeness as a natural property of the single-assignment setting.

In fact, a bounded notion of program verification as implemented in bounded model checking, which also relies on conversion to SA form, may also fit the same common foundation. The idea, which we will explore in future work, is to formalize this notion in a deductive setting, by obtaining a semantically justified bounded version of the VCGen of Sect. 4.

Acknowledgments. This work is financed by the ERDF-European Regional Development Fund through the Operational Programme for Competitiveness and Internationalisation - COMPETE 2020 Programme, and by National Funds through the FCT-Fundação para a Ciência e a Tecnologia (Portuguese Foundation for Science and

Technology) within project "POCI-01-0145-FEDER-006961". The first author is also sponsored by FCT grant SFRH/BD/52236/2013.

A A Translation to SA Form

We define a translation function that transforms an annotated program into SA form. We start by introducing some auxiliary definitions to deal with variable versions. Without loss of generality, we will assume that the universe of variables of the SA programs consists of two parts: the *variable identifier* and a *version* (a non-empty list of positive numbers). We let $\mathbf{Var}^{\text{SA}} = \mathbf{Var} \times \mathbb{N}^{+}$ be the set of SA variables, and we will write x_l to denote $(x, l) \in \mathbf{Var}^{\text{SA}}$. We write $\Sigma^{\text{SA}} = \mathbf{Var}^{\text{SA}} \to D$ for the set of states, with D being the interpretation domain.

Consider the *version function* $\mathcal{V} : \mathbf{Var} \to \mathbb{N}^{+}$. The function $\widehat{\mathcal{V}} : \mathbf{Var} \to \mathbf{Var}^{\text{SA}}$ is such that $\widehat{\mathcal{V}}(x) = x_{\mathcal{V}(x)}$. $\widehat{\mathcal{V}}$ is lifted to **Exp** and **Assert** in the obvious way, renaming the variables according to $\mathcal{V}$. Let $s \in \Sigma$ and $\mathcal{V} : \mathbf{Var} \to \mathbb{N}^{+}$. We define $\mathcal{V}(s) \in \mathbf{Var}^{\text{SA}} \rightharpoonup D$ as the partial function $[\widehat{\mathcal{V}}(x) \mapsto s(x) \mid x \in \mathbf{Var}]$. Moreover, for $s' \in \Sigma^{\text{SA}}$, $s' \oplus \mathcal{V}(s)$ denotes the overriding of s' by $\mathcal{V}(s)$.

The translation function T_{sa} is presented in Fig. 7. At the bottom we show the function that receives a triple and transforms it into the SA form. This function uses the auxiliary function shown on top (with the same name but different type) that receives the initial version of each variable identifier and the annotated program, and returns a pair with the final version of each variable identifier and the SA translated program. The definition of the latter function relies in turn on various auxiliary functions that deal with the version list and version functions, and also generate renaming commands. The functions are defined using Haskell-like syntax; we assume that the renaming sequences $\mathcal{I}$ and $\mathcal{U}$, defined in the case of while commands, follow some predefined order established over **Var** (any order will do).

We will now show that T_{sa} is indeed an SA translation. The full details of the proofs and a translation example can be found in [24]. Firstly, we prove that the T_{sa} translation preserves the operational semantics of the original programs. Let us first consider some lemmas.

Lemma 9. *Let* $\mathcal{V} \in \mathbf{Var} \to \mathbb{N}^{+}$, $s \in \Sigma$ *and* $s' \in \Sigma^{\text{SA}}$. *If* $\forall x \in \mathbf{Var}. s(x) = s'(\widehat{\mathcal{V}}(x))$, *then* $s' = s'_0 \oplus \mathcal{V}(s)$ *for some* $s'_0 \in \Sigma^{\text{SA}}$.

Lemma 10. *Let* $e \in \mathbf{Exp}$, $\phi \in \mathbf{Assert}$, $\mathcal{V} \in \mathbf{Var} \to \mathbb{N}^{+}$, $s \in \Sigma$ *and* $s' \in \Sigma^{\text{SA}}$.

1. $[\![\widehat{\mathcal{V}}(e)]\!](s' \oplus \mathcal{V}(s)) = [\![e]\!](s)$
2. $[\![\widehat{\mathcal{V}}(\phi)]\!](s' \oplus \mathcal{V}(s)) = [\![\phi]\!](s)$

Lemma 11. *Let* $C \in \mathbf{AComm}$ *and* $\mathcal{V} \in \mathbf{Var} \to \mathbb{N}^{+}$. *If* $T_{\mathsf{sa}}(\mathcal{V}, C) = (\mathcal{V}', C')$, *then for every* $x \notin \mathsf{Asgn}(C)$, $\mathcal{V}(x) = \mathcal{V}'(x)$.

Lemma 12. *Let* $C_t \in \mathbf{AComm}$, $\mathcal{V} \in \mathbf{Var} \to \mathbb{N}^{+}$, $s_i, s_f \in \Sigma$, $s', s'_f \in \Sigma^{\text{SA}}$, $\mathcal{V}' = \mathcal{V}[x \mapsto \mathsf{new}(\mathcal{V}(x)) \mid x \in \mathsf{Asgn}(C_t)]$, $T_{\mathsf{sa}}(\mathcal{V}', C_t) = (\mathcal{V}'', C'_t)$, $\mathcal{U} = [x_{\mathsf{new}(\mathcal{V}(x))} := x_{\mathcal{V}''(x)} \mid x \in \mathsf{Asgn}(C_t)]$. *If* $\langle \mathbf{while}\ b\ \mathbf{do}\ \lfloor C_t \rfloor, s_i \rangle \leadsto s_f$ *and*

$$
\begin{aligned}
T_{\mathsf{sa}} : (\mathbf{Var} \to \mathbb{N}^+) \times \mathbf{AComm} &\to (\mathbf{Var} \to \mathbb{N}^+) \times \mathbf{AComm}^{\mathrm{SA}} \\
T_{\mathsf{sa}}(\mathcal{V}, \mathbf{skip}) &= (\mathcal{V}, \mathbf{skip}) \\
T_{\mathsf{sa}}(\mathcal{V}, x := e) &= (\mathcal{V}[x \mapsto \mathsf{next}(\mathcal{V}(x))], x_{\mathsf{next}(\mathcal{V}(x))} := \widehat{\mathcal{V}}(e)) \\
T_{\mathsf{sa}}(\mathcal{V}, C_1; C_2) &= (\mathcal{V}'', C_1'; C_2') \\
&\quad \text{where } (\mathcal{V}', C_1') = T_{\mathsf{sa}}(\mathcal{V}, C_1) \\
&\quad \phantom{\text{where }} (\mathcal{V}'', C_2') = T_{\mathsf{sa}}(\mathcal{V}', C_2) \\
T_{\mathsf{sa}}(\mathcal{V}, \mathbf{if}\ b\ \mathbf{then}\ C_t\ \mathbf{else}\ C_f) &= (\mathsf{sup}(\mathcal{V}', \mathcal{V}''), \mathbf{if}\ \widehat{\mathcal{V}}(b)\ \mathbf{then}\ C_t'; \mathsf{merge}(\mathcal{V}', \mathcal{V}'')\ \mathbf{else}\ C_f'; \mathsf{merge}(\mathcal{V}'', \mathcal{V}')) \\
&\quad \text{where } (\mathcal{V}', C_t') = T_{\mathsf{sa}}(\mathcal{V}, C_t) \\
&\quad \phantom{\text{where }} (\mathcal{V}'', C_f') = T_{\mathsf{sa}}(\mathcal{V}, C_f) \\
T_{\mathsf{sa}}(\mathcal{V}, \mathbf{while}\ b\ \mathbf{do}\ \{\theta\}\ C) &= (\mathcal{V}''', \mathbf{for}\ (\mathcal{I}, \widehat{\mathcal{V}'}(b), \mathcal{U})\ \mathbf{do}\ \{\widehat{\mathcal{V}'}(\theta)\}\ \{C'\}; \mathsf{upd}(\mathsf{dom}(\mathcal{U}))) \\
&\quad \text{where } \mathcal{I} = [x_{\mathsf{new}(\mathcal{V}(x))} := x_{\mathcal{V}(x)} \mid x \in \mathsf{Asgn}(C)] \\
&\quad \phantom{\text{where }} \mathcal{V}' = \mathcal{V}[x \mapsto \mathsf{new}(\mathcal{V}(x)) \mid x \in \mathsf{Asgn}(C)] \\
&\quad \phantom{\text{where }} (\mathcal{V}'', C') = T_{\mathsf{sa}}(\mathcal{V}', C) \\
&\quad \phantom{\text{where }} \mathcal{U} = [x_{\mathsf{new}(\mathcal{V}(x))} := x_{\mathcal{V}''(x)} \mid x \in \mathsf{Asgn}(C)] \\
&\quad \phantom{\text{where }} \mathcal{V}''' = \mathcal{V}''[x \mapsto \mathsf{jump}(l) \mid x_l \in \mathsf{dom}(\mathcal{U})]
\end{aligned}
$$

$$\mathsf{next} : \mathbb{N}^+ \to \mathbb{N}^+ \qquad \mathsf{next}\ (h : t) = (h+1) : t$$

$$\mathsf{new} : \mathbb{N}^+ \to \mathbb{N}^+ \qquad \mathsf{new}\ l = 1 : l$$

$$\mathsf{jump} : \mathbb{N}^+ \to \mathbb{N}^+ \qquad \mathsf{jump}\ (i : j : t) = (j+1) : t$$

$$\mathsf{sup} : (\mathbf{Var} \to \mathbb{N}^+)^2 \to (\mathbf{Var} \to \mathbb{N}^+)$$

$$\mathsf{sup}\ (\mathcal{V}, \mathcal{V}')(x) = \begin{cases} \mathcal{V}(x) & \text{if } \mathcal{V}'(x) \prec \mathcal{V}(x) \\ \mathcal{V}'(x) & \text{otherwise} \end{cases}$$

$$\mathsf{merge} : (\mathbf{Var} \to \mathbb{N}^+)^2 \to \mathbf{Rnm}$$

$$\mathsf{merge}\ (\mathcal{V}, \mathcal{V}') = [x_{\mathcal{V}'(x)} := x_{\mathcal{V}(x)} \mid x \in \mathbf{Var} \wedge \mathcal{V}(x) \prec \mathcal{V}'(x)]$$

$$\mathsf{upd} : \mathcal{P}(\mathbf{Var}^{\mathrm{SA}}) \to \mathbf{Rnm}$$

$$\mathsf{upd}\ (X) = [x_{\mathsf{jump}(l)} := x_l \mid x_l \in X]$$

$$(h : t) \prec (h' : t') = h < h'$$

$$T_{\mathsf{sa}} : \mathbf{Assert} \times \mathbf{AComm} \times \mathbf{Assert} \to \mathbf{Assert}^{\mathrm{SA}} \times \mathbf{AComm}^{\mathrm{SA}} \times \mathbf{Assert}^{\mathrm{SA}}$$

$$T_{\mathsf{sa}}(\phi, C, \psi) = (\widehat{\mathcal{V}}(\phi), C', \widehat{\mathcal{V}'}(\psi)), \quad \text{where } (\mathcal{V}', C') = T_{\mathsf{sa}}(\mathcal{V}, C)\ , \text{ for some } \mathcal{V} \in \mathbf{Var} \to \mathbb{N}^+$$

Fig. 7. SA translation function

$\langle \mathbf{while}\ \mathcal{V}'(b)\ \mathbf{do}\ \{\lfloor \mathcal{W}(C_t') \rfloor; \mathcal{U}\}; \mathsf{upd}(\mathsf{dom}(\mathcal{U})), s' \oplus \mathcal{V}(s_i)\rangle \leadsto s_f'$, *then* $\forall x \in \mathbf{Var}.\, s_f(x) = s_f'(\widehat{\mathcal{V}'}(x))$.

Proposition 11. *Let* $C \in \mathbf{AComm}$, $\mathcal{V} \in \mathbf{Var} \to \mathbb{N}^+$, $s_i, s_f \in \Sigma$, $s', s_f' \in \Sigma^{\mathrm{SA}}$ *and* $T_{\mathsf{sa}}(\mathcal{V}, C) = (\mathcal{V}', C')$. *If* $\langle \lfloor C \rfloor, s_i\rangle \leadsto s_f$ *and* $\langle \lfloor \mathcal{W}(C') \rfloor, s' \oplus \mathcal{V}(s_i)\rangle \leadsto s_f'$, *then* $\forall x \in \mathbf{Var}.\, s_f(x) = s_f'(\widehat{\mathcal{V}'}(x))$.

Proof. By induction on the structure of C. □

Secondly, we prove that lifting the translation function to Hoare triples is sound, i.e., if the translated triple is valid then the original triple is also valid.

Lemma 13. *Let* $C \in \mathbf{AComm}$, $\mathcal{V} \in \mathbf{Var} \to \mathbb{N}^+$, *and* $s_i, s_f \in \Sigma$. *If* $\langle \lfloor C \rfloor, s_i\rangle \leadsto s_f$ *and* $T_{\mathsf{sa}}(\mathcal{V}, C) = (\mathcal{V}', C')$, *then* $\langle \lfloor \mathcal{W}(C') \rfloor, s_1' \oplus \mathcal{V}(s_i)\rangle \leadsto s_2' \oplus \mathcal{V}'(s_f)$, *for some* $s_1', s_2' \in \Sigma^{\mathrm{SA}}$.

Proof. By induction on the structure of C using Proposition 11. □

Proposition 12. *Let* $C \in \mathbf{AComm}$, $\phi, \psi \in \mathbf{Assert}$, $\mathcal{V} \in \mathbf{Var} \to \mathbb{N}^+$ *and* $T_{\mathsf{sa}}(\mathcal{V}, C) = (\mathcal{V}', C')$.
If $\models \{\widehat{\mathcal{V}}(\phi)\} \lfloor \mathcal{W}(C') \rfloor \{\widehat{\mathcal{V}'}(\psi)\}$, *then* $\models \{\phi\} \lfloor C \rfloor \{\psi\}$.

Proof. Follows from Lemmas 13 and 10 and Propositon 11. □

Finally, we will show that Hg-derivability is preserved, i.e. if a Hoare triple for an annotated program is derivable in Hg, then the translated triple is also derivable in Hg. Again we start by stating some lemmas.

Lemma 14. *Let* $\mathcal{V}, \mathcal{V}' \in \mathbf{Var} \to \mathbb{N}^+$ *and* $\psi \in \mathbf{Assert}$. *The following hold:*

1. $\vdash_{\mathsf{Hg}} \{\widehat{\mathcal{V}}(\psi)\}\, \mathsf{merge}(\mathcal{V}, \mathcal{V}')\, \{\widehat{\mathsf{sup}(\mathcal{V}, \mathcal{V}')}(\psi)\}$
2. $\vdash_{\mathsf{Hg}} \{\widehat{\mathcal{V}}(\psi)\}\, \mathsf{merge}(\mathcal{V}', \mathcal{V})\, \{\widehat{\mathsf{sup}(\mathcal{V}, \mathcal{V}')}(\psi)\}$

Lemma 15. *Let* $\mathcal{I} \in \mathbf{Rnm}$ *and* $\phi \in \mathbf{Assert}$. *Then* $\vdash_{\mathsf{Hg}} \{\phi\} \mathcal{I} \{\mathcal{I}^{-1}(\phi)\}$ *holds.*

Lemma 16. *Let* $\mathcal{V} \in \mathbf{Var} \to \mathbb{N}^+$, $C \in \mathbf{AComm}$, $\mathcal{V}' = \mathcal{V}[x \mapsto \mathsf{new}(\mathcal{V}(x)) \mid x \in \mathsf{Asgn}(C)]$, $T_{\mathsf{sa}}(\mathcal{V}', C) = (\mathcal{V}'', C')$ *and* $\mathcal{U} = [x_{\mathsf{new}(\mathcal{V}(x))} := x_{\mathcal{V}''(x)} \mid x \in \mathsf{Asgn}(C)]$. *The derivation* $\vdash_{\mathsf{Hg}} \{\widehat{\mathcal{V}''}(\theta)\} \mathcal{U} \{\widehat{\mathcal{V}'}(\theta)\}$ *holds.*

Lemma 17. *Let* $\mathcal{V} \in \mathbf{Var} \to \mathbb{N}^+$, $C \in \mathbf{AComm}$, $\mathcal{V}' = \mathcal{V}[x \mapsto \mathsf{new}(\mathcal{V}(x)) \mid x \in \mathsf{Asgn}(C)]$, $T_{\mathsf{sa}}(\mathcal{V}', C) = (\mathcal{V}'', C')$, $\mathcal{U} = [x_{\mathsf{new}(\mathcal{V}(x))} := x_{\mathcal{V}''(x)} \mid x \in \mathsf{Asgn}(C)]$ *and* $\mathcal{V}''' = \mathcal{V}''[x \mapsto \mathsf{jump}(l) \mid x_l \in \mathsf{dom}(\mathcal{U})]$. *The following derivation holds* $\vdash_{\mathsf{Hg}} \{\widehat{\mathcal{V}'}(\psi)\}\, \mathsf{upd}(\mathsf{dom}(\mathcal{U}))\, \{\widehat{\mathcal{V}'''}(\psi)\}$.

Proposition 13. *Let* $C \in \mathbf{AComm}$, $\phi, \psi \in \mathbf{Assert}$, $\mathcal{V} \in \mathbf{Var} \to \mathbb{N}^+$ *and* $T_{\mathsf{sa}}(\mathcal{V}, C) = (\mathcal{V}', C')$. *If* $\vdash_{\mathsf{Hg}} \{\phi\}\, C\, \{\psi\}$, *then* $\vdash_{\mathsf{Hg}} \{\widehat{\mathcal{V}}(\phi)\}\, \mathcal{W}(C')\, \{\widehat{\mathcal{V}'}(\psi)\}$.

Proof. By induction on the structure of $\vdash_{\mathsf{Hg}} \{\phi\}\, C\, \{\psi\}$. □

It is now immediate that T_{sa} conforms to Definition 6.

Proposition 14. *The* T_{sa} *function of Fig. 7 is an SA translation.*

Proof. Follows directly from Propositions 12 and 13. □

References

1. America, P., de Boer, F.: Proving total correctness of recursive procedures. Inf. Comput. **84**(2), 129–162 (1990)
2. Apt, K.R.: Ten years of Hoare's logic: a survey - part 1. ACM Trans. Program. Lang. Syst. **3**(4), 431–483 (1981)
3. Barnes, J.: High Integrity Software: The SPARK Approach to Safety and Security. Addison-Wesley, Boston (2003)

4. Barnett, M., Chang, B.-Y.E., DeLine, R., Jacobs, B., M. Leino, K.R.: Boogie: a modular reusable verifier for object-oriented programs. In: de Boer, F.S., Bonsangue, M.M., Graf, S., de Roever, W.-P. (eds.) FMCO 2005. LNCS, vol. 4111, pp. 364–387. Springer, Heidelberg (2006)
5. Barnett, M., Leino, K.R.M.: Weakest-precondition of unstructured programs. ACM SIGSOFT Softw. Eng. Notes **31**(1), 82–87 (2006)
6. Barnett, M., M. Leino, K.R., Schulte, W.: The Spec# programming system: an overview. In: Barthe, G., Burdy, L., Huisman, M., Lanet, J.-L., Muntean, T. (eds.) CASSIS 2004. LNCS, vol. 3362, pp. 49–69. Springer, Heidelberg (2005)
7. Baudin, P., Cuoq, P., Filliâtre, J.-C., Marché, C., Monate, B., Moy, Y., Prevosto, V.: ACSL: ANSI/ISO C specification language. In: CEA LIST and INRIA (2010)
8. Clarke, E., Kroning, D., Lerda, F.: A tool for checking ANSI-C programs. In: Jensen, K., Podelski, A. (eds.) TACAS 2004. LNCS, vol. 2988, pp. 168–176. Springer, Heidelberg (2004)
9. Stephen, A.: Cook: soundness and completeness of an axiom system for program verification. SIAM J. Comput. **7**(1), 70–90 (1978)
10. Correnson, L., Cuoq, P., Puccetti, A., Signoles, J.: Frama-C user manual (2010). http://frama-c.com
11. Cytron, R., Ferrante, J., Rosen, B.K., Wegman, M.N., Zadeck, F.K.: Efficiently computing static single assignment form and the control dependence graph. ACM Trans. Program. Lang. Syst. **13**(4), 451–490 (1991)
12. Dijkstra, E.W., Scholten, C.S.: Predicate calculus and program semantics. Springer, Scholten (1990)
13. Filliâtre, J.-C., Paskevich, A.: Why3 — where programs meet provers. In: Felleisen, M., Gardner, P. (eds.) ESOP 2013. LNCS, vol. 7792, pp. 125–128. Springer, Heidelberg (2013)
14. Flanagan, C., Saxe, J.B.: Avoiding exponential explosion: generating compact verification conditions. In: Proceedings of POpPL, pp. 193–205. ACM (2001)
15. Gordon, M., Collavizza, H.: Forward with Hoare. In: Roscoe, A.W., Jones, C.B., Wood, K.R. (eds.) Reflections on the Work of C.A.R. Hoare: History of Computing, pp. 101–121. Springer, London (2010)
16. Grigore, R., Charles, J., Fairmichael, F., Kiniry, J.: Strongest postcondition of unstructured programs. In: Proceedings of FTfJP, pp. 6:1–6:7. ACM (2009)
17. Hoare, C.A.R.: An axiomatic basis for computer programming. Commun. ACM **12**(10), 576–580 (1969)
18. Hoare, C.A.R.: Procedures and parameters: an axiomatic approach. In: Engeler, E. (ed.) Proceeedings of Symposium on Semantics of Algorithmic Languages. Lecture Notes in Mathematics, vol. 188, pp. 102–116. Springer, Heidelberg (1971)
19. Jhala, R., Majumdar, R.: Software model checking. ACM Comput. Surv. **41**(4), 21 (2009)
20. Kleymann, T.: Hoare logic and auxiliary variables. Formal Aspects Comput. **11**(5), 541–566 (1999)
21. Kroening, D.: Software verification. In: Biere, A., Heule, M., Van Maaren, H., Walsh, T. (eds.) Handbook of Satisfiability. Frontiers in Artificial Intelligence and Applications, vol. 185, pp. 505–532. IOS Press, Amsterdam (2009)
22. Rustan, K., Leino, M., Saxe, J.B., Stata, R.: Checking Java programs via guarded commands. In: Proceedings of ECOOP, pp. 110–111. Springer (1999)
23. Rustan, K., Leino, M.: Efficient weakest preconditions. Inf. Process. Lett. **93**(6), 281–288 (2005)
24. Loureno, C.B., Frade, M.J., Pinto, J.S.: A single-assignment translation for annotated programs. ArXiv e-prints (2016). http://arxiv.org/abs/1601.00584

25. Marché, C., Paulin-Mohring, C., Urbain, X.: The KRAKATOA tool for certification of JAVA/JAVACARD programs annotated in JML. J. Logic Algebraic Program. **58**(1–2), 89–106 (2004)
26. Reynolds, J.C.: Separation logic: a logic for shared mutable data structures. In: LICS, pp. 55–74. IEEE Computer Society (2002)
27. Vanbroekhoven, P., Janssens, G., Bruynooghe, M., Catthoor, F.: A practical dynamic single assignment transformation. ACM Trans. Des. Autom. Electron. Syst. **12**(4), 40 (2007)

Practical Optional Types for Clojure

Ambrose Bonnaire-Sergeant[1(✉)], Rowan Davies[2], and Sam Tobin-Hochstadt[1]

[1] Indiana University, Bloomington, USA
{abonnair,samth}@indiana.edu
[2] Omnia Team, Commonwealth Bank of Australia, Sydney, Australia
Rowan.Davies@cba.com.au

Abstract. Typed Clojure is an optional type system for Clojure, a dynamic language in the Lisp family that targets the JVM. Typed Clojure enables Clojure programmers to gain greater confidence in the correctness of their code via static type checking while remaining in the Clojure world, and has acquired significant adoption in the Clojure community. Typed Clojure repurposes Typed Racket's *occurrence typing*, an approach to statically reasoning about predicate tests, and also includes several new type system features to handle existing Clojure idioms.

In this paper, we describe Typed Clojure and present these type system extensions, focusing on three features widely used in Clojure. First, multimethods provide extensible operations, and their Clojure semantics turns out to have a surprising synergy with the underlying occurrence typing framework. Second, Java interoperability is central to Clojure's mission but introduces challenges such as ubiquitous `null`; Typed Clojure handles Java interoperability while ensuring the absence of null-pointer exceptions in typed programs. Third, Clojure programmers idiomatically use immutable dictionaries for data structures; Typed Clojure handles this with multiple forms of heterogeneous dictionary types. We provide a formal model of the Typed Clojure type system incorporating these and other features, with a proof of soundness. Additionally, Typed Clojure is now in use by numerous corporations and developers working with Clojure, and we present a quantitative analysis on the use of type system features in two substantial code bases.

1 Clojure with Static Typing

The popularity of dynamically-typed languages in software development, combined with a recognition that types often improve programmer productivity, software reliability, and performance, has led to the recent development of a wide variety of optional and gradual type systems aimed at checking existing programs written in existing languages. These include TypeScript [19] and Flow [11] for JavaScript, Hack [10] for PHP, and mypy [15] for Python among the optional

P. Thiemann (Ed.): ESOP 2016, LNCS 9632, pp. 68–94, 2016.
DOI: 10.1007/978-3-662-49498-1_4

```
(ann pname [(U File String) -> (U nil String)])
(defmulti pname class) ; multimethod dispatching on class of argument
(defmethod pname String [s] (pname (new File s))) ; String case
(defmethod pname File [f] (.getName f)) ; File case, static null check
(pname "STAINS/JELLY") ;=> "JELLY" :- (U nil Str)
```

Fig. 1. A simple typed Clojure program (delimiters: Java interoperation (green), type annotation (blue), function invocation (black), collection literal (red), other (gray)) (Color figure online)

systems, and Typed Racket [23], Reticulated Python [25], and GradualTalk [1] among gradually-typed systems.[1]

One key lesson of these systems, indeed a lesson known to early developers of optional type systems such as StrongTalk, is that type systems for existing languages must be designed to work with the features and idioms of the target language. Often this takes the form of a core language, be it of functions or classes and objects, together with extensions to handle distinctive language features.

We synthesize these lessons to present *Typed Clojure*, an optional type system for Clojure. Clojure is a dynamically typed language in the Lisp family—built on the Java Virtual Machine (JVM)—which has recently gained popularity as an alternative JVM language. It offers the flexibility of a Lisp dialect, including macros, emphasizes a functional style via immutable data structures, and provides interoperability with existing Java code, allowing programmers to use existing Java libraries without leaving Clojure. Since its initial release in 2007, Clojure has been widely adopted for "backend" development in places where its support for parallelism, functional programming, and Lisp-influenced abstraction is desired on the JVM. As a result, there is an extensive base of existing untyped programs whose developers can benefit from Typed Clojure, an experience we discuss in this paper.

Since Clojure is a language in the Lisp family, we apply the lessons of Typed Racket, an existing gradual type system for Racket, to the core of Typed Clojure, consisting of an extended λ-calculus over a variety of base types shared between all Lisp systems. Furthermore, Typed Racket's *occurrence typing* has proved necessary for type checking realistic Clojure programs.

However, Clojure goes beyond Racket in many ways, requiring several new type system features which we detail in this paper. Most significantly, Clojure supports, and Clojure developers use, **multimethods** to structure their code in extensible fashion. Furthermore, since Clojure is an untyped language, dispatch within multimethods is determined by application of dynamic predicates to argument values. Fortunately, the dynamic dispatch used by multimethods has surprising symmetry with the conditional dispatch handled by occurrence typing. Typed Clojure is therefore able to effectively handle complex and highly dynamic dispatch as present in existing Clojure programs.

[1] We use "gradual typing" for systems like Typed Racket with sound interoperation between typed and untyped code; Typed Clojure or TypeScript which don't enforce type invariants we describe as "optionally typed".

But multimethods are not the only Clojure feature crucial to type checking existing programs. As a language built on the Java Virtual Machine, Clojure provides flexible and transparent access to existing Java libraries, and **Clojure/Java interoperation** is found in almost every significant Clojure code base. Typed Clojure therefore builds in an understanding of the Java type system and handles interoperation appropriately. Notably, `null` is a distinct type in Typed Clojure, designed to automatically rule out null-pointer exceptions.

An example of these features is given in Fig. 1. Here, the `pname` multimethod dispatches on the `class` of the argument—for `Strings`, the first method implementation is called, for `Files`, the second. The `String` method calls a `File` constructor, returning a non-nil `File` instance—the `getName` method on `File` requires a non-nil target, returning a nilable type.

Finally, flexible, high-performance immutable dictionaries are the most common Clojure data structure. Simply treating them as uniformly-typed key-value mappings would be insufficient for existing programs and programming styles. Instead, Typed Clojure provides a flexible **heterogenous map** type, in which specific entries can be specified.

While these features may seem disparate, they are unified in important ways. First, they leverage the type system mechanisms inherited from Typed Racket—multimethods when using dispatch via predicates, Java interoperation for handling `null` tests, and heterogenous maps using union types and reasoning about subcomponents of data. Second, they are crucial features for handling Clojure code in practice. Typed Clojure's use in real Clojure deployments would not be possible without effective handling of these three Clojure features.

Our main contributions are as follows:

1. We motivate and describe Typed Clojure, an optional type system for Clojure that understands existing Clojure idioms.
2. We present a sound formal model for three crucial type system features: multi-methods, Java interoperability, and heterogenous maps.
3. We evaluate the use of Typed Clojure features on existing Typed Clojure code, including both open source and in-house systems.

The remainder of this paper begins with an example-driven presentation of the main type system features in Sect. 2. We then incrementally present a core calculus for Typed Clojure covering all of these features together in Sect. 3 and prove type soundness (Sect. 4). We then present an empirical analysis of significant code bases written in `core.typed`—the full implementation of Typed Clojure—in Sect. 5. Finally, we discuss related work and conclude.

2 Overview of Typed Clojure

We now begin a tour of the central features of Typed Clojure, beginning with Clojure itself. Our presentation uses the full Typed Clojure system to illustrate key type system ideas,[2] before studying the core features in detail in Sect. 3.

[2] Full examples: https://github.com/typedclojure/esop16.

2.1 Clojure

Clojure [13] is a Lisp that runs on the Java Virtual Machine with support for concurrent programming and immutable data structures in a mostly-functional style. Clojure provides easy interoperation with existing Java libraries, with Java values being like any other Clojure value. However, this smooth interoperability comes at the cost of pervasive `null`, which leads to the possibility of null pointer exceptions—a drawback we address in Typed Clojure.

2.2 Typed Clojure

A simple one-argument function `greet` is annotated with `ann` to take and return strings.

```
(ann  greet [Str -> Str])
(defn greet [n] (str "Hello, " n "!"))
(greet "Grace") ;=> "Hello, Grace!" :- Str
```

Providing `nil` (exactly Java's `null`) is a static type error—`nil` is not a string.

```
(greet nil) ; Type Error: Expected Str, given nil
```

Unions. To allow `nil`, we use *ad-hoc unions* (`nil` and `false` are logically false).

```
(ann  greet-nil [(U nil Str) -> Str])
(defn greet-nil [n] (str "Hello" (when n (str ", " n)) "!"))
(greet-nil "Donald") ;=> "Hello, Donald!" :- Str
(greet-nil nil)      ;=> "Hello!"         :- Str
```

Typed Clojure prevents well-typed code from dereferencing `nil`.

Flow Analysis. Occurrence typing [24] models type-based control flow. In `greetings`, a branch ensures `repeat` is never passed `nil`.

```
(ann  greetings [Str (U nil Int) -> Str])
(defn greetings [n i]
  (str "Hello, " (when i (apply str (repeat i "hello, "))) n "!"))
(greetings "Donald" 2)  ;=> "Hello, hello, hello, Donald!" :- Str
(greetings "Grace" nil) ;=> "Hello, Grace!"                :- Str
```

Removing the branch is a static type error—`repeat` cannot be passed `nil`.

```
(ann  greetings-bad [Str (U nil Int) -> Str])
(defn greetings-bad [n i]
; Expected Int, given (U nil Int)
  (str "Hello, " (apply str (repeat i "hello, ")) n "!"))
```

2.3 Java Interoperability

Clojure can interact with Java constructors, methods, and fields. This program calls the `getParent` on a constructed `File` instance, returning a nullable string.

```
(.getParent (new File "a/b"))  ;=> "a" :- (U nil Str)
```

Example 1

Typed Clojure can integrate with the Clojure compiler to avoid expensive reflective calls like getParent, however if a specific overload cannot be found based on the surrounding static context, a type error is thrown.

```
(fn [f] (.getParent f)) ; Type Error: Unresolved interop: getParent
```

Function arguments default to Any, which is similar to a union of all types. Ascribing a parameter type allows Typed Clojure to find a specific method.

```
(ann parent [(U nil File) -> (U nil Str)])
(defn parent [f] (if f (.getParent f) nil))
```

Example 2

The conditional guards from dereferencing nil, and—as before—removing it is a static type error, as typed code could possibly dereference nil.

```
(defn parent-bad-in [f :- (U nil File)]
  (.getParent f)) ; Type Error: Cannot call instance method on nil.
```

Typed Clojure rejects programs that assume methods cannot return nil.

```
(defn parent-bad-out [f :- File] :- Str
  (.getParent f)) ; Type Error: Expected Str, given (U nil Str).
```

Method targets can never be nil. Typed Clojure also prevents passing nil as Java method or constructor arguments by default—this restriction can be adjusted per method.

In contrast, JVM invariants guarantee constructors return non-null.[3]

```
(parent (new File s))
```

Example 3

2.4 Multimethods

Multimethods are a kind of extensible function—combining a *dispatch function* with one or more *methods*—widely used to define Clojure operations.

Value-based Dispatch. This simple multimethod takes a keyword (Kw) and says hello in different languages.

```
(ann hi [Kw -> Str]) ; multimethod type
(defmulti hi identity) ; dispatch function `identity`
(defmethod hi :en [_] "hello") ; method for `:en`
(defmethod hi :fr [_] "bonjour") ; method for `:fr`
(defmethod hi :default [_] "um...") ; default method
```

Example 4

When invoked, the arguments are first supplied to the dispatch function—identity—yielding a *dispatch value*. A method is then chosen based on the dispatch value, to which the arguments are then passed to return a value.

```
(map hi [:en :fr :bocce]) ;=> ("hello" "bonjour" "um...")
```

[3] http://docs.oracle.com/javase/specs/jls/se7/html/jls-15.html#jls-15.9.4.

For example, (hi :en) evaluates to *"hello"*—it executes the :en method because (= (identity :en) :en) is true and (= (identity :en) :fr) is false.

Dispatching based on literal values enables certain forms of method definition, but this is only part of the story for multimethod dispatch.

Class-based Dispatch. For class values, multimethods can choose methods based on subclassing relationships. Recall the multimethod from Fig. 1. The dispatch function class dictates whether the String or File method is chosen. The multimethod dispatch rules use isa?, a hybrid predicate which is both a subclassing check for classes and an equality check for other values.

```
(isa? :en :en)        ;=> true
(isa? String Object)  ;=> true
```

The current dispatch value and—in turn—each method's associated dispatch value is supplied to isa?. If exactly one method returns true, it is chosen. For example, the call (pname *"STAINS/JELLY"*) picks the String method because (isa? String String) is true, and (isa? String File) is not.

2.5 Heterogeneous Hash-Maps

The most common way to represent compound data in Clojure are immutable hash-maps, typicially with keyword keys. Keywords double as functions that look themselves up in a map, or return nil if absent.

```
(def breakfast {:en "waffles" :fr "croissants"})
(:en breakfast)     ;=> "waffles" :- Str
(:bocce breakfast) ;=> nil        :- nil
```

Example 5

HMap types describe the most common usages of keyword-keyed maps.

```
breakfast ; : - (HMap :mandatory {:en Str, :fr Str}, :complete? true)
```

This says :en and :fr are known entries mapped to strings, and the map is fully specified—that is, no other entries exist—by :complete? being true.

HMap types default to partial specification, with '{:en Str :fr Str} abbreviating (HMap :mandatory {:en Str, :fr Str}).

```
(ann lunch '{:en Str :fr Str})
(def lunch {:en "muffin" :fr "baguette"})
(:bocce lunch) ;=> nil :- Any ; less accurate type
```

Example 6

HMaps in Practice. The next example is extracted from a production system at CircleCI, a company with a large production Typed Clojure system (Sect. 5.2 presents a case study and empirical result from this code base).

Example 7

```
(defalias RawKeyPair ; extra keys disallowed
  (HMap :mandatory {:pub RawKey, :priv RawKey},
        :complete? true))
(defalias EncKeyPair ; extra keys disallowed
  (HMap :mandatory {:pub RawKey, :enc-priv EncKey}, :complete? true))

(ann enc-keypair [RawKeyPair -> EncKeyPair])
(defn enc-keypair [kp]
  (assoc (dissoc kp :priv) :enc-priv (encrypt (:priv kp))))
```

As `EncKeyPair` is fully specified, we remove extra keys like `:priv` via `dissoc`, which returns a new map that is the first argument without the entry named by the second argument. Notice removing `dissoc` causes a type error.

```
(defn enc-keypair-bad [kp] ; Type error: :priv disallowed
  (assoc kp :enc-priv (encrypt (:priv kp))))
```

2.6 HMaps and Multimethods, Joined at the Hip

HMaps and multimethods are the primary ways for representing and dispatching on data respectively, and so are intrinsically linked. As type system designers, we must search for a compositional approach that can anticipate any combination of these features.

Thankfully, occurrence typing, originally designed for reasoning about `if` tests, provides the compositional approach we need. By extending the system with a handful of rules based on HMaps and other functions, we can automatically cover both easy cases and those that compose rules in arbitrary ways.

Futhermore, this approach extends to multimethod dispatch by reusing occurrence typing's approach to conditionals and encoding a small number of rules to handle the `isa?`-based dispatch. In practice, conditional-based control flow typing extends to multimethod dispatch, and vice-versa.

We first demonstrate a very common, simple dispatch style, then move on to deeper structural dispatching where occurrence typing's compositionality shines.

HMaps and Unions. Partially specified HMap's with a common dispatch key combine naturally with ad-hoc unions. An `Order` is one of three kinds of HMaps.

```
(defalias Order "A meal order, tracking dessert quantities."
  (U '{:Meal ':lunch, :desserts Int} '{:Meal ':dinner :desserts Int}
     '{:Meal ':combo :meal1 Order :meal2 Order}))
```

The `:Meal` entry is common to each HMap, always mapped to a known keyword singleton type. It's natural to dispatch on the `class` of an instance—it's similarly natural to dispatch on a known entry like `:Meal`.

Example 8

```
(ann desserts [Order -> Int])
(defmulti desserts :Meal)  ; dispatch on :Meal entry
(defmethod desserts :lunch [o] (:desserts o))
(defmethod desserts :dinner [o] (:desserts o))
```

```
(defmethod desserts :combo [o]
  (+ (desserts (:meal1 o)) (desserts (:meal2 o))))

(desserts {:Meal :combo, :meal1 {:Meal :lunch :desserts 1},
          :meal2 {:Meal :dinner :desserts 2}}) ;=> 3
```

The `:combo` method is verified to only structurally recur on `Order`s. This is achieved because we learn the argument `o` must be of type `'{:Meal :combo}` since `(isa? (:Meal o) :combo)` is true. Combining this with the fact that `o` is an `Order` eliminates possibility of `:lunch` and `:dinner` orders, simplifying `o` to `'{:Meal ':combo :meal1 Order :meal2 Order}` which contains appropriate arguments for both recursive calls.

Nested Dispatch. A more exotic dispatch mechanism for `desserts` might be on the `class` of the `:desserts` key. If the result is a number, then we know the `:desserts` key is a number, otherwise the input is a `:combo` meal. We have already seen dispatch on `class` and on keywords in isolation—occurrence typing automatically understands control flow that combines its simple building blocks.

The first method has dispatch value `Long`, a subtype of `Int`, and the second method has `nil`, the sentinel value for a failed map lookup. In practice, `:lunch` and `:dinner` meals will dispatch to the `Long` method, but Typed Clojure infers a slightly more general type due to the definition of `:combo` meals.

Example 9

```
(ann desserts' [Order -> Int])
(defmulti desserts'
  (fn [o :- Order] (class (:desserts o))))
(defmethod desserts' Long [o]
;o :- (U '{:Meal (U ':dinner ':lunch), :desserts Int}
;
'{:Meal ':combo, :desserts Int, :meal1 Order, :meal2 Order})
  (:desserts o))
(defmethod desserts' nil [o]
  ; o :- '{:Meal ':combo, :meal1 Order, :meal2 Order}
  (+ (desserts' (:meal1 o)) (desserts' (:meal2 o))))
```

In the `Long` method, Typed Clojure learns that its argument is at least of type `'{:desserts Long}`—since `(isa? (class (:desserts o)) Long)` must be true. Here the `:desserts` entry *must* be present and mapped to a `Long`—even in a `:combo` meal, which does not specify `:desserts` as present or absent.

In the `nil` method, `(isa? (class (:desserts o)) nil)` must be true—which implies `(class (:desserts o))` is `nil`. Since lookups on missing keys return `nil`, either

- `o` has a `:desserts` entry to `nil`, like `:desserts nil`, or
- `o` is missing a `:desserts` entry.

We can express this type with the `:absent-keys` HMap option

```
(U '{:desserts nil} (HMap :absent-keys #{:desserts}))
```

This eliminates non-`:combo` meals since their `'{:desserts Int}` type does not agree with this new information (because `:desserts` is neither `nil` or absent).

From Multiple to Arbitrary Dispatch. Clojure multimethod dispatch, and Typed Clojure's handling of it, goes even further, supporting dispatch on multiple arguments via vectors. Dispatch on multiple arguments is beyond the scope of this paper, but the same intuition applies—adding support for multiple dispatch admits arbitrary combinations and nestings of it and previous dispatch rules.

3 A Formal Model of λ_{TC}

After demonstrating the core features of Typed Clojure, we link them together in a formal model called λ_{TC}. Building on occurrence typing, we incrementally add each novel feature of Typed Clojure to the formalism, interleaving presentation of syntax, typing rules, operational semantics, and subtyping.

3.1 Core Type System

We start with a review of occurrence typing [24], the foundation of λ_{TC}.

Expressions. Syntax is given in Fig. 2. Expressions e include variables x, values v, applications, abstractions, conditionals, and let expressions. All binding forms introduce fresh variables—a subtle but important point since our type environments are not simply dictionaries. Values include booleans b, nil, class literals C, keywords k, integers n, constants c, and strings s. Lexical closures $[\rho, \lambda x^{\tau}.e]_{\mathsf{c}}$ close value environments ρ—which map bindings to values—over functions.

Types. Types σ or τ include the top type $\top$, *untagged* unions $(\bigcup\ \overrightarrow{\tau})$, singletons $(\mathbf{Val}\, l)$, and class instances C. We abbreviate the classes **Boolean** to **B**, **Keyword** to **K**, **Nat** to **N**, **String** to **S**, and **File** to **F**. We also abbreviate the types $(\bigcup)$ to $\bot$, $(\mathbf{Val}\,\mathsf{nil})$ to **nil**, $(\mathbf{Val}\,\mathsf{true})$ to **true**, and $(\mathbf{Val}\,\mathsf{false})$ to **false**. The difference between the types $(\mathbf{Val}\, C)$ and C is subtle. The former is inhabited by class literals like **K** and the result of (*class* :a)—the latter by *instances* of classes, like a keyword literal :a, an instance of the type **K**. Function types $x{:}\sigma \xrightarrow[o]{\psi|\psi} \tau$ contain *latent* (terminology from [17]) propositions ψ, object o, and return type τ, which may refer to the function argument x. They are instantiated with the actual object of the argument in applications.

Objects. Each expression is associated with a symbolic representation called an *object*. For example, variable m has object m; (**class** (:lunch m)) has object $\mathbf{class}(\mathbf{key}_{:\mathsf{lunch}}(m))$; and 42 has the *empty* object $\emptyset$ since it is unimportant in our system. Figure 2 gives the syntax for objects o—non-empty objects $\pi(x)$ combine of a root variable x and a *path* π, which consists of a possibly-empty sequence of *path elements* (pe) applied right-to-left from the root variable. We use two path elements—**class** and $\mathbf{key}_k$—representing the results of calling *class* and looking up a keyword k, respectively.

e	$::= x \mid v \mid (e\ e) \mid \lambda x^{\tau}.e \mid (\textsf{if}\ e\ e\ e) \mid (\textsf{let}\ [x\ e]\ e)$	Expressions
v	$::= l \mid n \mid c \mid s \mid [\rho, \lambda x^{\tau}.e]_{\mathsf{c}}$	Values
c	$::= \mathit{class} \mid n?$	Constants
σ, τ	$::= \top \mid (\bigcup\ \overrightarrow{\tau}) \mid x{:}\tau \xrightarrow[o]{\psi\mid\psi} \tau \mid (\mathbf{Val}\,l) \mid C$	Types
l	$::= k \mid C \mid \textsf{nil} \mid b$	Value types
b	$::= \textsf{true} \mid \textsf{false}$	Boolean values
ψ	$::= \tau_{\pi(x)} \mid \overline{\tau}_{\pi(x)} \mid \psi \supset \psi \mid \psi \wedge \psi \mid \psi \vee \psi \mid \texttt{tt} \mid \texttt{ff}$	Propositions
o	$::= \pi(x) \mid \emptyset$	Objects
π	$::= \overrightarrow{pe}$	Paths
pe	$::= \mathbf{class} \mid \mathbf{key}_k$	Path elements
Γ	$::= \overrightarrow{\psi}$	Proposition environments
ρ	$::= \{\overrightarrow{x \mapsto v}\}$	Value environments

Fig. 2. Syntax of terms, types, propositions and objects

Propositions with a Logical System. In standard type systems, association lists often track the types of variables, like in LC-Let and LC-Local.

$$\textsc{LC-Let}\ \frac{\Gamma \vdash e_1 : \sigma \qquad \Gamma, x \mapsto \sigma \vdash e_2 : \tau}{\Gamma \vdash (\textsf{let}\ [x\ e_1]\ e_2) : \tau} \qquad \textsc{LC-Local}\ \frac{\Gamma(x) = \tau}{\Gamma \vdash x : \tau}$$

Occurrence typing instead pairs *logical formulas,* that can reason about arbitrary non-empty objects, with a *proof system.* The logical statement σ_x says variable x is of type σ.

$$\textsc{T0-Let}\ \frac{\Gamma \vdash e_1 : \sigma \qquad \Gamma, \sigma_x \vdash e_2 : \tau}{\Gamma \vdash (\textsf{let}\ [x\ e_1]\ e_2) : \tau} \qquad \textsc{T0-Local}\ \frac{\Gamma \vdash \tau_x}{\Gamma \vdash x : \tau}$$

In T0-Local, $\Gamma \vdash \tau_x$ appeals to the proof system to solve for τ.

We further extend logical statements to *propositional logic.* Figure 2 describes the syntax for propositions ψ, consisting of positive and negative *type propositions* about non-empty objects—$\tau_{\pi(x)}$ and $\overline{\tau}_{\pi(x)}$ respectively—the latter pronounced "the object $\pi(x)$ is *not* of type τ". The other propositions are standard logical connectives: implications, conjunctions, disjunctions, and the trivial ($\texttt{tt}$) and impossible ($\texttt{ff}$) propositions. The full proof system judgement $\Gamma \vdash \psi$ says *proposition environment* Γ proves proposition ψ.

Each expression is associated with two propositions—when expression e_1 is in test position like ($\textsf{if}\ e_1\ e_2\ e_3$), the type system extracts e_1's 'then' and 'else' proposition to check e_2 and e_3 respectively. For example, in ($\textsf{if}\ o\ e_2\ e_3$) we learn variable o is true in e_2 via o's 'then' proposition $\overline{(\bigcup\ \mathbf{nil}\ \mathbf{false})}_o$, and that o is false in e_3 via o's 'else' proposition $(\bigcup\ \mathbf{nil}\ \mathbf{false})_o$.

To illustrate, recall Example 8. The parameter o is of type **Order**, written $\mathbf{Order}_o$ as a proposition. In the :combo method, we know (:Meal o) is :combo,

$$\textsc{T-Local}\ \frac{\Gamma \vdash \tau_x \quad \sigma = (\cup\ \mathbf{nil}\ \mathbf{false})}{\Gamma \vdash x : \tau \ ;\ \overline{\sigma}_x | \sigma_x \ ;\ x} \qquad \textsc{T-Abs}\ \frac{\Gamma, \sigma_x \vdash e \Rightarrow e' : \sigma' \ ;\ \psi_+|\psi_- \ ;\ o \quad \tau = x{:}\sigma \xrightarrow[o]{\psi_+|\psi_-} \sigma'}{\Gamma \vdash \lambda x^\sigma.e \Rightarrow \lambda x^\sigma.e' : \tau \ ;\ \mathtt{tt}|\mathtt{ff} \ ;\ \emptyset}$$

$$\textsc{T-If}\ \frac{\Gamma \vdash e_1 \Rightarrow e_1' : \tau_1 \ ;\ \psi_{1+}|\psi_{1-} \ ;\ o_1 \quad \Gamma, \psi_{1+} \vdash e_2 \Rightarrow e_2' : \tau \ ;\ \psi_+|\psi_- \ ;\ o \quad \Gamma, \psi_{1-} \vdash e_3 \Rightarrow e_3' : \tau \ ;\ \psi_+|\psi_- \ ;\ o \quad e' = (\mathsf{if}\ e_1'\ e_2'\ e_3')}{\Gamma \vdash (\mathsf{if}\ e_1\ e_2\ e_3) \Rightarrow e' : \tau \ ;\ \psi_+|\psi_- \ ;\ o}$$

$$\textsc{T-Kw}\ \Gamma \vdash k : (\mathbf{Val}\, k) \ ;\ \mathtt{tt}|\mathtt{ff} \ ;\ \emptyset \qquad \textsc{T-Num}\ \Gamma \vdash n : \mathbf{N} \ ;\ \mathtt{tt}|\mathtt{ff} \ ;\ \emptyset$$

$$\textsc{T-Nil}\ \Gamma \vdash \mathsf{nil} : \mathbf{nil} \ ;\ \mathtt{ff}|\mathtt{tt} \ ;\ \emptyset \qquad \textsc{T-False}\ \Gamma \vdash \mathsf{false} : \mathbf{false} \ ;\ \mathtt{ff}|\mathtt{tt} \ ;\ \emptyset \qquad \textsc{T-Const}\ \Gamma \vdash c : \delta_\tau(c) \ ;\ \mathtt{tt}|\mathtt{ff} \ ;\ \emptyset$$

$$\textsc{T-Str}\ \Gamma \vdash s : \mathbf{S} \ ;\ \mathtt{tt}|\mathtt{ff} \ ;\ \emptyset \qquad \textsc{T-Class}\ \Gamma \vdash C : (\mathbf{Val}\, C) \ ;\ \mathtt{tt}|\mathtt{ff} \ ;\ \emptyset \qquad \textsc{T-True}\ \Gamma \vdash \mathsf{true} : \mathbf{true} \ ;\ \mathtt{tt}|\mathtt{ff} \ ;\ \emptyset$$

$$\textsc{T-Let}\ \frac{\Gamma \vdash e_1 \Rightarrow e_1' : \sigma \ ;\ \psi_{1+}|\psi_{1-} \ ;\ o_1 \quad \psi' = \overline{(\cup\ \mathbf{nil}\ \mathbf{false})}_x \supset \psi_{1+} \quad \psi'' = (\cup\ \mathbf{nil}\ \mathbf{false})_x \supset \psi_{1-} \quad \Gamma, \sigma_x, \psi', \psi'' \vdash e_2 \Rightarrow e_2' : \tau \ ;\ \psi_+|\psi_- \ ;\ o}{\Gamma \vdash (\mathsf{let}\ [x\ e_1]\ e_2) \Rightarrow (\mathsf{let}\ [x\ e_1']\ e_2') : \tau[o_1/x] \ ;\ \psi_+|\psi_-[o_1/x] \ ;\ o[o_1/x]}$$

$$\textsc{T-App}\ \frac{\Gamma \vdash e \Rightarrow e_1 : x{:}\sigma \xrightarrow[o_f]{\psi_{f+}|\psi_{f-}} \tau \ ;\ \psi_+|\psi_- \ ;\ o \quad \Gamma \vdash e' \Rightarrow e_1' : \sigma \ ;\ \psi'_+|\psi'_- \ ;\ o'}{\Gamma \vdash (e\ e') \Rightarrow (e_1\ e_1') : \tau[o'/x] \ ;\ \psi_{f+}|\psi_{f-}[o'/x] \ ;\ o_f[o'/x]}$$

$$\textsc{T-Subsume}\ \frac{\Gamma \vdash e \Rightarrow e' : \tau \ ;\ \psi_+|\psi_- \ ;\ o \quad \Gamma, \psi_+ \vdash \psi'_+ \quad \Gamma, \psi_- \vdash \psi'_- \quad \vdash \tau <: \tau' \quad \vdash o <: o'}{\Gamma \vdash e \Rightarrow e' : \tau' \ ;\ \psi'_+|\psi'_- \ ;\ o'}$$

Fig. 3. Core typing rules

based on multimethod dispatch rules. This is written $(\mathbf{Val}\ \mathsf{:combo})_{\mathbf{key}_{\mathsf{:Meal}}(o)}$, pronounced "the :Meal path of variable o is of type $(\mathbf{Val}\ \mathsf{:combo})$".

To attain the type of o, we must solve for τ in $\Gamma \vdash \tau_o$, under proposition environment $\Gamma = \mathbf{Order}_o, (\mathbf{Val}\ \mathsf{:combo})_{\mathbf{key}_{\mathsf{:Meal}}(o)}$ which deduces τ to be a :combo meal. The logical system *combines* pieces of type information to deduce more accurate types for lexical bindings—this is explained in Sect. 3.6.

Typing Judgment. We formalize our system following Tobin-Hochstadt and Felleisen [24]. The typing judgment $\Gamma \vdash e \Rightarrow e' : \tau \ ;\ \psi_+|\psi_- \ ;\ o$ says expression e rewrites to e', which is of type τ in the proposition environment Γ, with 'then' proposition ψ_+, 'else' proposition ψ_- and object o.

We write $\Gamma \vdash e \Rightarrow e' : \tau$ to mean $\Gamma \vdash e \Rightarrow e' : \tau \ ;\ \psi'_+|\psi'_- \ ;\ o'$ for some ψ'_+, ψ'_- and o', and abbreviate self rewriting judgements $\Gamma \vdash e \Rightarrow e : \tau \ ;\ \psi_+|\psi_- \ ;\ o$ to $\Gamma \vdash e : \tau \ ;\ \psi_+|\psi_- \ ;\ o$.

Typing Rules. The core typing rules are given as Fig. 3. We introduce the interesting rules with the complement number predicate as a running example.

$$\lambda d^\top.(\mathsf{if}\ (n?\ d)\ \mathsf{false}\ \mathsf{true}) \tag{1}$$

The lambda rule T-Abs introduces $\sigma_x = \top_d$ to check the body. With $\Gamma = \top_d$, T-If first checks the test $e_1 = (n?\ d)$ via the T-App rule, with three steps.

$$\textsc{S-UnionSuper}\quad \frac{\exists i.\ \vdash \tau <: \sigma_i}{\vdash \tau <: (\bigcup\ \overrightarrow{\sigma}^{i})} \qquad \textsc{S-UnionSub}\quad \frac{\overrightarrow{\vdash \tau_i <: \sigma}^{i}}{\vdash (\bigcup\ \overrightarrow{\tau}^{i}) <: \sigma} \qquad \textsc{S-FunMono}\quad \vdash x{:}\sigma \xrightarrow[o]{\psi_+|\psi_-} \tau <: \mathbf{Fn}$$

$$\textsc{S-Object}\quad \vdash C <: \mathbf{Object} \qquad \textsc{S-SClass}\quad \vdash (\mathbf{Val}\,C) <: \mathbf{Class} \qquad \textsc{S-SBool}\quad \vdash (\mathbf{Val}\,b) <: \mathbf{B}$$

$$\textsc{S-Fun}\quad \frac{\vdash \sigma' <: \sigma \qquad \vdash \tau <: \tau' \qquad \psi_+ \vdash \psi'_+ \qquad \psi_- \vdash \psi'_- \qquad \vdash o <: o'}{\vdash x{:}\sigma \xrightarrow[o]{\psi_+|\psi_-} \tau <: x{:}\sigma' \xrightarrow[o']{\psi'_+|\psi'_-} \tau'}$$

$$\textsc{S-Refl}\quad \vdash \tau <: \tau \qquad \textsc{S-Top}\quad \vdash \tau <: \top \qquad \textsc{S-SKw}\quad \vdash (\mathbf{Val}\,k) <: \mathbf{K}$$

Fig. 4. Core subtyping rules

$$\textsc{B-IfTrue}\quad \frac{\rho \vdash e_1 \Downarrow v_1 \qquad v_1 \neq \mathsf{false} \qquad v_1 \neq \mathsf{nil} \qquad \rho \vdash e_2 \Downarrow v}{\rho \vdash (\mathsf{if}\ e_1\ e_2\ e_3) \Downarrow v} \qquad \textsc{B-IfFalse}\quad \frac{\rho \vdash e_1 \Downarrow \mathsf{false}\ \text{ or }\ \rho \vdash e_1 \Downarrow \mathsf{nil} \qquad \rho \vdash e_3 \Downarrow v}{\rho \vdash (\mathsf{if}\ e_1\ e_2\ e_3) \Downarrow v}$$

Fig. 5. Select core semantics

First, in T-App the operator $e = n?$ is checked with T-Const, which uses δ_τ (Fig. 7, dynamic semantics in the supplemental material) to type constants. *n?* is a predicate over numbers, and *class* returns its argument's class.

Resuming $(n?\ d)$, in T-App the operand $e' = d$ is checked with T-Local as

$$\Gamma \vdash d : \top\ ;\ \overline{(\cup\ \mathbf{nil}\ \mathbf{false})}_d | (\cup\ \mathbf{nil}\ \mathbf{false})_d\ ;\ d \qquad (2)$$

which encodes the type, proposition, and object information about variables. The proposition $\overline{(\cup\ \mathbf{nil}\ \mathbf{false})}_d$ says "it is not the case that variable d is of type $(\cup\ \mathbf{nil}\ \mathbf{false})$"; $(\cup\ \mathbf{nil}\ \mathbf{false})_d$ says "d is of type $(\cup\ \mathbf{nil}\ \mathbf{false})$".

Finally, the T-App rule substitutes the operand's object o' for the parameter x in the latent type, propositions, and object. The proposition $\mathbf{N}_d$ says "d is of type $\mathbf{N}$"; $\overline{\mathbf{N}}_d$ says "it is not the case that d is of type $\mathbf{N}$". The object d is the symbolic representation of what the expression d evaluates to.

$$\Gamma \vdash (n?\ d) : \mathbf{B}\ ;\ \mathbf{N}_d | \overline{\mathbf{N}}_d\ ;\ \emptyset \qquad (3)$$

To demonstrate, the 'then' proposition—in T-App $\psi_+[o'/x]$—substitutes the latent 'then' proposition of $\delta_\tau(n?)$ with d, giving $\mathbf{N}_x[d/x] = \mathbf{N}_d$.

To check the branches of $(\mathsf{if}\ (n?\ d)\ \mathsf{false}\ \mathsf{true})$, T-If introduces $\psi_{1+} = \mathbf{N}_d$ to check $e_2 = \mathsf{false}$, and $\psi_{1-} = \overline{\mathbf{N}}_d$ to check $e_3 = \mathsf{true}$. The branches are first checked with T-False and T-True respectively, the T-Subsume premises $\Gamma, \psi_+ \vdash \psi'_+$ and $\Gamma, \psi_- \vdash \psi'_-$ allow us to pick compatible propositions for both branches.

$$\Gamma, \mathbf{N}_d \vdash \mathsf{false} : \mathbf{B}\ ;\ \overline{\mathbf{N}}_d | \mathbf{N}_d\ ;\ \emptyset$$
$$\Gamma, \overline{\mathbf{N}}_d \vdash \mathsf{true} : \mathbf{B}\ ;\ \overline{\mathbf{N}}_d | \mathbf{N}_d\ ;\ \emptyset$$

Finally T-Abs assigns a type to the overall function:

$$\vdash \lambda d^{\top}.(\mathsf{if}\ (n?\ d)\ \mathsf{false}\ \mathsf{true}) : d{:}\top \xrightarrow[\emptyset]{\overline{\mathbf{N}}_d|\mathbf{N}_d} \mathbf{B}\ ;\ \mathtt{tt}|\mathtt{ff}\ ;\ \emptyset$$

Subtyping. Figure 4 presents subtyping as a reflexive and transitive relation with top type $\top$. Singleton types are instances of their respective classes—boolean singleton types are of type **B**, class literals are instances of **Class** and keywords are instances of **K**. Instances of classes C are subtypes of **Object**. Function types are subtypes of **Fn**. All types except for **nil** are subtypes of **Object**, so $\top$ is similar to ($\bigcup$ **nil** **Object**). Function subtyping is contravariant left of the arrow—latent propositions, object and result type are covariant. Subtyping for untagged unions is standard.

Operational Semantics. We define the dynamic semantics for λ_{TC} in a big-step style using an environment, following [24]. We include both errors and a *wrong* value, which is provably ruled out by the type system. The main judgment is $\rho \vdash e \Downarrow \alpha$ which states that e evaluates to answer α in environment ρ. We chose to omit the core rules (included in supplemental material) however a notable difference is nil is a false value, which affects the semantics of if (Fig. 5).

3.2 Java Interoperability

We present Java interoperability in a restricted setting without class inheritance, overloading or Java Generics. We extend the syntax in Fig. 6 with Java field lookups and calls to methods and constructors. To prevent ambiguity between zero-argument methods and fields, we use Clojure's primitive "dot" syntax: field accesses are written $(.\ e\ fld)$ and method calls $(.\ e\ (mth\ \overrightarrow{e}))$.

In Example 1, `(.getParent (new File "a/b"))` translates to

$$(.\ (\mathsf{new}\ \mathbf{F}\ \text{“a/b”})\ (\mathsf{getParent})) \qquad (4)$$

But both the constructor and method are unresolved. We introduce *non-reflective* expressions for specifying exact Java overloads.

$$(.\ (\mathsf{new}_{[\mathbf{S}]}\ \mathbf{F}\ \ \text{“a/b”})\ (\mathsf{getParent}^{\mathbf{F}}_{[[],\mathbf{S}]})) \qquad (5)$$

From the left, the one-argument constructor for **F** takes a **S**, and the getParent method of **F** takes zero arguments and returns a **S**.

We now walk through this conversion.

Constructors. First we check and convert (new **F** "a/b") to ($\mathsf{new}_{[\mathbf{S}]}$ **F** "a/b"). The T-New typing rule checks and rewrites constructors. To check (new **F** "a/b") we first resolve the constructor overload in the class table—there is at most one to simplify presentation. With $C_1 = \mathbf{S}$, we convert to a nilable type the argument with $\tau_1 = (\bigcup\ \mathbf{nil}\ \mathbf{S})$ and type check "a/b" against τ_1. Typed Clojure defaults to allowing non-nilable arguments, but this can be overridden, so we model the more

$$
\begin{array}{llll}
e & ::= & \ldots (.\ e\ fld) \mid (.\ e\ (mth\ \overrightarrow{e})) \mid (\text{new}\ C\ \overrightarrow{e}) & \text{Expressions} \\
 & \mid & (.\ e\ fld^{C}_{C}) \mid (.\ e\ (mth^{C}_{[[\overrightarrow{C}],C]}\ \overrightarrow{e})) \mid (\text{new}_{[\overrightarrow{C}]}\ C\ \overrightarrow{e}) & \text{Non-reflective Expressions} \\
v & ::= & \ldots \mid C\ \{\overrightarrow{fld : v}\} & \text{Values} \\
ce & ::= & \{\mathsf{m} \mapsto \{\overrightarrow{mth \mapsto [[\overrightarrow{C}], C]}\}, \mathsf{f} \mapsto \{\overrightarrow{fld \mapsto C}\}, \mathsf{c} \mapsto \{[\overrightarrow{C}]\}\} & \text{Class descriptors} \\
\mathcal{CT} & ::= & \{\overrightarrow{C \mapsto ce}\} & \text{Class Table}
\end{array}
$$

T-New

$$
\frac{[\overrightarrow{C_i}] \in \mathcal{CT}[C][\mathsf{c}] \quad \overrightarrow{\mathsf{JT_{nil}}(C_i) = \tau_i} \quad \overrightarrow{\Gamma \vdash e_i \Rightarrow e'_i : \tau_i} \quad \mathsf{JT}(C) = \tau}{\Gamma \vdash (\text{new}\ C\overrightarrow{e_i}) \Rightarrow (\text{new}_{[\overrightarrow{C_i}]}\ C\ \overrightarrow{e'_i}) : \tau\ ;\ \mathtt{tt}|\mathtt{ff}\ ;\ \emptyset}
$$

T-Method

$$
\frac{\begin{array}{c}\Gamma \vdash e \Rightarrow e' : \sigma \quad \mathsf{TJ}(\sigma) = C_1 \quad mth \mapsto [[\overrightarrow{C_i}], C_2] \in \mathcal{CT}[C_1][\mathsf{m}] \\ \overrightarrow{\mathsf{JT_{nil}}(C_i) = \tau_i} \quad \overrightarrow{\Gamma \vdash e_i \Rightarrow e'_i : \tau_i} \quad \mathsf{JT_{nil}}(C_2) = \tau \quad \vdash \sigma <: \textbf{Object}\end{array}}{\Gamma \vdash (.\ e\ (mth\overrightarrow{e_i})) \Rightarrow (.\ e'\ (mth^{C_1}_{[[\overrightarrow{C_i}],C_2]}\ \overrightarrow{e'_i})) : \tau\ ;\ \mathtt{tt}|\mathtt{tt}\ ;\ \emptyset}
$$

T-Field

$$
\frac{\Gamma \vdash e \Rightarrow e' : \sigma \quad \vdash \sigma <: \textbf{Object} \quad \mathsf{TJ}(\sigma) = C_1 \quad fld \mapsto C_2 \in \mathcal{CT}[C_1][\mathsf{f}] \quad \mathsf{JT_{nil}}(C_2) = \tau}{\Gamma \vdash (.\ e\ fld) \Rightarrow (.\ e'\ fld^{C_1}_{C_2}) : \tau\ ;\ \mathtt{tt}|\mathtt{tt}\ ;\ \emptyset}
$$

$$
\begin{array}{lll}
\mathsf{JT_{nil}}(\textbf{Void}) = \textbf{nil} & \mathsf{JT}(\textbf{Void}) = \textbf{nil} & \mathsf{TJ}(\tau) = C \quad \text{if} \vdash \tau <: \mathsf{JT_{nil}}(C) \\
\mathsf{JT_{nil}}(C) = (\bigcup\ \textbf{nil}\ C) & \mathsf{JT}(C) = C &
\end{array}
$$

B-Field

$$
\frac{\rho \vdash e \Downarrow v \quad \mathsf{JVM_{getstatic}}[C_1, v_1, fld, C_2] = v}{\rho \vdash (.\ e\ fld^{C_1}_{C_2}) \Downarrow v}
$$

B-New

$$
\frac{\overrightarrow{\rho \vdash e_i \Downarrow v_i} \quad \mathsf{JVM_{new}}[C_1, [\overrightarrow{C_i}], [\overrightarrow{v_i}]] = v}{\rho \vdash (\text{new}_{[\overrightarrow{C_i}]}\ C\ \overrightarrow{e_i}) \Downarrow v}
$$

B-Method

$$
\frac{\rho \vdash e_m \Downarrow v_m \quad \overrightarrow{\rho \vdash e_a \Downarrow v_a} \quad \mathsf{JVM_{invokestatic}}[C_1, v_m, mth, [\overrightarrow{C_a}], [\overrightarrow{v_a}], C_2] = v}{\rho \vdash (.\ e_m\ (mth^{C_1}_{[[\overrightarrow{C_a}],C_2]}\ \overrightarrow{e_a})) \Downarrow v}
$$

Fig. 6. Java interoperability syntax, typing and operational semantics

$$
\begin{array}{ll}
\delta_\tau(class) = x{:}\top \xrightarrow[\mathbf{class}(x)]{\mathtt{tt}|\mathtt{tt}} (\bigcup\ \mathsf{nil}\ \textbf{Class}) \\
\delta_\tau(n?) = x{:}\top \xrightarrow[\emptyset]{\mathbf{N}_x|\overline{\mathbf{N}}_x} \mathbf{B}
\end{array}
$$

Fig. 7. Constant typing

general case. The return Java type **F** is converted to a non-nil Typed Clojure type $\tau = \mathbf{F}$ for the return type, and the propositions say constructors can never be false—constructors can never produce the internal boolean value that Clojure uses for false, or nil. Finally, the constructor rewrites to (new$_{[\mathsf{S}]}$ **F** "a/b").

Methods. Next we convert (. (new$_{[\mathsf{S}]}$ **F** "a/b") (getParent)) to the non-reflective expression (. (new$_{[\mathsf{S}]}$ **F** "a/b") (getParent$^{\mathbf{F}}_{[[],\mathsf{S}]}$)). The T-Method rule for unresolved methods checks (. (new$_{[\mathsf{S}]}$ **F** "a/b") (getParent)). We verify the target type $\sigma = \mathbf{F}$ is non-nil by T-New. The overload is chosen from the class table based on $C_1 = \mathbf{F}$—there is at most one. The nilable return type $\tau = (\bigcup\ \mathbf{nil}\ \mathbf{S})$ is given, and the entire expression rewrites to expression 5.

The T-Field rule (Fig. 6) is like T-Method, but without arguments.

The evaluation rules B-Field, B-New and B-Method (Fig. 6) simply evaluate their arguments and call the relevant JVM operation, which we do not model—Sect. 4 states our exact assumptions. There are no evaluation rules for reflective Java interoperability, since there are no typing rules that rewrite to reflective calls.

3.3 Multimethod Preliminaries: isa?

We now consider the isa? operation, a core part of the multimethod dispatch mechanism. Recalling the examples in Sect. 2.4, isa? is a subclassing test for classes, but otherwise is an equality test. The T-IsA rule uses IsAProps (Fig. 8), a metafunction which produces the propositions for isa? expressions.

To demonstrate the first IsAProps case, the expression (isa? (*class* x) $\mathbf{K}$) is true if x is a keyword, otherwise false. When checked with T-IsA, the object of the left subexpression $o = \mathbf{class}(x)$ (which starts with the **class** path element) and the type of the right subexpression $\tau = (\mathbf{Val}\,\mathbf{K})$ (a singleton class type) together trigger the first IsAProps case $\mathsf{IsAProps}(\mathbf{class}(x), (\mathbf{Val}\,\mathbf{K})) = \mathbf{K}_x|\overline{\mathbf{K}}_x$, giving propositions that correspond to our informal description $\psi_+|\psi_- = \mathbf{K}_x|\overline{\mathbf{K}}_x$.

The second IsAProps case captures the simple equality mode for non-class singleton types. For example, the expression (isa? x :en) produces true when x evaluates to :en, otherwise it produces false. Using T-IsA, it has the propositions $\psi_+|\psi_- = \mathsf{IsAProps}(x, (\mathbf{Val}\,\mathsf{:en})) = (\mathbf{Val}\,\mathsf{:en})_x|\overline{(\mathbf{Val}\,\mathsf{:en})}_x$ since $o = x and \tau = (\mathbf{Val}\,\mathsf{:en})$. The side condition on the second IsAProps case ensures we are in equality mode—if x can possibly be a class in (isa? x **Object**), IsAProps uses its conservative default case, since if x is a class literal, subclassing mode could be triggered. Capture-avoiding substitution of objects $[o/x]$ used in this case erases propositions that would otherwise have $\emptyset$ substituted in for their objects—it is defined in the appendix.

The operational behavior of isa? is given by B-IsA (Fig. 8). IsA explicitly handles classes in the second case.

3.4 Multimethods

Figure 8 presents *immutable* multimethods without default methods to ease presentation. Figure 9 translates the mutable Example 4 to λ_{TC}.

To check (defmulti $x{:}\,\mathbf{K} \to \mathbf{S}\ \lambda x^{\mathbf{K}}.x$), we note (defmulti σ e) creates a multimethod with *interface type* σ, and dispatch function e of type σ', producing a value of type (**Multi** σ σ'). The T-DefMulti typing rule checks the dispatch function, and verifies both the interface and dispatch type's domain agree. Our example checks with $\tau = \mathbf{K}$, interface type $\sigma = x{:}\,\mathbf{K} \to \mathbf{S}$, dispatch function type $\sigma' = x{:}\,\mathbf{K} \xrightarrow[x]{\mathtt{tt}|\mathtt{tt}} \mathbf{K}$, and overall type $(\mathbf{Multi}\, x{:}\,\mathbf{K} \to \mathbf{S}\ x{:}\,\mathbf{K} \xrightarrow[x]{\mathtt{tt}|\mathtt{tt}} \mathbf{K})$.

$$
\begin{array}{llr}
e & ::= \ldots \mid (\text{defmulti } \tau\ e) \mid (\text{defmethod } e\ e\ e) \mid (\text{isa? } e\ e) & \text{Expressions} \\
v & ::= \ldots \mid [v, t]_{\mathsf{m}} & \text{Values} \\
t & ::= \{\overrightarrow{v \mapsto v}\} & \text{Dispatch tables} \\
\sigma, \tau & ::= \ldots \mid (\mathbf{Multi}\,\tau\ \tau) & \text{Types}
\end{array}
$$

T-DefMulti

$$
\frac{\sigma = x{:}\tau \xrightarrow[o]{\psi_+|\psi_-} \tau' \qquad \sigma' = x{:}\tau \xrightarrow[o']{\psi'_+|\psi'_-} \tau'' \qquad \Gamma \vdash e \Rightarrow e' : \sigma'}{\Gamma \vdash (\text{defmulti } \sigma\ e) \Rightarrow (\text{defmulti } \sigma\ e') : (\mathbf{Multi}\,\sigma\ \sigma')\ ;\ \mathtt{tt}|\mathtt{ff}\ ;\ \emptyset}
$$

T-DefMethod

$$
\frac{\begin{array}{c}\tau_m = x{:}\tau \xrightarrow[o]{\psi_+|\psi_-} \sigma \qquad \tau_d = x{:}\tau \xrightarrow[o']{\psi'_+|\psi'_-} \sigma' \qquad \Gamma \vdash e_m \Rightarrow e'_m : (\mathbf{Multi}\,\tau_m\ \tau_d) \\ \Gamma \vdash e_v \Rightarrow e'_v : \tau_v \qquad \mathsf{IsAProps}(o', \tau_v) = \psi''_+|\psi''_- \\ \Gamma, \tau_x, \psi''_+ \vdash e_b \Rightarrow e'_b : \sigma\ ;\ \psi_+|\psi_-\ ;\ o \qquad e' = (\text{defmethod } e'_m\ e'_v\ \lambda x^{\tau}.e'_b)\end{array}}{\Gamma \vdash (\text{defmethod } e_m\ e_v\ \lambda x^{\tau}.e_b) \Rightarrow e' : (\mathbf{Multi}\,\tau_m\ \tau_d)\ ;\ \mathtt{tt}|\mathtt{ff}\ ;\ \emptyset}
$$

T-IsA

$$
\frac{\Gamma \vdash e \Rightarrow e_1 : \sigma\ ;\ \psi'_+|\psi'_-\ ;\ o \qquad \Gamma \vdash e' \Rightarrow e'_1 : \tau \qquad \mathsf{IsAProps}(o, \tau) = \psi_+|\psi_-}{\Gamma \vdash (\text{isa? } e\ e') \Rightarrow (\text{isa? } e_1\ e'_1) : \mathbf{B}\ ;\ \psi_+|\psi_-\ ;\ \emptyset}
$$

$$
\begin{array}{lll}
\mathsf{IsAProps}(\mathbf{class}(\pi(x)), (\mathbf{Val}\,C)) & = C_{\pi(x)}|\overline{C}_{\pi(x)} & \\
\mathsf{IsAProps}(o, (\mathbf{Val}\,l)) & = ((\mathbf{Val}\,l)_x|\overline{(\mathbf{Val}\,l)}_x)[o/x] & \text{if } l \neq C \\
\mathsf{IsAProps}(o, \tau) & = \mathtt{tt}|\mathtt{tt} & \text{otherwise}
\end{array}
$$

S-PMultiFn

$$
\frac{\vdash \sigma_t <: x{:}\sigma \xrightarrow[o]{\psi_+|\psi_-} \tau \qquad \vdash \sigma_d <: x{:}\sigma \xrightarrow[o']{\psi'_+|\psi'_-} \tau'}{\vdash (\mathbf{Multi}\,\sigma_t\ \sigma_d) <: x{:}\sigma \xrightarrow[o]{\psi_+|\psi_-} \tau}
$$

S-PMulti

$$
\frac{\vdash \sigma <: \sigma' \qquad \vdash \tau <: \tau'}{\vdash (\mathbf{Multi}\,\sigma\ \tau) <: (\mathbf{Multi}\,\sigma'\ \tau')}
$$

S-MultiMono

$$
\vdash (\mathbf{Multi}\,x{:}\sigma \xrightarrow[o]{\psi_+|\psi_-} \tau\ x{:}\sigma \xrightarrow[o']{\psi'_+|\psi'_-} \tau') <: \mathbf{Multi}
$$

B-DefMulti

$$
\frac{\rho \vdash e \Downarrow v_d \qquad v = [v_d, \{\}]_{\mathsf{m}}}{\rho \vdash (\text{defmulti } \tau\ e) \Downarrow v}
$$

B-DefMethod

$$
\frac{\rho \vdash e \Downarrow [v_d, t]_{\mathsf{m}} \qquad \rho \vdash e' \Downarrow v_v \qquad \rho \vdash e_f \Downarrow v_f \qquad v = [v_d, t[v_v \mapsto v_f]]_{\mathsf{m}}}{\rho \vdash (\text{defmethod } e\ e'\ e_f) \Downarrow v}
$$

$$
\begin{array}{l}
\mathsf{GM}(t, v_e) = v_f \text{ if } \overrightarrow{v_{fs}} = \{v_f\} \text{ where } \overrightarrow{v_{fs}} = \{v_f | v_k \mapsto v_f \in t \text{ and } \mathsf{IsA}(v_e, v_k) = \mathsf{true}\} \\
\mathsf{GM}(t, v_e) = \mathsf{err} \text{ otherwise}
\end{array}
$$

B-IsA

$$
\frac{\rho \vdash e_1 \Downarrow v_1 \qquad \rho \vdash e_2 \Downarrow v_2 \qquad \mathsf{IsA}(v_1, v_2) = v}{\rho \vdash (\text{isa? } e_1\ e_2) \Downarrow v}
\qquad
\begin{array}{lll}
\mathsf{IsA}(v, v) & = \mathsf{true} & v \neq C \\
\mathsf{IsA}(C, C') & = \mathsf{true} & \vdash C <: C' \\
\mathsf{IsA}(v, v') & = \mathsf{false} & \text{otherwise}
\end{array}
$$

B-BetaMulti

$$
\frac{\rho \vdash e \Downarrow [v_d, t]_{\mathsf{m}} \quad \rho \vdash e' \Downarrow v' \quad \rho \vdash (v_d\ v') \Downarrow v_e \quad \mathsf{GM}(t, v_e) = v_f \quad \rho \vdash (v_f\ v') \Downarrow v}{\rho \vdash (e\ e') \Downarrow v}
$$

Fig. 8. Multimethod syntax, typing and operational semantics

$$\begin{array}{l}(\text{let } [hi_0\ (\text{defmulti } x{:}\,\mathbf{K} \xrightarrow[\emptyset]{tt|tt} \mathbf{S}\ \lambda x^{\mathbf{K}}.x)]\\ \quad(\text{let } [hi_1\ (\text{defmethod } hi_0 \text{ :en } \lambda x^{\mathbf{K}}.\text{"hello"})]\\ \quad\quad(\text{let } [hi_2\ (\text{defmethod } hi_1 \text{ :fr } \lambda x^{\mathbf{K}}.\text{"bonjour"})]\\ \quad\quad\quad(hi_2 \text{ :en}))))\end{array}$$

Fig. 9. Multimethod example

Next, we show how to check (defmethod hi_0 :en $\lambda x^{\mathbf{K}}$."hello"). The expression (defmethod e_m e_v e_f) creates a new multimethod that extends multimethod e_m's dispatch table, mapping dispatch value e_v to method e_f. The T-DefMulti typing rule checks e_m is a multimethod with dispatch function type τ_d, then calculates the extra information we know based on the current dispatch value ψ''_+, which is assumed when checking the method body. Our example checks with e_m being of type $(\mathbf{Multi}\, x{:}\,\mathbf{K} \to \mathbf{S}\ x{:}\,\mathbf{K} \xrightarrow[x]{tt|tt} \mathbf{K})$ with $o' = x$ (from below the arrow on the right argument of the previous type) and $\tau_v = (\mathbf{Val}\text{ :en})$. Then $\psi''_+ = (\mathbf{Val}\text{ :en})_x$ from $\mathsf{IsAProps}(x, (\mathbf{Val}\text{ :en})) = (\mathbf{Val}\text{ :en})_x | \overline{(\mathbf{Val}\text{ :en})}_x$ (see Sect. 3.3). Since $\tau = \mathbf{K}$, we check the method body with $\mathbf{K}_x, (\mathbf{Val}\text{ :en})_x \vdash \text{"hello"} : \mathbf{S}\ ;\ tt|tt\ ;\ \emptyset$. Finally from the interface type τ_m, we know $\psi_+ = \psi_- = tt$, and $o = \emptyset$, which also agrees with the method body, above. Notice the overall type of a defmethod is the same as its first subexpression e_m.

It is worth noting the lack of special typing rules for overlapping methods—each method is checked independently based on local type information.

Subtyping. Multimethods are functions, via S-PMultiFn, which says a multimethod can be upcast to its interface type. Multimethod call sites are then handled by T-App via T-Subsume. Other rules are given in Fig. 8.

Semantics. Multimethod definition semantics are also given in Fig. 8. B-DefMulti creates a multimethod with the given dispatch function and an empty dispatch table. B-DefMethod produces a new multimethod with an extended dispatch table.

The overall dispatch mechanism is summarised by B-BetaMulti. First the dispatch function v_d is applied to the argument v' to obtain the dispatch value v_e. Based on v_e, the GM metafunction (Fig. 8) extracts a method v_f from the method table t and applies it to the original argument for the final result.

3.5 Precise Types for Heterogeneous Maps

Figure 10 presents heterogeneous map types. The type $(\mathbf{HMap}^{\mathcal{E}} \mathcal{M}\ \mathcal{A})$ contains $\mathcal{M}$, a map of *present* entries (mapping keywords to types), $\mathcal{A}$, a set of keyword keys that are known to be *absent* and tag $\mathcal{E}$ which is either $\mathcal{C}$ ("complete") if the map is fully specified by $\mathcal{M}$, and $\mathcal{P}$ ("partial") if there are *unknown* entries. The partially specified map of `lunch` in Example 6 is written $(\mathbf{HMap}^{\mathcal{P}}\{(\mathbf{Val}\text{ :en})\ \mathbf{S}, (\mathbf{Val}\text{ :fr})\ \mathbf{S}\}\ \{\})$ (abbreviated $\mathbf{Lu}$). The type of the

$$
\begin{array}{lll}
e & ::= \ldots \mid (\text{get } e\ e) \mid (\text{assoc } e\ e\ e) & \text{Expressions} \\
v & ::= \ldots \mid \{\} & \text{Values} \\
\tau & ::= \ldots \mid (\mathbf{HMap}^{\mathcal{E}}\ \mathcal{M}\ \mathcal{A}) & \text{Types} \\
\mathcal{M} & ::= \{\overrightarrow{k \mapsto \tau}\} & \text{HMap mandatory entries} \\
\mathcal{A} & ::= \{\overrightarrow{k}\} & \text{HMap absent entries} \\
\mathcal{E} & ::= \mathcal{C} \mid \mathcal{P} & \text{HMap completeness tags}
\end{array}
$$

T-AssocHMap

$$
\frac{\Gamma \vdash e \Rightarrow (\text{assoc } e'\ e'_k\ e'_v) : (\mathbf{HMap}^{\mathcal{E}}\ \mathcal{M}\ \mathcal{A}) \quad \Gamma \vdash e_k \Rightarrow e'_k : (\mathbf{Val}\, k) \quad \Gamma \vdash e_v \Rightarrow e'_v : \tau \quad k \notin \mathcal{A}}{\Gamma \vdash (\text{assoc } e\ e_k\ e_v) \Rightarrow (\text{assoc } e'\ e'_k\ e'_v) : (\mathbf{HMap}^{\mathcal{E}}\ \mathcal{M}[k \mapsto \tau]\ \mathcal{A})\ ;\ \mathtt{tt}|\mathtt{ff}\ ;\ \emptyset}
$$

T-GetHMap

$$
\frac{\Gamma \vdash e \Rightarrow e' : (\bigcup\ \overrightarrow{(\mathbf{HMap}^{\mathcal{E}}\ \mathcal{M}\ \mathcal{A})}^{i})\ ;\ \psi_{1+}|\psi_{1-}\ ;\ o \quad \Gamma \vdash e_k \Rightarrow e'_k : (\mathbf{Val}\, k) \quad \overrightarrow{\mathcal{M}[k] = \tau}^{i}}{\Gamma \vdash (\text{get } e\ e_k) \Rightarrow (\text{get } e'\ e'_k) : (\bigcup\ \overrightarrow{\tau}^{i})\ ;\ \mathtt{tt}|\mathtt{tt}\ ;\ \mathbf{key}_k(x)[o/x]}
$$

T-GetHMapAbsent

$$
\frac{\Gamma \vdash e \Rightarrow e' : (\mathbf{HMap}^{\mathcal{E}}\ \mathcal{M}\ \mathcal{A})\ ;\ \psi_{1+}|\psi_{1-}\ ;\ o \quad \Gamma \vdash e_k \Rightarrow e'_k : (\mathbf{Val}\, k) \quad k \in \mathcal{A}}{\Gamma \vdash (\text{get } e\ e_k) \Rightarrow (\text{get } e'\ e'_k) : \mathbf{nil}\ ;\ \mathtt{tt}|\mathtt{tt}\ ;\ \mathbf{key}_k(x)[o/x]}
$$

T-GetHMapPartialDefault

$$
\frac{\Gamma \vdash e \Rightarrow e' : (\mathbf{HMap}^{\mathcal{P}}\ \mathcal{M}\ \mathcal{A})\ ;\ \psi_{1+}|\psi_{1-}\ ;\ o \qquad \Gamma \vdash e_k \Rightarrow e'_k : (\mathbf{Val}\, k) \quad k \notin dom(\mathcal{M}) \quad k \notin \mathcal{A}}{\Gamma \vdash (\text{get } e\ e_k) \Rightarrow (\text{get } e'\ e'_k) : \top\ ;\ \mathtt{tt}|\mathtt{tt}\ ;\ \mathbf{key}_k(x)[o/x]}
$$

S-HMapMono

$$
\vdash (\mathbf{HMap}^{\mathcal{E}}\ \mathcal{M}\ \mathcal{A}) <: \mathbf{Map}
$$

S-HMapP

$$
\frac{\forall i.\ \mathcal{M}[k_i] = \sigma_i \text{ and } \vdash \sigma_i <: \tau_i}{\vdash (\mathbf{HMap}^{\mathcal{C}}\ \mathcal{M}\ \mathcal{A}') <: (\mathbf{HMap}^{\mathcal{P}}\ \{\overrightarrow{k \mapsto \tau}\}^{i}\ \mathcal{A})}
$$

S-HMap

$$
\frac{\forall i.\ \mathcal{M}[k_i] = \sigma_i \text{ and } \vdash \sigma_i <: \tau_i \qquad \mathcal{A}_1 \supseteq \mathcal{A}_2}{\vdash (\mathbf{HMap}^{\mathcal{E}}\ \mathcal{M}\ \mathcal{A}_1) <: (\mathbf{HMap}^{\mathcal{E}}\ \{\overrightarrow{k \mapsto \tau}\}^{i}\ \mathcal{A}_2)}
$$

B-Assoc

$$
\frac{\rho \vdash e \Downarrow m \qquad \rho \vdash e_k \Downarrow k \qquad \rho \vdash e_v \Downarrow v_v}{\rho \vdash (\text{assoc } e\ e_k\ e_v) \Downarrow m[k \mapsto v_v]}
$$

B-Get

$$
\frac{\rho \vdash e \Downarrow m \qquad \rho \vdash e' \Downarrow k \qquad k \in dom(m)}{\rho \vdash (\text{get } e\ e') \Downarrow m[k]}
$$

B-GetMissing

$$
\frac{\rho \vdash e \Downarrow m \qquad \rho \vdash e' \Downarrow k \qquad k \notin dom(m)}{\rho \vdash (\text{get } e\ e') \Downarrow \text{nil}}
$$

Fig. 10. HMap syntax, typing and operational semantics

$$
\begin{array}{l}
\mathsf{restrict}(\tau, \sigma) = \bot \ \text{ if } \nexists v.\ \vdash v : \tau\ ;\ \psi\ ;\ o \text{ and } \vdash v : \sigma\ ;\ \psi'\ ;\ o' \\
\mathsf{restrict}(\tau, \sigma) = \tau \ \text{ if } \vdash \tau <: \sigma \\
\mathsf{restrict}(\tau, \sigma) = \sigma \ \text{ otherwise}
\end{array}
\qquad
\begin{array}{l}
\mathsf{remove}(\tau, \sigma) = \bot \ \text{ if } \vdash \tau <: \sigma \\
\mathsf{remove}(\tau, \sigma) = \tau \ \text{ otherwise}
\end{array}
$$

Fig. 11. Restrict and remove

fully specified map `breakfast` in Example 5 elides the absent entries, written $(\mathbf{HMap}^{\mathcal{C}}\{(\mathbf{Val}\,\text{:en})\ \mathbf{S}, (\mathbf{Val}\,\text{:fr})\ \mathbf{S}\})$ (abbreviated **Bf**). To ease presentation, if an HMap has completeness tag $\mathcal{C}$ then $\mathcal{A}$ is elided and implicitly contains all keywords not in the domain of $\mathcal{M}$—dissociating keys is not modelled, so the set of absent entries otherwise never grows. Keys cannot be both present and absent.

The metavariable m ranges over the runtime value of maps $\{\overrightarrow{k \mapsto v}\}$, usually written $\{\overrightarrow{k\ v}\}$. We only provide syntax for the empty map literal, however when convenient we abbreviate non-empty map literals to be a series of assoc operations on the empty map. We restrict lookup and extension to keyword keys.

How to Check. A mandatory lookup is checked by T-GetHMap.

$$\lambda b^{\mathbf{Bf}}.(\mathsf{get}\ b\ \mathsf{:en})$$

The result type is **S**, and the return object is $\mathbf{key}_{\mathsf{:en}}(b)$. The object $\mathbf{key}_k(x)[o/x]$ is a symbolic representation for a keyword lookup of k in o. The substitution for x handles the case where o is empty.

$$\mathbf{key}_k(x)[y/x] = \mathbf{key}_k(y) \qquad \mathbf{key}_k(x)[\emptyset/x] = \emptyset$$

An absent lookup is checked by T-GetHMapAbsent.

$$\lambda b^{\mathbf{Bf}}.(\mathsf{get}\ b\ \mathsf{:bocce})$$

The result type is **nil**—since **Bf** is fully specified—with return object $\mathbf{key}_{\mathsf{:bocce}}(b)$.

A lookup that is not present or absent is checked by T-GetHMapPartial-Default.

$$\lambda u^{\mathbf{Lu}}.(\mathsf{get}\ u\ \mathsf{:bocce})$$

The result type is $\top$—since **Lu** has an unknown :bocce entry—with return object $\mathbf{key}_{\mathsf{:bocce}}(u)$. Notice propositions are erased once they enter a HMap type.

For presentational reasons, lookups on unions of HMaps are only supported in T-GetHMap and each element of the union must contain the relevant key.

$$\lambda u^{(\bigcup\ \mathbf{Bf}\,\mathbf{Lu})}.(\mathsf{get}\ u\ \mathsf{:en})$$

The result type is **S**, and the return object is $\mathbf{key}_{\mathsf{:en}}(u)$. However, lookups of :bocce on $(\bigcup\ \mathbf{Bf}\,\mathbf{Lu})$ maps are unsupported. This restriction still allows us to check many of the examples in Sect. 2—in particular we can check Example 8, as :Meal is in common with both HMaps, but cannot check Example 9 because a :combo meal lacks a :desserts entry. Adding a rule to handle Example 9 is otherwise straightforward.

Extending a map with T-AssocHMap preserves its completeness.

$$\lambda b^{\mathbf{Bf}}.(\mathsf{assoc}\ b\ \mathsf{:au}\ \text{“beans”})$$

The result type is $(\mathbf{HMap}^{\mathcal{C}}\{(\mathbf{Val}\,\mathsf{:en})\ \mathbf{S}, (\mathbf{Val}\,\mathsf{:fr})\ \mathbf{S}, (\mathbf{Val}\,\mathsf{:au})\ \mathbf{S}\})$, a complete map. T-AssocHMap also enforces $k \notin \mathcal{A}$ to prevent badly formed types.

Subtyping. Subtyping for HMaps designate **Map** as a common supertype for all HMaps. S-HMap says that HMaps are subtypes if they agree on $\mathcal{E}$, agree on mandatory entries with subtyping and at least cover the absent keys of the supertype. Complete maps are subtypes of partial maps as long as they agree on the mandatory entries of the partial map via subtyping (S-HMapP).

The semantics for get and assoc are straightforward.

$$
\begin{array}{ll}
\mathsf{update}((\bigcup\ \overrightarrow{\tau}), \nu, \pi) & = (\bigcup\ \overrightarrow{\mathsf{update}(\tau, \nu, \pi)}) \\
\mathsf{update}(\tau, (\mathbf{Val}\, C), \pi :: \mathbf{class}) & = \mathsf{update}(\tau, C, \pi) \\
\mathsf{update}(\tau, \nu, \pi :: \mathbf{class}) & = \tau \\
\mathsf{update}((\mathbf{HMap}^{\mathcal{E}}\ \mathcal{M}\ \mathcal{A}), \nu, \pi :: \mathbf{key}_k) & = (\mathbf{HMap}^{\mathcal{E}}\ \mathcal{M}[k \mapsto \mathsf{update}(\tau, \nu, \pi)]\ \mathcal{A}) \\
 & \quad \text{if } \mathcal{M}[k] = \tau \\
\mathsf{update}((\mathbf{HMap}^{\mathcal{E}}\ \mathcal{M}\ \mathcal{A}), \nu, \pi :: \mathbf{key}_k) & = \bot \quad \text{if } \vdash \mathbf{nil} \not<: \nu \text{ and } k \in \mathcal{A} \\
\mathsf{update}((\mathbf{HMap}^{\mathcal{P}}\ \mathcal{M}\ \mathcal{A}), \tau, \pi :: \mathbf{key}_k) & = (\cup\ (\mathbf{HMap}^{\mathcal{P}}\ \mathcal{M}[k \mapsto \tau]\ \mathcal{A}) \\
 & \qquad (\mathbf{HMap}^{\mathcal{P}}\ \mathcal{M}\ (\mathcal{A} \cup \{k\}))) \\
 & \quad \text{if } \vdash \mathbf{nil} <: \tau,\ k \notin dom(\mathcal{M}) \text{ and } k \notin \mathcal{A} \\
\mathsf{update}((\mathbf{HMap}^{\mathcal{P}}\ \mathcal{M}\ \mathcal{A}), \nu, \pi :: \mathbf{key}_k) & = (\mathbf{HMap}^{\mathcal{P}}\ \mathcal{M}[k \mapsto \mathsf{update}(\top, \nu, \pi)]\ \mathcal{A}) \\
 & \quad \text{if } \vdash \mathbf{nil} \not<: \nu,\ k \notin dom(\mathcal{M}) \text{ and } k \notin \mathcal{A} \\
\mathsf{update}(\tau, \nu, \pi :: \mathbf{key}_k) & = \tau \\
\mathsf{update}(\tau, \sigma, \epsilon) & = \mathsf{restrict}(\tau, \sigma) \\
\mathsf{update}(\tau, \overline{\sigma}, \epsilon) & = \mathsf{remove}(\tau, \sigma)
\end{array}
$$

Fig. 12. Type update (the metavariable ν ranges over τ and $\overline{\tau}$ (without variables), $\vdash \mathbf{nil} \not<: \overline{\tau}$ when $\vdash \mathbf{nil} <: \tau$, see Fig. 11 for restrict and remove.)

3.6 Proof System

The occurrence typing proof system uses standard propositional logic, except for where nested information is combined. This is handled by L-Update:

$$
\text{L-UPDATE}\quad \frac{\Gamma \vdash \tau_{\pi'(x)} \qquad \Gamma \vdash \nu_{\pi(\pi'(x))}}{\Gamma \vdash \mathsf{update}(\tau, \nu, \pi)_{\pi'(x)}}
$$

It says under Γ, if object $\pi'(x)$ is of type τ, and an extension $\pi(\pi'(x))$ is of possibly-negative type ν, then $\mathsf{update}(\tau, \nu, \pi)$ is $\pi'(x)$'s type under Γ.

Recall Example 8. Solving $\mathbf{Order}_o$, $(\mathbf{Val}\,\mathsf{:combo})_{\mathbf{key}_{\mathsf{:Meal}}(o)} \vdash \tau_o$ uses L-Update, where $\pi = \epsilon$ and $\pi' = [\mathbf{key}_{\mathsf{:Meal}}]$.

$$
\Gamma \vdash \mathsf{update}(\mathbf{Order}, (\mathbf{Val}\,\mathsf{:combo}), [\mathbf{key}_{\mathsf{:Meal}}])_o
$$

Since **Order** is a union of HMaps, we structurally recur on the first case of update (Fig. 12), which preserves π. Each initial recursion hits the first HMap case, since there is some τ such that $\mathcal{M}[k] = \tau$ and $\mathcal{E}$ accepts partial maps $\mathcal{P}$.

To demonstrate, :lunch meals are handled by the first HMap case and update to $(\mathbf{HMap}^{\mathcal{P}}\ \mathcal{M}[(\mathbf{Val}\,\mathsf{:Meal}) \mapsto \sigma']\ \{\})$ where $\sigma' = \mathsf{update}\ ((\mathbf{Val}\,\mathsf{:lunch}), (\mathbf{Val}\,\mathsf{:combo}), \epsilon)$ and $\mathcal{M} = \{(\mathbf{Val}\,\mathsf{:Meal}) \mapsto (\mathbf{Val}\,\mathsf{:lunch}), (\mathbf{Val}\,\mathsf{:desserts}) \mapsto \mathbf{N}\}$. σ' updates to $\bot$ via the penultimate update case, because restrict $((\mathbf{Val}\,\mathsf{:lunch}), (\mathbf{Val}\,\mathsf{:combo})) = \bot$ by the first restrict case. The same happens to :dinner meals, leaving just the :combo HMap.

In Example 9, $\Gamma \vdash \mathsf{update}(\mathbf{Order}, \mathbf{Long}, [\mathbf{class}, \mathbf{key}_{\mathsf{:desserts}}])_o$ updates the argument in the **Long** method. This recurs twice for each meal to handle the **class** path element.

We describe the other update cases. The first **class** case updates to C if *class* returns ($\mathbf{Val}\,C$). The second $\mathbf{key}_k$ case detects contradictions in absent keys. The third $\mathbf{key}_k$ case updates unknown entries to be mapped to τ or absent. The fourth $\mathbf{key}_k$ case updates unknown entries to be *present* when they do not overlap with **nil**.

4 Metatheory

We prove type soundness following Tobin-Hochstadt and Felleisen [24]. Our model is extended to include errors err and a *wrong* value, and we prove well-typed programs do not go wrong; this is therefore a stronger theorem than proved by Tobin-Hochstadt and Felleisen [24]. Errors behave like Java exceptions—they can be thrown and propagate "upwards" in the evaluation rules (err rules are deferred to the appendix).

Rather than modeling Java's dynamic semantics, a task of daunting complexity, we instead make our assumptions about Java explicit. We concede that method and constructor calls may diverge or error, but assume they can never go wrong (other assumptions given in the supplemental material).

Assumption 1 ($\mathsf{JVM}_{\mathsf{new}}$). *If* $\forall i.\ v_i = C_i\ \{\overrightarrow{fld_j : v_j}\}$ *or* $v_i = \mathsf{nil}$ *and* v_i *is consistent with* ρ *then either*

- $\mathsf{JVM}_{\mathsf{new}}[C, [\overrightarrow{C_i}], [\overrightarrow{v_i}]] = C\ \{\overrightarrow{fld_k : v_k}\}$ *which is consistent with* ρ,
- $\mathsf{JVM}_{\mathsf{new}}[C, [\overrightarrow{C_i}], [\overrightarrow{v_i}]] = \mathsf{err}$, *or*
- $\mathsf{JVM}_{\mathsf{new}}[C, [\overrightarrow{C_i}], [\overrightarrow{v_i}]]$ *is undefined.*

For the purposes of our soundness proof, we require that all values are *consistent.* Consistency (defined in the supplemental material) states that the types of closures are well-scoped—they do not claim propositions about variables hidden in their closures.

We can now state our main lemma and soundness theorem. The metavariable α ranges over v, err and *wrong*. Proofs are deferred to the supplemental material.

Lemma 1. *If* $\Gamma \vdash e' \Rightarrow e : \tau\ ;\ \psi_+|\psi_-\ ;\ o$, $\rho \models \Gamma$, ρ *is consistent, and* $\rho \vdash e \Downarrow \alpha$ *then either*

- $\rho \vdash e \Downarrow v$ *and all of the following hold:*
  1. *either* $o = \emptyset$ *or* $\rho(o) = v$,
  2. *either* $\mathsf{TrueVal}(v)$ *and* $\rho \models \psi_+$ *or* $\mathsf{FalseVal}(v)$ *and* $\rho \models \psi_-$,
  3. $\vdash v \Rightarrow v : \tau\ ;\ \psi'_+|\psi'_-\ ;\ o'$ *for some* ψ'_+, ψ'_- *and* o', *and*
  4. v *is consistent with* ρ, *or*
- $\rho \vdash e \Downarrow \mathsf{err}$.

Theorem 1 (Type Soundness). *If* $\Gamma \vdash e' \Rightarrow e : \tau\ ;\ \psi_+|\psi_-\ ;\ o$ *and* $\rho \vdash e \Downarrow v$ *then* $\vdash v \Rightarrow v : \tau\ ;\ \psi'_+|\psi'_-\ ;\ o'$ *for some* ψ'_+, ψ'_- *and* o'.

5 Experience

Typed Clojure is implemented as `core.typed` [2], which has seen wide usage.

5.1 Implementation

`core.typed` provides preliminary integration with the Clojure compilation pipeline, primarily to resolve Java interoperability.

The `core.typed` implementation extends this paper in several key areas to handle checking real Clojure code, including an implementation of Typed Racket's variable-arity polymorphism [22], and support for other Clojure idioms like datatypes and protocols. There is no integration with Java Generics, so only Java 1.4-style erased types are "trusted" by `core.typed`. Casts are needed to recover the discarded information, which—for collections—are then tracked via Clojure's universal sequence interface [14].

	feeds2imap	CircleCI
Total number of typed namespaces	11 (825 LOC)	87 (19,000 LOC)
Total number of `def` expressions	93	1834
• checked	52 (56%)	407 (22%)
• unchecked	41 (44%)	1427 (78%)
Total number of Java interactions	32	105
• static methods	5 (16%)	26 (25%)
• instance methods	20 (62%)	36 (34%)
• constructors	6 (19%)	38 (36%)
• static fields	1 (3%)	5 (5%)
Methods overriden to return non-nil	0	35
Methods overriden to accept nil arguments	0	1
Total HMap lookups	27	328
• resolved to mandatory key	20 (74%)	208 (64%)
• resolved to optional key	6 (22%)	70 (21%)
• resolved of absent key	0 (0%)	20 (6%)
• unresolved key	1 (4%)	30 (9%)
Total number of `defalias` expressions	18	95
• contained HMap or union of HMap type	7 (39%)	62 (65%)
Total number of checked `defmulti` expressions	0	11
Total number of checked `defmethod` expressions	0	89

Fig. 13. Typed Clojure features used in practice

5.2 Evaluation

Throughout this paper, we have focused on three interrelated type system features: heterogenous maps, Java interoperability, and multimethods. Our hypothesis is that these features are widely used in existing Clojure programs in interconnecting ways, and that handling them as we have done is required to type check realistic Clojure programs.

To evaluate this hypothesis, we analyzed two existing `core.typed` code bases, one from the open-source community, and one from a company that uses `core.typed` in production. For our data gathering, we instrumented the `core.typed` type checker to record how often various features were used (summarized in Fig. 13).

feeds2imap. feeds2imap[4] is an open source library written in Typed Clojure. It provides an RSS reader using the *javax.mail* framework.

Of 11 typed namespaces containing 825 lines of code, there are 32 Java interactions. The majority are method calls, consisting of 20 (62 %) instance methods and 5 (16 %) static methods. The rest consists of 1 (3 %) static field access, and 6 (19 %) constructor calls—there are no instance field accesses.

There are 27 lookup operations on HMap types, of which 20 (74 %) resolve to mandatory entries, 6 (22 %) to optional entries, and 1 (4 %) is an unresolved lookup. No lookups involved fully specified maps.

From 93 `def` expressions in typed code, 52 (56 %) are checked, with a rate of 1 Java interaction for 1.6 checked top-level definitions, and 1 HMap lookup to 1.9 checked top-level definitions. That leaves 41 (44 %) unchecked vars, mainly due to partially complete porting to Typed Clojure, but in some cases due to unannotated third-party libraries.

No typed multimethods are defined or used. Of 18 total type aliases, 7 (39 %) contained one HMap type, and none contained unions of HMaps—on further inspection there was no HMap entry used to dictate control flow, often handled by multimethods. This is unusual in our experience, and is perhaps explained by feeds2imap mainly wrapping existing *javax.mail* functionality.

CircleCI. CircleCI [7] provides continuous integration services built with a mixture of open- and closed-source software. Typed Clojure was used at CircleCI in production systems for two years [8], maintaining 87 namespaces and 19,000 lines of code, an experience we summarise in Sect. 5.3.

The CircleCI code base contains 11 checked multimethods. All 11 dispatch functions are on a HMap key containing a keyword, in a similar style to Example 8. Correspondingly, all 89 methods are associated with a keyword dispatch value. The argument type was in all cases a single HMap type, however, rather than a union type. In our experience from porting other libraries, this is unusual.

Of 328 lookup operations on HMaps, 208 (64 %) resolve to mandatory keys, 70 (21 %) to optional keys, 20 (6 %) to absent keys, and 30 (9 %) lookups are unresolved. Of 95 total type aliases defined with `defalias`, 62 (65 %) involved one or more HMap types. Out of 105 Java interactions, 26 (25 %) are static methods, 36 (34 %) are instance methods, 38 (36 %) are constructors, and 5 (5 %) are static fields. 35 methods are overriden to return non-nil, and 1 method overridden to accept nil—suggesting that `core.typed` disallowing `nil` as a method argument by default is justified.

[4] https://github.com/frenchy64/feeds2imap.clj.

Of 464 checked top-level definitions (which consists of 57 `defmethod` calls and 407 `def` expressions), 1 HMap lookup occurs per 1.4 top-level definitions, and 1 Java interaction occurs every 4.4 top-level definitions.

From 1834 `def` expressions in typed code, only 407 (22 %) were checked. That leaves 1427 (78 %) which have unchecked definitions, either by an explicit `:no-check` annotation or `tc-ignore` to suppress type checking, or the `warn-on-unannotated-vars` option, which skips `def` expressions that lack expected types via `ann`. From a brief investigation, reasons include unannotated third-party libraries, work-in-progress conversions to Typed Clojure, unsupported Clojure idioms, and hard-to-check code.

Lessons. Based on our empirical survey, HMaps and Java interoperability support are vital features used on average more than once per typed function. Multimethods are less common in our case studies. The CircleCI code base contains only 26 multimethods total in 55,000 lines of mixed untyped-typed Clojure code, a low number in our experience.

5.3 Further Challenges

After a 2 year trial, the second case study decided to disabled type checking [9]. They were supportive of the fundamental ideas presented in this paper, but primarily cited issues with the checker implementation in practice and would reconsider type checking if they were resolved. This is also supported by Fig. 13, where 78 % of `def` expressions are unchecked.

Performance. Rechecking files with transitive dependencies is expensive since all dependencies must be rechecked. We conjecture caching type state will significantly improve re-checking performance, though preserving static soundness in the context of arbitrary code reloading is a largely unexplored area.

Library Annotations. Annotations for external code are rarely available, so a large part of the untyped-typed porting process is reverse engineering libraries.

Unsupported Idioms. While the current set of features is vital to checking Clojure code, there is still much work to do. For example, common Clojure functions are often too polymorphic for the current implementation or theory to account for. The post-mortem [9] contains more details.

6 Related Work

Multimethods. Millstein [20] and collaborators present a sequence of systems [4,5,20] with statically-typed multimethods and modular type checking. In contrast to Typed Clojure, in these system methods declare the types of arguments that they expect which corresponds to exclusively using `class` as the dispatch function in Typed Clojure. However, Typed Clojure does not attempt to rule out failed dispatches.

Record Types. Row polymorphism [3,12,26], used in systems such as the OCaml object system, provides many of the features of HMap types, but defined using universally-quantified row variables. HMaps in Typed Clojure are instead designed to be used with subtyping, but nonetheless provide similar expressiveness, including the ability to require presence and absence of certain keys.

Dependent JavaScript [6] can track similar invariants as HMaps with types for JS objects. They must deal with mutable objects, they feature refinement types and strong updates to the heap to track changes to objects.

TeJaS [16], another type system for JavaScript, also supports similar HMaps, with the ability to record the presence and absence of entries, but lacks a compositional flow-checking approach like occurrence typing.

Typed Lua [18] has *table types* which track entries in a mutable Lua table. Typed Lua changes the dynamic semantics of Lua to accommodate mutability: Typed Lua raises a runtime error for lookups on missing keys—HMaps consider lookups on missing keys normal.

Java Interoperability in Statically Typed Languages. Scala [21] has nullable references for compatibility with Java. Programmers must manually check for `null` as in Java to avoid null-pointer exceptions.

Other Optional and Gradual Type Systems. Several other gradual type systems have been developed for existing dynamically-typed languages. Reticulated Python [25] is an experimental gradually typed system for Python, implemented as a source-to-source translation that inserts dynamic checks at language boundaries and supporting Python's first-class object system. Clojure's nominal classes avoids the need to support first-class object system in Typed Clojure, however HMaps offer an alternative to the structural objects offered by Reticulated. Similarly, Gradualtalk [1] offers gradual typing for Smalltalk, with nominal classes.

Optional types have been adopted in industry, including Hack [10], and Flow [11] and TypeScript [19], two extensions of JavaScript. These systems support limited forms of occurrence typing, and do not include the other features we present.

7 Conclusion

Optional type systems must be designed with close attention to the language that they are intended to work for. We have therefore designed Typed Clojure, an optionally-typed version of Clojure, with a type system that works with a wide variety of distinctive Clojure idioms and features. Although based on the foundation of Typed Racket's occurrence typing approach, Typed Clojure both extends the fundamental control-flow based reasoning as well as applying it to handle seemingly unrelated features such as multi-methods. In addition, Typed Clojure supports crucial features such as heterogeneous maps and Java interoperability while integrating these features into the core type system. Not only are each of these features important in isolation to Clojure and Typed

Clojure programmers, but they must fit together smoothly to ensure that existing untyped programs are easy to convert to Typed Clojure.

The result is a sound, expressive, and useful type system which, as implemented in `core.typed` with appropriate extensions, is suitable for typechecking a significant amount of existing Clojure programs. As a result, Typed Clojure is already successful: it is used in the Clojure community among both enthusiasts and professional programmers.

Our empirical analysis of existing Typed Clojure programs bears out our design choices. Multimethods, Java interoperation, and heterogeneous maps are indeed common in both Clojure and Typed Clojure, meaning that our type system must accommodate them. Furthermore, they are commonly used together, and the features of each are mutually reinforcing. Additionally, the choice to make Java's `null` explicit in the type system is validated by the many Typed Clojure programs that specify non-nullable types.

References

1. Allende, E., Callau, O., Fabry, J., Tanter, É., Denker, M.: Gradual typing for Smalltalk. Sci. Comput. Program. **96**, 52–69 (2014)
2. Bonnaire-Sergeant, A.: contributors, core.typed. https://github.com/clojure/core.typed
3. Cardelli, L., Mitchell, J.C.: Operations on records. Math. Struct. Comput. Sci. **1**, 3–48 (1991)
4. Chambers, C.: Object-oriented multi-methods in Cecil. In: Proceedings of the ECOOP (1992)
5. Chambers, C., Leavens, G.T.: Typechecking and modules for multi-methods. In: Proc. OOPSLA (1994)
6. Chugh, R., Herman, D., Jhala, R.: Dependent types for JavaScript. In: Proceedings of the OOPSLA (2012)
7. CircleCI: CircleCI. https://circleci.com
8. CircleCI: Why we're supporting Typed Clojure, and you should too! (September 2013). http://blog.circleci.com/supporting-typed-clojure/
9. CircleCI; O'Morain, M.: Why we're no longer using core.typed (September 2015). http://blog.circleci.com/why-were-no-longer-using-core-typed/
10. Facebook: Hack language specification. Technical report, Facebook (2014)
11. Facebook: Flow language specification. Technical report, Facebook (2015)
12. Harper, R., Pierce, B.: A record calculus based on symmetric concatenation. In: Proceedings of the POPL (1991)
13. Hickey, R.: The Clojure programming language. In: Proceedings of the DLS (2008)
14. Hickey, R.: Clojure sequence documentation (February 2015). http://clojure.org/sequences
15. Lehtosalo, J.: mypy. http://mypy-lang.org/
16. Lerner, B.S., Politz, J.G., Guha, A., Krishnamurthi, S.: TeJaS: retrofitting type systems for JavaScript. In: DLS 2013, Proceedings of the 9th Symposium on Dynamic Languages, pp. 1–16. ACM, New York, NY, USA (2013). http://doi.acm.org/10.1145/2508168.2508170
17. Lucassen, J.M., Gifford, D.K.: Polymorphic effect systems. In: Proceedings of the POPL (1988)

18. Maidl, A.M., Mascarenhas, F., Ierusalimschy, R.: Typed Lua: an optional type system for Lua. In: Proceedings of the Dyla (2014)
19. Microsoft: Typescript language specification. Technical report Version 1.4, Microsoft (2014)
20. Millstein, T., Chambers, C.: Modular statically typed multimethods. In: Information and Computation. pp. 279–303. Springer-Verlag (2002)
21. Odersky, M., Cremet, V., Dragos, I., Dubochet, G., Emir, B., McDirmid, S., Micheloud, S., Mihaylov, N., Schinz, M., Stenman, E., Spoon, L., Zenger, M., et al.: An overview of the Scala programming language, 2nd edn, Technical report, EPFL Lausanne, Switzerland (2006)
22. Strickland, T.S., Tobin-Hochstadt, S., Felleisen, M.: Practical variable-arity polymorphism. In: Castagna, G. (ed.) ESOP 2009. LNCS, vol. 5502, pp. 32–46. Springer, Heidelberg (2009)
23. Tobin-Hochstadt, S., Felleisen, M.: The design and implementation of Typed Scheme. In: Proceedings of the POPL (2008)
24. Tobin-Hochstadt, S., Felleisen, M.: Logical types for untyped languages. In: ICFP 2010, Proceedings of the ICFP (2010)
25. Vitousek, M.M., Kent, A.M., Siek, J.G., Baker, J.: Design and evaluation of gradual typing for Python. In: Proc. DLS (2014)
26. Wand, M.: Type inference for record concatenation and multiple inheritance (1989)

A Timed Process Algebra for Wireless Networks with an Application in Routing
(Extended Abstract)

Emile Bres[1,3], Rob van Glabbeek[1,2], and Peter Höfner[1,2(✉)]

[1] NICTA, Sydney, Australia
peter.hoefner@nicta.com.au
[2] Computer Science and Engineering, University of New South Wales, Sydney, Australia
[3] École Polytechnique, Paris, France

Abstract. This paper proposes a timed process algebra for wireless networks, an extension of the Algebra for Wireless Networks. It combines treatments of local broadcast, conditional unicast and data structures, which are essential features for the modelling of network protocols. In this framework we model and analyse the Ad hoc On-Demand Distance Vector routing protocol, and show that, contrary to claims in the literature, it fails to be loop free. We also present boundary conditions for a fix ensuring that the resulting protocol is indeed loop free.

1 Introduction

In 2011 we developed the *Algebra for Wireless Networks* (AWN) [10], a process algebra particularly tailored for Wireless Mesh Networks (WMNs) and Mobile Ad Hoc Networks (MANETs). Such networks are currently being used in a wide range of application areas, such as public safety and mining. They are self-organising wireless multi-hop networks that provide network communication without relying on a wired backhaul infrastructure. A significant characteristic of such networks is that they allow highly dynamic network topologies, meaning that network nodes can join, leave, or move within the network at any moment. As a consequence routing protocols have constantly to check for broken links, and to replace invalid routes by better ones.

To capture the typical characteristics of WMNs and MANETs, AWN offers a unique set of features: *conditional unicast* (a message transmission attempt with different follow-up behaviour depending on its success), *groupcast* (communication to a specific set of nodes), *local broadcast* (messages are received only by nodes within transmission range of the sender), and *data structure*. We are not aware of any other process algebra that provides all these features, and hence could not use any other algebra to model certain protocols for WMNs or MANETs in a straightforward fashion.[1] Case studies [9–11, 15] have shown

[1] A comparison between AWN and other process algebras can be found in [11, Sect. 11].

P. Thiemann (Ed.): ESOP 2016, LNCS 9632, pp. 95–122, 2016.
DOI: 10.1007/978-3-662-49498-1_5

that AWN provides the right level of abstraction to model full IETF protocols, such as the Ad hoc On-Demand Distance Vector (AODV) routing protocol [29]. AWN has been employed to formally model this protocol—thereby eliminating ambiguities and contradictions from the official specification, written in English Prose—and to reason about protocol behaviour and provide rigorous proofs of key protocol properties such as loop freedom and route correctness.

However, AWN abstracts from time. Analysing routing protocols without considering timing issues is useful in its own right; for AODV it has revealed many shortcomings in drafts as well as in the standard (e.g., [3,16,19]). Including time in a formal analysis, however, will pave the way to analyse protocols that repeat some procedures every couple of time units; examples are OLSR [7] and B.A.T.M.A.N. [26]. Even for a reactive protocol such as AODV, which does not schedule tasks regularly, it has been shown that timing aspects are important: if timing parameters are chosen poorly, some routes are not established since data that is stored locally at network nodes expires too soon and is erased [6]. Besides such shortcomings in "performance", also fundamental correctness properties like loop freedom can be affected by the treatment of time—as we will illustrate.

To enable time analyses of WMNs and MANETs, this paper proposes a *Timed (process) Algebra for Wireless Networks* (T-AWN), an extension of AWN. It combines AWN's unique set of features, such as local broadcast, with time.

In this framework we model and analyse the AODV routing protocol, and show that, contrary to claims in the literature, e.g., [30], it fails to be loop free, as data required for routing can expire. We also present boundary conditions for a fix ensuring that the resulting protocol is loop free.

Design Decisions. Prior to the development of T-AWN we had to make a couple of decisions.

Intranode Computations. In wireless networks sending a packet from one node to another takes multiple microseconds. Compared to these "slow" actions, time spent for internal (intranode) computations, such as variable assignments or evaluations of expressions, is negligible. We therefore postulate that only transmissions from one node to another take time.

This decision is debatable for processes that can perform infinite sequences of intranode computations without ever performing a durational action. In this paper (and in all applications), we restrict ourselves to *well-timed* processes in the spirit of [27], i.e., to processes where any infinite sequence of actions contains infinitely many time steps or infinitely many input actions, such as receiving an incoming packet.

But, in the same spirit as T-AWN assigns time to internode communications, it is more or less straightforward to assign times to other operations as well.

Guaranteed Message Receipt and Input Enabledness. A fundamental assumption underlying the semantics of (T-)AWN is that any broadcast message *is* received by all nodes within transmission range [11, Sect. 1].[2] This abstraction enables us to interpret a failure of route discovery (as documented for AODV in [11, Sect. 9]) as an imperfection in the protocol, rather than as a result of a chosen formalism not ensuring guaranteed receipt.

A consequence of this design decision is that in the operational semantics of (T-)AWN a broadcast of one node in a network needs to synchronise with some (in)activity of all other nodes in the network [11, Sect. 11]. If another node is within transmission range of the broadcast, the broadcast synchronises with a receive action of that node, and otherwise with a non-arrive transition, which signals that the node is out of range for this broadcast [11, Sect. 4.3].

A further consequence is that we need to specify our nodes in such a way that they are *input-enabled*, meaning that in any state they are able to receive messages from any other node within transmission range.

Since a transmission (broadcast, groupcast, or unicast) takes multiple units of time, we postulate that another node can only receive a message if it remains within transmission range during the whole period of sending.[3] A possible way to model the receive action that synchronises with a transmission such as a broadcast is to let it take the same amount of time as the broadcast action. However, a process that is busy executing a durational receive action would fail to be input-enabled, for it would not be able to start receiving another message before the ongoing message receipt is finished. For this reason, we model the receipt of a message as an instantaneous action that synchronises with the very end of a broadcast action.[4]

T-AWN Syntax. When designing or formalising a protocol in T-AWN, an engineer should not be bothered with timing aspects; except for functions and procedures that schedule tasks depending on the current time. Because of this, we use the syntax of AWN also for T-AWN; "extended" by a local timer `now`. Hence we can perform a timed analysis of any specification written in AWN, since they are also T-AWN specifications.

2 A Timed Process Algebra for Wireless Networks

In this section we propose T-AWN (Timed Algebra for Wireless Networks), an extension of the process algebra AWN [10, 11] with time. AWN itself is a variant

[2] In reality, communication is only half-duplex: a single-interface network node cannot receive messages while sending and hence messages can be lost. However, the CSMA protocol used at the link layer—not modelled by (T-)AWN—keeps the probability of packet loss due to two nodes (within range) sending at the same time rather low.

[3] To be precise, we forgive very short interruptions in the connection between two nodes—those that begin and end within the same unit of time.

[4] Another solution would be to assume that a broadcast-receiving process can receive multiple messages in parallel. In case the process is meant to add incoming messages to a message queue (as happens in our application to AODV), one can assume that a message that is being received in parallel is added to that queue as soon as its receipt is complete. However, such a model is equivalent to one in which only the very last stage of the receipt action is modelled.

of standard process algebras [2,4,18,23], tailored to protocols in wireless mesh networks, such as the Ad-hoc on Demand Distance Vector (AODV) routing protocol. In (T-)AWN, a WMN is modelled as an encapsulated parallel composition of network nodes. On each node several sequential processes may be running in parallel. Network nodes communicate with their direct neighbours—those nodes that are in transmission range—using either broadcast, groupcast or unicast. Our formalism maintains for each node the set of nodes that are currently in transmission range. Due to mobility of nodes and variability of wireless links, nodes can move in or out of transmission range. The encapsulation of the entire network inhibits communications between network nodes and the outside world, with the exception of the receipt and delivery of data packets from or to clients[5] of the modelled protocol that may be hooked up to various nodes.

In T-AWN we apply a discrete model of time, where each sequential process maintains a local variable `now` holding its local clock value—an integer. We employ only one clock for each sequential process. All sequential processes in a network synchronise in taking time steps, and at each time step all local clocks advance by one unit. For the rest, the variable `now` behaves as any other variable maintained by a process: its value can be read when evaluating guards, thereby making progress time-dependant, and any value can be assigned to it, thereby resetting the local clock.

In our model of a sequential process p running on a node, time can elapse only when p is transmitting a message to another node, or when p currently has no way to proceed—for instance, when waiting on input, or for its local clock to reach a specified value. All other actions of p, such as assigning values to variables, evaluating guards, communicating with other processes running on the same node, or communicating with clients of the modelled protocol hooked up at that node, are assumed to be an order of magnitude faster, and in our model take no time at all. Thus they are executed in preference to time steps.

2.1 The Syntax of T-AWN

The syntax of T-AWN is the same as the syntax of AWN [10,11], except for the presence of the variable `now` of the new type `TIME`. This brings the advantage that any specification written in AWN can be interpreted and analysed in a timed setting. The rest of this Sect. 2.1 is almost copied verbatim from the original articles about AWN [10,11].

A Language for Sequential Processes. The internal state of a process is determined, in part, by the values of certain data variables that are maintained by that process. To this end, we assume a data structure with several types, variables ranging over these types, operators and predicates. First order predicate logic yields terms (or *data expressions*) and formulas to denote data values and statements about them.[6] Our data structure always contains

[5] The application layer that initiates packet sending and/or awaits receipt of a packet.

[6] As operators we also allow *partial* functions with the convention that any atomic formula containing an undefined subterm evaluates to `false`.

the types TIME, DATA, MSG, IP and $\mathscr{P}$(IP) of *time values*, which we take to be integers (together with the special value ∞), *application layer data*, *messages*, *IP addresses*—or any other node identifiers—and *sets of IP addresses*. We further assume that there is a variable now of type TIME and a function newpkt : DATA $\times$ IP $\rightarrow$ MSG that generates a message with new application layer data for a particular destination. The purpose of this function is to inject data to the protocol; details will be given later.

In addition, we assume a type SPROC of *sequential processes*, and a collection of *process names*, each being an operator of type $\texttt{TYPE}_1 \times \cdots \times \texttt{TYPE}_n \rightarrow \texttt{SPROC}$ for certain data types $\texttt{TYPE}_i$. Each process name X comes with a *defining equation*

$$X(\texttt{var}_1, \ldots, \texttt{var}_n) \stackrel{def}{=} p\ ,$$

in which, for each $i = 1, \ldots, n$, $\texttt{var}_i$ is a variable of type $\texttt{TYPE}_i$ and p a *guarded*[7] *sequential process expression* defined by the grammar below. The expression p may contain the variables $\texttt{var}_i$ as well as X; however, all occurrences of data variables in p have to be *bound*. The choice of the underlying data structure and the process names with their defining equations can be tailored to any particular application of our language; our decisions made for modelling AODV are presented in Sect. 3. The process names are used to denote the processes that feature in this application, with their arguments $\texttt{var}_i$ binding the current values of the data variables maintained by these processes.

The *sequential process expressions* are given by the following grammar:

$$\begin{aligned} SP &::= X(\mathit{exp}_1, \ldots, \mathit{exp}_n) \mid [\varphi]SP \mid [\![\texttt{var} := \mathit{exp}]\!]SP \mid SP + SP \mid \\ &\quad\ \alpha.SP \mid \textbf{unicast}(\mathit{dest}, \mathit{ms}).SP \blacktriangleright SP \\ \alpha &::= \textbf{broadcast}(\mathit{ms}) \mid \textbf{groupcast}(\mathit{dests}, \mathit{ms}) \mid \textbf{send}(\mathit{ms}) \mid \\ &\quad\ \textbf{deliver}(\mathit{data}) \mid \textbf{receive}(\texttt{msg}) \end{aligned}$$

Here X is a process name, exp_i a data expression of the same type as $\texttt{var}_i$, φ a data formula, $\texttt{var} := \mathit{exp}$ an assignment of a data expression *exp* to a variable var of the same type, *dest*, *dests*, *data* and *ms* data expressions of types IP, $\mathscr{P}$(IP), DATA and MSG, respectively, and msg a data variable of type MSG.

The internal state of a sequential process described by an expression p in this language is determined by p, together with a *valuation* ξ associating data values $\xi(\texttt{var})$ to the data variables var maintained by this process. Valuations naturally extend to *ξ-closed* data expressions—those in which all variables are either bound or in the domain of ξ.

Given a valuation of the data variables by concrete data values, the sequential process $[\varphi]p$ acts as p if φ evaluates to true, and deadlocks if φ evaluates to false. In case φ contains free variables that are not yet interpreted as data values, values are assigned to these variables in any way that satisfies φ, if possible. The sequential process $[\![\texttt{var} := \mathit{exp}]\!]p$ acts as p, but under an updated

[7] An expression p is *guarded* if each call of a process name $X(\mathit{exp}_1, \ldots, \mathit{exp}_n)$ occurs with a subexpression $[\varphi]q$, $[\![\texttt{var} := \mathit{exp}]\!]q$, $\alpha.q$ or $\textbf{unicast}(\mathit{dest}, \mathit{ms}).q \blacktriangleright r$ of p.

valuation of the data variable `var`. The sequential process $p + q$ may act either as p or as q, depending on which of the two processes is able to act at all. In a context where both are able to act, it is not specified how the choice is made. The sequential process $\alpha.p$ first performs the action α and subsequently acts as p. The action **broadcast**(ms) broadcasts (the data value bound to the expression) ms to the other network nodes within transmission range, whereas **unicast**$(dest, ms).p \blacktriangleright q$ is a sequential process that tries to unicast the message ms to the destination $dest$; if successful it continues to act as p and otherwise as q. In other words, **unicast**$(dest, ms).p$ is prioritised over q; only if the action **unicast**$(dest, ms)$ is not possible, the alternative q will happen. It models an abstraction of an acknowledgment-of-receipt mechanism that is typical for unicast communication but absent in broadcast communication, as implemented by the link layer of relevant wireless standards such as IEEE 802.11 [20]. The process **groupcast**$(dests, ms).p$ tries to transmit ms to all destinations $dests$, and proceeds as p regardless of whether any of the transmissions is successful. Unlike **unicast** and **broadcast**, the expression **groupcast** does not have a unique counterpart in networking. Depending on the protocol and the implementation it can be an iterative unicast, a broadcast, or a multicast; thus **groupcast** abstracts from implementation details. The action **send**(ms) synchronously transmits a message to another process running on the same network node; this action can occur only when this other sequential process is able to receive the message. The sequential process **receive**(`msg`)$.p$ receives any message m (a data value of type `MSG`) either from another node, from another sequential process running on the same node or from the client hooked up to the local node. It then proceeds as p, but with the data variable `msg` bound to the value m. The submission of data from a client is modelled by the receipt of a message `newpkt`(d, dip), where the function `newpkt` generates a message containing the data d and the intended destination dip. Data is delivered to the client by **deliver**$(data)$.

A Language for Parallel Processes. *Parallel process expressions* are given by the grammar

$$PP ::= \xi, SP \mid PP \langle\langle PP ,$$

where SP is a sequential process expression and ξ a valuation. An expression ξ, p denotes a sequential process expression equipped with a valuation of the variables it maintains. The process $P \langle\langle Q$ is a parallel composition of P and Q, running on the same network node. An action **receive**(m) of P synchronises with an action **send**(m) of Q into an internal action τ, as formalised in Table 2. These receive actions of P and send actions of Q cannot happen separately. All other actions of P and Q, except time steps, including receive actions of Q and send actions of P, occur interleaved in $P \langle\langle Q$. Therefore, a parallel process expression denotes a parallel composition of sequential processes ξ, P with information flowing from right to left. The variables of different sequential processes running on the same node are maintained separately, and thus cannot be shared.

Though $\langle\!\langle$ only allows information flow in one direction, it reflects reality of WMNs. Usually two sequential processes run on the same node: $P \langle\!\langle Q$. The main process P deals with all protocol details of the node, e.g., message handling and maintaining the data such as routing tables. The process Q manages the queueing of messages as they arrive; it is always able to receive a message even if P is busy. The use of message queueing in combination with $\langle\!\langle$ is crucial in order to create input-enabled nodes (cf. Sect. 1).

A Language for Networks. We model network nodes in the context of a wireless mesh network by *node expressions* of the form $ip : PP : R$. Here $ip \in \mathtt{IP}$ is the *address* of the node, PP is a parallel process expression, and $R \subseteq \mathtt{IP}$ is the *range* of the node—the set of nodes that are currently within transmission range of ip.

A *partial network* is then modelled by a *parallel composition* $\|$ of node expressions, one for every node in the network, and a *complete network* is a partial network within an *encapsulation operator* $[\_]$ that limits the communication of network nodes and the outside world to the receipt and the delivery of data packets to and from the application layer attached to the modelled protocol in the network nodes. This yields the following grammar for network expressions:

$$N ::= [M] \qquad\qquad M ::= \; ip : PP : R \;\mid\; M\|M.$$

2.2 The Semantics of T-AWN

As mentioned in the introduction, the transmission of a message takes time. Since our main application assumes a wireless link and node mobility, the packet delivery time varies. Hence we assume a minimum time that is required to send a message, as well as an optional extra transmission time. In T-AWN the values of these parameters are given for each type of sending separately: $\mathtt{LB}$, $\mathtt{LG}$, and $\mathtt{LU}$, satisfying $\mathtt{LB}, \mathtt{LG}, \mathtt{LU} > 0$, specify the minimum bound, in units of time, on the duration of a broadcast, groupcast and unicast transmission; the optional additional transmission times are denoted by $\Delta\mathtt{B}$, $\Delta\mathtt{G}$ and $\Delta\mathtt{U}$, satisfying $\Delta\mathtt{B}, \Delta\mathtt{G}, \Delta\mathtt{U} \geq 0$. Adding up these parameters (e.g. $\mathtt{LB}$ and $\Delta\mathtt{B}$) yields maximum transmission times. We allow any execution consistent with these parameters. For all other actions our processes can take we postulate execution times of 0.

Sequential Processes. The structural operational semantics of T-AWN, given in Tables 1, 2, 3 and 4, is in the style of Plotkin [31] and describes how one internal state can evolve into another by performing an *action*.

A difference with AWN is that some of the transitions are time steps. On the level of node and network expressions they are labelled "tick" and the parallel composition of multiple nodes can perform such a transition iff each of those nodes can—see the third rule in Table 4. On the level of sequential and parallel process expressions, time-consuming transitions are labelled with *wait actions* from $\mathcal{W} = \{\mathrm{w}, \mathrm{ws}, \mathrm{wr}, \mathrm{wrs}\} \subseteq \mathrm{Act}$ and *transmission actions* from $\mathcal{R}\!:\!\mathcal{W} =$

$\{R\!:\!w_1 \mid w_1 \in \mathcal{W} \wedge R \subseteq \texttt{IP}\} \subseteq \text{Act}$. Wait actions $w_1 \in \mathcal{W}$ indicate that the system is waiting, possibly only as long as it fails to synchronise on a **receive** action (wr), a **send** action (ws) or both of those (wrs); actions $R\!:\!w_1$ indicate that the system is transmitting a message while the current transmission range of the node is $R \subseteq \texttt{IP}$. In the operational rule for choice ($+$) we combine any two wait actions $w_1, w_2 \in \mathcal{W}$ with the operator $\wedge$, which joins the conditions under which these wait actions can occur.

$\wedge$	w	wr	ws	wrs
w	w	wr	ws	wrs
wr	wr	wr	wrs	wrs
ws	ws	wrs	ws	wrs
wrs	wrs	wrs	wrs	wrs

In Table 1, which gives the semantics of sequential process expressions, a state is given as a pair ξ, p of a sequential process expression p and a valuation ξ of the data variables maintained by p. The set Act of actions that can be executed by sequential and parallel process expressions, and thus occurs as transition labels, consists of $R\!:$***cast**(m), **send**(m), **deliver**(d), **receive**(m), durational actions w_1 and $R\!:\!w_1$, and internal actions τ, for each choice of $R \subseteq \texttt{IP}$, $m \in \texttt{MSG}$, $d \in \texttt{DATA}$ and $w_1 \in \mathcal{W}$. Here $R\!:$***cast**(m) is the action of transmitting the message m, to be received by the set of nodes R, which is the intersection of the set of intended destinations with the nodes that are within transmission range throughout the transmission. We do not distinguish whether this message has been broadcast, groupcast or unicast—the differences show up merely in the value of R.

In Table 1 $\xi[\texttt{var} := v]$ denotes the valuation that assigns the value v to the variable var, and agrees with ξ on all other variables. We use $\xi[\texttt{now}{+}{+}]$ as an abbreviation for $\xi[\texttt{now} := \xi(\texttt{now}){+}1]$, the valuation ξ in which the variable now is incremented by 1. This describes the state of data variables after 1 unit of time elapses, while no other changes in data occurred. The empty valuation $\emptyset$ assigns values to no variables. Hence $\emptyset[\texttt{var}_i := v_i]_{i=1}^{n}$ is the valuation that *only* assigns the values v_i to the variables $\texttt{var}_i$ for $i = 1, \ldots, n$. Moreover, $\xi(\mathit{exp})\!\downarrow$, with exp a data expression, is the statement that $\xi(\mathit{exp})$ is defined; this might fail because exp contains a variable that is not in the domain of ξ or because exp contains a partial function that is given an argument for which it is not defined.

A state ξ, r is *unvalued*, denoted by $\xi(r)\!\uparrow$, if r has the form **broadcast**$(\mathit{ms}).p$, **groupcast**$(\mathit{dests}, \mathit{ms}).p$, **unicast**$(\mathit{dest}, \mathit{ms}).p$, **send**$(\mathit{ms}).p$, **deliver**$(\mathit{data}).p$, $[\![\texttt{var} := \mathit{exp}]\!]p$ or $X(\mathit{exp}_1, \ldots, \mathit{exp}_n)$ with either $\xi(\mathit{ms})$ or $\xi(\mathit{dests})$ or $\xi(\mathit{dest})$ or $\xi(\mathit{data})$ or $\xi(\mathit{exp})$ or some $\xi(\mathit{exp}_i)$ undefined. From such a state no progress is possible. However, the sixth last line in Table 1 does allow time to progress. We use $\xi(r)\!\downarrow$ to denote that a state is not unvalued.

Rule (rec) for process names in Table 1 is motivated and explained in [11, Sect. 4.1]. The variant (rec-w) of this rule for wait actions $w_1 \in \mathcal{W}$ has been modified such that the recursion is not yet unfolded while waiting. This simulates the behaviour of AWN where a process is only unwound if the first action of the process can be performed.

In the subsequent rules (grd) and ($\neg$grd) for variable-binding guards $[\varphi]$, the notation $\xi \xrightarrow{\varphi} \zeta$ says that ζ is an extension of ξ that satisfies φ: a valuation that agrees with ξ on all variables on which ξ is defined, and valuates the other variables occurring free in φ, such that the formula φ holds under ζ. All variables not free in φ and not evaluated by ξ are also not evaluated by ζ. Its negation

Table 1. Structural operational semantics for sequential process expressions

(bc)
$$\xi, \textbf{broadcast}(\mathit{ms}).p \xrightarrow{\tau} \xi, \mathtt{IP}: \textbf{*cast}(\xi(\mathit{ms}))[\mathtt{LB}, \mathtt{\Delta B}].p \blacktriangleright p \qquad (\text{if } \xi(\mathit{ms}){\downarrow})$$

(gc)
$$\xi, \textbf{groupcast}(\mathit{dests}, \mathit{ms}).p \xrightarrow{\tau} \xi, \xi(\mathit{dests}): \textbf{*cast}(\xi(\mathit{ms}))[\mathtt{LG}, \mathtt{\Delta G}].p \blacktriangleright p \qquad (\text{if } \xi(\mathit{dests}){\downarrow} \text{ and } \xi(\mathit{ms}){\downarrow})$$

(uc)
$$\xi, \textbf{unicast}(\mathit{dest}, \mathit{ms}).p \blacktriangleright q \xrightarrow{\tau} \xi, \{\xi(\mathit{dest})\}: \textbf{*cast}(\xi(\mathit{ms}))[\mathtt{LU}, \mathtt{\Delta U}].p \blacktriangleright q \qquad (\text{if } \xi(\mathit{dest}){\downarrow} \text{ and } \xi(\mathit{ms}){\downarrow})$$

(tr)
$$\xi, \mathit{dsts}: \textbf{*cast}(m)[n{+}1, o].p \blacktriangleright q \xrightarrow{R:\mathrm{w}} \xi[\mathtt{now}{+}{+}], (\mathit{dsts} \cap R): \textbf{*cast}(m)[n, o].p \blacktriangleright q \qquad (\forall R \subseteq \mathtt{IP})$$

(tr-o)
$$\xi, \mathit{dsts}: \textbf{*cast}(m)[n{+}1, o{+}1].p \blacktriangleright q \xrightarrow{R:\mathrm{w}} \xi[\mathtt{now}{+}{+}], (\mathit{dsts} \cap R): \textbf{*cast}(m)[n{+}1, o].p \blacktriangleright q \qquad (\forall R \subseteq \mathtt{IP})$$

(sc)
$$\xi, \mathit{dsts}: \textbf{*cast}(m)[0, o].p \blacktriangleright q \xrightarrow{\mathit{dsts}:\textbf{*cast}(m)} \xi, p \qquad (\text{if } \mathit{dsts} \neq \emptyset)$$

(¬sc)
$$\xi, \mathit{dsts}: \textbf{*cast}(m)[0, o].p \blacktriangleright q \xrightarrow{\mathit{dsts}:\textbf{*cast}(m)} \xi, q \qquad (\text{if } \mathit{dsts} = \emptyset)$$

(snd)
$$\xi, \textbf{send}(\mathit{ms}).p \xrightarrow{\textbf{send}(\xi(\mathit{ms}))} \xi, p \qquad (\text{if } \xi(\mathit{ms}){\downarrow})$$

(ws)
$$\xi, \textbf{send}(\mathit{ms}).p \xrightarrow{\mathrm{ws}} \xi[\mathtt{now}{+}{+}], \textbf{send}(\mathit{ms}).p \qquad (\text{if } \xi(\mathit{ms}){\downarrow})$$

(del)
$$\xi, \textbf{deliver}(\mathit{data}).p \xrightarrow{\textbf{deliver}(\xi(\mathit{data}))} \xi, p \qquad (\text{if } \xi(\mathit{data}){\downarrow})$$

(rcv)
$$\xi, \textbf{receive}(\mathtt{msg}).p \xrightarrow{\textbf{receive}(m)} \xi[\mathtt{msg} := m], p \qquad (\forall m \in \mathtt{MSG})$$

(wr)
$$\xi, \textbf{receive}(\mathtt{msg}).p \xrightarrow{\mathrm{wr}} \xi[\mathtt{now}{+}{+}], \textbf{receive}(\mathtt{msg}).p$$

(ass)
$$\xi, [\![\mathtt{var} := \mathit{exp}]\!]p \xrightarrow{\tau} \xi[\mathtt{var} := \xi(\mathit{exp})], p \qquad (\text{if } \xi(\mathit{exp}){\downarrow})$$

(w)
$$\xi, p \xrightarrow{\mathrm{w}} \xi[\mathtt{now}{+}{+}], p \qquad (\text{if } \xi(p){\uparrow})$$

(rec)
$$\frac{\emptyset[\mathtt{var}_i := \xi(\mathit{exp}_i)]_{i=1}^n, p \xrightarrow{a} \zeta, p'}{\xi, X(\mathit{exp}_1, \ldots, \mathit{exp}_n) \xrightarrow{a} \zeta, p'} \quad (X(\mathtt{var}_1, \ldots, \mathtt{var}_n) \stackrel{\mathit{def}}{=} p) \quad (\forall a \in \mathrm{Act} - \mathcal{W},\ \text{if } \xi(\mathit{exp}_i){\downarrow})$$

(rec-w)
$$\frac{\emptyset[\mathtt{var}_i := \xi(\mathit{exp}_i)]_{i=1}^n, p \xrightarrow{w_1} \zeta, p'}{\xi, X(\mathit{exp}_1, \ldots, \mathit{exp}_n) \xrightarrow{w_1} \xi[\mathtt{now}{+}{+}], X(\mathit{exp}_1, \ldots, \mathit{exp}_n)} \quad (X(\mathtt{var}_1, \ldots, \mathtt{var}_n) \stackrel{\mathit{def}}{=} p) \quad (\forall w_1 {\in} \mathcal{W},\ \text{if } \xi(\mathit{exp}_i){\downarrow})$$

(grd)
$$\frac{\xi \xrightarrow{\varphi} \zeta}{\xi, [\varphi]p \xrightarrow{\tau} \zeta, p}$$

(¬grd)
$$\frac{\xi \not\xrightarrow{\varphi}}{\xi, [\varphi]p \xrightarrow{\mathrm{w}} \xi[\mathtt{now}{+}{+}], [\varphi]p}$$

(alt-l)
$$\frac{\xi, p \xrightarrow{a} \zeta, p'}{\xi, p + q \xrightarrow{a} \zeta, p'}$$

(alt-r)
$$\frac{\xi, q \xrightarrow{a} \zeta, q'}{\xi, p + q \xrightarrow{a} \zeta, q'} \qquad (\forall a \in \mathrm{Act} - \mathcal{W})$$

(alt-w)
$$\frac{\xi, p \xrightarrow{w_1} \zeta, p' \quad \xi, q \xrightarrow{w_2} \zeta, q'}{\xi, p + q \xrightarrow{w_1 \wedge w_2} \zeta, p' + q'} \qquad (\forall w_1, w_2 \in \mathcal{W})$$

$\xi \not\xrightarrow{\varphi}$ says that no such extension exists, and thus that φ is false in the current state, no matter how we interpret the variables whose values are still undefined. If that is the case, the process $[\varphi]p$ will idle by performing the action w (of waiting) without changing its state, except that the variable now will be incremented.

Example 1. The process $[\![\mathtt{timeout} := \mathtt{now} + 2]\!][\mathtt{now} = \mathtt{timeout}]p$ first sets the variable `timeout` to 2 units after the current time. Then it encounters a guard that evaluates to `false`, and therefore takes a w-transition, twice. After two time units, the guard evaluates to `true` and the process proceeds as p.

The process **receive**(`msg`).p can receive any message m from the environment in which this process is running. As long as the environment does not provide a message, this process will wait. This is indicated by the transition labelled wr in Table 1. The difference between a wr-and a w-transition is that the former can be taken only when the environment does not synchronise with the **receive**-transition. In our semantics any state with an outgoing wr-transition also has an outgoing **receive**-transition (see Theorem 1), which conceptually has priority over the wr-transition. Likewise the transition labelled ws is only enabled in states that also admit a **send**-transition, and is taken only in a context where the **send**-transition cannot be taken.

Rules (alt-l) and (alt-r), defining the behaviour of the choice operator for non-wait actions are standard. Rule (alt-w) for wait actions says that a process $p + q$ can wait only if both p and q can wait; if one of the two arguments can make real progress, the choice process $p + q$ always chooses this progress over waiting. This is a direct generalisation of the law $p + \mathbf{0} = p$ of CCS [23]. As a consequence, a condition on the possibility of p or q to wait is inherited by $p+q$. This gives rise to the transition label wrs, that makes waiting conditional on the environment failing to synchronising with a **receive** as well as a **send**-transition. In understanding the target $\zeta, p'+q'$ of this rule, it is helpful to realise that whenever $\xi, p \xrightarrow{w_1} \zeta, q$, then $q = p$ and $\zeta = \xi[\mathtt{now}{+}{+}]$; see Proposition 1.

In order to give semantics to the transmission constructs (broadcast, groupcast, unicast), the language of sequential processes is extended with the auxiliary construct

$$dsts : {*}\mathbf{cast}(m)[n,o].SP \blacktriangleright SP\ ,$$

with $m \in \mathtt{MSG}$, $n, o \in \mathbb{N}$ and $dsts \subseteq \mathtt{IP}$. This is a variant of the **broadcast**-, **groupcast**- and **unicast**-constructs, describing intermediate states of the transmission of message m. The argument $dsts$ of ***cast** denotes those intended destinations that were not out of transmission range during the part of the transmission that already took place.

In a state $dsts$: ${*}\mathbf{cast}(m)[n,o].p \blacktriangleright q$ with $n > 0$ the transmission still needs between n and $n{+}o$ time units to complete. If $n = 0$ the actual ***cast**-transition will take place; resulting in state p if the message is delivered to at least one node in the network ($dsts$ is non-empty), and q otherwise.

Rule (gc) says that once a process commits to a **groupcast**-transmission, it is going to behave as $dsts$: ${*}\mathbf{cast}(m)[n,o]$ with time parameters $n :=$ `LG` and $o :=$ `ΔG`. The transmitted message m is calculated by evaluating the argument ms, and the transmission range $dsts$ of this ***cast** is initialised by evaluating the argument $dests$, indicating the intended destinations of the **groupcast**. Rules (bc) and (uc) for **broadcast** and **unicast** are the same, except that in the case of **broadcast** the intended destinations are given by the set `IP` of *all* possible destinations, whereas a **unicast** has only one intended destination. Moreover, only **unicast** exploits the difference in the continuation process depending on whether an intended destination is within transmission range. Subsequently, Rules (tr) and (tr-o) come into force; they allow time-consuming transmission steps to take place, each decrementing one of the time parameters n or o. Each time step of a transmission corresponds to a transition labelled $R\!:\!\mathrm{w}$, where R records the current transmission range. Since sequential processes store no information on transmission ranges—this information is added only when moving from process expressions to node expressions—at this stage of the description all possibilities for the transmission range need to be left open, and hence there is a transition labelled $R\!:\!\mathrm{w}$ for each choice of R.[8] When transitions for process expressions are inherited by node expressions, only one of the transitions labelled $R\!:\!\mathrm{w}$ is going to survive, namely the one where R equals the transmission range given by the node expression (cf. Rule (n-t) in Table 3). Upon doing a transition $R\!:\!\mathrm{w}$, the range *dsts* of the ***cast** is restricted to R. As soon as $n = 0$, regardless of the value of o, the transmission is completed by the execution of the action *dsts*: ***cast**(m) (Rules (sc) and $\neg$(sc)). Here the actual message m is passed on for synchronisation with **receive**-transitions of all nodes $ip \in dsts$.

This treatment of message transmission is somewhat different from the one in AWN. There, the rule $\xi, \mathbf{groupcast}(\mathit{dests}, \mathit{ms}).p \xrightarrow{\mathbf{groupcast}(\xi(\mathit{dests}),\xi(\mathit{ms}))} \xi, p$ describes the behaviour of the **groupcast** construct for sequential processes, and the rule

$$\frac{P \xrightarrow{\mathbf{groupcast}(D,m)} P'}{ip : P : R \xrightarrow{R\cap D\,:\,\mathbf{*cast}(m)} ip : P' : R}$$

lifts this behaviour from processes to nodes. In this last stage the **groupcast**-action is unified with the **broadcast**- and **unicast**-action into a ***cast**, at which occasion the range of the ***cast** is calculated as the intersection of the intended destinations D of the **groupcast** and the ones in transmission range R. In T-AWN, on the other hand, the conversion of **groupcast** to ***cast** happens already at the level of sequential processes.

Parallel Processes. Rules (p-al), (p-ar) and (p-a) of Table 2 are taken from AWN, and formalise the description of the operator $\langle\!\langle$ given in Sect. 2.1. Rule (p-w) stipulates under which conditions a process $P \langle\!\langle Q$ can do a wait action, and of which kind. Here $\langle\!\langle$ is also a partial binary function on the set $\mathcal{W}$, specified by the table on the right. The process $P \langle\!\langle Q$ can do a wait action only if both P and Q can do so. In case P can do a wr or a wrs-action, P can also do a **receive** and in case Q can do a ws or a wrs, Q can also do a **send**. When both these possibilities apply, the **receive** of P synchronises with the **send** of Q into a τ-step, which has priority over waiting. In the other 12 cases no synchronisation between P and Q is possible, and we

$\langle\!\langle$	w	wr	ws	wrs
w	w	wr	w	wr
wr	w	wr	–	–
ws	ws	wrs	ws	wrs
wrs	ws	wrs	–	–

[8] Similar to **receive**(msg).p having a transition for each possible incoming message m.

Table 2. Structural operational semantics for parallel process expressions

$$\text{(p-al)}\ \frac{P \xrightarrow{a} P'}{P \langle\!\langle Q \xrightarrow{a} P' \langle\!\langle Q} \left(\begin{array}{c}\forall a \neq \mathbf{receive}(m),\\ a \notin \mathcal{W}, a \notin \mathcal{R}\!:\!\mathcal{W}\end{array}\right) \qquad \text{(p-ar)}\ \frac{Q \xrightarrow{a} Q'}{P \langle\!\langle Q \xrightarrow{a} P \langle\!\langle Q'} \left(\begin{array}{c}\forall a \neq \mathbf{send}(m),\\ a \notin \mathcal{W}, a \notin \mathcal{R}\!:\!\mathcal{W}\end{array}\right)$$

$$\text{(p-a)}\ \frac{P \xrightarrow{\mathbf{receive}(m)} P' \quad Q \xrightarrow{\mathbf{send}(m)} Q'}{P \langle\!\langle Q \xrightarrow{\tau} P' \langle\!\langle Q'} \ (\forall m \in \mathtt{MSG}) \qquad \text{(p-w)}\ \frac{P \xrightarrow{w_1} P' \quad Q \xrightarrow{w_2} Q'}{P \langle\!\langle Q \xrightarrow{w_3} P' \langle\!\langle Q'}$$

$$\text{(p-tl)}\ \frac{P \xrightarrow{R:w_1} P' \quad Q \xrightarrow{w_2} Q'}{P \langle\!\langle Q \xrightarrow{R:w_3} P' \langle\!\langle Q'} \qquad \text{(p-tr)}\ \frac{P \xrightarrow{w_1} P' \quad Q \xrightarrow{R:w_2} Q'}{P \langle\!\langle Q \xrightarrow{R:w_3} P' \langle\!\langle Q'} \qquad \text{(p-t)}\ \frac{P \xrightarrow{R:w_1} P' \quad Q \xrightarrow{R:w_2} Q'}{P \langle\!\langle Q \xrightarrow{R:w_3} P' \langle\!\langle Q'}$$

$$(\forall w_1, w_2, w_3 \in \mathcal{W}, w_3 = w_1 \langle\!\langle w_2)$$

do obtain a wait action. Since a **receive**-action of P that does not synchronise with Q is dropped, so is the corresponding side condition of a wait action of P. Hence (within the remaining 12 cases) a wr of P is treated as a w, and a wrs as a ws. Likewise a ws of Q is treated as a w, and a wrs as a wr. This leaves 4 cases to be decided. In all four, we have $\mathrm{w}_1 \langle\!\langle \mathrm{w}_2 = \mathrm{w}_1 \wedge \mathrm{w}_2$.

Time steps $R\!:\!w_1$ are treated exactly like wait actions from $\mathcal{W}$ (cf. Rules (p-tl), (p-tr) and (p-t)). If for instance P can do a $R\!:\!\mathrm{w}$, meaning that it spends a unit of time on a transmission, while Q can do a wr, meaning that it waits a unit of time only when it does not receive anything from another source, the result is that $P \langle\!\langle Q$ can spend a unit of time transmitting something, but only as long as $P \langle\!\langle Q$ does not receive any message; if it does, the receive action of Q happens with priority over the wait action of Q, and thus occurs before P spends a unit of time transmitting.

Node and Network Expressions. The operational semantics of node and network expressions of Tables 3 and 4 uses transition labels tick, $R\!:\!\mathbf{*cast}(m)$, $H\neg K\!:\!\mathbf{arrive}(m)$, $ip\!:\!\mathbf{deliver}(d)$, $\mathbf{connect}(ip, ip')$, $\mathbf{disconnect}(ip, ip')$, τ and $ip\!:\!\mathbf{newpkt}(d, dip)$. As before, $m \in \mathtt{MSG}$, $d \in \mathtt{DATA}$, $R \subseteq \mathtt{IP}$, and $ip, ip' \in \mathtt{IP}$. Moreover, $H, K \subseteq \mathtt{IP}$ are sets of IP addresses.

The actions $R\!:\!\mathbf{*cast}(m)$ are inherited by nodes from the processes that run on these nodes (cf. Rule (n-sc)). The action $H\neg K\!:\!\mathbf{arrive}(m)$ states that the message m simultaneously arrives at all addresses $ip \in H$, and fails to arrive at all addresses $ip \in K$. The rules of Table 4 let a $R\!:\!\mathbf{*cast}(m)$-action of one node synchronise with an $\mathbf{arrive}(m)$ of all other nodes, where this $\mathbf{arrive}(m)$ amalgamates the arrival of message m at the nodes in the transmission range R of the $\mathbf{*cast}(m)$, and the non-arrival at the other nodes. Rules (n-rcv) and (n-dis) state that arrival of a message at a node happens if and only if the node receives it, whereas non-arrival can happen at any time. This embodies our assumption that, at any time, any message that is transmitted to a node within range of the sender is actually received by that node. (Rule (n-dis) may appear to say that any node ip has the option to disregard any message at any time. However, the encapsulation operator (below) prunes away all such disregard transitions that do not synchronise with a cast action for which ip is out of range.)

Table 3. Structural operational semantics for node expressions

$$\text{(n-sc)}\ \frac{P \xrightarrow{dsts:\mathbf{*cast}(m)} P'}{ip:P{:}R \xrightarrow{dsts:\mathbf{*cast}(m)} ip:P'{:}R} \qquad \text{(n-rcv)}\ \frac{P \xrightarrow{\mathbf{receive}(m)} P'}{ip:P{:}R \xrightarrow{\{ip\}\neg\emptyset:\mathbf{arrive}(m)} ip:P'{:}R}$$

$$\text{(n-del)}\ \frac{P \xrightarrow{\mathbf{deliver}(d)} P'}{ip:P{:}R \xrightarrow{ip:\mathbf{deliver}(d)} ip:P'{:}R} \qquad \text{(n-dis)}\ ip:P{:}R \xrightarrow{\emptyset\neg\{ip\}:\mathbf{arrive}(m)} ip:P{:}R$$

$$\text{(n-}\tau\text{)}\ \frac{P \xrightarrow{\tau} P'}{ip:P{:}R \xrightarrow{\tau} ip:P'{:}R} \qquad \text{(n-w)}\ \frac{P \xrightarrow{w_1} P'}{ip:P{:}R \xrightarrow{\text{tick}} ip:P'{:}R} \qquad \text{(n-t)}\ \frac{P \xrightarrow{R:w_1} P'}{ip:P{:}R \xrightarrow{\text{tick}} ip:P'{:}R} \quad (\forall w_1 \in \mathcal{W})$$

$$\text{(con)}\ ip{:}P{:}R \xrightarrow{\mathbf{connect}(ip,ip')} ip{:}P{:}R\cup\{ip'\} \qquad \text{(dis)}\ ip{:}P{:}R \xrightarrow{\mathbf{disconnect}(ip,ip')} ip{:}P{:}R-\{ip'\}$$

The action **send**(m) of a process does not give rise to any action of the corresponding node—this action of a sequential process cannot occur without communicating with a receive action of another sequential process running on the same node. Time-consuming actions w_1 and $R: w_1$, with $w_1 \in \mathcal{W}$, of a process are renamed into tick on the level of node expressions.[9] All we need to remember of these actions is that they take one unit of time. Since on node expressions the actions **send**(m) have been dropped, the side condition making the wait actions ws and wrs conditional on the absence of a **send**-action can be dropped as well. The priority of **receive**-actions over the wait action wr can now also be dropped, for in the absence of **send**-actions, **receive**-actions are entirely reactive. A node can do a **receive**-action only when another node, or the application layer, casts a message, and in this case that other node is not available to synchronise with a tick-transition.

Internal actions τ and the action ip:**deliver**(d) are simply inherited by node expressions from the processes that run on these nodes (Rules (n-τ) and (n-del)), and are interleaved in the parallel composition of nodes that makes up a network. Finally, we allow actions **connect**(ip, ip') and **disconnect**(ip, ip') for $ip, ip' \in \mathtt{IP}$ modelling a change in network topology. In this formalisation node ip' may be in the range of node ip, meaning that ip can send to ip', even when the reverse does not hold. For some applications, in particular the one to AODV in Sect. 3, it is useful to assume that ip' is in the range of ip if and only if ip is in the range of ip'. This symmetry can be enforced by adding the following rules to Table 3:

$$ip{:}P{:}R \xrightarrow{\mathbf{connect}(ip',ip)} ip{:}P{:}R\cup\{ip'\} \qquad ip{:}P{:}R \xrightarrow{\mathbf{disconnect}(ip',ip)} ip{:}P{:}R-\{ip'\}$$

$$\frac{ip \notin \{ip', ip''\}}{ip{:}P{:}R \xrightarrow{\mathbf{connect}(ip',ip'')} ip{:}P{:}R} \qquad \frac{ip \notin \{ip', ip''\}}{ip{:}P{:}R \xrightarrow{\mathbf{disconnect}(ip',ip'')} ip{:}P{:}R}$$

and replacing the rules in the third line of Table 4 for (dis)connect actions by

[9] Rule (n-t) ensures that only those $R{:}w_1$-transitions survive for which R is the current transmission range of the node.

Table 4. Structural operational semantics for network expressions

$$\text{(nw-tl/nw-tr)}\ \frac{M \xrightarrow{R:\textbf{*cast}(m)} M' \quad N \xrightarrow{H\neg K:\textbf{arrive}(m)} N'}{M\|N \xrightarrow{R:\textbf{*cast}(m)} M'\|N' \qquad N\|M \xrightarrow{R:\textbf{*cast}(m)} N'\|M'} \quad \left(\begin{array}{c}H\subseteq R,\\ K\cap R=\emptyset\end{array}\right)$$

$$\text{(arr)}\ \frac{M \xrightarrow{H\neg K:\textbf{arrive}(m)} M' \quad N \xrightarrow{H'\neg K':\textbf{arrive}(m)} N'}{M\|N \xrightarrow{(H\cup H')\neg(K\cup K'):\textbf{arrive}(m)} M'\|N'} \qquad \text{(tck)}\ \frac{M \xrightarrow{\text{tick}} M' \quad N \xrightarrow{\text{tick}} N'}{M\|N \xrightarrow{\text{tick}} M'\|N'}$$

$$\text{(nw-al)}\ \frac{M \xrightarrow{a} M'}{M\|N \xrightarrow{a} M'\|N} \qquad \text{(nw-ar)}\ \frac{N \xrightarrow{a} N'}{M\|N \xrightarrow{a} M\|N'} \qquad \text{(e-a)}\ \frac{M \xrightarrow{a} M'}{[M] \xrightarrow{a} [M']}$$

$$(\forall a \in \{ip\colon \textbf{deliver}(d), \tau, \textbf{connect}(ip, ip'), \textbf{disconnect}(ip, ip')\})$$

$$\text{(e-tck)}\ \frac{M \xrightarrow{\text{tick}} M'}{[M] \xrightarrow{\text{tick}} [M']} \qquad \text{(e-sc)}\ \frac{M \xrightarrow{R:\textbf{*cast}(m)} M'}{[M] \xrightarrow{\tau} [M']} \qquad \text{(e-np)}\ \frac{M \xrightarrow{\{ip\}\neg K:\textbf{arrive}(\texttt{newpkt}(d,dip))} M'}{[M] \xrightarrow{ip:\textbf{newpkt}(d,dip)} [M']}$$

$$\frac{M \xrightarrow{a} M' \quad N \xrightarrow{a} N'}{M\|N \xrightarrow{a} M'\|N'} \qquad \frac{M \xrightarrow{a} M'}{[M] \xrightarrow{a} [M']} \qquad \left(\forall a \in \left\{\begin{array}{c}\textbf{connect}(ip, ip'),\\ \textbf{disconnect}(ip, ip')\end{array}\right\}\right).$$

The main purpose of the encapsulation operator is to ensure that no messages will be received that have never been sent. In a parallel composition of network nodes, any action **receive**(m) of one of the nodes ip manifests itself as an action $H\neg K$: **arrive**(m) of the parallel composition, with $ip \in H$. Such actions can happen (even) if within the parallel composition they do not communicate with an action ***cast**(m) of another component, because they might communicate with a ***cast**(m) of a node that is yet to be added to the parallel composition. However, once all nodes of the network are accounted for, we need to inhibit unmatched arrive actions, as otherwise our formalism would allow any node at any time to receive any message. One exception however are those arrive actions that stem from an action **receive**(`newpkt`(d, dip)) of a sequential process running on a node, as those actions represent communication with the environment. Here, we use the function `newpkt`, which we assumed to exist.[10] It models the injection of new data d for destination `dip`.

The encapsulation operator passes through internal actions, as well as delivery of data to destination nodes, this being an interaction with the outside world (Rule (e-a)). ***cast**(m)-actions are declared internal actions at this level (Rule (e-sc)); they cannot be steered by the outside world. The connect and disconnect actions are passed through in Table 4 (Rule (e-a)), thereby placing them under control of the environment; to make them nondeterministic, their rules should have a τ-label in the conclusion, or alternatively **connect**(ip, ip') and **disconnect**(ip, ip') should be thought of as internal actions. Finally, actions **arrive**(m) are simply blocked by the encapsulation—they cannot occur without

[10] To avoid the function `newpkt` we could have introduced a new primitive **newpkt**, which is dual to **deliver**.

synchronising with a $*\mathbf{cast}(m)$—except for $\{ip\}\neg K : \mathbf{arrive}(\mathtt{newpkt}(d, dip))$ with $d \in \mathtt{DATA}$ and $dip \in \mathtt{IP}$ (Rule (e-np)). This action represents new data d that is submitted by a client of the modelled protocol to node ip, for delivery at destination dip.

Optional Augmentations to Ensure Non-blocking Broadcast. Our process algebra, as presented above, is intended for networks in which each node is *input enabled* [21], meaning that it is always ready to receive any message, i.e., able to engage in the transition $\mathbf{receive}(m)$ for any $m \in \mathtt{MSG}$—in the default version of T-AWN, network expressions are required to have this property. In our model of AODV (Sect. 3) we will ensure this by equipping each node with a message queue that is always able to accept messages for later handling—even when the main sequential process is currently busy. This makes our model input enabled and hence *non-blocking*, meaning that no sender can be delayed in transmitting a message simply because one of the potential recipients is not ready to receive it.

In [10,11] we additionally presented two versions of AWN without the requirement that all nodes need to be input enabled: one in which we kept the same operational semantics and simply accept blocking, and one were we added operational rules to avoid blocking, thereby giving up on the requirement that any broadcast message is received by all nodes within transmission range.

The first solution does not work for T-AWN, as it would give rise to *time deadlocks*, reachable states where time is unable to progress further.

The second solution is therefore our only alternative to requiring input enabledness for T-AWN. As in [10,11], it is implemented by the addition of the rule

$$\frac{P \overset{\mathbf{receive}(m)}{\not\longrightarrow}}{ip : P : R \xrightarrow{\{ip\}\neg\emptyset : \mathbf{arrive}(m)} ip : P : R}\ .$$

It states that a message may arrive at a node ip regardless whether the node is ready to receive it or not; if it is not ready, the message is simply ignored, and the process running on the node remains in the same state.

In [11, Sect. 4.5] also a variant of this idea is presented that avoids negative premises, yet leads to the same transition system. The same can be done to T-AWN in the same way, we skip the details and refer to [11, Sect. 4.5].

2.3 Results on the Process Algebra

In this section we list a couple of useful properties of our timed process algebra. In particular, we show that wait actions do not change the data state, except for the value of $\mathtt{now}$. Moreover, we show the absence of *time deadlocks*: a complete network N described by T-AWN always admits a transition, independently of the outside environment. More precisely, either $N \xrightarrow{\text{tick}}$, or $N \xrightarrow{ip:\mathbf{deliver}(d)}$ or $N \xrightarrow{\tau}$. We also show that our process algebra admits a translation into one without data structure. The operational rules of the translated process algebra are in the de Simone format [33], which immediately implies that strong bisimilarity is a congruence, and yields the associativity of our parallel operators. Last, we show that T-AWN and AWN are related by a simulation relation. Due to lack of space, most of the proofs are omitted, they can be found in Appendix of [5].

Proposition 1. *On the level of sequential processes, wait actions change only the value of the variable* now, *i.e.,* $\xi, p \xrightarrow{w_1} \zeta, q \Rightarrow (p = q \wedge \zeta = \xi[\texttt{now++}])$.

Proof Sketch. One inspects all rules of Table 1 that can generate w-steps, and then reasons inductively on the derivation of these steps.

Similarly, it can be observed that for transmission actions (actions from the set $\mathcal{R}:\mathcal{W}$) the data state does not change either; the process, however, changes. That means $\xi, p \xrightarrow{rw} \zeta, q \Rightarrow \zeta = \xi[\texttt{now++}]$ for all $rw \in \mathcal{R}:\mathcal{W}$. Furthermore, this result can easily be lifted to all other layers of our process algebra (with minor adaptations: for example on node expressions one has to consider tick actions).

To shorten the forthcoming definitions and properties we use the following abbreviations:

1. $P \xrightarrow{\textbf{rcv.}}$ iff $P \xrightarrow{\textbf{receive}(m)}$ for some $m \in \texttt{MSG}$,
2. $P \xrightarrow{\textbf{send}}$ iff $P \xrightarrow{\textbf{send}(m)}$ for some $m \in \texttt{MSG}$,
3. $P \xrightarrow{\textbf{wait}}$ iff $P \xrightarrow{w_1}$ for some $w_1 \in \mathcal{W}$,
4. $P \xrightarrow{\textbf{other}}$ iff $P \xrightarrow{a}$ for some $a \in$ Act not of the forms above,

where P is a parallel process expression—possibly incorporating the construct $dsts$: ***cast**$(m)[n, o].p$, but never in a +-context. Note that the last line covers also transmission actions $rw \in \mathcal{R}:\mathcal{W}$. The following result shows that the wait actions of a sequential process (with data evaluation) P are completely determined by the other actions P offers.

Theorem 1. *Let P be a state of a sequential process.*

1. $P \xrightarrow{\text{w}}$ *iff* $P \overset{\textbf{rcv.}}{\not\longrightarrow} \wedge P \overset{\textbf{send}}{\not\longrightarrow} \wedge P \overset{\textbf{other}}{\not\longrightarrow}$.
2. $P \xrightarrow{\text{wr}}$ *iff* $P \xrightarrow{\textbf{rcv.}} \wedge P \overset{\textbf{send}}{\not\longrightarrow} \wedge P \overset{\textbf{other}}{\not\longrightarrow}$.
3. $P \xrightarrow{\text{ws}}$ *iff* $P \overset{\textbf{rcv.}}{\not\longrightarrow} \wedge P \xrightarrow{\textbf{send}} \wedge P \overset{\textbf{other}}{\not\longrightarrow}$.
4. $P \xrightarrow{\text{wrs}}$ *iff* $P \xrightarrow{\textbf{rcv.}} \wedge P \xrightarrow{\textbf{send}} \wedge P \overset{\textbf{other}}{\not\longrightarrow}$.

Proof Sketch. The proof is by structural induction. It requires, however, a distinction between guarded terms (as defined in Footnote 7) and unguarded ones.

We could equivalently have omitted all transition rules involving wait actions from Table 1, and defined the wait transitions for sequential processes as described by Theorem 1 and Proposition 1. That our transition rules give the same result constitutes a sanity check of our operational semantics.

Theorem 1 does not hold in the presence of unguarded recursion. A counterexample is given by the expression $X()$ with $X() \overset{def}{=} X()$, for which we would have $X() \overset{\textbf{rcv.}}{\not\longrightarrow} \wedge X() \overset{\textbf{send}}{\not\longrightarrow} \wedge X() \overset{\textbf{other}}{\not\longrightarrow} \wedge X() \overset{\textbf{wait}}{\not\longrightarrow}$.

Lemma 1. *Let P be a state of a sequential or parallel process. If $P \xrightarrow{R:w_1}$ for some $R \subseteq \mathtt{IP}$ and $w_1 \in \mathcal{W}$ then $P \xrightarrow{R':w_1}$ for any $R' \subseteq \mathtt{IP}$.*

Observation 1. Let P be a state of a sequential process. If $P \xrightarrow{R:w_1}$ for some $w_1 \in \mathcal{W}$ then w_1 must be w and all outgoing transitions of P are labelled R': w.

For N a (partial) network expression, or a parallel process expression, write $N \xrightarrow{\textbf{inb}}$ iff $N \xrightarrow{a}$ with a of the form R: ***cast**(m), ip: **deliver**(d) (or **deliver**(d)) or τ—an *instantaneous non-blocking action.* Hence, for a parallel process expression P, $P \xrightarrow{\textbf{other}}$ iff $P \xrightarrow{\textbf{inb}}$ or $P \xrightarrow{R:w_1}$ for $w_1 \in \mathcal{W}$. Furthermore, write $P \xrightarrow{\textbf{time}}$ iff $P \xrightarrow{w_1}$ or $P \xrightarrow{R:w_1}$ for some $w_1 \in \mathcal{W}$. We now lift Theorem 1 to the level of parallel processes.

Theorem 2. *Let P be a state of a parallel process.*

1. $P \xrightarrow{\mathrm{w}} \vee P \xrightarrow{R:\mathrm{w}}$ *iff* $P \not\xrightarrow{\textbf{rcv.}} \wedge P \not\xrightarrow{\textbf{send}} \wedge P \not\xrightarrow{\textbf{inb}}$.
2. $P \xrightarrow{\mathrm{wr}} \vee P \xrightarrow{R:\mathrm{wr}}$ *iff* $P \xrightarrow{\textbf{rcv.}} \wedge P \not\xrightarrow{\textbf{send}} \wedge P \not\xrightarrow{\textbf{inb}}$.
3. $P \xrightarrow{\mathrm{ws}} \vee P \xrightarrow{R:\mathrm{ws}}$ *iff* $P \not\xrightarrow{\textbf{rcv.}} \wedge P \xrightarrow{\textbf{send}} \wedge P \not\xrightarrow{\textbf{inb}}$.
4. $P \xrightarrow{\mathrm{wrs}} \vee P \xrightarrow{R:\mathrm{wrs}}$ *iff* $P \xrightarrow{\textbf{rcv.}} \wedge P \xrightarrow{\textbf{send}} \wedge P \not\xrightarrow{\textbf{inb}}$.

Corollary 1. *Let P be a state of a parallel process. Then $P \xrightarrow{\textbf{time}}$ iff $P \not\xrightarrow{\textbf{inb}}$.* □

Lemma 2. *Let N be a partial network expression with L the set of addresses of the nodes of N. Then $N \xrightarrow{H\neg K:\,\textbf{arrive}(m)}$, for any partition $L = H \uplus K$ of L into sets H and K, and any $m \in \mathtt{MSG}$.*

Using this lemma, we can finally show one of our main results: an (encapsulated) network expression can perform a time-consuming action iff an instantaneous non-blocking action is not possible.

Theorem 3. *Let N be a partial or complete network expression. Then $N \xrightarrow{\mathrm{tick}}$ iff $N \not\xrightarrow{\textbf{inb}}$.*

Proof. We apply structural induction on N. First suppose N is a node expression ip: P: R. Then $N \xrightarrow{\mathrm{tick}}$ iff $P \xrightarrow{w_1} \vee P \xrightarrow{R:w_1}$ for some $w_1 \in \mathcal{W}$. By Lemma 1 this is the case iff $P \xrightarrow{w_1} \vee P \xrightarrow{R':w_1}$ for some $R' \subseteq \mathtt{IP}$ and $w_1 \in \mathcal{W}$, i.e., iff $P \xrightarrow{\textbf{time}}$. Moreover $N \xrightarrow{\textbf{inb}}$ iff $P \xrightarrow{\textbf{inb}}$. Hence the claim follows from Corollary 1.

Now suppose N is a partial network expression $M_1 \| M_2$. In case $M_i \not\xrightarrow{\textbf{inb}}$ for $i = 1, 2$ then $N \not\xrightarrow{\textbf{inb}}$. By induction $M_i \xrightarrow{\mathrm{tick}}$ for $i = 1, 2$, and hence $N \xrightarrow{\mathrm{tick}}$. Otherwise, $M_i \xrightarrow{\textbf{inb}}$ for $i = 1$ or 2. Now $N \xrightarrow{\textbf{inb}}$. In case $M_i \xrightarrow{\tau}$ or $M_i \xrightarrow{ip:\,\textbf{deliver}(d)}$ this follows from the third line of Table 4; if $M_i \xrightarrow{R:\,\textbf{*cast}(m)}$ it follows from the first line, in combination with Lemma 2. By induction $M_i \not\xrightarrow{\mathrm{tick}}$, and thus $N \not\xrightarrow{\mathrm{tick}}$.

Finally suppose that N is a complete network expression $[M]$. By the rules of Table 4 $N \xrightarrow{\mathrm{tick}}$ iff $M \xrightarrow{\mathrm{tick}}$, and $N \xrightarrow{\textbf{inb}}$ iff $M \xrightarrow{\textbf{inb}}$, so the claim follows from the case for partial network expressions. □

Corollary 2. *A complete network N described by T-AWN always admits a transition, independently of the outside environment, i.e., $\forall N, \exists a$ such that $N \xrightarrow{a}$ and $a \notin \{$**connect**(ip, ip'), **disconnect**(ip, ip'), $\mathtt{newpkt}(d, dip)\}$.*
More precisely, either $N \xrightarrow{\mathrm{tick}}$ or $N \xrightarrow{ip:\,\textbf{deliver}(d)}$ or $N \xrightarrow{\tau}$. □

Our process algebra admits a translation into one without data structures (although we cannot *describe* the target algebra without using data structures). The idea is to replace any variable by all possible values it can take. The target algebra differs from the original only on the level of sequential processes; the subsequent layers are unchanged. A formal definition can be found in Appendix of [5]. The resulting process algebra has a structural operational semantics in the (infinitary) *de Simone* format, generating the same transition system—up to strong bisimilarity, $\leftrightarroweq$—as the original, which provides some results 'for free'. For example, it follows that $\leftrightarroweq$, and many other semantic equivalences, are congruences on our language.

Theorem 4. *Strong bisimilarity is a congruence for all operators of T-AWN.*

This is a deep result that usually takes many pages to establish (e.g., [34]). Here we get it directly from the existing theory on structural operational semantics, as a result of carefully designing our language within the disciplined framework described by de Simone [33].

Theorem 5. $\langle\!\langle$ *is associative, and* $\|$ *is associative and commutative, up to* $\leftrightarroweq$.

Proof. The operational rules for these operators fit a format presented in [8], guaranteeing associativity up to $\leftrightarroweq$. The details are similar to the case for AWN, as elaborated in [10,11]; the only extra complication is the associativity of the operator $\langle\!\langle$ on $\mathcal{W}$, as defined on Page 12, which we checked automatically by means of the theorem prover Prover9 [22]. Commutativity of $\|$ follows by symmetry of the rules. □

Theorem 6. *Each AWN process P, seen as a T-AWN process, can be simulated by the AWN process P. Likewise, each AWN network N, seen as a T-AWN network, can be simulated by the AWN network N.*

Here a *simulation* refers to a *weak simulation* as defined in [14], but treating **(dis)connect**-actions as τ, and with the extra requirement that the data states maintained by related expressions are identical—except of course for the variables `now`, that are missing in AWN. Details can be found in Appendix of [5].

Thanks to Theorem 6, we can prove that all invariants on the data structure of a process expressed in AWN are still preserved when the process is interpreted as a T-AWN expression. As an application of this, an untimed version of AODV, formalised as an AWN process, has been proven loop free in [11,15]; the same system, seen as a T-AWN expression—and thus with specific execution times associated to uni-, group-, and broadcast actions—is still loop free when given the operational semantics of T-AWN.

3 Case Study: The AODV Routing Protocol

Routing protocols are crucial to the dissemination of data packets between nodes in WMNs and MANETs. Highly dynamic topologies are a key feature of WMNs and MANETs, due to mobility of nodes and/or the variability of wireless links.

This makes the design and implementation of robust and efficient routing protocols for these networks a challenging task. In this section we present a formal specification of the Ad hoc On-Demand Distance Vector (AODV) routing protocol. AODV [29] is a widely-used routing protocol designed for MANETs, and is one of the four protocols currently standardised by the IETF MANET working group[11]. It also forms the basis of new WMN routing protocols, including HWMP in the IEEE 802.11s wireless mesh network standard [20].

Our formalisation is based on an untimed formalisation of AODV [11,15], written in AWN, and models the exact details of the core functionality of AODV as standardised in IETF RFC 3561 [29]; e.g., route discovery, route maintenance and error handling. We demonstrate how T-AWN can be used to reason about critical protocol properties. As major outcome we demonstrate that AODV is *not* loop free, which is in contrast to common belief. Loop freedom is a critical property for any routing protocol, but it is particularly relevant and challenging for WMNs and MANETs. We close the section by discussing a fix to the protocol and prove that the resulting protocol is indeed loop free.

3.1 Brief Overview

AODV is a reactive protocol, which means that routes are established only on demand. If a node S wants to send a data packet to a node D, but currently does not know a route, it temporarily buffers the packet and initiates a route discovery process by broadcasting a route request (RREQ) message in the network. An intermediate node A that receives the RREQ message creates a routing table entry for a route towards node S referred to as a *reverse route*, and re-broadcasts the RREQ. This is repeated until the RREQ reaches the destination node D, or alternatively a node that knows a route to D. In both cases, the node replies by unicasting a corresponding route reply (RREP) message back to the source S, via a previously established reverse route. When forwarding RREP messages, nodes create a routing table entry for node D, called the *forward route*. When the RREP reaches the originating node D, a route from S to D is established and data packets can start to flow. Both forward and reverse routes are maintained in a routing table at every node—details are given below. In the event of link and route breaks, AODV uses route error (RERR) messages to notify the affected nodes: if a link break is detected by a node, it first invalidates all routes stored in the node's own routing table that actually use the broken link. Then it sends a RERR message containing the unreachable destinations to all (direct) neighbours using this route.

In AODV, a routing table consists of a list of entries—at most one for each destination—each containing the following information: (i) the destination IP address; (ii) the *destination sequence number*; (iii) the sequence-number-status flag—tagging whether the recorded sequence number can be trusted; (iv) a flag tagging the route as being valid or invalid—this flag is set to invalid when a link break is detected or the route's lifetime is reached; (v) the hop count, a metric to indicate the distance to the destination; (vi) the next hop, an IP address

[11] http://datatracker.ietf.org/wg/manet/charter/.

that identifies the next (intermediate) node on the route to the destination; (vii) a list of precursors, a set of IP addresses of those 1-hop neighbours that use this particular route; and (viii) the lifetime (expiration or deletion time) of the route. The destination sequence number constitutes a measure approximating the relative freshness of the information held—a higher number denotes newer information. The routing table is updated whenever a node receives an AODV control message (RREQ, RREP or RERR) or detects a link break.

During the lifetime of the network, each node not only maintains its routing table, it also stores its *own sequence number*. This number is used as a local "timer" and is incremented whenever a new route request is initiated. It is the source of the destination sequence numbers in routing tables of other nodes.

Full details of the protocol are outlined in the request for comments (RFC) [29].

3.2 Route Request Handling Handled Formally

Our formal model consists of seven processes: `AODV` reads a message from the message queue (modelled in process `QMSG`, see below) and, depending on the type of the message, calls other processes. Each time a message has been handled the process has the choice between handling another message, initiating the transmission of queued data packets or generating a new route request. `NEWPKT` and `PKT` describe all actions performed by a node when a data packet is received. The former process handles a newly injected packet. The latter describes all actions performed when a node receives data from another node via the protocol. `RREQ` models all events that might occur after a route request message has been received. Similarly, `RREP` describes the reaction of the protocol to an incoming route reply. `RERR` models the part of AODV that handles error messages. The last process `QMSG` queues incoming messages. Whenever a message is received, it is first stored in a message queue. When the corresponding node is able to handle a message, it pops the oldest message from the queue and handles it. An AODV network is an encapsulated parallel composition of node expressions, each with a different node address (identifier), and all initialised with the parallel composition $\texttt{AODV}(\dots) \langle\langle \texttt{QMSG}(\dots)$.

In this paper, we have room to present parts of the `RREQ` process only, depicted in Process 4[12]; the full formal specification of the entire protocol can be found in Appendix of [5]. There, we also discuss all differences between the untimed version of AODV, as formalised in [11,15], and the newly developed timed version. These differences mostly consist of setting expiration times for routing table entries and other data maintained by AODV, and handling the expiration of this data.

A route discovery in AODV is initiated by a source node broadcasting a RREQ message; this message is subsequently re-broadcast by other nodes. Process 4 shows major parts of our process algebra specification for handling a RREQ message received by a node *ip*. The incoming message carries eight parameters, including *hops*, indicating how far the RREQ had travelled so far, *rreqid*, an identifier for this request, *dip*, the destination IP address, and *sip*,

[12] The numbering scheme is consistent with the one in [5].

the sender of the incoming message; the parameters *ip*, *sn* and *rt*, storing the node's address, sequence number and routing table, as well as *rreqs* and *store*, are maintained by the process RREQ itself.

Before handling the incoming message, the process first updates *rreqs* (Line 1), a list of (unique) pairs containing the originator IP address *oip* and a route request identifier *rreqid* received within the last PATH_DISCOVERY_TIME: the update removes identifiers that are too old. Based on this list, the node then checks whether it has recently received a RREQ with the same *oip* and *rreqid*.

If this is the case, the RREQ message is ignored, and the protocol continues to execute the main AODV process (Lines 3–4). If the RREQ is new (Line 5), the process updates the routing table by adding a "reverse route" entry to *oip*, the originator of the RREQ, via node *sip*, with distance *hops*+1 (Line 6). If there already is a route to *oip* in the node's routing table *rt*, it is only updated with the new route if the new route is "better", i.e., fresher and/or shorter and/or replacing an invalid route. The lifetime of this reverse route is updated as well (Line 7): it is set to the maximum of the currently stored lifetime and the minimal lifetime, which is determined by $\texttt{now} + 2 \cdot \texttt{NET\_TRAVERSAL\_TIME} - 2 \cdot (hops + 1) \cdot \texttt{NODE\_TRAVERSAL\_TIME}$ [29, Page 17]. The process also adds the message to the list of known RREQs (Line 8).

Lines 10–22 (only shown in Appendix of [5]) deal with the case where the node receiving the RREQ is the intended destination, i.e., *dip*=*ip* (Line 10).

Process 4 Parts of the RREQ handling

```
RREQ(hops, rreqid, dip, dsn, dsk, oip, osn, sip , ip, sn, rt, rreqs, store) ≝
 1. ⟦exp_rreqs(rreqs, now)⟧
 2. (
 3.    [ (oip, rreqid, ∗) ∈ rreqs ]      /* the RREQ has been received previously */
 4.       AODV(ip, sn, rt, rreqs, store)      /* silently ignore RREQ, i.e., do nothing */
 5.    + [ (oip, rreqid, ∗) ∉ rreqs ]      /* the RREQ is new to this node */
 6.       ⟦rt := update(rt, (oip, osn, kno, val, hops + 1, sip, ∅, now + ACTIVE_ROUTE_TIMEOUT))⟧
 7.       ⟦rt := setTime_rt(rt, oip, now + 2 · NET_TRAVERSAL_TIME − 2 · (hops + 1) · NODE_TRAVERSAL_TIME)⟧
 8.       ⟦rreqs := rreqs ∪ {(oip, rreqid, now + PATH_DISCOVERY_TIME)}⟧      /* update rreqs */
 9.       (
10.          [ dip = ip ]      /* this node is the destination node */
11.             [...]
12.
23.          + [ dip ≠ ip ]      /* this node is not the destination node */
24.             (
25.                /* valid route to dip that is fresh enough */
26.                [ dip ∈ vD(rt) ∧ dsn ≤ sqn(rt,dip) ∧ sqnf(rt,dip) = kno ]
27.                   /* update rt by adding precursors */
28.                   ⟦rt := addpreRT(rt, dip, {sip})⟧
29.                   ⟦rt := addpreRT(rt, oip, {nhop(rt, dip)})⟧
30.                   /* unicast a RREP towards the oip of the RREQ */
31.                   unicast(nhop(rt, oip),
                               rrep(dhops(rt, dip), dip, sqn(rt, dip), oip, σ_time(rt, dip) − now, ip) .
32.                      AODV(ip, sn, rt, rreqs, store)
33.                   ▶ /* If the transmission is unsuccessful, a RERR message is generated */
34.                      [...]      /* update local data structure */
40.                      groupcast(pre, rerr(dests, ip)) . AODV(ip, sn, rt, rreqs, store)
41.                + [ dip ∉ vD(rt) ∨ sqn(rt,dip) < dsn ∨ sqnf(rt,dip) = unk ]      /* no fresh route */
42.                   /* no further update of rt */
43.                   broadcast(rreq(hops+1, rreqid, dip, max(sqn(rt, dip), dsn), dsk, oip, osn, ip)) .
44.                   AODV(ip, sn, rt, rreqs, store)
45.             )
46.       )
47. )
```

Lines 23–45 deal with the case where the node receiving the RREQ is not the destination, i.e., $dip \neq ip$ (Line 23). The node can respond to the RREQ with a corresponding RREP on behalf of the destination node *dip*, if its route to *dip* is "fresh enough" (Line 26). This means that (a) the node has a valid route to *dip*, (b) the destination sequence number in the node's current routing table entry (`sqn`(*rt*, *dip*)) is greater than or equal to the requested sequence number to *dip* in the RREQ message, and (c) the node's destination sequence number is trustworthy (`sqnf`(*rt*,*dip*)=`kno`). If these three conditions are met (Line 26), the node generates a RREP message, and unicasts it back to the originator node *oip* via the reverse route. Before unicasting the RREP message, the intermediate node updates the forward routing table entry to *dip* by placing the last hop node (*sip*) into the precursor list for that entry (Line 28). Likewise, it updates the reverse routing table entry to *oip* by placing the first hop `nhop`(*rt*, *dip*) towards *dip* in the precursor list for that entry (Line 29). To generate the RREP message, the process copies the sequence number for the destination *dip* from the routing table *rt* into the destination sequence number field of the RREP message and it places its distance in hops from the destination (`dhops`(*rt*, *dip*)) in the corresponding field of the new reply (Line 31). The RREP message is unicast to the next hop along the reverse route back to the originator of the corresponding RREQ message. If this unicast is successful, the process goes back to the AODV routine (Line 32). If the unicast of the RREP fails, we proceed with Lines 33–40, in which a route error (RERR) message is generated and sent. This conditional unicast is implemented in our model with the (T-)AWN construct **unicast**(*dest*, *ms*).$P \blacktriangleright Q$. In the latter case, the node sends a RERR message to all nodes that rely on the broken link for one of their routes. For this, the process first determines which destination nodes are affected by the broken link, i.e., the nodes that have this unreachable node listed as a next hop in the routing table (not shown in the shortened specification). Then, it invalidates any affected routing table entries, and determines the list of *precursors*, which are the neighbouring nodes that have a route to one of the affected destination nodes via the broken link. Finally, a RERR message is sent via groupcast to all these precursors (Line 40).

If the node is not the destination and there is either no route to the destination *dip* inside the routing table or the route is not fresh enough, the route request received has to be forwarded. This happens in Line 43. The information inside the forwarded request is mostly copied from the request received. Only the hop count is increased by 1 and the destination sequence number is set to the maximum of the destination sequence number in the RREQ packet and the current sequence number for *dip* in the routing table. In case *dip* is an unknown destination, `sqn`(*rt*, *dip*) returns the unknown sequence number 0.

To ensure that our time-free model from [11,15] accurately captures the intended behaviour of AODV [29], we spent a long time reading and interpreting the RFC, inspecting open-source implementations, and consulting network engineers. We now prove that our timed version of AODV behaves similar to our original formal specification, and hence (still) captures the intended behaviour.

Theorem 7. *The timed version of AODV (as sketched in this paper, and presented in [5]) is a proper extension of the untimed version (as presented in [11]). By this we mean that if all timing constants, such as* `ACTIVE_ROUTE_TIMEOUT`*, are set to* ∞*, and the maximal number of pending route request retries* `RREQ_RETRIES` *is set to* 1*, then the (T-AWN) transition systems of both versions of AODV are weakly bisimilar.*

Proof Sketch. First, one shows that the newly introduced functions, such as `exp_rreqs` and `setTime_rt` do not change the data state in case the time parameters equal ∞; and hence lead to transitions of the form $\xi, p \xrightarrow{\tau} \xi, p'$. This kind of transitions are the ones that make the bisimulation weak, since they do not occur in the formal specification of [11]. Subsequently, one proves that all other transitions are basically identical.

3.3 Loop Freedom

Loop freedom is a critical property for any routing protocol, but it is particularly relevant and challenging for WMNs and MANETs. "A routing-table loop is a path specified in the nodes' routing tables at a particular point in time that visits the same node more than once before reaching the intended destination" [12]. Packets caught in a routing loop can quickly saturate the links and have a detrimental impact on network performance.

For AODV and many other protocols sequence numbers are used to guarantee loop freedom. Such protocols usually claim to be loop free due to the use of monotonically increasing sequence numbers. For example, AODV "uses destination sequence numbers to ensure loop freedom at all times (even in the face of anomalous delivery of routing control messages), ..." [29]. It has been shown that sequence numbers do not a priori guarantee loop freedom [16]; for some plausible interpretations[13] of different versions of AODV, however, loop freedom has been proven [3,11,15,19,25,30,34,35][14]. With the exception of [3], all these papers consider only untimed versions of AODV. As mentioned in Sect. 1 untimed analyses revealed many shortcomings of AODV; hence they are necessary. At the same time, a timed analysis is required as well. [3] shows that the premature deletion of invalid routes, and a too quick restart of a node after a reboot, can yield routing loops. Since then, AODV has changed to such a degree that the examples of [3] do not apply any longer.

In [13], "it is shown that the use of a `DELETE_PERIOD` in the current AODV specification can result in loops". However, the loop constructed therein at any

[13] By a plausible interpretation of a protocol standard written in English prose we mean an interpretation that fills the missing bits, and resolves ambiguities and contradictions occurring in the standard in a sensible and meaningful way.

[14] The proofs in [3,30] are incorrect; the model of [34] does not capture the full behaviour of the routing protocol; and [35] is based on a subset of AODV that does not cover the "intermediate route reply" feature, a source of loops. In [25] a draft of a new version of AODV is modelled, without intermediate route reply. For a more detailed discussion see [15].

time passes through at least one invalid routing table entry. As such, it is not a routing loop in the sense of [11,15]—we only consider loops consisting of valid routing table entries, since invalid ones do not forward data packets. In a loop as in [13] data packets cannot be sent in circles forever.

a) C's entry for D has expired; B's has not b) B sends old data; C establishes loop

Fig. 1. Premature route expiration

It turns out that AODV as standardised in the RFC (and carefully formalised in Sect. 3.2 and the Appendix of [5]) is *not* loop free. A potential cause of routing loops, sketched in Fig. 1, is a situation where a node B has a valid routing table entry for a destination D (in Fig. 1 denoted D:val→C), but the next hop C no longer has a routing table entry for D (D:–), valid or invalid. In such a case, C might search for a new route to D and create a new routing table entry pointing to B as next hop, or to a node A upstream from B. We refer to this scenario as a case of *premature route expiration*.

A related scenario, which we also call premature route expiration, is when a node C sends a RREP message with destination D or a RREQ messages with originator D to a node B, but looses its route to D before that message arrives. This scenario can easily give rise to the scenario above.

Premature route expiration can be avoided by setting DELETE_PERIOD to ∞, which is essentially the case in the untimed version of AODV (cf. Theorem 7). In that case, no routing table entry expires or is erased. Hence, the situation where C no longer has a routing table entry for D is prevented.

In [11] we studied 5184 possible interpretations of the AODV RFC [29], a proliferation due to ambiguities, contradictions and cases of underspecification that could be resolved in multiple ways. In 5006 of these readings of the standard, including some rather plausible ones, we found routing loops, even when excluding all loops that are due to timing issues [11,16]. In [11,15,19] we have chosen a default reading of the RFC that avoids these loops, formalised it in AWN, and formally proved loop freedom, still assuming (implicitly) DELETE_PERIOD $= \infty$.

After taking this hurdle, the present paper continues the investigation by allowing arbitrary values for time parameters and for RREQ_RETRIES; hence dropping the simplifying assumption that DELETE_PERIOD $= \infty$.

One of our key results is that for the formalisation of AODV presented here, premature route expiration is the *only* potential source of routing loops. Under the assumption that premature route expiration does not occur, it turns out that, with minor modifications, the loop freedom proof of [11,15] applies to our timed model of AODV as well. A proof of this result is presented in Appendix of [5]. There, we revisit all the invariants from [11] that contribute to the loop-freedom proof, and determine which of them are still valid in the timed setting, and how others need to be modified.

It is trivial to find an example where premature route expiration does occur in AODV, and a routing loop ensues. This can happen when a message spends an inordinate amount of time in the queue of incoming messages of a node. However, this situation tends not to occur in realistic scenarios. To capture this, we now make the assumption that the transmission time of a message plus the period it spends in the queue of incoming messages of the receiving node, is bounded by `NODE_TRAVERSAL_TIME`. We also assume that the period a route request travels through the network is bounded by `NET_TRAVERSAL_TIME`.

These assumptions eliminate the "trivial" counterexample mentioned above. As we show in Appendix of [5], we now *almost* can prove an invariant that essentially says that premature route expiration does not occur. Following the methodology from [11,15,19], we establish our invariants by showing that they hold in all possible initial states of AODV, and are preserved under the transitions of our operation semantics, which correspond to the line numbers in our process algebraic specification.

We said "almost", because, as indicated in Appendix of [5], our main invariant is not preserved by five lines of our AODV specification. Additionally, we need to make the assumption that when a RREQ message is forwarded, the forwarding node has a valid routing table entry to the originator of the route request. This does not hold for our formalisation of AODV: in Process 4 no check is performed on *oip*, only the routing table to the destination node *dip* has to satisfy certain conditions (Lines 23 and 41).

It turns out that for each of these failures we can construct an example of premature route expiration, and, by that, a counterexample to loop freedom.

However, if we skip all five offending lines (or adapt them in appropriate ways) and make a small change to process RREQ that makes the above assumption valid,[15] we obtain a proof of loop freedom for the resulting version of AODV. This follows immediately from the invariants established in Appendix of [5].

4 Conclusion

In this paper we have proposed T-AWN, a timed process algebra for wireless networks. We are aware that there are many other timed process algebras, such as timed CCS [24], timed CSP [28,32], timed ACP [1], ATP [27] and TPL [17]. However, none of these algebras provides the unique set of features needed for modelling and analysing protocols for wireless networks (e.g. a conditional unicast).[16] These features are provided by (T-)AWN, though. Our treatment of time is based on design decisions that appear rather different from the ones in [1,24,27,28,32]. Our approach appears to be closest to [17], but avoiding the negative premises that play a crucial role in the operational semantics of [17].

We have illustrated the usefulness of T-AWN by analysing the Ad hoc On-Demand Distance Vector routing protocol, and have shown that, contrary to claims in the literature and to common belief, it fails to be loop free. We have also discussed boundary conditions for a fix ensuring that the resulting protocol is loop free.

---

15 The change basically introduces the test "$oip \in \mathtt{vD}(rt)$" in Line 41 or 9 of Process 4.

16 This is similar to the untimed situation. A detailed comparison between AWN and other process calculi for wireless networks is given in [11, Sect. 11.1]; this discussion can directly be transferred to the timed case.

Acknowledgement. NICTA is funded by the Australian Government through the Department of Communications and the Australian Research Council through the ICT Centre of Excellence Program.

References

1. Baeten, J., Bergstra, J.: Discrete time process algebra. Formal Aspects Comput. **8**(2), 188–208 (1996). doi:10.1007/BF01214556
2. Bergstra, J.A., Klop, J.W.: Observation of strains: algebra of communicating processes. In: de Bakker, J.W., Hazewinkel, M., Lenstra, J.K. (eds) Mathematics and Computer Science, CWI Monograpph 1, pp. 89–138. North-Holland (2011)
3. Bhargavan, K., Obradovic, D., Gunter, C.A.: Formal verification of standards for distance vector routing protocols. J. ACM **49**(4), 538–576 (2002). doi:10.1145/581771.581775
4. Bolognesi, T., Brinksma, E.: Introduction to the ISO Specification Language LOTOS. Comput. Netw. **14**, 25–59 (1987). doi:10.1016/0169-7552(87)90085-7
5. Bres, E., van Glabbeek, R.J., Höfner, P.: A Timed Process Algebra for Wireless Networks with an Application in Routing. Technical Report 9145, NICTA (2016). http://nicta.com.au/pub?id=9145
6. Chiyangwa, S., Kwiatkowska, M.: A timing analysis of AODV. In: Steffen, M., Zavattaro, G. (eds.) FMOODS 2005. LNCS, vol. 3535, pp. 306–321. Springer, Heidelberg (2005). doi:10.1007/11494881_20
7. Clausen, T., Jacquet, P.: Optimized Link State Routing Protocol (OLSR). RFC 3626 (Experimental), Network Working Group (2003). http://www.ietf.org/rfc/rfc3626.txt
8. Cranen, S., Mousavi, M.R., Reniers, M.A.: A rule format for associativity. In: van Breugel, F., Chechik, M. (eds.) CONCUR 2008. LNCS, vol. 5201, pp. 447–461. Springer, Heidelberg (2008). doi:10.1007/978-3-540-85361-9_35
9. Edenhofer, S., Höfner, P.: Towards a rigorous analysis of AODVv2 (DYMO). In: Rigorous Protocol Engineering (WRiPE 2012). IEEE (2012). doi:10.1109/ICNP.2012.6459942
10. Fehnker, A., van Glabbeek, R., Höfner, P., McIver, A., Portmann, M., Tan, W.L.: A process algebra for wireless mesh networks. In: Seidl, H. (ed.) Programming Languages and Systems. LNCS, vol. 7211, pp. 295–315. Springer, Heidelberg (2012). doi:10.1007/978-3-642-28869-2_15
11. Fehnker, A., van Glabbeek, R.J., Höfner, P., McIver, A.K., Portmann, M., Tan, W.L.: A Process Algebra for Wireless Mesh Networks used for Modelling, Verifying and Analysing AODV. Technical report 5513, NICTA (2013). http://arxiv.org/abs/1312.7645
12. Garcia-Luna-Aceves, J.J.: A unified approach to loop-free routing using distance vectors or link states. In: SIGCOMM 1989, SIGCOMM Computer Communication Review 19(4), pp. 212–223. ACM Press (1989). doi:10.1145/75246.75268
13. Garcia-Luna-Aceves, J.J., Rangarajan, H.: A new framework for loop-free on-demand routing using destination sequence numbers. In: MASS 2004, pp. 426–435. IEEE (2004). doi:10.1109/MAHSS.2004.1392182
14. van Glabbeek, R.J.: The linear time - branching time spectrum II; the semantics of sequential systems with silent moves. In: Best, E. (ed.) CONCUR 1993. LNCS, vol. 715, pp. 66–81. Springer, Heidelberg (1993). doi:10.1007/3-540-57208-2_6
15. Glabbeek, R.J., Höfner, P., Portmann, M., Tan, W.L.: Modelling and Verifying the AODV Routing Protocol. Distributed Computing (2016) (to appear)

16. van Glabbeek, R.J., Höfner, P., Tan, W.L., Portmann, M.: Sequence numbers do not guarantee loop freedom –AODV can yield routing loops–. In: MSWiM 2013, pp. 91–100. ACM Press (2013). doi:10.1145/2507924.2507943
17. Hennessy, M., Regan, T.: A process algebra for timed systems. Inf. Comput. **117**(2), 221–239 (1995). doi:10.1006/inco.1995.1041
18. Hoare, C.A.R.: Communicating Sequential Processes. Prentice Hall, Englewood Cliffs (1985)
19. Höfner, P., van Glabbeek, R.J., Tan, W.L., Portmann, M., McIver, A.K., Fehnker, A.: A Rigorous analysis of AODV and its variants. In: MSWiM 2012, pp. 203–212. ACM Press (2012). doi:10.1145/2387238.2387274
20. IEEE: IEEE Standard for Information Technology—Telecommunications and information exchange between systems—Local and metropolitan area networks — Specific requirements Part 11: Wireless LAN Medium Access Control (MAC) and Physical Layer (PHY) specifications Amendment 10: Mesh Networking (2011). doi:10.1109/IEEESTD.2011.6018236
21. Lynch, N., Tuttle, M.: An introduction to input/output automata. CWI-Q. **2**(3), 219–246 (1989). Centrum voor Wiskunde en Informatica, Amsterdam
22. McCune, W.W.: Prover9 and Mace4. http://www.cs.unm.edu/mccune/prover9. Accessed 10 October 2015
23. Milner, R.: Communication and Concurrency. Prentice Hall, Upper Saddle River (1989)
24. Moller, F., Tofts, C.: A temporal calculus of communicating systems. In: Baeten, J.C.M., Klop, J.W. (eds.) CONCUR 1990. LNCS, vol. 458, pp. 401–415. Springer, Heidelberg (1990). doi:10.1007/BFb0039073
25. Namjoshi, K.S., Trefler, R.J.: Loop freedom in AODVv2. In: Graf, S., Viswanathan, M. (eds.) FORTE 2015. LNCS, vol. 9039, pp. 98–112. Springer, Heidelberg (2015). doi:10.1007/978-3-319-19195-9_7
26. Neumann, A., Aichele, M., Lindner, C., Wunderlich, S.: Better Approach To Mobile Ad-hoc Networking (B.A.T.M.A.N.). Internet-Draft (Experimental), Network Working Group (2008). http://tools.ietf.org/html/draft-openmesh-b-a-t-m-a-n-00
27. Nicollin, X., Sifakis, J.: The algebra of timed processes, ATP: theory and application. Inf. Comput. **114**(1), 131–178 (1994). doi:10.1006/inco.1994.1083
28. Ouaknine, J., Schneider, S.: Timed CSP: a retrospective. Electronic Notes Theor. Comput. Sci. **162**, 273–276 (2006). doi:10.1016/j.entcs.2005.12.093
29. Perkins, C.E., Belding-Royer, E.M., Das, S.: Ad hoc On-Demand Distance Vector (AODV) Routing. RFC 3561 (Experimental), Network Working Group (2003). http://www.ietf.org/rfc/rfc3561.txt
30. Perkins, C.E., Royer, E.M.: Ad-hoc on-demand distance vector routing. In: Mobile Computing Systems and Applications (WMCSA 1999), pp. 90–100. IEEE (1999). doi:10.1109/MCSA.1999.749281
31. Plotkin, G.D.: A structural approach to operational semantics. J. Logic Algebraic Program. **60–61**, 17–139 (2004). doi:10.1016/j.jlap.2004.05.001. Originally appeared in (1981)
32. Reed, G., Roscoe, A.: A timed model for communicating sequential processes. In: Kott, L. (ed.) ICALP 1986. LNCS, vol. 226, pp. 314–323. Springer, Heidelberg (1986). doi:10.1007/3-540-16761-7_81
33. de Simone, R.: Higher-level synchronising devices in meije-SCCS. Theor. Comput. Sci. **37**, 245–267 (1985). doi:10.1016/0304-3975(85)90093-3

34. Singh, A., Ramakrishnan, C.R., Smolka, S.A.: A process calculus for Mobile Ad Hoc Networks. Sci. Comput. Program. **75**, 440–469 (2010). doi:10.1016/j.scico.2009.07.008
35. Zhou, M., Yang, H., Zhang, X., Wang, J.: The proof of AODV loop freedom. In: Wireless Communications & Signal Processing (WCSP 2009), IEEE (2009). doi:10.1109/WCSP.2009.5371479

Computing with Semirings and Weak Rig Groupoids

Jacques Carette[1(✉)] and Amr Sabry[2]

[1] McMaster University, Hamilton, Canada
carette@mcmaster.ca
[2] Indiana University, Bloomington, IN, USA
sabry@indiana.edu

Abstract. The original formulation of the Curry–Howard correspondence relates propositional logic to the simply-typed λ-calculus at three levels: the syntax of propositions corresponds to the syntax of types; the proofs of propositions correspond to programs of the corresponding types; and the normalization of proofs corresponds to the evaluation of programs. This rich correspondence has inspired our community for half a century and has been generalized to deal with more advanced logics and programming models. We propose a variant of this correspondence which is inspired by conservation of information and recent homotopy theoretic approaches to type theory.

Our proposed correspondence naturally relates semirings to reversible programming languages: the syntax of semiring elements corresponds to the syntax of types; the proofs of semiring identities correspond to (reversible) programs of the corresponding types; and equivalences between algebraic proofs correspond to meaning-preserving program transformations and optimizations. These latter equivalences are not ad hoc: the same way semirings arise naturally out of the structure of types, a categorical look at the structure of proof terms gives rise to (at least) a weak rig groupoid structure, and the coherence laws are exactly the program transformations we seek. Thus it is algebra, rather than logic, which finally leads us to our correspondence.

1 Introduction

Elementary building blocks of type theory include the empty type (⊥), the unit type (⊤), the sum type (⊎), and the product type (×). The traditional Curry–Howard correspondence which goes back to at least 1969 relates these types to logical propositions as follows: the type ⊥ corresponds to the absurd proposition with no proof; the type ⊤ corresponds to the trivially true proposition; the type $\tau_1 \uplus \tau_2$ corresponds to the disjunction of the corresponding propositions, and the type $\tau_1 \times \tau_2$ corresponds to the conjunction of the corresponding propositions. The following tautologies of propositional logic therefore give rise to functions witnessing the back-and-forth transformations:

$$\tau \uplus \tau \Leftrightarrow \tau$$
$$\tau \times \tau \Leftrightarrow \tau$$
$$(\tau_1 \times \tau_2) \uplus \tau_3 \Leftrightarrow (\tau_1 \uplus \tau_3) \times (\tau_2 \uplus \tau_3)$$

P. Thiemann (Ed.): ESOP 2016, LNCS 9632, pp. 123–148, 2016.
DOI: 10.1007/978-3-662-49498-1_6

This connection to logic, as inspiring as it is, only cares whether a type is inhabited or not. For example, when translated to the world of types, the second tautology above states that the type $\tau \times \tau$ is inhabited iff the type τ is. Furthermore, the proofs of the two implications give rise to two functions that produce an element from one type given an element of the other. This framework is however of no direct help if one is concerned with other, richer properties of types and their relationships. For example, type isomorphisms are an important relation between types that is more refined than mere inhabitance of types as they clearly distinguish $\tau \times \tau$ and τ.

The study of type isomorphisms became popular during at least two short periods: in the early 1990s when they were used to search large libraries [30], and in the mid 2000s when they were studied from a categorical perspective [11–13]. In the last few years, type isomorphisms became one of the central concepts in homotopy type theory (HoTT) [33], where type equivalences feature prominently. These connections exposed that there is even more interesting structure arising from type isomorphisms at higher levels. For example, let Bool abbreviate the type $\top \uplus \top$ and consider the two isomorphisms between the type Bool and itself. One of these is the identity and the other is the twist (negation) map. These isomorphisms are themselves "not equivalent" in a sense to be formalized.

The question we therefore ask is whether there is a natural correspondence, in the style of the Curry–Howard correspondence, between types and some existing mathematical entities, which would bring forth the structure of type isomorphisms and their equivalences at higher levels. We argue that, for the case of finite types, commutative semirings and their categorification are exactly these entities. In a broader sense, such a correspondence connects computation with mathematical structures common in topology and physics, thus opening the door for deeper and more fruitful interactions among these disciplines [1]. In more detail, because physical laws obey various conservation principles (including conservation of information), every computation is, at the physical level, an equivalence that preserves information. The idea that computation, at the logical and programming level, should also be based on "equivalences" (i.e., invertible processes) was originally motivated by such physical considerations [4,10,15,25,29,32]. More recently, the rising importance of energy conservation for both tiny mobile devices and supercomputers, the shrinking size of technology at which quantum effects become noticeable, and the potential for quantum computation and communication, are additional physical considerations adding momentum to such reversible computational models [7,14].

Outline. The next section discusses the correspondence between semirings and types at an intuitive informal level. Section 3 formalizes the notions of equivalences of types and equivalences of equivalences which are the semantic building blocks for the computational side of the Curry–Howard-style correspondence we aim for. Section 4 introduces a reversible programming language which exactly captures type equivalences. Section 5 lays the categorical foundation for developing a second language that exactly captures equivalences between equivalences. Section 6 introduces such a language. The remaining sections put our work in perspective, point out its limitations and directions for future work, and conclude.

We note that because the issues involved are quite subtle, the paper is partly an "unformalization" of an executable `Agda 2.4.2.4` package with the global `without-K` option enabled. The code is available at http://github.com// JacquesCarette/pi-dual/Univalence. We also make crucial use of a substantial library of categorical structures; we forked our copy from https://github.com/copumpkin/categories and augmented it with definitions for Groupoid, Rig Category and Bicategory. This fork is available from https://github.com/JacquesCarette/categories.

2 Informal Development

We explore the main ingredients that would constitute a Curry–Howard-like correspondence between (commutative) semirings and (constructive) type theory.

2.1 Semirings

We begin with the standard definition of commutative semirings.

Definition 1. *A* commutative semiring *sometimes called a* commutative rig *(ring without negative elements) consists of a set R, two distinguished elements of R named 0 and 1, and two binary operations + and ·, satisfying the following relations for any $a, b, c \in R$:*

$$
\begin{aligned}
0 + a &= a && (+\text{-}unit) \\
a + b &= b + a && (+\text{-}swap) \\
a + (b + c) &= (a + b) + c && (+\text{-}assoc) \\[1ex]
1 \cdot a &= a && (\cdot\text{-}unit) \\
a \cdot b &= b \cdot a && (\cdot\text{-}swap) \\
a \cdot (b \cdot c) &= (a \cdot b) \cdot c && (\cdot\text{-}assoc) \\[1ex]
0 \cdot a &= 0 && (\cdot\text{-}0) \\
(a + b) \cdot c &= (a \cdot c) + (b \cdot c) && (\cdot\text{-}+)
\end{aligned}
$$

If one were to focus on the *syntax* of the semiring elements, they would be described using the following grammar:

$$a, b ::= 0 \mid 1 \mid a + b \mid a \cdot b$$

This grammar corresponds to the grammar for the finite types in type theory:

$$\tau ::= \bot \mid \top \mid \tau_1 \uplus \tau_2 \mid \tau_1 \times \tau_2$$

We will show that this — so far — superficial correspondence scratches the surface of a beautiful correspondence of rich combinatorial structure.

2.2 Semiring Identities and Isomorphisms

Having matched the syntax of semiring elements and the syntax of types, we examine the computational counterpart of the semiring identities. When viewed from the type theory side, each semiring identity asserts that two types are "equal." For example, the identity ·-unit, i.e., $1 \cdot a = a$ asserts that the types $\top \times A$ and A are "equal." One way to express such an "equality" computationally is to exhibit two functions mediating between the two types and prove that these two functions are inverses. Specifically, we define:

$$\begin{array}{ll} \mathsf{f} : \top \times A \to A & \bar{\mathsf{f}} : A \to \top \times A \\ \mathsf{f}\ (\mathsf{tt}, x) = x & \bar{\mathsf{f}}\ x = (\mathsf{tt}, x) \end{array}$$

and prove $\mathsf{f} \circ \bar{\mathsf{f}} = \bar{\mathsf{f}} \circ \mathsf{f} = \mathsf{id}$. One could use this proof to "equate" the two types but, in our proof-relevant development, it is more appropriate to keep the identity of the types separate and speak of *isomorphisms.*

2.3 Proof Relevance

In the world of semirings, there are many proofs of $a + a = a + a$. Consider

$$\begin{array}{lll} \mathsf{pf}_1 : & a + a = a + a & \text{(because = is reflexive)} \\ \mathsf{pf}_2 : & a + a = a + a & \text{(using +-swap)} \end{array}$$

In some cases, we might not care *how* a semiring identity was proved and it might then be acceptable to treat pf_1 and pf_2 as "equal." But although these two proofs of $a + a = a + a$ look identical, they use different "justifications" and these justifications are clearly *not* "equal."

When viewed from the computational side, the situation is as follows. The first proof gives rise to one isomorphism using the self-inverse function id. The second proof gives rise to another isomorphism using another self-inverse function swap defined as:

$$\begin{array}{l} \mathsf{swap} : A \uplus B \to B \uplus A \\ \mathsf{swap}\ (\mathsf{inj}_1\ x) = \mathsf{inj}_2\ x \\ \mathsf{swap}\ (\mathsf{inj}_2\ x) = \mathsf{inj}_1\ x \end{array}$$

Now it is clear that even though both id and swap can be used to establish an isomorphism between $A \uplus A$ and itself, their actions are different. Semantically speaking, these two functions are different and no program transformation or optimization should ever identify them.

The discussion above should not however lead one to conclude that programs resulting from different proofs are always semantically different. Consider for example, the following two proofs of $(a + 0) + b = a + b$. To avoid clutter in this informal presentation, we omit the justifications that refer to the fact that = is a congruence relation:

$$\begin{array}{lll} \mathsf{pf}_3 : & (a + 0) + b = (0 + a) + b & \text{(using +-swap)} \\ & = a + b & \text{(using +-unit} \end{array}$$

$$\begin{array}{lll} \mathsf{pf}_4 : & (a + 0) + b = a + (0 + b) & \text{(using +-assoc)} \\ & = a + b & \text{(using +-unit)} \end{array}$$

On the computational side, the proofs induce the following two isomorphisms between $(A \uplus \bot) \uplus B$ and $A \uplus B$. The first isomorphism pf_3 takes the values in $(A \uplus \bot) \uplus B$ using the composition of the following two isomorphisms:

$$\begin{array}{ll}
\mathsf{f}_1 : (A \uplus \bot) \uplus B \to (\bot \uplus A) \uplus B & \overline{\mathsf{f}_1} : (\bot \uplus A) \uplus B \to (A \uplus \bot) \uplus B \\
\mathsf{f}_1(\mathsf{inj}_1\ (\mathsf{inj}_1\ x)) = \mathsf{inj}_1\ (\mathsf{inj}_2\ x) & \overline{\mathsf{f}_1}(\mathsf{inj}_1\ (\mathsf{inj}_2\ x)) = \mathsf{inj}_1\ (\mathsf{inj}_1\ x) \\
\mathsf{f}_1(\mathsf{inj}_2\ x) = \mathsf{inj}_2\ x & \overline{\mathsf{f}_1}(\mathsf{inj}_2\ x) = \mathsf{inj}_2\ x
\end{array}$$

$$\begin{array}{ll}
\mathsf{f}_2 : (\bot \uplus A) \uplus B \to A \uplus B & \overline{\mathsf{f}_2} : A \uplus B \to (\bot \uplus A) \uplus B \\
\mathsf{f}_2(\mathsf{inj}_1\ (\mathsf{inj}_2\ x)) = \mathsf{inj}_1\ x & \overline{\mathsf{f}_2}(\mathsf{inj}_1\ x) = \mathsf{inj}_1\ (\mathsf{inj}_2\ x) \\
\mathsf{f}_2(\mathsf{inj}_2\ x) = \mathsf{inj}_2\ x & \overline{\mathsf{f}_2}(\mathsf{inj}_2\ x) = \mathsf{inj}_2\ x
\end{array}$$

We calculate that composition corresponding to pf_3 as:

$$\begin{array}{ll}
\mathsf{f}_{12} : (A \uplus \bot) \uplus B \to A \uplus B & \overline{\mathsf{f}_{12}} : A \uplus B \to (A \uplus \bot) \uplus B \\
\mathsf{f}_{12}(\mathsf{inj}_1\ (\mathsf{inj}_1\ x)) = \mathsf{inj}_1\ x & \overline{\mathsf{f}_{12}}(\mathsf{inj}_1\ x) = \mathsf{inj}_1\ (\mathsf{inj}_1\ x) \\
\mathsf{f}_{12}(\mathsf{inj}_2\ x) = \mathsf{inj}_2\ x & \overline{\mathsf{f}_{12}}(\mathsf{inj}_2\ x) = \mathsf{inj}_2\ x
\end{array}$$

We can similarly calculate the isomorphism corresponding to pf_4 and verify that it is identical to the one above.

2.4 Summary

To summarize, there is a natural computational model that emerges from viewing types as syntax for semiring elements and semiring identities as type isomorphisms. The correspondence continues further between justifications for semiring identities and valid program transformations and optimizations. There is a long way however from noticing such a correspondence to formalizing it in such a way that a well-founded reversible programming language along with its accompanying program transformations and optimizations can be naturally extracted from the algebraic semiring structure. Furthermore, the correspondence between the algebraic manipulations in semirings and program transformations is so tight that it should be possible to conveniently move back and forth between the two worlds transporting results that are evident in one domain to the other. The remainder of the paper is about such a formalization and its applications.

3 Type Equivalences and Equivalences of Equivalences

The previous section used two informal notions of equivalence: between types, corresponding to semiring identities, and between programs, corresponding to proofs of semiring identities. We make this precise.

3.1 Type Equivalences

As a first approximation, Sect. 2.2 identifies two types when there is an isomorphism between them. The next section (Sect. 2.3) however reveals that we want to reason at a higher level about equivalences of such isomorphisms.

We therefore follow the HoTT approach and expose one of the functions forming the isomorphism in order to explicitly encode the precise way in which the two types are equivalent. Thus, the two equivalences between Bool and itself will be distinguished by the underlying witness of the isomorphism.

Technically our definition of type equivalence relies on quasi-inverses and homotopies defined next.[1]

Definition 2 (Homotopy). *Two functions* $f, g : A \to B$ *are* homotopic, *written* $f \sim g$, *if* $\forall x : A. f(x) = g(x)$. *In Agda, we write:*

```
_∼_ : ∀ {A : Set} {P : A → Set} → (f g : (x : A) → P x) → Set
_∼_ {A} f g = (x : A) → f x ≡ g x
```

where Set *is the universe of Agda types.*

In the HoTT world, there is a distinction between the identification of two functions $f \equiv g$, and two functions producing equal values on all inputs $f \sim g$: the two notions are traditionally identified but are only *equivalent* in the HoTT context.

Definition 3 (Quasi-inverse). *For a function* $f : A \to B$, *a* quasi-inverse *of* f *is a triple* (g, α, β), *consisting of a function* $g : B \to A$ *and two homotopies* $\alpha : f \circ g \sim \mathrm{id}_B$ *and* $\beta : g \circ f \sim \mathrm{id}_A$. *In Agda, we write:*

```
record isqinv {A : Set} {B : Set} (f : A → B) : Set where
  constructor qinv
  field
    g : B → A
    α : (f ∘ g) ∼ id
    β : (g ∘ f) ∼ id
```

The terminology "quasi-inverse" was chosen in the HoTT context as a reminder that this is a poorly-behaved notion by itself as the same function $f : A \to B$ may have multiple unequal quasi-inverses; however, up to homotopy, all quasi-inverses are equivalent. From a quasi-inverse, one can build an inverse (and vice-versa); however, in a proof-relevant setting, logical equivalence is insufficient.

Definition 4 (Equivalence of types). *Two types* A *and* B *are equivalent* $A \simeq B$ *if there exists a function* $f : A \to B$ *together with a quasi-inverse for* f. *In Agda, we write:*

```
_≃_ : Set → Set → Set
A ≃ B = Σ (A → B) isqinv
```

It is easy to prove that homotopies (for any given function space $A \to B$) are an equivalence relation. It is also straightforward to show that $\simeq$ is an equivalence relation by defining:

[1] For reasons beyond the scope of this paper, we do not use any of the definitions of equivalence which make it a *mere proposition*, as we want a definition which is syntactically symmetric.

$$\begin{aligned} \mathsf{id}{\simeq} &: A \simeq A \\ \mathsf{sym}{\simeq} &: (A \simeq B) \to (B \simeq A) \\ \mathsf{trans}{\simeq} &: (A \simeq B) \to (B \simeq C) \to (A \simeq C) \end{aligned}$$

The definition of equivalence allows us to formalize the presentation of Sect. 2.2 by proving that every commutative semiring identity is satisfied by types in the universe (Set) up to $\simeq$.

Theorem 1. *The collection of all types (*Set*) forms a commutative semiring (up to* $\simeq$*).*

Proof. As expected, the additive unit is $\bot$, the multiplicative unit is $\top$, and the two binary operations are $\uplus$ and $\times$. The relevant structure in Agda is:

```
typesCSR : CommutativeSemiring (Level.suc Level.zero) Level.zero
typesCSR = record {
  Carrier = Set ;
  _≈_ = _≃_ ; _+_ = _⊎_ ; _*_ = _×_ ;
  0# = ⊥ ; 1# = ⊤ ;
  isCommutativeSemiring = typesIsCSR }
```

The functions, homotopies, and quasi-inverses witnessing the explicit equivalences are defined within typesIsCSR and are straightforward. For future reference, we list some of these equivalences:

$$\begin{aligned} \mathsf{unite}_+{\simeq} &: (\bot \uplus A) \simeq A \\ \mathsf{unite}_+'{\simeq} &: (A \uplus \bot) \simeq A \\ \mathsf{swap}_+{\simeq} &: (A \uplus B) \simeq (B \uplus A) \\ \mathsf{assoc}_+{\simeq} &: ((A \uplus B) \uplus C) \simeq (A \uplus (B \uplus C)) \\ \_{\uplus\simeq}\_ &: (A \simeq C) \to (B \simeq D) \to ((A \uplus B) \simeq (C \uplus D)) \end{aligned}$$

3.2 Equivalences of Equivalences

In the terminology of Sect. 2.3, an equivalence $\simeq$ denotes a proof of a semiring identity. Thus the proofs pf_1, pf_2, pf_3, and pf_4 can be written formally as:

```
pf₁ pf₂ : {A : Set} → (A ⊎ A) ≃ (A ⊎ A)
pf₁ = id≃
pf₂ = swap₊≃

pf₃ pf₄ : {A B : Set} → ((A ⊎ ⊥) ⊎ B) ≃ (A ⊎ B)
pf₃ = trans≃ (swap₊≃ ⊎≃ id≃) (unite₊≃ ⊎≃ id≃)
pf₄ = trans≃ assoc₊≃ (id≃ ⊎≃ unite₊≃)
```

In order to argue that pf_3 and pf_4 are equivalent, we therefore need a notion of equivalence of equivalences. To motivate our definition below, we first consider the obvious idea of using $\simeq$ to relate equivalences. In that case, an equivalence of equivalences of type $(A \simeq B) \simeq (A \simeq B)$ would include functions f and g mapping between $(A \simeq B)$ and itself in addition to two homotopies α and β witnessing $(f \circ g) \sim \mathsf{id}$ and $(g \circ f) \sim \mathsf{id}$ respectively. Expanding the definition of a homotopy, we note that α and β would therefore attempt to compare equivalences (which include functions) using propositional equality $\equiv$. In other words, we need to resolve to homotopies again to compare these functions: two equivalences are equivalent if there exist homotopies between their underlying functions.[2]

Definition 5 (Equivalence of equivalences). *Two equivalences* $eq_1, eq_2 : A \simeq B$ *are themselves equivalent, written* $eq_1 \approxeq eq_2$*, if* $eq_1.f \sim eq_2.f$ *and* $eq_1.g \sim eq_2.g$*. In Agda, we write:*

```
record _≋_ {A B : Set} (eq₁ eq₂ : A ≃ B) : Set where
  constructor eq
  open isqinv
  field
    f≡ : proj₁ eq₁ ∼ proj₁ eq₂
    g≡ : g (proj₂ eq₁) ∼ g (proj₂ eq₂)
```

We could now verify that indeed $\mathsf{pf}_3 \approxeq \mathsf{pf}_4$. Such a proof exists in the accompanying code but requires a surprising amount of tedious infrastructure to present. We will have to wait until Sects. 5.1 and 6.4 to see this proof.

4 Programming with Equivalences

We have established and formalized a correspondence between semirings and types which relates semiring identities to the type equivalences of Definition 4. We have further introduced the infrastructure needed to reason about equivalences of equivalences so that we can reason about the relation between different proofs of the same semiring identity. As we aim to refine these relationships to a Curry–Howard-like correspondence, we now turn our attention to developing an actual programming language. The first step will be to introduce syntax that denotes type equivalences. Thus instead of having to repeatedly introduce functions and their inverses and proofs of homotopies, we will simply use a term language that exactly expresses type equivalences and nothing else.

4.1 Syntax of Π

In previous work, Bowman, James and Sabry [6,20] introduced the Π family of reversible languages whose only computations are isomorphisms between types. The simplest member of Π is exactly the language we seek for capturing type equivalences arising from semiring identities. The syntactic components of our language are as follows:

$$
\begin{array}{ll}
(\textit{Types}) & \tau ::= 0 \mid 1 \mid \tau_1 + \tau_2 \mid \tau_1 * \tau_2 \\
(\textit{Values}) & v ::= () \mid \mathsf{inl}\ v \mid \mathsf{inr}\ v \mid (v_1, v_2) \\
(\textit{Combinator types}) & \quad\ \tau_1 \leftrightarrow \tau_2 \\
(\textit{Terms and Combinators}) & c ::= [\textit{see Figs. 1 and 2}]
\end{array}
$$

[2] Strictly speaking, the g≡ component is redundant, from a logical perspective, as it is derivable. From a computational perspective, it is very convenient.

$$
\begin{array}{rcl}
id\!\leftrightarrow: & \tau \leftrightarrow \tau & : id\!\leftrightarrow \\
\\
unite_{+}l: & 0 + \tau \leftrightarrow \tau & : uniti_{+}l \\
swap_{+}: & \tau_1 + \tau_2 \leftrightarrow \tau_2 + \tau_1 & : swap_{+} \\
assocl_{+}: & \tau_1 + (\tau_2 + \tau_3) \leftrightarrow (\tau_1 + \tau_2) + \tau_3 & : assocr_{+} \\
\\
unite_{*}l: & 1 * \tau \leftrightarrow \tau & : uniti_{*}l \\
swap_{*}: & \tau_1 * \tau_2 \leftrightarrow \tau_2 * \tau_1 & : swap_{*} \\
assocl_{*}: & \tau_1 * (\tau_2 * \tau_3) \leftrightarrow (\tau_1 * \tau_2) * \tau_3 & : assocr_{*} \\
\\
absorbr: & 0 * \tau \leftrightarrow 0 & : factorzl \\
dist: & (\tau_1 + \tau_2) * \tau_3 \leftrightarrow (\tau_1 * \tau_3) + (\tau_2 * \tau_3) & : factor
\end{array}
$$

Fig. 1. Π-terms [6,20].

$$
\frac{\vdash c_1 : \tau_1 \leftrightarrow \tau_2 \quad \vdash c_2 : \tau_2 \leftrightarrow \tau_3}{\vdash c_1 \odot c_2 : \tau_1 \leftrightarrow \tau_3}
\qquad
\frac{\vdash c_1 : \tau_1 \leftrightarrow \tau_2 \quad \vdash c_2 : \tau_3 \leftrightarrow \tau_4}{\vdash c_1 \oplus c_2 : \tau_1 + \tau_3 \leftrightarrow \tau_2 + \tau_4}
$$

$$
\frac{\vdash c_1 : \tau_1 \leftrightarrow \tau_2 \quad \vdash c_2 : \tau_3 \leftrightarrow \tau_4}{\vdash c_1 \otimes c_2 : \tau_1 * \tau_3 \leftrightarrow \tau_2 * \tau_4}
$$

Fig. 2. Π-combinators.

The values classified by the finite types are the conventional ones: $()$ of type 1, $(\mathsf{inl}\ v)$ and $(\mathsf{inr}\ v)$ for injections into sum types, and (v_1, v_2) for product types.

Figure 1 gives the terms which correspond to the identities of commutative semirings. Each line of the figure introduces a pair of dual constants (where $id\!\leftrightarrow$, $swap_{+}$ and $swap_{*}$ are self-dual) that witness the type isomorphism in the middle. Figure 2 adds to that 3 combinators $\odot$, $\oplus$, and $\otimes$, which come from the requirement that $\leftrightarrow$ be transitive (giving a sequential composition operator $\odot$), and that $\leftrightarrow$ be a congruence for both $+$ and $*$ (giving a way to take sums and products of combinators using $\oplus$ and $\otimes$ respectively). This latter congruence requirement is classically invisible, but appears when being proof-relevant.

By construction, each term in the language has an inverse:

Definition 6 (Syntactic Inverse !). *Each Π-term $c : \tau_1 \leftrightarrow \tau_2$ has a syntactic inverse $!c : \tau_2 \leftrightarrow \tau_1$. We only show a few representative clauses:*

$$
\begin{array}{rclcrcl}
!id\!\leftrightarrow & = & id\!\leftrightarrow & \quad & !(c_1 \odot c_2) & = & !c_2 \ \odot\ !c_1 \\
!unite_{+}l & = & uniti_{+}l & & !(c_1 \oplus c_2) & = & !c_1 \ \oplus\ !c_2 \\
!uniti_{+}l & = & unite_{+}l & & !(c_1 \otimes c_2) & = & !c_1 \ \otimes\ !c_2
\end{array}
$$

4.2 Example Programs

The family of Π languages was previously introduced as standalone reversible programming languages. The fragment without recursive types discussed in this paper is universal for reversible boolean circuits [20]. With the addition of recursive types and trace operators [18], Π becomes a Turing-complete reversible language [6,20].

We illustrate the expressiveness of Π with a few small programs; we begin by defining the universe of types U:

```
data U : Set where
  ZERO  : U
  ONE   : U
  PLUS  : U → U → U
  TIMES : U → U → U
```

We then encode the type of booleans, write a few simple gates like the Toffoli gate [32], and use them to write a reversible full adder [19]:

```
BOOL : U
BOOL  = PLUS ONE ONE

BOOL² : U
BOOL² = TIMES BOOL BOOL

BOOL³ : U
BOOL³ = TIMES BOOL² BOOL

NOT : BOOL ↔ BOOL
NOT = swap₊

CNOT : BOOL² ↔ BOOL²
CNOT = dist ⊙ (id↔ ⊕ (id↔ ⊗ NOT)) ⊙ factor

TOFFOLI : TIMES BOOL BOOL² ↔ TIMES BOOL BOOL²
TOFFOLI = dist ⊙ (id↔ ⊕ (id↔ ⊗ CNOT)) ⊙ factor

PERES : BOOL³ ↔ BOOL³
PERES = (id↔ ⊗ NOT) ⊙ assocr⋆ ⊙ (id↔ ⊗ swap⋆) ⊙ TOFFOLI ⊙
  (id↔ ⊗ (NOT ⊗ id↔)) ⊙ TOFFOLI ⊙ (id↔ ⊗ swap⋆) ⊙
  (id↔ ⊗ (NOT ⊗ id↔)) ⊙ TOFFOLI ⊙ (id↔ ⊗ (NOT ⊗ id↔)) ⊙ assocl⋆

- Input: (z, ((n1, n2), cin)))
- Output: (g1, (g2, (sum, cout)))
F_ADDER : TIMES BOOL BOOL³ ↔ TIMES BOOL (TIMES BOOL BOOL²)
F_ADDER = swap⋆ ⊙ (swap⋆ ⊗ id↔) ⊙ assocr⋆ ⊙ swap⋆ ⊙ (PERES ⊗ id↔) ⊙
  assocr⋆ ⊙ (id↔ ⊗ swap⋆) ⊙ assocr⋆ ⊙ (id↔ ⊗ assocl⋆) ⊙
  (id↔ ⊗ PERES) ⊙ (id↔ ⊗ assocr⋆)
```

Although writing circuits using the raw syntax for combinators is tedious, the examples illustrate the programming language nature of Π. In other work, one can find a compiler from a conventional functional language to circuits [20], a systematic technique to translate abstract machines to Π [21], and a Haskell-like surface language [22] which can ease writing circuits. All that reinforces the first part of the title, i.e., that we can really compute with semirings.

4.3 Example Proofs

In addition to being a reversible programming language, Π is also a language for expressing proofs that correspond to semiring identities. Thus we can write variants of our proofs pf_1, pf_2, pf_3, and pf_4 from Sect. 2:

```
pf₁π pf₂π : {A : U} → PLUS A A ↔ PLUS A A
pf₁π = id↔
pf₂π = swap₊

pf₃π pf₄π : {A B : U} → PLUS (PLUS A ZERO) B ↔ PLUS A B
pf₃π = (swap₊ ⊕ id↔) ⊙ (unite₊l ⊕ id↔)
pf₄π = assocr₊ ⊙ (id↔ ⊕ unite₊l)
```

4.4 Semantics

We define the denotational semantics of Π to be type equivalences:

```
⟦_⟧ : U → Set
⟦ ZERO ⟧        = ⊥
⟦ ONE ⟧         = ⊤
⟦ PLUS t₁ t₂ ⟧  = ⟦ t₁ ⟧ ⊎ ⟦ t₂ ⟧
⟦ TIMES t₁ t₂ ⟧ = ⟦ t₁ ⟧ × ⟦ t₂ ⟧

c2equiv : {t₁ t₂ : U} → (c : t₁ ↔ t₂) → ⟦ t₁ ⟧ ≃ ⟦ t₂ ⟧
```

The function $[\![\cdot]\!]$ maps each type constructor to its Agda denotation. The function c2equiv confirms that every Π term encodes a type equivalence.

In previous work, we also defined an operational semantics for Π via forward and backward evaluators with the following signatures:

```
eval  : {t₁ t₂ : U} → (t₁ ↔ t₂) → ⟦ t₁ ⟧ → ⟦ t₂ ⟧
evalB : {t₁ t₂ : U} → (t₁ ↔ t₂) → ⟦ t₂ ⟧ → ⟦ t₁ ⟧
```

This operational semantics serves as an adequate semantic specification if one focuses solely on a programming language for reversible boolean circuits. It is straightforward to prove that eval and evalB are inverses of each other.

If, in addition, one is also interested in using Π for expressing semiring identities as type equivalences then the following properties are of more interest:

```
lemma0 : {t₁ t₂ : U} → (c : t₁ ↔ t₂) → (v : ⟦ t₁ ⟧) →
         eval c v ≡ proj₁ (c2equiv c) v

lemma1 : {t₁ t₂ : U} → (c : t₁ ↔ t₂) → (v : ⟦ t₂ ⟧) →
         evalB c v ≡ proj₁ (sym≃ (c2equiv c)) v
```

The two lemmas confirm that these type equivalences are coherent with respect to the operational semantics, i.e., that the operational and denotational semantics of Π coincide.

5 Categorification

We have seen two important ways of modeling equivalences between types: using back-and-forth functions that compose to the identity (Definition 4) and using a programming language tailored to only express isomorphisms between types (Sect. 4.1). In terms of our desired Curry–Howard-like correspondence, we have so far related the syntax of semiring elements to types and the proofs of semiring identities to programs of the appropriate types. The last important component of the Curry-Howard correspondence is to relate semiring proof transformations to program transformations.

We thus need to reason about equivalences of equivalences. Attempting to discover these when working directly with equivalences, or with the syntax of a programming language, proves quite awkward. It, however, turns out that the solution to this problem is evident if we first generalize our models of type equivalences to the categorical setting. As we explain, in the right class of categories, the objects represent types, the morphisms represent type equivalences, and the *coherence conditions* will represent equivalences of equivalences. Our task of modeling equivalences of equivalences then reduces to "reading off" the coherence conditions for each instance of the general categorical framework.

5.1 Monoidal Categories

As the details matter, we will be explicit about the definition of all the categorical notions involved. We begin with the conventional definitions for monoidal and symmetric monoidal categories.

Definition 7 (Monoidal Category). *A* monoidal category *[27] is a category with the following additional structure:*

- *a bifunctor $\otimes$ called the monoidal or tensor product,*
- *an object I called the unit object, and*
- *natural isomorphisms $\alpha_{A,B,C} : (A \otimes B) \otimes C \xrightarrow{\sim} A \otimes (B \otimes C)$, $\lambda_A : I \otimes A \xrightarrow{\sim} A$, and $\rho_A : A \otimes I \xrightarrow{\sim} A$, such that the two diagrams below (known as the* associativity pentagon *and the* triangle for unit*) commute.*

$$((A \otimes B) \otimes C) \otimes D \xrightarrow{\quad \alpha \quad} (A \otimes B) \otimes (C \otimes D)$$

$$\alpha \otimes \mathrm{id}_D \downarrow \qquad\qquad\qquad\qquad \downarrow \alpha$$

$$(A \otimes (B \otimes C)) \otimes D \qquad\qquad A \otimes (B \otimes (C \otimes D))$$

$$\alpha \searrow \qquad \swarrow \mathrm{id}_A \otimes \alpha$$

$$A \otimes ((B \otimes C) \otimes D)$$

$$(A \otimes I) \otimes B \xrightarrow{\quad \alpha \quad} A \otimes (I \otimes B)$$

$$\rho_A \otimes \mathrm{id}_B \searrow \qquad \swarrow \mathrm{id}_A \otimes \lambda_B$$

$$A \otimes B$$

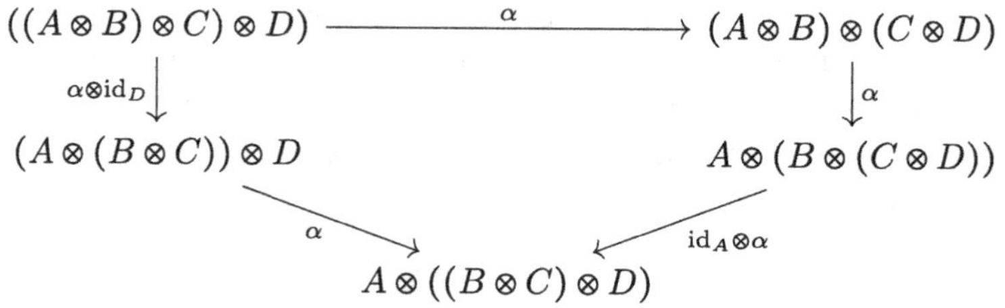

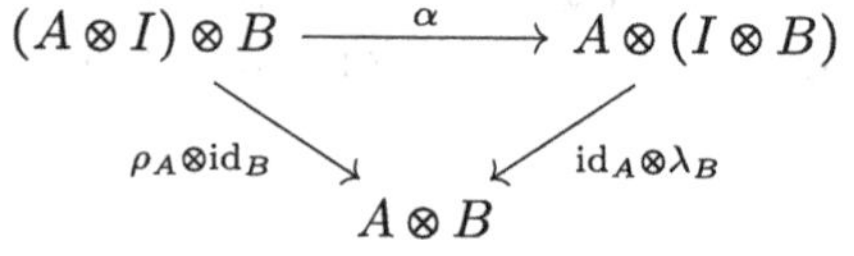

Definition 8 (Braided and Symmetric Monoidal Categories). *A monoidal category is* braided *if it has an isomorphism $\sigma_{A,B} : A \otimes B \xrightarrow{\sim} B \otimes A$ where σ is a natural transformation which satisfies the* unit *coherence triangle (below on the left) and the* bilinearity *hexagon below. A braided monoidal category is* symmetric *if it additionally satisfies the* symmetry *triangle (below on the right).*

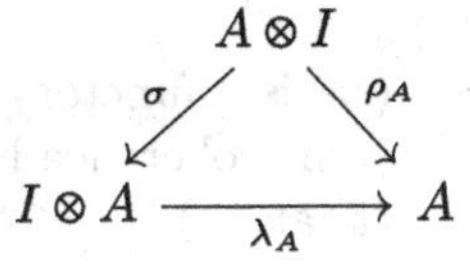

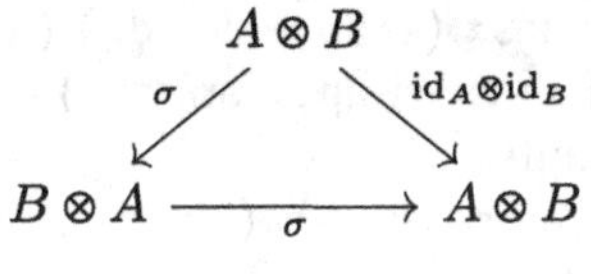

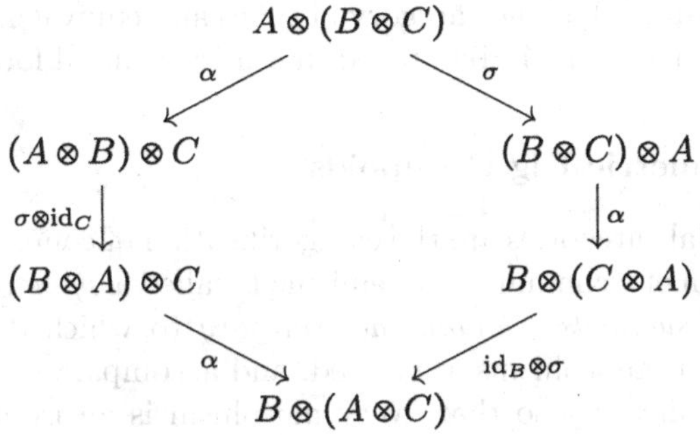

According to Mac Lane's coherence theorem, the triangle and pentagon coherence laws for monoidal categories are justified by the desire to equate any two isomorphisms built using σ, λ, and ρ and having the same source and target. Similar considerations justify the coherence laws for symmetric monoidal categories. It is important to note that the coherence conditions do *not* imply that every pair of parallel morphisms with the same source and target are equal. Indeed, as Dosen and Petric explain:

> In Mac Lane's second coherence result of [...], which has to do with symmetric monoidal categories, it is not intended that all equations between arrows of the same type should hold. What Mac Lane does can be described in logical terms in the following manner. On the one hand, he has an axiomatization, and, on the other hand, he has a model category where arrows are permutations; then he shows that his axiomatization is complete with respect to this model. It is no wonder that his coherence problem reduces to the completeness problem for the usual axiomatization of symmetric groups [9].

From a different perspective, Baez and Dolan [2] explain the source of these coherence laws as arising from homotopy theory. In this theory, laws are only imposed up to homotopy, with these homotopies satisfying certain laws, again only up to homotopy, with these higher homotopies satisfying their own higher coherence laws, and so on. Remarkably, they report, among other results, that the pentagon identity arises when studying the algebraic structure possessed by a space that is homotopy equivalent to a loop space and that the hexagon identity arises in the context of spaces homotopy equivalent to double loop spaces.

As a concrete example relating homotopies and coherence conditions, the homotopy between pf_3 and pf_4 discussed in Sect. 3.2 follows from the coherence conditions of symmetric monoidal categories as follows:

$$\begin{aligned}
\mathsf{pf}_3 &= \mathsf{trans}{\simeq}\ (\mathsf{swap}_{+}{\simeq}\ \uplus{\simeq}\ \mathsf{id}{\simeq})\ (\mathsf{unite}_{+}{\simeq}\ \uplus{\simeq}\ \mathsf{id}{\simeq}) \\
&\approxeq (\mathsf{trans}{\simeq}\ \mathsf{swap}_{+}{\simeq}\ \mathsf{unite}_{+}{\simeq})\ \uplus{\simeq}\ \mathsf{id}{\simeq} && (\uplus{\simeq} \text{ is a functor}) \\
&\approxeq \mathsf{unite}_{+}{}'{\simeq}\ \uplus{\simeq}\ \mathsf{id}{\simeq} && (\text{unit coherence law}) \\
&\approxeq \mathsf{trans}{\simeq}\ \mathsf{assoc}_{+}{\simeq}\ (\mathsf{id}{\simeq}\ \uplus{\simeq}\ \mathsf{unite}_{+}{\simeq}) && (\text{triangle}) \\
&= \mathsf{pf}_4
\end{aligned}$$

The derivation assumes that the category of types and equivalences is symmetric monoidal — a result which will be proved in a more general form in Theorem 2.

5.2 Weak Symmetric Rig Groupoids

Symmetric monoidal categories are the categorification of commutative monoids. The categorification of a commutative semiring is called a *symmetric rig category.* It is built from a *symmetric bimonoidal category* to which distributivity and absorption natural isomorphisms are added, and accompanying coherence laws. Since we can set things up so that every morphism is an isomorphism, it will also be a groupoid. Also, as the laws of the category only hold up to a higher equivalence, the entire setting is that of weak categories (aka bicategories).

There are several equivalent definitions of rig categories; we use the following from the nLab [28].

Definition 9 (Rig Category). *A* rig category *C is a category with a symmetric monoidal structure $(C, \oplus, 0)$ for addition and a monoidal structure $(C, \otimes, 1)$ for multiplication together with left and right distributivity natural isomorphisms:*

$$\begin{aligned}
d_\ell &: x \otimes (y \oplus z) \xrightarrow{\sim} (x \otimes y) \oplus (x \otimes z) \\
d_r &: (x \oplus y) \otimes z \xrightarrow{\sim} (x \otimes z) \oplus (y \otimes z)
\end{aligned}$$

and absorption/annihilation isomorphisms $a_l : x \otimes 0 \xrightarrow{\sim} 0$ and $a_r : 0 \otimes x \xrightarrow{\sim} 0$ satisfying coherence conditions [26] discussed below.

Definition 10 (Symmetric Rig Category). *A* symmetric rig category *is a rig category in which the multiplicative structure is symmetric.*

Definition 11 (Symmetric Rig Groupoid). *A* symmetric rig groupoid *is a symmetric rig category in which every morphism is invertible.*

The coherence conditions for rig categories were worked out by Laplaza [26]. Pages 31–35 of his paper report 24 coherence conditions numbered I to XXIV that vary from simple diagrams to quite complicated ones including a diagram with 9 nodes showing that two distinct ways of simplifying $(A \oplus B) \otimes (C \oplus D)$ to $(((A \otimes C) \oplus (B \otimes C)) \oplus (A \otimes D)) \oplus (B \otimes D)$ commute. The 24 coherence conditions are however not independent and it is sufficient to verify one of various smaller subsets, to be chosen depending on the situation. Generally speaking, the coherence laws appear rather obscure but they can be unpacked and "unformalized" to relatively understandable statements. They all express that two different means of getting between two equivalent types are equivalent. Thus we can give programming-oriented descriptions of these along the following lines:

I given $A \otimes (B \oplus C)$, swapping B and C then distributing (on the left) is the same as first distributing, then swapping the two summands;

II given $(A \oplus B) \otimes C$, first switching the order of the products then distributing (on the left) is the same as distributing (on the right) and then switching the order of both products;

IX given $(A \oplus B) \otimes (C \oplus D)$, we can either first distribute on the left, map right-distribution and finally associate, or we can go "the long way around" by right-distributing first, then mapping left-distribution, and then a long chain of administrative shuffles to get to the same point;

and so on.

Going through the details of the proof of the coherence theorem in [26] with a "modern" eye, one cannot help but think of Knuth-Bendix completion. Although it is known that the coherence laws for some categorical structures can be systematically derived in this way [3], it is also known that in the presence of certain structures (such as symmetry), Knuth-Bendix completion will not terminate. It would be interesting to know if there is indeed a systematic way to obtain these laws from the rewriting perspective but, as far as we know, there are no published results to that effect. The connections to homotopy theory cited by Baez and Dolan [2] (and mentioned in the previous section) appear to be the best hope for a rational reconstruction of the coherence laws.

5.3 The Symmetric Rig Groupoid of Types and Type Equivalences

We are now ready for the generalization of our model of types and type equivalences to a symmetric rig weak groupoid and this will, by construction, prove all equivalences between type equivalences like $\mathsf{pf}_3 \approx \mathsf{pf}_4$ that should be equated, while, again by construction, *not* identifying type equivalences like pf_1 and pf_2 that should not be equated.

Theorem 2. *The category whose objects are Agda types and whose morphisms are type equivalences is a symmetric rig groupoid.*

Proof. The definition of Category that we use is parametrized by an equivalence relation for its collection of morphisms between objects. Since we want a category with equivalences as morphisms, we naturally use $\approx$ for that notion of morphism-equality. These morphisms directly satisfy the axioms stated in the definitions of the various categories. The bulk of the work is in ensuring that the coherence conditions are satisfied up to homotopy. We only show the proof of one coherence condition, the first one in Laplaza's paper:

$$\begin{array}{ccc} A \otimes (B \oplus C) & \xrightarrow{\mathit{distl}} & (A \otimes B) \oplus (A \otimes C) \\ {\scriptstyle \mathrm{id}_A \otimes \mathit{swap}_+} \downarrow & & \downarrow {\scriptstyle \mathit{swap}_+} \\ A \otimes (C \oplus B) & \xrightarrow[\mathit{distl}]{} & (A \otimes C) \oplus (A \otimes B) \end{array}$$

We first have a lemma that shows that the two paths starting from the top left node are equivalent:

```
A×[B⊎C]→[A×C]⊎[A×B] : {A B C : Set} →
  (TE.distl ∘ (id {A = A} ×→ TE.swap₊ {B} {C})) ∼ (TE.swap₊ ∘ TE.distl)
A×[B⊎C]→[A×C]⊎[A×B] (x , inj₁ y) = refl
A×[B⊎C]→[A×C]⊎[A×B] (x , inj₂ y) = refl
```

The lemma asserts the that the two paths between $A \otimes (B \oplus C)$ and $(A \otimes C) \oplus (A \otimes B)$ are homotopic. To show that we have a groupoid, we also need to know that the converse lemma also holds, i.e. that reversing all arrows also gives a diagram for a homotopy, in other words:

```
[A×C]⊎[A×B]→A×[B⊎C] : {A B C : Set} →
  ((id ×→ TE.swap₊) ∘ TE.factorl) ∼ (TE.factorl ∘ TE.swap₊ {A × C} {A × B})
[A×C]⊎[A×B]→A×[B⊎C] (inj₁ x) = refl
[A×C]⊎[A×B]→A×[B⊎C] (inj₂ y) = refl
```

Finally we show that the forward equivalence and the backward equivalence are indeed related to the same diagram:

```
laplazaI = eq A×[B⊎C]→[A×C]⊎[A×B] [A×C]⊎[A×B]→A×[B⊎C]
```

where eq is the constructor for ≋. □

6 Programming with Equivalences of Equivalences

Following the lead of Sect. 4, we now develop an actual programming language whose terms denote equivalences of equivalences. Since we already have Π whose terms denote equivalences, what we actually need is a language whose terms denote equivalences of Π terms. One can think of such a language as a language for expressing valid program transformations and optimizations of Π programs. We will call the terms and combinators of the original Π language, level-0 terms, and the terms and combinators of the new language, level-1 terms.

As explained in the previous section, there is a systematic way to "discover" the level-1 terms which is driven by the coherence conditions. During our proofs, we collected all the level-1 terms that were needed to realize all the coherence conditions. This exercise suggested a refactoring of the original level-0 terms and a few iterations.

Let $c_1 : t_1 \leftrightarrow t_2$, $c_2 : t_2 \leftrightarrow t_3$, and $c_3 : t_3 \leftrightarrow t_4$:

$$c_1 \odot (c_2 \odot c_3) \Leftrightarrow (c_1 \odot c_2) \odot c_3$$
$$(c_1 \oplus (c_2 \oplus c_3)) \odot \mathit{assocl}_+ \Leftrightarrow \mathit{assocl}_+ \odot ((c_1 \oplus c_2) \oplus c_3)$$
$$(c_1 \otimes (c_2 \otimes c_3)) \odot \mathit{assocl}_* \Leftrightarrow \mathit{assocl}_* \odot ((c_1 \otimes c_2) \otimes c_3)$$
$$((c_1 \oplus c_2) \oplus c_3) \odot \mathit{assocr}_+ \Leftrightarrow \mathit{assocr}_+ \odot (c_1 \oplus (c_2 \oplus c_3))$$
$$((c_1 \otimes c_2) \otimes c_3) \odot \mathit{assocr}_* \Leftrightarrow \mathit{assocr}_* \odot (c_1 \otimes (c_2 \otimes c_3))$$
$$\mathit{assocr}_+ \odot \mathit{assocr}_+ \Leftrightarrow ((\mathit{assocr}_+ \oplus \mathit{id}{\leftrightarrow}) \odot \mathit{assocr}_+) \odot (\mathit{id}{\leftrightarrow} \oplus \mathit{assocr}_+)$$
$$\mathit{assocr}_* \odot \mathit{assocr}_* \Leftrightarrow ((\mathit{assocr}_* \otimes \mathit{id}{\leftrightarrow}) \odot \mathit{assocr}_*) \odot (\mathit{id}{\leftrightarrow} \otimes \mathit{assocr}_*)$$

Fig. 3. Signatures of level-1 Π-combinators: associativity

Let $a : t_1 \leftrightarrow t_2$, $b : t_3 \leftrightarrow t_4$, and $c : t_5 \leftrightarrow t_6$:

$$((a \oplus b) \otimes c) \odot \mathit{dist} \Leftrightarrow \mathit{dist} \odot ((a \otimes c) \oplus (b \otimes c))$$
$$(a \otimes (b \oplus c)) \odot \mathit{distl} \Leftrightarrow \mathit{distl} \odot ((a \otimes b) \oplus (a \otimes c))$$
$$((a \otimes c) \oplus (b \otimes c)) \odot \mathit{factor} \Leftrightarrow \mathit{factor} \odot ((a \oplus b) \otimes c)$$
$$((a \otimes b) \oplus (a \otimes c)) \odot \mathit{factorl} \Leftrightarrow \mathit{factorl} \odot (a \otimes (b \oplus c))$$

Fig. 4. Signatures of level-1 Π-combinators: distributivity and factoring

6.1 Revised Syntax of Level-0 Terms

The inspiration of symmetric rig groupoids suggested a refactoring of Π with the following additional level-0 combinators:

$$\begin{array}{rrcll} \mathit{unite}_+r : & \tau + 0 & \leftrightarrow & \tau & : \mathit{uniti}_+r \\ \mathit{unite}_*r : & \tau * 1 & \leftrightarrow & \tau & : \mathit{uniti}_*r \\ \mathit{absorbl} : & \tau * 0 & \leftrightarrow & 0 & : \mathit{factorzr} \\ \mathit{distl} : & \tau_1 * (\tau_2 + \tau_3) & \leftrightarrow & (\tau_1 * \tau_2) + (\tau_1 * \tau_3) & : \mathit{factorl} \end{array}$$

The added combinators are redundant, from an operational perspective, exactly because of the coherence conditions. They are however critical to the proofs, and in addition, they are often useful when representing circuits, leading to smaller programs with fewer redexes.

6.2 Syntax of Level-1 Terms

The big addition to Π is the level-1 combinators which are collected in Figs. 3, 4, 5, 6, 7, 8, 9, 10, 11 and 12. To avoid clutter we omit the names of the combinators (which are arbitrary) and omit some of the implicit type parameters. The reader should consult the code for full details.

Generally speaking, the level-1 combinators arise for the following reasons. About a third of the combinators come from the definition of the various natural isomorphisms $\alpha_{A,B,C}$, λ_A, ρ_A, $\sigma_{A,B}$, d_l, d_r, a_l and a_r. The first 4 natural isomorphisms actually occur twice, once for each of the symmetric monoidal structures at play. Each natural isomorphism is composed of 2 natural transformations (one in each direction) that must compose to the identity. This in

Let $c, c_1, c_2, c_3 : t_1 \leftrightarrow t_2$ and $c', c'' : t_3 \leftrightarrow t_4$:

$$id{\leftrightarrow} \odot c \Leftrightarrow c \qquad c \odot id{\leftrightarrow} \Leftrightarrow c \qquad c \odot !c \Leftrightarrow id{\leftrightarrow} \qquad !c \odot c \Leftrightarrow id{\leftrightarrow}$$

$$c \Leftrightarrow c \qquad \frac{c_1 \Leftrightarrow c_2 \quad c_2 \Leftrightarrow c_3}{c_1 \Leftrightarrow c_3} \qquad \frac{c_1 \Leftrightarrow c' \quad c_2 \Leftrightarrow c''}{c_1 \odot c_2 \Leftrightarrow c' \odot c''}$$

Fig. 5. Signatures of level-1 Π-combinators: identity and composition

Let $c_0 : 0 \leftrightarrow 0$, $c_1 : 1 \leftrightarrow 1$, and $c : t_1 \leftrightarrow t_2$:

$$\begin{array}{rr} \mathit{unite_+l} \odot c \Leftrightarrow (c_0 \oplus c) \odot \mathit{unite_+l} & \mathit{uniti_+l} \odot (c_0 \oplus c) \Leftrightarrow c \odot \mathit{uniti_+l} \\ \mathit{unite_+r} \odot c \Leftrightarrow (c \oplus c_0) \odot \mathit{unite_+r} & \mathit{uniti_+r} \odot (c \oplus c_0) \Leftrightarrow c \odot \mathit{uniti_+r} \\ \mathit{unite_*l} \odot c \Leftrightarrow (c_1 \otimes c) \odot \mathit{unite_*l} & \mathit{uniti_*l} \odot (c_1 \otimes c) \Leftrightarrow c \odot \mathit{uniti_+l} \\ \mathit{unite_*r} \odot c \Leftrightarrow (c \otimes c_1) \odot \mathit{unite_*r} & \mathit{uniti_*r} \odot (c \otimes c_1) \Leftrightarrow c \odot \mathit{uniti_*r} \end{array}$$

$$\mathit{unite_*l} \Leftrightarrow \mathit{distl} \odot (\mathit{unite_*l} \oplus \mathit{unite_*l})$$

$$\mathit{unite_+l} \Leftrightarrow \mathit{swap_+} \odot \mathit{uniti_+r} \qquad \mathit{unite_*l} \Leftrightarrow \mathit{swap_*} \odot \mathit{uniti_*r}$$

Fig. 6. Signatures of level-1 Π-combinators: unit

turn induces 4 coherence laws: two *naturality laws* which indicate that the combinator commutes with structure construction, and two which express that the resulting combinators are left and right inverses of each other. We note that the mere desire that $\oplus$ be a bifunctor induces 3 coherence laws. And then of course each "structure" (monoidal, braided, symmetric) comes with more, as outlined in the previous section, culminating with 13 additional coherence laws for the rig structure.

In our presentation, we group the level-1 combinators according to the dominant property of interest, e.g., associativity in Fig. 3, or according to the main two interacting properties, e.g., commutativity and associativity in Fig. 7. It is worth noting that most (but not all) of the properties involving only $\otimes$ were already

Let $c_1 : t_1 \leftrightarrow t_2$ and $c_2 : t_3 \leftrightarrow t_4$:

$$\mathit{swap_+} \odot (c_1 \oplus c_2) \Leftrightarrow (c_2 \oplus c_1) \odot \mathit{swap_+} \quad \mathit{swap_*} \odot (c_1 \otimes c_2) \Leftrightarrow (c_2 \otimes c_1) \odot \mathit{swap_*}$$

$$\begin{array}{c} (\mathit{assocr_+} \odot \mathit{swap_+}) \odot \mathit{assocr_+} \Leftrightarrow ((\mathit{swap_+} \oplus \mathit{id}{\leftrightarrow}) \odot \mathit{assocr_+}) \odot (\mathit{id}{\leftrightarrow} \oplus \mathit{swap_+}) \\ (\mathit{assocl_+} \odot \mathit{swap_+}) \odot \mathit{assocl_+} \Leftrightarrow ((\mathit{id}{\leftrightarrow} \oplus \mathit{swap_+}) \odot \mathit{assocl_+}) \odot (\mathit{swap_+} \oplus \mathit{id}{\leftrightarrow}) \\ (\mathit{assocr_*} \odot \mathit{swap_*}) \odot \mathit{assocr_*} \Leftrightarrow ((\mathit{swap_*} \otimes \mathit{id}{\leftrightarrow}) \odot \mathit{assocr_*}) \odot (\mathit{id}{\leftrightarrow} \otimes \mathit{swap_*}) \\ (\mathit{assocl_*} \odot \mathit{swap_*}) \odot \mathit{assocl_*} \Leftrightarrow ((\mathit{id}{\leftrightarrow} \otimes \mathit{swap_*}) \odot \mathit{assocl_*}) \odot (\mathit{swap_*} \otimes \mathit{id}{\leftrightarrow}) \end{array}$$

Fig. 7. Signatures of level-1 Π-combinators: commutativity and associativity

Let $c_1 : t_1 \leftrightarrow t_2$, $c_2 : t_3 \leftrightarrow t_4$, $c_3 : t_1 \leftrightarrow t_2$, and $c_4 : t_3 \leftrightarrow t_4$.
Let $a_1 : t_5 \leftrightarrow t_1$, $a_2 : t_6 \leftrightarrow t_2$, $a_3 : t_1 \leftrightarrow t_3$, and $a_4 : t_2 \leftrightarrow t_4$.

$$\frac{c_1 \Leftrightarrow c_3 \quad c_2 \Leftrightarrow c_4}{c_1 \oplus c_2 \Leftrightarrow c_3 \oplus c_4} \qquad \frac{c_1 \Leftrightarrow c_3 \quad c_2 \Leftrightarrow c_4}{c_1 \otimes c_2 \Leftrightarrow c_3 \otimes c_4}$$

$$\mathit{id}{\leftrightarrow} \oplus \mathit{id}{\leftrightarrow} \Leftrightarrow \mathit{id}{\leftrightarrow} \qquad \mathit{id}{\leftrightarrow} \otimes \mathit{id}{\leftrightarrow} \Leftrightarrow \mathit{id}{\leftrightarrow}$$

$$(a_1 \odot a_3) \oplus (a_2 \odot a_4) \Leftrightarrow (a_1 \oplus a_2) \odot (a_3 \oplus a_4)$$

$$(a_1 \odot a_3) \otimes (a_2 \odot a_4) \Leftrightarrow (a_1 \otimes a_2) \odot (a_3 \otimes a_4)$$

Fig. 8. Signatures of level-1 Π-combinators: functors

in Agda's standard library (in Data.Sum.Properties to be precise), whereas all properties involving only $\oplus$ were immediately provable due to η expansion. Nevertheless, for symmetry and clarity, we created a module Data.Prod.Properties to collect all of these. None of the mixed properties involved with distributivity and absorption were present, although the proofs for all of them were straightforward. Their statement, on the other hand, was at times rather complex (see Data.SumProd.Properties).

6.3 Example Level-1 Programs

A pleasant outcome of having the level-1 terms is that they also give rise to an interesting programming language which, in our context, can be viewed as a language for expressing transformations and optimizations of boolean circuits. We illustrate the idea with a few small examples.

Figures 3, 4, 5, 6, 7, 8, 9, 10, 11 and 12 contain rules to manipulate well-typed code fragments by rewriting them in a small-step fashion. In their textual form, the rules are certainly not intuitive. They however become "evidently correct" transformations on circuits when viewed diagrammatically. As an example, consider two arbitrary Π-combinators representing circuits of the given types:

$$\mathsf{c}_1 : \{B\ C : \mathsf{U}\} \rightarrow\ B \leftrightarrow C$$
$$\mathsf{c}_2 : \{A\ D : \mathsf{U}\} \rightarrow\ A \leftrightarrow D$$

Now consider the circuits p_1 and p_2 which use c_1 and c_2 as shown below:

$$\mathsf{p}_1\ \mathsf{p}_2 : \{\ A\ B\ C\ D : \mathsf{U}\ \} \rightarrow \mathsf{PLUS}\ A\ B \leftrightarrow \mathsf{PLUS}\ C\ D$$
$$\mathsf{p}_1 = \mathsf{swap}_+ \odot (\ \mathsf{c}_1 \oplus \mathsf{c}_2\ )$$
$$\mathsf{p}_2 = (\ \mathsf{c}_2 \oplus \mathsf{c}_1\ ) \odot \mathsf{swap}_+$$

As reversible circuits, p_1 and p_2 evaluate as follows. If p_1 is given the value $\mathsf{inl}\ a$, it first transforms it to $\mathsf{inr}\ a$, and then passes it to c_2. If p_2 is given the value $\mathsf{inl}\ a$, it first passes it to c_2 and then flips the tag of the result. Since c_2 is functorial, it must act polymorphically on its input and hence the two evaluations must produce the same result. The situation for the other possible input value is symmetric. This extensional reasoning is embedded once and for all in the proofs of coherence and distilled in a level-1 combinator (see the first combinator in Fig. 7):

$$\begin{aligned}\mathsf{swapl}_+\!\Leftrightarrow : \{t_1\ t_2\ t_3\ t_4 : \mathsf{U}\}\ \{c_1 : t_1 \leftrightarrow t_2\}\ \{c_2 : t_3 \leftrightarrow t_4\} \rightarrow \\ (\mathsf{swap}_+ \odot (c_1 \oplus c_2)) \Leftrightarrow ((c_2 \oplus c_1) \odot \mathsf{swap}_+)\end{aligned}$$

Categorically speaking, this combinator expresses exactly that the braiding $\sigma_{A,B}$ is a natural transformation, in other words that $\sigma_{A,B}$ must commute with $\oplus$. Pictorially, $\mathsf{swapl}_+\!\Leftrightarrow$ is a 2-path showing how the two programs can be transformed to one another. This can be visualized by imagining the connections as wires whose endpoints are fixed: holding the wires on the right side of the top path and flipping them produces the connection in the bottom path:

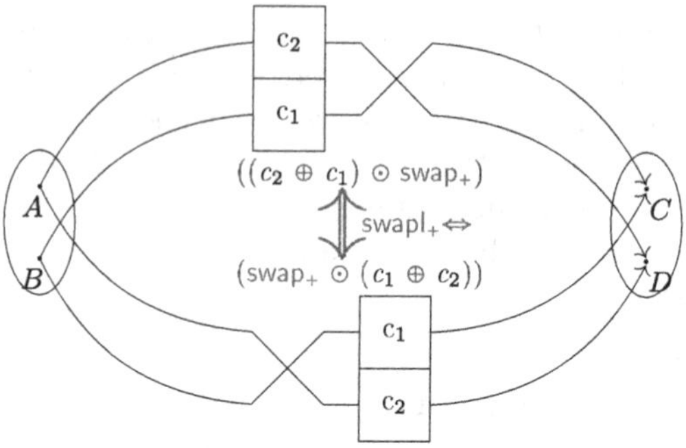

The fact that the current syntax is far from intuitive suggests that it might be critical to have either a diagrammatic interface similar to Quantomatic [8] (which only works for traced symmetric monoidal categories) or a radically different syntactic notation such as Penrose's abstract tensor notation [23,24].

$$\begin{aligned} unite_{+}r \oplus id\!\leftrightarrow &\Leftrightarrow assocr_{+} \odot (id\!\leftrightarrow \oplus\, unite_{+}l) \\ unite_{*}r \otimes id\!\leftrightarrow &\Leftrightarrow assocr_{*} \odot (id\!\leftrightarrow \otimes\, unite_{*}l) \end{aligned}$$

Fig. 9. Signatures of level-1 Π-combinators: unit and associativity

Let $c : t_1 \leftrightarrow t_2$:

$$(c \otimes id\!\leftrightarrow) \odot absorbl \Leftrightarrow absorbl \odot id\!\leftrightarrow \qquad (id\!\leftrightarrow \otimes c) \odot absorbr \Leftrightarrow absorbr \odot id\!\leftrightarrow$$

$$id\!\leftrightarrow \odot factorzl \Leftrightarrow factorzl \odot (id\!\leftrightarrow \otimes c) \qquad id\!\leftrightarrow \odot factorzr \Leftrightarrow factorzr \odot (c \otimes id\!\leftrightarrow)$$

$$absorbr \Leftrightarrow absorbl$$

$$absorbr \Leftrightarrow (distl \odot (absorbr \oplus absorbr)) \odot unite_{+}l$$

$$unite_{*}r \Leftrightarrow absorbr \qquad absorbl \Leftrightarrow swap_{*} \odot absorbr$$

$$absorbr \Leftrightarrow (assocl_{*} \odot (absorbr \otimes id\!\leftrightarrow)) \odot absorbr$$

$$(id\!\leftrightarrow \otimes absorbr) \odot absorbl \Leftrightarrow (assocl_{*} \odot (absorbl \otimes id\!\leftrightarrow)) \odot absorbr$$

$$id\!\leftrightarrow \otimes\, unite_{+}l \Leftrightarrow (distl \odot (absorbl \oplus id\!\leftrightarrow)) \odot unite_{+}l$$

Fig. 10. Signatures of level-1 Π-combinators: zero

$$((assocl_{+} \otimes id\!\leftrightarrow) \odot dist) \odot (dist \oplus id\!\leftrightarrow) \Leftrightarrow (dist \odot (id\!\leftrightarrow \oplus dist)) \odot assocl_{+}$$

$$assocl_{*} \odot distl \Leftrightarrow ((id\!\leftrightarrow \otimes distl) \odot distl) \odot (assocl_{*} \oplus assocl_{*})$$

$$\begin{aligned} (distl \odot (dist \oplus dist)) \odot assocl_{+} \Leftrightarrow\ & dist \odot (distl \oplus distl) \odot assocl_{+} \odot \\ & (assocr_{+} \oplus id\!\leftrightarrow) \odot \\ & ((id\!\leftrightarrow \oplus swap_{+}) \oplus id\!\leftrightarrow) \odot \\ & (assocl_{+} \oplus id\!\leftrightarrow) \end{aligned}$$

Fig. 11. Signatures of level-1 Π-combinators: associativity and distributivity

$$(id\leftrightarrow \otimes swap_+) \odot distl \Leftrightarrow distl \odot swap_+$$
$$dist \odot (swap_* \oplus swap_*) \Leftrightarrow swap_* \odot distl$$

Fig. 12. Signatures of level-1 Π-combinators: commutativity and distributivity

We conclude this section with a small but complete example showing how to prove the equivalence of two circuits implementing boolean negation. The first circuit uses the direct realization of boolean negation:

```
NOT1 : BOOL ↔ BOOL
NOT1 = Pi0.swap+
```

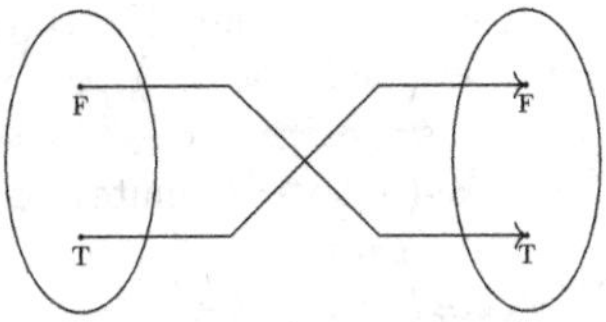

The second circuit is more convoluted:

```
NOT2 : BOOL ↔ BOOL
NOT2 =
  uniti⋆l ⊙
  Pi0.swap⋆ ⊙
  (Pi0.swap+ ⊗ id↔) ⊙
  Pi0.swap⋆ ⊙
  unite⋆l
```

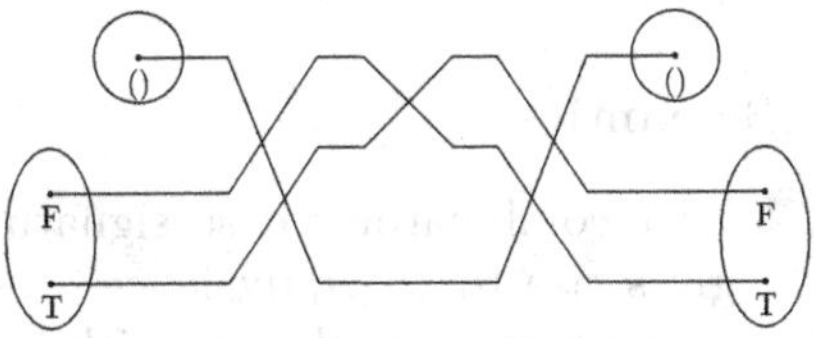

Here is a complete proof in level-1 Π using the small-step rewriting style that shows that the two circuits are equivalent. The proofs uses the names of the level-1 combinators from the accompanying code.

```
negEx : NOT2 ⇔ NOT1
negEx = uniti⋆l ⊙ (Pi0.swap⋆ ⊙ ((Pi0.swap+ ⊗ id↔) ⊙ (Pi0.swap⋆ ⊙ unite⋆l)))
    ⇔⟨ id⇔ ⊡ assoc⊙l ⟩
  uniti⋆l ⊙ ((Pi0.swap⋆ ⊙ (Pi0.swap+ ⊗ id↔)) ⊙ (Pi0.swap⋆ ⊙ unite⋆l))
    ⇔⟨ id⇔ ⊡ (swapl⋆⇔ ⊡ id⇔) ⟩
  uniti⋆l ⊙ (((id↔ ⊗ Pi0.swap+) ⊙ Pi0.swap⋆) ⊙ (Pi0.swap⋆ ⊙ unite⋆l))
    ⇔⟨ id⇔ ⊡ assoc⊙r ⟩
  uniti⋆l ⊙ ((id↔ ⊗ Pi0.swap+) ⊙ (Pi0.swap⋆ ⊙ (Pi0.swap⋆ ⊙ unite⋆l)))
    ⇔⟨ id⇔ ⊡ (id⇔ ⊡ assoc⊙l) ⟩
  uniti⋆l ⊙ ((id↔ ⊗ Pi0.swap+) ⊙ ((Pi0.swap⋆ ⊙ Pi0.swap⋆) ⊙ unite⋆l))
    ⇔⟨ id⇔ ⊡ (id⇔ ⊡ (linv⊙l ⊡ id⇔)) ⟩
  uniti⋆l ⊙ ((id↔ ⊗ Pi0.swap+) ⊙ (id↔ ⊙ unite⋆l))
    ⇔⟨ id⇔ ⊡ (id⇔ ⊡ idl⊙l) ⟩
  uniti⋆l ⊙ ((id↔ ⊗ Pi0.swap+) ⊙ unite⋆l)
    ⇔⟨ assoc⊙l ⟩
  (uniti⋆l ⊙ (id↔ ⊗ Pi0.swap+)) ⊙ unite⋆l
    ⇔⟨ unitil⋆⇔l ⊡ id⇔ ⟩
  (Pi0.swap+ ⊙ uniti⋆l) ⊙ unite⋆l
    ⇔⟨ assoc⊙r ⟩
  Pi0.swap+ ⊙ (uniti⋆l ⊙ unite⋆l)
    ⇔⟨ id⇔ ⊡ linv⊙l ⟩
  Pi0.swap+ ⊙ id↔
    ⇔⟨ idr⊙l ⟩
  Pi0.swap+ □
```

6.4 Example Level-1 Proof

In addition to proving circuit optimizations, we can also prove equivalences of semiring proofs. As discussed in Sect. 2.3, we expect pf₃π and pf₄π to be equivalent proofs. The following derivation shows the derivation using level-1 combinators:

```
pfEx : {A B : U} → pf₃π {A} {B} ⇔ pf₄π {A} {B}
pfEx {A} {B} =
  (Pi0.swap₊ ⊕ id↔) ⊙ (unite₊l ⊕ id↔)
    ⇔⟨ hom⊙⊕⇔ ⟩
  (Pi0.swap₊ ⊙ unite₊l) ⊕ (id↔ ⊙ id↔)
    ⇔⟨ resp⊕⇔  unite₊r-coh-r idl⊙l ⟩
  unite₊r ⊕ id↔
    ⇔⟨ triangle⊕l ⟩
  Pi0.assocr₊ ⊙ (id↔ ⊕ unite₊l) □
```

6.5 Semantics

Each level-1 combinator whose signature is in Figs. 3, 4, 5, 6, 7, 8, 9, 10, 11 and 12 gives rise to an equivalence of equivalences of types. Furthermore, the level-1 combinators are coherent with respect to the level-0 semantics. Formally, in Agda, we have:

```
cc2equiv :  {t₁ t₂ : U} {c₁ c₂ : t₁ ↔ t₂} (ce : c₁ ⇔ c₂) →
            PiEquiv.c2equiv c₁ ≋ PiEquiv.c2equiv c₂
```

In other words, equivalent programs exactly denote equivalent equivalences.

This is all compatible with the operational semantics as well, so that equivalent programs always give the same values; more amusingly, if we run one program then run an equivalent program backwards, we get the identity:

```
≋⇒≡ : {t₁ t₂ : U} (c₁ c₂ : t₁ ↔ t₂) (e : c₁ ⇔ c₂) → eval c₁ ∼ eval c₂
ping-pong : {t₁ t₂ : U} (c₁ c₂ : t₁ ↔ t₂) (e : c₁ ⇔ c₂) → (evalB c₂ ∘ eval c₁) ∼ id
```

It should be stressed that c_1 and c_2 can be arbitrarily complex programs (albeit equivalent), and still the above optimization property holds. So we have the promise of a very effective optimizer for such programs.

The next theorem is both trivial (as it holds by construction), and central to the correspondence: we distilled the level-1 combinators to make its proof trivial. It shows that the two levels of Π form a symmetric rig groupoid, thus capturing equivalences of types at level-0, and equivalences of equivalences at level-1.

Theorem 3. *The universe U and Π terms and combinators form a symmetric rig groupoid.*

Proof. The objects of the category are the syntax of finite types, and the morphisms are the Π terms and combinators. Short proofs establish that these morphisms satisfy the axioms stated in the definitions of the various categories. The bulk of the work is in ensuring that the coherence conditions are satisfied. As explained earlier in this section, this required us to add a few additional level-0 Π combinators and then to add a whole new layer of level-1 combinators witnessing enough equivalences of level-0 Π combinators to satisfy the coherence laws (see Figs. 3, 4, 5, 6, 7, 8, 9, 10, 11 and 12).

7 Conclusion

The traditional Curry-Howard correspondence is based on "mere logic (to use the HoTT terminology)." That is, it is based around *proof inhabitation*: two types, like two propositions, are regarded as "the same" when one is inhabited if and only if the other is. In that sense, the propositions A and $A \wedge A$, are indeed the same, as are the types T and $T \times T$. This is all centered around proof irrelevant mathematics.

What we have shown is that if we shift to proof relevant mathematics, computationally relevant equivalences, explicit homotopies, and algebra, something quite new emerges: an actual isomorphism between proof terms and reversible computations. Furthermore, what algebraic structure to use is not mysterious: it is exactly the algebraic structure of the semantics. In the case of finite types (with sums and products), this turns out to be commutative semirings.

But the Curry-Howard correspondence promises more: that proof transformations correspond to program transformations. In a proof irrelevant setting, this is rather awkward; similarly, in a extensional setting, program equivalence is a rather coarse concept. But, in our setting, both of these issues disappear. The key to proceed was to realize that there exist combinators which make equivalences look like a semiring, but do not actually have a semiring structure. The next insight is to "remember" that a monoidal category is really a model of a *typed monoid*; in a way, a monoidal category is a *categorified* monoid. So what we needed was a categorified version of commutative semirings. Luckily, this had already been done, in the form of Rig categories. Modifying this to have a weaker notion of equivalence and having all morphisms invertible was quite straightforward.

Again, being proof relevant mattered: it quickly became apparent that the *coherence laws* involved in weak Rig Groupoids were *exactly* the program equivalences that were needed. So rather than fumbling around finding various equivalences and hoping to stumble on enough of them to be complete, a systematic design emerged: given a 1-algebra of types parametrized by an equivalence $\simeq$, one should seek a 2-algebra (aka typed algebra, aka categorification of the given 1-algebra) that corresponds to it. The coherence laws then emerge as a complete set of program transformations. This, of course, clearly points the way to further generalizations.

The correspondence between rigs and types established in the paper provides a semantically well-founded approach to the representation, manipulation, and optimization of reversible circuits with the following main ingredients:

- reversible circuits are represented as terms witnessing morphisms between finite types in a symmetric rig groupoid;

- the term language for reversible circuits is universal; it could be used as a standalone point-free programming language or as a target for a higher-level language with a more conventional syntax;
- the symmetric rig groupoid structure ensures that programs can be combined using sums and products satisfying the familiar laws of these operations;
- the *weak* versions of the categories give us a second level of morphisms that relate programs to equivalent programs and is exactly captured in the coherence conditions of the categories; this level of morphisms also comes equipped with sums and products with the familiar laws and the coherence conditions capture how these operations interact with sequential composition;
- a sound and complete optimizer for reversible circuits can be represented as terms that rewrite programs in small steps witnessing this second level of morphisms.

From a much more general perspective, our result can be viewed as part of a larger programme aiming at a better integration of several disciplines most notably computation, topology, and physics. Computer science has traditionally been founded on models such as the λ-calculus which are at odds with the increasingly relevant physical principle of conservation of information as well as the recent foundational proposal of HoTT that identifies equivalences (i.e., reversible, information-preserving, functions) as a primary notion of interest.[3] Currently, these reversible functions are a secondary notion defined with reference to the full λ-calculus in what appears to be a detour. In more detail, current constructions start with the class of all functions $A \to B$, then introduce constraints to filter those functions which correspond to type equivalences $A \simeq B$, and then attempt to look for a convenient computational framework for effective programming with type equivalences. As we have shown, in the case of finite types, this is just convoluted since the collection of functions corresponding to type equivalences is the collection of isomorphisms between finite types and these isomorphisms can be inductively defined, giving rise to a well-behaved programming language and its optimizer.

More generally, reversible computational models — in which all functions have inverses — are known to be universal computational models [4] and more importantly they can be defined without any reference to irreversible functions, which ironically become the derived notion [17]. It is, therefore, at least plausible that a variant of HoTT based exclusively on reversible functions that directly correspond to equivalences would have better computational properties. Our current result is a step, albeit preliminary, in that direction as it only applies to finite types. However, it is plausible that this categorification approach can be generalized to accommodate higher-order functions. The intuitive idea is that our current development based on the categorification of the commutative semiring of the natural numbers might be generalizable to the categorification of the ring of integers or even to the categorification of the field of rational numbers. The

[3] The λ-calculus is not even suitable for keeping track of computational resources; linear logic [16] is a much better framework for that purpose but it does not go far enough as it only tracks "multiplicative resources" [31].

generalization to rings would introduce *negative types* and the generalization to fields would further introduce *fractional types*. It is even possible to conceive of more exotic types such as types with square roots and imaginary numbers by further generalizing the work to the field of *algebraic numbers*. These types have been shown to make sense in computations involving recursive datatypes such as trees that can be viewed as solutions to polynomials over type variables [5,12,13].

Acknowledgement. We would like sincerely thank the reviewers for their excellent and detailed comments. This material is based upon work supported by the National Science Foundation under Grant No. 1217454.

References

1. Baez, J., Stay, M.: Physics, topology, logic and computation: a Rosetta stone. arXiv:0903.0340 [quant-ph] (2009)
2. Baez, J.C., Dolan, J.: Categorification. In: Proceedings of Higher Category Theory, Contemporary Mathematics, vol. 230, pp. 1–36 (1998)
3. Beke, T.: Categorification, term rewriting and the Knuth-Bendix procedure. J. Pure Appl. Algebra **215**(5), 728–740 (2011)
4. Bennett, C.H.: Logical reversibility of computation. IBM J. Res. Dev. **17**, 525–532 (1973)
5. Blass, A.: Seven trees in one. J. Pure Appl. Algebra **103**, 1–21 (1995)
6. Bowman, W.J., James, R.P., Sabry, A.: Dagger traced symmetric monoidal categories and reversible programming. In: RC (2011)
7. DeBenedictis, E.P.: Reversible logic for supercomputing. In: Proceedings of the 2nd Conference on Computing Frontiers, CF 2005, pp. 391–402. ACM, New York (2005)
8. Dixon, L., Kissinger, A.: Open graphs and monoidal theories. arXiv:1011.4114 (2010)
9. Dosen, K., Petric, Z.: Proof-Theoretical Coherence. KCL Publications (College Publications), London (2004). http://www.mi.sanu.ac.yu/~kosta/coh.pdf
10. Feynman, R.: Simulating physics with computers. Int. J. Theoret. Phys. **21**, 467–488 (1982)
11. Fiore, M.P., di Cosmo, R., Balat, V.: Remarks on isomorphisms in typed calculi with empty and sum types. Ann. Pure Appl. Logic **141**(1–2), 35–50 (2006)
12. Fiore, M.: Isomorphisms of generic recursive polynomial types. In: POPL, pp. 77–88. ACM (2004)
13. Fiore, M., Leinster, T.: An objective representation of the Gaussian integers. J. Symbolic Comput. **37**(6), 707–716 (2004)
14. Frank, M.P.: Reversibility for efficient computing. Ph.D. thesis, Massachusetts Institute of Technology (1999)
15. Fredkin, E., Toffoli, T.: Conservative logic. Int. J. Theoret. Phys. **21**(3), 219–253 (1982)
16. Girard, J.-Y.: Linear logic. Theoret. Comput. Sci. **50**, 1–102 (1987)
17. Green, A.S., Altenkirch, T.: From reversible to irreversible computations. Electron. Notes Theoret. Comput. Sci. **210**, 65–74 (2008)
18. Hasegawa, M.: Recursion from cyclic sharing: traced monoidal categories and models of cyclic lambda calculi. In: TLCA, pp. 196–213 (1997)

19. Saiful Islam, Md.: A novel quantum cost efficient reversible full adder gate in nanotechnology. arXiv:1008.3533 (2010)
20. James, R.P., Sabry, A.: Information effects. In: POPL, pp. 73–84. ACM (2012)
21. James, R.P., Sabry, A.: Isomorphic interpreters from logically reversible abstract machines. In: RC (2012)
22. James, R.P., Sabry, A.: Theseus: a high-level language for reversible computation. In: Reversible Computation, Booklet of work-in-progress and short reports (2014)
23. Kissinger, A.: Abstract tensor systems as monoidal categories. arXiv:1308.3586 (2013)
24. Kissinger, A., Quick, D.: Tensors, !-graphs, and non-commutative quantum structures. arXiv:1412.8552 (2014)
25. Landauer, R.: Irreversibility and heat generation in the computing process. IBM J. Res. Dev. **5**, 183–191 (1961)
26. Laplaza, M.L.: Coherence for distributivity. In: Kelly, G.M., Laplaza, M., Lewis, G., Lane, S.M. (eds.) Coherence in Categories. LNM, vol. 281, pp. 29–65. Springer, Berlin (1972)
27. Mac Lane, S.: Categories for the Working Mathematician. Springer, New York (1971)
28. nLab: rig category (2015). http://ncatlab.org/nlab/show/rig+category
29. Peres, A.: Reversible logic and quantum computers. Phys. Rev. A **32**(6), 3266 (1985)
30. Rittri, M.: Using types as search keys in function libraries. In: FPCA (1989)
31. Sparks, Z., Sabry, A.: Superstructural reversible logic. In: 3rd International Workshop on Linearity (2014)
32. Toffoli, T.: Reversible computing. In: de Bakker, J., van Leeuwen, J. (eds.) Automata, Languages and Programming. LNCS, vol. 85, pp. 632–644. Springer, Heidelberg (1980)
33. Univalent Foundations Program: Homotopy Type Theory: Univalent Foundations of Mathematics. Princeton, Institute for Advanced Study (2013)

On Hierarchical Communication Topologies in the π-calculus

Emanuele D'Osualdo[1](✉) and C.-H. Luke Ong[2]

[1] TU Kaiserslautern, Kaiserslautern, Germany
dosualdo@cs.uni-kl.de
[2] University of Oxford, Oxford, UK
lo@cs.ox.ac.uk

Abstract. This paper is concerned with the shape invariants satisfied by the communication topology of π-terms, and the automatic inference of these invariants. A π-term P is *hierarchical* if there is a finite forest $\mathcal{T}$ such that the communication topology of every term reachable from P satisfies a $\mathcal{T}$-shaped invariant. We design a static analysis to prove a term hierarchical by means of a novel type system that enjoys decidable inference. The soundness proof of the type system employs a non-standard view of π-calculus reactions. The coverability problem for hierarchical terms is decidable. This is proved by showing that every hierarchical term is depth-bounded, an undecidable property known in the literature. We thus obtain an expressive static fragment of the π-calculus with decidable safety verification problems.

1 Introduction

Concurrency is pervasive in computing. A standard approach is to organise concurrent software systems as a dynamic collection of processes that communicate by message passing. Because processes may be destroyed or created, the number of processes in the system changes in the course of the computation, and may be unbounded. Moreover the messages that are exchanged may contain process addresses. Consequently the *communication topology* of the system—the hypergraph [19,20] connecting processes that can communicate directly—evolves over time. In particular, the connectivity of a process (i.e. its neighbourhood in this hypergraph) can change dynamically. The design and analysis of these systems is difficult: the dynamic reconfigurability alone renders verification problems undecidable. This paper is concerned with *hierarchical systems*, a new subclass of concurrent message-passing systems that enjoys decidability of safety verification problems, thanks to a shape constraint on the communication topology.

The π-calculus of Milner, Parrow and Walker [20] is a process calculus designed to model systems with a dynamic communication topology. In the π-calculus, processes can be spawned dynamically, and they communicate by exchanging messages along synchronous channels. Furthermore channel names can themselves be created dynamically, and passed as messages, a salient feature known as *mobility*, as this enables processes to modify their neighbourhood at runtime.

P. Thiemann (Ed.): ESOP 2016, LNCS 9632, pp. 149–175, 2016.
DOI: 10.1007/978-3-662-49498-1_7

It is well known that the π-calculus is a Turing-complete model of computation. Verification problems on π-terms are therefore undecidable in general. There are however useful fragments of the calculus that support automatic verification. The most expressive such fragment known to date is the *depth-bounded* π-calculus of Meyer [13]. Depth boundedness is a constraint on the shape of communication topologies. A π-term is *depth-bounded* if there is a number k such that every simple path[1] in the communication topology of every reachable π-term has length bounded by k. Meyer [15] proved that termination and coverability (a class of safety properties) are decidable for depth-bounded terms.

Unfortunately depth boundedness itself is an undecidable property [15], which is a serious impediment to the practical application of the depth-bounded fragment to verification. This paper offers a two-step approach to this problem. First we identify a (still undecidable) subclass of depth-bounded systems, called *hierarchical*, by a shape constraint on communication topologies (as opposed to numeric, as in the case of depth-boundedness). Secondly, by exploiting this richer structure, we define a type system, which in turn gives a *static* characterisation of an expressive and practically relevant fragment of the depth-bounded π-calculus.

Example 1 (Client-server pattern). To illustrate our approach, consider a simple system implementing a client-server pattern. A server S is a process listening on a channel s which acts as its address. A client C knows the address of a server and has a private channel c that represents its identity. When the client wants to communicate with the server, it asynchronously sends c along the channel s. Upon receipt of the message, the server acquires knowledge of (the address of) the requesting client; and spawns a process A to answer the client's request R asynchronously; the answer consists of a new piece of data, represented by a new name d, sent along the channel c. Then the server forgets the identity of the client and reverts to listening for new requests. Since only the requesting client knows c at this point, the server's answer can only be received by the correct client. Figure 1a shows the communication topology of a server and a client, in the three phases of the protocol.

The overall system is composed of an unbounded number of servers and clients, constructed according to the above protocol. The topology of a reachable configuration is depicted in Fig. 1b. While in general the topology of a mobile system can become arbitrarily complex, for such common patterns as client-server, the programmer often has a clear idea of the desired shape of the communication topology: there will be a number of servers, each with its cluster of clients; each client may in turn be waiting to receive a number of private replies. This suggests a hierarchical relationship between the names representing servers, clients and data, although the communication topology itself does not form a tree.

$\mathcal{T}$-compatibility and Hierarchical Terms. Recall that in the π-calculus there is an important relation between terms, $\equiv$, called *structural congruence*,

[1] A simple path is a path with no repeating edges.

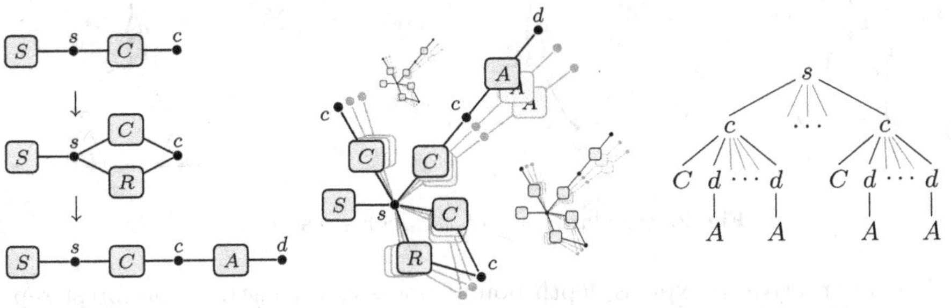

(a) the protocol (b) a reachable configuration (c) forest representation

Fig. 1. Evolution of the communication topology of a server interacting with a client. R represents a client's pending request and A a server's pending answer.

which equates terms that differ only in irrelevant presentation details, but not in behaviour. For instance, the structural congruence laws for restriction tell us that the order of restrictions is irrelevant—$\nu x.\,\nu y.P \equiv \nu y.\,\nu x.P$—and that the scope of a restriction can be extended to processes that do not refer to the restricted name—i.e., $(\nu x.P) \parallel Q \equiv \nu x.(P \parallel Q)$ when x does not occur free in Q—without altering the meaning of the term. The former law is called *exchange*, the latter is called *scope extrusion*.

Our first contribution is a formalisation in the π-calculus of the intuitive notion of hierarchy illustrated in Example 1. We shall often speak of the *forest representation* of a π-term P, forest(P), which is a version of the abstract syntax tree of P that captures the nesting relationship between the active restrictions of the term. (A restriction of a π-term is *active* if it is not in the scope of a prefix.) Thus the internal nodes of a forest representation are labelled with (active) restriction names, and its leaf nodes are labelled with the sequential subterms. Given a π-term P, we are interested in not just forest(P), but also forest(P') where P' ranges over the structural congruents of P, because these are all behaviourally equivalent representations. See Fig. 4 for an example of the respective forest representations of the structural congruents of a term. In our setting a hierarchy $\mathcal{T}$ is a *finite* forest of what we call *base types*. Given a finite forest $\mathcal{T}$, we say that a term P is *$\mathcal{T}$-compatible* if there is a term P', which is structurally congruent to P, such that the parent relation of forest(P') is consistent with the partial order of $\mathcal{T}$.

In Example 1 we would introduce base types srv, cl and data associated with the restrictions νs, νc and νd respectively, and we would like the system to be compatible to the hierarchy $\mathcal{T} = \mathsf{srv} \prec \mathsf{cl} \prec \mathsf{data}$, where $\prec$ is the is-parent-of relation. That is, we must be able to represent a configuration with a forest that, for instance, does not place a server name below a client name nor a client name below another client name. Such a representation is shown in Fig. 1c.

In the Example, we want every reachable configuration of the system to be compatible with the hierarchy. We say that a π-term P is *hierarchical* if there is a hierarchy $\mathcal{T}$ such that every term reachable from P is $\mathcal{T}$-compatible. Thus the hierarchy $\mathcal{T}$ is a shape invariant of the communication topology under reduction.

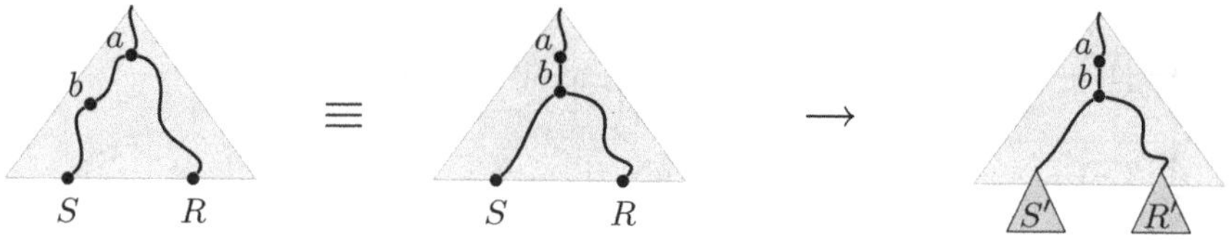

Fig. 2. Standard view of π-calculus reactions

It is instructive to express depth boundedness as a constraint on forest representation: a term P is depth-bounded if there is a constant k such that every term reachable from P has a structurally congruent P' whereby forest(P') has height bounded by k. It is straightforward to see that hierarchical terms are depth-bounded; the converse is however not true.

A Type System for Hierarchical Terms. While membership of the hierarchical fragment is undecidable, by exploiting the forest structure, we have devised a novel type system that guarantees the invariance of $\mathcal{T}$-compatibility under reduction. Furthermore type inference is decidable, so that the type system can be used to infer a hierarchy $\mathcal{T}$ with respect to which the input term is hierarchical. To the best of our knowledge, our type system is the first that can infer a shape invariant of the communication topology of a system.

The typing rules that ensure invariance of $\mathcal{T}$-compatibility under reduction arise from a new perspective of the π-calculus reaction, one that allows compatibility to a given hierarchy to be tracked more readily. Suppose we are presented with a $\mathcal{T}$-compatible term $P = C[S, R]$ where $C[\text{-},\text{-}]$ is the *reaction context*, and the two processes $S = \overline{a}\langle b\rangle.S'$ and $R = a(x).R'$ are ready to communicate over a channel a. After sending the message b, S continues as the process S', while upon receipt of b, R binds x to b and continues as $R'' = R'[b/x]$. Schematically, the traditional understanding of this transaction is: first extrude the scope of b to include R, then let them react, as shown in Fig. 2.

Instead, we seek to implement the reaction *without scope extrusion*: after the message is transmitted, the sender continues in-place as S', while R'' is split in two parts $R'_{\mathrm{mig}} \parallel R'_{\neg\mathrm{mig}}$, one that uses the message (the *migratable* part) and one that does not. As shown in Fig. 3, the migratable part of R'', R'_{mig}, is "installed" under b so that it can make use of the acquired name, while the non-migratable one, $R'_{\neg\mathrm{mig}}$, can simply continue in-place.

Crucially, the *reaction context*, $C[\text{-},\text{-}]$, is left unchanged. This means that if the starting term is $\mathcal{T}$-compatible, the reaction context of the *reactum* is $\mathcal{T}$-compatible as well. We can then focus on imposing constraints on the use of names of R' so that the migration does not result in R'_{mig} escaping the scope of previously bound names.

By using these ideas, our type system is able to statically accept π-calculus encodings of such system as that discussed in Example 1. The type system can be used, not just to *check* that a given $\mathcal{T}$ is respected by the behaviour of a term, but also to *infer* a suitable $\mathcal{T}$ when it exists. Once typability of a term

Fig. 3. $\mathcal{T}$-compatibility preserving reaction

is established, safety properties such as unreachability of error states, mutual exclusion or bounds on mailboxes, can be verified algorithmically. For instance, in Example 1, a coverability check can prove that each client can have at most one reply pending in its mailbox. To prove such a property, one needs to construct an argument that reasons about dynamically created names with a high degree of precision. This is something that counter abstraction and uniform abstractions based methods have great difficulty attaining.

Our type system is (necessarily) incomplete in that there are depth-bounded, or even hierarchical, systems that cannot be typed. The class of π-terms that can be typed is non-trivial, and includes terms which generate an unbounded number of names and exhibit mobility.

Outline. In Sect. 2 we review the π-calculus, depth-bounded terms, and related technical preliminaries. In Sect. 3 we introduce $\mathcal{T}$-compatibility and the hierarchical terms. We present our type system in Sect. 4. Section 5 discusses soundness of the type system. In Sect. 6 we give a type inference algorithm; and in Sect. 7 we present results on expressivity and discuss applications. We conclude with related and future work in Sects. 8 and 9. All missing definitions and proofs can be found in [5].

2 The π-calculus and the Depth-Bounded Fragment

2.1 Syntax and Semantics

We use a π-calculus with guarded replication to express recursion [17]. Fix a universe $\mathcal{N}$ of *names* representing channels and messages. The syntax is defined by the grammar:

$$
\begin{array}{rll}
\mathcal{P} \ni P, Q ::= \mathbf{0} \mid \nu x.P \mid P_1 \parallel P_2 \mid M \mid !M & \text{process} \\
M ::= M + M \mid \pi.P & \text{choice} \\
\pi ::= a(x) \mid \overline{a}\langle b \rangle \mid \tau & \text{prefix}
\end{array}
$$

Definition 1. *Structural congruence, $\equiv$, is the least relation that respects α-conversion of bound names, and is associative and commutative with respect* *to + (choice) and $\|$ (parallel composition) with* $\mathbf{0}$ *as the neutral element, and satisfies laws for restriction:* $\nu a.\mathbf{0} \equiv \mathbf{0}$ *and* $\nu a.\nu b.P \equiv \nu b.\nu a.P$*, and*

$$!P \equiv P \parallel !P \qquad \text{Replication}$$

$$P \parallel \nu a.Q \equiv \nu a.(P \parallel Q) \quad (\text{if } a \notin \text{fn}(P)) \qquad \text{Scope Extrusion}$$

In $P = \pi.Q$, we call Q the *continuation* of P and will often omit Q altogether when $Q = \mathbf{0}$. In a term $\nu x.P$ we will occasionally refer to P as the *scope* of x. The name x is bound in both $\nu x.P$, and in $a(x).P$. We will write $\text{fn}(P)$, $\text{bn}(P)$ and $\text{bn}_\nu(P)$ for the set of free, bound and restriction-bound names in P, respectively. A sub-term is *active* if it is not under a prefix. A name is active when it is bound by an active restriction. We write $\text{act}_\nu(P)$ for the set of active names of P. Terms of the form M and $!M$ are called *sequential*. We write $\mathcal{S}$ for the set of sequential terms, $\text{act}_\mathcal{S}(P)$ for the set of active sequential processes of P, and P^i for the parallel composition of i copies of P.

Intuitively, a sequential process acts like a thread running finite-control sequential code. A term $\boldsymbol{\tau}.(P \parallel Q)$ is the equivalent of spawning a process Q and continuing as P—although in this context the rôles of P and Q are interchangeable. Interaction is by *synchronous* communication over channels. An *input prefix* $a(x)$ is a blocking receive on the channel a binding the variable x to the message. An *output prefix* $\overline{a}\langle b\rangle$ is a blocking send of the message b along the channel a; here b is itself the name of a channel that can be used subsequently for further communication: an essential feature for mobility. A non-blocking send can be simulated by spawning a new process doing a blocking send. Restrictions are used to make a channel name private. A replication $!(\pi.P)$ can be understood as having a server that can spawn a new copy of P whenever a process tries to communicate with it. In other words it behaves like an infinite parallel composition $(\pi.P \parallel \pi.P \parallel \cdots)$.

For conciseness, we assume channels are unary (the extension to the polyadic case is straightforward). In contrast to process calculi without mobility, replication and systems of tail recursive equations are equivalent methods of defining recursive processes in the π-calculus [18, Sect. 3.1].

We rely on the following mild assumption, that the choice of names is unambiguous, especially when selecting a representative for a congruence class:

Name Uniqueness Assumption. *Each name in* P *is bound at most once and* $\text{fn}(P) \cap \text{bn}(P) = \emptyset$.

Normal Form. The notion of hierarchy, which is central to this paper, and the associated type system depend heavily on structural congruence. These are criteria that, given a structure on names, require the existence of a specific representative of the structural congruence class exhibiting certain properties. However, we cannot assume the input term is presented as that representative; even worse, when the structure on names is not fixed (for example, when inferring types) we cannot fix a representative and be sure that it will witness the desired properties. Thus, in both the semantics and the type system, we manipulate a neutral type of representative called *normal form*, which is a variant of the *standard form* [20].

In this way we are not distracted by the particular syntactic representation we are presented with.

We say that a term P is in *normal form* ($P \in \mathcal{P}_{\mathsf{nf}}$) if it is in standard form and each of its inactive subterms is also in normal form. Formally, normal forms are defined by the grammar

$$\mathcal{P}_{\mathsf{nf}} \ni N ::= \nu x_1.\cdots \nu x_n.(A_1 \parallel \cdots \parallel A_m)$$
$$A ::= \pi_1.N_1 + \cdots + \pi_n.N_n \mid !(\pi_1.N_1 + \cdots + \pi_n.N_n)$$

where the sequences $x_1 \dots x_n$ and $A_1 \dots A_m$ may be empty; when they are both empty the normal form is the term $\mathbf{0}$. We further assume w.l.o.g. that normal forms satisfy Name Uniqueness. Given a finite set of indexes $I = \{i_1, \dots, i_n\}$ we write $\prod_{i \in I} A_i$ for $(A_{i_1} \parallel \cdots \parallel A_{i_n})$, which is $\mathbf{0}$ when I is empty; and $\sum_{i \in I} \pi_i.N_i$ for $(\pi_{i_1}.N_{i_1} + \cdots + \pi_{i_n}.N_{i_n})$. This notation is justified by commutativity and associativity of the parallel and choice operators. Thanks to the structural laws of restriction, we also write $\nu X.P$ where $X = \{x_1, \dots, x_n\}$, or $\nu x_1\, x_2 \cdots x_n.P$, for $\nu x_1.\cdots \nu x_n.P$; or just P when X is empty. When X and Y are disjoint sets of names, we use juxtaposition for union.

Every process $P \in \mathcal{P}$ is structurally congruent to a process in normal form. The function $\mathrm{nf}\colon \mathcal{P} \to \mathcal{P}_{\mathsf{nf}}$, defined in [5], extracts, from a term, a structurally congruent normal form.

Given a process P with normal form $\nu X.\prod_{i \in I} A_i$, the *communication topology*[2] of P, written $\mathcal{G}[\![P]\!]$, is defined as the labelled hypergraph with X as hyperedges and I as nodes, each labelled with the corresponding A_i. An hyperedge $x \in X$ is connected with i just if $x \in \mathrm{fn}(A_i)$.

Semantics. We are interested in the reduction semantics of a π-term, which can be described using the following rule.

Definition 2 (Semantics of π-calculus). *The operational semantics of a term $P_0 \in \mathcal{P}$ is defined by the (pointed) transition system $(\mathcal{P}, \rightarrow, P_0)$ on π-terms, where P_0 is the initial term, and the transition relation, $\rightarrow \subseteq \mathcal{P}^2$, is defined by $P \rightarrow Q$ if either (i) to (iv) hold, or (v) and (vi) hold, where*

(i) $P \equiv \nu W.(S \parallel R \parallel C) \in \mathcal{P}_{\mathsf{nf}}$,
(ii) $S = (\overline{a}\langle b\rangle.\nu Y_s.S') + M_s$,
(iii) $R = (a(x).\nu Y_r.R') + M_r$,
(iv) $Q \equiv \nu W Y_s Y_r.(S' \parallel R'[b/x] \parallel C)$,
(v) $P \equiv \nu W.(\tau.\nu Y.P' \parallel C) \in \mathcal{P}_{\mathsf{nf}}$,
(vi) $Q \equiv \nu W Y.(P' \parallel C)$.

We define the set of reachable terms from P as $\mathrm{Reach}(P) := \{Q \mid P \rightarrow^* Q\}$, *writing $\rightarrow^*$ to mean the reflexive, transitive closure of $\rightarrow$. We refer to the restrictions, νY_s, νY_r and νY, as the restrictions* activated *by the transition $P \rightarrow Q$.*

Notice that the use of structural congruence in the definition of $\rightarrow$ takes unfolding replication into account.

[2] This definition arises from the "flow graphs" of [20]; see e.g. [15, p. 175] for a formal definition.

Example 2 (Client-server). We can model a variation of the client-server pattern sketched in the introduction, with the term $\nu s\, c.P$ where $P = !S \parallel !C \parallel !M$, $S = s(x).\nu d.\overline{x}\langle d\rangle$, $C = c(m).(\overline{s}\langle m\rangle \parallel m(y).\overline{c}\langle m\rangle)$ and $M = \tau.\nu m.\overline{c}\langle m\rangle$. The term $!S$ represents a server listening to a port s for a client's requests. A request is a channel x that the client sends to the server for exchanging the response. After receiving x the server creates a new name d and sends it over x. The term $!M$ creates unboundedly many clients, each with its own private mailbox m. A client on a mailbox m repeatedly sends requests to the server and concurrently waits for the answer on the mailbox before recursing.

In the following examples, we use CCS-style nullary channels, which can be understood as a shorthand: $c.P := c(x).P$ and $\overline{c}.P := \nu x.\overline{c}\langle x\rangle.P$ where $x \notin \mathrm{fn}(P)$.

Example 3 (Resettable counter). A counter with reset is a process reacting to messages on three channels *inc*, *dec* and *rst*. An *inc* message increases the value of the counter, a *dec* message decreases it or causes a deadlock if the counter is zero, and a *rst* message resets the counter to zero. This behaviour is exhibited by the process $C_i = !\,\big(p_i(t).\big(inc_i.(\overline{t} \parallel \overline{p_i}\langle t\rangle) + dec_i.(t.\overline{p_i}\langle t\rangle) + rst_i.(\nu t'_i.\overline{p_i}\langle t'_i\rangle)\big)\big)$. Here, the number of processes $\overline{t}$ in parallel with $\overline{p_i}\langle t\rangle$ represents the current value of the counter i. A system $\big(\nu p_1\, t_1.(C_1 \parallel \overline{p_1}\langle t_1\rangle) \parallel \nu p_2\, t_2.(C_2 \parallel \overline{p_2}\langle t_2\rangle)\big)$ can for instance simulate a two-counter machine when put in parallel with a finite control process sending signals along the channels inc_i, dec_i and rst_i.

Example 4 (Unbounded ring). Let $R = \nu m.\nu s_0.(M \parallel \overline{m}\langle s_0\rangle \parallel \overline{s_0})$, $S = !(s.\overline{n})$ and $M = !\,\big(m(n).s_0.\nu s.(S \parallel \overline{m}\langle s\rangle \parallel \overline{s})\big)$. The term R implements an unboundedly growing ring. It initialises the ring with a single "master" node pointing at itself (s_0) as the next in the ring. The term M, implementing the master node's behaviour, waits on s_0 and reacts to a signal by creating a new slave with address s connected with the previous next slave n. A slave S simply propagates the signals on its channel to the next in the ring.

2.2 Forest Representation of Terms

In the technical developement of our ideas, we will manipulate the structure of terms in non-trivial ways. When reasoning about these manipulations, a term is best viewed as a forest representing (the relevant part of) its abstract syntax tree. Since we only aim to capture the active portion of the term, the active sequential subterms are the leaves of its forest view. Parallel composition corresponds to (unordered) branching, and names introduced by restriction are represented by internal (non-leaf) nodes.

A *forest* is a simple, acyclic, directed graph, $f = (N_f, \prec_f)$, where the edge relation $n_1 \prec_f n_2$ means "n_1 is the parent of n_2". We write $\leq_f$ and $<_f$ for the reflexive transitive and the transitive closure of $\prec_f$ respectively. A *path* is a sequence of nodes, $n_1 \ldots n_k$, such that for each $i < k$, $n_i \prec_f n_{i+1}$. Henceforth we drop the subscript f from $\prec_f, \leq_f$ and $<_f$ (as there is no risk of confusion),

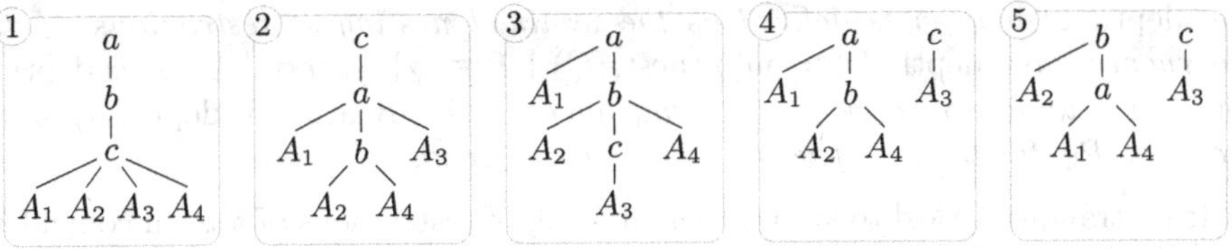

Fig. 4. Examples of forests in $\mathcal{F}[\![P]\!]$ where $P = \nu\, a\, b\, c.(A_1 \parallel A_2 \parallel A_3 \parallel A_4)$, $A_1 = a(x)$, $A_2 = b(x)$, $A_3 = c(x)$ and $A_4 = \overline{a}\langle b \rangle$.

and assume that all forests are finite. Thus every node has a unique path to a root (and that root is unique).

An *L-labelled forest* is a pair $\varphi = (f_\varphi, \ell_\varphi)$ where f_φ is a forest and $\ell_\varphi \colon N_\varphi \to L$ is a labelling function on nodes. Given a path $n_1 \dots n_k$ of f_φ, its *trace* is the induced sequence $\ell_\varphi(n_1) \dots \ell_\varphi(n_k)$. By abuse of language, a *trace* is an element of L^* which is the trace of some path in the forest.

We define L-labelled forests inductively from the empty forest $(\emptyset, \emptyset)$. We write $\varphi_1 \uplus \varphi_2$ for the disjoint union of forests φ_1 and φ_2, and $l[\varphi]$ for the forest with a single root, which is labelled with $l \in L$, and whose children are the respective roots of the forest φ. Since the choice of the set of nodes is irrelevant, we will always interpret equality between forests up to isomorphism (i.e. a bijection on nodes respecting parent and labeling).

Definition 3 (Forest representation). *We represent the structural congruence class of a term $P \in \mathcal{P}$ with the set of labelled forests $\mathcal{F}[\![P]\!] := \{\mathrm{forest}(Q) \mid Q \equiv P\}$ with labels in $\mathrm{act}_\nu(P) \uplus \mathrm{act}_\mathcal{S}(P)$ where $\mathrm{forest}(Q)$ is defined as*

$$\mathrm{forest}(Q) := \begin{cases} (\emptyset, \emptyset) & \text{if } Q = \mathbf{0} \\ Q[(\emptyset, \emptyset)] & \text{if } Q \text{ is sequential} \\ x[\mathrm{forest}(Q')] & \text{if } Q = \nu x.Q' \\ \mathrm{forest}(Q_1) \uplus \mathrm{forest}(Q_2) & \text{if } Q = Q_1 \parallel Q_2 \end{cases}$$

Note that leaves (and only leaves) are labelled with sequential processes.

The restriction height, $\mathrm{height}_\nu(\mathrm{forest}(P))$, *is the length of the longest path formed of nodes labelled with names in* $\mathrm{forest}(P)$.

In Fig. 4 we show some of the possible forest representations of an example term.

2.3 Depth-Bounded Terms

Definition 4 (Depth-bounded term [13]). *The* nesting of restrictions *of a term is given by the function*

$$\mathrm{nest}_\nu(M) := \mathrm{nest}_\nu(!M) := \mathrm{nest}_\nu(\mathbf{0}) := 0$$
$$\mathrm{nest}_\nu(\nu x.P) := 1 + \mathrm{nest}_\nu(P)$$
$$\mathrm{nest}_\nu(P \parallel Q) := \max(\mathrm{nest}_\nu(P), \mathrm{nest}_\nu(Q)).$$

The depth *of a term is defined as the minimal nesting of restrictions in its congruence class,* $\mathrm{depth}(P) := \min\{\mathrm{nest}_\nu(Q) \mid P \equiv Q\}$*. A term* $P \in \mathcal{P}$ *is* depth-bounded *if there exists* $k \in \mathbb{N}$ *such that for each* $Q \in \mathrm{Reach}(P)$*,* $\mathrm{depth}(Q) \leq k$*. We write* $\mathcal{P}_{\mathsf{db}}$ *for the set of terms with bounded depth.*

It is straightforward to see that the nesting of restrictions of a term coincides with the height of its forest representation, i.e., for every $P \in \mathcal{P}$, $\mathrm{nest}_\nu(P) = \mathrm{height}_\nu(\mathrm{forest}(P))$.

Example 5 (Depth-bounded term). The term in Example 2 is depth-bounded: all the reachable terms are congruent to terms of the form

$$Q_{ijk} = \nu\, s\, c.\big(P \parallel N^i \parallel Req^j \parallel Ans^k\big)$$

for some $i, j, k \in \mathbb{N}$ where $N = \nu\, m.\overline{c}\langle m\rangle$, $Req = \nu\, m.(\overline{s}\langle m\rangle \parallel m(y).\overline{c}\langle m\rangle)$ and $Ans = \nu\, m.(\nu\, d.\overline{m}\langle d\rangle \parallel m(y).\overline{c}\langle m\rangle)$. For any i, j, k, $\mathrm{nest}_\nu(Q_{ijk}) \leq 4$.

Example 6 (Depth-unbounded term). Consider the term in Example 4 and the following run:

$$\begin{aligned} R &\to^* \nu\, m\, s_0.(M \parallel \nu\, s_1.(!(s_1.\overline{s_0}) \parallel \overline{m}\langle s_1\rangle \parallel \overline{s_1})) \\ &\to^* \nu\, m\, s_0.(M \parallel \nu\, s_1.(!(s_1.\overline{s_0}) \parallel \nu\, s_2.(!(s_2.\overline{s_1}) \parallel \overline{m}\langle s_2\rangle \parallel \overline{s_2}))) \to^* \dots \end{aligned}$$

The scopes of s_0, s_1, s_2 and the rest of the instantiations of $\nu\, s$ are inextricably nested, thus R has unbounded depth: for each $n \geq 1$, a term with depth n is reachable.

Depth boundedness is a semantic notion. Because the definition is a universal quantification over reachable terms, analysis of depth boundedness is difficult. Indeed the membership problem is undecidable [15]. In the communication topology interpretation, depth has a tight relationship with the maximum length of the simple paths. A path $v_1 e_1 v_2 \dots v_n e_n v_{n+1}$ in $\mathcal{G}[\![P]\!]$ is *simple* if it does not repeat hyper-edges, i.e., $e_i \neq e_j$ for all $i \neq j$. A term is depth-bounded if and only if there exists a bound on the length of the simple paths of the communication topology of each reachable term [13]. This allows terms to grow unboundedly in *breadth*, i.e., the degree of hyper-edges in the communication topology.

A term P is *embeddable* in a term Q, written $P \preceq Q$, if $P \equiv \nu\, X.\prod_{i \in I} A_i \in \mathcal{P}_{\mathsf{nf}}$ and $Q \equiv \nu\, XY.(\prod_{i \in I} A_i \parallel R) \in \mathcal{P}_{\mathsf{nf}}$ for some term R. In [13] the term embedding ordering, $\preceq$, is shown to be both a simulation relation on π-terms, and an effective well-quasi ordering on depth-bounded terms. This makes the transition system $(\mathrm{Reach}(P)/_{\equiv}, \to/_{\equiv}, P)$ a *well-structured transition system* (WSTS) [1,8] under the term embedding ordering. Consequently a number of verification problems are decidable for terms in $\mathcal{P}_{\mathsf{db}}$.

Theorem 1 (Decidability of termination [13]). *The termination problem for depth-bounded terms, which asks, given a term* $P_0 \in \mathcal{P}_{\mathsf{db}}$*, if there is an infinite sequence* $P_0 \to P_1 \to \dots$*, is decidable.*

Theorem 2 (Decidability of coverability [13,25]). *The coverability problem for depth-bounded terms, which asks, given a term* $P \in \mathcal{P}_{\mathsf{db}}$ *and a query* $Q \in \mathcal{P}$*, if there exists* $P' \in \mathrm{Reach}(P)$ *such that* $Q \preceq P'$*, is decidable.*

3 $\mathcal{T}$-compatibility and Hierarchical Terms

A hierarchy is specified by a finite forest $(\mathcal{T}, \prec)$. In order to formally relate *active* restrictions in a term to nodes of the hierarchy $\mathcal{T}$, we annotate restrictions with types. For the moment we view types abstractly as elements of a set $\mathbb{T}$, equipped with a map base: $\mathbb{T} \to \mathcal{T}$. An annotated restriction $\nu(x:\tau)$ where $\tau \in \mathbb{T}$ will be associated with the node base(τ) in the hierarchy $\mathcal{T}$. Elements of $\mathbb{T}$ are called *types*, and those of $\mathcal{T}$ are called *base types*. In the simplest case and, especially for Sect. 3, we may assume $\mathbb{T} = \mathcal{T}$ and base$(t) = t$. In Sect. 4 we will consider a set $\mathbb{T}$ of types generated from $\mathcal{T}$, and a non-trivial base map.

Definition 5 (Annotated term). *A* $\mathbb{T}$-annotated π-term *(or simply* annotated π-term*)* $P \in \mathcal{P}^{\mathbb{T}}$ *has the same syntax as ordinary π-terms except that restrictions take the form $\nu(x:\tau)$ where $\tau \in \mathbb{T}$. In the abbreviated form νX, X is a set of annotated names $(x:\tau)$.*

Structural congruence, $\equiv$, of annotated terms, is defined by Definition 1, with the proviso that the type annotations are invariant under α-conversion and replication. For example, $!\,(\pi.\,\nu\,(x:\tau).P) \equiv \pi.\,\nu\,(x:\tau).P \parallel !\,(\pi.\,\nu\,(x:\tau).P)$ and $\nu\,(x:\tau).P \equiv \nu\,(y:\tau).P[y/x]$; observe that the annotated restrictions that occur in a replication unfolding are necessarily inactive.

The forest representation of an annotated π-term is obtained from Definition 3 by replacing the case of $Q = \nu\,(x:\tau).Q'$ by

$$\text{forest}(\nu\,(x:\tau).Q') := (x,t)[\text{forest}(Q')]$$

where base$(\tau) = t$. Thus the forests in $\mathcal{F}[\![P]\!]$ have labels in $(\text{act}_\nu(P) \times \mathcal{T}) \uplus \text{act}_{\mathcal{S}}(P)$. We write $\mathcal{F}_{\mathcal{T}}$ for the set of forests with labels in $(\mathcal{N} \times \mathcal{T}) \uplus \mathcal{S}$. We write $\mathcal{P}_{\mathsf{nf}}^{\mathbb{T}}$ for the set of $\mathbb{T}$-annotated π-terms in normal form.

The definition of the transition relation of annotated terms, $P \to Q$, is obtained from Definition 2, where W, Y_s, Y_r and Y are now sets of annotated names, by replacing clauses (iv) and (vi) by

(iv') $Q \equiv \nu W Y_s' Y_r'.(S' \parallel R'[b/x] \parallel C)$ *(vi')* $Q \equiv \nu W Y'.(P' \parallel C)$

respectively, such that $Y_s \restriction \mathcal{N} = Y_s' \restriction \mathcal{N}$, $Y_r \restriction \mathcal{N} = Y_r' \restriction \mathcal{N}$, and $Y \restriction \mathcal{N} = Y \restriction \mathcal{N}$, where $X \restriction \mathcal{N} := \{x \in \mathcal{N} \mid \exists \tau.(x:\tau) \in X\}$. I.e. the type annotation of the names that are activated by the transition (i.e. those from Y_s, Y_r and Y) are not required to be preserved in Q. (By contrast, the annotation of every active restriction in P is preserved by the transition.) While in this context inactive annotations can be ignored by the transitions, they will be used by the type system in Sect. 4, to establish invariance of $\mathcal{T}$-compatible.

Now we are ready to explain what it means for an annotated term P to be $\mathcal{T}$-compatible: there is a forest in $\mathcal{F}[\![P]\!]$ such that every trace of it projects to a chain in the partial order $\mathcal{T}$.

Definition 6 ($\mathcal{T}$-compatibility). *Let $P \in \mathcal{P}^{\mathbb{T}}$ be an annotated π-term. A forest $\varphi \in \mathcal{F}[\![P]\!]$ is* $\mathcal{T}$-compatible *if for every trace $((x_1,t_1)\ldots(x_k,t_k)\,A)$ in φ it holds that $t_1 < t_2 < \ldots < t_k$. The π-term P is* $\mathcal{T}$-compatible *if $\mathcal{F}[\![P]\!]$ contains a $\mathcal{T}$-compatible forest. A term is* $\mathcal{T}$-shaped *if each of its subterms is $\mathcal{T}$-compatible.*

As a property of annotated terms, $\mathcal{T}$-compatibility is by definition invariant under structural congruence.

A term $P' \in \mathcal{P}^{\mathbb{T}}$ is a *type annotation* (or simply *annotation*) of $P \in \mathcal{P}$ if its *type-erasure*, written $\ulcorner P \urcorner$, coincides with P. (We omit the obvious definition of type-erasure.) A *consistent annotation* of a transition of terms, $P \to Q$, is a choice function that, given an annotation P' of P, returns an annotation Q' of Q such that $P' \to Q'$. Note that it follows from the definition that the annotation of every active restriction in P' is preserved in Q'. The effect of the choice function is therefore to pick a possibly new annotation for each restriction in Q' that is activated by the transition. Thus, given a semantics $(\mathcal{P}, \to, P)$ of a term P, and an annotation P' of P, and a consistent annotation for every transition of the semantics, there is a well-defined pointed transition system $(\mathcal{P}^{\mathbb{T}}, \to', P')$ such that every transition sequence of the former lifts to a transition sequence of the latter. We call $(\mathcal{P}^{\mathbb{T}}, \to', P')$ a *consistent annotation* of the semantics $(\mathcal{P}, \to, P)$.

Definition 7 (Hierarchical term). *A term $P \in \mathcal{P}$ is* hierarchical *if there exist a finite forest $\mathcal{T} = \mathbb{T}$ and a consistent annotation $(\mathcal{P}^{\mathbb{T}}, \to', P')$ of the semantics $(\mathcal{P}, \to, P)$ of P, such that all terms reachable from P' are $\mathcal{T}$-compatible.*

Example 7. The term in Examples 2 and 5 is hierarchical: take the hierarchy $\mathcal{T} = \mathsf{s} \prec \mathsf{c} \prec \mathsf{m} \prec \mathsf{d}$ and annotate each name in Q_{ijk} as follows: $s\!:\!\mathsf{s}$, $c\!:\!\mathsf{c}$, $m\!:\!\mathsf{m}$ and $d\!:\!\mathsf{d}$. The annotation is consistent, and forest(Q_{ijk}) is $\mathcal{T}$-compatible for all i,j and k.

Example 4 gives an example of a term that is not hierarchical. The forest representation of the reachable terms shown in Example 6 does not have a bounded height, which means that if $\mathcal{T}$ has n base types, there is a reachable term with a representation of height bigger than n, which implies that there will be a path repeating a base type.

Let us now study this fragment. First it is easy to see that invariance of $\mathcal{T}$-compatibility under reduction $\to$, for some finite $\mathcal{T}$, puts a bound $|\mathcal{T}|$ on the height of the $\mathcal{T}$-compatible reachable forests, and consequently a bound on depth.

Theorem 3. *Every hierarchical term is depth-bounded. The converse is false.*

Thanks to Theorem 2, an immediate corollary of Theorem 3 is that coverability and termination are decidable for hierarchical terms.

Unfortunately, like the depth-bounded fragment, membership of the hierarchical fragment is undecidable. The proof is by adapting the argument for the undecidability of depth boundedness [15].

Lemma 1. *Every terminating π-term is hierarchical.*

Proof. Since the transition system of a term, quotiented by structural congruence, is finitely branching, by König's lemma the computation tree of a terminating term is finite, so it contains finitely many reachable processes and therefore finitely many names. Take the set of all (disambiguated) active names of the reachable terms and fix an arbitrary total order $\mathcal{T}$ on them. The consistent annotation with $(x : x)$ for each name will prove the term hierarchical.

Theorem 4. *Determining whether an arbitrary π-term is hierarchical, is undecidable.*

Proof. The π-calculus is Turing-complete, so termination is undecidable. Suppose we had an algorithm to decide if a term is hierarchical. Then we could decide termination of an arbitrary π-term by first checking if the term is hierarchical; if the answer is yes, we can decide termination for it by Theorem 1, otherwise we know that it is not terminating by Lemma 1.

Theorem 4—and the corresponding version for depth-bounded terms—is a serious impediment to any practical application of hierarchical terms to verification: when presented with a term to verify, one has to prove that it belongs to one of the two fragments, manually, before one can apply the relevant algorithms.

While the two fragments have a lot in common, hierarchical systems have a richer structure, which we will exploit to define a type system that can prove a term hierarchical, in a feasible, sound but incomplete way. Thanks to the notion of hierarchy, we are thus able to statically capture an expressive fragment of the π-calculus that enjoys decidable coverability.

4 A Type System for Hierarchical Topologies

The purpose of this section is to devise a static check to determine if a term is hierarchical. To do so, we define a type system, parametrised over a forest $\mathcal{T}$, which satisfies subject reduction. Furthermore we prove that if a term is typable then $\mathcal{T}$-shapedness is preserved by reduction of the term. Typability together with $\mathcal{T}$-shapedness of the initial term would then prove the term hierarchical.

As we have seen in the introduction, the typing rules make use of a new perspective on π-calculus reactions. Take the term $\nu a.(\nu b.\overline{a}\langle b\rangle.S \parallel \nu c.a(x).R)$ where $\nu a.(\nu b.[-] \parallel \nu c.[-])$ is the *reaction context*. Standardly the synchronisation of the two sequential processes over a is preceded by an extrusion of the scope of b to include $\nu c.a(x).R$, followed by the actual reaction:

$$\begin{aligned}\nu a.(\,\nu b.(\overline{a}\langle b\rangle.S) \parallel \nu c.a(x).R) &\equiv \nu a.\,\nu b.(\overline{a}\langle b\rangle.S \parallel \nu c.a(x).R) \\ &\to \nu a.\,\nu b.(S \parallel \nu c.(R[b/x]))\end{aligned}$$

This dynamic reshuffling of scopes is problematic for establishing invariance of $\mathcal{T}$-compatibility under reduction: notice how νc is brought into the scope of νb, possibly disrupting $\mathcal{T}$-compatibility. (For example, the preceding reduction would break $\mathcal{T}$-compatibility of the forest representations if the tree $\mathcal{T}$ is either $a \prec c \prec b$ or $b \succ a \prec c$.) We therefore adopt a different view. After the message is transmitted, the sender continues in-place as S, while R is split into two parts $R_{\mathrm{mig}} \parallel R_{\neg\mathrm{mig}}$, one that uses the message (the *migratable* one) and one that does not. The migratable portion R_{mig} is "installed" under νb so that it can make use of the acquired name, while the non-migratable one can simply continue in-place:

$$\nu a.(\,\nu b.(\overline{a}\langle b\rangle.S) \parallel \nu c.a(x).R) \to \nu a.(\,\nu b.(S \parallel R_{\mathrm{mig}}[b/x]) \parallel \nu c.R_{\neg\mathrm{mig}})$$

Crucially, the *reaction context*, $\nu a.(\nu b.[-] \parallel \nu c.[-])$, is unchanged. This means that if the starting term is $\mathcal{T}$-compatible, the context of the *reactum* is $\mathcal{T}$-compatible as well. Naturally, this only makes sense if R_{mig} does not use c. Thus our typing rules impose constraints on the use of names of R so that the migration does not result in R_{mig} escaping the scope of bound names such as c.

The formal definition of "migratable" is subtle. Consider the term

$$\nu f.a(x).\, \nu c\, d\, e.\big(\overline{x}\langle c\rangle \parallel \overline{c}\langle d\rangle \parallel \overline{a}\langle e\rangle.\overline{e}\langle f\rangle\big)$$

Upon synchronisation with $\nu b.\overline{a}\langle b\rangle$, surely $\overline{x}\langle c\rangle$ will need to be put under the scope of νb after substituting b for x, hence the first component of the continuation, $\overline{x}\langle c\rangle$, is migratable. However this implies that the scope of νc will need to be placed under νb, which in turn implies that $\overline{c}\langle d\rangle$ needs to be considered migratable as well. On the other hand, $\nu e.\overline{a}\langle e\rangle.\overline{e}\langle f\rangle$ must be placed in the scope of f, which may not be known by the sender, so it is not considered migratable. The following definition makes these observations precise.

Definition 8 (Linked to, tied to, migratable). *Given a normal form* $P = \nu X.\prod_{i\in I} A_i$ *we say that* A_i *is* linked to A_j in P, *written* $i \leftrightarrow_P j$, *if* $\mathrm{fn}(A_i) \cap \mathrm{fn}(A_j) \cap X \neq \emptyset$. *We define the* tied-to *relation as the transitive closure of* $\leftrightarrow_P$. *I.e.* A_i *is* tied to A_j, *written* $i \frown_P j$, *if* $\exists k_1, \dots, k_n \in I.\, i \leftrightarrow_P k_1 \leftrightarrow_P k_2 \dots \leftrightarrow_P k_n \leftrightarrow_P j$, *for some* $n \geq 0$. *Furthermore, we say that a name* y *is* tied to A_i in P, *written* $y \lhd_P i$, *if* $\exists j \in I.\, y \in \mathrm{fn}(A_j) \wedge j \frown_P i$. *Given an input-prefixed normal form* $a(y).P$ *where* $P = \nu X.\prod_{i\in I} A_i$, *we say that* A_i is migratable in $a(y).P$, *written* $\mathrm{Mig}_{a(y).P}(i)$, *if* $y \lhd_P i$.

These definitions have an intuitive meaning with respect to the communication topology of a normal form P: two sequential subterms are linked if they are connected by an hyperedge in the communication topology of P, and are tied to each other if there exists a path between them.

The following lemma indicates how the tied-to relation fundamentally constrains the possible shape of the forest of a term.

Lemma 2. *Let* $P = \nu X.\prod_{i\in I} A_i \in \mathcal{P}_{\mathsf{nf}}$, *if* $i \frown_P j$ *then if a forest* $\varphi \in \mathcal{F}[\![P]\!]$ *has leaves labelled with* A_i *and* A_j *respectively, they belong to the same tree in* φ *(i.e., have a common ancestor in* φ*).*

Example 8. Take the normal form $P = \nu a\ b\ c.(A_1 \parallel A_2 \parallel A_3 \parallel A_4)$ where $A_1 = a(x)$, $A_2 = b(x)$, $A_3 = c(x)$ and $A_4 = \overline{a}\langle b\rangle$. We have $1 \leftrightarrow_P 4$, $2 \leftrightarrow_P 4$, therefore $1 \frown_P 2 \frown_P 4$ and $a \lhd_P 2$. In Fig. 4 we show some of the forests in $\mathcal{F}[\![P]\!]$. Forest 1 represents $\mathrm{forest}(P)$. The fact that A_1, A_2 and A_4 are tied is reflected by the fact that none of the forests place them in disjoint trees. Now suppose we select only the forests in $\mathcal{F}[\![P]\!]$ that respect the hierarchy $a \prec b$: in all the forests in this set, the nodes labelled with A_1, A_2 and A_4 have a as common ancestor (as in forests 1, 2, 3 and 4). In particular, in these forests A_2 is necessarily a descendent of a even if a is not one of its free names.

In Sect. 3 we introduced annotations in a rather abstract way by means of a generic domain of types $\mathbb{T}$. In Definition 7 we ask for the existence of an annotation for the semantics of a term. Specifically, one can decide an arbitrary annotation for each active name. A type system however will examine the term statically, which means that it needs to know what could be a possible annotation for a variable, i.e., the name bound in an input action. This information is directly related to the notion of data-flow, that is the set of names that are bound to a variable during runtime. Since a static method cannot capture this information precisely, we make use of *sorts* [18], also known as *simple types*, to approximate it. The annotation of a restriction will carry not only which base type should be associated with its instances, but also instructions on how to annotate the messages received or sent through those instances. Concretely, we define

$$\mathbb{T} \ni \tau ::= t \mid t[\tau]$$

where $t \in \mathcal{T}$ is a base type.

A name with type t cannot be used as a channel but can be used as a message; a name with type $t[\tau]$ can be used to transmit a name of type τ. We will write $\text{base}(\tau)$ for t when $\tau = t[\tau']$ or $\tau = t$. By abuse of notation we write, for a set of types X, $\text{base}(X)$ for the set of base types of the types in X.

As is standard, we keep track of the types of free names by means of a typing environment. An environment Γ is a partial map from names to types, which we will write as a set of *type assignments*, $x : \tau$. Given a set of names X and an environment Γ, we write $\Gamma(X)$ for the set $\{\Gamma(x) \mid x \in X \cap \text{dom}(\Gamma)\}$. Given two environments Γ and Γ' with $\text{dom}(\Gamma) \cap \text{dom}(\Gamma') = \emptyset$, we write $\Gamma\Gamma'$ for their union. For a type environment Γ we define

$$\min_{\mathcal{T}}(\Gamma) := \{(x : \tau) \in \Gamma \mid \forall (y : \tau') \in \Gamma.\, \text{base}(\tau') \nless \text{base}(\tau)\}.$$

A judgement $\Gamma \vdash_{\mathcal{T}} P$ means that $P \in \mathcal{P}_{\mathsf{nf}}^{\mathbb{T}}$ can be typed under assumptions Γ, over the hierarchy $\mathcal{T}$; we say that P is *typable* if $\Gamma \vdash_{\mathcal{T}} P$ is provable for some Γ and $\mathcal{T}$. An arbitrary term $P \in \mathcal{P}^{\mathbb{T}}$ is said to be *typable* if its normal form is. The typing rules are presented in Fig. 5.

The type system presents several non-standard features. First, it is defined on normal forms as opposed to general π-terms. This choice is motivated by the fact that different syntactic presentations of the same term may be misleading when trying to analyse the relation between the structure of the term and $\mathcal{T}$. The rules need to guarantee that a reduction will not break $\mathcal{T}$-compatibility, which is a property of the congruence class of the term. As justified by Lemma 2, the scope of names in a congruence class may vary, but the tied-to relation puts constraints on the structure that must be obeyed by all members of the class. Therefore the type system is designed around this basic concept, rather than the specific scoping of any representative of the structural congruence class. Second, no type information is associated with the typed term, only restricted names hold type annotations. Third, while the rules are compositional, the constraints

$$\frac{\forall i \in I.\, \Gamma, X \vdash_{\mathcal{T}} A_i \qquad \forall i \in I.\, \forall x{:}\tau_x \in X.\, x \lhd_P i \implies \mathrm{base}(\Gamma(\mathrm{fn}(A_i))) < \mathrm{base}(\tau_x)}{\Gamma \vdash_{\mathcal{T}} \nu X.\prod_{i\in I} A_i}\ \textsc{Par}$$

$$\frac{\forall i \in I.\, \Gamma \vdash_{\mathcal{T}} \pi_i.P_i}{\Gamma \vdash_{\mathcal{T}} \sum_{i\in I}\pi_i.P_i}\ \textsc{Choice} \qquad \frac{\Gamma \vdash_{\mathcal{T}} A}{\Gamma \vdash_{\mathcal{T}} !A}\ \textsc{Repl} \qquad \frac{\Gamma \vdash_{\mathcal{T}} P}{\Gamma \vdash_{\mathcal{T}} \tau.P}\ \textsc{Tau}$$

$$\frac{a{:}t_a[\tau_b] \in \Gamma \qquad b{:}\tau_b \in \Gamma \qquad \Gamma \vdash_{\mathcal{T}} Q}{\Gamma \vdash_{\mathcal{T}} \overline{a}\langle b\rangle.Q}\ \textsc{Out}$$

$$\frac{a{:}t_a[\tau_x] \in \Gamma \qquad \Gamma, x{:}\tau_x \vdash_{\mathcal{T}} \nu X.\prod_{i\in I} A_i \qquad \mathrm{base}(\tau_x) < t_a \vee \big(\forall i \in I.\ \mathrm{Mig}_{a(x).P}(i) \implies \mathrm{base}(\Gamma(\mathrm{fn}(A_i) \setminus \{a\})) < t_a\big)}{\Gamma \vdash_{\mathcal{T}} a(x).\nu X.\prod_{i\in I} A_i}\ \textsc{In}$$

Fig. 5. A type system for hierarchical terms. The term P stands for $\nu X.\prod_{i\in I} A_i$.

on base types have a global flavour due to the fact that they involve the structure of $\mathcal{T}$ which is a global parameter of typing proofs.

Let us illustrate intuitively how the constraints enforced by the rules guarantee preservation of $\mathcal{T}$-compatibility. Consider the term

$$P = \nu e\, a.\Big(\nu b.\big(\overline{a}\langle b\rangle.A_0\big) \parallel \nu d.\big(a(x).Q\big)\Big)$$

with $Q = \nu c.(A_1 \parallel A_2 \parallel A_3)$, $A_0 = b(y)$, $A_1 = \overline{x}\langle c\rangle$, $A_2 = c(z).\overline{a}\langle e\rangle$ and $A_3 = \overline{a}\langle d\rangle$. Let $\mathcal{T}$ be the forest with $t_e \prec t_a \prec t_b \prec t_c$ and $t_a \prec t_d$, where t_x is the base type of the (omitted) annotation of the restriction νx, for $x \in \{a, b, c, d, e\}$. The reader can check that forest(P) is $\mathcal{T}$-compatible.

In the traditional understanding of mobility, we would interpret the communication of b over a as an application of scope extrusion to include $\nu d.\big(a(x).Q\big)$ in the scope of b and then syncronisation over a with the application of the substitution $[b/x]$ to Q; note that the substitution is only valid because the scope of b has been extended to include the receiver.

Our key observation is that we can instead interpret this communication as a migration of the subcomponents of Q that do get their scopes changed by the reduction, from the scope of the receiver to the scope of the sender. For this operation to be sound, the subcomponents of Q migrating to the sender's scope cannot use the names that are in the scope of the receiver but not of the sender.

In our specific example, after the synchronisation between the prefixes $\overline{a}\langle b\rangle$ and $a(x)$, b is substituted to x in A_1 resulting in the term $A_1' = \overline{b}\langle c\rangle$ and A_0, A_1', A_2 and A_3 become active. The scope of A_0 can remain unchanged as it cannot know more names than before as a result of the communication. By contrast, A_1 now knows b as a result of the substitution $[b/x]$: A_1 needs to migrate under the scope of b. Since A_1 uses c as well, the scope of c needs to be moved under b; however A_2 uses c so it needs to migrate under b with the scope of c. A_3 instead does not use neither b nor c so it can avoid migration and its scope remains unaltered.

This information can be formalised using the tied-to relation: on one hand, A_1 and A_2 need to be moved together because $1 \frown_Q 2$ and they need to be moved because $x \lhd_Q 1, 2$. On the other hand, A_3 is not tied to neither A_1 nor A_2 in Q and does not know x, thus it is not migratable. After reduction, our view of the reactum is the term

$$\nu a.\Big(\nu b.(A_0 \parallel \nu c.(A_1' \parallel A_2)) \parallel \nu d.A_3\Big)$$

the forest of which is $\mathcal{T}$-compatible. Rule Par, applied to A_1 and A_2, ensures that c has a base type that can be nested under the one of b. Rule In does not impose constraints on the base types of A_3 because A_3 is not migratable. It does however check that the base type of e is an ancestor of the one of a, thus ensuring that both receiver and sender are already in the scope of e. The base type of a does not need to be further constrained since the fact that the synchronisation happened on it implies that both the receiver and the sender were already under its scope; this implies, by $\mathcal{T}$-compatibility of P, that c can be nested under a.

We now describe the purpose of the rules of the type system in more detail. Most of the rules just drive the derivation through the structure of the term. The crucial constraints are checked by Par, In and Out.

The Out *Rule.* The main purpose of rule Out is enforcing types to be consistent with the dataflow of the process: the type of the argument of a channel a must agree with the types of all the names that may be sent over a. This is a very coarse sound over-approximation of the dataflow; if necessary it could be refined using well-known techniques from the literature but a simple approach is sufficient here to type interesting processes.

The Par *Rule.* Rule Par is best understood imagining the normal form to be typed, P, as the continuation of a prefix $\pi.P$. In this context a reduction exposes each of the active sequential subterms of P which need to have a place in a $\mathcal{T}$-compatible forest for the reactum. The constraint in Par can be read as follows. A "new" leaf A_i may refer to names already present in the forests of the reaction context; these names are the ones mentioned in both $\mathrm{fn}(A_i)$ and Γ. Then we must be able to insert A_i so that we can find these names in its path. However, A_i must belong to a tree containing all the names in X that are tied to it in P. So by requiring every name tied to A_i to have a base type greater than any name in the context that A_i may refer to, we make sure that we can insert the continuation in the forest of the context without violating $\mathcal{T}$-compatibility. Note that $\Gamma(\mathrm{fn}(A_i))$ contains only types that annotate names both in Γ and $\mathrm{fn}(A_i)$, that is, names which are not restricted by X and are referenced by A_i (and therefore come from the context).

The In *Rule.* Rule In serves two purposes: on the one hand it requires the type of the messages that can be sent through a to be consistent with the use of the variable x which will be bound to the messages; on the other hand, it constrains

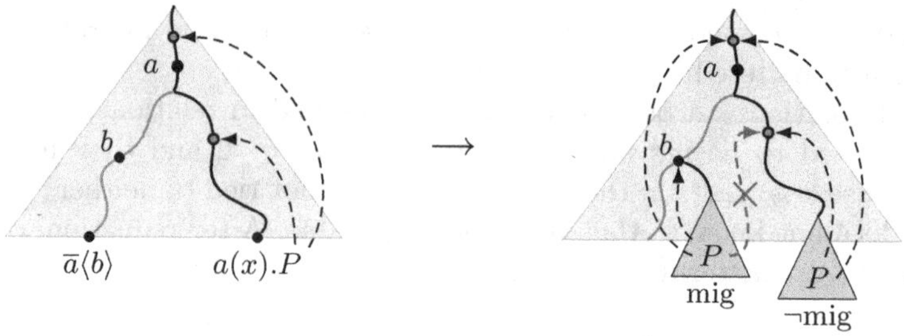

Fig. 6. Explanation of constraints imposed by rule IN. The dashed lines represent references to names restricted in the reduction context.

the base types of a and x so that synchronisation can be performed without breaking $\mathcal{T}$-compatibility.

The second purpose is achieved by distinguishing two cases, represented by the two disjuncts of the condition on base types of the rule. In the first case, the base type of the message is an ancestor of the base type of a in $\mathcal{T}$. This implies that in any $\mathcal{T}$-compatible forest representing $a(x).P$, the name b sent as message over a is already in the scope of P. Under this circumstance, there is no real mobility, P does not know new names by the effect of the substitution $[b/x]$, and the $\mathcal{T}$-compatibility constraints to be satisfied are in essence unaltered.

The second case is more complicated as it involves genuine mobility. This case also requires a slightly non-standard feature: not only do the premises predicate on the direct subcomponents of an input prefixed term, but also on the direct subcomponents of the continuation. This is needed to be able to separate the continuation in two parts: the one requiring migration and the one that does not. The situation during execution is depicted in Fig. 6. The non migratable sequential terms behave exactly as the case of the first disjunct: their scope is unaltered. The migratable ones instead are intended to be inserted as descendents of the node representing the message b in the forest of the reaction context.

For this to be valid without rearrangement of the forest of the context, we need all the names in the context that are referenced in the migratable terms, to be also in the scope at b; we make sure this is the case by requiring the free names of any migratable A_i that are from the context (i.e. in Γ) to have base types smaller than the base type of a. The set $\mathrm{base}(\Gamma(\mathrm{fn}(A_i) \setminus \{a\}))$ indeed represents the base types of the names in the reaction context referenced in a migratable continuation A_i. In fact a is a name that needs to be in the scope of both the sender and the receiver at the same time, so it needs to be a common ancestor of sender and receiver in any $\mathcal{T}$-compatible forest. Any name in the reaction context and in the continuation of the receiver, with a base type smaller than the one of a, will be an ancestor of a—and hence of the sender, the receiver and the node representing the message—in any $\mathcal{T}$-compatible forest. Clearly, remembering a is not harmful as it must be already in the scope of receiver and sender, so we exclude it from the constraint.

Example 9. Take the normal form in Example 2. Let us fix $\mathcal{T}$ to be the forest $\mathsf{s} \prec \mathsf{c} \prec \mathsf{m} \prec \mathsf{d}$ and annotate the normal form with the following types: $s : \tau_s = \mathsf{s}[\tau_m]$, $c : \tau_c = \mathsf{c}[\tau_m]$, $m : \tau_m = \mathsf{m}[\mathsf{d}]$ and $d : \mathsf{d}$. We want to prove $\emptyset \vdash_{\mathcal{T}} \nu\, s\, c.P$. We can apply rule PAR: in this case there are no conditions on types because, being the environment empty, we have $\mathrm{base}(\emptyset(\mathrm{fn}(A))) = \emptyset$ for every active sequential term A of P. Let $\Gamma = \{(s : \tau_s), (c : \tau_c)\}$. The rule requires $\Gamma \vdash_{\mathcal{T}} !S$, $\Gamma \vdash_{\mathcal{T}} !C$ and $\Gamma \vdash_{\mathcal{T}} !M$, which can be proved by proving typability of S, C and M under Γ by rule REPL.

To prove $\Gamma \vdash_{\mathcal{T}} S$ we apply rule IN; we have $s : \mathsf{s}[\tau_m] \in \Gamma$ and we need to prove that $\Gamma, x : \tau_m \vdash_{\mathcal{T}} \nu\, d.\overline{x}\langle d \rangle$. No constraints on base types are generated at this step since the migratable sequential term $\nu\, d.\overline{x}\langle d \rangle$ does not contain free variables typed by Γ making $\Gamma(\mathrm{fn}(\nu\, d.\overline{x}\langle d \rangle) \setminus \{a\}) = \Gamma(\{x\})$ empty. Next, $\Gamma, x : \tau_m \vdash_{\mathcal{T}} \nu\, d.\overline{x}\langle d \rangle$ can be proved by applying rule PAR which amounts to checking $\Gamma, x : \tau_m, d : \mathsf{d} \vdash_{\mathcal{T}} \overline{x}\langle d \rangle.\mathbf{0}$ (by a simple application of OUT and the axiom $\Gamma, x : \tau_m, d : \mathsf{d} \vdash_{\mathcal{T}} \mathbf{0}$) and verifying the condition—true in $\mathcal{T}$—$\mathrm{base}(\tau_m) < \mathrm{base}(\tau_d)$: in fact d is tied to $\overline{x}\langle d \rangle$ and, for $\Gamma' = \Gamma \cup \{x : \tau_m\}$, $\mathrm{base}(\Gamma'(\mathrm{fn}(\overline{x}\langle d \rangle))) = \mathrm{base}(\Gamma'(\{x, d\})) = \mathrm{base}(\{\tau_m\})$. The proof for $\Gamma \vdash_{\mathcal{T}} M$ is similar and requires $\mathsf{c} < \mathsf{m}$ which is true in $\mathcal{T}$.

Finally, we can prove $\Gamma \vdash_{\mathcal{T}} C$ using rule IN; both the two continuations $A_1 = \overline{s}\langle m \rangle$ and $A_2 = m(y).\overline{c}\langle m \rangle$ are migratable in C and since $\mathrm{base}(\tau_m) < \mathrm{base}(\tau_c)$ is false we need the other disjunct of the condition to be true. This amounts to checking that $\mathrm{base}(\Gamma(\mathrm{fn}(A_1) \setminus \{c\})) = \mathrm{base}(\Gamma(\{s, m\})) = \mathrm{base}(\{\tau_s\}) = \mathsf{s} < \mathsf{c}$ (note $m \notin \mathrm{dom}(\Gamma)$) and $\mathrm{base}(\Gamma(\mathrm{fn}(A_a) \setminus \{c\})) = \mathrm{base}(\Gamma(\emptyset)) < \mathsf{c}$ (that holds trivially).

To complete the typing we need to show $\Gamma, m : \tau_m \vdash_{\mathcal{T}} A_1$ and $\Gamma, m : \tau_m \vdash_{\mathcal{T}} A_2$. The former can be proved by a simple application of OUT which does not impose further constraints on $\mathcal{T}$. The latter is proved by applying IN which requires $\mathrm{base}(\tau_c) < \mathsf{m}$, which holds in $\mathcal{T}$.

Note how, at every step, there is only one rule that applies to each subproof.

Example 10. The term Example 4 is not typable under any $\mathcal{T}$. To see why, one can build the proof tree without assumptions on $\mathcal{T}$ by assuming that each restriction $\nu\, x$ has base type t_x. When typing $\overline{m}\langle s \rangle$ we deduce that $t_s = t_n$, which is in contradiction with the constraint that $t_n < t_s$ required by rule PAR when typing $\nu\, s.(S \parallel \overline{m}\langle s \rangle \parallel \overline{s})$.

5 Soundness of the Type System

We now establish the soundness of the type system. Theorem 5 will show how typability is preserved by reduction. Theorem 6 establishes the main property of the type system: if a term is typable then $\mathcal{T}$-shapedness is invariant under reduction. This allows us to conclude that if a term is $\mathcal{T}$-shaped and typable, then every term reachable from it will be $\mathcal{T}$-shaped.

The subtitution lemma states that substituting names without altering the types preserves typability.

Lemma 3 (Substitution). *Let $P \in \mathcal{P}_{\mathsf{nf}}^{\mathbb{T}}$ and Γ be a typing environment such that $\Gamma(a) = \Gamma(b)$. Then it holds that if $\Gamma \vdash_{\mathcal{T}} P$ then $\Gamma \vdash_{\mathcal{T}} P[b/a]$.*

Before we state the main theorem, we define the notion of P-safe type environment, which is a simple restriction on the types that can be assigned to names that are free at the top-level of a term.

Definition 9 (P-safe environment). *A type environment Γ is said to be* P-safe *if for each $x \in \mathrm{fn}(P)$ and $(y : \tau) \in \mathrm{bn}_\nu(P)$, $\mathrm{base}(\Gamma(x)) < \mathrm{base}(\tau)$.*

Theorem 5 (Subject Reduction). *Let P and Q be two terms in $\mathcal{P}_{\mathsf{nf}}^{\mathbb{T}}$ and Γ be a P-safe type environment. If $\Gamma \vdash_{\mathcal{T}} P$ and $P \to Q$, then $\Gamma \vdash_{\mathcal{T}} Q$.*

The proof is by careful analysis of how the typing proof for P can be adapted to derive a proof for Q. The only difficulty comes from the fact that some of the subterms of P will appear in Q with a substitution applied. However, typability of P ensures that we are only substituting names for names with the same type, thus allowing us to apply Lemma 3.

To establish that $\mathcal{T}$-shapedness is invariant under reduction for typable terms, we will need to show that starting from a typable $\mathcal{T}$-shaped term P, any step will reduce it to a (typable) $\mathcal{T}$-shaped term. The hypothesis of $\mathcal{T}$-compatibility of P can be used to extract a $\mathcal{T}$-compatible forest φ from $\mathcal{F}[\![P]\!]$. While many forests in $\mathcal{F}[\![P]\!]$ can be witnesses of the $\mathcal{T}$-compatibility of P, we want to characterise the shape of a witness that *must* exist if P is $\mathcal{T}$-compatible. The proof of invariance relies on selecting a φ that does not impose unnecessary hierarchical dependencies among names. Such forest is identified by $\Phi_{\mathcal{T}}(\mathrm{nf}(P))$: it is the shallowest among all the $\mathcal{T}$-compatible forests in $\mathcal{F}[\![P]\!]$.

Definition 10 ($\Phi_{\mathcal{T}}$). *The function $\Phi_{\mathcal{T}} \colon \mathcal{P}_{\mathsf{nf}}^{\mathbb{T}} \to \mathcal{F}_{\mathcal{T}}$ is defined inductively as*

$$\Phi_{\mathcal{T}}(\textstyle\prod_{i \in I} A_i) := \biguplus_{i \in I} \{A_i[]\}$$

$$\Phi_{\mathcal{T}}(P) := \Big(\biguplus \big\{(x, \mathrm{base}(\tau))[\Phi_{\mathcal{T}}(\nu Y_x . \textstyle\prod_{j \in I_x} A_j)] \mid (x : \tau) \in \min_{\mathcal{T}}(X)\big\}\Big) \uplus \Phi_{\mathcal{T}}(\nu Z . \textstyle\prod_{r \in R} A_r)$$

where $X \neq \emptyset$, $P = \nu X . \prod_{i \in I} A_i$ $I_x = \{i \in I \mid x \lhd_P i\}$ and

$$Y_x = \{(y : \tau) \in X \mid \exists i \in I_x . \, y \in \mathrm{fn}(A_i)\} \setminus \min_{\mathcal{T}}(X)$$
$$Z = X \setminus \big(\textstyle\bigcup_{(x : \tau) \in \min_{\mathcal{T}}(X)} Y_x \cup \{x : \tau\}\big)$$
$$R = I \setminus \big(\textstyle\bigcup_{(x : \tau) \in \min_{\mathcal{T}}(X)} I_x\big)$$

Forest 4 of Fig. 4 is $\Phi_{\mathcal{T}}(P)$ when every restriction νx has base type x (for $x \in \{a, b, c\}$) and $\mathcal{T}$ is the forest with nodes a, b and c and a single edge $a \prec b$.

Lemma 4. *Let $P \in \mathcal{P}_{\mathsf{nf}}^{\mathbb{T}}$. Then:*

(a) $\Phi_{\mathcal{T}}(P)$ is a $\mathcal{T}$-compatible forest;
(b) $\Phi_{\mathcal{T}}(P) \in \mathcal{F}[\![P]\!]$ if and only if P is $\mathcal{T}$-compatible;
(c) if $P \equiv Q \in \mathcal{P}^{\mathbb{T}}$ then $\Phi_{\mathcal{T}}(P) \in \mathcal{F}[\![Q]\!]$ if and only if Q is $\mathcal{T}$-compatible.

Theorem 6 (Invariance of $\mathcal{T}$-shapedness). *Let P and Q be terms in $\mathcal{P}_{\mathsf{nf}}^{\mathbb{T}}$ such that $P \to Q$ and Γ be a P-safe environment such that $\Gamma \vdash_{\mathcal{T}} P$. Then, if P is $\mathcal{T}$-shaped then Q is $\mathcal{T}$-shaped.*

The key of the proof is (a) the use of $\Phi_{\mathcal{T}}(P)$ to extract a specific $\mathcal{T}$-compatible forest, (b) the definition of a way to insert the subtrees of the continuations of the reacting processes in the forest of reaction context, in a way that preserves $\mathcal{T}$-compatibility. Thanks to the constraints of the typing rules, we will always be able to find a valid place in the reaction context where to attach the trees representing the reactum.

6 Type Inference

In this section we will show that it is possible to take any non-annotated normal form P and derive a forest $\mathcal{T}$ and an annotated version of P that can be typed under $\mathcal{T}$.

Inference for simple types has already been proved decidable in [9,24]. In our case, since our types are not recursive, the algorithm concerned purely with the constraints imposed by the type system of the form $\tau_x = t[\tau_y]$ is even simpler. The main difficulty is inferring the structure of $\mathcal{T}$.

Let us first be more specific on assigning simple types. The number of ways a term P can be annotated with types are infinite, simply from the fact that types allow an arbitrary nesting as in t, $t[t]$, $t[t[t]]$ and so on. We observe that, however, there is no use annotating a restriction with a type with nesting deeper than the size of the program: the type system cannot inspect more deeply nested types. Thanks to this observation we can restrict ourselves to annotations with bounded nesting in the type's structure. This also gives a bound on the number of base types that need to appear in the annotated term. Therefore, there are only finitely many possible annotations and possible forests under which P can be proved typably hierarchical. A naïve inference algorithm can then enumerate all of them and type check each.

Theorem 7 (Decidability of inference). *Given a normal form $P \in \mathcal{P}_{\mathsf{nf}}$, it is decidable if there exists a finite forest $\mathcal{T}$, a $\mathcal{T}$-annotated version $P' \in \mathcal{P}^{\mathbb{T}}$ of P and a P'-safe environment Γ such that P' is $\mathcal{T}$-shaped and $\Gamma \vdash_{\mathcal{T}} P'$.*

While enumerating all the relevant forests, annotations and environments is impractical, more clever strategies for inference exist.

We start by annotating the term with type variables: each name x gets typed with a type variable t_x. Then we start the type derivation, collecting all the constraints on types along the way. If we can find a $\mathcal{T}$ and type expressions to associate to each type variable, so that these constraints are satisfied, the process can be typed under $\mathcal{T}$.

By inspecting rules PAR and IN we observe that all the "tied-to" and "migratable" predicates do not depend on $\mathcal{T}$ so for any given P, the type constraints can be expressed simply by conjunctions and disjunctions of two kinds of basic predicates:

1. *data-flow constraints* of the form $\mathsf{t}_x = t_x[\mathsf{t}_y]$ where t_x is a base type variable;
2. *base type constraints* of the form $\mathrm{base}(\mathsf{t}_x) < \mathrm{base}(\mathsf{t}_y)$ which correspond to constraints over the corresponding base type variables, e.g. $t_x < t_y$.

Note that the P-safety condition on Γ translates to constraints of the second kind. The first kind of constraint can be solved using unification in linear time. If no solution exists, the process cannot be typed. This is the case of processes that cannot be *simply typed.* If unification is successful we get a set of equations over base type variables. Any assignment of those variables to nodes in a suitable forest that satisfies the constraints of the second kind would be a witness of typability. An example of the type inference in action can be found in [5].

First we note that if there exists a $\mathcal{T}$ which makes P typable and $\mathcal{T}$-compatible, then there exists a $\mathcal{T}'$ which does the same but is a linear chain of base types (i.e. a single tree with no branching). To see how, simply take $\mathcal{T}'$ to be any topological sort of $\mathcal{T}$.

Now, suppose we are presented with a set $\mathcal{C}$ of constraints of the form $t < t'$ (no disjuctions). One approach for solving them could be based on reductions to SAT or CLP(FD). We instead outline a direct algorithm. If the constraints are acyclic, i.e. it is not possible to derive $t < t$ by transitivity, then there exists a finite forest satisfying the constraints, having as nodes the base type variables. To construct such forest, we can first represent the constraints as a graph with the base type variables as vertices and an edge between t and t' just when $t < t' \in \mathcal{C}$. Then we can check the graph for acyclicity. If the test fails, the constraints are unsatisfiable. Otherwise, any topological sort of the graph will represent a forest satisfying $\mathcal{C}$.

We can modify this simple procedure to support constraints including disjuctions by using backtracking on the disjuncts. Every time we arrive at an acyclic assignment, we can check for $\mathcal{T}$-shapedness (which takes linear time) and in case the check fails we can backtrack again.

To speed up the backtracking algorithm, one can merge the acyclicity test with the $\mathcal{T}$-compatibility check. Acyclicity can be checked by constructing a topological sort of the constraints graph. Every time we produce the next node in the sorting, we take a step in the construction of $\Phi(P)$ using the fact that the currently produced node is the minimal base type among the remaining ones. We can then backtrack as soon as a choice contradicts $\mathcal{T}$-compatibility.

The complexity of the type checking problem is easily seen to be linear in the size of the program. This proves, in conjnuction with the finiteness of the candidate guesses for $\mathcal{T}$ and annotations, that the type inference problem is in NP. We conjecture that inference is also NP-hard.

We implemented the above algorithm in a tool called 'James Bound' (jb), available at http://github.com/bordaigorl/jamesbound.

7 Expressivity and Verification

7.1 Expressivity

Typably hierarchical terms form a rather expressive fragment. Apart from including common patterns as the client-server one, they generalise powerful models of computation with decidable properties.

Relations with variants of CCS are the easiest to establish: CCS can be seen as a syntactic subset of π-calculus when including 0-arity channels, which are very easily dealt with by straightforward specialisations of the typing rules for actions. One very expressive, yet not Turing-powerful, variant is CCS$^!$ [10] which can be seen as our π-calculus without mobility. Indeed, every CCS$^!$ process is typably hierarchical [4, Sect. 11.4].

Reset nets can be simulated by using resettable counters as defined in Example 3. The full encoding can be found in [5]. The encoding preserves coverability but not reachability.

CCS$^!$ was recently proven to have decidable reachability [10] so it is reasonable to ask whether reachability is decidable for typably hierarchical terms.

We show this is not the case by introducing a weak encoding of Minsky machines (in [5]). The encoding is weak in the sense that not all of the runs represent real runs of the encoded Minsky machine; however with reachability one can distinguish between the reachable terms that are encodings of reachable configurations and those which are not. We therefore reduce reachability of Minsky machines to reachability of typably hierarchical terms.

Theorem 8. *The reachability problem is undecidable for (typably) hierarchical terms.*

Theorem 8 can be used to clearly separate the (typably) hierarchical fragment from other models of concurrent computation as Petri Nets, which have decidable reachability and are thus less expressive.

7.2 Applications

Although reachability is not decidable, coverability is often quite enough to prove non-trivial safety properties. To illustrate this point, let us consider Example 2 again. In our example, each client waits for a reply reaching its mailbox before issuing another request; moreover the server replies to each request with a single message. Together, these observations suggest that the mailboxes of each client will contain at most one message at all times. To automatically verify this property we could use a coverability algorithm for depth-bounded systems: since the example is typable, it is depth-bounded and such algorithm is guaranteed to terminate with a correct answer. To formulate the property as a coverability problem, we can ask for coverability of the following query: $\nu s\, m.(!S \parallel m(y).\overline{c}\langle m\rangle \parallel \nu d.\overline{m}\langle d\rangle \parallel \nu d'.\overline{m}\langle d'\rangle)$. This is equivalent to asking whether a term is reachable that embeds a server connected with a client with a mailbox containing two messages. The query is not coverable and therefore we proved our property.[3]

Other examples of coverability properties are variants of secrecy properties. For instance, the coverability query $\nu s\, m\, m'.(!S \parallel m(y).\overline{c}\langle m\rangle \parallel m'(y).\overline{c}\langle m'\rangle \parallel \nu d.(\overline{m}\langle d\rangle \parallel \overline{m'}\langle d\rangle))$ encodes the property "can two different clients receive the same message?", which cannot happen in our example.

It is worth noting that this level of accuracy for proving such properties automatically is uncommon. Many approaches based on counter abstraction [7, 23] or CFA-style abstractions [6] would collapse the identities of clients by not distinguishing between different mailbox addresses. Instead a single counter is typically used to record the number of processes in the same control state and of messages. In our case, abstracting the mailbox addresses away has the effect of making the bounds on the clients' mailboxes unprovable in the abstract model.

A natural question at this point is: how can we go about verifying terms which cannot be typed, as the ring example? Coverability algorithms can be applied to untypable terms and they yield sound results when they terminate. But termination is not guaranteed, as the term in question may be depth-unbounded.

However, even a failed typing attempt may reveal interesting information about the structure of a term. For instance, in Example 10 one may easily see that the cyclic dependencies in the constraints are caused by the names representing the "next" process identities. In the general case heuristics can be employed to automatically identify a minimal set of problematic restrictions. Once such restrictions are found, a counter abstraction could be applied *to those restrictions only* yielding a term that simulates the original one but introducing some spurious behaviour. Type inference can be run again on the abstracted term; on failure, the process can be repeated, until a hierarchical abstraction is obtained. This abstract model can then be model checked instead of the original term, yielding sound but possibly imprecise results.

8 Related Work

Depth boundedness in the π-calculus was first proposed in [13] where it is proved that depth-bounded systems are well-structured transition systems. In [25] it is further proved that (forward) coverability is decidable even when the depth bound k is not known *a priori*. In [26] an approximate algorithm for computing the *cover set*—an over-approximation of the set of reachable terms—of a system of depth bounded by k is presented. All these analyses rely on the assumption of depth boundedness and may even require a known bound on the depth to terminate.

[3] To fully prove a bound on the mailbox capacity one may need to also ask another coverability question for the case where the two messages bear the same data-value d.

Several other interesting fragments of the π-calculus have been proposed in the literature, such as name bounded [11], mixed bounded [16], and structurally stationary [14]. Typically defined by a non-trivial condition on the set of reachable terms – a *semantic* property, membership becomes undecidable. Links with Petri nets via encodings of proper subsets of depth-bounded systems have been explored in [16]. Our type system can prove depth boundedness for processes that are breadth and name unbounded, and which cannot be simulated by Petri nets. In [2], Amadio and Meyssonnier consider fragments of the asynchronous π-calculus and show that coverability is decidable for the fragment with no mobility and bounded number of active sequential processes, via an encoding to Petri nets. Typably hierarchical systems can be seen as an extension of the result for a synchronous π-calculus with unbounded sequential processes and a restricted form of mobility.

Recently Hüchting et al. [12] proved several relative classification results between fragments of π-calculus. Using Karp-Miller trees, they presented an algorithm to decide if an arbitrary π-term is bounded in depth by a given k. The construction is based on an (accelerated) exploration of the state space of the π-term, with non primitive recursive complexity, which makes it impractical. By contrast, our type system uses a very different technique leading to a quicker algorithm, at the expense of precision. Our forest-structured types can also act as specifications, offering more intensional information to the user than just a bound k.

Our types are based on Milner's sorts for the π-calculus [9,18], later refined into I/O types [21] and their variants [22]. Based on these types is a system for termination of π-terms [3] that uses a notion of levels, enabling the definition of a lexicographical ordering. Our type system can also be used to determine termination of π-terms in an approximate but conservative way, by using it in conjunction with Theorem 1. Because the respective orderings between types of the two approaches are different in conception, we expect the terminating fragments isolated by the respective systems to be incomparable.

9 Future Directions

The type system we presented in Sect. 4 is conservative: the use of simple types, for example, renders the analysis context-insensitive. Although we have kept the system simple so as to focus on the novel aspects, a number of improvements are possible. First, the extension to the polyadic case is straightforward. Second, the type system can be made more precise by using subtyping and polymorphism to refine the analysis of control and data flow. Third, the typing rule for replication introduces a very heavy approximation: when typing a subterm, we have no information about which other parts of the term (crucially, which restrictions) may be replicated. By incorporating some information about which names can be instantiated unboundedly in the types, the precision of the analysis can be greatly improved. The formalisation and validation of these extensions is a topic of ongoing research.

Another direction worth exploring is the application of this machinery to heap manipulating programs and security protocols verification.

Acknowledgement. We would like to thank Damien Zufferey for helpful discussions on the nature of depth boundedness, and Roland Meyer for insightful feedback on a previous version of this paper.

References

1. Abdulla, P.A., Cerans, K., Jonsson, B., Tsay, Y.: General decidability theorems for infinite-state systems. In: Symposium on Logic in Computer Science, pp. 313–321. IEEE Computer Society (1996)
2. Amadio, R.M., Meyssonnier, C.: On decidability of the control reachability problem in the asynchronous π-calculus. Nordic J. Comput. **9**(2), 70–101 (2002)
3. Deng, Y., Sangiorgi, D.: Ensuring termination by typability. Inf. Comput. **204**(7), 1045–1082 (2006)
4. D'Osualdo, E.: Verification of Message Passing Concurrent Systems. Ph.D. thesis, University of Oxford (2015). http://ora.ox.ac.uk/objects/uuid:f669b95b-f760-4de9-a62a-374d41172879
5. D'Osualdo, E., Ong, C.-H.L.: On hierarchical communication topologies in the pi-calculus. CoRR (2016). http://arxiv.org/abs/1601.01725
6. D'Osualdo, E., Kochems, J., Ong, C.-H.L.: Automatic verification of Erlang-style concurrency. In: Logozzo, F., Fähndrich, M. (eds.) Static Analysis. LNCS, vol. 7935, pp. 454–476. Springer, Heidelberg (2013)
7. Emerson, E.A., Trefler, R.J.: From asymmetry to full symmetry: new techniques for symmetry reduction in model checking. In: Pierre, L., Kropf, T. (eds.) CHARME 1999. LNCS, vol. 1703, pp. 142–157. Springer, Heidelberg (1999)
8. Finkel, A., Schnoebelen, P.: Well-structured transition systems everywhere! Theor. Comput. Sci. **256**(1–2), 63–92 (2001)
9. Gay, S.J.: A sort inference algorithm for the polyadic π-calculus. In: Deusen, M.S.V., Lang, B. (eds.) Principles of Programming Languages (POPL), pp. 429–438. ACM Press (1993)
10. He, C.: The decidability of the reachability problem for $CCS^!$. In: Katoen, J.-P., König, B. (eds.) CONCUR 2011. LNCS, vol. 6901, pp. 373–388. Springer, Heidelberg (2011)
11. Hüchting, R., Majumdar, R., Meyer, R.: A theory of name boundedness. In: D'Argenio, P.R., Melgratti, H. (eds.) CONCUR 2013 – Concurrency Theory. LNCS, vol. 8052, pp. 182–196. Springer, Heidelberg (2013)
12. Hüchting, R., Majumdar, R., Meyer, R.: Bounds on mobility. In: Baldan, P., Gorla, D. (eds.) CONCUR 2014. LNCS, vol. 8704, pp. 357–371. Springer, Heidelberg (2014)
13. Meyer, R.: On boundedness in depth in the π-calculus. In: IFIP International Conference on Theoretical Computer Science, IFIP TCS, pp. 477–489 (2008)
14. Meyer, R.: A theory of structural stationarity in the π-calculus. Acta Informatica **46**(2), 87–137 (2009)
15. Meyer, R.: Structural stationarity in the π-calculus. Ph.D. thesis, University of Oldenburg (2009)

16. Meyer, R., Gorrieri, R.: On the relationship between π-calculus and finite place/transition Petri nets. In: Bravetti, M., Zavattaro, G. (eds.) CONCUR 2009. LNCS, vol. 5710, pp. 463–480. Springer, Heidelberg (2009)
17. Milner, R.: Functions as processes. Math. Struct. Comput. Sci. **2**(02), 119–141 (1992)
18. Milner, R.: The polyadic pi-calculus: a tutorial. Technical Report CS-LFCS-91-180, University of Edinburgh (1993)
19. Milner, R.: Communicating and Mobile Systems: the π-Calculus. Cambridge University Press, Cambridge (1999)
20. Milner, R., Parrow, J., Walker, D.: A calculus of mobile processes, I, II. Inf. Comput. **100**(1), 1–77 (1992)
21. Pierce, B.C., Sangiorgi, D.: Typing and subtyping for mobile processes. In: Symposium on Logic in Computer Science, pp. 376–385 (1993)
22. Pierce, B.C., Sangiorgi, D.: Behavioral equivalence in the polymorphic pi-calculus. J. ACM **47**(3), 531–584 (2000)
23. Pnueli, A., Xu, J., Zuck, L.D.: Liveness with $(0, 1, \infty)$-counter abstraction. In: Brinksma, E., Larsen, K.G. (eds.) CAV 2002. LNCS, vol. 2404, pp. 107–122. Springer, Heidelberg (2002)
24. Vasconcelos, V.T., Honda, K.: Principal typing schemes in a polyadic π-calculus. In: Best, E. (ed.) CONCUR 1993. LNCS, vol. 715, pp. 524–538. Springer, Heidelberg (1993)
25. Wies, T., Zufferey, D., Henzinger, T.A.: Forward analysis of depth-bounded processes. In: Ong, L. (ed.) FOSSACS 2010. LNCS, vol. 6014, pp. 94–108. Springer, Heidelberg (2010)
26. Zufferey, D., Wies, T., Henzinger, T.A.: Ideal abstractions for well-structured transition systems. In: Kuncak, V., Rybalchenko, A. (eds.) VMCAI 2012. LNCS, vol. 7148, pp. 445–460. Springer, Heidelberg (2012)

Modular Termination Verification for Non-blocking Concurrency

Pedro da Rocha Pinto[1(✉)], Thomas Dinsdale-Young[2], Philippa Gardner[1], and Julian Sutherland[1]

[1] Imperial College London, London, UK
{pmd09,pg,jhs110}@doc.ic.ac.uk
[2] Aarhus University, Aarhus, Denmark
tyoung@cs.au.dk

Abstract. We present Total-TaDA, a program logic for verifying the total correctness of concurrent programs: that such programs both terminate and produce the correct result. With Total-TaDA, we can specify constraints on a thread's concurrent environment that are necessary to guarantee termination. This allows us to verify total correctness for non-blocking algorithms, e.g. a counter and a stack. Our specifications can express lock- and wait-freedom. More generally, they can express that one operation cannot impede the progress of another, a new non-blocking property we call *non-impedance*. Moreover, our approach is modular. We can verify the operations of a module independently, and build up modules on top of each other.

1 Introduction

The problem of understanding and proving the correctness of programs has been considered at least since Turing [21]. When proving a program, it is not just important to know that it will give the right answer, but also that the program terminates. This is especially challenging for concurrent programs. When multiple threads are changing some shared resource, knowing if each thread terminates can often depend on the behaviour of the other threads and even on the scheduler that decides which thread should run at a particular moment.

If we prove that a concurrent program only produces the right answer, we establish *partial correctness*. Many recent developments have been made in program logics for partial correctness of concurrent programs [5,11,16,17,19,22]. These logics emphasise a *modular* approach, which allows us to decouple the verification of a module's clients and its implementation. Each operation of the module is proven in isolation, and the reasoning is local to the thread. To achieve this, these logics abstract the interference between a thread and its environment.

These logics have been applied to reason about fine-grained concurrency, which is characterised by the use of low-level synchronisation operations (such as compare-and-swap). A well-known class of fine-grained concurrent programs is that of *non-blocking* algorithms. With non-blocking algorithms, suspension of a thread cannot halt the progress of other threads: the progress of a single thread

P. Thiemann (Ed.): ESOP 2016, LNCS 9632, pp. 176–201, 2016.
DOI: 10.1007/978-3-662-49498-1_8

cannot require another thread to be scheduled. Thus if the interference from the environment is suitably restricted, the operations are guaranteed to terminate.

If we prove that a program produces the correct results and also always completes in a finite time, we establish *total correctness*. Turing [21] and Floyd [6] introduced the use of well-founded relations, combined with partial-correctness arguments, to prove the termination of sequential programs. The same technique is general enough to prove concurrent programs too. However, previous applications of this technique in the concurrent setting, which we discuss in Sect. 7, do not support straight-forward reasoning about clients.

In this paper, we extend a particular concurrent program logic, TaDA [16], with well-founded termination reasoning. With the resulting logic, Total-TaDA, we can prove total correctness of fine-grained concurrent programs. The novelty of our approach is in using TaDA's abstraction mechanisms to specify constraints on the environment necessary to ensure termination. It retains the modularity of TaDA and abstracts the internal termination arguments. We demonstrate our approach on counter and stack algorithms.

We observe that Total-TaDA can be used to verify standard non-blocking properties of algorithms. However, our specifications capture more: we propose the concept of *non-impedance* that our specifications suggest. We say that one operation *impedes* another if the second can be prevented from terminating by repeated concurrent invocations of the first. This concept seems important to the design and use of non-blocking algorithms where we have some expectation about how clients use the algorithm, and what progress guarantees they expect.

TaDA. TaDA introduced a new form of specification, given by *atomic triples*, which supports local, modular reasoning and can express constraints on the concurrent environment. Simple atomic triples have the following form:

$$\vdash \mathbb{V}x \in X.\, \langle p(x) \rangle\ \mathbb{C}\ \langle q(x) \rangle$$

Intuitively, the specification states that the program $\mathbb{C}$ atomically updates $p(x)$ to $q(x)$ for an arbitrary $x \in X$. As we are in a concurrent setting, while $\mathbb{C}$ is executing, there might be interference from the environment before the atomic update. The pseudo-quantifier $\mathbb{V}$ restricts the interference: before the atomic update, the environment must maintain $p(x)$, but it is allowed to change the parameter as long as it stays within X; after the atomic update, the environment is not constrained. This specification thus provides a contract between the client of $\mathbb{C}$ and the implementation: the client can assume that the precondition holds for some $x \in X$ until it performs the update.

Using the atomic triple, an increment operation of a counter is specified as:[1]

$$\vdash \mathbb{V}n \in \mathbb{N}.\, \big\langle \mathsf{C}(s, \mathtt{x}, n) \big\rangle\ \mathtt{incr(x)}\ \big\langle \mathsf{C}(s, \mathtt{x}, n+1) \land \mathsf{ret} = n \big\rangle$$

The internal structure of the counter is abstracted using the abstract predicate [14] $\mathsf{C}(s, x, n)$, which states that there is a counter at address x with value

[1] The parameter s of the abstract predicate was mistakenly abstracted in [16]. Technically, it is not possible to abstract it by existentially quantifying in the precondition of the atomic triple.

n and s abstracts implementation specific information about the counter. The specification says that the `incr` atomically increments the counter by 1. The environment is allowed to update the counter to any value of n as long as it is a natural number. The specification enforces obligations on both the client and the implementation: the client must guarantee that the counter is not destroyed and that its value is a natural number until the atomic update occurs; and the implementation must guarantee that it does not change the value of the counter until it performs the specified atomic action. Working at the abstraction of the counter means that each operation can be verified without knowing the rest of the operations of the module. Consequently, modules can be extended with new operations without having to re-verify the existing operations. Additionally, the implementation of `incr` can be replaced by another implementation that satisfies the same specification, without needing to re-verify the clients that make use of the counter. While atomic triples are expressive, they do not guarantee termination. In particular, an implementation could block, deadlock or live-lock and still be considered correct.

Non-blocking Algorithms. In general, guaranteeing the termination of concurrent programs is a difficult problem. In particular, termination could depend on the behaviour of the scheduler (whether or not it is *fair*) and of other threads that might be competing for resources. We focus on non-blocking programs. Non-blocking programs have the benefit that their termination is not dependent on the behaviour of the scheduler.

There are two common non-blocking properties: *wait-freedom* [8] and *lock-freedom* [13]. Wait-freedom requires that operations complete irrespective of the interference caused by other threads: termination cannot depend on the amount of interference caused by the environment. Lock-freedom is less restrictive. It requires that, when multiple threads are performing operations, then at least one of them must make progress. This means that a thread might never terminate if the amount of interference caused by the environment is unlimited.

TaDA is well suited to reasoning about interference between threads. In particular, we can write specifications that limit the amount of interference caused by the client, and so guarantee termination of lock-free algorithms. We will see how both wait-freedom and lock-freedom can be expressed in Total-TaDA.

Termination. Well-founded relations provide a general way to prove termination. In particular, Floyd [6] used well-founded relations to prove the termination of sequential programs. In fact, it is sufficient to use ordinal numbers [3] without losing expressivity. A 'Hoare-style' while rule, using ordinals and adapted from Floyd's work, has the form:

$$\frac{\forall \gamma \leq \alpha.\ \vdash_\tau \{p(\gamma) \land \mathbb{B}\}\ \mathbb{C}\ \{\exists \beta.\, p(\beta) \land \beta < \gamma\}}{\vdash_\tau \{p(\alpha)\}\ \texttt{while}\ (\mathbb{B})\ \mathbb{C}\ \{\exists \beta.\, p(\beta) \land \neg\mathbb{B} \land \beta \leq \alpha\}}$$

The loop invariant $p(\gamma)$ is parametrised by an ordinal γ (the *variant*) which is decreased by every execution of the loop body $\mathbb{C}$. Because ordinals cannot have infinite descending chains, the loop must terminate in a finite number of steps.

This proof rule allows termination reasoning to be localised to the individual loops in the program. In this paper, we extend TaDA with termination based on ordinal numbers, using the while rule given above.

Total-TaDA. We obtain the program logic Total-TaDA by modifying TaDA to have a total-correctness semantics. The details are given in Sect. 3. With Total-TaDA, we can specify and verify non-blocking algorithms. Wait-free operations always terminate, independently of the operations performed by the environment. For lock-free operations however, we need to restrict the amount of interference the environment can cause in order to guarantee termination. Our key insight is that, as well as bounding the number of iterations of loops, ordinals can bound the interference on a module. This allows us to give total-correctness specifications for lock-free algorithms. In Sect. 2, we specify and verify lock-free implementations of a counter. The specification introduces ordinals to bound the number of times a client may update the counter. This makes it possible to guarantee that the lock-free increment operation will terminate, since either it will succeed or some other concurrent increment will succeed. As the number of increments is bounded, the operation must eventually succeed.

Total-TaDA retains the modularity of TaDA. In particular, we can verify the termination of clients of modules using the total-correctness specifications, without reference to the implementation. We show an example of this in Sect. 2.2. Since the client only depends on the specification, we can replace the implementation. In Sect. 2.3 we show that two different implementations of a counter satisfy the same total-correctness specification. With Total-TaDA we can verify the operations of a module independently, exploiting locality.

As a case study for Total-TaDA, we show how to specify and verify both functional correctness and termination of Treiber's stack in Sect. 4. In Sect. 5, we discuss the implications of a total-correctness semantics for the soundness proof of Total-TaDA. In Sect. 6, we show how lock-freedom and wait-freedom can be expressed with Total-TaDA specifications. We also introduce the concept of non-impedance in Sect. 6.3 and argue for its value in specifying non-blocking algorithms. We discuss related work in Sect. 7 and future directions in Sect. 8.

2 Motivating Examples: Counters

We introduce Total-TaDA by providing specifications of the operations of a counter module. We justify the specifications by using them to reason about two clients, one sequential and one concurrent. We show how two different implementations can be proved to satisfy the specification.

Our underlying programming language is a concurrent while language with functions, allocation and the atomic assignment $\mathtt{x} := E$, read $E := [E]$, write $[E] := E$ and compare-and-swap $\mathtt{x} := \mathtt{CAS}(E, E, E)$, where expressions E have no side effects. Consider a counter module with a constructor `makeCounter` and two operations: `incr` that increments the value of the counter by 1 and returns its previous value; and `read` that returns the value of the counter. We give an implementation in Fig. 1a, and an alternative implementation of `incr` in Fig. 1b.

```
function makeCounter() {
  x := alloc(1);
  [x] := 0;
  return x;
}

function read(x) {
  v := [x];
  return v;
}
```

```
function incr(x) {
  b := 0;
  while (b = 0) {
    v := [x];
    b := CAS(x, v, v + 1);
  }
  return v;
}
```

(a) Spin counter operations.

```
function incr(x) {
  n := 0; b := 0;
  while (b = 0) {
    if (n = 0) {
      v := [x];
      b := CAS(x, v, v + 1);
      n := random();
    } else {
      n := n − 1;
    }
  }
  return v;
}
```

(b) Backoff increment.

Fig. 1. Counter module implementations.

2.1 Abstract Specification

The Total-TaDA specification for the makeCounter() operation is a Hoare triple with a total-correctness interpretation:

$$\forall\alpha.\ \vdash_\tau \{\mathsf{emp}\}\ \mathtt{x} := \mathtt{makeCounter()}\ \{\exists s.\,\mathsf{C}(s, \mathtt{x}, 0, \alpha)\}$$

The counter predicate is extended with an ordinal parameter, α, that provides a bound on the amount of interference the counter can sustain. When the value of the counter is updated, the ordinal α must decrease.

The operation allocates a new counter, with value 0, and allows the client to pick an initial ordinal α. If a finite bound on the number of updates is already determined, then that is an appropriate choice for the ordinal. However, it could be that the bound is determined by subsequent (non-deterministic) operations, in which case an infinite ordinal should be used. For example, consider the following client program:

```
x := makeCounter();
m := random();
while (m > 0) {
  incr(x); m := m − 1;
}
```

Here, the number of increments is bounded by the (finite) value returned by random, but it is not determined when the counter is constructed. Choosing $\alpha = \omega$ (the first infinite ordinal) is appropriate in this case: the first increment can decrease the ordinal from ω to $\mathtt{m} - 1$, while subsequent increments simply decrement the ordinal by 1.

The increment operation is specified as follows:

$$\forall\beta.\ \vdash_\tau \mathbb{V} n \in \mathbb{N}, \alpha.\quad \langle \mathsf{C}(s, \mathtt{x}, n, \alpha) \wedge \alpha > \beta(n, \alpha) \rangle \quad \mathtt{incr(x)} \quad \langle \mathsf{C}(s, \mathtt{x}, n+1, \beta(n, \alpha)) \wedge \mathsf{ret} = n \rangle$$

The specification resembles the partial-correctness specification given in the introduction, but with the addition of the ordinal α and the function β. The client chooses how to decrease the ordinal by providing a function β that determines the new ordinal in terms of the old ordinal and previous value of the counter. The condition $\alpha > \beta(n, \alpha)$ requires the client to guarantee that such a decrease is possible. (So, for example, the client could not use the specification in a situation where the concurrent environment might reduce the ordinal to zero.) The implementation may rely on the fact that a counter's ordinal cannot be increased to guarantee termination.

The read operation is specified as follows:

$$\vdash_\tau \mathbb{V} n \in \mathbb{N}, \alpha. \left\langle \mathsf{C}(s, \mathtt{x}, n, \alpha) \right\rangle \mathtt{read(x)} \left\langle \mathsf{C}(s, \mathtt{x}, n, \alpha) \wedge \mathsf{ret} = n \right\rangle$$

Unlike the increment, the read operation does not affect the ordinal. This means that the client is not bounded with respect to the number of reads it performs. Such a specification is possible for operations that do not impede the progress of other operations. In this case, `read` does not impede `incr` or `read`.

Finally, we give an axiom that allows the client to decrease the ordinal without requiring any physical operation.

$$\forall s, n, \alpha, \beta < \alpha. \mathsf{C}(s, \mathtt{x}, n, \alpha) \implies \mathsf{C}(s, \mathtt{x}, n, \beta)$$

This is possible because the ordinals do not have any concrete representation in memory. They are just a logical mechanism to limit the amount of interference over a resource.

The ordinal parameter is exposed in the specification of the counter to allow the implementation to guarantee that its loops terminate. In a wait-free implementation it would not be necessary to expose the ordinal parameter. For this counter, the read operation is wait-free, while the increment operation is lock-free, since termination depends on bounding the number of interfering increments.

2.2 Clients

Sequential Client. Consider a program that creates a counter and contains two nested loops. As in the previous example, the outer loop runs a finite but randomly determined number of times. The inner loop also runs a randomly determined number of times, and increments the counter on each iteration. Figure 2 shows this client, together with its total-correctness proof.

The while rule is used for each of the loops: for the outer loop, the variant is `n`; for the inner loop, the variant is `m`. Since the number of iterations of each loop is determined before it is run, the variants need only be considered up to finite ordinals (*i.e.* natural numbers). (We could modify the code to use a single loop that conditionally decrements `n` (and randomises `m`) or decrements `m`. This variation would require a transfinite ordinal for the variant.)

As well as enforcing loop termination, ordinals play a role as a parameter to the C predicate, which must be decreased on each increment. When we create

```
{emp}
x := makeCounter();
{∃s. C(s, x, 0, ω²)}
n := random();
{∃s. C(s, x, 0, ω · n)}
while (n > 0) {
  ∀γ. {∃s, v. C(s, x, v, ω · n) ∧ γ = n ∧ n > 0}
    m := random();
    {∃s, v. C(s, x, v, ω · (n − 1) + m) ∧ γ = n ∧ n > 0}
    while (m > 0) {                                              ⎫
      ∀δ. {∃s, v. C(s, x, v, ω · (n − 1) + m) ∧ δ = m ∧ m > 0}   ⎪
        incr(x);                                                 ⎪ Frame:
        {∃s, v. C(s, x, v, ω · (n − 1) + m − 1) ∧ δ = m > 0}     ⎪ γ = n ∧ n > 0
        m := m − 1;                                              ⎪
        {∃s, ζ, v. C(s, x, v, ω · (n − 1) + m) ∧ ζ = m ∧ ζ < δ}  ⎪
    }                                                            ⎭
    {∃s, v. C(s, x, v, ω · (n − 1)) ∧ γ = n ∧ n > 0}
    n := n − 1;
    {∃s, β, v. C(s, x, v, ω · n) ∧ β = n ∧ β < γ}
}
{∃s, v. C(s, x, v, 0)}
```

Fig. 2. Proof of a sequential client of the counter.

the counter, we choose ω^2 as the initial ordinal. We have seen that ω allows us to decrement the counter a non-deterministic (but finite) number of times. We want to repeat this a non-deterministic (but finite) number of times, so $\omega \cdot \omega = \omega^2$ is the appropriate ordinal. Once the number $\mathtt{n}$ of iterations of the outer loop is determined, we decrease this to $\omega \cdot \mathtt{n}$ by using the axiom provided by the counter module. Similarly, when $\mathtt{m}$ is chosen, we decrease the ordinal from $\omega \cdot \mathtt{n} = \omega \cdot (\mathtt{n} - 1) + \omega$ to $\omega \cdot (\mathtt{n} - 1) + \mathtt{m}$.

Concurrent Client. Consider a program that creates two threads, each of which increments the counter a finite but unbounded number of times. We again prove this client using the abstract specification of the counter. The proof is given in Fig. 3. In this example, the counter is shared between the two threads, which may concurrently update it. To reason about sharing, we use a *shared region.*

As in TaDA, a shared region encapsulates some resource that is available to multiple threads. Threads can access the resource when performing (abstractly) atomic operations, such as `incr`. The region presents an abstract state, and defines a protocol that determines how the region may be updated. Ghost resources, called *guards*, are associated with transitions in the protocol. The guards for a region form a partial commutative monoid with the operation $\bullet$, which is lifted by $*$ in assertions. In order for a thread to make a particular update, it must have ownership of a guard associated with the corresponding transition. All guards are allocated along with the region they are associated with.

For the concurrent client, we introduce a region with type name **CClient**. This region encapsulates the shared counter. Accordingly, the region type is parametrised by the address of the counter. The abstract state of the region records the current value of the counter.

There are two types of guard resources associated with **CClient** regions. The guard $\textsc{Inc}(m, \beta, \pi)$ provides capability to increment the counter. Conceptually, multiple threads may have $\textsc{Inc}$ guards, and a fractional permission $\pi \in (0, 1]$ (in the style of [2]) is used to keep track of these capabilities. The parameter m expresses the *local contribution* to the value of the counter — the actual value is the sum of the local contributions. The ordinal parameter β represents a local bound on the number of increments. Again, the actual bound is a sum of the local bounds. Standard ordinal addition is inconvenient since it is not commutative; we use the natural (or Hessenberg) sum [9], denoted $\oplus$, which is associative, commutative, and monotone in its arguments.

To allow the $\textsc{Inc}$ guard to be shared among threads, we impose the following equivalence on guards:

$$\textsc{Inc}(n + m, \alpha \oplus \beta, \pi_1 + \pi_2) = \textsc{Inc}(n, \alpha, \pi_1) \bullet \textsc{Inc}(m, \beta, \pi_2)$$

where $n \geq 0$, $m \geq 0$ and $1 \geq \pi_1 + \pi_2 > 0$. This equivalence expresses that $\textsc{Inc}$ guards can be split (or joined), preserving the total contribution to the value of the counter, ordinal bound and permission.

The second type of guard resource is $\textsc{Total}(n, \alpha)$, which tracks the actual value of the counter n and ordinal α. These values should match the totals for the $\textsc{Inc}$ guards, which we enforce by requiring the following implication to hold:

$$\textsc{Total}(n, \alpha) \bullet \textsc{Inc}(m, \beta, 1) \text{ defined} \implies n = m \wedge \alpha = \beta$$

We wish to allow the contributions recorded in $\textsc{Inc}$ guards to change, but to do so we must simultaneously update the $\textsc{Total}$ guard, as expressed by the following equivalence:

$$\textsc{Total}(n + m, \alpha \oplus \beta) \bullet \textsc{Inc}(m, \beta, \pi) = \textsc{Total}(n + m', \alpha \oplus \beta') \bullet \textsc{Inc}(m', \beta', \pi)$$

(We have constructed an instance of the authoritative monoid of Iris [11].)

The possible states of **CClient** regions are the natural numbers $\mathbb{N}$, representing the value of the shared counter, together with the distinguished state $\circ$, representing that the region is no longer required. The protocol for a region is specified by a guarded transition system, which describes how the abstract state may be updated in atomic steps, and which guard resources are required to do so. The transitions for **CClient** regions are as follows:

$$\textsc{Inc}(m, \gamma, \pi) : n \rightsquigarrow n + 1 \qquad \textsc{Inc}(m, \gamma, 1) : n \rightsquigarrow \circ$$

This specifies that any thread with an $\textsc{Inc}$ guard may increment the value of the counter, and a thread owning the full $\textsc{Inc}$ guard may dispose of the region.

It remains to define the interpretation of the region states:

$$I(\mathbf{CClient}_r(s, x, n)) \triangleq \exists \alpha.\, \mathsf{C}(s, x, n, \alpha) * [\textsc{Total}(n, \alpha)]_r$$
$$I(\mathbf{CClient}_r(s, x, \circ)) \triangleq \mathsf{True}$$

$$
\begin{array}{c}
\{\mathsf{emp}\} \\
\mathtt{x} := \mathtt{makeCounter}(); \\
\{\exists s.\, \mathsf{C}(s, \mathtt{x}, 0, \omega \oplus \omega)\} \\
\{\exists s, r.\, \mathbf{CClient}_r(s, \mathtt{x}, 0) * [\textsc{Inc}(0, \omega \oplus \omega, 1)]_r\}
\end{array}
$$

$$
\left.
\begin{array}{l}
\{\exists s, v.\, \mathbf{CClient}_r(s, \mathtt{x}, v) * [\textsc{Inc}(0, \omega, \tfrac{1}{2})]_r \wedge 0 \leq v\} \\
\mathtt{n} := \mathtt{random}();\ \mathtt{i} := 0; \\
\{\exists s, v.\, \mathbf{CClient}_r(s, \mathtt{x}, v) * [\textsc{Inc}(\mathtt{i}, \mathtt{n}, \tfrac{1}{2})]_r \wedge 0 \leq v \wedge \mathtt{i} = 0\} \\
\mathtt{while}\ (\mathtt{i} < \mathtt{n})\ \{ \\
\quad \forall \beta.\ \left\{\begin{array}{l} \exists s, v.\, \mathbf{CClient}_r(s, \mathtt{x}, v) * [\textsc{Inc}(\mathtt{i}, \beta, \tfrac{1}{2})]_r \wedge \mathtt{i} \leq v \\ \wedge\, \mathtt{i} < \mathtt{n} \wedge \beta = \mathtt{n} - \mathtt{i} \end{array}\right\} \\
\qquad \mathtt{incr}(\mathtt{x});\ \mathtt{i} := \mathtt{i} + 1; \\
\qquad \left\{\begin{array}{l} \exists s, \delta, v.\, \mathbf{CClient}_r(s, \mathtt{x}, v) * [\textsc{Inc}(\mathtt{i}, \delta, \tfrac{1}{2})]_r \wedge \mathtt{i} \leq v \\ \wedge\, \mathtt{i} \leq \mathtt{n} \wedge \delta = \mathtt{n} - \mathtt{i} \wedge \delta < \beta \end{array}\right\} \\
\} \\
\{\exists s, v.\, \mathbf{CClient}_r(s, \mathtt{x}, v) * [\textsc{Inc}(\mathtt{n}, 0, \tfrac{1}{2})]_r\}
\end{array}
\right\|
\begin{array}{l}
\left\{\begin{array}{l} \exists s, v.\, \mathbf{CClient}_r(s, \mathtt{x}, v) \\ *\, [\textsc{Inc}(0, \omega, \tfrac{1}{2})]_r \end{array}\right\} \\
\mathtt{m} := \mathtt{random}(); \\
\mathtt{j} := 0; \\
\mathtt{while}\ (\mathtt{j} < \mathtt{m})\ \{ \\
\quad \mathtt{incr}(\mathtt{x}); \\
\quad \mathtt{j} := \mathtt{j} + 1; \\
\} \\
\left\{\begin{array}{l} \exists s, v.\, \mathbf{CClient}_r(s, \mathtt{x}, v) \\ *\, [\textsc{Inc}(\mathtt{m}, 0, \tfrac{1}{2})]_r \end{array}\right\}
\end{array}
$$

$$
\begin{array}{c}
\{\exists s, r.\, \mathbf{CClient}_r(s, \mathtt{x}, \mathtt{n} + \mathtt{m}) * [\textsc{Inc}(\mathtt{n} + \mathtt{m}, 0, 1)]_r\} \\
\{\exists s.\, \mathsf{C}(s, \mathtt{x}, \mathtt{n} + \mathtt{m}, 0)\}
\end{array}
$$

Fig. 3. Proof of a concurrent client of the counter.

By interpreting the state $\circ$ as True, we allow a thread transitioning into that state to acquire the counter that previously belonged to the region. (This justifies the last step of the proof in Fig. 3.)

The proof rule that allows us to use the atomic specification of the `incr` operation to update the shared region is the $\mathsf{use\ atomic}$ rule, inherited from TaDA. A simplified version of the rule is as follows:

$$
\frac{\forall x \in X.\, (x, f(x)) \in \mathcal{T}_{\mathbf{t}}(\mathrm{G})^* \qquad \vdash_\tau \mathbb{W} x \in X.\, \langle I(\mathbf{t}_a(x)) * [\mathrm{G}]_a \rangle\ \mathbb{C}\ \langle I(\mathbf{t}_a(f(x))) * q \rangle}{\vdash_\tau \{\exists x \in X.\, \mathbf{t}_a(x) * [\mathrm{G}]_a\}\ \mathbb{C}\ \{\exists x \in X.\, \mathbf{t}_a(f(x)) * q\}}
$$

In the conclusion of the rule, the abstract state of the region a (of type $\mathbf{t}$) is updated according to the function f. The first premiss requires that this update is allowed by the transition system for the region, given the guard resources available (G). The second premiss requires that the program $\mathbb{C}$ (abstractly) atomically performs the corresponding update on the concrete state of the region.

The $\{\}$-assertions in Total-TaDA are required to be stable. That is, the region states must account for the possible changes that the concurrent environment could make, under the assumption that it has guards that are compatible with those of the thread. This is why, for instance, in Fig. 3 the state of the **CClient** region is always existentially quantified.

2.3 Implementations

We prove the total correctness of the two distinct increment implementations against the abstract specification given in Sect. 2.1.

Spin Counter Increment. Consider `incr` shown in Fig. 1a. Note that the read, write and compare-and-swap operations are atomic. We want to prove the total correctness of `incr` against the atomic specification. The first step is to give a concrete interpretation of the abstract predicate $\mathsf{C}(s, x, n, \alpha)$. We introduce a new region type, **Counter**, with only one non-empty guard, G. The abstract states of the region are pairs of the form (n, α), where n is the value of the counter and α is a bound on the number of increments. All transitions are guarded by G with the transition:

$$\mathrm{G} : \forall n \in \mathbb{N}, m \in \mathbb{N}, \alpha > \beta.\, (n, \alpha) \rightsquigarrow (n + m, \beta)$$

The transition requires that updates to the state of the region must decrease the ordinal. This allows us to effectively bound interference, which is necessary to guarantee the termination of the loop in `incr`.

The interpretation of the `Counter` region states is defined as follows:

$$I(\mathbf{Counter}_r(x, n, \alpha)) \triangleq x \mapsto n$$

The expression $x \mapsto n$ asserts that there exists a heap cell with address x and value n. Note that α is not represented in the concrete heap, as it is not part of the program. We use it solely to ensure that the number of operations is finite.

We define the interpretation of the abstract predicate as follows:

$$\mathsf{C}(r, x, n, \alpha) \triangleq \mathbf{Counter}_r(x, n, \alpha) * [\mathrm{G}]_r$$

The abstract predicate $\mathsf{C}(r, x, n, \alpha)$ asserts that there is a **Counter** region with identifier r, address x, and with abstract state (n, α). Furthermore, it encapsulates exclusive ownership of the guard G, and so embodies exclusive permission to update the counter. (Note that the type of the first parameter of C, which is abstract to the client, is instantiated as RId.)

The specification for the increment is atomic and as such, we use the make atomic rule from TaDA. A slightly simplified version of the rule is as follows:

$$\frac{\begin{array}{c}\{(x, y) \mid x \in X, y \in Q(x)\} \subseteq \mathcal{T}_{\mathbf{t}}(\mathrm{G})^* \\ a : x \in X \rightsquigarrow Q(x) \vdash_{\tau} \left\{\exists x \in X.\, \mathbf{t}_a(x) * a \Mapsto \blacklozenge\right\}\ \mathbb{C}\ \left\{\exists x \in X, y \in Q(x).\, a \Mapsto (x, y)\right\}\end{array}}{\vdash_{\tau} \forall\!\!\!\forall x \in X.\, \left\langle \mathbf{t}_a(x) * [\mathrm{G}]_a \right\rangle\ \mathbb{C}\ \left\langle \exists y \in Q(x).\, \mathbf{t}_a(y) * [\mathrm{G}]_a \right\rangle}$$

This rule establishes in its conclusion that $\mathbb{C}$ atomically updates region a from some state $x \in X$ to some state $y \in Q(x)$. The first premiss requires that the available guard G permits this update, according to the transition system. The second premiss essentially establishes that $\mathbb{C}$ will perform a single atomic update on region a, corresponding to the required update. The *atomicity context* $a : x \in X \rightsquigarrow Q(x)$ records the update we require. The program is given the atomic tracking resource $a \Mapsto \blacklozenge$ initially (in place of the guard G); this resource permits a single update to the region in accordance with the atomicity context, while at the same time guaranteeing that the region's state will remain within X. When the single update occurs, the atomic tracking resource simultaneously changes to record the actual update performed: $a \Mapsto (x, y)$.

The make atomic rule of Total-TaDA is just the same as that of TaDA. The only difference is that termination is enforced. Whereas in TaDA it would be

$\forall \beta.\, \mathbb{W} n \in \mathbb{N}, \alpha.$

$\langle \mathsf{C}(s, \mathtt{x}, n, \alpha) \land \alpha > \beta(n, \alpha) \rangle$

abstract; substitute $s = r$

$\langle \mathbf{Counter}_r(\mathtt{x}, n, \alpha) * [\mathrm{G}]_r \land \alpha > \beta(n, \alpha) \rangle$

make atomic

$r : (n, \alpha) \land n \in \mathbb{N} \land \alpha > \beta(n, \alpha) \rightsquigarrow (n + 1, \beta(n, \alpha)) \vdash_\tau$

$\{\exists n \in \mathbb{N}, \alpha.\, \mathbf{Counter}_r(\mathtt{x}, n, \alpha) * r \Rrightarrow \blacklozenge \land \alpha > \beta(n, \alpha)\}$

`b := 0;`

$\{\exists n \in \mathbb{N}, \alpha.\, \mathbf{Counter}_r(\mathtt{x}, n, \alpha) * r \Rrightarrow \blacklozenge \land \mathtt{b} = 0 \land \alpha > \beta(n, \alpha)\}$

`while (b = 0) {`

$\forall \gamma.$

$\{\exists n \in \mathbb{N}, \alpha.\, \mathbf{Counter}_r(\mathtt{x}, n, \alpha) * r \Rrightarrow \blacklozenge \land \mathtt{b} = 0 \land \gamma \geq \alpha > \beta(n, \alpha)\}$

open region

$\mathbb{W} n \in \mathbb{N}, \alpha.$

$\langle \mathtt{x} \mapsto n \land \gamma \geq \alpha > \beta(n, \alpha) \rangle$

`v := [x];`

$\langle \mathtt{x} \mapsto n \land \mathtt{v} = n \land \gamma \geq \alpha > \beta(n, \alpha) \land (n > \mathtt{v} \Rightarrow \gamma > \alpha) \rangle$

$\left\{\begin{array}{l} \exists n \in \mathbb{N}, \alpha.\, \mathbf{Counter}_r(\mathtt{x}, n, \alpha) * r \Rrightarrow \blacklozenge \land \\ \gamma \geq \alpha > \beta(n, \alpha) \land n \geq \mathtt{v} \land (n > \mathtt{v} \Rightarrow \gamma > \alpha) \end{array}\right\}$

update region

$\mathbb{W} n \in \mathbb{N}, \alpha.$

$\langle \mathtt{x} \mapsto n \land \gamma \geq \alpha > \beta(n, \alpha) \land n \geq \mathtt{v} \land (n > \mathtt{v} \Rightarrow \gamma > \alpha) \rangle$

`b := CAS(x, v, v + 1);`

$\left\langle \begin{array}{l} \alpha > \beta(n, \alpha) \land \underline{\text{if}}\ \mathtt{b} = 0\ \underline{\text{then}}\ \gamma > \alpha \land \mathtt{x} \mapsto n \\ \quad \underline{\text{else}}\ \mathtt{x} \mapsto n + 1 \land \mathtt{v} = n \end{array} \right\rangle$

$\left\{\begin{array}{l} \exists n \in \mathbb{N}, \alpha.\, \gamma \geq \alpha > \beta(n, \alpha) \land \underline{\text{if}}\ \mathtt{b} = 0\ \underline{\text{then}} \begin{pmatrix} \mathbf{Counter}_r(\mathtt{x}, n, \alpha) \\ * r \Rrightarrow \blacklozenge \land \gamma > \alpha \end{pmatrix} \\ \quad \underline{\text{else}}\ r \Rrightarrow ((\mathtt{v}, \alpha), (\mathtt{v} + 1, \beta(n, \alpha))) \end{array}\right\}$

`}`

$\{\exists n \in \mathbb{N}, \alpha.\, r \Rrightarrow ((n, \alpha), (n + 1, \beta(n, \alpha))) \land \mathtt{v} = n\}$

`return v;`

$\{\exists n \in \mathbb{N}, \alpha.\, r \Rrightarrow ((n, \alpha), (n + 1, \beta(n, \alpha))) \land \mathsf{ret} = n\}$

$\langle \mathbf{Counter}_r(\mathtt{x}, n + 1, \beta(n, \alpha)) * [\mathrm{G}]_r \land \mathsf{ret} = n \rangle$

$\langle \mathsf{C}(s, \mathtt{x}, n, \beta(n, \alpha)) \land \mathsf{ret} = n \rangle$

Fig. 4. Proof of total correctness of increment.

possible for an abstract atomic operation to loop forever without performing its atomic update, in Total-TaDA it is guaranteed to eventually perform the update.

A proof of the increment implementation is shown in Fig. 4. The atomicity context allows the environment to modify the abstract state of the counter. However, it makes no restriction on the number of times. The **Counter** transition system enforces that the ordinal α must decrease every time the value of the counter is increased. This means that the number of times the region's abstract state is updated is finite. Our loop invariant is parametrised with a variant γ that takes the value of α at the beginning of each loop iteration. When we first read the value of the counter n, we can assert: $n > \mathtt{v} \Rightarrow \gamma > \alpha$.

If the compare-and-swap operation fails, the value of the counter has changed. This can only happen in accordance with the region's transition system, and so the ordinal parameter α must have decreased. As such, the invariant still holds but for a lower ordinal, $\alpha < \gamma$. We are localising the termination argument for the loop, by relating the local variant with the ordinal parametrising the region.

If the compare-and-swap succeeds, then we record our update from $(\mathtt{v}, \alpha)$ to $(\mathtt{v} + 1, \beta(\mathtt{v}, \alpha))$, where β is the function chosen by the client that determines how the ordinal is reduced. The make atomic rule allows us to export this update in the postcondition of the whole operation.

Backoff Increment. Consider a different implementation of the increment operation, given in Fig. 1b. Like the previous implementation, it loops attempting to perform the operation. However, if the compare-and-swap fails due to contention, it waits for a random number of iterations before retrying.

Despite the differences to the previous increment, the specification is the same. In fact, we can give the same interpretation for the abstract predicate $\mathsf{C}(x, n, \alpha)$, and the same guards and regions that were used for the previous implementation. (Since this is the case, a counter module could provide *both* of these operations: the proof system guarantees that they work correctly together.)

The main difference in the proof is that each iteration of the loop depends on not only the amount of interference on the counter, but also on the variable $\mathtt{n}$ that is randomised when the compare-and-swap fails. Any random number will be smaller than ω, and the maximum amount of times that the compare-and-swap can fail is α, the parameter of the C predicate. This is because α is a bound on the number of times the counter can be incremented. We therefore use $\omega \cdot \alpha + \mathtt{n}$ as the upper bound on the number of loop iterations.

Let γ be equal to $\omega \cdot \alpha + \mathtt{n}$ at the start of the loop iteration. At each loop iteration, we have two cases, when $\mathtt{n} = 0$ or otherwise. In the first case we try to perform the increment by doing a compare-and-swap. If the compare-and-swap succeeds, then the increment occurs and the loop will exit. If it fails, then the environment must have decreased α. This means that $\gamma \geq \omega \cdot \alpha + \omega$ for the new value of α. We then set $\mathtt{n}$ to be a new random number, which is less than ω, and end up with $\gamma > \omega \cdot \alpha + \mathtt{n}$. In the second case of the loop iteration, we simply decrement $\mathtt{n}$ by 1 and we know that $\gamma > \omega \cdot \alpha + \mathtt{n}$ for the new value of $\mathtt{n}$. The proof of the backoff increment is shown in Fig. 5.

3 Logic

Total-TaDA is a Hoare logic which, for the first time, can be used to prove total correctness for fine-grained non-blocking concurrent programs. The logic is essentially the same as for TaDA, simply adapted to incorporate termination analysis using ordinals in a standard way.

Total-TaDA assertions, ranged over by $p, q, \ldots$, are constructed from the standard assertions of separation logic [15], plus abstract predicates, region predicates and tokens, examples of which are given in Sect. 2. The Total-TaDA proof judgement has the form:

$$\mathcal{A} \vdash_\tau \mathbb{V}x \in X.\, \langle p_p \mid p(x) \rangle\ \mathbb{C}\ \ \exists\!\!\exists y \in Y.\, \langle q_p(x, y) \mid q(x, y) \rangle.$$

In our examples, the atomicity context $\mathcal{A}$ describes an update to a single region. In general, $\mathcal{A}$ may describe updates to multiple regions (although only one

abstract; substitute $s = r$

make atomic

$$\forall \beta.\ \mathbb{V}n \in \mathbb{N}, \alpha.$$
$$\langle \mathsf{C}(s, \mathtt{x}, n, \alpha) \wedge \alpha > \beta(n, \alpha) \rangle$$
$$\langle \mathbf{Counter}_r(\mathtt{x}, n, \alpha) * [\mathrm{G}]_r \wedge \alpha > \beta(n, \alpha) \rangle$$
$$r : (n, \alpha) \wedge n \in \mathbb{N} \wedge \alpha > \beta(n, \alpha) \rightsquigarrow (n+1, \beta(n, \alpha)) \vdash_\tau$$
$$\{\exists n \in \mathbb{N}, \alpha.\ \mathbf{Counter}_r(\mathtt{x}, n, \alpha) * r \Rrightarrow \blacklozenge \wedge \alpha > \beta(n, \alpha)\}$$
$$\mathtt{n} := 0; \mathtt{b} := 0;$$
$$\{\exists n \in \mathbb{N}, \alpha.\ \mathbf{Counter}_r(\mathtt{x}, n, \alpha) * r \Rrightarrow \blacklozenge \wedge \mathtt{n} = 0 \wedge \mathtt{b} = 0 \wedge \alpha > \beta(n, \alpha)\}$$
$$\mathtt{while}\ (\mathtt{b} = 0)\ \{$$
$$\forall \gamma.$$
$$\{\exists n \in \mathbb{N}, \alpha.\ \mathbf{Counter}_r(\mathtt{x}, n, \alpha) * r \Rrightarrow \blacklozenge \wedge \mathtt{b} = 0 \wedge \gamma \geq \omega \cdot \alpha + \mathtt{n} \wedge \alpha > \beta(n, \alpha)\}$$
$$\mathtt{if}\ (\mathtt{n} = 0)\ \{$$
$$\{\exists n \in \mathbb{N}, \alpha.\ \mathbf{Counter}_r(\mathtt{x}, n, \alpha) * r \Rrightarrow \blacklozenge \wedge \gamma \geq \omega \cdot \alpha \wedge \alpha > \beta(n, \alpha)\}$$

open region

$$\mathbb{V}n \in \mathbb{N}, \alpha.$$
$$\langle \mathtt{x} \mapsto n \wedge \gamma \geq \omega \cdot \alpha \wedge \alpha > \beta(n, \alpha) \rangle$$
$$\mathtt{v} := [\mathtt{x}];$$
$$\langle \mathtt{x} \mapsto n \wedge \mathtt{v} = n \wedge \gamma \geq \omega \cdot \alpha \wedge \alpha > \beta(n, \alpha) \wedge (n > \mathtt{v} \Rightarrow \gamma \geq \omega \cdot \alpha + \omega) \rangle$$
$$\left\{ \begin{array}{l} \exists n \in \mathbb{N}, \alpha.\ \mathbf{Counter}_r(\mathtt{x}, n, \alpha) * r \Rrightarrow \blacklozenge \wedge \gamma \geq \omega \cdot \alpha \wedge \alpha > \beta(n, \alpha) \\ \wedge\, n \geq \mathtt{v} \wedge (n > \mathtt{v} \Rightarrow \gamma \geq \omega \cdot \alpha + \omega) \end{array} \right\}$$

update region

$$\mathbb{V}n \in \mathbb{N}, \alpha.$$
$$\langle \mathtt{x} \mapsto n \wedge \gamma \geq \omega \cdot \alpha \wedge \alpha > \beta(n, \alpha) \wedge n \geq \mathtt{v} \wedge (n > \mathtt{v} \Rightarrow \gamma \geq \omega \cdot \alpha + \omega) \rangle$$
$$\mathtt{b} := \mathtt{CAS}(\mathtt{x}, \mathtt{v}, \mathtt{v}+1);$$
$$\left\langle \begin{array}{l} \alpha > \beta(n, \alpha) \wedge \underline{\text{if}}\ \mathtt{b} = 0\ \underline{\text{then}}\ \gamma \geq \omega \cdot \alpha + \omega \wedge \mathtt{x} \mapsto n \\ \quad \underline{\text{else}}\ \mathtt{x} \mapsto n+1 \wedge \mathtt{v} = n \end{array} \right\rangle$$
$$\left\{ \begin{array}{l} \exists n \in \mathbb{N}, \alpha.\ \alpha > \beta(n, \alpha) \wedge \underline{\text{if}}\ \mathtt{b} = 0\ \underline{\text{then}} \begin{pmatrix} \mathbf{Counter}_r(\mathtt{x}, n, \alpha) * r \Rrightarrow \blacklozenge \\ \wedge\, \gamma \geq \omega \cdot \alpha + \omega \end{pmatrix} \\ \quad \underline{\text{else}}\ r \Rrightarrow ((\mathtt{v}, \alpha), (\mathtt{v}+1, \beta(n, \alpha))) \end{array} \right\}$$
$$\mathtt{n} := \mathtt{random}();$$
$$\left\{ \begin{array}{l} \exists n \in \mathbb{N}, \alpha.\ \alpha > \beta(n, \alpha) \wedge \underline{\text{if}}\ \mathtt{b} = 0\ \underline{\text{then}} \begin{pmatrix} \mathbf{Counter}_r(\mathtt{x}, n, \alpha) * r \Rrightarrow \blacklozenge \\ \wedge\, \gamma > \omega \cdot \alpha + \mathtt{n} \end{pmatrix} \\ \quad \underline{\text{else}}\ r \Rrightarrow ((\mathtt{v}, \alpha), (\mathtt{v}+1, \beta(n, \alpha))) \end{array} \right\}$$
$$\}\ \mathtt{else}\ \{$$
$$\left\{ \begin{array}{l} \exists n \in \mathbb{N}, \alpha.\ \mathbf{Counter}_r(\mathtt{x}, n, \alpha) * r \Rrightarrow \blacklozenge \\ \wedge\, \mathtt{b} = 0 \wedge \gamma \geq \omega \cdot \alpha + \mathtt{n} \wedge \alpha > \beta(n, \alpha) \end{array} \right\}$$
$$\mathtt{n} := \mathtt{n} - 1;$$
$$\left\{ \begin{array}{l} \exists n \in \mathbb{N}, \alpha.\ \mathbf{Counter}_r(\mathtt{x}, n, \alpha) * r \Rrightarrow \blacklozenge \\ \wedge\, \mathtt{b} = 0 \wedge \gamma > \omega \cdot \alpha + \mathtt{n} \wedge \alpha > \beta(n, \alpha) \end{array} \right\}$$
$$\}$$
$$\left\{ \begin{array}{l} \exists n \in \mathbb{N}, \alpha.\ \alpha > \beta(n, \alpha) \wedge \underline{\text{if}}\ \mathtt{b} = 0\ \underline{\text{then}} \begin{pmatrix} \mathbf{Counter}_r(\mathtt{x}, n, \alpha) * r \Rrightarrow \blacklozenge \\ \wedge\, \gamma > \omega \cdot \alpha + \mathtt{n} \end{pmatrix} \\ \quad \underline{\text{else}}\ r \Rrightarrow ((\mathtt{v}, \alpha), (\mathtt{v}+1, \beta(n, \alpha))) \end{array} \right\}$$
$$\}$$
$$\{\exists n \in \mathbb{N}, \alpha, .\ r \Rrightarrow ((n, \alpha), (n+1, \beta(n, \alpha))) \wedge \mathtt{v} = n\}$$
$$\mathtt{return}\ \mathtt{v};$$
$$\{\exists n \in \mathbb{N}, \alpha.\ r \Rrightarrow ((n, \alpha), (n+1, \beta(n, \alpha))) \wedge \mathsf{ret} = n\}$$
$$\langle \mathbf{Counter}_r(\mathtt{x}, n+1, \beta(n, \alpha)) * [\mathrm{G}]_r \wedge \mathsf{ret} = n \rangle$$
$$\langle \mathsf{C}(s, \mathtt{x}, n, \beta(n, \alpha)) \wedge \mathsf{ret} = n \rangle$$

Fig. 5. Proof of total correctness of backoff increment.

update to each).[2] The pre- and postconditions are split into a private part (the p_p and $q_p(x, y)$) and a public part (the $p(x)$ and $q(x, y)$). The idea is that the command may make multiple, non-atomic updates to the private part, but must only make a single atomic update to the public part. Before the atomic update, the environment is allowed to change the public part of the state, but only by changing the parameter x of p which must remain within X. After the atomic update, the specification makes no constraint on how the environment modifies the public state. All that is known is that, immediately after the atomic update, the public and private parts satisfy the postcondition for a common value of y. The private assertions in our judgements must be *stable*: that is, they must account for any updates other threads could have sufficient resources to perform.

The non-atomic Hoare triple $\vdash_\tau \{p\} \mathbb{C} \{q\}$ is syntactic sugar for the judgement $\vdash_\tau \langle p \mid \mathsf{true}\rangle \mathbb{C} \langle q \mid \mathsf{true}\rangle$. The atomic triple $\vdash_\tau \mathbb{V}x \in X. \langle p(x)\rangle \mathbb{C} \langle q(x)\rangle$ is syntactic sugar for the judgement $\vdash_\tau \mathbb{V}x \in X. \langle \mathsf{true} \mid p(x)\rangle \mathbb{C} \langle \mathsf{true} \mid q(x)\rangle$.

We give an overview of the key Total-TaDA proof rules that deal with termination and atomicity in Fig. 6. The while rule enforces that the number of times that the loop body can run is finite. The rule allows us to perform a while loop if we can guarantee that each loop iteration decreases the ordinal parametrising the invariant p. By the finite-chain property of ordinals, there cannot be an infinite number of iterations.

The parallel rule and the frame rule are analogous to those for separation logic. The parallel rule allows us to split resources among two threads as long as the resources of one thread are not touched by the other thread. The frame rule allows us to add the frame resources to the pre- and postcondition, which are untouched by the command. Our frame rule separately adds to both the private and public parts. Note that the frame for the public part may be parametrised by the $\mathbb{V}$-bound variable x.

The next three rules allow us to access the contents of a shared region by using an atomic command. With all of the rules, the update to the shared region must be atomic, so its interpretation is in the public part of the premiss. (The region is in the public part in the conclusion also, but may be moved by weakening.)

The open region rule allows us to access the contents of a shared region without updating its abstract state. The command may change the concrete state of the region, so long as the abstract state is preserved.

The use atomic rule allows us to update the abstract state of a shared region. To do so, we need a guard that permits this update. This rule takes a $\mathbb{C}$ which (abstractly) atomically updates the region a from some state $x \in X$ to the state $f(x)$. It requires the guard G for the region, which allows the update according to the transition system, as established by one of the premisses. Another premiss states that the command $\mathbb{C}$ performs the update described by the transition system of region a in an atomic way. This allows us to conclude that the region a is updated atomically by the command $\mathbb{C}$. Note that the command is not

[2] We have omitted region levels, analogous to those in TaDA, in our judgements to simplify our presentation. They prevent a region from being opened twice within a single branch of the proof tree, which unsoundly duplicates resources.

while rule

$$\frac{\forall \gamma \leq \alpha.\, \mathcal{A} \vdash_{\tau} \{p(\gamma) \wedge \mathbb{B}\}\ \mathbb{C}\ \{\exists \beta.\, p(\beta) \wedge \beta < \gamma\}}{\mathcal{A} \vdash_{\tau} \{p(\alpha)\}\ \texttt{while}\ (\mathbb{B})\ \mathbb{C}\ \{\exists \beta.\, p(\beta) \wedge \neg\mathbb{B} \wedge \beta \leq \alpha\}}$$

parallel rule

$$\frac{\forall i \in \{1,2\}.\, \mathcal{A} \vdash_{\tau} \{p_i\}\ \mathbb{C}_i\ \{q_i\}}{\mathcal{A} \vdash_{\tau} \{p_1 * p_2\}\ \mathbb{C}_1 \parallel \mathbb{C}_2\ \{q_1 * q_2\}}$$

frame rule

$$\frac{\mathcal{A} \vdash_{\tau} \mathbb{V}x \in X.\langle p_p \,|\, p(x)\rangle\ \mathbb{C}\ \ \exists\!\!\exists y \in Y.\langle q_p(x,y) \,|\, q(x,y)\rangle}{\mathcal{A} \vdash_{\tau} \mathbb{V}x \in X.\langle r' * p_p \,|\, r(x) * p(x)\rangle\ \mathbb{C}\ \ \exists\!\!\exists y \in Y.\langle r' * q_p(x,y) \,|\, r(x) * q(x,y)\rangle}$$

open region rule

$$\frac{\mathcal{A} \vdash_{\tau} \mathbb{V}x \in X.\langle p_p \,|\, I(\mathbf{t}_a(x)) * p(x)\rangle\ \mathbb{C}\ \ \exists\!\!\exists y \in Y.\langle q_p(x,y) \,|\, I(\mathbf{t}_a(x)) * q(x,y)\rangle}{\mathcal{A} \vdash_{\tau} \mathbb{V}x \in X.\langle p_p \,|\, \mathbf{t}_a(x) * p(x)\rangle\ \mathbb{C}\ \ \exists\!\!\exists y \in Y.\langle q_p(x,y) \,|\, \mathbf{t}_a(x) * q(x,y)\rangle}$$

use atomic rule

$$\frac{\begin{array}{c} a \notin \mathcal{A} \qquad \forall x \in X.\, (x, f(x)) \in \mathcal{T}_{\mathbf{t}}(\mathrm{G})^{*} \\ \mathcal{A} \vdash_{\tau} \mathbb{V}x \in X.\langle p_p \,|\, I(\mathbf{t}_a(x)) * p(x) * [\mathrm{G}]_a\rangle\ \mathbb{C}\ \ \exists\!\!\exists y \in Y.\langle q_p(x,y) \,|\, I(\mathbf{t}_a(f(x))) * q(x,y)\rangle \end{array}}{\mathcal{A} \vdash_{\tau} \mathbb{V}x \in X.\langle p_p \,|\, \mathbf{t}_a(x) * p(x) * [\mathrm{G}]_a\rangle\ \mathbb{C}\ \ \exists\!\!\exists y \in Y.\langle q_p(x,y) \,|\, \mathbf{t}_a(f(x)) * q(x,y)\rangle}$$

update region rule

$$\frac{\mathcal{A} \vdash_{\tau} \begin{array}{c} \mathbb{V}x \in X.\langle p_p \,|\, I(\mathbf{t}_a(x)) * p(x)\rangle \\ \mathbb{C} \\ \exists\!\!\exists y \in Y.\langle q_p(x,y) \,|\, \exists z \in Q(x).\, I(\mathbf{t}_a(z)) * q_1(x,y,z) \vee I(\mathbf{t}_a(x)) * q_2(x,y)\rangle \end{array}}{a : x \in X \rightsquigarrow Q(x), \mathcal{A} \vdash_{\tau} \begin{array}{c} \mathbb{V}x \in X.\langle p_p \,|\, \mathbf{t}_a(x) * p(x) * a \Rightarrow \blacklozenge\rangle \\ \mathbb{C} \\ \exists\!\!\exists y \in Y.\left\langle q_p(x,y) \,\middle|\, \begin{array}{c} \exists z \in Q(x).\, \mathbf{t}_a(z) * q_1(x,y,z) * a \Rightarrow (x,z) \\ \vee\, \mathbf{t}_a(x) * q_2(x,y) * a \Rightarrow \blacklozenge \end{array}\right\rangle \end{array}}$$

make atomic rule

$$\frac{\begin{array}{c} a \notin \mathcal{A} \quad \{(x,y) \mid x \in X, y \in Q(x)\} \subseteq \mathcal{T}_{\mathbf{t}}(\mathrm{G})^{*} \\ a : x \in X \rightsquigarrow Q(x), \mathcal{A} \vdash_{\tau} \\ \{p_p * \exists x \in X.\, \mathbf{t}_a(x) * a \Rightarrow \blacklozenge\}\ \mathbb{C}\ \{\exists x \in X, y \in Q(x).\, q_p(x,y) * a \Rightarrow (x,y)\} \end{array}}{\mathcal{A} \vdash_{\tau} \mathbb{V}x \in X.\langle p_p \,|\, \mathbf{t}_a(x) * [\mathrm{G}]_a\rangle\ \mathbb{C}\ \ \exists\!\!\exists y \in Q(x).\langle q_p(x,y) \,|\, \mathbf{t}_a(y) * [\mathrm{G}]_a\rangle}$$

Fig. 6. A selection of proof rules of Total-TaDA.

operating at the same level of abstraction as the region a. Instead it is working at a lower level of abstraction, which means that if it is atomic at that level it will also be atomic at the region a level.

The update region rule similarly allows us to update the abstract state of a shared region, but this time the authority comes from the atomicity context instead of a guard. In order to perform such an update, the atomic update to the region must not already have happened, indicated by $a \Rightarrow \blacklozenge$ in the precondition of the conclusion. In the postcondition, there are two cases: either the appropriate update happened, or no update happened. If it did happen, the new state of the region is some $z \in Q(x)$, and both x and z are recorded in the atomicity tracking resource. If it did not, then both the region's abstract state and the atomicity tracking resource are unchanged. The premiss requires the command to make a corresponding update to the concrete state of the region. The atomicity context and tracking resource are not in the premiss; they serve to record information about the atomic update that is performed for use further down the proof tree.

$$\forall \alpha.\ \vdash_\tau \{\mathsf{emp}\}\ \mathbf{makeStack}()\ \{\exists s \in \mathbb{T}_1, t \in \mathbb{T}_2.\, \mathsf{Stack}(s, \mathsf{ret}, [], t, \alpha)\}$$

$$\forall \beta.\ \vdash_\tau \mathbb{W} vs, t, \alpha. \langle \mathsf{Stack}(s, \mathtt{x}, vs, t, \alpha) \wedge \alpha > \beta(vs, \alpha)\rangle \\ \mathbf{push}(\mathtt{x}, \mathtt{v}) \\ \langle \exists t'.\, \mathsf{Stack}(s, \mathtt{x}, \mathtt{v} : vs, t', \beta(vs, \alpha))\rangle$$

$$\vdash_\tau \mathbb{W} vs, t, \alpha. \quad \langle \mathsf{Stack}(s, \mathtt{x}, vs, t, \alpha)\rangle \\ \mathbf{pop}(\mathtt{x}) \\ \left\langle \begin{array}{l} \underline{\mathbf{if}}\ vs = []\ \underline{\mathbf{then}}\ \mathsf{Stack}(s, \mathtt{x}, vs, t, \alpha) \wedge \mathsf{ret} = 0 \\ \underline{\mathbf{else}}\ \exists vs', t'.\, \mathsf{Stack}(s, \mathtt{x}, vs', t', \alpha) \wedge vs = \mathsf{ret} : vs' \end{array} \right\rangle$$

Fig. 7. Stack operation specifications.

Finally, we revisit the make atomic rule, which elaborates on the version presented in Sect. 2.3. As before, a guard in the conclusion must permit the update in accordance with the transition system for the region. This is replaced in the premiss by the atomicity context and atomicity tracking resource, which tracks the occurrence of the update. One difference is the inclusion of the private state, which is effectively preserved between the premiss and the conclusion. A second difference is the $\exists\!\!\exists$-binding of the resulting state of the atomic update. This allows the private state to reflect the result of the update.

4 Case Study: Treiber's Stack

We now consider a version of Treiber's stack [20] to demonstrate how Total-TaDA can be applied to verify the total correctness of larger modules.

4.1 Specification

In Fig. 7, we give the specification of the lock-free stack operations. This is a Total-TaDA specification satisfiable by a reasonable non-blocking implementation. As with the counter, the predicate representing the stack is parametrised by an ordinal that bounds the number of operations on the stack, in order to guarantee termination. The $\mathsf{Stack}(s, x, vs, t, \alpha)$ predicate has five parameters: the address of the stack x; its contents vs; an ordinal α that decreases every time a push operation is performed; and two parameters, s and t that range over abstract types $\mathbb{T}_1$ and $\mathbb{T}_2$ respectively. These last two parameters encapsulate implementation-specific information about the configuration of the stack (s is invariant, while t may vary) and hence their types are abstract to the client.

The constructor returns an empty stack, parametrised by an arbitrary ordinal chosen by the client. The push operation atomically adds an element to the head of the stack. The pop operation atomically removes one element from the head of the stack, if one is available (*i.e.* the stack is non-empty); otherwise it will simply return 0. (As this stack is non-blocking, it would not be possible for the pop operation to wait for the stack to become non-empty.)

Note that the ordinal parametrising the stack is not required to decrease when popping the stack. This means that the stack operations cannot be starved by an

```
function makeStack() {
  x := alloc(1);
  [x] := 0;
  return x;
}
```

```
function push(x, v) {
  y := alloc(2);
  [y.value] := v;
  do {
    z := [x];
    [y.next] := z;
    b := CAS(x, z, y);
  } while (b = 0);
}
```

```
function pop(x) {
  do {
    y := [x];
    if (y = 0) { return 0; }
    z := [y.next];
    b := CAS(x, y, z);
  } while (b = 0);
  v := [y.value];
  return v;
}
```

Fig. 8. Treiber's stack operations.

unbounded number of pop invocations. This need not be the case in general for a lock-free stack, but it is true for Treiber's stack. We discuss the ramifications of this kind of specification further in Sect. 6.3.

4.2 Implementation

Figure 8 gives an implementation of the stack operations based on Treiber's stack [20]. The stack is represented as a heap cell containing a pointer (the head pointer) to a singly-linked list of the values on the stack.

Values are pushed onto the stack by allocating a new node holding the value to be pushed and a pointer to the old head of the stack. A compare-and-swap operation updates the old head of the stack to point to the new node. If the operation fails, it will be because the head of the stack has changed, and so the operation is retried.

Values are popped from the stack by moving the head pointer one step along the list. Again, a compare-and-swap operation is used for this update, so if the head of the stack changes the operation can be retried. If the stack is empty (*i.e.* the head points to 0), then pop simply returns 0, without affecting the stack.

4.3 Correctness

To prove correctness of the implementation, we introduce predicates to represent the linked list:

$$\mathsf{list}(x, ns) \triangleq (x = 0 \land ns = []) \lor (\exists v, l.\, \mathsf{node}(x, v, l) * \mathsf{list}(l, ns') \land ns = (x, v) : ns')$$

$$\mathsf{node}(n, v, l) \triangleq n.\mathtt{value} \mapsto v * n.\mathtt{next} \mapsto l$$

It is important to the correctness of the algorithm that nodes that have been popped can never reappear as the head of the stack. To account for this, in our representation of the stack we track the set of previously popped nodes, and ensure that they are disjoint from the nodes in the stack. The $\mathsf{stack}(x, ns, ds)$ predicate therefore consists of a list starting at address x, with contents ns, and a disjoint set of nodes ds (the discarded nodes):

$$\mathsf{stack}(x, ns, ds) \triangleq \mathsf{list}(x, ns) * \bigotimes_{(n,v) \in ds} \mathsf{node}(n, v, \_)$$

We define a region type **TStack** to hold the shared data-structure. The type is parametrised by the address of the stack, and its abstract state consists of a list of nodes in the stack ns, a set of popped nodes ds, and an ordinal α. The **TStack** region type has the following interpretation:

$$I(\mathbf{TStack}_r(x, ns, ds, \alpha)) \triangleq \exists y.\, x \mapsto y * \mathsf{stack}(y, ns, ds)$$

We use a single guard G to give threads permissions to push and pop the stack. The transition system is given as follows:

$$\mathrm{G} : \forall n, v, ns, ds, \alpha, \beta < \alpha.\, (ns, ds, \alpha) \rightsquigarrow ((n, v) : ns, ds, \beta)$$
$$\mathrm{G} : \forall n, v, ns, ds, \alpha.\, ((n, v) : ns, ds, \alpha) \rightsquigarrow (ns, (n, v) \uplus ds, \alpha)$$

The first action allows us to add an element to the head of the stack. The second action allows us to remove the top element of the stack, adding it to the set of discarded nodes. There is no explicit transition for the pop on the empty stack, since this operation does not change the abstract state.

Note that for every transition $(ns, ds, \alpha) \rightsquigarrow (ns', ds', \alpha')$, we have $2{\cdot}\alpha + |ns| > 2 \cdot \alpha' + |ns'|$. Pushing decreases the ordinal, but extends the length of the stack by 1; popping maintains the ordinal, but decreases the length of the stack. This property allows us to use $2 \cdot \alpha + |ns|$ as a variant in the compare-and-swap loops, since it is guaranteed to decrease under any interference.

The abstract predicate $\mathsf{Stack}(s, x, vs, t, \alpha)$ combines the region and the guard:

$$\mathsf{Stack}(r, x, vs, (ns, ds), \alpha) \triangleq \mathbf{TStack}_r(x, ns, ds, \alpha) * [\mathrm{G}]_r \wedge vs = \mathsf{snds}(ns)$$

The function snds returns the list of elements of the second elements of the list of pairs ns. Consequently, vs is the list of values on the stack, rather than pairs of address and value.

The proof for pop is given in Fig. 9. When the stack is non-empty, if the compare-and-swap fails then another thread must have succeeded in updating the stack, and so reduced the ordinal or the length of the stack; by basing the loop variant on the ordinal and stack length, we can guarantee that the operation will eventually succeed. The proof for push is given in the technical report [18].

5 Soundness

The proof of soundness of Total-TaDA is similar to that for TaDA [16] and based on the Views Framework [4]. We use the same model for assertions as that for TaDA. We also use a similar semantic judgement, $\models$, which ensures that the concrete behaviours of programs simulate the abstract behaviours represented by the specifications. The key distinction is that, whereas in TaDA the judgement is defined coinductively (as a greatest fixed point), in Total-TaDA the judgement is defined inductively (as a least fixed point). This means that TaDA admits executions that never terminate, while Total-TaDA requires executions to always terminate: that is, reach a base-case of the inductive definition.

The soundness proof consists of lemmas that justify each of the proof rules for the semantic judgement. Most of the Total-TaDA rules have similar proofs to

$$\mathbb{W} vs, t, \alpha.$$
$$\langle \mathsf{Stack}(s, \mathtt{x}, vs, t, \alpha) \rangle$$

abstract; substitute $s = r$, $t = (ns, ds)$

$$\langle \mathbf{TStack}_r(\mathtt{x}, ns, ds, \alpha) * [\mathrm{G}]_r \wedge vs = \mathsf{snds}(ns) \rangle$$

make atomic

$$r : (ns, ds, \alpha) \rightsquigarrow \underline{\text{if}}\ ns = []\ \underline{\text{then}}\ (ns, ds, \alpha)\ \underline{\text{else}}\ (ns', (n, v) \uplus ds, \alpha) \wedge ns = (n, v) : ns' \vdash_\tau$$
$$\{ \exists ns, ds, \alpha.\ \mathbf{TStack}_r(\mathtt{x}, ns, ds, \alpha) * r \Rrightarrow \blacklozenge \}$$

do {

$$\forall \gamma.$$
$$\{ \exists ns, ds, \alpha.\ \mathbf{TStack}_r(\mathtt{x}, ns, ds, \alpha) * r \Rrightarrow \blacklozenge \wedge \gamma \geq 2 \cdot \alpha + |ns| \}$$

update region

$$\mathbb{W} ns, ds, \alpha.\ \langle \exists w.\ \mathtt{x} \mapsto w * \mathsf{stack}(w, ns, ds) \wedge \gamma \geq 2 \cdot \alpha + |ns| \rangle$$

`y := [x];`

$$\left\langle \begin{array}{l} \mathtt{x} \mapsto \mathtt{y} * \mathsf{stack}(\mathtt{y}, ns, ds) \wedge \gamma \geq 2 \cdot \alpha + |ns| \wedge \\ \underline{\text{if}}\ \mathtt{y} = 0\ \underline{\text{then}}\ ns = []\ \underline{\text{else}}\ \exists v.\ (\mathtt{y}, v) = \mathsf{head}(ns) \end{array} \right\rangle$$

$$\left\{ \begin{array}{l} \exists ns, ds, \alpha.\ \underline{\text{if}}\ \mathtt{y} = 0\ \underline{\text{then}}\ r \Rrightarrow (([], ds, \alpha), ([], ds, \alpha)) \\ \quad \underline{\text{else}}\ \exists v. \left(\begin{array}{l} \mathbf{TStack}_r(\mathtt{x}, ns, ds, \alpha) * r \Rrightarrow \blacklozenge \wedge (\mathtt{y}, v) \in ns +\!\!+\ ds \wedge \\ \gamma \geq 2 \cdot \alpha + |ns| \wedge \mathsf{head}(ns) \neq (\mathtt{y}, v) \Rightarrow \gamma > 2 \cdot \alpha + |ns| \end{array} \right) \end{array} \right\}$$

if (y = 0) {

return 0; $\{ \exists ds, \alpha.\ r \Rrightarrow (([], ds, \alpha), ([], ds, \alpha)) \wedge \mathsf{ret} = 0 \}$

}

$$\left\{ \begin{array}{l} \exists ns, ds, v, \alpha.\ \mathbf{TStack}_r(\mathtt{x}, ns, ds, \alpha) * r \Rrightarrow \blacklozenge \wedge (\mathtt{y}, v) \in ns +\!\!+\ ds \wedge \\ \gamma \geq 2 \cdot \alpha + |ns| \wedge \mathsf{head}(ns) \neq (\mathtt{y}, v) \Rightarrow \gamma > 2 \cdot \alpha + |ns| \end{array} \right\}$$

`z := [y.next];`

$$\left\{ \begin{array}{l} \exists ns, ds, \alpha.\ \mathbf{TStack}_r(\mathtt{x}, ns, ds, \alpha) * r \Rrightarrow \blacklozenge \wedge \gamma \geq 2 \cdot \alpha + |ns| \wedge \\ \left(\begin{array}{l} (\exists v, v', ns'.\ ns = [(\mathtt{y}, v), (\mathtt{z}, v')] +\!\!+\ ns') \vee (\exists v.\ ns = [(\mathtt{y}, v)] \wedge \mathtt{z} = 0) \\ \vee (\exists v.\ (\mathtt{y}, v) \in ns +\!\!+\ ds \wedge \mathsf{head}(ns) \neq (\mathtt{y}, v) \wedge \gamma > 2 \cdot \alpha + |ns|) \end{array} \right) \end{array} \right\}$$

update region

$$\mathbb{W} ns, ds, \alpha.$$
$$\left\langle \begin{array}{l} \exists w.\ \mathtt{x} \mapsto w * \mathsf{stack}(w, ns, ds) \wedge \gamma \geq 2 \cdot \alpha + |ns| \wedge \\ \left(\begin{array}{l} (\exists v, v', ns'.\ ns = [(\mathtt{y}, v), (\mathtt{z}, v')] +\!\!+\ ns') \\ \vee (\exists v.\ ns = [(\mathtt{y}, v)] \wedge \mathtt{z} = 0) \\ \vee (\exists v.\ (\mathtt{y}, v) \in ns +\!\!+\ ds \wedge \mathsf{head}(ns) \neq (\mathtt{y}, v) \wedge \gamma > 2 \cdot \alpha + |ns|) \end{array} \right) \end{array} \right\rangle$$

`b := CAS(x, y, z);`

$$\left\langle \begin{array}{l} \underline{\text{if}}\ \mathtt{b} = 0\ \underline{\text{then}}\ \exists w.\ \mathtt{x} \mapsto w * \mathsf{stack}(w, ns, ds) \wedge \gamma > 2 \cdot \alpha + |ns| \\ \quad \underline{\text{else}}\ \exists v, ns'.\ \mathtt{x} \mapsto \mathtt{z} * \mathsf{stack}(\mathtt{z}, ns', (\mathtt{y}, v) \uplus ds) \wedge ns = (\mathtt{y}, v) : ns' \end{array} \right\rangle$$

$$\left\{ \begin{array}{l} \exists ns, ds, \alpha.\ \gamma \geq 2 \cdot \alpha + |ns| \wedge \\ \underline{\text{if}}\ \mathtt{b} = 0\ \underline{\text{then}}\ \mathbf{TStack}_r(\mathtt{x}, ns, ds, \alpha) * r \Rrightarrow \blacklozenge \wedge \gamma > 2 \cdot \alpha + |ns| \\ \quad \underline{\text{else}} \left(\begin{array}{l} \exists v, ns', ds', \alpha'.\ (\mathtt{y}, v) \in ds' \wedge \mathbf{TStack}_r(\mathtt{x}, ns', ds', \alpha') \\ \quad * r \Rrightarrow (((\mathtt{y}, v) : ns, ds, \alpha), (ns, (\mathtt{y}, v) \uplus ds), \alpha) \end{array} \right) \end{array} \right\}$$

} **while** (b = 0);

$$\left\{ \begin{array}{l} \exists v, ns, ds, \alpha, ns', ds', \alpha'.\ (\mathtt{y}, v) \in ds' \wedge \mathbf{TStack}_r(\mathtt{x}, ns', ds', \alpha') \\ * r \Rrightarrow (((\mathtt{y}, v) : ns, ds, \alpha), (ns, (\mathtt{y}, v) \uplus ds, \alpha)) \end{array} \right\}$$

`v := [y.value];` $\{ \exists ns, ds, \alpha.\ r \Rrightarrow (((\mathtt{y}, \mathtt{v}) : ns, ds, \alpha), (ns, (\mathtt{y}, \mathtt{v}) \uplus ds, \alpha)) \}$

return v; $\{ \exists y, ns, ds, \alpha.\ r \Rrightarrow (((y, \mathsf{ret}) : ns, ds, \alpha), (ns, (y, \mathsf{ret}) \uplus ds), \alpha) \}$

$$\left\langle \begin{array}{l} \underline{\text{if}}\ vs = []\ \underline{\text{then}}\ \mathbf{TStack}_r(\mathtt{x}, ns, ds, \alpha) * [\mathrm{G}]_r \wedge vs = \mathsf{snds}(ns) \wedge \mathsf{ret} = 0 \\ \quad \underline{\text{else}} \left(\begin{array}{l} \exists ns', vs', y.\ \mathbf{TStack}_r(\mathtt{x}, ns', (y, \mathsf{ret}) \uplus ds, \alpha) * [\mathrm{G}]_r \\ \quad \wedge vs' = \mathsf{snds}(ns') \wedge ns = (y, \mathsf{ret}) : ns' \end{array} \right) \end{array} \right\rangle$$

$$\left\langle \begin{array}{l} \underline{\text{if}}\ vs = []\ \underline{\text{then}}\ \mathsf{Stack}(s, \mathtt{x}, vs, t, \alpha) \wedge \mathsf{ret} = 0 \\ \quad \underline{\text{else}}\ \exists vs', t'.\ \mathsf{Stack}(s, \mathtt{x}, vs', t', \alpha) \wedge vs = \mathsf{ret} : vs' \end{array} \right\rangle$$

Fig. 9. Proof of total correctness of Treiber's stack pop operation.

the corresponding TaDA rules, but proceed by induction instead of coinduction. Of course, the while rule is different, since termination does not follow trivially. We sketch the proof for while. All details are in the technical report [18].

Lemma 1 (While Rule). *Let α be an ordinal. If, for all $\gamma \leq \alpha$,*

$$\mathcal{A} \vDash_\tau \{p(\gamma) \wedge \mathbb{B}\}\ \mathbb{C}\ \{\exists \beta.\, p(\beta) \wedge \beta < \gamma\},\ \textit{then} \quad (1)$$

$$\mathcal{A} \vDash_\tau \{p(\alpha)\}\ \texttt{while}\ (\mathbb{B})\ \mathbb{C}\ \{\exists \beta.\, p(\beta) \wedge \neg\mathbb{B} \wedge \beta \leq \alpha\}. \quad (2)$$

Proof. The proof is by transfinite induction on α. As the inductive hypothesis (IH), assume that the lemma holds for all $\delta < \alpha$. The program $\texttt{while}\ (\mathbb{B})\ \mathbb{C}$ has two possible reductions, which do not affect the state, depending on the truth value of the loop test. Consequently, to show (2), it is sufficient to establish:

$$\mathcal{A} \vDash_\tau \{p(\alpha) \wedge \mathbb{B}\}\ \mathbb{C}; \texttt{while}\ (\mathbb{B})\ \mathbb{C}\ \{\exists \beta.\, p(\beta) \wedge \neg\mathbb{B} \wedge \beta \leq \alpha\} \quad (3)$$

$$\mathcal{A} \vDash_\tau \{p(\alpha) \wedge \neg\mathbb{B}\}\ \texttt{skip}\ \{\exists \beta.\, p(\beta) \wedge \neg\mathbb{B} \wedge \beta \leq \alpha\} \quad (4)$$

(4) holds trivially. To establish (3), (1) gives $\mathcal{A} \vDash_\tau \{p(\alpha) \wedge \mathbb{B}\}\ \mathbb{C}\ \{\exists \delta.\, p(\delta) \wedge \delta < \alpha\}$. For all $\delta < \alpha$, IH gives $\mathcal{A} \vDash_\tau \{p(\delta)\}\ \texttt{while}\ (\mathbb{B})\ \mathbb{C}\ \{\exists \beta.\, p(\beta) \wedge \neg\mathbb{B} \wedge \beta \leq \delta\}$, and hence $\mathcal{A} \vDash_\tau \{\exists \delta.\, p(\delta) \wedge \delta < \alpha\}\ \texttt{while}\ (\mathbb{B})\ \mathbb{C}\ \{\exists \beta.\, p(\beta) \wedge \neg\mathbb{B} \wedge \beta \leq \alpha\}$. Now (3) follows using the analogous sequential composition lemma in the technical report [18]. □

6 Non-blocking Properties

Non-blocking properties are used to characterise concurrent algorithms that guarantee progress. A *lock-free* algorithm guarantees global progress: an individual thread might fail to make progress, but only because some other thread does make progress. A *wait-free* algorithm guarantees local progress: every thread makes progress when it is scheduled. We consider how non-blocking properties can be formalised using Total-TaDA.

6.1 Lock-Freedom

We have described lock-freedom in terms of an informal notion of "progress". In order to properly characterise modules as lock-free, we need a more formal definition. We can characterise global progress for a module as follows: at any time, eventually either a pending operation will be completed or another operation will be begun. If we assume that the number of threads is bounded, then as long as there are pending module operations, some operation will eventually complete. (If the number of threads is unbounded, then there is no guarantee that any operation will complete, even if it is scheduled arbitrarily often, since additional operations can always begin.)

Based on this observation, Gotsman *et al.* [7] reduced lock-freedom to the termination of a simple class of programs, the bounded most-general clients (BMGCs) of a module. Hoffmann *et al.* [10] generalised the result to apply to algorithms where the identity or number of threads is significant. An (m, n)-bounded general client consists of m threads which each invoke n module operations in sequence. If all such bounded general clients (for every n and m)[3] terminate, then the module is lock free.

Definition 1. *Consider a module $\mathcal{M}$ with initialiser* `init` *and a set of operations O. Define the following sets of programs:*

$$T_n = \{\mathsf{op}_1; \ldots ; \mathsf{op}_n \mid \mathsf{op}_i \in O\} \qquad C_{m,n} = \{\mathtt{init}; (t_1 \| \ldots \| t_m) \mid t_i \in T_n\}.$$

Theorem 1 (Hoffmann et al. [10]). *Given a module $\mathcal{M}$, if, for all m and n, every program $c \in C_{m,n}$ terminates, then $\mathcal{M}$ is lock free.*

Using this theorem, we define a specification pattern for Total-TaDA that guarantees lock-freedom and follows easily from the typical specifications we establish for lock-free modules.

Theorem 2. *Given a module $\mathcal{M}$ and some abstract predicate* M *(with two abstract parameters and an ordinal parameter), suppose that the following specifications are provable:*

$$\forall \alpha.\ \vdash_\tau \{\mathsf{true}\}\ \mathtt{init}\ \{\exists s, u.\, \mathsf{M}(s, u, \alpha)\}$$
$$\forall \mathsf{op} \in O. \forall \beta.\ \vdash_\tau \mathbb{V}\alpha, u. \langle \mathsf{M}(s, u, \alpha) \wedge \alpha > \beta(\alpha)\rangle\ \mathsf{op}\ \langle \exists u'.\, \mathsf{M}(s, u', \beta(\alpha))\rangle.$$

Then $\mathcal{M}$ is lock-free.

Proof. By Theorem 1, it is sufficient to show that, for arbitrary m, n and $c \in C_{m,n}$, the program c terminates.Fix the number of threads m.

We define a region type $\mathbf{M}$ whose abstract states consist of vectors $\bar{x} \in \mathbb{N}^m$. (We denote by x_i, for $1 \leq i \leq m$, the i-th component of vector $\bar{x}$. We denote by $\sum \bar{x}$ the sum $\sum_{i=1}^{i=m} x_i$.) Region states are interpreted as follows: $I(\mathbf{M}_a(s, \bar{x})) \triangleq \exists u.\, \mathsf{M}(s, u, \sum \bar{x})$. The guard algebra for $\mathbf{M}$ consists of m distinct guards $\mathrm{G}_1, \ldots, \mathrm{G}_m$. The state transition system for $\mathbf{M}$ allows a thread holding guard G_i to decrease the i-th component of the abstract state:

$$\mathrm{G}_i : (\forall j \neq i.\, x_j = y_j) \wedge x_i > y_i \wedge \bar{x} \rightsquigarrow \bar{y}.$$

For $1 \leq i \leq m$, arbitrary n, and $\mathsf{op} \in O$, using the use atomic rule, we have

$$\frac{\mathbb{V}k, u.\, \langle \mathsf{M}(s, u, k + n + 1)\rangle\ \mathsf{op}\ \langle \exists u'.\, \mathsf{M}(s, u', k + n)\rangle}{\{\exists s, \bar{x}.\, \mathbf{M}_a(s, \bar{x}) * [\mathrm{G}_i]_a \wedge x_i = n + 1\}\ \mathsf{op}\ \{\exists s, \bar{x}.\, \mathbf{M}_a(s, \bar{x}) * [\mathrm{G}_i]_a \wedge x_i = n\}}$$

Applying this specification repeatedly (by induction), we have for arbitrary $t \in T_n$

$$\vdash_\tau \{\exists s, \bar{x}.\, \mathbf{M}_a(s, \bar{x}) * [\mathrm{G}_i]_a \wedge x_i = n\}\ t\ \{\mathsf{true}\}$$

Let $c = \mathtt{init}; (t_1 \| \ldots \| t_m) \in C_{m,n}$ be arbitrary. We derive $\vdash_\tau \{\mathsf{true}\}\ c\ \{\mathsf{true}\}$ easily by choosing $n \cdot m$ as the initial ordinal and creating an $\mathbf{M}$-region with initial state $(n, \ldots, n)$. Consequently, c terminates, as required. □

It is straightforward to apply Theorem 2 to the modules we have considered.

[3] The bounded *most-general* client may be seen as the program which non-deterministically chooses among all bounded general clients.

6.2 Wait-Freedom

Whereas lock-freedom only requires that *some* thread makes progress, wait-freedom requires that *every* thread makes progress (provided that it is not permanently descheduled). In terms of operations, this requires that each operation of a module should complete within a finite number of steps. Since Total-TaDA specifications guarantee that operations terminate, it is simple to describe a specification that implies that a module is wait-free.

Theorem 3. *Given a module* $\mathcal{M}$ *and some abstract predicate* M *(with two abstract parameters), suppose that the following specifications are provable:*

$$\vdash_\tau \{\mathsf{true}\}\ \mathtt{init}\ \{\exists s,t.\,\mathsf{M}(s,u)\} \qquad \forall \mathsf{op} \in O.\ \vdash_\tau \mathbb{V}u.\,\langle \mathsf{M}(s,u)\rangle\ \mathtt{op}\ \langle \exists u'.\,\mathsf{M}(s,u')\rangle.$$

Then $\mathcal{M}$ *is wait-free.*

Proof. The specifications imply that M is an invariant which is established by the initialiser and preserved at all times by the module operations. Furthermore, all of the module operations terminate, assuming the environment maintains M invariant. Consequently, all of the module operations terminate in the context of an environment calling module operations: the module is wait-free. □

Lock-freedom can only be applied to a module as a whole, since it relates to global progress. Wait-freedom, by contrast, relates to local progress — that the operations of *each* thread terminate — and so it is meaningful to consider an individual operation to be wait-free in a context where other operations may be lock-free or even blocking. By combining (partial-correctness) TaDA and Total-TaDA specifications (indicated by $\vdash$ and $\vdash_\tau$ respectively), we can give a specification pattern that guarantees wait-freedom for a specific module operation.

Theorem 4. *Given a module* $\mathcal{M}$ *and some abstract predicate* M *(with two abstract parameters), suppose that the following specifications are provable:*

$$\vdash \{\mathsf{true}\}\ \mathtt{init}\ \{\exists s,u.\,\mathsf{M}(s,u)\} \qquad \vdash_\tau \mathbb{V}u.\,\langle \mathsf{M}(s,u)\rangle\ \mathtt{op}\ \langle \exists u'.\,\mathsf{M}(s,u')\rangle$$
$$\forall \mathsf{op}' \in O.\ \vdash \mathbb{V}u.\,\langle \mathsf{M}(s,u)\rangle\ \mathtt{op}'\ \langle \exists u'.\,\mathsf{M}(s,u')\rangle$$

Then `op` *is wait-free.*

Proof. As before, M is a module invariant; `op` is guaranteed to terminate with this invariant, therefore it is wait-free. □

The specifications required by Theorem 4 do not follow from those given for our examples. However, where applicable, the proofs can easily be adapted. For instance, to show that the `read` operation of the counter is wait-free, we would remove the ordinals from the region definition, and abstract the value of the counter. This breaks the termination proof for the increment operations, but we can adapt it to a partial-correctness proof in TaDA. The termination proof for `read` does not depend on the ordinal parameter of the region, and so we can still establish total correctness, as required.

6.3 Non-impedance

Recall the counter specification from Sect. 2.1. If we abstract the value and address of the counter (which are irrelevant to termination), the specification becomes:

$$\forall \alpha.\ \vdash_\tau \{\mathsf{emp}\}\ \mathtt{x} := \mathtt{makeCounter}()\ \{\exists s \in \mathbb{T}_1, u \in \mathbb{T}_2.\, \mathsf{C}(s, u, \alpha)\}$$
$$\vdash_\tau \mathbb{V} u, \alpha.\, \big\langle \mathsf{C}(s, u, \alpha) \big\rangle\ \mathtt{read(x)}\ \big\langle \mathsf{C}(s, u, \alpha) \big\rangle$$
$$\forall \beta.\ \vdash_\tau \mathbb{V} u, \alpha.\, \big\langle \mathsf{C}(s, u, \alpha) \wedge \alpha > \beta(\alpha) \big\rangle\ \mathtt{incr(x)}\ \big\langle \exists u'.\, \mathsf{C}(s, u', \beta(\alpha)) \big\rangle$$

Since the `read` operation does not change the ordinal, it implies that both the `read` and `incr` operations will terminate in a concurrent environment that performs an unbounded number of `read`s. This suggests an alternative approach to characterising lock-free modules in terms of which operations *impede* each other — that is, which operations may prevent the termination of an operation if infinitely many of them are invoked during a (fair) execution of the operation. Our specification implies that `read` does not impede either `read` or `incr`. This is expressed by edges 1 and 2 in the following non-impedance graph:

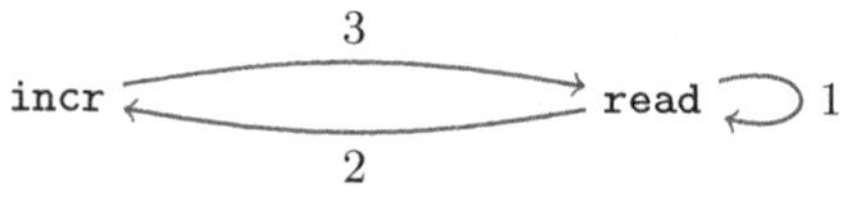

Note that the above specifications for the counter do not by themselves imply that `incr` does not impede `read` (edge 3). This can be demonstrated by considering an alternative implementation of `read`, that satisfies the specification but is not wait-free:

```
do {
  v := [x]; w := [x];
} while (v ≠ w);
return v;
```

Recall that we can prove that `read` is wait-free by giving a different specification as in Theorem 4. An operation is wait-free exactly when every operation does not impede it. For `read`, this is expressed by edges 1 and 3 in the above graph.

The stack specification in Fig. 7, much like the counter specification, implies that `pop` does not impede either `push` or `pop`:

The `pop` operation, however, may be impeded by `push`.

The non-impedance relationships implied by the stack specification are important for clients. For instance, consider a producer-consumer scenario in which the stack is used to communicate data from producers to consumers. When no data is available, consumers may simply loop attempting to pop the stack. If the `pop` operation could impede `push`, then producers might be starved by consumers. In this situation, we could not guarantee that the system would make progress. This suggests that non-impedance, which is captured by Total-TaDA specifications, can be an important property of non-blocking algorithms.

7 Related Work

Hoffmann *et al.* [10] introduced a concurrent separation logic for verifying total correctness. By adapting the most-general-client approach of Gotsman *et al.* [7], they establish that modules are lock-free. (They do not, however, establish functional correctness.) This method involves a thread passing "tokens" to other threads whose lock-free operations are impeded by modifications to the shared state. Subsequent approaches [1,12] also use some form of tokens that are used up in loops or function calls. These approaches require special proof rules for the tokens. When these approaches restrict to dealing with finite numbers of tokens, support for unbounded non-determinism (as in the backoff increment example of Fig. 5) is limited. In Total-TaDA such token passing is not necessary. Instead, we require the client to provide a general (ordinal) limit on the amount of impeding interference. Consequently, we can guarantee the termination of loops with standard proof rules.

Liang *et al.* [12] have developed a proof theory for termination-preserving refinement, applying it to verify linearisability and lock-freedom. Their approach constrains impedance by requiring that impeding actions correspond to progress at the abstract level. In Total-TaDA, such constraints are made by requiring that impeding actions decrease an ordinal associated with a shared region. Their approach does not freely combine lock-free and wait-free specifications whereas, with Total-TaDA, we can reason about lock- and wait-freedom in combination, and more subtle conditions such as non-impedance. For example, we can show when a read operation of a lock-free data-structure is wait-free. Their specifications establish termination-preserving refinement (given a context, if the abstract program is guaranteed to terminate, then so is the concrete), whereas Total-TaDA specifications establish termination (in a context, the program will terminate).

Boström and Müller [1] have introduced an approach that can verify termination and progress properties of concurrent programs. The approach supports blocking concurrency and non-terminating programs, which Total-TaDA does not. However, the approach does not aim at racy concurrent programs and cannot deal with any of the examples shown in the paper. Furthermore, the relationship between termination and lock- and wait-freedom is not considered.

Of the above approaches, none covers total functional correctness for fine-grained concurrent programs. With Total-TaDA we can reason about clients that use modules, without their implementation details. Moreover, with Total-TaDA it is easy to verify module operations independently, with respect to a common abstraction, rather than considering a whole module at once. Finally, our approach to specification is unique in supporting lock- and wait-freedom simultaneously, as well as expressing more subtle conditions such as non-impedance.

8 Conclusions and Future Work

We have introduced Total-TaDA, a program logic that provides local, modular reasoning for proving the termination and functional correctness of non-blocking concurrent programs. With our abstract specifications, clients can reason about total correctness without needing to know about the underlying implementation. Different implementations, satisfying the same specification, can have different termination arguments, but these arguments are not exposed to the clients. By using ordinals to bound interference, our specifications can express traditional non-blocking properties. Moreover, they capture a new notion of *non-impedance*: that one operation does not set back the progress of another.

We have claimed that our approach supports modular reasoning, and substantiated this by reasoning about implementations and clients of modules. We provide further examples in the technical report [18]. In particular, we specify a non-blocking map and verify two implementations, based on lists and hash tables, with the second making use of the first through the abstract specification. We also implement a set specification on top of the map.

Blocking. Many concurrent modules make use of *blocking*, for example by using semaphores or monitors. Properties such as starvation-freedom can be expressed in terms of termination, but require the assumption of a fair scheduler. Some aspects of our approach are likely to apply here. However, it is also necessary to constrain future behaviours, for instance, to specify that a lock that has been acquired will be released in a finite time. This might be achieved with a program logic that can reason explicitly about continuations.

Non-termination. Some programs, such as operating systems, are designed not to terminate. Such programs should still continually perform useful work. It would be interesting to extend Total-TaDA to specify and verify progress properties of non-terminating systems. Progress can be seen as localised termination, so the same reasoning techniques should apply. However, a different approach to specification will be necessary to express and verify these properties.

Acknowledgements. We thank Bart Jacobs, Hongjin Liang, Peter Müller and the anonymous referees for useful feedback. This research was supported by EPSRC Programme Grants EP/H008373/1 and EP/K008528/1, by the "ModuRes" Sapere Aude Advanced Grant from The Danish Council for Independent Research for the Natural Sciences (FNU) and the "Automated Verification for Concurrent Programs" Individual Postdoc Grant from The Danish Council for Independent Research for Technology and Production Sciences (FTP).

References

1. Boström, P., Müller, P.: Modular verification of finite blocking in non-terminating programs. In: Boyland, J.T. (ed.) 29th European Conference on Object-Oriented Programming, vol. 37, pp. 639–663. Schloss Dagstuhl-Leibniz-Zentrum fuer Informatik, Dagstuhl (2015)
2. Boyland, J.: Checking interference with fractional permissions. In: Cousot, R. (ed.) Static Analysis. LNCS, vol. 2694, pp. 55–72. Springer, Heidelberg (2003)
3. Cantor, G.: Beiträge zur begründung der transfiniten mengenlehre. Mathematische Annalen **49**(2), 207–246 (1897). http://dx.doi.org/10.1007/BF01444205
4. Dinsdale-Young, T., Birkedal, L., Gardner, P., Parkinson, M., Yang, H.: Views: compositional reasoning for concurrent programs. In: POPL, pp. 287–300 (2013)

5. Dinsdale-Young, T., Dodds, M., Gardner, P., Parkinson, M.J., Vafeiadis, V.: Concurrent abstract predicates. In: D'Hondt, T. (ed.) ECOOP 2010. LNCS, vol. 6183, pp. 504–528. Springer, Heidelberg (2010)
6. Floyd, R.W.: Assigning meanings to programs. In: Proceedings of the American Mathematical Society Symposia on Applied Mathematics, vol. 19, pp. 19–31 (1967)
7. Gotsman, A., Cook, B., Parkinson, M., Vafeiadis, V.: Proving that non-blocking algorithms don't block. In: POPL, pp. 16–28 (2009)
8. Herlihy, M.: Wait-free synchronization. ACM Trans. Program. Lang. Syst. **13**(1), 124–149 (1991)
9. Hessenberg, G.: Grundbegriffe der Mengenlehre. Abhandlungen der Fries'schen Schule / Neue Folge. Vandenhoeck & Ruprecht, Göttingen (1906)
10. Hoffmann, J., Marmar, M., Shao, Z.: Quantitative reasoning for proving lock-freedom. In: 2013 28th Annual IEEE/ACM Symposium on Logic in Computer Science (LICS), pp. 124–133. IEEE (2013)
11. Jung, R., Swasey, D., Sieczkowski, F., Svendsen, K., Turon, A., Birkedal, L., Dreyer, D.: Iris: monoids and invariants as an orthogonal basis for concurrent reasoning. In: POPL, pp. 637–650 (2015)
12. Liang, H., Feng, X., Shao, Z.: Compositional verification of termination-preserving refinement of concurrent programs. In: Proceedings of the Joint Meeting of the Twenty-Third EACSL Annual Conference on Computer Science Logic (CSL) and the Twenty-Ninth Annual ACM/IEEE Symposium on Logic in Computer Science (LICS), p. 65. ACM (2014)
13. Massalin, H., Pu, C.: A lock-free multiprocessor os kernel. SIGOPS Oper. Syst. Rev. **26**, 108 (1992)
14. Parkinson, M., Bierman, G.: Separation logic and abstraction. In: POPL, pp. 247–258 (2005)
15. Reynolds, J.C.: Separation logic: a logic for shared mutable data structures. In: 2002 Proceedings 17th Annual IEEE Symposium on Logic in Computer Science, pp. 55–74. IEEE (2002)
16. da Rocha Pinto, P., Dinsdale-Young, T., Gardner, P.: Tada: a logic for time and data abstraction. In: Jones, R. (ed.) ECOOP 2014. LNCS, vol. 8586, pp. 207–231. Springer, Heidelberg (2014)
17. da Rocha Pinto, P., Dinsdale-Young, T., Gardner, P.: Steps in modular specifications for concurrent modules (invited tutorial paper). Electron. Notes Theor. Comput. Sci. **319**, 3–18 (2015)
18. da Rocha Pinto, P., Dinsdale-Young, T., Gardner, P., Sutherland, J.: Modular termination verification for non-blocking concurrency. Technical report, Imperial College London (2016)
19. Svendsen, K., Birkedal, L.: Impredicative concurrent abstract predicates. In: Shao, Z. (ed.) ESOP 2014 (ETAPS). LNCS, vol. 8410, pp. 149–168. Springer, Heidelberg (2014)
20. Treiber, R.K.: Systems programming: coping with parallelism. Technical report RJ 5118, IBM Almaden Research Center, April 1986
21. Turing, A.M.: Checking a large routine. In: Report of a Conference on High Speed Automatic Calculating Machines, pp. 67–69 (1949). http://www.turingarchive.org/browse.php/B/8
22. Turon, A., Dreyer, D., Birkedal, L.: Unifying refinement and hoare-style reasoning in a logic for higher-order concurrency. In: ICFP, pp. 377–390 (2013)

Call-By-Push-Value from a Linear Logic Point of View

Thomas Ehrhard(✉)

CNRS, IRIF, UMR 8243, Univ Paris Diderot, Sorbonne Paris Cité,
75205 Paris, France
thomas.ehrhard@pps.univ-paris-diderot.fr

Abstract. We present and study a simple Call-By-Push-Value lambda-calculus with fix-points and recursive types. We explain its connection with Linear Logic by presenting a denotational interpretation of the language in any model of Linear Logic equipped with a notion of embedding retraction pairs. We consider the particular case of the Scott model of Linear Logic from which we derive an intersection type system for our calculus and prove an adequacy theorem. Last, we introduce a fully polarized version of this calculus which turns out to be a term language for a large fragment of LLP and refines lambda-mu.

1 Introduction

Linear Logic (LL) has been introduced as a refinement of Intuitionistic Logic: in [14], Girard proposed a very simple and natural translation of intuitionistic logic and of the lambda-calculus in LL. From a categorical point of view, as explained in [28], this translation corresponds to the construction of the Kleisli category of the exponential comonad "!" of LL. An adequate categorical axiomatization of the denotational models of LL has been then provided in [3], see also [26] for a very complete and detailed picture.

In [14], another possible translation of intuitionistic formulas strangely called "boring" is mentioned. It appeared later that, just as the original Girard's translation corresponds to the call-by-name (CBN) evaluation strategy of the lambda-calculus, the "boring" translation corresponds to the call-by-value (CBV) reduction strategy, see in particular [24]. Indeed, a first observation is that this latter translation does not preserve all β-reductions, but only those respecting a CBV discipline. More deeply, domain-theoretic denotational models of the lambda-calculus arising through the original Girard translation, that is, arising as Kleisli categories of the exponential comonad, enjoy an adequacy property expressing that a term reduces to a "value" (a head-normal term, say) iff its interpretation is different from $\bot$. A similar property holds for the CBV translation (now, a closed value is an abstraction) with respect to the CBV reduction strategy.

P. Thiemann (Ed.): ESOP 2016, LNCS 9632, pp. 202–228, 2016.
DOI: 10.1007/978-3-662-49498-1_9

Both translations give a particularly preeminent role to the Kleisli category of the "!" comonad. This is obvious for the original CBN translation but it is also true for the CBV translation if we consider that the "!" functor defines a strong monad on the cartesian closed Kleisli category: then the CBV translation coincides with Moggi's interpretation of the CBV lambda-calculus in a CCC equipped with a computational monad [27].

So LL provides a common setting where both CBN and CBV can be faithfully interpreted. In spite of its appealing symmetries and its high degree of asynchrony, the syntax of LL proof nets is complex and does not seem to be a convenient starting point for the design of programming languages; it is rather a powerful tool for analyzing the operational and denotational properties of programming languages. It seems therefore natural to look for lambda-calculi admitting a translation in LL and where both CBN and CBV can be embedded, factorizing the two translations mentioned above.

Levy introduced a lambda-calculus subsuming both CBN and CBV: the *Call-By-Push-Value* lambda-calculus. We propose a similar functional calculus where both CBN and CBV can be encoded and features a simple connection with LL. For reasons which will become clear later, we call it *half-polarized lambda-calculus* (Λ_{HP}). Our calculus is actually isomorphic to (a sub-calculus) of SFPL [25]. It bears some similarities with the adjoint calculus of [2], though we do not need linear variables. It is also close to the Enriched Effect Calculus [10].

The LL exponential "!" allows to turn a term of type A into a term of type $!A$ which is duplicable and discardable, by means of an operation called *promotion*. This discardability and duplicability is made possible by the structural rules $!A$ is equipped with. It was already observed by Girard in [15] (and probably much earlier) that the property of "being equipped with structural rules" is preserved by the $\otimes$ and $\oplus$ connectives of LL. This observation can be made more accurate as follows: a "type equipped with structural rules" is a coalgebra for the "!" connective, that is, an object of the Eilenberg-Moore category of "!", and this category admits $\oplus$ as coproduct and $\otimes$ as cartesian product. This category is not a CCC in general but contains the CCC Kleisli category of "!" as a full sub-category (remember that the Kleisli category is the category of free !-coalgebras). The Eilenberg-Moore category of "!" was used crucially by Girard to give a semantics to a classical sequent calculus and by other authors (see for instance [21]) to interpret classical extensions of the lambda-calculus such as Parigot's $\lambda\mu$-calculus.

Replacing the Kleisli category with this larger Eilenberg-Moore category when interpreting the lambda-calculus has other major benefits. Consider for instance the interpretation of ordinary PCF in an LL-induced categorical model, that is, in the Kleisli category of the "!" comonad of a categorical model $\mathcal{L}$ of LL. The simplest and most natural interpretation for the type of natural numbers is $\mathsf{N} = 1 \oplus 1 \oplus \cdots$ (ω copies of the unit 1 of the tensor product). But 1 has a canonical structure of !-coalgebra (because $1 = !\top$ where $\top$ is the terminal object of $\mathcal{L}$) and this is therefore also true of N, as a coproduct of coalgebras. This means that we have a well behaved morphism $\mathrm{h}_{\mathsf{N}} \in \mathcal{L}(\mathsf{N}, !\mathsf{N})$ which allows to turn any morphism $f \in \mathcal{L}_!(\mathsf{N}, X)$ of the Kleisli CCC $\mathcal{L}_!$ where we interpret

PCF into a *linear* morphism $f\,\mathsf{h}_{\mathsf{N}} \in \mathcal{L}(\mathsf{N}, X)$. Operationally, this means that, in spite of the fact that PCF is a CBN language and that its interpretation in $\mathcal{L}_!$ is a CBN interpretation, we can deal with the terms of ground type in a CBV fashion. For instance we can replace the ordinary PCF "if zero" conditional with the following more sensible one:

$$\frac{\mathcal{P} \vdash M : \iota \qquad \mathcal{P} \vdash N : \sigma \qquad \mathcal{P}, x : \iota \vdash N' : \sigma}{\mathcal{P} \vdash \mathsf{if}(M, N, x \cdot N') : \sigma}$$

with the reduction rules

$$\mathsf{if}(\underline{0}, N, x \cdot N') \to N \qquad \mathsf{if}(\underline{n+1}, N, x \cdot N') \to N' \left[\underline{n}/x\right]$$
$$M \to M' \Rightarrow \mathsf{if}(M, N, x \cdot N') \to \mathsf{if}(M', N, x \cdot N')$$

The denotational interpretation of $\mathsf{if}(M, N, x \cdot N')$ uses crucially the coalgebra structure h_{N} of N. This idea is also reminiscent of Krivine's *storage operators* [20] which allow a CBV discipline for data types in a globally CBN calculus.

Call-By-Push-Value and Λ_{HP} generalize this idea. We consider two classes of types: the *positive types* $\varphi, \psi \dots$ and the larger class of *general types* $\sigma, \tau, \dots$ Just as in [15], positive types correspond to objects of $\mathcal{L}^!$ whereas general types are just objects of $\mathcal{L}$. Of course there is an obvious way of considering a positive type as a general one by simply forgetting its coalgebra structure. There is also a way of turning a general type into a positive one using "!", and positive types are stable under sums $\oplus$ and product $\otimes$. In Girard's CBN translation, $\sigma \Rightarrow \tau$ (where $\Rightarrow$ is intuitionistic implication) becomes $!\sigma \multimap \tau$: *the main idea of* Λ_{HP} *is to generalize this idea by allowing to replace* $!\sigma$ *with an arbitrary positive type* φ. Therefore, the implication of Λ_{HP} is linear: all the required non-linearity is provided by the positivity of the premise. Accordingly all variables have positive types. This is also why we use a new notation $\langle M \rangle N$ for the application of M to N, to stress the fact that this application is linear.

There is however a subtlety which does not occur in CBN: consider a term M of type σ with one free variable x of positive type φ. Consider also a closed term N of type φ. The interpretation of M is a morphism $f \in \mathcal{L}(\varphi, \sigma)$ (identifying types with their interpretation) and the interpretation of N is a morphism $g \in \mathcal{L}(1, \varphi)$. There is no reason however for g to belong to $\mathcal{L}^!(1, \varphi)$ and so we cannot be sure that $f\,g$ (we use simple juxtaposition to denote composition of morphisms in $\mathcal{L}$) will coincide with the interpretation of $M\,[N/x]$. Indeed, for that substitutivity property to hold, we would need g to be duplicable and discardable which is the case if we can make sure that $g \in \mathcal{L}^!(1, \varphi)$, but does not hold in general. It is here that the syntactic notion of *value* comes in: if $\varphi = !\sigma$ then N is a value if $N = R^!$ (a promotion of a term R of type σ), if $\varphi = \varphi_1 \otimes \varphi_2$ then N is a value if $N = \langle V_1, V_2 \rangle$ where V_i is a value of type φ_i, and similarly for sums. The main property of values is that their interpretations are coalgebra morphisms: if N is a value then $g \in \mathcal{L}^!(1, \varphi)$. This is why, in Λ_{HP}, β reduction is restricted to the case where the argument is a value. This also means that in $\langle \lambda x^{\varphi}\, M \rangle N$ we need to reduce N to a value before reducing the β-redex. If, for instance, the reduction of N diverges without reaching a value then the reduction of $\langle \lambda x^{\varphi} M \rangle N$ diverges even if M does not use x, just as in CBV.

Positive types are also stable under fix-points if we assume that the objects of $\mathcal{L}$ can be equipped with a notion of embedding-retraction pairs, which is usually the case in categories of domains. Under the assumption that this new category has all countable filtered colimits and that the functors interpreting types are continuous, it is easy to prove that all "positive types with parameters" have fix-points which are themselves positive types. The presence of "!" as an explicit type constructor in Λ_{HP} allows to define lazy recursive types such as $\rho = \varphi \otimes !\rho$ where φ is a given type: ρ is the type of streams of elements of type φ. At the level of terms, the construction which introduces an "!" is the aforementioned construction $R^!$ which corresponds to the well known (generalized) promotion of LL aka *exponential box*; this construction corresponds here to *thunks* or *suspensions*. In this stream type ρ the box construction is crucially used to postpone the evaluation of the tail of the stream. The box can be opened (that is, the thunk can be forced) by means of an explicit *dereliction* syntactic construct $\mathsf{der}(M)$ which can be applied to any term M of type $!\sigma$ for some σ and which corresponds exactly to the usual dereliction rule of LL.

Contents. We define a version of Λ_{HP} featuring positive and ordinary types, recursive positive types and a fix-point operator for terms. Since many data types can be defined easily in this language (ordinary integers, lazy integers, lists, streams, various kinds of finite and infinite trees...), it widely encompasses PCF and is closer to FPC [13], with the additional feature of allowing to freely combine CBV and CBN. We define the syntax of the language, provide a typing system and a simple operational semantics which is "weak" in the sense that reduction is forbidden under λs and within boxes (more general reductions can of course be defined but, just as in CBV, a let construction or new reduction rules as in [4] should be added).

We do not describe the embeddings of the CBN and CBV lambda-calculi into Λ_{HP} because they are very similar to the corresponding embeddings into CBPV, described in [22]. It will be fully described in a longer version of this paper.

Then we recall the general definition of a categorical model of LL (with fix-point operators), of its Eilenberg-Moore category and we describe the additional categorical structure which will allow to interpret recursive positive types. To illustrate the connection of Λ_{HP} with LL without introducing a syntax for LL proofs[1], we describe the interpretation of Λ_{HP} in such a categorical model of LL and state a Soundness Theorem.

This categorical semantics is a special case of Levy's adjunction semantics of [22] for CBPV. One of the interests of this LL-based semantics is that it admits extensions in various exciting directions (Ludics, Differential LL, Light LL etc.) on which we think that Λ_{HP} will shed a new light. There is another good reason for considering this semantics: it gives a standard way of building the "category of values" as $\mathcal{L}^!$, starting from a "linear" category $\mathcal{L}$ which is usually much simpler. This is typically the case when $\mathcal{L}$ is the category of coherence spaces and linear

[1] This would be very interesting but would require more space.

maps; in this case it is not easy to give a direct, domain-theoretic description of $\mathcal{L}^!$. The Scott semantics described in Sect. 4 is a remarkable exception where $\mathcal{L}^!$ can be seen as a category of predomains and Scott continuous functions.

We also provide a description of this Scott semantical interpretation as a very simple "intersection" typing system and prove an adequacy theorem (which can be understood as a normalization theorem for this typing system). This result is important as it shows that our weak reduction semantics for Λ_{HP} is complete in the sense that if a closed term is equivalent to a value in any equivalence relation compatible with the denotational semantics, then it weakly reduces to a value. Next we introduce a fully polarized version Λ_{LLP} of our calculus, a system which is closer to Levy's original CBPV although it generalizes it by allowing "classical" constructions borrowed from Parigot's $\lambda\mu$-calculus and is deeply related with Laurent's Polarized Linear Logic LLP. Last we define an encoding of Λ_{HP} into Λ_{LLP} and outline its basic features.

Our initial motivation for introducing Λ_{LLP} was to combine our representation of data as !-coalgebra morphisms in Λ_{HP} with the representation of stacks (continuations) as !-coalgebra morphisms in the semantics of classical calculi such as the CBN $\lambda\mu$-calculus. Λ_{LLP} is presented in the $\lambda\mu\tilde{\mu}$ style [7] and further developed in [8]. We think that it provides a satisfactory answer to our quest and deserves further study. Independently, Pierre-Louis Curien introduced recently in the unpublished note [5] a similar formalism for representing Levy's original CBPV (Curien's calculus however is intuitionistic whereas ours is classical).

2 Syntax

Types are given by the following BNF syntax. We define by mutual induction two kinds of types: *positive types* and *general types*, given type variables ζ, ξ...:

$$\text{positive types} \quad \varphi, \psi, \ldots := !\sigma \mid \varphi \otimes \psi \mid \varphi \oplus \psi \mid \zeta \mid \mathsf{Fix}\,\zeta \cdot \varphi \tag{1}$$

$$\text{general types types} \quad \sigma, \tau \ldots := \varphi \mid \varphi \multimap \sigma \mid \top \tag{2}$$

More constructions could be added for general types, as in CBPV (such as products or recursive types), we do not so here by lack of space. We consider the types up to the equation $\mathsf{Fix}\,\zeta \cdot \varphi = \varphi\left[(\mathsf{Fix}\,\zeta \cdot \varphi)/\zeta\right]$.

Terms are given by the following BNF syntax, given variables $x, y, \ldots$:

$$\begin{aligned} M, N \ldots := x \mid M^! \mid \langle M, N \rangle \mid \mathsf{in}_1 M \mid \mathsf{in}_2 M \\ \mid \lambda x^\varphi\, M \mid \langle M \rangle N \mid \mathsf{case}(M, x_1 \cdot N_1, x_2 \cdot N_2) \\ \mid \mathsf{pr}_1 M \mid \mathsf{pr}_2 M \mid \mathsf{der}(M) \mid \mathsf{fix}\, x^{!\sigma}\, M \end{aligned}$$

This calculus can be seen as a special case of Levy's CBPV [22] in which the type constructor F is kept implicit (and U is "!"). Section 5 proposes a version of CBPV where F is "?", taking benefit of this for introducing constructs related to classical logic.

The notion of substitution is defined as usual. Figure 1 provides the typing rules for these terms. A typing context is an expression $\mathcal{P} = (x_1 : \varphi_1, \ldots, x_k : \varphi_k)$ where all types are positive and the x_is are pairwise distinct variables.

$$\frac{\mathcal{P} \vdash M : \sigma}{\mathcal{P} \vdash M^! : !\sigma} \qquad \frac{\mathcal{P} \vdash M_1 : \varphi_1 \qquad \mathcal{P} \vdash M_2 : \varphi_2}{\mathcal{P} \vdash \langle M_1, M_2 \rangle : \varphi_1 \otimes \varphi_2} \qquad \frac{\mathcal{P} \vdash M : \varphi_i}{\mathcal{P} \vdash \mathsf{in}_i M : \varphi_1 \oplus \varphi_2}$$

$$\frac{}{\mathcal{P}, x : \varphi \vdash x : \varphi} \qquad \frac{\mathcal{P}, x : \varphi \vdash M : \sigma}{\mathcal{P} \vdash \lambda x^{\varphi}\, M : \varphi \multimap \sigma} \qquad \frac{\mathcal{P} \vdash M : \varphi \multimap \sigma \qquad \mathcal{P} \vdash N : \varphi}{\mathcal{P} \vdash \langle M \rangle N : \sigma}$$

$$\frac{\mathcal{P} \vdash M : !\sigma}{\mathcal{P} \vdash \mathsf{der}(M) : \sigma} \qquad \frac{\mathcal{P}, x : !\sigma \vdash M : \sigma}{\mathcal{P} \vdash \mathsf{fix}\, x^{!\sigma}\, M : \sigma}$$

$$\frac{\mathcal{P} \vdash M : \varphi_1 \oplus \varphi_2 \qquad \mathcal{P}, x_1 : \varphi_1 \vdash M_1 : \sigma \qquad \mathcal{P}, x_2 : \varphi_2 \vdash M_2 : \sigma}{\mathcal{P} \vdash \mathsf{case}(M, x_1 \cdot M_1, x_2 \cdot M_2) : \sigma}$$

$$\frac{\mathcal{P} \vdash M : \varphi_1 \otimes \varphi_2}{\mathcal{P} \vdash \mathsf{pr}_i M : \varphi_i}$$

Fig. 1. Typing system for Λ_{HP}

Remark 1. It might seem strange to the reader acquainted with LL that the rules introducing the $\otimes$ connective and eliminating the $\multimap$ connective have an "additive" handling of typing contexts (the same typing context $\mathcal{P}$ occurs in both premises): our contexts are not linear. The reason for this becomes clear in Sect. 3 where positive types are interpreted as !-coalgebras, which are equipped with morphisms allowing to interpret the structural rules of weakening and contraction. This is why typing contexts involve positive types only.

We define now a *weak* reduction relation on terms, meaning that we never reduce within a "box" $M^!$ or under a λ. *Values* are particular Λ_{HP} terms (they are not a new syntactic category) defined by the following BNF syntax:

$$V, W \ldots := x \mid M^! \mid \langle V, W \rangle \mid \mathsf{in}_1 V \mid \mathsf{in}_2 V\,.$$

Remark 2. A closed value is simply a tree whose leaves are "boxes" or "thunks" $M^!$ (where the M's are arbitrary well typed closed terms) and whose internal nodes are either unary nodes bearing an index 1 or 2, or ordered binary nodes.

Figure 2 defines weak reduction $\to_{\mathsf{w}}$.

Proposition 1. *The reduction $\to_{\mathsf{w}}$ enjoys subject reduction and Church-Rosser.*

The first statement is a straightforward verification using a Substitution Lemma that we do not state. The second one is easy: $\to_{\mathsf{w}}$ has the diamond property.

Proposition 2. *Any value is $\to_{\mathsf{w}}$-normal. If φ is a positive type, $\vdash M : \varphi$ and M is $\to_{\mathsf{w}}$-normal, then M is a value.*

This is easy. In the second statement M has to be closed (the term $\langle \mathsf{der}(x) \rangle V$ is normal, is not a value and can be given a positive type).

$$\frac{}{\mathsf{der}(M^!) \to_{\mathsf{w}} M} \qquad \frac{}{\langle \lambda x^{\varphi}\, M\rangle V \to_{\mathsf{w}} M\,[V/x]} \qquad \frac{}{\mathsf{pr}_i\langle V_1, V_2\rangle \to_{\mathsf{w}} V_i}$$

$$\frac{}{\mathsf{fix}\, x^{!\sigma}\, M \to_{\mathsf{w}} M\,\left[(\mathsf{fix}\, x^{!\sigma}\, M)^!/x\right]} \qquad \frac{M \to_{\mathsf{w}} M'}{\mathsf{der}(M) \to_{\mathsf{w}} \mathsf{der}(M')}$$

$$\frac{M \to_{\mathsf{w}} M'}{\langle M\rangle N \to_{\mathsf{w}} \langle M'\rangle N} \qquad \frac{N \to_{\mathsf{w}} N'}{\langle M\rangle N \to_{\mathsf{w}} \langle M\rangle N'}$$

$$\frac{M \to_{\mathsf{w}} M'}{\mathsf{pr}_i M \to_{\mathsf{w}} \mathsf{pr}_i M'} \qquad \frac{M_1 \to_{\mathsf{w}} M_1'}{\langle M_1, M_2\rangle \to_{\mathsf{w}} \langle M_1', M_2\rangle} \qquad \frac{M_2 \to_{\mathsf{w}} M_2'}{\langle M_1, M_2\rangle \to_{\mathsf{w}} \langle M_1, M_2'\rangle}$$

$$\frac{}{\mathsf{case}(\mathsf{in}_i V, x_1 \cdot M_1, x_2 \cdot M_2) \to_{\mathsf{w}} M_i\,[V/x_i]} \qquad \frac{M \to_{\mathsf{w}} M'}{\mathsf{in}_i M \to_{\mathsf{w}} \mathsf{in}_i M'}$$

$$\frac{M \to_{\mathsf{w}} M'}{\mathsf{case}(M, x_1 \cdot M_1, x_2 \cdot M_2) \to_{\mathsf{w}} \mathsf{case}(M', x_1 \cdot M_1, x_2 \cdot M_2)}$$

Fig. 2. Weak reduction axioms and rules for Λ_{HP}

2.1 Examples

Given any type σ, we define $\Omega^\sigma = \mathsf{fix}\, x^{!\sigma}\, \mathsf{der}(x)$ which satisfies $\vdash \Omega^\sigma : \sigma$. It is clear that $\Omega^\sigma \to_{\mathsf{w}} \mathsf{der}((\Omega^\sigma)^!) \to_{\mathsf{w}} \Omega^\sigma$ so that we can consider Ω^σ as the ever-looping program of type σ.

Unit type and natural numbers. We define a unit type 1 by $1 = !\top$, and we set $* = (\Omega^\top)^!$. We define the type ι of unary natural numbers by $\iota = 1 \oplus \iota$ (by this we mean that $\iota = \mathsf{Fix}\,\zeta \cdot (1 \oplus \zeta)$). We define $\underline{0} = \mathsf{in}_1 *$ and $\underline{n+1} = \mathsf{in}_2 \underline{n}$ so that we have $\mathcal{P} \vdash \underline{n} : \iota$ for each $n \in \mathbb{N}$.

Then, given a term M, we define the term $\mathsf{suc}(M) = \mathsf{in}_2 M$, so that we have

$$\frac{\mathcal{P} \vdash M : \iota}{\mathcal{P} \vdash \mathsf{suc}(M) : \iota}$$

Last, given terms M, N_1 and N_2 and a variable x, we define an "ifz" conditional by $\mathsf{if}(M, N_1, x \cdot N_2) = \mathsf{case}(M, z \cdot N_1, x \cdot N_2)$ where z is not free in N_1, so that

$$\frac{\mathcal{P} \vdash M : \iota \qquad \mathcal{P} \vdash N_1 : \sigma \qquad \mathcal{P}, x : \iota \vdash N_2 : \sigma}{\mathcal{P} \vdash \mathsf{if}(M, N_1, x \cdot N_2) : \sigma}$$

Streams. Let φ be a positive type and S_φ be the positive type defined by $\mathsf{S}_\varphi = \varphi \otimes !\mathsf{S}_\varphi$, that is $\mathsf{S}_\varphi = \mathsf{Fix}\,\zeta \cdot (\varphi \otimes !\zeta)$. We can define a term M such that $\vdash M : \mathsf{S}_\varphi \multimap \iota \multimap \varphi$ which computes the nth element of a stream:

$$M = \mathsf{fix}\, f^{!(\mathsf{S}_\varphi \multimap \iota \multimap \varphi)}\, \lambda x^{\mathsf{S}_\varphi}\, \lambda y^{\iota}\, \mathsf{if}(y, \mathsf{pr}_1 x, z \cdot \langle \mathsf{der}(f)\rangle \mathsf{der}(\mathsf{pr}_2 x)\, z)$$

Conversely, we can define a term N such that $\vdash N : !(\iota \multimap \varphi) \multimap \mathsf{S}_\varphi$ which turns a function into a stream.

$$N = \mathsf{fix}\, F^{!(!(\iota \multimap \varphi) \multimap \mathsf{S}_\varphi)}\, \lambda f^{!(\iota \multimap \varphi)}\, \langle \langle \mathsf{der}(f)\rangle \underline{0}, (\langle \mathsf{der}(F)\rangle (\lambda x^{\iota}\, \langle \mathsf{der}(f)\rangle \mathsf{suc}(x))^!)^! \rangle$$

Observe that the recursive call of F is encapsulated into a box, which makes the construction lazy.

Lists. There are various possibilities for defining a type of lists of elements of a positive type φ. The simplest definition is $\lambda_0 = 1 \oplus (\varphi \otimes \lambda_0)$. This corresponds to the ordinary ML type of lists. But we can also define $\lambda_1 = 1 \oplus (\varphi \otimes !\lambda_1)$ and then we have a type of lazy lists (or terminable streams) where the tail of the list is computed only when required.

We could also consider $\lambda_2 = 1 \oplus (!\sigma \otimes \lambda_2)$ which allows to manipulate lists of objects of type σ (which can be a general type) without accessing their elements.

3 Denotational Semantics

The kind of denotational models we are interested in in this paper are those induced by a model of LL, in the spirit of Girard's seminal work [15] on the semantics of the classical system LC where positive formulas are interpreted as $\otimes$-comonoids; this interpretation is further developed *e.g.* in [21]. We use here exactly the same idea for interpreting positive types.

We first recall the general categorical definition of a model of LL implicit in [14], our main reference here is [26] to which we also refer for the rich bibliography on this general topic.

3.1 Models of Linear Logic

A model of LL consists of the following data.

- A category $\mathcal{L}$.
- A symmetric monoidal structure $(\otimes, 1, \lambda, \rho, \alpha, \sigma)$ which is assumed to be closed: $\otimes$ is a functor $\mathcal{L}^2 \to \mathcal{L}$, 1 an object of $\mathcal{L}$, $\lambda_X \in \mathcal{L}(1 \otimes X, X)$, $\rho_X \in \mathcal{L}(X \otimes 1, X)$, $\alpha_{X,Y,Z} \in \mathcal{L}((X \otimes Y) \otimes Z, X \otimes (Y \otimes Z))$ and $\sigma_{X,Y} \in \mathcal{L}(X \otimes Y, Y \otimes X)$ are natural isomorphisms satisfying coherence diagrams that we do not record here. We use $X \multimap Y$ for the object of linear morphisms from X to Y, ev for the evaluation morphism which belongs to $\mathcal{L}((X \multimap Y) \otimes X, Y)$ and cur for the linear curryfication map $\mathcal{L}(Z \otimes X, Y) \to \mathcal{L}(Z, X \multimap Y)$.
- An object $\perp$ of $\mathcal{L}$ such that the natural morphism $\eta_X = \mathrm{cur}(\mathrm{ev}\,\sigma_{X \multimap \perp, X}) \in \mathcal{L}(X, (X \multimap \perp) \multimap \perp)$ is an iso for each object X (one says that $\mathcal{L}$ is a $*$-autonomous category[2]). We use $X^\perp$ for the object $X \multimap \perp$ of $\mathcal{L}$.
- The category $\mathcal{L}$ is assumed to be cartesian. We use $\top$ for the terminal object, & for the cartesian product and pr_i for the projections. It follows by $*$-autonomy that $\mathcal{L}$ has also all finite coproducts. We use 0 for the initial object, $\oplus$ for the coproduct and in_i for the injections. Given an object X of $\mathcal{L}$, we use in^X for the unique element of $\mathcal{L}(0, X)$.

---

[2] Though not essential for interpreting Λ_{HP}, this assumption is natural as it holds in the concrete models we have in mind and it simplifies the interpretation of Λ_{LLP}, the calculus of Sect. 5.

- We are also given a comonad $!\_ : \mathcal{L} \to \mathcal{L}$ with counit $\mathrm{der}_X \in \mathcal{L}(!X, X)$ (called dereliction) and comultiplication $\mathrm{dig}_X \in \mathcal{L}(!X, !!X)$ (called digging).
- And a strong symmetric monoidal structure for the functor $!\_$, from the symmetric monoidal category $(\mathcal{L}, \&)$ to the symmetric monoidal category $(\mathcal{L}, \otimes)$. This means that we are given an iso $\mathrm{m}^0 \in \mathcal{L}(1, !\top)$ and a natural iso $\mathrm{m}^2_{X,Y} \in \mathcal{L}(!X \otimes !Y, !(X \mathbin{\&} Y))$ which satisfy commutations that we do not record here. We also require a coherence condition relating m^2 and dig.

We use $?\_$ for the "De Morgan dual" of $!\_$: $?X = (!(X^\perp))^\perp$ and similarly for morphisms. It is a monad on $\mathcal{L}$ with unit der'_X and multiplication dig'_X defined straightforwardly, using der_Y and dig_Y.

Lax monoidality. It follows that we can define a lax symmetric monoidal structure for the functor $!\_$ from the symmetric monoidal category $(\mathcal{L}, \otimes)$ to itself. This means that we can define a morphism $\mu^0 \in \mathcal{L}(1, !1)$ and a natural transformation $\mu^2_{X,Y} \in \mathcal{L}(!X \otimes !Y, !(X \otimes Y))$ which satisfy some coherence diagrams whose main consequence is that we can canonically extend this natural transformation to the case of n-ary tensors:

$$\mu^{(n)}_{X_1,\dots,X_N} \in \mathcal{L}(!X_1 \otimes \cdots \otimes !X_n, !(X_1 \otimes \cdots \otimes X_n))$$

in a way which is compatible with the symmetric monoidal structure of $\mathcal{L}$ (and allows us to write things just as if $\otimes$ were strictly associative).

The Eilenberg-Moore category. It is then standard to define the category $\mathcal{L}^!$ of !-coalgebras. An object of this category is a pair $P = (\underline{P}, \mathrm{h}_P)$ where $\underline{P} \in \mathsf{Obj}(\mathcal{L})$ and $\mathrm{h}_P \in \mathcal{L}(\underline{P}, !\underline{P})$ is such that $\mathrm{der}_{\underline{P}}\, \mathrm{h}_P = \mathrm{Id}$ and $\mathrm{dig}_{\underline{P}}\, \mathrm{h}_P = !\mathrm{h}_P\, \mathrm{h}_P$.

Given two such coalgebras P and Q, an element of $\mathcal{L}^!(P, Q)$ is an $f \in \mathcal{L}(\underline{P}, \underline{Q})$ such that $\mathrm{h}_Q\, f = !f\, \mathrm{h}_P$. Identities and composition are defined in the obvious way. The functor $!\_$ can then be seen as a functor from $\mathcal{L}$ to $\mathcal{L}^!$: this functor maps X to the coalgebra $(!X, \mathrm{dig}_X)$ and a morphism $f \in \mathcal{L}(X, Y)$ to the coalgebra morphism $!f \in \mathcal{L}^!((!X, \mathrm{dig}_X), (!Y, \mathrm{dig}_Y))$. This functor is right adjoint to the forgetful functor $\mathsf{U} : \mathcal{L}^! \to \mathcal{L}$ which maps a !-coalgebra P to $\underline{P}$ and a morphism f to itself. Given $f \in \mathcal{L}(\underline{P}, X)$, we use $f^! \in \mathcal{L}^!(P, !X)$ for the morphism associated with f by this adjunction, one has $f^! = !f\, \mathrm{h}_P$. If $g \in \mathcal{L}^!(Q, P)$, we have

$$f^!\, g = (f\, g)^! \tag{3}$$

The object 1 of $\mathcal{L}$ induces an object of $\mathcal{L}^!$, still denoted as 1, namely $(1, \mu^0)$.

Given two objects P and Q of $\mathcal{L}^!$, one defines an object $P \otimes Q$ of $\mathcal{L}^!$ by setting $\underline{P \otimes Q} = \underline{P} \otimes \underline{Q}$ and by defining $\mathrm{h}_{P \otimes Q}$ as a composition of morphisms:

$$\underline{P} \otimes \underline{Q} \xrightarrow{\mathrm{h}_P \otimes \mathrm{h}_Q} !\underline{P} \otimes !\underline{Q} \xrightarrow{\mu^2_{\underline{P},\underline{Q}}} !(\underline{P} \otimes \underline{Q})$$

Any object P of $\mathcal{L}^!$ can be equipped with a canonical structure of commutative comonoid. This means that we can define a morphism $\mathrm{w}_P \in \mathcal{L}^!(P, 1)$ and a morphism $\mathrm{c}_P \in \mathcal{L}^!(P, P \otimes P)$ which satisfy the commutations of Fig. 3.

$$\begin{array}{ccc} \underline{P} & \xrightarrow{c_P} & \underline{P}\otimes\underline{P} \\ & \searrow^{\lambda_{\underline{P}}^{-1}} & \downarrow{\scriptstyle w_P\otimes\underline{P}} \\ & & 1\otimes\underline{P} \end{array} \qquad \begin{array}{ccccc} \underline{P} & \xrightarrow{c_P} & \underline{P}\otimes\underline{P} & \xrightarrow{c_P\otimes\underline{P}} & (\underline{P}\otimes\underline{P})\otimes\underline{P} \\ {\scriptstyle c_P}\downarrow & & & & \downarrow{\scriptstyle \alpha_{\underline{P},\underline{P},\underline{P}}} \\ \underline{P}\otimes\underline{P} & & \xrightarrow{\underline{P}\otimes c_P} & & \underline{P}\otimes(\underline{P}\otimes\underline{P}) \end{array} \qquad \begin{array}{ccc} \underline{P} & \xrightarrow{c_P} & \underline{P}\otimes\underline{P} \\ & \searrow^{c_P} & \downarrow{\scriptstyle \sigma_{\underline{P},\underline{P}}} \\ & & \underline{P}\otimes\underline{P} \end{array}$$

Fig. 3. Commutative $\otimes$-comonoid

One can check a stronger property, namely that 1 is the terminal object of $\mathcal{L}^!$ and that $P \otimes Q$ (equipped with projections defined in the obvious way using w_Q and w_P) is the cartesian product of P and Q in $\mathcal{L}^!$; the proof consists of surprisingly long computations for which we refer again to [26].

It is also important to notice that, if the family $(P_i)_{i\in I}$ of objects of $\mathcal{L}^!$ is such that the family $(\underline{P_i})_{i\in I}$ admits a coproduct $(\bigoplus_{i\in I}\underline{P_i}, (\mathrm{in}_i)_{i\in I})$ in $\mathcal{L}$, then it admits a coproduct in $\mathcal{L}^!$. This coproduct $P = \bigoplus_{i\in I} P_i$ is defined by $\underline{P} = \bigoplus_{i\in I}\underline{P_i}$, with a structure map h_P defined by the fact that, for each $i \in I$, $h_P\,\mathrm{in}_i$ is the following composition of morphisms:

$$\underline{P_i} \xrightarrow{h_{P_i}} !\underline{P_i} \xrightarrow{!\mathrm{in}_i} !\underline{P}$$

Fix-point operators. For any object X, we assume to be given a morphism $\mathrm{fix}_X \in \mathcal{L}(!(!X \multimap X), X)$ such that the following diagram commutes

$$\begin{array}{ccc} !(!X \multimap X) & \xrightarrow{c_{!X}} & !(!X \multimap X)\otimes !(!X \multimap X) \\ & & \downarrow{\scriptstyle \mathrm{der}_{!X\multimap X}\otimes \mathrm{fix}^!_X} \\ & \searrow^{\mathrm{fix}_X} & (!X \multimap X)\otimes !X \\ & & \downarrow{\scriptstyle \mathrm{ev}} \\ & & X \end{array}$$

Remark 3. It might seem natural to require stronger uniformity conditions inspired by the notion of *Conway operator* [30]. This does not seem to be necessary as far as soundness of our semantics is concerned even if the fix-point operators arising in concrete models satisfy these further properties.

3.2 Embedding-Retraction Pairs

We introduce the categorical assumptions used to interpret fix-points of types.

We assume that 0 and $\top$ are isomorphic; these isos being unique, we assume that 0 and $\top$ are the same objects[3].

[3] This is true in many concrete models. It implies that any hom-set $\mathcal{L}(X,Y)$ has a distinguished element which coincides with the least element $\bot$ in denotational models based on domains or games. So this identification is typical of models featuring partial morphisms, which is required here because of the availability of fix-point operators for types and for programs.

We assume to be given a category $\mathcal{L}_\subseteq$ such that $\mathsf{Obj}(\mathcal{L}_\subseteq) = \mathsf{Obj}(\mathcal{L})$ together with a functor $\mathsf{F} : \mathcal{L}_\subseteq \to \mathcal{L}^{\mathsf{op}} \times \mathcal{L}$ such that $\mathsf{F}(X) = (X, X)$ and for which we use the notation $(\varphi^-, \varphi^+) = \mathsf{F}(\varphi)$. We assume that $\varphi^-\, \varphi^+ = \mathrm{Id}_X$. We define E (for *embedding*) as the functor $\mathrm{pr}_2\, \mathsf{F} : \mathcal{L}_\subseteq \to \mathcal{L}$. We assume moreover that the following properties hold.

- The category $\mathcal{L}_\subseteq$ has all countable filtered colimits and these colimits are preserved by E.
- 0 is initial in $\mathcal{L}_\subseteq$ with $\mathsf{E}\theta^X = \mathsf{in}^X$ if θ^X is the unique element of $\mathcal{L}_\subseteq(0, X)$.
- There is a continuous functor[4] $\otimes_\subseteq : \mathcal{L}_\subseteq^2 \to \mathcal{L}_\subseteq$ which behaves as $\otimes$ on objects and satisfies $(\varphi \otimes_\subseteq \psi)^+ = \varphi^+ \otimes \psi^+$ and $(\varphi \otimes_\subseteq \psi)^- = \varphi^- \otimes \psi^-$. We use the same notation $\otimes$ for the functor $\otimes_\subseteq$. We make similar assumptions for $\oplus$ and $!\_$.
- There is a continuous functor $\mathcal{N} : \mathcal{L}_\subseteq \to \mathcal{L}_\subseteq$ such that $\mathcal{N}(X) = X^\perp$, $\mathcal{N}(\varphi)^+ = (\varphi^-)^\perp$ and $\mathcal{N}(\varphi)^- = (\varphi^+)^\perp$. We simply denote $\mathcal{N}(\varphi)$ as $\varphi^\perp$; remember that this operation is covariant.

So we can define a continuous covariant functor $\multimap : \mathcal{L}_\subseteq^2 \to \mathcal{L}_\subseteq$ by $X \multimap Y = (X \otimes Y^\perp)^\perp$ and $\varphi \multimap \psi = (\varphi \otimes \psi^\perp)^\perp$, so that $(\varphi \multimap \psi)^+ = \varphi^- \multimap \psi^+$ and $(\varphi \multimap \psi)^- = \varphi^+ \multimap \psi^-$ in $\mathcal{L}$.

We need to extend this notion of embedding-retraction pair to !-coalgebras because we want to define fix-points of positive types. Let $\mathcal{L}^!_\subseteq$ be the category whose objects are those of $\mathcal{L}^!$ and where

$$\mathcal{L}^!_\subseteq(P, Q) = \{\varphi \in \mathcal{L}_\subseteq(\underline{P}, \underline{Q}) \mid \varphi^+ \in \mathcal{L}^!(P, Q)\}\,.$$

In this definition, it is important *not to require* φ^- to be a coalgebra morphism. We still use U for the obvious forgetful functor $\mathcal{L}^!_\subseteq \to \mathcal{L}_\subseteq$. Observe that $\otimes$ and $\oplus$ define functors $(\mathcal{L}^!_\subseteq)^2 \to \mathcal{L}^!_\subseteq$ and that $!\_$ defines a functor $\mathcal{L}_\subseteq \to \mathcal{L}^!_\subseteq$.

Let J be a countable filtered category and let $\mathcal{E} : J \to \mathcal{L}^!_\subseteq$ be a functor. Let X be the colimit of the functor $\mathsf{U}\,\mathcal{E}$ in $\mathcal{L}_\subseteq$ and let $(\varphi_i \in \mathcal{L}_\subseteq(\mathsf{U}\mathcal{E}(i), X))_{i\in J}$ be the corresponding colimit cocone. We know that $(\varphi_i^+ \in \mathcal{L}(\mathsf{U}\mathcal{E}(i), X))_{i\in J}$ is a colimit cocone in $\mathcal{L}$. In particular, to prove that two morphisms $g, g' \in \mathcal{L}(X, Y)$ are equal, it suffices to prove that $g\,\varphi_i^+ = g'\,\varphi_i^+$ for each $i \in J$.

We want to equip X with a coalgebra structure $h \in \mathcal{L}(X, !X)$. For this, due to this universal property, it suffices to define a cocone $(f_i \in \mathcal{L}(\mathsf{U}\mathcal{E}(i), !X))_{i\in J}$. We set $f_i = !\varphi_i^+\, \mathrm{h}_{\mathcal{E}(i)}$ and h is completely characterized by the fact that $h\,\varphi_i^+ = f_i$ for each $i \in J$.

Let us prove that $\mathrm{der}_X\, h = \mathrm{Id}_X$. We have $\mathrm{der}_X\, h\,\varphi_i^+ = \mathrm{der}_X\, !\varphi_i^+\, \mathrm{h}_{\mathcal{E}(i)} = \varphi_i^+\, \mathrm{der}_{\underline{\mathcal{E}(i)}}\, h_{\mathcal{E}(i)} = \varphi_i^+$ and the result follows from the universal property. The equation $\mathrm{dig}_X\, h = !h\, h$ is proven similarly: we have $\mathrm{dig}_X\, h\,\varphi_i^+ = \mathrm{dig}_X\, !\varphi_i^+\, \mathrm{h}_{\mathcal{E}(i)} = !!\varphi_i^+\, \mathrm{dig}_{\underline{\mathcal{E}(i)}}\, \mathrm{h}_{\mathcal{E}(i)} = !!\varphi_i^+\, !\mathrm{h}_{\mathcal{E}(i)}\, \mathrm{h}_{\mathcal{E}(i)} = !f_i\, \mathrm{h}_{\mathcal{E}(i)}$ and $!h\, h\,\varphi_i^+ = !h\, !\varphi_i^+\, \mathrm{h}_{\mathcal{E}(i)} = !f_i\, \mathrm{h}_{\mathcal{E}(i)}$.

So we have proven that $\mathcal{E}$ has a colimit in the category $\mathcal{L}^!$ of coalgebras. A functor $\Phi : \mathcal{M}_1 \times \cdots \times \mathcal{M}_n \to \mathcal{M}$ (where $\mathcal{M}$ and the $\mathcal{M}_i$s belong to $\{\mathcal{L}_\subseteq, \mathcal{L}^!_\subseteq\}$) is continuous if it commutes with countable filtered colimits.

[4] That is, a directed colimits preserving functor.

Proposition 3. *The functors* $\otimes$ *and* $\oplus$ *from* $(\mathcal{L}^!_\subseteq)^2$ *to* $\mathcal{L}^!_\subseteq$ *are continuous. The functor* $!\_ : \mathcal{L}_\subseteq \to \mathcal{L}^!_\subseteq$ *is continuous. The functor* $\multimap : (\mathcal{L}_\subseteq)^2 \to \mathcal{L}_\subseteq$ *is continuous.*

Immediate consequence of our hypotheses and of the above considerations.

Theorem 1. *Let* $\Phi : (\mathcal{L}^!_\subseteq)^{n+1} \to \mathcal{L}^!_\subseteq$ *be continuous. There is a continuous* $\mathit{Fix}(\Phi) : (\mathcal{L}^!_\subseteq)^n \to \mathcal{L}^!_\subseteq$ *which is naturally isomorphic to* $\Phi \circ \langle \mathrm{Id}^n, \mathit{Fix}(\Phi)\rangle$.

Proof. Let $\boldsymbol{P} = (P_1, \dots, P_n)$ be a tuple of objects of $\mathcal{L}^!$. Consider the functor $\Phi_{\boldsymbol{P}} : \mathcal{L}^!_\subseteq \to \mathcal{L}^!_\subseteq$ defined by $\Phi_{\boldsymbol{P}}(P) = \Phi(\boldsymbol{P}, P)$ and similarly for morphisms. Consider the set of natural numbers equipped with the usual order relation as a filtered category ($\mathbb{N}(n,m)$ has one element $l_{n,m}$ if $n \leq m$ and is empty otherwise). We define a functor $\mathcal{E} : \mathbb{N} \to \mathcal{L}^!_\subseteq$ as follows. First, we set $\mathcal{E}(i) = \Phi^i_{\boldsymbol{P}}(0)$. For each i, we define $\varphi_0 = \theta^{\mathcal{E}(1)}$ and then we set $\varphi_{i+1} = \Phi_{\boldsymbol{P}}(\varphi_i)$. Then, given $i, j \in \mathbb{N}$ such that $i \leq j$, we set $\mathcal{E}(l_{i,j}) = \varphi_{j-1} \cdots \varphi_i$. We define $\mathrm{Fix}(\Phi)(\boldsymbol{P})$ as the colimit of this functor $\mathcal{E}$ in $\mathcal{L}^!_\subseteq$. By standard categorical methods using the universal property of colimits, we extend this operation to a continuous functor $\mathrm{Fix}(\Phi) : (\mathcal{L}^!_\subseteq)^n \to \mathcal{L}^!_\subseteq$ which satisfies the required condition by continuity of Φ. □

3.3 Interpreting Types and Terms

With any positive type φ and any repetition-free list $\boldsymbol{\zeta} = (\zeta_1, \dots, \zeta_n)$ of type variables containing all free variables of φ we associate a continuous functor $[\varphi]^!_{\boldsymbol{\zeta}} : (\mathcal{L}^!_\subseteq)^n \to \mathcal{L}^!_\subseteq$ and with any general type σ and any list $\boldsymbol{\zeta} = (\zeta_1, \dots, \zeta_n)$ of pairwise distinct type variables containing all free variables of σ we associate a continuous functor $[\sigma]_{\boldsymbol{\zeta}} : (\mathcal{L}^!_\subseteq)^n \to \mathcal{L}_\subseteq$. We give the definition on objects, the definition on morphisms being similar.

$$
\begin{aligned}
&[\zeta_i]^!_{\boldsymbol{\zeta}}(\boldsymbol{P}) = P_i \qquad && [!\sigma]^!_{\boldsymbol{\zeta}}(\boldsymbol{P}) = !([\sigma]_{\boldsymbol{\zeta}}(\boldsymbol{P}))\\
&[\varphi \otimes \psi]^!_{\boldsymbol{\zeta}}(\boldsymbol{P}) = [\varphi]^!_{\boldsymbol{\zeta}}(\boldsymbol{P}) \otimes [\psi]^!_{\boldsymbol{\zeta}}(\boldsymbol{P}) &&\\
&[\varphi \oplus \psi]^!_{\boldsymbol{\zeta}}(\boldsymbol{P}) = [\varphi]^!_{\boldsymbol{\zeta}}(\boldsymbol{P}) \oplus [\psi]^!_{\boldsymbol{\zeta}}(\boldsymbol{P}) &&\\
&[\mathsf{Fix}\,\zeta \cdot \varphi]^!_{\boldsymbol{\zeta}} = \mathrm{Fix}([\varphi]^!_{\boldsymbol{\zeta},\zeta}) && [\top]_{\boldsymbol{\zeta}}(\boldsymbol{P}) = \top \quad \text{(the terminal object of } \mathcal{L})\\
&[\varphi]_{\boldsymbol{\zeta}} = \mathsf{U}\,[\varphi]^!_{\boldsymbol{\zeta}} && [\varphi \multimap \sigma]_{\boldsymbol{\zeta}}(\boldsymbol{P}) = (\underline{[\varphi]^!_{\boldsymbol{\zeta}}(\boldsymbol{P})}) \multimap ([\sigma]_{\boldsymbol{\zeta}}(\boldsymbol{P}))
\end{aligned}
$$

When we write $[\sigma]$ or $[\varphi]^!$ (without subscript), we assume implicitly that the types σ and φ have no free type variables. Then $[\sigma]$ is an object of $\mathcal{L}$ and $[\varphi]^!$ is an object of $\mathcal{L}^!$.

From now on, we assume that the only isos of $\mathcal{L}_\subseteq$ are the identity maps. This means in particular that the isos resulting from Theorem 1 are identities. This assumption is necessary because we have no roll/unroll syntactic constructs of terms associated with fixpoints of types. It holds in many concrete models, and in particular in the Scott model of Sect. 4.

Interpreting terms. Given a typing context $\mathcal{P} = (x_1 : \varphi_1, \dots, x_n : \varphi_n)$, we define $[\mathcal{P}]^!$ as the object $[\varphi_1]^! \otimes \cdots \otimes [\varphi_n]^!$ of $\mathcal{L}^!$. Notice that $\underline{[\mathcal{P}]^!} = [\varphi_1] \otimes \cdots \otimes [\varphi_n]$. We denote this object of $\mathcal{L}$ as $[\mathcal{P}]$.

Given a term M, a typing context $\mathcal{P} = (x_1 : \varphi_1, \dots, x_n : \varphi_n)$ and a type σ such that $\mathcal{P} \vdash M : \sigma$, we define $[M]_{\mathcal{P}} \in \mathcal{L}([\mathcal{P}], [\sigma])$ by induction on the typing derivation of M, that is, on M. Indeed, given a term M and a typing context $\mathcal{P}$, there is at most one type σ and one derivation of $\mathcal{P} \vdash M : \sigma$ (and this derivation is isomorphic to M).

Remark 4. A crucial observation is that $\mathcal{L}^!([\mathcal{P}]^!, [\varphi]^!) \subseteq \mathcal{L}([\mathcal{P}], [\varphi])$ for any positive type φ. Hence, for a term M such that $\mathcal{P} \vdash M : \varphi$, it may happen, *but it is not necessarily the case*, that $[M]_{\mathcal{P}} \in \mathcal{L}^!([\mathcal{P}]^!, [\varphi]^!)$. The terms M which have this property are duplicable and discardable, and the main property of values is that they belong to this semantically defined class of terms. Let us call such terms *$\mathcal{L}$-regular.*

We define $[M]_{\mathcal{P}}$ by induction on the typing derivation, that is, on M.

If $M = x_i$ for $1 \leq i \leq n$, then $[M]_{\mathcal{P}} = \mathrm{pr}_i \in \mathcal{L}^!([\mathcal{P}]^!, [P_i]^!)$. Remember indeed that $[\mathcal{P}]^!$ is the cartesian product of $[P_1]^!, \dots, [P_n]^!$ in $\mathcal{L}^!$. Observe that M is *$\mathcal{L}$-regular*.

Assume that $M = N^!$ and $\sigma = !\tau$ with $\mathcal{P} \vdash N : \tau$. By inductive hypothesis we have $[N]_{\mathcal{P}} \in \mathcal{L}(\underline{[\mathcal{P}]^!}, [\tau])$ and hence we can set $[M]_{\mathcal{P}} = [N]^!_{\mathcal{P}} \in \mathcal{L}^!([\mathcal{P}]^!, ![\tau])$ so that M is *$\mathcal{L}$-regular*.

Assume that $M = \langle M_1, M_2 \rangle$ and $\sigma = \varphi_1 \otimes \varphi_2$ with $\mathcal{P} \vdash M_i : \varphi_i$ for $i = 1, 2$. By inductive hypothesis we have defined $[M_i]_{\mathcal{P}} \in \mathcal{L}([\mathcal{P}], [\varphi_i])$ for $i = 1, 2$. Since $[\mathcal{P}] = \underline{[\mathcal{P}]^!}$ we have a contraction morphism $\mathrm{c}_{[\mathcal{P}]^!} \in \mathcal{L}^!([\mathcal{P}]^!, [\mathcal{P}]^! \otimes [\mathcal{P}]^!)$ so that we can set $[M] = ([M_1]_{\mathcal{P}} \otimes [M_2]_{\mathcal{P}})\, \mathrm{c}_{[\mathcal{P}]^!} \in \mathcal{L}([\mathcal{P}], [\sigma])$. Hence if M_1 and M_2 are *$\mathcal{L}$-regular*, then M is *$\mathcal{L}$-regular*.

Assume that $M = \mathsf{in}_i N$ (for $i = 1$ or $i = 2$)) and $\sigma = \varphi_1 \oplus \varphi_2$. By inductive hypothesis we have $[N]_{\mathcal{P}} \in \mathcal{L}([\mathcal{P}], [\varphi_i])$ and since we have $\mathrm{in}_i \in \mathcal{L}^!([\varphi_i]^!, [\varphi_1]^! \oplus [\varphi_2]^!)$ it makes sense to set $[M]_{\mathcal{P}} = \mathrm{in}_i\, [N]_{\mathcal{P}} \in \mathcal{L}([\mathcal{P}], [\sigma])$. Observe that if N is *$\mathcal{L}$-regular* then so is M.

Assume that $M = \lambda x^{\varphi} N$ and $\sigma = \varphi \multimap \tau$ with $\mathcal{P}, x : \varphi \vdash N : \tau$. By inductive hypothesis we have $[N]_{\mathcal{P}, x:\varphi} \in \mathcal{L}([\mathcal{P}] \otimes [\varphi], [\tau])$ and we set $[M]_{\mathcal{P}} = \mathrm{cur}([N]_{\mathcal{P}, x:\varphi}) \in \mathcal{L}([\mathcal{P}], [\varphi] \multimap [\tau])$. Of course, even if τ is positive and N is *$\mathcal{L}$-regular*, M is not *$\mathcal{L}$-regular*, simply because its type is not positive.

Assume that $M = \langle N \rangle R$ with $\mathcal{P} \vdash N : \varphi \multimap \sigma$ and $\mathcal{P} \vdash R : \varphi$ for some positive type φ. By inductive hypothesis we have $[N]_{\mathcal{P}} \in \mathcal{L}([\mathcal{P}], [\varphi] \multimap [\sigma])$ and $[R]_{\mathcal{P}} \in \mathcal{L}([\mathcal{P}], [\varphi])$. Since $[\mathcal{P}] = \underline{[\mathcal{P}]^!}$ we have a contraction morphism $\mathrm{c}_{[\mathcal{P}]^!} \in \mathcal{L}^!([\mathcal{P}]^!, [\mathcal{P}]^! \otimes [\mathcal{P}]^!)$ so that we can set $[M]_{\mathcal{P}} = \mathrm{ev}\, ([N]_{\mathcal{P}} \otimes [R]_{\mathcal{P}})\, \mathrm{c}_{[\mathcal{P}]^!} \in \mathcal{L}([\mathcal{P}], [\sigma])$.

Assume that $M = \mathsf{case}(N, x_1 \cdot R_1, x_2 \cdot R_2)$ with $\mathcal{P} \vdash N : \varphi_1 \oplus \varphi_2$ and $\mathcal{P}, x_i : \varphi_i \vdash R_i : \sigma$ for $i = 1, 2$. By inductive hypothesis we have $[M]_{\mathcal{P}} \in \mathcal{L}([\mathcal{P}], [\varphi_1] \oplus [\varphi_2])$ and $[R_i]_{\mathcal{P}, x_i:\varphi_i} \in \mathcal{L}([\mathcal{P}] \otimes [\varphi_i], [\sigma])$ for $i = 1, 2$. By the universal property of the coproduct $\oplus$ in $\mathcal{L}$ and by the fact that the functor $[\mathcal{P}] \otimes \_$ is a left adjoint, there is exactly one morphism $f \in \mathcal{L}([\mathcal{P}] \otimes ([\varphi_1] \oplus [\varphi_2]), [\sigma])$ such that $f\, ([\mathcal{P}] \otimes \mathrm{in}_i) = [R_i]_{\mathcal{P}, x_i:\varphi_i}$ for $i = 1, 2$. Then we set $[M]_{\mathcal{P}} = f\, ([\mathcal{P}] \otimes [N]_{\mathcal{P}})\, \mathrm{c}_{[\mathcal{P}]^!}$.

Assume that $M = \mathsf{pr}_i N$ and $\sigma = \varphi_i$ for $i = 1$ or $i = 2$, with $\mathcal{P} \vdash N : \varphi_1 \otimes \varphi_2$. By inductive hypothesis we have $[N]_{\mathcal{P}} \in \mathcal{L}([\mathcal{P}], [\varphi_1] \otimes [\varphi_2])$. Then remember that we have the projection $\mathrm{pr}_i \in \mathcal{L}^!([\varphi_1]^! \otimes [\varphi_2]^!, [\varphi_i]^!)$ so that we can set $[M]_{\mathcal{P}} = \mathrm{pr}_i\, [N]_{\mathcal{P}} \in \mathcal{L}([\mathcal{P}], [\varphi_i])$.

Assume that $M = \mathsf{der}(N)$ with $\mathcal{P} \vdash N :!\sigma$. Then we have $\mathsf{der}_{[\sigma]} \in \mathcal{L}(![\sigma], [\sigma])$ so that we can set $[M]_{\mathcal{P}} = \mathsf{der}_{[\sigma]}\,[N]_{\mathcal{P}} \in \mathcal{L}([\mathcal{P}], [\sigma])$.

Assume that $M = \mathsf{fix}\, x^{!\sigma}\, N$ so that $\mathcal{P}, x :!\sigma \vdash N : \sigma$. By inductive hypothesis we have $\mathsf{cur}([N]_{\mathcal{P},x:!\sigma}) \in \mathcal{L}([\mathcal{P}]^!, ![\sigma] \multimap [\sigma])$ and hence $(\mathsf{cur}([N]_{\mathcal{P},x:!\sigma}))^! \in \mathcal{L}^!([\mathcal{P}], !(![\sigma] \multimap [\sigma]))$ so that we can set $[M]_{\mathcal{P}} = \mathsf{fix}\,(\mathsf{cur}([N]_{\mathcal{P},x:!\sigma}))^! \in \mathcal{L}([\mathcal{P}], [\sigma])$.

Proposition 4. *If $\mathcal{P} \vdash V : \varphi$ and V is a value, then V is $\mathcal{L}$-*regular*, that is* $[V]_{\mathcal{P}} \in \mathcal{L}^!([\mathcal{P}]^!, [\varphi]^!)$.

The proof is a straightforward verification (in the definition of the interpretation of terms we have singled out the constructions which preserve *$\mathcal{L}$-regular*ity). The main operational feature of *$\mathcal{L}$-regular* terms is that they enjoy the following substitutivity property.

Proposition 5 (Substitution Lemma). *Assume that $\mathcal{P}, x : \varphi \vdash M : \sigma$ and $\mathcal{P} \vdash N : \varphi$, and assume that N is $\mathcal{L}$-*regular*. Then we have*

$$[M\,[N/x]]_{\mathcal{P}} = [M]_{\mathcal{P},x:\varphi}\,([\mathcal{P}] \otimes [N]_{\mathcal{P}})\,\mathsf{c}_{[\mathcal{P}]^!}$$

Proof. Induction on M using in an essential way the *$\mathcal{L}$-regular*ity of N. Let us consider two cases to illustrate this point. Assume first that $M = R^!$ and $\sigma = !\tau$, with $\mathcal{P}, x : \varphi \vdash R : \tau$ so that $[R]_{\mathcal{P},x:\varphi} \in \mathcal{L}([\mathcal{P}] \otimes [\varphi], [\sigma])$. Then we have $[M\,[N/x]]_{\mathcal{P}} = [R\,[N/x]^!]_{\mathcal{P}} = ([R\,[N/x]]_{\mathcal{P}})^! = ([R]_{\mathcal{P},x:\varphi}\,([\mathcal{P}] \otimes [N]_{\mathcal{P}})\,\mathsf{c}_{[\mathcal{P}]})^!$ by inductive hypothesis. We obtain the contended equation by applying Eq. (3) and the fact that $[\mathcal{P}] \otimes [N]_{\mathcal{P}}$ is a coalgebra morphism since N is *$\mathcal{L}$-regular*, and the fact that $\mathsf{c}_{[\mathcal{P}]}$ is also a coalgebra morphism.

Let us also consider the case $M = \langle M_1, M_2 \rangle$ and $\sigma = \varphi_1 \otimes \varphi_2$ with $\mathcal{P}, x : \varphi \vdash M_i : \varphi_i$ for $i = 1, 2$ so that $[M_i]_{\mathcal{P},x:\varphi} \in \mathcal{L}([\mathcal{P}] \otimes [\varphi], [\varphi_i])$ for $i = 1, 2$. We have

$$\begin{aligned}
[M\,[N/x]]_{\mathcal{P}} &= [\langle M_1\,[N/x]\,, M_2\,[N/x]\rangle]_{\mathcal{P}}\\
&= ([M_1\,[N/x]]_{\mathcal{P}} \otimes [M_2\,[N/x]]_{\mathcal{P}})\,\mathsf{c}_{[\mathcal{P}]^! \otimes [\varphi]^!}\\
&= (([M_1]_{\mathcal{P},x:\varphi}\,([\mathcal{P}] \otimes [N]_{\mathcal{P}})) \otimes ([M_2]_{\mathcal{P},x:\varphi}\,([\mathcal{P}] \otimes [N]_{\mathcal{P}})))\\
&\quad \mathsf{c}_{[\mathcal{P}]^! \otimes [\varphi]^!}\\
&= ([M_1]_{\mathcal{P}} \otimes [M_2]_{\mathcal{P}})\,\mathsf{c}_{[\mathcal{P}]^!}\,([\mathcal{P}] \otimes [N]_{\mathcal{P}})
\end{aligned}$$

using the inductive hypothesis, naturality of contraction in $\mathcal{L}^!$ and the fact that $([\mathcal{P}] \otimes [N]_{\mathcal{P}})$ is a coalgebra morphism since N is *$\mathcal{L}$-regular*. The other cases are handled similarly. □

Theorem 2 (Soundness). *If $\mathcal{P} \vdash M : \sigma$ and $M \to_{\mathsf{w}} M'$ then $[M]_{\mathcal{P}} = [M']_{\mathcal{P}}$.*

Proof. By induction on the derivation that $M \to_{\mathsf{w}} M'$, using the Substitution Lemma and the *$\mathcal{L}$-regular*ity of values.

4 Scott Semantics

Usually, in a model $\mathcal{L}$ of LL, an object X of $\mathcal{L}$ can be endowed with several different structures of !-coalgebras which makes the category $\mathcal{L}^!$ difficult to describe simply (in contrast with the Kleisli category used for interpreting PCF; its objects are those of $\mathcal{L}$). In the Scott model of LL however, every object of the linear category has exactly one structure of !-coalgebra as we shall see now. This is certainly a distinctive feature of this model. Such a property does not hold for instance in coherence spaces. A nice outcome of these observations will be a very simple intersection typing system for Λ_{HP}.

Remark 5. As explained in [11], this semantics of LL has been independently discovered by several authors, see for instance [18,31]. The same model is also considered in [23] Sect. 5.5.4 to interpret may non-determinism in CBPV. Our model allows therefore to interpret the corresponding non-deterministic extension of Λ_{HP} and the proof of adequacy of Sect. 4.4[5] can easily be extended to this language. This will be explained thoroughly in a forthcoming paper.

4.1 The Scott Semantics of LL

We introduce a "linear" category **Polr** of preorders and relations. A preorder is a pair $S = (|S|, \leq_S)$ where $|S|$ is an at most countable set and $\leq_S$ (written $\leq$ when no confusion is possible) is a preorder relation on $|S|$. Given two preorders S and T, a morphism from S to T is a $f \subseteq |S| \times |T|$ such that, if $(a, b) \in f$ and $(a', b') \in |S| \times |T|$ satisfy $a \leq_S a'$ and $b' \leq_S b$, then $(a', b') \in f$. The relational composition of two morphisms is still a morphism and the identity morphism at S is $\mathrm{Id}_S = \{(a, a') \mid a' \leq_S a\}$.

Given an object S in **Polr**, the set $\mathsf{Ini}(S)$ of downwards closed subsets of $|S|$, ordered by inclusion, is a complete lattice which is ω-prime-algebraic (and all such lattices are of that shape up to iso). **Polr** is equivalent to the category of ω-prime algebraic complete lattices and linear maps (functions preserving all lubs).

Monoidal structure and cartesian product. The object 1 is $(\{*\}, =)$ and given preorders S and T we set $S \otimes T = (|S| \times |T|, \leq_S \times \leq_T)$. The tensor product of morphisms is defined in the obvious way. The isos defining the monoidal structure are easy to define. Then one defines $S \multimap T$ by $|S \multimap T| = |S| \times |T|$ and $(a', b') \leq_{S \multimap T} (a, b))$ if $a \leq a'$ and $b' \leq b$. The linear evaluation morphism $\mathrm{ev} \in \mathbf{Polr}((S \multimap T) \otimes S, T)$ is given by $\mathrm{ev} = \{(((a', b), a), b') \mid b' \leq b \text{ and } a' \leq a\}$. If $f \in \mathbf{Polr}(U \otimes S, T)$ then $\mathrm{cur}(f) \in \mathbf{Polr}(U, S \multimap T)$ is defined by moving parentheses. This shows that **Polr** is closed. It is *-autonomous, with $\bot = 1$ as dualizing object. Observe that $S^\bot$ is simply $|S|$ equipped with $\geq_S$ as preorder relation $\leq_{S^\bot}$.

[5] This adequacy result can probably be seen as a special case of the general adequacy results of [23].

Given a countable family of objects $(S_i)_{i\in I}$, the cartesian product S is defined by $|S| = \bigcup_{i\in I}\{i\} \times |S_i|$ with $(i,a) \leq (j,b)$ if $i = j$ and $a \leq b$. Projections are defined by $\mathrm{pr}_i = \{((i,a),a') \mid a' \leq a\}$. Tupling of morphisms is defined as in **Rel**. Coproducts are defined similarly.

Exponential. One sets $!S = (\mathcal{P}_{\mathrm{fin}}(|S|), \leq)$ with $u \leq u'$ if $\forall a \in u\, \exists a' \in u'\; a \leq_S a'$ (where $\mathcal{P}_{\mathrm{fin}}(E)$ is the set of all finite subsets of E). Given $f \in \mathbf{Polr}(S,T)$, one defines $!f$ as $\{(u,v) \in |!S| \times |!T| \mid \forall b \in v\, \exists a \in u\; (a,b) \in f\}$. It is easy to prove that this defines a functor $\mathbf{Polr} \to \mathbf{Polr}$. Then one sets $\mathrm{der}_S = \{(u,a) \mid \exists a' \in u\; a \leq a'\} \in \mathbf{Polr}(!S,S)$ and $\mathrm{dig}_S = \{(u,\{u_1,\dots,u_n\}) \mid u_1 \cup \cdots \cup u_n \leq_{!S} u\} \in \mathbf{Polr}(!S,!!S)$. This defines a comonad $\mathbf{Polr} \to \mathbf{Polr}$. The Seely isos are given by $\mathrm{m}^0 = \{(*,\emptyset)\} \in \mathbf{Polr}(1,!\top)$ and $\mathrm{m}^2_{S,T} = \{((u,v),w) \mid w \leq_{!(S\&T)} \{1\} \times u \cup \{2\} \times v\} \in \mathbf{Polr}(!S \otimes !T, !(S \mathbin{\&} T))$.

Each object S has a fix-point operator $\mathrm{fix}_S \in \mathbf{Polr}(!(!S \multimap S), S)$ which is defined as a least fix-point: $\mathrm{fix}_S = \{(w,a) \mid \exists (u',a') \in w\; a \leq a'$ and $\forall a'' \in u'\; (w,a'') \in \mathrm{fix}_S\}$.

4.2 The Category of !-coalgebras

The first main observation is that each object of **Polr** has exactly one structure of !-coalgebra. The proofs will be given in a longer version of this paper.

Theorem 3. *Let S be an object of* **Polr**. *Then (S, p_S) is a !-coalgebra, where $\mathrm{p}_S = \{(a,u) \in |S| \times |!S| \mid \forall a' \in u\; a' \leq a\}$. Moreover, if P is a !-coalgebra, then $\mathrm{h}_P = \mathrm{p}_{\underline{P}}$.*

Morphisms of !-coalgebras. Now that we know that the objects of $\mathbf{Polr}^!$ are those of **Polr**, we turn our attention to morphisms. When we consider a preorder S as an object of $\mathbf{Polr}^!$, we always mean the object (S, p_S) described above.

With any preorder S, we have associated an ω-prime algebraic complete lattice $\mathsf{Ini}(S)$. We associate now with such a preorder an ω-algebraic cpo $\mathsf{Idl}(S)$ which is the ideal completion of S: an element of $\mathsf{Idl}(S)$ is a subset ξ of $|S|$ such that ξ is non-empty, downwards closed and directed (meaning that if $a, a' \in \xi$ then there is $a'' \in \xi$ such that $a, a' \leq_S a''$). We equip $\mathsf{Idl}(S)$ with the inclusion partial order relation.

Lemma 1. *For any preorder S, the partially ordered set $\mathsf{Idl}(S)$ is a cpo which has countably many compact elements. Moreover, for any $\xi \in \mathsf{Idl}(S)$, the set of compact elements $\xi_0 \in \mathsf{Idl}(S)$ such that $\xi_0 \subseteq \xi$ is directed and ξ is the lub of that set. In general, $\mathsf{Idl}(S)$ has no minimum element.*

Theorem 4. *Given preorders S and T, there is a bijective and functorial correspondence between $\mathbf{Polr}^!(S,T)$ and the set of Scott continuous functions from $\mathsf{Idl}(S)$ to $\mathsf{Idl}(T)$. Moreover, this correspondence is an order isomorphism when Scott-continuous functions are equipped with the usual pointwise ordering relation and $\mathbf{Polr}^!(S,T)$ is equipped with the inclusion order on relations.*

Let **Predom** be the category whose objects are the preorders and where a morphism from S to T is a Scott continuous function from $\mathsf{Idl}(S)$ to $\mathsf{Idl}(T)$. We have seen that $\mathbf{Polr}^!$ and **Predom** are equivalent categories (isomorphic indeed). It is easy to retrieve directly the fact that **Predom** has products and sums: the product of S and T is $S \otimes T$ (and indeed, it is easy to check that $\mathsf{Idl}(S \otimes T) \simeq \mathsf{Idl}(S) \times \mathsf{Idl}(T)$) and their sum is $S \oplus T$ and indeed $\mathsf{Idl}(S \oplus T) \simeq \mathsf{Idl}(S) + \mathsf{Idl}(T)$, the disjoint union of the predomains $\mathsf{Idl}(S)$ and $\mathsf{Idl}(T)$. This predomain has no minimum element as soon as $|S|$ and $|T|$ are non-empty. Observe also that $\mathsf{Idl}(!S) = \mathsf{Ini}(S)$: one retrieves the fact that the Kleisli category of the ! comonad is the category of preorders and Scott continuous functions between the associated lattices.

Inclusions and embedding-retraction pairs. We define a category $\mathbf{Polr}_{\subseteq}$ as follows: the objects are those of **Polr** and $\mathbf{Polr}_{\subseteq}(S,T)$ is a singleton $\{\varphi_{S,T}\}$ if $|S| \subseteq |T|$ and $\forall a, a' \in |S|\ a \leq_S a' \Leftrightarrow a \leq_T a'$ (and then we write $S \subseteq T$) and is empty otherwise. So $(\mathbf{Polr}_{\subseteq}, \subseteq)$ is a partially ordered class. The functor F is defined as follows: if $S \subseteq T$ then $\varphi^+_{S,T} = \{(a,b) \in |S| \times |T| \mid b \leq_T a\}$ and $\varphi^-_{S,T} = \{(b,a) \in |T| \times |S| \mid a \leq_T b\}$; this definition is functorial and $\varphi^-_{S,T}\, \varphi^+_{S,T} = \mathrm{Id}_S$. The partially ordered class $\mathbf{Polr}_{\subseteq}$ is complete in the sense that any directed family of objects[6] $(S_i)_{i \in J}$ has a lub S given by $|S| = \cup_{i \in J} |S_i|$ and $a \leq_S a'$ if $a \leq_{S_i} a'$ for some i; we denote this preorder as $\cup_{i \in J} S_i$. The operations $\otimes$, $\oplus$ and $!\_$ are monotone and Scott-continuous operations on this partially ordered class.

Lemma 2. *Assume that* $S_1 \subseteq S_2$ *and let* $f_i \in \mathbf{Polr}(S_i, T)$ *for* $i = 1, 2$. *Then* $f_1 = f_2\, \varphi^+_{S_1,S_2}$ *iff* $f_1 = f_2 \cap |S_1 \multimap T|$.

Given a directed family $(S_i)_{i \in J}$ in $\mathbf{Polr}_{\subseteq}$ and setting $S = \cup_{i \in J} S_i$, one proves easily using Lemma 2 that the cone $(\varphi^+_{S_i,S} \in \mathbf{Polr}(S_i, S))_{i \in J}$ is a colimit cone in **Polr**. Consider indeed a family of morphisms $(f_i \in \mathbf{Polr}(S_i, T))_{i \in J}$ such that $i \leq j \Rightarrow f_i = f_j\, \varphi^+_{S_i,S_j}$, that is $f_i = f_j \cap |S_i \multimap T|$. Then $f = \cup_{i \in J} f_i$ is the unique element of $\mathbf{Polr}(S,T)$ such that $f\, \varphi^+_{S_i,S} = f_i$ for each $i \in J$. So the category $\mathbf{Polr}_{\subseteq}$ satisfies all the axioms of Sect. 3.2.

As explained in that section, this allows to define fixpoints of positive types. As a first example consider the type of flat natural numbers $\iota = \mathsf{Fix}\zeta \cdot (1 \oplus \zeta)$ where $1 = !\top$, so that $|1| = \{\emptyset\}$. Up to renaming we have $|[\iota]| = \mathbb{N}$ and $n \leq_{[\iota]} n'$ iff $n = n'$. The coalgebraic structure of this positive type is given by $\mathrm{h}_{[\iota]} = \{(n, \emptyset) \mid n \in \mathbb{N}\} \cup \{(n, \{n\}) \mid n \in \mathbb{N}\}$. Consider now the type $\rho = \mathsf{Fix}\zeta \cdot (1 \oplus (\iota \otimes !\zeta))$ of lazy lists of flat natural numbers. The interpretation S of this type is the least fix-point of the continuous functor (that is, the Scott continuous functional) $[1 \oplus (\iota \otimes !\zeta)]_\zeta : \mathbf{Polr}_{\subseteq} \to \mathbf{Polr}_{\subseteq}$. So $|S| = \cup_{n=0}^{\infty} U_n$ where $(U_n)_{n \in \mathbb{N}}$ is the monotone sequence of sets defined by $U_0 = \emptyset$ and $U_{n+1} = \{\emptyset\} \cup (\mathbb{N} \times \mathcal{P}_{\mathrm{fin}}(U_n))$ (this is a disjoint union). The preorder relation on $|S|$ is given by: $\emptyset \leq_S a$ iff

[6] Because we are dealing with a partially ordered class, we can replace general filtered categories with directed posets.

$a = \emptyset$ and $(n, u) \leq_S a$ iff $a = (n, u')$ and $\forall b \in u \exists b' \in u'\ b \leq_S b'$. This preorder relation defines the coalgebraic structure of this positive type.

4.3 Scott Semantics as a Typing System

It is interesting to present the Scott semantics of terms as a typing system, in the spirit of Coppo-Dezani Intersection Types, see [19]. A *semantic context* is a sequence $\Phi = (x_1 : a_1 : \varphi_1, \ldots, x_n : a_n : \varphi_n)$ where $a_i \in [\varphi_i]$ for each i, its *underlying typing context* is $\underline{\Phi} = (x_1 : \varphi_1, \ldots, x_n : \varphi_n)$ and its *underlying tuple* is $\langle \Phi \rangle = (a_1, \ldots, a_k) \in [\underline{\Phi}]$. The typing rules are given in Fig. 4, the intended meaning of these rules is made clear in Proposition 7.

$$\frac{a' \leq_{[\varphi]} a}{\Phi, x : a : \varphi \vdash x : a' : \varphi} \qquad \frac{u \in \mathcal{P}_{\mathrm{fin}}(|[\sigma]|) \qquad \forall a \in u \quad \Phi \vdash M : a : \sigma}{\Phi \vdash M^! : u : !\sigma}$$

$$\frac{\Phi \vdash M_1 : a_1 : \varphi_1 \qquad \Phi \vdash M_2 : a_2 : \varphi_2}{\Phi \vdash \langle M_1, M_2 \rangle : (a_1, a_2) : \varphi_1 \otimes \varphi_2}$$

$$\frac{\Phi \vdash M : a : \varphi_i}{\Phi \vdash \mathsf{in}_i M : (i, a) : \varphi_1 \oplus \varphi_2} \qquad \frac{\Phi \vdash M : (a, b) : \varphi \multimap \sigma \qquad \Phi \vdash N : a : \varphi}{\Phi \vdash \langle M \rangle N : b : \sigma}$$

$$\frac{\Phi \vdash M : (1, a) : \varphi_1 \oplus \varphi_2 \qquad \Phi, x_1 : a : \varphi_1 \vdash N_1 : b : \sigma \qquad \underline{\Phi}, x_2 : \varphi_2 \vdash N_2 : \sigma}{\Phi \vdash \mathsf{case}(M, x_1 \cdot N_1, x_2 \cdot N_2) : b : \sigma}$$

$$\frac{\Phi \vdash M : (2, a) : \varphi_1 \oplus \varphi_2 \qquad \underline{\Phi}, x_1 : \varphi_1 \vdash N_1 : \sigma \qquad \Phi, x_2 : a : \varphi_2 \vdash N_2 : b : \sigma}{\Phi \vdash \mathsf{case}(M, x_1 \cdot N_1, x_2 \cdot N_2) : b : \sigma}$$

$$\frac{\Phi \vdash M : (a_1, a_2) : \varphi_1 \otimes \varphi_2}{\Phi \vdash \mathsf{pr}_i M : a_i : \varphi_i} \qquad \frac{\Phi \vdash M : \{a\} : !\sigma}{\Phi \vdash \mathsf{der}(M) : a : \sigma}$$

$$\frac{\Phi, x : u : !\sigma \vdash M : a : \sigma \qquad \forall b \in u \quad \Phi \vdash \mathsf{fix}\, x^{!\sigma}\, M : b : \sigma}{\Phi \vdash \mathsf{fix}\, x^{!\sigma}\, M : a : \sigma}$$

Fig. 4. Scott semantics as a typing system

A simple induction on typing derivation trees shows that this typing system is "monotone" as usually for intersection type systems. We write $\Phi \leq \Phi'$ if $\Phi = (x_1 : a_1 : \varphi_1, \ldots, x_n : a_n : \varphi_n)$, $\Phi' = (x_1 : a_1' : \varphi_1, \ldots, x_n : a_n' : \varphi_n)$ and $a_i \leq_{[\varphi_i]} a_i'$ for $i = 1, \ldots, n$.

Proposition 6. *If* $\Phi \vdash M : a : \sigma$, $a' \leq_{[\sigma]} a$ *and* $\Phi \leq \Phi'$ *then* $\Phi' \vdash M : a' : \sigma$.

Using this property, one can prove that this deduction system describes exactly the Scott denotational semantics of Λ_{HP}.

Proposition 7. *Given* $a_1 \in [\varphi_1], \ldots, a_n \in [\varphi_n]$ *and* $a \in [\sigma]$, *one has* $(a_1, \ldots, a_n, a) \in [M]_{x_1:\sigma_n,\ldots,x_1:\sigma_n}$ *iff* $x_1 : a_1 : \varphi_1, \ldots, x_n : a_n : \varphi_n \vdash M : a : \sigma$.

$$|u|_{\mathsf{v}}^{!\sigma} = \{N^! \mid N \in \bigcap_{a\in u} |a|^\sigma\}$$
$$|(a_1,a_2)|_{\mathsf{v}}^{\varphi_1\otimes\varphi_2} = \{\langle V_1,V_2\rangle \mid V_i \in |a_i|_{\mathsf{v}}^{\varphi_i} \text{ for } i=1,2\}$$
$$|(i,a)|_{\mathsf{v}}^{\varphi_1\oplus\varphi_2} = \{\mathsf{in}_i V \mid V \in |a|_{\mathsf{v}}^{\varphi_i}\}$$
$$|a|^\varphi = \{M \mid \vdash M : \varphi \text{ and } \exists V \in |a|_{\mathsf{v}}^{\varphi}\ M \to_{\mathsf{w}}^* V\}$$
$$|(a,b)|^{\varphi\multimap\sigma} = \{M \mid \vdash M : \varphi \multimap \sigma \text{ and } \forall V \in |a|_{\mathsf{v}}^{\varphi}\ \langle M\rangle V \in |b|^\sigma\}$$

Fig. 5. Interpretation of points as sets of terms in Λ_{HP}

The proof also uses crucially the fact that all structural operations (weakening, contraction, dereliction, promotion) admit a very simple description in terms of the preorder relation on objects thanks to Theorem 3; for instance the contraction morphism of an object S (seen as an object of $\mathbf{Polr}^!$) is $\mathrm{c}_S = \{(a,(a_1,a_2)) \mid a_i \le a \text{ for } i=1,2\}$.

4.4 Adequacy

Our goal now is to prove that, if a closed term M of positive type φ has a non-empty interpretation, that is, if there is $a \in |[\varphi]|$ such that $\vdash M : a : \varphi$, then the reduction $\to_{\mathsf{w}}$ starting from M terminates. We use a semantic method adapted *e.g.* from the presentation of the *reducibility* method in [19].

Given a type σ and an $a \in [\sigma]$, we define a set $|a|^\sigma$ of terms M such that $\vdash M : \sigma$ (so these terms are all closed). The definition is by induction on the structure of the point a (and not on the type σ, whose definition involves fix-points and is therefore not well-founded in general).

Given a positive type φ and $a \in [\varphi]$, we define $|a|_{\mathsf{v}}^{\varphi}$ as a set of *closed values* V such that $\vdash V : \varphi$ and given a general type σ and $a \in [\sigma]$, we define $|a|^\sigma$ as a set of closed terms M such that $\vdash M : \sigma$. The definitions are by mutual induction and are given in Fig. 5. Observe that for a value V such that $\vdash V : \varphi$ and for $a \in [\varphi]$, the statements $V \in |a|^\varphi$ and $V \in |a|_{\mathsf{v}}^{\varphi}$ are equivalent because V is normal for the $\to_{\mathsf{w}}$ reduction.

Lemma 3. *If $M \to_{\mathsf{w}} M' \in |a|^\sigma$ then $M \in |a|^\sigma$.*

Proof. By induction on the structure of a. If $\sigma = \varphi$, the property follows readily from the definition. Assume that $\sigma = \varphi \multimap \tau$ and $a = (b,c)$. Assume that $M \to_{\mathsf{w}} M' \in |a|^\sigma$. Let $V \in |b|_{\mathsf{v}}^{\varphi}$, we have $\langle M\rangle V \to_{\mathsf{w}} \langle M'\rangle V$ and $\langle M'\rangle V \in |c|^\tau$ by definition of $|\varphi \multimap \tau|^{(b,c)}$. The announced property follows by inductive hypothesis. □

Lemma 4. *Let σ be a type and let $a, a' \in |[\sigma]|$ be such that $a \le_{[\sigma]} a'$. Then $|a|^\sigma \supseteq |a'|^\sigma$. If σ is positive, we have $|a|_{\mathsf{v}}^{\sigma} \supseteq |a'|_{\mathsf{v}}^{\sigma}$.*

Theorem 5. *Let $\Phi = (x_1 : a_1 : \varphi_1, \dots, x_k : a_k : \varphi_k)$ and assume that $\Phi \vdash M : a : \sigma$. Then for any family of closed values $(V_i)_{i=1}^k$ such that $V_i \in |a_i|^{\varphi_i}$ one has $M\,[V_1/x_1, \dots, V_k/x_k] \in |a|^\sigma$.*

So if $\vdash M : \varphi$ and $[M] \neq \emptyset$ we have $M \to_{\mathsf{w}}^{*} V$ for a value V. Let us say that two closed terms M_1, M_2 such that $\vdash M_i : \sigma$ for $i = 1, 2$ are observationally equivalent if for all closed term C of type $!\sigma \multimap 1$, $\langle C \rangle M_1^! \to_{\mathsf{w}}^{*} *$ iff $\langle C \rangle M_2^! \to_{\mathsf{w}}^{*} *$. As usual, Theorem 5 allows to prove that if $[M_1] = [M_2]$ then M_1 and M_2 are observationally equivalent.

Another important consequence of Theorem 5 is a "completeness" property of the weak reduction of Fig. 2 which can be stated as follows. Let $\simeq$ be an equivalence relation on terms which contains $\to_{\mathsf{w}}^{*}$ and is compatible with the semantics of Sect. 3.3 in the sense that, if $\mathcal{P} \vdash M_i : \sigma$ for $i = 1, 2$ and $M_1 \simeq M_2$, then $[M_1]_{\mathcal{P}} = [M_2]_{\mathcal{P}}$ in any model $\mathcal{L}$. Assume that $\vdash M : \varphi$ and $\vdash V : \varphi$ for a closed term M and a closed value V, and assume that $M \simeq V$. Then $M \to_{\mathsf{w}}^{*} V'$ where V' is a value such that $V \simeq V'$. Indeed $[V]$ is non-empty in the Scott model of Sect. 4, let $a \in [V]$. By our hypothesis we have $a \in [M]$ and hence $M \in |a|^{\varphi}$, meaning that $M \to_{\mathsf{w}}^{*} V'$ for some $V' \in |\varphi|_{\mathsf{v}}^{a}$. By our assumptions we have $M \simeq V'$ and hence $V' \simeq V$.

5 A Fully Polarized Calculus

In Λ_{HP} positive types are interpreted as !-coalgebras, and general types are simply interpreted as objects of the underlying linear category: in some sense, this system is half-polarized and is intuitionistic for that reason. In a fully polarized system we would expect non-positive types to be negative, that is, linear duals of !-coalgebras. This system would feature syntactic constructions related to classical logic such as call/cc, the price to pay being a more complicated encoding of data-types.

It is quite easy to turn our hierarchy of types (1) and (2) into a polarized one:

$$\varphi, \psi, \ldots := !\sigma \mid \varphi \otimes \psi \mid \varphi \oplus \psi \mid \zeta \mid \mathsf{Fix}\,\zeta \cdot \varphi \quad \text{(positive)} \tag{4}$$

$$\sigma, \tau \ldots := ?\varphi \mid \varphi \multimap \sigma \mid \top \quad \text{(negative)} \tag{5}$$

Accordingly we introduce a polarized syntax for expressions featuring five mutually recursive syntactic categories.

$$\begin{aligned}
P, Q \ldots &:= x \mid N^! \mid \langle P_1, P_2 \rangle \mid \mathsf{in}_i P \quad \text{(positive terms)} \\
M, N, \ldots &:= \mathsf{der}\, P \mid \lambda x^{\varphi}\, M \mid \mu\alpha^{\sigma}\, c \mid \mathsf{fix}\, x^{!\sigma}\, M \quad \text{(negative terms)} \\
\pi, \rho \ldots &:= \alpha \mid \eta^! \mid P \cdot \pi \quad \text{(positive contexts)} \\
\eta, \theta \ldots &:= \mathsf{der}\, \pi \mid \mathsf{pr}_i\, \eta \mid [\eta_1, \eta_2] \mid \tilde{\mu} x^{\varphi}\, c \quad \text{(negative contexts)} \\
c, d \ldots &:= P * \eta \mid M * \pi \quad \text{(commands, cuts)}
\end{aligned}$$

Intuitively, positive terms correspond to data, negative terms to programs, negative contexts to patterns (apart from the negative context $\tilde{\mu} x^{\varphi}\, c$ which generalizes the concept of "closure") and positive contexts to evaluation environments.

The typing rules correspond to a large fragment of LLP, see [21][7], and are given in Fig. 6.

Let us say that an expression e is well typed in typing contexts $\mathcal{P} = (x_1 : \varphi_1, \ldots, x_n : \varphi_n)$, $\mathcal{N} = (\alpha_1 : \sigma_1, \ldots, \alpha_k : \sigma_k)$ if e is a positive term P and $\mathcal{P} \vdash P : \varphi \,|\, \mathcal{N}$ for some type φ, if e is a negative term M and $\mathcal{P} \vdash M : \sigma \,|\, \mathcal{N}$ for some type σ, if e is a positive context π and $\mathcal{P} \,|\, \pi : \sigma \vdash \mathcal{N}$ for some type σ, if e is a negative context η and $\mathcal{P} \,|\, \eta : \varphi \vdash \mathcal{N}$ for some type φ and if e is a command c and $\mathcal{P} \vdash c \,|\, \mathcal{N}$. In the four first cases, φ (resp. σ) is *the type of* e. Observe that, when it exists, this type is completely determined by e, $\mathcal{P}$ and $\mathcal{N}$ (the typing rules are syntax-directed).

5.1 Operational Semantics

The weak reduction rules are given in Fig. 7. All redexes are commands and it is crucial to observe that there are no critical pairs. Specifically, there is no command which is simultaneously of shape $M * \pi$ and $P * \tilde{\mu} x^{\varphi}\, c$ because in the former the term is negative whereas it is positive in the latter. In particular the "Lafont critical pair" $\mu\alpha^{\theta}\, c * \tilde{\mu} x^{\theta}\, d$ cannot occur since θ cannot be positive and negative!.

Remark 6. In this weak reduction paradigm, we only reduce commands. A sequence of reduction alternates therefore sequences of *positive commands* of shape $P * \eta$ where a piece of data P is explored by a pattern η with sequences of *negative commands* $M * \pi$ where a program M is executed in an evaluation context π. The transition from the execution phase to the pattern-matching phase is realized by the reduction rule (6) and the converse by (10). We retrieve the basic idea of *focusing* of [1] and of Ludics, [16], that "positive" means passive and "negative", active (many other authors should be mentioned here of course).

We also consider a general reduction relation $\to$ on expressions which is defined by allowing the application of the rules of Fig. 7 *anywhere* in an expression as well as the two following $\mu\eta$ reduction rules: $\mu\alpha^{\sigma}\,(M * \alpha) \to M$ if α does not occur free in M and $\tilde{\mu} x^{\varphi}\,(x * \eta) \to \eta$ if x does not occur free in η.

Proposition 8. *If e is typable in contexts $\mathcal{P}, \mathcal{N}$ and $e \to e'$ then e' is typable in contexts $\mathcal{P}, \mathcal{N}$, belongs to the same syntactic category as e and has the same type as e (when it applies).*

The proof is a straightforward verification. As usual one has first to state and prove a Substitution Lemma.

The reduction $\to$ on Λ_{LLP} enjoys Church-Rosser as we shall see in a longer paper. The denotational semantics that we outline now gives us another proof that this calculus is sound.

[7] In a Sequent Calculus presentation, with double-sided sequents contrarily to most presentations of LLP in the literature. Our syntax is based on the $\lambda\mu\tilde{\mu}$ presentation of sequent calculus-oriented classical lambda-calculi due to [7].

$$\frac{}{\mathcal{P}, x : \varphi \vdash x : \varphi \,|\, \mathcal{N}} \quad \frac{\mathcal{P} \vdash N : \sigma \,|\, \mathcal{N}}{\mathcal{P} \vdash N^! : !\sigma \,|\, \mathcal{N}} \quad \frac{\mathcal{P} \vdash P_1 : \varphi_1 \,|\, \mathcal{N} \qquad \mathcal{P} \vdash P_1 : \varphi_2 \,|\, \mathcal{N}}{\mathcal{P} \vdash \langle P_1, P_2 \rangle : \varphi_1 \otimes \varphi_2 \,|\, \mathcal{N}}$$

$$\frac{\mathcal{P} \vdash P : \varphi_i \,|\, \mathcal{N}}{\mathcal{P} \vdash \mathsf{in}_i P : \varphi_1 \oplus \varphi_2 \,|\, \mathcal{N}} \quad \frac{\mathcal{P} \vdash P : \varphi \,|\, \mathcal{N}}{\mathcal{P} \vdash \mathsf{der}\, P : ?\varphi \,|\, \mathcal{N}} \quad \frac{\mathcal{P}, x : \varphi \vdash M : \sigma \,|\, \mathcal{N}}{\mathcal{P} \vdash \lambda x^{\varphi}\, M : \varphi \multimap \sigma \,|\, \mathcal{N}}$$

$$\frac{\mathcal{P} \vdash c \,|\, \alpha : \sigma, \mathcal{N}}{\mathcal{P} \vdash \mu\alpha^{\sigma}\, c : \sigma \,|\, \mathcal{N}} \quad \frac{\mathcal{P}, x : !\sigma \vdash M : \sigma \,|\, \mathcal{N}}{\mathcal{P} \vdash \mathsf{fix}\, x^{!\sigma}\, M : \sigma \,|\, \mathcal{N}}$$

$$\frac{}{\mathcal{P} \,|\, \alpha : \sigma \vdash \alpha : \sigma, \mathcal{N}} \quad \frac{\mathcal{P} \,|\, \eta : \varphi \vdash \mathcal{N}}{\mathcal{P} \,|\, \eta^! : ?\varphi \vdash \mathcal{N}} \quad \frac{\mathcal{P} \vdash P : \varphi \,|\, \mathcal{N} \qquad \mathcal{P} \,|\, \pi : \sigma \vdash \mathcal{N}}{\mathcal{P} \,|\, P \cdot \pi : \varphi \multimap \sigma \vdash \mathcal{N}}$$

$$\frac{\mathcal{P} \,|\, \pi : \sigma \vdash \mathcal{N}}{\mathcal{P} \,|\, \mathsf{der}\, \pi : !\sigma \vdash \mathcal{N}} \quad \frac{\mathcal{P} \,|\, \eta : \varphi_i \vdash \mathcal{N}}{\mathcal{P} \,|\, \mathsf{pr}_i \eta : \varphi_1 \otimes \varphi_2 \vdash \mathcal{N}}$$

$$\frac{\mathcal{P} \,|\, \eta_1 : \varphi_1 \vdash \mathcal{N} \qquad \mathcal{P} \,|\, \eta_2 : \varphi_2 \vdash \mathcal{N}}{\mathcal{P} \,|\, [\eta_1, \eta_2] : \varphi_1 \oplus \varphi_2 \vdash \mathcal{N}} \quad \frac{\mathcal{P}, x : \varphi \vdash c \,|\, \mathcal{N}}{\mathcal{P} \,|\, \tilde{\mu} x^{\varphi}\, c : \varphi \vdash \mathcal{N}}$$

$$\frac{\mathcal{P} \vdash P : \varphi \,|\, \mathcal{N} \qquad \mathcal{P} \,|\, \eta : \varphi \vdash \mathcal{N}}{\mathcal{P} \vdash P * \eta \,|\, \mathcal{N}} \quad \frac{\mathcal{P} \vdash M : \sigma \,|\, \mathcal{N} \qquad \mathcal{P} \,|\, \pi : \sigma \vdash \mathcal{N}}{\mathcal{P} \vdash M * \pi \,|\, \mathcal{N}}$$

Fig. 6. Typing rules for Λ_{LLP}: positive terms, negative terms, positive contexts, negative contexts and commands

$$\mathsf{der}\, P * \eta^! \to_{\mathsf{w}} P * \eta \tag{6}$$
$$\lambda x^{\varphi}\, M * P \cdot \pi \to_{\mathsf{w}} M\,[P/x] * \pi \tag{7}$$
$$\mu\alpha^{\sigma}\, c * \pi \to_{\mathsf{w}} c\,[\pi/\alpha] \tag{8}$$
$$\mathsf{fix}\, x^{!\sigma}\, M * \pi \to_{\mathsf{w}} M\left[(\mathsf{fix}\, x^{!\sigma}\, M)^!/x\right] * \pi \tag{9}$$
$$M^! * \mathsf{der}\, \pi \to_{\mathsf{w}} M * \pi \tag{10}$$
$$\langle P_1, P_2 \rangle * \mathsf{pr}_i \eta \to_{\mathsf{w}} P_i * \eta \tag{11}$$
$$\mathsf{in}_i P * [\eta_1, \eta_2] \to_{\mathsf{w}} P * \eta_i \tag{12}$$
$$P * \tilde{\mu} x^{\varphi}\, c \to_{\mathsf{w}} c\,[P/x] \tag{13}$$

Fig. 7. Reduction rules for Λ_{LLP}

5.2 Denotational Semantics

Assume to be given a model of LL $\mathcal{L}$ as specified in Sect. 3. With any positive type φ, negative type σ and sequence of pairwise distinct type variables $\boldsymbol{\zeta} = (\zeta_1, \ldots, \zeta_n)$ containing all free variables of φ and σ, we associate the continuous functors $[\varphi]_{\boldsymbol{\zeta}}, [\![\sigma]\!]_{\boldsymbol{\zeta}} : (\mathcal{L}^!_{\subseteq})^n \to \mathcal{L}^!_{\subseteq}$ defined in Fig. 8 on objects, the definition on

$$[\zeta_i]_\varsigma(\boldsymbol{P}) = P_i \qquad [!\sigma]_\varsigma(\boldsymbol{P}) = !(\underline{[\![\sigma]\!]_\varsigma(\boldsymbol{P})}^\perp)$$
$$[\varphi \otimes \psi]_\varsigma(\boldsymbol{P}) = [\varphi]_\varsigma(\boldsymbol{P}) \otimes [\psi]_\varsigma(\boldsymbol{P})$$
$$[\varphi \oplus \psi]_\varsigma(\boldsymbol{P}) = [\varphi]_\varsigma(\boldsymbol{P}) \oplus [\psi]_\varsigma(\boldsymbol{P})$$
$$[\mathsf{Fix}\,\zeta \cdot \varphi]_\varsigma = \mathrm{Fix}([\varphi]_{\varsigma,\zeta}) \qquad [\![\top]\!]_\varsigma(\boldsymbol{P}) = 0$$
$$[\![?\varphi \;{}_\varsigma(\boldsymbol{P}) = !(\underline{[\varphi]_\varsigma(\boldsymbol{P})}^\perp) \qquad [\![\varphi \multimap \sigma]\!]_\varsigma(\boldsymbol{P}) = [\varphi]_\varsigma(\boldsymbol{P}) \otimes [\![\sigma]\!]_\varsigma(\boldsymbol{P})$$

Fig. 8. Semantics of types in Λ_{LLP}

morphisms being similar[8]. With any positive terms and contexts P and π with $\mathcal{P} \vdash P : \varphi \,|\, \mathcal{N}$ and $\mathcal{P} \,|\, \pi : \sigma \vdash \mathcal{N}$ we associate coalgebra morphisms $[P]_{\mathcal{P},\mathcal{N}} \in \mathcal{L}^!([\mathcal{P}] \otimes [\![\mathcal{N}]\!], [\varphi])$ and $[\pi]_{\mathcal{P},\mathcal{N}} \in \mathcal{L}^!([\mathcal{P}] \otimes [\![\mathcal{N}]\!], [\![\sigma]\!])$ and with any negative terms and contexts M and η with $\mathcal{P} \vdash M : \sigma \,|\, \mathcal{N}$ and $\mathcal{P} \,|\, \eta : \varphi \vdash \mathcal{N}$ we associate morphisms $[M]_{\mathcal{P},\mathcal{N}} \in \mathcal{L}(\underline{[\mathcal{P}]} \otimes \underline{[\![\mathcal{N}]\!]}, \underline{[\![\sigma]\!]}^\perp)$ and $[\eta]_{\mathcal{P},\mathcal{N}} \in \mathcal{L}(\underline{[\mathcal{P}]} \otimes \underline{[\![\mathcal{N}]\!]}, \underline{[\varphi]}^\perp)$. Last, with any command c such that $\mathcal{P} \vdash c \,|\, \mathcal{N}$ we associate a morphism $[c]_{\mathcal{P},\mathcal{N}} \in \mathcal{L}(\underline{[\mathcal{P}]} \otimes \underline{[\![\mathcal{N}]\!]}, \perp)$.

The interpretation of positive terms is defined as for Λ_{HP} (see Sect. 3.3). Negative terms: the interpretation of $\mathsf{der}\,P$ uses the dereliction morphism in $\mathcal{L}(\underline{[\varphi]}, ?\underline{[\varphi]})$, the interpretation of $\lambda x^\varphi\, M$ and of $\mathsf{fix}\, x^{!\sigma}\, M$ is defined as in Λ_{HP} (replacing $[\sigma]$ with $\underline{[\![\sigma]\!]}^\perp$) and we provide the interpretation of $\mu\alpha^\sigma\, c$: assume that $\mathcal{P} \vdash c \,|\, \mathcal{N}, \alpha : \sigma$ so that $[c]_{\mathcal{P},\mathcal{N},\alpha:\sigma} \in \mathcal{L}(\underline{[\mathcal{P}]} \otimes \underline{[\![\mathcal{N}]\!]} \otimes \underline{[\![\sigma]\!]}, \perp)$ and we set $[\mu\alpha^\sigma\, c]_{\mathcal{P},\mathcal{N}} = \mathrm{cur}[c]_{\mathcal{P},\mathcal{N},\alpha:\sigma}$. Positive contexts: we deal only with one case. Assume that $\mathcal{P} \vdash P : \varphi \,|\, \mathcal{N}$ and $\mathcal{P} \,|\, \pi : \sigma \vdash \mathcal{N}$. We have $[P]_{\mathcal{P},\mathcal{N}} \in \mathcal{L}^!([\mathcal{P}] \otimes [\![\mathcal{N}]\!], [\varphi])$ and $[\pi]_{\mathcal{P},\mathcal{N}} \in \mathcal{L}^!([\mathcal{P}] \otimes [\![\mathcal{N}]\!], [\![\sigma]\!])$ so that we can set $[P \cdot \pi]_{\mathcal{P},\mathcal{N}} = ([P]_{\mathcal{P},\mathcal{N}} \otimes [\pi]_{\mathcal{P},\mathcal{N}})\, \mathrm{c}_{[\mathcal{P}] \otimes [\![\mathcal{N}]\!]}$ whose codomain is $[\varphi] \otimes [\![\sigma]\!] = [\![\varphi \multimap \sigma]\!]$ as required. The interpretation of α uses a projection and the interpretation of $\eta^!$ uses a promotion. Negative contexts: assume that $\mathcal{P} \,|\, \pi : \sigma \vdash \mathcal{N}$, then $[\pi]_{\mathcal{P},\mathcal{N}} \in \mathcal{L}^!([\mathcal{P}] \otimes [\![\mathcal{N}]\!], [\![\sigma]\!])$ so we set $[\mathsf{der}\,\pi]_{\mathcal{P},\mathcal{N}} = \mathrm{der}'_{[\![\sigma]\!]}\, [\pi]_{\mathcal{P},\mathcal{N}} \in \mathcal{L}(\underline{[\mathcal{P}]} \otimes \underline{[\![\mathcal{N}]\!]}, ?\underline{[\![\sigma]\!]})$ which makes sense since $?\underline{[\![\sigma]\!]} = \underline{[!\sigma]}^\perp$ (see Fig. 8). The interpretation of $\mathsf{pr}_i\, \eta$ uses $\mathrm{pr}_i^\perp \in \mathcal{L}(\underline{[\varphi_i]}^\perp, (\underline{[\varphi_1]} \otimes \underline{[\varphi_2]})^\perp)$. To define $[[\eta_1, \eta_2]]_{\mathcal{P},\mathcal{N}}$ we simply use the pairing operation associated with the cartesian product & of $\mathcal{L}$ (warning: *not* of $\mathcal{L}^!$!) which is the linear “De Morgan” dual of the coproduct $\oplus$ of $\mathcal{L}$. The interpretation of $\tilde{\mu} x^\varphi\, c$ uses a linear curryfication. Commands: assume that $\mathcal{P} \vdash P : \varphi \,|\, \mathcal{N}$ and $\mathcal{P} \,|\, \eta : \varphi \vdash \mathcal{N}$ so that $[P]_{\mathcal{P},\mathcal{N}} \in \mathcal{L}^!([\mathcal{P}] \otimes [\![\mathcal{N}]\!], [\varphi]) \subseteq \mathcal{L}(\underline{[\mathcal{P}]} \otimes \underline{[\![\mathcal{N}]\!]}, \underline{[\varphi]})$ and $[\eta]_{\mathcal{P},\mathcal{N}} \in \mathcal{L}(\underline{[\mathcal{P}]} \otimes \underline{[\![\mathcal{N}]\!]}, \underline{[\varphi]}^\perp)$ and we set $[P * \eta]_{\mathcal{P},\mathcal{N}} = \mathrm{ev}\,([\eta]_{\mathcal{P},\mathcal{N}} \otimes [P]_{\mathcal{P},\mathcal{N}})\, \mathrm{c}_{[\mathcal{P}] \otimes [\![\mathcal{N}]\!]}$. The interpretation of $M * \pi$ is similar.

Proposition 9. *Assume that* $\mathcal{P} \vdash P : \varphi \,|\, \mathcal{N}$ *and that* e *is a well-typed expression in typing contexts* $x : \varphi, \mathcal{P}, \mathcal{N}$. *Then we have* $[e\,[P/x]]_{\mathcal{P},\mathcal{N}} = [e]_{x:\varphi,\mathcal{P},\mathcal{N}}\,([P]_{\mathcal{P},\mathcal{N}} \otimes$

[8] Notice that the interpretation of a negative type is actually the semantics of its linear negation; we adopt this convention in order to avoid the explicit introduction of negative objects in the model. This is possible because we have assumed that $\mathcal{L}$ is $*$-autonomous.

$$\zeta^+ = \zeta \qquad (!\sigma)^+ = !(\sigma^-)$$
$$(\varphi_1 \otimes \varphi_2)^+ = \varphi_1^+ \otimes \varphi_2^+ \qquad (\varphi_1 \oplus \varphi_2)^+ = \varphi_1^+ \oplus \varphi_2^+$$
$$(\mathsf{Fix}\,\zeta \cdot \varphi)^+ = \mathsf{Fix}\,\zeta \cdot \varphi^+$$
$$\varphi^- = ?(\varphi^+) \qquad (\varphi \multimap \sigma)^- = \varphi^+ \multimap \sigma^-$$

Fig. 9. Translation of types

Id) $\mathsf{c}_{[\mathcal{P}]\otimes[\![\mathcal{N}]\!]}$. *Assume that* $\mathcal{P} \,|\, \pi : \sigma \vdash \mathcal{N}$ *and that* e *is a well-typed expression in typing contexts* $\mathcal{P}$, $\mathcal{N}, \alpha : \sigma$. *Then we have* $[e\,[\pi/\alpha]]_{\mathcal{P},\mathcal{N}} = [e]_{\mathcal{P},\mathcal{N},\alpha:\sigma}\,(\mathrm{Id} \otimes [\pi]_{\mathcal{P},\mathcal{N}})\,\mathsf{c}_{[\mathcal{P}]\otimes[\![\mathcal{N}]\!]}$.

Theorem 6. *If* e *is a well-typed expression in typing contexts* $\mathcal{P}$, $\mathcal{N}$ *and if* $e \to e'$ *then* $[e]_{\mathcal{P},\mathcal{N}} = [e']_{\mathcal{P},\mathcal{N}}$.

The proof is routine, using Proposition 9.

Given a negative type σ, observe that $\Omega^\sigma = \mathsf{fix}\, x^{!\sigma}\,(\mu\alpha^\sigma\,(x * \mathsf{der}\,\alpha))$ is a closed negative term of type σ. A consequence of Theorem 6 is that Λ_{LLP} is sound in the sense that the reflexive and transitive closure of $\to$ does not equate *e.g.* the two booleans $\mathsf{in}_1(\Omega^\top)^!$ and $\mathsf{in}_2(\Omega^\top)^!$ (closed positive terms of type $!\top \oplus !\top$). Indeed it is easy to build models where these constants have distinct interpretations (for instance the Scott model **Polr** of Sect. 4).

5.3 Translating Λ_{HP} into Λ_{LLP}

With any positive type φ of Λ_{HP} we associate a positive type φ^+ of Λ_{LLP} and with any general type σ we associate a negative type of Λ_{LLP}. The translation does almost nothing apart adding a few "?" to make sure that σ^- is negative, see Fig. 9. Given a Λ_{HP} typing context $\mathcal{P} = (x_1 : \varphi_1, \ldots, x_n : \varphi_n)$, we set $\mathcal{P}^+ = (x_1 : \varphi_1^+, \ldots, x_n : \varphi_n^+)$. With any term M of Λ_{HP} such that $\mathcal{P} \vdash M : \sigma$ one associates a term M^- of Λ_{LLP} such that $\mathcal{P}^+ \vdash M^- : \sigma^- \,|$. We give two cases of this translation, the complete translation will be given in a longer paper.

If $M = \langle N \rangle R$ with $\mathcal{P} \vdash N : \varphi \multimap \sigma$ and $\mathcal{P} \vdash R : \varphi$ then by inductive hypothesis, $\mathcal{P}^+ \vdash N^- : \varphi^+ \multimap \sigma^- \,|$ and $\mathcal{P}^+ \vdash R^- : ?\varphi^+ \,|$. We have $\mathcal{P}^+, x : \varphi^+ \,|\, x \cdot \alpha : \varphi^+ \multimap \sigma^- \vdash \alpha : \sigma^-$, hence $\mathcal{P}^+, x : \varphi^+ \vdash N^- * (x \cdot \alpha) \,|\, \alpha : \sigma^-$. Therefore we have $\mathcal{P}^+ \,|\, \mu x^{\varphi^+}\, N^- * (x \cdot \alpha) : \varphi^+ \vdash \alpha : \sigma^-$ so that $\mathcal{P}^+ \,|\, (\mu x^{\varphi^+}\, N^- * (x \cdot \alpha))^! : ?\varphi^+ \vdash \alpha : \sigma^-$ and we set $\langle N \rangle R^- = \mu\alpha^{\sigma^-}\,(R^- * (\mu x^{\varphi^+}\, N^- * (x \cdot \alpha))^!)$.

If $M = \langle M_1, M_2 \rangle$ there are two possible translations (similar phenomena occur in CPS translation, see for instance [29]), a *left first* translation and a *right first* translation. We give the first one, the other one being obtained by swapping the roles of M_1 and M_2. We assume that $\mathcal{P} \vdash M_i : \varphi_i$ and hence $\mathcal{P}^+ \vdash M_i^- : ?\varphi_i^+ \,|$ for $i = 1, 2$. We have $\mathcal{P}^+, x_2 : \varphi_2^+ \,|\, \tilde{\mu} x_1^{\varphi_1^+}\, \mathsf{der}\,\langle x_1, x_2 \rangle * \alpha : \varphi_1^+ \vdash \alpha : ?(\varphi_1^+ \otimes \varphi_2^+)$, hence $\mathcal{P}^+, x_2 : \varphi_2^+ \vdash M_1^- * (\tilde{\mu} x_1^{\varphi_1^+}\, \mathsf{der}\,\langle x_1, x_2 \rangle * \alpha)^! \,|\, \alpha : ?(\varphi_1^+ \otimes \varphi_2^+)$ and hence we set $\langle M_1, M_2 \rangle^- = \mu\alpha^{?(\varphi_1^+ \otimes \varphi_2^+)}\, M_2^- * \left(\tilde{\mu} x_2^{\varphi_2^+}\, M_1^- * (\tilde{\mu} x_1^{\varphi_1^+}\, \mathsf{der}\,\langle x_1, x_2 \rangle * \alpha)^!\right)^!$.

Given a Λ_{HP} value V such that $\mathcal{P} \vdash V : \varphi$, one defines straightforwardly a positive term V^+ of Λ_{LLP} such that $\mathcal{P}^+ \vdash V^+ : \varphi^+ \mid$: one sets $(M^!)^+ = (M^-)^!$, $\langle V_1, V_2\rangle^+ = \langle V_1^+, V_1^+\rangle$ and similarly for the other cases.

Lemma 5. *If $\mathcal{P} \vdash V : \varphi$ in Λ_{HP} and if V is a value then $V^- \to_{\mathsf{w}}^* \mathsf{der}\,(V^+)$.*

Lemma 6. *If $\mathcal{P}, x : \varphi \vdash M : \sigma$ and $\mathcal{P} \vdash V : \varphi$ in Λ_{HP} (with V being a value) then $M\,[V/x]^- \to_{\mathsf{w}}^* M^-\,[V^+/x]$.*

Proof. Induction on M, using Lemma 5 when $M = x$. □

Theorem 7. *If $\mathcal{P} \vdash M : \sigma$ in Λ_{HP} then $\mathcal{P}^+ \vdash M^- : \sigma^- \mid$. Moreover, if $M \to_{\mathsf{w}} M'$ then there is a negative term R of Λ_{LLP} such that $M^- \to^* R$ and $M'^- \to^* R$.*

As a consequence, using confluence of $\to^*$ in Λ_{LLP}, one proves that, if $M \to^* M'$ in Λ_{HP} there is a negative term R of Λ_{LLP} such that $M^- \to^* R$ and $M'^- \to^* R$ (induction on the length of the reduction $M \to^* M'$). This shows that Λ_{HP} embeds in Λ_{LLP} by a translation $M \mapsto M^-$ which is compatible with the operational semantics. In the long version of this paper, we will also describe a simple relation between the semantics of M and of M^-.

Conclusion. The half-polarized and fully polarized calculi proposed in this paper admit LL-based models featuring non-trivial computational effects such as non-deterministic or probabilistic computations [9] (with full abstraction properties [12]). One can accommodate other effects by extending the language with monad type constructions interpreted as monads acting on $\mathcal{L}$ and featuring a strength, in the spirit of [17], as we will explain in a forthcoming paper.

I would like to thank the referees for their insightful suggestions and comments. I also would like to mention the work [6] which shares some features with ours (in particular an emphasis on the resource modality "!"); these papers have been written independently and simultaneously.

This work has been partly funded by the French-Chinese project ANR-11-IS02-0002 and NSFC 61161130530 *Locali*.

References

1. Andreoli, J.-M.: Logic programming with focusing proofs in linear logic. J. Logic Comput. **2**(3), 297–347 (1992)
2. Benton, P.N., Wadler, P.: Linear logic, monads and the lambda calculus. In: Proceedings of 11th Annual IEEE Symposium on Logic in Computer Science, New Brunswick, New Jersey, USA, July 27–30, pp. 420–431. IEEE Computer Society (1996)
3. Bierman, G.M.: What is a categorical model of intuitionistic linear logic? In: Dezani-Ciancaglini, M., Plotkin, G. (eds.) TLCA 1995. LNCS, vol. 902, pp. 78–93. Springer, Heidelberg (1995)
4. Carraro, A., Guerrieri, G.: A semantical and operational account of call-by-value solvability. In: Muscholl, A. (ed.) FOSSACS 2014 (ETAPS). LNCS, vol. 8412, pp. 103–118. Springer, Heidelberg (2014)

5. Curien, P.-L.: Call-By-Push-Value in system L style. Unpublished note (2015)
6. Curien, P.-L., Fiore, M., Munch-Maccagnoni, G.: A theory of effects and resources: adjunction models and polarised calculi. In: Proceedings of POpPL (2015, To appear) (2016)
7. Curien, P.-L., Herbelin, H.: The duality of computation. In: Odersky, M., Wadler, P. (eds.) Proceedings of the Fifth ACM SIGPLAN International Conference on Functional Programming (ICFP 2000), Montreal, Canada, September 18–21, pp. 233–243. ACM (2000)
8. Curien, P.-L., Munch-Maccagnoni, G.: The duality of computation under focus. In: Calude, C.S., Sassone, V. (eds.) TCS 2010. IFIP AICT, vol. 323, pp. 165–181. Springer, Heidelberg (2010)
9. Danos, V., Ehrhard, T.: Probabilistic coherence spaces as a model of higher-order probabilistic computation. Inf. Comput. **152**(1), 111–137 (2011)
10. Egger, J., Møgelberg, R.E., Simpson, A.: The enriched effect calculus: syntax and semantics. J. Logic Comput. **24**(3), 615–654 (2014)
11. Ehrhard, T.: The scott model of linear logic is the extensional collapse of its relational model. Theor. Comput. Sci. **424**, 20–45 (2012)
12. Ehrhard, T., Tasson, C., Pagani, M.: Probabilistic coherence spaces are fully abstract for probabilistic PCF. In: Jagannathan, S., Sewell, P. (eds.) POPL, pp. 309–320. ACM (2014)
13. Fiore, M.P., Plotkin, G.D.: An axiomatization of computationally adequate domain theoretic models of FPC. In: Proceedings of the Ninth Annual Symposium on Logic in Computer Science (LICS 1994), Paris, France, July 4–7, pp. 92–102. IEEE Computer Society (1994)
14. Girard, J.-Y.: Linear logic. Theor. Comput. Sci. **50**, 1–102 (1987)
15. Girard, J.-Y.: A new constructive logic: classical logic. Math. Struct. Comput. Sci. **1**(3), 225–296 (1991)
16. Girard, J.-Y.: Locus solum. Math. Struct. Comput. Sci. **11**(3), 301–506 (2001)
17. Hasegawa, M.: Linearly used effects: monadic and CPS transformations into the linear lambda calculus. In: Hu, Z., Rodríguez-Artalejo, M. (eds.) FLOPS 2002. LNCS, vol. 2441, pp. 167–182. Springer, Heidelberg (2002)
18. Huth, M.: Linear domains and linear maps. In: Main, M.G., Melton, A.C., Mislove, M.W., Schmidt, D., Brookes, S.D. (eds.) MFPS 1993. LNCS, vol. 802, pp. 438–453. Springer, Heidelberg (1994)
19. Krivine, J.-L.: Lambda-Calculus, Types and Models. Ellis Horwood Series in Computers and Their Applications. Ellis Horwood, Translation by René Cori from French 1990 (edn.) (Masson) (1993)
20. Krivine, J.-L.: A general storage theorem for integers in call-by-name λ-calculus. Theor. Comput. Sci. **129**, 79–94 (1994)
21. Laurent, O., Regnier, L.: About translations of classical logic into polarized linear logic. In: Proceedings of 18th IEEE Symposium on Logic in Computer Science (LICS 2003), pp. 22–25, Ottawa, Canada, pp. 11–20. IEEE Computer Society, June 2003
22. Levy, P.B.: Adjunction models for call-by-push-value with stacks. Electron. Notes Theor. Comput. Sci. **69**, 248–271 (2002)
23. Levy, P.B.: Call-By-Push-Value: A Functional/Imperative Synthesis. Semantics Structures in Computation, vol. 2. Springer, Heidelberg (2004)
24. Maraist, J., Odersky, M., Turner, D.N., Wadler, P.: Call-by-name, call-by-value, call-by-need and the linear lambda calculus. Theor. Comput. Sci. **228**(1–2), 175–210 (1999)

25. Marz, M., Rohr, A., Streicher, T.: Full Abstraction and Universality via Realisability. In: 14th Annual IEEE Symposium on Logic in Computer Science, Trento, Italy, July 2–5, pp. 174–182. IEEE Computer Society, (1999)
26. Melliès, P.-A.: Categorical semantics of linear logic. In: Curien, P.-L., Herbelin, H., Krivine, J.-L., Melliès, P.-A. (eds.) Interactive Models of Computation and Program Behaviour, vol. 27. Panoramas et Synthèses, Socièté Mathèmatique de France, Marseille (2009)
27. Moggi, E.: Computational lambda-calculus and monads. In: Proceedings of the 4th Annual IEEE Symposium on Logic in Computer Science. IEEE Computer Society (1989)
28. Seely, R.A.G.: Linear logic, *-autonomous categories and cofree coalgebras. Contem. Math. **92** (1989). American Mathematical Society
29. Selinger, P.: Control categories and duality: on the categorical semantics of the lambda-mu calculus. Math. Struct. Comput. Sci. **11**(2), 207–260 (2001)
30. Simpson, A.K., Plotkin, G.D.: Complete axioms for categorical fixed-point operators. In: 15th Annual IEEE Symposium on Logic in Computer Science, Santa Barbara, California, USA, 26–29 June, pp. 30–41. IEEE Computer Society (2000)
31. Winskel, G.: A linear metalanguage for concurrency. In: Haeberer, A.M. (ed.) AMAST 1998. LNCS, vol. 1548, pp. 42–58. Springer, Heidelberg (1998)

Visible Type Application

Richard A. Eisenberg(✉), Stephanie Weirich(✉), and Hamidhasan G. Ahmed

University of Pennsylvania, Philadelphia, USA
{eir,sweirich}@cis.upenn.edu, hamidhasan14@gmail.com

Abstract. The Hindley-Milner (HM) type system automatically infers the types at which polymorphic functions are used. In HM, the inferred types are unambiguous, and every expression has a principal type. Type annotations make HM compatible with extensions where complete type inference is impossible, such as higher-rank polymorphism and type-level functions. However, programmers cannot use annotations to explicitly provide type arguments to polymorphic functions, as HM requires type instantiations to be inferred.

We describe an extension to HM that allows visible type application. Our extension requires a novel type inference algorithm, yet its declarative presentation is a simple extension to HM. We prove that our extended system is a conservative extension of HM and admits principal types. We then extend our approach to a higher-rank type system with bidirectional type-checking. We have implemented this system in the Glasgow Haskell Compiler and show how our approach scales in the presence of complex type system features.

1 Introduction

The Hindley-Milner (HM) type system [7,13,18] achieves remarkable concision. While allowing a strong typing discipline, a program written in HM need not mention a single type. The brevity of HM comes at a cost, however: HM programs *must* not mention a single type. While this rule has long been relaxed by allowing visible type annotations (and even requiring them for various type system extensions), it remains impossible for languages based on HM, such as OCaml and Haskell, to use *visible type application* when calling a polymorphic function.[1]

This restriction makes sense in the HM type system, where visible type application is unnecessary, as all type instantiations can be determined via unification. Suppose the function *id* has type $\forall\, a.\ a \rightarrow a$. If we wished to visibly instantiate the type variable a (in a version of HM extended with type annotations), we could write the expression $(id :: Int \rightarrow Int)$. This annotation forces the type

[1] Syntax elements appearing in a programmer's source code are often called *explicit*, in contrast to *implicit* terms, which are inferred by the compiler. However, the implicit/explicit distinction also can indicate whether terms are computationally significant [19]. Our work applies only to the inferred vs. specified distinction, so we use *visible* to refer to syntax elements appearing in source code.

P. Thiemann (Ed.): ESOP 2016, LNCS 9632, pp. 229–254, 2016.
DOI: 10.1007/978-3-662-49498-1_10

Declarative	Syntax-directed	
HM (§4.1)	C (§5.1)	from Damas and Milner [8] and Clément et al. [5]
HMV (§4.2)	V (§5.2)	HM types with visible type application
B (§6.2)	SB (§6.1)	Higher-rank types with visible type application

Fig. 1. The type systems studied in this paper

checker to unify the provided type $\mathit{Int} \to \mathit{Int}$ with the type $a \to a$, concluding that type a should be instantiated with Int.

However, this annotation is a roundabout way of providing information to the type checker. It would be much more direct if programmers could provide type arguments explicitly, writing the expression $\mathit{id}\ @\mathit{Int}$ instead.

Why do we want visible type application? In the Glasgow Haskell Compiler (GHC) – which is based on HM but extends it significantly – there are two main reasons:

First, type instantiation cannot always be determined by unification. Some Haskell features, such as type classes [28] and GHC's type families [3,4,11], do not allow the type checker to unambiguously determine type arguments from an annotation. The current workaround for this issue is the *Proxy* type which clutters implementations and requires careful foresight by library designers. Visible type application improves such code. (See Sect. 2.)

Second, even when type arguments *can* be determined from an annotation, this mechanism is not always friendly to developers. For example, the variable to instantiate could appear multiple times in the type, leading to a long annotation. Partial type signatures help [29], but they do not completely solve the problem.[2]

Although the idea seems straightforward, adding visible type applications to the HM type system requires care, as we describe in Sect. 3. In particular, we observe that we can allow visible type application only at certain types: those with *specified type quantification*, known to the programmer via type annotation. Such types may be instantiated either visibly by the programmer, or when possible, invisibly through inference.

This paper presents a systematic study of the integration of visible type application within the HM typing system. In particular, the contributions of this paper are the four novel type systems (HMV, V, SB, B), summarized in Fig. 1. These systems come in pairs: a declarative version that justifies the compositionality of our extensions and a syntax-directed system that explains the structure of our type inference algorithm.

- System HMV extends the declarative version of the HM type system with a single, straightforward new rule for visible type application. In support of this feature, it also includes two other extensions: scoped type variables and a distinction between specified and generalized type quantification. The importance of this system is that it demonstrates that visible type application can be added orthogonally to the HM type system, an observation that we found obvious only in hindsight.

[2] The extended version of this paper [12] contains an example of this issue.

- System V is a syntax-directed version of HMV. This type system directly corresponds to a type inference algorithm, called $\mathcal{V}$. Although Algorithm $\mathcal{V}$ works differently than Algorithm $\mathcal{W}$ [8], it retains the ability to calculate principal types. The key insight is that we can *delay* the instantiation of type variables until necessary. We prove that System V is sound and complete with respect to HMV, and that Algorithm $\mathcal{V}$ is sound and complete with respect to System V. These results show the principal types property for HMV.
- System SB is a syntax-directed bidirectional type system with higher-rank types, *i.e.* higher-rank types. In extending GHC with visible type application, we were required to consider the interactions of System V with all of the many type system extensions featured in GHC. Most interactions are orthogonal, as expected from the design of V. However, GHC's extension to support higher-rank types [23] changes its type inference algorithm to be bidirectional. System SB shows that our approach in designing System V straightforwardly extends to a bidirectional system. System SB's role in this paper is twofold: to show how our approach to visible type application meshes well with type system extensions, and to be the basis for our implementation in GHC.
- System B is a novel, simple declarative specification of System SB. We prove that System SB is sound and complete with respect to System B. A similar declarative specification was not present in prior work [23]; this paper shows that an HM-style presentation is possible even in the case of higher-rank systems.

Our visible type application extension is part of GHC 8.0. The extended version [12] describes this implementation and elaborates on interactions between our algorithm and other features of GHC.[3]

2 Why Visible Type Application?

Before we discuss how to extend HM type systems with visible type application, we first elaborate on why we would like this feature in the first place.

When a Haskell library author wishes to give a client the ability to control type variable instantiation, the current workaround is the standard library's *Proxy* type.

```
data Proxy a = Proxy
```

However, as we shall see, programming with *Proxy* is noisy and painfully indirect. With built-in visible type application, these examples are streamlined and easier to work with.[4] In the following example and throughout this paper,

[3] Although the type inference algorithm in this paper uses unification to determine type instantiations, following Damas's Algorithm $\mathcal{W}$ [7], the results in this paper are applicable to GHC's implementation based on constraint-solving. What matters here is how constraints are generated (specified by the syntax-directed versions of type systems) not how they are solved.

[4] Visible type application has been a GHC feature request since 2011. See https://ghc.haskell.org/trac/ghc/ticket/5296.

unadorned code blocks are accepted by GHC 7.10, blocks with a solid gray bar at the left are ill-typed, and blocks with a gray background are accepted only by our implementation of visible type application.

Resolving Type Class Ambiguity. Suppose a programmer wished to normalize the representation of expression text by running it through a parser and then pretty printer. The *normalize* function below maps the string `"7 - 1 * 0 + 3 / 3"` to `"((7 - (1 * 0)) + (3 / 3))"`, resolving precedence and making the meaning clear.[5]

```
normalize :: String → String
normalize x = show ((read :: String → Expr) x)
```

However, the designer of this function cannot make it polymorphic in a straightforward way. Adding a polymorphic type signature results in an ambiguous type, which GHC rightly rejects, as it cannot infer the instantiation for *a* at call sites.

```
normalizePoly :: ∀ a. (Show a, Read a) ⇒ String → String
normalizePoly x = show ((read :: String → a) x)
```

Instead, the programmer must add a *Proxy* argument, which is never evaluated, to allow clients of this polymorphic function to specify the parser and pretty-printer to use

```
normalizeProxy :: ∀ a. (Show a, Read a)
               ⇒ Proxy a → String → String
normalizeProxy _ x = show ((read :: String → a) x)
normalizeExpr :: String → String
normalizeExpr = normalizeProxy (Proxy :: Proxy Expr)
```

With visible type application, we can write these two functions more directly:[6]

```
normalize :: ∀ a. (Show a, Read a) ⇒ String → String
normalize x = show (read @a x)
normalizeExpr :: String → String
normalizeExpr = normalize @Expr
```

[5] This example uses the following functions from the standard library,

```
show :: ∀ a. Show a ⇒ a → String
read :: ∀ a. Read a ⇒ String → a
```

as well as user-defined instances of the *Show* and *Read* classes for the type *Expr*.

[6] Our new extension `TypeApplications` implies the extension `AllowAmbiguousTypes`, which allows our updated *normalize* definition to be accepted.

Although the *show*/*read* ambiguity is somewhat contrived, proxies are indeed useful in more sophisticated APIs. For example, suppose a library designer would like to allow users to choose the representation of an internal data structure to best meet the needs of their application. If the type of that data structure is not included in the input and output types of the API, then a *Proxy* argument is a way to give this control to clients.[7]

Other Examples. More practical examples of the need for visible type application require a fair amount of build-up to motivate the need for the intricate types involved. We have included two larger examples in the extended version [12]. One builds from recent work on deferring constraints until runtime [2] and the other on translating a dependently typed program from Agda [16] into Haskell.

3 Our Approach to Visible Type Application

Visible type application seems like a straightforward extension, but adding this feature – both to GHC and to the HM type system that it is based on – turned out to be more difficult and interesting than we first anticipated. In particular, we encountered two significant questions.

3.1 Just *What* are the Type Parameters?

The first problem is that it is not always clear what the type parameters to a polymorphic function are!

One aspect of the HM type system is that it permits expressions to be given multiple types. For example, the identity function for pairs,

$$pid\ (x, y) = (x, y)$$

can be assigned any of the following most general types:

$$\begin{array}{ll} (1)\ \forall\, a\ b. & (a, b) \to (a, b) \\ (2)\ \forall\, a\ b. & (b, a) \to (b, a) \\ (3)\ \forall\, c\ a\ b. & (a, b) \to (a, b) \end{array}$$

All of these types are principal; no type above is more general than any other. However, the type of the expression,

$$pid\ @Int\ @Bool$$

is very different depending on which "equivalent" type is chosen for *pid*:

$$\begin{array}{lll} & (Int, Bool) \to (Int, Bool) & \text{-- } pid \text{ has type (1)} \\ & (Bool, Int) \to (Bool, Int) & \text{-- } pid \text{ has type (2)} \\ \forall\, b. & (Bool, b) \to (Bool, b) & \text{-- } pid \text{ has type (3)} \end{array}$$

[7] See http://stackoverflow.com/questions/27044209/haskell-why-use-proxy.

Class constraints do not have a fixed ordering in types, and it is possible that a type variable is mentioned *only* in a constraint. Which of the following is preferred?

$$\forall\, r\ m\ w\ a.\ (\mathit{MonadReader}\ r\ m, \mathit{MonadWriter}\ w\ m) \Rightarrow a \rightarrow m\ a$$
$$\forall\, w\ m\ r\ a.\ (\mathit{MonadWriter}\ w\ m, \mathit{MonadReader}\ r\ m) \Rightarrow a \rightarrow m\ a$$

Equality constraints and GADTs can add new quantified variables. Should we prefer the type $\forall\, a.\ a \rightarrow a$ or the equivalent type $\forall\, a\ b.\ (a \sim b) \Rightarrow a \rightarrow b$?

Type abbreviations mean that quantifying variables as they appear can be ambiguous without also specifying how type abbreviations are used and when they are expanded. Suppose

$$\textbf{type}\ \mathit{Phantom}\ a = \mathit{Int}$$
$$\textbf{type}\ \mathit{Swap}\ a\ b = (b, a)$$

Should we prefer $\forall\, a\ b.\ \mathit{Swap}\ a\ b \rightarrow \mathit{Int}$ or $\forall\, b\ a.\ \mathit{Swap}\ a\ b \rightarrow \mathit{Int}$? Similarly, should we prefer $\forall\, a.\ \mathit{Phantom}\ a \rightarrow \mathit{Int}$ or $\mathit{Int} \rightarrow \mathit{Int}$?

Fig. 2. Why specified polytypes?

Of course, there are ad hoc mechanisms for resolving this ambiguity. We could try to designate one of the above types (1–3) as the real principal type for *pid*, perhaps by disallowing the quantification of unused variables (ruling out type 3 above) and by enforcing an ordering on how variables are quantified (preferring type 1 over type 2 above). Our goal would be to make sure that each expression has a *unique* principal type, with respect to its quantified type variables. However, in the context of the full Haskell language, this strategy fails. There are just too many ways that types that are not α-equivalent can be considered equivalent by HM. See Fig. 2 for a list of language features that cause difficulties.

In the end, although it may be possible to resolve all of these ambiguities, we prefer not to. That approach leads to a system that is fragile (a new extension could break the requirement that principal types are unique up to α-equivalence), difficult to explain to programmers (who must be able to determine which type is principal) and difficult to reason about.

Our Solution: Specified Polytypes. Our system is designed around the following principle:

> *Only user-specified type parameters can be instantiated via explicit type applications.*

In other words, we allow visible type application to instantiate a polytype only when that type is given by a user annotation. This restriction follows in a long line of work requiring user annotations to support advanced type system features [14,22,23]. We refer to variables quantified in type annotations as *specified variables*, distinct from compiler-generated quantified variables, which we call *generalized variables*.

There is one nuance to this rule in practice. Haskell allows programming to omit variable quantification, allowing a type signature like

$$\mathit{const} :: a \to b \to a \quad \text{-- NB: no } \forall$$

Are these variables specified? We have decided that they are. There is a very easy rule at work here: just order the variables left-to-right as the user wrote them. We thus consider variables from type signatures to be specified, even when not bound by an explicit ∀.

3.2 Is Our Extension Compatible with the Rest of the Type System?

We do not want to extend just the type inference algorithm that GHC uses. We would also like to extend its *specification*, which is rooted in HM. This way, we will have a concise description (and better understanding) of what programs type check, and a simple way to reason about the properties of the type system.

Our first attempt to add type application to GHC was based on our understanding of Algorithm $\mathcal{W}$, the standard algorithm for HM type inference. This algorithm instantiates polymorphic functions only at occurrences of variables. So, it seems that the only new form we need to allow is a visible type right after variable occurrences:

$$x\ @\tau_1 \ldots @\tau_n$$

However, this extension is not very robust to code refactoring. For example, it is not closed under substitution. If type application is only allowed at variables, then we cannot substitute for this variable and expect the code to still type check. Therefore our algorithm should allow visible type applications at other expression forms. But where else makes sense?

For example, it seems sensible to allow a type instantiation is after a polymorphic type annotation (such an annotation certainly specifies the type of the expression):

$$(\lambda x \to x :: \forall\, a\, b.\, (a, b) \to (a, b))\ @\mathit{Int}$$

Likewise, we should also allow a visible instantiation after a **let** to enable refactoring:[8]

$$(\textbf{let}\ y = ((\lambda x \to x) :: \forall\, a\, b.\, (a, b) \to (a, b))\ \textbf{in}\ y)\ @\mathit{Int}$$

However, how do we know that we have identified all sites where visible type applications should be allowed? Furthermore, we may have identified them all for core HM, but what happens when we go to the full language of GHC, which includes features that may expose new potential sites?

[8] In fact, the Haskell 2010 Report [15] *defines* type annotations by expanding to a **let**-declaration with a signature.

One way to think about this issue in a principled way is to develop a compositional specification of the type system, which allows type application for *any* expression that can be assigned a polytype. Then, if our algorithm is complete with respect to this specification, we will know that we have allowed type applications in all of the appropriate places. This specification is itself useful in its own right, as we will have a concise description (and better understanding) of what programs type check and a simple way to reason about the properties of the type system.

Once we started thinking of specifications, we found that Algorithm $\mathcal{W}$ could not be matched up with the compositional specification that we wanted. That led us to reconsider our algorithm and develop a new approach to HM type inference.

Our Solution: Lazy Instantiation for Specified Polytypes. Our new type inference algorithm, which we call Algorithm $\mathcal{V}$, is based on the following design principle:

> *Delay instantiation of "specified" type parameters until absolutely necessary.*

Although Algorithm $\mathcal{W}$ instantiates all polytypes immediately, it need not do so. In fact, it is possible to develop a sound and complete alternative implementation of the HM type system that does not do this immediate instantiation. Instead, instantiation is done only on demand, such as when a polymorphic function is applied to arguments. Lazy instantiation has been used in (non-HM) type inference before [10] and may be folklore; however this work contains the first proof that it can be used to implement the HM type system.

In the next section, we give this algorithm a simple specification, presented as a small extension of HM's existing declarative specification. We then continue with a syntax-directed account of the type system, characterizing where lazy instantiations actually must occur during type checking.

4 HM with Visible Type Application

To make our ideas precise, we next review the declarative specification of the HM type system [7,13,18] (which we call System HM), and then show how to extend this specification with visible type arguments.

4.1 System HM

The grammar of System HM is shown in Fig. 3. The expression language comprises the Curry-style typed λ-calculus with the addition of numeric literals (of type *Int*) and **let**-expressions. Monotypes are as usual, but we diverge from standard notation in type schemes as they quantify over a possibly-empty *set* of type variables. Here, we write these type variables in braces to emphasize

HM

Metavariables: x, y term variables; a, b, c type variables; n numeric literals

$$
\begin{array}{lll}
e & ::= x \mid \lambda x.\, e \mid e_1\, e_2 & \text{expressions} \\
 & \quad \mid n \mid \textbf{let}\ x = e_1\ \textbf{in}\ e_2 & \\
\tau & ::= a \mid \tau_1 \rightarrow \tau_2 \mid \mathit{Int} & \text{monotypes} \\
\sigma & ::= \forall\{\overline{a}\}.\,\tau & \text{type schemes} \\
\Gamma & ::= \cdot \mid \Gamma, x{:}\sigma & \text{contexts}
\end{array}
$$

HMV

This grammar extends HM:

$$
\begin{array}{lll}
e & ::= \ldots \mid e\,@\tau \mid (\Lambda\overline{a}.e : \upsilon) & \text{expressions} \\
\tau & ::= \ldots & \text{monotypes} \\
\upsilon & ::= \tau \mid \forall a.\,\upsilon & \text{spec. polytypes} \\
\sigma & ::= \upsilon \mid \forall\{a\}.\,\sigma & \text{type schemes} \\
\Gamma & ::= \cdot \mid \Gamma, x{:}\sigma \mid \Gamma, a & \text{contexts}
\end{array}
$$

We write $(e : \upsilon)$ to mean $(\Lambda \cdot .e : \upsilon)$, $\mathit{ftv}(\sigma)$ to be the set of type variables free in σ, and lift ftv to contexts with $\mathit{ftv}(\overline{x{:}\sigma}, \overline{a})$ to be $\overline{a} \cup \bigcup_i \mathit{ftv}(\sigma_i)$.

Fig. 3. Grammars for Systems HM and HMV

that they should be considered order-independent. We sometimes write τ for the type scheme $\forall\{\,\}.\tau$ with an empty set of quantified variables and write $\forall\{a\}.\forall\{\overline{b}\}.\tau$ to mean $\forall\{a, \overline{b}\}.\tau$. Here – and throughout this paper – we liberally use the Barendregt convention that bound variables are always distinct from free variables.

The declarative typing rules for System HM appear in Fig. 4. (The figure also includes the definition for our extended system, called System HMV, described in Sect. 4.2.) System HM is not syntax-directed; rules HM_Gen and HM_Sub can apply anywhere.

So that we can better compare this system with others in the paper, we make two changes to the standard HM rules. Neither of these changes are substantial; our version types the same programs as the original.[9] First, in HM_Let, we allow the type of a **let** expression to be a polytype σ, instead of restricting it to be a monotype τ. We discuss this change further in Sect. 5.2. Second, we replace the usual instantiation rule with HM_Sub. This rule allows the type of any expression to be converted to any less general type in one step (as determined by the subsumption relation $\sigma_1 \leq_{\mathsf{hm}} \sigma_2$). Note that in rule HM_InstG the lists of variables $\overline{a}_1$ and $\overline{a}_2$ need not be the same length.

4.2 System HMV: HM with Visible Types

System HMV is an extension of System HM, adding visible type application. A key detail in its design is its separation of specified type variables from those arising from generalization, as initially explored in Sect. 3.1. Types may be generalized at any time in HMV, quantifying over a variable free in a type but not free in the typing context. The type variable generalized in this manner is *not* specified, as the generalization takes place absent any direction from the programmer. By contrast, a type variable mentioned in a type annotation *is* specified, precisely because it is written in the program text.

[9] Both ways of the equivalence proof proceed by induction, liberally using instantiation, generalization, and subsumption to bridge the gap between the two systems.

$\boxed{\Gamma \vdash_{hm} e : \sigma}$ Typing rules for System HM

$$\frac{x{:}\sigma \in \Gamma}{\Gamma \vdash_{hm} x : \sigma}\text{HM\_VAR} \qquad \frac{\Gamma, x{:}\tau_1 \vdash_{hm} e : \tau_2}{\Gamma \vdash_{hm} \lambda x.\, e : \tau_1 \to \tau_2}\text{HM\_ABS}$$

$$\frac{\Gamma \vdash_{hm} e_1 : \tau_1 \to \tau_2 \qquad \Gamma \vdash_{hm} e_2 : \tau_1}{\Gamma \vdash_{hm} e_1\, e_2 : \tau_2}\text{HM\_APP} \qquad \frac{}{\Gamma \vdash_{hm} n : \mathit{Int}}\text{HM\_INT}$$

$$\frac{\Gamma \vdash_{hm} e_1 : \sigma_1 \qquad \Gamma, x{:}\sigma_1 \vdash_{hm} e_2 : \sigma_2}{\Gamma \vdash_{hm} \mathbf{let}\ x = e_1\ \mathbf{in}\ e_2 : \sigma_2}\text{HM\_LET}$$

$$\frac{\Gamma \vdash_{hm} e : \sigma \qquad a \notin ftv(\Gamma)}{\Gamma \vdash_{hm} e : \forall\{a\}.\sigma}\text{HM\_GEN} \qquad \frac{\Gamma \vdash_{hm} e : \sigma_1 \qquad \sigma_1 \leq_{hm} \sigma_2}{\Gamma \vdash_{hm} e : \sigma_2}\text{HM\_SUB}$$

$\boxed{\sigma_1 \leq_{hm} \sigma_2}$ HM subsumption

$$\frac{\tau_1[\overline{\tau}/\overline{a}_1] = \tau_2 \qquad \overline{a}_2 \notin ftv(\forall\{\overline{a}_1\}.\, \tau_1)}{\forall\{\overline{a}_1\}.\, \tau_1 \leq_{hm} \forall\{\overline{a}_2\}.\, \tau_2}\text{HM\_INSTG}$$

$\boxed{\Gamma \vdash_{hmv} e : \sigma}$ Extra typing rules for System HMV

$$\frac{\Gamma \vdash \tau \qquad \Gamma \vdash_{hmv} e : \forall a.\, \upsilon}{\Gamma \vdash_{hmv} e\, @\tau : \upsilon[\tau/a]}\text{HMV\_TAPP} \qquad \frac{\Gamma \vdash \upsilon \qquad \upsilon = \forall \overline{a}, \overline{b}.\, \tau \qquad \Gamma, \overline{a} \vdash_{hmv} e : \tau \qquad \overline{a}, \overline{b} \notin ftv(\Gamma)}{\Gamma \vdash_{hmv} (\Lambda \overline{a}.e : \upsilon) : \upsilon}\text{HMV\_ANNOT}$$

$\boxed{\sigma_1 \leq_{hmv} \sigma_2}$ HMV subsumption

$$\frac{\tau_1[\overline{\tau}/\overline{b}] = \tau_2}{\forall \overline{a}, \overline{b}.\, \tau_1 \leq_{hmv} \forall \overline{a}.\, \tau_2}\text{HMV\_INSTS} \qquad \frac{\upsilon_1[\overline{\tau}/\overline{a}_1] \leq_{hmv} \upsilon_2 \qquad \overline{a}_2 \notin ftv(\forall\{\overline{a}_1\}.\, \upsilon_1)}{\forall\{\overline{a}_1\}.\, \upsilon_1 \leq_{hmv} \forall\{\overline{a}_2\}.\, \upsilon_2}\text{HMV\_INSTG}$$

$\boxed{\Gamma \vdash \upsilon}$ Type well-formedness

$$\frac{ftv(\upsilon) \subseteq \Gamma}{\Gamma \vdash \upsilon}\text{TY\_SCOPED}$$

Fig. 4. Typing rules for Systems HM and HMV

The grammar of System HMV appears in Fig. 3. The type language is enhanced with a new intermediate form υ that quantifies over an ordered list of type variables. (We sometimes write $\forall a. \forall b.\, \tau$ as $\forall a, b.\, \tau$.) This form sits between type schemes and monotypes; σs contain υs, which then contain τs.[10] Thus the full form of a type scheme σ can be written as $\forall\{\overline{a}\}, \overline{b}.\, \tau$, including both a set of

[10] The grammar for System HMV redefines several metavariables. These metavariables then have (slightly) different meanings in different sections of this paper, but disambiguation should be clear from context. In analysis relating systems with different grammars (for example, in Lemma 1), the more restrictive grammar takes precedence.

$\forall\{a,b\}.\,a \to b \leq_{\mathsf{hmv}} \forall\{a\}.\,a \to a$	Works the same as $\leq_{\mathsf{hm}}$ for type schemes
$\forall a,b.\,a \to b \leq_{\mathsf{hmv}} \mathit{Int} \to \mathit{Int}$	Can instantiate specified vars
$\forall a,b.\,a \to b \leq_{\mathsf{hmv}} \forall a.\,a \to \mathit{Int}$	Can instantiate only a *tail* of the specified vars
$\forall a,b.\,a \to b \leq_{\mathsf{hmv}} \forall\{a,b\}.\,a \to b$	Variables can be regeneralized
$\forall a,b.\,a \to b \leq_{\mathsf{hmv}} \forall\{b\}.\,\mathit{Int} \to b$	Right-to-left nature of HMV_INSTS forces regeneralization
$\forall a,b.\,a \to b \not\leq_{\mathsf{hmv}} \forall b.\,\mathit{Int} \to b$	Known vars are instantiated from the right, never the left
$\forall\{a\}.\,a \to a \not\leq_{\mathsf{hmv}} \forall a.\,a \to a$	Specified quantification is more general than generalized quantification

Fig. 5. Examples of HMV subsumption relation

generalized variables $\{\overline{a}\}$ and a list of specified variables $\overline{b}$. Note that order never matters for generalized variables (they are in a set) while order does certainly matter for specified variables (the list specifies their order). We say that υ is the metavariable for *specified polytypes*, distinct from *type schemes* σ.

Expressions in HMV include two new forms: $e\,@\tau$ instantiates a specified type variable with a monotype τ, while $(\Lambda\overline{a}.e : \upsilon)$ allows us to annotate an expression with its type, potentially binding scoped type variables if the type is polymorphic. Requiring a type annotation in concert with scoped type variable binding ensures that the order of quantification is specified: the type annotation is a specified polytype υ. We do not allow annotation by type schemes σ: if the user writes the type, all quantified variables are considered specified.

Typing contexts Γ in HMV are enhanced with the ability to store type variables. This feature is used to implement scoped type variables, where the type variables $\overline{a}$, bound in $\Lambda\overline{a}.e$, are available for use in types occurring within e.

Typing Rules. The type system of HMV includes all of the rules of HM plus the new rules and relation shown at the bottom of Fig. 4. The HMV rules inherited from System HM are modified to recur back to System HMV relations: in effect, replace all hm subscripts with hmv subscripts. Note, in particular, rule HM_SUB; in System HMV, this rule refers to the $\sigma_1 \leq_{\mathsf{hmv}} \sigma_2$ relation, described below.

The most important addition to this type system is HMV_TAPP, which enables visible type application when the type of the expression is quantified over a specified type variable.

A type annotation $(\Lambda\overline{a}.e : \upsilon)$, typed with HMV_ANNOT, allows an expression to be assigned a specified polytype. We require the specified polytype to have the form $\forall\overline{a},\overline{b}.\,\tau$; that is, a prefix of the specified polytype's quantified variables must be the type variables scoped in the expression.[11] The inner expression e is then checked at type τ, with the type variables $\overline{a}$ (but not the $\overline{b}$) in scope. Types that appear in expressions (such as in type annotations and explicit type applications) may mention only type variables that are currently in scope.

[11] Note that the Barendregt convention allows bound variables to α-vary, so only the number of scoped type variables is important.

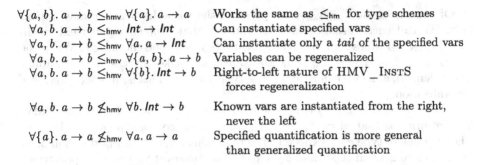

Of course, in the $\Gamma, \overline{a} \vdash_{\mathsf{hmv}} e : \tau$ premise, the variables $\overline{a}$ and $\overline{b}$ may appear in τ. We call such variables *skolems* and say that *skolemizing* υ yields τ. In effect, these variables form new type constants when type-checking e. When the expression e has type τ, we know that e cannot make any assumptions about the skolems $\overline{a}, \overline{b}$, so we can assign e the type $\forall \overline{a}, \overline{b}.\, \tau$. This is, in effect, *specified* generalization.

The relation $\sigma_1 \leq_{\mathsf{hmv}} \sigma_2$ (Fig. 4) implements subsumption for System HMV. The intuition is that, if $\sigma_1 \leq_{\mathsf{hmv}} \sigma_2$, then an expression of type σ_1 can be used wherever one of type σ_2 is expected. For type schemes, the standard notion of σ_1 being a more general type than σ_2 is sufficient. However for specified polytypes, we must be more cautious.

Suppose an expression $x \; @\tau_1 \; @\tau_2$ type checks, where x has type $\forall a, b.\, \upsilon_1$. The subsumption rule means that we can arbitrarily change the type of x to some υ, as long as $\upsilon \leq_{\mathsf{hmv}} \forall a, b.\, \upsilon_1$. Therefore, υ must be of the form $\forall a, b.\, \upsilon_2$ so that $x \; @\tau_1 \; @\tau_2$ will continue to instantiate a with τ_1 and b with τ_2. Accordingly, we cannot, say, allow subsumption to reorder specified variables.

However, it is safe to allow *some* instantiation of specified variables as part of subsumption, as in rule HMV_INSTS. Examine this rule closely: it instantiates variables *from the right*. This odd-looking design choice is critical. Continuing the example above, υ could also be of the form $\forall a, b, c.\, \upsilon_3$. In this case, the additional specified variable c causes no trouble – it need not be instantiated by a visible application. But we cannot allow instantiation *left-to-right* as that would allow the visible type arguments to skip instantiating a or b.

Further examples illustrating $\leq_{\mathsf{hmv}}$ appear in Fig. 5.

4.3 Properties of System HMV

We wish System HMV to be a conservative extension of System HM. That is, any expression that is well-typed in HM should remain well-typed in HMV, and any expression not well-typed in HM (but written in the HM subset of HMV) should also not be well-typed in HMV.

Lemma 1 (Conservative Extension for HMV). *Suppose Γ and e are both expressible in HM; that is, they do not include any type instantiations, type annotations, scoped type variables, or specified polytypes. Then, $\Gamma \vdash_{\mathsf{hm}} e : \sigma$ if and only if $\Gamma \vdash_{\mathsf{hmv}} e : \sigma$.*

This property follows directly from the definition of HMV as an extension of HM. Note, in particular, that no HM typing rule is changed in HMV and that the $\leq_{\mathsf{hmv}}$ relation contains $\leq_{\mathsf{hm}}$; furthermore, the new rules all require constructs not found in HM.

We also wish to know that making generalized variables into specified variables does not disrupt types:

Lemma 2 (Extra knowledge is harmless). *If $\Gamma, x{:}\forall\{\overline{a}\}.\, \tau \vdash_{\mathsf{hmv}} e : \sigma$, then $\Gamma, x{:}\forall \overline{a}.\, \tau \vdash_{\mathsf{hmv}} e : \sigma$.*

This property follows directly from the context generalization lemma below, noting that $\forall \overline{a}.\, \tau \leq_{\mathsf{hmv}} \forall\{\overline{a}\}.\, \tau$.

Lemma 3 (Context generalization for HMV). *If $\Gamma \vdash_{\mathsf{hmv}} e : \sigma$ and $\Gamma' \leq_{\mathsf{hmv}} \Gamma$, then $\Gamma' \vdash_{\mathsf{hmv}} e : \sigma$.*

This lemma is proved in the extended version [12].

In practical terms, Lemma 2 means that if an expression contains **let** $x = e_1$ **in** e_2, and the programmer figures out the type assigned to x (say, $\forall\{\overline{a}\}.\,\tau$) and then includes that type in an annotation (as **let** $x = (e_1 : \forall\overline{a}.\,\tau)$ **in** e_2), the outer expression's type does not then change.

However, note that, by design, context generalization is not as flexible for specified polytypes as it is for type schemes. In other words, suppose the following expression type-checks.

$$\mathbf{let}\ x = ((\lambda y \to y) :: \forall\ a\ b.\ (a, b) \to (a, b))\ \mathbf{in}\ \ldots$$

The programmer cannot then replace the type annotation with the type $\forall\ a.\ a \to a$, because x may be used with visible type applications. This behavior may be surprising, but it follows directly from the fact that $\forall\ a.\ a \to a \not\leq_{\mathsf{hmv}} \forall\ a\ b.\ (a, b) \to (a, b)$.

Finally, we would also like to show that HMV retains the principal types property, defined with respect to the enhanced subsumption relation $\sigma_1 \leq_{\mathsf{hmv}} \sigma_2$.

Theorem 4 (Principal types for HMV). *For all terms e well-typed in a context Γ, there exists a type scheme σ_{p} such that $\Gamma \vdash_{\mathsf{hmv}} e : \sigma_{\mathrm{p}}$ and, for all σ such that $\Gamma \vdash_{\mathsf{hmv}} e : \sigma$, $\sigma_{\mathrm{p}} \leq_{\mathsf{hmv}} \sigma$.*

Before we can prove this, we first must show how to extend HM's type inference algorithm (Algorithm $\mathcal{W}$ [8]) to include visible type application. Once we do so, we can prove that this new algorithm always computes principal types.

5 Syntax-Directed Versions of HM and HMV

The type systems in the previous section declare when programs are well-formed, but they are fairly far removed from an algorithm. In particular, the rules HM_Gen and HM_Sub can appear at any point in a typing derivation.

5.1 System C

We can explain the HM type system in a more algorithmic manner by using a syntax-directed specification, called System C, in Fig. 6. This version of the type system, derived from Clément et al. [5], clarifies exactly where generalization and instantiation occur during type checking. Notably, instantiation occurs only at the usage of a variable, and generalization occurs only at a **let**-binding. These rules are syntax-directed because the conclusion of each rule in the main judgment $\Gamma \vdash_{\mathsf{c}} e : \tau$ is syntactically distinct. Thus, from the shape of an expression, we can determine the shape of its typing derivation.

However, the judgment $\Gamma \vdash_{\mathsf{c}} e : \tau$ is still not quite an algorithm: it makes nondeterministic guesses. For example, in the rule C_Abs, the type τ_1 is guessed;

$\boxed{\Gamma \vdash_{\mathsf{c}} e : \tau}$ Typing rules for System C

$$\frac{x{:}\forall\{\overline{a}\}.\,\tau \in \Gamma}{\Gamma \vdash_{\mathsf{c}} x : \tau[\overline{\tau}/\overline{a}]}\,\text{C\_VAR} \qquad \frac{\Gamma, x{:}\tau_1 \vdash_{\mathsf{c}} e : \tau_2}{\Gamma \vdash_{\mathsf{c}} \lambda x.\, e : \tau_1 \rightarrow \tau_2}\,\text{C\_ABS}$$

$$\frac{\Gamma \vdash_{\mathsf{c}} e_1 : \tau_1 \rightarrow \tau_2 \qquad \Gamma \vdash_{\mathsf{c}} e_2 : \tau_1}{\Gamma \vdash_{\mathsf{c}} e_1\, e_2 : \tau_2}\,\text{C\_APP} \qquad \frac{}{\Gamma \vdash_{\mathsf{c}} n : \mathsf{Int}}\,\text{C\_INT}$$

$$\frac{\Gamma \vdash^{gen}_{\mathsf{c}} e_1 : \sigma \qquad \Gamma, x{:}\sigma \vdash_{\mathsf{c}} e_2 : \tau_2}{\Gamma \vdash_{\mathsf{c}} \mathbf{let}\ x = e_1\ \mathbf{in}\ e_2 : \tau_2}\,\text{C\_LET}$$

$\boxed{\Gamma \vdash^{gen}_{\mathsf{c}} e : \sigma}$ Generalization for System C

$$\frac{\overline{a} = \mathit{ftv}(\tau) \setminus \mathit{ftv}(\Gamma) \qquad \Gamma \vdash_{\mathsf{c}} e : \tau}{\Gamma \vdash^{gen}_{\mathsf{c}} e : \forall\{\overline{a}\}.\,\tau}\,\text{C\_GEN}$$

Fig. 6. Syntax-directed version of the HM type system

there is no indication in the expression what the choice for τ_1 should be. The advantage of studying a syntax-directed system such as System C is that doing so separates concerns: System C fixes the structure of the typing derivation (and of any implementation) while leaving monotype-guessing as a separate problem. Algorithm $\mathcal{W}$ deduces the monotypes via unification, but a constraint-based approach [25,27] would also work.

5.2 System V: Syntax-Directed Visible Types

Just as System C is a syntax-directed version of HM, we can also define System V, a syntax-directed version of HMV (Fig. 7). However, although we could define HMV by a small addition to HM (two new rules, plus subsumption), the difference between System C and System V is more significant.

Like System C, System V uses multiple judgments to restrict where generalization and instantiation can occur. In particular, the system allows an expression to have a type scheme only as a result of generalization (using the judgment $\Gamma \vdash^{gen}_{\mathsf{v}} e : \sigma$). Generalization is, once again, available only in **let**-expressions.

However, the main difference that enables visible type annotation is the separation of the main typing judgment into two: $\Gamma \vdash_{\mathsf{v}} e : \tau$ and $\Gamma \vdash^{*}_{\mathsf{v}} e : \upsilon$. The key idea is that, sometimes, we need to be lazy about instantiating specified type variables so that the programmer has a chance to add a visible instantiation. Therefore, the system splits the rules into a judgment $\vdash_{\mathsf{v}}$ that requires e to have a monotype, and those in $\vdash^{*}_{\mathsf{v}}$ that can retain specified quantification.

The first set of rules in Fig. 7, as in System C, infers a monotype for the expression. The premises of the rule V_ABS uses this same judgment, for example, to require that the body of an abstraction have a monotype. All expressions can be assigned a monotype; if the first three rules do not apply, the last rule V_INSTS infers a polytype instead, then instantiates it to yield a monotype. Because implicit instantiation happens all at once in this rule, we do not need

$\boxed{\Gamma \vdash_{\mathsf{v}} e : \tau}$ Monotype checking for System V

$$\frac{\Gamma, x{:}\tau_1 \vdash_{\mathsf{v}} e : \tau_2}{\Gamma \vdash_{\mathsf{v}} \lambda x.\, e : \tau_1 \to \tau_2}\text{V\_Abs} \qquad \frac{\Gamma \vdash_{\mathsf{v}} e_1 : \tau_1 \to \tau_2 \qquad \Gamma \vdash_{\mathsf{v}} e_2 : \tau_1}{\Gamma \vdash_{\mathsf{v}} e_1\, e_2 : \tau_2}\text{V\_App}$$

$$\frac{}{\Gamma \vdash_{\mathsf{v}} n : \mathit{Int}}\text{V\_Int} \qquad \frac{\Gamma \vdash^{*}_{\mathsf{v}} e : \forall \overline{a}.\, \tau \quad \text{no other rule matches}}{\Gamma \vdash_{\mathsf{v}} e : \tau[\overline{\tau}/\overline{a}]}\text{V\_InstS}$$

$\boxed{\Gamma \vdash^{*}_{\mathsf{v}} e : \upsilon}$ Specified polytype checking for System V

$$\frac{x{:}\forall\{\overline{a}\}.\,\upsilon \in \Gamma}{\Gamma \vdash^{*}_{\mathsf{v}} x : \upsilon[\overline{\tau}/\overline{a}]}\text{V\_Var} \qquad \frac{\Gamma \vdash^{gen}_{\mathsf{v}} e_1 : \sigma_1 \qquad \Gamma, x{:}\sigma_1 \vdash^{*}_{\mathsf{v}} e_2 : \upsilon_2}{\Gamma \vdash^{*}_{\mathsf{v}} \textbf{let}\, x = e_1 \,\textbf{in}\, e_2 : \upsilon_2}\text{V\_Let}$$

$$\frac{\Gamma \vdash \tau \quad \Gamma \vdash^{*}_{\mathsf{v}} e : \forall a.\, \upsilon}{\Gamma \vdash^{*}_{\mathsf{v}} e\,@\tau : \upsilon[\tau/a]}\text{V\_TApp} \qquad \frac{\Gamma \vdash \upsilon \qquad \upsilon = \forall \overline{a}, \overline{b}.\, \tau \quad \Gamma, \overline{a} \vdash_{\mathsf{v}} e : \tau \qquad \overline{a}, \overline{b} \notin \mathit{ftv}(\Gamma)}{\Gamma \vdash^{*}_{\mathsf{v}} (\Lambda\overline{a}.e : \upsilon) : \upsilon}\text{V\_Annot}$$

$$\frac{\Gamma \vdash_{\mathsf{v}} e : \tau \quad \text{no other rule matches}}{\Gamma \vdash^{*}_{\mathsf{v}} e : \tau}\text{V\_Mono}$$

$\boxed{\Gamma \vdash^{gen}_{\mathsf{v}} e : \sigma}$ Generalization for System V

$$\frac{\overline{a} = \mathit{ftv}(\upsilon) \setminus \mathit{ftv}(\Gamma) \qquad \Gamma \vdash^{*}_{\mathsf{v}} e : \upsilon}{\Gamma \vdash^{gen}_{\mathsf{v}} e : \forall\{\overline{a}\}.\,\upsilon}\text{V\_Gen}$$

Fig. 7. Typing rules for System V

to worry about instantiating specified variables out of order, as we did in System HMV.

The second set of rules (the $\vdash^{*}_{\mathsf{v}}$ judgment) allows e to be assigned a specified polytype. Note that the premise of rule V_TApp uses this judgment.

Rule V_Var is like rule C_Var: both look up a variable in the environment and instantiate its generalized quantified variables. The difference is that C_Var's types can contain *only* generalized variables; System V's types can have specified variables after the generalized ones. Yet we instantiate only the generalized ones in the V_Var rule, lazily preserving the specified ones.

Rule V_Let is likewise similar to C_Let. The only difference is that the result type is not restricted to be a monotype. By putting V_Let in the $\vdash^{*}_{\mathsf{v}}$ judgment and returning a specified polytype, we allow the following judgment to hold:

$$\cdot \vdash_{\mathsf{v}} (\textbf{let}\, x = (\lambda y.\, y : \forall a.\, a \to a)\, \textbf{in}\, x)\,@\mathit{Int} : \mathit{Int} \to \mathit{Int}$$

The expression above would be ill-typed in a system that restricted the result of a **let**-expression to be a monotype. It is for this reason that we altered System HM to include a polytype in its HM_Let rule, for consistency with HMV.

Rule V_ANNOT is identical to rule HMV_ANNOT. It uses the $\vdash_{\mathsf{v}}$ judgment in its premise to force instantiation of all quantified type variables before regeneralizing to the specified polytype υ. In this way, the V_ANNOT rule is effectively able to reorder specified variables. Here, reordering is acceptable, precisely because it is user-directed.

Finally, if an expression form cannot yield a specified polytype, rule V_MONO delegates to $\vdash_{\mathsf{v}}$ to find a monotype for the expression.

5.3 Relating System V to System HMV

Systems HMV and V are equivalent; they type check the same set of expressions. We prove this correspondence using the following two theorems.

Theorem 5 (Soundness of V against HMV)

1. *If* $\Gamma \vdash_{\mathsf{v}} e : \tau$, *then* $\Gamma \vdash_{\overline{\mathsf{h}}\mathsf{mv}} e : \tau$.
2. *If* $\Gamma \vdash^{*}_{\mathsf{v}} e : \upsilon$, *then* $\Gamma \vdash_{\overline{\mathsf{h}}\mathsf{mv}} e : \upsilon$.
3. *If* $\Gamma \vdash^{gen}_{\mathsf{v}} e : \sigma$, *then* $\Gamma \vdash_{\overline{\mathsf{h}}\mathsf{mv}} e : \sigma$.

Theorem 6 (Completeness of V against HMV). *If* $\Gamma \vdash_{\overline{\mathsf{h}}\mathsf{mv}} e : \sigma$, *then there exists* σ' *such that* $\Gamma \vdash^{gen}_{\mathsf{v}} e : \sigma'$ *where* $\sigma' \leq_{\mathsf{hmv}} \sigma$.

The proofs of these theorems appear in the extended version [12].

Having established the equivalence of System V with System HMV, we can note that Lemma 2 ("Extra knowledge is harmless") carries over from HMV to V. This property is quite interesting in the context of System V. It says that a typing context where all type variables are specified admits all the same expressions as one where some type variables are generalized. In System V, however, specified and generalized variables are instantiated via different mechanisms, so this is a powerful theorem indeed.

It is mechanical to go from the statement of System V in Fig. 7 to an algorithm. In the extended version [12], we define Algorithm $\mathcal{V}$ which implements System V, analogous to Algorithm $\mathcal{W}$ which implements System C. We then prove that Algorithm $\mathcal{V}$ is sound and complete with respect to System V and that Algorithm $\mathcal{V}$ finds principal types. Linking the pieces together gives us the proof of the principal types property for System HMV (Theorem 4). Furthermore, Algorithm $\mathcal{V}$ is guaranteed to terminate, yielding this theorem:

Theorem 7. *Type-checking System V is decidable.*

6 Higher-Rank Type Systems

We now extend the design of System HMV to include *higher-rank polymorphism* [17]. This extension allows function parameters to be used at multiple types. Incorporating this extension is actually quite straightforward. We include this extension to show that our framework for visible type application is indeed easy to extend – the syntax-directed system we study in this section is essentially a merge of System V and the bidirectional system from our previous work [23]. This system is also the basis for our implementation in GHC.

As an example, the following function does not type check in the vanilla Hindley-Milner type system, assuming *id* has type $\forall\ a.\ a \rightarrow a$.

$$\textbf{let}\ foo = \lambda f \rightarrow (f\,3, f\ True)\ \textbf{in}\ foo\ id$$

Yet, with the `RankNTypes` language extension and the following type annotation, GHC is happy to accept

$$\begin{array}{l}\textbf{let}\ foo :: (\forall\ a.\ a \rightarrow a) \rightarrow (Int, Bool) \\ \quad\ foo = \lambda f \rightarrow (f\,3, f\ True) \\ \textbf{in}\ foo\ id\end{array}$$

Visible type application means that higher-rank arguments can also be explicitly instantiated. For example, we can instantiate lambda-bound identifiers:

$$\begin{array}{l}\textbf{let}\ foo :: (\forall\ a.\ a \rightarrow a) \rightarrow (Int \rightarrow Int, Bool) \\ \quad\ foo = \lambda f \rightarrow (f\,@Int, f\ True) \\ \textbf{in}\ foo\ id\end{array}$$

Higher-rank types also mean that visible instantiations can occur after other arguments are passed to a function. For example, consider this alternative type for the *pair* function:

$$\begin{array}{l}pair :: \forall\ a.\ a \rightarrow \forall\ b.\ b \rightarrow (a, b) \\ pair = \lambda x\ y \rightarrow (x, y)\end{array}$$

If *pair* has this type, we can instantiate *b* after providing the first component for the pair, thus:

$$\begin{array}{l}bar = pair\ \texttt{'x'}\ @Bool \\ \quad \text{-- } bar \text{ inferred to have type } Bool \rightarrow (Char, Bool)\end{array}$$

In the rest of this section, we provide the technical details of these language features and discuss their interactions. In contrast to the presentation above, we present the syntax-directed higher-rank system first. We do so for two reasons: understanding a bidirectional system requires thinking about syntax, and thus the syntax-directed system seems easier to understand; and we view the declarative system as an expression of properties – or a set a metatheorems – about the higher-rank type system.

6.1 System SB: Syntax-Directed Bidirectional Type Checking

Figures 8 and 9 show System SB, the higher-rank, bidirectional analogue of System V, supporting predicative higher-rank polymorphism and visible type application.

This system shares the same expression language of Systems HMV and V, retaining visible type application and type annotations. However, types in System SB may have non-prenex quantification. The body of a specified polytype

The grammar for SB extends that for System HMV (Fig. 3):

$e ::= \dots$	expressions	$\rho ::= \tau \mid \upsilon_1 \to \rho_2$	rho-types
$\tau ::= \dots$	monotypes	$\phi ::= \tau \mid \upsilon_1 \to \upsilon_2$	phi-types
$\Gamma ::= \cdot \mid \Gamma, x{:}\sigma \mid \Gamma, a$	contexts	$\upsilon ::= \phi \mid \forall a.\, \upsilon$	specified polytypes
		$\sigma ::= \upsilon \mid \forall \{a\}.\, \sigma$	type schemes

$\boxed{\Gamma \vdash_{\mathsf{sb}} e \Rightarrow \phi}$ Synthesis of types without top-level quantifiers

$$\frac{\Gamma, x{:}\tau \vdash^{*}_{\mathsf{sb}} e \Rightarrow \upsilon}{\Gamma \vdash_{\mathsf{sb}} \lambda x.\, e \Rightarrow \tau \to \upsilon}\text{SB\_ABS} \qquad \frac{\Gamma \vdash^{*}_{\mathsf{sb}} e \Rightarrow \forall \overline{a}.\, \phi \quad \text{no other rule matches}}{\Gamma \vdash_{\mathsf{sb}} e \Rightarrow \phi[\overline{\tau}/\overline{a}]}\text{SB\_INSTS}$$

$$\frac{}{\Gamma \vdash_{\mathsf{sb}} n \Rightarrow \mathit{Int}}\text{SB\_INT}$$

$\boxed{\Gamma \vdash^{*}_{\mathsf{sb}} e \Rightarrow \upsilon}$ Synthesis of specified polytypes

$$\frac{x{:}\forall\{\overline{a}\}.\, \upsilon \in \Gamma}{\Gamma \vdash^{*}_{\mathsf{sb}} x \Rightarrow \upsilon[\overline{\tau}/\overline{a}]}\text{SB\_VAR} \qquad \frac{\Gamma \vdash_{\mathsf{sb}} e_1 \Rightarrow \upsilon_1 \to \upsilon_2 \quad \Gamma \vdash^{*}_{\mathsf{sb}} e_2 \Leftarrow \upsilon_1}{\Gamma \vdash^{*}_{\mathsf{sb}} e_1\ e_2 \Rightarrow \upsilon_2}\text{SB\_APP}$$

$$\frac{\Gamma \vdash \tau \quad \Gamma \vdash^{*}_{\mathsf{sb}} e \Rightarrow \forall a.\, \upsilon}{\Gamma \vdash^{*}_{\mathsf{sb}} e\, @\tau \Rightarrow \upsilon[\tau/a]}\text{SB\_TAPP} \qquad \frac{\Gamma \vdash \upsilon \quad \upsilon = \forall \overline{a}, \overline{b}.\, \phi \quad \Gamma, \overline{a} \vdash^{*}_{\mathsf{sb}} e \Leftarrow \phi \quad \overline{a}, \overline{b} \notin \mathit{ftv}(\Gamma)}{\Gamma \vdash^{*}_{\mathsf{sb}} (\Lambda \overline{a}.e : \upsilon) \Rightarrow \upsilon}\text{SB\_ANNOT}$$

$$\frac{\Gamma \vdash^{gen}_{\mathsf{sb}} e_1 \Rightarrow \sigma_1 \quad \Gamma, x{:}\sigma_1 \vdash^{*}_{\mathsf{sb}} e_2 \Rightarrow \upsilon_2}{\Gamma \vdash^{*}_{\mathsf{sb}} \mathbf{let}\ x = e_1\ \mathbf{in}\ e_2 \Rightarrow \upsilon_2}\text{SB\_LET} \qquad \frac{\Gamma \vdash_{\mathsf{sb}} e \Rightarrow \phi \quad \text{no other rule matches}}{\Gamma \vdash^{*}_{\mathsf{sb}} e \Rightarrow \phi}\text{SB\_PHI}$$

$\boxed{\Gamma \vdash^{gen}_{\mathsf{sb}} e \Rightarrow \sigma}$ Synthesis with generalization

$$\frac{\Gamma \vdash^{*}_{\mathsf{sb}} e \Rightarrow \upsilon \quad \overline{a} = \mathit{ftv}(\upsilon) \setminus \mathit{ftv}(\Gamma)}{\Gamma \vdash^{gen}_{\mathsf{sb}} e \Rightarrow \forall\{\overline{a}\}.\, \upsilon}\text{SB\_GEN}$$

$\boxed{\Gamma \vdash_{\mathsf{sb}} e \Leftarrow \rho}$ Checking against types without top-level quantifiers

$$\frac{\Gamma \vdash^{gen}_{\mathsf{sb}} e_1 \Rightarrow \sigma_1 \quad \Gamma, x{:}\sigma_1 \vdash_{\mathsf{sb}} e_2 \Leftarrow \rho_2}{\Gamma \vdash_{\mathsf{sb}} \mathbf{let}\ x = e_1\ \mathbf{in}\ e_2 \Leftarrow \rho_2}\text{SB\_DLET}$$

$$\frac{\Gamma, x{:}\upsilon_1 \vdash^{*}_{\mathsf{sb}} e \Leftarrow \rho_2}{\Gamma \vdash_{\mathsf{sb}} \lambda x.\, e \Leftarrow \upsilon_1 \to \rho_2}\text{SB\_DABS} \qquad \frac{\Gamma \vdash^{*}_{\mathsf{sb}} e \Rightarrow \upsilon_1 \quad \upsilon_1 \leq_{\mathsf{dsk}} \rho_2 \quad \text{no other rule matches}}{\Gamma \vdash_{\mathsf{sb}} e \Leftarrow \rho_2}\text{SB\_INFER}$$

$\boxed{\Gamma \vdash^{*}_{\mathsf{sb}} e \Leftarrow \upsilon}$ Checking against specified polytypes

$$\frac{\mathit{prenex}(\upsilon) = \forall \overline{a}.\, \rho \quad \overline{a} \notin \mathit{ftv}(\Gamma) \quad \Gamma \vdash_{\mathsf{sb}} e \Leftarrow \rho}{\Gamma \vdash^{*}_{\mathsf{sb}} e \Leftarrow \upsilon}\text{SB\_DEEPSKOL}$$

Fig. 8. Syntax-directed bidirectional type system

$\boxed{\sigma_1 \leq_{\mathsf{b}} \sigma_2}$ **Higher-rank instantiation**

$$\frac{}{\tau \leq_{\mathsf{b}} \tau}\text{B\_REFL} \qquad \frac{\upsilon_3 \leq_{\mathsf{b}} \upsilon_1 \qquad \upsilon_2 \leq_{\mathsf{b}} \upsilon_4}{\upsilon_1 \to \upsilon_2 \leq_{\mathsf{b}} \upsilon_3 \to \upsilon_4}\text{B\_FUN}$$

$$\frac{\phi_1[\overline{\tau}/\overline{b}] \leq_{\mathsf{b}} \phi_2}{\forall \overline{a}, \overline{b}.\, \phi_1 \leq_{\mathsf{b}} \forall \overline{a}.\, \phi_2}\text{B\_INSTS} \qquad \frac{\upsilon_1[\overline{\tau}/\overline{a}] \leq_{\mathsf{b}} \upsilon_2 \qquad \overline{b} \notin \mathit{ftv}(\forall\{\overline{a}\}.\, \upsilon_1)}{\forall\{\overline{a}\}.\, \upsilon_1 \leq_{\mathsf{b}} \forall\{\overline{b}\}.\, \upsilon_2}\text{B\_INSTG}$$

$\boxed{\phi_1 \leq^*_{\mathsf{dsk}} \rho_2}$ **Subsumption, after deep skolemization**

$$\frac{}{\tau \leq^*_{\mathsf{dsk}} \tau}\text{DSK\_REFL} \qquad \frac{\upsilon_3 \leq_{\mathsf{dsk}} \upsilon_1 \qquad \upsilon_2 \leq_{\mathsf{dsk}} \rho_4}{\upsilon_1 \to \upsilon_2 \leq^*_{\mathsf{dsk}} \upsilon_3 \to \rho_4}\text{DSK\_FUN}$$

$\boxed{\sigma_1 \leq_{\mathsf{dsk}} \upsilon_2}$ **Deep skolemization**

$$\frac{\mathit{prenex}(\upsilon_2) = \forall \overline{c}.\, \rho_2 \qquad \phi_1[\overline{\tau}/\overline{a}][\overline{\tau}'/\overline{b}] \leq^*_{\mathsf{dsk}} \rho_2}{\forall\{\overline{a}\}, \overline{b}.\, \phi_1 \leq_{\mathsf{dsk}} \upsilon_2}\text{DSK\_INST}$$

Define $\mathit{prenex}(\upsilon) = \forall \overline{a}.\, \rho$ as follows:

$$\begin{aligned}
\mathit{prenex}(\forall \overline{a}.\, \tau) &= \forall \overline{a}.\, \tau \\
\mathit{prenex}(\forall \overline{a}.\, \upsilon_1 \to \upsilon_2) &= \forall \overline{a}, \overline{b}.\, \upsilon_1 \to \rho_2 \\
\text{where } \forall \overline{b}.\, \rho_2 &= \mathit{prenex}(\upsilon_2)
\end{aligned}$$

Examples:

$\forall a.\, a \to \forall b.\, b \to b \leq_{\mathsf{b}} \mathit{Int} \to \mathit{Bool} \to \mathit{Bool}$	Can instantiate non-top-level vars
$\forall a.\, a \to \forall b.\, b \to b \leq_{\mathsf{b}} \mathit{Int} \to \forall b.\, b \to b$	Not all vars must be instantiated
$\forall a.\, a \to \forall b.\, b \to b \leq_{\mathsf{b}} \forall a.\, a \to \mathit{Bool} \to \mathit{Bool}$	Can skip a top-level quantifier
$(\mathit{Int} \to \mathit{Int}) \to \mathit{Bool} \leq_{\mathsf{b}} (\forall a.\, a \to a) \to \mathit{Bool}$	Contravariant instantiation
$\mathit{Int} \to \forall a, b.\, a \to b \not\leq_{\mathsf{b}} \mathit{Int} \to \forall b.\, \mathit{Bool} \to b$	Spec. vars are inst'd from the right
$\mathit{Int} \to \forall a.\, a \to a \not\leq_{\mathsf{b}} \forall a.\, \mathit{Int} \to a \to a$	Cannot move $\forall$ for spec. vars
$\mathit{Int} \to \forall a, b.\, a \to b \leq_{\mathsf{dsk}} \mathit{Int} \to \forall b.\, \mathit{Bool} \to b$	$\leq_{\mathsf{dsk}}$ can inst. spec. vars in any order
$\mathit{Int} \to \forall a.\, a \to a \leq_{\mathsf{dsk}} \forall a.\, \mathit{Int} \to a \to a$	Spec. $\forall$ can move with $\leq_{\mathsf{dsk}}$
$(\mathit{Int} \to \forall b.\, b \to b) \to \mathit{Int} \leq_{\mathsf{dsk}} (\forall a, b.\, a \to b \to b) \to \mathit{Int}$	Contravariant out-of-order inst.
$\forall\{a\}.\, a \to a \leq_{\mathsf{dsk}} \forall a.\, a \to a$	Same handling of spec. and gen. vars

Fig. 9. Higher-rank subsumption relations

υ is now a *phi-type* ϕ: a type that has no top-level quantification but may have quantification to the left or to the right of arrows. Note also that these inner quantified types are υs, not σs. In other words, non-prenex quantification is over only *specified* variables, never generalized ones. As we will see, inner quantified types are introduced only by user annotation, and thus there is no way the system could produce an inner type scheme, even if the syntactic restriction were not in place.

The grammar also defines *rho-types* ρ, which also have no top-level quantification, but do allow inner quantification to the *left* of arrows. We convert specified polytypes (which may quantify to the right of arrows) to corresponding rho-types by means of the *prenex* operation, which appears in Fig. 9.

System SB is defined by five mutually recursive judgments: $\Gamma \vdash_{\mathsf{sb}} e \Rightarrow \phi$, $\Gamma \vdash^{*}_{\mathsf{sb}} e \Rightarrow \upsilon$, and $\Gamma \vdash^{gen}_{\mathsf{sb}} e \Rightarrow \sigma$ are synthesis judgments, producing the type as an output; $\Gamma \vdash_{\mathsf{sb}} e \Leftarrow \rho$ and $\Gamma \vdash^{*}_{\mathsf{sb}} e \Leftarrow \upsilon$ are checking judgments, requiring the type as an input.

Type Synthesis. The synthesis judgments are very similar to the judgments from System V, ignoring direction arrows. The differences stem from the non-prenex quantification allowed in SB. The level of similarity is unsurprising, as the previous systems essentially all work only in synthesis mode; they derive a type given an expression. The novelty of a bidirectional system is its ability to propagate information about specified polytypes toward the leaves of an expression.

Type Checking. Rule SB_DAbs is what makes the system higher-rank. The checking judgment $\Gamma \vdash_{\mathsf{sb}} e \Leftarrow \rho$ pushes in a rho-type, with no top-level quantification. Thus, SB_DAbs can recognize an arrow type $\upsilon_1 \to \rho_2$. Propagating this type into an expression $\lambda x.\ e$, SB_DAbs uses the type υ_1 as x's type when checking e. This is the only place in system SB where a lambda-term can abstract over a variable with a polymorphic type. Note that the synthesis rule SB_Abs uses a monotype for the type of x.[12]

Rule SB_Infer mediates between the checking and synthesis judgments. When no checking rule applies, we synthesize a type and then check it according to the $\leq_{\mathsf{dsk}}$ deep skolemization relation, taken directly from previous work and shown in Fig. 9. For brevity, we do not explain the details of this relation here, instead referring readers to Peyton Jones et al. [23, Sect. 4.6] for much deeper discussion. However, we note that there is a design choice to be made here; we could have also used Odersky–Läufer's slightly less expressive higher-rank subsumption relation [21] instead. We present the system with deep skolemization for backwards compatibility with GHC. See the extended version [12] for a discussion of this alternative.

The entry point into the type checking judgments is through the $\Gamma \vdash^{*}_{\mathsf{sb}} e \Leftarrow \upsilon$ judgment. This judgment has just one rule, SB_DeepSkol. The rule skolemizes all type variables appearing at the top-level and to the right of arrows. Skolemizing here is necessary to expose a rho-type to the $\Gamma \vdash_{\mathsf{sb}} e \Leftarrow \rho$ judgment, so that rule SB_DAbs can fire.[13] The reason this rule requires deep skolemization

[12] Higher-rank systems can also include an "annotated abstraction" form, $\lambda x{:}\upsilon.\ e$. This form allows higher-rank types to be synthesized for lambda expressions as well as checked. However, this form is straightforward to add but is not part of GHC, which uses patterns (beyond the scope of this paper) to bind variables in abstractions. Therefore we omit the annotated abstraction form from our formalism.

[13] Our choice to skolemize before SB_DLet is arbitrary, as SB_DLet does not interact with the propagated type.

$\boxed{\Gamma \vdash_{\mathsf{b}} e \Rightarrow \sigma}$ Synthesis rules for System B

$$\frac{x{:}\sigma \in \Gamma}{\Gamma \vdash_{\mathsf{b}} x \Rightarrow \sigma}\text{B\_VAR} \qquad \frac{\Gamma, x{:}\tau \vdash_{\mathsf{b}} e \Rightarrow \upsilon}{\Gamma \vdash_{\mathsf{b}} \lambda x.\, e \Rightarrow \tau \rightarrow \upsilon}\text{B\_ABS}$$

$$\frac{\Gamma \vdash_{\mathsf{b}} e_1 \Rightarrow \upsilon_1 \rightarrow \upsilon_2 \qquad \Gamma \vdash_{\mathsf{b}} e_2 \Leftarrow \upsilon_1}{\Gamma \vdash_{\mathsf{b}} e_1\, e_2 \Rightarrow \upsilon_2}\text{B\_APP} \qquad \frac{}{\Gamma \vdash_{\mathsf{b}} n \Rightarrow \mathsf{Int}}\text{B\_INT}$$

$$\frac{\Gamma \vdash_{\mathsf{b}} e_1 \Rightarrow \sigma_1 \qquad \Gamma, x{:}\sigma_1 \vdash_{\mathsf{b}} e_2 \Rightarrow \sigma}{\Gamma \vdash_{\mathsf{b}} \mathbf{let}\, x = e_1\, \mathbf{in}\, e_2 \Rightarrow \sigma}\text{B\_LET}$$

$$\frac{\Gamma \vdash_{\mathsf{b}} e \Rightarrow \sigma \qquad a \notin \mathit{ftv}(\Gamma)}{\Gamma \vdash_{\mathsf{b}} e \Rightarrow \forall\{a\}.\sigma}\text{B\_GEN} \qquad \frac{\Gamma \vdash_{\mathsf{b}} e \Rightarrow \sigma_1 \qquad \sigma_1 \leq_{\mathsf{b}} \sigma_2}{\Gamma \vdash_{\mathsf{b}} e \Rightarrow \sigma_2}\text{B\_SUB}$$

$$\frac{\Gamma \vdash \tau \qquad \Gamma \vdash_{\mathsf{b}} e \Rightarrow \forall a.\upsilon}{\Gamma \vdash_{\mathsf{b}} e\,@\tau \Rightarrow \upsilon[\tau/a]}\text{B\_TAPP} \qquad \frac{\Gamma \vdash \upsilon \qquad \upsilon = \forall\overline{a}, \overline{b}.\phi \qquad \Gamma, \overline{a} \vdash_{\mathsf{b}} e \Leftarrow \phi \qquad \overline{a}, \overline{b} \notin \mathit{ftv}(\Gamma)}{\Gamma \vdash_{\mathsf{b}} (\Lambda\overline{a}.e : \upsilon) \Rightarrow \upsilon}\text{B\_ANNOT}$$

$\boxed{\Gamma \vdash_{\mathsf{b}} e \Leftarrow \upsilon}$ Checking rules for System B

$$\frac{\Gamma, x{:}\upsilon_1 \vdash_{\mathsf{b}} e \Leftarrow \upsilon_2}{\Gamma \vdash_{\mathsf{b}} \lambda x.\, e \Leftarrow \upsilon_1 \rightarrow \upsilon_2}\text{B\_DABS} \qquad \frac{\Gamma \vdash_{\mathsf{b}} e_1 \Rightarrow \sigma_1 \qquad \Gamma, x{:}\sigma_1 \vdash_{\mathsf{b}} e_2 \Leftarrow \upsilon}{\Gamma \vdash_{\mathsf{b}} \mathbf{let}\, x = e_1\, \mathbf{in}\, e_2 \Leftarrow \upsilon}\text{B\_DLET}$$

$$\frac{\Gamma \vdash_{\mathsf{b}} e \Leftarrow \upsilon \qquad a \notin \mathit{ftv}(\Gamma)}{\Gamma \vdash_{\mathsf{b}} e \Leftarrow \forall a.\upsilon}\text{B\_SKOL} \qquad \frac{\Gamma \vdash_{\mathsf{b}} e \Rightarrow \sigma_1 \qquad \sigma_1 \leq_{\mathsf{dsk}} \upsilon_2}{\Gamma \vdash_{\mathsf{b}} e \Leftarrow \upsilon_2}\text{B\_INFER}$$

Fig. 10. System B

instead of top-level skolemization is subtle, but this choice is not due to visible type application or lazy instantiation; the same choice is made in prior work [23, ruleGEN2 of Fig. 8]. We refer readers to the extended version [12] for the details.

6.2 System B: Declarative Specification

Figure 10 shows the typing rules of System B, a declarative system that accepts the same programs as System SB. This declarative type system itself is a novel contribution of this work. (The systems presented in related work [10,21,23] are more similar to SB than to B.)

Although System B is *bidirectional*, it is also *declarative*. In particular, the use of generalization (B_GEN), subsumption (B_SUB), skolemization (B_SKOL), and mode switching (B_INFER), can happen arbitrarily in a typing derivation. Understanding what expressions are well-typed does not require knowing precisely when these operations take place.

The subsumption rule (B_SUB) in the synthesis judgment corresponds to HMV_SUB from HMV. However, the novel subsumption relation $\leq_{\mathsf{b}}$ used by this rule, shown at the top of Fig. 9, is *different* from the $\leq_{\mathsf{dsk}}$ deep skolemization relation used in System SB. This $\sigma_1 \leq_{\mathsf{b}} \sigma_2$ judgment extends the action of $\leq_{\mathsf{hmv}}$ to higher-rank types: in particular, it allows subsumption for generalized type variables (which can be quantified only at the top level) and instantiation (only) for specified type variables. We could say that this judgment enables *inner instantiation* because instantiations are not restricted to top level. See also the examples at the bottom of Fig. 9.

In contrast, rule B_INFER (in the checking judgment) uses the stronger of the two subsumption relations $\leq_{\mathsf{dsk}}$. This rule appears at precisely the spot in the derivation where a specified type from synthesis mode meets the specified type from checking mode. The relation $\leq_{\mathsf{dsk}}$ subsumes $\leq_{\mathsf{b}}$; that is, $\sigma_1 \leq_{\mathsf{b}} \upsilon_2$ implies $\sigma_1 \leq_{\mathsf{dsk}} \upsilon_2$.

Properties of System B and SB. We can show that Systems SB and B admit the same expressions.

Lemma 8 (Soundness of System SB)

1. *If* $\Gamma \vdash_{\mathsf{sb}} e \Rightarrow \phi$ *then* $\Gamma \vdash_{\mathsf{b}} e \Rightarrow \phi$.
2. *If* $\Gamma \vdash^{*}_{\mathsf{sb}} e \Rightarrow \upsilon$ *then* $\Gamma \vdash_{\mathsf{b}} e \Rightarrow \upsilon$.
3. *If* $\Gamma \vdash^{gen}_{\mathsf{sb}} e \Rightarrow \sigma$ *then* $\Gamma \vdash_{\mathsf{b}} e \Rightarrow \sigma$.
4. *If* $\Gamma \vdash^{*}_{\mathsf{sb}} e \Leftarrow \upsilon$ *then* $\Gamma \vdash_{\mathsf{b}} e \Leftarrow \upsilon$.
5. *If* $\Gamma \vdash_{\mathsf{sb}} e \Leftarrow \rho$ *then* $\Gamma \vdash_{\mathsf{b}} e \Leftarrow \rho$.

Lemma 9 (Completeness of System SB)

1. *If* $\Gamma \vdash_{\mathsf{b}} e \Rightarrow \sigma$ *then* $\Gamma \vdash^{gen}_{\mathsf{sb}} e \Rightarrow \sigma'$ *where* $\sigma' \leq_{\mathsf{b}} \sigma$.
2. *If* $\Gamma \vdash_{\mathsf{b}} e \Leftarrow \upsilon$ *then* $\Gamma \vdash^{*}_{\mathsf{sb}} e \Leftarrow \upsilon$.

What is the role of System B? In our experience, programmers tend to prefer the syntax-directed presentation of the system because that version is more algorithmic. As a result, it can be easier to understand why a program type checks (or doesn't) by reasoning about System SB.

However, the fact that System B is sound and complete with respect to System SB provides properties that we can use to reason about SB. The main difference between the two is that System B divides subsumption into two different relations. The weaker $\leq_{\mathsf{b}}$ can be used at any time during synthesis, but it can only instantiate (but not generalize) specified variables. The stronger $\leq_{\mathsf{dsk}}$ is used at only the check/synthesis boundary but can generalize and reorder specified variables.

The connection between the two systems tells us that B_SUB is *admissible* for SB. As a result, when refactoring code, we need not worry about precisely where a type is instantiated, as we see here that instantiation need not be determined syntactically.

Likewise, the proof also shows that System B (and System SB) is flexible with respect to the instantiation relation $\leq_{\mathsf{b}}$ in the context. As in System HMV, this result implies that making generalized variables into specified variables does not disrupt types.

Lemma 10 (Context Generalization). *Suppose* $\Gamma' \leq_{\mathsf{b}} \Gamma$.

1. *If* $\Gamma \vdash_{\mathsf{b}} e \Rightarrow \sigma$ *then there exists* $\sigma' \leq_{\mathsf{b}} \sigma$ *such that* $\Gamma' \vdash_{\mathsf{b}} e \Rightarrow \sigma'$.
2. *If* $\Gamma \vdash_{\mathsf{b}} e \Leftarrow \upsilon$ *and* $\upsilon \leq_{\mathsf{b}} \upsilon'$ *then* $\Gamma' \vdash_{\mathsf{b}} e \Leftarrow \upsilon'$.

Proofs of these properties appear in the extended version [12].

6.3 Integrating Visible Type Application with GHC

System SB is the direct inspiration for the type-checking algorithm used in our version of GHC enhanced with visible type application. It is remarkably straightforward to implement the system described here within GHC; accounting for the behavior around imported functions (Sect. 3.1) was the hardest part. The other interactions (the difference between this paper's scoped type variables and GHC's, how specified type variables work with type classes, etc.) are generally uninteresting; see the extended version [12] for further comments.

One pleasing synergy between visible type application and GHC concerns GHC's recent *partial type signature* feature [29]. This feature allows wildcards, written with an underscore, to appear in types; GHC infers the correct replacement for the wildcard. These work well in visible type applications, allowing the user to write @_ as a visible type argument where GHC can infer the argument. For example, if *f* has type $\forall\ a\ b.\ a \rightarrow b \rightarrow (a, b)$, then we can write *f* @_ @[*Int*] *True* [] to let GHC infer that *a* should be *Bool* but to visibly instantiate *b* to be [*Int*]. Getting partial type signatures to work in the new context of visible type applications required nothing more than hooking up the pieces.

7 Related Work and Conclusions

Explicit Type Arguments. The F# language [26] permits explicit type arguments in function applications and method invocations. These explicit arguments, typically mandatory, are used to resolve ambiguity in type-dependent operations. However, the properties of this feature have not been studied.

Implicit Arguments in Dependently-Typed Languages. Languages such as Coq [6], Agda [20], Idris [1] and Twelf [24] are not based on the HM type system, so their designs differ from Systems HMV and B. However, they do support invisible arguments. In these languages, an invisible argument is not necessarily a type; it could be any argument that can be inferred by the type checker.

Coq, Agda, and Idris require all quantification, including that for invisible arguments, to be specified by the user. These languages do not support generalization, i.e., automatically determining that an expression should quantify over an invisible argument (in addition to any visible ones). They differ in how they specify the visibility of arguments, yet all of them provide the ability to override an invisibility specification and provide such arguments visibly. These languages also provide a facility for *named* invisible arguments, allowing users to specify argument values by name instead of by position. This choice means that α-equivalent types are no longer fully interchangeable. Though we have not studied this possibility deeply, we conjecture that formally specifying a named-argument system would encounter many of the same subtleties (in particular, requiring two different subsumption relations in the metatheory) that we encountered with positional arguments.

Twelf, on the other hand, supports invisible arguments via generalization and visible arguments via specification. Although it is easy to convert between the two versions, there is no way to visibly provide an invisible argument as we have done. Instead, the user must rely on type annotations to control instantiations.

Specified vs. Generalized Variables. Dreyer and Blume's work on specifying ML's type system and inference algorithm in the presence of modules [9] introduces a separation of (what we call) specified and generalized variables. Their work focuses on the type parameters to ML functors, finding inconsistencies between the ML language specification and implementations. They conclude that the ML specification as written is hard to implement and propose a new one. Their work includes a type system that allows functors to have invisible arguments alongside their visible ones. This specification is easier to implement, as they demonstrate.

Their work has similarities to ours in the separation of classes of variables and the need to alter the specification to make type inference reasonable. Interestingly, they come from the opposite direction from ours, adding invisible arguments in a place where arguments previously were all visible. However, despite these surface similarities, we have not found a deeper connection between our work and theirs.

Predicative, Higher-Rank Type Systems. As we have already indicated, Systems B and SB are directly inspired by GHC's design for higher-rank types [23]. However, in this work we have redesigned the algorithm to use lazy instantiation and have made a distinction between specified polytypes and generalized polytypes. Furthermore, we have pushed the design further, providing a declarative specification for the type system.

Our work is also closely related to recent work on using a bidirectional type system for higher-rank polymorphism by Dunfield and Krishnaswami [10], called DK below. The closest relationship is between their declarative system (Fig. 4 in their paper) and our System SB (Fig. 8). The most significant difference is that the DK system never generalizes. All polymorphic types in their system are specified; functions must have a type annotation to be polymorphic. Consequently, DK uses a different algorithm for type checking than the one proposed in this work. Nevertheless, it defers instantiations of specified polymorphism, like our algorithm.

Our relation $\leq_{\mathsf{dsk}}$, which requires two specified polytypes, is similar to the DK subsumption relation. The DK version is slightly weaker as it does not use deep skolemization; but that difference is not important in this context. Another minor difference is that System SB uses the $\Gamma \vdash_{\mathsf{sb}} e \Rightarrow \phi$ judgment to syntactically guide instantiation whereas the the DK system uses a separate application judgment form. System B – and the metatheory of System SB – also includes implicit subsumption $\leq_{\mathsf{b}}$, which does not have an analogue in the DK system. A more extended comparison with the DK system appears in the extended version [12].

Conclusion. This work extends the HM type system with visible type application, while maintaining important properties of that system that make it useful for functional programmers. Our extension is fully backwards compatible with previous versions of GHC. It retains the principal types property, leading to robustness during refactoring. At the same time, our new systems come with simple, compositional specifications.

While we have incorporated visible type application with all existing features of GHC, we do not plan to stop there. We hope that our mix of specified polytypes and type schemes will become a basis for additional type system extensions, such as impredicative types, type-level lambdas, and dependent types.

Acknowledgments. Thanks to Simon Peyton Jones, Dimitrios Vytiniotis, Iavor Diatchki, Adam Gundry, Conor McBride, Neel Krishnaswami, and Didier Rémy for helpful discussion and feedback.

References

1. Brady, E.: Idris, a general-purpose dependently typed programming language: design and implementation. J. Funct. Prog. **23**, 552–593 (2013)
2. Buiras, P., Vytiniotis, D., Alejandro Russo, H.: Mixing static and dynamic typing for information-flow control in Haskell. In: International Conference on Functional Programming, ICFP 2015. ACM (2015)
3. Chakravarty, M.M.T., Keller, G., Peyton Jones, S.: Associated type synonyms. In: International Conference on Functional Programming, ICFP 2005. ACM (2005)
4. Chakravarty, M.M.T., Keller, G., Peyton Jones, S., Marlow, S.: Associated types with class. In: ACM SIGPLAN-SIGACT Symposium on Principles of Programming Languages (2005)
5. Clément, D., Despeyroux, T., Kahn, G., Joëlle Despeyroux, A.: simple applicative language : Mini-ML. In: Conference on LISP and Functional Programming, LFP 1986. ACM (1986)
6. Coq development team. The Coq proof assistant reference manual. LogiCal Project. Version 8.0 (2004). http://coq.inria.fr
7. Damas, L.: Type Assignment in Programming Languages. PhD thesis, University of Edinburgh (1985)
8. Damas, L., Milner, R.: Principal type-schemes for functional programs. In: Symposium on Principles of Programming Languages, POPL 1982. ACM (1982)
9. Dreyer, D., Blume, M.: Principal type schemes for modular programs. In: De Nicola, R. (ed.) ESOP 2007. LNCS, vol. 4421, pp. 441–457. Springer, Heidelberg (2007)

10. Dunfield, J., Krishnaswami, N.R.: Complete and easy bidirectional typechecking for higher-rank polymorphism. In: International Conference on Functional Programming, ICFP 2013. ACM (2013)
11. Eisenberg, R.A., Vytiniotis, D., Peyton Jones, S., Weirich, S.: Closed type families with overlapping equations. In: Principles of Programming Languages, POPL 2014. ACM (2014)
12. Eisenberg, R.A., Weirich, S., Ahmed, H.: Visible type application (extended version) (2015). http://www.seas.upenn.edu/~sweirich/papers/type-app-extended.pdf
13. Hindley, J.R.: The principal type-scheme of an object in combinatory logic. Trans. Am. Math. Soc. **146**, 29–60 (1969)
14. Le Botlan, D., Rémy, D.: ML^F: Raising ML to the power of System F. In: International Conference on Functional Programming. ACM (2003)
15. Marlow, S. (ed.): Haskell language report (2010)
16. McBride, C.: Agda-curious? Keynote. In: ICFP 2012 (2012)
17. McCracken, N.: The typechecking of programs with implicit type structure. In: Kahn, G., MacQueen, D.B., Plotkin, G. (eds.) Semantics of Data Types. LNCS, vol. 173, pp. 301–315. Springer, Heidelberg (1984)
18. Milner, R.: A theory of type polymorphism in programming. J. Comput. Syst. Sci. **17**, 348–375 (1978)
19. Miquel, A.: The implicit calculus of constructions. In: Abramsky, S. (ed.) TLCA 2001. LNCS, vol. 2044, pp. 344–359. Springer, Heidelberg (2001)
20. Norell, U.: Towards a practical programming language based on dependent type theory. PhD thesis, Department of Computer Science and Engineering, Chalmers University of Technology, SE-412 96 Göteborg, Sweden, September 2007
21. Odersky, M., Läufer, K.: Putting type annotations to work. In: Symposium on Principles of Programming Languages, POPL 1996. ACM (1996)
22. Peyton Jones, S., Vytiniotis, D., Weirich, S., Washburn, G.: Simple unification-based type inference for GADTs. In: International Conference on Functional Programming, ICFP 2006. ACM (2006)
23. Peyton Jones, S., Vytiniotis, D., Weirich, S., Shields, M.: Practical type inference for arbitrary-rank types. J. Func. Program. **17**(1), 1–82 (2007)
24. Pfenning, F., Schürmann, C.: System description: Twelf - a meta-logical framework for deductive systems. In: Ganzinger, H. (ed.) CADE 1999. LNCS (LNAI), vol. 1632, pp. 202–206. Springer, Heidelberg (1999)
25. Pottier, F., Rémy, D.: The Essence of ML Type Inference. In: Pierce, B.C. (ed.) Advanced Topics in Types and Programming Languages, pp. 387–489. The MIT Press (2005)
26. Syme, D.: The F# 2.0 Language Specification. Microsoft Research and the Microsoft Developer Division (2012). http://fsharp.org/specs/language-spec/2.0/FSharpSpec-2.0-April-2012.pdf
27. Vytiniotis, D., Peyton Jones, S., Schrijvers, T., Sulzmann, M.: OutsideIn(X) modular type inference with local assumptions. J. Funct. Program. **21**(4–5), 333–412 (2011)
28. Wadler, P., Blott, S.: How to make ad-hoc polymorphism less ad-hoc. In: POPL, pp. 60–76. ACM (1989)
29. Winant, T., Devriese, D., Piessens, F., Schrijvers, T.: Partial type signatures for haskell. In: Flatt, M., Guo, H.-F. (eds.) PADL 2014. LNCS, vol. 8324, pp. 17–32. Springer, Heidelberg (2014)

Automatically Splitting a Two-Stage Lambda Calculus

Nicolas Feltman(✉), Carlo Angiuli, Umut A. Acar, and Kayvon Fatahalian

Carnegie Mellon University, Pittsburgh, USA
nfeltman@cs.cmu.edu

Abstract. Staged programming languages assign a stage to each program expression and evaluate each expression in its assigned stage. A common use of staged languages is to describe programs where inputs arrive at different times or rates. In this paper we present an algorithm for statically *splitting* these mixed-staged programs into two unstaged, but dependent, programs where the outputs of the first program can be efficiently reused across multiple invocations of the second. While previous algorithms for performing this transformation (also called *pass separation* and *data specialization*) were limited to operate on simpler, imperative languages, we define a splitting algorithm for an explicitly-two-stage, typed lambda calculus λ^{12} with a $\bigcirc$ modality denoting computation at a later stage, and a ∇ modality noting purely first-stage code. Most notably, the algorithm splits mixed-stage recursive and higher-order functions. We prove the dynamic correctness of our splitting algorithm with respect to a partial-evaluation semantics, and mechanize this proof in Twelf. We also implement the algorithm in a prototype compiler, and demonstrate that the ability to split programs in a language featuring recursion and higher-order features enables non-trivial algorithmic transformations that improve code efficiency and also facilitates modular expression of staged programs.

1 Introduction

Consider a function F which, given $x, y_1, \ldots, y_m$, computes $f(x, y_i)$ for each y_i:

fun $F(x, y_1, y_2 \cdots, y_m)$ =
  $f(x, y_1); f(x, y_2); \ldots; f(x, y_m)$

Observe that this implementation would be wasteful if $f(x, y_i)$ does a significant amount of work that does not depend on y_i. In such a case, it would be advantageous to find the computations in f that depend only on x and then stage execution of f so they are performed only once at the beginning of F.

Jørring and Scherlis classify automatic program staging transformations, such as the one described above, as forms of *frequency reduction* or *precomputation* [15]. To perform frequency reduction, one identifies and hoists computations that are performed multiple times, in order to compute them only once.

P. Thiemann (Ed.): ESOP 2016, LNCS 9632, pp. 255–281, 2016.
DOI: 10.1007/978-3-662-49498-1_11

```
datatype list = Empty
              | Cons of int * list

fun part (p, Empty) =(0,Empty,Empty)
  | part (p, Cons (h,t)) =
    let val (n,le,ri) = part (p,t)
    in if h < p
       then (n+1,Cons(h,le),ri)
       else (n,le,Cons(h,ri))

qsel: list * int -> int
fun qsel (Empty, k) = 0
  | qsel (Cons ht, k) =
    let val (i,le,ri) = part ht in
    case compare k i of
      LT => qsel (le, k)
    | EQ => #1 ht
    | GT => qsel (ri, k-i-1)
```

(a) Unstaged quickselect.

```
@gr{
datatype list = Empty
              | Cons of int * list
fun part (p, Empty) = ...
}

qss : ∇list * ○int -> ○int
fun qss (gr{Empty},_) = next {0}
  | qss (gr{Cons ht},next{k}) =
    let
      @gr{val (i0,le,ri) = part ht}
      val next{i} = hold gr{i0}
    in next{
    case compare k i of
      LT => prev {
            qss (gr{le}, next{k})}
    | EQ => prev {hold gr{#1 ht}}
    | GT => prev {
        qss (gr{ri}, next{k-i-1})}
    }
```

(b) Staged quickselect in λ^{12}.

Fig. 1. Quickselect: traditional and staged.

To perform precomputation, one identifies computations that can be performed in advance and does so—for example, at compile time if the relevant inputs are statically known.

One common precomputation technique is partial evaluation [9,13], which relies on dynamic compilation to specialize functions to known argument values. Going back to our example, if f specializes to a particular v, written f_v, such that $f(v, y) = f_v(y)$, then F can be specialized to v as

fun $F_v(y_1, y_2, \ldots, y_m)$ =
  $f_v(y_1); f_v(y_2); \ldots; f_v(y_m)$.

This eliminates the need to compute m times those parts of $f(v, -)$ which do not depend on the second argument.

Closely related to partial evaluation is *metaprogramming*, where known values represent program code to be executed in a later stage [4,5,20,28]. Metaprogramming enables fine-grained control over specialization by requiring explicit *staging annotations* that mark the stage of each expression.

While simple forms of frequency reduction include standard compiler optimizations such as loop hoisting and common subexpression elimination, Jørring and Scherlis proposed the more general transformation of *splitting* a program into multiple subfunctions (called pass separation in [15]). In our example, splitting transforms the function f into two others f_1 and f_2 such that $f(x, y_i) = f_2(f_1(x), y_i)$. Then we evaluate F by evaluating f_1 on x, and using the result z to evaluate the second function on each y_i.

```
fun F_multipass(x, y1, y2, ..., ym) =
  let z = f1(x) in f2(z, y1); f2(z, y2); ...; f2(z, ym)
```

The key difference between splitting and partial evaluation (or metaprogramming) is that the former can be performed without access to the first argument x; $F_{\text{multipass}}$ works for any x, while F_v is defined only for $x = v$. Therefore, unlike partial evaluation, splitting is a static program transformation ("metastatic" in partial evaluation terminology) and does not require dynamic code generation.

Prior work on partial evaluation and metaprogramming has demonstrated automatic application of these techniques on higher order functional languages. In contrast, automatic splitting transformations have been limited to simpler languages [8,11,16,22].

In this paper, we present a splitting algorithm for λ^{12}, a two-staged typed lambda calculus in the style of Davies [4], with support for recursion and first-class functions. Like Davies, λ^{12} uses a $\bigcirc$ modality to denote computation in the second stage, but to aid splitting we also add a ∇ modality to denote purely first-stage computations. The dynamic semantics Sect. 3 of λ^{12} are that of Davies, modified to provide an eager behavior between stages, which we believe is more intuitive in the context of splitting. We then prove the correctness of our splitting algorithm Sect. 4 for λ^{12} with respect to the semantics. Finally, we discuss our implementation of this splitting algorithm Sect. 5 and demonstrate its power and behavior for a number of staged programs ranging from straight-line arithmetic operations to recursive and higher-order functions Sect. 6.

We also demonstrate that splitting a recursive mixed-stage f yields an f_1 which computes a recursive data structure and an f_2 which traverses that structure in light of information available at the second stage. In the case of the quickselect algorithm, which we discuss next, the split code executes asymptotically faster than an unstaged evaluation of f.

2 Overview

Suppose that we wish to perform a series of order statistics queries on a list `l`. To this end, we can use the quickselect algorithm [12], which given a list `l` and an integer `k`, returns the element of `l` with rank `k` (i.e. the kth-largest element). As implemented in an ML-like language in Fig. 1(a), `qs` partitions `l` using the first element as a pivot and then recurs on one of the two resulting sides, depending on the relationship of `k` to the size `i` of the first half, in order to find the desired element. If the index is out of range, a default value of `0` is returned. Assuming that the input list, with size n, is uniformly randomly ordered (which can be achieved by pre-permuting it), `qs` runs in expected $\Theta(n)$ time. Using `qs`, we can perform m different order statistics queries with ranks `k1`, ..., `km` as follows:

```
(qs l k1, qs l k2, ..., qs l km)
```

Unfortunately, this approach requires $\Theta(n \cdot m)$ time.

We can attempt to improve on this algorithm by factoring out computations shared between these calls to `qs`. In particular, we can construct a binary search tree out of `l`, at cost $\Theta(n \log n)$, and then simply look for the `k`th leftmost element of that tree. Doing lookups efficiently, in $\Theta(\log n)$ time, requires one more innovation—augmenting the tree by storing at each node the size of its left subtree. Thus in total this approach has expected runtime $\Theta(n \log n + m \log n)$.

Is this method, wherein we precompute a data structure, better than the direct $\Theta(mn)$ method? The answer depends on the relationship between the number of lookups m and the size of the list n. If m is constant, then the direct method is superior for sufficiently large n. This is because the precomputed method does unnecessary work sorting parts of the list where there are no query points. However, if the number of queries grows with the size of the list, specifically in $\omega(\log n)$, then the precomputed method will be asymptotically faster.

Rewriting algorithms in this way—to precompute some intermediate results that depend on constant (or infrequently-varying) inputs—is non-trivial, as it requires implementing more complex data structures and algorithms. In this paper, we present a splitting algorithm which does much of this task automatically.

2.1 Staging

The idea behind staged programming is to use staging annotations—in our case, guided by types—to indicate the stage of each subterm.

In Fig. 1(b) we show a staged version of `qs`, called `qss`, where first-stage code is colored red, and second-stage blue. In `qss`, we regard the input list `l` as arriving in the first stage (with type ∇list, a list "now"), the input rank `k` as arriving in the second stage (with type $\bigcirc$int, an integer in the "future"), and the result as being produced in the second stage (with type $\bigcirc$int).

`qss` is obtained from `qs` by wrapping certain computations with `prev` and `next`, signaling transitions between first- and second-stage code. Additionally, `gr` (*ground*) annotations mark certain first-stage components as being purely first-stage, rather than mixed-stage. We also use a function `hold : ∇int -> ◯int`, to promote first-stage integers to second-stage integers. Our type system ensures that the staging annotations in `qss` are consistent, in the sense that computations marked as first-stage cannot depend on ones marked as second-stage.

The process of automatically adding staging annotations to unstaged code, called *binding time analysis*, has been the subject of extensive research Sect. 7. In this paper, we do not consider this problem, instead assuming that the annotations already exist. In the case of `qss`, we have specifically chosen annotations which maximize the work performed in the first stage.

2.2 Splitting Staged Programs

In the rest of this section, we present a high-level overview of the main ideas behind our splitting algorithm, applied to `qss`. Splitting `qss` yields a two-part program that creates a probabilistically balanced, augmented binary search tree as an intermediate data structure. In particular, its first part (`qs1`) constructs

```
datatype tree = Leaf
              | Branch of int * int * tree * tree

datatype list = Empty
              | Cons of int * list
fun part (p : int, l : list) = ...

fun qs1 (l : list) : tree =
  case l of
    Empty => Leaf
  | Cons ht =>
      let val (i,le,ri) = part ht in
      Branch (i,#1 ht,qs1 le,qs1 ri)
```

```
fun qs2 (p : tree, k : int) :int=
  case p of
    Leaf => 0
  | Branch (i,h,p1,p2) =>
      case compare k i of
        LT => qs2 (p1,k)
      | EQ => h
      | GT => qs2 (p2,k-i-1)
```

Fig. 2. Two-pass implementation of quickselect.

such a binary search tree and its second part (qs2) traverses the tree, using the embedded size information to find the element of the desired rank. The code for qs1 and qs2 is in Fig. 2.

Our splitting algorithm scans qss for first-stage computations, gathering them into qs1. Given l, this function performs these computations and places the information needed by the subsequent function into a boundary data structure. In particular, qs1 performs all recursive calls and evaluates all instances of part (since it depends only on l). It produces a boundary data structure that collects the results from these recursive calls, tagged by the branch (LT, EQ, or GT) in which that call occurred. Since the recursive calls occur in two different branches (LT and GT) the boundary structure is a binary tree. Lastly, it records i (the size of the left subtree) and #1 ht (the pivot/head of the list) in the boundary structure, because those computations are *held* for use in the second stage. The final result is a binary search tree augmented with size information, and whose keys are the pivots.

Our splitting algorithm simultaneously scans qss for second-stage computations, gathering them into qs2. This function is given the boundary data structure and the rank k, and it finishes the computation. Now that k is known, the conditional on compare k i can be evaluated, choosing which recursive call of qss is actually relevant for this k. Since the boundary data structure contains the first-stage data for *all* of the recursive calls, performing these comparisons essentially walks the tree, using the rank along with the size data i to look up the kth leftmost node in the tree.

3 λ^{12} Statics and Dynamics

We express two-stage programs as terms in λ^{12}, a typed, modal lambda calculus. Although λ^{12} describes computations that occur in two stages, we find it helpful for the specification of splitting to codify terms using one of three *worlds*. A world is essentially a slightly finer classification than a stage. Whereas there is only one

$$
\begin{array}{rl}
\text{Worlds} & w ::= \mathbb{1M} \mid \mathbb{1G} \mid \mathbb{2} \\
\{\mathbb{1M},\mathbb{2}\}\text{-Types} & \tau ::= \text{unit} \mid \tau \times \tau \mid \tau \rightarrow \tau \mid \alpha \mid \mu\alpha.\tau \mid \tau + \tau \\
& \tau_{\mathbb{M}} ::= \text{unit} \mid \tau_{\mathbb{M}} \times \tau_{\mathbb{M}} \mid \tau_{\mathbb{M}} \rightarrow \tau_{\mathbb{M}} \mid \alpha \mid \mu\alpha.\tau_{\mathbb{M}} \mid \bigcirc\tau \mid \nabla\tau \\
\text{Contexts} & \Gamma ::= \bullet \mid \Gamma, x_w : \tau_w \; @ \; w \\
\text{Terms} & e_w ::= \texttt{app(}e_w\texttt{;}e_w\texttt{)} \mid \texttt{<}e_w\texttt{,}e_w\texttt{>} \mid \texttt{pi1(}e_w\texttt{)} \mid \texttt{pi2(}e_w\texttt{)} \\
& \quad \mid \texttt{inl(}e_w\texttt{)} \mid \texttt{inr(}e_w\texttt{)} \mid \texttt{case(}e_w\texttt{;}x.e_w\texttt{;}x.e_w\texttt{)} \\
& \quad \mid \texttt{roll(}e_w\texttt{)} \mid \texttt{unroll(}e_w\texttt{)} \\
& e_{\mathbb{M}} ::= \underline{v} \mid \texttt{next(}e_{\mathbb{2}}\texttt{)} \mid \texttt{gr(}e_{\mathbb{G}}\texttt{)} \mid \texttt{letg(}e_{\mathbb{M}}\texttt{;}x_{\mathbb{G}}.e_{\mathbb{M}}\texttt{)} \\
& \quad \mid \texttt{caseg(}e_{\mathbb{M}}\texttt{;}x_{\mathbb{M}}.e_{\mathbb{M}}\texttt{;}x_{\mathbb{M}}.e_{\mathbb{M}}\texttt{)} \\
& e_{\mathbb{G}} ::= \underline{u} \\
& e_{\mathbb{2}} ::= \underline{q} \mid \texttt{prev(}e_{\mathbb{M}}\texttt{)} \mid \texttt{fn(}x_{\mathbb{2}}\texttt{.}x_{\mathbb{2}}\texttt{.}e_{\mathbb{2}}\texttt{)} \\
\text{Partial Values} & v ::= x_{\mathbb{M}} \mid \texttt{<>} \mid \texttt{fn(}x_{\mathbb{M}}\texttt{.}x_{\mathbb{M}}\texttt{.}e_{\mathbb{M}}\texttt{)} \mid \texttt{<}v,v\texttt{>} \mid \texttt{roll(}v\texttt{)} \\
& \quad \mid \texttt{inl(}v\texttt{)} \mid \texttt{inr(}v\texttt{)} \mid \texttt{next(}y\texttt{)} \mid \texttt{gr(}v\texttt{)} \\
\text{Ground Values} & u ::= x_{\mathbb{G}} \mid \texttt{<>} \mid \texttt{fn(}x_{\mathbb{G}}\texttt{.}x_{\mathbb{G}}\texttt{.}e_{\mathbb{G}}\texttt{)} \mid \texttt{<}u,u\texttt{>} \mid \texttt{roll(}u\texttt{)} \mid \texttt{inl(}u\texttt{)} \mid \texttt{inr(}u\texttt{)} \\
\text{Residuals} & q ::= x_{\mathbb{2}} \mid \texttt{<>} \mid \texttt{fn(}x_{\mathbb{2}}\texttt{.}x_{\mathbb{2}}\texttt{.}q\texttt{)} \mid \texttt{app(}q\texttt{;}q\texttt{)} \mid \texttt{<}q,q\texttt{>} \mid \texttt{pi1(}q\texttt{)} \mid \texttt{pi2(}q\texttt{)} \\
& \quad \mid \texttt{roll(}q\texttt{)} \mid \texttt{unroll(}q\texttt{)} \mid \texttt{inl(}q\texttt{)} \mid \texttt{inr(}q\texttt{)} \mid \texttt{case(}q\texttt{;}x_{\mathbb{2}}.q\texttt{;}x_{\mathbb{2}}.q\texttt{)}
\end{array}
$$

Fig. 3. $\lambda^{\mathbb{12}}$ abstract syntax. Subscript-w rules apply at all worlds.

world, $\mathbb{2}$, for second-stage computations, there are two worlds corresponding to the first stage: $\mathbb{1M}$ for *mixed* first-stage computations, which may contain second-stage subterms within `next` blocks, and $\mathbb{1G}$ for *ground* first-stage computations, which may not. The distinction between these two first-stage worlds is necessary for the splitting algorithm to produce efficient outputs and will be discussed in Sect. 4.6.

The abstract syntax of $\lambda^{\mathbb{12}}$ is presented as a grammar in Fig. 3. To simplify the upcoming translation in Sect. 4, we have chosen to statically distinguish between values and general computations, using an underline constructor ("$\underline{v}$") which explicitly note the parts of a computation that have been reduced to a value.[1] Moreover, the value/computation distinction interacts non-trivially with the three possible world classifications. As a result, we end up with six classes of term in the grammar.

The key feature of all three forms of value is that they have no remaining work in the first stage. That is, all of the first-stage portions of a value are fully reduced (except the bodies of first-stage functions). In the case of values at $\mathbb{1G}$, which we call *ground values*, this collapses to just the standard notion of values in a monostage language. In the case of values at $\mathbb{2}$, which we call *residuals*, this collapses to just standard monostage terms. Lastly, values at $\mathbb{1M}$ end up with more of a mixed character, so we call them *partial values*.

[1] In this presentation, the value/computation distinction is encoded intrinsically at the syntactic level. However, we found it more convenient in the formal Twelf implementation to maintain the distinction with an extrinsic judgement.

$$\frac{\Gamma \vdash v : A @ w}{\Gamma \vdash \underline{v} : A @ w} \qquad \frac{\cdot}{\Gamma \vdash \texttt{<>} : \texttt{unit} @ w} \qquad \frac{\Gamma, f : A \to B @ w, x : A @ w \vdash e : B @ w}{\Gamma \vdash \texttt{fn}(f.x.e) : A \to B @ w}$$

$$\frac{\Gamma \vdash e_1 : A \to B @ w \quad \Gamma \vdash e_2 : A @ w}{\Gamma \vdash \texttt{app}(e_1;e_2) : B @ w} \qquad \frac{\Gamma \vdash e_1 : A @ w \quad \Gamma \vdash e_2 : B @ w}{\Gamma \vdash \texttt{<}e_1, e_2\texttt{>} : A \times B @ w}$$

$$\frac{\Gamma \vdash e : A \times B @ w}{\Gamma \vdash \texttt{pi1}(e) : A @ w} \qquad \frac{\Gamma \vdash e : A \times B @ w}{\Gamma \vdash \texttt{pi2}(e) : B @ w} \qquad \frac{\Gamma \vdash e : \mu\alpha.\tau @ w}{\Gamma \vdash \texttt{unroll}(e) : [\mu\alpha.\tau/\alpha]\tau @ w}$$

$$\frac{\Gamma \vdash e : A @ w}{\Gamma \vdash \texttt{inl}(e) : A + B @ w} \qquad \frac{\Gamma \vdash e : B @ w}{\Gamma \vdash \texttt{inr}(e) : A + B @ w} \qquad \frac{\Gamma \vdash e : [\mu\alpha.\tau/\alpha]\tau @ w}{\Gamma \vdash \texttt{roll}(e) : \mu\alpha.\tau @ w}$$

$$\frac{\Gamma \vdash e_1 : A + B @ w \quad \Gamma, x_2 : A @ w \vdash e_2 : C @ w \quad \Gamma, x_3 : B @ w \vdash e_3 : C @ w}{\Gamma \vdash \texttt{case}(e_1;x_2.e_2;x_3.e_3) : C @ w}$$

$$\frac{\Gamma \vdash e : A @ \mathbb{2}}{\Gamma \vdash \texttt{next}(e) : \bigcirc A @ \mathbb{1M}} \qquad \frac{\Gamma \vdash e : \bigcirc A @ \mathbb{1M}}{\Gamma \vdash \texttt{prev}(e) : A @ \mathbb{2}} \qquad \frac{\Gamma \vdash e : A @ \mathbb{1G}}{\Gamma \vdash \texttt{gr}(e) : \nabla A @ \mathbb{1M}}$$

$$\frac{\Gamma \vdash e_1 : \nabla A @ \mathbb{1M} \quad \Gamma, x : A @ \mathbb{1G} \vdash e_2 : B @ \mathbb{1M}}{\Gamma \vdash \texttt{letg}(e_1;x.e_2) : B @ \mathbb{1M}} \qquad \frac{\Gamma \vdash e_1 : \nabla(A+B) @ \mathbb{1M} \quad \Gamma, x_2 : \nabla A @ \mathbb{1M} \vdash e_2 : C @ \mathbb{1M} \quad \Gamma, x_3 : \nabla B @ \mathbb{1M} \vdash e_3 : C @ \mathbb{1M}}{\Gamma \vdash \texttt{caseg}(e_1;x_2.e_2;x_3.e_3) : C @ \mathbb{1M}}$$

Fig. 4. λ^{12} statics, split into standard rules and staged rules.

3.1 Statics

The typing judgment $\Gamma \vdash e : A @ w$, defined in Fig. 4, means that e has type A at world w, in the context Γ.

All three worlds contain unit, product, function, sum and recursive types defined in the usual fashion. These "standard" features can only be constructed from subterms of the same world, and variables can only be used at the same world where they were introduced. Thus differing worlds (and hence, differing stages of computation) only interact by means of the $\bigcirc$ and ∇ type formers. These modalities are internalizations of worlds $\mathbb{2}$ and $\mathbb{1G}$, respectively, as types at world $\mathbb{1M}$.

At the term level, `next` blocks can be used to form future computations: given a term e of type A at world $\mathbb{2}$, $\texttt{next}(e)$ has type $\bigcirc A$ at $\mathbb{1M}$. This essentially encapsulates e as a computation that will be evaluated in the future, and it provides a handle (of type $\bigcirc A$) now to that eventual value. Computations at $\mathbb{1M}$ can shuffle this handle around as a value, but the future result it refers to cannot be accessed. This is because the only way to eliminate a $\bigcirc$ wrapper is by using a `prev`, which yields an A at $\mathbb{2}$. This feature was adapted from linear temporal logic, via [4], and ensures that there can be no flow of information from the second stage to the first.

∇A is a type in world $\mathbb{1M}$ which classifies purely-first-stage computations of type A. Given a world $\mathbb{1G}$ term e of type A, $\texttt{gr}(e)$ has type ∇A at world $\mathbb{1M}$.

(e is guaranteed not to contain second-stage computations because $\bigcirc$ types are not available in world $\mathbb{1G}$.) An e of type ∇A at $\mathbb{1M}$ can be unwrapped as an A at $\mathbb{1G}$ using the $\texttt{letg}(e;x.e')$ construct, which binds $x : A @ \mathbb{1G}$ in a $\mathbb{1M}$ term e'. This allows us to compute under ∇—for example, given a $p : \nabla(A \times B) @ \mathbb{1M}$, the term $\texttt{letg}(p;x.\texttt{gr}(\texttt{pi1}(x)))$ computes its first projection, of type ∇A. This elimination form, in contrast to that of $\bigcirc$, does not permit world $\mathbb{1M}$ subterms within any world $\mathbb{1G}$ term.

These features are sufficient to ensure that mixed code does not leak into ground code, however they also prevent information from ever escaping a ∇ wrapper. So to allow the latter behavior but not the former, we introduce the $\texttt{caseg}(e;x.e_1;x.e_2)$ construct, whose predicate is of type $\nabla(A + B)$ and whose branches are world $\mathbb{1M}$ terms open on ∇A and ∇B respectively. This essentially allows code at $\mathbb{1M}$ to inspect an injection tag within a ∇.

Although products and functions are restricted to types at the same world, $\bigcirc$ allows construction of "mixed-stage" products and functions. For example, `qss` is a function at world $\mathbb{1M}$ which takes a $\nabla\text{list} \times \bigcirc\text{int}$ (a purely-first-stage list and a second-stage integer) to a $\bigcirc$int (a second-stage computation of an integer).

The example code in this paper uses an extension of the formalized λ^{12}. In particular, it makes liberal use of ints and various functions on these, as well as a function `hold`() which takes a ∇int to a $\bigcirc$int.[2]

3.2 Dynamics

The central tenet of a staged language is that first-stage code should be evaluated entirely before second-stage code. Accordingly, our dynamics operates in two passes. The first pass takes an input top-level program $e : A @ \mathbb{2}$ and reduces all of its first-stage (worlds $\mathbb{1M}$ and $\mathbb{1G}$) subterms in place, eventually resulting in a residual $\underline{q}$. The second pass further reduces this residual. Since q is monostage by definition, this second pass is standard unstaged evaluation and is not described in further detail in this paper. Moreover, for the purposes of these dynamics, we consider a top level program to always be typed at world $\mathbb{2}$.

Since $e : A@\mathbb{2}$ may be constructed out of terms at other worlds, our dynamics requires notions of values and steps that are specialized to each world. The rules for all parts of first-pass evaluation are given in Fig. 5. In this and later figures, we extensively use an $\mathcal{S}[\text{-}]$ construction to indicate a *shallow* evaluation context which looks a single level deep.

World $\mathbb{2}$. Steps at world $\mathbb{2}$ are given by the judgment $e \overset{2}{\hookrightarrow} e'$. Since first pass evaluation should not reduce stage two terms, this judgment does nothing but traverse e to find `prev` blocks, under which it performs in-place reductions. A world $\mathbb{2}$ term is done evaluating when it has the form $\underline{q}$, where q is a residual.

2 `hold`() is definable in λ^{12} given an inductive definition of ints. In practice, we provide both ints and `hold`() as primitives. It is sensible to extend `hold`() to all base types and to products and sums thereof. This is related to the notion of *mobility* ([19]).

Shallow Reductions, $e \overset{w}{\longrightarrow} e'$		
e	e'	w
$<\underline{v_1}, \underline{v_2}>$	$\underline{<v_1, v_2>}$	all
$\texttt{pi1}(\underline{<v_1, v_2>})$	$\underline{v_1}$	$1\mathbb{G}, 1\mathbb{M}$
$\texttt{pi2}(\underline{<v_1, v_2>})$	$\underline{v_2}$	$1\mathbb{G}, 1\mathbb{M}$
$\texttt{pi1}(\underline{v})$	$\underline{\texttt{pi1}(v)}$	2
$\texttt{pi2}(\underline{v})$	$\underline{\texttt{pi2}(v)}$	2
$\texttt{app}(\underline{\texttt{fn}(f.x.e)};\underline{v})$	$[\texttt{fn}(f.x.e), v/f, x]e$	$1\mathbb{G}, 1\mathbb{M}$
$\texttt{app}(\underline{v_1};\underline{v_2})$	$\underline{\texttt{app}(v_1;v_2)}$	2
$\texttt{inl}(\underline{v})$	$\underline{\texttt{inl}(v)}$	all
$\texttt{inr}(\underline{v})$	$\underline{\texttt{inr}(v)}$	all
$\texttt{case}(\underline{\texttt{inl}(v)};x_2.e_2;\cdot)$	$[v/x_2]e_2$	$1\mathbb{G}, 1\mathbb{M}$
$\texttt{case}(\underline{\texttt{inr}(v)};\cdot;x_3.e_3)$	$[v/x_3]e_3$	$1\mathbb{G}, 1\mathbb{M}$
$\texttt{roll}(\underline{v})$	$\underline{\texttt{roll}(v)}$	all
$\texttt{unroll}(\underline{\texttt{roll}(v)})$	$\underline{v}$	$1\mathbb{G}, 1\mathbb{M}$
$\texttt{unroll}(\underline{v})$	$\underline{\texttt{unroll}(v)}$	2
$\texttt{case}(\underline{e_1};x_2.\underline{e_2};x_3.\underline{e_3})$	$\underline{\texttt{case}(e_1;x_2.e_2;x_3.e_3)}$	2
$\texttt{next}(\underline{y})$	$\underline{\texttt{next}(y)}$	$1\mathbb{M}$
$\texttt{prev}(\underline{\texttt{next}(y)})$	y	2
$\texttt{gr}(\underline{v})$	$\underline{\texttt{gr}(v)}$	$1\mathbb{M}$
$\texttt{letg}(\underline{\texttt{gr}(v)};x.e)$	$[v/x]e$	$1\mathbb{M}$
$\texttt{caseg}(\underline{\texttt{gr}(\texttt{inl}(v))};x_2.e_2;\cdot)$	$[\texttt{gr}(v)/x_2]e_2$	$1\mathbb{M}$
$\texttt{caseg}(\underline{\texttt{gr}(\texttt{inr}(v))};\cdot;x_3.e_3)$	$[\texttt{gr}(v)/x_3]e_3$	$1\mathbb{M}$

Shallow Contexts, $\mathcal{S}$ $\textsf{vc}_w$	
$\mathcal{S}[\text{-}]$	w
$<\text{-}, e>$	all
$<\underline{v}, \text{-}>$	all
$\texttt{pi1}(\text{-})$	all
$\texttt{pi2}(\text{-})$	all
$\texttt{fn}(f.x.\text{-})$	2
$\texttt{app}(\text{-};e)$	all
$\texttt{app}(\underline{v};\text{-})$	all
$\texttt{inl}(\text{-})$	all
$\texttt{inr}(\text{-})$	all
$\texttt{roll}(\text{-})$	all
$\texttt{unroll}(\text{-})$	all
$\texttt{case}(\text{-};x_2.e_2;x_3.e_3)$	all
$\texttt{case}(\underline{v_1};x_2.\text{-};x_3.e_3)$	2
$\texttt{case}(\underline{v_1};x_2.\underline{v_2};x_3.\text{-})$	2
$\texttt{caseg}(\text{-};x_2.e_2;x_3.e_3)$	$1\mathbb{M}$
$\texttt{letg}(\text{-};x.e)$	$1\mathbb{M}$

$$\frac{e \overset{w}{\longrightarrow} e'}{e \overset{w}{\hookrightarrow} e'} \quad \frac{e \overset{w}{\hookrightarrow} e' \quad \mathcal{S}\ \textsf{vc}_w}{\mathcal{S}[e] \overset{w}{\hookrightarrow} \mathcal{S}[e']} \quad \frac{e \overset{1\mathbb{G}}{\hookrightarrow} e'}{\texttt{gr}(e) \overset{1\mathbb{M}}{\hookrightarrow} \texttt{gr}(e')} \quad \frac{e \overset{2}{\hookrightarrow} e'}{\texttt{next}(e) \overset{1\mathbb{M}}{\hookrightarrow} \texttt{next}(e')} \quad \frac{e \overset{1\mathbb{M}}{\hookrightarrow} e'}{\texttt{prev}(e) \overset{2}{\hookrightarrow} \texttt{prev}(e')}$$

$$\frac{q \text{ not a variable}}{\texttt{next}(\underline{q}) \nearrow [\![q/y]\!]\texttt{next}(\underline{y})} \quad \frac{e \nearrow [\![q/y]\!]e'}{\texttt{prev}(e) \overset{2}{\hookrightarrow} \texttt{let}(y;q.\texttt{prev}(e'))} \quad \frac{e \nearrow [\![q/y]\!]e' \quad \mathcal{S}\ \textsf{vc}_{1\mathbb{M}}}{\mathcal{S}[e] \nearrow [\![q/y]\!]\mathcal{S}[e']}$$

Fig. 5. First-pass evaluation of λ^{12} dynamics. The judgement $e \overset{w}{\hookrightarrow} e'$ indicates that e takes a step to e' in the first pass; $\overset{w}{\longrightarrow}$ and $\mathcal{S}$ $\textsf{vc}_w$ are helper judgements.

To be a residual, a term must have no first-stage subterms (equivalently, no prevs), even within the body of a function or branches of a case. This implies that $\overset{2}{\hookrightarrow}$ must proceed underneath second-stage binders.

World $1\mathbb{G}$. Since the ground fragment of the language is not dependent on other worlds, the semantics of ground is just that of a monostage language. Thus, $e \overset{1\mathbb{G}}{\hookrightarrow} e'$ traverses into subterms to find the left-most unevaluated code where it performs a reduction. A ground value u comprises only units, injections, tuples, and functions, where the body of the function may be any ground term.

World $1\mathbb{M}$. Like its ground counterpart, the $1\mathbb{M}$ step judgment, $e \overset{1\mathbb{M}}{\hookrightarrow} e'$, finds the left-most unevaluated subterm and performs a reduction. It also descends into gr and next blocks, using one of the other two step judgements ($\overset{1\mathbb{G}}{\hookrightarrow}$ or $\overset{2}{\hookrightarrow}$) there.

The value form for $\mathbb{1M}$, called a partial value, comprises units, tuples, functions, **gr** blocks of ground values, and **next** blocks containing *only a stage two variable.* This strong requirement ensures that second-stage computations are not duplicated when partial values are substituted for a variable. This is a departure from the staged semantics of [4,27]. Whereas those semantics interpret values of type $\bigcirc A$ to mean "code of type A that can be executed in the future," ours interprets $\bigcirc A$ to mean "a reference to a value that will be accessible in the future." This contrast stems from differing goals: metaprogramming explicitly intends to model code manipulating code, whereas our applications feel more natural with an eager interpretation of `next`. One consequence of the stronger requirement on partial values is that a new kind of step is necessary to put terms into that form. To illustrate, consider:

```
prev{(fn x : ○int => e') (next{e})}
```

We could reduce this to $\texttt{prev}([\texttt{next}(e)/x]e'$, but this may potentially duplicate an expensive computation e depending on how many times x appears in e'. Instead, we choose to *hoist* e outside, binding it to a temporary variable y, and substituting that variable instead:

```
let val y = e in prev{[next{y}/x]e'}
```

This behavior is implemented by the $e \nearrow [\![q/y]\!]e'$ judgment, called a *hoisting step.* We read this as saying that somewhere within e there was a subterm q which needs to be hoisted out, yielding the new term e' which has a new variable y where q used to be. These steps occur when a `next` block has contents that are a residual but (to prevent loops) not when those contents are already a variable. In essence, the rules for hoisting steps operate by "bubbling up" a substitution to the innermost containing `prev`, where it is reified into a `let` statement.[3]

Consider the following example, where `P` has type $\nabla(\text{unit} + \text{unit})$,

```
caseg P of _ => next{0} | _ => next{1}
```

Depending on what `P` evaluates to in the first stage, the whole term will step to either `next{0}` or `next{1}`. In this sense, we can see `case` (at world $\mathbb{1M}$) and `caseg` as the constructs that facilitate all cross-stage communication.

3.3 Type Safety

The statics and dynamics of λ^{12} are related by the type safety theorems below, again annotated by world. In all cases, Γ may be any list of variable bindings at world $\mathbb{2}$, representing the second-stage binders under which we are evaluating. Note how the progress theorem for world $\mathbb{1M}$ states that every well-typed term must take either a standard step or a hoisting step.

Theorem 1 (Progress)

– *If* $\Gamma \vdash e : A \mathbin{@} \mathbb{1M}$, *then either* e *has the form* $\underline{v}$, *or* $e \overset{\mathbb{1M}}{\hookrightarrow} e'$, *or* $e \nearrow [\![q/y]\!]e'$.

[3] Because a program is a term at $\mathbb{2}$, this `prev` always exists. Otherwise, the semantics would need a mechanism to accumulate the bindings that hoisting steps create.

– *If* $\Gamma \vdash e : A \,@\, \mathbb{1G}$*, then either* e *has the form* $\underline{u}$*, or* $e \overset{\mathbb{1G}}{\hookrightarrow} e'$.
– *If* $\Gamma \vdash e : A \,@\, \mathbb{2}$*, then either* e *has the form* $\underline{q}$*, or* $e \overset{\mathbb{2}}{\hookrightarrow} e'$.

Theorem 2 (Preservation)

– *If* $\Gamma \vdash e : A \,@\, \mathbb{1M}$ *and* $e \nearrow [\![q/y]\!]e'$*,*
then $\Gamma \vdash q : B \,@\, \mathbb{2}$ *and* $\Gamma, y : B \,@\, \mathbb{2} \vdash e' : A \,@\, \mathbb{1M}$.
– *If* $\Gamma \vdash e : A \,@\, w$ *and* $e \overset{w}{\hookrightarrow} e'$*, then* $\Gamma \vdash e' : A \,@\, w$.

3.4 Evaluating Staged Programs

Multistage functions, such as `qss` from Sect. 2, can be represented as terms with a type fitting the pattern $A \to \bigcirc(B \to C)$ at $\mathbb{1M}$.[4] To apply such a function f to arguments $a : A \,@\, \mathbb{1M}$ and $b : B \,@\, \mathbb{2}$, simply evaluate the program:

```
prev{f a} b
```

Moreover, the reuse of first-stage computations across multiple second-stage computations can even be encoded within λ^{12}. The following program runs many order statistics queries `k1`, ..., `km` on the same list:

```
prev{ let val list = gr{[7,4,2,5,9,...,3]} in
next{ let fun lookup k = prev{qss (list,next{k})}
      in (lookup k1,...,lookup km)}}
```

Observe that this code evaluates `qss` only once and substiutes its result into the body of the function `lookup`, which is then called many times in the second stage.

4 Splitting Algorithm

The goal of a stage splitting translation is to send a program $\mathcal{P}$ in a multistage language to an equivalent form $\mathcal{P}'$ where the stages are seperated at the top level. More specifically, $\mathcal{P}$ and $\mathcal{P}'$ should produce the same answer under their respective semantics.

Since λ^{12} has three classes of multistage term, our splitting algorithm has three forms: $e \overset{2}{\rightsquigarrow} \{p|l.r\}$ for $\mathbb{2}$-terms, $e \overset{\mathbb{1M}}{\rightsquigarrow} \{c|l.r\}$ for $\mathbb{1M}$-terms, and $v \hookrightarrow \{i;q\}$ for partial values. In each form the output has two parts, corresponding to the first-stage (p, c, and i) and second-stage ($l.r$, and q) content of the input. Note that there's no need to provide forms of splitting for ground terms or residuals, since those classes of term are already monostage by construction.

The rules of the three splitting judgements are given in Figs. 6 and 7. Since the rules are simply recursive on the structure of the term, the splitting algorithm runs in linear time on the size of the input program. Splitting is defined for all well-typed inputs Theorem 3, and it produces unique results Theorem 4. That is, each splitting judgement defines a total function.

[4] We can rewrite `qss` in this curried form, or apply a higher-order currying function.

Theorem 3 (Splitting Totality)

- *For term* e*, if* $\Gamma \vdash e : A\ @\mathbb{2}$*, then* $e \overset{2}{\rightsquigarrow} \{p|l.r\}$.
- *For term* e*, if* $\Gamma \vdash e : A\ @\mathbb{1M}$*, then* $e \overset{\mathbb{1M}}{\rightsquigarrow} \{c|l.r\}$.
- *For partial value* v*, if* $\Gamma \vdash v : A\ @\mathbb{1M}$*, then* $v \hookrightarrow \{i\,;q\}$.

Theorem 4 (Splitting Uniqueness)

- *If* $e \overset{2}{\rightsquigarrow} \{p|l.r\}$ *and* $e \overset{2}{\rightsquigarrow} \{p'|l'.r'\}$*, then* $p = p'$*, and* $l.r = l'.r'$.
- *If* $e \overset{\mathbb{1M}}{\rightsquigarrow} \{p|l.r\}$ *and* $e \overset{\mathbb{1M}}{\rightsquigarrow} \{c'|l'.r'\}$*, then* $c = c'$*, and* $l.r = l'.r'$.
- *If* $v \hookrightarrow \{i\,;q\}$ *and* $v \hookrightarrow \{i'\,;q'\}$*, then* $i = i'$ *and* $q = q'$.

We prove these theorems by straightforward induction on the typing derivation and simultaneous induction on the splitting derivations, respectively.

4.1 Outputs of Splitting

Splitting a top level program $e : A @ \mathbb{2}$, via $\overset{2}{\rightsquigarrow}$, yields $\{p|l.r\}$. Like e, this output is evaluated in two passes. The first pass reduces p to the value b and plugs this result in for l to produce $[b/l]r$; the second pass evaluates $[b/l]r$. The relationship between the two stages in this case is thus like a pipeline, which is why we write them with a '|' in between. Since execution of the first pass serves to generate input for the second pass, we say p is a *precomputation* that produces a *boundary value* (b) for the *resumer* ($l.r$).

Splitting a partial value v, via $\hookrightarrow$, yields $\{i\,;q\}$. Since partial values, by definition, have no remaining work in the first pass and since transfer of information between the stages occurs in the first pass of evalution, we know that the second-stage components of v can no longer depend on its first-stage components. Analogously, this must also hold for the output of splitting, which is why q—unlike the resumer of world $\mathbb{2}$ term splitting—is not open on a variable. Thus, i and q are operationally independent, but they represent the complementary portions of v that are relevant to each stage. We call i the *immediate value* and q the residual.

For any $e : A\ @\ \mathbb{1M}$, splitting e via $\overset{\mathbb{1M}}{\rightsquigarrow}$ yields the pair of monostage terms $\{c\,|\,l.r\}$. This output form is essentially a hybrid of the previous two. Because e is a term, c needs to produces a boundary value b to be passed to the resumer ($l.r$) And since e types at world $\mathbb{1M}$, it has an eventual result at the first stage as well as the second, and so it must produce an immediate value i. The term c meets both of these responsibilities by reducing to the tuple $<i, b>$, and so we call it a *combined term*.

4.2 World 2 Term Splitting

The dynamic correctness of the splitting translation requires that the simple evaluate-and-plug semantics on the output produces the same answer as the staged semantics of the previous section. That is, $[b/l]r$ (the *applied resumer*) should be equivalent to the residual q produced by direct evaluation, $e \overset{2}{\hookrightarrow} \cdots \overset{2}{\hookrightarrow} \underline{q}$.

This condition is stated more precisely as Theorem 5, where "$e \Downarrow v$" indicates standard monostage reduction of the term e to the value v, and "$\equiv$" indicates a monostage equivalence, which is defined in Fig. 8.

Theorem 5 (End-to-End Correctness). *If* $\cdot \vdash e : A \,@\, \mathbb{2}$, $e \overset{2}{\hookrightarrow} \cdots \overset{2}{\hookrightarrow} \underline{q}$, *and* $e \overset{2}{\rightsquigarrow} \{p|l.r\}$, *then* $p \Downarrow b$ *and* $[b/l]r \equiv q$.

We prove Theorem 5 by induction on the steps of evaluation. In the base case, where e is already a residual of the form $\underline{q}$, we know $\underline{q} \overset{2}{\rightsquigarrow} \{\underline{\texttt{<>}}|\_.q\}$, so by uniqueness of splitting, $p = \texttt{<>}$ and $r = q$. From here, we can directly derive $\underline{\texttt{<>}} \Downarrow \texttt{<>}$ and $q \equiv q$.

In the recursive case, where the evaluation takes at least one step, we have $e \overset{2}{\hookrightarrow} e' \overset{2}{\hookrightarrow} \cdots \overset{2}{\hookrightarrow} \underline{q}$ as well as $\cdot \vdash e : A \,@\, \mathbb{2}$ and $e \overset{2}{\rightsquigarrow} \{p|l.r\}$. By preservation and totality of splitting, we know $\cdot \vdash e' : A \,@\, \mathbb{2}$ and $e' \overset{2}{\rightsquigarrow} \{p'|l'.r'\}$. From here, the inductive hypothesis yields $p' \Downarrow b'$ and $[b'/l']r' \equiv q$. All that we now require is $p \Downarrow b$ and $[b/l]r \equiv [b'/l']r'$, To close this gap we introduce Lemma 1, which essentially states that any single step is correct, and whose proof will concern the rest of this section.

Lemma 1 (Single Step Correctness)

- *If* $e \overset{2}{\hookrightarrow} e'$, $e \overset{2}{\rightsquigarrow} \{p|l.r\}$, $e' \overset{2}{\rightsquigarrow} \{p'|l'.r'\}$, *and* $p' \Downarrow b'$, *then* $p \Downarrow b$ *and* $[b/l]r \equiv [b'/l']r'$.
- *If* $e \overset{\mathbb{1M}}{\hookrightarrow} e'$, $e \overset{\mathbb{1M}}{\rightsquigarrow} \{c|l.r\}$, $e' \overset{\mathbb{1M}}{\rightsquigarrow} \{c'|l'.r'\}$, *and* $c' \Downarrow \texttt{<}i, b'\texttt{>}$, *then* $c \Downarrow \texttt{<}i, b\texttt{>}$ *and* $[b/l]r \equiv [b'/l']r'$.

After invocation of that new lemma, we can derive $[b/l]r \equiv [b'/l']r' \equiv q$ directly. In order to prove Lemma 1, we will need to state analogous version for steps at $\mathbb{1M}$, since the various kinds of multistage term in λ^{12} are mutually dependent. Thus, this section proceeds by covering the definition of splitting at $\mathbb{1M}$, starting with the value form at that world.

4.3 Partial Value Splitting

To provide intuition about the behavior of partial value splitting, consider the following partial value:

```
(next{y}, (gr{injL 7}, next{y}))
```

To construct the value i representing its first-stage components, splitting first redacts all second-stage (blue) parts, along with the surrounding **next** annotations. The resulting "holes" in the term are replaced with unit values.

```
((), (gr{injL 7},()))
```

Finally, partial value splitting drops **gr** annotations, yielding:

```
((), (injL 7,()))
```

$$\frac{\cdot}{x \hookrightarrow \{x;x\}} \qquad \frac{\cdot}{\texttt{<>} \hookrightarrow \{\texttt{<>};\texttt{<>}\}} \qquad \frac{\cdot}{\texttt{gr}(m) \hookrightarrow \{m;\texttt{<>}\}} \qquad \frac{\cdot}{\texttt{next}(y) \hookrightarrow \{\texttt{<>};y\}}$$

$$\frac{v_1 \hookrightarrow \{i_1;q_1\} \quad v_2 \hookrightarrow \{i_2;q_2\}}{\texttt{<}v_1,v_2\texttt{>} \hookrightarrow \{\texttt{<}i_1,i_2\texttt{>};\texttt{<}q_1,q_2\texttt{>}\}} \qquad \frac{v \hookrightarrow \{i;q\} \quad \mathcal{S}[\text{-}] \in \{\texttt{inl(-)},\texttt{inr(-)},\texttt{roll(-)}\}}{\mathcal{S}[v] \hookrightarrow \{\mathcal{S}[i];q\}}$$

$$\frac{e \overset{\mathbb{1M}}{\rightsquigarrow} \{c \,|\, l.r\}}{\texttt{fn}(f.x.e) \hookrightarrow \{\texttt{fn}(f.x.\texttt{let}(c;\texttt{<}x,y\texttt{>}.\texttt{<}x,\texttt{roll}(y)\texttt{>}));\texttt{fn}(f.\texttt{<}x,\texttt{roll}(l)\texttt{>}.r)\}}$$

Fig. 6. Partial value splitting rules.

To construct the residual q (corresponding to second-stage computations) partial value splitting redacts all **gr** blocks (replacing them with unit) and **next** annotations:

```
(y, ((),y))
```

A precise definition of the partial value splitting relation is given in Fig. 6. In some regards, the formulation of partial value splitting is arbitrary. For instance, we chose to replace "holes" with unit values, but in fact we could have used any value there and it would make no difference in the end. There are however, at least some parts of the definition that are not arbitrary. Importantly, partial value splitting must not lose any meaningful information, such as injection tags.

4.4 World 𝟙M Term Splitting

The correctness of 𝟙M term splitting with respect to a $\overset{\mathbb{1M}}{\hookrightarrow}$ step is given in Lemma 1. It's very similar to the world 𝟚 version, in that the reduction of the first stage part of e' should imply reduction of the first stage part of e, and that the resulting applied resumers should be equivalent. But split forms at 𝟙M have one more piece of output than those at 𝟚, namely the immediate value i. Lemma 1 accounts for this by saying that that immediate value must be exactly identical on both sides of the step.

The correctness of 𝟙M term splitting with respect to hoisting steps is given in Lemma 2. Because hoisting steps are nothing but rearrangement of second-stage code, this lemma can use the strong requirement of identical combined terms.

Lemma 2 (Hoisting Step Correctness). *If* $e \nearrow [\![q/y]\!]e'$, $e \overset{\mathbb{1M}}{\rightsquigarrow} \{c|l.r\}$, *and* $e' \overset{\mathbb{1M}}{\rightsquigarrow} \{c'|l'.r'\}$, *then* $c = c'$, *and* $l.r \equiv l'.\texttt{let}(q;y.r')$.

4.5 Example Cases

In this section, we consider a few exemplar cases from the proof of Lemma 1.

Reduction of `pi1`. Define $C = \texttt{let}(\underline{\texttt{<<}i_1,i_2\texttt{>},\texttt{<>>}};\texttt{<}y,z\texttt{>}.\texttt{<pi1}(\underline{y}),\underline{z}\texttt{>})$ and $E = \texttt{pi1}(\underline{\texttt{<}v_1,v_2\texttt{>}})$. We are given $E \overset{\mathbb{1M}}{\hookrightarrow} \underline{v_1}$, $E \overset{\mathbb{1M}}{\rightsquigarrow} \{C|l.\texttt{pi1}(\underline{\texttt{<}q_1,q_2\texttt{>}})\}$, and $\underline{v_1} \overset{\mathbb{1M}}{\rightsquigarrow} \{\underline{\texttt{<}i_1,\texttt{<>>}}|\_.\underline{q_1}\}$, and we need to show $C \Downarrow \texttt{<}i_1,\texttt{<>>}$ and $\texttt{pi1}(\underline{\texttt{<}q_1,q_2\texttt{>}}) \equiv q_1$.

$$\frac{v \hookrightarrow \{i;q\}}{\underline{v} \overset{\mathbb{1M}}{\rightsquigarrow} \{\underline{\langle i, \langle\rangle\rangle} \mid \_.q\}} \qquad \frac{e \overset{\mathbb{1M}}{\rightsquigarrow} \{c \mid l.r\} \quad \mathcal{S}[\text{-}] \in \{\texttt{inl(-)}, \texttt{inr(-)}, \texttt{roll(-)}, \texttt{unroll(-)}\}}{\mathcal{S}[e] \overset{\mathbb{1M}}{\rightsquigarrow} \{\texttt{let}(c;\langle y, z\rangle.\langle \mathcal{S}[\underline{y}], \underline{z}\rangle) \mid l.r\}}$$

$$\frac{e \overset{\mathbb{2}}{\rightsquigarrow} \{p \mid l.r\}}{\texttt{next}(e) \overset{\mathbb{1M}}{\rightsquigarrow} \{\langle\langle\rangle, p\rangle \mid l.r\}} \qquad \frac{e \overset{\mathbb{1M}}{\rightsquigarrow} \{c \mid l.r\} \quad \mathcal{S}[\text{-}] \in \{\texttt{pi1(-)}, \texttt{pi2(-)}\}}{\mathcal{S}[e] \overset{\mathbb{1M}}{\rightsquigarrow} \{\texttt{let}(c;\langle y, z\rangle.\langle \mathcal{S}[\underline{y}], \underline{z}\rangle) \mid l.\mathcal{S}[r]\}}$$

$$\frac{e_1 \overset{\mathbb{1M}}{\rightsquigarrow} \{c_1 \mid l_1.r_1\} \quad e_2 \overset{\mathbb{1M}}{\rightsquigarrow} \{c_2 \mid l_2.r_2\}}{\langle e_1, e_2\rangle \overset{\mathbb{1M}}{\rightsquigarrow} \left\{\begin{array}{l} \left(\begin{array}{l} \texttt{let}(c_1;\langle y_1, z_1\rangle. \\ \texttt{let}(c_2;\langle y_2, z_2\rangle. \\ \underline{\langle\langle y_1, y_2\rangle, \langle z_1, z_2\rangle\rangle})) \end{array}\right) \\ \mid \langle l_1, l_2\rangle.\langle r_1, r_2\rangle \end{array}\right\}}$$

$$\frac{e_1 \overset{\mathbb{1M}}{\rightsquigarrow} \{c_1 \mid l_1.r_1\} \quad e_2 \overset{\mathbb{1M}}{\rightsquigarrow} \{c_2 \mid l_2.r_2\}}{\begin{array}{l}\texttt{app}(e_1;e_2) \overset{\mathbb{1M}}{\rightsquigarrow} \\ \left\{\begin{array}{l} \left(\begin{array}{l} \texttt{let}(c_1;\langle y_1, z_1\rangle. \\ \texttt{let}(c_2;\langle y_2, z_2\rangle. \\ \texttt{let}(\texttt{app}(y_1;y_2);\langle y_3, z_3\rangle. \\ \underline{\langle y_3, \langle z_1, z_2, z_3\rangle\rangle}))) \end{array}\right) \\ \mid \langle l_1, l_2, l_3\rangle.\texttt{app}(\underline{r_1};\underline{\langle r_2, l_3\rangle}) \end{array}\right\}\end{array}}$$

$$\frac{\cdot}{\texttt{gr}(e) \overset{\mathbb{1M}}{\rightsquigarrow} \{\langle e, \langle\rangle\rangle \mid \_.\langle\rangle\}} \qquad \frac{e_1 \overset{\mathbb{1M}}{\rightsquigarrow} \{c_1 \mid l_1.r_1\} \quad e_2 \overset{\mathbb{1M}}{\rightsquigarrow} \{c_2 \mid l_2.r_2\}}{\begin{array}{l}\texttt{letg}(e_1;x.e_2) \overset{\mathbb{1M}}{\rightsquigarrow} \\ \left\{\begin{array}{l} \texttt{let}(c_1;\langle x, z_1\rangle.\texttt{let}(c_2;\langle y_2, z_2\rangle.\langle y_2, \langle z_1, z_2\rangle\rangle)) \\ \mid \langle l_1, l_2\rangle.\texttt{let}(r_1;\_.r_2) \end{array}\right\}\end{array}}$$

$$\frac{e_1 \overset{\mathbb{1M}}{\rightsquigarrow} \{c_1 \mid l_1.r_1\} \quad e_2 \overset{\mathbb{1M}}{\rightsquigarrow} \{c_2 \mid l_2.r_2\} \quad e_3 \overset{\mathbb{1M}}{\rightsquigarrow} \{c_3 \mid l_3.r_3\}}{\begin{array}{l}\texttt{caseg}(e_1;x_2.e_2;x_3.e_3) \overset{\mathbb{1M}}{\rightsquigarrow} \\ \left\{\begin{array}{l} \left(\begin{array}{l} \texttt{let}(c_1;\langle y_1, z_1\rangle. \\ \texttt{case}(y_1; \\ \quad x_2.\texttt{let}(c_2;\langle y_2, z_2\rangle.\underline{\langle y_2, \langle z_1, \texttt{inl}(z_2)\rangle\rangle}); \\ \quad x_3.\texttt{let}(c_3;\langle y_3, z_3\rangle.\underline{\langle y_3, \langle z_1, \texttt{inr}(z_3)\rangle\rangle}))) \end{array}\right) \\ \mid \langle l_1, l_b\rangle.(r_1;\texttt{case}(\underline{l_b};l_2.[\langle\rangle/x_2]r_2;l_3.[\langle\rangle/x_3]r_3)) \end{array}\right\}\end{array}}$$

$$\frac{\cdot}{\underline{q} \overset{\mathbb{2}}{\rightsquigarrow} \{\underline{\langle\rangle} \mid \_.q\}} \qquad \frac{e \overset{\mathbb{1M}}{\rightsquigarrow} \{c \mid l.r\}}{\texttt{prev}(e) \overset{\mathbb{2}}{\rightsquigarrow} \{\texttt{pi2}(c) \mid l.r\}}$$

$$\frac{e \overset{\mathbb{2}}{\rightsquigarrow} \{p \mid l.r\} \quad \mathcal{S}[\text{-}] \in \{\texttt{pi1(-)}, \texttt{pi2(-)}, \texttt{inl(-)}, \texttt{inr(-)}, \texttt{roll(-)}, \texttt{unroll(-)}, \texttt{fn}(f.x.\text{-})\}}{\mathcal{S}[e] \overset{\mathbb{2}}{\rightsquigarrow} \{p \mid l.\mathcal{S}[r]\}}$$

$$\frac{e_1 \overset{\mathbb{2}}{\rightsquigarrow} \{p_1 \mid l_1.r_1\} \quad e_2 \overset{\mathbb{2}}{\rightsquigarrow} \{p_2 \mid l_2.r_2\} \quad \mathcal{S}[\text{-},\text{-}] \in \{\langle\text{-},\text{-}\rangle, \texttt{app(-;-)}, \texttt{let}(\text{-};x.\text{-})\}}{\mathcal{S}[e_1, e_2] \overset{\mathbb{2}}{\rightsquigarrow} \{\langle p_1, p_2\rangle \mid \langle l_1, l_2\rangle.\mathcal{S}[r_1, r_2]\}}$$

$$\frac{e_1 \overset{\mathbb{2}}{\rightsquigarrow} \{p_1 \mid l_1.r_1\} \quad e_2 \overset{\mathbb{2}}{\rightsquigarrow} \{p_2 \mid l_2.r_2\} \quad e_3 \overset{\mathbb{2}}{\rightsquigarrow} \{p_3 \mid l_3.r_3\}}{\texttt{case}(e_1;x_2.e_2;x_3.e_3) \overset{\mathbb{2}}{\rightsquigarrow} \{\langle p_1, p_2, p_3\rangle \mid \langle l_1, l_2, l_3\rangle.\texttt{case}(r_1;x_2.r_2;x_3.r_3)\}}$$

Fig. 7. Splitting rules for terms at $\mathbb{1M}$ and $\mathbb{2}$.

$$\frac{\cdot}{e \equiv e} \qquad \frac{e \equiv e'}{e' \equiv e} \qquad \frac{e \equiv e' \quad e' \equiv e''}{e \equiv e''} \qquad \frac{e \xrightarrow{\mathbb{1}\mathbb{G}} e'}{e \equiv e'} \qquad \frac{\cdot}{\mathtt{let}(q;x.\underline{x}) \equiv q}$$

$$\frac{e \equiv e' \quad \mathcal{S}[\text{-}] \in \left\{\begin{array}{l} \mathtt{pi1}(\text{-}), \mathtt{pi2}(\text{-}), \mathtt{inl}(\text{-}), \mathtt{inr}(\text{-}), \mathtt{roll}(\text{-}), \mathtt{unroll}(\text{-}), \mathtt{fn}(f.x.\text{-}), \\ \langle \text{-}, e\rangle, \langle e, \text{-}\rangle, \mathtt{app}(\text{-};e), \mathtt{app}(e;\text{-}), \mathtt{let}(e;x.\text{-}), \mathtt{let}(\text{-};x.e), \\ \mathtt{case}(\text{-};x_2.e_2;x_3.e_3), \mathtt{case}(e_1;x_2.\text{-};x_3.e_3), \mathtt{case}(e_1;x_2.e_2;x_3.\text{-}), \end{array}\right\}}{\mathcal{S}[e] \equiv \mathcal{S}[e']}$$

$$\frac{\mathcal{S}[\text{-}] \in \{\mathtt{pi1}(\text{-}), \mathtt{pi2}(\text{-}), \langle \text{-}, e\rangle, \langle \underline{v}, \text{-}\rangle, \mathtt{app}(\text{-};e), \mathtt{app}(\underline{v};\text{-}), \mathtt{case}(\text{-};x_2.e_2;x_3.e_3)\}}{\mathcal{S}[\mathtt{let}(q;x.e)] \equiv \mathtt{let}(q;x.\mathcal{S}[e])}$$

Fig. 8. Monostage equivalence relation, including reduction, congruence, and let-transposition rules. Since the $\mathbb{1}\mathbb{G}$ fragment of λ^{12} is monostage, we simply use $e \xrightarrow{\mathbb{1}\mathbb{G}} e'$ to mean any standard reduction from e to e'.

Both of these can be derived directly. This pattern, where the outputs can be directly derived, extends to the `pi2` and `prev` reduction rules and all value promotion rules.

Reduction of Application. Let

$$\begin{aligned} E &= \mathtt{app}(\underline{\mathtt{fn}(f.x.e)};\underline{v}), \\ E' &= [\mathtt{fn}(f.x.e), v/f, x]e, \\ I &= \mathtt{fn}(f.x.\mathtt{let}(c;\langle x, y\rangle.\langle x, \mathtt{roll}(y)\rangle)), \\ Q &= \mathtt{fn}(f.\langle x, \mathtt{roll}(l)\rangle.r), \text{ and} \end{aligned} \qquad C = \left[\begin{array}{l} \mathtt{let}(\underline{\langle I, \langle\rangle\rangle};\langle y_1, z_1\rangle. \\ \mathtt{let}(\underline{\langle i_1, \langle\rangle\rangle};\langle y_2, z_2\rangle. \\ \mathtt{let}(\mathtt{app}(\underline{y_1};\underline{y_2});\langle y_3, z_3\rangle. \\ \underline{\langle y_3, \langle z_1, z_2, z_3\rangle\rangle})))\end{array}\right].$$

We are given $E \xhookrightarrow{\mathbb{1}\mathbb{M}} E'$, $E \overset{\mathbb{1}\mathbb{M}}{\rightsquigarrow} \{C|\langle \_, \_, l\rangle.\mathtt{app}(\underline{Q};\underline{\langle q_1, l\rangle})\}$, $E' \overset{\mathbb{1}\mathbb{M}}{\rightsquigarrow} \{[I, i_1/f, x]c|l.[Q, q_1/f, x]r\}$, and $[I, i_1/f, x]c \Downarrow \langle i, b\rangle$. From this, we can derive $C \Downarrow \langle i, \langle\langle\rangle, \langle\rangle, \mathtt{roll}(b)\rangle\rangle$ and $\mathtt{app}(\underline{Q};\underline{\langle q_1, \mathtt{roll}(b)\rangle}) \equiv [Q, q_1, b/f, x, l]r$ directly. This pattern applies to all of the other reduction rules involving substitution, namely those for `caseg`, and `letg`.

Compatibility of `pi1`*at* $\mathbb{2}$. By the case, we are given $\mathtt{pi1}(e) \xhookrightarrow{\mathbb{2}} \mathtt{pi1}(e')$, $\mathtt{pi1}(e) \overset{\mathbb{2}}{\rightsquigarrow} \{p|l.\mathtt{pi1}(r)\}$, $\mathtt{pi1}(e') \overset{\mathbb{2}}{\rightsquigarrow} \{p'|l'.\mathtt{pi1}(r')\}$, and $p' \Downarrow b'$. Inversion of the first three yields $e \xhookrightarrow{\mathbb{2}} e'$, $e \overset{\mathbb{2}}{\rightsquigarrow} \{p|l.r\}$, and $e' \overset{\mathbb{2}}{\rightsquigarrow} \{p'|l'.r'\}$. Using Lemma 1 inductively gives $p \Downarrow b$ and $[b/l]r \equiv [b'/l']r$. From this, $[b/l]\mathtt{pi1}(r) \equiv [b'/l']\mathtt{pi1}(r)$ can be derived directly. This pattern generalizes to all world $\mathbb{2}$ compatibility rules.

Compatibility of `pi1` *at* $\mathbb{1}\mathbb{M}$. By the case, we are given $\mathtt{pi1}(e) \xhookrightarrow{\mathbb{1}\mathbb{M}} \mathtt{pi1}(e')$, $\mathtt{pi1}(e) \overset{\mathbb{1}\mathbb{M}}{\rightsquigarrow} \{\mathtt{let}(c;\langle y, z\rangle.\langle \mathtt{pi1}(\underline{y}), \underline{z}\rangle)|l.\mathtt{pi1}(r)\}$, $\mathtt{pi1}(e') \overset{\mathbb{1}\mathbb{M}}{\rightsquigarrow} \{\mathtt{let}(c';\langle y, z\rangle.\langle \mathtt{pi1}(\underline{y}), \underline{z}\rangle)|l'.\mathtt{pi1}(r')\}$, and $\mathtt{let}(c';\langle y, z\rangle.\langle \mathtt{pi1}(\underline{y}), \underline{z}\rangle) \Downarrow \langle i, b'\rangle$. Inversion of the first three yields $e \xhookrightarrow{\mathbb{1}\mathbb{M}} e'$, $e \overset{\mathbb{1}\mathbb{M}}{\rightsquigarrow} \{c|l.r\}$, and $e' \overset{\mathbb{1}\mathbb{M}}{\rightsquigarrow} \{c'|l'.r'\}$, and inversion of the reduction yields, for some i_2, $c' \Downarrow \langle\langle i, i_2\rangle, b'\rangle$. Using Lemma 1 inductively gives $c \Downarrow \langle\langle i, i_2\rangle, b\rangle$ and

$[b/l]r \equiv [b'/l']r$. From this, we can derive $\texttt{let}(c;<y,z>.<\texttt{pi1}(\underline{y}),\underline{z}>) \Downarrow <i,b>$ and $[b/l]\texttt{pi1}(r) \equiv [b'/l']\texttt{pi1}(r)$ directly. This pattern generalizes to all world $\mathbb{1M}$ compatibility rules.

Compatibility of `gr`. We are given $\texttt{gr}(e) \overset{\mathbb{1M}}{\hookrightarrow} \texttt{gr}(e')$, $\texttt{gr}(e) \overset{\mathbb{1M}}{\rightsquigarrow} \{<e,\underline{<>}>|\_.\underline{<>}\}$, $\texttt{gr}(e') \overset{\mathbb{1M}}{\rightsquigarrow} \{<e',\underline{<>}>|\_.\underline{<>}\}$, and $<e',\underline{<>}> \Downarrow <i,<>>$. Inversion of the step and reduction yield $e \overset{\mathbb{1G}}{\hookrightarrow} e'$ and $e' \Downarrow i$. As a simple property of monostage reduction (which $\overset{\mathbb{1G}}{\hookrightarrow}$ is), we know $e \Downarrow i$. From here, we can derive $<e,\underline{<>}> \Downarrow <i,<>>$ and $\underline{<>} \equiv \underline{<>}$ directly.

4.6 Role of World $\mathbb{1G}$

The splitting algorithm described in the previous subsections operates purely on the local structure of λ^{12} terms. One artifact of this design is that splitting $\mathbb{1M}$ terms may generate resumers containing unnecessary logic. For example, the rule for splitting $\mathbb{1M}$ `caseg` terms inserts the tag from the `caseg` argument into the boundary value, then decodes this tag in the resumer. This logic occurs regardless of whether the terms forming the branches of the `caseg` contain second-stage computations. Worse, if this `caseg` appeared in the body of a recursive function with no other second-stage computations, splitting would generate a resumer with (useless) recursive calls.

An illustrative example is the `part` function in the quickselect example of Sect. 6.3. If `part` were defined at $\mathbb{1M}$ then (like `qs`) it would split into two functions `part1` and `part2`, the latter of which recursively computes the (trivial) second-stage component of `part`'s result. Moreover, `qs2` would call `part2`, just as `qs1` calls `part1`:

```
fun qs2 (p : tree, k : int) : int =
... | Branch (i,h,p1,p2) =>
  let val () = part2 ((),()) in
  case compare k i of ...
```

Rather than attempt global optimization of the outputs of splitting, we instead leverage the type system to indicate when a term contains no second-stage computations by adding a third world $\mathbb{1G}$ whose terms are purely first-stage. Defining `part` in this world is tantamount to proving it has no second-stage computations, allowing splitting to avoid generating the resumer `part2` and calling it from `qs2`.

Since direct staged term evaluation Sect. 3 reduces all first-stage terms to value forms without any remaining stage two work, the distinction between $\mathbb{1M}$ and $\mathbb{1G}$ is unnecessary. In contrast, when performing program transformations before the first-stage inputs are known, it is valuable to form a clear distinction between ground and mixed terms. This was similarly observed in prior work seeking to implement self-applicable partial evaluators [17,18]. While this paper assumes that ground annotations already exist in the input, it may be possible to use binding-time analysis techniques to automatically insert them. Ground is also similar to the validity mechanism in ML5 [19].

4.7 Typing the Boundary Data Structure

One of the central features of our splitting algorithm is that it encodes the control flow behavior of the original staged program into the boundary data structure. For instance, the `case` and `caseg` splitting rules put injection tags on the boundary based on which branch was taken, and the `fn` rule adds a roll tag to the boundary. As a result, the boundary value passed between the two output programs has a (potentially recursive) structure like a tree or list.

This structure can be described with a type; for instance, the staged quick-select yields a binary search tree. Indeed, for most of our examples in Sect. 6, inferring this type is straight-forward. However, we do not yet have a formal characterization of these boundary types that is defined for all $\lambda^{\mathbb{1}2}$ programs, though we plan to pursue this in future work.[5]

5 Implementation

We have encoded the type system, dynamic semantics, splitting algorithm, and output semantics in Twelf, as well as all of the theorems of Sects. 3 and 4, and their proofs. We also have a Standard ML implementation of the $\lambda^{\mathbb{1}2}$ language, a staged interpreter, the splitting algorithm, and an interpreter for split programs. This implementation extends the language described in Sect. 3 with ints, bools, `let` statements, n-ary sums and products, datatype and function declarations, and deep pattern matching (including `next`() and `gr`() patterns). The code snippets in this paper are written in our concrete syntax, using these additional features when convenient. Our expanded syntax allows staging annotations around declarations. For example,

```
@gr{
  datatype list = Empty | Cons of int * list
  fun part (...) = ...
}
fun qss (...) = ...
```

declares the `list` datatype and `part` function at world $\mathbb{1}\mathbb{G}$, by elaborating into:

```
val gr{Empty} = gr{roll (inj ...)}
val gr{Cons} = gr{fn (...) => roll (inj ...)}
val gr{part} = gr{fn (...) => ...}
val qss = fn (...) => ...
```

In the splitting algorithm, we perform a number of optimizations which drastically improve the readability of split programs. For example, we split patterns directly, instead of first translating them into lower-level constructs. We also take advantage of many local simplifications, most notably, not pairing precomputations when one is known to be `<>`.

[5] Observe that in the outputs of splitting we could have omitted the `roll` tag from functions or replaced `inl`(a) and `inr`(b) with <0, a> and <1, b>, and the proof of correctness would still have gone through. We chose the tags, however, in order to keep the typed interpretation more natural, even in absence of a formal result.

6 Examples of Splitting

Now we investigate the behavior of our splitting algorithm on several examples. The split code that follows is the output of our splitting implementation; for clarity, we have performed some minor optimizations and manually added type annotations (including datatype declarations and constructor names), as our algorithm does not type its output.

6.1 Dot Product

Our first example, dot, appears in [16]. dot is a first-order, non-recursive function—precisely the sort of code studied in prior work on pass separation for imperative languages. dot takes the dot product of two three-dimensional vectors, where the first two coordinates are first-stage, and the last coordinate is second-stage.

```
type vec = ∇int * ∇int * ○int
// dot : vec * vec -> ○int
fun dot ((gr{x1},gr{y1},next{z1}),(gr{x2},gr{y2},next{z2})) =
  next{ prev{hold gr{(x1*x2) + (y1*y2)}} + (z1*z2)}
```

The body of dot is an int term at world 2 containing an int computation of (x1*x2) + (y1*y2) which is promoted from world 1G to world 2. We would expect the first stage of the split program to take the first two coordinates of each vector and perform that first-stage computation; and the second stage to take the final coordinates and the result of the first stage, then multiply and add. Our algorithm splits dot into the two functions:

```
fun dot1 ((x1,y1,()), (x2,y2,()))    = ((), (x1*x2)+(y1*y2))
fun dot2 ((((),(),z1),((),(),z2)),l) = l+(z1*z2)
```

As expected, dot1 returns (x1*x2)+(y1*y2) as the precomputation, and dot2 adds that precomputation to the products of the final coordinates. This is exactly what is done in [16], though they write the precomputation into a mutable cache.

6.2 Exponentiation by Squaring

Our next example, exp, is a mainstay of the partial evaluation literature (for example, in [13]). exp recursively computes b^e using exponentiation by squaring, where e is known at the first stage, and b is known at the second stage.

```
fun exp (next{b} : ○int , gr{e} : ∇int) =
 if      gr{e == 0}          then next{1}
 else if gr{e mod 2 == 0} then exp(next{b*b},gr{e/2})
 else                             next{b*prev{exp(next{b*b},gr{(e-1)/2})}}
```

Because exp is a recursive function whose conditionals test the parity of the exponent argument, the sequence of branches taken corresponds exactly to the binary representation of e. Partially evaluating exp with e eliminates all of the conditionals, selecting and expanding the appropriate branch in each case.

Our algorithm, on the other hand, produces:

```
datatype binnat = Zero
                | Even of binnat
                | Odd of binnat

fun exp1 (b : unit, e : int) =
  if      e == 0        then ((), Zero)
  else if e mod 2 == 0 then ((), Even (#2 (exp1 ((), e/2))))
  else                       ((), Odd  (#2 (exp1 ((), (e-1)/2))))

fun exp2 ((b : int, e : unit), l : binnat) =
    case l of
      Zero => 1
    | Even n => exp2 ((b*b, ()), n)
    | Odd n => b * exp2 ((b*b, ()), n)
```

exp1 recursively performs parity tests on e, but unlike exp, it simply computes a data structure (a binnat) recording which branches were taken. exp2 takes b and a binnat l, and uses l to determine how to compute with b.

Of course, the binnat computed by exp1 is precisely the binary representation of e! While partial evaluation realizes exp's control-flow dependency on a fixed e by recursively expanding its branches in place, we explicitly record this dependency generically over all e by creating a boundary data structure. This occurs in the $\overset{1M}{\rightsquigarrow}$ rule for case, which emits a tag corresponding to the taken branch in the precomputation, and cases on it (as l_b) in the residual.

Because splitting exp does not eliminate its conditionals, partial evaluation is more useful in this case. (Notice, however, that partially evaluating exp2 on a binnat is essentially the same as partially evaluating exp on the corresponding int.) Nevertheless, splitting exp still demonstrates how our algorithm finds interesting data structures latent in the structure of recursive functions.

6.3 Quickselect

Let us return to the quickselect algorithm, which we discussed at length in Sect. 2. (The code is in Fig. 1(b).) qss finds the kth largest element of a list l by recursively partitioning the list by its first element, then recurring on the side containing the kth largest element. l is first-stage and k is second-stage.

Stage-splitting qss produces:

```
datatype tree = Leaf | Branch of int * tree * int * tree
datatype list = Empty | Cons of int * list

fun part ((p,l):int*list) : (int*list*list) =
  case l of Empty => (0,Empty, Empty)
```

```
  | Cons (h,t) =>
      let val (n,left,right) = part (p,t) in
      if h<p then (n+1,Cons(h,left),right)
             else (n,left,Cons(h,right))

fun qs1 (l : list, k : unit) =
  ((), case l of Empty => Leaf
       | Cons (h,t) => Branch (
           let val (n,left,right) = part (h,t) in
           (n, #2 (qs1 left k), h, #2 (qs1 right k))))

fun qs2 (((), k : int), p : tree) =
  case p of Leaf => 0
  | Branch (n,left,h,right) =>
      case compare k n of
        LT => qs2 (((), k), left)
      | EQ => h
      | GT => qs2 (((), k-n-1), right)
```

This is nearly identical to the cleaned-up code we presented in Fig. 2, except we do not suppress the trivial inputs and outputs of `qs1` and `qs2`.

The function `qs1` partitions l, but since the comparison with k (to determine which half of l to recur on) is at the second stage, it simply recurs on *both* halves, pairing up the results along with h (the head of l) and n (the size of the left half). `qs2` takes k and this tree p, and uses k to determine how to traverse p.

How does our splitting algorithm generate binary search trees and a traversal algorithm? The $\overset{2}{\rightsquigarrow}$ rule for `case` tuples up the precomputations for its branches, and in the residual, selects the residual corresponding to the appropriate branch. The tree is implicit in the structure of the code; ordinarily, the quickselect algorithm only explores a single branch, but the staging annotations force the entire tree to be built.

This is an instance where stage-splitting is more practical than partial evaluation; if l is large, partially evaluating `quickselect` requires runtime generation of a huge amount of code simultaneously encoding the tree and traversal algorithm. (Avoiding the code blowup, by not expanding some calls to `part`, would result in duplicating first-stage computations.)

Note that the recursive `part` function is defined within a `gr` annotation. As explained in Sect. 4.6, defining `part` at $\mathbb{1M}$ would cause it to split in a way that incurs extra cost at the second stage. In this case, that cost would be $\Theta(n)$ in the size of the input list, enough to overpower the asymptotic speedup gained elsewhere. With `gr` annotations, however, this can be prevented.

As discussed in Sect. 2, `qs1` performs $\Theta(n \log n)$ expected work per call, whereas `qs2` performs $\Theta(\log n)$ expected work. This results in a net speedup over standard quickselect if we perform many (specifically, $\omega(\log n)$) queries on the same list—precisely the topic of our next example.

6.4 Mixed-Stage Map Combinator

As a lambda calculus, one of the strengths of λ^{12} is that it can express combinators as higher order functions. In this example, we consider just such a combinator: `tmap`, which turns a function of type ∇`list` $*\bigcirc$`int` $\rightarrow \bigcirc$`int` into one of type ∇`list` $*\bigcirc$`list2` $\rightarrow \bigcirc$`list2`, by mapping over the second argument.[6]

```
@next{ datatype list2 = Empty2 | Cons2 of int * list2 }

fun tmap (f : ∇list * ○int -> ○int) (l : ∇list, q : ○list2) =
  next{ let fun m Empty2        = Empty2
              | m (Cons2(h,t)) = Cons2(prev{f (l,next{h})}, m t)
        in m prev{q}}
val mapqss = tmap qss
```

Importantly, `tmap f` performs the first-stage part of `f` once and second-stage part of `f` many times. This was discussed in the context of partial evaluation in Sect. 3.4, but it is especially clear when we look at the output of splitting:

```
fun tmap1 f = (fn (l,()) => ((),#2 (f (l,()))),())
val (mapqss1,()) = tmap1 qs1

datatype list2 = Empty2 | Cons2 of int * list2
fun tmap2 (f,()) ((l,q), p : tree) =
  let fun m Empty2 = Empty2
        | m (Cons2(h,t)) = Cons2(f ((l,h), p), m t)
  in m q
val mapqss2 = tmap2 (qs2, ())
```

Indeed, observe that the argument `f` (for which `qs1` is later substituted) of `tmap1` is called only once, whereas the corresponding argument `f` (for which `qs2` is later substituted) in `tmap2` is evaluated once per element in the query list `q`.

6.5 Composing Graphics Pipeline Programs

Composable staged programs are particularly important the domain of real-time graphics. This need arises because modern graphics architectures actually *require* that graphics computations be structured as a pipeline of stages which perform increasingly fine-grained computations (e.g., per-object, per-screen region, per-pixel), where computations in later stages use the results of an earlier stage multiple times [26].

The standard way to program these graphics pipelines is to define one program (usually called a *shader*) per stage. In other words, the programmer is expected to write their multi-stage programs in an already split form. This requirement results in complex code where invariants must hold across different

---

[6] λ^{12} doesn't have a way to "share" datatype declarations between stages, so we define `list2` to be a list of integers at the second stage.

stages and local changes to the logic of one stage may require changes to that of upstream stages. This harms composition and modularity. Graphics researchers therefore have suggested using mechanisms like our stages [8,11,22] to express graphics program logic, including representing entire pipeline as a single multi-stage function [8].

As a language, λ^{12} is well suited for specification of such functions, and we give a simple example below. In it, we consider a graphics pipeline program to be a staged function that takes an object definition in the first stage (`object`) and a pixel coordinate in the second stage ($\bigcirc$`coord`), and emits the color of the object at the specified pixel ($\bigcirc$`color`). Given two such multistage functions, we then define a combinator that multiplies their results pointwise in the second stage.[7]

```
datatype object = ...
@next{  type coord = int * int
        type color = ...         }
type pipeline = object * ◯coord -> ◯color

fun shade (refl : pipeline, albedo : pipeline) : pipeline =
  fn (obj : object, next{xy} : ◯coord) =>
      prev{refl (obj,next{xy})} * prev{albedo (obj,next{xy})}
```

Prior work [8] lacks the ability to define such combinators, because it does not support higher order functions.

7 Related Work

Frequency reduction and precomputation are common techniques for both designing algorithms and performing compiler optimizations [15]. The idea behind precomputation is to identify computations that can be performed earlier (e.g., at compile time) if their inputs are available statically and perform them at that earlier time. Dynamic algorithms, partial evaluation, and incremental computation are all examples of precomputation techniques. The idea behind frequency reduction is to identify computations that are performed multiple times and pull them ahead so that they can be performed once and used later as needed. Dynamic programming, loop hoisting, and splitting (presented here) are all examples of frequency reduction techniques.

Precomputation techniques. Perhaps one of the most studied examples of precomputation is partial evaluation, which distinguishes between static (compile-time) and dynamic (runtime) stages. Given a program and values for all static

[7] Although this is a general pointwise multiplication combinator, the variable names suggest a possible interpretation of the inputs and output: the first input function calculates the albedo of an object (a measure of how much light it reflects), the second input calculates the object's incoming light, and so the output (the product of these terms) is a function that calculates the outgoing light from an object.

inputs, partial evaluation generates a specialized program by performing computations that depend only on the static inputs [13]. We refer the reader to the book by Jones, Gommard, and Sestoft for a comprehensive discussion of partial evaluation work until the early 90's [14].

Early approaches to partial evaluation can be viewed as operating in two stages: binding time analysis and program specialization. For a multivariate program with clearly marked static and dynamic arguments, binding-time analysis identifies all the parts of the program that can be computed by the knowledge of static arguments. Using this information and the values of static arguments, program specialization specializes the original program to a partially-evaluated one that operates on many different dynamic arguments. This approach has been applied to construct partial evaluators for a number of languages such as Scheme [2,3].

Researchers have explored other staging transformations that, like splitting, partition an input two-stage program into two components, one corresponding to each stage. In particular, *binding time separation* [18] (also called *program bifurcation* [6]) has been used as a preprocessor step in partial evaluators, allowing efficient specialization of programs with mixed-stage data structures without changes to the specializer itself. Notably, the grammar-based binding-time specifications used in binding time separation are capable of describing data structures with purely-static, purely-dynamic, and mixed-stage content, much like the type system of $\lambda^{\mathbb{12}}$ (though this correspondence is less clear without our addition of $\mathbb{1G}$ and ∇).

However unlike splitting, where the goal is to emit code where first-stage results are computed once and then reused in multiple invocations of second-stage execution, the second (dynamic) function produced by binding time separation does not use the results of the first; instead, it has access to the first-stage inputs and recomputes all required first-stage computations. As noted by Knoblock and Ruf [16], it may be possible to modify the program bifurcation algorithm to cache and reuse the intermediate results, but this was never attempted. Alternatively, our algorithm could potentially be used as the basis of a general bifurcation algorithm in a partial evaluator.

Experience with binding time analysis showed that it can be difficult to control, leading to programs whose performance was difficult to predict. This led to investigations based on type systems for making the stage of computations explicit in programs [10,21] and writing "metaprograms" that, when evaluated at a stage, yield a new program to be evaluated at the next stage. Davies [4] presented a logical construction of binding-time type systems by deriving a type system via the Curry-Howard correspondence applied to temporal logic. Davies and Pfenning proposed a new type system for staged computation based on a particular fragment of modal logic [5]. The work on MetaML extended type-based techniques to a full-scale language by developing a statically typed programming language based on ML that enables the programmer to express programs with multiple stages [27,28]. MetaML's type system is similar to Davies [4] but extends it in several important ways. Nanevksi and Pfenning further extended the these techniques by allowing free variables to occur within staged computations [20].

The type-system of λ^{12} is closely related to this later line of work on metaprogramming and staged computation. The specific extension to the typed lambda calculus that we use here is based on the $\bigcirc$ modality of Davies [5]. Our types differ in the restriction to two stages and the addition of ∇; however, the key difference between our work and this prior work is that we instead focus on the problem of splitting.

Another class of precomputation techniques is incremental computation, where a program can efficiently respond to small changes in its inputs by only recomputing parts of the computation affected by the changes [1,7,23,24]. However, unlike splitting, incremental computation does not require fixing any of its inputs and, in the general case, allows for all program inputs to change. Thus, the benefits of incremental computation depend on what changes to inputs are made. For example, while it is possible to apply incremental computation to the quickselect example in Sect. 2, techniques would unfold the quickselect function based on the demanded ranks, potentially incurring linear time cost at each step of the algorithm (as opposed to the logarithmic result produced by splitting). Moreover, incremental computation techniques must also maintain sophisticated data structures dynamically at run time to track what computations must be performed.

Stage Splitting. Algorithms for stage splitting have appeared in the literature under the names *pass separation* [15] and *data specialization* [16]. Perhaps the closest work to ours is the algorithm for data specialization given by Knoblock and Ruf [16], which also seeks to statically split an explicitly staged program into two stages. However, they only consider a simple first-order language and straight-line programs. Their work also treats all computations guarded by second-stage conditionals as second-stage computations, which would prevent optimization (via splitting) of programs such as quickselect.

As noted in Sect. 6.5, splitting algorithms have also been a topic of interest in programming systems for computer graphics, where, to achieve high performance, programs are manually separated into components by frequency of execution corresponding to graphics hardware pipeline stages. The software engineering challenges of modifying multiple per-stage programs have led to suggestions of writing graphics programs in an explicitly-staged programming language [8,11,22] and deferring the task of pass separation to the compiler. However, all prior splitting efforts in computer graphics, like that of Knoblock and Ruf [16], have been limited to simple, imperative languages.

Defunctionalization. Defunctionalization [25] is a program transformation that eliminates high-order functions and replaces them with lower order functions that manipulate a data structure encoding the original control flow. This operation has similarity to our splitting transformation, which eliminates staging in a program by encoding control flow in a data structure passed between the stage one and stage two outputs. It would interesting to explore the possibility of a semantics-preserving transformation to convert a staged program into a higher-order form, and then applying defunctionalization to obtain our results.

8 Conclusion

This paper presents a splitting algorithm for $\lambda^{\mathbb{1}\mathbb{2}}$, a two-staged typed lambda calculus with support for recursion and first-class functions. The type system of $\lambda^{\mathbb{1}\mathbb{2}}$ uses three worlds $\mathbb{1}\mathbb{M}$, $\mathbb{1}\mathbb{G}$, and $\mathbb{2}$ to classify code by its stage, with the modalities $\bigcirc$ and ∇ providing internalizations of second-stage code and ground first-stage code to the mixed world. We present a dynamic semantics that evaluates terms in two passes and provides an eager interpretation of `next` via hoisting steps. We prove the correctness of our splitting algorithm against the dynamic semantics, and implement this proof in Twelf. Finally, we discuss our implementation of $\lambda^{\mathbb{1}\mathbb{2}}$ and its splitting algorithm and analyze their behavior for a number of staged programs, including those with higher-order and recursive functions.

Looking forward, we are interested in investigating the behavior of splitting in the presence of richer language features such as mutation, polymorphism, parallel constructs, and more than two stages. Also while we have proven the dynamic correctness of our splitting algorithm, we do not yet have a characterization of the types of the output or of the cost behavior of output terms.

References

1. Acar, U.A., Blelloch, G.E., Blume, M., Harper, R., Tangwongsan, K.: An experimental analysis of self-adjusting computation. ACM Trans. Prog. Lang. Sys. **32**(1), 3:1–3:53 (2009)
2. Bondorf, A., Danvy, O.: Automatic autoprojection of recursive equations with global variable and abstract data types. Sci. Comput. Program. **16**(2), 151–195 (1991)
3. Consel, C.: New insights into partial evaluation: the schism experiment. In: Ganzinger, H. (ed.) ESOP '88. Lecture Notes in Computer Science, vol. 300, pp. 236–246. Springer, Heidelberg (1988)
4. Davies, R.: A temporal-logic approach to binding-time analysis. In: LICS, pp. 184–195 (1996)
5. Davies, R., Pfenning, F.: A modal analysis of staged computation. J. ACM **48**(3), 555–604 (2001)
6. De Niel, A., Bevers, E., De Vlaminck, K.: Program bifurcation for a polymorphically typed functional language. SIGPLAN Not. **26**(9), 142–153 (1991)
7. Demers, A., Reps, T., Teitelbaum, T.: Incremental evaluation of attribute grammars with application to syntax-directed editors. In: Principles of Programming Languages, pp. 105–116 (1981)
8. Foley, T., Hanrahan, P.: Spark: modular, composable shaders for graphics hardware. ACM Trans. Graph. **30**(4), 107:1–107:12 (2011)
9. Futamura, Y.: Partial evaluation of computation process - an approach to a compiler-compiler. Syst. Comput. Controls **2**(5), 45–50 (1971)
10. Gomard, C.K., Jones, N.D.: A partial evaluator for the untyped lambda-calculus. J. Funct. Program. **1**(1), 21–69 (1991)
11. He, Y., Gu, Y., Fatahalian, K.: Extending the graphics pipeline with adaptive, multi-rate shading. ACM Trans. Graph. **33**(4), 142:1–142:12 (2014)
12. Hoare, C.A.R.: Algorithm 65: find. Commun. ACM **4**(7), 321–322 (1961)

13. Jones, N.D.: An introduction to partial evaluation. ACM Comput. Surv. **28**(3), 480–503 (1996)
14. Jones, N.D., Gomard, C.K., Sestoft, P.: Partial Evaluation and Automatic Program Generation. Prentice Hall International Series in Computer Science. Prentice Hall, UPPER SADDLE RIVER (1993)
15. Jørring, U., Scherlis, W.L.: Compilers and staging transformations. In: Proceedings of the 13th ACM SIGACT-SIGPLAN Symposium on Principles of Programming Languages. POPL 1986, NY, USA, pp. 86–96. ACM, New York (1986)
16. Knoblock, T.B., Ruf, E.: Data specialization. In: Proceedings of the ACM SIGPLAN 1996 Conference on Programming Language Design and Implementation. PLDI 1996, NY, USA, pp. 215–225. ACM, New York (1996)
17. Mogensen, T.A.: Binding time analysis for polymorphically typed higher order languages. In: Díaz, J., Orejas, F. (eds.) TAPSOFT 1989. LNCS, vol. 352, pp. 298–312. Springer, Heidelberg (1989). Volume 2: Advanced Seminar on Foundations of Innovative Software Development II and Colloquium on Current Issues in Programming Languages
18. Mogensen, T.A.: Separating binding times in language specifications. In: Proceedings of the Fourth International Conference on Functional Programming Languages and Computer Architecture. FPCA 1989, NY, USA, pp. 12–25. ACM, New York (1989)
19. Murphy VII, T., Crary, K., Harper, R.: Distributed control flow with classical modal logic. In: Ong, L. (ed.) CSL 2005. LNCS, vol. 3634, pp. 51–69. Springer, Heidelberg (2005)
20. Nanevski, A., Pfenning, F.: Staged computation with names and necessity. J. Funct. Program. **15**(5), 893–939 (2005)
21. Nielson, F., Nielson, H.R.: Two-level Functional Languages. Cambridge University Press, New York (1992)
22. Proudfoot, K., Mark, W.R., Tzvetkov, S., Hanrahan, P.: A real-time procedural shading system for programmable graphics hardware. In: Proceedings of the 28th Annual Conference on Computer Graphics and Interactive Techniques. SIGGRAPH 2001, pp. 159–170. ACM (2001)
23. Pugh, W., Teitelbaum, T.: Incremental computation via function caching. In: Principles of Programming Languages, pp. 315–328 (1989)
24. Ramalingam, G., Reps, T.: A categorized bibliography on incremental computation. In: Principles of Programming Languages, pp. 502–510 (1993)
25. Reynolds, J.C.: Definitional interpreters for higher-order programming languages. In: Proceedings of the ACM Annual Conference. ACM 1972, NY, USA, vol. 2, pp. 717–740. ACM, New York (1972)
26. Segal, M., Akeley, K.: The OpenGL Graphics System: A Specification (Version 4.0). The Khronos Group, Inc., Beaverton (2010)
27. Taha, W.: Multi-Stage Programming: Its Theory and Applications. Ph.D. thesis, Oregon Graduate Institute of Science and Technology(1999)
28. Taha, W., Sheard, T.: Multi-stage programming with explicit annotations. In: Proceedings of the 1997 ACM SIGPLAN Symposium on Partial Evaluation and Semantics-based Program Manipulation. PEPM 1997 (1997)

Probabilistic NetKAT

Nate Foster[1(✉)], Dexter Kozen[1], Konstantinos Mamouras[2], Mark Reitblatt[1], and Alexandra Silva[3]

[1] Cornell University, New York, USA
jnfoster@cs.cornell.edu
[2] University of Pennsylvania, Philadelphia, USA
[3] University College London, London, UK

Abstract. This paper presents a new language for network programming based on a probabilistic semantics. We extend the NetKATlanguage with new primitives for expressing probabilistic behaviors and enrich the semantics from one based on deterministic functions to one based on measurable functions on sets of packet histories. We establish fundamental properties of the semantics, prove that it is a conservative extension of the deterministic semantics, show that it satisfies a number of natural equations, and develop a notion of approximation. We present case studies that show how the language can be used to model a diverse collection of scenarios drawn from real-world networks.

1 Introduction

Formal specification and verification of networks has become a reality in recent years with the emergence of network-specific programming languages and property-checking tools. Programming languages like Frenetic [11], Pyretic [35], Maple [51], FlowLog [37], and others are enabling programmers to specify the intended behavior of a network in terms of high-level constructs such as Boolean predicates and functions on packets. Verification tools like Header Space Analysis [21], VeriFlow [22], and NetKAT [12] are making it possible to check properties such as connectivity, loop freedom, and traffic isolation automatically.

However, despite many notable advances, these frameworks all have a fundamental limitation: they model network behavior in terms of deterministic packet-processing functions. This approach works well enough in settings where the network functionality is simple, or where the properties of interest only concern the forwarding paths used to carry traffic. But it does not provide satisfactory accounts of more complicated situations that often arise in practice:

- **Congestion:** the network operator wishes to calculate the expected degree of congestion on each link given a model of the demands for traffic.
- **Failure:** the network operator wishes to calculate the probability that packets will be delivered to their destination, given that devices and links fail with a certain probability.

K. Mamouras—Work performed at Cornell University.

P. Thiemann (Ed.): ESOP 2016, LNCS 9632, pp. 282–309, 2016.
DOI: 10.1007/978-3-662-49498-1_12

- **Randomized Forwarding:** the network operator wishes to use randomized routing schemes such as equal cost multi-path routing (ECMP) or Valiant load balancing (VLB) to balance load across multiple paths.

Overall, there is a mismatch between the realities of modern networks and the capabilities of existing reasoning frameworks. This paper presents a new framework, Probabilistic NetKAT (ProbNetKAT), that is designed to bridge this gap.

Background. As its name suggests, ProbNetKAT is based on NetKAT, a network programming language developed in prior work [1,12,47]. NetKAT is an extension of Kleene algebra with tests (KAT), an algebraic system for propositional verification of imperative programs that has been extensively studied for nearly two decades [25]. At the level of syntax, NetKAT offers a rich collection of intuitive constructs including: conditional tests; primitives for modifying packet headers and encoding topologies; and sequential, parallel, and iteration operators. The semantics of the language can be understood in terms of a denotational model based on functions from packet histories to sets of packet histories (where a history records the path through the network taken by a packet) or equivalently, using an equational deductive system that is sound and complete with respect to the denotational semantics. NetKAT has a PSPACE decision procedure that exploits the coalgebraic structure of the language and can solve many verification problems automatically [12]. Several practical applications of NetKAT have been developed, including algorithms for testing reachability and non-interference, a syntactic correctness proof for a compiler that translates programs to hardware instructions for SDN switches, and a compiler that handles source programs written against virtual topologies [47].

Challenges. Probabilistic NetKAT enriches the semantics of NetKAT so that programs denote functions that yield probability distributions on sets of packet histories. Although this change is simple at the surface, it enables adding powerful primitives such as random choice, which can be used to handle the scenarios above involving congestion, failure, and randomized forwarding. At the same time, it creates significant challenges because the semantics must be extended to handle probability distributions while preserving the intuitive meaning of NetKAT's existing programming constructs. A number of important questions do not have obvious answers: Should the semantics be based on discrete or continuous distributions? How should it handle operators such as parallel composition that combine multiple distributions into a single distribution? Do suitable fixpoints exist that can be used to provide semantics for iteration?

Approach. Our development of a semantics for ProbNetKAT follows a classic approach: we first define a suitable mathematical space of objects and then identify semantic objects in this space that serve as denotations for each of the syntactic constructs in the language. Our semantics is based on Markov kernels over sets of packet histories. To a first approximation, these can be thought of as functions that produce a probability distribution on sets of packet histories, but the properties of Markov kernels ensure that important operators such as sequential composition behave as expected. The parallel composition operator is particularly interesting, since it must combine disjoint and overlapping distributions (the latter models multicast), as is the Kleene star operator, since it requires showing that fixpoints exist.

Evaluation. To evaluate our design, we prove that the probabilistic semantics of ProbNetKAT is a conservative extension of the standard NetKAT semantics. This is a crucial point of our work: the language developed in this paper is based on NetKAT, which in turn is an extension of KAT, a well-established framework for program verification. Hence, this work can be seen as the next step in the modular development of an expressive network programming language, with increasingly sophisticated set of features, based on a sound and long-standing mathematical foundation. We also develop a number of case studies that illustrate the use of the semantics on examples inspired by real-world scenarios. These case studies model congestion, failure, and randomization, as discussed above, as well as a gossip protocol that disseminates information through a network.

Contributions. Overall, the contributions of this paper are as follows:

- We present the design of ProbNetKAT, the first language-based framework for specifying and verifying probabilistic network behavior.
- We define a formal semantics for ProbNetKAT based on Markov kernels, prove that it conservatively extends the semantics of NetKAT, and develop a notion of approximation between programs.
- We develop a number of case studies that illustrate the use of ProbNetKAT on real-world examples.

Outline. The rest of this paper is organized as follows: Sect. 2 introduces the basic ideas behind ProbNetKAT through an example; Sect. 3 reviews concepts from measure theory needed to define the semantics; Sect. 4 and Sect. 5 present the syntax and semantics of ProbNetKAT; Sect. 6 illustrates the semantics by proving conservativity and some natural equations; Sect. 8 discusses applications of the semantics to real-world examples. We discuss related work in Sect. 9 and conclude in Sect. 10. Proofs and further semantic details can be found in the extended version of this paper [13].

2 Overview

This section introduces ProbNetKAT using a simple example and discusses some of the key challenges in designing the language.

Preliminaries. A *packet* π is a record with fields x_1 to x_k ranging over standard header fields (Ethernet and IP addresses, TCP ports, etc.) as well as special switch and port fields indicating its network location: $\{x_1 = n_1, \ldots, x_k = n_k\}$. We write $\pi(x)$ for value of π's x field and $\pi[n/x]$ for the packet obtained from π by setting the x field to n. We often abbreviate the switch field as sw. A *packet history* σ is a non-empty sequence of packets $\pi_1 : \pi_2 : \cdots : \pi_m$, listed from youngest to oldest. Operationally, only the *head packet* π_1 exists in the network, but in the semantics we keep track of the packet's history to enable precise specification of forwarding along specific paths. We write $\pi : \eta$ for the history with head π and (possibly empty) tail η and H for the set of all histories.

Example. Consider the network shown in Fig. 1 with six switches arranged into a "barbell" topology. Suppose the network operator wants to configure the switches to forward traffic on the two left-to-right paths from I_1 to E_1 and I_2 to E_2. We can implement this in ProbNetKAT as follows:

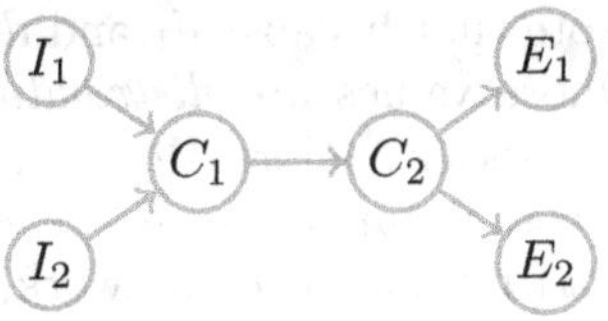

Fig. 1. Barbell topology.

$$p \triangleq (sw = I_1; \mathtt{dup}; sw \leftarrow C_1; \mathtt{dup}; sw \leftarrow C_2; \mathtt{dup}; sw \leftarrow E_1) \mathbin{\&}$$
$$(sw = I_2; \mathtt{dup}; sw \leftarrow C_1; \mathtt{dup}; sw \leftarrow C_2; \mathtt{dup}; sw \leftarrow E_2)$$

Because it only uses deterministic constructs, this program can be modeled as a function $f \in 2^H \rightarrow 2^H$ on sets of packet histories: the input represents the initial set of in-flight packets while the output represents the final set of results produced by the program—the empty set is produced when the input packets are dropped (e.g., in a firewall) and a set with more elements than the input set is produced when some input packets are copied (e.g., in multicast). Our example program consists of tests ($sw = I_1$), which filter the set of input packets, retaining only those whose head packets satisfy the test; modifications ($sw \leftarrow C_1$), which change the value of one of the fields in the head packet; duplication (dup), which archives the current value of the head packet in the history; and sequential (;) and parallel (&) composition operators. In this instance, the tests are mutually exclusive so the parallel composition behaves like a disjoint union operator.

Now suppose the network operator wants to calculate not just *where* traffic is routed but also *how much* traffic is sent across each link. The deterministic semantics we have seen so far calculates the trajectories that packets take through the network. Hence, for a given set of inputs, we can use the semantics to calculate the set of output histories and then count how many packets traversed each link, yielding an upper bound on congestion. But now suppose we want to *predict* the amount of congestion that could be induced from a model that encodes expectations about the set of possible inputs. Such models, which are often represented as traffic matrices, can be built from historical monitoring data using a variety of statistical techniques [34]. Unfortunately, even simple calculations of how much congestion is likely to occur on a given link cannot be performed using the deterministic semantics.

Returning to the example, suppose that we wish to represent the following traffic model in ProbNetKAT: in each time period, the number of packets originating at I_1 is either 0, 1 or 2, with equal probability, and likewise for I_2. Let π_1 to π_4 be distinct packets, and write $\pi_{I_j,i}!$ for the sequence of assignments that produces the packet π_i located at switch I_j. We can encode the distributions at I_1 and I_2 using the following ProbNetKAT terms:[1]

$$d_1 \triangleq \mathtt{drop} \oplus \pi_{I_1,1}! \oplus (\pi_{I_1,1}! \mathbin{\&} \pi_{I_1,2}!)$$
$$d_2 \triangleq \mathtt{drop} \oplus \pi_{I_2,3}! \oplus (\pi_{I_2,3}! \mathbin{\&} \pi_{I_2,4}!)$$

[1] An expression $p_1 \oplus \cdots \oplus p_n$ means that one of the p_i should be chosen at random with uniform probability and executed.

Note that because d_1 and d_2 involve probabilistic choice, they denote functions whose values are *distributions* on sets of histories rather than simply sets of histories as before. However, because they do not contain tests, they are actually constant functions, so we can treat them as distributions. For the full input distribution to the network, we combine d_1 and d_2 independently using parallel composition: $d \triangleq d_1 \,\&\, d_2$.

To calculate a distribution that encodes the amount of congestion on network links, we can push the input distribution d through the forwarding policy p using sequential composition: $d; p$. This produces a distribution on sets of histories. In this example, there are nine such sets, where we write $I_{1,1}$ to indicate that π_1 was processed at I_1, and similarly for the other switches and packets,

$$
\begin{array}{l}
\{\},\\
\{E_{1,1}{:}C_{2,1}{:}C_{1,1}{:}I_{1,1}\},\\
\{E_{1,1}{:}C_{2,1}{:}C_{1,1}{:}I_{1,1},\ E_{1,2}{:}C_{2,2}{:}C_{1,2}{:}I_{1,2}\},\\
\{E_{2,3}{:}C_{2,3}{:}C_{1,3}{:}I_{2,3}\},\\
\{E_{2,3}{:}C_{2,3}{:}C_{1,3}{:}I_{2,3},\ E_{2,4}{:}C_{2,4}{:}C_{1,4}{:}I_{2,4}\},\\
\{E_{1,1}{:}C_{2,1}{:}C_{1,1}{:}I_{1,1},\ E_{2,3}{:}C_{2,3}{:}C_{1,3}{:}I_{2,3}\}\\
\{E_{1,1}{:}C_{2,1}{:}C_{1,1}{:}I_{1,1},\ E_{1,2}{:}C_{2,2}{:}C_{1,2}{:}I_{1,2},\ E_{2,3}{:}C_{2,3}{:}C_{1,3}{:}I_{2,3}\}\\
\{E_{1,1}{:}C_{2,1}{:}C_{1,1}{:}I_{1,1},\ E_{2,3}{:}C_{2,3}{:}C_{1,3}{:}I_{2,3},\ E_{2,4}{:}C_{2,4}{:}C_{1,4}{:}I_{2,4}\}\\
\{E_{1,1}{:}C_{2,1}{:}C_{1,1}{:}I_{1,1},\ E_{1,2}{:}C_{2,2}{:}C_{1,2}{:}I_{1,2},\ E_{2,3}{:}C_{2,3}{:}C_{1,3}{:}I_{2,3},\ E_{2,4}{:}C_{2,4}{:}C_{1,4}{:}I_{2,4}\}
\end{array}
$$

and the output distribution is uniform, each set occurring with probability 1/9. Now suppose we wish to calculate the expected number of packets traversing the link ℓ from C_1 to C_2. We can filter the output distribution on the set

$$b \triangleq \{\sigma \mid C_{2,i}{:}C_{1,i} \in \sigma \text{ for some } i\}$$

and ask for the expected size of the result. The filtering is again done by composition, viewing b as an extended test. (In this example, all histories traverse ℓ, so b actually has no effect.) The expected number of packets traversing ℓ is given by integration:

$$\int_{a \in 2^H} |a| \cdot [\![d; p; b]\!](da) = 2.$$

Hence, even in a simple example where forwarding is deterministic, our semantics for ProbNetKAT is quite useful: it enables making predictions about quantitative properties such as congestion, which can be used to provision capacity, inform traffic engineering algorithms, or calculate the risk that service-level agreements may be violated. More generally, ProbNetKAT can be used to express much richer behaviors such as randomized routing, faulty links, gossip, etc., as shown by the examples presented in Sect. 8.

Challenges. We faced several challenges in formulating the semantics of ProbNetKAT in a satisfactory way. The deterministic semantics of NetKAT [1,12] interprets programs as packet-processing functions on sets of packet histories. This is different enough from other probabilistic models in the literature that it was not obvious how to apply standard approaches. On the one hand, we wanted to extend the deterministic semantics conservatively—i.e., a ProbNetKAT program that makes no probabilistic choices should behave the same as under the deterministic NetKAT semantics. This goal was achieved (Theorem 2) using the notion of a *Markov kernel*, well known from previous work in probabilistic semantics [10, 24, 39]. Among other things, conservativity enables using NetKAT axioms to reason about deterministic sub-terms of ProbNetKAT programs. On the other hand, when moving to the probabilistic domain, several properties enjoyed by the deterministic version were lost, and great care was needed to formulate the new semantics correctly. Most notably, it is no longer the case that the meaning of a program on an input set of packet histories is uniquely determined by its action on individual histories (Sect. 6.4). The parallel composition operator (&), which supplants the union operator (+) of NetKAT, is no longer idempotent except when applied to deterministic programs (Lemma 1(vi)), and distributivity no longer holds in general (Lemma 4). Nevertheless, the semantics provides a powerful means of reasoning that is sufficient to derive many interesting and useful properties of networks (Sect. 8).

Perhaps the most challenging theoretical problem was the formulation of the semantics of iteration (*). In the deterministic version, the iteration operator can be defined as a sum of powers. In ProbNetKAT, this approach does not work, as it requires that parallel composition be idempotent. Hence, we formulate the semantics of iteration in terms of an infinite stochastic process. Giving denotational meaning to this operational construction required an intricate application of the Kolmogorov extension theorem. This formulation gives a canonical solution to an appropriate fixpoint equation as desired (Theorem 1). However the solution is not unique, and it is not a least fixpoint in any natural ordering that we are aware of.

Another challenge was the observation that in the presence of both duplication (dup) and iteration (*), models based on discrete distributions do not suffice, and it is necessary to base the semantics on an uncountable state space with continuous measures and sequential composition defined by integration. Most models in the literature only deal with discrete distributions, with a few notable exceptions (e.g. [10, 23, 24, 38, 39]). To see why a discrete semantics suffices in the absence of either duplication or iteration note that H is a countable set. Without iteration, we could limit our attention to distributions on finite subsets of H, which are also countable. Similarly, with iteration but without duplication, the set of histories that could be generated by a program is actually finite. Hence a discrete semantics would suffice in that case as well, even though iterative processes would not necessarily converge after finitely many steps as with deterministic processes. However, in the presence of both duplication and iteration, infinite sets and continuous measures are unavoidable (Sect. 6.3), although in specific applications, discrete distributions sometimes suffice.

3 Measure Theory Primer

This section introduces the background mathematics necessary to understand the semantics of ProbNetKAT. Because ProbNetKAT requires continuous probability distributions, we review some basic measure theory. See Halmos [17], Chung [5], or Rao [42] for a more thorough treatment.

Overview. Measures are a generalization of the concepts of length or volume of Euclidean geometry to other spaces, and form the basis of continuous probability theory. In this section, we explain what it means for a space to be *measurable*, show how to construct measurable spaces, and give basic operations and constructions on measurable spaces including Lebesgue integration with respect to a measure and the construction of product spaces. We also define the crucial notion of *Markov kernels*, the analog of Markov transition matrices for finite-state stochastic processes, which form the basis of our semantics for ProbNetKAT.

Measurable Spaces and Measurable Functions. A *σ-algebra* $\mathcal{B}$ on a set S is a collection of subsets of S containing $\emptyset$ and closed under complement and countable union (hence also closed under countable intersection). A pair $(S, \mathcal{B})$ where S is a set and $\mathcal{B}$ is a σ-algebra on S is called a *measurable space*. If the σ-algebra is obvious from the context, we simply say that S is a measurable space. For a measurable space $(S, \mathcal{B})$, we say that a subset $A \subseteq S$ is *measurable* if it is in $\mathcal{B}$. For applications in probability theory, elements of S and $\mathcal{B}$ are often called *outcomes* and *events*, respectively.

If $\mathcal{F}$ is a collection of subsets of a set S, then we define $\sigma(\mathcal{F})$, the σ-algebra *generated* by $\mathcal{F}$, to be the smallest σ-algebra that contains $\mathcal{F}$. That is,

$$\sigma(\mathcal{F}) \triangleq \bigcap\{\mathcal{A} \mid \mathcal{F} \subseteq \mathcal{A} \,\text{and}\, \mathcal{A} \,\text{is a}\, \sigma\text{−algebra}\}.$$

Note that $\sigma(\mathcal{F})$ is well-defined, since the intersection is nonempty (we have that $\mathcal{F} \subseteq \mathcal{P}(S)$, and $\mathcal{P}(S)$ is a σ-algebra). If $(S, \mathcal{B})$ is a measurable space and $\mathcal{B} = \sigma(\mathcal{F})$, we say that the space is *generated* by $\mathcal{F}$.

Let $(S, \mathcal{B}_S)$ and $(T, \mathcal{B}_T)$ be measurable spaces. A function $f : S \to T$ is *measurable* if the inverse image $f^{-1}(B) = \{x \in S \mid f(x) \in B\}$ of every measurable subset $B \subseteq T$ is a measurable subset of S. For the particular case where T is generated by the collection $\mathcal{F}$, we have the following criterion for measurability: f is measurable if and only if $f^{-1}(B)$ is measurable for every $B \in \mathcal{F}$.

Measures. A *measure* on $(S, \mathcal{B})$ is a countably additive map $\mu : \mathcal{B} \to \mathbb{R}$. The condition that the map be *countably additive* stipulates that if $A_i \in \mathcal{B}$ is a countable set of pairwise disjoint events, then $\mu(\bigcup_i A_i) = \sum_i \mu(A_i)$. Equivalently, if A_i is a countable chain of events, that is, if $A_i \subseteq A_j$ for $i \leq j$, then $\lim_i \mu(A_i)$ exists and is equal to $\mu(\bigcup_i A_i)$. A measure is a *probability measure* if $\mu(A) \geq 0$ for all $A \in \mathcal{B}$ and $\mu(S) = 1$. By convention, $\mu(\emptyset) = 0$.

For every $a \in S$, the Dirac measure on a is the probability measure:

$$\delta_a(A) = \begin{cases} 1, & a \in A, \\ 0, & a \notin A. \end{cases}$$

A measure is *discrete* if it is a countable weighted sum of Dirac measures.

Markov Kernels. Again let $(S, \mathcal{B}_S)$ and $(T, \mathcal{B}_T)$ be measurable spaces. A function $P : S \times \mathcal{B}_T \to \mathbb{R}$ is called a *Markov kernel* (also called a Markov transition, measurable kernel, stochastic kernel, stochastic relation, etc.) if

- for fixed $A \in \mathcal{B}_T$, the map $\lambda s.P(s,A) : S \to \mathbb{R}$ is a measurable function on $(S, \mathcal{B}_S)$; and
- for fixed $s \in S$, the map $\lambda A.P(s,A) : \mathcal{B}_T \to \mathbb{R}$ is a probability measure on $(T, \mathcal{B}_T)$.

These properties allow integration on the left and right respectively.

The measurable spaces and Markov kernels form a category, the *Kleisli category of the Giry monad*; see [10,38,39]. In this context, we occasionally write $P : (S, \mathcal{B}_S) \to (T, \mathcal{B}_T)$ or just $P : S \to T$. Composition is given by integration: for $P : S \to T$ and $Q : T \to U$,

$$(P \,;\, Q)(s, A) = \int_{t \in T} P(s, dt) \cdot Q(t, A).$$

Associativity of composition is essentially Fubini's theorem (see Chung [5] or Halmos [17]). Markov kernels were first proposed as a model of probabilistic while programs by Kozen [24].

Deterministic Kernels. A Markov kernel $P : S \to T$ is *deterministic* if for every $s \in S$, there is an $f(s) \in T$ such that

$$P(s, A) = \delta_{f(s)}(A) = \delta_s(f^{-1}(A)) = \chi_A(f(s)).$$

where χ_A is the characteristic function of A. The function $f : S \to T$ is necessarily measurable. Conversely, every measurable function gives a deterministic kernel. Thus, the and the measurable functions are in one-to-one correspondence.

4 Syntax

ProbNetKAT extends NetKAT [1,12], which is itself based on Kleene algebra with tests (KAT) [25], a generic equational system for reasoning about partial correctness of programs.

4.1 Kleene Algebra (KA) & Kleene Algebra with Tests (KAT)

A *Kleene algebra* (KA) is an algebraic structure $(K, +, \cdot, {}^*, 0, 1)$, where K is an idempotent semiring under $(+, \cdot, 0, 1)$, and $p^* \cdot q$ is the least solution of the affine linear inequality $p \cdot r + q \leq r$, where $p \leq q$ is shorthand for $p + q = q$, and similarly for $q \cdot p^*$. A *Kleene algebra with tests* (KAT) is a two-sorted algebraic structure, $(K, B, +, \cdot, {}^*, 0, 1, \neg)$, where $\neg$ is a unary operator defined only on B, such that

- $(K, +, \cdot, {}^*, 0, 1)$ is a Kleene algebra,
- $(B, +, \cdot, \neg, 0, 1)$ is a Boolean algebra, and
- $(B, +, \cdot, 0, 1)$ is a subalgebra of $(K, +, \cdot, 0, 1)$.

The elements of B and K are usually called *tests* and *actions*.

Naturals

$$n \in 0 \mid 1 \mid 2 \mid \ldots$$

Fields

$$x ::= x_1 \mid \cdots \mid x_k$$

Packets

$$\pi ::= \{x_1 = n_1, \cdots, x_k = n_k\}$$

Histories

$$\sigma, \tau ::= \pi : \eta$$
$$\eta ::= \langle\rangle \mid \pi : \eta$$

Extended Tests

$$t \subseteq H$$
$$\texttt{skip} \triangleq H$$
$$\texttt{drop} \triangleq \varnothing$$
$$x = n \triangleq \{\pi : \eta \mid \pi(x) = n\}$$

Tests

$a ::=$	t	*Extended test*
$\mid$	$a_1 \mathbin{\&} a_2$	*Disjunction*
$\mid$	$a_1 ; a_2$	*Conjunction*
$\mid$	$\overline{a}$	*Negation*

Actions

$p ::=$	a	*Test*
$\mid$	$x \leftarrow n$	*Modification*
$\mid$	$p_1 \mathbin{\&} p_2$	*Parallel Composition*
$\mid$	$p_1 ; p_2$	*Sequential Composition*
$\mid$	$p_1 \oplus_r p_2$	*Probabilistic Choice*
$\mid$	p^*	*Iteration*
$\mid$	**dup**	*Duplication*

Fig. 2. ProbNetKAT syntax.

The axioms of KA and KAT (both elided here) capture natural conditions such as associativity of $\cdot$; see the original paper by Kozen for a complete listing [25]. Note that the KAT axioms do not hold for arbitrary ProbNetKAT programs—e.g., parallel composition is not idempotent—although they do hold for the deterministic fragment of the language.

4.2 NetKAT Syntax

NetKAT [1,12] extends KAT with network-specific primitives for filtering, modifying, and forwarding packets, along with additional axioms for reasoning about programs built using those primitives. Formally, NetKAT is KAT with atomic tests $x = n$ and actions $x \leftarrow n$ and dup. The test $x = n$ checks whether field x of the current packet contains the value n; the assignment $x \leftarrow n$ assigns the value n to the field x in the current packet; the action dup duplicates the packet in the packet history, which provides a way to keep track of the path the packet takes through the network. In NetKAT, we write ; instead of $\cdot$, `skip` instead of 1, and `drop` instead of 0, to capture their intuitive use as programming constructs. We often use juxtaposition to indicate sequential composition in examples. As an example to illustrate the main features of NetKAT, the expression

$$sw = 6 \; ; \; pt = 8 \; ; \; dst \leftarrow 10.0.1.5 \; ; \; pt \leftarrow 5$$

encodes the command: "For all packets located at port 8 of switch 6, set the destination address to 10.0.1.5 and forward it out on port 5."

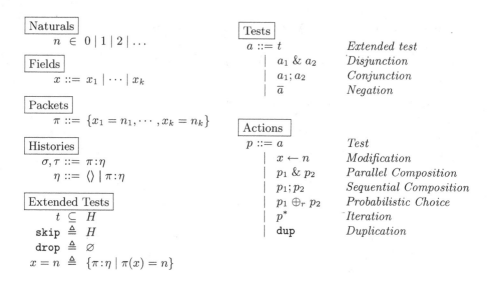

$$[\![x \leftarrow n]\!](\pi{:}\eta) = \{\pi[n/x]{:}\eta\}$$

$$[\![x = n]\!](\pi{:}\eta) = \begin{cases} \{\pi{:}\eta\}, & \pi(x) = n \\ \varnothing, & \pi(x) \neq n \end{cases}$$

$$[\![\mathtt{dup}]\!](\pi{:}\eta) = \{\pi{:}\pi{:}\eta\}$$

$$[\![\mathtt{skip}]\!](\sigma) = \{\sigma\}$$

$$[\![\mathtt{drop}]\!](\sigma) = \varnothing$$

$$[\![p + q]\!](\sigma) = [\![p]\!](\sigma) \cup [\![q]\!](\sigma)$$

$$[\![p\,;q]\!](\sigma) = \textstyle\bigcup_{\tau \in [\![p]\!](\sigma)} [\![q]\!](\tau)$$

$$[\![p^*]\!](\sigma) = \textstyle\bigcup_n [\![p^n]\!](\sigma)$$

$$[\![\bar{a}]\!](\sigma) = \begin{cases} \{\sigma\}, & \text{if } [\![a]\!](\sigma) = \varnothing \\ \varnothing, & \text{if } [\![a]\!](\sigma) = \{\sigma\} \end{cases}$$

Fig. 3. NetKAT semantics: primitive actions and tests (left); KAT operations (right).

4.3 ProbNetKAT Syntax

ProbNetKAT extends NetKAT with several new operations, as shown in the grammar in Fig. 2:

- A *random choice* operation $p \oplus_r q$, where p and q are expressions and r is a real number in the interval $[0, 1]$. The expression $p \oplus_r q$ intuitively behaves according to p with probability r and q with probability $1 - r$. We frequently omit the subscript r, in which case r is understood to implicitly be $1/2$.
- A *parallel composition* operation $p \,\&\, q$, where p and q are expressions. The expression $p \,\&\, q$ intuitively says to perform both p and q, making any probabilistic choices in p and q independently, and combine the results. The operation & serves the same purpose as + in NetKAT and replaces it syntactically. We use the notation & to distinguish it from +, which is used in the semantics to add measures and measurable functions as in [23,24].
- *Extended tests* t which generalize NetKAT's tests by allowing them to operate on the entire packet history rather than simply the head packet. Formally an extended test t is just an element of 2^H. The extended test `skip` is defined as the set of all packet histories and `drop` is the empty set. An atomic test $x = n$ is defined as the set of all histories σ where the x field of the head packet of σ is n. As we saw in Sect. 2, extended tests are often useful for reasoning probabilistically about properties such as congestion.

Although ProbNetKAT is based on KAT, it is important to keep in mind that because the semantics is probabilistic, many familiar KAT equations no longer hold. For example, idempotence of parallel composition does not hold in general. We will however prove that ProbNetKAT conservatively extends NetKAT, so it follows that the NetKAT axioms hold on the deterministic fragment.

5 Semantics

The standard semantics of (non-probabilistic) NetKAT interprets expressions as packet-processing functions. As defined in Fig. 2, a packet π is a record whose fields assign constant values n to fields x and a packet history σ is a nonempty sequence of packets $\pi_1{:}\pi_2{:}\cdots{:}\pi_k$, listed from youngest to oldest. Recall that operationally, only the head packet π_1 exists in the network, but we keep track of the history to enable precise specification of forwarding along specific paths.

5.1 NetKAT Semantics

Formally, a (non-probabilistic) NetKAT term p denotes a function

$$[\![p]\!] : H \to 2^H,$$

where H is the set of all packet histories. Intuitively, the function $[\![p]\!]$ takes an input packet history σ and produces a set of output packet histories $[\![p]\!](\sigma)$.

The semantics of NetKAT is shown in Fig. 3. The test $x = n$ drops the packet if the test is not satisfied and otherwise passes it through unaltered. Put another way, tests behave like filters. The dup construct duplicates the head packet π, yielding a fresh copy that can be modified by other constructs. Hence, the dup construct can be used to encode paths through the network, with each occurrence of dup marking an intermediate hop. Note that $+$ behaves like a disjunction operation when applied to tests and like a union operation when applied to actions. Similarly, ; behaves like a conjunction operation when applied to tests and like a sequential composition when applied to actions. Negation is only ever applied to tests, as is enforced by the syntax of the language.

5.2 Sets of Packet Histories as a Measurable Space

To give a denotational semantics to ProbNetKAT, we must first identify a suitable space of mathematical objects. Because we want to reason about probability distributions over sets of network paths, we construct a *measurable space* (as defined in Sect. 3) from sets of packet histories, and then define the semantics using Markov kernels on this space. The powerset 2^H of packet histories H forms a topological space with topology generated by basic clopen sets,

$$B_\tau = \{a \in 2^H \mid \tau \in a\}, \ \tau \in H.$$

This space is homeomorphic to the *Cantor space*, the topological product of countably many copies of the discrete two-element space. In particular, it is also compact. Let $\mathcal{B} \subseteq 2^{2^H}$ be the Borel sets of this topology. This is the smallest σ-algebra containing the sets B_τ. The measurable space $(2^H, \mathcal{B})$ with outcomes 2^H and events $\mathcal{B}$ provides a foundation for interpreting ProbNetKAT programs as Markov kernels $2^H \to 2^H$.

5.3 The Operation &

Next, we define an operation on measures that will be needed to define the semantics of ProbNetKAT's parallel composition operator. Parallel composition differs in some important ways from NetKAT's union operator—intuitively, union merely combines the sets of packet histories generated by its arguments, whereas parallel composition must somehow combine measures on sets of packet histories, which is a more intricate operation. For example, while union is idempotent, parallel composition is not in general.

Operationally, the & operation on measures can be understood as follows: given measures μ and ν, to compute $\mu \,\&\, \nu$, we sample μ and ν independently to get two subsets of H, then take their union. The probability of an event $A \in \mathcal{B}$ is the probability that this union is in A. Formally, given $\mu, \nu \in \mathcal{M}$, let $\mu \times \nu$ be the product measure on the product space $2^H \times 2^H$. The union operation $\bigcup : 2^H \times 2^H \to 2^H$ is continuous and therefore measurable, so we can define:

$$(\mu \,\&\, \nu)(A) \triangleq (\mu \times \nu)(\{(a,b) \mid a \cup b \in A\}). \tag{5.1}$$

Intuitively, this is the probability that the union $a \cup b$ of two independent samples taken with respect to μ and ν lies in A. The & operation enjoys a number of useful properties, as captured by the following lemma:

Lemma 1. *(i) & is associative and commutative.*
(ii) & is linear in both arguments.
(iii) $(\delta_a \,\&\, \mu)(A) = \mu(\{b \mid a \cup b \in A\})$.
(iv) $\delta_a \,\&\, \delta_b = \delta_{a \cup b}$.
(v) $\delta_\emptyset$ *is a two-sided identity for &.*
(vi) $\mu \,\&\, \mu = \mu$ *iff* $\mu = \delta_a$ *for some* $a \in 2^H$.

There is an infinitary version of & that works on countable multisets of measures, but we will not need it in this paper.

5.4 ProbNetKAT Semantics

Now we are ready to define the semantics of ProbNetKAT itself. Every ProbNetKAT term p denotes a Markov kernel

$$[\![p]\!] : 2^H \times \mathcal{B} \to \mathbb{R}$$

which can be curried as

$$[\![p]\!] : 2^H \to \mathcal{B} \to \mathbb{R}$$

Intuitively, the term p, given an input $a \in 2^H$, produces an output according to the distribution $[\![p]\!](a)$. We can think of running the program p with input a as a probabilistic experiment, and the value $[\![p]\!](a, A) \in \mathbb{R}$ is the probability that the outcome of the experiment lies in $A \in \mathcal{B}$. The measure $[\![p]\!](a)$ is not necessarily discrete (Sect. 6.3): its total weight is always 1, although the probability of any given singleton may be 0.

The semantics of the atomic operations is defined as follows for $a \in 2^H$:

$$\begin{aligned}
[\![x \leftarrow n]\!](a) &= \delta_{\{\pi[n/x]:\eta \,\mid\, \pi:\eta \in a\}} \\
[\![x = n]\!](a) &= \delta_{\{\pi:\eta \,\mid\, \pi:\eta \in a,\ \pi(x)=n\}} \\
[\![\mathtt{dup}]\!](a) &= \delta_{\{\pi:\pi:\eta \,\mid\, \pi:\eta \in a\}} \\
[\![\mathtt{skip}]\!](a) &= \delta_a \\
[\![\mathtt{drop}]\!](a) &= \delta_\emptyset
\end{aligned}$$

These are all deterministic terms, and as such, they correspond to measurable functions $f : 2^H \to 2^H$. In each of these cases, the function f is completely determined by its action on singletons, and indeed by its action on the head packet of the unique element of each of those singletons. Note that if no elements of a satisfy the test $x = n$, the result is $\delta_\emptyset$, which is the Dirac measure on the emptyset, not the constant 0 measure. The semantics of the parallel/sequential composition and random choice operators is defined as follows:

$$[\![p \,\&\, q]\!](a) = [\![p]\!](a) \,\&\, [\![q]\!](a)$$
$$[\![p \,;\, q]\!](a) = [\![q]\!]([\![p]\!](a))$$
$$[\![p \oplus_r q]\!](a) = r[\![p]\!](a) + (1-r)[\![q]\!](a)$$

Note that composition requires us to extend $[\![q]\!]$ to allow measures as inputs. It is not surprising that this extension is needed: in NetKAT, the semantics is similarly extended to handle sets of histories. Here, the extension is done by integration, as described in Sect. 3:

$$[\![q]\!](\mu) \triangleq \lambda A. \int_{a \in 2^H} [\![q]\!](a, A) \cdot \mu(da), \quad \text{for } \mu \text{ a measure on } 2^H.$$

Both phenomena are consequences of sequential composition taking place in the Kleisli category of the powerset and Giry monads respectively.

5.5 Semantics of Iteration

To complete the semantics, we must define the semantics of the Kleene star operator. This turns out to be quite challenging, because the usual definition of star as a sum of powers does not work with ProbNetKAT. Instead, we define an infinite stochastic process and show that it satisfies the essential fixpoint equation that Kleene star is expected to obey (Theorem 1).

Consider the following infinite stochastic process. Starting with $c_0 \in 2^H$, create a sequence $c_0, c_1, c_2, \ldots$ inductively. After n steps, say we have constructed $c_0, \ldots, c_n$. Let c_{n+1} be the outcome obtained by sampling 2^H according to the distribution $[\![p]\!](c_n)$. Continue this process forever to get an infinite sequence $c_0, c_1, c_2, \ldots \in (2^H)^\omega$. Take the union of the resulting sequence $\bigcup_n c_n$ and ask whether it is in A. The probability of this event is taken to be $[\![p^*]\!](c_0, A)$. This intuitive operational definition can be justified denotationally. However, the formal development is quite technical and depends on an application of the Kolmogorov extension theorem—see the full version of this paper [13].

The next theorem shows that the iteration operator satisfies a natural fixpoint equation. In fact, this property was the original motivation behind the operational definition we just gave. It can be used to describe the iterated processing performed by a network (Sect. 8), and to define the semantics of loops (Sect. 5.6).

Theorem 1. $[\![p^*]\!] = [\![\texttt{skip} \,\&\, pp^*]\!]$.

Proof. To determine the probability $[\![p^*]\!](c_0, A)$, we sample $[\![p]\!](c_0)$ to get an outcome c_1, then run the protocol $[\![p^*]\!]$ on c_1 to obtain a set c, then ask whether $c_0 \cup c \in A$. Thus

$$\begin{aligned}
[\![p^*]\!](c_0, A) &= \int_{c_1} [\![p]\!](c_0, dc_1) \cdot [\![p^*]\!](c_1, \{c \mid c_0 \cup c \in A\}) \\
&= [\![p^*]\!]([\![p]\!](c_0))(\{c \mid c_0 \cup c \in A\}) \\
&= (\delta_{c_0} \;\&\; [\![p^*]\!]([\![p]\!](c_0)))(A) \qquad \text{by Lemma 1(iii)} \\
&= ([\![\mathtt{skip}]\!](c_0) \;\&\; [\![pp^*]\!](c_0))(A) \\
&= [\![\mathtt{skip} \;\&\; pp^*]\!](c_0, A).
\end{aligned}$$

□

Note that this equation does not uniquely determine $[\![p^*]\!]$ uniquely. For example, it can be shown that a probability measure μ is a solution of $[\![\mathtt{skip}^*]\!](\pi) = [\![\mathtt{skip} \;\&\; \mathtt{skip} \;;\; \mathtt{skip}^*]\!](\pi)$ if and only if $\mu(B_\pi) = 1$. That is, π appears in the output set of $[\![\mathtt{skip}^*]\!](\pi)$ with probability 1. Also note that unlike KAT and NetKAT, $[\![p^*]\!]$ is *not* the same as the infinite sum of powers $[\![\&_n\, p^n]\!]$. The latter fails to capture the sequential nature of iteration in the presence of probabilistic choice.

5.6 Extended Tests

ProbNetKAT's *extended tests* generalize NetKAT's tests, which are predicates on the head packet in a history, to predicates over the entire history. An extended test is an element $t \in 2^H$ used as a deterministic program with semantics

$$[\![t]\!](a) \triangleq \delta_{a \cap t}.$$

A test $x = n$ is a special case in which $t = \{\pi{:}\eta \mid \pi(x) = n\}$. For every extended test there is a corresponding measure:

$$[\![t]\!](\mu) = \lambda A.\mu(\{a \mid a \cap g \in A\}).$$

Using this construct, we can define encodings of conditionals and loops in the standard way:

$$\mathsf{if}\, b\, \mathsf{then}\, p\, \mathsf{else}\, q = bp \;\&\; \bar{b}q \qquad\qquad \mathsf{while}\, b\, \mathsf{do}\, p = (bp)^*\bar{b}.$$

Importantly, unlike treatments involving subprobability measures found in previous work [24,38], the output here is always a probability measure, even if the program does not halt. For example, the output of the program while true do skip is the Dirac measure $\delta_\emptyset$.

6 Properties

Having defined the semantics of ProbNetKAT in terms of Markov kernels, we now develop some essential properties that provide further evidence in support of our semantics.

- We prove that ProbNetKAT is a conservative extension of NetKAT—i.e., every deterministic ProbNetKAT program behaves like the corresponding NetKAT program.
- We present some additional properties enjoyed by ProbNetKAT programs.
- We show that ProbNetKAT programs can generate continuous measures from discrete inputs, which shows that our use of Markov kernels is truly necessary and that no semantics based on discrete measures would suffice.
- Finally, we present a tempting alternative "uncorrelated" semantics and show that it is inadequate for defining the semantics of ProbNetKAT.

6.1 Conservativity of the Extension

Although ProbNetKAT extends NetKAT with new probabilistic operators, the addition of these operators does not affect the behavior of purely deterministic programs. We will prove that this property is indeed true of our semantics—i.e., ProbNetKAT is a conservative extension of NetKAT.

First, we show that programs that do not use choice are deterministic:

Lemma 2. *All syntactically deterministic ProbNetKAT programs p (those without an occurrence of $\oplus_r$) are (semantically) deterministic. That is, for any $a \in 2^H$, the distribution $[\![p]\!](a)$ is a point mass.*

Next we show that the semantics agree on deterministic programs. Let $[\![\cdot]\!]_{\mathrm{N}}$ and $[\![\cdot]\!]_{\mathrm{P}}$ denote the semantic maps for NetKAT and ProbNetKAT respectively.

Theorem 2. *For deterministic programs, ProbNetKAT semantics and NetKAT semantics agree in the following sense. For $a \in 2^H$, define $[\![p]\!]_{\mathrm{N}}(a) = \bigcup_{\tau \in a} [\![p]\!]_{\mathrm{N}}(\tau)$. Then for any $a, b \in 2^H$ we have $[\![p]\!]_{\mathrm{N}}(a) = b$ if and only if $[\![p]\!]_{\mathrm{P}}(a) = \delta_b$.*

Using the fact that the NetKAT axioms are sound and complete [1, Theorems 1 and 2], we immediately obtain the following corollary:

Corollary 1. *The NetKAT axioms are sound and complete for deterministic ProbNetKAT programs.*

Besides providing further evidence that our probabilistic semantics captures the intended behavior, these theorems also have a pragmatic benefit: they allow us to use NetKAT to reason about deterministic terms in ProbNetKAT programs.

6.2 Further Properties

Next, we identify several natural equations that are satisfied by ProbNetKAT programs. The first two equations show that drop is a left and right unit for the parallel composition operator &:

$$[\![p \,\&\, \mathtt{drop}]\!] = [\![p]\!] = [\![\mathtt{drop} \,\&\, p]\!]$$

This equation makes intuitive sense as deterministically dropping all inputs should have no affect when composed in parallel with any other program. The next equation states that $\oplus_r$ is idempotent:

$$[\![p \oplus_r p]\!] = [\![p]\!]$$

Again, this equation makes sense intuitively as randomly choosing between p and itself is the same as simply executing p. The next few equations show that parallel composition is associative and commutative:

$$[\![(p \mathbin{\&} q) \mathbin{\&} s]\!] = [\![p \mathbin{\&} (q \mathbin{\&} s)]\!]$$
$$[\![p \mathbin{\&} q]\!] = [\![q \mathbin{\&} p]\!]$$

The next equation shows that the arguments to random choice can be exchanged, provided the bias is complemented:

$$[\![p \oplus_r q]\!] = [\![q \oplus_{1-r} p]\!]$$

The final equation describes how to reassociate expressions involving random choice, which is not associative in general. However, by explicitly keeping track of biases, we can obtain an equation that captures a kind of associativity:

$$[\![\left(p \oplus_{\frac{a}{a+b}} q\right) \oplus_{\frac{a+b}{a+b+c}} s]\!] = [\![p \oplus_{\frac{a}{a+b+c}} \left(q \oplus_{\frac{b}{b+c}} s\right)]\!]$$

Next we develop some additional properties involving deterministic programs.

Lemma 3. *Let p be a deterministic program with $[\![p]\!](a) = \delta_{f(a)}$. The function $f : 2^H \to 2^H$ is measurable, and for any measure μ, we have $[\![p]\!](\mu) = \mu \circ f^{-1}$.*

As we have seen in Lemma 1(vi), & is not idempotent except in the deterministic case. Neither does sequential composition distribute over & in general. However, if the term being distributed is deterministic, then the property holds:

Lemma 4. *If p is deterministic, then*

$$[\![p(q \mathbin{\&} r)]\!] = [\![pq \mathbin{\&} pr]\!] \qquad\qquad [\![(q \mathbin{\&} r)p]\!] = [\![qp \mathbin{\&} rp]\!].$$

Neither equation holds unconditionally.

Finally, consider the program $\texttt{skip} \oplus_r \texttt{dup}$. This program does nothing with probability r and duplicates the head packet with probability $1 - r$, where $r \in [0, 1)$. We can show that independent of r, the value of the iterated program on any single packet π is the point mass

$$[\![(\texttt{skip} \oplus_r \texttt{dup})^*]\!](\pi) = \delta_{\{\pi^n \mid n \geq 1\}}. \tag{6.1}$$

6.3 A Continuous Measure

Without the Kleene star operator or dup, a ProbNetKAT program can generate only a discrete measure. This raises the question of whether it is possible to generate a continuous measure at all, even in the presence of * and dup. This question is important, because with only discrete measures, we would have no need for measure theory or integrals and the semantics would be significantly simpler. It turns out that the answer to this question is yes, it is possible to generate a continuous measure, therefore discrete measures do not suffice.

To see why, let π_0 and π_1 be distinct packets and let p be the program that changes the current packet to either π_0 or π_1 with equal probability. Then consider the program, p ; $(\mathsf{dup} ; p)^*$. Operationally, it first sets the input packet to either 0 or 1 with equal probability, then repeats the following steps forever:

(i) output the current packet,
(ii) duplicate the current packet, and
(iii) set the new current packet to π_0 or π_1 with equal probability.

This procedure produces outcomes a with exactly one packet history of every length and linearly ordered by the suffix relation. Thus each possible outcome a corresponds to a complete path in an infinite binary tree. Moreover, the probability that a history τ is generated is $2^{-|\tau|}$, thus any particular set is generated with probability 0, because the probability that a set is generated cannot be greater than the probability that any one of its elements is generated.

Theorem 3. *Let μ be the measure $[\![p ; (\mathsf{dup} ; p)^*]\!](0)$.*

(i) For $\tau \in H$, the probability that τ is a member of the output set is $2^{-|\tau|}$.
(ii) Two packet histories of the same length are generated with probability 0.
(iii) $\mu(\{a\}) = 0$ for all $a \in 2^H$, thus μ is a continuous measure.

For the proof, see the full version of this paper [13].

In fact, the measure μ is the uniform measure on the subspace of 2^H consisting of all sets that contain exactly one history of each length and are linearly ordered by the suffix relation. This subspace is homeomorphic to the Cantor space.

6.4 Uncorrelated Semantics

It is tempting to consider a weaker *uncorrelated semantics*

$$[p] : 2^H \to [0,1]^H$$

in which $[p](a)(\tau)$ gives the probability that τ is contained in the output set on input a. Indeed, this semantics can be obtained from the standard ProbNetKAT semantics as follows:

$$[p](a)(\tau) \triangleq [\![p]\!](a)(B_\tau).$$

However, although it is simpler in that it does not require continuous measures, one loses correlation between packets. Worse, it is not compositional, as the following example shows. Let π_0, π_1 be two packets and consider the programs $\pi_0! \oplus \pi_1!$ and $(\pi_0! \mathbin{\&} \pi_1!) \oplus \mathtt{drop}$, where $\pi!$ is the program that sets the current packet to π. Both programs have the same uncorrelated meaning:

$$[\![\pi_0! \oplus \pi_1!]\!](a)(\pi) = [\![(\pi_0! \mathbin{\&} \pi_1!) \oplus \mathtt{drop}]\!](a)(\pi) = \tfrac{1}{2}$$

for $\pi \in \{\pi_0, \pi_1\}$ and $a \neq \emptyset$ and 0 otherwise. But their standard meanings differ:

$$[\![\pi_0! \oplus \pi_1!]\!](a) = \tfrac{1}{2}\delta_{\{\pi_0\}} + \tfrac{1}{2}\delta_{\{\pi_1\}}$$
$$[\![(\pi_0! \mathbin{\&} \pi_1!) \oplus \mathtt{drop}]\!](a) = \tfrac{1}{2}\delta_{\{\pi_0,\pi_1\}} + \tfrac{1}{2}\delta_{\emptyset},$$

Moreover, composing on the right with $\pi_0!$ yields $\delta_{\{\pi_0\}}$ and $\frac{1}{2}\delta_{\{\pi_0\}} + \frac{1}{2}\delta_{\emptyset}$, respectively, which have different uncorrelated meanings as well. Thus we have no choice but to reject the uncorrelated semantics as a viable alternative.

7 Approximation

In this section we show that every program can be approximated arbitrarily closely by a loop-free program, using a suitable notion of approximation for the iterates of a loop. Intuitively, this explains why in many real-world scenarios it suffices to only keep track of finite and discrete distributions. Approximation in the context of bisimulation of Markov processes has been studied previously by a number of other authors [8–10,28,38,39].

7.1 Weak Convergence of $p^{(M)}$ to p^*

In Sect. 5.5, we defined $[\![p^*]\!]$ operationally in terms of an infinite process. To get $[\![p^*]\!](c_0, A)$, we compute an infinite sequence $c_0, c_1, \ldots$ where in the nth step we sample c_n to get c_{n+1}. Then we take the union of the c_n and ask whether it is in A. We proved that the resulting kernel exists and satisfies $[\![p^*]\!] = [\![\mathtt{skip} \mathbin{\&} p \mathbin{;} p^*]\!]$.

Now let $c_0, c_1, \ldots, c_{m-1}$ be the outcome of the first m steps of this process, and let $[\![p^{(m)}]\!](c_0, A)$ be the probability that $\bigcup_{n=0}^{m-1} c_n \in A$. This gives an approximation to $[\![p^*]\!](c_0, A)$. Formally, define

$$p^{(0)} = \mathtt{skip} \qquad\qquad p^{(n+1)} = \mathtt{skip} \mathbin{\&} p \mathbin{;} p^{(n)}.$$

Note that $p^{(n)}$ is not p^n, nor is it $p^0 \mathbin{\&} \cdots \mathbin{\&} p^n$.

The appropriate notion of convergence in this setting is *weak convergence*. A sequence of measures μ_n converge weakly to a measure μ if for all bounded continuous real-valued functions f, the expected values of f with respect to the measures μ_n converge to the expected value of f with respect to μ. The following theorem captures the relationship between the approximations of an iterated program and the iterated program itself:

Theorem 4. *The measures $[\![p^{(m)}]\!](c)$ converge weakly to $[\![p^*]\!](c)$.*

See the full version of this paper for the proof [13].

7.2 Approximation by *-Free Programs

We have observed that *-free programs only generate finite discrete distributions on finite inputs. In this section we show that every program is weakly approximated to arbitrary precision by *-free programs. The approximating programs are obtained by replacing each p^* with $p^{(m)}$ for sufficiently large m.

This explains why we see only finite discrete distributions in most applications. In most cases, we start with finite sets and iterate only finitely many times. For instance, this will happen whenever there is a bound on the number of occurrences of dup in any string generated by the program as a regular expression. So although the formal semantics requires continuous distributions and integration, in many real-world scenarios we only need finite and discrete distributions.

Theorem 5. *For every ProbNetKAT program p, there is a sequence of *-free programs that converge weakly to p.*

The proof uses Theorem 4 and the fact that all program constructors are continuous with respect to weak convergence.

8 Applications

In this section, we demonstrate the expressiveness of ProbNetKAT's probabilistic operators and power of its semantics by presenting three case studies drawn from scenarios that commonly arise in real-world networks. Specifically, we show how ProbNetKAT can be used to model and analyze expected delivery in the presence of failures, expected congestion with randomized routing schemes, and expected convergence with gossip protocols. To the best of our knowledge, ProbNetKAT is the first high-level network programming language that adequately handles these and other examples involving probabilistic behavior.

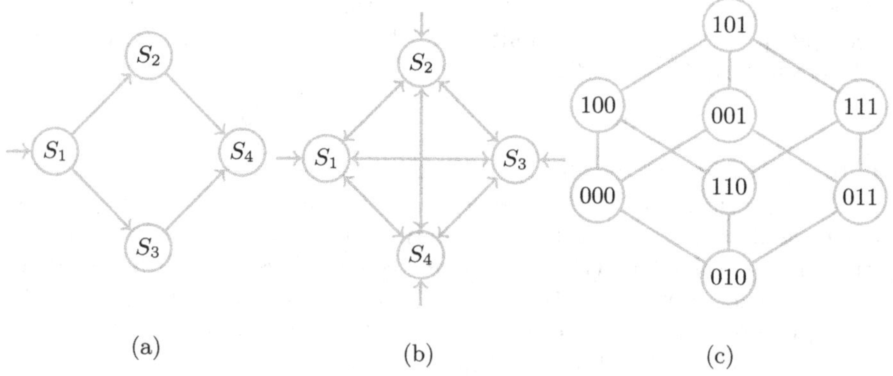

Fig. 4. Topologies used in case studies: (a) fault tolerance, (b) load balancing, and (c) gossip protocols.

8.1 Fault Tolerance

Failures are a fact of life in real-world networks. Devices and links fail due to factors ranging from software and hardware bugs to interference from the environment such as loss of power or cables being severed. A recent empirical study of data center networks by Gill et al. [14] found that failures occur frequently and can cause issues ranging from degraded performance to service disruptions. Hence, it important for network operators to be able to understand the impact of failures—e.g., they may elect to use routing schemes that divide traffic over many diverse paths in order to minimize the impact of any given failure.

We can encode failures in ProbNetKAT using random choice and `drop`: the idiom $p \oplus_d \texttt{drop}$ encodes a program that succeeds and executes p with probability d, or fails and executes `drop` with probability $1 - d$. Note that since `drop` produces no packets, it accurately models a device or link that has crashed. We can then compute the probability that traffic will be delivered under an arbitrary forwarding scheme.

As a concrete example, consider the topology depicted in Fig. 4(a), with four switches connected in a diamond. Suppose that we wish to forward traffic from S_1 to S_4 and we know that the link between S_1 and S_2 fails with 10 % probability (for simplicity, in this example, we will assume that the switches and all other links are reliable). What is the probability that a packet that originates at S_1 will be successfully delivered to S_4, as desired?

Obviously the answer to this question depends on the configuration of the network—using different forwarding paths will lead to different outcomes. To investigate this question, we will encode the overall behavior of the network using several terms: a term p that encodes the local forwarding behavior of the switches; a term t that encodes the forwarding behavior of the network topology; and a term e that encodes the network egresses.

The standard way to model a link ℓ is as the sequential composition of terms that (i) test the location (i.e., switch and port) at one end of the link; (ii) duplicate the head packet, and (iii) update the location to the other end of the link. However, because we are only concerned with end-to-end packet delivery in this example, we can safely elide the `dup` term. Hence, using the idiom discussed above, we would model a link ℓ that fails with probability $1 - d$ as $\ell \oplus_d \texttt{drop}$. Hence, since there is a 10 % probability of failure of the link $S_1 \rightarrow S_2$, we encode the topology t as follows:

$$\begin{aligned} t \triangleq & (sw = S_1; pt = 2; ((sw \leftarrow S_2; pt \leftarrow 1) \oplus_{.9} \texttt{drop})) \\ & \& \ (sw = S_1; pt = 3; sw \leftarrow S_3; pt \leftarrow 1) \\ & \& \ (sw = S_2; pt = 4; sw \leftarrow S_4; pt \leftarrow 2) \\ & \& \ (sw = S_3; pt = 4; sw \leftarrow S_4; pt \leftarrow 3). \end{aligned}$$

Here, we adopt the convention that each port is named according to the identifier of the switch it connects to—e.g., port 1 on switch S_2 connects to switch S_1.

Next, we define the local forwarding policy p that encodes the behavior on switches. Suppose that we forward traffic from S_1 to S_4 via S_2. Then p would be defined as follows: $p \triangleq (sw = S_1; pt \leftarrow 2)$ & $(sw = S_2; pt \leftarrow 4)$ Finally, the egress predicate e is simply: $e \triangleq sw = S_4$.

The complete network program is then $(p; t)^*; e$. That is, the network alternates between forwarding on switches and topology, iterating these steps until the packet is either dropped or exits the network.

Using our semantics for ProbNetKAT, we can evaluate this program on a packet starting at S_1: unsurprisingly, we obtain a distribution in which there is a 90 % chance that the packet is delivered to S_4 and a 10 % chance it is dropped.

Going a step further, we can model a more fault-tolerant forwarding scheme that divides traffic across multiple paths to reduce the impact of any single failure. The following program p' divides traffic evenly between S_2 and S_3:

$$p' \triangleq (sw = S_1; (pt \leftarrow 2 \oplus pt \leftarrow 3)) \ \& \ (sw = S_2; pt \leftarrow 4) \ \& \ (sw = S_3; pt \leftarrow 4)$$

As expected, evaluating this policy on a packet starting at S_1 gives us a 95 % chance that the packet is delivered to S_4 and only a 5 % chance that it is dropped. The positive effect with respect to failures has also been observed in previous work on randomized routing [53].

8.2 Load Balancing

In many networks, operators must balance demands for traffic while optimizing for various criteria such as minimizing the maximum amount of congestion on any given link. An attractive approach to these traffic engineering problems is to use routing schemes based on randomization: the operator computes a collection of paths that utilize the full capacity of the network and then maps incoming traffic flows onto those paths randomly. By spreading traffic over a diverse set of paths, such schemes ensure that (in expectation) the traffic will closely approximate the optimal solution, even though they only require a static set of paths in the core of the network.

Valiant load balancing (VLB) [49] is a classic randomized routing scheme that provides low expected congestion for any feasible demands in a full mesh. VLB forwards packets using a simple two-phase strategy: in the first phase, the ingress switch forwards the packet to a randomly selected neighbor, without considering the the packet's ultimate destination; in the second phase, the neighbor forwards the packet to the egress switch that is connected to the destination.

Consider the four-node mesh topology shown in Fig. 4(b). To encode this behavior, we assume that each switch has ports named $1, 2, 3, 4$, that port i on switch i connects to the outside world, and that all other ports j connect to switch j. We can write a ProbNetKAT program for this load balancing scheme by splitting it into two parts, one for each phase of routing. VLB often requires that traffic be tagged in each phase so that switches know when to forward it randomly or deterministically, but in this example, we can use topological information to distinguish the phases. Packets coming in from the outside (port i on switch i) are forwarded randomly, and packets on internal ports are forwarded deterministically.

We model the initial (random) phase with a term p_1:

$$p_1 \triangleq \mathop{\&}_{k=1}^{4} (sw = k; pt = k; \bigoplus_{j \neq k} pt \leftarrow j).$$

Here we tacitly use an n-ary version of $\oplus$ that chooses each each summand with equal probability.

Similarly, we can model the second (deterministic) phase with a term p_2:

$$p_2 \triangleq \left(\mathop{\&}_{k=1}^{4} (sw = k; pt \neq k) \right); \left(\mathop{\&}_{k=1}^{4} (dst = k; pt \leftarrow k) \right)$$

Note that the guards $sw = k; pt \neq k$ restrict to second-phase packets. The overall switch term p is simply $p_1 \ \& \ p_2$.

The topology term t is encoded with **dup** terms to record the paths, as described in Sect. 8.1.

The power of VLB is its ability to route $nr/2$ load in a network with n switches and internal links with capacity r. In our example, $n = 4$ and r is 1 packet, so we can route 2 packets of random traffic with no expected congestion. We can model this demand with a term d that generates two packets with random origins and random destinations (writing $\pi_{i,j,k}!$ for a sequence of assignments setting the switch to i, the port to j, and the identifier to k):

$$d \triangleq (\bigoplus_{k=1}^{4} (\pi_{k,k,0}!) \ \& \ \bigoplus_{k=1}^{4} (\pi_{k,k,1}!)); (\bigoplus_{k=1}^{4} dst \leftarrow k)$$

The full network program to analyze is then $d; (p; t)^*; p$. We can use similar techniques as in the congestion example from Sect. 2 to reason about congestion. We first define a random variable to extract the information we care about. Let $X_{\max}$ be a random variable equal to the maximum number of packets traversing a single internal link. By using the semantics as in Sect. 2, we can calculate that the expected value of $X_{\max}$ is 1 packet—i.e., there is no congestion.

8.3 Gossip Protocols

Gossip (or epidemic) protocols are randomized algorithms that are often used to efficiently disseminate information in large-scale distributed systems [7]. An attractive feature of gossip protocols and other epidemic algorithms is that they are able to rapidly converge to a consistent global state while only requiring bounded worst-case communication. Operationally, a gossip protocol proceeds in loosely synchronized rounds: in each round, every node communicates with a randomly selected peer and the nodes update their state using information shared during the exchange. For example, in a basic anti-entropy protocol, a "rumor" is injected into the system at a single node and spreads from node to node through pair-wise communication. In practice, such protocols can rapidly disseminate information in well-connected graphs with high probability.

We can use ProbNetKAT to model the convergence of gossip protocols. We introduce a single packet to model the "rumor" being gossiped by the system: when a node receives the packet, it randomly selects one of its neighbors to infect (by sending it the packet), and also sends a copy back to itself to maintain the infection. In gossip terminology, this would be characterized as a "push" protocol since information propagates from the node that initiates the communication to the recipient rather than the other way around.

We can make sure the nodes do not send out more than one infection packet per round by using a single incoming port (port 0) on each switch and exploiting ProbNetKAT's set semantics: because infection packets are identical modulo location, multiple infection packets arriving at the same port are identified.

Rounds	$E[X_{\mathsf{infected}}]$
0	1.00
1	2.00
2	3.33
3	4.86
4	6.25
5	7.17
6	7.66

Fig. 5. Gossip results.

To simplify the ProbNetKAT program, we assume that the network topology is a hypercube, as shown in Fig. 4(c). The program for gossiping on a hypercube is highly uniform—assuming that switches are numbered in binary, we can randomly select a neighbor by flipping a single bit.

The fragment of the switch program p for switch 000 is as follows:

$$sw = 000; ((pt \leftarrow 001 \oplus pt \leftarrow 010 \oplus pt \leftarrow 100) \,\&\, pt \leftarrow 0).$$

The overall forwarding policy is obtained by combining analogous fragments for the other switches using parallel composition.

Encoding the topology of the hypercube as t, we can then analyze $(p;t)^*$ and calculate the expected number of infected nodes after a given number of rounds X_{infected} using the ProbNetKAT semantics. The results for the first few rounds are shown in Fig. 5. This captures the usual behavior of a push-based gossip protocol.

9 Related Work

Work related to ProbNetKAT can be divided into two categories: (i) models and semantics for probabilistic programs and (i) domain-specific frameworks for specifying and reasoning about network programs. This section summarizes the most relevant pieces of prior work in each of these categories.

9.1 Probabilistic Programming

Computational models and logics for probabilistic programming have been extensively studied for many years. Denotational and operational semantics for probabilistic while programs were first studied by Kozen [23]. Early logical systems for reasoning about probabilistic programs were proposed in a sequence of separate papers by Saheb-Djahromi, Ramshaw, and Kozen [24,41,44]. There are also numerous recent efforts [15,16,26,28,36]. Our semantics for ProbNetKAT builds on the foundation developed in these papers and extends it to the new domain of network programming.

Probabilistic programming in the context of artificial intelligence has also been extensively studied in recent years [2,43]. However, the goals of this line of work are different than ours in that it focuses on Bayesian inference.

Probabilistic automata in several forms have been a popular model going back to the early work of Paz [40], as well as many other recent efforts [31,45, 46]. Probabilistic automata are a suitable operational model for probabilistic programs and play a crucial role in the development of decision procedures for bisimulation equivalence, logics to reason about behavior, in the synthesis of probabilistic programs, and in model checking procedures [4,8,20,27,29]. In the present paper, we do not touch upon any of these issues so the connections to probabilistic automata theory are thin. However, we expect they will play an important role in our future work—see below.

Denotational models combining probability and nondeterminism have been proposed in papers by several authors [19,32,48,50], and general models for labeled Markov processes, primarily based on Markov kernels, have been studied extensively [10,38,39]. Because ProbNetKAT does not have nondeterminism, we have not encountered the extra challenges arising in the combination of nondeterministic and probabilistic behavior.

All the above mentioned systems provide semantics and logical formalisms for specifying and reasoning about state-transition systems involving probabilistic choice. A crucial difference between our work and these efforts is in that our model is not really a state-transition model in the usual sense, but rather a packet-filtering model that filters, modifies, and forwards packets. Expressions denote functions that consume sets of packet histories as input and produce probability distributions of sets of packet histories as output. As demonstrated by our example applications, this view is appropriate for modeling the functionality of packet-switching networks. It has its own peculiarities and is different enough from standard state-based computation that previous semantic models in the literature do not immediately apply. Nevertheless, we have drawn much inspiration from the literature and exploited many similarities to provide a powerful formalism for modeling probabilistic behavior in packet-switching networks.

9.2 Network Programming

Recent years have seen an incredible growth of languages and systems for programming and reasoning about networks. Network programming languages such as Frenetic [11], Pyretic [35], Maple [51], NetKAT [1], and FlowLog [37] have introduced high-level abstractions and semantics that enable programmers to reason precisely about the behavior of networks. However, as mentioned previously, all of these language are based on deterministic packet-processing functions, and do not handle probabilistic traffic models or forwarding policies. Of all these frameworks, NetKAT is the most closely related as ProbNetKAT builds directly on its features.

In addition to programming languages, a number of network verification tools have been developed, including Header Space Analysis [21], VeriFlow [22], the NetKAT verifier [12], and Libra [52]. Similar to the network programming languages described above, these tools only model deterministic networks and verify deterministic properties.

Network calculus is a general framework for analyzing network behavior using tools from queuing theory [6]. It models the low-level behavior of network devices in significant detail, including features such as traffic arrival rates, switch propagation delays, and the behaviors of components like buffers and queues. This enables reasoning about quantitative properties such as latency, bandwidth, congestion, etc. Past work on network calculus can be divided into two branches: deterministic [30] and stochastic [18]. Like ProbNetKAT, the stochastic branch of network calculus provides tools for reasoning about the probabilistic behavior, especially in the presence of statistical multiplexing. However, network calculus is generally known to be difficult to use, since it can require the use of external facts from queuing theory to establish many desired results. In contrast, ProbNetKAT is a self-contained, language-based framework that offers general programming constructs and a complete denotational semantics.

10 Conclusion

Previous work [1,12] has described NetKAT, a language and logic for specifying and reasoning about the behavior of packet-switching networks. In this paper we have introduced ProbNetKAT, a conservative extension of NetKAT with constructs for reasoning about the probabilistic behavior of such networks. To our knowledge, this is the first language-based framework for specifying and verifying probabilistic network behavior. We have developed a formal semantics for ProbNetKAT based on Markov kernels and shown that the extension is conservative over NetKAT. We have also determined the appropriate notion of approximation and have shown that every ProbNetKAT program is arbitrarily closely approximated by loop-free programs. Finally, we have presented several case studies that illustrate the use of ProbNetKAT on real-world examples.

Our examples have used the semantic definitions directly in the calculation of distributions, fault tolerance, load balancing, and a probabilistic gossip protocol. Although we have exploited several general properties of our system in these arguments, we have made no attempt to assemble them into a formal deductive system or decision procedure as was done previously for NetKAT [1,12]. These questions remain topics for future investigation. We are hopeful that the coalgebraic perspective developed in [12] will be instrumental in obtaining a sound and complete axiomatization and a practical decision procedure for equivalence of ProbNetKAT expressions.

As a more practical next step, we would like to augment the existing NetKAT compiler [47] with tools for handling the probabilistic constructs of ProbNetKAT along with a formal proof of correctness. Features such as OpenFlow [33] "group tables" support for simple forms of randomization and emerging platforms such as P4 [3] offer additional flexibility. Hence, there already exist machine platforms that could serve as a compilation target for (restricted fragments of) ProbNetKAT.

Another interesting question is whether it is possible to learn ProbNetKAT programs from traces of a system, enabling active learning of running network policies. Such a capability would have many applications. For example, learning algorithms might be useful for detecting compromised nodes in a network. Alternatively, a network operator might use information from `traceroute` to learn a model that provides partial information about the paths from their own network to another autonomous system on the Internet.

Acknowledgments. The authors wish to thank the members of the Cornell PLDG and DIKU COPLAS group for insightful discussions and helpful comments. Our work is supported by the National Security Agency; the National Science Foundation under grants CNS-1111698, CNS-1413972, CCF-1422046, CCF-1253165, and CCF-1535952; the Office of Naval Research under grant N00014-15-1-2177; the Dutch Research Foundation (NWO) under project numbers 639.021.334 and 612.001.113; and gifts from Cisco, Facebook, Google, and Fujitsu.

References

1. Anderson, C., Foster, N., Guha, A., Jeannin, J., Kozen, D., Schlesinger, C., Walker, D.: NetKAT: semantic foundations for networks. In: *POPL 2014*, ACM (2014)
2. Borgström, J., Gordon, A.D., Greenberg, M., Margetson, J., Van Gael, J.: Measure transformer semantics for Bayesian machine learning. In: Barthe, G. (ed.) ESOP 2011. LNCS, vol. 6602, pp. 77–96. Springer, Heidelberg (2011)
3. Bosshart, P., Daly, D., et al.: P4: programming protocol-independent packet processors. ACM SIGCOMM Comput. Commun. Rev. **44**(3), 87–95 (2014)
4. Cattani, S., Segala, R.: Decision algorithms for probabilistic bisimulation. In: Brim, L., Jančar, P., Křetínský, M., Kučera, A. (eds.) CONCUR 2002. LNCS, vol. 2421, pp. 371–385. Springer, Heidelberg (2002)
5. Chung, K.L.: A Course in Probability Theory, 2nd edn. Academic Press, New York (1974)
6. Cruz, R.: A calculus for network delay, parts I and II. IEEE Trans. Inf. Theor. **37**(1), 114–141 (1991)
7. Demers, A., Gealy, M., Greene, D., Hauser, C., Irish, W., Larson, J., Manning, S., Shenker, S., Sturgis, H., Swinehart, D., Terry, D., Woods, D.: Epidemic algorithms for replicated database maintenance. In: *PODC 1987*, ACM (1987)
8. Desharnais, J., Edalat, A., Panangaden, P.: Bisimulation for labelled Markov processes. Inf. Comput. **179**(2), 163–193 (2002)
9. Desharnais, J., Gupta, V., Jagadeesan, R., Panangaden, P.: A metric for labelled Markov processes. Theor. Comput. Sci. **318**(3), 323–354 (2004)
10. Doberkat, E.: Stochastic Relations: Foundations for Markov Transition Systems. Studies in Informatics. Chapman Hall, New York (2007)
11. Foster, N., Harrison, R., Freedman, M., Monsanto, C., Rexford, J., Story, A., Walker, D.: Frenetic: a network programming language. In: *ICFP 2011*, ACM (2011)

12. Foster, N., Kozen, D., Milano, M., Silva, A., Thompson, L.: A coalgebraic decision procedure for NetKAT. In: *POPL 2015*, ACM (2015)
13. Foster, N., Kozen, D., Mamouras, K., Reitblatt, M., Silva, A.: Probabilistic NetKAT (full version). http://hdl.handle.net/1813/40335
14. Gill, P., Jain, N., Nagappan, N.: Understanding network failures in data centers: measurement, analysis, and implications. In: SIGCOMM 2011, ACM (2011)
15. Gordon, A., Henzinger, T., Nori, A., Rajamani, S.: Probabilistic programming. In: ICSE 2014, IEEE (2014)
16. Gretz, F., Jansen, N., Kaminski, B., Katoen, J., McIver, A., Olmedo, F.: Conditioning in probabilistic programming. MFPS 2015 Electron. Notes Theor. Comput. Sci. **319**, 199–216 (2015)
17. Halmos, P.R.: Measure Theory. Van Nostrand, New York (1950)
18. Jiang, Y.: A basic stochastic network calculus. In: SIGCOMM 2006, ACM (2006)
19. Jones, C.: Probabilistic nondeterminism. Ph.D. thesis, Edinburgh University (1990)
20. Jonsson, B., Larsen, K.G.: Specification and refinement of probabilistic processes. In: LICS 1991, IEEE (1991)
21. Kazemian, P., Varghese, G., McKeown, N.: Header space analysis: static checking for networks. In: NSDI 2012, USENIX (2012)
22. Khurshid, A., Zou, X., Zhou, W., Caesar, M., Godfrey, P.: VeriFlow: verifying network-wide invariants in real time. In: NSDI 2013, USENIX (2013)
23. Kozen, D.: Semantics of probabilistic programs. JCSS **22**, 328–350 (1981)
24. Kozen, D.: A probabilistic PDL. JCSS **30**(2), 162–178 (1985)
25. Kozen, D.: Kleene algebra with tests. TOPLAS **19**(3), 427–443 (1997)
26. Kozen, D., Mardare, R., Panangaden, P.: Strong completeness for Markovian logics. In: Chatterjee, K., Sgall, J. (eds.) MFCS 2013. LNCS, vol. 8087, pp. 655–666. Springer, Heidelberg (2013)
27. Kwiatkowska, M., Norman, G., et al.: Symbolic model checking for probabilistic timed automata. Inf. Comput. **205**(7), 1027–1077 (2007)
28. Larsen, K.G., Mardare, R., Panangaden, P.: Taking It to the limit: approximate reasoning for Markov processes. In: Rovan, B., Sassone, V., Widmayer, P. (eds.) MFCS 2012. LNCS, vol. 7464, pp. 681–692. Springer, Heidelberg (2012)
29. Larsen, K., Skou, A.: Bisimulation through probabilistic testing. Inf. Comput. **94**, 456–471 (1991)
30. Le Boudec, J., Thiran, P.: Network Calculus: A Theory of Deterministic Queuing Systems for the Internet. Springer-Verlag, Heidelberg (2001)
31. McIver, A., Cohen, E., Morgan, C., Gonzalia, C.: Using probabilistic Kleene algebra pKA for protocol verification. JLAP **76**(1), 90–111 (2008)
32. McIver, A., Morgan, C.: Abstraction, Refinement and Proof for Probabilistic Systems. Springer, New York (2005)
33. McKeown, N., Anderson, T., et al.: Openflow: enabling innovation in campus networks. SIGCOMM CCR **38**(2), 69–74 (2008)
34. Medina, A., Taft, N., Salamatian, K., Bhattacharyya, S., Diot, C.: Traffic matrix estimation: existing techniques and new directions. In: SIGCOMM 2002, ACM (2002)
35. Monsanto, C., Reich, J., Foster, N., Rexford, J., Walker, D.: Composing software defined networks. In NSDI 2013, USENIX (2013)
36. Morgan, C., McIver, A., Seidel, K.: Probabilistic predicate transformers. TOPLAS **18**(3), 325–353 (1996)
37. Nelson, T., Ferguson, A., Scheer, M., Krishnamurthi, S.: Tierless programming and reasoning for software-defined networks. In: NSDI 2014, USENIX (2014)

38. Panangaden, P.: Probabilistic relations. In: School of Computer Science, McGill University, Montreal, pp. 59–74 (1998)
39. Panangaden, P.: Labelled Markov Processes. Imperial College Press, London (2009)
40. Paz, A.: Introduction to Probabilistic Automata. Academic Press, Orlando (1971)
41. Ramshaw, L.H.: Formalizing the analysis of algorithms. Ph.D. thesis, Stanford University (1979)
42. Rao, M.M.: Measure Theory and Integration. Wiley-Interscience, New York (1987)
43. Roy, D.: Computability, inference and modeling in probabilistic programming. Ph.D. thesis, Massachusetts Institute of Technology (2011)
44. Saheb-Djahromi, N.: Probabilistic LCF. In: Winkowski, J. (ed.) Mathematical Foundations of Computer Science 1978. Lecture Notes in Computer Science, vol. 64, pp. 442–451. Springer, Heidelberg (1978)
45. Segala, R.: Probability and nondeterminism in operational models of concurrency. In: Baier, C., Hermanns, H. (eds.) CONCUR 2006. LNCS, vol. 4137, pp. 64–78. Springer, Heidelberg (2006)
46. Segala, R., Lynch, N.A.: Probabilistic simulations for probabilistic processes. NJC **2**, 250–273 (1995)
47. Smolka, S., Eliopoulos, S., Foster, N., Guha, A.: A fast compiler for NetKAT. In: ICFP 2015, ACM (2015)
48. Tix, R., Keimel, K., Plotkin, G.: Semantic domains for combining probability and nondeterminism. ENTCS **222**, 3–99 (2009)
49. Valiant, L.: A scheme for fast parallel communication. SIAM J. Comput. **11**(2), 350–361 (1982)
50. Varacca, D., Winskel, G.: Distributing probability over non-determinism. Math. Struct. Comput. Sci. **16**(1), 87–113 (2006)
51. Voellmy, A., Wang, J., Yang, Y., Ford, B., Hudak, P.: Maple: simplifying SDN programming using algorithmic policies. In: SIGCOMM (2013)
52. Zeng, H., Zhang, S., et al.: Libra: divide and conquer to verify forwarding tables in huge networks. In: NSDI (2014)
53. Rui, Z.-S., McKeown, N.: Designing a predictable internet backbone with valiant load-balancing. In: de Meer, H., Bhatti, N. (eds.) IWQoS 2005. LNCS, vol. 3552, pp. 178–192. Springer, Heidelberg (2005)

Coordinated Concurrent Programming in SYNDICATE

Tony Garnock-Jones(✉) and Matthias Felleisen

Northeastern University, Boston, MA, USA
tonyg@ccs.neu.edu

Abstract. Most programs interact with the world: via graphical user interfaces, networks, etc. This form of interactivity entails concurrency, and concurrent program components must coordinate their computations. This paper presents SYNDICATE, a novel design for a coordinated, concurrent programming language. Each concurrent component in SYNDICATE is a functional actor that participates in scoped conversations. The medium of conversation arranges for message exchanges and coordinates access to common knowledge. As such, SYNDICATE occupies a novel point in this design space, halfway between actors and threads.

1 From Interaction to Concurrency and Coordination

Most programs must interact with their context. Interactions often start as reactions to external events, such as a user's gesture or the arrival of a message. Because nobody coordinates the multitude of external events, a program must notice and react to events in a concurrent manner. Thus, a sequential program must de-multiplex the sequence of events and launch the appropriate concurrent component for each event. Put differently, these interacting programs consist of concurrent components, even in sequential languages.

Concurrent program components must coordinate their computations to realize the overall goals of the program. This coordination takes two forms: the exchange of knowledge and the establishment of frame conditions. In addition, coordination must take into account that reactions to events may call for the creation of new concurrent components or that existing components may disappear due to exceptions or partial failures. In short, coordination poses a major problem to the proper design of effective communicating, concurrent components.

This paper presents SYNDICATE, a novel language for coordinated concurrent programming. A SYNDICATE program consists of functional actors that participate in precisely scoped conversations. So-called *networks* coordinate these conversations. When needed, they apply a functional actor to an event and its current state; in turn, they receive a new state plus descriptions of actions. These actions may represent messages for other participants in the conversations or assertions for a common space of knowledge.

Precise scoping implies a separation of distinct conversations, and hence existence of multiple networks. At the same time, an actor in one network may have

P. Thiemann (Ed.): ESOP 2016, LNCS 9632, pp. 310–336, 2016.
DOI: 10.1007/978-3-662-49498-1_13

Programs	$P \in \mathbb{P}$	$::=$	$\mathsf{actor}\ f\ u\ \vec{a} \mid \mathsf{net}\ \vec{P}$
Leaf functions	$f \in \mathbb{F}$	$=$	$\mathbb{E} \times \mathbb{V} \longrightarrow_{total} \vec{\mathbb{A}} \times \mathbb{V} + \mathbb{E}\mathrm{rr}$
Values	$u, v \in \mathbb{V}$		(first-order data; numbers, strings, lists, trees, sets, etc.)
Events	$e \in \mathbb{E}$	$::=$	$\langle c \rangle \mid \pi$
Actions	$a \in \mathbb{A}$	$::=$	$\langle c \rangle \mid \pi \mid P$
Assertions	$c, d \in \mathbb{S}$	$::=$	$u \mid ?c \mid {\downharpoonleft}c$
Assertion sets	$\pi \in \Pi$	$=$	$\mathcal{P}(\mathbb{S})$

Fig. 1. Syntax of SYNDICATE Programs

to communicate with an actor in a different network. To accommodate such situations, SYNDICATE allows the embedding of one network into another as if the first were just an actor within the second. In other words, networks simultaneously scope and compose conversations. The resulting tree-structured shape of networked conversations corresponds both to tree-like arrangements of containers and processes in modern operating systems and to the nesting of layers in network protocols [1]. SYNDICATE thus unifies the programming techniques of distributed programming with those of coordinated concurrent programming.

By construction, SYNDICATE networks also manage resources. When a new actor appears in a conversation, a network allocates the necessary resources. When an actor fails, it deallocates the associated resources. In particular, it retracts all shared state associated with the actor, thereby making the failure visible to interested participants. SYNDICATE thus solves notorious problems of service discovery and resource management in the coordination of communicating components.

In sum, SYNDICATE occupies a novel point in the design space of coordinated concurrent (functional) components (Sect. 2), sitting firmly between a thread-based world with sharing and local-state-only, message-passing actors. Our design for SYNDICATE includes two additional contributions: an efficient protocol for incrementally maintaining the common knowledge base and a trie-based data structure for efficiently indexing into it (Sect. 3). Finally, our paper presents evaluations concerning the fundamental performance characteristics of SYNDICATE as well as its pragmatics (Sects. 4 and 5).

2 SYNDICATE

SYNDICATE is a new language directly inspired by our previous work on Network Calculus (NC) [2]. It generalizes NC's "observation" mechanism into a means of asserting and monitoring common group state. In SYNDICATE, NC's subscriptions are a special case of general assertions, which simplifies the syntax, semantics and programming model. SYNDICATE thus supports Actor-style point-to-point, NC-style multicast, and a novel form of assertion-set-based communication in a uniform mechanism. This section describes SYNDICATE using mathematical syntax and semantics. It includes examples and concludes with theorems about SYNDICATE's key properties. The remainder of the paper reports on our prototype implementations based on Javascript [3] and Racket [4].

2.1 Abstract SYNDICATE Syntax and Informal Semantics

Figure 1 displays the syntax of SYNDICATE programs. Each program P consists of a single actor: either a *leaf actor* or a *network actor*. A leaf actor has the shape actor $f\ u\ \vec{a}$, comprising not only its event-transducing behavior function f but also a piece of actor-private state u and a sequence of initial actions $\vec{a}$. A network actor creates a group of communicating actors, and consists of a sequence of programs prefixed with the keyword `net`.

Leaf actor functions consume an event plus their current state. The function computes a sequence of desired actions plus a state value. Behavior functions are total, though termination via an exception is acceptable. We call the latter a crash. These constraints are reflected in the type associated with f; see Fig. 1.

In the λ-calculus, a program is usually a combination of an inert part—a function value—and an input value. In SYNDICATE, delivering an event to an actor is analogous to such an application. However, the pure λ-calculus has no analogue of the actions produced by SYNDICATE actors.

A SYNDICATE actor may produce actions like those in the traditional Actor model, namely sending messages $\langle c \rangle$ and spawning new actors P, but it may also produce *state change notifications* π. The latter convey sets of assertions an actor wishes to publish in its network's *shared dataspace*. Each such set completely replaces all previous assertions made by that actor; to retract an assertion, the actor issues a state change notification action lacking the assertion concerned.

We take the liberty of using wildcard $\star$ as a form of assertion set comprehension. For now, when we write expressions such as $\{(\mathtt{a}, \star)\}$, we mean the set of all pairs having the atom a on the left. Similarly, $\{?\star\}$ means $\{?c \mid c \in \mathbb{S}\}$. Clearly, implementers must take pains to keep representations of sets specified in this manner tractable. We discuss this issue in more detail in Sect. 3.

When an actor issues an assertion of shape $?c$, it expresses an interest in being informed of all assertions c. In other words, an assertion $?c$ acts as a subscription to c. Similarly, $??c$ specifies interest in being informed about assertions of shape $?c$, and so on. The network sends a state change notification *event* to an actor each time the set of assertions matching the actor's interests changes.

An actor's subscriptions are assertions like any other. State change notifications thus give an actor control over its subscriptions as well as over any other information it wishes to make available to its peers or acquire from them.

Our examples use a mathematical notation to highlight the essential aspects of SYNDICATE's coordination abilities without dwelling on language details. We use *italic* text to denote variables and `monospace` to denote literal atoms and strings. In places where SYNDICATE demands a sequence of values, for example the $\vec{a}$ in an actor action, our language supplies a single list value $[a_1, ..., a_n]$. We include list comprehensions $[a \mid a \in \mathbb{A}, P(a), ...]$ because actors frequently need to construct, filter, and transform sequences of values. Similarly, we add syntax for sets $\{c_1, ..., c_n\}$, including set comprehensions $\{c \mid c \in \mathbb{S}, P(c), ...\}$, and for tuples $(v_1, ..., v_n)$, to represent the sets and tuples needed by SYNDICATE. We write constructors for actions and events just as in SYNDICATE: that is, $\langle\cdot\rangle$ constructs a message event or action; $?\cdot$, an "interest" assertion; $\downharpoonleft\cdot$, a cross-layer assertion; and actor and net, actions which spawn new actors.

We define functions using patterns over the language's values. For example, the leaf function definition

$$\mathit{box}\ \langle(\texttt{set}, \mathit{id}, v_c)\rangle\ v_o = ([\{?(\texttt{set}, \mathit{id}, \star), (\texttt{value}, \mathit{id}, v_c)\}], v_c)$$

introduces a function *box* that expects two arguments: a SYNDICATE message and an arbitrary value. The $\langle(\texttt{set}, \mathit{id}, v_c)\rangle$ pattern for the former says it must consist of a triple with set on the left and arbitrary values in the center and right field. The function yields a pair whose left field is a sequence of actions and whose right one is its new state value v_c. The sequence of actions consists of only one element: a state change notification action bearing an assertion set. The assertion set is written in part using a wildcard denoting an infinite set, and in part using a simple value. The resulting assertion set thus contains not only the triple $(\texttt{value}, \mathit{id}, v_c)$ but also the infinite set of all ?-labelled triples with set on the left and with *id* in the middle.

2.2 Some SYNDICATE Programs

Suppose we wish to create an actor X with an interest in the price of milk. Here is how it might be written:

$$\textsf{actor}\ f_X\ u_X\ [\{?(\texttt{price}, \texttt{milk}, \star)\}]$$

Its initial action is a state change notification containing the assertion set

$$\{?(\texttt{price}, \texttt{milk}, c) \mid c \in \mathbb{S}\}$$

If some peer Y previously asserted $(\texttt{price}, \texttt{milk}, 1.17)$, this assertion is immediately delivered to X in a state change notification event. Infinite sets of interests thus act as *query patterns* over the shared dataspace.

Redundant assertions do not cause change notifications. If actor Z subsequently also asserts $(\texttt{price}, \texttt{milk}, 1.17)$, no notification is sent to X, since X has already been informed that $(\texttt{price}, \texttt{milk}, 1.17)$ has been asserted. However, if Z instead asserts $(\texttt{price}, \texttt{milk}, 9.25)$, then a change notification is sent to X containing *both* asserted prices.

Symmetrically, it is not until the last assertion of shape $(\texttt{price}, \texttt{milk}, p)$ for some particular p is retracted from the network that X is sent a notification about the lack of assertions of shape $(\texttt{price}, \texttt{milk}, p)$.

When an actor crashes, all its assertions are automatically retracted. By implication, if no other actor is making the same assertions at the time, then peers interested in the crashing actor's assertions are sent a state change notification event informing them of the retraction(s).

For a different example, consider an actor representing a shared mutable reference cell holding a number. A new box is created by choosing a name *id* and launching the actor

$$\textsf{actor}\ \mathit{box}\ 0\ [\{?(\texttt{set}, \mathit{id}, \star), (\texttt{value}, \mathit{id}, 0)\}]$$

The new actor's first action asserts both its interest in **set** messages labelled with *id* as well as the fact that the **value** of box *id* is currently 0. Its behavior is given by the function *box* from Sect. 2.1. Upon receipt of a **set** message bearing a new value v_c, the actor replaces its private state value with v_c and constructs a single action specifying the new set of facts the actor wants to assert. This new set of facts includes the unchanged **set**-message subscription as well as a new **value** fact, thereby replacing v_o with v_c in the shared dataspace.

To read the value of the box, clients either include an appropriate assertion in their initially declared interests or issue it later:

$$\mathsf{actor}\ \mathit{boxClient}\ ()\ [\{?(\mathtt{value}, \mathit{id}, \star)\}]$$

As corresponding facts come and go in response to actions taken by the box actor they are forwarded to interested parties. For example, an actor that increments the number held in the box each time it changes would be written

$$\mathit{boxClient}\ \{(\mathtt{value}, \mathit{id}, v)\}\ ()\ = ([\langle(\mathtt{set}, \mathit{id}, v+1)\rangle], ())$$

Our next example demonstrates *demand matching*. The need to measure demand for some service and allocate resources in response appears in different guises in a wide variety of concurrent systems. Here, we imagine a client, A, beginning a conversation with some service by adding (**hello**, A) to the shared dataspace. In response, the service should create a worker actor to talk to A.

The "listening" part of the service is spawned as follows:

$$\mathsf{actor}\ \mathit{demandMatcher}\ \emptyset\ [\{?(\mathtt{hello}, \star)\}]$$

Its behavior function is defined as follows:

$$\mathit{demandMatcher}\ \pi_{new}\ \pi_{old} = ([\mathit{mkWorker}\ x \mid (\mathtt{hello}, x) \in \pi_{new} - \pi_{old}], \pi_{new})$$

The actor-private state of *demandMatcher*, π_{old}, is the set of currently-asserted **hello** tuples.[1] The incoming event, π_{new}, is the newest version of that set from the environment. The demand matcher performs set subtraction to determine newly-appeared requests and calls a helper function *mkWorker* to produce a matching service actor for each:

$$\mathit{mkWorker}\ x = \mathsf{actor}\ \mathit{worker}\ (\mathit{initialStateFor}\ x)\ (\mathit{initialActionsFor}\ x)$$

Thus, when (**hello**, A) first appears as a member of π_{new}, the demand matcher invokes *mkWorker* A, which yields a request to create a new worker actor that talks to client A. The conversation between A and the new worker proceeds from there. A more sophisticated implementation of demand matching might maintain a pool of workers, allocating incoming conversation requests as necessary.

Our final example demonstrates an architectural pattern seen in operating systems, web browsers, and cloud computing. Figure 2 sketches the architecture of a SYNDICATE program implementing a word processing application with multiple open documents, alongside other applications and a *file server* actor. The "Kernel" network is at the bottom of this tree-like representation of containment.

[1] Our implementations of SYNDICATE internalise assertion sets as *tries* (Sect. 3.3).

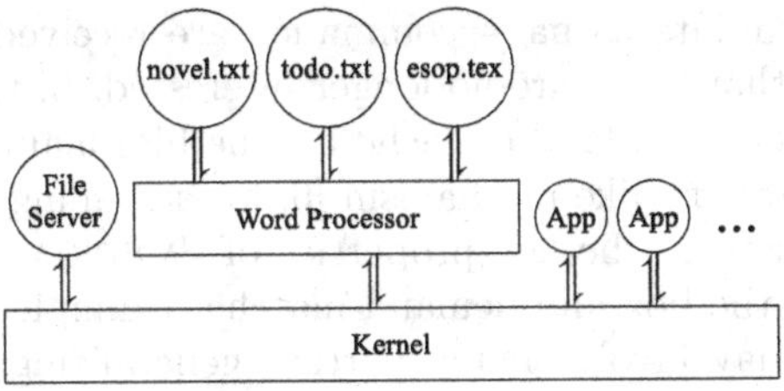

Fig. 2. Layered file server / Word processor architecture

The hierarchical nature of SYNDICATE means that each network has a containing network in turn. Actors may interrogate and augment assertions in the dataspaces of containing networks by prefixing assertions relating to the nth relative network layer with n harpoons $\downharpoonleft$. SYNDICATE networks relay $\downharpoonleft$-labelled assertions outward and relay assertions matching $\downharpoonleft$-labelled interests inward.

In this example, actors representing open documents communicate directly with each other—via a local network scoped to the word processor—and only indirectly with other actors in the system. When the actor for a document decides that it is time to save its content to the file system, it issues a message such as

$$\langle \downharpoonleft(\texttt{save}, \text{“}\texttt{novel.txt}\text{”}, \text{“}\texttt{Call me Ishmael.}\text{”})\rangle$$

into its local network. The harpoon ($\downharpoonleft$) signals that, like a system call in regular software applications, the message is intended to be relayed to the *next outermost* network—the medium connecting the word processing application as a whole to its peers. Once the message is relayed, the message

$$\langle(\texttt{save}, \text{“}\texttt{novel.txt}\text{”}, \text{“}\texttt{Call me Ishmael.}\text{”})\rangle$$

is issued into the outer network, where it may be processed by the file server. The harpoon is removed as part of the relaying operation, and no further harpoons remain, indicating that the message should be processed *here*, at this network.

The file server responds to two protocols, one for writing files and one for reading file contents and broadcasting changes to files as they happen. These protocols are articulated as two subscriptions:

$$\{?(\texttt{save}, \star, \star), ??(\texttt{contents}, \star, \star)\}$$

The first indicates interest in `save` messages. When a `save` message is received, the server stores the updated file content.

The second indicates interest in *subscriptions* in the shared dataspace, an interest in *interest* in file contents. This is how the server learns that peers wish to be kept informed of the contents of files under its control. The file server is told each time some peer asserts interest in the contents of a file. In response, it asserts facts of the form

$$(\texttt{contents}, \text{“}\texttt{novel.txt}\text{”}, \text{“}\texttt{Call me Ishmael.}\text{”})$$

and keeps them up-to-date as `save` commands are received, finally retracting them when it learns that peers are no longer interested. In this way, the shared dataspace not only acts as a kind of cache for the files maintained on disk, but also doubles as an `inotify`-like mechanism [6] for signalling changes in files.

Our examples illustrate the key properties of SYNDICATE and their unique combination. Firstly, the box and demand-matcher examples show that SYNDICATE conversations may involve many parties, generalizing the Actor model's point-to-point conversations. At the same time, the file server example shows that SYNDICATE conversations are more precisely bounded than those of traditional Actors. Each of its networks crisply delimits its contained conversations, each of which may therefore use a task-appropriate language of discourse.

Secondly, all three examples demonstrate the shared-dataspace aspect of SYNDICATE. Assertions made by one actor can influence other actors, but cannot directly alter or remove assertions made by others. The box's content is made visible through an assertion in the dataspace, and any actor that knows *id* can retrieve the assertion. The demand-matcher responds to changes in the dataspace that denote the existence of new conversations. The file server makes file contents available through assertions in the (outer) dataspace, in response to clients placing subscriptions in that dataspace.

Finally, SYNDICATE places an upper bound on the lifetimes of entries in the shared space. Items may be asserted and retracted by actors at will in response to incoming events, but when an actor crashes, all of its assertions are automatically retracted. If the box actor were to crash during a computation, the assertion describing its content would be visibly withdrawn, and peers could take some compensating action. The demand matcher can be enhanced to monitor *supply* as well as demand and to take corrective action if some worker instance exits unexpectedly. The combination of this temporal bound on assertions with SYNDICATE's state change notifications gives good failure-signalling and fault-tolerance properties, improving on those seen in Erlang [7].

2.3 Formal SYNDICATE Semantics

Figure 3a shows the syntax of SYNDICATE machine configurations, along with a metafunction boot, which loads programs in $\mathbb{P}$ into starting machine states in Σ.

The reduction relation operates on actor states $\Sigma = \overrightarrow{e} \triangleright B \triangleright \overrightarrow{a}$, which are triples of a sequence of events $\overrightarrow{e}$ destined for the actor, the actor's behavior and state B, and a sequence of actions $\overrightarrow{a}$ issued by the actor and destined for processing by its containing network. The behavior and state of leaf actors is a pair (f, u); the behavior of a network actor is determined by the reduction rules of SYNDICATE, and its state is a *configuration*.

Network Configurations C comprise three registers: a sequence of actions to be performed $\overrightarrow{(k, a)}$, each labelled with some *location* k denoting the origin of the action; the current contents of the shared dataspace R; and a sequence of actors $\overrightarrow{\ell \mapsto \Sigma}$ residing within the configuration. Each actor is assigned a locally-unique *label* ℓ, scoped strictly to the configuration and meaningless outside. Labels are

Configurations	$C \in \mathbb{C}$	$::= [\overrightarrow{(k,a)}\ ;\ R\ ;\ \vec{A}]$	
Actors	$A \in \mathbb{O}$	$::= \ell \mapsto \Sigma$	
Actor States	$\Sigma \in \mathbb{\Sigma}$	$::= \vec{e} \triangleright B \triangleright \vec{a}$	
Behaviors	$B \in \mathbb{B}$	$::= (f,u) \mid C$	
Shared Dataspaces	$R \in \mathbb{R}$	$= \mathcal{P}(\mathit{Lift}(\mathbb{L}) \times \mathbb{S})$	
Locations	$j,k \in \mathit{Lift}(\mathbb{L})$	$::= \ell \mid \downharpoonright$	
Local Labels	$\ell \in \mathbb{L}$	$= \mathbb{N}$	
Events	$e \in \mathbb{E}$	$::= \langle c \rangle \mid \pi$	
Actions	$a \in \mathbb{A}$	$::= \langle c \rangle \mid \pi \mid P$	

$$\mathsf{boot} : \mathbb{P} \rightarrow \mathbb{\Sigma}$$
$$\mathsf{boot}\,(\mathsf{actor}\, f\, u\, \vec{a}) = \cdot \triangleright (f,u) \triangleright \vec{a}$$
$$\mathsf{boot}\,(\mathsf{net}\, \vec{P}) = \cdot \triangleright [\overrightarrow{(\downharpoonright, P)}\ ;\ \emptyset\ ;\ \cdot] \triangleright \cdot$$

(a)

$$A_Q \in \mathbb{O}_Q ::= \ell \mapsto \Sigma_Q$$
$$\Sigma_Q \in \mathbb{\Sigma}_Q ::= \vec{e} \triangleright B \triangleright \cdot$$

Quiescent Terms

$$C_I \in \mathbb{C}_I ::= [\cdot\ ;\ R\ ;\ \vec{A_I}]$$
$$A_I \in \mathbb{O}_I ::= \ell \mapsto \Sigma_I$$
$$\Sigma_I \in \mathbb{\Sigma}_I ::= \cdot \triangleright B_I \triangleright \cdot$$
$$B_I \in \mathbb{B}_I ::= (f,u) \mid C_I$$

Inert Terms

(b)

Fig. 3. Evaluation syntax and inert and quiescent terms of SYNDICATE

never made visible to leaf actors: they are an internal matter, used solely as part of the behavior of network actors. The locations marking each queued action in the configuration are either the labels of some contained actor or the special location $\downharpoonright$ denoting an action resulting from some external force, such as an event arriving from the configuration's containing configuration.

The reduction relation drives actors toward *quiescent* and even *inert* states. Figure 3b defines these syntactic classes, which are roughly analogous to values in the call-by-value λ-calculus. An actor is quiescent when its sequence of actions is empty, and it is inert when, besides being quiescent, it has no more events to process and cannot take any further internal reductions.

The reductions and metafunctions of SYNDICATE are shown in Figs. 4 and 5. Rules notify-leaf and exception deliver an event to a leaf actor and update its state based on the results. An exception results in the failing actor becoming inert and issuing a synthesised action retracting all its previous assertions.

Rule notify-net delivers an event to a *network* actor. Not only is the arriving event labelled with the special location $\downharpoonright$ before being enqueued, it is transformed by the metafunction inp, which prepends a harpoon marker to each assertion contained in the event. This marks the assertions as pertaining to the next outermost network, rather than to the local network.

Rule gather reads from the outbound action queue of an actor in a network. It labels each action with the label of the actor before enqueueing it in the network's pending action queue for processing.

The newtable rule is central. A queued state change notification action (k, π) not only replaces assertions associated with location k in the shared dataspace but also inserts a state change notification *event* into the event queues of interested local actors via the metafunction bc (short for "broadcast"). Because k may have made assertions labelled with $\downharpoonright$, newtable also prepares a state change notification for the wider environment, using the out metafunction.

$$\vec{e}e_0 \triangleright (f,u) \triangleright \vec{a} \longrightarrow \vec{e} \triangleright (f,u') \triangleright \vec{a}'\vec{a} \quad \text{when } f(e_0,u) = (\vec{a}', u') \qquad \textsf{(notify-leaf)}$$

$$\vec{e}e_0 \triangleright (f,u) \triangleright \vec{a} \longrightarrow \cdot \triangleright (\lambda eu.(\cdot,u),u) \triangleright \emptyset\,\vec{a} \quad \text{when } f(e_0,u) \in \mathbb{E}\mathrm{rr} \qquad \textsf{(exception)}$$

$$\vec{e}e_0 \triangleright [\,\cdot\,; R; \overrightarrow{A_I}] \triangleright \vec{a} \longrightarrow \vec{e} \triangleright [(\downharpoonleft, \mathsf{inp}(e_0)); R; \overrightarrow{A_I}] \triangleright \vec{a} \qquad \textsf{(notify-net)}$$

$$\begin{array}{l} \vec{e} \triangleright [\qquad \overrightarrow{(k,a)}; R; \overrightarrow{A_Q}(\ell \mapsto \vec{e}' \triangleright B \triangleright \vec{a}'a'')\vec{A}] \triangleright \vec{a} \longrightarrow \\ \vec{e} \triangleright [(\ell,a'')\,\overrightarrow{(k,a)}; R; \overrightarrow{A_Q}(\ell \mapsto \vec{e}' \triangleright B \triangleright \vec{a}' \quad)\vec{A}] \triangleright \vec{a} \end{array} \qquad \textsf{(gather)}$$

$$\begin{array}{l} \vec{e} \triangleright [\overrightarrow{(k',a)}(k,\pi); R \quad ; \overrightarrow{A_Q} \quad] \triangleright \quad \vec{a} \longrightarrow \\ \vec{e} \triangleright [\overrightarrow{(k',a)} \quad ; R \oplus (k,\pi); \overrightarrow{\mathsf{bc}(k,\pi,R,A_Q)}] \triangleright \mathsf{out}(k,\pi,R)\,\vec{a} \end{array} \qquad \textsf{(newtable)}$$

$$\begin{array}{l} \vec{e} \triangleright [\overrightarrow{(k',a)}(k,\langle c\rangle); R; \overrightarrow{A_Q} \quad] \triangleright \quad \vec{a} \longrightarrow \\ \vec{e} \triangleright [\overrightarrow{(k',a)} \quad ; R; \overrightarrow{\mathsf{bc}(k,\langle c\rangle,R,A_Q)}] \triangleright \mathsf{out}(k,\langle c\rangle,R)\,\vec{a} \end{array} \qquad \textsf{(message)}$$

$$\vec{e} \triangleright [\overrightarrow{(k',a)}(k,P); R; \overrightarrow{A_Q}] \triangleright \vec{a} \longrightarrow \vec{e} \triangleright [\overrightarrow{(k',a)}; R; \overrightarrow{A_Q}(\ell \mapsto \mathsf{boot}(P))] \triangleright \vec{a} \qquad \textsf{(spawn)}$$

where ℓ distinct from k, every k', and the labels of every A_Q

$$\frac{\Sigma_Q \longrightarrow \Sigma'}{\vec{e} \triangleright [\,\cdot\,; R; \overrightarrow{A_I}(\ell \mapsto \Sigma_Q)\overrightarrow{A_Q}] \triangleright \vec{a} \longrightarrow \vec{e} \triangleright [\,\cdot\,; R; \overrightarrow{A_Q}\overrightarrow{A_I}(\ell \mapsto \Sigma')] \triangleright \vec{a}} \qquad \textsf{(schedule)}$$

Fig. 4. Reduction semantics of Syndicate

Rule message performs send-message actions $\langle c\rangle$. The bc metafunction is again used to deliver the message to interested peers, and out relays the message on to the containing network if it happens to be labelled with $\downharpoonleft$.

The bc metafunction computes the consequences of an action for a given actor. When it deals with a state change notification, the entire aggregate shared dataspace R is projected according to the asserted interests of each actor. The results of the projection are assembled into a state change notification. When bc deals with a message, a message event $\langle c\rangle$ is enqueued for an actor with local label ℓ only if it has previously asserted interest in c; that is, if $(\ell, ?c) \in R$.

The out metafunction never produces an action for transmission to the outer network when the cause of the call to out is an action from the outer network. Without this rule, configurations would never become inert.

The spawn rule allocates a fresh local label ℓ and places the configuration to be spawned into the collection of local actors, alongside its siblings.

Finally, the schedule rule allows quiescent, non-inert contained actors to take a step and rotates the sequence of actors as it does so. Variations on this rule can express different scheduling policies. For example, sorting the sequence decreasing by event queue length prioritizes heavily-loaded actors.

2.4 Properties

Two theorems capture invariants that support the design of and reasoning about effective protocols for Syndicate programs. Theorem 1 assures programmers

$$\oplus : \mathbb{R} \times (\mathit{Lift}(\mathbb{L}) \times \Pi) \longrightarrow \mathbb{R}$$
$$R \oplus (k, \pi) = \{(j, c) \mid (j, c) \in R,\ j \neq k\} \cup \{(k, c) \mid c \in \pi\}$$

$$\mathsf{bc} : \mathit{Lift}(\mathbb{L}) \times \mathbb{E} \times \mathbb{R} \times \mathbb{O}_Q \longrightarrow \mathbb{O}$$
$$\mathsf{bc}(k,\ \pi,\ R^{old},\ \ell \mapsto \vec{e} \triangleright B \triangleright \cdot) = \begin{cases} \ell \mapsto \pi^{new}\,\vec{e} \triangleright B \triangleright \cdot & \text{when } \pi^{new} \neq \pi^{old} \\ \ell \mapsto \quad \vec{e} \triangleright B \triangleright \cdot & \text{when } \pi^{new} = \pi^{old} \end{cases}$$
$$\text{where } R^{new} = R^{old} \oplus (k, \pi)$$
$$\pi^{new} = \{c \mid (j, c) \in R^{new},\ (\ell, ?c) \in R^{new}\}$$
$$\pi^{old} = \{c \mid (j, c) \in R^{old},\ (\ell, ?c) \in R^{old}\}$$
$$\mathsf{bc}(k,\ \langle c \rangle,\ R,\ \ell \mapsto \vec{e} \triangleright B \triangleright \cdot) = \begin{cases} \ell \mapsto \langle c \rangle \vec{e} \triangleright B \triangleright \cdot & \text{when } (\ell, ?c) \in R \text{ and either } k = \downarrow \\ & \quad\text{or } \neg\exists d \text{ s.t. } c = \downarrow d \\ \ell \mapsto \quad \vec{e} \triangleright B \triangleright \cdot & \text{otherwise} \end{cases}$$

$$\mathsf{inp} : \mathbb{E} \longrightarrow \mathbb{A}$$
$$\mathsf{inp}(\pi) = \{\downarrow c \mid c \in \pi\}$$
$$\mathsf{inp}(\langle c \rangle) = \langle \downarrow c \rangle$$

$$\mathsf{out} : \mathit{Lift}(\mathbb{L}) \times \mathbb{E} \times \mathbb{R} \longrightarrow \vec{\mathbb{A}}$$
$$\mathsf{out}(\downarrow, \_, \_) = \cdot \qquad \text{(empty sequence of actions)}$$
$$\mathsf{out}(\ell, \pi, R) = \{c \mid (j, \downarrow c) \in R \oplus (\ell, \pi),\ j \neq \downarrow\} \qquad \text{(sequence of single } \pi \text{ action)}$$
$$\mathsf{out}(\ell, \langle c \rangle, \_) = \begin{cases} \langle d \rangle & \text{when } c = \downarrow d \\ \cdot & \text{otherwise} \end{cases}$$

Fig. 5. Metafunctions for semantics

that the network does not invalidate any reasoning about causality that they incorporate into their protocol designs. Theorem 2 makes a causal connection between the actions of an actor and the events it subsequently receives. It expresses the *purpose* of the network: to keep actors informed of exactly the assertions and messages relevant to their interests as those interests change.

Theorem 1 (Order preservation). *If an actor produces action A before action B, then A is interpreted by the network before B. Events are enqueued atomically with interpretation of the action that causes them. If event C for actor ℓ is enqueued before event D, also for ℓ, then C is delivered before D.*

Proof (Sketch). The reduction rules consistently move items one-at-a-time from the front of one queue to the back of another, and events are only enqueued during action interpretation. □

Theorem 2 (Causality). *If π_ℓ is the* most recently interpreted *state change notification action from actor ℓ in some network, then events e subsequently enqueued for ℓ are bounded by π_ℓ. That is, if $e = \pi'$, then $\pi' \subseteq \{c \,|\, ?c \in \pi_\ell\}$; if $e = \langle d \rangle$, then $?d \in \pi_\ell$.*

Proof (Sketch). Interpretation of π_ℓ updates R so that $\{c \mid (\ell, c) \in R\} = \pi_\ell$. The ℓ-labelled portion of R is not altered until the next state change notification from ℓ is interpreted. The updated R is used in bc to compute events for ℓ in response to interpreted actions; the rest follows from the definition of bc. □

3 Efficiency Considerations

Taking Sect. 2.3 literally implies that SYNDICATE networks convey entire sets of assertions to and fro every time the dataspace changes. While wholesale transmission is a convenient illusion, it is intractable as an implementation strategy. Because the *change* in state from one moment to the next is usually small, actors and networks transmit redundant information with each action and event. In short, SYNDICATE needs an incremental semantics (Sect. 3.1).

Relatedly, while many actors find natural expression in terms of whole sets of assertions, some are best expressed in terms of reactions to changes in state. Supporting a change-oriented interface between leaf actors and their networks simplifies the programmer's task in these cases (Sect. 3.2).

Regardless of how programmers articulate leaf actors, an implementation of SYNDICATE requires fast computation of the overlap between one actor's actions and the declared interests of others. From the definitions of bc and out we know that the chosen data representation must support a variety of set operations on, and between, assertion sets and shared dataspaces. These structures may include wildcards, making them infinite. Choice of data structure for these sets is key to an efficient SYNDICATE implementation (Sect. 3.3).

3.1 Deriving an Incremental Semantics for SYNDICATE

Starting from the definitions of Sect. 2, we replace assertion-set events with *patches*. Patches allow incremental maintenance of the shared dataspace without materially changing the semantics in other respects. When extended to code in leaf actors, they permit incremental computation in response to changes.

The required changes to SYNDICATE's program syntax are small: we replace assertion sets π with patches Δ in the syntax of events and actions.

$$\begin{aligned} \text{Events } e \in \mathbb{E} &::= \langle c \rangle \mid \Delta \\ \text{Actions } a \in \mathbb{A} &::= \langle c \rangle \mid \Delta \mid P \\ \text{Patches } \Delta \in \mathbb{\Delta} &::= \frac{\pi_{add}}{\pi_{del}} \quad \text{where } \pi_{add} \cap \pi_{del} = \emptyset \end{aligned}$$

All other definitions from Fig. 1 remain the same. The configuration syntax is as before, except that queued events and actions now use patches instead of assertion sets. Behavior functions, too, exchange patches with their callers.

Patches denote changes in assertion sets. They are intended to be applied to some existing set of assertions. The notation is chosen to resemble a substitution, with elements to be added to the set written above the line and those to be removed below. We require that a patch's two sets be disjoint.

To match the exchange of patches for assertion sets, we replace the newtable reduction rule from Fig. 4 with a rule for applying patches:

$$\overrightarrow{e} \triangleright [\overrightarrow{(k',a)}(k, \frac{\pi_{add}}{\pi_{del}})\, ;\, R\, ;\, \overrightarrow{A_Q}] \triangleright \overrightarrow{a} \quad \longrightarrow$$
$$\overrightarrow{e} \triangleright [\overrightarrow{(k',a)}\, ;\, R \oplus (k, \Delta')\, ;\, \overrightarrow{\mathsf{bc}_{\Delta}(k, \Delta', R, A_Q)}] \triangleright \mathsf{out}(k, \Delta', R)\overrightarrow{a} \qquad (\mathsf{patch})$$

where

$$\Delta' = \frac{\pi_{add} - \{c \mid (k,c) \in R\}}{\pi_{del} \cap \{c \mid (k,c) \in R\}}$$

The effect of the definition of Δ' is to render harmless any attempt by k to add an assertion it has already added or retract an assertion that is not asserted.

The $\oplus$ operator, defined in Fig. 5 for wholesale assertion-set updates, is straightforwardly adapted to patches:

$$R \oplus (k, \frac{\pi_{add}}{\pi_{del}}) = R \cup \{(k,c) \mid c \in \pi_{add}\} - \{(k,c) \mid c \in \pi_{del}\}$$

The inp metafunction is likewise easily adjusted:

$$\mathsf{inp}(\frac{\pi_{add}}{\pi_{del}}) = \frac{\{\downharpoonleft c \mid c \in \pi_{add}\}}{\{\downharpoonleft c \mid c \in \pi_{del}\}}$$

It is the out metafunction that requires deep surgery. We must take care not only to correctly relabel assertions in the resulting patch but to signal only true changes to the aggregate set of assertions of the entire network:

$$\mathsf{out}(\ell, \frac{\pi_{add}}{\pi_{del}}, R) = \frac{\{c \mid \downharpoonleft c \in \pi_{add} - \pi_{\ell\downharpoonleft}\}}{\{c \mid \downharpoonleft c \in \pi_{del} - \pi_{\ell\downharpoonleft}\}}$$
$$\text{where } \pi_{\ell\downharpoonleft} = \{c \mid (j,c) \in R, j \neq \ell, j \neq \downharpoonleft\}$$

The definition of $\pi_{\ell\downharpoonleft}$ here is analogous to that of $\pi_{\bullet}$ in the definition of bc_{Δ}, which also filters R to compute a mask applied to the patch. There is one key difference between $\pi_{\bullet}$ and $\pi_{\ell\downharpoonleft}$. Assertions learned as feedback from the containing network (i.e., those labelled with $\downharpoonleft$ in R) are discarded when computing the aggregate set $\pi_{\ell\downharpoonleft}$ of local assertions pertaining to the containing network. While a contained actor's assertions feed directly into the assertions made by the group as a whole, those received from the containing network must not.

The metafunction bc_{Δ} (Fig. 6) constructs a state change notification tailored to the interests of the given actor ℓ. The notification describes the net change to the shared dataspace caused by actor k's patch action—as far as that change is relevant to the interests of ℓ. The patch Δ_{fb} that bc_{Δ} constructs as feedback when $\ell = k$ differs from the patch Δ_{other} delivered to k's peers. While assertions made by k's peers do not change during the reduction, k's assertions do. Not only must new assertions in π_{add} be considered as potentially worthy of inclusion, but new subscriptions in π_{add} must be given the opportunity to examine the entirety of the aggregate state. Similar considerations arise for π_{del}.

$$\mathsf{bc}_\Delta : \mathit{Lift}(\mathbb{L}) \times \mathbb{\Delta} \times \mathbb{R} \times \mathbb{O}_Q \longrightarrow \mathbb{O}$$

$$\mathsf{bc}_\Delta(k, \frac{\pi_{add}}{\pi_{del}}, R^{old}, \ell \mapsto \vec{e} \triangleright B \triangleright \cdot) = \begin{cases} \ell \mapsto \Delta_{fb} & \vec{e} \triangleright B \triangleright \cdot \quad \text{if } \ell = k \text{ and } \Delta_{fb} \neq \frac{\emptyset}{\emptyset} \\ \ell \mapsto \Delta_{other} & \vec{e} \triangleright B \triangleright \cdot \quad \text{if } \ell \neq k \text{ and } \Delta_{other} \neq \frac{\emptyset}{\emptyset} \\ \ell \mapsto & \vec{e} \triangleright B \triangleright \cdot \quad \text{otherwise} \end{cases}$$

$$\text{where } \Delta_{fb} = \frac{\{c \mid c \in \pi_{\bullet add},\ (\ell, ?c) \in R^{new}\} \cup \{c \mid c \in (\pi_\circ \cup \pi_{\bullet add} - \pi_{\bullet del}),\ ?c \in \pi_{add}\}}{\{c \mid c \in \pi_{\bullet del},\ (\ell, ?c) \in R^{old}\} \cup \{c \mid c \in \pi_\circ,\ ?c \in \pi_{del}\}}$$

$$\Delta_{other} = \frac{\{c \mid c \in \pi_{\bullet add},\ (\ell, ?c) \in R^{old}\}}{\{c \mid c \in \pi_{\bullet del},\ (\ell, ?c) \in R^{old}\}} \qquad \pi_\bullet = \{c \mid (j, c) \in R^{old},\ j \neq k\}$$

$$R^{new} = R^{old} \oplus (\ell, \frac{\pi_{add}}{\pi_{del}}) \qquad \pi_{\bullet add} = \pi_{add} - \pi_\bullet$$

$$\pi_\circ = \{c \mid (j, c) \in R^{old}\} \qquad \pi_{\bullet del} = \pi_{del} - \pi_\bullet$$

Fig. 6. Definition of bc_Δ metafunction

The final change adjusts the exception rule to produce $\frac{\emptyset}{\{\star\}} \in \Delta$ instead of $\emptyset \in \pi$ as the action that retracts all outstanding assertions of a crashing process:

$$\vec{e}\, e_0 \triangleright (f, u) \triangleright \vec{a} \longrightarrow \cdot \triangleright (\lambda eu.(\cdot, u), u) \triangleright \frac{\emptyset}{\{\star\}}\ \vec{a} \text{ when } f(e_0, u) \in \mathbb{E}\mathrm{rr} \quad (\mathsf{exception_I})$$

Equivalence Theorem. Programs using the incremental protocol and semantics are not directly comparable to those using the monolithic semantics of the previous section. Each variation uses a unique language for communication between networks and actors. However, any two assertion sets π_1 and π_2 can be equivalently represented by π_1 and a patch $\frac{\pi_2 - \pi_1}{\pi_1 - \pi_2}$, because $\pi_2 = \pi_1 \cup (\pi_2 - \pi_1) - (\pi_1 - \pi_2)$ and $(\pi_2 - \pi_1) \cap (\pi_1 - \pi_2) = \emptyset$.

This idea suggests a technique for embedding an actor communicating via the monolithic protocol into a network that uses the incremental protocol. Specifically, the actor *integrates* the series of incoming patches to obtain knowledge about the state of the world, and *differentiates* its outgoing assertion sets with respect to previous assertion sets.

Every monolithic leaf actor can be translated into an equivalent incremental actor by composing its behavior function with a wrapper that performs this on-the-fly integration and differentiation. The reduction rules ensure that, if every monolithic leaf actor in a program is translated into an incremental actor in this way, each underlying monolithic-protocol behavior function receives events and emits actions *identical* to those seen in the run of the unmodified program using the monolithic semantics.

Let us imagine hierarchical configurations as trees like the one in Fig. 2. Each actor and each network becomes a node, and each edge represents the pair of queues connecting an actor to its container. For a monolithic-protocol configuration to be equivalent to an incremental-protocol configuration, it must have the same tree shape and equivalent leaf actors with identical private states. Furthermore, at each internal monolithic node (i.e., at each network), the shared dataspace set must be identical to that in the corresponding incremental node. Finally, events and actions queued along a given edge on the monolithic side must have the same *effects* as those queued on the corresponding incremental edge. If these conditions are satisfied, then reduction of the monolithic configuration proceeds in lockstep with the equivalent incremental configuration, and equivalence is preserved at each step.

While dataspace equality is simple set equality, comparing the effects of monolithic and incremental action queues calls for technical definitions. Corresponding slots in the queues must contain either identical message-send actions, spawn actions that result in equivalent actors, or state change notifications that have the same effect on the shared dataspace in the container. Comparing event queues is similar, except that instead of requiring state change notifications to have identical effects on the shared dataspace, we require that they instead identically modify the *perspective* on the shared dataspace that the actor they are destined for has been accumulating.

We write $\Sigma_{\mathtt{M}} \approx \Sigma_{\mathtt{I}}$ to denote equivalence between monolithic and incremental states, and use M and I subscripts for monolithic and incremental constructs generally. We write $[\![P_{\mathtt{M}}]\!]$ to denote the translation of a monolithic-protocol program into the incremental-protocol language using the wrapping technique sketched above. The translation maintains additional state with each leaf actor in order to compute patches from assertion sets and vice versa and to expose information required for judging equivalence between the two kinds of machine state. Where a leaf actor has private state u in an untranslated program, it has state (u, π_i, π_o) in the translated program. The new registers π_i and π_o are the actor's most recently delivered and produced assertion sets, respectively.

Theorem 3 (Incremental Protocol Equivalence). *For every monolithic program $P_{\mathtt{M}}$, if there exists $\Sigma_{\mathtt{M}}$ such that $\mathsf{boot}(P_{\mathtt{M}}) \longrightarrow_{\mathtt{M}}^{n} \Sigma_{\mathtt{M}}$ for some $n \in \mathbb{N}$, then there exists a unique $\Sigma_{\mathtt{I}}$ such that $\mathsf{boot}([\![P_{\mathtt{M}}]\!]) \longrightarrow_{\mathtt{I}}^{n} \Sigma_{\mathtt{I}}$ and $\Sigma_{\mathtt{M}} \approx \Sigma_{\mathtt{I}}$.*

Proof (Sketch). We first define $(\!|P_{\mathtt{M}}|\!)$ to mean augmentation of the monolithic program with the same additional registers as provided by $[\![P_{\mathtt{M}}]\!]$. Second, we define an equivalence between translated and untranslated monolithic machine states that ignores the extra registers, and prove that reduction respects this equivalence. Third, we prove that $(\!|P_{\mathtt{M}}|\!)$ and $[\![P_{\mathtt{M}}]\!]$ reduce in lockstep, and that equivalence between translated monolithic and incremental states is preserved by reduction. Finally, we prove that the two notions of equivalence together imply the desired equivalence. The full proof takes the form of a Coq script, available via www.ccs.neu.edu/racket/pubs/#esop16-gjf. □

3.2 Programming with the Incremental Protocol

The incremental protocol occasionally simplifies programming of leaf actors, and it often improves their efficiency. Theorem 3 allows programmers to choose on an actor-by-actor basis which protocol is most appropriate for a given task.

For example, the demand-matcher example from Sect. 2.2 can be implemented in a *locally-stateless* manner using patch-based state change notifications. It is no longer forced to maintain a record of the most recent set of active conversations, and thus no set subtraction is required. Instead, it can rely upon the added and removed sets in patch events it receives from its network:

$$\mathsf{actor}\ \mathit{demandMatcher}\ ()\ \left[\frac{\{?(\mathtt{hello},\star)\}}{\emptyset}\right]$$

$$\mathit{demandMatcher}\ \frac{\pi_{add}}{\pi_{del}}\ () = ([\mathit{mkWorker}\ x \mid (\mathtt{hello}, x) \in \pi_{add}], ())$$

More generally, Theorem 4 can free actors written using the incremental protocol from maintaining sets of assertions they have "seen before"; they may rely on the network to unambiguously signal (dis)appearance of assertions.

Theorem 4 (Duplicate-freedom). *For all pairs of events* $e = \frac{\pi_1}{\pi_2}$ *and* $e' = \frac{\pi_3}{\pi_4}$ *delivered to an actor,* $c \in \pi_1 \cap \pi_3$ *only if some event* $\frac{\pi_5}{\pi_6}$ *was delivered between* e *and* e'*, where* $c \in \pi_6$*. Symmetrically,* c *cannot be retracted twice without being asserted in the interim.*

Proof (Sketch). The patch rule prunes patch actions against R to ensure that only real changes are passed on in events. R itself is then updated to incorporate the patch so that subsequent patches can be accurately pruned in turn. □

3.3 Tries for Efficient Dataspace Implementation

Our implementations of SYNDICATE use a novel *trie*-based [8] associative map structure, making it possible to compute metafunctions such as bc, bc_Δ and out efficiently. These tries index SYNDICATE dataspaces, assertion sets, and patches. When a network routes an event, it matches the event's assertions against the assertions laid out along the paths of the trie to find the actors interested in the event. The trie-based organization of the dataspace allows the network to rapidly discard irrelevant portions of the search space.

While a trie must use sequences of tokens as keys, we wish to key on trees. Hence, we must map our tree-shaped assertions, which have both hierarchical and linear structure, to sequences of tokens that encode both forms of structure. To this end, we reinterpret assertions as sequences of tokens by reading them left to right and inserting distinct "push" and "pop" tokens $\ll$ and $\gg$ to mark entry to, and exit from, nested subsequences.[2]

Figure 7 shows the syntax of values, patterns, and tries, and Fig. 8 shows how we read patterns and values as token sequences. A value may be an atom x or a tuple of values $(v, w, ...)$. Patterns extend values with wildcard $\star$; hence, every value is a pattern. Tries involve three kinds of node:

[2] Inspired by Alur and Madhusudan's work on *nested-word automata* [9].

$$\begin{array}{rrl} \text{Values} & v, w \in \mathbb{V} ::= & x \mid (v, w, ...) \\ \text{Patterns} & p, q \in \mathbb{Q} ::= & x \mid (p, q, ...) \mid \star \\ \text{Atoms} & x, y, z \in \mathbb{X} & \text{Integers, Strings, Symbols, etc.} \\ \text{Tokens} & \sigma \in \mathbb{K} ::= & x \mid \ll \mid \gg \mid \star \\ \text{Tries} & r \in \mathbb{T} ::= & \mathsf{ok}(\{j, k, ...\}) \mid \mathsf{br}(\overrightarrow{\sigma \mapsto r}) \mid \mathsf{tl}(r) \end{array}$$

Fig. 7. Values, Patterns and Tries

$$\begin{aligned} [\![\cdot]\!] &: \mathbb{Q} \longrightarrow \vec{\mathbb{K}} \\ [\![x]\!] &= x \\ [\![(p, q, ...)]\!] &= \ll [\![p]\!]\ [\![q]\!]\ \ldots \gg \\ [\![\star]\!] &= \star \end{aligned}$$

Example: $[\![$ (**sale**,**milk**, (1,pt), (1.17,**USD**)) $]\!] =$
$\ll$ **sale milk** $\ll$ 1 pt $\gg$ $\ll$ 1.17 **USD** $\gg$ $\gg$

Fig. 8. Compiling patterns (and values) to token sequences.

$\mathsf{ok}(\{j, k, ...\})$ is a leaf. The tokens along the path from the root of the trie to this leaf represent assertions made by actors at locations $\{j, k, ...\}$. The locations are a set because more than one actor may be making the same assertion at the same time.

$\mathsf{br}(\overrightarrow{\sigma \mapsto r})$ is a branch node, with edges labelled with tokens σ leading to nested tries r.

$\mathsf{tl}(r)$ nodes are ephemeral. During routing computations, they arise from specializing an edge $\star \mapsto r$ to $\ll\ \mapsto \mathsf{tl}(r)$, and they disappear as soon as a matching generalization is possible. As such, they match balanced sequences of tokens until an unmatched $\gg$ appears, and then continue as r.

For example, consider the dataspace where actor 1 has asserted the (infinite) assertion set $\{(a, \star)\}$ and actor 3 has asserted $\{(\star, b)\}$. Its trie representation is

$$\begin{aligned} \mathsf{br}(\ll \mapsto \mathsf{br}(a \mapsto &\mathsf{br}(b \mapsto \mathsf{br}(\gg \mapsto \mathsf{ok}(\{1,3\})), \\ &\quad\ \star \mapsto \mathsf{br}(\gg \mapsto \mathsf{ok}(\{1\}))), \\ \star \mapsto &\mathsf{br}(b \mapsto \mathsf{br}(\gg \mapsto \mathsf{ok}(\{3\}))))) \end{aligned}$$

If actor 2 wishes to assert $\{(\star, \star)\}$, the network receives the trie

$$\mathsf{br}(\ll \mapsto \mathsf{br}(\star \mapsto \mathsf{br}(\star \mapsto \mathsf{br}(\gg \mapsto \mathsf{ok}(\{2\})))))$$

and computes the union of this trie with its current dataspace during processing of the newtable rule, yielding the updated dataspace trie

$$\begin{aligned} \mathsf{br}(\ll \mapsto \mathsf{br}(a \mapsto &\mathsf{br}(b \mapsto \mathsf{br}(\gg \mapsto \mathsf{ok}(\{1,2,3\})), \\ &\quad\ \star \mapsto \mathsf{br}(\gg \mapsto \mathsf{ok}(\{1,2\}))), \\ \star \mapsto &\mathsf{br}(b \mapsto \mathsf{br}(\gg \mapsto \mathsf{ok}(\{2,3\})), \\ &\quad\ \star \mapsto \mathsf{br}(\gg \mapsto \mathsf{ok}(\{2\}))))) \end{aligned}$$

$$route : \overrightarrow{(\mathbb{K}\backslash\star)} \times \mathbb{T} \longrightarrow \mathcal{P}(Lift(\mathbb{L}))$$

$$route(\cdot, r) = \begin{cases} locations & \text{if } r = \mathsf{ok}(locations) \\ \emptyset & \text{otherwise} \end{cases}$$

$$route(\sigma'\vec{\sigma}, \mathsf{ok}(locations)) = \emptyset$$

$$route(\sigma'\vec{\sigma}, \mathsf{br}(h)) = \begin{cases} \emptyset & \text{if } h = \emptyset \\ route(\vec{\sigma}, get(h, \sigma')) & \text{if } h \neq \emptyset \end{cases}$$

$$route(\gg \vec{\sigma}, \mathsf{tl}(r)) = route(\vec{\sigma}, r)$$

$$route(\ll \vec{\sigma}, \mathsf{tl}(r)) = route(\vec{\sigma}, \mathsf{tl}(\mathsf{tl}(r)))$$

$$route(x\vec{\sigma}, \mathsf{tl}(r)) = route(\vec{\sigma}, \mathsf{tl}(r))$$

$$get(h, \sigma) = \begin{cases} r & \text{if } (\sigma \mapsto r) \in h \\ \mathsf{br}(\emptyset) & \text{if } (\sigma \mapsto r) \notin h \text{ and } \sigma = \star \\ \mathsf{tl}(get(h, \star)) & \text{if } (\sigma \mapsto r) \notin h \text{ and } \sigma = \ll \\ untl(get(h, \star)) & \text{if } (\sigma \mapsto r) \notin h \text{ and } \sigma = \gg \\ get(h, \star) & \text{if } (\sigma \mapsto r) \notin h \text{ and } \sigma \notin \{\star, \ll, \gg\} \end{cases}$$

$$untl(r) = \begin{cases} r' & \text{if } r = \mathsf{tl}(r') \\ \mathsf{br}(\emptyset) & \text{otherwise} \end{cases}$$

Fig. 9. Message routing using tries.

Routing of *messages* is done with the *route* function of Fig. 9. Evaluating $route([\![v]\!], r)$ yields the set of locations in r to which a message $\langle v \rangle$ should be sent. If a specific token is not found in a branch, *route* takes the $\star$ branch, if one exists. No backtracking is needed. Notice what happens when $\ll$ is to be matched against $\mathsf{br}(h)$ where $\ll \notin dom(h)$ and $\star \mapsto r \in h$. The result of $get(h, \ll)$ is $\mathsf{tl}(r)$, which requires the matcher to consume tokens until a matching $\gg$ is seen before continuing to match the rest of the input against r.

Routing of *state change notifications* requires finding all actors making assertions that *overlap* an assertion set or patch. Our implementation relies on a set intersection calculation, as does the subsequent filtering needed before enqueueing a patch event for an actor. Such set operations on trie maps are computed by *combine* (Fig. 10). Its third argument determines the operation. For example, supplying f_{union} computes trie union by lifting actor-location-set union to tries:

$$f_{union}(\mathsf{ok}(\alpha_1), \mathsf{ok}(\alpha_2)) = \mathsf{ok}(\alpha_1 \cup \alpha_2)$$
$$f_{union}(\mathsf{ok}(\alpha_1), \mathsf{br}(\emptyset)) = \mathsf{ok}(\alpha_1)$$
$$f_{union}(\mathsf{br}(\emptyset), \mathsf{ok}(\alpha_2)) = \mathsf{ok}(\alpha_2)$$

Analogous definitions yield trie subtraction and trie intersection, but *combine* also generalizes beyond simple set operations. For example, we use it to compute values such as $\pi_{\bullet add}$, (part of bc_Δ, Fig. 6), in a single pass over π_{add} and R.

Implementation of our tries and the functions operating upon them requires care. While the algorithms shown in Figs. 9 and 10 are correct, an implementation

$$combine : \mathbb{T} \times \mathbb{T} \times (\mathbb{T} \times \mathbb{T} \to \mathbb{T}) \to \mathbb{T}$$
$$combine(r_1, r_2, f) = g(r_1, r_2)$$
$$\text{where } g(\mathsf{tl}(r_1), \mathsf{tl}(r_2)) = \begin{cases} \mathsf{tl}(g(r_1, r_2)) & \text{when } g(r_1, r_2) \neq \mathsf{br}(\emptyset) \\ \mathsf{br}(\emptyset) & \text{otherwise} \end{cases}$$
$$g(\mathsf{tl}(r_1), r_2) = g(expand(r_1), r_2)$$
$$g(r_1, \mathsf{tl}(r_2)) = g(r_1, expand(r_2))$$
$$g(\mathsf{ok}(\alpha_1), r_2) = f(\mathsf{ok}(\alpha_1), r_2)$$
$$g(r_1, \mathsf{ok}(\alpha_2)) = f(r_1, \mathsf{ok}(\alpha_2))$$
$$g(\mathsf{br}(h_1), \mathsf{br}(h_2)) = \mathsf{br}(dedup(\{g(get(h_1, \sigma), get(h_2, \sigma)) \mid \sigma \in dom(h_1) \cup dom(h_2)\}))$$

$$expand : \mathbb{T} \longrightarrow \mathbb{T}$$
$$expand(r) = \mathsf{br}(\{\star \mapsto \mathsf{tl}(r),\ \gg \mapsto r\})$$

$$dedup : (\mathbb{K} \mapsto \mathbb{T}) \longrightarrow (\mathbb{K} \mapsto \mathbb{T})$$
$$dedup(h) = \{\sigma \mapsto r \mid \sigma \mapsto r \in h, distinct(\sigma, r, h)\}$$

$$distinct : \mathbb{K} \times \mathbb{T} \times (\mathbb{K} \mapsto \mathbb{T}) \longrightarrow 2$$
$$distinct(\star, r, h) = (r \neq \mathsf{br}(\emptyset))$$
$$distinct(\ll, r, h) = \begin{cases} r' \neq get(h, \star) & \text{if } r = \mathsf{tl}(r') \\ r \neq \mathsf{br}(\emptyset) & \text{otherwise} \end{cases}$$
$$distinct(\gg, r, h) = (r \neq untl(get(h, \star)))$$
$$distinct(x, r, h) = (r \neq get(h, \star))$$

Fig. 10. Operations on tries.

must apply three important optimizations, not shown here for lack of space, to be performant. First, *combine*'s g must, if possible, avoid iterating over both h_1 and h_2 when its two arguments are both br. For most applications of *combine*, g treats the larger of the two as a base against which the smaller of the two is applied. Second, efficient implementation of *distinct* from Fig. 10 relies on cheaply testing equality between tries. To address this, we *hash-cons* [10] to force pointer-equality to hold exactly when set equality holds for our tries. Finally, we use smart constructors extensively to enforce invariants that would otherwise be distributed throughout the codebase.

4 Pragmatics of SYNDICATE's Performance

While the unicast, address-based routing of Actors makes an efficient implementation straightforward, SYNDICATE's multicast messages place new demands on implementations. Furthermore, SYNDICATE offers communication via assertions, and in order to provide a usable service we must discover the boundaries of acceptable performance for this new medium.

4.1 Reasoning About Routing Time and Delivery Time

For messaging protocols using address-based routing, computation of the set of recipients ("routing") should take time in $\tilde{O}(|\mathit{address}|)$. More general messaging protocols effectively use more of each message as address information. In such cases, routing time should be bounded by $\tilde{O}(|\mathit{message}|)$. In either case, noting that $|\mathit{address}| \leq |\mathit{message}|$, delivery to all n interested recipients ("delivery") should take time in $\tilde{O}(n)$, for $\tilde{O}(|\mathit{message}| + n)$ overall processing time. Actor-style unicast messaging is then a special case, where the address is the target process ID, the size of the message body is irrelevant, and $n = 1$.

Communication via assertions happens through state change notifications. Programmers might reasonably expect that routing time should be bounded by the number of assertions in each notification, which is why the incremental semantics using patches instead of full sets is so important. A complication arises, however, when one considers that patches written using wildcards refer to *infinite* sets of assertions. Our trie-based representation of assertion sets takes care to represent such infinite sets tractably, but the programmer cannot assume a routing time bounded by the size of the *representation* of the notification. To see this, consider that asserting $\star$ forces a traversal of the entirety of the ?-prefixed portion of the dataspace to discover *every* active interest.

Fortunately, routing time *can* be bounded by the size of the representation of the *intersection* of the patch being processed with the dataspace itself. When processing a patch $\frac{\pi_{add}}{\pi_{del}}$ to a dataspace R, our function *combine* (Fig. 10) explores R only along paths that are in π_{add} or π_{del}. When reasoning about routing time, therefore, programmers must set their expectations based on both the patches being issued and the assertions established in the environment to be modified by each patch. After routing has identified the n actors to receive state change notifications, the associated delivery time is in $\tilde{O}(n)$, just as for messages.

4.2 Measuring SYNDICATE Performance

Notwithstanding the remarks above, we cannot yet make precise statements about complexity bounds on routing and delivery costs in SYNDICATE. The difficulty is the complex interaction between the protocol chosen by the SYNDICATE programmer and the data structures and algorithms used to represent and manipulate assertion sets in the SYNDICATE implementation.

We can, however, measure the performance of our Racket-based SYNDICATE implementation on representative protocols. For example, we expect that:

1. simple actor-style unicast messaging performs in $\tilde{O}(1)$;
2. multicast messaging performs within $\tilde{O}(|\mathit{message}| + n)$;
3. state change notification performance can be understood; and
4. SYNDICATE programs can smoothly interoperate with the "real world."

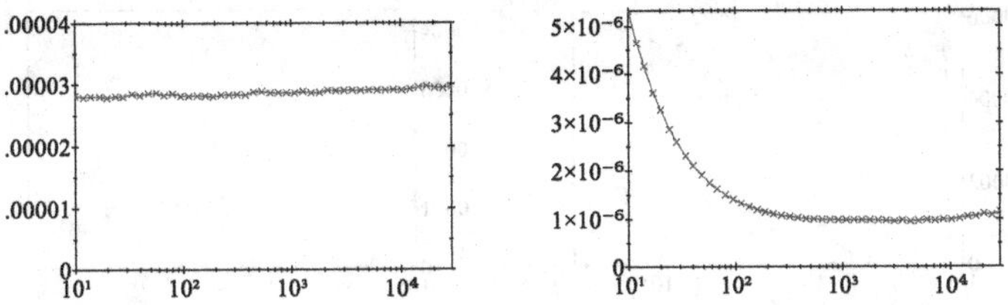

(a) Unicast (b) Broadcast

Fig. 11. Message routing and delivery latencies, sec/msg vs. k

Unicast Messaging. We demonstrate a unicast, actor-like protocol using a simple "ping-pong" program. The program starts k actors in a single SYNDICATE network, with the ith peer asserting the subscription $?(\texttt{ping}, \star, i)$. When it receives a message $(\texttt{ping}, j, i)$, it replies by sending $(\texttt{ping}, i, j)$. Once all k peers have started, a final process numbered $k+1$ starts and exchanges messages with one of the others until ten seconds have elapsed. It then records the overall mean message delivery latency.

Figure 11a shows message latency as a function of the number of actors. Each point along the x-axis corresponds to a complete run with a specific value for k. It confirms that, as expected, total routing and delivery latency is roughly $\tilde{O}(1)$.

Broadcast Messaging. To analyze the behavior of broadcasting, we measure a variation on the "ping-pong" program which broadcasts each ping to all k participants. Each *sent* message results in k *delivered* messages. Figure 11b shows mean latency of each delivery against k. This latency is comprised of a fixed per-delivery cost along with that delivery's share of a fixed *per-transmission* routing cost. In small groups, the fixed routing cost is divided among few actors, while in large groups it is divided among many, becoming an infinitesimal contributor to overall delivery latency. Latency of each delivery, then, is roughly $\tilde{O}(\frac{1}{k}+1)$. Aggregating to yield latency for each transmission gives $\tilde{O}(1+k)$, as expected.

State Change Notifications. Protocols making use of state change notifications fall into one of two categories: either the number of assertions relevant to an actor's interests depends on the number of actors in the group, or it does not. Hence, we measure one of each kind of protocol.

The first program uses a protocol with assertion sets independent of group size. A single "publishing" actor asserts the set $\{\texttt{A}\}$, a single atom, and k "subscribers" are started, each asserting $\{?\texttt{A}\}$. Exactly k patch events $\frac{\{\texttt{A}\}}{\emptyset}$ are delivered. Each event has constant, small size, no matter the value of k.

The second program demonstrates a protocol sensitive to group size, akin to a "chatroom" protocol. The program starts k "peer" actors in total. The ith peer asserts a patch containing both $(\texttt{presence}, i)$ and $?(\texttt{presence}, \star)$. It thereby informs peers of its own existence while observing the presence of every other actor in the network. Consequently, it initially receives a patch indicating its

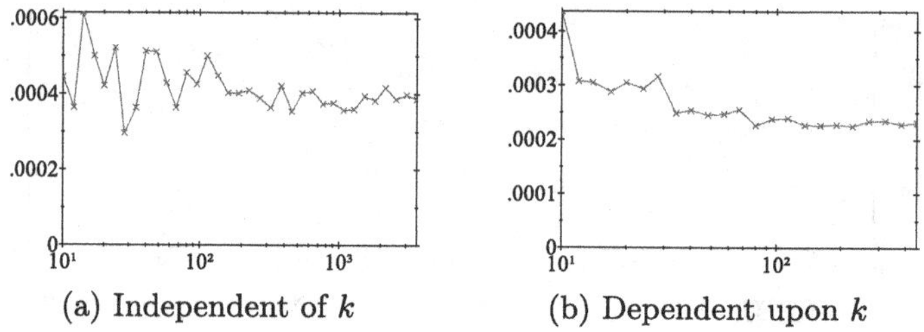

Fig. 12. State change notification cost, sec/notification vs. k

own presence along with that of the $i-1$ previously-started peers, followed by $k-i-1$ patches, one at a time as each subsequently-arriving peer starts up.

Measuring the time-to-inertness of differently-sized examples of each program and dividing by the number of state change notification events delivered shows that in both cases the processing required to compute and deliver each state change notification is roughly constant even as k varies (Fig. 12).

Communication with the Outside World. An implementation of a TCP/IP "echo" service validates our claim that SYNDICATE can effectively structure a concurrent program that interacts with the wider world, because this service is a typical representative of many network server applications.

A "driver" actor provides a pure SYNDICATE interface to socket functionality. A new connection is signalled by a new assertion. The program responds by spawning an actor for the connection. When the connection closes, the "driver" retracts the assertion, and the per-connection actor reacts by terminating.

The scalability of the server is demonstrated by gradually ramping up the number of active connections. Our client program alternates between adding new connections and performing work spread evenly across all open connections. During each connection-opening phase, it computes the mean per-connection time taken for the server to become ready for work again after handling the batch of added connections. Figure 13 plots the value of k, the total number of connections at the end of a phase, on the (logarithmic) x-axis; on the y-axis, it records mean seconds taken for the server to handle each new arrival. The marginal cost of each additional connection remains essentially constant and small, though the results are noisy and subject to GC effects.

5 Pragmatics of SYNDICATE Programming

SYNDICATE's networks support both publish-subscribe interaction [5] and continuous queries [11,12] over dataspaces. To demonstrate the benefits of this dual arrangement, we report highlights of Racket and Javascript SYNDICATE implementations of two new case studies: a rudimentary TCP/IP stack and a GUI-based text entry widget, respectively.

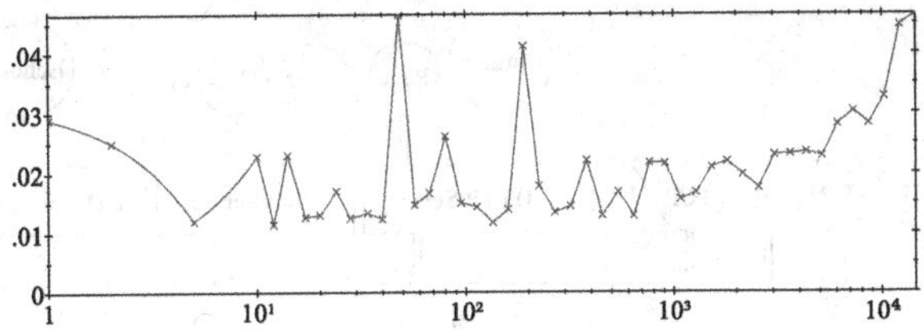

Fig. 13. Marginal cost of additional connections, sec/conn. vs. k

TCP/IP Stack. Our TCP/IP stack (Fig. 14) is structured similarly to a traditional operating system, with "kernel" services available in an outermost layer and each application running in its own nested network. Applications thus remain isolated by default, able to access Ethernet, IP, or TCP services on demand, and able to interact with peers via the Kernel-layer network as they see fit.

Our demo configuration includes a simple "hit counter" single-page HTTP application, a TCP/IP-based chat server, and a simple UDP packet echo server. The code for the chat server was originally written as a standalone program using a SYNDICATE interface to the kernel's TCP/IP stack. It needed nothing more than a change of environment to run against our stack, since our stack shares its protocol of assertions and messages with the SYNDICATE kernel interface.

Placing configuration information in the shared dataspace encourages a design that automatically adapts as the configuration changes. Actors receive their initial configuration settings through the same mechanism that informs them of later updates. For example, the IP routing table is configured by placing an assertion for each route into the Kernel-layer network. An assertion such as

$$(\texttt{gateway}, 0.0.0.0/0, 192.168.1.1, \texttt{wlan0})$$

specifies a default route via gateway 192.168.1.1 over ethernet interface `wlan0`. IP interfaces self-configure in response to such assertions. An actor is spawned for each interface. Each such actor asserts a tuple announcing its own existence. The ARP implementation responds to these, using a demand-matcher to spawn an ARP driver instance for each announced interface. If a route is removed, the corresponding IP interface actor reacts by terminating. Its assertions are removed, causing termination of the matching ARP driver instance in turn.

Each ARP driver instance maintains a cache of mappings between IP addresses and Ethernet MAC addresses, which it publishes into the shared dataspace. Actors forwarding IP datagrams query the shared dataspace to discover the MAC address for the next hop by asserting a new interest. For example, $?(\texttt{arpQuery}, 10.2.3.4, \star)$ requests the MAC address associated with IP address 10.2.3.4. When the ARP driver sees a query for an IP address not in the cache, it sends ARP packets to discover the needed information and asserts results into the dataspace as they arrive. Thus, if 10.2.3.4 is at MAC address m, $(\texttt{arpQuery}, 10.2.3.4, m)$ is ultimately asserted, and the forwarding actor can

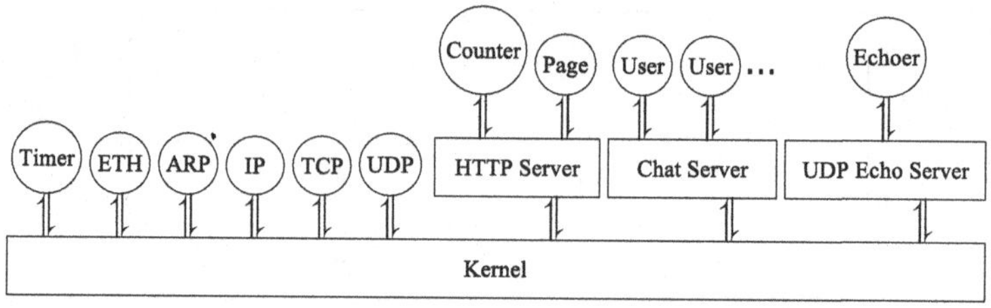

Fig. 14. Layering of TCP/IP stack implementation

address its Ethernet packet. The idea is general; a similar protocol could be used to proxy queries and cache query results for a relational database.

Assertions in shared dataspaces can be used to represent resource demand and supply. We have already seen how the IP and ARP drivers spawn actors in response to demand for their services. Another example is found in the port allocation services that manage TCP and UDP port numbers. Each established TCP or UDP endpoint claims its port via assertion, and the allocation services monitor such assertions in order to avoid collisions and reclaim released ports.

Finally, assertions can be used to solve startup ordering problems and arrange for the clean shutdown of services. Several actors must coordinate to produce a complete, working IP interface. Each asserts its readiness to the next in line via a tuple declaring the fact. Any actor depending on service X can simply monitor the dataspace for assertions of the form "service X is ready" before publishing its own readiness. By contrast, languages such as Java [13, Sect. 12.4] and C++ [14, Sect. 3.6.2] solve their static initializer ordering problems via complex ad-hoc rules, which sometimes leave ordering unspecified.

Text Entry Widget. Following Samimi [15], we constructed a simple text entry GUI control. Samimi's design proceeds in two stages. In the first, it calls for two components: one representing the *model* of a text field, including its contents and cursor position, and one acting as the *view*, responsible for drawing the widget and interpreting keystrokes. In the second stage, a *search* component is added, responsible for searching the current content of the model for a pattern and collaborating with the view to highlight the results.

Our browser-hosted solution naturally has an actor for each of the three components. The model actor maintains the current contents and cursor position as assertions in the shared dataspace. The view actor observes these assertions and, when they change, updates the display. It also subscribes to keystroke events and translates them into messages understandable to the model actor. The addition of the search actor necessitates no changes to the model actor. The search actor observes the assertion of the current content of the field in the same way the view actor does. If it finds a matching substring, it asserts this fact. The view actor must observe these assertions and highlight any corresponding portion of text.

6 Related Work

SYNDICATE draws directly on Network Calculus [2], which, in turn, has borrowed elements from Actor models [16–18], process calculi [19–23], and actor languages such as Erlang [7], Scala [24], E [25] and AmbientTalk [26].

This work makes a new connection to shared-dataspace *coordination models* [27], including languages such as Linda [28] and Concurrent ML (CML) [29]. Linda's tuplespaces correspond to SYNDICATE's dataspaces, but Linda is "generative," meaning that its tuples take on independent existence once created. SYNDICATE's assertions instead exist only as long as some actor continues to assert them, which provides a natural mechanism for managing resources and dealing with partial failures (Sect. 2). Linda research on failure-handling focuses mostly on atomicity and transactions [30], though Rowstron introduces *agent wills* [31] and uses them to build a fault-tolerance mechanism. Turning to multiple tuplespaces, the Linda variants KLAIM [32] and LIME [33] offer multiple spaces and different forms of mobility. Papadopoulos [34] surveys the many other variations; SYNDICATE's non-mobile, hierarchical, nameless actors and networks occupy a hitherto unexplored point in this design space.

CML [29,35] is a combinator language for coordinating I/O and concurrency, available in SML/NJ and Racket [4, version 6.2.1, Sect. 11.2.1]. CML uses synchronous channels to coordinate preemptively-scheduled threads in a shared-memory environment. Like SYNDICATE, CML treats I/O, communication, and synchronization uniformly. In contrast to SYNDICATE, CML is at heart *transactional*. Where CML relies on garbage collection of threads and explicit "abort" handlers to release resources involved in rolled-back transactions, SYNDICATE monitors assertions of interest to detect situations when a counterparty is no longer interested in the outcome of a particular action. CML's threads inhabit a single, unstructured shared-memory space; it has no equivalent of SYNDICATE's process isolation and layered media.

The routing problem faced by SYNDICATE is a recurring challenge in networking, distributed systems, and coordination languages. Tries matching prefixes of *flat* data find frequent application in IP datagram routing [36] and are also used for topic-matching in industrial publish-subscribe middleware [5,37]. We do not know of any other uses of tries exploiting visibly-pushdown languages [9,38] (VPLs) for simultaneously evaluating multiple patterns over semi-structured data (such as the language of our assertions), though Mozafari et al. [39] compile single XPath queries into NFAs using VPLs in a complex event processing setting. A cousin to our technique is YFilter [40], which uses tries to aggregate multiple XPath queries into a single NFA for routing XML documents to collections of subscriptions. Depth in their tries corresponds to depth in the XML document; depth in ours, to *position* in the input tree. More closely related are the tries of Hinze [41], keyed by type-directed preorder readings of tree-shaped values. Hinze's tries rely on types and lack wildcards.

7 Conclusion

Programmers constantly invent and re-invent design patterns that help them address the lack of coordination mechanisms in their chosen languages. Even the most recent implementations of actors fail to integrate the observer pattern, conversations among groups of actors, and partial failure recovery. Instead programmers fake these using administrative actors and brittle work-arounds.

SYNDICATE provides a blueprint for eliminating these problems once and for all. Its shared dataspace directly provides the observer pattern and simultaneously enables clearly delimited conversations; data sharing automatically takes care of failures. Our incremental semantics for SYNDICATE explains how to implement the language in a uniformly efficient, scalable way.

Acknowledgements. This work was supported in part by the DARPA CRASH program and several NSF grants. The authors would like to thank the anonymous reviewers for their suggestions, which greatly improved this paper. In addition, we thank Sam Tobin-Hochstadt and Sam Caldwell as well as the participants of NU PLT's coffee round for their helpful feedback.

Resources. Benchmarks, proof scripts, links to our implementations, and supplemental materials are available via www.ccs.neu.edu/racket/pubs/#esop16-gjf.

References

1. Day, J.: Patterns in Network Architecture: A Return to Fundamentals. Prentice Hall, Indianapolis (2008)
2. Garnock-Jones, T., Tobin-Hochstadt, S., Felleisen, M.: The network as a language construct. In: European Symposium on Programming, pp. 473–492 (2014)
3. ECMA: ECMA-262: ECMAScrippt 2015 Language Specification. 6th edn. Ecma International (2015)
4. Flatt, M., PLT:Reference: Racket.Technical Report PLT-TR-2010-1, PLT Inc. (2010). http://racket-lang.org/tr1/
5. Eugster, P.T., Felber, P.A., Guerraoui, R., Kermarrec, A.M.: The many faces of publish/subscribe. ACM Comp. Surv. **35**(2), 114–131 (2003)
6. Love, R.: Kernel korner: Intro to inotify. Linux J. **2005**(139), 8 (2005)
7. Armstrong, J.: Making reliable distributed systems in the presence of software errors. Ph.D. thesis, Royal Institute of Technology, Stockholm (2003)
8. Fredkin, E.: Trie memory. Comm. ACM **3**(9), 490–499 (1960)
9. Alur, R., Madhusudan, P.: Adding nesting structure to words. J. ACM **56**(3), 16:1–16:43 (2009)
10. Goubault, J.: Implementing functional languages with fast equality, sets and maps: an exercise in hash consing. Bull S.A. Research Center, Technical report (1994)
11. Terry, D., Goldberg, D., Nichols, D., Oki, B.: Continuous queries over append-only databases. ACM SIGMOD Record **21**, 321–330 (1992)
12. Babcock, B., Babu, S., Datar, M., Motwani, R., Widom, J.: Models and issues in data stream systems. In: Symposium on Principles of Database Systems, Madison, Wisconsin (2002)

13. Gosling, J., Joy, B., Steele Jr, G.L., Bracha, G., Buckley, A.: The Java Language Specification, Java SE 7 edn. Addison-Wesley Professional, Redwood (2013)
14. ISO: ISO/IEC 14882: 2011 Information technology – Programming languages – C++. International Organization for Standardization (2012)
15. Samimi, H.: A Distributed Text Field in Bloom (2013). http://www.hesam.us/cs/cooplangs/textfield.pdf
16. Agha, G.A., Mason, I.A., Smith, S.F., Talcott, C.L.: A foundation for Actor computation. J. Func. Prog. **7**(1), 1–72 (1997)
17. Callsen, C.J., Agha, G.: Open heterogeneous computing in ActorSpace. J. Parallel Distrib. Comput. **21**(3), 289–300 (1994)
18. Varela, C.A., Agha, G.: A hierarchical model for coordination of concurrent activities. In: Ciancarini, P., Wolf, A.L. (eds.) COORDINATION 1999. LNCS, vol. 1594, pp. 166–182. Springer, Heidelberg (1999)
19. Caires, L., Vieira, H.T.: Analysis of service oriented software systems with the Conversation Calculus. In: Seventh International Conference on Formal Aspects of Component Software, pp. 6–33 (2010)
20. Vieira, H.T., Caires, L., Seco, J.C.: The conversation calculus: a model of service-oriented computation. In: Drossopoulou, S. (ed.) ESOP 2008. LNCS, vol. 4960, pp. 269–283. Springer, Heidelberg (2008)
21. Cardelli, L., Gordon, A.D.: Mobile ambients. Theor. Comput. Sci. **240**(1), 177–213 (2000)
22. Fournet, C., Gonthier, G.: The Join Calculus: a language for distributed mobile programming. In: Applied Semantics: International Summer School (2000)
23. Sangiorgi, D., Walker, D.: The Pi-Calculus: A Theory of Mobile Processes. Cambridge University Press, Cambridge (2003)
24. Haller, P., Odersky, M.: Scala actors: unifying thread-based and event-based programming. Theor. Comput. Sci. **410**(2–3), 202–220 (2009)
25. Miller, M.S.: Robust composition: Towards a unified approach to access control and concurrency control. Ph.D. thesis, Johns Hopkins University (2006)
26. Van Cutsem, T., Gonzalez Boix, E., Scholliers, C., Lombide Carreton, A., Harnie, D., Pinte, K., De Meuter, W.: AmbientTalk: programming responsive mobile peer-to-peer applications with actors. Comput. Lang. Syst. Struct. **40**(3–4), 112–136 (2014)
27. Gelernter, D., Carriero, N.: Coordination languages and their significance. Comm. ACM **35**(2), 97–107 (1992)
28. Gelernter, D.: Generative communication in Linda. ACM Trans. Program. Lang. Syst. **7**(1), 80–112 (1985)
29. Reppy, J.H.: CML: a higher-order concurrent language. In: Conference on Programming Language Design and Implementation, pp. 293–305 (1991)
30. Bakken, D.E., Schlichting, R.D.: Supporting fault-tolerant parallel programming in Linda. IEEE Trans. Parallel Dist. Syst. **6**(3), 287–302 (1995)
31. Rowstron, A.: Using agent wills to provide fault-tolerance in distributed shared memory systems. In: Parallel and Distributed Processing, pp. 317–324 (2000)
32. De Nicola, R., Ferrari, G., Pugliese, R.: Klaim: a kernel language for agents interaction and mobility. IEEE Trans. Softw. Eng. **24**(5), 315–330 (1998)
33. Murphy, A.L., Picco, G.P., Roman, G.C.: LIME: A coordination model and middleware supporting mobility of hosts and agents. ACM Trans. Softw. Eng. Methodol. **15**(3), 279–328 (2006)
34. Papadopoulos, G.A., Arbab, F.: Coordination models and languages. Adv. Comput. **46**, 329–400 (1998)

35. Reppy, J.H.: Concurrent Programming in ML. Cambridge University Press, Cambridge (1999)
36. Sklower, K.: A tree-based packet routing table for Berkeley Unix. In: USENIX Winter Conference (1991)
37. Baldoni, R., Querzoni, L., Virgillito, A.: Distributed event routing in publish/subscribe communication systems: a survey. Technical Report 15–05, Dipartimento di Informatica e Sistemistica, Università di Roma "La Sapienzia" (2005)
38. Alur, R.: Marrying words and trees. In: Symposium on Principles of Database Systems, pp. 233–242 (2007)
39. Mozafari, B., Zeng, K., Zaniolo, C.: High-performance complex event processing over XML streams. In: ACM SIGMOD International Conference on Management of Data, pp. 253–264 (2012)
40. Diao, Y., Altinel, M., Franklin, M.J., Zhang, H., Fischer, P.: Path sharing and predicate evaluation for high-performance XML filtering. ACM Trans. Database Syst. **28**(4), 467–516 (2003)
41. Hinze, R.: Generalizing generalized tries. J. Func. Prog. **10**(4), 327–351 (2000)

An Application of Computable Distributions to the Semantics of Probabilistic Programming Languages

Daniel Huang[1(✉)] and Greg Morrisett[2]

[1] Harvard SEAS, Cambridge, MA, USA
dehuang@fas.harvard.edu
[2] Cornell University, Ithaca, NY, USA
greg.morrisett@cornell.edu

Abstract. Most probabilistic programming languages for Bayesian inference give either operational semantics in terms of sampling, or denotational semantics in terms of measure-theoretic distributions. It is important that we can relate the two, given that practitioners often reason both analytically (*e.g.*, density) as well as algorithmically (*i.e.*, in terms of sampling) about distributions. In this paper, we give denotational semantics to a functional language extended with continuous distributions and show that by restricting attention to *computable distributions*, we can realize a corresponding sampling semantics.

Keywords: Probabilistic programs · Computable distributions · Semantics

1 Introduction

Probabilistic programming for Bayesian inference hopes to simplify probabilistic modeling by (1) providing a programming language for users to formally specify probabilistic models and (2) automating the task of inferring model parameters given observed data.

A natural interpretation of these probabilistic programs is as a sampler (*e.g.*, [9,35]). In essence, we can view a probabilistic program as describing a sampling procedure encoding how one believes observed data is generated. The flexibility of sampling has inspired embeddings of probabilistic primitives in full-fledged programming languages, including Scheme and Scala (*e.g.*, [9,23]). However, languages based on sampling often avoid the basic question of what it means to sample from a continuous distribution. For instance, these languages either have semantics given by an implementation in a host-language (*e.g.*, [9]), or use an abstract machine that assumes reals and primitive continuous distributions [21].

Another approach grounds the semantics of probabilistic programs in measure theory, which is the foundation of probability theory (*e.g.*, [3,29]). Measure theory provides a rigorous definition of conditioning, and a uniform treatment

P. Thiemann (Ed.): ESOP 2016, LNCS 9632, pp. 337–363, 2016.
DOI: 10.1007/978-3-662-49498-1_14

of discrete and continuous distributions. For instance, measure-theoretic probability makes sense of why the probability of obtaining any sample from an (absolutely) continuous distribution is zero, as well what it means to observe a probability zero event. These situations are encountered frequently in practice, as many models incorporate both continuous distributions and observation of real-valued data. Consequently, measure-theoretic semantics have been proposed as a generalization of sampling semantics (*e.g.*, [3]). However, this approach also has its drawbacks. First, measure theory has been developed without programming language constructs in mind (*e.g.*, recursion and higher-order functions), unlike standard denotational semantics. Hence, languages based on measure theory often omit language features (*e.g.*, [3]) or develop new meta-theory (*e.g.*, [29]). Second, measure-theoretic semantics must also develop a corresponding operational theory. For instance, Toronto *et al.* [29] give denotational semantics and later show how to implement a sound approximation of their ideal semantics because it is not directly implementable.

In this paper, we address the shortcomings of these existing approaches, and give denotational semantics to a functional language with continuous distributions that uses largely standard semantic constructs, and make the connection to a faithful sampling implementation. Our approach is motivated by *Type-2 computable distributions*, which admit *Type-2 computable* sampling procedures.[1] Computable distributions have been defined and studied in the context of Type-2 (Turing) machines and algorithmic randomness (*e.g.*, [6,7,31]). Their implications for probabilistic programs have also been hinted at in the literature (*e.g.*, [1,5]). Hence, we will recast these ideas in the context of high-level probabilistic languages for Bayesian inference.

There are advantages to giving semantics with computable distributions in mind, instead of directly using measure-theoretic distributions. First, every computable distribution admits a *sampling algorithm*, which operates on input bit-randomness (*e.g.*, a stream of coin flips) instead of requiring black-box primitives that generate Uniformly distributed values. Indeed, a computable distribution is completely characterized by a *sampling algorithm* (see Proposition 1), which reflects the intuition that we can express a distribution by describing how to sample from it. Second, we can use results from computability theory to guide the design of such a language. In particular, Ackerman *et al.* show that computing a conditional distribution is akin to solving the Halting problem [1]. Thus, our language provides only conditioning operators for restricted settings. Finally, computable distributions can be represented as ordinary program values. This means that we can use standard programming language meta-theory, and it enables us to scale our approach to probabilistic languages embedded in full-fledged programming languages proposed by the machine learning community (*e.g.*, [9,23]).

However, our approach has some limitations. As we already mentioned above, conditioning is not computable in general so we do not give semantics to a

[1] Because we will use the phrase "Type-2 computable" frequently, we will sometimes abbreviate it to just "computable" when it is clear from context that we are referring to Type-2 computability.

generic conditioning operator (see Sect. 5). Nonetheless, the situation where we do give semantics to conditioning corresponds to an effective version of Bayes rule, which is central to Bayesian inference in practice. Second, even though our approach gives realizable semantics, it is not necessarily efficient because algorithms that operate on computable distributions compute by enumeration. It would be interesting to see if we can efficiently implement algorithms that compute approximately with computable distributions, but this is not in scope for this paper.

2 The Basic Idea

We begin by expanding upon the issues involved in giving semantics to probabilistic programming languages. In order to focus on the probabilistic aspect, we informally consider simple, first-order languages without recursion, extended with discrete and continuous distributions.

We start with adding discrete distributions with finite support to a programming language (*e.g.*, [25]), and illustrate how sampling and distribution semantics can coincide. A distribution with finite support assigns positive probability to a finite number of values in its domain. We can interpret a type $\texttt{Dist}\ \alpha$ as a *probability mass function*, which maps values of type α (written $\mathcal{V}[\![\alpha]\!]$) to a probability in the interval $[0,1]$, such that the probabilities sum to 1. A discrete distribution is completely characterized by its probability mass function.

$$\text{(Finite discrete)}\quad \mathcal{V}[\![\texttt{Dist}\ \alpha]\!] \triangleq \mathcal{V}[\![\alpha]\!] \to [0,1] \quad \text{where } |\mathcal{V}[\![\alpha]\!]| \text{ finite}$$

As others have observed, probabilities form a monad (*e.g.*, [8,25]). Monadic bind $x \leftarrow e_1\ ;\ e_2$ re-weights the probability mass function of e_2 by summing over all possible values e_1 can take on and re-weighting according to its probability. We write the expression denotation function as $\mathcal{E}[\![\Gamma \vdash e : \alpha]\!]\rho \in \mathcal{V}[\![\alpha]\!]$ under a well-typed environment ρ (w.r.t. Γ). Below, let $f_1 = \mathcal{E}[\![\Gamma \vdash e_1 : \texttt{Dist}\ \alpha_1]\!]\rho$ be the denotation of e_1.

$$\begin{aligned}\text{(Denotational)}\quad & \mathcal{E}[\![\Gamma \vdash x \leftarrow e_1\ ;\ e_2 : \texttt{Dist}\ \alpha_2]\!]\rho\ (v_2) \triangleq \\ & \sum_{v_1 \in \text{dom}(f_1)} \mathcal{E}[\![\Gamma, x : \alpha_1 \vdash e_2 : \texttt{Dist}\ \alpha_2]\!]\rho[x \mapsto v_1]\ (v_2) \cdot (f_1(v_1))\end{aligned}$$

Alternatively, we can interpret monadic bind $x \leftarrow e_1\ ;\ e_2$ as sampling: "draw a sample according to distribution e_1, bind the value to variable x, and continue with distribution e_2." We can express sampling $\mathcal{S}[\![\Gamma \vdash e : \alpha]\!]\rho : 2^\omega \to \mathcal{V}[\![\alpha]\!]$ as bind in a state monad (written $\leftarrow_s$) whose state is a stream of bit-randomness 2^ω.

$$\text{(Sampling)}\quad \mathcal{S}[\![x \leftarrow e_1\ ;\ e_2]\!]\rho \triangleq v \leftarrow_s \mathcal{S}[\![e_1]\!]\rho\ ;\ \mathcal{S}[\![e_2]\!]\rho[x \mapsto v]$$

If we restrict the probabilities to be rational, then everything is discrete and finite, which coincides with traditional notions of computation. We can relate sampling to the denotational view as

$$\mathbf{P}(\mathcal{S}[\![e]\!]\rho = v) = \mathcal{E}[\![\Gamma \vdash e : \alpha]\!]\rho\ (v)$$

where the probability $\mathbf{P}(\cdot)$ is with respect to the distribution on the input bit-randomness.

Next, we can consider *continuous* distributions in the context of a probabilistic language. One approach is to interpret $\texttt{Dist}\ \alpha$ as a measure-theoretic distribution (*e.g.*, [3]). A *measure* $\mu : \mathcal{F} \to [0, \infty]$ on X maps a (measurable) set $A \in \mathcal{F}$, where $\mathcal{F}$ is a certain collection of subsets of X called a σ-algebra, to a non-negative real number, such that μ is countably additive and $\mu(\emptyset) = 0$. Then, a *probability measure* or *probability distribution* is a measure μ such that the mass of the entire space is 1 (*i.e.*, $\mu(X) = 1$).

$$\text{(Measure)} \quad \mathcal{V}[\![\texttt{Dist}\ \alpha]\!] \triangleq \mathcal{F} \to [0,1] \quad \text{where } \mathcal{F} \text{ is a } \sigma\text{-algebra}$$

We can use monadic bind again, but now the re-weighting is accomplished by a (Lebesgue) integral.

$$\text{(Denotational)} \quad \mathcal{E}[\![\Gamma \vdash x \leftarrow e_1\ ;\ e_2 : \texttt{Dist}\ \alpha_2]\!]\rho(A) \triangleq$$
$$\int (\lambda v.\ \mathcal{E}[\![\Gamma, x : \alpha_1 \vdash e_2 : \texttt{Dist}\ \alpha_2]\!]\rho[x \mapsto v](A)) d(\mathcal{E}[\![\Gamma \vdash e_1 : \texttt{Dist}\ \alpha_1]\!]\rho)$$

Sampling has the same form as before. We can relate the sampling with the denotational view as the push-forward of μ_{iid} (distribution on 2^ω corresponding to independent and identically distributed (i.i.d.) fair coin flips) with respect to the sampling function.

$$\mu_{\text{iid}} \circ \mathcal{S}[\![e]\!]\rho^{-1} = \mathcal{E}[\![e]\!]\rho$$

Note that we could have also used the push-forward to relate the denotational view for the discrete case. Unlike the finite discrete case, we cannot implement $\mathcal{S}[\![\cdot]\!]\rho$ for all continuous distributions on a Turing machine. There are a countable number of Turing machine configurations, but an uncountable number of continuous distributions.

In this paper, we propose to address the gap between a denotational semantics with continuous distributions and an algorithmic sampling interpretation using Type-2 computable distributions. To this end, we will present a core probabilistic language extending PCF with distributions and give it semantics using largely standard techniques. Because we want the denotational semantics to be easily relatable to a sampling semantics, we will be restricted to considering only distributions on topological spaces (in this paper, computable metric spaces) instead of measurable spaces (*i.e.*, the tuple $(X, \mathcal{F})$ of a set and a σ-algebra) used in standard measure-theoretic probability. Thus, our semantics can support only Borel measures, *i.e.*, a measure defined uniquely on the open sets of the topology. Nonetheless, this covers a wide class of distributions used in practice, including familiar continuous distributions on the reals $\mathbb{R}$ (*e.g.*, Uniform, Gaussian, and etc.) and (infinite) products of reals.

After we give the semantics, we will identify a subset of the denotations as corresponding to Type-2 computable objects. Importantly, we can implement Type-2 computable operators in a standard programming language. Thus, we will provide an implementation of the sampling semantics as a Haskell library.

Moreover, the semantics of conditioning (when computable) can be given as a program that computes the conditional distribution (see Sect. 5). Hence, we can also give semantics to conditioning as a library function. We will see that we can write familiar probabilistic programs with familiar reasoning principles. Because we do not need anything beyond standard language semantics, our approach can also be used to give semantics to probabilistic languages embedded in full-fledged languages proposed and used by the machine learning community (*e.g.*, [9,23,35]).

3 Background on Computability and Distributions

In this section, we introduce background on Type-2 computability (see Type Two Theory of Effectivity or TTE [32]), which can be used to provide a notion of computability on reals and distributions. The background will primarily be useful for connecting the denotational semantics to an implementation of the sampling semantics (see Sect. 4.2). We start by illustrating the basic idea behind Type-2 computability using computable reals.

Intuitively, a real is computable if we can *enumerate* it's binary expansion. Of course, a Turing machine algorithm can only enumerate a finite prefix of the expansion in a finite amount of time. Thus, Type-2 computability extends the conventional notion of algorithm (which terminates) to account for computing on bit-streams. A *Type-2 algorithm* is specified using conventional Turing machine code (*i.e.*, with finite set of states and finite state transition specification) and computes (partial) bit-stream functions (*i.e.*, $g_M : \{0,1\}^\omega \rightharpoonup \{0,1\}^\omega$) such that finite prefixes of the output are determined by finite prefixes of the input (called the *finite prefix property.*) This captures the intuition that a Type-2 algorithm computes a function to arbitrary precision in finite time using a finite amount of input, even though computing the entire output bit-stream cannot be done in finite time. Now that we have clarified what we mean by enumerate, we can return to computable reals.

More formally, a real $x \in \mathbb{R}$ is *computable* if we can enumerate a fast Cauchy sequence of rationals that converges to x. Recall that a sequence $(q_n)_{n\in\mathbb{N}}$ is *Cauchy* if for every $\epsilon > 0$, there is an N such that $d(q_n, q_m) < \epsilon$ for every $n, m > N$. Thus, the elements of a Cauchy sequence become closer and closer to one another as we traverse the sequence. When $d(q_n, q_{n+1}) < 2^{-n}$ for all n, we call $(q_n)_{n\in\mathbb{N}}$ a *fast Cauchy sequence.* Hence, the representation of a computable real as a fast Cauchy sequence evokes the idea of enumerating it's binary expansion.

As an example of a computable real, consider π and one possible series expansion of it below [2].

$$\pi = \sum_{k=0}^{\infty} \frac{1}{16^k} \left[\frac{4}{8k+1} - \frac{2}{8k+4} - \frac{1}{8k+5} - \frac{1}{8k+6} \right]$$

An algorithm can use the above series expansion and a rate of convergence to obtain a fast Cauchy sequence (*e.g.*, the BPP algorithm [2]).

A function $f : \mathbb{R} \to \mathbb{R}$ is *computable* if given a fast Cauchy encoding of $x \in \mathbb{R}$, there is an algorithm that outputs a fast Cauchy sequence of $f(x)$. For example, addition $+ : \mathbb{R} \times \mathbb{R} \to \mathbb{R}$ is computable because an algorithm can add the (Cauchy) input sequences element-wise to obtain a (Cauchy) output sequence. Next, we introduce computable metric spaces, which can be used to generalize the ideas above to computable distributions.

As a reminder, *metric space* (X, d) is a set X equipped with a *metric* $d : X \times X \to \mathbb{R}$. A metric induces a collection of sets called *(open) balls*, where a ball centered at $c \in X$ with radius $r \in R$ is the set of points within r of c, *i.e.*, $B(c, r) = \{x \in X \mid d(c, x) < r\}$. In this paper, the topology we associate with a metric space will be the one induced by the collection of balls. Hence, a Borel measure will assign probabilities to open balls. For example, $(\mathbb{R}, d_{\text{Euclid}})$ gives the familiar Euclidean topology on the reals $\mathbb{R}$ (with Euclidean distance d_{Euclid}) and a Borel distribution on the reals assigns probabilities to open intervals.

To define a computable metric space, we need some additional properties on (X, d). First, we must be able to approximate elements of X using elements from a simpler, countable set S. This way, we can encode an element $s \in S$ as a finite sequence of bits and an element $x \in X$ as the stream of bits corresponding to a sequence of elements of S that converges to x. More formally, we say S is *dense* in X if for every $x \in X$, there is a sequence $(s_n)_{n \in \mathbb{N}}$ that converges to x, where $s_n \in S$ for every n. Second, (X, d) should be *complete*, *i.e.*, every Cauchy sequence comprised of elements from X also converges to a point in X. Putting this together gives the definition of a computable metric space.

Definition 1 *[12, Definition 2.4.1]. A* computable metric space *is a tuple (X, d, S) such that*

- *(X, d) is a complete metric space.*
- *S is a countable, dense subset of X with a fixed numbering.*
- *For all $i, j \in \mathbb{N}$, $d(s_i, s_j)$ is computable, uniformly in $\langle i, j \rangle$ (*i.e.*, the function $(i, j) \mapsto d(s_i, s_j)$ is computable), where $\langle \cdot, \cdot \rangle : \mathbb{N} \times \mathbb{N} \to \mathbb{N}$ is a pairing function.*

The computable reals we gave at the beginning corresponds to the computable metric space $(\mathbb{R}, d_{\text{Euclid}}, \mathbb{Q})$.

A computable distribution over the computable metric space (X, d, S) can be defined as a computable point in the computable metric space $(\mathcal{M}(X), d_\rho, \mathcal{D}(S))$, where $\mathcal{M}(X)$ is the set of Borel probability measures on a computable metric space (X, d, S), d_ρ is the Prokhorov metric (see [12, Definition 4.1.1.]), and $\mathcal{D}(S)$ is the class of distributions with finite support at ideal points S and rational masses (see [12, Proposition 4.1.1]). For instance, the sequence below converges to the standard Uniform distribution on the interval $(0, 1)$.

$$\{0 \mapsto \frac{1}{2}, \frac{1}{2} \mapsto \frac{1}{2}\}, \{0 \mapsto \frac{1}{4}, \frac{1}{4} \mapsto \frac{1}{4}, \frac{2}{4} \mapsto \frac{1}{4}, \frac{3}{4} \mapsto \frac{1}{4}\}, \ldots,$$

Thus, a Uniform distribution can be seen as the limit of a sequence of increasingly finer discrete, Uniform distributions. Although the idea of a computable distribution as a computable point is fairly intuitive for the standard Uniform distribution, it may be less insightful for more complicated distributions.

Alternatively, we can think of a computable distribution on a computable metric space (X, d, S) in terms of sampling, *i.e.*, as a (Type-2) computable function $\{0,1\}^\omega \to X$. To make this more concrete, we sketch an algorithm that samples from the standard Uniform. The idea is to generate a value that can be queried for more precision instead of a sample x in its entirety. Thus, a sampling algorithm will interleave flipping coins with outputting an element to the desired precision, such that the sequence of outputs $(s_n)_{n \in \mathbb{N}}$ converges to a sample.

For instance, one binary digit of precision for a standard Uniform corresponds to obtaining the point 1/2 because it is within 1/2 of any point in the unit interval. Demanding another digit of precision produces either 1/4 or 3/4 according to the result of a fair coin flip. This is encoded below using the function `bisect`, which recursively bisects an interval n times, starting with $(0, 1)$, using the random bit-stream u to select which interval to recurse on.

$$\text{uniform} : (\texttt{Nat} \to \texttt{Bool}) \to (\texttt{Nat} \to \texttt{Rat})$$
$$\text{uniform} \triangleq \lambda u.\ \lambda n.\ \texttt{bisect}\ u\ 0\ 1\ n$$

In the limit, we obtain a single point corresponding to the sample.

The sampling view is equivalent to the definition of a computable distribution in terms of computable metric spaces. From a practical perspective, this means we can implement probabilistic programs as samplers and still capture the class of computable distributions. For completeness, we state the equivalence below. First, a *computable probability space* [12, Definition 5.0.1] $(\mathcal{X}, \mu)$ is a pair where $\mathcal{X}$ is a computable metric space and μ is a computable distribution. A function $s : (\mathcal{X}, \mu) \to (\mathcal{Y}, \nu)$ is *measure-preserving* if $\nu(A) = \mu(s^{-1}(A))$ for all measurable A. We call a distribution μ on $\mathcal{X}$ *samplable* if there is a computable function $s : (2^\omega, \mu_{\text{iid}}) \to (\mathcal{X}, \mu)$ such that s is computable on $\text{dom}(s)$ of full-measure and is measure-preserving.

Proposition 1 *(Computable iff samplable). A distribution $\mu \in \mathcal{M}(X)$ on computable metric space (X, d, S) is computable iff it is samplable (see [4, Lemmas 2 and 3]).*

4 Semantics

In this section, we describe a core probabilistic language based on PCF and give it semantics using largely standard constructs (see [34]). The semantics of distributions will be given in terms of both valuations (a topological variant of distributions) and samplers. After we give the semantics, we identify a subset of the denotations as Type-2 computable, and give an implementation of the sampling semantics as a Haskell library. We will refer to Haskell plus the library as λ_{CD}.

4.1 A Core Language and Its Semantics

Syntax. The core language extends a basic functional language (PCF with pairs) with reals (constants c) and distributions (constants d). The core language does not have a primitive for conditioning on a distribution. Instead, we will add conditioning as a library function later (see Sect. 5).

$$\begin{aligned} \alpha &::= \text{PCF types} + \text{pairs} \mid \texttt{Real} \mid \texttt{Samp}\ \alpha \\ e &::= \text{PCF exp} + \text{pairs} \mid c \mid d \mid e \oplus e \mid \texttt{return}\ e \mid x \leftarrow e\ ;\ e \end{aligned}$$

The primitives $\oplus$ provide primitive operations on reals. The expressions $\texttt{return}\ e$ and $x \leftarrow e_1\ ;\ e_2$ can be thought of as return and bind in the sampling monad. The type `Real` refers to reals and the type $\texttt{Samp}\ \alpha$ refers to distributions. The typing rules are standard. The type $\texttt{Samp}\ \alpha$ is well-formed if values of type α support the operations required of a computable metric space. In this language, this includes naturals $\mathbb{N}$, reals $\mathbb{R}$, and products of computable metric spaces.

Interpretation of Types. The interpretation of types will use both complete partial orders (CPO's) and computable metric spaces. The former is a standard structure from denotational semantics used to give meaning to recursion. The latter was introduced in the background and are the spaces that we consider distributions on.

To start, we introduce basic notation for constructing CPO's that will be used to give the interpretation of types $\mathcal{V}[\![\cdot]\!]$. The construction $\text{Disc}(X)$ equips the set X with the discrete order. $D_\perp$ creates a lifted domain with underlying set $\{\lfloor d \rfloor \mid d \in D\} \cup \{\perp\}$ with the usual lifted ordering. The CPO construction $D \Rightarrow E$ creates the CPO of continuous functions between CPO's D and E.

The interpretation of types $\mathcal{V}[\![\cdot]\!]$ is defined by induction on types. We give the interpretation of basic types (sans distributions $\texttt{Samp}\ \alpha$) below following a call-by-name evaluation strategy (to better match the Haskell implementation.)

$$\begin{aligned} \mathcal{V}[\![\texttt{Nat}]\!] &\triangleq \text{Disc}(\mathbb{N})_\perp \\ \mathcal{V}[\![(\alpha_1, \alpha_2)]\!] &\triangleq (\mathcal{V}[\![\alpha_1]\!] \times \mathcal{V}[\![\alpha_2]\!])_\perp \\ \mathcal{V}[\![\alpha_1 \to \alpha_2]\!] &\triangleq (\mathcal{V}[\![\alpha_1]\!] \Rightarrow \mathcal{V}[\![\alpha_2]\!])_\perp \\ \mathcal{V}[\![\texttt{Real}]\!] &\triangleq \text{Disc}(\mathbb{R})_\perp \end{aligned}$$

The interpretation of basic PCF types is standard. The reals $\mathbb{R}$ are given the discrete order (information ordering). In order to give the interpretation of $\texttt{Samp}\ \alpha$, we will need to write the space of distributions on $\mathcal{V}[\![\alpha]\!]$ as a CPO. To this end, we will use valuations, a topological variation of a distribution.

A *valuation* $\nu : \mathcal{O}(X) \to [0,1]$ is a function that assigns to each open set of a topological space $(X, \mathcal{O}(X))$ a probability, such that it is strict ($\nu(\emptyset) = 0$), monotone, and modular ($\nu(U) + \nu(V) = \nu(U \cup V) + \nu(U \cap V)$ for every open U and V). The type of a valuation can be given as a CPO. To see this, let $\mathcal{O}^{\subseteq}(X)$ be the open sets on a space X ordered by set inclusion and let $[0,1]^{\uparrow}$ be the interval $[0,1]$ ordered by $\leq$. Then, a valuation can be seen as an element of the CPO $\mathcal{O}^{\subseteq}(X) \Rightarrow [0,1]^{\uparrow}$. A valuation is similar to a measure (hence, topological variant of distribution), but a valuation does not necessarily satisfy countable additivity. A valuation that does is called a *ω-continuous valuation*, where ω-continuous means $\nu(\cup_{n\in\mathbb{N}} O_n) = \sup_{n\in\mathbb{N}} \nu(O_n)$ for O_n open for $n \in \mathbb{N}$. Indeed, every Borel measure μ on $\mathcal{X}$ can be restricted to a *ω-continuous valuation* $\mu|_{\mathcal{O}(X)} : [\mathcal{O}^{\subseteq}(X) \Rightarrow [0,1]^{\uparrow}]$. Moreover, a computable distribution can be identified with a ω-continuous valuation (see [12, Proposition 4.2.1] and [28]). Now, we can proceed to interpret $\texttt{Samp}\ \alpha$.

One idea used in the study of probabilistic powerdomains is to use valuations to put distributions on CPO's (see [13]) using the CPO's Scott topology. For example, a valuation on the CPO Disc(ℕ) results in the powerset $2^{\mathbb{N}}$, which is the σ-algebra associated with distributions on the naturals. However, we cannot apply a valuation in this manner to Disc(ℝ) to obtain a familiar continuous distribution used in statistics. For example, a valuation on the Scott topology derived from the CPO Disc(ℝ) results in the powerset $2^{\mathbb{R}}$, which is not the Borel σ-algebra on ℝ. Instead, we will start with the topology of a computable metric spaces which includes familiar continuous distributions, and then derive a CPO from it to support recursion.

To this end, we will use the *specialization preorder* (written S), which orders $x \sqsubseteq y$ if every open set that contains x also contains y, to convert a topological space $(X, \mathcal{O}(X))$ into a preordered set. Intuitively, $x \sqsubseteq y$ if x contains less information than y. We can always find an open ball that separates two distinct points x and y (the distance between two distinct points is positive) in a computable metric space. Hence, the specialization preorder of a computable metric space always gives the discrete order (information ordering), and hence degenerately, a CPO. For example, the specialization preorder of the computable metric space $(\mathbb{R}, d, \mathbb{Q})$ is Disc(ℝ). We can now start to put this together to convert a computable metric space into a CPO.

We write $\mathcal{V}^M[\![\cdot]\!]$ to associate a well-formed type with a computable metric space, defined by induction on well-formed types.

$$\mathcal{V}^M[\![\texttt{Nat}]\!] \triangleq (\mathbb{N}, d_{\text{discrete}}, \mathbb{N})$$
$$\mathcal{V}^M[\![\texttt{Real}]\!] \triangleq (\mathbb{R}, d_{\text{Euclid}}, \mathbb{Q})$$
$$\mathcal{V}^M[\![(\alpha_1, \alpha_2)]\!] \triangleq \mathcal{V}^M[\![\alpha_1]\!] \times \mathcal{V}^M[\![\alpha_2]\!]$$

The interpretation of naturals and reals are standard. The interpretation of a product $\mathcal{V}^M[\![(\alpha_1, \alpha_2)]\!]$ forms the product of computable metric spaces $\mathcal{V}^M[\![\alpha_1]\!]$ and $\mathcal{V}^M[\![\alpha_2]\!]$. As one last step, we will need to handle ⊥ for recursion. One can check the specialization preorder of the topology $\mathcal{O}(\lfloor X \rfloor) \cup \{\lfloor X \rfloor \cup \{\bot\}\}$ produces $\text{Disc}(X)_\bot$. We will write L to lift a computable metric space.

The interpretation of the type $\texttt{Samp}\ \alpha$ is a pair of a valuation and a sampling function realizing the valuation, where $\texttt{psh}_\alpha$ computes the push-forward measure and relates the valuation component to the sampling component. Below, let $D \times_F E$ be the CPO $\{(d,e) \in D \times E \mid F(e) = d\}$ with a product ordering, where F is a continuous function, and 2^ω is the CPO of continuous functions between Disc(ℕ) and Disc({0, 1}).

$$\mathcal{V}[\![\texttt{Samp}\ \alpha]\!] \triangleq [\mathcal{O}^{\subseteq}(S \circ L(\mathcal{V}^M[\![\alpha]\!])) \Rightarrow [0,1]^{\uparrow}] \times_{\texttt{psh}_\alpha} (2^\omega \Rightarrow S \circ L(\mathcal{V}^M[\![\alpha]\!])_\perp)\ .$$

This explicitly relates the valuation component to the sampling function component. We will see the implementation of the sampling semantics will identify $2^\omega \Rightarrow S \circ L(\mathcal{V}^M[\![\alpha]\!])_\perp$ with a Type-2 computable sampling algorithm.

The denotation of the sampler contains an extra lifting to distinguish $\texttt{bot} : \texttt{Samp}\ \alpha$ from $\texttt{return bot} : \texttt{Samp}\ \alpha$, where $\mathcal{E}[\![\texttt{bot}]\!]\rho = \perp$. In the former, we obtain the bottom valuation, which assigns 0 mass to every open set. This corresponds to the sampling function $\lambda u \in 2^\omega.\ \perp$. In the latter, we obtain the valuation that assigns 0 mass to every open set, except for $\{\lfloor X \rfloor \cup \perp\}$ which is assigned mass 1. This corresponds to the sampling function $\lambda u \in 2^\omega.\ \lfloor \perp \rfloor$.

Semantics. The expression denotation function $\mathcal{E}[\![\Gamma \vdash e : \alpha]\!]\rho \in \mathcal{V}[\![\alpha]\!]$ is defined by induction on the typing derivation. The denotation is also parameterized by a global environment Υ that interprets constants c and primitive distributions d. The following notation will be used for writing the semantics. We lift a function using $\dagger \in (D \Rightarrow E_\perp) \Rightarrow (D_\perp \Rightarrow E_\perp)$, defined in the usual way. The function $\text{lift}(d) = \lfloor d \rfloor$ lifts an element. Finally, the notation let $x = e_1$ in e_2 is a strict let binding.

Now, we describe the expression denotation function. The semantics of the PCF expressions are standard and are not shown.

$$\begin{aligned}
\mathcal{E}[\![\Gamma \vdash c : \texttt{Real}]\!]\rho &\triangleq \Upsilon(c) \\
\mathcal{E}[\![\Gamma \vdash e_1 \oplus e_2 : \texttt{Real}]\!]\rho &\triangleq \mathcal{E}[\![e_1]\!]\rho \oplus_\perp \mathcal{E}[\![e_2]\!]\rho \\
\mathcal{E}[\![\Gamma \vdash d : \texttt{Samp}\ \alpha]\!]\rho &\triangleq \Upsilon(d) \\
\mathcal{E}[\![\Gamma \vdash \texttt{return}\ e : \texttt{Samp}\ \alpha]\!]\rho &\triangleq (\lambda U.\ 1_U(\mathcal{E}[\![e]\!]\rho), \lambda u.\ \lfloor \mathcal{E}[\![e]\!]\rho \rfloor) \\
\mathcal{E}[\![\Gamma \vdash x \leftarrow e_1\ ;\ e_2 : \texttt{Samp}\ \alpha_2]\!]\rho &= (\lambda U.\ \int h_U\ d\mu, g^\dagger \circ f) \quad \text{where}
\end{aligned}$$

$$\begin{aligned}
\mu &= \pi_1(\mathcal{E}[\![e_1]\!]\rho) \\
h_U &= \lambda v.\ \pi_1(\mathcal{E}[\![e_2]\!]\rho[x \mapsto v])(U) \\
f &= \lambda u.\ \text{let } v = \pi_2(\mathcal{E}[\![e_1]\!]\rho)(u_e) \text{ in } \lfloor (v, u_o) \rfloor \\
g &= \lambda(v, w).\ \pi_2(\mathcal{E}[\![e_2]\!]\rho[x \mapsto v])(w)
\end{aligned}$$

The operations $\oplus_\perp$ correspond to strict primitives on reals. The denotation of $\texttt{return}\ e$ is a point mass valuation centered at $\mathcal{E}[\![e]\!]\rho$, which corresponds to a sampler that ignores the input bit-randomness and returns $\mathcal{E}[\![e]\!]\rho$. The meaning of $x \leftarrow e_1\ ;\ e_2$ also gives a valuation and a sampler. In the former, we reweigh $\mathcal{E}[\![e_2]\!]\rho[x \mapsto \cdot]$ according to the valuation $\mathcal{E}[\![e_1]\!]\rho$. In the sampling view, we first split the input bit-randomness u into two bit streams u_e and u_o, corresponding to the bits of u with even indices and the bits of u with odd indices respectively. We run the sampler denoted by e_1 on the input u_e to produce a sample v, and pass the unused bit-randomness u_o. Then, we run the sampler $\pi_2(\mathcal{E}[\![e_2]\!]\rho[x \mapsto v])$ with x bound to v on the bit-randomness u_o.

Properties. We need to check that the semantics we gave above is well-defined, particularly for the cases corresponding to manipulating distributions.

Recall that the interpretation of `Samp` α is a pair of a valuation ν and a sampling function s, such that the push-forward of s is equivalent to ν. Thus, for the meaning of `return` e, we will need to argue that a sampler that ignores its input randomness is equivalent to a point mass valuation. For the meaning of $x \leftarrow e_1 \; ; \; e_2$, we will need to relate a composition of sampling functions to a reweighing by integration. The first sampling function passes input bits that are unconsumed to the second sampling function. We can state this formally below.

Lemma 1 *(Push). Let X and Y be computable metric spaces.*

1. *Let* $f \in 2^\omega \Rightarrow (S \circ L(X))_\bot$ *be a constant function,* i.e., $f(u) = \lfloor d \rfloor$ *for every* u. *Then,* $\boldsymbol{psh}(f) = \lambda U.\, 1_U(d)$
2. *Let* $f \in 2^\omega \Rightarrow (S \circ L(X) \times 2^\omega)_\bot$ *such that* $\boldsymbol{psh}(f) = \boldsymbol{psh}((\mathit{lift} \circ \pi_1)^\dagger \circ f) \otimes \mu_{iid}$ *(independence) and* $g \in S \circ L(X) \times 2^\omega \Rightarrow (S \circ L(Y))_\bot$. *Then,*

$$\boldsymbol{psh}(g^\dagger \circ f) = \lambda U. \int \lambda v.\, \boldsymbol{psh}(g(v))(U)\; d(\boldsymbol{psh}((\mathit{lift} \circ \pi_1)^\dagger \circ f))$$

Consequently, the expression denotation function is well-defined.

Lemma 2 *(Denotation well-defined). If* $\Gamma \vdash e : \alpha$, *then* $\mathcal{E}[\![e]\!]\rho \in \mathcal{V}[\![\alpha]\!]$.

We now restrict the interpretation of types to consider Type-2 computability. Importantly, we can implement the restriction in a standard programming language. Below, we give the interpretation of types $\mathcal{V}^c[\![\cdot]\!]$ restricted to Type-2 computable objects.

$$\mathcal{V}^c[\![\texttt{Real}]\!] \triangleq \{r \in \mathcal{V}[\![\texttt{Real}]\!] \mid r \text{ is Type-2 computable or } r = \bot\}$$
$$\mathcal{V}^c[\![\texttt{Samp}\ \alpha]\!] \triangleq \{(\nu, s) \in \mathcal{V}[\![\texttt{Samp}\ \alpha]\!] \mid \text{for Type-2 computable } u,\ s(u) \text{ is Type-2 computable on dom}(s) \text{ or } s(u) = \bot\}$$

We restrict the reals to the computable reals by choosing the Type-2 computable subset. The distributions are restricted to those sampling functions $2^\omega \Rightarrow (S \circ L(\mathcal{V}^M[\![\alpha]\!]))_\bot$ that are Type-2 computable. As a reminder, a Type-2 computable function $f : 2^\omega \to L(\mathcal{V}^M[\![\alpha]\!])$ transforms finite prefixes of an input in 2^ω into a fast Cauchy sequence in $\mathcal{V}^M[\![\alpha]\!]$. Hence, there are (continuous CPO) sampling functions in the unrestricted denotational semantics that do not satisfy this property.

The expression denotation function is still well-defined, assuming that our global environment only contains Type-2 computable elements and functions. Informally, it follows because Type-2 computable functions are closed under composition. For instance, the composition of Type-2 computable sampling algorithms will be Type-2 computable.

Lemma 3 *(Denotation well-defined). If* $\Gamma \vdash e : \alpha$, *then* $\mathcal{E}[\![e]\!]\rho \in \mathcal{V}^c[\![\alpha]\!]$.

In the next section, we will implement the sampling semantics as a Haskell library.

```
module A (approx, anth, CMetrizable, enum, metric) where
approx :: (Nat -> a) -> A a      -- fast Cauchy sequence
anth :: A a -> Nat -> a

class CMetrizable a where
    enum :: [a]                  -- countable, dense subset
    metric :: a -> a -> A Rat    -- computable metric

newtype A a = A { getA :: Nat -> a }

module CompDistLib (sampler) where
type RandBits = Nat -> Bool
type Samp = State RandBits
sampler :: (CMetrizable a) => (RandBits -> a) -> Samp a
```

Fig. 1. Library interface

We end by giving familiar laws justified by the denotational semantics. For example, the type Samp α satisfies the monad laws and commutativity, where $\equiv$ means equivalence in distribution. This follows the monadic structure of standard probability as others have observed (*e.g.*, [8]). For commutativity, we require that x is not free in e_2 and that y is not free in e_1.

$$
\begin{array}{rcll}
x' \leftarrow \texttt{return}\, x \,;\, f\ x' & \equiv & f\ x & \text{(left identity)}\\
x \leftarrow e \,;\, \texttt{return}\, x & \equiv & e & \text{(right identity)}\\
x \leftarrow e \,;\, y \leftarrow f\ x \,;\, g\ y & \equiv & y \leftarrow (x \leftarrow e \,;\, f\ x) \,;\, g\ y & \text{(bind associativity)}\\
x \leftarrow e_1 \,;\, y \leftarrow e_2 \,;\, f\ x\ y & \equiv & y \leftarrow e_2 \,;\, x \leftarrow e_1 \,;\, f\ x\ y & \text{(commutativity)}
\end{array}
$$

These laws have an operational sampling interpretation. For example, the associativity of bind says that an algorithm can re-associate the sampling steps, provided that there are no dependencies, and still obtain samples from the same distribution. Commutativity says that if two distributions are independent, then a sampler can sample them in either order. Of course, re-associating or commuting produces samplers that consume input randomness differently, but the distribution induced by the samplers will be equivalent.

4.2 Computable Distributions as a Library

We now present a Haskell library (Fig. 1) for expressing samplers that implements the ideas from the previous section. In particular, we will show that we can implement the sampling semantics in Haskell without assuming reals or primitive continuous distributions.

The module A contains operations for computable metric spaces. First, the type A α models an element of a computable metric space. It can be read as an approximation by a sequence of values of type α. For example, a computable real can be given the type CReal $\triangleq$ A Rat, meaning it is a sequence of rationals that converges to a real. We can form values of type `A` α using `approx`, which requires us to check that the function we are coercing describes a fast Cauchy sequence, and project out approximations using `anth`.

To form `A` α, values of type α should support the operations required of a computable metric space. We can indicate the required operations using Haskell's type-class mechanism.

```
class CMetrizable a where
    enum :: [a]
    metric :: a -> a -> A Rat
```

When we implement an instance of `CMetrizable`, we should check that the implementation of `enum` enumerates a dense subset and `metric` computes a metric as a computable metric space requires (see Sect. 3). Below, we give an instance of `A Rat` for computable reals.

```
instance CMetrizable Rat where
    enum = 0 : [ toRational m / 2^n
               | n <- [1..]
               , m <- [-2^n * n..2^n * n]
               , odd m || abs m > 2^n * (n-1) ]
    metric x y = A (\_ -> abs (x - y))
```

This instance enumerates the dyadic rationals (powers of 2), which are a dense subset of the reals. Note that there are many other choices here for the dense enumeration.[2] In this instance, we can actually compute the metric as a dyadic rational, whereas a computable metric requires the weaker condition that we can compute the metric as a computable real.

Next, we can use the module `A` to implement computable operations on commonly used types. This reifies the computable primitives $\oplus$ from the core language as a library function. For example, a library for computable reals will contain the `CMetrizable` instance implementation above and other computable functions. However, some operations are not realizable (*e.g.*, equality) and so this module does not contain all operations one may want to perform on reals.

```
module RealLib (CReal, pi, ...) where
import A
import CompDistLib

type CReal = A Rat
instance CMetrizable Rat where ...

pi :: A Rat
(+) :: A Rat -> A Rat -> A Rat
exp :: A Rat -> A Rat
...
```

Next, we give constructs for expressing distributions described in the module `CompDistLib`. The type of sampling algorithms `Samp` α is an instance of the state monad.

[2] Algorithms that operate on computable metric spaces compute by enumeration so the algorithm is sensitive to the choice of enumeration.

```
type RandBits = Nat -> Bool
type Samp = State RandBits
```

The threaded state is an infinite bit-stream of randomness, where each bit is i.i.d. according to a Bernoulli distribution (*i.e.*, fair coin flip). An algorithm consumes this bit-stream to generate samples.

By reusing the state monad, we automatically obtain monadic bind and return from the Haskell standard library. Bind corresponds to sampling, where the sampling monad `Samp` α threads the bit-stream of randomness. Return corresponds to a deterministic computation because the computation ignores the bit-stream. Instead of building in primitive distributions, we provide an introduction form `sampler` that coerces an arbitrary sampling function, constrained to types α that have a `CMetrizable` instance. We should call `sampler` only on sampling functions realizing Type-2 computable sampling algorithms.

```
sampler :: (CMetrizable a) => (RandBits -> a) -> Samp a
sampler f = State (\u -> let (u_e, u_o) = split u in
                         return (f u_e, u_o))
    where split u = (\n -> u (2 * n), \n -> u (2 * n + 1))
```

The function `split` splits an input bit-stream of randomness into two, non-overlapping bit-streams of randomness and will be used to ensure that primitive distributions built from `sampler` have access to fresh bit-streams of randomness. Thus, `sampler` first splits the input randomness `u`. Then, it runs the input sampling function f on `u_e`, and threads the unused portion `u_o` through for the rest of the computation. At this point, we are done describing the implementation of the semantics. We end with a few examples.

First, note that we can express distributions that are not (strictly) Type-2 computable—recall from the definition that computable distributions are normalized (see Sect. 3). Consider the program below, where `bot` = `bot` (*i.e.*, `bot` is a computation that does not terminate) and `bernoulli` is a Bernoulli distribution:

```
maybeLoop :: Samp Bool
maybeLoop = do
  b <- bernoulli
  if b then return bot else bernoulli
```

This program diverges 1/2 the time and returns a fair coin flip the other 1/2 according to Haskell semantics. Hence, it does not generate a sample with probability 1 so it cannot be a Type-2 computable distribution. Later when we add conditioning to λ_{CD} as a library function implementing a Type-2 conditioning algorithm, we will not give semantics to conditioning on un-normalized distributions because the Type-2 algorithm assumes the distribution is normalized. Distributions such as `maybeLoop` that fail to generate a sample with positive probability are not useful in the context of Bayesian inference. Hence, we are fine not giving semantics to conditioning on these distributions.

Next, we show how to use the library to encode continuous distributions. To start, we fill in the sketch of the standard Uniform distribution from before using `sampler`. As a reminder, we need to convert a random bit-stream into a sequence of (dyadic) rational approximations.

```
std_uni :: Samp CReal
std_uni = sampler (\u -> A (\n -> bisect (n+1) u 0 1 0))
    where
      bisect n u (l :: Rat) (r :: Rat) m =
          if m < n
          then (if u m
                then bisect n u l (midpt l r) (m+1)
                else bisect n u (midpt l r) r (m+1))
          else midpt l r
      midpt l r = l + (r - l) / 2
```

The function `bisect` repeatedly bisects an interval specified by (`l`, `r`). By construction, the sampler produces a sequence of dyadic rationals. We can see that this sampling function is uniformly distributed because it inverts the binary expansion specified by the uniformly distributed input bit-stream. Once we have the Uniform distribution, we can encode other primitive distributions (*e.g.*, Normal, Exponential, and etc.) as transformations of the Uniform as in standard statistics using return and bind.

For example, we give an encoding of the standard Normal distribution using the Marsaglia polar transformation, which diverges with probability 0:

```
std_normal :: Samp CReal
std_normal = do
  u1 <- uniform (-1) 1
  u2 <- uniform (-1) 1
  s <- return (u1 * u1 + u2 * u2)
  if s < 1
  then return (u1 * sqrt (- log s / s))
  else std_normal
```

The distribution `uniform` (-1) 1 is the Uniform distribution on the interval $(-1, 1)$ and can be encoded by shifting and scaling a draw from `std_uniform`. We can check that this distribution is samplable. First, we check that the algorithm produces a sample with probability 1 by showing that both $s = 1$ (by absolute continuity) and divergence (by Borel-Cantelli) occur with probability 0. Note that the operation `<` semi-decides both $<$ and $>$, where we are guaranteed with probability 1 that equality does not hold. Next, the algorithm is measure-preserving because `uniform` (-1) 1 is a samplable distribution and compositions of computable functions preserve measure. Hence, we can conclude that this distribution is samplable.

5 Conditioning

Conditioning is the core operation of Bayesian inference. As we alluded to earlier, conditioning is not computable in general [1]. We could use a more abstract definition of conditioning used in measure theory, but it would be undesirable if the semantics of conditioning for a probabilistic programming language was not computable given that one of its goals is to automate inference. Instead, we take a library approach, which requires the client to provide an implementation of a conditioning algorithm and limits us to situations where conditioning is computable. Hence, the semantics of our core language remains unchanged.

5.1 Preliminaries

We begin with background on conditioning in the context of Bayesian inference before moving to conditioning in the measure-theoretic and computable settings. A Bayesian model puts a distribution on the product space $\Theta \times D$, where Θ is the space of parameters and D is the space of observations. Observing a particular value $d \in D$ restricts the domain of the distribution to that subspace, resulting in a distribution on parameters given the data d. More formally, the objective of Bayesian inference is to compute the *posterior distribution* $p(\theta \mid d)$ (function of θ for fixed d) given a *joint distribution* $p(d, \theta)$ and observed data $d \in D$. The notation $p(\cdot)$ refers to the density of a distribution, but it is common (in statistics) to refer to $p(\cdot)$ as a distribution as we have done above. The *density* of a distribution μ with respect to a distribution ν is an integrable function f such that $\mu(A) = \int_A f d\nu$ for every measurable A. Thus, a density along with the underlying measure ν (often Lebesgue measure) determines a measure. The joint and posterior are related with *Bayes' rule*:

$$p(\theta \mid d) = \frac{p(d, \theta)}{\int p(d, \theta) d\theta} \propto p(d \mid \theta) p(\theta),$$

where $p(\theta)$ is called the *prior distribution* and $p(d \mid \theta)$ is called the *likelihood*. The posterior distribution $p(\theta \mid d)$ is a *conditional distribution*.

Conditioning can be defined in more abstract settings when we do not have densities. First, we need to introduce additional measure-theoretic definitions. A tuple $(\Omega, \mathcal{F}, \mu)$ is called a *probability space*, where $(\Omega, \mathcal{F})$ is a measurable space and μ is a measure. We will omit the underlying σ-algebra and measure when they are unambiguous from context. A function $f : \Omega_1 \to \Omega_2$ is *measurable* if $f^{-1}(B)$ is measurable for measurable B. In the case of metric spaces, the measurable sets are generated by the open balls so measurable functions are a superset of the continuous functions. A *random variable* that takes on values in a probability space S is a measurable function $X : \Omega \to S$. The *distribution* of a random variable X, written $\mathbf{P}[X \in \cdot]$, is defined as the push-forward of the underlying measure, *i.e.*, $\mathbf{P}[X \in A] = \mu(X^{-1}(A))$ for all measurable A. We write $X \sim \mu$ to indicate that the random variable X is distributed according to μ.

Now, we can give definitions for conditioning in the measure-theoretic setting. We will not give the most general definition of conditioning as conditional expectation, choosing to restrict the scope to the case that also applies in the computable setting [1]. In the following, let X and Y be random variables in computable metric spaces S and T respectively. In addition, let $\mathcal{B}_T$ be the (Borel) σ-algebra on T and let $\mathbf{P}_X$ be the distribution of X. A measurable function

```
module Conditioning where
import A
import CompDistLib
import RealLib

newtype BndDens a b =
    BndDens { getDens :: (A a -> A b -> CReal, Rat) }

-- Requires comp. dist. and bounded conditional density
obs_dens :: forall u v y.
    (CMetrizable u, CMetrizable v, CMetrizable y) =>
    Samp (A (u, v)) -> BndDens u y -> A y -> Samp (A (u, v))
```

Fig. 2. An interface for conditioning.

$\mathbf{P}[Y \in B \mid X]$ for B measurable is a *version* of the *conditional probability of* $Y \in B$ *given* X when

$$\mathbf{P}(X \in A, Y \in B) = \int_A \mathbf{P}[Y \in B \mid X] d\mathbf{P}_X$$

for all measurable A. A *probability kernel* is a function $\kappa : S \times \mathcal{B}_T \to [0,1]$ such that $\kappa(s, \cdot)$ is a Borel measure on T for every $s \in S$, and $\kappa(\cdot, B)$ is measurable for every measurable B. A *regular conditional probability* is then a probability kernel κ such that $\mathbf{P}(X \in A, Y \in B) = \int \kappa(x, B)\mathbf{P}_X(dx)$, where A and B are measurable.

These definitions have computable versions.

Definition 2 *(Computable probability kernel [1, Definition 4.2]). Let S and T be computable metric spaces, and $\mathcal{B}_T$ be the σ-algebra on T. A probability kernel $\kappa : S \times \mathcal{B}_T \to [0,1]$ is computable if $\kappa(\cdot, A)$ is a lower semi-computable function for every r.e. open $A \in \sigma(\mathcal{B}_T)$.*

Definition 3 *(Computable conditional distribution [1, Definition 4.7]). Let X and Y be random variables in computable metric spaces S and T. Let κ be a version of $\mathbf{P}[Y \mid X]$ (notation for $\mathbf{P}[Y \in \cdot \mid X]$). Then $\mathbf{P}[Y \mid X]$ is computable if κ is computable on a $\mathbf{P}_X$ measure-one subset.*

Thus, a non-computable conditional distribution is one for which *every* version is non-computable.

5.2 Conditioning

Now, we add conditioning as a library to λ_{CD} (Fig. 2). λ_{CD} provides only a restricted conditioning operation `obs_dens`, which requires a conditional density. We will see that the computability of `obs_dens` corresponds to an effective version of Bayes' rule, which is central to Bayesian inference, and hence, widely applicable in practice. We have given only one conditioning primitive here, but it is possible to identify other situations where conditioning is computable and add those to the conditioning library. For example, conditioning on positive probability events is computable (see [7, Proposition 3.1.2]).

The library provides the conditioning operation `obs_dens`, which enables us to condition on *continuous*-valued data when a bounded and computable conditional density is available.

Proposition 2 *[1, Corollary 8.8]. Let U, V and Y be computable random variables, where Y is independent of V given U. Let $p_{Y \mid U}(y \mid u)$ be a conditional density of Y given U that is bounded and computable. Then the conditional distribution $\mathbf{P}[(U, V) \mid Y]$ is computable.*

The bounded and computable conditional density enables the following integral to be computed, which is in essence Bayes' rule. A version of the conditional distribution $\mathbf{P}((U, V) \mid Y)$ is

$$\kappa_{(U,V) \mid Y}(y, B) = \frac{\int_B p_{Y \mid U}(y \mid u) d\mathbf{P}_{(U,V)}}{\int p_{Y \mid U}(y \mid u) d\mathbf{P}_{(U,V)}}$$

where B is a Borel set in the space associated with $U \times V$.

Another interpretation of the restricted situation is that our observations have been corrupted by independent smooth noise [1, Corollary 8.9]. To see this, let U be the random variable corresponding to our ideal model of how the data was generated, V be the random variable corresponding to the model parameters, and Y be the random variable corresponding to the corrupted data we observe. Notice that the model (U, V) is not required to have a density and can be an arbitrary computable distribution. Indeed, probabilistic programming systems proposed by the machine learning community impose a similar restriction (*e.g.*, [9,35]).

Now, we describe `obs_dens`, starting with its type signature. Let the type `BndDens` α β represent a bounded computable density:

```
newtype BndDens a b =
    BndDens { getDens :: (A a -> A b -> CReal, Rat) }
```

Conditioning thus takes a samplable distribution, a bounded computable density describing how observations have been corrupted, and returns a samplable distribution representing the conditional. In the context of Bayesian inference, it does not make sense to condition distributions such as `maybeLoop` that diverge with positive probability. Hence, we do not give semantics to conditioning on those distributions.

Now, we give a sketch of its implementation. In essence, it is a λ_{CD} program that implements the proof that conditioning is computable in this restricted setting. This is possible because results in computability theory have computable realizers.[3]

[3] That is, we implement the Type-2 machine code as a Haskell program. The implementation relies on Haskell's imprecise exceptions mechanism [22] to express the modulus of continuity of a computable function (see Andrej Bauer's blog http://math.andrej.com/2006/03/27/sometimes-all-functions-are-continuous).

```
obs_dens :: forall u v y.
    (CMetrizable u, CMetrizable v, CMetrizable y) =>
    Samp (A (u, v)) -> BndDens u y -> A y -> Samp (A (u, v))
obs_dens dist (BndDens (dens, bnd)) d =
    let f :: A (u, v) -> CReal = \x -> dens (afst x) d
        mu :: Prob (u, v) = stc dist
        nu :: Prob (u, v) = \bs ->
              let num   = integrate_bnd_dom mu f bnd bs
                  denom = integrate_bnd mu f bnd
              in map fst (cauchy_to_lu (num / denom))
    in
      cts nu
```

The parameter `dist` corresponds to the joint distribution of the model (both model parameters and likelihood), `dens` corresponds to a bounded conditional density describing how observation of data has been corrupted by independent noise, and `d` is the observed data. Next, we informally describe the undefined functions in the sketch. The functions `stc` and `cts` witness the computable isomorphism between samplable and computable distributions. The functions `integrate_bnd_dom` and `integrate_bnd` compute an integral (see [12, Proposition 4.3.1]), and correspond to an effective Lebesgue integral. `cauchy_to_lu` converts a Cauchy description of a computable real into an enumeration of lower and upper bounds.

Because `obs_dens` works with conditional densities, we do not need to worry about the Borel paradox. The Borel paradox shows that we can obtain different conditional distributions by conditioning on equivalent probability zero events [26]. In addition, note that it is not possible to create a boolean value that distinguishes two probability zero events in λ_{CD}. For instance, the operator `==` implementing equality on reals returns false if two reals are provably not-equal and diverges otherwise because equality is not decidable.

Now, we give an encoding in λ_{CD} of an example by Ackerman et al. [1] that shows that conditioning is not always computable. Similar to other results in computability theory, the example demonstrates that an algorithm computing the conditional distribution would also solve the Halting problem.

```
non_comp :: Samp (Nat, CReal)
non_comp = do
  n <- geometric (1/2)
  c <- bernoulli (1/3)
  u <- uniform 0 1
  v <- uniform 0 1
  x <- return (approx (\k -> dk k (tm_halts_within_k n k)))
  return (n, x)
    where dk k m | m > k = anth v k
                 | m = k = c
                 | m < k = anth u (k - m - 1)
```

The Uniform distribution `uniform` generates approximations via dyadic rationals. The distributions `geometric` and `bernoulli` correspond to Geometric and

Bernoulli distributions. The function `tm_halts_within_k` accepts a natural n specifying the n-th Turing machine and a natural k describing the number of steps to run the machine for, and returns the number of steps the n-th Turing machine halts in or k if it cannot tell. Upon inspection, we see the function `dk` produces the binary expansion (as a dyadic rational) of a computable real, using `tm_halts_within_k` to select different bits of the binary expansion of u or v, or the bit c. Thus, it is computable. However, it is not possible to compute the conditional distribution $P(N \mid X)$, where the random variable N corresponds to the program variable n and X to x, because we would compute the Halting set.

6 Examples

In this section, we give additional examples of distributions in λ_{CD}, including a non-parametric prior (a distribution on a countable number of parameters) and a singular distribution (neither discrete nor continuous). This highlights the expressiveness of λ_{CD} and demonstrates how to apply the reasoning principles from before.

Geometric Distribution. Consider the encoding of a Geometric distribution with bias 1/2, which returns the number of Bernoulli trials until a success.

```
geometric :: SampT Nat
geometric = do
  b <- bernoulli (1/2)
  if b
  then return 1
  else do
    n <- geometric
    return (n + 1)
```

Our denotational view shows that the code encodes the Geometric distribution, where μ_B is a Bernoulli distribution and μ^n corresponds to n un-foldings of `geometric`. To see this, we can proceed by induction on n and use the induction hypothesis that μ^n is the measure $\{0\} \mapsto 0, \{1\} \mapsto (1/2), \ldots, \{n\} \mapsto (1/2)^n$.

$$\mathcal{E}[\![\texttt{geometric}]\!]\rho = \lambda U. \sup_n \int \lambda v. \begin{cases} 1_U(1) & \text{if } v = t \\ \int \lambda w.\ 1_U(w+1) d\mu^n & \text{otherwise} \end{cases} d\mu_B$$

$$= \lambda U. \sup_n (1_U(1)\frac{1}{2} + \sum_{w=0}^{\infty} 1_U(w+1)\mu^n(\{w\}))$$

Non-parametric Prior. We give two different encodings of the Dirichlet process, a prior distribution used in mixture models where the number of mixtures is unknown (*e.g.*, [19]). The Dirichlet process $\text{DP}(\alpha, G_0)$ is a distribution on distributions—a draw produces a discrete distribution with support determined by G_0, the based distribution, and mass according to α, the concentration parameter. The Dirichlet process can be represented in multiple ways, where each representation illuminates different properties. One representation is called the

Blackwell-MacQueen urn scheme (see [19]), which describes how to sample from the distribution resulting from a draw of the Dirichlet process. Thus, we can imagine it describing the following process:

$$G \sim \mathrm{DP}(\alpha, G_0)$$
$$\theta_n \mid G \sim G \text{ for } n \in \mathbb{N} .$$

The conditional distribution of θ_n is

$$\theta_n \mid \theta_{1:n-1} \sim \frac{\alpha}{\alpha+n-1} G_0 + \frac{1}{\alpha+n-1} \sum_{j=1}^{n-1} 1_{\theta_j} \text{ for } n \in \mathbb{N} ,$$

which shows that the base distribution G_0 determines the support and α determines how often we select a new point from G_0 to put mass on. We can encode the conditional distribution in λ_{CD}.

```
urn' :: CReal -> Samp a -> [a] -> Samp a
urn' alpha g0 prev =
    let l = length prev
        n :: Integer = (toInteger l) + 1
        w = 1 / (fromInteger n - 1 + alpha)
        ws = replicate l w ++ [alpha]
        d = disc_id ws
    in do
      c <- d
      if c == n - 1
      then g0
      else return (prev !! (fromInteger c))
```

We can put our reasoning principles to work to argue that `urn'` encodes the conditional distributions. First, we can use a distributional view of the monadic block of `urn'` under an environment ρ, where $\mu = \mathcal{E}[\![\texttt{d}]\!]\rho$.

$$\mathcal{E}[\![\texttt{c} \leftarrow \texttt{d ; if c == n-1 then g0 else return (prev !! c)}]\!]\rho = \lambda U.$$
$$\int \lambda v.\pi_1 \circ \begin{cases} \mathcal{E}[\![\texttt{g0}]\!]\rho[c \mapsto v](U) & \text{if } \mathcal{E}[\![\texttt{c == n-1}]\!]\rho[c \mapsto v] \\ \mathcal{E}[\![\texttt{return (prev !! c)}]\!]\rho[c \mapsto v](U) & \text{otherwise} \end{cases} d\mu$$

Next, substituting away the `let` bindings (justified by Haskell semantics) implies that $\mathcal{E}[\![d]\!]\rho$ is the discrete distribution

$$0 \mapsto \frac{1}{\alpha+n-1}, \ldots, n-2 \mapsto \frac{1}{\alpha+n-1}, n-1 \mapsto \frac{\alpha}{\alpha+n-1} .$$

This reduces the previous integral to the summation

$$\lambda U. \sum_{j=0}^{n-2} \frac{1}{\alpha+n-1} \mathcal{E}[\![\texttt{return (prev !! c)}]\!]\rho[c \mapsto j](U)$$
$$+ \frac{\alpha}{\alpha+n-1} \mathcal{E}[\![\texttt{g0}]\!]\rho[c \mapsto n-1](U) ,$$

where $\mathcal{E}[\![\texttt{g0}]\!]\rho$ is the base distribution G_0. Rewriting this in statistical notation gives the desired result

$$\mathcal{E}[\![\texttt{urn' alpha g0 prev}]\!]\rho \sim \frac{\alpha}{\alpha+n-1}G_0 + \frac{\sum_{j=1}^{n-1}}{\alpha+n-1}1_{\texttt{prev}_j}\ .$$

Next, we can describe the entire infinite sequence using lazy monadic lists

```
data MList m a = Nil | Cons a (m (MList m a))
```

and analogoulsy define common operations expected of lists such as `iterate`, `map`, and `tail`.

```
urn :: forall a. CReal -> Samp a -> Samp (MList a)
urn alpha g0 =
    let f :: ((a, [a]) -> Samp a) = return . fst)
        g (_, acc) = do
          x <- urn' alpha g0 acc
          return (x, acc ++ [x])
    in do
      x0 <- g0
      xs <- ML.map f (ML.iterate g (return (x0, [])))
      ML.tail xs
```

Expressing the resulting conditional distribution for each n gives

$$\mathcal{E}[\![\texttt{urn alpha g0}]\!]\rho_n \mid \mathcal{E}[\![\texttt{urn alpha g0}]\!]\rho_{1:n-1} \sim \frac{\alpha}{\alpha+n-1}G_0 + \frac{\sum_{j=1}^{n-1}}{\alpha+n-1}1_{\texttt{psh}(\mathcal{E}[\![\texttt{urn alpha g0}]\!]\rho)_j}\ .$$

Alternatively, there is a constructive representation known as the stick-breaking construction (see [19]) that gives the structure of the discrete distribution directly. We describe a process that gives $G \sim \mathrm{DP}(\alpha, G_0)$. First, let random variables $\beta_k \sim \mathrm{Beta}(1, \alpha)$ be distributed according to the Beta distribution for $k \in \mathbb{N}$. Next, define $\pi_k = \beta_k \prod_{i=1}^{k-1}(1-\beta_i)$ for $k \in \mathbb{N}$. Let $X_k \sim G_0$ for $k \in \mathbb{N}$. The result G is $\sum_{k=1}^{\infty} \pi_k 1_{X_k}(\cdot)$. We can encode the stick-breaking construction in λ_{CD}, where `ML.@:` is synonymously `ML.Cons` and `ML.!!!` indexes a lazy monadic list. The function `mdisc_id` samples an index according to an input lazy monad list specifying probabilities.

```
sticks :: CReal -> Samp a -> Samp a
sticks alpha g0 = do
  xs <- ML.repeat g0
  pis <- weights 1
  c <- mdisc_id pis
  xs ML.!!! fromInteger c
    where
      weights :: CReal -> Samp (MList CReal)
      weights left = do
        v <- beta 1 alpha
        return ((v * left) ML.@: (weights (left * (1 - v))))
```

We can follow a similar pattern to reason about the urn representation. For instance, we can analyze this function compositionally as before by reasoning that $c \leftarrow$ `mdisc_id pis xs ; ML.!!! fromInteger c` selects a sample from `xs` according to the weights `pis`. Finally, we can combine this with showing that `weights` generates the weights π_k.

The encodings show that we can use probabilistic and standard program reasoning principles at the same time. Because we checked that each program encoded their respective representation, we also obtain that sampling `sticks` an infinite number of times is equivalent to `urn` because both encode the Dirichlet process. This might seem strange because the urn encoding has more sequential dependencides than the stick-breaking representation. The equivalence relies on a probabilistic concept called *exchangeability*, which asserts the existence of a conditionally independent representation if the distribution is invariant under all finite permutations. Exchangeability has been studied in the Type-2 setting [5] and it would be interesting to see if we can lift those results into λ_{CD}.

Singular Distribution. Next, we give an encoding of the Cantor distribution. The Cantor distribution is singular so it is not a mixture of a discrete component and a component with a density. The distribution can be defined recursively. It starts by trisecting the unit interval, and placing half the mass on the leftmost interval and the other half on the rightmost interval, leaving no mass for the middle, continuing in the same manner with each remaining interval that has positive probability. We can encode the Cantor distribution in λ_{CD} be directly transforming a random bit-stream into a sequence of approximations.

```
cantor :: Samp CReal
cantor = sampler (\u -> approx (\n -> go u 0 1 0 n))
    where go u (left :: Rat) (right :: Rat) n m =
              let pow = 3 ^^ (-n) in
              if (n < m)
              then (if u n
                    then go u left (left + pow) (n + 1) m
                    else go u (right - pow) right (n + 1) m)
              else right - (1 / 2) * pow
```

The sampling algorithm keeps track of which interval it is currently in specified by `left` and `right`. If the current bit is 1, we trisect the left interval. Otherwise, we trisect the rightmost interval. Crucially, the number of trisections is bounded by the precision we would like to generate the sample to. We could express the Cantor distribution in a measure-theoretic language with recursion, but we would need to trisect infinitely to express the distribution exactly.

7 Related Work

The semantics of probabilistic programs have been studied outside the context of Bayesian inference, in particular, to look at non-determinism and probabilistic algorithms. For instance, Kozen [15] gives both a sampling semantics and denotational semantics to a first-order imperative language. Instead of CPO constructions, the denotational semantics uses constructs from analysis, and recovers order-theoretic structure to support recursion. In the functional setting, researchers have studied *probabilistic powerdomains*, which put *distributions* on CPO's so that the space of distributions themselves forms a CPO. For example, Saheb [27] introduces the probabilistic powerdomain on CPO's by considering probability measures. Jones [13] considers powerdomains of valuations on CPO's instead and shows that this results in CPO's that have more desirable properties reminiscent of standard domains (*e.g.*, ω-algebraic). The work on powerdomains typically does not consider continuous distributions (we obtain the topology from a computable metric space as opposed to the Scott-topology of a CPO) or Bayesian inference.

Semantics for probabilistic programs have also been studied with machine learning applications in mind. Ramsey *et al.* give denotational semantics to a higher-order language without recursion extended with discrete distributions using the probability monad, and shows how to efficiently implement probabilistic queries [25]. Borgström *et al.* [3] uses measure theory to give denotational semantics to a first-order language without recursion using measure transformers. The main focus of the work is to ensure that the semantics of conditioning on events of 0 probability is well-defined. Toronto et al. [29] propose another measure-theoretic approach for a first-order language with recursion by interpreting probabilistic programs as pre-image computations of measurable functions to support conditioning. They do not use standard constructs from denotational semantics, and thus, do not handle recursion with a fixed-point construction. Instead, their target is a variant of lambda calculus extended with set-theoretic operations (λ_{ZFC}). Park *et al.* [21] give an operational semantics to an ML-like language in terms of sampling functions, but uses an idealized abstract machine. Hence, they also use the observation that a continuous distribution is characterized by a sampling procedure, but do not explore connections to a denotational approach nor the (faithful) realizability of their operational semantics.

Probabilistic languages have also been proposed to study inference, and typically have been given operational semantics. Some languages restrict to expressing well-established abstractions, such as factor graphs and Bayesian networks, in order to automate standard inference algorithms. In this restricted setting, they are given semantics in terms of the abstractions they express. For instance, the Bugs system [16] provides a language for users to specify Bayesian networks and implements Gibbs sampling, a Markov Chain Monte Carlo sampling algorithm used in practice that reduces the problem of sampling from a multivariate conditional distribution into sampling from multiple univariate conditional distributions. Several other probabilistic programming languages similar to Bugs have been developed for expressing factor graphs (*e.g.*, [10,17,18]) and directed models (*e.g.*, [11,30]), and automate inference using standard algorithms, including message passing and HMC sampling.

Other researchers extend Turing-complete languages with the ability to sample from primitive distributions (*e.g.*, [9,14,20,23,24,33,35]) and have been proposed to study inference in this richer setting. These languages have operational semantics given in terms of an inference method implemented in the host language. Examples include Stochastic Lisp [14] and Ibal [24] which only have discrete distributions. Others add *continuous* distributions, including Church [9] which embeds in Scheme and Fiagro [23] which embeds in Scala. The Church language performs inference by sampling program traces. Other languages have built upon this, including Probabilistic Matlab [33], Probabilistic C [35], and R2 [20], each proposing a different method to improve the efficiency of sampling program traces.

8 Discussion

In summary, we show that we can give sampling semantics to a high-level probabilistic language for Bayesian inference that corresponds to a natural denotational view. Our approach, by acknowledging the limits of computability, gives a semantics that corresponds to the intuition of probabilistic programs encoding generative models as samplers. In particular, Type-2 computability makes sense (*i.e.*, algorithmically) of sampling from continuous distributions as well as the difficulty of supporting a generic conditioning primitive. Moreover, we have shown that many ideas such as the ones in the probabilistic powerdomains can also be applied to give semantics to modern probabilistic languages designed for Bayesian inference. We end with a few directions for future work.

First, as we mentioned previously, algorithms that operate on computable distributions (and reals) are not necessarily efficient. In many practical situations, it is not necessary to compute to arbitrary precision as Type-2 computability demands, but *enough* precision. It would be interesting to see if we can efficiently implement an approximate semantics in this relaxed setting. Second, our approach has not been designed with inference in mind. The language λ_{CD} is perhaps too expressive—we can express distributions that are not meaningful for inference (*e.g.*, `maybeLoop`) and singular distributions that have limited applications (*e.g.*, Cantor distribution). It would be interesting to explore restricted language designs where we have guaranteed efficient inference.

Acknowledgements. This work was supported by Oracle Labs. We would like to thank Nate Ackerman, Stephen Chong, Jean-Baptiste Tristan, Dexter Kozen, Dan Roy, and our anonymous reviewers for helpful discussions and feedback.

References

1. Ackerman, N.L., Freer, C.E., Roy, D.M.: Noncomputable conditional distributions. In: Proceedings of the IEEE 26th Annual Symposium on Logic in Computer Science, LICS 2011, pp. 107–116. IEEE Computer Society, Washington, DC (2011)
2. Bailey, D., Borwein, P., Plouffe, S.: On the Rapid Computation of Various Polylogarithmic Constants. Math. Comput. **66**(218), 903–913 (1997)
3. Borgström, J., Gordon, A.D., Greenberg, M., Margetson, J., Van Gael, J.: Measure transformer semantics for bayesian machine learning. In: Barthe, G. (ed.) ESOP 2011. LNCS, vol. 6602, pp. 77–96. Springer, Heidelberg (2011)

4. Freer, C.E., Roy, D.M.: Posterior distributions are computable from predictive distributions. In: Teh, Y.W., Titterington, D.M. (eds.) Proceedings of the Thirteenth International Conference on Artificial Intelligence and Statistics (AISTATS-10), vol. 9, pp. 233–240 (2010)
5. Freer, C.E., Roy, D.M.: Computable de finetti measures. Ann. Pure. Appl. Logic **163**(5), 530–546 (2012)
6. Gács, P.: Uniform test of algorithmic randomness over a general space. Theor. Comput. Sci. **341**(1), 91–137 (2005)
7. Galatolo, S., Hoyrup, M., Rojas, C.: Effective symbolic dynamics, random points, statistical behavior, complexity and entropy. Inf. Comput. **208**(1), 23–41 (2010)
8. Giry, M.: A categorical approach to probability theory. In: Banaschewski, B. (ed.) Categorical Aspects of Topology and Analysis, pp. 68–85. Springer, Heidelberg (1982)
9. Goodman, N.D., Mansinghka, V.K., Roy, D., Bonawitz, K., Tenenbaum, J.B.: Church: A language for generative models. In: Proceedings of the 24th Conference on Uncertainty in Artificial Intelligence, UAI , pp. 220–229 (2008)
10. Hershey, S., Bernstein, J., Bradley, B., Schweitzer, A., Stein, N., Weber, T., Vigoda, B.: Accelerating Inference: towards a full Language, Compiler and Hardware stack. CoRR abs/1212.2991 (2012)
11. Hoffman, M.D., Gelman, A.: The No-U-Turn sampler: adaptively setting path lengths in hamiltonian monte carlo. J. Mach. Learn. Res. **15**, 1351–1381 (2013)
12. Hoyrup, M., Rojas, C.: Computability of probability measures and Martin-Löf randomness over metric spaces. Inf. Comput. **207**(7), 830–847 (2009)
13. Jones, C., Plotkin, G.: A probabilistic powerdomain of evaluations. In: Proceedings of the Fourth Annual Symposium on Logic in Computer Science, pp. 186–195. IEEE Press, Piscataway (1989)
14. Koller, D., McAllester, D., Pfeffer, A.: Effective bayesian inference for stochastic programs. In: Proceedings of the 14th National Conference on Artificial Intelligence (AAAI), pp. 740–747 (1997)
15. Kozen, D.: Semantics of probabilistic programs. J. Comput. Syst. Sci. **22**(3), 328–350 (1981)
16. Lunn, D., Spiegelhalter, D., Thomas, A., Best, N.: The BUGS project: Evolution, critique and future directions. Statistic in Medicine (2009)
17. McCallum, A., Schultz, K., Singh, S.: Factorie: Probabilistic programming via imperatively defined factor graphs. Adv. Neural Inf. Process. Syst. **22**, 1249–1257 (2009)
18. Minka, T., Guiver, J., Winn, J., Kannan, A.: Infer.NET 2.3, Microsoft Research Cambridge (2009)
19. Neal, R.M.: Markov chain sampling methods for Dirichlet process mixture models. J. Comput. Graph. Stat. **9**(2), 249–265 (2000)
20. Nori, A.V., Hur, C.-K., Rajamani, S.K., Samuel, S.: R2: An efficient MCMC sampler for probabilistic programs. In: AAAI Conference on Artificial Intelligence (2014)
21. Park, S., Pfenning, F., Thrun, S.: A probabilistic language based upon sampling functions. In: Proceedings of the 32Nd ACM SIGPLAN-SIGACT Symposium on Principles of Programming Languages, POPL 2005, pp. 171–182. ACM, New York (2005)
22. Jones, S.P., Reid, A., Henderson, F., Hoare, T., Marlow, S.: A semantics for imprecise exceptions. In: Proceedings of the ACM SIGPLAN Conference on Programming Language Design and Implementation, PLDI 1999, pp. 25–36. ACM, New York (1999)

23. Pfeffer, A.: Creating and manipulating probabilistic programs with figaro. In: 2nd International Workshop on Statistical Relational AI (2012)
24. Pfeffer, A.: IBAL: a probabilistic rational programming language. In: Proceedings of the 17th International Joint Conference on Artificial Intelligence - vol. 1, IJCAI 2001, pp. 733–740. Morgan Kaufmann Publishers Inc., San Francisco (2001)
25. Ramsey, N., Pfeffer, A.: Stochastic lambda calculus and monads of probability distributions. In: Proceedings of the 29th ACM SIGPLAN-SIGACT Symposium on Principles of Programming Languages, POPL 2002, pp. 154–165. ACM, New York (2002)
26. Rao, M.M., Swift, R.J.: Probability Theory with Applications. Springer-Verlag New York Inc, Secaucus (2006)
27. Saheb-Djahromi, N.: CPO's of measures for nondeterminism. Theor. Comput. Sci. **12**(1), 19–37 (1980)
28. Schröder, M.: Admissible representations for probability measures. Math. Logic Q. **53**(4–5), 431–445 (2007)
29. Toronto, N., McCarthy, J., Van Horn, D.: Running probabilistic programs backwards. In: Vitek, J. (ed.) ESOP 2015. LNCS, vol. 9032, pp. 53–79. Springer, Heidelberg (2015)
30. Tristan, J.-B., Huang, D., Tassarotti, J., Pocock, A.C., Green, S., Steele, G.L.: Augur: data-parallel probabilistic modeling. In: Advances in Neural Information Processing Systems, pp. 2600–2608 (2014)
31. Weihrauch, K.: Computability on the probability measures on the Borel sets of the unit interval. Theor. Comput. Sci. **219**(1), 421–437 (1999)
32. Weihrauch, K.: Computable Analysis: An Introduction. Springer-Verlag New York Inc, Secaucus (2000)
33. Wingate, D., Stuhlmller, A., Goodman, N.D.: Lightweight implementations of probabilistic programming languages via transformational compilation. In: Artificial Intelligence and Statistics, AISTATS 2011 (2011)
34. Winskel, G.: The Formal Semantics of Programming Languages: An Introduction. MIT Press, Cambridge (1993)
35. Wood, F., van de Meent, J.W., Mansinghka, V.: A new approach to probabilistic programming inference. In: Proceedings of the 17th International Conference on Artificial Intelligence and Statistics, pp. 2–46 (2014)

Weakest Precondition Reasoning for Expected Run–Times of Probabilistic Programs

Benjamin Lucien Kaminski(✉), Joost-Pieter Katoen(✉), Christoph Matheja(✉), and Federico Olmedo(✉)

Software Modeling and Verification Group, RWTH Aachen University, Ahornstraße 55, 52074 Aachen, Germany
{benjamin.kaminski,katoen,matheja, federico.olmedo}@cs.rwth-aachen.de

Abstract. This paper presents a wp–style calculus for obtaining bounds on the expected run–time of probabilistic programs. Its application includes determining the (possibly infinite) expected termination time of a probabilistic program and proving positive almost–sure termination—does a program terminate with probability one in finite expected time? We provide several proof rules for bounding the run–time of loops, and prove the soundness of the approach with respect to a simple operational model. We show that our approach is a conservative extension of Nielson's approach for reasoning about the run–time of deterministic programs. We analyze the expected run–time of some example programs including a one–dimensional random walk and the coupon collector problem.

Keywords: Probabilistic programs · Expected run–time · Positive almost–sure termination · Weakest precondition · Program verification

1 Introduction

Since the early days of computing, randomization has been an important tool for the construction of algorithms. It is typically used to convert a deterministic program with bad worst–case behavior into an efficient randomized algorithm that yields a correct output with high probability. The Rabin–Miller primality test, Freivalds' matrix multiplication, and the random pivot selection in Hoare's quicksort algorithm are prime examples. Randomized algorithms are conveniently described by probabilistic programs. On top of the usual language constructs, probabilistic programming languages offer the possibility of sampling values from a probability distribution. Sampling can be used in assignments as well as in Boolean guards.

The interest in probabilistic programs has recently been rapidly growing. This is mainly due to their wide applicability [10]. Probabilistic programs are

This work was supported by the Excellence Initiative of the German federal and state government.

P. Thiemann (Ed.): ESOP 2016, LNCS 9632, pp. 364–389, 2016.
DOI: 10.1007/978-3-662-49498-1_15

for instance used in security to describe cryptographic constructions and security experiments. In machine learning they are used to describe distribution functions that are analyzed using Bayesian inference. The sample program

$$C_{geo}\colon\ \ b := 1;\ \texttt{while}\,(b = 1)\,\{b :\approx 1/2 \cdot \langle 0 \rangle + 1/2 \cdot \langle 1 \rangle\}$$

for instance flips a fair coin until observing the first heads (i.e. 0). It describes a geometric distribution with parameter $1/2$.

The run–time of probabilistic programs is affected by the outcome of their coin tosses. Technically speaking, the run–time is a random variable, i.e. it is t_1 with probability p_1, t_2 with probability p_2 and so on. An important measure that we consider over probabilistic programs is then their *average* or *expected* run–time (over all inputs). Reasoning about the expected run–time of probabilistic programs is surprisingly subtle and full of nuances. In classical sequential programs, a single diverging program run yields the program to have an infinite run–time. This is not true for probabilistic programs. They may admit arbitrarily long runs while having a finite expected run–time. The program C_{geo}, for instance, does admit arbitrarily long runs as for any n, the probability of not seeing a heads in the first n trials is always positive. The expected run–time of C_{geo} is, however, finite.

In the classical setting, programs with finite run–times can be sequentially composed yielding a new program again with finite run–time. For probabilistic programs this does not hold in general. Consider the pair of programs

$$C_1\colon\ x := 1;\ b := 1;\ \texttt{while}\,(b = 1)\,\{b :\approx 1/2 \cdot \langle 0 \rangle + 1/2 \cdot \langle 1 \rangle;\ x := 2x\}\quad \text{and}$$
$$C_2\colon\ \texttt{while}\,(x > 0)\,\{x := x - 1\}.$$

The loop in C_1 terminates on average in two iterations; it thus has a finite expected run–time. From any initial state in which x is non–negative, C_2 makes x iterations, and thus its expected run–time is finite, too. However, the program $C_1; C_2$ has an *infinite* expected run–time—even though it almost–surely terminates, i.e. it terminates with probability one. Other subtleties can occur as program run–times are very sensitive to variations in the probabilities occurring in the program.

Bounds on the expected run–time of randomized algorithms are typically obtained using a detailed analysis exploiting classical probability theory (on expectations or martingales) [9,22]. This paper presents an alternative approach, based on formal program development and verification techniques. We propose a wp–style calculus à la Dijkstra for obtaining bounds on the expected run–time of probabilistic programs. The core of our calculus is the transformer ert, a quantitative variant of Dijkstra's wp–transformer. For a program C, $\mathsf{ert}\,[C]\,(f)\,(\sigma)$ gives the expected run–time of C started in initial state σ under the assumption that f captures the run–time of the computation following C. In particular, $\mathsf{ert}\,[C]\,(\mathbf{0})\,(\sigma)$ gives the expected run–time of program C on input σ (where $\mathbf{0}$ is the constantly zero run–time). Transformer ert is defined inductively on the program structure. We prove that our transformer conservatively extends Nielson's approach [23] for reasoning about the run–time of deterministic programs. In addition we show that $\mathsf{ert}\,[C]\,(f)\,(\sigma)$ corresponds to the expected run–time in a simple operational model for our probabilistic programs based on Markov Decision Processes (MDPs). The main contribution is a set of proof rules for obtaining (upper and lower) bounds on the expected run–time of loops. We apply our approach for analyzing the expected run–time of some example programs including a one–dimensional random walk and the coupon collector problem [20].

We finally point out that our technique enables determining the (possibly infinite) expected time until termination of a probabilistic program and proving (universal) *positive almost–sure termination*—does a program terminate with probability one in finite expected time (on all inputs)? It has been recently shown [16] that the universal positive almost–sure termination problem is Π_3^0–complete, and thus strictly harder to solve than the universal halting problem for deterministic programs. To the best of our knowledge, the formal verification framework in this paper is the first one that is proved sound and can handle both positive almost–sure termination and infinite expected run–times.

Related work. Several works apply wp–style– or Floyd–Hoare–style reasoning to study quantitative aspects of classical programs. Nielson [23,24] provides a Hoare logic for determining upper bounds on the run–time of deterministic programs. Our approach applied to such programs yields the tightest upper bound on the run–time that can be derived using Nielson's approach. Arthan *et al.* [1] provide a general framework for sound and complete Hoare–style logics, and show that an instance of their theory can be used to obtain upper bounds on the run–time of while programs. Hickey and Cohen [13] automate the average–case analysis of deterministic programs by generating a system of recurrence equations derived from a program whose efficiency is to be analyzed. They build on top of Kozen's seminal work [18] on semantics of probabilistic programs. Berghammer and Müller–Olm [3] show how Hoare–style reasoning can be extended to obtain bounds on the closeness of results obtained using approximate algorithms to the optimal solution. Deriving space and time consumption of deterministic programs has also been considered by Hehner [11]. Formal reasoning about probabilistic programs goes back to Kozen [18], and has been developed further by Hehner [12] and McIver and Morgan [19]. The work by Celiku and McIver [5] is perhaps the closest to our paper. They provide a wp–calculus for obtaining performance properties of probabilistic programs, including upper bounds on expected run–times. Their focus is on refinement. They do neither provide a soundness result of their approach nor consider lower bounds. We believe that our transformer is simpler to work with in practice, too. Monniaux [21] exploits abstract interpretation to automatically prove the probabilistic termination of programs using exponential bounds on the tail of the distribution. His analysis can be used to prove the soundness of experimental statistical methods to determine the average run–time of probabilistic programs. Brazdil *et al.* [4] study the run–time of probabilistic programs with unbounded recursion by considering probabilistic pushdown automata (pPDAs). They show (using martingale theory) that for every pPDA the probability of performing a long run decreases exponentially (polynomially) in the length of the run, iff the pPDA has a finite (infinite) expected runtime. As opposed to our program verification technique, [4] considers reasoning at the operational level. Fioriti and Hermanns [8] recently proposed a typing scheme for deciding almost-sure termination. They showed, amongst others, that if a program is well-typed, then it almost surely terminates. This result does not cover positive almost-sure-termination.

Organization of the paper. Section 2 defines our probabilistic programming language. Section 3 presents the transformer ert and studies its elementary properties such as continuity. Section 4 shows that the ert transformer coincides with the expected run–time in an MDP that acts as operational model of our programs. Section 5 presents two sets of proof rules for obtaining upper and lower bounds on the expected run–time of loops. In Sect. 6, we show that the ert transformer is a conservative extension of Nielson's approach for obtaining upper bounds on deterministic programs. Section 7 discusses two case studies in detail. Section 8 concludes the paper.

The proofs of the main facts are included in the body of the paper. The remaining proofs and the calculations omitted in Sect. 7 are included in an extended version of the paper [17].

2 A Probabilistic Programming Language

In this section we present the probabilistic programming language used throughout this paper, together with its run–time model. To model probabilistic programs we employ a standard imperative language à la Dijkstra's Guarded Command Language [7] with two distinguished features: we allow distribution expressions in assignments and guards to be probabilistic. For instance, we allow for probabilistic assignments like

$$y :\approx \texttt{Unif}[1 \ldots x]$$

which endows variable y with a uniform distribution in the interval $[1 \ldots x]$. We allow also for a program like

$$x := 0;\ \texttt{while}\ \big(p \cdot \langle \mathsf{true} \rangle + (1-p) \cdot \langle \mathsf{false} \rangle\big)\ \{x := x + 1\}$$

which uses a probabilistic loop guard to simulate a geometric distribution with success probability p, i.e. the loop guard evaluates to true with probability p and to false with the remaining probability $1-p$.

Formally, the set of *probabilistic programs* pProgs is given by the grammar

C ::=		`empty`	empty program
	|	`skip`	effectless operation
	|	`halt`	immediate termination
	|	$x :\approx \mu$	probabilistic assignment
	|	$C; C$	sequential composition
	|	$\{C\} \,\square\, \{C\}$	non–deterministic choice
	|	`if` (ξ) $\{C\}$ `else` $\{C\}$	probabilistic conditional
	|	`while` (ξ) $\{C\}$	probabilistic while loop

Here x represents a *program variable* in Var, μ a *distribution expression* in DExp, and ξ a distribution expression over the truth values, i.e. a *probabilistic guard*, in DExp. We assume distribution expressions in DExp to represent discrete probability distributions with a (possibly *infinite*) support of total probability mass 1. We use $p_1 \cdot \langle a_1 \rangle + \cdots + p_n \cdot \langle a_n \rangle$ to denote the distribution expression that assigns probability p_i to a_i. For instance, the distribution expression $1/2 \cdot \langle \mathsf{true} \rangle + 1/2 \cdot \langle \mathsf{false} \rangle$ represents the toss of a fair coin. Deterministic expressions over program variables such as $x - y$ or $x - y > 8$ are special instances of distribution expressions—they are understood as Dirac probability distributions[1].

To describe the different language constructs we first present some preliminaries. A *program state* σ is a mapping from program variables to values in Val. Let $\Sigma \triangleq \{\sigma \mid \sigma : \mathsf{Var} \to \mathsf{Val}\}$ be the set of program states. We assume an interpretation function $[\![\cdot]\!] : \mathsf{DExp} \to (\Sigma \to \mathcal{D}(\mathsf{Val}))$ for distribution expressions, $\mathcal{D}(\mathsf{Val})$ being the set of discrete probability distributions over Val. For $\mu \in \mathsf{DExp}$, $[\![\mu]\!]$ maps each program state to a probability distribution of values. We use $[\![\mu : v]\!]$ as a shorthand for the function mapping each program state σ to the probability that distribution $[\![\mu]\!](\sigma)$ assigns to value v, i.e. $[\![\mu : v]\!](\sigma) \triangleq \mathsf{Pr}_{[\![\mu]\!](\sigma)}(v)$, where Pr denotes the probability operator on distributions over values.

We now present the effects of pProgs programs and the run–time model that we adopt for them. `empty` has no effect and its execution consumes no time. `skip` has also no effect but consumes, in contrast to `empty`, one unit of time. `halt` aborts any further program execution and consumes no time. $x :\approx \mu$ is a probabilistic assignment that samples a value from $[\![\mu]\!]$ and assigns it to variable x; the sampling and assignment consume (altogether) one unit of time. $C_1; C_2$ is the sequential composition of programs C_1 and C_2. $\{C_1\} \Box \{C_2\}$ is a non–deterministic choice between programs C_1 and C_2; we take a demonic view where we assume that out of C_1 and C_2 we execute the program with the greatest run–time. $\texttt{if}\,(\xi)\,\{C_1\}\,\texttt{else}\,\{C_2\}$ is a probabilistic conditional branching: with probability $[\![\xi : \mathsf{true}]\!]$ program C_1 is executed, whereas with probability $[\![\xi : \mathsf{false}]\!] = 1 - [\![\xi : \mathsf{true}]\!]$ program C_2 is executed; evaluating (or more rigorously, sampling a value from) the probabilistic guard requires an additional unit of time. $\texttt{while}\,(\xi)\,\{C\}$ is a probabilistic while loop: with probability $[\![\xi : \mathsf{true}]\!]$ the loop body C is executed followed by a recursive execution of the loop, whereas with probability $[\![\xi : \mathsf{false}]\!]$ the loop terminates; as for conditionals, each evaluation of the guard consumes one unit of time.

Example 1 (Race between tortoise and hare). The probabilistic program

$$
\begin{array}{l}
h :\approx 0;\, t :\approx 30;\\
\texttt{while}\,(h \le t)\,\{\\
\quad \texttt{if}\,\left(1/2 \cdot \langle \mathsf{true} \rangle + 1/2 \cdot \langle \mathsf{false} \rangle\right)\,\{h :\approx h + \texttt{Unif}[0 \ldots 10]\}\\
\quad \texttt{else}\,\{\texttt{empty}\};\\
\quad t :\approx t + 1\\
\},
\end{array}
$$

[1] A Dirac distribution assigns the total probability mass, i.e. 1, to a single point.

adopted from [6], illustrates the use of the programming language. It models a race between a hare and a tortoise (variables h and t represent their respective positions). The tortoise starts with a lead of 30 and in each step advances one step forward. The hare with probability $1/2$ advances a random number of steps between 0 and 10 (governed by a uniform distribution) and with the remaining probability remains still. The race ends when the hare passes the tortoise. △

We conclude this section by fixing some notational conventions. To keep our program notation consistent with standard usage, we use the standard symbol $:=$ instead of $:\approx$ for assignments whenever μ represents a Dirac distribution given by a deterministic expressions over program variables. For instance, in the program in Example 1 we write $t := t + 1$ instead of $t :\approx t + 1$. Likewise, when ξ is a probabilistic guard given as a deterministic Boolean expression over program variables, we use $[\![\xi]\!]$ to denote $[\![\xi\colon \mathsf{true}]\!]$ and $[\![\neg\xi]\!]$ to denote $[\![\xi\colon \mathsf{false}]\!]$. For instance, we write $[\![b = 0]\!]$ instead of $[\![b = 0\colon \mathsf{true}]\!]$.

3 A Calculus of Expected Run–Times

Our goal is to associate to any program C a function that maps each state σ to the average or expected run–time of C started in initial state σ. We use the functional space of *run–times*

$$\mathbb{T} \triangleq \{f \mid f\colon \Sigma \to \mathbb{R}^{\infty}_{\geq 0}\}$$

to model such functions. Here, $\mathbb{R}^{\infty}_{\geq 0}$ represents the set of non–negative real values extended with ∞. We consider run–times as a mapping from program states to real numbers (or ∞) as the expected run–time of a program may depend on the initial program state.

We express the run–time of programs using a continuation–passing style by means of the transformer

$$\mathsf{ert}[\,\cdot\,]\colon \mathsf{pProgs} \to (\mathbb{T} \to \mathbb{T}).$$

Concretely, $\mathsf{ert}\,[C]\,(f)\,(\sigma)$ gives the expected run–time of program C from state σ assuming that f captures the run–time of the computation that follows C. Function f is usually referred to as *continuation* and can be thought of as being evaluated in the final states that are reached upon termination of C. Observe that, in particular, if we set f to the constantly zero run–time, $\mathsf{ert}\,[C]\,(\mathbf{0})\,(\sigma)$ gives the expected run–time of program C on input σ.

The transformer ert is defined by induction on the structure of C following the rules in Table 1. The rules are defined so as to correspond to the run–time model introduced in Sect. 2. That is, $\mathsf{ert}\,[C]\,(\mathbf{0})$ captures the expected number of assignments, guard evaluations and `skip` statements. Most rules in Table 1 are self–explanatory. ert[`empty`] behaves as the identity since `empty` does not modify the program state and its execution consumes no time. On the other hand, ert[`skip`] adds one unit of time since this is the time required by the execution of `skip`. ert[`halt`] yields always the constant run–time $\mathbf{0}$ since `halt` aborts

Table 1. Rules for defining the expected run–time transformer ert. **1** is the constant run–time $\lambda\sigma.1$. $\mathsf{E}_\eta(h) \triangleq \sum_v \mathsf{Pr}_\eta(v) \cdot h(v)$ represents the expected value of (random variable) h w.r.t. distribution η. For $\sigma \in \Sigma$, $f[x/v](\sigma) \triangleq f(\sigma[x/v])$, where $\sigma[x/v]$ is the state obtained by updating in σ the value of x to v. $\max\{f_1, f_2\} \triangleq \lambda\sigma. \max\{f_1(\sigma), f_2(\sigma)\}$ represents the point–wise lifting of the max operator over $\mathbb{R}^\infty_{\geq 0}$ to the function space of run–times. $\mathsf{lfp}\, X\centerdot F(X)$ represents the least fixed point of the transformer $F\colon \mathbb{T} \to \mathbb{T}$.

C	$\mathsf{ert}[C](f)$
`empty`	f
`skip`	$\mathbf{1} + f$
`halt`	$\mathbf{0}$
$x :\approx \mu$	$\mathbf{1} + \lambda\sigma\centerdot \mathsf{E}_{[\![\mu]\!](\sigma)}(\lambda v.\, f[x/v](\sigma))$
$C_1;\, C_2$	$\mathsf{ert}[C_1](\mathsf{ert}[C_2](f))$
$\{C_1\} \Box \{C_2\}$	$\max\{\mathsf{ert}[C_1](f), \mathsf{ert}[C_2](f)\}$
`if` $(\xi)\ \{C_1\}$ `else` $\{C_2\}$	$\mathbf{1} + [\![\xi : \mathsf{true}]\!] \cdot \mathsf{ert}[C_1](f) + [\![\xi : \mathsf{false}]\!] \cdot \mathsf{ert}[C_2](f)$
`while` $(\xi)\ \{C'\}$	$\mathsf{lfp}\, X\centerdot\, \mathbf{1} + [\![\xi : \mathsf{false}]\!] \cdot f + [\![\xi : \mathsf{true}]\!] \cdot \mathsf{ert}[C'](X)$

any subsequent program execution (making their run–time irrelevant) and consumes no time. The definition of ert on random assignments is more involved: $\mathsf{ert}[x :\approx \mu](f)(\sigma) = 1 + \sum_v \mathsf{Pr}_{[\![\mu]\!](\sigma)}(v) \cdot f(\sigma[x/v])$ is obtained by adding one unit of time (due to the distribution sampling and assignment of the value sampled) to the sum of the run–time of each possible subsequent execution, weighted according to their probabilities. $\mathsf{ert}[C_1;\, C_2]$ applies $\mathsf{ert}[C_1]$ to the expected run–time obtained from the application of $\mathsf{ert}[C_2]$. $\mathsf{ert}[\{C_1\} \Box \{C_2\}]$ returns the maximum between the run–time of the two branches. $\mathsf{ert}[$`if` $(\xi)\ \{C_1\}$ `else` $\{C_2\}]$ adds one unit of time (on account of the guard evaluation) to the weighted sum of the run–time of the two branches. Lastly, the ert of loops is given as the least fixed point of a run–time transformer defined in terms of the run–time of the loop body.

Remark. We stress that the above run–time model is a design decision for the sake of concreteness. All our developments can easily be adapted to capture alternative models. These include, for instance, the model where only the number of assignments in a program run or the model where only the number of loop iterations are of relevance. We can also capture more fine–grained models, where for instance the run–time of an assignment depends on the *size* of the distribution expression being sampled.

Example 2 (Truncated geometric distribution). To illustrate the effects of the ert transformer consider the program in Fig. 1. It can be viewed as modeling a truncated geometric distribution: we repeatedly flip a fair coin until observing

$$
\begin{aligned}
C_{trunc}\colon\ & \texttt{if}\ \left(1/2\cdot\langle\mathsf{true}\rangle + 1/2\cdot\langle\mathsf{false}\rangle\right)\ \{succ := \mathsf{true}\}\ \texttt{else}\ \{\\
&\qquad \texttt{if}\ \left(1/2\cdot\langle\mathsf{true}\rangle + 1/2\cdot\langle\mathsf{false}\rangle\right)\ \{succ := \mathsf{true}\}\\
&\qquad \texttt{else}\ \{succ := \mathsf{false}\}\\
&\ \}
\end{aligned}
$$

Fig. 1. Program modeling a truncated geometric distribution

the first heads or completing the second unsuccessful trial. The calculation of the expected run–time $\mathsf{ert}\left[C_{trunc}\right](\mathbf{0})$ of program C_{trunc} goes as follows:

$$
\begin{aligned}
&\mathsf{ert}\left[C_{trunc}\right](\mathbf{0})\\
&\quad= \mathbf{1} + \tfrac{1}{2}\cdot \mathsf{ert}\left[succ := \mathsf{true}\right](\mathbf{0})\\
&\qquad\quad + \tfrac{1}{2}\cdot \mathsf{ert}\left[\texttt{if}\ (\ldots)\ \{succ := \mathsf{true}\}\ \texttt{else}\ \{succ := \mathsf{false}\}\right](\mathbf{0})\\
&\quad= \mathbf{1} + \tfrac{1}{2}\cdot \mathbf{1} + \tfrac{1}{2}\cdot\left(\mathbf{1} + \tfrac{1}{2}\cdot \mathsf{ert}\left[succ := \mathsf{true}\right](\mathbf{0}) + \tfrac{1}{2}\cdot \mathsf{ert}\left[succ := \mathsf{false}\right](\mathbf{0})\right)\\
&\quad= \mathbf{1} + \tfrac{1}{2}\cdot \mathbf{1} + \tfrac{1}{2}\cdot\left(\mathbf{1} + \tfrac{1}{2}\cdot \mathbf{1} + \tfrac{1}{2}\cdot \mathbf{1}\right) \;=\; \tfrac{\mathbf{5}}{\mathbf{2}}
\end{aligned}
$$

Therefore, the execution of C_{trunc} takes, on average, 2.5 units of time. △

Note that the calculation of the expected run–time in the above example is straightforward as the program at hand is loop–free. Computing the run–time of loops requires the calculation of least fixed points, which is generally not feasible in practice. In Sect. 5, we present invariant–based proof rules for reasoning about the run–time of loops.

The ert transformer enjoys several algebraic properties. To formally state these properties we make use of the point–wise order relation "$\preceq$" between run–times: given $f, g \in \mathbb{T}$, $f \preceq g$ iff $f(\sigma) \leq g(\sigma)$ for all states $\sigma \in \Sigma$.

Theorem 1 (Basic properties of the ert transformer). *For any program $C \in \mathsf{pProgs}$, any constant run–time $\mathbf{k} = \lambda\sigma.k$ for $k \in \mathbb{R}_{\geq 0}$, any constant $r \in \mathbb{R}_{\geq 0}$, and any two run–times $f, g \in \mathbb{T}$ the following properties hold:*

Monotonicity:	$f \preceq g \implies \mathsf{ert}\left[C\right](f) \preceq \mathsf{ert}\left[C\right](g)$;
Propagation of constants:	$\mathsf{ert}\left[C\right](\mathbf{k} + f) = \mathbf{k} + \mathsf{ert}\left[C\right](f)$ *provided C is* halt*–free*;
Preservation of ∞ :	$\mathsf{ert}\left[C\right](\infty) = \infty$ *provided C is* halt*–free*;
Sub–additivity:	$\mathsf{ert}\left[C\right](f + g) \preceq \mathsf{ert}\left[C\right](f) + \mathsf{ert}\left[C\right](g)$; *provided C is fully probabilistic*;[2]
Scaling:	$\mathsf{ert}\left[C\right](r\cdot f) \succeq \min\{1, r\}\cdot \mathsf{ert}\left[C\right](f)$; $\mathsf{ert}\left[C\right](r\cdot f) \preceq \max\{1, r\}\cdot \mathsf{ert}\left[C\right](f)$.

[2] A program is called *fully probabilistic* if it contains no non–deterministic choices.

Proof. Monotonicity follows from continuity (see Lemma 1 below). The remaining proofs proceed by induction on the program structure; see [17] for details. □

We conclude this section with a technical remark regarding the well–definedness of the ert transformer. To guarantee that ert is well–defined, we must show the existence of the least fixed points used to define the run–time of loops. To this end, we use a standard denotational semantics argument (see e.g. [26, Chap. 5]): First we endow the set of run–times $\mathbb{T}$ with the structure of an ω–complete partial order (ω–cpo) with bottom element. Then we use a continuity argument to conclude the existence of such fixed points.

Recall that $\preceq$ denotes the point–wise comparison between run–times. It easily follows that $(\mathbb{T}, \preceq)$ defines an ω–cpo with bottom element $\mathbf{0} = \lambda\sigma.0$ where the supremum of an ω–chain $f_1 \preceq f_2 \preceq \cdots$ in $\mathbb{T}$ is also given point–wise, i.e. as $\sup_n f_n \triangleq \lambda\sigma.\ \sup_n f_n(\sigma)$. Now we are in a position to establish the continuity of the ert transformer:

Lemma 1 (Continuity of the ert transformer). *For every program C and every ω–chain of run–times $f_1 \preceq f_2 \preceq \cdots$,*

$$\mathsf{ert}\,[C]\,(\sup_n f_n) \quad = \quad \sup_n \mathsf{ert}\,[C]\,(f_n)\,.$$

Proof. By induction on the program structure; see [17] for details. □

Lemma 1 implies that for each program $C \in \mathsf{pProgs}$, guard $\xi \in \mathsf{DExp}$, and run–time $f \in \mathbb{T}$, function $F_f(X) = \mathbf{1} + [\![\xi : \mathsf{false}]\!] \cdot f + [\![\xi : \mathsf{true}]\!] \cdot \mathsf{ert}\,[C]\,(X)$ is also continuous. The Kleene Fixed Point Theorem then ensures that the least fixed point $\mathsf{ert}\,[\texttt{while}\,(\xi)\,\{C\}]\,(f) = \mathsf{lfp}\,F_f$ exists and the expected run–time of loops is thus well-defined.

Finally, as the aforementioned function F_f is frequently used in the remainder of the paper, we define:

Definition 1 (Characteristic functional of a loop). *Given program $C \in \mathsf{pProgs}$, probabilistic guard $\xi \in \mathsf{DExp}$, and run–time $f \in \mathbb{T}$, we call*

$$F_f^{\langle \xi, C\rangle} \colon \mathbb{T} \to \mathbb{T},\ X \mapsto \mathbf{1} + [\![\xi \colon \mathsf{false}]\!] \cdot f + [\![\xi \colon \mathsf{true}]\!] \cdot \mathsf{ert}\,[C]\,(X)$$

the characteristic functional *of loop* $\texttt{while}\,(\xi)\,\{C\}$ *with respect to* f.

When C and ξ are understood from the context, we usually omit them and simply write F_f for the characteristic functional associated to $\texttt{while}\,(\xi)\,\{C\}$ with respect to run–time f. Observe that under this definition, the ert of loops can be recast as

$$\mathsf{ert}\,[\texttt{while}\,(\xi)\,\{C\}]\,(f) \quad = \quad \mathsf{lfp}\,F_f^{\langle \xi, C\rangle}\,.$$

This concludes our presentation of the ert transformer. In the next section we validate the transformer's definition by showing a soundness result with respect to an operational model of programs.

4 An Operational Model for Expected Run–Times

We prove the soundness of the expected run–time transformer with respect to a simple operational model for our probabilistic programs. This model will be given in terms of a Markov Decision Process (MDP, for short) whose collected reward corresponds to the run–time. We first briefly recall all necessary notions. A more detailed treatment can be found in [2, Chap. 10]. A *Markov Decision Process* is a tuple $\mathfrak{M} = (\mathcal{S},\, \mathit{Act},\, \mathbf{P},\, s_0,\, \mathit{rew})$ where $\mathcal{S}$ is a countable set of states, Act is a (finite) set of actions, $\mathbf{P}\colon \mathcal{S}\times \mathit{Act}\times\mathcal{S} \to [0,1]$ is the transition probability function such that for all states $s \in \mathcal{S}$ and actions $\alpha \in \mathit{Act}$,

$$\sum_{s'\in\mathcal{S}} \mathbf{P}(s,\alpha,s') \in \{0,1\}\ ,$$

$s_0 \in \mathcal{S}$ is the initial state, and $\mathit{rew}\colon \mathcal{S} \to \mathbb{R}_{\geq 0}$ is a reward function. Instead of $\mathbf{P}(s,\alpha,s') = p$, we usually write $s \xrightarrow{\alpha} s' \vdash p$. An MDP $\mathfrak{M}$ is a *Markov chain* if no non–deterministic choice is possible, i.e. for each pair of states $s, s' \in \mathcal{S}$ there exists exactly one $\alpha \in \mathit{Act}$ with $\mathbf{P}(s,\alpha,s') \neq 0$.

A *scheduler* for $\mathfrak{M}$ is a mapping $\mathfrak{S}\colon \mathcal{S}^+ \to \mathit{Act}$, where $\mathcal{S}^+$ denotes the set of non–empty finite sequences of states. Intuitively, a scheduler resolves the non–determinism of an MDP by selecting an action for each possible sequence of states that has been visited so far. Hence, a scheduler $\mathfrak{S}$ induces a Markov chain which is denoted by $\mathfrak{M}_{\mathfrak{S}}$. In order to define the expected reward of an MDP, we first consider the reward collected along a path. Let $\mathrm{Paths}^{\mathfrak{M}_{\mathfrak{S}}}$ ($\mathrm{Paths}^{\mathfrak{M}}_{\mathit{fin}}$) denote the set of all (finite) paths π ($\hat{\pi}$) in $\mathfrak{M}_{\mathfrak{S}}$. Analogously, let $\mathrm{Paths}^{\mathfrak{M}_{\mathfrak{S}}}(s)$ and $\mathrm{Paths}^{\mathfrak{M}_{\mathfrak{S}}}_{\mathit{fin}}(s)$ denote the set of all infinite and finite paths in $\mathfrak{M}_{\mathfrak{S}}$ starting in state $s \in \mathcal{S}$, respectively. For a finite path $\hat{\pi} = s_0 \ldots s_n$, the *cumulative reward* of $\hat{\pi}$ is defined as

$$\mathit{rew}(\hat{\pi}) \;\triangleq\; \sum_{k=0}^{n-1} \mathit{rew}(s_k).$$

For an infinite path π, the cumulative reward of reaching a non–empty set of target states $T \subseteq \mathcal{S}$, is defined as $\mathit{rew}(\pi, \Diamond T) \triangleq \mathit{rew}(\pi(0)\ldots\pi(n))$ if there exists an n such that $\pi(n) \in T$ and $\pi(i) \notin T$ for $0 \leq i < n$ and $\mathit{rew}(\pi, \Diamond T) \triangleq \infty$ otherwise. Moreover, we write $\Pi(s,T)$ to denote the set of all finite paths $\hat{\pi} \in \mathrm{Paths}^{\mathfrak{M}_{\mathfrak{S}}}_{\mathit{fin}}(s)$, $s \in \mathcal{S}$, with $\hat{\pi}(n) \in T$ for some $n \in \mathbb{N}$ and $\hat{\pi}(i) \notin T$ for $0 \leq i < n$. The probability of a finite path $\hat{\pi}$ is

$$\Pr^{\mathfrak{M}_{\mathfrak{S}}}\{\hat{\pi}\} \;\triangleq\; \prod_{k=0}^{|\hat{\pi}|-1} \mathbf{P}(s_k, \mathfrak{S}(s_1,\ldots,s_k), s_{k+1}).$$

The *expected reward* that an MDP $\mathfrak{M}$ eventually reaches a non–empty set of states $T \subseteq \mathcal{S}$ from a state $s \in \mathcal{S}$ is defined as follows. If

$$\inf_{\mathfrak{S}} \Pr^{\mathfrak{M}_{\mathfrak{S}}}\{s \models \Diamond T\} \;=\; \inf_{\mathfrak{S}} \sum_{\hat{\pi}\in\Pi(s,T)} \Pr^{\mathfrak{M}_{\mathfrak{S}}}\{\hat{\pi}\} \;<\; 1$$

$$\frac{}{\langle \downarrow,\, \sigma\rangle \xrightarrow{\tau} \langle\, \mathit{sink}\,\rangle \vdash 1}\ \text{[terminated]} \qquad \frac{}{\langle\, \mathit{sink}\,\rangle \xrightarrow{\tau} \langle\, \mathit{sink}\,\rangle \vdash 1}\ \text{[sink]}$$

$$\frac{}{\langle \texttt{empty},\, \sigma\rangle \xrightarrow{\tau} \langle \downarrow,\, \sigma\rangle \vdash 1}\ \text{[empty]} \qquad \frac{}{\langle \texttt{skip},\, \sigma\rangle \xrightarrow{\tau} \langle \downarrow,\, \sigma\rangle \vdash 1}\ \text{[skip]}$$

$$\frac{}{\langle \texttt{halt},\, \sigma\rangle \xrightarrow{\tau} \langle\, \mathit{sink}\,\rangle \vdash 1}\ \text{[halt]} \qquad \frac{[\![\mu\colon v]\!](\sigma) = p > 0}{\langle x :\approx \mu,\, \sigma\rangle \xrightarrow{\tau} \langle \downarrow,\, \sigma\,[x/v]\rangle \vdash p}\ \text{[pr–assgn]}$$

$$\frac{\langle C_1,\, \sigma\rangle \xrightarrow{\alpha} \langle C_1',\, \sigma'\rangle \vdash p,\ \alpha \in \mathit{Act} \quad 0 < p \leq 1}{\langle C_1; C_2,\, \sigma\rangle \xrightarrow{\alpha} \langle C_1'; C_2,\, \sigma'\rangle \vdash p}\ [\text{seq}_1] \qquad \frac{}{\langle \downarrow; C_2,\, \sigma\rangle \xrightarrow{\tau} \langle C_2,\, \sigma\rangle \vdash 1}\ [\text{seq}_2]$$

$$\frac{}{\langle \{C_1\} \,\square\, \{C_2\},\, \sigma\rangle \xrightarrow{L} \langle C_1,\, \sigma\rangle \vdash 1}\ [\square\text{–}L] \qquad \frac{}{\langle \{C_1\} \,\square\, \{C_2\},\, \sigma\rangle \xrightarrow{R} \langle C_2,\, \sigma\rangle \vdash 1}\ [\square\text{–}R]$$

$$\frac{[\![\xi\colon \mathsf{true}]\!](\sigma) = p > 0}{\langle \texttt{if}\ (\xi)\ \{C_1\}\ \texttt{else}\ \{C_2\},\, \sigma\rangle \xrightarrow{\tau} \langle C_1,\, \sigma\rangle \vdash p}\ \text{[if–true]}$$

$$\frac{[\![\xi\colon \mathsf{false}]\!](\sigma) = p > 0}{\langle \texttt{if}\ (\xi)\ \{C_1\}\ \texttt{else}\ \{C_2\},\, \sigma\rangle \xrightarrow{\tau} \langle C_2,\, \sigma\rangle \vdash p}\ \text{[if–false]}$$

$$\frac{}{\langle \texttt{while}\ (\xi)\ \{C\},\, \sigma\rangle \xrightarrow{\tau} \langle \texttt{if}\ (\xi)\ \{C; \texttt{while}\ (\xi)\ \{C\}\}\ \texttt{else}\ \{\texttt{empty}\},\, \sigma\rangle \vdash 1}\ \text{[while]}$$

Fig. 2. Rules for the transition probability function of operational MDPs.

then $\mathsf{ExpRew}^{\mathfrak{M}}(s \models \Diamond T) \triangleq \infty$. Otherwise,

$$\mathsf{ExpRew}^{\mathfrak{M}}(s \models \Diamond T) \ \triangleq\ \sup_{\mathfrak{S}} \sum_{\hat{\pi} \in \Pi(s,T)} \Pr^{\mathfrak{M}_{\mathfrak{S}}}\{\hat{\pi}\} \cdot \mathit{rew}(\hat{\pi}).$$

We are now in a position to define an operational model for our probabilistic programming language. Let $\downarrow$ denote a special symbol indicating successful termination of a program.

Definition 2 (The operational MDP of a program). *Given program* $C \in \mathsf{pProgs}$, *initial program state* $\sigma_0 \in \Sigma$, *and continuation* $f \in \mathbb{T}$, *the* operational MDP *of* C *is given by* $\mathfrak{M}^f_{\sigma_0}[\![C]\!] = (\mathcal{S},\, \mathit{Act},\, \mathbf{P},\, s_0,\, \mathit{rew})$, *where*

- $\mathcal{S} \triangleq ((\mathsf{pProgs} \cup \{\downarrow\} \cup \{\downarrow; C \mid C \in \mathsf{pProgs}\}) \times \Sigma) \cup \{\langle\, \mathit{sink}\,\rangle\}$,
- $\mathit{Act} \triangleq \{L,\, \tau,\, R\}$,
- *the transition probability function* $\mathbf{P}$ *is given by the rules in Fig. 2,*
- $s_0 \triangleq \langle C,\, \sigma_0\rangle$, *and*
- $\mathit{rew} : \mathcal{S} \to \mathbb{R}_{\geq 0}$ *is the reward function defined according to Table 2.*

Since the initial state of the MDP $\mathfrak{M}^f_{\sigma_0}[\![C]\!]$ of a program C with initial state σ_0 is uniquely given, instead of $\mathsf{ExpRew}^{\mathfrak{M}^f_{\sigma_0}[\![C]\!]}(\langle C,\, \sigma_0\rangle \models \Diamond T)$ we simply write

$$\mathsf{ExpRew}^{\mathfrak{M}^f_{\sigma}[\![C]\!]}(T)\,.$$

Table 2. Definition of the reward function $rew\colon \mathcal{S} \to \mathbb{R}_{\geq 0}$ of operational MDPs.

s	$rew(s)$
$\langle \downarrow, \sigma\rangle$	$f(\sigma)$
$\langle \texttt{skip}, \sigma\rangle$, $\langle x :\approx \mu, \sigma\rangle$, $\langle \texttt{if}\,(\xi)\,\{C_1\}\,\texttt{else}\,\{C_2\}, \sigma\rangle$	1
$\langle\, sink \rangle$, $\langle \texttt{empty}, \sigma\rangle$, $\langle \texttt{halt}, \sigma\rangle$, $\langle \downarrow ;\, C_2, \sigma\rangle$, $\langle \{C_1\} \,\Box\, \{C_2\}, \sigma\rangle$, $\langle \texttt{while}\,(\xi)\,\{C\}, \sigma\rangle$	0
$\langle C_1;\, C_2, \sigma\rangle$	$rew(\langle C_1, \sigma\rangle)$

The rules in Fig. 2 defining the transition probability function of a program's MDP are self–explanatory. Since only guard evaluations, assignments and `skip` statements are assumed to consume time, i.e. have a positive reward, we assign a reward of 0 to all other program statements. Moreover, note that all states of the form $\langle \texttt{empty}, \sigma\rangle$, $\langle \downarrow, \sigma\rangle$ and $\langle\, sink \rangle$ are needed, because an operational MDP is defined with respect to a given continuation $f \in \mathbb{T}$. In case of $\langle \texttt{empty}, \sigma\rangle$, a reward of 0 is collected and after that the program successfully terminates, i.e. enters state $\langle \downarrow, \sigma\rangle$ where the continuation f is collected as reward. In contrast, since no state other than $\langle\, sink \rangle$ is reachable from the unique sink state $\langle\, sink \rangle$, the continuation f is not taken into account if $\langle\, sink \rangle$ is reached without reaching a state $\langle \downarrow, \sigma\rangle$ first. Hence the operational MDP directly enters $\langle\, sink \rangle$ from a state of the form $\langle \texttt{halt}, \sigma\rangle$.

Example 3 (MDP of C_{trunc}). Recall the probabilistic program C_{trunc} from Example 2. Figure 3 depicts the MDP $\mathfrak{M}_\sigma^f[\![C_{trunc}]\!]$ for an arbitrary fixed state $\sigma \in \Sigma$ and an arbitrary continuation $f \in \mathbb{T}$. Here labeled edges denote the value of the transition probability function for the respective states, while the reward of each state is provided in gray next to the state. To improve readability, edge labels are omitted if the probability of a transition is 1. Moreover, $\mathfrak{M}_\sigma^f[\![C_{trunc}]\!]$ is a Markov chain, because C_{trunc} contains no non-deterministic choice.

A brief inspection of Fig. 3 reveals that $\mathfrak{M}_\sigma^f[\![C_{trunc}]\!]$ contains three finite paths $\hat{\pi}_{\mathsf{true}}$, $\hat{\pi}_{\mathsf{false\ true}}$, $\hat{\pi}_{\mathsf{false\ false}}$ that eventually reach state $\langle\, sink \rangle$ starting from the initial state $\langle C_{trunc}, \sigma\rangle$. These paths correspond to the results of the two probabilistic guards in C. Hence the expected reward of $\mathfrak{M}_\sigma^f[\![C]\!]$ to eventually reach $T = \{\langle\, sink \rangle\}$ is given by

$$
\begin{aligned}
&\mathsf{ExpRew}^{\mathfrak{M}_\sigma^f[\![C_{trunc}]\!]}(T) \\
&\quad= \sup\nolimits_{\mathfrak{S}} \textstyle\sum_{\hat{\pi} \in \Pi(s,T)} \Pr^{\mathfrak{M}_{\mathfrak{S}}}\{\hat{\pi}\} \cdot rew(\hat{\pi}) \\
&\quad= \textstyle\sum_{\hat{\pi} \in \Pi(s,T)} \Pr^{\mathfrak{M}}\{\hat{\pi}\} \cdot rew(\hat{\pi}) \qquad (\mathfrak{M}_\sigma^f[\![C_{trunc}]\!] = \mathfrak{M} \text{ is a Markov chain}) \\
&\quad= \Pr^{\mathfrak{M}}\{\hat{\pi}_{\mathsf{true}}\} \cdot rew(\hat{\pi}_{\mathsf{true}}) \;+\; \Pr^{\mathfrak{M}}\{\hat{\pi}_{\mathsf{false\ true}}\} \cdot rew(\hat{\pi}_{\mathsf{false\ true}}) \\
&\qquad + \Pr^{\mathfrak{M}}\{\hat{\pi}_{\mathsf{false\ false}}\} \cdot rew(\hat{\pi}_{\mathsf{false\ false}})
\end{aligned}
$$

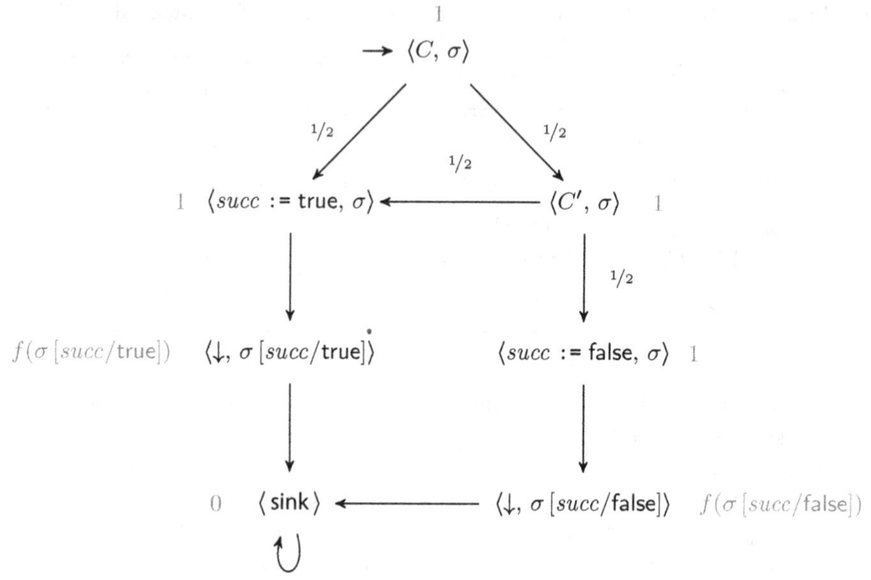

Fig. 3. The operational MDP $\mathfrak{M}_\sigma^f[\![C_{trunc}]\!]$ corresponding to the program in Example 3. C' denotes the subprogram $\texttt{if}\,(1/2\cdot\langle\mathsf{true}\rangle + 1/2\cdot\langle\mathsf{false}\rangle)\,\{succ := \mathsf{true}\}\,\texttt{else}\,\{succ := \mathsf{false}\}$.

$$
\begin{aligned}
&= \left(\tfrac{1}{2}\cdot 1\cdot 1\right)\cdot\left(1+1+f(\sigma\,[succ/\mathsf{true}])\right)\\
&\quad + \left(\tfrac{1}{2}\cdot\tfrac{1}{2}\cdot 1\cdot 1\right)\cdot\left(1+1+1+f(\sigma\,[succ/\mathsf{true}])\right)\\
&\quad + \left(\tfrac{1}{2}\cdot\tfrac{1}{2}\cdot 1\cdot 1\right)\cdot\left(1+1+1+f(\sigma\,[succ/\mathsf{false}])\right)\\
&= 1+\tfrac{1}{2}\cdot f(\sigma\,[succ/\mathsf{true}]) + \tfrac{1}{4}\cdot\left(6+f(\sigma\,[succ/\mathsf{true}])+f(\sigma\,[succ/\mathsf{false}])\right)\\
&= \tfrac{5}{2} + \tfrac{3}{4}\cdot f(\sigma\,[succ/\mathsf{true}]) + \tfrac{1}{4}\cdot f(\sigma\,[succ/\mathsf{false}]).
\end{aligned}
$$

Observe that for $f = \mathbf{0}$, the expected reward $\mathsf{ExpRew}^{\mathfrak{M}_\sigma^f[\![C_{trunc}]\!]}(T)$ and the expected run–time $\mathsf{ert}\,[C]\,(f)\,(\sigma)$ (cf. Example 2) coincide, both yielding $5/2$. △

The main result of this section is that ert precisely captures the expected reward of the MDPs associated to our probabilistic programs.

Theorem 2 (Soundness of the ert transformer). *Let* $\xi \in \mathsf{DExp}$, $C \in \mathsf{pProgs}$, *and* $f \in \mathbb{T}$. *Then, for each* $\sigma \in \Sigma$, *we have*

$$\mathsf{ExpRew}^{\mathfrak{M}_\sigma^f[\![C]\!]}(\langle\, sink \rangle) \;=\; \mathsf{ert}\,[C]\,(f)\,(\sigma)\;.$$

Proof. By induction on the program structure; see [17] for details. □

5 Expected Run–Time of Loops

Reasoning about the run–time of loop–free programs consists mostly of syntactic reasoning. The run–time of a loop, however, is given in terms of a least fixed point. It is thus obtained by fixed point iteration but need not be reached within a finite number of iterations. To overcome this problem we next study invariant–based proof rules for approximating the run–time of loops.

We present two families of proof rules which differ in the kind of the invariants they build on. In Sect. 5.1 we present a proof rule that rests on the presence of an invariant approximating the entire run–time of a loop in a global manner, while in Sect. 5.2 we present two proof rules that rely on a parametrized invariant that approximates the run–time of a loop in an incremental fashion. Finally in Sect. 5.3 we discuss how to improve the run–time bounds yielded by these proof rules.

5.1 Proof Rule Based on Global Invariants

The first proof rule that we study allows upper–bounding the expected run–time of loops and rests on the notion of *upper invariants.*

Definition 3 (Upper invariants). *Let $f \in \mathbb{T}$, $C \in \mathsf{pProgs}$ and $\xi \in \mathsf{DExp}$. We say that $I \in \mathbb{T}$ is an* upper invariant *of loop* $\mathtt{while}\,(\xi)\,\{C\}$ *with respect to f iff*

$$1 + [\![\xi : \mathsf{false}]\!] \cdot f + [\![\xi : \mathsf{true}]\!] \cdot \mathsf{ert}\,[C]\,(I) \;\preceq I$$

or, equivalently, iff $F_f^{\langle \xi, C\rangle}(I) \preceq I$, where $F_f^{\langle \xi, C\rangle}$ is the characteristic functional.

The presence of an upper invariant of a loop readily establishes an upper bound of the loop's run–time.

Theorem 3 (Upper bounds from upper invariants). *Let $f \in \mathbb{T}$, $C \in \mathsf{pProgs}$ and $\xi \in \mathsf{DExp}$. If $I \in \mathbb{T}$ is an upper invariant of* $\mathtt{while}\,(\xi)\,\{C\}$ *with respect to f then*

$$\mathsf{ert}\,[\mathtt{while}\,(\xi)\,\{C\}]\,(f) \;\preceq\; I.$$

Proof. The crux of the proof is an application of Park's Theorem[3] [25] which, given that $F_f^{\langle \xi, C\rangle}$ is continuous (see Lemma 1), states that

$$F_f^{\langle \xi, C\rangle}(I) \preceq I \implies \mathsf{lfp}\, F_f^{\langle \xi, C\rangle} \preceq I.$$

The left–hand side of the implication stands for I being an upper invariant, while the right–hand side stands for $\mathsf{ert}\,[\mathtt{while}\,(\xi)\,\{C\}]\,(f) \preceq I$. □

Notice that if the loop body C is itself loop–free, it is usually fairly easy to verify that some $I \in \mathbb{T}$ is an upper invariant, whereas *inferring* the invariant is—as in standard program verification—one of the most involved part of the verification effort.

[3] If $H : \mathcal{D} \to \mathcal{D}$ is a continuous function over an ω–cpo $(\mathcal{D}, \sqsubseteq)$ with bottom element, then $H(d) \sqsubseteq d$ implies $\mathsf{lfp}\, H \sqsubseteq d$ for every $d \in \mathcal{D}$.

Example 4 (Geometric distribution). Consider loop

$$C_{\mathsf{geo}}: \ \texttt{while}\,(c=1)\,\{c :\approx 1/2 \cdot \langle 0 \rangle + 1/2 \cdot \langle 1 \rangle\}\,.$$

From the calculations below we conclude that $I = \mathbf{1} + [\![c=1]\!] \cdot \mathbf{4}$ is an upper invariant with respect to $\mathbf{0}$:

$$\begin{aligned}
&\mathbf{1} + [\![c \neq 1]\!] \cdot \mathbf{0} + [\![c=1]\!] \cdot \mathsf{ert}\,[c :\approx 1/2 \cdot \langle 0 \rangle + 1/2 \cdot \langle 1 \rangle]\,(I) \\
&\quad = \mathbf{1} + [\![c=1]\!] \cdot \left(\mathbf{1} + \tfrac{1}{2} \cdot I\,[c/0] + \tfrac{1}{2} \cdot I\,[c/1]\right) \\
&\quad = \mathbf{1} + [\![c=1]\!] \cdot \big(\mathbf{1} + \tfrac{1}{2} \cdot \underbrace{(\mathbf{1} + [\![0=1]\!] \cdot \mathbf{4})}_{=\mathbf{1}} + \tfrac{1}{2} \cdot \underbrace{(\mathbf{1} + [\![1=1]\!] \cdot \mathbf{4})}_{=\mathbf{5}}\big) \\
&\quad = \mathbf{1} + [\![c=1]\!] \cdot \mathbf{4} \ = \ I \ \preceq \ I
\end{aligned}$$

Then applying Theorem 3 we obtain

$$\mathsf{ert}\left[C_{\mathsf{geo}}\right](\mathbf{0}) \ \preceq \ \mathbf{1} + [\![c=1]\!] \cdot \mathbf{4}.$$

In words, the expected run–time of C_{geo} is at most 5 from any initial state where $c = 1$ and at most 1 from the remaining states. △

The invariant–based technique to reason about the run–time of loops presented in Theorem 3 is complete in the sense that there always exists an upper invariant that establishes the exact run–time of the loop at hand.

Theorem 4. *Let* $f \in \mathbb{T}$, $C \in \mathsf{pProgs}$, $\xi \in \mathsf{DExp}$. *Then there exists an upper invariant* I *of* $\texttt{while}\ (\xi)\ \{C\}$ *with respect to* f *such that* $\mathsf{ert}\,[\texttt{while}\,(\xi)\,\{C\}]\,(f) = I$.

Proof. The result follows from showing that $\mathsf{ert}\,[\texttt{while}\,(\xi)\,\{C\}]\,(f)$ is itself an upper invariant. Since $\mathsf{ert}\,[\texttt{while}\,(\xi)\,\{C\}]\,(f) = \mathsf{lfp}\,F_f^{\langle \xi, C \rangle}$ this amounts to showing that

$$F_f^{\langle \xi, C \rangle}\left(\mathsf{lfp}\,F_f^{\langle \xi, C \rangle}\right) \ \preceq \ \mathsf{lfp}\,F_f^{\langle \xi, C \rangle}\,,$$

which holds by definition of lfp. □

Intuitively, the proof of this theorem shows that $\mathsf{ert}\,[\texttt{while}\,(\xi)\,\{C\}]\,(f)$ itself is the tightest upper invariant that the loop admits.

5.2 Proof Rules Based on Incremental Invariants

We now study a second family of proof rules which builds on the notion of ω–invariants to establish *both* upper and lower bounds for the run–time of loops.

Definition 4 (ω–invariants). *Let* $f \in \mathbb{T}$, $C \in \mathsf{pProgs}$ *and* $\xi \in \mathsf{DExp}$. *Moreover let* $I_n \in \mathbb{T}$ *be a run–time parametrized by* $n \in \mathbb{N}$. *We say that* I_n *is a* lower ω–invariant *of loop* $\texttt{while}\,(\xi)\,\{C\}$ *with respect to* f *iff*

$$F_f^{\langle \xi, C \rangle}(\mathbf{0}) \succeq I_0 \qquad \textit{and} \qquad F_f^{\langle \xi, C \rangle}(I_n) \succeq I_{n+1} \quad \textit{for all}\ n \geq 0.$$

Dually, we say that I_n *is an* upper ω–invariant *iff*

$$F_f^{\langle \xi, C \rangle}(\mathbf{0}) \preceq I_0 \qquad \textit{and} \qquad F_f^{\langle \xi, C \rangle}(I_n) \preceq I_{n+1} \quad \textit{for all}\ n \geq 0.$$

Intuitively, a lower (resp. upper) ω–invariant I_n represents a lower (resp. upper) bound for the expected run–time of those program runs that finish within $n+1$ iterations, weighted according to their probabilities. Therefore we can use the asymptotic behavior of I_n to approximate from below (resp. above) the expected run–time of the entire loop.

Theorem 5 (Bounds from) ω–invariants). *Let $f \in \mathbb{T}$, $C \in$ pProgs, $\xi \in$ DExp.*

1. *If I_n is a lower ω–invariant of* $\mathtt{while}\,(\xi)\,\{C\}$ *with respect to f and $\lim_{n\to\infty} I_n$ exists[4], then*
$$\mathsf{ert}\left[\mathtt{while}\,(\xi)\,\{C\}\right](f) \succeq \lim_{n\to\infty} I_n.$$
2. *If I_n is an upper ω–invariant of* $\mathtt{while}\,(\xi)\,\{C\}$ *with respect to f and $\lim_{n\to\infty} I_n$ exists, then*
$$\mathsf{ert}\left[\mathtt{while}\,(\xi)\,\{C\}\right](f) \preceq \lim_{n\to\infty} I_n.$$

Proof. We prove only the case of lower ω–invariants since the other case follows by a dual argument. Let F_f be the characteristic functional of the loop with respect to f. Let $F_f^0 = \mathbf{0}$ and $F_f^{n+1} = F_f(F_f^n)$. By the Kleene Fixed Point Theorem, $\mathsf{ert}\left[\mathtt{while}\,(\xi)\,\{C\}\right](f) = \sup_n F_f^n$ and since $F_f^0 \preceq F_f^1 \preceq \ldots$ forms an ω–chain, by the Monotone Sequence Theorem[5], $\sup_n F_f^n = \lim_{n\to\infty} F_f^n$. Then the proof follows from showing that $F_f^{n+1} \succeq I_n$. We prove this by induction on n. The base case $F_f^1 \succeq I_0$ holds because I_n is a lower ω–invariant. For the inductive case we reason as follows:
$$F_f^{n+2} = F_f\big(F_f^{n+1}\big) \succeq F_f(I_n) \succeq I_{n+1}.$$
Here the first inequality follows by I.H. and the monotonicity of F_f (recall that $\mathsf{ert}[C]$ is monotonic by Theorem 1), while the second inequality holds because I_n is a lower ω–invariant. □

Example 5 (Lower bounds for C_{geo}). Reconsider loop C_{geo} from Example 4. Now we use Theorem 5.1. to show that $\mathbf{1} + [\![c=1]\!] \cdot \mathbf{4}$ is also a lower bound of its run–time. To this end we first show that $I_n = \mathbf{1} + [\![c=1]\!] \cdot (\mathbf{4} - \mathbf{3/2^n})$ is a lower ω–invariant of the loop with respect to $\mathbf{0}$:

$$\begin{aligned} F_{\mathbf{0}}(\mathbf{0}) &= \mathbf{1} + [\![c \neq 1]\!] \cdot \mathbf{0} + [\![c=1]\!] \cdot \mathsf{ert}\left[c :\approx 1/2\langle 0\rangle + 1/2\langle 1\rangle\right](\mathbf{0}) \\ &= \mathbf{1} + [\![c=1]\!] \cdot \left(\mathbf{1} + \tfrac{1}{2}\cdot \mathbf{0}\,[c/0] + \tfrac{1}{2}\cdot \mathbf{0}\,[c/1]\right) \\ &= \mathbf{1} + [\![c=1]\!] \cdot \mathbf{1} \;=\; \mathbf{1} + [\![c=1]\!] \cdot (\mathbf{4} - \mathbf{3/2^0}) \;=\; I_0 \succeq I_0 \end{aligned}$$

$$\begin{aligned} F_{\mathbf{0}}(I_n) &= \mathbf{1} + [\![c \neq 1]\!] \cdot \mathbf{0} + [\![c=1]\!] \cdot \mathsf{ert}\left[c :\approx 1/2\langle 0\rangle + 1/2\langle 1\rangle\right](I_n) \\ &= \mathbf{1} + [\![c=1]\!] \cdot \left(\mathbf{1} + \tfrac{1}{2}\cdot I_n\,[c/0] + \tfrac{1}{2}\cdot I_n\,[c/1]\right) \end{aligned}$$

[4] Limit $\lim_{n\to\infty} I_n$ is to be understood pointwise, on $\mathbb{R}_{\geq 0}^{\infty}$, i.e. $\lim_{n\to\infty} I_n = \lambda\sigma. \lim_{n\to\infty} I_n(\sigma)$ and $\lim_{n\to\infty} I_n(\sigma) = \infty$ is considered a valid value.

[5] If $\langle a_n\rangle_{n\in\mathbb{N}}$ is an increasing sequence in $\mathbb{R}_{\geq 0}^{\infty}$, then $\lim_{n\to\infty} a_n$ coincides with supremum $\sup_n a_n$.

$$= \mathbf{1} + [\![c = 1]\!] \cdot \left(\mathbf{1} + \tfrac{1}{2} \cdot (\mathbf{1} + \mathbf{0}) + \tfrac{1}{2} \cdot (\mathbf{1} + (\mathbf{4} - \tfrac{\mathbf{3}}{\mathbf{2^n}}))\right)$$

$$= \mathbf{1} + [\![c = 1]\!] \cdot (\mathbf{4} - \tfrac{\mathbf{3}}{\mathbf{2^{n+1}}}) \;=\; I_{n+1} \;\succeq\; I_{n+1}$$

Then from Theorem 5.1 we obtain

$$\mathsf{ert}\left[C_{\mathsf{geo}}\right](\mathbf{0}) \;\succeq\; \lim_{n\to\infty} \left(\mathbf{1} + [\![c = 1]\!] \cdot (\mathbf{4} - \tfrac{\mathbf{3}}{\mathbf{2^n}})\right) \;=\; \mathbf{1} + [\![c = 1]\!] \cdot \mathbf{4}.$$

Combining this result with the upper bound $\mathsf{ert}\left[C_{\mathsf{geo}}\right](\mathbf{0}) \preceq \mathbf{1} + [\![c = 1]\!] \cdot \mathbf{4}$ established in Example 4 we conclude that $\mathbf{1} + [\![c = 1]\!] \cdot \mathbf{4}$ is the exact run–time of C_{geo}. Observe, however, that the above calculations show that I_n is both a lower and an upper ω–invariant (exact equalities $F_0(\mathbf{0}) = I_0$ and $F_0(I_n) = I_{n+1}$ hold). Then we can apply Theorem 5.1 and 5.2 simultaneously to derive the exact run–time without having to resort to the result from Example 4.

Invariant Synthesis. In order to synthesize invariant $I_n = \mathbf{1} + [\![c = 1]\!] \cdot (\mathbf{4} - \mathbf{3}/\mathbf{2^n})$, we proposed template $I_n = \mathbf{1} + [\![c = 1]\!] \cdot a_n$ and observed that under this template the definition of lower ω–invariant reduces to $a_0 \leq 1$, $a_{n+1} \leq 2 + \frac{1}{2} a_n$, which is satisfied by $a_n = 4 - 3/2^n$. △

Now we apply Theorem 5.1 to a program with infinite expected run–time.

Example 6 (Almost–sure termination at infinite expected run–time). Recall the program from the introduction:

```
C :  1:  x := 1; b := 1;
     2:  while (b = 1) {b :≈ 1/2⟨0⟩ + 1/2⟨1⟩; x := 2x};
     3:  while (x > 0) {x := x − 1}
```

Let C_i denote the i-th line of C. We show that $\mathsf{ert}[C](\mathbf{0}) \succeq \infty$.[6] Since

$$\mathsf{ert}[C](\mathbf{0}) \;=\; \mathsf{ert}[C_1](\mathsf{ert}[C_2](\mathsf{ert}[C_3](\mathbf{0})))$$

we start by showing that

$$\mathsf{ert}[C_3](\mathbf{0}) \;\succeq\; \mathbf{1} + [\![x > 0]\!] \cdot 2x$$

using lower ω–invariant $J_n = \mathbf{1} + [\![n > x > 0]\!] \cdot 2x + [\![x \geq n]\!] \cdot (2n - 1)$. We omit here the details of verifying that J_n is a lower ω–invariant. Next we show that

$$\begin{aligned}\mathsf{ert}[C_2](\mathbf{1} + [\![x > 0]\!] \cdot 2x) \;\succeq\; & \mathbf{1} + [\![b \neq 1]\!] \cdot (\mathbf{1} + [\![x > 0]\!] \cdot 2x) \\ & + [\![b = 1]\!] \cdot (\mathbf{7} + [\![x > 0]\!] \cdot \infty)\end{aligned}$$

by means of the lower ω–invariant

$$I_n \;=\; \mathbf{1} + [\![b \neq 1]\!] \cdot (\mathbf{1} + [\![x > 0]\!] \cdot 2x) + [\![b = 1]\!] \cdot \left(\mathbf{7} - \tfrac{\mathbf{5}}{\mathbf{2^n}} + n \cdot [\![x > 0]\!] \cdot 2x\right).$$

[6] Note that while this program terminates with probability one, the expected run–time to achieve termination is infinite.

Let F be the characteristic functional of loop C_2 with respect to $\mathbf{1} + [\![x > 0]\!] \cdot 2x$. The calculations to establish that I_n is a lower ω–invariant now go as follows:

$$\begin{aligned} F(\mathbf{0}) = {} & \mathbf{1} + [\![b \neq 1]\!] \cdot (\mathbf{1} + [\![x > 0]\!] \cdot 2x) \\ & + [\![b = 1]\!] \cdot \Big(\mathbf{1} + \tfrac{1}{2} \cdot (\mathbf{1} + \mathbf{0}\,[x, b/2x, 0]) + \tfrac{1}{2} \cdot (\mathbf{1} + \mathbf{0}\,[x, b/2x, 1])\Big) \\ = {} & \mathbf{1} + [\![b \neq 1]\!] \cdot (\mathbf{1} + [\![x > 0]\!] \cdot 2x) + [\![b = 1]\!] \cdot \big(\mathbf{1} + \tfrac{1}{2} \cdot \mathbf{1} + \tfrac{1}{2} \cdot \mathbf{1}\big) \\ = {} & \mathbf{1} + [\![b \neq 1]\!] \cdot (\mathbf{1} + [\![x > 0]\!] \cdot 2x) + [\![b = 1]\!] \cdot \mathbf{2} = I_0 \succeq I_0 \end{aligned}$$

$$\begin{aligned} F(I_n) = {} & \mathbf{1} + [\![b \neq 1]\!] \cdot (\mathbf{1} + [\![x > 0]\!] \cdot 2x) \\ & + [\![b = 1]\!] \cdot \Big(\mathbf{1} + \tfrac{1}{2} \cdot (\mathbf{1} + I_n\,[x, b/2x, 0]) + \tfrac{1}{2} \cdot (\mathbf{1} + I_n\,[x, b/2x, 1])\Big) \\ = {} & \mathbf{1} + [\![b \neq 1]\!] \cdot (\mathbf{1} + [\![x > 0]\!] \cdot 2x) \\ & + [\![b = 1]\!] \cdot \Big(\mathbf{1} + \tfrac{1}{2} \cdot (\mathbf{3} + [\![2x > 0]\!] \cdot 4x) + \tfrac{1}{2} \cdot \Big(\mathbf{9} - \tfrac{\mathbf{5}}{\mathbf{2^n}} + n \cdot [\![2x > 0]\!] \cdot 4x\Big)\Big) \\ = {} & \mathbf{1} + [\![b \neq 1]\!] \cdot (\mathbf{1} + [\![x > 0]\!] \cdot 2x) \\ & + [\![b = 1]\!] \cdot \Big(\mathbf{7} - \tfrac{\mathbf{5}}{\mathbf{2^{n+1}}} + (n{+}1) \cdot [\![x > 0]\!] \cdot 2x\Big) \\ = {} & I_{n+1} \succeq I_{n+1} \end{aligned}$$

Now we can complete the run–time analysis of program C:

$$\begin{aligned} & \mathsf{ert}\,[C]\,(\mathbf{0}) \\ & \quad = \mathsf{ert}\,[C_1]\,(\mathsf{ert}\,[C_2]\,(\mathsf{ert}\,[C_3]\,(\mathbf{0}))) \\ & \quad \succeq \mathsf{ert}\,[C_1]\,\big(\mathbf{1} + [\![b \neq 1]\!] \cdot (\mathbf{1} + [\![x > 0]\!] \cdot 2x) + [\![b = 1]\!] \cdot (\mathbf{7} + [\![x > 0]\!] \cdot \boldsymbol{\infty})\big) \\ & \quad = \mathsf{ert}[x \mathrel{:=} 1]\Big(\mathsf{ert}[b \mathrel{:=} 1]\Big(\mathbf{1} + [\![b \neq 1]\!] \cdot (\mathbf{1} + [\![x > 0]\!] \cdot 2x) \\ & \qquad\qquad + [\![b = 1]\!] \cdot (\mathbf{7} + [\![x > 0]\!] \cdot \boldsymbol{\infty})\Big)\Big) \\ & \quad = \mathsf{ert}\,[x \mathrel{:=} 1]\,(\mathbf{8} + [\![x > 0]\!] \cdot \boldsymbol{\infty}) = \mathbf{8} + \boldsymbol{\infty} = \boldsymbol{\infty} \end{aligned}$$

Overall, we obtain that the expected run–time of the program C is infinite even though it terminates with probability one. Notice furthermore that sub–programs `while` $(b = 1)\ \{b :\approx {}^1\!/\!_2\langle 0\rangle + {}^1\!/\!_2\langle 1\rangle\,;\ x \mathrel{:=} 2x\}$ and `while` $(x > 0)\ \{x \mathrel{:=} x - 1\}$ have expected run–time $\mathbf{1} + [\![b]\!] \cdot \mathbf{4}$ and $\mathbf{1} + [\![x > 0]\!] \cdot 2x$, respectively, i.e. both have a finite expected run–time.

Invariant synthesis. In order to synthesize the ω–invariant I_n of loop C_2 we propose the template $I_n = \mathbf{1} + [\![b \neq 1]\!] \cdot \big(\mathbf{1} + [\![x > 0]\!] \cdot 2x\big) + [\![b = 1]\!] \cdot \big(a_n + b_n \cdot [\![x > 0]\!] \cdot 2x\big)$ and from the definition of lower ω–invariants we obtain $a_0 \leq 2$, $a_{n+1} \leq {}^7\!/\!_2 + {}^1\!/\!_2 \cdot a_n$ and $b_0 \leq 0$, $b_{n+1} \leq 1 + b_n$. These recurrences admit solutions $a_n = 7 - {}^5\!/\!_{2^n}$ and $b_n = n$. △

As the proof rule based on upper invariants, the proof rules based on ω-invariants are also complete: Given loop `while` $(\xi)\ \{C\}$ and run–time f, it is enough to consider the ω-invariant $I_n = F_f^{n+1}$, where F_f^n is defined as in the proof of

Theorem 5 to yield the exact run–time $\mathsf{ert}\,[\mathtt{while}\,(\xi)\,\{C\}]\,(f)$ from an application of Theorem 5. We formally capture this result by means of the following theorem:

Theorem 6. *Let $f \in \mathbb{T}$, $C \in \mathsf{pProgs}$ and $\xi \in \mathsf{DExp}$. Then there exists a (both lower and upper) ω–invariant I_n of $\mathtt{while}\,(\xi)\,\{C\}$ with respect to f such that $\mathsf{ert}\,[\mathtt{while}\,(\xi)\,\{C\}]\,(f) = \lim_{n\to\infty} I_n$.*

Theorem 6 together with Theorem 4 shows that the set of invariant–based proof rules presented in this section are complete. Next we study how to refine invariants to make the bounds that these proof rules yield more precise.

5.3 Refinement of Bounds

An important property of both upper and lower bounds of the run–time of loops is that they can be easily refined by repeated application of the characteristic functional.

Theorem 7 (Refinement of bounds). *Let $f \in \mathbb{T}$, $C \in \mathsf{pProgs}$ and $\xi \in \mathsf{DExp}$. If I is an upper (resp. lower) bound of $\mathsf{ert}\,[\mathtt{while}\,(\xi)\,\{C\}]\,(f)$ and $F_f^{\langle \xi, C\rangle}(I) \preceq I$ (resp. $F_f^{\langle \xi, C\rangle}(I) \succeq I$), then $F_f^{\langle \xi, C\rangle}(I)$ is also an upper (resp. lower) bound, at least as precise as I.*

Proof. If I is an upper bound of $\mathsf{ert}\,[\mathtt{while}\,(\xi)\,\{C\}]\,(f)$ we have $\mathsf{lfp}\, F_f^{\langle \xi, C\rangle} \preceq I$. Then from the monotonicity of $F_f^{\langle \xi, C\rangle}$ (recall that ert is monotonic by Theorem 1) and from $F_f^{\langle \xi, C\rangle}(I) \preceq I$ we obtain

$$\mathsf{ert}\,[\mathtt{while}\,(\xi)\,\{C\}]\,(f) \;=\; \mathsf{lfp}\, F_f^{\langle \xi, C\rangle} \;=\; F_f^{\langle \xi, C\rangle}(\mathsf{lfp}\, F_f^{\langle \xi, C\rangle}) \;\preceq\; F_f^{\langle \xi, C\rangle}(I) \;\preceq\; I,$$

which means that $F_f^{\langle \xi, C\rangle}(I)$ is also an upper bound, possibly tighter than I. The case for lower bounds is completely analogous. □

Notice that if I is an upper invariant of $\mathtt{while}\,(\xi)\,\{C\}$ then I fulfills all necessary conditions of Theorem 7. In practice, Theorem 7 provides a means of iteratively improving the precision of bounds yielded by Theorems 3 and 5, as for instance for upper bounds we have

$$\mathsf{ert}\,[\mathtt{while}\,(\xi)\,\{C\}]\,(f) \;\preceq\; \cdots \;\preceq\; F_f^{\langle \xi, C\rangle}\left(F_f^{\langle \xi, C\rangle}(I)\right) \;\preceq\; F_f^{\langle \xi, C\rangle}(I) \;\preceq I.$$

If I_n is an upper (resp. lower) ω-invariant, applying Theorem 7 requires checking that $F_f^{\langle \xi, C\rangle}(L) \preceq L$ (resp. $F_f^{\langle \xi, C\rangle}(L) \succeq L$), where $L = \lim_{n\to\infty} I_n$. This proof obligation can be discharged by showing that I_n forms an ω-chain, i.e. that $I_n \preceq I_{n+1}$ for all $n \in \mathbb{N}$.

6 Run–Time of Deterministic Programs

The notion of expected run–times as defined by ert is clearly applicable to deterministic programs, i.e. programs containing neither probabilistic guards nor probabilistic assignments nor non–deterministic choice operators. We show that the ert of deterministic programs coincides with the tightest upper bound on the run–time that can be derived in an extension of Hoare logic [14] due to Nielson [23,24].

In order to compare our notion of ert to the aforementioned calculus we restrict our programming language to the language dProgs of deterministic programs considered in [24] which is given by the following grammar:

$$C \quad ::= \quad \texttt{skip} \mid x := E \mid C; C \mid \texttt{if}\,(\xi)\,\{C\}\,\texttt{else}\,\{C\} \mid \texttt{while}\,(\xi)\,\{C\}\ ,$$

where E is a *deterministic* expression and ξ is a *deterministic* guard, i.e. $[\![E]\!](\sigma)$ and $[\![\xi]\!](\sigma)$ are Dirac distributions for each $\sigma \in \Sigma$. For simplicity, we slightly abuse notation and write $[\![E]\!](\sigma)$ to denote the unique value $v \in \mathsf{Val}$ such that $[\![E\colon v]\!](\sigma) = 1$.

For deterministic programs, the MDP $\mathfrak{M}^{\mathbf{0}}_{\sigma}[\![C]\!]$ of a program $C \in \mathsf{dProgs}$ and a program state $\sigma \in \Sigma$ is a labeled transition system. In particular, if a terminal state of the form $\langle\downarrow, \sigma'\rangle$ is reachable from the initial state of $\mathfrak{M}^{\mathbf{0}}_{\sigma}[\![C]\!]$, it is unique. Hence we may capture the effect of a deterministic program by a partial function $\mathbb{C}[\![\,\cdot\,]\!](\,\cdot\,) : \mathsf{dProgs} \times \Sigma \rightharpoonup \Sigma$ mapping each $C \in \mathsf{dProgs}$ and $\sigma \in \Sigma$ to a program state $\sigma' \in \Sigma$ if and only if there exists a state $\langle\downarrow, \sigma'\rangle$ that is reachable in the MDP $\mathfrak{M}^{\mathbf{0}}_{\sigma}[\![C]\!]$ from the initial state $\langle C, \sigma\rangle$. Otherwise, $\mathbb{C}[\![C]\!](\sigma)$ is undefined.

Nielson [23,24] developed an extension of the classical Hoare calculus for total correctness of programs in order to establish additionally upper bounds on the run–time of programs. Formally, a *correctness property* is of the form

$$\{\, P \,\}\; C \;\{\, E \Downarrow Q \,\}\ ,$$

where $C \in \mathsf{dProgs}$, E is a deterministic expression over the program variables, and P, Q are (first–order) assertions. Intuitively, $\{\, P \,\}\; C \;\{\, E \Downarrow Q \,\}$ is valid, written $\models_E \{\, P \,\}\; C \;\{\, E \Downarrow Q \,\}$, if and only if there exists a natural number k such that for each state σ satisfying the precondition P, the program C terminates after at most $k \cdot [\![E]\!](\sigma)$ steps in a state satisfying postcondition Q. In particular, it should be noted that E is evaluated in the *initial* state σ.

Figure 4 is taken verbatim from [24] except for minor changes to match our notation. Most of the inference rules are self–explanatory extensions of the standard Hoare calculus for total correctness of deterministic programs [14] which is obtained by omitting the gray parts.

The run–time of skip and $x := E$ is one time unit. Since guard evaluations are assumed to consume no time in this calculus, any upper bound on the run–time of both branches of a conditional is also an upper bound on the run–time of the conditional itself (cf. rule [if]). The rule of consequence allows to increase an already proven upper bound on the run–time by an arbitrary constant factor. Furthermore, the run–time of two sequentially composed programs C_1 and C_2

$$\frac{}{\{\, P \,\}\ \texttt{skip}\ \{\, 1 \Downarrow P \,\}}\ [\text{skip}] \qquad \frac{}{\{\, Q\,[x/\llbracket E \rrbracket] \,\}\ x \texttt{ := } E\ \{\, 1 \Downarrow Q \,\}}\ [\text{assgn}]$$

$$\frac{\{\, P \wedge E_2' = u \,\}\ C_1\ \{\, E_1 \Downarrow Q \wedge E_2 \le u \,\} \quad \{\, Q \,\}\ C_2\ \{\, E_2 \Downarrow R \,\}}{\{\, P \,\}\ C_1; C_2\ \{\, E_1 + E_2' \Downarrow R \,\}}\ [\text{seq}]$$

where u is a fresh logical variable

$$\frac{\{\, P \wedge \xi \,\}\ C_1\ \{\, E \Downarrow Q \,\} \quad \{\, P \wedge \neg\xi \,\}\ C_2\ \{\, E \Downarrow Q \,\}}{\{\, P \,\}\ \texttt{if}\ (\xi)\ \{C_1\}\ \texttt{else}\ \{C_2\}\ \{\, E \Downarrow Q \,\}}\ [\text{if}]$$

$$\frac{\{\, P(z+1) \wedge E' = u \,\}\ C\ \{\, E_1 \Downarrow P(z)\ \wedge\ E \le u \,\}}{\{\, \exists z \text{.}\ P(z) \,\}\ \texttt{while}\ (\xi)\ \{C\}\ \{\, E \Downarrow P(0) \,\}}\ [\text{while}]$$

where $z \in \mathbb{N}$, $P(z+1) \Rightarrow \xi\ \wedge\ E \ge E_1 + E'$, $P(0) \Rightarrow \neg\xi\ \wedge\ E \ge 1$ and u is a fresh logical variable

$$\frac{\{\, P' \,\}\ C\ \{\, E' \Downarrow Q' \,\}}{\{\, P \,\}\ C\ \{\, E \Downarrow Q \,\}}\ [\text{cons}]$$

where $P \Rightarrow P'\ \wedge\ E' \le k \cdot E$ for some $k \in \mathbb{N}$ and $Q' \Rightarrow Q$

Fig. 4. Inference system for order of magnitude of run–time of deterministic programs according to Nielson [23].

is, intuitively, the sum of their run–times E_1 and E_2. However, run–times are expressions which are evaluated in the initial state. Thus, the run–time of C_2 has to be expressed in the initial state of $C_1; C_2$. Technically, this is achieved by adding a fresh (and hence universally quantified) variable u that is an upper bound on E_2 and at the same time is equal to a new expression E_2' in the precondition of $C_1; C_2$. Then, the run–time of $C_1; C_2$ is given by the sum $E_1 + E_2'$.

The same principle is applied to each loop iteration. Here, the run–time of the loop body is given by E_1 and the run–time of the remaining z loop iterations, E', is expressed in the initial state by adding a fresh variable u. Then, any upper bound of $E \ge E_1 + E'$ is an upper bound on the run–time of z loop iterations.

We denote provability of a correctness property $\{\, P \,\}\ C\ \{\, E \Downarrow Q \,\}$ and a total correctness property $\{\, P \,\}\ C\ \{\, \Downarrow Q \,\}$ in the standard Hoare calculus by $\vdash_E \{\, P \,\}\ C\ \{\, E \Downarrow Q \,\}$ and $\vdash \{\, P \,\}\ C\ \{\, \Downarrow Q \,\}$, respectively.

Theorem 8 (Soundness of ert for deterministic programs). *For all $C \in$ dProgs and assertions P, Q, we have*

$$\vdash \{\, P \,\}\ C\ \{\, \Downarrow Q \,\}\ \textit{implies}\ \vdash_E \{\, P \,\}\ C\ \{\, \mathsf{ert}\,[C]\,(\mathbf{0}) \Downarrow Q \,\}.$$

Proof. By induction on the program structure; see [17] for details.

Intuitively, this theorem means that for every terminating deterministic program, the ert is an upper bound on the run–time, i.e. ert is sound with respect to the inference system shown in Fig. 4. The next theorem states that no tighter bound can be derived in this calculus. We cannot get a more precise relationship, since we assume guard evaluations to consume time.

Theorem 9 (Completeness of ert w.r.t. Nielson). *For all $C \in dProgs$, assertions P, Q and deterministic expressions E, $\vdash_E \{ P \} \; C \; \{ E \Downarrow Q \}$ implies that there exists a natural number k such that for all $\sigma \in \Sigma$ satisfying P, we have*

$$\mathsf{ert}\,[C]\,(\mathbf{0})\,(\sigma) \;\leq\; k \cdot (\llbracket E \rrbracket(\sigma)) \; .$$

Proof. By induction on the program structure; see [17] for details. □

Theorem 8 together with Theorem 9 shows that our notion of ert is a conservative extension of Nielson's approach for reasoning about the run–time of deterministic programs. In particular, given a correctness proof of a deterministic program C in Hoare logic, it suffices to compute $\mathsf{ert}\,[C]\,(\mathbf{0})$ in order to obtain a corresponding proof in Nielson's proof system.

7 Case Studies

In this section we use our ert–calculus to analyze the run–time of two well–known randomized algorithms: the *One–Dimensional (Symmetric) Random Walk* and the *Coupon Collector Problem.*

7.1 One–Dimensional Random Walk

Consider program

$$P_{rw}: \;\; x := 10;\; \mathtt{while}\,(x > 0)\,\{x :\approx 1/2 \cdot \langle x{-}1\rangle + 1/2 \cdot \langle x{+}1\rangle\} \; ,$$

which models a one–dimensional walk of a particle which starts at position $x = 10$ and moves with equal probability to the left or to the right in each turn. The random walk stops if the particle reaches position $x = 0$. It can be shown that the program terminates with probability one [15] but requires, on average, an infinite time to do so. We now apply our ert–calculus to formally derive this run–time assertion.

The expected run–time of P_{rw} is given by

$$\mathsf{ert}\,[P_{rw}]\,(\mathbf{0}) \;=\; \mathsf{ert}\,[x := 10]\,(\mathsf{ert}\,[\mathtt{while}\,(x > 0)\,\{C\}]\,(\mathbf{0})) \; ,$$

where C stands for the probabilistic assignment in the loop body. Thus, we need to first determine run–time $\mathsf{ert}\,[\mathtt{while}\,(x > 0)\,\{C\}]\,(\mathbf{0})$. To do so we propose

$$I_n \;=\; \mathbf{1} + \llbracket 0 < x \leq n \rrbracket \cdot \infty$$

as a lower ω–invariant of loop $\mathtt{while}\;(x > 0)\,\{C\}$ with respect to $\mathbf{0}$; detailed calculations for verifying that I_n is indeed a lower ω–invariant can be found in the extended version of the paper [17]. Theorem 5 then states that

$$\mathsf{ert}\,[\mathtt{while}\,(x > 0)\,\{C\}]\,(\mathbf{0}) \succeq \lim_{n\to\infty} \mathbf{1} + \llbracket 0 < x \leq n \rrbracket \cdot \infty = \mathbf{1} + \llbracket 0 < x \rrbracket \cdot \infty.$$

Altogether we have

$$\begin{aligned}\mathsf{ert}\left[P_{rw}\right](\mathbf{0}) &= \mathsf{ert}\left[x := 10\right]\left(\mathsf{ert}\left[\mathtt{while}\,(x > 0)\,\{C\}\right](\mathbf{0})\right)\\ &\succeq \mathsf{ert}\left[x := 10\right]\left(\mathbf{1} + [\![0 < x]\!] \cdot \infty\right)\\ &= \mathbf{1} + \left(\mathbf{1} + [\![0 < x]\!] \cdot \infty\right)[x/10]\\ &= \mathbf{1} + (\mathbf{1} + 1 \cdot \infty) \;=\; \infty,\end{aligned}$$

which says that $\mathsf{ert}\left[P_{rw}\right](\mathbf{0}) \succeq \infty$. Since the reverse inequality holds trivially, we conclude that $\mathsf{ert}\left[P_{rw}\right](\mathbf{0}) = \infty$.

7.2 The Coupon Collector Problem

Now we apply our ert–calculus to solve the Coupon Collector Problem. This problem arises from the following scenario[7]: Suppose each box of cereal contains one of N different coupons and once a consumer has collected a coupon of each type, he can trade them for a prize. The aim of the problem is determining the average number of cereal boxes the consumer should buy to collect all coupon types, assuming that each coupon type occurs with the same probability in the cereal boxes.

The problem can be modeled by program C_{cp} below:

```
cp := [0, ..., 0]; i := 1; x := N
while (x > 0) {
    while (cp[i] ≠ 0) {
        i :≈ Unif[1...N]
    };
    cp[i] := 1; x := x − 1
}
```

Array cp is initialized to 0 and whenever we obtain the first coupon of type i, we set $cp[i]$ to 1. The outer loop is iterated N times and in each iteration we collect a new—unseen—coupon type. The collection of the new coupon type is performed by the inner loop.

We start the run–time analysis of C_{cp} introducing some notation. Let C_{in} and C_{out}, respectively, denote the inner and the outer loop of C_{cp}. Furthermore, let $\#col \triangleq \sum_{i=1}^{N} [cp[i] \neq 0]$ denote the number of coupons that have already been collected.

Analysis of the inner loop. For analyzing the run–time of the outer loop we need to refer to the run–time of its body, with respect to an arbitrary continuation $g \in \mathbb{T}$. Therefore, we first analyze the run–time of the inner loop C_{in}. We propose

[7] The problem formulation presented here is taken from [20].

the following lower and upper ω–invariant for the inner loop C_{in}:

$$J^g_{\mathrm{n}} = \mathbf{1} + [cp[i] = 0] \cdot g + [cp[i] \neq 0] \cdot \sum_{k=0}^{n} \left(\frac{\#col}{N}\right)^k \left(\mathbf{2} + \frac{1}{N} \sum_{j=1}^{N} [\![cp[j] = 0]\!] \cdot g[i/j]\right).$$

Moreover, we write J^g for the same invariant where n is replaced by ∞. A detailed verification that J^g_{n} is indeed a lower and upper ω–invariant is provided in the extended version of the paper [17]. Theorem 5 now yields

$$J^g = \lim_{n\to\infty} J^g_{\mathrm{n}} \preceq \mathsf{ert}\,[C_{\mathrm{in}}]\,(g) \preceq \lim_{n\to\infty} J^g_{\mathrm{n}} = J^g. \qquad (\star)$$

Since the run–time of a deterministic assignment $x := E$ is

$$\mathsf{ert}\,[x := E]\,(f) = \mathbf{1} + f\,[x/E]\,, \qquad (✠)$$

the expected run–time of the body of the outer loop reduces to

$$\begin{aligned} &\mathsf{ert}\,[C_{\mathrm{in}}\,;\; cp[i] := 1;\; x := x-1]\,(g) && (\dagger)\\ &= \mathbf{2} + \mathsf{ert}\,[C_{\mathrm{in}}]\,(g[x/x-1,\; cp[i]/1]) && (\text{by } ✠)\\ &= \mathbf{2} + J^{g[x/x-1,\, cp[i]/1]} && (\text{by } \star)\\ &= \mathbf{2} + J^{g}[x/x-1,\; cp[i]/1]. \end{aligned}$$

Analysis of the outer loop. Since program C_{cp} terminates right after the execution of the outer loop C_{out}, we analyze the run–time of the outer loop C_{out} with respect to continuation $\mathbf{0}$, i.e. $\mathsf{ert}\,[C_{out}]\,(\mathbf{0})$. To this end we propose

$$I_n = \mathbf{1} + \sum_{\ell=0}^{n} [x > \ell] \cdot \left(\mathbf{3} + [n \neq 0] + 2 \cdot \sum_{k=0}^{\infty} \left(\frac{\#col + \ell}{N}\right)^k\right) - 2 \cdot [cp[i] = 0] \cdot [x > 0] \cdot \sum_{k=0}^{\infty} \left(\frac{\#col}{N}\right)^k$$

as both an upper and lower ω–invariant of C_{out} with respect to $\mathbf{0}$. A detailed verification that I_n is an ω-invariant is found in the extended version of the paper [17]. Now Theorem 5 yields

$$I = \lim_{n\to\infty} I_n \preceq \mathsf{ert}\,[C_{\mathrm{out}}]\,(\mathbf{0}) \preceq \lim_{n\to\infty} I_n = I, \qquad (\ddagger)$$

where I denotes the same invariant as I_n with n replaced by ∞.

Analysis of the overall program. To obtain the overall expected run–time of program C_{cp} we have to account for the initialization instructions before the outer loop. The calculations go as follows:

$$
\begin{aligned}
&\mathsf{ert}\,[C_{cp}]\,(\mathbf{0}) \\
&\quad = \mathsf{ert}\,[cp := [0,\dots,0]\,;\, i := 1\,;\, x := N\,;\, C_{\text{out}}]\,(\mathbf{0}) \\
&\quad = \mathbf{3} + \mathsf{ert}\,[C_{\text{out}}]\,(\mathbf{0})\,[x/N, i/1, cp[1]/0,\dots,cp[N]/0] && \text{(by ✠)} \\
&\quad = \mathbf{3} + I[x/N, i/1, cp[1]/0,\dots,cp[N]/0] && \text{(by ‡)} \\
&\quad = \mathbf{4} + [N > 0] \cdot \left(4N + 2\sum_{\ell=1}^{N-1}\left(\sum_{k=0}^{\infty}\left(\tfrac{\ell}{N}\right)^k\right)\right) \\
&\quad = \mathbf{4} + [N > 0] \cdot \left(4N + 2\sum_{\ell=1}^{N-1}\tfrac{N}{\ell}\right) && \left(\begin{array}{l}\text{geom. series and}\\ \text{sum reordering}\end{array}\right) \\
&\quad = \mathbf{4} + [N > 0] \cdot 2N \cdot (\mathbf{2} + \mathcal{H}_{N-1}),
\end{aligned}
$$

where $\mathcal{H}_{N-1} \triangleq 0 + 1/1 + 1/2 + 1/3 + \cdots + 1/N-1$ denotes the $(N-1)$-th harmonic number. Since the harmonic numbers approach asymptotically to the natural logarithm, we conclude that the coupon collector algorithm C_{cp} runs in expected time $\Theta(N \cdot \log(N))$.

8 Conclusion

We have studied a wp–style calculus for reasoning about the expected run–time and positive almost–sure termination of probabilistic programs. Our main contribution consists of several sound and complete proof rules for obtaining upper as well as lower bounds on the expected run–time of loops. We applied these rules to analyze the expected run–time of a variety of example programs including the well-known coupon collector problem. While finding invariants is, in general, a challenging task, we were able to guess correct invariants by considering a few loop unrollings most of the time. Hence, we believe that our proof rules are natural and widely applicable.

Moreover, we proved that our approach is a conservative extension of Nielson's approach for reasoning about the run–time of deterministic programs and that our calculus is sound with respect to a simple operational model.

Acknowledgement. We thank Gilles Barthe for bringing to our attention the coupon collector problem as a particularly intricate case study for formal verification of expected run–times and Thomas Noll for bringing to our attention Nielson's Hoare logic.

References

1. Arthan, R., Martin, U., Mathiesen, E.A., Oliva, P.: A general framework for sound and complete Floyd-Hoare logics. ACM Trans. Comput. Log. **11**(1), 7 (2009)
2. Baier, C., Katoen, J.: Principles of Model Checking. MIT Press, Cambridge (2008)
3. Berghammer, R., Müller-Olm, M.: Formal development and verification of approximation algorithms using auxiliary variables. In: Bruynooghe, M. (ed.) LOPSTR 2004. LNCS, vol. 3018, pp. 59–74. Springer, Heidelberg (2004)
4. Brázdil, T., Kiefer, S., Kucera, A., Vareková, I.H.: Runtime analysis of probabilistic programs with unbounded recursion. J. Comput. Syst. Sci. **81**(1), 288–310 (2015)

5. Celiku, O., McIver, A.K.: Compositional specification and analysis of cost-based properties in probabilistic programs. In: Fitzgerald, J.S., Hayes, I.J., Tarlecki, A. (eds.) FM 2005. LNCS, vol. 3582, pp. 107–122. Springer, Heidelberg (2005)
6. Chakarov, A., Sankaranarayanan, S.: Probabilistic program analysis with martingales. In: Sharygina, N., Veith, H. (eds.) CAV 2013. LNCS, vol. 8044, pp. 511–526. Springer, Heidelberg (2013)
7. Dijkstra, E.W.: A Discipline of Programming. Prentice Hall, Upper Saddle River (1976)
8. Fioriti, L.M.F., Hermanns, H.: Probabilistic termination: soundness, completeness, and compositionality. In: Principles of Programming Languages (POPL), pp. 489–501. ACM (2015)
9. Frandsen, G.S.: Randomised Algorithms. Lecture Notes. University of Aarhus, Denmark (1998)
10. Gordon, A.D., Henzinger, T.A., Nori, A.V., Rajamani, S.K.: Probabilistic programming. In: Future of Software Engineering (FOSE), pp. 167–181. ACM (2014)
11. Hehner, E.C.R.: Formalization of time and space. Formal Aspects Comput. **10**(3), 290–306 (1998)
12. Hehner, E.C.R.: A probability perspective. Formal Aspects Comput. **23**(4), 391–419 (2011)
13. Hickey, T., Cohen, J.: Automating program analysis. J. ACM **35**(1), 185–220 (1988)
14. Hoare, C.A.R.: An axiomatic basis for computer programming. Commun. ACM **12**(10), 576–580 (1969)
15. Hurd, J.: A formal approach to probabilistic termination. In: Carreño, V.A., Muñoz, C.A., Tahar, S. (eds.) TPHOLs 2002. LNCS, vol. 2410, pp. 230–245. Springer, Heidelberg (2002)
16. Kaminski, B.L., Katoen, J.-P.: On the hardness of almost–Sure termination. In: Italiano, G.F., Pighizzini, G., Sannella, D.T. (eds.) MFCS 2015. LNCS, vol. 9234, pp. 307–318. Springer, Heidelberg (2015)
17. Kaminski, B.L., Katoen, J.P., Matheja, C., Olmedo, F.: Weakest precondition reasoning for expected run-times of probabilistic programs. ArXiv e-prints (2016). http://arxiv.org/abs/1601.01001
18. Kozen, D.: Semantics of probabilistic programs. J. Comput. Syst. Sci. **22**(3), 328–350 (1981)
19. McIver, A., Morgan, C.: Abstraction Refinement and Proof for Probabilistic Systems. Monographs in Computer Science. Springer, New York (2004)
20. Mitzenmacher, M., Upfal, E.: Probability and Computing: Randomized Algorithms and Probabilistic Analysis. Cambridge University Press, Cambridge (2005)
21. Monniaux, D.: An abstract analysis of the probabilistic termination of programs. In: Cousot, P. (ed.) SAS 2001. LNCS, vol. 2126, pp. 111–126. Springer, Heidelberg (2001)
22. Motwani, R., Raghavan, P.: Randomized Algorithms. Cambridge University Press, Cambridge (1995)
23. Nielson, H.R.: A Hoare-like proof system for analysing the computation time of programs. Sci. Comput. Program. **9**(2), 107–136 (1987)
24. Nielson, H.R., Nielson, F.: Semantics with Applications: An Appetizer. Undergraduate Topics in Computer Science. Springer, London (2007)
25. Wechler, W.: Universal Algebra for Computer Scientists. EATCS Monographs on Theoretical Computer Science, vol. 25. Springer, Heidelberg (1992)
26. Winskel, G.: The Formal Semantics of Programming Languages: An Introduction. MIT Press, Cambridge (1993)

Improving Floating-Point Numbers: A Lazy Approach to Adaptive Accuracy Refinement for Numerical Computations

Hideyuki Kawabata[1(✉)] and Hideya Iwasaki[2]

[1] Hiroshima City University,
3-4-1 Ozuka-Higashi, Asa-Minami-Ku, Hiroshima 731-3194, Japan
kawabata@hiroshima-cu.ac.jp
[2] The University of Electro-Communications,
1-5-1 Chofugaoka, Chofu, Tokyo 182-8585, Japan
iwasaki@cs.uec.ac.jp

Abstract. Numerical computation using floating-point numbers is prone to accuracy degradation due to round-off errors and cancellation of significant digits. Although multiple-precision arithmetic might alleviate this problem, it is difficult to statically decide the optimal degree of precision for each operation in a program. This paper presents a solution to this problem: the partial results in floating-point representations are incrementally improved using adaptive control. This process of adaptive accuracy refinement is implemented using lazy lists, each one containing a sequence of floating-point numbers with gradually improving accuracies. The computation process is driven by the propagation of demand for more accurate results. The concept of this *improving floating-point number* (IFN) mechanism was experimentally implemented in two ways: as a Haskell library and as a pure C library. Despite the simple approach, the results for numerical problems demonstrated the effectiveness of this mechanism.

Keywords: Improving floating-point numbers · Accurate numerical computation · Lazy evaluation · Haskell library

1 Introduction

Obtaining accurate results from numerical computation is not an easy task. Since real values cannot be represented correctly using a fixed number of digits, ordinary numerical computation is carried out using approximated representations of numbers. Programmers have to be fully aware that computation based on approximated numbers can easily degrade the accuracy of the result unexpectedly.

In *floating-point representation* using base 2, each value is denoted as $s \times m \times 2^e$, where s, m, and e are the *sign*, *mantissa*, and *exponent*, respectively. The mantissa (also called *significant digits*) is particularly important since it affects the precision of each number. There are many cases in which the mantissa of a resultant value has few meaningful digits, or even no digit, due to the accumulation of round-off errors or catastrophic cancellation [1].

P. Thiemann (Ed.): ESOP 2016, LNCS 9632, pp. 390–418, 2016.
DOI: 10.1007/978-3-662-49498-1_16

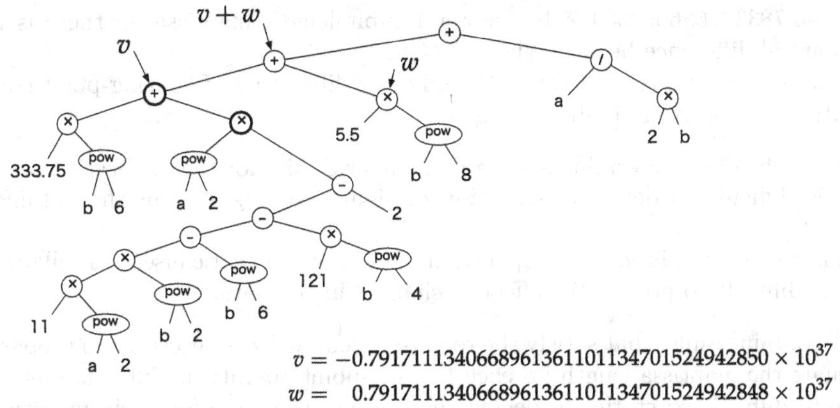

Fig. 1. Tree representation of Rump's example. Catastrophic cancellation happens at node labeled "$v + w$" if an insufficient number of bits are used for computation.

Multiple-precision floating-point arithmetic such as that defined in IEEE 754 [2] has been used to avoid catastrophic cancellation, and some processors have been designed to support multiple-precision arithmetic. In addition, arbitrary-precision arithmetic operations can be performed by using libraries such as the GNU MPFR library [3].

However, even if multiple-precision floating-point numbers are used, the accuracy of the computational results cannot be guaranteed. A simple example of this is *Rump's example* [4] (Fig. 1):

$$y = 333.75b^6 + a^2(11a^2b^2 - b^6 - 121b^4 - 2) + 5.5b^8 + a/(2b)\ . \qquad (1)$$

If $a = 77617$ and $b = 33096$, $a^2 = 5.5b^2 + 1$ holds. Thus, (1) is transformed to

$$y = -2 + a/(2b) = -54767/66192 \doteqdot -0.827396059946821368 14.$$

However, calculating this equation using double-precision numbers yields $y = -1.1805916207174113 \times 10^{21}$, which is far from the correct answer. This inaccuracy is due to catastrophic cancellation of significant digits. In fact, a completely useless value is produced by the addition of two numbers with absolute values that are almost the same (the leading 36 digits in their decimal are identical) and the signs are opposite at the node labeled "$v + w$" in Fig. 1.

The result of quadruple-precision computation of (1) using the MPFR library is $y = 1.172603940053179$, and the result with higher precision computation with 122 bits for the mantissa of each number is $y = -0.8273960599468214$, which is sufficiently accurate. However, a closer look at the computational process reveals that a 122-bit length for *all* operations is too much — only two operations (indicated by thick circles in Fig. 1) are critical enough to require a 122-bit mantissa. For other operations, quadruple-precision numbers suffice.

Next, let us slightly change the value of b. The results of (1) with $a = 77617$ and $b = 33095$ are $y = -4.7833916866560586 \times 10^{32}$ for double-precision and

$y = -4.783391686660554 \times 10^{32}$ for a 122-bit length mantissa — there is no substantial difference between them.

This small example illustrates the inherent difficulties of floating-point computation with a fixed number of digits.

- It is difficult to determine a suitable number of bits for each operation.
- It is difficult to detect cancellation of significant digits from the obtained result.
- It is difficult to pinpoint the operations in a program that caused cancellation.
- It is difficult to predict the effect of changes in the data.

To obtain results that satisfy the required accuracy, it is necessary to properly estimate the mantissa length for each floating-point operation. Unfortunately, it is quite difficult to statically decide the optimal precision for each operation. Thus, we take a *dynamic* approach; the partial results in floating-point representations are incrementally improved using adaptive control. This *adaptive accuracy refinement* process requires tracing of accumulated errors and application of suitable strategies to remove inaccurate values.

In this paper, we present a mechanism for adaptive accuracy refinement of computational results. It uses lazy lists, each one containing an infinite sequence of specially designed floating-point numbers with gradually improving accuracies. These numbers are approximations of the same real value and are ordered on the basis of what we call "accuracy." In computation using this mechanism, "referring to the next value" corresponds to obtaining a better (more accurate) value via recomputation of subexpressions, which are propagated to dependent operands automatically. In principle, computation using this *improving floating-point number* (IFN) mechanism is applicable to any numerical algorithm.

To get the flavor how our IFN mechanism works, let us return to Rump's example. Here, we use our implementation of the mechanism in Haskell, which will be described in Sect. 3. First, we define the function *rump* in Haskell.

```
rump :: Fractional t => t -> t -> t
rump a b = 333.75 * b^6 + a^2 * (11 * a^2 * b^2 - b^6 - 121 * b^4 - 2)
           + 5.5 * b^8 + a / (2 * b)
```

The following is a GHCi session that calls *rump* for *Double* numbers (incorrect value is returned) and then calls *rump* for IFNs.

```
*Main> rump 77617 33096
-1.1805916207174113e21
*Main> let qs = rump (77617 :: IFN) (33096 :: IFN)
*Main> accurateValue 32 qs
-0.827396059946821 x 10 ^ (0) : ac=55
*Main> accurateValue 128 qs
-0.827396059946821368141165095479816292000 x 10 ^ (0) : ac=130
```

Once we bind the result of *rump* that uses IFN computation to the variable *qs*, we can obtain an arbitrary accuracy of the resultant value by giving the desired accuracy to the library function *accurateValue*.

The contributions of the work reported in this paper are summarized as follows:

- Our proposed IFN mechanism achieves adaptive accuracy refinement for the computation of each subexpression in the entire expression. This enables the user to easily obtain a computational result with the desired accuracy without cancellation of significant digits. In contrast to computation using a fixed number of bits such as with functions in the MPFR library, computation using the IFN mechanism can be done using only a sufficient number of bits for each subexpression. Note that "sufficient number of bits" varies with the subexpression; the number of bits for each subexpression is automatically adjusted.
- We formalize an IFN as a list of specially represented floating-point numbers that approximate the same real value and for which the accuracies are improved. On the basis of this concept, we define unary / binary operators and basic mathematical functions on IFNs, the results of which are also IFNs.
- An experimental IFN library was implemented as both a Haskell library and a pure C library. The lazy evaluation facility of Haskell facilitated implementation of the Haskell library in a quite natural manner because computation using IFNs proceeds in response to demands for "more accurate" values of the IFN of interest. A C version of the library was developed to cope with the performance problem of the Haskell library. Application of these libraries to numerical problems for which it is difficult to obtain precise answers by using *Double* numbers demonstrated the effectiveness of the proposed IFN mechanism.

The organization of this paper is as follows. Section 2 outlines the concept of our IFN mechanism and the adaptive refinement of subexpressions using IFNs. In Sect. 3, we describe the details of IFNs, floating-point numbers for IFNs, and arithmetic operations for IFNs. In Sect. 4, support for logical expressions is discussed. In Sect. 5, issues related to implementing IFN libraries are considered. Section 6 describes several numerical examples demonstrating the effectiveness and applicability of our IFN mechanism. In Sect. 7, we discuss a few IFN-related issues. Related work is covered in Sect. 8. Finally, we conclude with a brief summary in Sect. 9.

Throughout this paper, we use Haskell [5] with some extra typesetting features to describe the design of IFN libraries. Though some datatypes in Sects. 3 and 4 are defined naively for the sake of conciseness, our practical IFN Haskell library uses more efficient implementation by means of Haskell's foreign function interface (FFI), as described in Sect. 5.

2 Improving Floating-Point Numbers

To improve the accuracy of floating-point computations of an expression by adaptive and appropriate accuracy refinements of its subexpressions, we introduce the concept of *improving floating-point numbers*. Intuitively speaking, an IFN is an infinite sequence of floating-point values, each of which approximates the same real value v, i.e., the ideal result of the computation. The further to the right the value is in the sequence, the closer it is to v.

The basic idea of IFNs came from the notion of "improving sequences" [6,7], which is a finite monotonic sequence of approximation values of a final value that are gradually improved in accordance with an ordering relation. However, IFNs are different from improving sequences because IFNs are *infinite* sequences.

Hereafter, we denote a floating-point number by q. Each q is associated with an integer that represents its accuracy, which we denote by $ac\ q$. We represent an IFN by using a lazy list of q's.

$$qs = [q_0, q_1, q_2, \ldots]$$

Since accuracies are improved in an IFN, the relation $ac\ q_i < ac\ q_{i+1}$ holds for all $i \geq 0$. To see why an IFN has to be infinite, consider the case in which $v = 5/7$. Since $5/7 = (0.101101...)_2$, instances of IFNs that represent v could be

$$[(0.1)_2, (0.11)_2, (0.110)_2, (0.1011)_2, (0.10111)_2, (0.101110)_2, \ldots]$$
$$[(0.110)_2, (0.101110)_2, (0.101101110)_2, \ldots].$$

In any case, an infinite sequence is capable of expressing arbitrary accuracies naturally.

The floating-point values in an IFN are forced from left to right. If all q_i's $(i \leq k)$ have been forced and q_j's $(k < j)$ have not been forced yet, the *current value* of this IFN is q_k, and its current accuracy is $ac\ q_k$. If the current accuracy is unsatisfactory, q_{k+1} is forced, and the current value is set to q_{k+1}. This process is repeated until the desired accuracy is obtained.

To see how the computation in terms of IFNs proceeds, let us consider a simple example: addition of v and w. Suppose that v corresponds to $ps = [p_0, p_1, \ldots, p_h, \ldots]$ where its current value is p_h, and w corresponds to $qs = [q_0, q_1, \ldots, q_k, \ldots]$ where its current value is q_k. Also suppose that $v + w$ corresponds to $rs = [r_0, r_1, \ldots, r_l, \ldots]$ where we have already computed $r_0, r_1, \ldots, r_l$ by using $p_0, p_1, \ldots, p_h, q_0, q_1, \ldots, q_k$. If we are not satisfied with $ac\ r_l$, we want to compute r_{l+1} to obtain better accuracy. If the next values of ps and qs (p_{h+1} and q_{k+1}) are judged to be necessary, we force them and compute r_{l+1} by using both p_{h+1} and q_{k+1}. It is worth noting that the computation of r_{l+1} has to produce a value with better accuracy than r_l. If ps is the result of another computation, say multiplication of ps' and ps'', forcing p_{h+1} induces other floating-point values in ps' and ps'' to be forced. In this way, the entire computation is driven by the propagation of the demands for the next values in IFNs. This kind of demand-driven computation can be naturally described on the basis of lazy evaluation. We thus used Haskell to build a prototype IFN library. As we describe in later sections, there are several design choices in a practical implementation.

3 Adaptive Accuracy Refinement with IFNs

3.1 Floating-Point Datatype

Let us define datatype Q for floating-point numbers:

$$\textbf{data}\ Q = Q\ \{\ sign :: Int,\ mantissa :: [Int],\ expo :: Int\ \}$$

where *sign*, *mantissa*, and *expo* are the sign, mantissa, and exponent, respectively; *sign* is either 1 or −1, and *mantissa* is a finite list for which the elements are either 0 or 1. We assume that q is an instance of Q.

Functions *ac* and *lenM* are defined as follows.

$$\begin{aligned} ac,\ lenM &:: \ Q \to Int \\ ac\ q &= lenM\ q - expo\ q \\ lenM\ q &= length\ (mantissa\ q) \end{aligned}$$

Each q is associated with two real values, $\langle q \rangle$ and $\{q\}$:

$$\langle q \rangle = (sign\ q) \times \left(\frac{b_1}{2^1} + \frac{b_2}{2^2} + \cdots + \frac{b_n}{2^n} \right) \times 2^e, \quad \{q\} = \frac{1}{2^{n+1}} \times 2^e,$$

where $e = expo\ q$, $[b_1, b_2, \ldots, b_n] = mantissa\ q$, and $n = lenM\ q$. Using $\langle q \rangle$ and $\{q\}$, we define the relation between a real value v and q. If v satisfies the following inequality, we say that a floating-point number q is an *approximation* of v and write $v \leftarrow\!\!\prec q$. We also say that v is *properly represented* by q if $v \leftarrow\!\!\prec q$ holds.

$$\langle q \rangle - \{q\}\ \leq v \leq\ \langle q \rangle + \{q\}$$

Note that for each q, the range within which a real value being properly represented by q should reside is rigorously defined only by q. Here, the following property holds:

$$\{q\} = \frac{1}{2^{(ac\ q)+1}}.$$

This means that the accuracy of q, $ac\ q$, indicates the width of the range in which real values approximated by q can reside. A larger $ac\ q$ indicates that q represents a real v satisfying $v \leftarrow\!\!\prec q$ more precisely.

Example 1. Consider the following three floating-point numbers q, q', and q''. For q and q', equations $\langle q \rangle = \langle q' \rangle$ and $ac\ q = ac\ q'$ hold. In addition, for any real v, $v \leftarrow\!\!\prec q \Longleftrightarrow v \leftarrow\!\!\prec q'$. However, for q and q'', $\langle q \rangle = \langle q'' \rangle$, but $ac\ q < ac\ q''$. For any real v, $v \leftarrow\!\!\prec q'' \Longrightarrow v \leftarrow\!\!\prec q$ but $v \leftarrow\!\!\prec q \not\Longrightarrow v \leftarrow\!\!\prec q''$.

$$\begin{aligned} q\ &= Q\ \{\ sign = 1,\ mantissa = [1,1,0,0],\ expo = -2\} \\ q'\ &= Q\ \{\ sign = 1,\ mantissa = [0,0,0,1,1,0,0],\ expo = 1\} \\ q'' &= Q\ \{\ sign = 1,\ mantissa = [1,1,0,0,0,0,0,0,0],\ expo = -2\} \end{aligned}$$

Here, let us define *left-shifting* and *right-shifting*. Suppose q_1, q_2, and q_3 are instances of Q:

$$q_1 = Q\ \{\ sign = s,\ \ mantissa = [b_1, b_2, \ldots, b_n],\ \ expo = e\}$$
$$q_2 = Q\ \{\ sign = s,\ \ mantissa = [b_{m+1}, b_{m+2}, \ldots, b_n],\ \ expo = e - m\}$$
$$q_3 = Q\ \{\ sign = s,\ \ mantissa = [\underbrace{0, 0, \ldots, 0}_{m}, b_1, b_2, \ldots, b_n],\ \ expo = e + m\}$$

Left-shifting q_1 by m digits leads to q_2, where $lenM\ q_2 = n - m$, and right-shifting q_2 by m digits leads to q_3, where $lenM\ q_3 = n + m$. Note that right-shifting does not change real values associated with Q, i.e., $\langle q_1 \rangle = \langle q_3 \rangle$ and $\{q_1\} = \{q_3\}$. If $b_1 = b_2 = \cdots = b_m = 0$ and $b_{m+1} \neq 0$, left-shifting q_1 by m digits removes all leading zeros of the mantissa of q_1. We call the removal of leading zeros of the mantissa by left-shifting *normalization*. Normalization also does not change real values associated with Q. In Example 1, q and q' have the same representation under normalization.

3.2 Definition of IFNs

An IFN is an infinite list of Q's instances $qs = [q_0, q_1, q_2, \ldots]$ that satisfies two conditions:

- $ac\ q_i < ac\ q_{i+1}$ holds for all $i \geq 0$, and
- there is a real value v that satisfies $v \leftarrowtail q_i$ for all $i \geq 0$.[1]

If every element of an IFN qs properly represents a real v, i.e., $v \leftarrowtail q_i$ for all $i \geq 0$, we say that *qs is an IFN with respect to v* and write $v \leftarrowtail qs$ by overloading the relation symbol $\leftarrowtail$. Since IFNs are infinite lists, $v \leftarrowtail qs \wedge w \leftarrowtail qs \Longrightarrow v = w$.

Now let us define datatype *IFN* for IFNs in Haskell.

$$\textbf{type}\ IFN = [Q]$$

An IFN instance can be generated from a literal in a program by using

$$\begin{array}{lcl} genIFNfromString & :: & String \rightarrow IFN \\ genIFNfromString\ s & = & map\ (\backslash n \rightarrow fromString\ n\ s)\ [initN,\ initN + diffN\ ..] \end{array}$$

The function $fromString :: Int \rightarrow String \rightarrow Q$ generates an instance of Q that approximates a given number in a string representation with a designated length the mantissa. *initN* and *diffN* are respectively the initial length of the mantissa and the difference between the lengths of the mantissas of consecutive elements in the returned IFN. As will be described in Sect. 5.2 in detail, the values of *initN* and *diffN* and the way in which the IFNs are generated greatly affect the performance of the IFN library.

Given an IFN, we can obtain an instance of Q for which the accuracy is equal to or greater than a specified value by using the *accurateValue* function.

$$\begin{array}{l} accurateValue \quad :: Int \rightarrow IFN \rightarrow Q \\ accurateValue\ a\ qs = head\ (dropWhile\ \ (\backslash q \rightarrow ac\ q < a)\ qs) \end{array}$$

[1] The condition is weaker than the following: $\langle q_i \rangle - \{q_i\} \leq \langle q_{i+1} \rangle - \{q_{i+1}\} < \langle q_{i+1} \rangle + \{q_{i+1}\} \leq \langle q_i \rangle + \{q_i\}$; i.e., each successive floating-point number does not necessarily denote a sub-interval of the previous one.

We call functions that accept IFNs as operands and returns an IFN *IFN operators*. When a program is constructed by composition of IFN operators, results at any level of accuracy can be obtained by using *accurateValue*.

3.3 Floating-Point Arithmetic Operators for Q

Arithmetic operators for Q are expected to satisfy several conditions. That is, for any q_1 and q_2 and real v_1 and v_2,

$$\begin{aligned} v_1 \leftarrowtail q_1 &\Longrightarrow -v_1 \leftarrowtail negQ\ q_1 \\ v_1 \leftarrowtail q_1 \wedge v_2 \leftarrowtail q_2 &\Longrightarrow v_1 + v_2 \leftarrowtail addQ\ q_1\ q_2 \\ v_1 \leftarrowtail q_1 \wedge v_2 \leftarrowtail q_2 &\Longrightarrow v_1 \times v_2 \leftarrowtail mulQ\ q_1\ q_2 \\ v_1 \leftarrowtail q_1 \wedge v_2 \leftarrowtail q_2 &\Longrightarrow v_1 / v_2 \leftarrowtail divQ\ q_1\ q_2, \end{aligned}$$

where *negQ*, *addQ*, *mulQ*, and *divQ* correspond to real operators $-$ (unary minus), $+$, $\times$, and $/$, respectively.

We define *negQ* as follows. It is easy to check that the above condition for *negQ* holds since $\langle negQ\ q_1 \rangle = -\langle q_1 \rangle$ and $\{negQ\ q_1\} = \{q_1\}$.

$$\begin{aligned} &negQ\ :: Q \rightarrow Q \\ &negQ\ q = Q\ \{\ sign = -\ (sign\ q),\ mantissa = mantissa\ q,\ expo = expo\ q\ \} \end{aligned}$$

We have to be careful in defining binary operators for Q because simple definitions would not satisfy the above conditions.

Example 2. Let us consider addition operators for Q. We can readily define a function for variable-precision addition, *simpleAddQ*, such that *simpleAddQ* $q_1\ q_2$ is an instance of Q satisfying $\langle simpleAddQ\ q_1\ q_2 \rangle = \langle q_1 \rangle + \langle q_2 \rangle$. Now, for the following instances of Q, $v_1 \leftarrowtail q_1$ and $v_2 \leftarrowtail q_2$ hold where $v_1 = (0.7813)_{10}$ and $v_2 = (0.3907)_{10}$. However, $v_1 + v_2 = (1.1720)_{10} \not\leftarrowtail q_{1+2} =$ *simpleAddQ* $q_1\ q_2$.

$$\begin{aligned} q_1 &= Q\ \{\ sign = 1,\ mantissa = [1,1,0,1],\ expo = 0\} \\ q_2 &= Q\ \{\ sign = 1,\ mantissa = [1,1,0,1],\ expo = -1\} \\ q_{1+2} &= Q\ \{\ sign = 1,\ mantissa = [1,0,0,1,1,1],\ expo = 1\} \end{aligned}$$

In contrast, "rounding" of q_{1+2} with a mantissa length of 3 yields q'_{1+2}, which satisfies the relation $v_1 + v_2 \leftarrowtail q'_{1+2}$.

$$q'_{1+2} = Q\ \{\ sign = 1,\ mantissa = [1,0,1],\ expo = 1\}$$

Rounding of Q is defined as follows. Let q_a, q_b, and q_c be instances of Q:

$$\begin{aligned} q_a &= Q\ \{\ sign = s,\ mantissa = [b_1, b_2, \ldots, b_r, b_{r+1}, \ldots, b_n],\ expo = e\} \\ q_b &= Q\ \{\ sign = s,\ mantissa = [b_1, b_2, \ldots, b_r],\ expo = e\} \\ q_c &= Q\ \{\ sign = s,\ mantissa = [\underbrace{0, 0, \ldots, 0}_{r-1}, b_{r+1}],\ expo = e\}. \end{aligned}$$

Then, rounding of q_a at r-th digit is computed as *simpleAddQ* $q_b\ q_c$.

As illustrated in the above example, "proper" floating-point operators apparently do not generate results with a very long mantissa. Let us denote the rounded representation of q at the r-th digit as $roundQ\ q\ r$. In Example 2, $q'_{1+2} = roundQ\ q_{1+2}\ 3$.

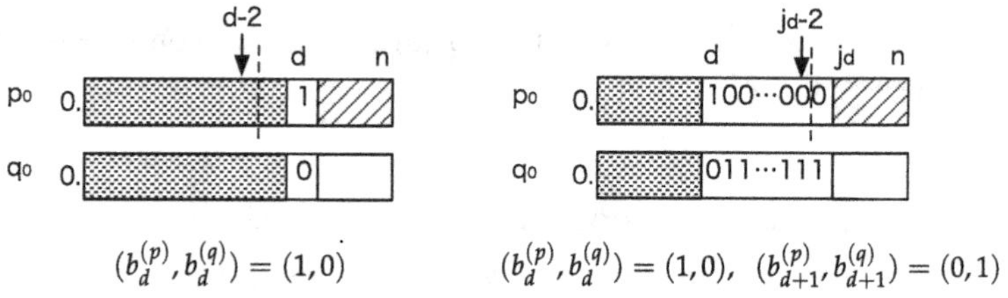

Fig. 2. Position of mantissa to be rounded to construct $r_0 = p_0 \sqcup_0 q_0$. Bits in shaded rectangles of p_0 and q_0 are the same. Other bits that are not explicitly shown are arbitrary. If $(b_{d+1}^{(p)}, b_{d+1}^{(q)}) = (0, 1)$, j_d is defined as in the right figure.

Now we show the definition of *addQ* in terms of *simpleAddQ* used in Example 2. First we briefly describe a binary operator $\sqcup$ of type $Q \to Q \to Q$, which is defined using another binary operator $\sqcup_0$ of type $Q \to Q \to Q$. Suppose that two Qs, namely p_0 and q_0, are as follows:

$$p_0 = Q\ \{\ sign = s_p,\ mantissa = [b_1^{(p)}, b_2^{(p)}, \ldots, b_n^{(p)}],\ expo = e\}$$
$$q_0 = Q\ \{\ sign = s_q,\ mantissa = [b_1^{(q)}, b_2^{(q)}, \ldots, b_n^{(q)}],\ expo = e\}.$$

Then, $r_0 = p_0 \sqcup_0 q_0$ is an instance of Q such that among all qs that satisfy both $\langle p_0 \rangle \longleftarrow q$ and $\langle q_0 \rangle \longleftarrow q$, r_0 gives the maximum of $ac\ q$ for most cases. The function $\sqcup_0$ is defined as follows.

- Case $\langle p_0 \rangle > \langle q_0 \rangle \geq 0$ or $\langle p_0 \rangle < \langle q_0 \rangle \leq 0$: Suppose the following expressions hold, as shown in Fig. 2:

$$\begin{cases} b_i^{(p)} = b_i^{(q)}, & i = 1, \ldots, d-1 \\ b_i^{(p)} \neq b_i^{(q)}, & i = d. \end{cases}$$

  Note that $(b_d^{(p)}, b_d^{(q)}) = (1, 0)$. Here, we suppose $d \geq 3$ assuming that p_0 and q_0 are appropriately shifted beforehand. Now, if $d < n$ and $(b_{d+1}^{(p)}, b_{d+1}^{(q)}) = (0, 1)$, then $r_0 = roundQ\ p_0\ (j_d - 2)$, where j_d is the smallest integer satisfying $j_d > d + 1$ and $(b_{j_d}^{(p)}, b_{j_d}^{(q)}) \neq (0, 1)$. If $d = n$ or $(b_{d+1}^{(p)}, b_{d+1}^{(q)}) \neq (0, 1)$, then $r_0 = roundQ\ p_0\ (d - 2)$.
- Case $\langle q_0 \rangle > \langle p_0 \rangle \geq 0$or $\langle q_0 \rangle < \langle p_0 \rangle \leq 0$: Exchange p_0 and q_0 and apply the previous case.
- Case $|\langle p_0 \rangle| = |\langle q_0 \rangle| > 0$: If $\langle p_0 \rangle = \langle q_0 \rangle$, $r_0 = p_0 = q_0$. If $\langle p_0 \rangle = -\langle q_0 \rangle$, $r_0 = roundQ\ p_0\ (d - 2)$, where the first $d - 1$ digits of $mantissa\ p_0$ are zeros and the d-th digit is 1.

– Case $|\langle p_0\rangle| = |\langle q_0\rangle| = 0$: $r_0 = p_0 = q_0$.

Now, the binary operator $\sqcup$ is defined using $\sqcup_0$ and appropriate shifting to support an arbitrary exponent: if $q_3 = q_1 \sqcup q_2$, q_3 is an instance of Q such that, among all qs that satisfy both $\langle q_1\rangle \leftarrow\!\!\prec q$ and $\langle q_2\rangle \leftarrow\!\!\prec q$, q_3 gives the maximum of $ac\ q$ for most cases. Then, $addQ\ q_1\ q_2$ is defined as $(simpleAddQ\ h\ d) \sqcup (simpleAddQ\ h\ (negQ\ d))$, where $h = simpleAddQ\ q_1\ q_2$, $d = simpleAddQ\ d_1\ d_2$, $\langle d_1\rangle = \{q_1\}$, and $\langle d_2\rangle = \{q_2\}$. The above condition for $addQ$ holds because the following equations hold.

$$\begin{aligned}\langle simpleAddQ\ h\ d\rangle &= \langle h\rangle + \langle d\rangle = (\langle q_1\rangle + \{q_1\}) + (\langle q_2\rangle + \{q_2\})\\ \langle simpleAddQ\ h\ (negQ\ d)\rangle &= \langle h\rangle - \langle d\rangle = (\langle q_1\rangle - \{q_1\}) + (\langle q_2\rangle - \{q_2\})\end{aligned}$$

Note that the d_1 and d_2 instances of Q are easily constructed and that the entire computation of $addQ$ can be done without evaluating real values $\langle q_1\rangle$, $\langle q_2\rangle$, $\{q_1\}$, and $\{q_2\}$.

Likewise, $mulQ$ can be defined. First, we define $simpleMulQ$, where $simpleMulQ\ q_1\ q_2$ is an instance of Q such that $\langle simpleMulQ\ q_1\ q_2\rangle = \langle q_1\rangle \times \langle q_2\rangle$. Then, for q_1 and q_2 such that $\langle q_1\rangle > 0$ and $\langle q_2\rangle > 0$, $mulQ\ q_1\ q_2$ is defined as

$$\begin{aligned}&(simpleAddQ\ (simpleAddQ\ h\ d_3)\ (simpleAddQ\ d_1\ d_2))\\ &\quad \sqcup (simpleAddQ\ (simpleAddQ\ h\ (negQ\ d_1))\ (simpleAddQ\ (negQ\ d_2)\ d_3),\end{aligned}$$

where $h = simpleMulQ\ q_1\ q_2$, $d_1 = simpleMulQ\ q_1\ d'_1$, $d_2 = simpleMulQ\ q_1\ d'_2$, $\langle d'_1\rangle = \{q_2\}$, $\langle d'_2\rangle = \{q_1\}$, and $\langle d_3\rangle = \{q_1\} \times \{q_2\}$. The definitions of $mulQ$ for other cases are similar.

We can also define $divQ$ in a similar manner; its definition is omitted due to space limitation.

As described above, binary Q operators such as $addQ$ and $mulQ$ are constructed using raw arithmetic operators such as $simpleAddQ$ and $simpleMulQ$ and a binary operator $\sqcup$ for accuracy management. The raw operators are expected to be built with highly tuned variable-precision libraries such as MPFR.

3.4 Unary IFN Operator: Negation

Negation of an IFN is constructed as follows:

$negIFN :: IFN \rightarrow IFN$
$negIFN = map\ negQ$

If qs is an IFN with respect to a real v, $negIFN\ qs$ should be an IFN with respect to $-v$. First, the ordering of accuracy can be preserved if

$$ac\ q < ac\ q' \Longrightarrow ac\ (negQ\ q) < ac\ (negQ\ q')$$

holds. The $negQ$ defined in Sect. 3.3 satisfies this condition because $ac\ (negQ\ p) = ac\ p$. In addition, $\langle negQ\ p\rangle = -\langle p\rangle$. Thus, $negIFN$ is indeed a proper IFN operator for negation.

3.5 Binary IFN Operators

First, we define addition of two IFNs.

$$
\begin{array}{l}
addIFN \quad :: IFN \rightarrow IFN \rightarrow IFN \\
addIFN \quad = addIFN'\ a_{\mathrm{init}}\ \textbf{where}\ a_{\mathrm{init}} = \text{minimum value of } Int \\
addIFN' \quad :: Int \rightarrow IFN \rightarrow IFN \rightarrow IFN \\
addIFN'\ a\ (p{:}ps)\ (q{:}qs) \\
\quad \mid ac\ p < ac\ q = \textbf{if}\ a' \leq a\ \textbf{then}\ addIFN'\ a\ ps\ (q{:}qs) \\
\qquad\qquad\qquad\qquad\quad \textbf{else}\ r : addIFN'\ a'\, ps\ (q{:}qs) \\
\quad \mid ac\ p > ac\ q = \textbf{if}\ a' \leq a\ \textbf{then}\ addIFN'\ a\ (p{:}ps)\ qs \\
\qquad\qquad\qquad\qquad\quad \textbf{else}\ r : addIFN'\ a'(p{:}ps)\ qs \\
\quad \mid \textbf{otherwise} = \textbf{if}\ a' \leq a\ \textbf{then}\ addIFN'\ a\ ps\ qs \\
\qquad\qquad\qquad\qquad\quad \textbf{else}\ r : addIFN'\ a'\, ps\ qs \\
\qquad\qquad \textbf{where}\ r = addQ\ p\ q \\
\qquad\qquad\qquad\quad a' = ac\ r
\end{array}
$$

The function $addIFN'$ keeps the current accuracy (the accuracy of the current value) in its first argument and uses it to ensure that the accuracy of the next value in the resultant IFN is improved.[2]

One may wonder whether recursive application of *addIFN'* while obtaining "the next value" might not terminate. However, *addIFN* is shown to work properly as follows.

Let us examine the behavior of *addIFN*. Suppose we are adding two IFNs, $ps = [p_0, p_1, \ldots]$ and $qs = [q_0, q_1, \ldots]$, and the result is $[r_0, r_1, \ldots] = addIFN\ ps\ qs$, which has a current value of $r_i = addQ\ p_j\ q_k$. If r_{i+1} is forced, $addIFN'$ behaves as follows:

- If $ac\ p_j < ac\ q_k$, the candidate for r_{i+1} is $addQ\ p_{j+1}\ q_k$. In this case, the inequality $min\ (ac\ p_j)\ (ac\ q_k) < min\ (ac\ p_{j+1})\ (ac\ q_k)$ holds. If $ac\ r_i < ac\ (addQ\ p_{j+1}\ q_k)$, then r_{i+1} is readily available as $addQ\ p_{j+1}\ q_k$. On the other hand, if $ac\ r_i \geq ac\ (addQ\ p_{j+1}\ q_k)$, searching for appropriate operands continues.
- If $ac\ p_j > ac\ q_k$, the candidate for r_{i+1} is $addQ\ p_j\ q_{k+1}$. Here, $min\ (ac\ p_j)\ (ac\ q_k) < min\ (ac\ p_j)\ (ac\ q_{k+1})$ holds. If $ac\ r_i \geq ac\ (addQ\ p_j\ q_{k+1})$, searching for appropriate operands continues.
- If $ac\ p_j = ac\ q_k$, the candidate for r_{i+1} is $addQ\ p_{j+1}\ q_{k+1}$. In this case, $min\ (ac\ p_j)\ (ac\ q_k) < min\ (ac\ p_{j+1})\ (ac\ q_{k+1})$ holds. If $ac\ r_i \geq ac\ (addQ\ p_{j+1}\ q_{k+1})$, searching for appropriate operands continues.

Here we show that the search terminates and that r_{i+1} is eventually available. *addQ* has the following property; its derivation is omitted for the sake of brevity:

$$min\,(ac\,p)\ (ac\,q) - 3 \leq ac\,(addQ\,p\,q) \leq min\,(ac\,p)\ (ac\,q) - 1,$$

[2] The inequality $a' \leq a$ in the definition of *addIFN'* can be modified to enhance performance; see Sect. 5.2 for details.

where p and q are normalized instances of Q. From this inequality, we can see that $addQ\ p\ q$ depends on the value of $min\ (ac\ p)\ (ac\ q)$. The following property is also derived from the above inequality:

$$min\ (ac\ p)\ (ac\ q) < min\ (ac\ p')\ (ac\ q') - 2 \Longrightarrow ac\ (addQ\ p\ q) < ac\ (addQ\ p'\ q').$$

As described above, calculating the next value by using *addIFN'* is done on the basis of the ascending order of the value of $min\ (ac\ p)\ (ac\ q)$ without an upper limit. Thus, the accuracy of $addQ\ p\ q$ can be greater than any designated integer. As a result, the above property guarantees the termination of *addIFN'*. In summary, *addIFN* is a proper IFN operator for addition.

Next, we define multiplication of two IFNs.

$$
\begin{array}{ll}
mulIFN & :: IFN \rightarrow IFN \rightarrow IFN \\
mulIFN & = mulIFN'\ a_{\mathrm{init}}\ \textbf{where}\ a_{\mathrm{init}} = \text{minimum value of}\ Int \\
mulIFN' & :: Int \rightarrow IFN \rightarrow IFN \rightarrow IFN \\
\multicolumn{2}{l}{mulIFN'\ a\ (p{:}ps)\ (q{:}qs)} \\
\quad \mid\ lenM\ p < lenM\ q & = \textbf{if}\ a' \leq a\ \textbf{then}\ mulIFN'\ a\ ps\ (q{:}qs) \\
 & \qquad\qquad \textbf{else}\ r : mulIFN'\ a'ps\ (q{:}qs) \\
\quad \mid\ lenM\ p > lenM\ q & = \textbf{if}\ a' \leq a\ \textbf{then}\ mulIFN'\ a\ (p{:}ps)\ qs \\
 & \qquad\qquad \textbf{else}\ r : mulIFN'\ a'(p{:}ps)\ qs \\
\quad \mid\ \textbf{otherwise} & = \textbf{if}\ a' \leq a\ \textbf{then}\ mulIFN'\ a\ ps\ qs \\
 & \qquad\qquad \textbf{else}\ r : mulIFN'\ a'ps\ qs \\
\qquad\qquad \textbf{where}\ r & = mulQ\ p\ q \\
\qquad\qquad\quad a' & = ac\ r
\end{array}
$$

To show that *mulIFN* works properly, first we show that *mulIFN'* searches for appropriate operands for use in calculating "the next value" in such a way that the value of $f\ p\ q = ac\ p + ac\ q - max\ (lenM\ p)\ (lenM\ q)$ increases, where p and q are instances of Q that are used to calculate $mulQ\ p\ q$.

Suppose we are multiplying two IFNs, $ps = [p_0, p_1, \ldots]$ and $qs = [q_0, q_1, \ldots]$, and the result is $[r_0, r_1, \ldots] = mulIFN\ ps\ qs$, which has a current value of $r_i = mulQ\ p_j\ q_k$. The behavior of *mulIFN'* when r_{i+1} is forced is as follows:

- If $lenM\ p_j < lenM\ q_k$, the candidate for r_{i+1} is $mulQ\ p_{j+1}\ q_k$. Let us examine the value of $f\ p_{j+1}\ q_k - f\ p_j\ q_k$. If $lenM\ p_{j+1} > lenM\ q_k$, then

$$
\begin{aligned}
f\ p_{j+1}\ q_k - f\ p_j\ q_k &= ac\ p_{j+1} - ac\ p_j - lenM\ p_{j+1} + lenM\ q_k \\
&= (expo\ p_j - expo\ p_{j+1}) + (lenM\ q_k - lenM\ p_j) > 0
\end{aligned}
$$

since $expo\ p_j \geq expo\ p_{j+1}$. On the other hand, if $lenM\ p_{j+1} \leq lenM\ q_k$, then

$$f\ p_{j+1}\ q_k - f\ p_j\ q_k = ac\ p_{j+1} - ac\ p_j - lenM\ q_k + lenM\ q_k > 0.$$

If $ac\ r_i < ac\ (mulQ\ p_{j+1}\ q_k)$, then r_{i+1} is readily available as $mulQ\ p_{j+1}\ q_k$. If $ac\ r_i \geq ac\ (mulQ\ p_{j+1}\ q_k)$, searching for appropriate operands continues.
- If $lenM\ p_j > lenM\ q_k$, $f\ p_j\ q_{k+1} > f\ p_j\ q_k$ can be shown similarly. If $ac\ r_i \geq ac\ (mulQ\ p_j\ q_{k+1})$, searching for appropriate operands continues.

- If $lenM\ p_j = lenM\ q_k$, $f\ p_{j+1}\ q_{k+1} > f\ p_j\ q_k$ can be shown similarly. If $ac\ r_i \geq ac\ (mulQ\ p_{j+1}\ q_{k+1})$, searching for appropriate operands continues.

Now, letting p, p', q, and q' be normalized instances of Q, the property of *mulQ*, the derivation of which is omitted for the sake of brevity, is summarized as

$$f\ p\ q < f\ p'\ q' - 2 \Longrightarrow ac\ (mulQ\ p\ q) < ac\ (mulQ\ p'\ q').$$

The above property guarantees that $ac\ (mulQ\ p\ q)$ can be greater than any designated integer. Thus, as described above, the termination of *mulIFN'* is guaranteed. In summary, *mulIFN* is a proper IFN operator for multiplication.

subIFN is defined by a composition of *addIFN* and *negIFN*.

$$\begin{aligned} &subIFN && :: IFN \rightarrow IFN \rightarrow IFN \\ &subIFN\ ps\ qs && = addIFN\ ps\ (negIFN\ qs) \end{aligned}$$

Division operator *divIFN* can be essentially constructed in the same way.

3.6 Basic Mathematical Functions for IFN

In this section, we briefly sketch the implementation of basic mathematical functions for IFN such as exponential (*expIFN*), square root (*sqrtIFN*), logarithmic (*logIFN*), and trigonometric (*sinIFN*, *cosIFN*, etc.) functions. Each IFN function is constructed using corresponding arithmetic operators for Q, e.g., *expQ* for *expIFN* and *sqrtQ* for *sqrtIFN*. As described in Sect. 3.3, these mathematical functions should satisfy the following conditions:

$$\begin{aligned} v \leftarrowtail q &\Longrightarrow e^v \leftarrowtail expQ\ q \\ v \leftarrowtail q \wedge v \geq 0 &\Longrightarrow \sqrt{v} \leftarrowtail sqrtQ\ q \\ v \leftarrowtail q \wedge v > 0 &\Longrightarrow \log\ v \leftarrowtail logQ\ q \\ v \leftarrowtail q &\Longrightarrow \sin\ v \leftarrowtail sinQ\ q, \end{aligned}$$

where v is a real value and q is an instance of Q. To implement the Q functions, we make use of the MPFR functions. Note that the result of each MPFR function is guaranteed to be the nearest possible floating-point value assuming that its inputs are exact values [3].

Monotonic (and continuous) functions including *expQ*, *sqrtQ*, and *logQ* can be easily implemented. Since the exact upper and lower bounds for which q (an instance of Q) properly represents are readily obtained from q, the projected range can be computed using a unary MPFR function, and the corresponding Q value can be generated using the operator $\sqcup$. For example, *expQ* can be defines as:

$$\begin{aligned} &expQ && :: Q \rightarrow Q \\ &expQ\ \ q && = l \sqcup u \\ &\quad \textbf{where}\ l && = simpleExpQ\ (simpleAddQ\ q\ (negQ\ d)) \\ &\quad\quad\ \ u && = simpleExpQ\ (simpleAddQ\ q\ d) \\ &\quad\quad\ \ d && = Q\ \{\ sign = 1,\ mantissa = [1],\ expo = -\ ac\ q\ \} \end{aligned}$$

where *simpleExpQ* corresponds to the square root function of MPFR. Note that $\{q\} = \langle d \rangle$.

The functions described here are unary. The definitions of monotonic IFN functions are straightforward; e.g., $expIFN = map\ expQ$.

Non-monotonic functions such as trigonometric functions are not as easy to implement as monotonic ones. The implementation of continuous functions such as *sinQ* and *cosQ* requires special treatment for the maximum and / or minimum values in the range of each Q. If the accuracy of an input value is too low, the corresponding range could be $(-1, 1)$. Other trigonometric functions such as *tanQ* can be composed of other functions. Although such special treatment has to be taken into consideration, non-monotonic functions can be implemented by using MPFR functions (although we have not yet implemented them in the current IFN library.)

To construct non-monotonic IFN functions, the resultant lazy list must be filtered such that its elements are in ascending order of accuracy. For example, *sinIFN* can be defined as follows:

$$
\begin{aligned}
&sinIFN && :: \ IFN \rightarrow IFN \\
&sinIFN && = \ sinIFN'\ a_{\text{init}} \ \textbf{where}\ a_{\text{init}} = -1 \\
&sinIFN' && :: \ Int \rightarrow IFN \rightarrow IFN \\
&sinIFN'\ a\ (p{:}ps) && = \ \textbf{if}\ a' \leq a\ \textbf{then}\ sinIFN'\ a\ ps\ \textbf{else}\ r : sinIFN'\ a'\ ps \\
&\qquad \textbf{where}\ r && = \ sinQ\ p \\
&\qquad\qquad a' && = \ ac\ r
\end{aligned}
$$

3.7 Precision and Accuracy

In ordinary floating-point computations, the word "precision" usually denotes the number of (meaningful) digits in the mantissa. Precision thus implies the relative error of each floating-point number. In contrast, we use "accuracy" for the index of preciseness of each floating-point number of Q. As defined in Sect. 3.1, the accuracy of a floating-point number q of type Q, $ac\ q$, is an indicator of the absolute error of q. In the strict sense, precision and accuracy are different. However, phrases used in the context of numerical computation such as "precision improvement" and "accuracy improvement" imply the same meaning. Hereafter, we use the "precision" and "accuracy" interchangeably unless otherwise stated.

4 Logical Expressions with IFNs

4.1 Treatment of Logical Expressions

The preciseness of the results of numerical computations does not depend only on the accuracy of the arithmetic operations. For some numerical methods including iterative solving and truncated summation of an infinite series, control transfers are required to terminate the computation. Thus, correct evaluation of branch conditions, i.e., logical expressions, dependent on the results of floating-point arithmetic is crucial.

Logical expressions have type *Bool*. Since there is no "more precise *True*," or "*True* but very close to *False*," a logical expression should return a simple Boolean value. Boolean values should not change even when adaptive accuracy refinement is applied to arithmetic expressions. This means that accurate comparisons of floating-point values have to be done immediately.

Zero-testing for a floating-point value is not as easy as one might think. It might not be enough to simply look at the mantissa of floating-point numbers. Recall that every floating-point number is simply an approximation of a real value. In fact, algorithms dependent on the result of equality checking are considered to be improper when writing numerical programs. Nevertheless, two numbers are frequently compared.

Taking the above into account, our design decision is summarized as follows:

- True zero is separately treated throughout the computation.
- Zero-testing is done in accordance with an auxiliary parameter.

4.2 Introduction of True Zeros

Here we introduce the idea of *true zeros*. A true zero is generated when a literal constant zero appears in a program. In addition, a true zero can be the result of an operation on Q. For example, we can extend *mulQ* so that $mulQ\ q\ z = z$, where z is a true zero. A true zero is never generated from an operation when all operands are not true zeros.

To treat true zeros, we extend the datatype Q:

$$\textbf{data}\ Q = Q\ \{\ sign :: Int,\ \ mantissa :: [\,Int\,],\ \ expo :: Int,\ \ zeroFlag :: Bool\ \}$$

We let Q include *zeroFlag*, which represents whether the value is a true zero. Notice that we do not care about the values of *sign*, *mantissa*, and *expo* for a true zero because any operation on Q can be defined without them.

As for IFN operators, if we define $ac\ z = \infty$ and $lenM\ z = \infty$ for a true zero z, no modification for the IFN operators defined in Sects. 3.4 and 3.5 is required. In fact, when a true zero appears as the current value in an IFN, the next value need not be accessed because there should be no better value.

As a result of this separate handling of true zeros, a true zero can appear only as the first element in a lazy list, and the subsequent elements are never accessed. This property can be used for optimization in the implementation of IFN operators. For example, $addIFN\ ps\ qs$ can be defined to return ps immediately if the first element of qs is a true zero.

4.3 Zero-Testing and Equality Testing

Besides true zero, it is practically convenient to capture very small computational results as "approximated zero." Here, *tol* is an integer called *tolerance* that is used to judge whether to treat a value as zero.

If we assume that the q instance of Q is normalized, a zero-testing function can be defined as:

$$
\begin{array}{llll}
\mathit{zeroQ} :: Q \to \mathit{Int} \to \mathit{Int} & & & \\
\mathit{zeroQ}\ q\ \mathit{tol} & \mid \mathit{zeroFlag}\ q & \| \quad \mathit{expo}\ q < \mathit{tol} & = 1 \\
& \mid \mathit{mantissa}\ q \neq [\,] & \&\& \quad \mathit{expo}\ q \geq \mathit{tol} & = -1 \\
& \mid \textbf{otherwise} & & = 0
\end{array}
$$

$\mathit{zeroQ}\ q\ \mathit{tol} = 0$ indicates that $\langle q \rangle = 0$ but $\mathit{expo}\ q$ is too large to treat q as zero.

By using *zeroQ*, a zero-testing function for IFNs with tolerance *tol* can be defined as:

$$
\begin{array}{lll}
\mathit{zeroIFN} :: \mathit{IFN} \to \mathit{Int} \to \mathit{Bool} & & \\
\mathit{zeroIFN}\ (q{:}qs)\ \ \mathit{tol} & \mid \mathit{zeroQ}\ q\ \mathit{tol} == 1 & = \mathit{True} \\
& \mid \mathit{zeroQ}\ q\ \mathit{tol} == -1 & = \mathit{False} \\
& \mid \textbf{otherwise} & = \mathit{zeroIFN}\ qs\ \mathit{tol}
\end{array}
$$

zeroIFN uses adaptive accuracy refinement on a given IFN. *zeroIFN* stops for any IFN. Letting $v \leftarrowtail qs$, the relationship between an IFN *qs* and an integer *tol* is

$$
\begin{cases}
\mathit{zeroIFN}\ qs\ \mathit{tol} = \mathit{True} & \Longrightarrow |v| < 2^{tol-1} \\
\mathit{zeroIFN}\ qs\ \mathit{tol} = \mathit{False} & \Longrightarrow |v| \geq 2^{tol-1}.
\end{cases}
$$

Equality testing of two IFNs is defined as follows.

$$
\begin{array}{lll}
\mathit{equalIFN} & :: & \mathit{IFN} \to \mathit{IFN} \to \mathit{Int} \to \mathit{Bool} \\
\mathit{equalIFN}\ ps\ qs\ \mathit{tol} & = & \mathit{zeroIFN}\ (\mathit{subIFN}\ ps\ qs)\ \mathit{tol}
\end{array}
$$

where *subIFN* is an IFN operator defined in Sect. 3.5.

The relationship among *ps*, *qs*, and *tol* is

$$
\begin{cases}
\mathit{equalIFN}\ ps\ qs\ \mathit{tol} = \mathit{True} & \Longrightarrow |v - w| < 2^{tol-1} \\
\mathit{equalIFN}\ ps\ qs\ \mathit{tol} = \mathit{False} & \Longrightarrow |v - w| \geq 2^{tol-1},
\end{cases}
$$

where $v \leftarrowtail ps$ and $w \leftarrowtail qs$. Note that *equalIFN* does not test true equality; it tests only the approximate equality of two IFNs.

4.4 Comparison Between Two IFNs

A comparison function that judges whether an IFN is less than another is defined as:

$$
\begin{array}{ll}
\mathit{lessIFN} & :: \mathit{IFN} \to \mathit{IFN} \to \mathit{Int} \to \mathit{Bool} \\
\mathit{lessIFN}\ \ (p{:}ps)\ \ (q{:}qs)\ \ \mathit{tol} & \\
\quad \mid \langle p \rangle + \{p\} < \langle q \rangle - \{q\} & = \mathit{True} \\
\quad \mid \langle p \rangle - \{p\} \geq \langle q \rangle + \{q\} & = \mathit{False} \\
\quad \mid \mathit{zeroQ}\ (\mathit{addQ}\ q\ (\mathit{negQ}\ p))\ \mathit{tol} == 1 & = \mathit{False} \\
\quad \mid \mathit{ac}\ p > \mathit{ac}\ q & = \mathit{lessIFN}\ (p{:}ps)\ \ qs\ \ \mathit{tol} \\
\quad \mid \mathit{ac}\ p < \mathit{ac}\ q & = \mathit{lessIFN}\ ps\ (q{:}\ qs)\ \ \mathit{tol} \\
\quad \mid \textbf{otherwise} & = \mathit{lessIFN}\ ps\ qs\ \ \mathit{tol}
\end{array}
$$

lessIFN uses adaptive accuracy refinement on a given IFN, and stops for any IFN as well as *zeroIFN*. The relationship between *ps*, *qs* and *tol* is

$$\begin{cases} \mathit{lessIFN}\ ps\ qs\ tol = \mathit{True} \Longrightarrow v + 2^{tol-1} \leq w \\ \mathit{lessIFN}\ ps\ qs\ tol = \mathit{False} \Longrightarrow v + 2^{tol-1} > w, \end{cases}$$

where $v \leftarrow\!\prec ps$ and $w \leftarrow\!\prec qs$.

Other comparison operators can be defined using *lessIFN*:

```
lesseqIFN, greaterIFN, greatereqIFN  :: IFN → IFN → Int → Bool
lesseqIFN                            :: IFN → IFN → Int → Bool
lesseqIFN  (p:ps)  (q:qs)  tol
  | ⟨p⟩ + {p} < ⟨q⟩ − {q}                = True
  | ⟨p⟩ − {p} ≥ ⟨q⟩ + {q}                = False
  | zeroQ (addQ q (negQ p)) tol == 1     = True
  | ac p > ac q                          = lesseqIFN (p:ps) qs tol
  | ac p < ac q                          = lesseqIFN ps (q:qs) tol
  | otherwise                            = lesseqIFN ps qs tol
greaterIFN ps qs tol                     = not (lesseqIFN ps qs tol)
greatereqIFN ps qs tol                   = not (lessIFN ps qs tol)
```

5 Detailed Design and Implementation of Primitives

In Sects. 3 and 4, we presented the principle of IFN and the basic design of primitives in the IFN library. In fact, the functions in Haskell presented in previous sections could literally constitute a set of library primitives. However, the data structures and algorithms used in their codes are not suitable for high-speed computation. In this section, we discuss implementation issues and the detailed design of primitives.

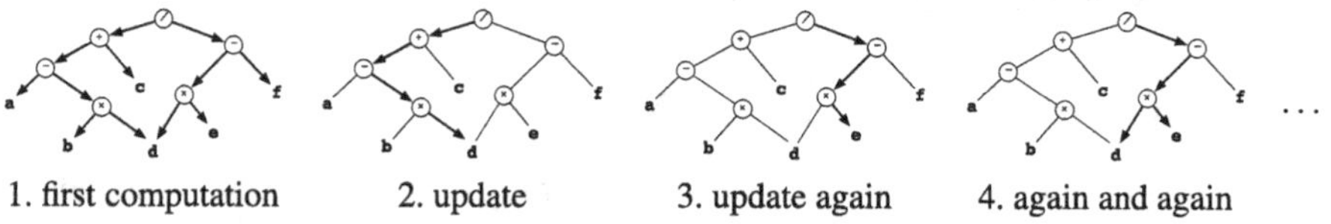

Fig. 3. Adaptive precision refinement in naive way. Arrows along edges depict propagation of order for recomputation.

5.1 Adaptive Accuracy Refinement for IFN Computations

Control of Adaptive Accuracy Refinement. In previous sections, we described the basic design of IFNs. An IFN does not know whether its current value is sufficiently accurate; this can be judged only at the root of the computation tree. If the root judges that the accuracy of the IFN's current value at the root is unsatisfactory, it issues a demand for "recomputation for a more accurate value" to its child (or children) on the basis of the definition of the operation (e.g., *addIFN*) at the root. This recomputation demand is propagated down to the (part of the) leaves. Every node that receives the demand produces the next more accurate value in the IFN stream it returns. The entire computation proceeds as a repetition of this *accuracy refinement process*.

The accuracy refinement process, illustrated in Fig. 3, starts only if the resulting precision does not meet the user's requirement. The demand for recomputation is propagated all the way to one or more leaves, and the values at the nodes on the paths from the leaves to the root are updated. This process is iterated until the resultant value at the root is sufficiently accurate. Even though recomputation is done only at nodes of a subtree in each iteration, the repetition process is inherently inefficient.

In fact, the accuracy refinement process could be performed too many times because each node in the computation tree is not informed of the required accuracies of the value it produces (in the IFN stream). Our approach to reducing this inefficiency is to advise each node of the required accuracy of the value it produces when propagating the demand for a more accurate value. Although the required accuracy at the root is not actually required at other nodes, we use the accuracy given by the user as the lower limit at each node of the computation tree. Although this is a simple heuristic approach, it works well for many cases from our experience.

Setting Initial Accuracy of IFNs. To control the initial precisions of the IFNs at the nodes and leaves of the computation tree, we introduce datatype *IFNgen* for constructing the computation tree.

type $IFNgen = Int \rightarrow IFN$

IFNgen is a function type that accepts an accuracy and generates an IFN for which the initial element's accuracy is defined by the argument. Numerical programs are constructed using "*IFNgen* operators" instead of IFN operators. This modification is realizable by replacing several primitives as follows:

$$
\begin{aligned}
&addIFN \quad\quad :: IFNgen \rightarrow IFNgen \rightarrow IFNgen\\
&addIFN\ v\ w\ a = addIFN'\ a\ (v\ a)\ (w\ a)
\end{aligned}
$$

$$
\begin{aligned}
&genIFNfromString \quad :: String \rightarrow IFNgen\\
&genIFNfromString\ s\ a = map\ f\ [a,\ a{+}\ diffN\ ..]\\
&\qquad\qquad \textbf{where}\ f\ n = fromString\ (fromIntegral\ n)\ s
\end{aligned}
$$

$$
\begin{aligned}
&accurateValue \quad :: Int \rightarrow IFNgen \rightarrow Q\\
&accurateValue\ a\ v = head\ \$\ dropWhile(\backslash q \rightarrow ac\ q < a)\ (v\ a)
\end{aligned}
$$

Although the types of primitives change, the whole course of computation is consistently replaced, and the numerical programs prepared by the user do not need to be modified.

With *IFNgen*, the result accuracy required by the user is propagated all the way through the edges of the computation tree to the leaves. With this functionality, the modification of the accuracy required for operands at each IFN operator can be controlled in detail by using an appropriate function, *nextAccuracy*, that returns, given the current accuracy, the next accuracy to be attained. For example, *addIFN* can be defined as follows:

```
addIFN          :: IFNgen → IFNgen → IFNgen
addIFN v w a = let a′= nextAccuracy a in addIFN′ a (v a′) (w a′)
```

Conversion of an *IFN*-based library to an *IFNgen*-based library causes subtle but non-ignorable problems. When computation trees are constructed on the basis of *IFNgen*, the nodes of the tree are type *IFNgen* functions that generate specific IFNs at run-time. Therefore, even though the generator of type *IFNgen* is referred to by multiple *IFNgen* operators as the generator of the operands, the IFNs generated at run-time are not shared. The use of non-shared IFNs means that complicated numerical programs that utilize iterative algorithms and / or matrix computations are unfeasible because of the blowup of duplicated computations.

To share IFNs among IFNgen operators, we use a static storage area to save once-generated IFNs. This mechanism is achieved by modifying several primitives as follows. Each *IFNgen* operator creates a reference *IORef Maybe IFN* when it is first evaluated, and the created IFNs are written into it. Note that the user's program does not need not to be modified.

```
import Data.IORef
saveIFN   :: IFNgen → IFNgen
saveIFN f = unsafePerformIO $ do
    ref ← newIORef Nothing
    let f′ a = unsafePerformIO $ do
                t ← readIORef ref
                case t of
                  Nothing → do let v = f a
                               writeIORef ref (Just v)
                               return v
                  Just v′  → do let newv = dropWhile (\n → ac n < a) v′
                               return newv
    return f′

addIFN     :: IFNgen → IFNgen → IFNgen
addIFN v w = saveIFN $ \a → let a′= f a in addIFN′ a (v a′) (w a′)

genIFNfromString   :: String → IFNgen
genIFNfromString s = saveIFN $ \a → map f [a, a + diffN..]
         where f n = fromString (fromIntegral n) s
```

5.2 Configuration of IFNs

The definition of IFN is very simple as described in Sect. 3.2. To optimize performance, we can design IFN operators as follows:

- The accuracy of each IFN's initial element for literal values can be set higher than the user's required accuracy for the total results.
- The difference in accuracy between the elements of each IFN for literal values can be increased, or even the sequence can be defined on the basis of a geometric series.
- A lower limit on accuracy refinement can be imposed for each IFN operator.

In our experience, these modifications and parameter settings greatly affect the performance of numerical programs. However, it is difficult to determine the optimal configuration. If the accuracy of each IFN's initial element for literals is too large, useless computations to obtain too accurate values by variable-length floating-point operations might take a very long time. However, if it is too small, there could be a huge number of iterations for adaptive accuracy refinement, resulting in a great amount of time to obtain accurate results. The settings for other items in the list above also affect computational cost. Deciding the appropriate configuration remains for future work.

5.3 Structure of Datatype Q and Design of Q Operators

The datatype definition of Q presented in Sect. 3.1 was introduced for the sake of concise explanation of the idea of IFNs and is not sufficient for efficient implementation of IFNs. It is quite natural to define Q in terms of variable-length floating point representation in C. Thus, we decided to use the MPFR library [3] for this purpose. We used the MPFR data structure *__mpfr_struct* to construct Q in C and used MPFR routines like *mpfr_add* to define Q operators such as *simpleAddQ*. The definition of Q in C is as follows.

```
typedef struct {
  __mpfr_struct *_mp;
  bool _zeroFlag;
} Q;
```

We used Boehm's GC library for memory management of C objects. By using Haskell's foreign function interface (FFI) and the *Foreign* and *Foreign.Concurrent* modules, we made Haskell's GC cooperate with Boehm's GC.

5.4 Implementation in C Without General-Purpose Garbage Collectors

The adaptive accuracy refinement functionality of the IFN library relies greatly on the lazy evaluation of infinite lists. However, because the dynamic structure constructed at run-time is fairly simple, general-purpose garbage collectors are not necessary (or may be unsuitable). Objects created at run-time do not cyclically reference to each other, and the point of destruction of an IFN's elements in the course of execution is predeterminable. Thus, an implementation of the IFN library in C with its own memory management, such as collection by reference counting, may outperform the awkward cooperation of Haskell's and Boehm's GC facilities described in Sect. 5.4, especially for complicated problems.

On the basis of this perspective, we implemented a version of the IFN library completely in C without general-purpose garbage collectors. IFN cells and other objects such as instances of Q and their mantissas are managed by using a set of ring buffers.

6 Numerical Experiments

Examples presented in this section demonstrate the potential and applicability of adaptive accuracy refinement using IFNs. The results are compared with those of programs using other computable real arithmetic libraries, namely Exact Real Arithmetic (ERA) (version 1.0) [8] and iRRAM (version 2013_01) [9].

ERA is a Haskell library for computable real numbers developed by David Lester [8]. In the library, a computable real, say x, is represented by a function f of type $Int \to Integer$, where the following inequality holds for all $i :: Int, i \geq 0$.

$$\frac{f\ i - 1}{2^i} < x < \frac{f\ i + 1}{2^i}$$

Once f is constructed, the user can obtain an approximated value of x that possesses the desired accuracy. Numerical operators are built on type *CReal*. For example, addition is essentially defined as follows.

data *CReal* = *CR* (*Int* → *Integer*)
(+) :: *CReal* → *CReal* → *CReal*
(*CR* x') + (*CR* y') = *CR* (\p → *round_uk* ((x' (p + 2) + y'(p + 2)) % 4))
where *round_uk* x = *floor* (x + 1 % 2)

Although the implementation is done in quite a small number of lines, ERA is thought to be the fastest among computable real libraries implemented in Haskell [10]. ERA is not based on the idea of adaptive refinement of accuracy — it does not need it. However, to obtain a final result with user-defined accuracy, much computation on integers may be required.

iRRAM is a C++ library for computable real numbers [9]. Each variable of type *REAL* is constructed with a multiple-precision number and information on its absolute error. Errors are accumulated during the course of computation, and if the error in the resultant value exceeds the user's request, the entire computation is repeated with a significantly better precision iRRAM uses external multiple-precision libraries such as MPFR. It was the "clear winner" of a competition among several systems for exact arithmetic held at CCA 2000 [11].

Note that IFN libraries are still prototypes and have much room for optimization. Although the comparison among the libraries reported here was done mainly on the basis of performance, the aim was not to determine a "winner" but to clarify the characteristics of the libraries.

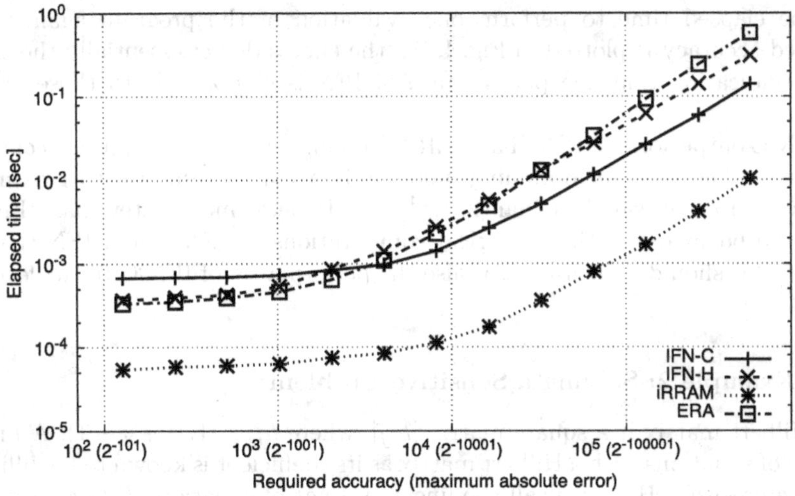

Fig. 4. Performance of libraries for Rump's example. For IFN-C and IFN-H, required accuracies were from 128 to 524,288 (i.e., required absolute errors were from 2^{-129} to $2^{-524289}$). For ERA and iRRAM, required number of decimal digits for result ranged from 38 to 157,826.

6.1 Environment

All programs were run on a MacBook Pro (Intel Core i7 3 GHz with 16GB memory) running OS X 10.10.3. We used two versions of the IFN library. One was implemented in Haskell (IFN-H), described in Sects. 5.1 and 5.3, and the other was implemented in C (IFN-C), described in Sect. 5.4. Both used MPFR [3].

Application programs were written in Haskell for IFN-H and ERA, in C for IFN-C, and in C++ for iRRAM. The Haskell programs given to IFN-H and ERA were the same, and the C and C++ programs were equivalent to the Haskell programs.

The software versions were GHC 7.8.4, Boehm GC 7.4.2 (for IFN-H), GCC 4.8.4, MPFR 3.1.1, and GMP 5.1.1.

6.2 Example 1: Simple Expression

Rump's example (1) was evaluated for accuracies from 128 to 524,288, where required absolute errors were from 2^{-129} to $2^{-524289}$. For ERA and iRRAM, required accuracy was translated into required number of decimal digits for the result, and it ranged from 38 to 157,826. The program used for Haskell was as follows, where type T was *IFNgen* for IFN-H and *CReal* for ERA.

rump (77617:: *T*) (33096:: *T*)
where
  rump a b = ...

The elapsed time to perform one evaluation of the program against the required accuracy is plotted in Fig. 4. All the curves depict essentially the same trend, indicating that the performance of IFN is comparable to those of the others.

IFN-C outperformed IFN-H and ERA for a higher range of required accuracy. However, when used for obtaining moderately accurate results with maximum absolute errors of, say, less than 2^{-1024}, IFN-H performed better than IFN-C. Since the behaviors of the numerical computations of IFN-C and IFN-H were the same, it should be possible to raise the performance of IFN-C to the level of IFN-H.

6.3 Example 2: Solving a Sensitive Problem

The Hilbert matrix is a square matrix $[h_{ij}]$, where $h_{ij} = 1/(i + j - 1)$. A linear system of equations with a Hilbert matrix as its coefficient is known to be difficult to solve precisely. Here, we call the linear systems of equations *Hilbert systems.* We solved Hilbert systems of several sizes requiring several accuracies. We used LU factorization algorithm without pivoting. The C and C++ programs for IFN-C and iRRAM were written as follows. The Haskell programs for IFN-H and ERA were written using mutable arrays offered by *Data.Array.IO*.

for $k = 1, \ ..., \ n$
  for $i = k + 1, \ ..., \ n$
    $a_{ik} \leftarrow a_{ik} / a_{kk}$
    for $j = k + 1, \ ..., \ n$
      $a_{ij} \leftarrow a_{ij} - a_{ik} a_{kj}$

As shown in Fig. 5, the behavior of IFN-C was similar to that of iRRAM. Although clear differences are apparent, IFN-C can be said to be comparable to iRRAM. IFN-H performed as well as IFN-C. However, there was substantial performance degradation of IFN-H for large problems. This is probably because the cost of garbage collection increased with the problem size.

The poor performance of ERA might be because the computed values of common subexpressions were not shared in the overall computation. Although the same functions were used at nodes in the computation tree, the fact that multiple invocations of these functions did not share the results caused an explosion in the amount of computation. A computational real arithmetic library of this type is thus difficult to use in algorithms that perform iterations or matrix computations.

Effects of the Accuracy Control Strategy. Here, we show the results for Hilbert systems with 64 unknowns for several configuration patterns (cf. Sect. 5.2). The experiments were done using IFN-C. The choices used were as follows:

1. The accuracy of the first element's in each IFN for literal values was set as either

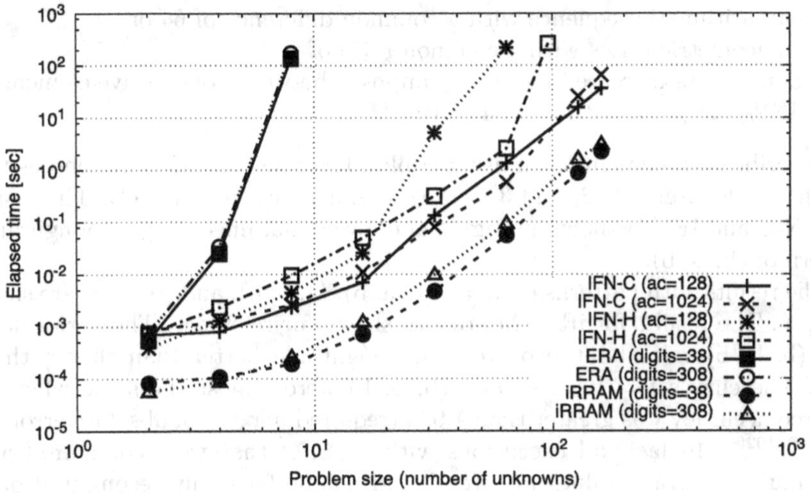

Fig. 5. Solving linear equations with Hilbert matrix. Required accuracies were 128 and 1024 (i.e., required maximum absolute errors were 2^{-129} and 2^{-1025}). For ERA and iRRAM, required correct figures in decimal were 38 and 308.

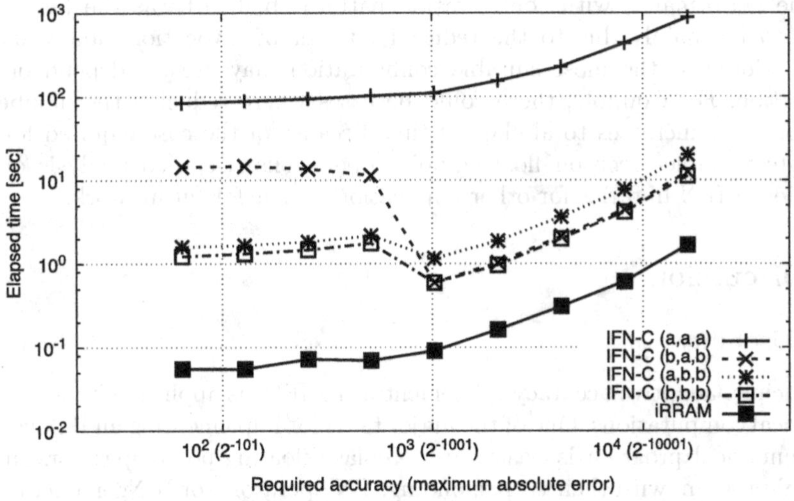

Fig. 6. Solving linear equations with Hilbert matrix of size 64 × 64. Required accuracies for IFN-C were from 64 to 16,384 (i.e., required absolute errors were from 2^{-65} to 2^{-16385}). For iRRAM, required number of decimal digits for the result ranged from 20 to 4,932. IFN-C performance was evaluated for four configurations.

(a) the accuracy required for the result or
(b) twice the required accuracy.

2. The pattern to increase the accuracy of each IFN for literal values was set as either

   (a) an arithmetic sequence with a common difference of 64 or
   (b) a geometric series with a common ratio of 2.
3. The minimum increase in accuracy imposed between consecutive elements in all IFNs was set as either (a) 4 or (b) 32.

We describe each configuration using triples; for example, (a, b, a) denotes that the choices for items 1, 2, and 3 are (a), (b), and (a), respectively. The results for IFN-C and IFN-H shown in Figs. 4 and 5 were obtained with a configuration pattern of (b, b, b).

The results with patterns (a, a, a), (b, a, b), (a, b, b), and (b, b, b) are shown in Fig. 6. The results for iRRAM are also shown for reference. The performance with (b, b, b) was about two orders of magnitude better than that with (a, a, a). The curves for (b, a, b) and (b, b, b) were almost the same when the required accuracy was greater than 1,024 (required maximum absolute error less than 2^{-1025}). In fact, all executions with (b, _, _) that were configured with large initial accuracy values for literals did not perform any recomputation in the range of requirements, including (b, b, a) and (b, a, b), which are not shown in Fig. 6. When moderate accuracy was required, items 2 and 3 both have to be (b). Although not shown in Fig. 6, the result with (b, b, a) was very close to that of (b, a, b).

The performance with configuration pattern (b, b, b) was the best. This seems to be mainly due to the reduced number of invocations for recomputation. However, the most suitable configuration may greatly depend on the application. For example, there could be cases where reducing the number of computations increases total elapsed time because of the cost required for too accurate variable-precision floating-point operations. Detailed analysis of the behavior of IFN libraries for other applications is left for future work.

7 Discussion

7.1 Usability

In principle, adaptive accuracy refinement using IFNs is applicable to almost all numerical computations. One of the major tasks for implementing an IFN version of a numerical program is basically to replace floating-point operators in the original program with their corresponding IFN operators (or IFNgen operators). As for the Haskell library we developed, since the *IFN* datatype is declared as instances of number-related type classes such as *Num* and *Fractional*, the user can use normal arithmetic operators such as $+$, $*$ without any knowledge of the internal details of IFNs.

7.2 Applicability

IFNs can be used to solve any type of numerical problem. As demonstrated in Sect. 6, evaluation of complex expressions and matrix computations can be carried out.

Usage of IFNs simply enables the user to eliminate errors caused by the usage of fixed length floating-point representations. When IFNs are used for programs derived from an approximated modeling process such as truncation, discretization, and any style of simplification, the accuracy of the results is not guaranteed. In addition, because the accuracy of zero-testing depends on the external parameter, the accuracy of the entire result can also depend on the parameter. This includes iterative algorithms such as the Newton-Raphson method, which require comparison of (computed) real values to control the execution.

7.3 Performance

Compared to arithmetic on the basis of a fixed-number of bits such as *Double*, IFN arithmetic has inherent and significant overhead caused by operators on Q (e.g., *addQ*), operators on IFNs (e.g., *addIFN*) and the control of demand driven computation.

The properties of IFN operators enable the user to obtain computational results for expressions composed of basic arithmetic operations with the desired accuracies. However, expressions that would cause catastrophic cancellations of significant digits (if *Double* numbers were used) could take a long computational time with IFNs.

The results of our experimental implementation of IFN libraries (Sect. 6) show the potential of IFNs. Although current versions of IFN libraries cannot be used to solve large problems, we think there is much room for improvement in terms of computational speed. Rearrangement of the many bit-wise operations required for post-processing of $\sqcup$ in each Q operator may be one way to reduce computational time.

8 Related Work

The basic idea of IFNs came from the notion of *improving sequences* [6,7]. An improving sequence is a finite monotonic sequence of approximation values of a final value that are improved gradually in accordance with an ordering relation. Programs constructed with improving sequences offers many opportunities to eliminate too accurate computation. The effectiveness of improving sequences has been demonstrated for combinatorial optimization problems. IFNs are different from improving sequences because IFNs are specialized and *infinite* streams representing real numbers

Dynamic detection of catastrophic cancellation of significant digits can be realized by monitoring each normalization process of the resultant values in floating-point arithmetic (an example of a vector processor with cancellation detectors is presented elsewhere [12]).

Sophisticated tools for detecting precision degradation have been proposed [13,14]. They use *shadow values* calculated using higher precision arithmetic, so the results are presumably better. By using the tools, the occurrence of cancellation can be detected and causes of the errors can be analyzed. However, accuracy of the results will never be guaranteed by those tools.

An option other than floating-point arithmetic for carrying out precise numerical computation is classical rational arithmetic. Each value is represented by a pair of integers, i.e., a numerator and a denominator. While it can be used to evaluate simple expressions like Rump's example (Sect. 1), it may not be suitable for complicated programs due to huge computational cost. Approximation by a kind of rounding may be needed.

Interval arithmetic, in which each value is represented by upper and lower bounds, is another tool for accuracy-aware numerical computation [1]. Analyses of complicated functions and linear systems based on special facilities for precise inner product computation have been carried out [15]. Our floating-point representation of Q can be considered a virtual interval representation. The feasibility of adaptive refinement with interval arithmetic based on lazy evaluation has been indirectly confirmed by our research.

Exact real computer arithmetic has been studied for decades [16]. To deal with reals, a number of representations have been considered, such as continued fraction representation [17,18], linear fractional transformations for exact arithmetic [19], radix representations with negative digits, non-integral or irrational bases, and nested sequences of rational intervals [20]. In scaled-integer representation [21], reals are represented by functions, and each arithmetic operation consists of the application and construction of functions with rational computation for coefficients. Some of those adopt lazy stream implementation in which each infinite stream represents a real. Although we have not examined in them detail, several libraries have been implemented [8,9,22–24]. Compared to previous approaches, ours is simple and thus has many design choices for the details. The most significant difference between IFNs and others is that each approximate value is represented as a precision-guaranteed floating-point number. In that sense, an IFN can be seen as a sequence of intervals. It can also be seen as a kind of Cauchy sequence although different from ordinary definitions of Cauchy sequences for computable real arithmetic.

9 Conclusion

We have demonstrated a means of adaptive refinement based on lazy evaluation for accurate floating-point numerical computations. We presented the idea of improving floating-point numbers (IFNs) to encapsulate adaptive refinement processes into lazy lists. Computations using IFNs was described in detail. Numerical results based on implementations in Haskell and C demonstrated the effectiveness of the approach.

Future work includes optimization, design of supporting tools, and numerical evaluation on a larger scale of complicated numerical problems.

Acknowledgments. The first author thanks Toshiaki Kitamura and Mizuki Yokoyama for their useful discussions. The authors thank the anonymous reviewers for their detailed comments. This work was supported in part by an HCU Grant for Special Academic Research (General Studies) under Grant No.1030301.

References

1. Knuth, D.E.: The Art of Computer Programming, Sect. 4.2.2, 3rd edn. Addison-Wesley, Boston (1997)
2. Microprocessor Standards Committee of the IEEE Computer Society: IEEE Standard for Floating-Point Arithmetic. IEEE Standard 754 (2008)
3. The GNU MPFR Library. http://www.mpfr.org
4. Rump, S.M.: Algorithms for verified inclusion. In: Moore, R. (ed.) Reliability in Computing, Perspectives in Computing, pp. 109–126. Academic Press, New York (1988)
5. Bird, R.: Introduction to Functional Programming Using Haskell, 2nd edn. Prentice Hall, Englewood Cliffs (1998)
6. Morimoto, T., Takano, Y., Iwasaki, H.: Instantly turning a naive exhaustive search into three efficient searches with pruning. In: Hanus, M. (ed.) PADL 2007. LNCS, vol. 4354, pp. 65–79. Springer, Heidelberg (2007)
7. Iwasaki, H., Morimoto, T., Takano, Y.: Pruning with improving sequences in lazy functional programs. Higher-Order Symbolic Comput. **24**, 281–309 (2011)
8. Lester, D.: ERA: Exact Real Arithmetic, version 1.0 (2000). http://hackage.haskell.org/package/numbers-3000.2.0.1/docs/Data-Number-CReal.html
9. Müller, N.T.: The iRRAM: exact arithmetic in C++. In: Blank, J., Brattka, V., Hertling, P. (eds.) CCA 2000. LNCS, vol. 2064, p. 222. Springer, Heidelberg (2001)
10. Haskell wiki, Applications and Libraries / Mathematics, Sect. 3.2.2.2. http://www.haskell.org/haskellwiki/Applications_and_libraries/Mathematics#Dynamic_precision_by_lazy_evaluation
11. Blanck, J.: Exact real arithmetic systems: results of competition. In: Blank, J., Brattka, V., Hertling, P. (eds.) CCA 2000. LNCS, vol. 2064, p. 389. Springer, Heidelberg (2001)
12. Aniya, S., Kitamura, T.: A performance improvement for floating-point arithmetic unit with precision degradation detection. In: The 17th Workshop on Synthesis And System Integration of Mixed Information Technologies (SASIMI 2012), pp. 490–491 (2012)
13. Jeffrey, K.H., Lam, M.O., Stewart, G.W.: Dynamic floating-point cancellation detection. In: WHIST 2011 (2011)
14. Benz, F., Hildebrandt, A., Hack, S.: A dynamic program analysis to find floating-point accuracy problems. In: SIGPLAN Notices, PLDI 2012, vol. 47, No. 6, pp. 453–462 (2012)
15. Jansen, P., Weidner, P.: High-accuracy arithmetic software – some tests of the ACRITH problem-solving routines. ACM Trans. Math. Softw. **12**(1), 62–70 (1986)
16. Gowland, P., Lester, D.R.: A survey of exact arithmetic implementations. In: Blank, J., Brattka, V., Hertling, P. (eds.) CCA 2000. LNCS, vol. 2064, pp. 30–47. Springer, Heidelberg (2001)
17. Gosper, W.: Continued fractions (1972). http://www.inwap.com/pdp10/hbaker/hakmem/cf.html
18. Vuillemin, J.: Exact real computer arithmetic with continued fractions. IEEE Trans. Comput. **39**, 1087–1105 (1990)
19. Potts, P.: Exact real arithmetic using Möbius transformations, Ph.D. thesis, Department of Computing, Imperial College of Science, Technology and Medicine, University of London. http://www.doc.ic.ac.uk/%7Eae/papers.html
20. Escardó, M.: Introduction to exact numerical computation, Notes for a tutorial at ISSAC (2000). http://www.cs.bham.ac.uk/%7Emhe/issac

21. Boehm, H.-J., Cartwright, R., Riggle, M., O'Donnell, M.J.: Exact real arithmetic: a case study in higher order programming. In: ACM Symposium on Lisp and Functional Programming, pp. 162–173 (1986)
22. Guy, M.: bignum / BigFloat (2007). http://bignum.sourceforge.net/
23. Edalat, A.: Exact real number computation using linear fractional transformations, Final Report on EPSRC grant GR/L43077/01 (2001)
24. Lambov, B.: RealLib: an efficient implementation of exact real arithmetic. Math. Struct. Comput. Sci. **17**, 81–98 (2007)

Needle & Knot: Binder Boilerplate Tied Up

Steven Keuchel[1(✉)], Stephanie Weirich[2], and Tom Schrijvers[3]

[1] Ghent University, Ghent, Belgium
steven.keuchel@ugent.be
[2] University of Pennsylvania, Philadelphia, USA
sweirich@cis.upenn.edu
[3] KU Leuven, Leuven, Belgium
tom.schrijvers@cs.kuleuven.be

Abstract. To lighten the burden of programming language mechanization, many approaches have been developed that tackle the substantial boilerplate which arises from variable binders. Unfortunately, the existing approaches are limited in scope. They typically do not support complex binding forms (such as multi-binders) that arise in more advanced languages, or they do not tackle the boilerplate due to mentioning variables and binders in relations. As a consequence, the human mechanizer is still unnecessarily burdened with binder boilerplate and discouraged from taking on richer languages.

This paper presents Knot, a new approach that substantially extends the support for binder boilerplate. Knot is a highly expressive language for natural and concise specification of syntax with binders. Its meta-theory constructively guarantees the coverage of a considerable amount of binder boilerplate for well-formed specifications, including that for well-scoping of terms and context lookups. Knot also comes with a code generator, Needle, that specializes the generic boilerplate for convenient embedding in Coq and provides a tactic library for automatically discharging proof obligations that frequently come up in proofs of weakening and substitution lemmas of type-systems.

Our evaluation shows, that Needle & Knot significantly reduce the size of language mechanizations (by 40 % in our case study). Moreover, as far as we know, Knot enables the most concise mechanization of the POPLmark Challenge (1a + 2a) and is two-thirds the size of the next smallest. Finally, Knot allows us to mechanize for instance dependently-typed languages, which is notoriously challenging because of dependent contexts and mutually-recursive sorts with variables.

1 Introduction

The meta-theory of programming language semantics and type-systems is highly complex due to the management of many details. Formal proofs are long and prone to subtle errors that can invalidate large amounts of work. In order to guarantee the correctness of formal meta-theory, techniques for mechanical formalization in proof-assistants have received much attention in recent years.

P. Thiemann (Ed.): ESOP 2016, LNCS 9632, pp. 419–445, 2016.
DOI: 10.1007/978-3-662-49498-1_17

This paper targets the syntactic approach to programming language metatheory, invented by Wright and Felleisen [42] and popularized by Pierce [25]. An important issue that arises in such formalizations is the treatment of variable binding which typically comprises the better part of the formalization. Most of this variable binding infrastructure is repetitive and tedious boilerplate. By boilerplate we mean mechanical operations and lemmas that appear in many languages, such as: (1) common operations like calculating the sets of free variables or the domain of a typing context, appending contexts and substitutions; (2) lemmas about operations like commutation of substitutions or the interaction between the free-variable calculation and substitution; and (3) lemmas about the well-scoping of terms and preservation of well-scoping under operations.

To alleviate researchers from this burden, multiple approaches have been developed to capture the structure of variable binding and generically take care of the associated boilerplate. These include specification languages of syntax with binding and scoping rules [33], tools or reflection libraries that generate code for proof assistants from specifications [7,27,32], generic programming libraries that implement boilerplate using datatype generic functions and proofs [18] and meta-languages that have built-in support for syntax with binding [22,24,35].

Yet, despite the multitude of existing approaches, the scope of the available support is still rather limited. Most approaches do not cover rich-binding forms (such as patterns or declaration lists) or the advanced scoping rules (like sequential and recursive scopes) of more complex languages. Those that do still leave most of the boilerplate up to the developer. As a consequence, only drastic simplifications of languages are mechanized, in order to fit the mold of existing tools and make the development cost affordable. For example, multi-variable binders are replaced by single-variable binders and polymorphic languages by monomorphic sublanguages to avoid dealing with multiple distinct namespaces. Obviously, there is a very real danger that these simplifications gloss over actual problems in the original language and give a false sense of security.

This work greatly improves the support for binder boilerplate in the mechanization of programming languages in two dimensions. First, we support a rich class of abstract syntaxes with binders involving advanced binding forms, complex scoping rules and mutually recursive sorts with variables. Secondly, the supported boilerplate for this class goes beyond term-related functions and lemmas: it also generically covers contexts and well-scopedness predicates.

For this purpose, we provide KNOT, a language to concisely and naturally specify the abstract syntax and rich binding structure of programming languages. From such a KNOT specification, our NEEDLE tool generates the corresponding COQ code as well as all the derived boilerplate. Our specific contributions are:

1. We present KNOT, a new approach to automate the treatment of variable binding boilerplate. KNOT is a natural and concise specification language for syntax with binders. KNOT is highly expressive, supporting multi-binders, advanced scoping rules and mutually recursive sorts with variables.
2. We prove that any well-formed KNOT specification is guaranteed to produce a considerable amount of binder boilerplate operations and lemmas that include

the usual term-level interaction lemmas, but also lemmas for contexts and context lookups and for weakening, strengthening and substitution lemmas of well-scopedness relations. Our mechanized proof consists of a constructive generic implementation which in particular deals with the challenges of mutually recursive definitions.

3. Alongside the generic implementation, we provide NEEDLE, a convenient code generator that produces specialized boilerplate for easy embedding in larger COQ formalizations. NEEDLE also provides a library of tactics to simplify and automatically discharge well-scopedness proof obligations.
4. We demonstrate the usefulness of KNOT with two case studies.
   (a) We show that the KNOT-based approach is on average 40 % smaller than the unassisted approach in a case-study of type-safety mechanizations for 10 languages.
   (b) We compare the KNOT solution of the POPLMARK challenge (1A + 2A) to 7 other solutions. Ours is by far the smallest.

The code for NEEDLE and the Coq developments (compatible with Coq 8.4 and 8.5) are available at https://users.ugent.be/~skeuchel/knot.

2 Overview

This section gives an overview of the variable binding boilerplate that arises when proving type preservation of typed programming languages. For this purpose, we use $F_\times$ (i.e., System F with products and destructuring pattern bindings) as the running example. In the following, we elaborate the different steps of the formalization and point out where variable binding boilerplate arises.

2.1 Syntax: Variable Representation

Figure 1 (top) shows the first step in the formalization: the syntax of $F_\times$. Notice that patterns can be nested and can bind an arbitrary number of variables at once. In this grammar the scoping rules are left implicit. The intended rules are that in a type or term abstraction the variable scopes over the body e and in a pattern binding the variables bound by the pattern scope over e_2 but not e_1.

The syntax raises the first variable-related issue: how to concretely represent variables, an issue that is side-stepped in Fig. 1 (top). Traditionally, one would use identifiers for variables. However, when formalizing meta-theory this representation requires reasoning modulo α-equivalence of terms to an excruciating extent. It is therefore inevitable to choose a different representation.

The goal of this paper is neither to develop a new approach to variable binding nor to compare existing ones, but rather to scale the generic treatment of a single approach to realistic languages. For this purpose, we choose de Bruijn representations [9], motivated by two main reasons. First, reasoning with de Bruijn representations is well-understood and, in particular, the representation of pattern binding and scoping rules is also well-understood [10,15].

α, β ::=		type variable	p ::=		pattern
x, y ::=		term variable		$\mid x$	variable pattern
Γ, Δ ::=		type environment		$\mid p_1, p_2$	pair pattern
	$\mid \epsilon$	empty env	e ::=		term
	$\mid \Gamma, \alpha$	type binding		$\mid x$	term variable
	$\mid \Gamma, x : \tau$	term binding		$\mid \lambda x : \tau . e$	term abstraction
τ, σ ::=		type		$\mid e_1\ e_2$	application
	$\mid \alpha$	type variable		$\mid \Lambda\alpha . e$	type abstraction
	$\mid \tau \to \tau$	function type		$\mid e\ [\tau]$	type application
	$\mid \tau_1 \times \tau_2$	product type		$\mid e_1, e_2$	pair
	$\mid \forall \alpha . \tau$	universal type		$\mid$ **case** e_1 **of** $p \to e_2$	pattern binding

$E ::= \mathit{enil}$	$T ::= \mathit{tvar}\ n$	$t ::= \mathit{var}\ n$	$\mid \mathit{tyapp}\ t\ T$
$\mid \mathit{etvar}\ E$	$\mid \mathit{tarr}\ T_1\ T_2$	$\mid \mathit{abs}\ T\ t$	$\mid \mathit{prod}\ t_1\ t_2$
$\mid \mathit{evar}\ E\ T$	$\mid \mathit{tprod}\ T_1\ T_2$	$\mid \mathit{app}\ t_1\ t_2$	$\mid$ **case** $t_1\ p\ t_2$
$p ::= \mathit{pvar}$	$\mid \mathit{tall}\ T$	$\mid \mathit{tyabs}\ t$	
$\mid \mathit{pprod}\ p_1\ p_2$			

Fig. 1. $F_\times$ syntax and de Bruijn representation

Second, the functions related to variable binding, the statements of properties of these functions and their proofs have highly regular structures with respect to the abstract syntax and the scoping rules of the language. This helps us in treating boilerplate generically and automating proofs.

The term grammar in Fig. 1 (bottom) encodes a de Bruijn representation of $F_\times$. The variable occurrences of binders have been removed in this representation and the referencing occurrences of type and term variables are replaced by de Bruijn indices n. These de Bruijn indices point directly to their binders: The index n points to the nth enclosing binding position. For instance, the $F_\times$ expression for the polymorphic swap function

$$\Lambda\alpha.\Lambda\beta.\lambda x : (\alpha, \beta).\textbf{case}\ x\ \textbf{of}\ (x1, x2) \to (x2, x1)$$

is represented by the de Bruijn term

$$\begin{array}{l} \mathit{tyabs}\ (\mathit{tyabs}\ (\mathit{abs}\ (\mathit{tprod}\ (\mathit{tvar}\ 1)\ (\mathit{tvar}\ 0)) \\ \quad (\textbf{case}\ (\mathit{var}\ 0)\ (\mathit{pprod}\ \mathit{pvar}\ \mathit{pvar})\ (\mathit{prod}\ (\mathit{var}\ 0)\ (\mathit{var}\ 1))))) \end{array}$$

Again, the order in which de Bruijn indices are bound and the scoping rules are left implicit in the term grammar. Our specification language Knot for de Bruijn terms from Sect. 3 will make order of binding and scoping rules explicit.

A second example is $\mathit{tyabs}\ (\mathit{tyabs}\ (\mathit{abs}\ (\mathit{tvar}\ 1)\ (\mathit{abs}\ (\mathit{tvar}\ 0)\ (\mathit{var}\ 1)))$ for the polymorphic *const* function $\Lambda\alpha.\Lambda\beta.\lambda x{:}\alpha.\lambda y{:}\beta.x$. We use different namespaces for term and type variables and treat indices for variables from distinct namespaces independently: The index for the type variable β that is used in the inner *abs* is 0 and not 1, because we only count the number of binders for the corresponding namespace and not binders for other namespaces.

2.2 Semantics: Shifting and Substitution

The next step in the formalization is to develop the typical semantic relations for the language of study. In the case of $F_\times$, these comprise a small-step call-by-value operational semantics, as well as a well-scopedness relation for types, a typing relation for terms and a typing relation for patterns. The operational semantics defines the evaluation of term- and type-abstraction by means of β-reduction.

$$(\lambda x.e_1)\ e_2 \longrightarrow_\beta [x \mapsto e_2]\ e_1 \qquad (\Lambda\alpha.e)\ \tau \longrightarrow_\beta [\alpha \mapsto \tau]\ e$$

This requires the first boilerplate for the de Bruijn representation: substitution of type variables in types, terms and contexts, and of term variables in terms.

It is necessary to define *weakening*s first, that adapts the indices of free variables in a term e when its context Γ is changed, e.g. when traversing into the right-hand side of a pattern binding that binds Δ variables: $\Gamma \vdash e \rightsquigarrow \Gamma, \Delta \vdash e$.

To only adapt free variables but not bound variables in e, we implement *weakening* by reducing it to a more general operation called *shifting* that implements insertion of a single variable in the middle of a context [10,25]

$$\Gamma, \Delta \vdash e \rightsquigarrow \Gamma, x, \Delta \vdash e \qquad \Gamma, \Delta \vdash e \rightsquigarrow \Gamma, \alpha, \Delta \vdash e$$

In total, we need to implement four shift functions to adapt type-variable indices in types, terms and contexts and term-variable indices in terms.

Table 1. Lines of Coq code for the $F_\times$ meta-theory mechanization.

	Useful		Boilerplate	
Syntax	28	(4.1 %)	0	(0 %)
Semantics	62	(9.2 %)	149	(22.1 %)
Theorems	140	(20.7 %)	296	(43.9 %)
Total	230	(34.0 %)	445	(66.0 %)

2.3 Theorems: Commutation, Weakening and Preservation

Given the definitions from the previous subsection, we are ready to define the semantics and type system of $F_\times$ and move on to formulate and prove type soundness for $F_\times$. We refrain from formulating it here explicitly. The proof of type soundness involves the usual lemmas for canonical forms, typing inversion, pattern-matching definedness as well as progress and preservation [42]. To prove these lemmas, we require a second set of variable binding boilerplate:

- Interaction lemmas for the shift, weaken and substitution operations. These include commutation lemmas for two operations working on distinct indices and the cancellation of a subst and a shift working on the same variables (cf. Sect. 6). In the case of $F_\times$, we only need interaction lemmas for type-variable operations to prove the preservation lemma, but in general these may also involve interactions between two operations in distinct namespaces.

- Weakening and strengthening lemmas about context lookups which in particular need additional interaction lemmas for context concatenation.
- We need to define well-scopedness of types with respect to a context and prove weakening and strengthening properties and the preservation of well-scopedness under well-scoped type-variable substitution.

2.4 Summary

Table 1 summarizes the effort required to formalize type soundness of $F_{\times}$ in the Coq proof assistant in terms of the de Bruijn representation. It lists the lines of Coq code for the three different parts of the formalization discussed above, divided in binder-related "boilerplate" and the other "useful" code. The table clearly shows that the boilerplate constitutes about two thirds of the formalization. The boilerplate lemmas in particular, while individually fairly short, make up the bulk of the boilerplate and close to half of the whole formalization.

Of course, very similar variable binder boilerplate arises in the formalization of other languages, where it requires a similar unnecessarily large development effort. For instance, Rossberg et al. [30] report that 400 out of 500 lemmas of their mechanization in the locally-nameless style [6] were tedious boilerplate lemmas.

Fortunately, there is much regularity to the boilerplate: it follows the structure of the language's abstract syntax and its scoping rules. Many earlier works have already exploited this fact in order to automatically generate or generically define part of the boilerplate for simple languages.

2.5 Our Solution: Needle and Knot

The aim of this work is to considerably extend the support for binder boilerplate in language mechanizations on two accounts. First, we go beyond simple single variable binders and tackle complex binding structures, like the nested pattern matches of $F_{\times}$, recursively and sequentially scoped binders, mutually recursive binders, heterogeneous binders, etc. Secondly, we cover a larger extent of the boilerplate than earlier works, specifically catering to contexts, context lookups and well-scopedness relations.

Our approach consists of a specification language, called Knot, that allows concise and natural specifications of abstract syntax of programming languages and provides rich binding structure. We provide generic definitions and lemmas for the variable binding boilerplate that apply to every well-formed Knot specification. Finally, we complement the generic approach with a code generator, called Needle, that specializes the generic definitions and allows manual customization and extension.

We follow two important principles: Firstly, even though in its most general form, syntax with binders has a monadic structure [3–5], Knot restricts itself to free monadic structures. This allows us to define substitution and all related boilerplate generically and encompasses the vast majority of languages.

Secondly, we hide as much as possible the underlying concrete representation of de Bruijn indices as natural numbers. Instead, we provide an easy-to-use

Labels

S, T	*Sort label*	α, β, γ	*Namespace label*
K	*Constructor label*	x, y, z	*Meta-variable*
E	*Env label*	f	*Function label*
s, t	*Sort field*		

Declarations and definitions

spec	$::= \overline{\mathit{decl}}$	*Specification*
decl	$::= \mathit{namedecl} \mid \mathit{sortdecl} \mid \mathit{fundecl} \mid \mathit{envdecl}$	*Declaration*
$\mathit{namedecl}$	$::= \mathbf{namespace}\, \alpha : S$	*Namespace*
$\mathit{sortdecl}$	$::= \mathbf{sort}\, S := \overline{\mathit{ctordecl}}$	*Sort*
$\mathit{ctordecl}$	$::= K\,(x@\alpha) \mid K\,\overline{(x : \alpha)}\,\overline{([bs]s : S)}$	*Ctor decl.*
bs	$::= \overline{\mathit{bsi}}$	*Binding spec.*
bsi	$::= x \mid f\, s$	*Bind. spec. item*
$\mathit{fundecl}$	$::= \mathbf{fun}\, f : S \rightarrow [\overline{\alpha}] := \overline{\mathit{funclause}}$	*Function*
$\mathit{funclause}$	$::= K\, \overline{x}\, \overline{s} \rightarrow \mathit{bs}$	*Function clause*
$\mathit{envdecl}$	$::= \mathbf{env}\, E := \overline{\mathit{envclause}}$	*Environment*
$\mathit{envclause}$	$::= \alpha \mapsto \overline{S}$	*Env. clause*

Fig. 2. The syntax of KNOT

interface that admits only sensible operations and prevents proofs from going astray. In particular, we rule out comparisons using inequalities and decrements, and any reasoning using properties of these operations.

3 The Knot Specification Language

This section introduces KNOT, our language for specifying the abstract syntax of programming languages and associated variable binder information. The advantage of specifying programming languages in KNOT is straightforward: the variable binder boilerplate comes for free for any well-formed KNOT specification.

The syntax of KNOT allows programming languages to be expressed in terms of different syntactic sorts, term constructors for these sorts and binding specifications for these term constructors. The latter specify the number of variables that are bound by the term constructors as well as their scoping rules.

3.1 Knot Syntax

Figure 2 shows the grammar of KNOT. A KNOT specification *spec* of a language consists of variable namespace declarations *namedecl*, syntactic sort declarations *sortdecl*, function declarations *fundecl* and environment declarations *envdecl*.

A namespace declaration introduces a new namespace α and associates it with a particular sort S. This expresses that variables of namespace α can be substituted for terms of sort S. It is possible to associate multiple namespaces with a single sort.

A declaration of S comes with two kinds of constructor declarations *ctordecl*. Variable constructors $K\ (x@\alpha)$ hold a variable reference in the namespace α. These are the only constructors where variables can appear free. Regular constructors $K\,\overline{(x:\alpha)}\,\overline{(s:S)}$ contain named variable bindings $\overline{(x:\alpha)}$ and named subterms $\overline{(s:S)}$. Meta-variables x and field names s scope over the constructor declaration. For the sake of presentation, we assume that the variable bindings precede subterms. The distinction between variable and regular constructors follows straightforwardly from our free-monadic view on syntax. This rules out languages for normal forms, but as they require custom behavior (renormalization) during substitution [31,40] their substitution-related boilerplate cannot be defined generically anyway.

Each subterm s is preceded by a binding specification bs that stipulates which variable bindings are brought in scope of s. The binding specification consists of a list of items bsi. An item is either a meta-variable x that refers to a singleton variable binding of the constructor or the invocation of a function f, that computes which variables in siblings or the same subterm are brought in scope of s. Functions serve in particular to specify multi-binders in binding specifications. In regular programming languages the binding specifications will often be empty and can be omitted.

Functions are defined by function declarations *fundecl*. The type signature $f : S \to [\overline{\alpha}]$ denotes that function f operates on terms of sort S and yields variables in namespaces $\overline{\alpha}$. The function itself is defined by exhaustive case analysis on a term of sort S. A crucial property of Knot is the enforcement of lexical scoping: shifting and substituting variables does not change the scoping of bound variables. To achieve this, functions cannot be defined for sorts that have variable constructors.

Environments E represent a list of variables that are in scope and associate them with additional data such as typing information. To this end, an environment declaration *envdecl* consists of clauses $\alpha \mapsto \overline{S}$ that stipulate that variables in namespace α are associated to terms of sorts $\overline{S}$.

3.2 Examples

Several examples of rich binder forms now illustrate Knot's expressive power. Figure 3 (top) shows the Knot specification of $F_\times$. We start with the declaration of two namespaces: *Tyv* for type variables and *Tmv* for term variables, which is followed by the declarations of $F_\times$'s three sorts: types, patterns and terms. For readability, we omit empty binding specifications. The Knot specification contains only four non-empty binding specifications: universal quantification for types and type abstraction for terms bind exactly one type variable, the lambda abstraction for terms binds exactly one term variable and the pattern match binds *bind* p variables in t_2 where *bind* is a function defined on patterns.

Figure 3 (bottom) shows the specification of a simply-typed lambda calculus with recursive let definitions as they are found in the Haskell programming

```
namespace Tyv : Ty
namespace Tmv : Term

sort Ty :=
  | TVar (X@Tyv)                    | TProd (T1 T2 : Ty)
  | TArr (T1 T2 : Ty)               | TAll  (X : Tyv) ([X]T : Ty)
sort Term := Var (x@Tmv)
  | App (t1 t2 : Term)              | Abs (x : Tmv) (T : Ty) ([x]t : Term)
  | TApp (t : Term) (T : Ty)        | TAbs (X : Tyv) ([X]t1 : Term)
  | Prod  (t1 t2 : Term)            | Case (t1 : Term) (p : Pat) ([bind p]t2 : Term)
sort Pat   := PVar (x : Tmv)        | PProd (p1 p2 : Pat)
fun bind : Pat → [Tmv] :=
  | PVar x → x                      | PProd p1 p2 → bind p1, bind p2
env Env :=
  | (x : Tmv) ↦ (T : Ty)            | (X : Tyv) ↦  % nothing associated
```

```
namespace Tmv : Term
sort Ty :=    Top     | Arr   (T1 T2 : Ty)
sort Term := Var (x@Tmv)
  | App (t1 t2 : Term) | Abs   (x : Tmv) (T : Ty) ([x]t : Term)
  | Let  ([bind ds]ds : Decls) ([bind ds]t : Term)
sort Decls := Nil      | Cons (x : Tmv) (t : Term) (ds : Decls)
fun bind : Decls → [Tmv] :=
  | Nil →   []         | Cons x t ds → x, bind ds
env Env := (x : Tmv) ↦ (T : Ty)
```

Fig. 3. Example specifications of $F_\times$ and λ_{letrec}

language. The auxiliary function *bind* collects the variables bound by a declaration list *ds*. In the term constructor *Let*, we specify that the variables of *ds* are not only bound in the body *t* but also recursively in *ds* itself.

Figure 4 (top) shows the specification of a lambda calculus with first-order dependent types as presented by Aspinall and Hofmann [26]. In this language, terms and types are mutually recursive and have distinct namespaces. Type variables can be declared in the context with a specific kind K but are never bound in the syntax.

The calculus presented in Fig. 4 (top) uses telescopic abstractions. Telescopes were invented to model dependently typed systems [10]. They are lists of variables together with their types $x_1 : T_1, \ldots, x_n : T_n$ where each variable scopes over subsequent types. In the abstract syntax, the sequential scoping is captured in the binding specification of the recursive position of the *TCons* constructor. In the lambda abstraction case *Abs* and the dependent function type constructor *Pi* the variables of a telescope are bound simultaneously in the body.

$$\begin{array}{ll}
\textbf{namespace}\ \mathit{Tyv} : \mathit{Ty} & \\
\textbf{namespace}\ \mathit{Tmv} : \mathit{Term} & \\
\textbf{sort}\ \mathit{Kind} := \mathit{Star} & \mid \mathit{KPi}\ (x : \mathit{Tmv})\ (T : \mathit{Ty})\ ([x]K : \mathit{Kind}) \\
\textbf{sort}\ \mathit{Ty} \ \ := \mathit{TVar}\ (X @ \mathit{Tyv}) & \\
\quad \mid \mathit{TApp}\ (T : \mathit{Ty})\ (t : \mathit{Term}) & \mid \mathit{TPi}\ (x : \mathit{Tmv})\ (T_1 : \mathit{Ty})\ ([x]\, T_2 : \mathit{Ty}) \\
\textbf{sort}\ \mathit{Term} := \mathit{Var}\ \ (x @ \mathit{Tmv}) & \\
\quad \mid \mathit{App}\ \ (t_1\ t_2 : \mathit{Term}) & \mid \mathit{Abs}\ (x : \mathit{Tmv})\ (T : \mathit{Ty})\ ([x]t : \mathit{Term}) \\
\textbf{env}\ \mathit{Env} := (X : \mathit{Tyv}) \mapsto (K : \mathit{Kind}) \mid (x : \mathit{Tmv}) \mapsto (T : \mathit{Ty}) &
\end{array}$$

$$\begin{array}{ll}
\textbf{namespace}\ \mathit{Tmv} : \mathit{Term} & \\
\textbf{sort}\ \mathit{Term} := \ \mathit{Var}\ (x @ \mathit{Tmv}) & \\
\quad \mid \mathit{App}\ (t : \mathit{Term})\ (ts : \mathit{Terms}) \mid \mathit{Abs}\ (d : \mathit{Tele})\ ([\mathit{bind}\ \ d]t : \mathit{Term}) & \\
\quad \mid \mathit{Pi}\ \ \ (d : \mathit{Tele})\ ([\mathit{bind}\ \ d]t : \mathit{Term}) & \\
\textbf{sort}\ \mathit{Terms} := \mathit{Nil} & \mid \mathit{Cons}\ \ \ (t : \mathit{Term})\ (ts : \mathit{Terms}) \\
\textbf{sort}\ \mathit{Tele} := \ \ \ \mathit{TNil} & \mid \mathit{TCons}\ (x : \mathit{Tmv})\ (T : \mathit{Term})\ ([x]d : \mathit{Tele}) \\
\textbf{fun}\ \mathit{bind} : \mathit{Tele} \to [\mathit{Tmv}] := \ \mid \mathit{TNil} \to [\,] \mid \mathit{TCons}\ x\ T\ d \to x, \mathit{bind}\ \ d & \\
\textbf{env}\ \mathit{Env} := \mathit{etm} : (x : \mathit{Tmv}) \mapsto (T : \mathit{Term}) &
\end{array}$$

Fig. 4. Example specifications of λLF and λ_{tele}

3.3 Well-Formed *Knot* Specifications

In this section, we generally define well-formedness of specifications that in particular ensures that meta-variables and field names in binding specifications are always bound and that binding specifications are well-typed. To do so, we make use of several kinds of global information. The global environment V contains the mapping from namespaces to the associated sort. The function environment Φ contains the type signatures for all functions $f : S \to \overline{\alpha}$.

The global function *depsOf* maps sort S to the set of namespaces $\overline{\alpha}$ that S depends on. For example, in $F_\times$ terms depend on both type and term variables, but types only depend on type variables. *depsOf* is the least function that fulfill two conditions:

1. For each variable constructor $(K : \alpha \to S)$: $\alpha \in \mathit{depsOf}\ S$,
2. and for each regular constructor $(K : \overline{\alpha}\,\overline{T} \to S)$: $\mathit{depsOf}\ T_i \subseteq \mathit{depsOf}\ S \quad (\forall i)$.

The function *depsOf* induces a subordination relation on sorts similar to subordination in Twelf [22,38]. We will use *depsOf* in the definition of syntactic operations to avoid recursing into subterms in which no variables of interest are to be found and for subordination-based strengthening lemmas.

Figure 5 defines the well-formedness relation $\vdash \mathit{spec}$ for Knot specifications. The single rule WfSpec expresses that a specification is well-formed if each of the constructor declarations inside the sort declarations is and the meta-environment V contains exactly the declared namespaces.

$$
\begin{array}{lll}
V & ::= \overline{\alpha : S} & \text{Var. assoc.} \\
\Phi & ::= \overline{f : S \to [\alpha]} & \text{Function env.} \\
L & ::= \overline{x : \alpha}, \overline{s : S} & \text{Local env.}
\end{array}
$$

$\boxed{\vdash spec}$

$$
\frac{V = \overline{\alpha : S} \qquad \overline{\overline{\vdash_T \; ctordecl}}}{\vdash \overline{\textbf{namespace}\ \alpha : S}\ \overline{\textbf{sort}\ T := \overline{ctordecl}}}\ \textsc{WfSpec}
$$

$\boxed{\vdash_S \; ctordecl}$

$$
\frac{\alpha : S \in V}{\vdash_S K\,(x@\alpha)}\ \textsc{WfVar}
\qquad
\frac{\forall j.(\overline{x : \alpha}, \overline{t : T}) \vdash bs_j : depsOf\ T_j}{\vdash_S K\ \overline{(x : \alpha)}\ \overline{([bs]t : T)}}\ \textsc{WfReg}
$$

$\boxed{L \vdash bs : \overline{\alpha}}$ $\boxed{L \vdash bsi : \overline{\alpha}}$

$$
\frac{\forall j. L \vdash bsi_j : \overline{\alpha}}{L \vdash \overline{bsi} : \overline{\alpha}}\ \textsc{WfBs}
\qquad
\frac{(x : \beta) \in L \quad \beta \in \overline{\alpha}}{L \vdash x : \overline{\alpha}}\ \textsc{WfSng}
\qquad
\frac{(s : S) \in L \quad \overline{\beta} \subseteq \overline{\alpha} \quad f : S \to [\overline{\beta}] \in \Phi}{L \vdash f\ s : \overline{\alpha}}\ \textsc{WfCall}
$$

Fig. 5. Well-formed specifications

The auxiliary well-sorting relation $\vdash_S ctordecl$ denotes that constructor declaration *ctordecl* has sort S. There are two rules for this relation, one for each constructor form. Rule WfVar requires that the associated sort of the variable namespace matches the sort of the constructor. Rule WfReg handles regular constructors. It builds a constructor-local meta-environment L for meta-variables with their namespace $x : \alpha$ and fields with their sorts $s : S$. The binding specifications of all fields and all functions defined on S are checked against L.

The relation $L \vdash bs : \overline{\alpha}$ in Fig. 5 denotes that binding specification *bs* is typed heterogeneously with elements from namespaces $\overline{\alpha}$. By rule WfBs a binding specification is well-typed if each of its items is well-typed.

Rule WfSng regulates the well-typing of a singleton variable binding. It is well-typed if the namespace β of the binding is among the namespaces $\overline{\alpha}$. Correspondingly, the rule WfCall states that a function call $f\ s$ is well-typed if the namespace set $\overline{\beta}$ of the function is a subset of $\overline{\alpha}$.

In addition to the explicitly formulated well-formedness requirements of Fig. 5, we also require a number of simple consistency properties:

1. Constructor names are not repeated for different constructor declarations.
2. Field names are not repeated in a constructor declaration.
3. For each namespace α there is a unique variable constructor declaration $K\ \alpha$.
4. Function declarations are exhaustive and not overlapping.
5. There is at most one environment clause per namespace.

The first two requirements avoid ambiguity and follow good practice. The third requirement expresses that every variable belongs to one sort and there is only one way, i.e., one term constructor, to inject it in that sort. The fourth

n, m	$::= 0 \mid S\ n$		de Bruijn index
u, v, w	$::= K\ n \mid K\ \overline{u}$		Sort term
Γ, Δ	$::= [\,] \mid \Gamma \triangleright_\alpha \overline{u}$		Environment term

Fig. 6. Grammars of raw de Bruijn terms

requirement ensures that functions are total. Finally, the last requirement avoids ambiguity by associating variables from a namespace with only one kind of data.

4 Knot Semantics

The previous section has introduced the KNOT specification language for abstract syntax. This section generically defines the semantics of the language in terms of a de Bruijn representation, declare the abstract syntax that is valid with respect to the specification and define the semantics of binding specifications. We assume a given well-formed specification *spec* in the rest of this section.

4.1 Term Semantics

We assume that information about constructors is available in a global environment. We use $(K : \alpha \to S)$ for looking up the type of a variable constructor and $(K : \overline{\alpha} \to \overline{T} \to S)$ for retrieving the fields types of regular constructors.

Figure 6 contains a term grammar for raw terms of sorts and environments. A sort term consists of either a constructor applied to a de Bruijn index or a term constructor applied to other sort terms. An environment term is either and empty environment or the cons of an environment and a list of associated sort terms. The cons is additionally tagged with a namespace α. It is straightforward to define a well-sortedness judgement $\vdash u : S$ for raw sort terms and $\vdash \Gamma : E$ for raw environment terms. See also the well-scopedness relation in Fig. 8 that refines well-sortedness.

4.2 Binding Specification Semantics

The binding specification $[\,bs\,]\ t$ for a particular subterm t of a given term constructor K defines the variables that are brought into scope in t. For example, the binding specification of the pattern-matching case of $F_\times$ in Fig. 3 states that the pattern variables are bound in the body by means of a function *bind* that collects these variables. We need to define an interpretation of binding specifications and functions that we can use in the definitions of boilerplate functions.

Figure 7 defines the interpretation $[\![\ bs\ ]\!]_\vartheta$ of bs as a meta-level evaluation. Interpretation is always performed in the context of a particular constructor K. This is taken into account in the interpretation function: the parameter $\vartheta : \overline{t \mapsto u}$ is a mapping from field labels to concrete subterms.

Traditionally, one would use a natural number to count the number of variables that are being bound. Instead, we use heterogeneous variable lists

$$hvl, h, d ::= 0 \mid S_\alpha\ h \quad \text{Heterogeneous var. list}$$

$$\boxed{[\![\ \_\ ]\!]\_ :: bs \to \overline{t \mapsto u} \to h}$$

$$\begin{aligned}
[\![\ \epsilon\ ]\!]_\vartheta &= 0 \\
[\![\ bs, x_\alpha\ ]\!]_\vartheta &= [\![\ bs\ ]\!]_\vartheta + 1_\alpha \\
[\![\ bs, f\ t_i\ ]\!]_\vartheta &= [\![\ bs\ ]\!]_\vartheta + [\![\ f\ ]\!](\vartheta\ t_i)
\end{aligned}$$

$$\boxed{[\![\ \_\ ]\!] :: f \to u \to h}$$

$$\begin{aligned}
&[\![\ f\ ]\!](K\ \overline{u}) = [\![\ bs_i\ ]\!]_\vartheta \\
&\quad \mathbf{where}\ f\ (K\ \overline{x}\ \overline{t}) = \overline{bs_i} \in spec \\
&\quad\quad \vartheta := \overline{t \mapsto u}
\end{aligned}$$

$$\boxed{domain :: \Gamma \to h}$$

$$\begin{aligned}
domain\ [\,] &= 0 \\
domain\ (\Gamma \rhd_\alpha \overline{u}) &= domain\ \Gamma + 1_\alpha
\end{aligned}$$

$$\boxed{\_ + \_ :: h \to h \to h}$$

$$\begin{aligned}
h\ + 0 &= h \\
h1 + S_\alpha\ h2 &= S_\alpha\ (h1 + h2)
\end{aligned}$$

Fig. 7. Interpretation of binding specifications and functions

hvl – a refinement of natural numbers – defined in Fig. 7 for dealing with heterogeneous contexts: each successor S_α is tagged with a namespace α to keep track of the number and order of variables of different namespaces. This allows us to model languages with heterogeneous binders, i.e. that bind variables of different namespaces at the same time, for which reordering the bindings is undesirable.

In case the binding specification item is a single-variable binding, the result is a one with the correct tag. In the interesting case of a function call $f\ t_i$, the evaluation pattern matches on the corresponding subterm $\vartheta\ t_i$ and interprets the right-hand side of the appropriate function clause with respect to the new subterms. Note that we have ruled out function definitions for variable constructors. Thus, we do not need to handle that case here.

The *hvl*s are term counterparts of environments from which the associated information has been dropped. The function *domain* in Fig. 7 makes this precise by calculating the underlying *hvl* of an environment term. In the following, we use the extension of addition from natural numbers to concatenation $\_+\_$ of *hvl*s – defined in Fig. 7 – and implicitly use its associativity property. In contrast, concatenation is not commutative. We mirror the convention of extending environments to the right at the level of *hvl* and will always add new variables on the right-hand side of concatenation.

4.3 Well-Scopedness

Part of the semantics is the well-scopedness of terms. It is current practice to define well-scopedness with respect to a typing environment: a term is well-scoped iff all of its free variables are bound in the environment. The environment is extended when going under binders. For example, when going under the binder of a lambda abstraction with a type-signature the conventional rule is:

$$\frac{\Gamma, x : \tau \vdash e}{\Gamma \vdash \lambda\,(x : \tau).e}$$

$\boxed{h \vdash_\alpha n}$

$$\frac{}{S_\alpha\ h \vdash_\alpha 0}\ \textsc{WsZero} \qquad \frac{h \vdash_\alpha n}{S_\alpha\ h \vdash_\alpha S\ n}\ \textsc{WsHom} \qquad \frac{\alpha \neq \beta \quad h \vdash_\alpha n}{S_\beta\ h \vdash_\alpha n}\ \textsc{WsHet}$$

$\boxed{h \vdash u : S}$

$$\frac{h \vdash_\alpha n \qquad K : \alpha \to S}{K\ n : S}\ \textsc{WsVar} \qquad \frac{K : \overline{x : \alpha} \to \overline{[bs]t : T} \to S \quad \vartheta = \overline{t \mapsto u} \quad h + [\![bs_i]\!]_\vartheta \vdash u_i : T_i \quad (\forall i)}{h \vdash K\ \overline{u} : S}\ \textsc{WsCtor}$$

$\boxed{h \vdash \Gamma : E}$

$$\frac{}{h \vdash [\,] : E}\ \textsc{WsNil} \qquad \frac{E : \alpha \to \overline{T} \qquad h \vdash \Gamma \quad h + \mathit{domain}\ \Gamma \vdash u_i : T_i \quad (\forall i)}{h \vdash (\Gamma \triangleright_\alpha \overline{u}) : E}\ \textsc{WsCons}$$

Fig. 8. Well-scopedness of terms

The rule follows the intention that the term variable should be of the given type. In this regard, well-scopedness is already a lightweight type-system. However, it is problematic for Knot to establish this intention or in general establish what the associated data in the environment should be. Furthermore, we allow the user to define different environments with potentially incompatible associated data. Hence, instead we define well-scopedness by using domains of environments. In fact, this is all we need to establish well-scopedness.

Figure 8 defines the well-scopedness relation on de Bruijn indices as well as sort and environment terms. The relation $h \vdash_\alpha n$ denotes that n is a well-scoped de Bruijn index for namespace α with respect to the variables in h. This is a refinement of $n < h$ in which only the successors for namespace α in h are taken into account. This is accomplished by rule WsHom which strips away one successor in the homogeneous case and rule WsHet that simply skips successors in the heterogeneous case. Rule WsZero forms the base case for $n = 0$ which requires that h has a successor tagged with α.

Rule WsVar delegates well-scopedness of variable constructors to the well-scopedness of the index in the appropriate namespace. In rule WsCtor, the heterogeneous variable list h is extended for each subterm u_i with the result of evaluating its binding specification bs_i.

The relation $h \vdash \Gamma$ defines the well-scopedness of environment terms with respect to previously existing variables h. We will also write $\vdash \Gamma$ as short-hand for $0 \vdash \Gamma$. Note in particular that rule WsCons extends h with the *domain* of the existing bindings when checking the well-scopedness of associated data.

5 Infrastructure Operations

In this section, we generically define common infrastructure operations generically over all terms of a specifications. This includes shifting and substitution in sort and environment terms and lookups in environments.

$$c ::= 0 \mid S\ c \quad \text{Cutoffs}$$

$$\boxed{\mathit{weaken}_\alpha :: c \to h \to c}$$

$$\begin{array}{l}
\mathit{weaken}_\alpha\ c\ 0 \qquad\quad = c \\
\mathit{weaken}_\alpha\ c\ (S_\beta\ h) = \\
\quad \textbf{if } \alpha = \beta \\
\qquad \textbf{then } S\ (\mathit{weaken}_\alpha\ c\ h) \\
\qquad \textbf{else } \mathit{weaken}_\alpha\ c\ h
\end{array}$$

$$\boxed{\mathit{shift}_{\mathbb{N}} :: c \to n \to n}$$

$$\begin{array}{l}
\mathit{shift}_{\mathbb{N}}\ 0 \qquad n \qquad = S\ n \\
\mathit{shift}_{\mathbb{N}}\ (S\ c)\ 0 \qquad = 0 \\
\mathit{shift}_{\mathbb{N}}\ (S\ c)\ (S\ n) = S\ (\mathit{shift}_{\mathbb{N}}\ c\ n)
\end{array}$$

$$\boxed{\mathit{weaken} :: u \to h \to u}$$

$$\begin{array}{l}
\mathit{weaken}\ u\ 0 \qquad\quad = u \\
\mathit{weaken}\ u\ (S_\alpha\ h) = \\
\quad \mathit{shift?}_\alpha\ 0\ (\mathit{weaken}\ u\ h)
\end{array}$$

$$\boxed{\mathit{shift}_\alpha :: c \to u \to u}$$

$$\begin{array}{l}
\mathit{shift}_\alpha\ c\ (K\ n) = \\
\quad \textbf{if } K : \alpha \to S \\
\qquad \textbf{then } K\ (\mathit{shift}_{\mathbb{N}}\ c\ n) \\
\qquad \textbf{else } K\ n \\
\mathit{shift}_\alpha\ c\ (K\ \overline{u}) = \\
\qquad \overline{K\ \mathit{shift?}_\alpha\ (\mathit{weaken}_\alpha\ c\ [\![\ bs\ ]\!]_\vartheta)\ u} \\
\quad \textbf{where} \\
\qquad K\ \overline{x}\ (\overline{[bs]\ t : T}) \in \mathit{spec} \\
\qquad \vartheta = \overline{t \mapsto u}
\end{array}$$

$$\boxed{\mathit{shift?}_\alpha :: c \to u \to u}$$

$$\begin{array}{l}
\mathit{shift?}_\alpha\ c\ u = \\
\quad \textbf{if } \alpha \in \mathit{depsOf}\ u \\
\qquad \textbf{then } \mathit{shift}_\alpha\ c\ u \textbf{ else } u
\end{array}$$

Fig. 9. Shifting of terms

5.1 Shifting

Shifting adapts indices when a variable x is inserted into the context.

$$\Gamma, \Delta \vdash e \rightsquigarrow \Gamma, (x : \tau), \Delta \vdash e$$

Indices in e for α-variables in Γ need to be incremented to account for the new variable while indices for variables in Δ remain unchanged. The *shift* function is defined in Fig. 9 implements this. It is parameterized over the namespace α of variable x in which the shift is performed. It takes a *cut-off* parameter c that is the number of α-variable bindings in Δ. In case of a variable constructor $K : \alpha \to S$, the index is shifted using the $\mathit{shift}_{\mathbb{N}}$ function. For variable constructors of other namespaces, we keep the index unchanged. In the case of a regular constructor, we need to calculate the cut-offs for the recursive calls. This is done by evaluating the binding specification bs and weakening the cut-off. Using the calculated cut-offs, the $\mathit{shift?}_\alpha$ function can proceed recursively on the subterms that depend on the namespace α.

Instead of using the traditional arithmetical implementation

$$\textbf{if } n < c \textbf{ then } n \textbf{ else } n + 1$$

we use an equivalent recursive definition of $\mathit{shift}_{\mathbb{N}}$ that inserts the successor constructor *at the right place*. This follows the inductive structure of Δ which facilitates inductive proofs on Δ.

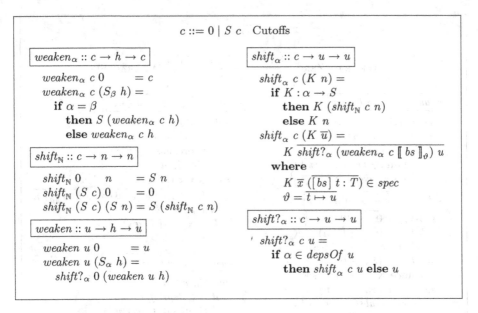

$$x ::= 0 \mid S_\alpha\ x \quad \text{Trace}$$

$\boxed{\vdash_\alpha x}$

$$\frac{}{\vdash_\alpha 0}\ \textsc{WfTraceZero} \qquad \frac{\vdash_\alpha n \qquad \beta \in \mathit{depsOf}\ \alpha}{\vdash_\alpha S\ n}\ \textsc{WfTraceSucc}$$

$\boxed{\mathit{weaken}_\alpha :: x \to h \to x}$

$$\begin{aligned}
&\mathit{weaken}_\alpha\ c\ 0 = c\\
&\mathit{weaken}_\alpha\ c\ (S_\beta\ h) =\\
&\quad \textbf{if}\ \beta \in \mathit{depsOf}\ \alpha\\
&\quad\quad \textbf{then}\ S_\beta\ (\mathit{weaken}_\alpha\ x\ h)\\
&\quad\quad \textbf{else}\ \mathit{weaken}_\alpha\ x\ h
\end{aligned}$$

$\boxed{\mathit{subst}_{\alpha,\mathrm{N}} :: v \to x \to n \to u}$

$$\begin{aligned}
&\mathit{subst}_{\alpha,\mathrm{N}}\ v\ 0\quad 0 = v\\
&\mathit{subst}_{\alpha,\mathrm{N}}\ v\ 0\quad (S\ n) = K\ n\\
&\quad \textbf{where}\ K : \alpha \to T \in \mathit{spec}\\
&\mathit{subst}_{\alpha,\mathrm{N}}\ v\ (S_\alpha\ x)\ 0 = K\ 0\\
&\quad \textbf{where}\ K : \alpha \to T \in \mathit{spec}\\
&\mathit{subst}_{\alpha,\mathrm{N}}\ v\ (S_\alpha\ x)\ (S\ n) =\\
&\quad \mathit{weaken}\ (\mathit{substN}\ v\ x\ n)\ 1_\alpha\\
&\mathit{subst}_{\alpha,\mathrm{N}}\ v\ (S_\beta\ x)\ n =\\
&\quad \mathit{weaken}\ (\mathit{substN}\ v\ x\ n)\ 1_\beta
\end{aligned}$$

$\boxed{\mathit{subst}_\alpha :: v \to x \to u \to u}$

$$\begin{aligned}
&\mathit{subst}_\alpha\ v\ x\ (K\ n) =\\
&\quad \textbf{if}\ K : \alpha \to S\\
&\quad\quad \textbf{then}\ \mathit{subst}_{\alpha,\mathrm{N}}\ v\ x\ n\\
&\quad\quad \textbf{else}\ K\ n\\
&\mathit{subst}_\alpha\ v\ x\ (K\ \overline{u}) =\\
&\quad\quad K\ \overline{\mathit{subst?}_\alpha\ v\ (\mathit{weaken}_\alpha\ x\ [\![\ bs\ ]\!]_\vartheta)\ u}\\
&\quad \textbf{where}\\
&\quad\quad K\ \overline{x}\ (\overline{[bs]\ t : T}) \in \mathit{spec}\\
&\quad\quad \vartheta = \overline{t \mapsto u}
\end{aligned}$$

$\boxed{\mathit{subst?}_\alpha :: v \to x \to u \to u}$

$$\begin{aligned}
&\mathit{subst?}_\alpha\ v\ x\ u =\\
&\quad \textbf{if}\ \alpha \in \mathit{depsOf}\ u\\
&\quad\quad \textbf{then}\ \mathit{subst}_\alpha\ v\ x\ u\\
&\quad\quad \textbf{else}\ u
\end{aligned}$$

Fig. 10. Substitution of terms

Weakening. Weakening is the transportation of a term e from a context Γ to a bigger context Γ, Δ where variables are only added at the end.

$$\Gamma \vdash e \rightsquigarrow \Gamma, \Delta \vdash e$$

Figure 9 shows the implementation of weaken_α that iterates the 1-place $\mathit{shift?}_\alpha$ function. Its second parameter h is the domain of Δ; the range of Δ is not relevant for weakening.

5.2 Substitution

Next, we define substitution of a single variable x for a term e in some other term e' generically. In the literature, two commonly used variants can be found.

1. The first variant keeps the invariant that e and e' are in the same context and immediately weakens e when passing under a binder while traversing e' to keep this invariant. It corresponds to the substition lemma

$$\frac{\Gamma, \Delta \vdash e : \sigma \qquad \Gamma, x : \sigma, \Delta \vdash e' : \tau}{\Gamma, \Delta \vdash \{x \mapsto e\}\ e' : \tau}$$

2. The second variant keeps the invariant that e' is in a weaker context than e. It defers weakening of e until the variable positions are reached to keep the invariant and performs shifting if the variable is substituted. It corresponds to the substitution lemma

$$\frac{\Gamma \vdash e : \sigma \qquad \Gamma, x : \sigma, \Delta \vdash e' : \tau}{\Gamma, \Delta \vdash [x \mapsto e]\ e' : \tau}$$

Both variants were already present in de Bruijn's seminal paper [9], but the first variant has enjoyed more widespread use. However, we will use the second variant because it has the following advantages:

1. It supports the more general case of languages with a dependent context:

$$\frac{\Gamma \vdash e : \sigma \qquad \Gamma, x : \sigma, \Delta \vdash e' : \tau}{\Gamma, [x \mapsto e]\ \Delta \vdash [x \mapsto e]\ e' : [x \mapsto e]\ \tau}$$

2. The parameter e is constant while recursing into e' and hence it can also be moved outside of inductions on the structure of e. Proofs become slightly simpler because we do not need to reason about any changes to s when going under binders.

For the definition of substitution, we again need to use a refinement of natural numbers, a different one from before: we need to keep track of variable bindings of the namespaces to transport e into the context of e', i.e. those in *depsOf* S where S is the sort of e. Figure 10 contains the refinement, which we call "traces", a well-formedness condition that expresses the namespace restriction and a $weaken_\alpha$ function for traces.

Figure 10 also contains the definition of substitution. Like for shift, we define substitution by three functions. The function $subst_{\alpha,\mathbb{N}}\ v\ x\ n$ defines the operation for namespace α on indices by recursing on x and case distinction on n. If the index and the trace match, then the result is the term v. If the index n is strictly smaller or strictly larger than the trace x, then $subst_{\alpha,\mathbb{N}}$ constructs a term using the variable constructor for α. In the recursive cases, $subst_{\alpha,\mathbb{N}}$ performs the necessary shifts when coming out of the recursion in the same order in which the binders have been crossed. This avoids a multiplace *weaken* on terms.

The substitution $subst_\alpha$ traverses terms to the variable positions and weakens the trace according to the binding specification. As previously discussed v remains unchanged. The function $subst?_\alpha$ only recurses into the term if it is interesting to do so.

5.3 Environment Lookups

The paramount infrastructure operation on environments is the lookup of variables and their associated data. Lookup is a partial function. For that reason, we define it as a relation $(n : \overline{u}) \in_\alpha \Gamma$ that witnesses that looking up the index n

$$\boxed{(n : \overline{u}) \in_\alpha \Gamma} \qquad \frac{\textit{domain}\ \Gamma \vdash u_i \quad (\forall i)}{(0 : \overline{\textit{weaken}\ u\ 1_\alpha}) \in_\alpha (\Gamma \rhd_\alpha \overline{u})}\ \text{InHere}$$

$$\frac{(n : \overline{u}) \in_\alpha \Gamma}{(\textit{weaken}_\alpha\ n\ 1_\beta : \overline{\textit{weaken}\ u\ 1_\beta}) \in_\alpha (\Gamma \rhd_\beta \overline{v})}\ \text{InThere}$$

Fig. 11. Environment lookup

of namespace α in the environment term Γ is valid and that $\overline{u}$ is the associated data. Figure 11 contains the definition.

Rule InHere forms the base case where $n = 0$. In this case the environment term needs to be a cons for namespace α. Note that well-scopedness of the associated data is included as a premise. This reflects common practice of annotating variable cases with with well-scopedness conditions. By moving it into the lookup itself, we free the user from dealing with this obligation explicitly. We need to *weaken* the result of the lookup to account for the binding.

Rule InThere encodes the case that the lookup is not the last cons of the environment. The rule handles both the homogeneous $\alpha = \beta$ and the heterogeneous case $\alpha \neq \beta$ by means of weakening the index n. The associated data is also shifted to account for the new β binding.

6 Infrastructure Lemmas

Programming language mechanizations typically rely on many boilerplate properties of the infrastructure operations that we introduced in the previous section. To further reduce the hand-written boilerplate, we have set up the Knot specification language in such a way that it provides all the necessary information to generically state and prove a wide range of these properties.[1] Below we briefly summarize the three different kinds of ubiquitous lemmas that we cover. In general, it is quite challenging to tackle these boilerplate lemmas generically because their exact statements, and in particular which premises are needed, depend highly on the *depsOf* function and also on the dependencies of the associated data in environments.

Interaction Lemmas. Formalizations involve a number of interaction boilerplate lemmas between *shift*, *weaken* and *subst*. These lemmas are for example needed in weakening and substitution lemmas for typing relations. Two operation always commute when they are operating on different variables and a shifting followed by a substitution on the same variable cancel each other out:

$$\textit{subst}_\alpha\ v\ 0\ \alpha\ (\textit{shift}_\alpha\ 0\ \alpha\ u) = u.$$

[1] In fact, we provide more such lemmas than any other framework based on first-order representations – see Sect. 9.

Well-Scopedness. The syntactic operations preserve well-scoping. This includes shifting, weakening and substitution lemmas. If a sort does not depend on the namespace of the substitute, we can formulate a strengthening lemma instead:

$$\frac{h + 1_\alpha \vdash u : S \qquad \alpha \notin \mathit{depsOf}\ S}{h \vdash u : S}$$

Environment Lookup. Lemmas for shifting, weakening and strengthening for environment lookups form the variable cases for corresponding lemmas of typing relations. These lemmas also explain how the associated data in the context is changed. For operating somewhere deep in the context we use relations, like for example $\Gamma_1 \xhookrightarrow{c}_\alpha \Gamma_2$ which denotes that Γ_2 is the result after inserting a new α variable at cutoff position c in Γ_1. The shifting lemma for lookups is then:

$$\frac{\Gamma_1 \xhookrightarrow{c}_\alpha \Gamma_2 \qquad (n : \overline{u}) \in_\alpha \Gamma_1}{(\mathit{shift}_{\mathbb{N}}\ c\ n : \overline{\mathit{shift?}_\alpha\ c\ u}) \in_\alpha \Gamma_2}$$

7 Implementation

This section briefly describes our two implementations of KNOT. The first is a generic implementation that acts as a constructive proof of the boilerplate's existence for all well-formed specifications. The second, called NEEDLE, is a code generator that is better suited to practical mechanization.

7.1 The Generic Knot Implementation

We implemented the boilerplate functions generically for all well-formed KNOT specifications in about 4.3k lines of Coq by employing datatype-generic programming techniques [8]. Following our free monad principle, we capture de Bruijn terms in a free monadic structure that is parameterized by namespaces and whose underlying functor covers the regular constructors of sorts. To model the underlying functors, we use the universe of finitary containers [1,13,14,19] Finitary containers closely model our specification language: a set of shapes (constructors) with a finite number of fields. We use an indexed [2] version to model mutually recursive types and use a higher-order presentation to obtain better induction principles for which we assume functional extensionality[2]. We implemented boilerplate operations and lemmas for this universe generically.

7.2 The Needle Code Generator

While the generic Coq definitions presented in the previous sections are satisfactory from a theoretical point of view, they are less so from a pragmatic perspective. The reason is that the generic code only covers the variable binder

[2] However, the code based on our generator NEEDLE does not assume any axioms.

boilerplate; the rest of a language's formalization still needs to be developed manually. Developing the latter part directly on the generic form is cumbersome. Working with conversion functions is possible but often reveals too much of the underlying generic representation. As observed by Lee et al. [18], this happens in particular when working with generic predicates.

For this reason, we also implemented a code generation tool, called NEEDLE that generates all the boilerplate in a language-specific non-generic form. NEEDLE takes a KNOT specification and generates Coq code: the inductive definitions of a de Bruijn representation of the object language and the corresponding specialized boilerplate definitions, lemmas and proofs. Both proof terms and proof scripts are generated. NEEDLE is implemented in about 11k lines of Haskell.

Soundness. We have not formally established that NEEDLE always generates type-correct code or that the proof scripts always succeed. Nevertheless, a number of important implementation choices bolster the confidence in NEEDLE's correctness: First, the generic-programming based implementation is evidence for the existence of type-sound boilerplate definitions and proofs for for every language specified with KNOT.

Secondly, the generic implementation contains a small proof-term DSL featuring only the basic properties of equality such as symmetry, reflexivity, transitivity and congruence and additionally stability and associativity lemmas as axioms. The induction steps of proofs on the structure of terms or on the structure of well-scopedness relation on terms in the generic implementation elaborate to this DSL first and then adhere to its soundness lemma. Subsequently, we ported the proof term elaboration to NEEDLE. Hence, we have formally established the correctness of elaboration functions but not their Haskell implementations.

Thirdly, lemmas for which we generate proof scripts follow the structure of the generic proofs. In particular, this includes all induction proofs on natural number- or list-like data because these are less fragile than induction proofs on terms. A companion library contains tactics specialized for each kind of lemma that performs the same proof steps as the generic proof.

Finally and more pragmatically, we have implemented a test suite of KNOT specifications for NEEDLE that contains a number of languages with advanced binding constructs including languages with mutually recursive and heterogeneous binders, recursive scoping and dependently-typed languages with interdependent namespaces for which correct code is generated.

Nevertheless, the above does not rule out trivial points of failure like name clashes between definitions in the code and the Coq standard library or software bugs in the code generator. Fortunately, when the generated code is loaded in Coq, Coq still performs a type soundness check to catch any issues. In short, soundness never has to be taken at face value.

Table 2. Size statistics of the meta-theory mechanizations.

		Specification			Lemmas			Total		
		Ess.	Bpl.	KNOT	Ess.	Terms	Ctxs	Manual	KNOT	
(1)	λ	44	39	42	43	0	23	149	83	(55.7 %)
(2)	$\lambda_{\times}$	85	67	82	117	0	47	316	198	(62.7 %)
(3)	F	54	102	53	60	127	111	454	118	(26.0 %)
(4)	$F_{\times}$	91	149	93	140	138	158	676	269	(39.8 %)
(5)	F_{seq}	103	164	99	137	153	174	731	247	(33.8 %)
(6)	$F_{<:}$	70	124	69	268	128	178	768	289	(37.6 %)
(7)	$F_{<:,\times}$	114	163	112	402	139	243	1061	476	(44.9 %)
(8)	$F_{<:,\mathrm{rcd}}$	214	234	199	646	161	292	1547	831	(53.7 %)
(9)	λ_{ω}	101	95	100	355	128	108	787	504	(64.0 %)
(10)	F_{ω}	124	106	123	415	129	108	882	591	(67.0 %)

8 Case Studies

This sections demonstrates the benefits of the KNOT approach with two case studies. First, we compare fully manual versus KNOT-based mechanizations of type-safety proofs for 10 languages. Second, we compare KNOT's solution of the POPLMARK challenge against various existing ones.

8.1 Manual vs. Knot Mechanizations

We compare manual against KNOT-based mechanization of type safety for 10 textbook calculi: (1) the simply-typed lambda calculus, (2) the simply-typed lambda calculus with products, (3) System F, (4) System F with products, (5) System F with sequential lets, (6) System $F_{<:}$ as in the POPLMARK challenge 1A + 2A, (7) System $F_{<:}$ with binary products, (8) System $F_{<:}$ with records as in the POPLMARK challenge 1B + 2B, (9) the simply-typed lambda calculus with type-operators, and (10) System F with type-operators.

For each language, we have two COQ formalizations: one developed without tool support and one that uses NEEDLE's generated code. Table 2 gives a detailed overview of the code sizes (LoC) of the different parts of the formalization for each language and the total and relative amount of boilerplate code.

The *Specification* column comprises the language specifications. For the manual approach, it is split into an *essential* part and a *boilerplate* part. The former comprises the abstract syntax declarations (including binding specifications), the evaluation rules, typing contexts and typing rules and is also captured (slightly more concisely) in the KNOT specification. The latter consists of context lookups for the variable typing rule as well as shifting and substitution operators, that are necessary to define β-reduction and, if supported by the language, type application; all of this boilerplate is generated by NEEDLE and thus not counted towards the KNOT-based mechanization.

The essential meta-theoretical *Lemmas* for type-safety are weakening and substitution lemmas for the typing relations, typing and value inversion as well as progress and preservation and where applicable this includes: pattern-matching definedness, reflexivity and transitivity of subtyping and the Church-Rosser property for type reductions.

We separate the binder boilerplate in these formalizations into two classes:

1. Term-related boilerplate consists of interaction lemmas discussed in Sect. 6 and other interaction lemmas between shifting, weakening and the size of terms. This is absent form the mechanizations of λ and $\lambda_\times$ that do not require them. In all other cases, NEEDLE derives the necessary lemmas. This is about 140 lines of code for each language. The size depends mainly on the number of namespaces, the number of syntactic sorts and the dependency structure between them, which is roughly the same for these languages.
2. The boilerplate context lemmas consist of weakening, strengthening and substitution lemmas for term well-scopedness relations and for context lookups. The size depends on the number of namespaces that are handled by the context. In the cases where only single-variable binding is used, we can skip weakening and strengthening lemmas related to multi-binders.

Summary. Table 2 clearly shows that KNOT provides substantial savings in each of the language formalizations, ranging up to 74 % for System F. Note that these formalizations of type safety use only a fraction of the lemmas generated by NEEDLE. For instance, none of the above formalization uses any of the interaction lemmas for terms that are generated.

8.2 Comparison of Approaches

Because it is the most widely implemented benchmark for mechanizing metatheory, we use parts 1A + 2A of the POPLMARK challenge to compare our work with that of others. These parts prove type-safety for System $F_{<:}$ with algorithmic subtyping. As they involve only single-variable bindings, they are manageable for most existing approaches (though they do not particularly put KNOT's expressivity to the test). Figure 12 compares 9 different solutions:

- Charguéraud's [11] developments use the locally-nameless representation and come with proof automation for this representation.
- Vouillon [39] presents a self-contained de Bruijn solution.
- Our manual version from Sect. 8.1.
- GMETA [18] is a datatype-generic library supporting both de Bruijn indices and the locally-nameless representation.
- LNGEN [7] is a code-generator that produces Coq code for the locally-nameless representation from an Ott specification.
- AUTOSUBST [32] is a Coq tactic library for de Bruijn indices.
- Our KNOT solution from Sect. 8.1.

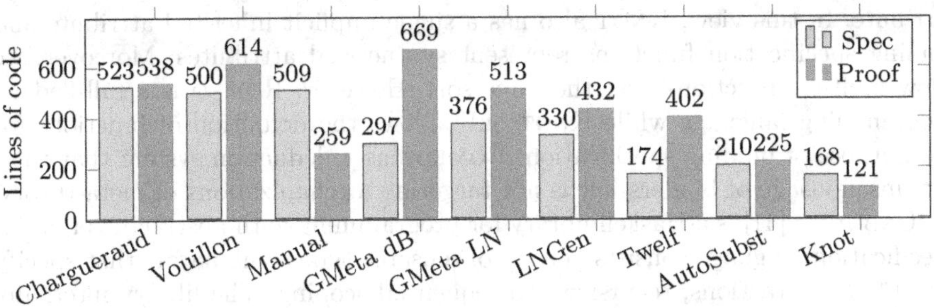

Fig. 12. Sizes (in LoC) of POPLMARK solutions

The figure provides the size (in LoC) for each solution. The LoC counts, generated by *coqwc*, are separated into *proof* scripts and other *spec*ification lines, except for the TWELF solution were we made the distinction manually. We excluded both library code and generated code. The AUTOSUBST and KNOT formalizations are significantly smaller than the others due to the uniformity of weakening and substitution lemmas. KNOT's biggest savings compared to AUTOSUBST come from the generation of well-scopedness relations and the automation of well-scopedness proof obligations. In summary, the KNOT solution is the smallest solutions we are aware of.

9 Related Work

For lack of space, we cover only work on specification languages for variable binding, and systems and tools for reasoning about syntax with binders.

9.1 Specification Languages

The OTT tool [33] allows the definition of concrete programming language syntax and inductive relations on terms. Its binding specifications have inspired those of KNOT. The main difference is that KNOT allows heterogeneous binding specification functions instead of being restricted to homogeneous ones. While OTT generates datatype and function definitions for abstract syntax in multiple proof assistants, support for lemmas is absent.

The Cαml tool [28] defines a specification language for abstract syntax with binding specifications from which it generates OCaml definitions and substitutions. A single abstraction construct allows atoms appearing in one subterm to be bound in another. However this rules out nested abstractions and therefore, the telescopic lambdas of Fig. 4 cannot be encoded directly in Cαml. We are not aware of any work that uses Cαml for the purpose of mechanization.

ROMEO [34] is a programming language that checks for safe handling of variables in programs. ROMEO's specification language is based on the concept of attribute grammars [16] with a single implicit inherited and synthesized attribute. In this view, KNOT also has a single implicit inherited attribute and binding specification functions represent synthesized attributes. Moreover, we allow multiple functions over the same sort. However, ROMEO is a full-fledged programming language while KNOT only allows the definition of functions for the purpose of binding specification. ROMEO has a deduction system that rules out unsafe usage of binders but is not targeting mechanizations of meta-theory.

UNBOUND [41] is a Haskell library for programming with abstract syntax. Its specification language consists of a set of reusable type combinators that specify variables, abstractions, recursive and sequential scoping. The library internally uses a locally nameless approach to implement the binding boilerplate which is hidden from the user. The library also has a combinator called *Shift* which allows to skip enclosing abstractions. This form of non-linear scoping is not supported by KNOT. However, the objective of UNBOUND is to eliminate boilerplate in meta-programs and not meta-theoretic reasoning.

Knot focuses on the kind of abstract syntax representations that are common in mechanizations, which are usually fully resolved and desugared variants of the concrete surface syntax of a language. More work is needed to specify surface languages with complex name resolutions algorithms. In this vein, it would be interesting to extend Knot to synthesize scope graphs [21,37], which are a recent development to address name resolution in a syntax independent manner.

9.2 Tools for First-Order Representations

Aydemir and Weirich [7] created LNGEN, a tool that generates locally-nameless COQ definitions from an OTT specification. It takes care of boilerplate syntax operations, local closure predicates and lemmas. It supports multiple namespaces but restricts itself to single-variable binders.

The DBGEN tool [27] generates de Bruijn representations and boilerplate code. It supports multiple namespaces, mutually recursive definitions and, to a limited extent, multi-variable binders: one can specify that n variables are to be bound in a field, with n either a natural number literal or a natural number field of the constructor. It generates all basic interaction lemmas, but does not deal with well-scopedness or contexts.

GMETA [18] is a framework for first-order representations of variable binding developed by Lee et al. It is implemented as a library in COQ that makes use of datatype-generic programming concepts to implement syntactic operations and well-scopedness predicates generically. GMETA allows multiple namespaces but is restricted to the single-variable case. The system does not follow our free monad principle to model namespaces explicitly, but rather establishes the connection at variable binding and reference positions by comparing the structure representation of sorts for equality. This raises the question whether the universe models syntax adequately when different sorts have the same structure.

GMETA contains a reusable library for contexts of one or two sorts. In the case of two sorts, e.g. term and type variables, the binding of type variables can be telescopic which is enough to address the POPLMARK challenge. Hence, GMETA captures the structure of terms generically, but not the structure of contexts and the accompanying library implements only two instances, but admittedly the ones that are used the most.

AutoSubst [32] is a Coq library that derives boilerplate automatically by reflection using Coq's built-in tactics language. It supports variable binding annotations in the datatype declarations but is limited to single variable bindings and directly recursive definitions. AutoSubst derives parallel substitution operations which is particularly useful for proofs that rely on more machinery for substitutions than type-safety proofs like logical relation proofs for normalization, parametricity or full-abstraction. We do not support parallel substitutions yet, but plan to do so in the future.

9.3 Languages for Mechanization

Several languages have direct support for variable binding. Logical frameworks such as Abella [12], Hybrid [20], Twelf [22] and Beluga [24] are specifically designed to reason about logics and programming languages. Their specialized meta-logic encourages the use of higher-order abstract syntax (HOAS) to represent object-level variable binding with meta-variable bindings. The advantage is that facts about substitution, α-equivalence and well-scoping are inherited from the meta-language. These systems also allow the definition of higher-order judgements to get substitution lemmas for free if the object-language context admits exchange [29]. If it does not admit exchange, the context can still be modeled explicitly [17,23]. For the POPLmark challenge for instance this becomes necessary to isolate a variable in the middle of the context for narrowing.

Despite the large benefits of these systems, they are generally limited to single variable binding and other constructs like patterns or recursive lets have to be encoded by transforming the object language [29].

Nominal Isabelle [36] is an extension of the Isabelle/HOL framework with support for nominal terms which provides α-equivalence for free. At the moment, the system is limited to single variable binding but support for richer binding structure is planned [35].

10 Conclusion

This paper has presented a new approach to mechanizing meta-theory based on Knot, a specification language for syntax with variable binding, and Needle, an infrastructure code generator. Our work distinguishes itself from earlier work on two accounts. First, it covers a wider range of binding constructs featuring rich binding forms and advanced scoping rules. Secondly, it covers a larger extent of the boilerplate functions and lemmas needed for mechanizations. In future work, we want to include support for typing relations.

Acknowledgements. Thanks to the anonymous reviewers for helping to improve the presentation. This work has been funded by the Transatlantic partnership for Excellence in Engineering (TEE) and by the Flemish Fund for Scientific Research (FWO).

References

1. Abbott, M., Altenkirch, T., Ghani, N.: Categories of containers. In: Gordon, A.D. (ed.) FOSSACS 2003. LNCS, vol. 2620, pp. 23–38. Springer, Heidelberg (2003)
2. Altenkirch, T., Morris, P.: Indexed containers. In: LICS 2009, pp. 277–285 (2009)
3. Altenkirch, T., Chapman, J., Uustalu, T.: Monads need not be endofunctors. In: Ong, L. (ed.) FOSSACS 2010. LNCS, vol. 6014, pp. 297–311. Springer, Heidelberg (2010)
4. Altenkirch, T., Chapman, J., Uustalu, T.: Relative monads formalised. J. Formalized Reasoning **7**(1), 1–43 (2014). http://jfr.unibo.it/article/view/4389. ISSN: 1972-5787
5. Altenkirch, T., Reus, B.: Monadic presentations of lambda terms using generalized inductive types. In: Flum, J., Rodríguez-Artalejo, M. (eds.) CSL 1999. LNCS, vol. 1683, pp. 453–468. Springer, Heidelberg (1999)
6. Aydemir, B., Charguéraud, A., Pierce, B.C., Pollack, R., Weirich, S.: Engineering formal metatheory. In: POPL 2008. ACM (2008)
7. Aydemir, B., Weirich, S.: LNgen: Tool support for locally nameless representations. Technical report, UPenn (2010)
8. Backhouse, R., Jansson, P., Jeuring, J., Meertens, L.: Generic programming. In: Swierstra, S.D., Oliveira, J.N. (eds.) AFP 1998. LNCS, vol. 1608, pp. 28–115. Springer, Heidelberg (1999)
9. de Bruijn, N.: Lambda calculus notation with nameless dummies, a tool for automatic formula manipulation, with application to the church-rosser theorem. Indagationes Math. (Proc.) **75**(5), 381–392 (1972)
10. de Bruijn, N.G.: Telescopic mappings in typed lambda calculus. Inf. Comput. **91**(2), 189–204 (1991). doi:10.1016/0890-5401(91)90066-B. http://www.sciencedirect.com/science/article/pii/089054019190066B
11. Charguéraud, A.: http://www.chargueraud.org/softs/ln/ (Accessed 02 July 2015)
12. Gacek, A.: The abella interactive theorem prover (system description). In: Armando, A., Baumgartner, P., Dowek, G. (eds.) IJCAR 2008. LNCS (LNAI), vol. 5195, pp. 154–161. Springer, Heidelberg (2008)
13. Gambino, N., Hyland, M.: Wellfounded trees and dependent polynomial functors. In: Berardi, S., Coppo, M., Damiani, F. (eds.) TYPES 2003. LNCS, vol. 3085, pp. 210–225. Springer, Heidelberg (2004)
14. Jaskelioff, M., Rypacek, O.: An investigation of the laws of traversals. In: MSFP 2012, pp. 40–49 (2012)
15. Keuchel, S., Jeuring, J.T.: Generic conversions of abstract syntax representations. In: WGP 2012. ACM (2012)
16. Knuth, D.E.: Semantics of context-free languages. Math. Syst. Theor. **2**(2), 127–145 (1968)
17. Lee, D.K., Crary, K., Harper, R.: Towards a mechanized metatheory of standard ml, pp. 173–184. POPL 2007. ACM (2007)
18. Lee, G., Oliveira, B.C.D.S., Cho, S., Yi, K.: GMeta: a generic formal metatheory framework for first-order representations. In: Seidl, H. (ed.) Programming Languages and Systems. LNCS, vol. 7211, pp. 436–455. Springer, Heidelberg (2012)
19. Moggi, E., Bell, G., Jay, C.: Monads, shapely functors and traversals. ENTCS 29, CTCS 1999, pp. 187–208 (1999)
20. Momigliano, A., Martin, A.J., Felty, A.P.: Two-level hybrid: a system for reasoning using higher-order abstract syntax. In: ENTCS (2008)

21. Neron, P., Tolmach, A., Visser, E., Wachsmuth, G.: A theory of name resolution. In: Vitek, J. (ed.) ESOP 2015. LNCS, vol. 9032, pp. 205–231. Springer, Heidelberg (2015)
22. Pfenning, F., Schürmann, C.: System description: twelf - a meta-logical framework for deductive systems. In: Ganzinger, H. (ed.) CADE 1999. LNCS (LNAI), vol. 1632, pp. 202–206. Springer, Heidelberg (1999)
23. Pientka, B., Dunfield, J.: Programming with proofs and explicit contexts, pp. 163–173. PPDP 2008. ACM (2008)
24. Pientka, B., Dunfield, J.: Beluga: a framework for programming and reasoning with deductive systems (system description). In: Giesl, J., Hähnle, R. (eds.) IJCAR 2010. LNCS, vol. 6173, pp. 15–21. Springer, Heidelberg (2010)
25. Pierce, B.C.: Types and Programming Languages. MIT Press, Cambridge (2002)
26. Pierce, B.C.: Advanced Topics in Types and Programming Languages. MIT Press, Cambridge (2005)
27. Polonowski, E.: Automatically generated infrastructure for de bruijn syntaxes. In: Blazy, S., Paulin-Mohring, C., Pichardie, D. (eds.) ITP 2013. LNCS, vol. 7998, pp. 402–417. Springer, Heidelberg (2013)
28. Pottier, F.: An overview of Cαml. Electron. Notes Theoret. Comput. Sci. **148**(2), 27–52 (2006). doi:10.1016/j.entcs.2005.11.039. http://www.sciencedirect.com/science/article/pii/S1571066106001253. ISSN: 1571-0661
29. The Twelf Project: The Twelf Wiki. http://twelf.org/wiki (Accessed: 14 October 2015)
30. Rossberg, A., Russo, C.V., Dreyer, D.: F-ing modules. In: TLDI 2010. ACM (2010)
31. Sabry, A., Felleisen, M.: Reasoning about programs in continuation-passing style. LSC **6**(3–4), 289–360 (1993)
32. Schäfer, S., Tebbi, T., Smolka, G.: Autosubst: reasoning with de bruijn terms and parallel substitutions. In: Zhang, X., Urban, C. (eds.) ITP 2015. Lecture Notes in Computer Science, vol. 9236, pp. 359–374. Springer, Heidelberg (2015)
33. Sewell, P., Nardelli, F.Z., Owens, S., Peskine, G., Ridge, T., Sarkar, S., Strniša, R.: Ott: effective tool support for the working semanticist. JFP **20**(1), 71–122 (2010)
34. Stansifer, P., Wand, M.: Romeo: a system for more flexible binding-safe programming. In: ICFP 2014, pp. 53–65. ACM (2014)
35. Urban, C., Kaliszyk, C.: General bindings and alpha-equivalence in nominal Isabelle. In: Barthe, G. (ed.) ESOP 2011. LNCS, vol. 6602, pp. 480–500. Springer, Heidelberg (2011)
36. Urban, C., Tasson, C.: Nominal techniques in Isabelle/HOL. In: Nieuwenhuis, R. (ed.) CADE 2005. LNCS (LNAI), vol. 3632, pp. 38–53. Springer, Heidelberg (2005)
37. Van Antwerpen, H., Néron, P., Tolmach, A., Visser, E., Wachsmuth, G.: A Constraint Language for Static Semantic Analysis based on Scope Graphs. Technical report, TU Delft (2015)
38. Virga, R.: Higher-order rewriting with dependent types. Ph.D. thesis, Carnegie Mellon University Pittsburgh, PA (1999)
39. Vouillon, J.: A solution to the poplmark challenge based on de bruijn indices. JAR **49**(3), 327–362 (2012)
40. Watkins, K., Cervesato, I., Pfenning, F., Walker, D.W.: A concurrent logical framework: the propositional fragment. In: Berardi, S., Coppo, M., Damiani, F. (eds.) TYPES 2003. LNCS, vol. 3085, pp. 355–377. Springer, Heidelberg (2004)
41. Weirich, S., Yorgey, B.A., Sheard, T.: Binders unbound. In: ICFP 2011. ACM (2011)
42. Wright, A., Felleisen, M.: A syntactic approach to type soundness. Inf. Comput. **115**(1), 38–94 (1994)

On the Relative Expressiveness of Higher-Order Session Processes

Dimitrios Kouzapas[1], Jorge A. Pérez[2(✉)], and Nobuko Yoshida[3]

[1] University of Glasgow, Glasgow, UK
[2] University of Groningen, Groningen, The Netherlands
j.a.perez@rug.nl
[3] Imperial College London, London, UK

Abstract. By integrating constructs from the λ-calculus and the π-calculus, in *higher-order process calculi* exchanged values may contain processes. This paper studies the relative expressiveness of $\mathsf{HO}\pi$, the higher-order π-calculus in which communications are governed by *session types*. Our main discovery is that HO, a subcalculus of $\mathsf{HO}\pi$ which lacks name-passing and recursion, can serve as a new core calculus for session-typed higher-order concurrency. By exploring a new bisimulation for HO, we show that HO can encode $\mathsf{HO}\pi$ fully abstractly (up to typed contextual equivalence) more precisely and efficiently than the first-order session π-calculus (π). Overall, under session types, $\mathsf{HO}\pi$, HO, and π are equally expressive; however, $\mathsf{HO}\pi$ and HO are more tightly related than $\mathsf{HO}\pi$ and π.

1 Introduction

Type-preserving compilations are important in the design of functional and object-oriented languages: type information has been used to, e.g., justify code optimizations and reason about programs [18,21,38]. A vast literature on *expressiveness* in concurrency theory also studies compilations (or *encodings*) [8,10,16,26,31]: they are used to transfer reasoning techniques across calculi, and to implement process constructs using simpler ones. In this work, we study *relative expressiveness* via *type-preserving encodings* for $\mathsf{HO}\pi$, a *higher-order* process language that integrates message-passing concurrency with functional features. We consider source and target calculi coupled with *session types* [11] denoting interaction protocols. Building on untyped frameworks for relative expressiveness [10], we propose type preservation as a new criterion for *precise encodings*. We identify HO, a new core calculus for higher-order session concurrency without name passing. We show that HO can encode $\mathsf{HO}\pi$ precisely and efficiently. Requiring type preservation makes this encoding far from trivial: we crucially exploit advances on session type duality [2,3] and recent characterisations of typed contextual equivalence [14]. We develop a full hierarchy of variants of $\mathsf{HO}\pi$ based on precise encodings: our encodings are type-preserving and fully abstract up to typed behavioural equalities. Figure 1 illustrates this hierarchy; the variants of $\mathsf{HO}\pi$ are explained next.

P. Thiemann (Ed.): ESOP 2016, LNCS 9632, pp. 446–475, 2016.
DOI: 10.1007/978-3-662-49498-1_18

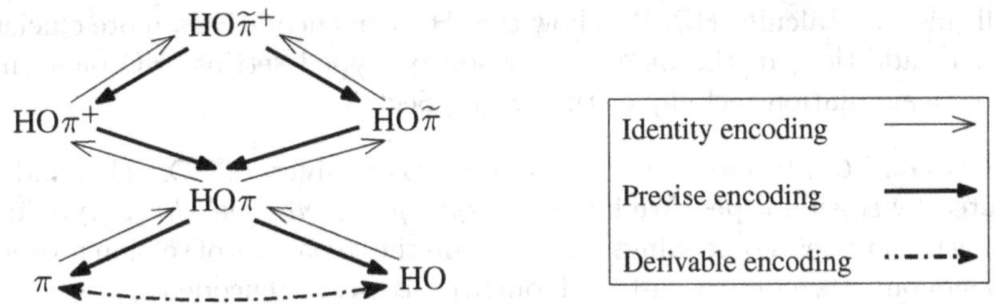

Fig. 1. Encodability in higher-order sessions. Precise encodings are defined in Definition 15.

Context. In *session-based concurrency*, interactions are organised into *sessions*, basic communication units. Interaction patterns can then be abstracted as *session types* [11], against which specifications may be checked. Session type $?(U);S$ (resp. $!\langle U\rangle;S$) describes a protocol that first receives (resp. sends) a value of type U and then continues as protocol S. Also, given an index set I, types $\&\{l_i : S_i\}_{i\in I}$ and $\oplus\{l_i : S_i\}_{i\in I}$ define, respectively, external and internal choice constructs for a labelled choice mechanism; types $\mu t.S$ and end denote recursive and completed protocols, respectively. In the π-calculus, session types describe the intended interactive behaviour of the names in a process [11].

Session-based concurrency has also been casted in higher-order process calculi which, by combining features from the λ-calculus and the π-calculus, enable the exchange of values that may contain processes [9,22]. The higher-order calculus with sessions studied here, called $\mathsf{HO}\pi$, can specify protocols involving *code mobility*: it includes constructs for synchronisation along shared names, session communication (value passing, labelled choice) along linear names, recursion, (first-order) abstractions and applications. That is, values in communications include names but also (first-order) abstractions—functions from name identifiers to processes. (In contrast, we rule out *higher-order* abstractions—functions from processes to processes.) Abstractions can be linear or shared; their types are denoted $C{\multimap}\diamond$ and $C{\rightarrow}\diamond$, respectively (C denotes a name). In $\mathsf{HO}\pi$ we may have processes with a session type such as, e.g.,

$$S = \&\{up : ?(C{\multimap}\diamond); !\langle \mathsf{ok}\rangle; \mathsf{end}\ ,\ down : !\langle C{\rightarrow}\diamond\rangle; !\langle \mathsf{ok}\rangle; \mathsf{end}\ ,\ quit : !\langle \mathsf{bye}\rangle; \mathsf{end}\}\,.$$

S is the type of a server that offers ($\&$) three different behaviours to a client: to *upload* a linear function, to *download* a shared function, or to *quit* the protocol. Following a client's selection ($\oplus$), the server sends a message (ok or bye) before closing the session.

Expressiveness of $\mathsf{HO}\pi$. We study the type-preserving, relative expressivity of $\mathsf{HO}\pi$. As expected from known literature in the untyped setting [32], the first-order session π-calculus [11] (here denoted π) can encode $\mathsf{HO}\pi$ preserving session types. In this paper, our *main discovery* is that $\mathsf{HO}\pi$ without name-passing and recursion can serve as a core calculus for higher-order session concurrency.

We call this core calculus HO. We show that HO can encode HOπ more efficiently than π. In addition, in the higher-order session typed setting, HO offers more tractable bisimulation techniques than π (cf. Sect. 5.2).

Challenges and Contributions. We assess the expressivity of HOπ, HO, and π as delineated by session types. We introduce *type-preserving encodings*: type information is used to define encodings and to retain the semantics of session protocols. Indeed, not only we require well-typed source processes are encoded into well-typed target processes: we demand that session type constructs (input, output, branching, select) used to type the source process are preserved by the typing of the target process. This criterion is included in our notion of *precise encoding* (Definition 15), which extends encodability criteria for untyped processes with *full abstraction*. Full abstraction results are stated up to two behavioural equalities that characterise barbed congruence: *characteristic bisimilarity* ($\approx^{\mathtt{C}}$, defined in [14]) and *higher-order bisimilarity* ($\approx^{\mathtt{H}}$), introduced in this work. It turns out that $\approx^{\mathtt{H}}$ offers more direct reasoning than $\approx^{\mathtt{C}}$. Using precise encodings we establish strong correspondences between HOπ and its variants—see below.

One main contribution is an encoding of HOπ into HO (Sect. 7.1). Since HO lacks both name-passing and recursion, this encoding involves two *key challenges*:

a. In known (typed) encodings of name-passing into process-passing [36] only the output capability of names can be sent—a received name cannot be used in later inputs. This is far too limiting in HOπ, where session names may be passed around (*delegation*) and types describe interaction *structures*, rather than "loose" name capabilities.
b. Known encodings of recursion in untyped higher-order calculi do not carry over to session typed calculi such as HOπ, because linear abstractions cannot be copied/duplicated. Hence, the discipline of session types limits the possibilities for representing infinite behaviours—even simple forms, such as input-guarded replication.

Our encoding overcomes these two obstacles, as we discuss in Sect. 2.

Additional technical contributions include: (i) the encodability of HO into π (Sect. 7.2); (ii) extensions of our encodability results to richer settings (Sect. 8); (iii) a non encodability result showing that shared names strictly add expressive power to session calculi (Sect. 7.4). In essence, (i) extends known results for untyped processes [32] to the session typed setting. Concerning (ii), we develop extensions of our encodings to

- The extension of HOπ with *higher-order* abstractions (HOπ^+);
- The extension of HOπ with polyadic name passing and abstraction (HO$\tilde{\pi}$);
- The super-calculus of HOπ^+ and HO$\tilde{\pi}$ (HO$\tilde{\pi}^+$), equivalent to the calculus in [22].

Figure 1 summarises our encodability results: they connect HOπ with existing higher-order process calculi [22], and highlight the status of HO as the core calculus for session concurrency. Finally, to our knowledge we are the first to prove the non encodability result (iii), exploiting session determinacy and typed equivalences.

Outline. Section 2 overviews key ideas of the precise encoding of $\mathsf{HO}\pi$ into π. Section 3 presents $\mathsf{HO}\pi$ and its subcalculi (HO and π); Sect. 4 summarises their session type system. Section 5 presents behavioural equalities for $\mathsf{HO}\pi$: we recall definitions of barbed congruence and characteristic bisimilarity [14], and introduce higher-order bisimilarity. We show that these three typed relations coincide (Theorem 2). Section 6 defines *precise encodings* by extending encodability criteria for untyped processes. Section 7 gives precise encodings of $\mathsf{HO}\pi$ into HO and of $\mathsf{HO}\pi$ into π (Theorems 3 and 4). Mutual encodings between π and HO are derivable; all these calculi are thus equally expressive. Via empirical and formal comparisons between these two precise encodings, in Sect. 7.3 we establish that $\mathsf{HO}\pi$ and HO are more tightly related than $\mathsf{HO}\pi$ and π (Theorem 5). Moreover, we prove the impossibility of encoding communication along shared names using linear names (Theorem 6). In Sect. 8 we show encodings of $\mathsf{HO}\pi^+$ and $\mathsf{HO}\tilde{\pi}$ into $\mathsf{HO}\pi$ (Theorems 7 and 8). Section 9 collects concluding remarks and reviews related works. Omitted definitions and proofs are in [15].

2 Overview: Encoding Name Passing into Process Passing

A Precise Encoding of Name-Passing into Process-Passing. As mentioned above, our encoding of $\mathsf{HO}\pi$ into HO (Sect. 7.1) should (a) enable the communication of arbitrary names, as required to represent delegation, and (b) address the fact that linearity of session types limits the possibilities for representing infinite behaviour. To encode name passing into HO we "pack" the name to be sent into an abstraction; upon reception, the receiver "unpacks" this object following a precise protocol on a fresh session:

$$[\![a!\langle b\rangle.P]\!] = a!\langle \lambda z.\; z?(x).(x\, b)\rangle.[\![P]\!]$$
$$[\![a?(x).Q]\!] = a?(y).(\nu\, s)(y\, s \mid \overline{s}!\langle \lambda x.\, [\![Q]\!]\rangle.\mathbf{0})$$

Above, a, b are names and s and $\overline{s}$ are linear session names (*endpoints*). Processes $a!\langle V\rangle.P$ and $a?(x).P$ denote output and input at a; abstractions and applications are denoted $\lambda x.P$ and $(\lambda x.P)a$. Processes $(\nu\, s)(P)$ and $\mathbf{0}$ represent hiding and inaction. Thus, following a communication on a, a (deterministic) reduction between s and $\overline{s}$ guarantees that b is properly unpacked by means of abstraction passing and appropriate applications. Notice that the above encoding requires three extra reduction steps to mimic a name communication step in $\mathsf{HO}\pi$. Also, an output action in the source process is translated into an output action in the encoded process (and similarly for input). This is key to ensure the preservation of session type operators mentioned above (cf. Definition 13).

As hinted at above, a challenge in encoding $\mu X.P$ is preserving linearity of session names. Intuitively, we encode the recursion body P as an abstraction $\lambda\tilde{x}.\llbracket P\rrbracket_\sigma$ in which each session name of P (included in set σ) is converted into a name variable in $\tilde{x}$. Since $\lambda\tilde{x}.\llbracket P\rrbracket_\sigma$ does not mention (linear) session names, we may embed it into a "duplicator" process which implements recursion using higher-order communication [40]. The encoding of the recursion variable

X invokes this duplicator in a by-need fashion: it receives $\lambda\tilde{x}.\,\llbracket P \rrbracket_\sigma$ and uses two copies of it: one copy allows us to obtain P through the application of the session names of P; the other allows us to invoke the duplicator when needed. Interestingly, for this encoding to work we require non-tail recursive session types; this exploits recent advances on the theory of duality for session types [2,3].

A Plausible Encoding That is Not Precise. Our notion of *precise encoding* (Definition 15) requires the translation of both process and types; it admits only process mappings that preserve session types *and* are fully abstract. Thus, our encodings not only exhibit strong behavioural correspondences, but also relate source and target processes with consistent communication structures described by session types. These requirements are demanding and make our developments far from trivial. In particular, requiring type preservation may rule out other plausible encoding strategies. To illustrate this point, consider the following alternative encoding of name-passing into HO:[1]

$$\llbracket a?(x).Q \rrbracket^u = a!\langle \lambda x.\,\llbracket Q \rrbracket^u \rangle.\mathbf{0}$$
$$\llbracket a!\langle b \rangle.P \rrbracket^u = a?(x).(x\,b \mid \llbracket P \rrbracket^u)$$

Intuitively, the encoding of input takes the initiative by sending an abstraction containing the encoding of its continuation Q; the encoding of output applies this received value to name b. Hence, this mapping entails a "role inversion": outputs are translated into inputs, and inputs are translated into outputs. Although fairly reasonable, we will see that the encoding $\llbracket\cdot\rrbracket^u$ is *not type preserving.* Consequently, it is also not *precise.* Since individual prefixes (input, output, branching, select) represent actions in a structured communication sequence (i.e., a protocol abstracted by a session type), the encoding $\llbracket\cdot\rrbracket^u$ would simply alter the meaning of the session protocol in the source language.

3 Higher-Order Session π-Calculi

We introduce the *higher-order session π-calculus* (HOπ). We define syntax, operational semantics, and its sub-calculi (π and HO). A type system and behavioural equivalences are introduced in Sects. 4 and 5. Extensions of HOπ with higher-order abstractions and polyadicity (noted HOπ^+ and HO$\tilde{\pi}$, respectively) are discussed in Sect. 8.

$$u,w ::= n \mid x,y,z \qquad n ::= a,b \mid s,\overline{s} \qquad V,W ::= u \mid \boxed{\lambda x.P}$$
$$P,Q ::= u!\langle V\rangle.P \mid u?(x).P \mid u\triangleleft l.P \mid u\triangleright\{l_i : P_i\}_{i\in I} \mid \boxed{V\,u} \mid P \mid Q \mid (\nu n)P \mid \mathbf{0} \mid X \mid \mu X.P$$

Fig. 2. Syntax of HOπ. While HO lacks shaded constructs, π lacks boxed constructs.

[1] This encoding was suggested by a reviewer of a previous version of this paper.

3.1 HOπ: Syntax, Operational Semantics, and Subcalculi

Syntax. The syntax of HOπ is defined in Fig. 2. HOπ it is a subcalculus of the language studied in [22]. It is also a variant of the language that we investigated in [14], which includes higher-order value applications.

Names $a, b, c, \ldots$ (resp. $s, \overline{s}, \ldots$) range over shared (resp. session) names. Names $m, n, t, \ldots$ are session or shared names. Dual endpoints are $\overline{n}$ with $\overline{\overline{s}} = s$ and $\overline{a} = a$. Variables are denoted with $x, y, z, \ldots$, and recursive variables are denoted with $X, Y \ldots$. An abstraction $\lambda x. P$ is a process P with name parameter x. *Values* V, W include identifiers $u, v, \ldots$ and abstractions $\lambda x. P$ (first- and higher-order values, resp.).

Process terms $P, Q, \ldots$ include usual prefixes for sending/receiving values V. Processes $u \triangleleft l.P$ and $u \triangleright \{l_i : P_i\}_{i \in I}$ are the usual session processes for selecting and branching [11]. Process $V\, u$ is the application which substitutes name u on the abstraction V. Typing ensures that V is not a name. Recursion $\mu X.P$ binds the recursive variable X in P. Constructs for inaction $\mathbf{0}$, parallel composition $P_1 \mid P_2$, and name restriction $(\nu\, n)P$ are standard. Session name restriction $(\nu\, s)P$ simultaneously binds endpoints s and $\overline{s}$ in P. Functions $\mathtt{fv}(P)$ and $\mathtt{fn}(P)$ denote the sets of free variables and names. We assume V in $u!\langle V\rangle.P$ does not include free recursive variables X. If $\mathtt{fv}(P) = \emptyset$, we call P *closed*.

Operational Semantics. The *operational semantics* of HOπ is defined in terms of a reduction relation, denoted $\longrightarrow$ and given in Fig. 3 (top). We briefly describe the rules. Rule [App] defines name application. Rule [Pass] defines a shared interaction at n (with $\overline{n} = n$) or a session interaction. Rule [Sel] is the standard rule for labelled choice/selection. Other rules are standard π-calculus rules. Reduction is closed under *structural congruence*, noted $\equiv$ (cf. Fig. 3, bottom). We assume the expected extension of $\equiv$ to values V. We write $\longrightarrow^*$ for a multi-step reduction.

$$(\lambda x. P)\, u \longrightarrow P\{u/x\} \quad \text{[App]} \qquad n!\langle V\rangle.P \mid \overline{n}?(x).Q \longrightarrow P \mid Q\{V/x\} \quad \text{[Pass]}$$

$$n \triangleleft l_j.Q \mid \overline{n} \triangleright \{l_i : P_i\}_{i \in I} \longrightarrow Q \mid P_j \;\; (j \in I) \quad \text{[Sel]} \qquad P \longrightarrow P' \Rightarrow (\nu n)P \longrightarrow (\nu n)P' \quad \text{[Res]}$$

$$P \longrightarrow P' \;\Rightarrow\; P \mid Q \longrightarrow P' \mid Q \quad \text{[Par]} \qquad P \equiv Q \longrightarrow Q' \equiv P' \;\Rightarrow\; P \longrightarrow P' \quad \text{[Cong]}$$

$$P \mid \mathbf{0} \equiv P \quad P_1 \mid P_2 \equiv P_2 \mid P_1 \quad P_1 \mid (P_2 \mid P_3) \equiv (P_1 \mid P_2) \mid P_3 \quad (\nu n)\mathbf{0} \equiv \mathbf{0}$$

$$P \mid (\nu n)Q \equiv (\nu n)(P \mid Q) \; (n \notin \mathtt{fn}(P)) \quad \mu X.P \equiv P\{\mu X.P/X\} \quad P \equiv Q \text{ if } P \equiv_\alpha Q$$

Fig. 3. Operational semantics of HOπ.

Subcalculi. As motivated in the introduction, we define two *subcalculi* of HOπ:

- The *core higher-order session calculus*, denoted HO, lacks recursion and name passing; its formal syntax is obtained from Fig. 2 by excluding constructs in grey .

- The *session π-calculus*, denoted π, lacks higher-order communication but includes recursion; its formal syntax is obtained from Fig. 2 *by excluding constructs in* $\boxed{\text{boxes}}$.

Let $\mathsf{C} \in \{\mathsf{HO}\pi, \mathsf{HO}, \pi\}$. We write $\mathsf{C}^{-\mathsf{sh}}$ to denote the calculus C without shared names: we delete a, b from n. In Sect. 7 we shall demonstrate that $\mathsf{HO}\pi$, HO, and π have the same expressivity, and that C is strictly more expressive than $\mathsf{C}^{-\mathsf{sh}}$.

4 Session Types for HOπ

We define a session type system for $\mathsf{HO}\pi$ and state *type soundness* (Theorem 1), its main property. Our system distills the key features of [22,23] and so it is simpler.

The syntax of types of $\mathsf{HO}\pi$ follows. We write $\diamond$ to denote the process type.

$$U ::= C \mid \boxed{L} \qquad C ::= S \mid \langle S \rangle \mid \boxed{\langle L \rangle} \qquad L ::= C{\rightarrow}\diamond \mid C{\multimap}\diamond$$
$$S ::= !\langle U \rangle; S \mid ?(U); S \mid \oplus\{l_i : S_i\}_{i \in I} \mid \&\{l_i : S_i\}_{i \in I} \mid \mu \mathsf{t}.S \mid \mathsf{t} \mid \mathsf{end}$$

Value type U includes first-order types C and higher-order types L. Types $C{\rightarrow}\diamond$ and $C \multimap \diamond$ denote *shared* and *linear* higher-order types, respectively. Session types, denoted by S, follow the standard binary session type syntax [11], with the extension that carried types U may be higher-order. Shared channel types are denoted $\langle S \rangle$ and $\langle L \rangle$. Types of HO exclude C from value types U; the types of π exclude $\boxed{L}$ and $\boxed{\langle L \rangle}$. From each $\mathsf{C} \in \{\mathsf{HO}\pi, \mathsf{HO}, \pi\}$, $\mathsf{C}^{-\mathsf{sh}}$ excludes shared name types ($\langle S \rangle$ and $\langle L \rangle$), from name type C.

We write S dual S' if S is the *dual* of S'. Intuitively, session type duality is obtained by dualising ! by ?, ? by !, ⊕ by &, and &by ⊕, including the fixed point construction. We use the *co-inductive* definition of duality given in [2].

We consider shared, linear, and session *environments*, denoted Γ, Λ, and Δ, resp.:

$$\begin{aligned}
\Gamma &::= \emptyset \mid \Gamma \cdot x : C{\rightarrow}\diamond \mid \Gamma \cdot u : \langle S \rangle \mid \Gamma \cdot u : \langle L \rangle \mid \Gamma \cdot X : \Delta \\
\Lambda &::= \emptyset \mid \Lambda \cdot x : C{\multimap}\diamond \\
\Delta &::= \emptyset \mid \Delta \cdot u : S
\end{aligned}$$

Γ maps variables and shared names to value types, and recursive variables to session environments; it admits weakening, contraction, and exchange principles. Λ maps variables to linear higher-order types; Δ maps session names to session types. Both Λ and Δ are only subject to exchange. Domains of Γ, Λ and Δ are assumed pairwise distinct. $\Delta_1 \cdot \Delta_2$ is the disjoint union of Δ_1 and Δ_2. We focus on *balanced* session environments:

Definition 1 (Balanced). *We say that a session environment* Δ *is* balanced *if whenever* $s : S_1, \overline{s} : S_2 \in \Delta$ *then* S_1 dual S_2.

$$\text{(PROM)}\ \frac{\Gamma;\emptyset;\emptyset \vdash V \triangleright C{\multimap}\diamond}{\Gamma;\emptyset;\emptyset \vdash V \triangleright C{\rightarrow}\diamond} \qquad \text{(EPROM)}\ \frac{\Gamma;\Lambda\cdot x : C{\multimap}\diamond;\Delta \vdash P \triangleright \diamond}{\Gamma\cdot x : C{\rightarrow}\diamond;\Lambda;\Delta \vdash P \triangleright \diamond} \qquad \text{(ABS)}\ \frac{\Gamma;\Lambda;\Delta_1 \vdash P \triangleright \diamond \quad \Gamma;\emptyset;\Delta_2 \vdash x \triangleright C}{\Gamma\backslash x;\Lambda;\Delta_1\backslash\Delta_2 \vdash \lambda x.P \triangleright C{\multimap}\diamond}$$

$$\text{(APP)}\ \frac{U = C{\multimap}\diamond \vee C{\rightarrow}\diamond \quad \Gamma;\Lambda;\Delta_1 \vdash V \triangleright U \quad \Gamma;\emptyset;\Delta_2 \vdash u \triangleright C}{\Gamma;\Lambda;\Delta_1\cdot\Delta_2 \vdash V u \triangleright \diamond} \qquad \text{(SEND)}\ \frac{u : S \in \Delta_1\cdot\Delta_2 \quad \Gamma;\Lambda_1;\Delta_1 \vdash P \triangleright \diamond \quad \Gamma;\Lambda_2;\Delta_2 \vdash V \triangleright U}{\Gamma;\Lambda_1\cdot\Lambda_2;((\Delta_1\cdot\Delta_2)\backslash u : S)\cdot u : !\langle U\rangle;S \vdash u!\langle V\rangle.P \triangleright \diamond}$$

$$\text{(RCV)}\ \frac{\Gamma;\Lambda_1;\Delta_1\cdot u : S \vdash P \triangleright \diamond \quad \Gamma;\Lambda_2;\Delta_2 \vdash x \triangleright U}{\Gamma\backslash x;\Lambda_1\cdot\Lambda_2;\Delta_1\backslash\Delta_2\cdot u : ?(U);S \vdash u?(x).P \triangleright \diamond}$$

$$\text{(REQ)}\ \frac{\Gamma;\emptyset;\emptyset \vdash u \triangleright U_1 \quad \Gamma;\Lambda;\Delta_1 \vdash P \triangleright \diamond \quad \Gamma;\emptyset;\Delta_2 \vdash V \triangleright U_2 \quad (U_1 = \langle S\rangle \wedge U_2 = S) \vee (U_1 = \langle L\rangle \wedge U_2 = L)}{\Gamma;\Lambda;\Delta_1\cdot\Delta_2 \vdash u!\langle V\rangle.P \triangleright \diamond}$$

$$\text{(ACC)}\ \frac{\Gamma;\emptyset;\emptyset \vdash u \triangleright U_1 \quad \Gamma;\Lambda_1;\Delta_1 \vdash P \triangleright \diamond \quad \Gamma;\Lambda_2;\Delta_2 \vdash x \triangleright U_2 \quad (U_1 = \langle S\rangle \wedge U_2 = S) \vee (U_1 = \langle L\rangle \wedge U_2 = L)}{\Gamma\backslash x;\Lambda_1\backslash\Lambda_2;\Delta_1\backslash\Delta_2 \vdash u?(x).P \triangleright \diamond}$$

Fig. 4. Selected typing rules for HOπ.

Given the above intuitions for environments, the typing judgements for values V and processes P are self-explanatory. They are denoted $\Gamma;\Lambda;\Delta \vdash V \triangleright U$ and $\Gamma;\Lambda;\Delta \vdash P \triangleright \diamond$.

Figure 4 gives selected typing rules; see [15] for a full account. The shared type $C{\rightarrow}\diamond$ is derived using rule (PROM) only if the value has a linear type with an empty linear environment. Rule (EPROM) allows us to freely use a shared type variable as linear. Abstraction values are typed with rule (ABS). Application typing is governed by rule (APP): we expect the type C of an application name u to match the type of the application variable x (i.e., $C \multimap \diamond$ or $C \rightarrow \diamond$). In rule (SEND), the type U of value V should appear as a prefix in the session type $!\langle U\rangle;S$ of u. Rule (RCV) is its dual. Rules (REQ) and (ACC) type interaction along shared names; the type of the sent/received object (S and L, resp.) should match the type of the sent/received subject ($\langle S\rangle$ and $\langle L\rangle$, resp.).

Definition 2. *We define the relation $\longrightarrow$ on session environments as:*

$$\Delta\cdot s : !\langle U\rangle;S_1\cdot\overline{s} : ?(U);S_2 \longrightarrow \Delta\cdot s : S_1\cdot\overline{s} : S_2$$
$$\Delta\cdot s : \oplus\{l_i : S_i\}_{i\in I}\cdot\overline{s} : \&\{l_i : S'_i\}_{i\in I} \longrightarrow \Delta\cdot s : S_k\cdot\overline{s} : S'_k \ (k \in I)$$

We state type soundness for HOπ; it implies type soundness for HO, π, and $\mathsf{C}^{-\mathsf{sh}}$.

Theorem 1 (Type Soundness). Suppose $\Gamma;\emptyset;\Delta \vdash P \triangleright \diamond$ with Δ balanced. Then $P \longrightarrow P'$ implies $\Gamma;\emptyset;\Delta' \vdash P' \triangleright \diamond$ and $\Delta = \Delta'$ or $\Delta \longrightarrow \Delta'$ with Δ' balanced.

5 Behavioural Theory for HOπ

We first define reduction-closed, barbed congruence ($\cong$, Definition 7) as the reference equivalence relation for HOπ processes. We then define two characterisations of $\cong$: *characteristic* and *higher-order bisimilarities* (denoted $\approx^{\mathtt{C}}$ and $\approx^{\mathtt{H}}$, cf. Definitions 8 and 9).

5.1 Reduction-Closed, Barbed Congruence ($\cong$)

We consider *typed relations* $\Re$ that relate closed terms whose session environments are balanced and *confluent:*

Definition 3 (Session Environment Confluence). *Let* $\longrightarrow^*$ *denote multi-step reduction as in Definition 2. We denote* $\Delta_1 \rightleftharpoons \Delta_2$ *if there exists* Δ *such that* $\Delta_1 \longrightarrow^* \Delta$ *and* $\Delta_2 \longrightarrow^* \Delta$.

Definition 4 (Typed Relation). *We say that* $\Gamma; \emptyset; \Delta_1 \vdash P \triangleright \diamond \; \Re \; \Gamma; \emptyset; \Delta_2 \vdash Q \triangleright \diamond$ *is a* typed relation *whenever* P *and* Q *are closed;* Δ_1 *and* Δ_2 *are balanced; and* $\Delta_1 \rightleftharpoons \Delta_2$. *We write* $\Gamma; \Delta_1 \vdash P \; \Re \; \Delta_2 \vdash Q$ *for the typed relation* $\Gamma; \emptyset; \Delta_1 \vdash P \triangleright \diamond \; \Re \; \Gamma; \emptyset; \Delta_2 \vdash Q \triangleright \diamond$.

As usual, a *barb* $\downarrow_n$ is an observable on an output prefix with subject n [20]. A *weak barb* $\Downarrow_n$ is a barb after zero or more reduction steps. Typed barbs $\downarrow_n$ (resp. $\Downarrow_n$) occur on typed processes $\Gamma; \emptyset; \Delta \vdash P \triangleright \diamond$. When n is a session name we require that its dual endpoint $\overline{n}$ is not present in the session environment Δ:

Definition 5 (Barbs). *Let* P *be a closed process. We define:*

1. $P \downarrow_n$ *if* $P \equiv (\nu \tilde{m})(n!\langle V \rangle.P_2 \mid P_3), n \notin \tilde{m}$.
2. $\Gamma; \Delta \vdash P \downarrow_n$ *if* $\Gamma; \emptyset; \Delta \vdash P \triangleright \diamond$ *with* $P \downarrow_n$ *and* $\overline{n} \notin \mathsf{dom}(\Delta)$.
   $\Gamma; \Delta \vdash P \Downarrow_n$ *if* $P \longrightarrow^* P'$ *and* $\Gamma; \Delta' \vdash P' \downarrow_n$.

To define a congruence relation, we introduce the family $\mathbb{C}$ of contexts:

Definition 6 (Context). *A context* $\mathbb{C}$ *is defined as:*

$$\begin{aligned}\mathbb{C} ::= & - \mid u!\langle V \rangle.\mathbb{C} \mid u?(x).\mathbb{C} \mid u!\langle \lambda x.\mathbb{C} \rangle.P \mid (\nu n)\mathbb{C} \mid (\lambda x.\mathbb{C})u \mid \mu X.\mathbb{C} \\ \mid & \; \mathbb{C} \mid P \mid P \mid \mathbb{C} \mid u \triangleleft l.\mathbb{C} \mid u \triangleright \{l_1 : P_1, \cdots, l_i : \mathbb{C}, \cdots, l_n : P_n\}\end{aligned}$$

Notation $\mathbb{C}[P]$ *replaces the hole* $-$ *in* $\mathbb{C}$ *with* P.

We define reduction-closed, barbed congruence [12].

Definition 7 (Barbed Congruence). *Typed relation* $\Gamma; \Delta_1 \vdash P \; \Re \; \Delta_2 \vdash Q$ *is a* reduction-closed, barbed congruence *whenever:*

1. *If* $P \longrightarrow P'$ *then there exist* Q', Δ_1', Δ_2' *such that* $Q \longrightarrow^* Q'$ *and* $\Gamma; \Delta_1' \vdash P' \; \Re \; \Delta_2' \vdash Q'$;
2. *If* $\Gamma; \Delta_1 \vdash P \downarrow_n$ *then* $\Gamma; \Delta_2 \vdash Q \Downarrow_n$;
3. *For all* $\mathbb{C}$, *there exist* Δ_1'', Δ_2'' *such that* $\Gamma; \Delta_1'' \vdash \mathbb{C}[P] \; \Re \; \Delta_2'' \vdash \mathbb{C}[Q]$;
4. *The symmetric cases of 1 and 2.*

The largest such relation is denoted with $\cong$.

5.2 Two Equivalence Relations: $\approx^{\mathsf{C}}$ and $\approx^{\mathsf{H}}$

A Typed Labelled Transition System. In [14] we have characterised reduction-closed, barbed congruence for $\mathsf{HO}\pi$ via a typed relation called *characteristic bisimilarity*. Its definition uses a *typed* labelled transition system (LTS) informed by session types. Given a label ℓ (a visible action or τ), we write $\Gamma;\emptyset;\Delta \vdash P \stackrel{\ell}{\longmapsto} \Delta' \vdash P'$ to denote (strong) transitions. Weak transitions are as expected: we write $\Longmapsto$ for the reflexive, transitive closure of $\stackrel{\tau}{\longmapsto}$, $\stackrel{\ell}{\Longmapsto}$ for $\Longmapsto\stackrel{\ell}{\longmapsto}\Longmapsto$, and $\stackrel{\hat{\ell}}{\Longmapsto}$ for $\stackrel{\ell}{\Longmapsto}$ if $\ell \neq \tau$ and $\Longmapsto$ otherwise. Intuitively, the transitions of a typed process should be enabled by its associated typing:

$$\text{if } P \stackrel{\ell}{\longmapsto} P' \text{ and } (\Gamma,\Delta) \stackrel{\ell}{\longmapsto} (\Gamma,\Delta') \text{ then } \Gamma;\emptyset;\Delta \vdash P \stackrel{\ell}{\longmapsto} \Delta' \vdash P'.$$

As an example of how types enable transitions, consider the rule for input:

$$\frac{\overline{s} \notin \mathsf{dom}(\Delta) \qquad \Gamma;\Lambda';\Delta' \vdash V \triangleright U \qquad V = m \vee V \equiv [U]_{\mathsf{c}} \vee V \equiv \lambda x.\, t?(y).(y\, x) \text{ with } t \text{ fresh}}{(\Gamma;\Lambda;\Delta\cdot s:?(U);S) \stackrel{s?\langle V\rangle}{\longmapsto} (\Gamma;\Lambda\cdot\Lambda';\Delta\cdot\Delta'\cdot s:S)}$$

This rule states that a session environment can input a value if such a value is typed with an input prefix and is either a name m, a *characteristic value* $[U]_{\mathsf{c}}$, or a *trigger value* (the abstraction $\lambda x.\, t?(y).(y\, x)$). A characteristic value is the simplest process that inhabits a type (here, the type U carried by the input prefix). The above rule is used to limit the input actions that can be observed from a session input prefix. For more details on the typed LTS and the characteristic process definition see [14]. Moreover, we define a *(first-order) trigger process*:

$$t \Leftarrow V\!:\!U \stackrel{\mathsf{def}}{=} t?(x).(\nu\, s)([\![?(U);\mathsf{end}]\!]^s \mid \overline{s}!\langle V\rangle.\mathbf{0}) \tag{1}$$

The trigger process $t \Leftarrow V\!:\!U$ is is defined as a process input prefixed on a fresh name t: it applies a value on the *characteristic process* $[\![?(U);\mathsf{end}]\!]^s$ (see [14] for details).

Characterising $\cong$. We define *characteristic* and *higher-order* bisimilarities. While higher-order bisimilarity is a new equality, characteristic bisimilarity was introduced in [14].

Definition 8 (Characteristic Bisimilarity). *A typed relation* $\mathfrak{R}$ *is called a* characteristic bisimulation *if for all* $\Gamma;\Delta_1 \vdash P_1 \;\mathfrak{R}\; \Delta_2 \vdash Q_1$

1. *Whenever* $\Gamma;\Delta_1 \vdash P_1 \stackrel{(\nu\,\tilde{m}_1)n!\langle V_1:U\rangle}{\longmapsto} \Delta_1' \vdash P_2$*, there exist* Q_2*,* V_2*,* Δ_2' *such that* $\Gamma;\Delta_2 \vdash Q_1 \stackrel{(\nu\,\tilde{m}_2)n!\langle V_2:U\rangle}{\Longmapsto} \Delta_2' \vdash Q_2$ *and, for fresh* t*,*

$$\Gamma;\Delta_1'' \vdash (\nu\,\tilde{m}_1)(P_2 \mid t \Leftarrow V_1\!:\!U_1) \;\mathfrak{R}\; \Delta_2'' \vdash (\nu\,\tilde{m}_2)(Q_2 \mid t \Leftarrow V_2\!:\!U_2)$$

2. *For all* $\Gamma;\Delta_1 \vdash P_1 \overset{\ell}{\longmapsto} \Delta_1' \vdash P_2$ *such that* ℓ *is not an output, there exist* Q_2, Δ_2' *such that* $\Gamma;\Delta_2 \vdash Q_1 \overset{\hat{\ell}}{\Longmapsto} \Delta_2' \vdash Q_2$ *and* $\Gamma;\Delta_1' \vdash P_2 \;\Re\; \Delta_2' \vdash Q_2$*; and*
3. *The symmetric cases of 1 and 2.*

The largest such bisimulation is called characteristic bisimilarity *and denoted by* $\approx^{\mathsf{C}}$.

Interestingly, for reasoning about $\mathsf{HO}\pi$ processes we can also exploit the simpler *higher-order bisimilarity.* We replace triggers as in (1) with *higher-order triggers*:

$$t \hookleftarrow V \overset{\mathtt{def}}{=} t?(x).(\nu\, s)(x\, s \mid \bar{s}!\langle V\rangle.\mathbf{0}) \tag{2}$$

We may then define:

Definition 9 (Higher-Order Bisimilarity). *Higher-order bisimilarity, denoted by* $\approx^{\mathtt{H}}$*, is defined by replacing Clause (1) in Definition 8 with the following clause:*

Whenever $\Gamma;\Delta_1 \vdash P_1 \overset{(\nu\,\tilde{m}_1)n!\langle V_1\rangle}{\longmapsto} \Delta_1' \vdash P_2$ *then there exist* Q_2, V_2, Δ_2' *such that* $\Gamma;\Delta_2 \vdash Q_1 \overset{(\nu\,\tilde{m}_2)n!\langle V_2\rangle}{\Longmapsto} \Delta_2' \vdash Q_2$ *and, for fresh* t,
$\Gamma;\Delta_1'' \vdash (\nu\,\tilde{m}_1)(P_2 t \hookleftarrow V_1) \;\Re\; \Delta_2'' \vdash (\nu\,\tilde{m}_2)(Q_2 \mid t \hookleftarrow V_2)$

We state the following important result, which attests the significance of $\approx^{\mathtt{H}}$:

Theorem 2. *Typed relations* $\cong$, $\approx^{\mathtt{H}}$, *and* $\approx^{\mathsf{C}}$ *coincide for* $\mathsf{HO}\pi$ *processes.*

Proof. Coincidence of $\cong$ and $\approx^{\mathsf{C}}$ was established in [14]. Coincidence of $\approx^{\mathtt{H}}$ with $\cong$ and $\approx^{\mathsf{C}}$ is a new result: see [15] for details. □

Remark 1 (Comparison between $\approx^{\mathtt{H}}$ *and* $\approx^{\mathsf{C}}$*).* The key difference between $\approx^{\mathtt{H}}$ and $\approx^{\mathsf{C}}$ is in the trigger process considered. Because of the application in (2), $\approx^{\mathtt{H}}$ cannot be used to reason about processes in π. In contrast, $\approx^{\mathsf{C}}$ is more general: it can uniformly input characteristic, first- or higher-order values. This convenience comes at a price: the definition of (1) requires information on the type of V; in contrast, the higher-order trigger (2) is more generic and simple, as it works independently of the given type.

An up-to technique. Processes that do not use shared names are deterministic. The following up-to technique, based on determinacy properties, will be useful in proofs (Sect. 7). Recall that $\Gamma;\Delta \vdash P \overset{\tau}{\longmapsto} \Delta' \vdash P'$ denotes an internal (typed) transition.

Notation 1 (Deterministic Transitions). *We distinguish two kinds of* τ*-transitions:* session transitions, *noted* $\Gamma;\Delta \vdash P \overset{\tau_s}{\longmapsto} \Delta' \vdash P'$, *and* β-transitions, *noted* $\Gamma;\Delta \vdash P \overset{\tau_\beta}{\longmapsto} \Delta' \vdash P'$. *Intuitively,* $\overset{\tau_s}{\longmapsto}$ *results from a session communication (i.e., synchronization between two dual endpoints), while* $\overset{\tau_\beta}{\longmapsto}$ *results from an application. We write* $\Gamma;\Delta \vdash P \overset{\tau_d}{\longmapsto} \Delta' \vdash P'$ *to denote a session transition or a* β*-transition. See [15] for definitions of* $\overset{\tau_\beta}{\longmapsto}$ *and* $\overset{\tau_s}{\longmapsto}$.

We have the following determinacy property; see [15] for details.

Lemma 1 (τ-Inertness). *(1) Let $\Gamma;\Delta \vdash P \stackrel{\tau_d}{\longmapsto} \Delta' \vdash P'$ be a deterministic transition, with balanced Δ. Then $\Gamma;\Delta \vdash P \cong \Delta' \vdash P'$ with $\Delta \longrightarrow^* \Delta'$ balanced. (2) Let P be an $\mathsf{HO}\pi^{-\mathsf{sh}}$ process. Assume $\Gamma;\emptyset;\Delta \vdash P \triangleright \diamond$. Then $P \longrightarrow^* P'$ implies $\Gamma;\Delta \vdash P \cong \Delta' \vdash P'$ with $\Delta \longrightarrow^* \Delta'$.*

We use Lemma 1 to prove Theorem 6, the negative result stated in Sect. 7.4. This property also enables us to define the following up-to technique, useful in full abstraction proofs. We write $\stackrel{\tau_d}{\Longmapsto}$ to denote a (possibly empty) sequence of deterministic steps $\stackrel{\tau_d}{\longmapsto}$.

Lemma 2 (Up-to Deterministic Transition). *Let $\Gamma;\Delta_1 \vdash P_1 \,\Re\, \Delta_2 \vdash Q_1$ such that if whenever:*

1. *$\forall (\nu\, \tilde{m}_1)n!\langle V_1\rangle$ such that $\Gamma;\Delta_1 \vdash P_1 \stackrel{(\nu\, \tilde{m}_1)n!\langle V_1\rangle}{\longmapsto} \Delta_3 \vdash P_3$ implies that $\exists Q_2, V_2$ such that $\Gamma;\Delta_2 \vdash Q_1 \stackrel{(\nu\, \tilde{m}_2)n!\langle V_2\rangle}{\Longmapsto} \Delta_2' \vdash Q_2$ and $\Gamma;\Delta_3 \vdash P_3 \stackrel{\tau_d}{\Longmapsto} \Delta_1' \vdash P_2$ and for fresh t: $\Gamma;\Delta_1'' \vdash (\nu\, \tilde{m}_1)(P_2 \mid t \hookleftarrow V_1) \,\Re\, \Delta_2'' \vdash (\nu\, \tilde{m}_2)(Q_2 \mid t \hookleftarrow V_2)$.*
2. *$\forall \ell \neq (\nu\, \tilde{m})n!\langle V\rangle$ such that $\Gamma;\Delta_1 \vdash P_1 \stackrel{\ell}{\longmapsto} \Delta_3 \vdash P_3$ implies that $\exists Q_2$ such that $\Gamma;\Delta_1 \vdash Q_1 \stackrel{\hat{\ell}}{\Longmapsto} \Delta_2' \vdash Q_2$ and $\Gamma;\Delta_3 \vdash P_3 \stackrel{\tau_d}{\Longmapsto} \Delta_1' \vdash P_2$ and $\Gamma;\Delta_1' \vdash P_2 \,\Re\, \Delta_2' \vdash Q_2$.*
3. *The symmetric cases of 1 and 2.*

Then $\Re \subseteq \approx^H$.

6 Criteria for Typed Encodings

We define the formal notion of *encoding* by extending to a typed setting existing criteria for untyped processes (as in, e.g., [8,10,16,24,26,27,30,41]). We first define a typed calculus parametrised by a syntax, operational semantics, and typing. Based on this definition, in Sects. 7 and 8 we define concrete instances of (higher-order) typed calculi.

Definition 10 (Typed Calculus). *A typed calculus $\mathcal{L}$ is a tuple $\langle \mathsf{C}, \mathcal{T}, \stackrel{\tau}{\longmapsto}, \approx, \vdash\rangle$ where C and $\mathcal{T}$ are sets of processes and types, respectively; also, $\stackrel{\tau}{\longmapsto}$, $\approx$, and $\vdash$ denote a transition system, a typed equivalence, and a typing system for C, respectively.*

As we explain later, we write $\stackrel{\tau}{\longmapsto}$ to denote an operational semantics defined in terms of τ-transitions (to characterise reductions). Our notion of encoding considers mappings on both processes and types; these are denoted $[\![\cdot]\!]$ and $(\!|\cdot|\!)$, respectively:

Definition 11 (Typed Encoding). *Consider typed calculi $\mathcal{L}_1 = \langle \mathsf{C}_1, \mathcal{T}_1, \stackrel{\tau}{\longmapsto}_1, \approx_1, \vdash_1\rangle$ and $\mathcal{L}_2 = \langle \mathsf{C}_2, \mathcal{T}_2, \stackrel{\tau}{\longmapsto}_2, \approx_2, \vdash_2\rangle$. Given mappings $[\![\cdot]\!] : \mathsf{C}_1 \to \mathsf{C}_2$ and $(\!|\cdot|\!) : \mathcal{T}_1 \to \mathcal{T}_2$, we write $\langle [\![\cdot]\!], (\!|\cdot|\!)\rangle : \mathcal{L}_1 \to \mathcal{L}_2$ to denote the* typed encoding *of $\mathcal{L}_1$ into $\mathcal{L}_2$.*

Mapping $(\!\cdot\!)$ extends to typing environments, e.g., $(\Delta \cdot u : S) = (\Delta) \cdot u : (S)$. We introduce syntactic criteria for typed encodings. Let σ denote a substitution of names for names (a renaming, as usual). Given environments Δ and Γ, we write $\sigma(\Delta)$ and $\sigma(\Gamma)$ to denote the effect of applying σ on the domains of Δ and Γ (clearly, $\sigma(\Gamma)$ concerns only shared names in Γ: process and recursive variables in Γ are not affected by σ).

Definition 12 (Syntax Preservation). *We say that typed encoding* $\langle [\![\cdot]\!], (\cdot) \rangle : \mathcal{L}_1 \to \mathcal{L}_2$ *is* syntax preserving *if it is:*

1. Homomorphic wrt parallel, *if* $(\Gamma); \emptyset; (\Delta_1 \cdot \Delta_2) \vdash_2 [\![P_1 \mid P_2]\!] \triangleright \diamond$ *then* $(\Gamma); \emptyset; (\Delta_1) \cdot (\Delta_2) \vdash_2 [\![P_1]\!] \mid [\![P_2]\!] \triangleright \diamond$.
2. Compositional wrt restriction, *if* $(\Gamma); \emptyset; (\Delta) \vdash_2 [\![(\nu n)P]\!] \triangleright \diamond$ *then* $(\Gamma); \emptyset; (\Delta) \vdash_2 (\nu n)[\![P]\!] \triangleright \diamond$.
3. Name invariant, *if* $(\sigma(\Gamma)); \emptyset; (\sigma(\Delta)) \vdash_2 [\![\sigma(P)]\!] \triangleright \diamond$ *then* $\sigma((\Gamma)); \emptyset; \sigma((\Delta)) \vdash_2 \sigma([\![P]\!]) \triangleright \diamond$, *for any injective renaming of names* σ.

Homomorphism wrt parallel (used in, e.g., [26,27]) expresses that encodings should preserve the distributed topology of source processes. This criterion is appropriate for both encodability and non encodability results; in our setting, it is induced by rules for typed composition. Compositionality wrt restriction is also supported by typing and is useful in our encodability results (Sect. 7). The name invariance criterion follows [10,16].

We now state *type preservation*, a static criterion on the mapping $(\cdot) : \mathcal{T}_1 \to \mathcal{T}_2$: it ensures that type operators are preserved. The source and target languages that we consider here share five (session) type operators: input, output, recursion (binary operators); selection and branching (n-ary operators). Type preservation enables us to focus on mappings $(\cdot)$ that always translate a type operator into itself. This is key to retain the meaning of structured protocols: as session types operators abstract communication behaviour, type preserving encodings help us maintain behaviour across translations.

Definition 13 (Type Preservation). *The typed encoding* $\langle [\![\cdot]\!], (\cdot) \rangle : \mathcal{L}_1 \to \mathcal{L}_2$ *is* type preserving *if for every k-ary type operator* op *in* $\mathcal{T}_1$ *it holds that*

$$(\mathsf{op}(T_1, \cdots, T_k)) = \mathsf{op}((T_1), \cdots, (T_k))$$

Example 1. Following the discussion in Sect. 2, let $(\cdot)_u$ be a mapping on session types such that $(!\langle U\rangle; S)_u = ?((U)_u); (S)_u$ and $(?(U); S)_u = !\langle (U)_u\rangle; (S)_u$ (other type operators are translated homomorphically). That is, $(\cdot)_u$ translates the output type operator into an input type operator (and viceversa). Therefore, $(\cdot)_u$ does not satisfy type preservation.

Next we define semantic criteria for typed encodings:

Definition 14 (Semantic Preservation). *Consider two typed calculi* $\mathcal{L}_1$ *and* $\mathcal{L}_2$*, defined as* $\mathcal{L}_1 = \langle \mathsf{C}_1, \mathcal{T}_1, \overset{\tau}{\longmapsto}_1, \approx_1, \vdash_1 \rangle$ *and* $\mathcal{L}_2 = \langle \mathsf{C}_2, \mathcal{T}_2, \overset{\tau}{\longmapsto}_2, \approx_2, \vdash_2 \rangle$. *We say that the encoding* $\langle [\![\cdot]\!], (\cdot) \rangle : \mathcal{L}_1 \to \mathcal{L}_2$ *is* semantic preserving *if it satisfies the properties below.*

1. Type Soundness: *if* $\Gamma;\emptyset;\Delta \vdash_1 P \triangleright \diamond$ *then* $(\Gamma);\emptyset;(\Delta) \vdash_2 [\![P]\!] \triangleright \diamond$, *for any* P *in* C_1.
2. Barb Preserving: *if* $\Gamma;\Delta \vdash_1 P \downarrow_n$ *then* $(\Gamma);(\Delta) \vdash_2 [\![P]\!] \Downarrow_n$.
3. Operational Correspondence: *If* $\Gamma;\emptyset;\Delta \vdash_1 P \triangleright \diamond$ *then*
   (a) *Completeness: If* $\Gamma;\Delta \vdash_1 P \stackrel{\tau}{\longmapsto}_1 \Delta' \vdash_1 P'$ *then* $\exists Q, \Delta''$ *s.t.*
   (i) $(\Gamma);(\Delta) \vdash_2 [\![P]\!] \Longmapsto_2 (\Delta'') \vdash_2 Q$
   and (ii) $(\Gamma);(\Delta'') \vdash_2 Q \approx_2 (\Delta') \vdash_2 [\![P']\!]$.
   (b) *Soundness: If* $(\Gamma);(\Delta) \vdash_2 [\![P]\!] \Longmapsto_2 (\Delta') \vdash_2 Q$ *then* $\exists P', \Delta''$ *s.t.*
   (i) $\Gamma;\Delta \vdash_1 P \stackrel{\tau}{\longmapsto}_1 \Delta'' \vdash_1 P'$
   and (ii) $(\Gamma);(\Delta'') \vdash_2 [\![P']\!] \approx_2 (\Delta') \vdash_2 Q$.
4. Full Abstraction: $\Gamma;\Delta \vdash_1 P \approx_1 \Delta' \vdash_1 Q$ *if and only if* $(\Gamma);(\Delta) \vdash_2 [\![P]\!] \approx_2 (\Delta') \vdash_2 [\![Q]\!]$.

Together with type preservation (Definition 13), type soundness is a distinguishing criterion in our notion of encoding. Barb preservation, related to success sensitiveness in [10], is convenient in our developments as all considered calculi have the same notion of barb. Operational correspondence, standardly divided into completeness and soundness, is also based on [10]; it relies on τ-transitions (reductions). Completeness ensures that a step of the source process is mimicked by a step of its associated encoding; soundness is its converse. Above, operational correspondence is stated in generic terms. It is worth stressing that the operational correspondence statements for our encodings are tailored to the specifics of each encoding, and so they are actually stronger than the criteria given above (see Propositions 3, 6, 10, 13 and [15] for details). Finally, following [27,32,45], we consider full abstraction as an encodability criterion: this leads to stronger encodability results.

We introduce *precise* and *minimal* encodings. While we state strong positive encodability results in terms of *precise* encodings, to prove the non-encodability result in Sect. 7.4, we appeal to the weaker *minimal* encodings.

Definition 15 (Typed Encodings: Precise and Minimal). *We say that the typed encoding* $\langle [\![\cdot]\!], (\cdot) \rangle : \mathcal{L}_1 \to \mathcal{L}_2$ *is* precise, *if it is syntax, type, and semantic preserving (Definitions 12, 13, 14). We say that the encoding is* minimal, *if it is syntax preserving (Definition 12), barb preserving (Definition 14-2), and operationally complete (Definition 14-3(a)).*

The following property will come in handy in Sect. 8:

Proposition 1. *Let* $\langle [\![\cdot]\!]^1, (\cdot)^1 \rangle : \mathcal{L}_1 \to \mathcal{L}_2$ *and* $\langle [\![\cdot]\!]^2, (\cdot)^2 \rangle : \mathcal{L}_2 \to \mathcal{L}_3$ *be two precise encodings. Then their composition, denoted* $\langle [\![\cdot]\!]^2 \circ [\![\cdot]\!]^1, (\cdot)^2 \circ (\cdot)^1 \rangle : \mathcal{L}_1 \to \mathcal{L}_3$, *is precise.*

7 Expressiveness Results

We first present two precise encodings: (1) higher-order communication with recursion and name-passing ($\mathsf{HO}\pi$) into higher-order communication without name-passing nor recursion (HO) (Sect. 7.1); and (2) HOπ into the first-order calculus with name-passing with recursion (π) (Sect. 7.2). We then compare these encodings (Sect. 7.3). Moreover, in Sect. 7.4 we state our impossibility result for shared/linear names. We consider the typed calculi (cf. Definition 10):

$$\mathcal{L}_{\mathsf{HO}\pi} = \langle \mathsf{HO}\pi, \mathcal{T}_1, \overset{\tau}{\longmapsto}, \approx^{\mathtt{H}}, \vdash \rangle \quad \mathcal{L}_{\mathsf{HO}} = \langle \mathsf{HO}, \mathcal{T}_2, \overset{\tau}{\longmapsto}, \approx^{\mathtt{H}}, \vdash \rangle \quad \mathcal{L}_{\pi} = \langle \pi, \mathcal{T}_3, \overset{\tau}{\longmapsto}, \approx^{\mathtt{C}}, \vdash \rangle$$

where: $\mathcal{T}_1$, $\mathcal{T}_2$, and $\mathcal{T}_3$ are sets of types of HOπ, HO, and π, respectively. The typing $\vdash$ is defined in Sect. 4. The LTSs follow the intuitions given in Sect. 5.2. Moreover, $\approx^{\mathtt{H}}$ is as in Definition 9, and $\approx^{\mathtt{C}}$ is as in Definitions 8.

7.1 From HOπ to HO

HO is expressive enough to precisely encode HOπ. As discussed above, the main challenges are to encode (1) name passing and (2) recursion, for which we only use abstraction passing. As explained in Sect. 2, for (1), we pass an abstraction which enables to use the name upon application. For (2), we copy a process upon reception; passing around linear abstractions is delicate because they cannot be copied. To handle linearity, we define the following auxiliary mapping $\llfloor \cdot \rrfloor_\sigma$ from processes with free names to processes without free names (but with free variables instead):

Definition 16 (Auxiliary Mapping). *Let $|\cdot| : 2^{\mathcal{N}} \longrightarrow \mathcal{V}^\omega$ denote a map of sequences of lexicographically ordered names to sequences of variables, defined inductively as: $|\epsilon| = \epsilon$ and $|n \cdot \tilde{m}| = x_n \cdot |\tilde{m}|$. Also, let σ be a set of session names. Figure 5 defines an auxiliary mapping $\llfloor \cdot \rrfloor_\sigma$: HO $\to$ HO.*

Let P be an HOπ process with $\mathtt{fn}(P) = \{n_1, \cdots, n_k\}$. Intuitively, our encoding $[\![\cdot]\!]^1_f$ exploits the abstraction $\lambda x_1, \cdots, x_k. \llfloor [\![P]\!]^1_f \rrfloor_\emptyset$, where $|n_j| = x_j$, for all $j \in \{1, \ldots, k\}$:

Definition 17 (Typed Encoding of HOπ into HO). *Let f be a map from process variables to sequences of name variables. The typed encoding $\langle [\![\cdot]\!]^1_f, (\cdot)^1 \rangle : \mathcal{L}_{\mathsf{HO}\pi} \to \mathcal{L}_{\mathsf{HO}}$ is given in Fig. 6. Mapping $(\cdot)^1$ on types homomorphically extends to environments Δ and Γ, with $(\Gamma \cdot X : \Delta_1)^1 = (\Gamma)^1 \cdot z_X : (S_1, \ldots, S_m, S^*) \!\to\! \diamond$ where S^* is defined as $\mu \mathsf{t}.?((S_1, \ldots, S_m, \mathsf{t}) \!\to\! \diamond)$; $\mathbf{end}$ provided that $\Delta_1 = \{n_i : S_i\}_{1 \le i \le m}$.*

$$\llfloor \mathbf{0} \rrfloor_\sigma \overset{\mathsf{def}}{=} \mathbf{0} \qquad \llfloor n!\langle \lambda x.\, Q\rangle.P \rrfloor_\sigma \overset{\mathsf{def}}{=} u!\langle \lambda x.\llfloor Q\rrfloor_\sigma\rangle.\llfloor P\rrfloor_\sigma \qquad \llfloor (\nu n)P \rrfloor_\sigma \overset{\mathsf{def}}{=} (\nu n)\llfloor P\rrfloor_{\sigma\cdot n}$$

$$\llfloor P \mid Q \rrfloor_\sigma \overset{\mathsf{def}}{=} \llfloor P\rrfloor_\sigma \mid \llfloor Q\rrfloor_\sigma \qquad \llfloor x n \rrfloor_\sigma \overset{\mathsf{def}}{=} x u \qquad \llfloor (\lambda x.Q) n \rrfloor_\sigma \overset{\mathsf{def}}{=} (\lambda x.\llfloor Q\rrfloor_\sigma) u$$

$$\llfloor n?(x).P \rrfloor_\sigma \overset{\mathsf{def}}{=} u?(x).\llfloor P\rrfloor_\sigma \quad \llfloor n \triangleleft l.P \rrfloor_\sigma \overset{\mathsf{def}}{=} u \triangleleft l.\llfloor P\rrfloor_\sigma \quad \llfloor n \triangleright \{l_i : P_i\}_{i\in I} \rrfloor_\sigma \overset{\mathsf{def}}{=} u \triangleright \{l_i : \llfloor P_i\rrfloor_\sigma\}_{i\in I}$$

In all cases: $u = n$ if $n \in \sigma$; otherwise $u = x_n$.

Fig. 5. Auxiliary mapping used to encode HOπ into HO (Definition 16).

Types:

$$\lfloor S \rfloor^1 \stackrel{\text{def}}{=} (?(\langle\!\langle S \rangle\!\rangle^1 \multimap \diamond); \text{end}) \multimap \diamond \qquad \lfloor \langle S \rangle \rfloor^1 \stackrel{\text{def}}{=} (?(\langle \langle\!\langle S \rangle\!\rangle^1 \rangle \to \diamond); \text{end}) \multimap \diamond$$

$$\lfloor \langle L \rangle \rfloor^1 \stackrel{\text{def}}{=} (?(\langle \langle\!\langle L \rangle\!\rangle^1 \rangle \to \diamond); \text{end}) \multimap \diamond \qquad \lfloor C \multimap \diamond \rfloor^1 \stackrel{\text{def}}{=} \langle\!\langle C \rangle\!\rangle^1 \multimap \diamond \qquad \lfloor C \to \diamond \rfloor^1 \stackrel{\text{def}}{=} \langle\!\langle C \rangle\!\rangle^1 \to \diamond$$

$$\langle\!\langle \langle S \rangle \rangle\!\rangle^1 \stackrel{\text{def}}{=} \langle \langle\!\langle S \rangle\!\rangle^1 \rangle \qquad \langle\!\langle \langle L \rangle \rangle\!\rangle^1 \stackrel{\text{def}}{=} \langle \langle\!\langle L \rangle\!\rangle^1 \rangle$$

$$\langle\!\langle !\langle U \rangle; S \rangle\!\rangle^1 \stackrel{\text{def}}{=} !\langle \lfloor U \rfloor^1 \rangle; \langle\!\langle S \rangle\!\rangle^1 \qquad \langle\!\langle ?(U); S \rangle\!\rangle^1 \stackrel{\text{def}}{=} ?(\lfloor U \rfloor^1); \langle\!\langle S \rangle\!\rangle^1$$

$$\langle\!\langle \oplus\{l_i : S_i\}_{i\in I} \rangle\!\rangle^1 \stackrel{\text{def}}{=} \oplus\{l_i : \langle\!\langle S_i \rangle\!\rangle^1\}_{i\in I} \qquad \langle\!\langle \&\{l_i : S_i\}_{i\in I} \rangle\!\rangle^1 \stackrel{\text{def}}{=} \&\{l_i : \langle\!\langle S_i \rangle\!\rangle^1\}_{i\in I}$$

$$\langle\!\langle \mathsf{t} \rangle\!\rangle^1 \stackrel{\text{def}}{=} \mathsf{t} \qquad \langle\!\langle \mu \mathsf{t}.S \rangle\!\rangle^1 \stackrel{\text{def}}{=} \mu \mathsf{t}.\langle\!\langle S \rangle\!\rangle^1 \qquad \langle\!\langle \text{end} \rangle\!\rangle^1 \stackrel{\text{def}}{=} \text{end}$$

Terms:

$$[\![u!\langle w \rangle.P]\!]^1_f \stackrel{\text{def}}{=} u!\langle \lambda z.\, z?(x).(x\, w) \rangle.[\![P]\!]^1_f \qquad [\![u?(x{:}C).Q]\!]^1_f \stackrel{\text{def}}{=} u?(y).(\nu\, s)(y\, s \mid \overline{s}!\langle \lambda x.\, [\![Q]\!]^1_f \rangle.\mathbf{0})$$

$$[\![u!\langle \lambda x.\, Q \rangle.P]\!]^1_f \stackrel{\text{def}}{=} u!\langle \lambda x.\, [\![Q]\!]^1_f \rangle.[\![P]\!]^1_f \qquad [\![u?(x{:}L).P]\!]^1_f \stackrel{\text{def}}{=} u?(x).[\![P]\!]^1_f$$

$$[\![s \triangleleft l.P]\!]^1_f \stackrel{\text{def}}{=} s \triangleleft l.[\![P]\!]^1_f \qquad [\![s \triangleright \{l_i{:}P_i\}_{i\in I}]\!]^1_f \stackrel{\text{def}}{=} s \triangleright \{l_i : [\![P_i]\!]^1_f\}_{i\in I}$$

$$[\![\mathbf{0}]\!]^1_f \stackrel{\text{def}}{=} \mathbf{0} \qquad [\![(\nu\, n)P]\!]^1_f \stackrel{\text{def}}{=} (\nu\, n)[\![P]\!]^1_f$$

$$[\![x\, u]\!]^1_f \stackrel{\text{def}}{=} x\, u \qquad [\![(\lambda x.\, Q)\, u]\!]^1_f \stackrel{\text{def}}{=} (\lambda x.\, [\![Q]\!]^1_f)\, u$$

$$[\![P \mid Q]\!]^1_f \stackrel{\text{def}}{=} [\![P]\!]^1_f \mid [\![Q]\!]^1_f$$

$$[\![\mu X.P]\!]^1_f \stackrel{\text{def}}{=} (\nu\, s)(\overline{s}!\langle \lambda(\|\tilde{n}\|, y).\, y?(z_X).\llbracket [\![P]\!]^1_{f,\{X\to\tilde{n}\}} \rrbracket_{\emptyset} \rangle.\mathbf{0} \mid s?(z_X).[\![P]\!]^1_{f,\{X\to\tilde{n}\}}) \quad (\tilde{n} = \text{fn}(P))$$

$$[\![X]\!]^1_f \stackrel{\text{def}}{=} (\nu\, s)(z_X\, (\tilde{n}, s) \mid \overline{s}!\langle \lambda(\|\tilde{n}\|, y).\, z_X\, (\|\tilde{n}\|, y) \rangle.\mathbf{0}) \quad (\tilde{n} = f(X))$$

Above fn(P) denotes a lexicographically ordered sequence of free names in P. The input bound variable x is annotated by a type to distinguish first- and higher-order cases.

Fig. 6. Encoding of HOπ into HO (Definition 17).

Note that Δ in $X : \Delta$ is mapped to a non-tail recursive session type with variable z_X. Non-tail recursive session types were studied in [2,3]; to our knowledge, this is the first application in the context of higher-order session types. For simplicity, we use polyadic name abstractions. A precise encoding of polyadicity into HO is given in Sect. 8.

Key elements in Fig. 6 are encodings of *name passing* ($[\![u!\langle w \rangle.P]\!]^1_f$ and $[\![u?(x).P]\!]^1_f$) and *recursion* ($[\![\mu X.P]\!]^1_f$ and $[\![X]\!]^1_f$). As motivated in Sect. 2, a name w is passed as an input-guarded abstraction; on the receiver side, the encoding i) receives the abstraction; ii) applies to it a fresh endpoint s; iii) uses the dual endpoint $\overline{s}$ to send the continuation P as an abstraction. Thus, name substitution is achieved via name application. As for recursion, to encode $\mu X.P$ we first record a mapping from recursive variable X to process variable z_X. Then, using $\llbracket \cdot \rrbracket_\sigma$ in Definition 16, we encode the recursion body P as a name abstraction in which free names of P are converted into name variables. (Notice that P is first encoded into HO and then transformed using mapping $\llbracket \cdot \rrbracket_\sigma$.) Subsequently, this higher-order value is embedded in an input-guarded "duplicator" process. We encode X in such a way that it simulates recursion unfolding by invoking the duplicator in a by-need fashion. That is, upon reception, the HO abstraction encoding P is duplicated: one copy is used to reconstitute the original recursion body P (through the application of $\mathtt{fn}(P)$); another copy is used to re-invoke the duplicator when needed. We illustrate the encoding by means of an example.

Example 2 (The Encoding $[\![\cdot]\!]^1_f$ At Work). Let $P = \mu X.a!\langle m\rangle.X$ be an $\mathsf{HO}\pi$ process. Its encoding into HO is given next; notice that $f = \emptyset$ and $f' = X \to x_a x_m$.

$$[\![P]\!]^1_f = (\nu\, s_1)(s_1?(x).[\![a!\langle m\rangle.X]\!]^1_{f'} \mid \overline{s_1}!\langle \lambda(x_a, x_m, z).\, z?(x).\llbracket\!\lfloor [\![a!\langle m\rangle.X]\!]^1_{f'} \rfloor\!\rrbracket_\emptyset\rangle.\mathbf{0})$$

$$[\![a!\langle m\rangle.X]\!]^1_{f'} = a!\langle \lambda z.\, z?(x).(x\, m)\rangle.(\nu\, s_2)(x\,(a, m, s_2) \mid \overline{s_2}!\langle \lambda(x_a, x_m, z).\, x\,(x_a, x_m, z)\rangle.\mathbf{0})$$

$$\llbracket\!\lfloor [\![a!\langle m\rangle.X]\!]^1_{f'} \rfloor\!\rrbracket_\emptyset = x_a!\langle \lambda z.\, z?(x).(x\, x_m)\rangle.(\nu\, s_2)(x\,(x_a, x_m, s_2) \mid \overline{s_2}!\langle \lambda(x_a, x_m, z).\, x\,(x_a, x_m, z)\rangle.\mathbf{0})$$

That is, by writing V to denote the process

$$\lambda(x_a, x_m, z).\, z?(x).x_a!\langle \lambda z.\, z?(x).(x\, x_m)\rangle.(\nu\, s_2)(x\,(x_a, x_m, s_2) \mid \overline{s_2}!\langle \lambda(x_a, x_m, z).\, x\,(x_a, x_m, z)\rangle.\mathbf{0})$$

we would have

$$[\![P]\!]^1_f = (\nu\, s_1)(s_1?(x).a!\langle \lambda z.\, z?(x).(x\, m)\rangle.(\nu\, s_2)(x\,(a, m, s_2) \mid \overline{s_2}!\langle \lambda(x_a, x_m, z).\, x\,(x_a, x_m, z)\rangle.\mathbf{0}) \mid \overline{s_1}!\langle V\rangle.\mathbf{0})$$

Next we illustrate the behaviour of $[\![P]\!]^1_f$; below ℓ stands for $a!\langle \lambda z.\, z?(x).(x\, m)\rangle$.

$$\begin{aligned}
[\![P]\!]^1_f &\equiv (\nu\, s_1)(\overline{s_1}!\langle V\rangle.\mathbf{0} \mid s_1?(x).a!\langle \lambda z.\, z?(x).(x\, m)\rangle.(\nu\, s_2)(\overline{s_2}!\langle \lambda(x_a, x_m, z).\\
&\qquad x\,(x_a, x_m, z)\rangle.\mathbf{0}) \mid x\,(a, m, s_2))\\
&\overset{\tau}{\longmapsto} a!\langle \lambda z.\, z?(x).(x\, m)\rangle.(\nu\, s_2)(\overline{s_2}!\langle V\rangle.\mathbf{0} \mid s_2?(x).a!\langle \lambda z.\, z?(x).(x\, m)\rangle.\\
&\qquad (\nu\, s_3)(\overline{s_3}!\langle \lambda(x_a, x_m, z).\, x\,(x_a, x_m, z)\rangle.\mathbf{0}) \mid x\,(a, m, s_3))\\
&\equiv_\alpha a!\langle \lambda z.\, z?(x).(x\, m)\rangle.(\nu\, s_1)(\overline{s_1}!\langle V\rangle.\mathbf{0} \mid s_1?(x).a!\langle \lambda z.\, z?(x).(x\, m)\rangle.\\
&\qquad (\nu\, s_2)(\overline{s_2}!\langle \lambda(x_a, x_m, z).\, x\,(x_a, x_m, z)\rangle.\mathbf{0}) \mid x\,(a, m, s_2))\\
&\equiv a!\langle \lambda z.\, z?(x).(x\, m)\rangle.[\![\mu X.a!\langle m\rangle.X]\!]^1_f \overset{\ell}{\longmapsto} [\![\mu X.a!\langle m\rangle.X]\!]^1_f.
\end{aligned}$$

We now describe the properties of the encoding. Directly from Fig. 6 we may state:

Proposition 2 ($\mathsf{HO}\pi$ into HO: Type Preservation). *The encoding from $\mathcal{L}_{\mathsf{HO}\pi}$ into $\mathcal{L}_{\mathsf{HO}}$ (cf. Definition 17) is type preserving.*

Now, we state operational correspondence with respect to reductions; the full statement (and proof) can be found in [15].

Proposition 3 ($\mathsf{HO}\pi$ into HO: Operational Correspondence - Excerpt). *Let P be an $\mathsf{HO}\pi$ process such that $\Gamma; \emptyset; \Delta \vdash P \triangleright \diamond$.*

1. *Completeness: Suppose $\Gamma; \Delta \vdash P \overset{\tau}{\longmapsto} \Delta' \vdash P'$. Then we have:*
   (a) If $P' \equiv (\nu\, \tilde{m})(P_1 \mid P_2\{m/x\})$ then $\exists R$ s.t.

$$(\Gamma)^1; (\Delta)^1 \vdash [\![P]\!]^1_f \overset{\tau}{\longmapsto} (\Delta)^1 \vdash (\nu\, \tilde{m})([\![P_1]\!]^1_f \mid R), \text{ and}$$

$$(\Gamma)^1; (\Delta)^1 \vdash (\nu\, \tilde{m})([\![P_1]\!]^1_f \mid R) \overset{\tau_\beta}{\longmapsto}\overset{\tau_s}{\longmapsto}\overset{\tau_\beta}{\longmapsto} (\Delta)^1 \vdash (\nu\, \tilde{m})([\![P_1]\!]^1_f \mid [\![P_2]\!]^1_f\{m/x\}).$$

(b) *If* $P' \equiv (\nu\,\tilde{m})(P_1 \mid P_2\{\lambda y.\,Q/x\})$ *then*
$(\Gamma)^1; (\Delta)^1 \vdash [\![P]\!]^1_f \overset{\tau}{\longmapsto} (\Delta_1)^1 \vdash (\nu\,\tilde{m})([\![P_1]\!]^1_f \mid [\![P_2]\!]^1_f\{\lambda y.\,[\![Q]\!]^1_\emptyset/x\})$.

(c) *If* $P' \not\equiv (\nu\,\tilde{m})(P_1 \mid P_2\{m/x\}) \wedge P' \not\equiv (\nu\,\tilde{m})(P_1 \mid P_2\{\lambda y.\,Q/x\})$ *then*
$(\Gamma)^1; (\Delta)^1 \vdash [\![P]\!]^1_f \overset{\tau}{\longmapsto} (\Delta'_1)^1 \vdash [\![P']\!]^1_f$.

2. *Soundness: Suppose* $(\Gamma)^1; (\Delta)^1 \vdash [\![P]\!]^1_f \overset{\tau}{\longmapsto} (\Delta')^1 \vdash Q$. *Then* $\Delta' = \Delta$ *and either*
   (a) $\exists P'$ *s.t.* $\Gamma; \Delta \vdash P \overset{\tau}{\longmapsto} \Delta \vdash P'$, *and* $Q = [\![P']\!]^1_f$.
   (b) $\exists P_1, P_2, x, m, Q'$ *s.t.* $\Gamma; \Delta \vdash P \overset{\tau}{\longmapsto} \Delta \vdash (\nu\,\tilde{m})(P_1 \mid P_2\{m/x\})$, *and*
   $(\Gamma)^1; (\Delta)^1 \vdash Q \overset{\tau_\beta}{\longmapsto}\overset{\tau_s}{\longmapsto}\overset{\tau_\beta}{\longmapsto} (\Delta)^1 \vdash [\![P_1]\!]^1_f \mid [\![P_2\{m/x\}]\!]^1_f$

Observe how we can explicitly distinguish the role of finite, deterministic reductions ($\overset{\tau_s}{\longmapsto}$ and $\overset{\tau_\beta}{\longmapsto}$, defined in Notation 1) in both soundness and completeness statements.

The typed operational correspondence given above is an important component in the proof of *full abstraction*, which we state next.

Proposition 4 (HOπ into HO: Full Abstraction). *Let* P_1, Q_1 *be* HOπ *processes.*
$\Gamma; \Delta_1 \vdash P_1 \approx^H \Delta_2 \vdash Q_1$ *if and only if* $(\Gamma)^1; (\Delta_1)^1 \vdash [\![P_1]\!]^1_f \approx^H (\Delta_2)^1 \vdash [\![Q_1]\!]^1_f$.

We may state the main result of this section. See [15] for details.

Theorem 3 (Precise Encoding of HOπ into HO). *The encoding from* $\mathcal{L}_{\mathsf{HO}\pi}$ *into* $\mathcal{L}_{\mathsf{HO}}$ *(cf. Definition 17) is precise.*

7.2 From HOπ to π

We now discuss the precise encodability of HOπ into π; the non trivial issue is encoding higher-order communication, which is present in HOπ but not in π. We closely follow Sangiorgi's encoding [33,36], which represents the exchange of a process with the exchange of a fresh *trigger name*. Trigger names may then be used to activate copies of the process, which becomes a persistent resource represented by an input-guarded replication. We cast this strategy in the setting of session-typed communications. In the presence of session names (which are linear and cannot be replicated), our approach uses replicated names as triggers for shared resources and non-replicated names for linear resources (cf. $[\![u!\langle \lambda x.\,Q\rangle.P]\!]^2$).

Definition 18 (Typed Encoding of HOπ into π). *The typed encoding* $\langle [\![\cdot]\!]^2, (\cdot)^2\rangle : \mathcal{L}_{\mathsf{HO}\pi} \to \mathcal{L}_\pi$ *is defined in Fig. 7.*

Observe how $[\![(\lambda x.\,P)\,u]\!]^2$ naturally induces a name substitution. We describe key properties of this encoding. First, type preservation and operational correspondence:

Proposition 5 (HOπ into π: Type Preservation). *The encoding from* $\mathcal{L}_{\mathsf{HO}\pi}$ *into* $\mathcal{L}_\pi$ *(cf. Definition 18) is type preserving.*

Types:

$$\langle\!\langle !\langle S \multimap \diamond\rangle; S_1 \rangle\!\rangle^2 \stackrel{\text{def}}{=} !\langle\langle ?(\langle\!\langle S \rangle\!\rangle^2); \mathsf{end}\rangle\rangle; \langle\!\langle S_1 \rangle\!\rangle^2 \qquad \langle\!\langle ?(S \multimap \diamond); S_1 \rangle\!\rangle^2 \stackrel{\text{def}}{=} ?(\langle ?(\langle\!\langle S \rangle\!\rangle^2); \mathsf{end}\rangle); \langle\!\langle S_1 \rangle\!\rangle^2$$

Terms:

$$[\![u!\langle \lambda x.\, Q\rangle.P]\!]^2 \stackrel{\text{def}}{=} \begin{cases} (\nu a)(u!\langle a\rangle.([\![P]\!]^2 \mid *\, a?(y).y?(x).[\![Q]\!]^2)) & (s \notin \mathtt{fn}(Q)) \\ (\nu a)(u!\langle a\rangle.([\![P]\!]^2 \mid a?(y).y?(x).[\![Q]\!]^2)) & (\text{otherwise}) \end{cases}$$

$$[\![u?(x).P]\!]^2 \stackrel{\text{def}}{=} u?(x).[\![P]\!]^2$$

$$[\![x u]\!]^2 \stackrel{\text{def}}{=} (\nu s)(x!\langle s\rangle.\bar{s}!\langle u\rangle.\mathbf{0})$$

$$[\![(\lambda x.\, P)\, u]\!]^2 \stackrel{\text{def}}{=} (\nu s)(s?(x).[\![P]\!]^2 \mid \bar{s}!\langle u\rangle.\mathbf{0})$$

Notice: $*P$ means $\mu X.(P \mid X)$. Elided mappings are homomorphic.

Fig. 7. Encoding of HOπ into π (Definition 18).

Proposition 6 (HOπ into π: Operational Correspondence - Excerpt). *Let P be an HOπ process such that $\Gamma; \emptyset; \Delta \vdash P \triangleright \diamond$.*

1. *Completeness: Suppose $\Gamma; \Delta \vdash P \stackrel{\ell}{\longmapsto} \Delta' \vdash P'$. Then either:*
   (a) *If $\ell = \tau$ then one of the following holds:*
   - $(\Gamma)^2; (\Delta)^2 \vdash [\![P]\!]^2 \stackrel{\tau}{\longmapsto} (\Delta')^2 \vdash (\nu \tilde{m})([\![D]\!]^P_1 2 \mid (\nu a)([\![D]\!]^P_2 2\{a/x\} \mid *\ a?(y).$ $y?(x).[\![Q]\!]^2$ *for some P_1, P_2, Q;*
   - $(\Gamma)^2; (\Delta)^2 \vdash [\![P]\!]^2 \stackrel{\tau}{\longmapsto} (\Delta')^2 \vdash (\nu \tilde{m})([\![D]\!]^P_1 2 \mid (\nu s)([\![D]\!]^P_2 2\{\bar{s}/x\} \mid s?(y).y?(x).$ $[\![Q]\!]^2$, *for some P_1, P_2, Q;*
   - $(\Gamma)^2; (\Delta)^2 \vdash [\![P]\!]^2 \stackrel{\tau}{\longmapsto} (\Delta')^2 \vdash [\![P']\!]^2$

   (b) *If $\ell = \tau_\beta$ then $(\Gamma)^2; (\Delta)^2 \vdash [\![P]\!]^2 \stackrel{\tau_s}{\longmapsto} (\Delta')^2 \vdash [\![P']\!]^2$.*
2. *Suppose $(\Gamma)^2; (\Delta)^2 \vdash [\![P]\!]^2 \stackrel{\tau}{\longmapsto} (\Delta')^2 \vdash R$.*
   Then $\exists P'$ such that $P \stackrel{\tau}{\longmapsto} P'$ and $(\Gamma)^2; (\Delta')^2 \vdash [\![P']\!]^2 \approx^H (\Delta')^2 \vdash R$.

Exploiting the above properties (type preservation, typed operational correspondence), we can show that our typed encoding is fully abstract and precise.

Proposition 7 (HOπ to π: Full Abstraction). *Let P_1, Q_1 be HOπ processes. $\Gamma; \Delta_1 \vdash P_1 \approx^H \Delta_2 \vdash Q_1$ if and only if $(\Gamma)^2; (\Delta_1)^2 \vdash [\![P_1]\!]^2 \approx^C (\Delta_2)^2 \vdash [\![Q_1]\!]^2$.*

Theorem 4 (Precise Encoding of HOπ into π). *The encoding from $\mathcal{L}_{\mathsf{HO}\pi}$ into $\mathcal{L}_\pi$ (cf. Definition 18) is precise.*

7.3 Comparing Precise Encodings

The precise encodings in Sects. 7.1 and 7.2 confirm that HO and π constitute two important sources of expressiveness in HOπ. This naturally begs the question: which of the two sub-calculi is more tightly related to HOπ? We argue, both empirically and formally, that when compared to π, HO is more economical and satisfies tighter correspondences.

Empirical Comparison: Reduction Steps. We first contrast the way in which (a) the encoding from **HOπ** to **HO** (Sect. 7.1) translates processes with name passing; (b) the encoding from **HOπ** to π (Sect. 7.2) translates processes with abstraction passing. Consider the **HOπ** processes:

$$P_1 = s!\langle a\rangle.\mathbf{0} \mid \overline{s}?(x).(x!\langle s_1\rangle.\mathbf{0} \mid \ldots \mid x!\langle s_n\rangle.\mathbf{0}) \qquad P_2 = s!\langle \lambda x.\, P\rangle.\mathbf{0} \mid \overline{s}?(x).(x\, s_1 \mid \ldots \mid x\, s_n)$$

P_1 features *pure* name passing (no abstraction-passing), whereas P_2 involves *pure* abstraction passing (no name passing). In both cases, the intended communication on s leads to n usages of the communication object (name a in P_1, abstraction $\lambda x.\, P$ in P_2). Consider now the reduction steps from P_1 and P_2:

$$P_1 \overset{\tau}{\longmapsto} a!\langle s_1\rangle.\mathbf{0} \mid \ldots \mid a!\langle s_n\rangle.\mathbf{0}$$

$$P_2 \overset{\tau}{\longmapsto} (\lambda x.\, P)\, s_1 \mid \ldots \mid (\lambda x.\, P)\, s_n \quad \underbrace{\overset{\tau_\beta}{\longmapsto}\overset{\tau_\beta}{\longmapsto}\cdots\overset{\tau_\beta}{\longmapsto}}_{n} \quad P\{s_1/x\} \mid \ldots \mid P\{s_1/x\}$$

By considering the encoding of P_1 into **HO** we obtain:

$$\begin{aligned}
[\![P_1]\!]^1_f = \;& s!\langle \lambda z.\, z?(y).y\, a\rangle.\mathbf{0} \mid \\
& \overline{s}?(x).(\nu\, t)(x\, t \mid \overline{t}!\langle \lambda x.\, (x!\langle \lambda z.\, z?(y).y\, s_1\rangle.\mathbf{0} \mid \ldots \mid x!\langle \lambda z.\, z?(y).y\, s_n\rangle.\mathbf{0})\rangle.\mathbf{0}) \\
\overset{\tau_s}{\longmapsto}\overset{\tau_\beta}{\longmapsto}\;& (\nu\, t)(t?(y).y\, a \mid \overline{t}!\langle \lambda x.\, (x!\langle \lambda z.\, z?(y).y\, s_1\rangle.\mathbf{0} \mid \ldots \mid x!\langle \lambda z.\, z?(y).y\, s_n\rangle.\mathbf{0})\rangle.\mathbf{0}) \\
\overset{\tau_s}{\longmapsto}\overset{\tau_\beta}{\longmapsto}\;& a!\langle \lambda z.\, z?(y).y\, s_1\rangle.\mathbf{0} \mid \ldots \mid a!\langle \lambda z.\, z?(y).y\, s_n\rangle.\mathbf{0}
\end{aligned}$$

Now, we encode P_2 into π:

$$\begin{aligned}
[\![P_2]\!]^2 \;=\;& (\nu\, b)(s!\langle b\rangle.\mathbf{0} \mid *\; b?(y).y?(x).P) \mid \\
& \overline{s}?(x).((\nu\, s)(x!\langle s\rangle.\overline{s}!\langle s_1\rangle.\mathbf{0}) \mid \ldots \mid (\nu\, s)(x!\langle s\rangle.\overline{s}!\langle s_n\rangle.\mathbf{0})) \\
\overset{\tau_s}{\longmapsto}\overset{\tau_s}{\longmapsto}\overset{\tau_s}{\longmapsto}\;& (\nu\, b)(*\, b?(y).y?(x).P \mid P\{s_1/x\} \mid \ldots \mid (\nu\, s)(b!\langle s\rangle.\overline{s}!\langle s_n\rangle.\mathbf{0})) \\
\Longmapsto_{2*(n-1)}\;& (\nu\, b)(*\, b?(y).y?(x).P \mid P\{s_1/x\} \mid \ldots \mid P\{s_n/x\})
\end{aligned}$$

Clearly, encoding P_1 into **HO** is more economical than encoding P_2 into π. Not only moving to a pure higher-order setting requires less reduction steps than in the first-order concurrency of π; in the presence of shared names, moving to a first-order setting brings the need of setting up and handling replicated processes which will eventually lead to garbage (stuck) processes (cf. $*\, b?(y).y?(x).P$ above). In contrast, the mechanism present in **HO** works efficiently regardless of the linear or shared properties of the name that is "packed" into the abstraction. The use of β-transitions guarantees local synchronizations, which are arguably more economical than point-to-point, session synchronizations.

It is useful to move our comparison to a purely linear setting. Consider processes:

$$Q_1 = s'!\langle s\rangle.\mathbf{0} \mid \overline{s'}?(x).x!\langle a\rangle.\mathbf{0} \overset{\tau}{\longmapsto} s!\langle a\rangle.\mathbf{0} \qquad Q_2 = s!\langle \lambda x.\, P\rangle.\mathbf{0} \mid \overline{s}?(x).x\, a \overset{\tau}{\longmapsto}\overset{\tau}{\longmapsto} P\{a/x\}$$

Q_1 is a π process; Q_2 is an HO processs. If we consider their encodings into HO and π, respectively, we obtain:

$$\begin{array}{rcl}
[\![Q_1]\!]^1_f & = & s'!\langle \lambda z.\, z?(y).y\, s\rangle.\mathbf{0} \mid \overline{s'}?(x).(\nu\, t)(x\, t \mid \bar{t}!\langle \lambda x.\, x!\langle \lambda z.\, z?(y).y\, a\rangle.\mathbf{0}\rangle.\mathbf{0}) \\
& \overset{\tau_s}{\longmapsto}\overset{\tau_\beta}{\longmapsto} & (\nu\, t)(t?(y).y\, s \mid \bar{t}!\langle \lambda x.\, x!\langle \lambda z.\, z?(y).y\, a\rangle.\mathbf{0}\rangle.\mathbf{0}) \\
& \overset{\tau_s}{\longmapsto} & \lambda x.\, x!\langle \lambda z.\, z?(y).y\, a\rangle.\mathbf{0}\, s \ \overset{\tau_\beta}{\longmapsto} \ s!\langle \lambda z.\, z?(y).y\, a\rangle.\mathbf{0} \\
[\![Q_2]\!]^2 & = & (\nu\, t)(s!\langle t\rangle.\mathbf{0} \mid \bar{t}?(y).y?(x).P) \mid \bar{s}?(x).(\nu\, s)(x!\langle s\rangle.\bar{s}!\langle a\rangle.\mathbf{0}) \\
& \overset{\tau_s}{\longmapsto}\overset{\tau_s}{\longmapsto} & (\nu\, s)(s?(x).P \mid \bar{s}!\langle a\rangle.\mathbf{0}) \ \overset{\tau_s}{\longmapsto} \ P\{a/x\}
\end{array}$$

In this case, the encoding $[\![\cdot]\!]^2$ is more efficient, as it induces less reduction steps. Therefore, considering a fragment of HOπ without shared communications (linearity only) has consequences in terms of reduction steps. Notice that we prove that linear communications do not suffice to encode shared communications (Sect. 7.4).

Formal Comparison: Labelled Transition Correspondence. We now formally establish differences between $[\![\cdot]\!]^1_f$ and $[\![\cdot]\!]^2$. To this end, we introduce an extra encodability criterion: a form of operational correspondence for *visible actions.* Below we write ℓ_1, ℓ_2 to denote actions different from τ and $\overset{\ell}{\longmapsto}$ to denote an LTS. As actions from different calculi may be different, we also consider a mapping on action labels, denoted $\{\cdot\}$:

Definition 19 (Labelled Correspondence / Tight Encodings). *Consider typed calculi $\mathcal{L}_1$ and $\mathcal{L}_2$, defined as $\mathcal{L}_1 = \langle \mathsf{C}_1, \mathcal{T}_1, \overset{\ell_1}{\longmapsto}_1, \approx_1, \vdash_1\rangle$ and $\mathcal{L}_2 = \langle \mathsf{C}_2, \mathcal{T}_2, \overset{\ell_2}{\longmapsto}_2, \approx_2, \vdash_2\rangle$. The encoding $\langle [\![\cdot]\!], (\cdot)\rangle : \mathcal{L}_1 \to \mathcal{L}_2$ satisfies* labelled operational correspondence *if it satisfies:*

1. *If $\Gamma;\Delta \vdash_1 P \overset{\ell_1}{\longmapsto}_1 \Delta' \vdash_1 P'$ then $\exists Q, \Delta'', \ell_2$ s.t. (i) $(\Gamma);(\Delta) \vdash_2 [\![P]\!] \overset{\ell_2}{\Longrightarrow}_2 (\Delta'') \vdash_2 Q$; (ii) $\ell_2 = \{\ell_1\}$; (iii) $(\Gamma);(\Delta'') \vdash_2 Q \approx_2 (\Delta') \vdash_2 [\![P']\!]$.*
2. *If $(\Gamma);(\Delta) \vdash_2 [\![P]\!] \overset{\ell_2}{\Longrightarrow}_2 (\Delta') \vdash_2 Q$ then $\exists P', \Delta'', \ell_1$ s.t. (i) $\Gamma;\Delta \vdash_1 P \overset{\ell_1}{\longmapsto}_1 \Delta'' \vdash_1 P'$; (ii) $\ell_2 = \{\ell_1\}$; (iii) $(\Gamma);(\Delta'') \vdash_2 [\![P']\!] \approx_2 (\Delta') \vdash_2 Q$.*

A tight encoding *is a typed encoding which is precise (Definition 15) and that also satisfies labelled operational correspondence as above.*

We may formally state that HOπ and HO are more closely related than HOπ and π:

Theorem 5 (HO Tightly Encodes HOπ). *While the encoding of* HOπ *into* HO *(Definition 17) is tight, the encoding of* HOπ *into π (Definition 18) is not tight.*

To substantiate the above claim, we show that the encoding $[\![\cdot]\!]^1_f$ enjoys labelled operational correspondence, whereas $[\![\cdot]\!]^2$ does not. Consider the following mapping:

$$\{(\nu\,\tilde{m}_1)n!\langle m\rangle\}^1 \stackrel{\text{def}}{=} (\nu\,\tilde{m}_1)n!\langle \lambda z.\, z?(x).x\,m\rangle \qquad \{n?\langle m\rangle\}^1 \stackrel{\text{def}}{=} n?\langle \lambda z.\, z?(x).x\,m\rangle$$
$$\{(\nu\,\tilde{m})n!\langle \lambda x.\, P\rangle\}^1 \stackrel{\text{def}}{=} (\nu\,\tilde{m})n!\langle \lambda x.\, [\![P]\!]^1_{\emptyset}\rangle \qquad \{n?\langle \lambda x.\, P\rangle\}^1 \stackrel{\text{def}}{=} n?\langle \lambda x.\, [\![P]\!]^1_{\emptyset}\rangle$$
$$\{n \oplus l\}^1 \stackrel{\text{def}}{=} n \oplus l \qquad \{n\&l\}^1 \stackrel{\text{def}}{=} n\&l$$

Then the following result, a complement of Proposition 3, holds:

Proposition 8 (Labelled Transition Correspondence, HOπ into HO). *Let P be an HOπ process. If $\Gamma;\emptyset;\Delta \vdash P \triangleright \diamond$ then:*

1. *Suppose $\Gamma;\Delta \vdash P \stackrel{\ell_1}{\longmapsto} \Delta' \vdash P'$. Then we have:*
   (a) *If $\ell_1 \in \{(\nu\,\tilde{m})n!\langle m\rangle, (\nu\,\tilde{m})n!\langle \lambda x.\, Q\rangle, s\oplus l, s\&l\}$ then $\exists \ell_2$ s.t.*
   $(\Gamma)^1;(\Delta)^1 \vdash [\![P]\!]^1_f \stackrel{\ell_2}{\longmapsto} (\Delta')^1 \vdash [\![P']\!]^1_f$ *and* $\ell_2 = \{\ell_1\}^1$.
   (b) *If $\ell_1 = n?\langle \lambda y.\, Q\rangle$ and $P' = P_0\{\lambda y.\, Q/x\}$ then $\exists \ell_2$ s.t.*
   $(\Gamma)^1;(\Delta)^1 \vdash [\![P]\!]^1_f \stackrel{\ell_2}{\longmapsto} (\Delta')^1 \vdash [\![P_0]\!]^1_f\{\lambda y.\, [\![Q]\!]^1_{\emptyset}/x\}$ *and* $\ell_2 = \{\ell_1\}^1$.
   (c) *If $\ell_1 = n?\langle m\rangle$ and $P' = P_0\{m/x\}$ then $\exists \ell_2, R$ s.t. $(\Gamma)^1;(\Delta)^1 \vdash [\![P]\!]^1_f \stackrel{\ell_2}{\longmapsto} (\Delta')^1 \vdash R$,*
   with $\ell_2 = \{\ell_1\}^1$, and $(\Gamma)^1;(\Delta')^1 \vdash R \stackrel{\tau_\beta}{\longmapsto}\stackrel{\tau_s}{\longmapsto}\stackrel{\tau_\beta}{\longmapsto} (\Delta')^1 \vdash [\![P_0]\!]^1_f\{m/x\}$.
2. *Suppose $(\Gamma)^1;(\Delta)^1 \vdash [\![P]\!]^1_f \stackrel{\ell_2}{\longmapsto} (\Delta')^1 \vdash Q$. Then we have:*
   (a) *If $\ell_2 \in \{(\nu\,\tilde{m})n!\langle \lambda z.\, z?(x).(x\,m)\rangle, (\nu\,\tilde{m})n!\langle \lambda x.\, R\rangle, s\oplus l, s\&l\}$ then $\exists \ell_1, P'$ s.t.*
   $\Gamma;\Delta \vdash P \stackrel{\ell_1}{\longmapsto} \Delta' \vdash P'$, $\ell_1 = \{\ell_2\}^1$, *and* $Q = [\![P']\!]^1_f$.
   (b) *If $\ell_2 = n?\langle \lambda y.\, R\rangle$ then either:*
      (i) *$\exists \ell_1, x, P', P''$ s.t.*
      $\Gamma;\Delta \vdash P \stackrel{\ell_1}{\longmapsto} \Delta' \vdash P'\{\lambda y.\, P''/x\}$, $\ell_1 = \{\ell_2\}^1$, $[\![P'']\!]^1_{\emptyset} = R$, *and* $Q = [\![P']\!]^1_f$.
      (ii) *$R \equiv y?(x).(x\,m)$ and $\exists \ell_1, z, P'$ s.t. $\Gamma;\Delta \vdash P \stackrel{\ell_1}{\longmapsto} \Delta' \vdash P'\{m/z\}$,*
      $\ell_1 = \{\ell_2\}^1$, *and* $(\Gamma)^1;(\Delta')^1 \vdash Q \stackrel{\tau_\beta}{\longmapsto}\stackrel{\tau_s}{\longmapsto}\stackrel{\tau_\beta}{\longmapsto} (\Delta'')^1 \vdash [\![P'\{m/z\}]\!]^1_f$

The analog of Proposition 8 does not hold for the encoding of HOπ into π. Consider the HOπ process:

$$\Gamma;\emptyset;\Delta \vdash s!\langle \lambda x.\, P\rangle.\mathbf{0} \triangleright \diamond \stackrel{s!\langle \lambda x.\, P\rangle}{\longmapsto} \emptyset \vdash \mathbf{0} \not\longmapsto$$

with $\lambda x.\, P$ being a linear value. We translate it into a π process:

$$(\Gamma)^2;\emptyset;(\Delta)^2 \vdash (\nu\, a)(s!\langle a\rangle.\mathbf{0} \mid a?(y).y?(x).P) \triangleright \diamond \stackrel{s!\langle a\rangle}{\longmapsto} \Delta' \vdash a?(y).y?(x).P \triangleright \diamond \stackrel{a?\langle V\rangle}{\longmapsto} \ldots$$

The resulting processes have a mismatch both in the typing environment ($\Delta' \neq (\emptyset)^2$) and in the actions that they can subsequently observe: the first process cannot perform any action, while the second process can perform actions of the encoding of $\lambda x.\, P$.

7.4 A Negative Result

As most session calculi, $\mathsf{HO}\pi$ includes communication on both shared and linear names. The former enables non determinism, unrestricted behaviour; the latter allows to represent deterministic, linear communication structures. The expressiveness of shared names is also illustrated by our encoding from $\mathsf{HO}\pi$ into π (Fig. 7). This result begs the question: can we represent shared name interaction using session name interaction? It turns out that shared names add expressiveness to $\mathsf{HO}\pi$: we prove the non existence of a minimal encoding (cf. Definition 15) of shared name interaction into linear interaction.

Theorem 6. *There is no minimal encoding from π to $\mathsf{HO}\pi^{-\mathsf{sh}}$. Hence, for any $\mathsf{C}_1, \mathsf{C}_2 \in \{\mathsf{HO}\pi, \mathsf{HO}, \pi\}$, there is no minimal encoding from $\mathcal{L}_{\mathsf{C}_1}$ into $\mathcal{L}_{\mathsf{C}_2^{-\mathsf{sh}}}$.*

By Definitions 17 and 18 and Propositions 3 and 4, we have:

Corollary 1. *Let $\mathsf{C}_1, \mathsf{C}_2 \in \{\mathsf{HO}\pi, \mathsf{HO}, \pi\}$. There is a precise encoding of $\mathcal{L}_{\mathsf{C}_1^{-\mathsf{sh}}}$ in $\mathcal{L}_{\mathsf{C}_2^{-\mathsf{sh}}}$.*

8 Extensions: Higher-Order Abstractions and Polyadicity

Here we extend $\mathsf{HO}\pi$ in two directions: (i) $\mathsf{HO}\pi^+$ extends $\mathsf{HO}\pi$ with higher-order applications/abstractions; (ii) $\mathsf{HO}\tilde{\pi}$ extends $\mathsf{HO}\pi$ with polyadicity. In both cases, we detail the required modifications in syntax and types. Using encoding composability (Proposition 1), the two extensions may be combined into $\mathsf{HO}\tilde{\pi}^+$: the polyadic extension of $\mathsf{HO}\pi^+$.

$\mathsf{HO}\pi$*with Higher-Order Abstractions ($\mathsf{HO}\pi^+$) and with Polyadicity ($\mathsf{HO}\tilde{\pi}$).* We first introduce $\mathsf{HO}\pi^+$, the extension of $\mathsf{HO}\pi$ with higher-order abstractions and applications. This is the calculus that we studied in [14]. The syntax of $\mathsf{HO}\pi^+$ is obtained from Fig. 2 by extending $V\,u$ to $V\,W$, where W is a higher-order value. As for the reduction semantics, we keep the rules in Fig. 3, except for [App] which is replaced by

$$(\lambda x.\,P)\,V \longrightarrow P\{V/x\}$$

The syntax of types is modified as follows: $L \;::=\; U \!\rightarrow\! \diamond \;\mid\; U \!\multimap\! \diamond$. These types can be easily accommodated in the type system in Sect. 4: we replace C by U in [Abs] and C by U' in [App]. Subject reduction (Theorem 1) holds for $\mathsf{HO}\pi^+$ (cf. [14])

The calculus $\mathsf{HO}\tilde{\pi}$ extends $\mathsf{HO}\pi$ with polyadic name passing $\tilde{n}$ and $\lambda\tilde{x}.\,Q$ in the syntax of values V. The operational semantics is kept unchanged, with the expected use of the simultaneous substitution $\{\tilde{V}/\tilde{x}\}$. The type syntax is extended to:

$$L \;::=\; \tilde{C} \!\rightarrow\! \diamond \;\mid\; \tilde{C} \!\multimap\! \diamond \qquad S \;::=\; !\langle\tilde{U}\rangle;S \;\mid\; ?(\tilde{U});S \;\mid\; \cdots$$

As in [22,23], the type system for $\mathsf{HO}\tilde{\pi}$ disallows a shared name that directly carries polyadic shared names.

By combining $\mathsf{HO}\pi^+$ and $\mathsf{HO}\widetilde{\pi}$ into a single calculus we obtain $\mathsf{HO}\widetilde{\pi}^+$: the extension of $\mathsf{HO}\pi$ allows *both* higher-order abstractions/aplications and polyadicity.

Precise Encodings of $\mathsf{HO}\pi^+$ *and* $\mathsf{HO}\widetilde{\pi}$ *into* $\mathsf{HO}\pi$. We give encodings of $\mathsf{HO}\pi^+$ into $\mathsf{HO}\pi$ and into $\mathsf{HO}\widetilde{\pi}$, and show that they are precise. We use encoding composition (Proposition 1) to encode $\mathsf{HO}\widetilde{\pi}^+$ into HO and π. We consider the following typed calculi (cf. Definition 10):

- $\mathcal{L}_{\mathsf{HO}\pi^+} = \langle \mathsf{HO}\pi^+, \mathcal{T}_4, \overset{\ell}{\longmapsto}, \approx^{\mathtt{H}}, \vdash \rangle$, where $\mathcal{T}_4$ is a set of types of $\mathsf{HO}\pi^+$; the typing $\vdash$ is defined in Sect. 4 with extended rules [Abs] and [App].
- $\mathcal{L}_{\mathsf{HO}\widetilde{\pi}} = \langle \mathsf{HO}\widetilde{\pi}, \mathcal{T}_5, \overset{\ell}{\longmapsto}, \approx^{\mathtt{H}}, \vdash \rangle$, where $\mathcal{T}_5$ is the set of types of $\mathsf{HO}\widetilde{\pi}$; the typing $\vdash$ is defined in in Sect. 4 with polyadic types.

First, the typed encoding $\langle [\![\cdot]\!]^3, (\!(\cdot)\!)^3 \rangle : \mathsf{HO}\pi^+ \to \mathsf{HO}\pi$ is defined in Fig. 8. It satisfies the following properties:

Proposition 9 ($\mathsf{HO}\pi^+$ into $\mathsf{HO}\pi$: Type Preservation). *The encoding from* $\mathcal{L}_{\mathsf{HO}\pi^+}$ *into* $\mathcal{L}_{\mathsf{HO}\pi}$ *(cf. Fig. 8) is type preserving.*

Proposition 10 (Operational Correspondence: From $\mathsf{HO}\pi^+$ to $\mathsf{HO}\pi$-Excerpt). *Let P be an $\mathsf{HO}\pi^+$ process such that $\Gamma; \emptyset; \Delta \vdash P$.*

1. *Completeness: $\Gamma; \Delta \vdash P \overset{\ell}{\longmapsto} \Delta' \vdash P'$ implies*
   (a) *If $\ell = \tau_\beta$ then $(\!(\Gamma)\!)^3; (\!(\Delta)\!)^3 \vdash [\![P]\!]^3 \overset{\tau}{\longmapsto} \Delta'' \vdash R$ and $(\!(\Gamma)\!)^3; (\!(\Delta')\!)^3 \vdash [\![P']\!]^3 \approx^H \Delta'' \vdash R$, for some R;*
   (b) *If $\ell = \tau$ and $\ell \neq \tau_\beta$ then $(\!(\Gamma)\!)^3; (\!(\Delta)\!)^3 \vdash [\![P]\!]^3 \overset{\ell}{\longmapsto} (\!(\Delta')\!)^3 \vdash [\![P']\!]^3$.*
2. *Soundness: $(\!(\Gamma)\!)^3; (\!(\Delta)\!)^3 \vdash [\![P]\!]^3 \overset{\tau}{\longmapsto} (\!(\Delta'')\!)^3 \vdash Q$ implies either*
   (a) *$\Gamma; \Delta \vdash P \overset{\tau}{\longmapsto} \Delta' \vdash P'$ with $Q \equiv [\![P']\!]^3$*
   (b) *$\Gamma; \Delta \vdash P \overset{\tau_\beta}{\longmapsto} \Delta' \vdash P'$ and $(\!(\Gamma)\!)^3; (\!(\Delta'')\!)^3 \vdash Q \overset{\tau_\beta}{\longmapsto} (\!(\Delta'')\!)^3 \vdash [\![P']\!]^3$.*

Types :

$$(\!(L \to \diamond)\!)^3 \overset{\text{def}}{=} ?(\!(\!(L)\!)^3); \mathsf{end} \to \diamond \qquad (\!(!\langle L \to \diamond \rangle; S)\!)^3 \overset{\text{def}}{=} !\langle (\!(L \to \diamond)\!)^3 \rangle; (\!(S)\!)^3$$

$$(\!(L \multimap \diamond)\!)^3 \overset{\text{def}}{=} ?(\!(\!(L)\!)^3); \mathsf{end} \multimap \diamond \qquad (\!(?(L \to \diamond); S)\!)^3 \overset{\text{def}}{=} ?(\!(\!(L \to \diamond)\!)^3); (\!(S)\!)^3$$

Terms :

$$\{\!\{x\}\!\}^3 \overset{\text{def}}{=} x$$

$$\{\!\{\lambda x : L.\, P\}\!\}^3 \overset{\text{def}}{=} \lambda z.\, z?(x).[\![P]\!]^3$$

$$[\![(x : L)\, V]\!]^3 \overset{\text{def}}{=} (\nu\, s)(x\, s \mid \overline{s}!\langle \{\!\{V\}\!\}^3 \rangle.\mathbf{0})$$

$$[\![u!\langle \lambda x : L.\, Q \rangle.P]\!]^3 \overset{\text{def}}{=} u!\langle \{\!\{\lambda x.\, Q\}\!\}^3 \rangle.[\![P]\!]^3$$

$$[\![(\lambda x : L.\, P)\, V]\!]^3 \overset{\text{def}}{=} (\nu\, s)(s?(x).[\![P]\!]^3 \mid \overline{s}!\langle \{\!\{V\}\!\}^3 \rangle.\mathbf{0})$$

Mappings for elided processes and types are homomorphic.

Fig. 8. Encoding of $\mathsf{HO}\pi^+$ into $\mathsf{HO}\pi$.

Proposition 11 (Full Abstraction. From $\mathsf{HO}\pi^+$ to $\mathsf{HO}\pi$). *Let P, Q be $\mathsf{HO}\pi^+$ processes with $\Gamma;\emptyset;\Delta_1 \vdash P \triangleright \diamond$ and $\Gamma;\emptyset;\Delta_2 \vdash Q \triangleright \diamond$. Then $\Gamma;\Delta_1 \vdash P \approx^H \Delta_2 \vdash Q$ if and only if $(\Gamma)^3;(\Delta_1)^3 \vdash [\![P]\!]^3 \approx^H (\Delta_2)^3 \vdash [\![Q]\!]^3$*

Using the above propositions, Theorems 3 and 4, and Proposition 1, we derive the following:

Theorem 7 (Encoding $\mathsf{HO}\pi^+$ into $\mathsf{HO}\pi$). *The encoding from $\mathcal{L}_{\mathsf{HO}\pi^+}$ into $\mathcal{L}_{\mathsf{HO}\pi}$ (cf. Fig. 8) is precise. Hence, the encodings from $\mathcal{L}_{\mathsf{HO}\pi^+}$ to $\mathcal{L}_{\mathsf{HO}}$ and $\mathcal{L}_{\pi}$ are also precise.*

Second, we define the typed encoding $\langle [\![\cdot]\!]^4, (\!(\cdot)\!)^4 \rangle : \mathsf{HO}\tilde{\pi} \to \mathsf{HO}\pi$ in Fig. 9. For simplicity, we give the dyadic case (tuples of length 2); the general case is as expected. The encoding of $\mathsf{HO}\tilde{\pi}$ satisfies the following properties:

Proposition 12 ($\mathsf{HO}\tilde{\pi}$ into $\mathsf{HO}\pi$: Type Preservation). *The encoding from $\mathcal{L}_{\mathsf{HO}\tilde{\pi}}$ into $\mathcal{L}_{\mathsf{HO}\pi}$ (cf. Fig. 9) is type preserving.*

Proposition 13 (Operational Correspondence: From $\mathsf{HO}\tilde{\pi}$ to $\mathsf{HO}\pi$-Excerpt). *Let $\Gamma;\emptyset;\Delta \vdash P$.*

1. *Completeness: $\Gamma;\Delta \vdash P \overset{\ell}{\longmapsto} \Delta' \vdash P'$ implies*
   (a) *If $\ell = \tau_\beta$ then $(\Gamma)^4;(\Delta)^4 \vdash [\![P]\!]^4 \overset{\tau_\beta}{\longmapsto}\overset{\tau_s}{\longmapsto}\overset{\tau_s}{\longmapsto} (\Delta')^4 \vdash [\![P']\!]^4$*
   (b) *If $\ell = \tau$ then $(\Gamma)^4;(\Delta)^4 \vdash [\![P]\!]^4 \overset{\tau}{\longmapsto}\overset{\tau}{\longmapsto}\overset{\tau}{\longmapsto} (\Delta')^4 \vdash [\![P']\!]^4$*
2. *Soundness: $(\Gamma)^4;(\Delta)^4 \vdash [\![P]\!]^4 \overset{\ell}{\longmapsto} (\Delta_1)^4 \vdash P_1$ implies*
   (a) *If $\ell = \tau_\beta$ then $\Gamma;\Delta \vdash P \overset{\tau_\beta}{\longmapsto} \Delta' \vdash P'$ and $(\Gamma)^4;(\Delta_1)^4 \vdash P_1 \overset{\tau_s}{\longmapsto}\overset{\tau_s}{\longmapsto} (\Delta')^4 \vdash (P')^4$*
   (b) *If $\ell = \tau$ then $\Gamma;\Delta \vdash P \overset{\tau}{\longmapsto} \Delta' \vdash P'$ and $(\Gamma)^4;(\Delta_1)^4 \vdash P_1 \overset{\tau}{\longmapsto}\overset{\tau}{\longmapsto}\overset{\tau}{\longmapsto} (\Delta')^4 \vdash (P')^4$*

Types:

$$
\begin{aligned}
(\!(!\langle S_1,S_2\rangle;S)\!)^4 &\stackrel{\mathsf{def}}{=} !\langle(\!(S_1)\!)^4\rangle;!\langle(\!(S_2)\!)^4\rangle;(\!(S)\!)^4\\
(\!(!\langle L\rangle;S)\!)^4 &\stackrel{\mathsf{def}}{=} !\langle(\!(L)\!)^4\rangle;(\!(S)\!)^4\\
(\!((C_2,C_2)\!\to\!\diamond)\!)^4 &\stackrel{\mathsf{def}}{=} (?(\!(C_1)\!)^4);?(\!(C_2)\!)^4);\mathbf{end})\!\to\!\diamond\\
(\!((C_1,C_2)\!\multimap\!\diamond)\!)^4 &\stackrel{\mathsf{def}}{=} (?(\!(C_1)\!)^4);?(\!(C_2)\!)^4);\mathbf{end})\!\multimap\!\diamond
\end{aligned}
$$

Terms:

$$
\begin{aligned}
[\![u!\langle u_1,u_2\rangle.P]\!]^4 &\stackrel{\mathsf{def}}{=} u!\langle u_1\rangle.u!\langle u_2\rangle.[\![P]\!]^4\\
[\![u!\langle \lambda(x_1,x_2).\,Q\rangle.P]\!]^4 &\stackrel{\mathsf{def}}{=} u!\langle \lambda z.\,z?(x_1).z?(x_2).[\![Q]\!]^4\rangle.[\![P]\!]^4\\
[\![x\,(u_1,u_2)]\!]^4 &\stackrel{\mathsf{def}}{=} (\nu\, s)(x\, s \mid \overline{s}!\langle u_1\rangle.\overline{s}!\langle u_2\rangle.\mathbf{0})\\
[\![(\lambda(x_1,x_2).\,P)\,(u_1,u_2)]\!]^4 &\stackrel{\mathsf{def}}{=} (\nu\, s)(s?(x_1).s?(x_2).[\![P]\!]^4 \mid \overline{s}!\langle u_1\rangle.\overline{s}!\langle u_2\rangle.\mathbf{0})
\end{aligned}
$$

The input cases are defined as the output cases by replacing ! by ?. Elided mappings for processes and types are homomorphic.

Fig. 9. Encoding of $\mathsf{HO}\tilde{\pi}$ (dyadic case) into $\mathsf{HO}\pi$.

Proposition 14 (Full Abstraction: From $\mathsf{HO}\vec{\pi}$ to $\mathsf{HO}\pi$). *Let P, Q be $\mathsf{HO}\vec{\pi}$ processes with $\Gamma;\emptyset;\Delta_1 \vdash P \triangleright \diamond$ and $\Gamma;\emptyset;\Delta_2 \vdash Q \triangleright \diamond$. Then we have:*
$\Gamma;\Delta_1 \vdash P \approx^H \Delta_2 \vdash Q$ if and only if $(\Gamma)^4;(\Delta_1)^4 \vdash [\![P]\!]^4 \approx^H (\Delta_2)^4 \vdash [\![Q]\!]^4$.

Using the above propositions, Theorems 3 and 4, and Proposition 1, we derive the following:

Theorem 8 (Encoding of $\mathsf{HO}\vec{\pi}$ into $\mathsf{HO}\pi$). *The encoding from $\mathcal{L}_{\mathsf{HO}\vec{\pi}}$ into $\mathcal{L}_{\mathsf{HO}\pi}$ (cf. Fig. 9) is precise. Hence, the encodings from $\mathcal{L}_{\mathsf{HO}\vec{\pi}}$ to $\mathcal{L}_{\mathsf{HO}}$ and $\mathcal{L}_{\pi}$ are also precise.*

By combining Theorems 7 and 8, we can extend preciseness to the super-calculus $\mathsf{HO}\vec{\pi}^+$.

9 Concluding Remarks and Related Work

We have thoroughly studied the expressivity of the higher-order π-calculus with sessions, here denoted $\mathsf{HO}\pi$. Unlike most previous works, we have carried out our study in the setting of *session types*. Types not only delineate and enable encodings; they inform the techniques required to reason about such encodings. Our results cover a wide spectrum of features intrinsic to higher-order concurrency: pure process-passing (first- and higher-order abstractions), name-passing, polyadicity, linear/shared communication (cf. Fig. 1). Remarkably, the discipline embodied by session types turns out to be fundamental to show that all these languages are equally expressive, up to strong typed bisimilarities. Indeed, although our encodings may be used in an untyped setting, session type information is critical to establish key properties for preciseness, in particular full abstraction.

Related Work. There is a vast literature on expressiveness for process calculi; we refer to [28] and [29, Sect. 2.3] for surveys. Our study casts known results [32] into a session typed setting, and offers new encodability results. Our work stresses the view of "encodings as protocols", namely session protocols which enforce linear and shared disciplines for names, a distinction little explored in previous works. This distinction enables us to obtain refined operational correspondence results (cf. Propositions. 3, 6, 10, 13). We showed that HO suffices to encode the first-order session calculus [11], here denoted π. To our knowledge, this is a new result; its significance is stressed by the demanding encodability criteria considered, in particular full abstraction up to typed bisimilarities ($\approx^{\mathtt{H}}/\approx^{\mathtt{C}}$, cf. Propositions 4 and 7). This encoding is relevant in a broader setting, as known encodings of name-passing into higher-order calculi [4,19,36,42,44] require limitations in source/target languages, do not consider types, and/or fail to satisfy strong encodability criteria (see below). We also showed that HO can encode $\mathsf{HO}\pi$ and its extension with higher-order applications ($\mathsf{HO}\pi^+$). Thus, all these calculi are equally expressive with fully abstract encodings (up to $\approx^{\mathtt{H}}/\approx^{\mathtt{C}}$). These appear to be the first results of this kind.

Early works on (relative) expressiveness appealed to different notions of encoding. Later on, proposals of abstract frameworks which formalise the notion of encoding and state associated syntactic/semantic criteria were put forward; recent proposals include [8,10,30,31,41]. Our formulation of precise encoding (Definition 15) builds upon existing proposals (e.g., [10,16,26]) to account for the session types associated to **HO**π.

Early expressiveness studies for higher-order calculi are [32,39]; recent works include [4,16,17,42,43]. Due to the close relationship between higher-order process calculi and functional calculi, encodings of (variants of) the λ-calculus into the π-calculus (see, e.g., [1,7,33,37,46]) are also related. Sangiorgi's encoding of the higher-order π-calculus into the π-calculus [32] is fully abstract with respect to reduction-closed, barbed congruence. We have shown in Sect. 7.2 that the analogue of Sangiorgi's encoding for the session typed setting also satisfies full abstraction (up to $\approx^{\mathtt{H}}/\approx^{\mathtt{C}}$, cf. Proposition 6). A basic form of input/output types is used in [35], where the encoding in [32] is casted in the asynchronous setting, with output and applications coalesced in a single construct. Building upon [35], a simply typed encoding for synchronous processes is given in [36]; the reverse encoding (i.e., first-order communication into higher-order processes) is also studied for an asynchronous, localised π-calculus (only the output capability of names can be sent around). The work [34] studies hierarchies for calculi with *internal* first-order mobility and with higher-order mobility without name-passing (similarly as the subcalculus **HO**). The hierarchies are defined according to the order of types needed in typing. Via fully abstract encodings, it is shown that that name- and process-passing calculi with equal order of types have the same expressiveness.

Other related works are [4,17,19,42]. The paper [4] gives a fully abstract encoding of the π-calculus into Homer, a higher-order calculus with explicit locations, local names, and nested locations. The paper [19] presents a *reflective* calculus with a "quoting" operator: names are quoted processes and represent the code of a process; name-passing is then a way of passing the code of a process. This reflective calculus can encode both first- and higher-order π-calculus. Building upon [40], the work [42] studies the (non)encodability of the untyped π-calculus into a higher-order π-calculus with a powerful name relabelling operator, which is essential to encode name-passing. The paper [44] defines an encoding of the (untyped) π-calculus without relabeling. This encoding is quite different from the one in Sect. 7.1: in [44] names are encoded using polyadic name abstractions (called *pipes*); guarded replication enables infinite behaviours. While our encoding satisfies full abstraction, the encoding in [44] does not: only divergence-reflection and operational correspondence (soundness and completeness) properties are established. Soundness is stated up-to *pipe-bisimilarity*, an equivalence tailored to the encoding strategy; the authors of [44] describe this result as "weak".

A core higher-order calculus is studied in [17]: it lacks restriction, name passing, output prefix, and replication/recursion. Still, this subcalculus of **HO** is Turing equivalent. The work [16] extends this core calculus with restriction, output prefix, and polyadicity; it shows that synchronous communication can encode asynchronous communication, and that process passing polyadicity induces an expressiveness hierarchy. The paper [43] complements [16] by studying the expressivity of second-order process abstractions. Polyadicity is shown to induce an expressiveness hierarchy; also, by adapting the encoding in [32], process abstractions are encoded into name abstractions. In contrast, here we give a fully abstract encoding of $\mathsf{HO}\widetilde{\pi}^{+}$ into HO that preserves session types; this improves [16,43] by enforcing linearity disciplines on process behaviour. The focus of [16,42–44] is on untyped, higher-order processes; they do not address communication disciplined by (session) type systems.

Within session types, the works [5,6] encode binary sessions into a linearly typed π-calculus. While [6] gives an encoding of π into a linear calculus (an extension of [1]), the work [5] gives operational correspondence (without full abstraction) for the first- and higher-order π-calculi into [13]. By the result of [6], $\mathsf{HO}\pi^{+}$ is encodable into the linearly typed π-calculi. The syntax of $\mathsf{HO}\pi$ is a subset of that in [22,23]. The work [22] develops a higher-order session calculus with process abstractions and applications; it admits the type $U = U_1 \rightarrow U_2 \ldots U_n \rightarrow \diamond$ and its linear type U^1 which corresponds to $\tilde{U}{\rightarrow}\diamond$ and $\tilde{U}{\multimap}\diamond$ in a super-calculus of $\mathsf{HO}\pi^{+}$ and $\mathsf{HO}\widetilde{\pi}$. Our results show that the calculus in [22] is not only expressed but also reasoned in HO via precise encodings (with a limited form of arrow types: $C{\rightarrow}\diamond$ and $C{\multimap}\diamond$). The recent work [25] studies two encodings: from PCF with an effect system into a session-typed π-calculus, and its reverse. The reverse encoding is used to implement session channel passing in Concurrent Haskell. In future work we plan to use the core calculi studied in this paper to implement higher-order communication efficiently into Concurrent Haskell without losing its expressiveness.

Acknowledgments. We have benefited from feedback from the users of the Moca mailing list, in particular Greg Meredith and Xu Xian. We are grateful to the anonymous reviewers for their useful remarks and suggestions. This work has been partially sponsored by the Doctoral Prize Fellowship, EPSRC EP/K011715/1, EPSRC EP/K034413/1, and EPSRC EP/L00058X/1, EU project FP7-612985 UpScale, and EU COST Action IC1201 BETTY. Pérez is also affiliated to the NOVA Laboratory for Computer Science and Informatics (NOVA LINCS), Universidade Nova de Lisboa, Portugal.

References

1. Berger, M., Honda, K., Yoshida, N.: Sequentiality and the π-calculus. In: Abramsky, S. (ed.) TLCA 2001. LNCS, vol. 2044, pp. 29–45. Springer, Heidelberg (2001)
2. Bernardi, G., Dardha, O., Gay, S.J., Kouzapas, D.: On duality relations for session types. In: Maffei, M., Tuosto, E. (eds.) TGC 2014. LNCS, vol. 8902, pp. 51–66. Springer, Heidelberg (2014)
3. Bono, V., Padovani, L.: Typing copyless message passing. LMCS **8**(1), 1–50 (2012)
4. Bundgaard, M., Hildebrandt, T.T., Godskesen, J.C.: A cps encoding of name-passing in higher-order mobile embedded resources. Theor. Comput. Sci. **356**(3), 422–439 (2006)
5. Dardha, O., Giachino, E., Sangiorgi, D.: Session types revisited. In: Proceedings of PPDP 2012, pp. 139–150. ACM (2012)

6. Demangeon, R., Honda, K.: Full abstraction in a subtyped pi-calculus with linear types. In: Katoen, J.-P., König, B. (eds.) CONCUR 2011. LNCS, vol. 6901, pp. 280–296. Springer, Heidelberg (2011)
7. Fu, Y.: Variations on mobile processes. Theor. Comput. Sci. **221**(1–2), 327–368 (1999)
8. Fu, Y., Lu, H.: On the expressiveness of interaction. Theor. Comput. Sci. **411** (11–13), 1387–1451 (2010)
9. Gay, S.J., Vasconcelos, V.T.: Linear type theory for asynchronous session types. J. Funct. Program. **20**(1), 19–50 (2010)
10. Gorla, D.: Towards a unified approach to encodability and separation results for process calculi. Inf. Comput. **208**(9), 1031–1053 (2010)
11. Honda, K., Vasconcelos, V.T., Kubo, M.: Language primitives and type discipline for structured communication-based programming. In: Hankin, C. (ed.) ESOP 1998. LNCS, vol. 1381, p. 122. Springer, Heidelberg (1998)
12. Honda, K., Yoshida, N.: On reduction-based process semantics. TCS **151**(2), 437–486 (1995)
13. Kobayashi, N., Pierce, B.C., Turner, D.N.: Linearity and the Pi-Calculus. TOPLAS **21**(5), 914–947 (1999)
14. Kouzapas, D., Pérez, J.A., Yoshida, N.: Characteristic bisimulation for higher-order session processes. In: CONCUR 2015. LIPIcs, vol. 42, pp. 398–411, Dagstuhl, Germany (2015)
15. Kouzapas, D., Pérez, J.A., Yoshida, N.: Full version of this paper. Technical report, Imperial College / University of Groningen (2015). http://arxiv.org/abs/1502.02585
16. Lanese, I., Pérez, J.A., Sangiorgi, D., Schmitt, A.: On the expressiveness of polyadic and synchronous communication in higher-order process calculi. In: Abramsky, S., Gavoille, C., Kirchner, C., Meyer auf der Heide, F., Spirakis, P.G. (eds.) ICALP 2010. LNCS, vol. 6199, pp. 442–453. Springer, Heidelberg (2010)
17. Lanese, I., Pérez, J.A., Sangiorgi, D., Schmitt, A.: On the expressiveness and decidability of higher-order process calculi. Inf. Comput. **209**(2), 198–226 (2011)
18. League, C., Shao, Z., Trifonov, V.: Type-preserving compilation of Featherweight Java. ACM Trans. Program. Lang. Syst. **24**(2), 112–152 (2002)
19. Meredith, L.G., Radestock, M.: A reflective higher-order calculus. Electr. Notes Theor. Comput. Sci. **141**(5), 49–67 (2005)
20. Milner, R., Sangiorgi, D.: Barbed bisimulation. In: Kuich, W. (ed.) ICALP 1992. LNCS, vol. 623, pp. 685–695. Springer, Heidelberg (1992)
21. Morrisett, J.G., Walker, D., Crary, K., Glew, N.: From system F to typed assembly language. ACM Trans. Program. Lang. Syst. **21**(3), 527–568 (1999)
22. Mostrous, D., Yoshida, N.: Two session typing systems for higher-order mobile processes. In: Della Rocca, S.R. (ed.) TLCA 2007. LNCS, vol. 4583, pp. 321–335. Springer, Heidelberg (2007)
23. Mostrous, D., Yoshida, N.: Session typing and asynchronous subtying for higher-order π-Calculus. Inf. Comput. **241**, 227–263 (2015)
24. Nestmann, U.: What is a "good" encoding of guarded choice? Inf. Comput. **156** (1–2), 287–319 (2000)
25. Orchard, D., Yoshida, N.: Effects as sessions, sessions as effects. In: POPL. ACM (2016)
26. Palamidessi, C.: Comparing the expressive power of the synchronous and asynchronous pi-calculi. MSCS **13**(5), 685–719 (2003)

27. Palamidessi, C., Saraswat, V.A., Valencia, F.D., Victor, B.: On the expressiveness of linearity vs persistence in the asychronous pi-calculus. Proc. LICS **2006**, 59–68 (2006)
28. Parrow, J.: Expressiveness of process algebras. Electr. Notes Theor. Comput. Sci. **209**, 173–186 (2008)
29. Pérez, J.A.: Higher-Order Concurrency: Expressiveness and Decidability Results. PhD thesis, University of Bologna (2010)
30. Peters, K., Nestmann, U., Goltz, U.: On distributability in process calculi. In: Felleisen, M., Gardner, P. (eds.) ESOP 2013. LNCS, vol. 7792, pp. 310–329. Springer, Heidelberg (2013)
31. Peters, K., van Glabbeek, R.J.: Analysing and comparing encodability criteria. In: Proceedings of EXPRESS/SOS. EPTCS, vol. 190, pp. 46–60 (2015)
32. Sangiorgi, D.: Expressing Mobility in Process Algebras: First-Order and Higher Order Paradigms. PhD thesis, University of Edinburgh (1992)
33. Sangiorgi, D.: The lazy lambda calculus in a concurrency scenario. In: 7th LICS Conference, pp. 102–109. IEEE Computer Society Press (1992)
34. Sangiorgi, D.: π-calculus, internal mobility and agent-passing calculi. TCS **167**(2), 235–274 (1996)
35. Sangiorgi, D.: Asynchronous process calculi: the first- and higher-order paradigms. Theor. Comput. Sci. **253**(2), 311–350 (2001)
36. Sangiorgi, D., Walker, D.: The π-Calculus: A Theory of Mobile Processes. Cambridge University Press, Cambridge (2001)
37. Sangiorgi, D., Xu, X.: Trees from functions as processes. In: Baldan, P., Gorla, D. (eds.) CONCUR 2014. LNCS, vol. 8704, pp. 78–92. Springer, Heidelberg (2014)
38. Shao, Z., Appel, A.W.: A type-based compiler for standard ML. In: Proceedings of PLDI 1995, pp. 116–129. ACM (1995)
39. Thomsen, B.: Calculi for Higher Order Communicating Systems. PhD thesis, Department of Computer Science, Imperial College (1990)
40. Thomsen, B.: Plain CHOCS: a second generation calculus for higher order processes. Acta Informatica **30**(1), 1–59 (1993)
41. van Glabbeek, R.J.: Musings on encodings and expressiveness. In Proceedings of EXPRESS/SOS. EPTCS, vol. 89, pp. 81–98 (2012)
42. Xu, X.: Distinguishing and relating higher-order and first-order processes by expressiveness. Acta Informatica **49**(7–8), 445–484 (2012)
43. Xu, X., Yin, Q., Long, H.: On the expressiveness of parameterization in process-passing. In: Tuosto, E., Ouyang, C. (eds.) WS-FM 2013. LNCS, vol. 8379, pp. 147–167. Springer, Heidelberg (2014)
44. Xu, X., Yin, Q., Long, H.: On the computation power of name parameterization in higher-order processes. In: Proceedings of ICE. EPTCS, vol. 189, pp. 114–127 (2015)
45. Yoshida, N.: Graph types for monadic mobile processes. In: Chandru, V., Vinay, V. (eds.) FSTTCS 1996. LNCS, vol. 1180, pp. 371–386. Springer, Heidelberg (1996)
46. Yoshida, N., Berger, M., Honda, K.: Strong normalisation in the pi -calculus. Inf. Comput. **191**(2), 145–202 (2004)

A Classical Realizability Model for a Semantical Value Restriction

Rodolphe Lepigre(✉)

LAMA, UMR 5127 - CNRS, Université Savoie Mont Blanc, Chambéry, France
rodolphe.lepigre@univ-smb.fr

Abstract. We present a new type system with support for proofs of programs in a call-by-value language with control operators. The proof mechanism relies on observational equivalence of (untyped) programs. It appears in two type constructors, which are used for specifying program properties and for encoding dependent products.The main challenge arises from the lack of expressiveness of dependent products due to the value restriction. To circumvent this limitation we relax the syntactic restriction and only require equivalence to a value.The consistency of the system is obtained semantically by constructing a classical realizability model in three layers (values, stacks and terms).

1 Introduction

In this work we consider a new type system for a call-by-value language, with control operators, polymorphism and dependent products. It is intended to serve as a theoretical basis for a proof assistant focusing on program proving, in a language similar to OCaml or SML. The proof mechanism relies on dependent products and equality types $t \equiv u$, where t and u are (possibly untyped) terms of the language. Equality types are interpreted as $\top$ if the denoted equivalence holds and as $\bot$ otherwise.

In our system, proofs are written using the same language as programs. For instance, a pattern-matching corresponds to a case analysis in a proof, and a recursive call to the use of an induction hypothesis. A proof is first and foremost a program, hence we may say that we follow the "program as proof" principle, rather than the usual "proof as program" principle. In particular, proofs can be composed as programs and with programs to form proof tactics.

Programming in our language is similar to programming in any dialect of ML. For example, we can define the type of unary natural numbers, and the corresponding addition function.

```
type nat = Z[] | S[nat]
let rec add n m = match n with
  | Z[]   → m
  | S[nn] → S[add nn m]
```

We can then prove properties of addition such as `add Z[] n` $\equiv$ `n` for all `n` in `nat`. This property can be expressed using a dependent product over `nat` and an equality type.

P. Thiemann (Ed.): ESOP 2016, LNCS 9632, pp. 476–502, 2016.
DOI: 10.1007/978-3-662-49498-1_19

```
let addZeroN n:nat : (add Z[] n ≡ n) = 8<
```

The term 8< (to be pronounced "scissors") can be introduced whenever the goal is derivable from the context with equational reasoning. Our first proof is immediate since we have add Z[] n ≡ n by definition of add.

Let us now show that add n Z[] ≡ n for every n in nat. Although the statement of this property is similar to the previous one, its proof is slightly more complex and requires case analysis and induction.

```
let rec addNZero n:nat : (add n Z[] ≡ n) =
  match n with
  | Z[]   → 8<
  | S[nn] → let r = addNZero nn in 8<
```

In the S[nn] case, the induction hypothesis (i.e. add nn Z[] ≡ nn) is obtained by a recursive call. It is then used to conclude the proof using equational reasoning. Note that in our system, programs that are considered as proofs need to go through a termination checker. Indeed, a looping program could be used to prove anything otherwise. The proofs addZeroN and addNZero are obviously terminating, and hence valid.

Several difficulties arise when combining call-by-value evaluation, side-effects, dependent products and equality over programs. Most notably, the expressiveness of dependent products is weakened by the value restriction: elimination of dependent product can only happen on arguments that are syntactic values. In other words, the typing rule

$$\frac{\Gamma \vdash t : \Pi_{a:A}\, B \qquad \Gamma \vdash u : A}{\Gamma \vdash t\, u : B[a := u]}$$

cannot be proved safe if u is not a value. This means, for example, that we cannot derive a proof of add (add Z[] Z[]) Z[] ≡ add Z[] Z[] by applying addNZero (which has type Πn:nat (add n Z[] ≡ n)) to add Z[] Z[] since it is not a value. The restriction affects regular programs in a similar way. For instance, it is possible to define a list concatenation function append with the following type.

$$\Pi\texttt{n:nat}\,\Pi\texttt{m:nat List(n)} \Rightarrow \texttt{List(m)} \Rightarrow \texttt{List(add n m)}$$

However, the append function cannot be used to implement a function concatenating three lists. Indeed, this would require being able to provide append with a non-value natural number argument of the form add n m.

Surprisingly, the equality types and the underlying observational equivalence relation provide a solution to the lack of expressiveness of dependent products. The value restriction can be relaxed to obtain the rule

$$\frac{\Gamma, u \equiv v \vdash t : \Pi_{a:A}\, B \qquad \Gamma, u \equiv v \vdash u : A}{\Gamma, u \equiv v \vdash t\, u : B[a := u]}$$

which only requires u to be equivalent to some value v. The same idea can be applied to every rule requiring value restriction. The obtained system is conservative over the one with the syntactic restriction. Indeed, finding a value equivalent to a term that is already a value can always be done using the reflexivity of the equivalence relation.

Although the idea seems simple, proving the soundness of the new typing rules semantically is surprisingly subtle. A model is built using classical realizability techniques in which the interpretation of a type A is spread among two sets: a set of values $[\![A]\!]$ and a set of terms $[\![A]\!]^{\perp\perp}$. The former contains all values that should have type A. For example, $[\![\mathtt{nat}]\!]$ should contain the values of the form `S[S[...Z[]...]]`. The set $[\![A]\!]^{\perp\perp}$ is the completion of $[\![A]\!]$ with all the terms behaving like values of $[\![A]\!]$ (in the observational sense). To show that the relaxation of the value restriction is sound, we need the values of $[\![A]\!]^{\perp\perp}$ to also be in $[\![A]\!]$. In other words, the completion operation should not introduce new values. To obtain this property, we need to extend the language with a new, non-computable instruction internalizing equivalence. This new instruction is only used to build the model, and will not be available to the user (nor will it appear in an implementation).

2 About Effects and Value Restriction

A soundness issue related to side-effects and call-by-value evaluation arose in the seventies with the advent of ML. The problem stems from a bad interaction between side-effects and Hindley-Milner polymorphism. It was first formulated in terms of references [30, Sect. 2], and many alternative type systems were designed (e.g. [4,14,15,29]). However, they all introduced a complexity that contrasted with the elegance and simplicity of ML's type system (for a detailed account, see [31, Sect. 2] and [5, Sect. 2]).

A simple and elegant solution was finally found by Andrew Wright in the nineties. He suggested restricting generalization in let-bindings[1] to cases where the bound term is a syntactic value [30,31]. In slightly more expressive type systems, this restriction appears in the typing rule for the introduction of the universal quantifier. The usual rule

$$\frac{\Gamma \vdash t : A \qquad X \notin FV(\Gamma)}{\Gamma \vdash t : \forall X\, A}$$

cannot be proved safe (in a call-by-value system with side-effects) if t is not a syntactic value. Similarly, the elimination rule for dependent product (shown previously) requires value restriction. It is possible to exhibit a counter-example breaking the type safety of our system if it is omitted [13].

In this paper, we consider control structures, which have been shown to give a computational interpretation to classical logic by Timothy Griffin [6]. In 1991,

[1] In ML the polymorphism mechanism is strongly linked with let-bindings. In OCaml syntax, they are expressions of the form `let x = u in t`.

Robert Harper and Mark Lillibridge found a complex program breaking the type safety of ML extended with Lisp's *call/cc* [7]. As with references, value restriction solves the inconsistency and yields a sound type system. Instead of using control operators like *call/cc*, we adopt the syntax of Michel Parigot's $\lambda\mu$-calculus [24]. Our language hence contains a new binder $\mu\alpha\, t$ capturing the continuation in the μ-variable α. The continuation can then be restored in t using the syntax $u * \alpha$[2]. In the context of the $\lambda\mu$-calculus, the soundness issue arises when evaluating $t\,(\mu\alpha\, u)$ when $\mu\alpha\, u$ has a polymorphic type. Such a situation cannot happen with value restriction since $\mu\alpha\, u$ is not a value.

3 Main Results

The main contribution of this paper is a new approach to value restriction. The syntactic restriction on terms is replaced by a semantical restriction expressed in terms of an observational equivalence relation denoted $(\equiv)$. Although this approach seems simple, building a model to prove soundness semantically (Theorem 6) is surprisingly subtle. Subject reduction is not required here, as our model construction implies type safety (Theorem 7). Furthermore our type system is consistent as a logic (Theorem 8).

In this paper, we restrict ourselves to a second order type system but it can easily be extended to higher-order. Types are built from two basic sorts of objects: *propositions* (the types themselves) and *individuals* (untyped terms of the language). Terms appear in a restriction operator $A \upharpoonright t \equiv u$ and a membership predicate $t \in A$. The former is used to define the equality types (by taking $A = \top$) and the latter is used to encode dependent product.

$$\Pi_{a:A} B \quad := \quad \forall a (a \in A \Rightarrow B)$$

Overall, the higher-order version of our system is similar to a Curry-style HOL with ML programs as individuals. It does not allow the definition of a type which structure depends on a term (e.g. functions with a variable number of arguments). Our system can thus be placed between HOL (a.k.a. F_ω) and the pure calculus of constructions (a.k.a. *CoC*) in (a Curry-style and classical version of) Barendregt's λ-cube.

Throughout this paper we build a realizability model à la Krivine [12] based on a call-by-value abstract machine. As a consequence, formulas are interpreted using three layers (values, stacks and terms) related via orthogonality (Definition 9). The crucial property (Theorem 4) for the soundness of semantical value restriction is that

$$\phi^{\perp\perp} \cap \Lambda_v = \phi$$

for every set of values ϕ (closed under $(\equiv)$). Λ_v denotes the set of all values and $\phi^{\perp}$ (resp. $\phi^{\perp\perp}$) the set of all stacks (resp. terms) that are compatible with every value in ϕ (resp. stacks in $\phi^{\perp}$). To obtain a model satisfying this property, we need to extend our programming language with a term $\delta_{v,w}$ which reduction depends on the observational equivalence of two values v and w.

[2] This was originally denoted $[\alpha]u$.

4 Related Work

To our knowledge, combining call-by-value evaluation, side-effects and dependent products has never been achieved before. At least not for a dependent product fully compatible with effects and call-by-value. For example, the Aura language [10] forbids dependency on terms that are not values in dependent applications. Similarly, the $F^\star$ language [28] relies on (partial) let-normal forms to enforce values in argument position. Daniel Licata and Robert Harper have defined a notion of positively dependent types [16] which only allow dependency over strictly positive types. Finally, in language like ATS [32] and DML [33] dependent types are limited to a specific index language.

The system that seems the most similar to ours is NuPrl [2], although it is inconsistent with classical reasoning. NuPrl accommodates an observational equivalence ($\sim$) (Howe's "squiggle" relation [8]) similar to our ($\equiv$) relation. It is partially reflected in the syntax of the system. Being based on a Kleene style realizability model, NuPrl can also be used to reason about untyped terms.

The central part of this paper consists in a classical realizability model construction in the style of Jean-Louis Krivine [12]. We rely on a call-by-value presentation which yields a model in three layers (values, terms and stacks). Such a technique has already been used to account for classical ML-like polymorphism in call-by-value in the work of Guillaume Munch-Maccagnoni [21][3]. It is here extended to include dependent products.

The most actively developed proof assistants following the Curry-Howard correspondence are Coq and Agda [18,22]. The former is based on Coquand and Huet's calculus of constructions and the latter on Martin-L?f's dependent type theory [3,17]. These two constructive theories provide dependent types, which allow the definition of very expressive specifications. Coq and Agda do not directly give a computational interpretation to classical logic. Classical reasoning can only be done through the definition of axioms such as the law of the excluded middle. Moreover, these two languages are logically consistent, and hence their type-checkers only allow terminating programs. As termination checking is a difficult (and undecidable) problem, many terminating programs are rejected. Although this is not a problem for formalizing mathematics, this makes programming tedious.

The TRELLYS project [1] aims at providing a language in which a consistent core can interact with type-safe dependently-typed programming with general recursion. Although the language defined in [1] is call-by-value and allows effect, it suffers from value restriction like Aura [10]. The value restriction does not appear explicitly but is encoded into a well-formedness judgement appearing as the premise of the typing rule for application. Apart from value restriction, the main difference between the language of the TRELLYS project and ours resides in the calculus itself. Their calculus is Church-style (or explicitly typed) while ours is Curry-style (or implicitly typed). In particular, their terms and types

[3] Our Theorem 4 seems unrelated to Lemma 9 in Munch-Maccagnoni's work [21].

are defined simultaneously, while our type system is constructed on top of an untyped calculus.

Another similar system can be found in the work of Alexandre Miquel [20], where propositions can be classical and Curry-style. However the rest of the language remains Church style and does not embed a full ML-like language. The PVS system [23] is similar to ours as it is based on classical higher-order logic. However this tool does not seem to be a programming language, but rather a specification language coupled with proof checking and model checking utilities. It is nonetheless worth mentioning that the undecidability of PVS's type system is handled by generating proof obligations. Our system will take a different approach and use a non-backtracking type-checking and type-inference algorithm.

5 Syntax, Reduction and Equivalence

The language is expressed in terms of a *Krivine Abstract Machine* [11], which is a stack-based machine. It is formed using four syntactic entities: values, terms, stacks and processes. The distinction between terms and values is specific to the call-by-value presentation, they would be collapsed in call-by-name. We require three distinct countable sets of variables:

- $\mathcal{V}_\lambda = \{x, y, z...\}$ for λ-variables,
- $\mathcal{V}_\mu = \{\alpha, \beta, \gamma...\}$ for μ-variables (also called stack variables) and
- $\mathcal{V}_\iota = \{a, b, c...\}$ for term variables. Term variables will be bound in formulas, but never in terms.

We also require a countable set $\mathcal{L} = \{l, l_1, l_2...\}$ of labels to name record fields and a countable set $\mathcal{C} = \{C, C_1, C_2...\}$ of constructors.

Definition 1. *Values, terms, stacks and processes are mutually inductively defined by the following grammars. The names of the corresponding sets are displayed on the right.*

$$v, w ::= x \mid \lambda x\, t \mid C[v] \mid \{l_i = v_i\}_{i\in I} \qquad (\Lambda_v)$$

$$t, u ::= a \mid v \mid t\, u \mid \mu\alpha\, t \mid p \mid v.l \mid case_v\ [C_i[x_i] \to t_i]_{i\in I} \mid \delta_{v,w} \qquad (\Lambda)$$

$$\pi, \rho ::= \alpha \mid v.\pi \mid [t]\pi \qquad (\Pi)$$

$$p, q ::= t * \pi \qquad (\Lambda \times \Pi)$$

Terms and values form a variation of the $\lambda\mu$-calculus [24] enriched with ML-like constructs (i.e. records and variants). For technical purposes that will become clear later on, we extend the language with a special kind of term $\delta_{v,w}$. It will only be used to build the model and is not intended to be accessed directly by the user. One may note that values and processes are terms. In particular, a process of the form $t * \alpha$ corresponds exactly to a named term $[\alpha]t$ in the most usual presentation of the $\lambda\mu$-calculus. A stack can be either a stack variable, a value pushed on top of a stack, or a stack frame containing a term on top of a stack. These two constructors are specific to the call-by-value presentation, only one would be required in call-by-name.

Remark 1. We enforce values in constructors, record fields, projection and case analysis. This makes the calculus simpler because only β-reduction will manipulate the stack. We can define syntactic sugars such as the following to hide the restriction from the programmer.

$$t.l \;:=\; (\lambda x\, x.l)\, t \qquad\qquad C[t] \;:=\; (\lambda x\, C[x])\, t$$

Definition 2. *Given a value, term, stack or process ψ we denote $FV_\lambda(\psi)$ (resp. $FV_\mu(\psi)$, $TV(\psi)$) the set of free λ-variables (resp. free μ-variables, term variables) contained in ψ. We say that ψ is closed if it does not contain any free variable of any kind. The set of closed values and the set of closed terms are denoted Λ_v^* and Λ^* respectively.*

Remark 2. A stack, and hence a process, can never be closed as they always at least contain a stack variable.

5.1 Call-by-Value Reduction Relation

Processes form the internal state of our abstract machine. They are to be thought of as a term put in some evaluation context represented using a stack. Intuitively, the stack π in the process $t * \pi$ contains the arguments to be fed to t. Since we are in call-by-value the stack also handles the storing of functions while their arguments are being evaluated. This is why we need stack frames (i.e. stacks of the form $[t]\pi$). The operational semantics of our language is given by a relation $(\succ)$ over processes.

Definition 3. *The relation $(\succ) \subseteq (\Lambda \times \Pi)^2$ is defined as the smallest relation satisfying the following reduction rules.*

$$\begin{array}{rcll}
t\, u * \pi & \succ & u * [t]\pi & \\
v * [t]\pi & \succ & t * v.\pi & \\
\lambda x\, t * v.\pi & \succ & t[x:=v] * \pi & \\
\mu\alpha\, t * \pi & \succ & t[\alpha:=\pi] * \pi & \\
p * \pi & \succ & p & \\
\{l_i = v_i\}_{i\in I}.l_k * \pi & \succ & v_k * \pi & k \in I \\
case_{C_k[v]}\; [C_i[x_i] \to t_i]_{i\in I} * \pi & \succ & t_k[x_k:=v] * \pi & k \in I
\end{array}$$

We will denote $(\succ^+)$ its transitive closure, $(\succ^*)$ its reflexive-transitive closure and $(\succ^k)$ its k-fold application.

The first three rules are those that handle β-reduction. When the abstract machine encounters an application, the function is stored in a stack-frame in order to evaluate its argument first. Once the argument has been completely computed, a value faces the stack-frame containing the function. At this point the function can be evaluated and the value is stored in the stack ready to be consumed by the function as soon as it evaluates to a λ-abstraction. A capture-avoiding substitution can then be performed to effectively apply the argument to the function. The fourth and fifth rules handle the classical part of computation. When a μ-abstraction is reached, the current stack (i.e. the current evaluation context) is captured and substituted for the corresponding μ-variable. Conversely, when a process is reached, the current stack is thrown away and evaluation resumes with the process. The last two rules perform projection and case analysis in the expected way. Note that for now, states of the form $\delta_{v,w} * \pi$ are unaffected by the reduction relation.

Remark 3. For the abstract machine to be simpler, we use right-to-left call-by-value evaluation, and not the more usual left-to-right call-by-value evaluation.

Lemma 1. *The reduction relation ($\succ$) is compatible with substitutions of variables of any kind. More formally, if p and q are processes such that $p \succ q$ then:*

- *for all $x \in \mathcal{V}_\lambda$ and $v \in \Lambda_v$, $p[x := v] \succ q[x := v]$,*
- *for all $\alpha \in \mathcal{V}_\mu$ and $\pi \in \Pi$, $p[\alpha := \pi] \succ q[\alpha := \pi]$,*
- *for all $a \in \mathcal{V}_\iota$ and $t \in \Lambda$, $p[a := t] \succ q[a := t]$.*

Consequently, if σ is a substitution for variables of any kind and if $p \succ q$ (resp. $p \succ^* q$, $p \succ^+ q$, $p \succ^k q$) then $p\sigma \succ q\sigma$ (resp. $p\sigma \succ^* q\sigma$, $p\sigma \succ^+ q\sigma$, $p\sigma \succ^k q\sigma$).

Proof. Immediate case analysis on the reduction rules.

We are now going to give the vocabulary that will be used to describe some specific classes of processes. In particular we need to identify processes that are to be considered as the evidence of a successful computation, and those that are to be recognised as expressing failure.

Definition 4. *A process $p \in \Lambda \times \Pi$ is said to be:*

- final *if there is a value $v \in \Lambda_v$ and a stack variable $\alpha \in \mathcal{V}_\mu$ such that $p = v * \alpha$,*
- δ-like *if there are values $v, w \in \Lambda_v$ and a stack $\pi \in \Pi$ such that $p = \delta_{v,w} * \pi$,*
- blocked *if there is no $q \in \Lambda \times \Pi$ such that $p \succ q$,*
- stuck *if it is not final nor δ-like, and if for every substitution σ, $p\sigma$ is blocked,*
- non-terminating *if there is no blocked process $q \in \Lambda \times \Pi$ such that $p \succ^* q$.*

Lemma 2. *Let p be a process and σ be a substitution for variables of any kind. If p is δ-like (resp. stuck, non-terminating) then $p\sigma$ is also δ-like (resp. stuck, non-terminating).*

Proof. Immediate by definition.

Lemma 3. *A stuck state is of one of the following forms, where $k \notin I$.*

$$C[v].l * \pi \qquad (\lambda x\ t).l * \pi \qquad C[v] * w.\pi \qquad \{l_i = v_i\}_{i \in I} * v.\pi$$

$$case_{\lambda x\ t}\ [C_i[x_i] \to t_i]_{i \in I} * \pi \qquad case_{\{l_i = v_i\}_{i \in I}}\ [C_j[x_j] \to t_j]_{j \in J} * \pi$$

$$case_{C_k[v]}\ [C_i[x_i] \to t_i]_{i \in I} * \pi \qquad \{l_i = v_i\}_{i \in I}.l_k * \pi$$

Proof. Simple case analysis.

Lemma 4. *A blocked process $p \in \Lambda \times \Pi$ is either stuck, final, δ-like, or of one of the following forms.*

$$x.l * \pi \qquad x * v.\pi \qquad case_x\ [C_i[x_i] \to t_i]_{i \in I} * \pi \qquad a * \pi$$

Proof. Straight-forward case analysis using Lemma 3.

5.2 Reduction of $\delta_{v,w}$ and Equivalence

The idea now is to define a notion of observational equivalence over terms using a relation $(\equiv)$. We then extend the reduction relation with a rule reducing a state of the form $\delta_{v,w} * \pi$ to $v * \pi$ if $v \not\equiv w$. If $v \equiv w$ then $\delta_{v,w}$ is stuck. With this rule reduction and equivalence will become interdependent as equivalence will be defined using reduction.

Definition 5. *Given a reduction relation R, we say that a process $p \in \Lambda \times \Pi$ converges, and write $p \Downarrow_R$, if there is a final state $q \in \Lambda \times \Pi$ such that pR^*q (where R^* is the reflexive-transitive closure of R). If p does not converge we say that it diverges and write $p \Uparrow_R$. We will use the notations $p \Downarrow_i$ and $p \Uparrow_i$ when working with indexed notation symbols like $(\twoheadrightarrow_i)$.*

Definition 6. *For every natural number i we define a reduction relation $(\twoheadrightarrow_i)$ and an equivalence relation $(\equiv_i)$ which negation will be denoted $(\not\equiv_i)$.*

$$(\twoheadrightarrow_i) = (\succ) \cup \{(\delta_{v,w} * \pi, v * \pi) \mid \exists j < i, v \not\equiv_j w\}$$

$$(\equiv_i) = \{(t, u) \mid \forall j \leq i, \forall \pi, \forall \sigma, t\sigma * \pi \Downarrow_j \Leftrightarrow u\sigma * \pi \Downarrow_j\}$$

It is easy to see that $(\twoheadrightarrow_0) = (\succ)$. For every natural number i, the relation $(\equiv_i)$ is indeed an equivalence relation as it can be seen as an intersection of equivalence relations. Its negation can be expressed as follows.

$$(\not\equiv_i) = \{(t, u), (u, t) \mid \exists j \leq i, \exists \pi, \exists \sigma, t\sigma * \pi \Downarrow_j \wedge u\sigma * \pi \Uparrow_j\}$$

Definition 7. *We define a reduction relation $(\twoheadrightarrow)$ and an equivalence relation $(\equiv)$ which negation will be denoted $(\not\equiv)$.*

$$(\twoheadrightarrow) = \bigcup_{i \in \mathbb{N}} (\twoheadrightarrow_i) \qquad (\equiv) = \bigcap_{i \in \mathbb{N}} (\equiv_i)$$

These relations can be expressed directly (i.e. without the need of a union or an intersection) in the following way.

$$(\equiv) = \{(t, u) \mid \forall i, \forall \pi, \forall \sigma, t\sigma * \pi \Downarrow_i \Leftrightarrow u\sigma * \pi \Downarrow_i\}$$
$$(\not\equiv) = \{(t, u), (u, t) \mid \exists i, \exists \pi, \exists \sigma, t\sigma * \pi \Downarrow_i \wedge u\sigma * \pi \Uparrow_i\}$$
$$(\twoheadrightarrow) = (\succ) \cup \{(\delta_{v,w} * \pi, v * \pi) \mid v \not\equiv w\}$$

Remark 4. Obviously $(\twoheadrightarrow_i) \subseteq (\twoheadrightarrow_{i+1})$ and $(\equiv_{i+1}) \subseteq (\equiv_i)$. As a consequence the construction of $(\twoheadrightarrow_i)_{i\in\mathbb{N}}$ and $(\equiv_i)_{i\in\mathbb{N}}$ converges. In fact $(\twoheadrightarrow)$ and $(\equiv)$ form a fixpoint at ordinal ω. Surprisingly, this property is not explicitly required.

Theorem 1. *Let t and u be terms. If $t \equiv u$ then for every stack $\pi \in \Pi$ and substitution σ we have $t\sigma * \pi \Downarrow_{\twoheadrightarrow} \Leftrightarrow u\sigma * \pi \Downarrow_{\twoheadrightarrow}$.*

Proof. We suppose that $t \equiv u$ and we take $\pi_0 \in \Pi$ and a substitution σ_0. By symmetry we can assume that $t\sigma_0 * \pi_0 \Downarrow_{\twoheadrightarrow}$ and show that $u\sigma_0 * \pi_0 \Downarrow_{\twoheadrightarrow}$. By definition there is $i_0 \in \mathbb{N}$ such that $t\sigma_0 * \pi_0 \Downarrow_{i_0}$. Since $t \equiv u$ we know that for every $i \in \mathbb{N}$, $\pi \in \Pi$ and substitution σ we have $t\sigma * \pi \Downarrow_i \Leftrightarrow u\sigma * \pi \Downarrow_i$. This is true in particular for $i = i_0$, $\pi = \pi_0$ and $\sigma = \sigma_0$. We hence obtain $u\sigma_0 * \pi_0 \Downarrow_{i_0}$ which give us $u\sigma_0 * \pi_0 \Downarrow_{\twoheadrightarrow}$.

Remark 5. The converse implication is not true in general: taking $t = \delta_{\lambda x\, x,\{\}}$ and $u = \lambda x\, x$ gives a counter-example. More generally $p \Downarrow_{\twoheadrightarrow} \Leftrightarrow q \Downarrow_{\twoheadrightarrow}$ does not necessarily imply $p \Downarrow_i \Leftrightarrow q \Downarrow_i$ for all $i \in \mathbb{N}$.

Corollary 1. *Let t and u be terms and π be a stack. If $t \equiv u$ and $t * \pi \Downarrow_{\twoheadrightarrow}$ then $u * \pi \Downarrow_{\twoheadrightarrow}$.*

Proof. Direct consequence of Theorem 1 using π and an empty substitution.

5.3 Extensionality of the Language

In order to be able to work with the equivalence relation $(\equiv)$, we need to check that it is extensional. In other words, we need to be able to replace equals by equals at any place in terms without changing their observed behaviour. This property is summarized in the following two theorems.

Theorem 2. *Let v and w be values, E be a term and x be a λ-variable. If $v \equiv w$ then $E[x := v] \equiv E[x := w]$.*

Proof. We are going to prove the contrapositive so we suppose $E[x := v] \not\equiv E[x := w]$ and show $v \not\equiv w$. By definition there is $i \in \mathbb{N}$, $\pi \in \Pi$ and a substitution σ such that $(E[x := v])\sigma * \pi \Downarrow_i$ and $(E[x := w])\sigma * \pi \Uparrow_i$ (up to symmetry). Since we can rename x in such a way that it does not appear in $dom(\sigma)$, we can suppose $E\sigma[x := v\sigma] * \pi \Downarrow_i$ and $E\sigma[x := w\sigma] * \pi \Uparrow_i$. In order to show $v \not\equiv w$ we need to find $i_0 \in \mathbb{N}$, $\pi_0 \in \Pi$ and a substitution σ_0 such that $v\sigma_0 * \pi_0 \Downarrow_{i_0}$ and $w\sigma_0 * \pi_0 \Uparrow_{i_0}$ (up to symmetry). We take $i_0 = i$, $\pi_0 = [\lambda x\, E\sigma]\pi$ and $\sigma_0 = \sigma$. These values are suitable since by definition $v\sigma_0 * \pi_0 \twoheadrightarrow_{i_0} E\sigma[x := v\sigma] * \pi \Downarrow_{i_0}$ and $w\sigma_0 * \pi_0 \twoheadrightarrow_{i_0} E\sigma[x := w\sigma] * \pi \Uparrow_{i_0}$.

Lemma 5. *Let s be a process, t be a term, a be a term variable and k be a natural number. If $s[a := t] \Downarrow_k$ then there is a blocked state p such that $s \succ^* p$ and either*

- *$p = v * \alpha$ for some value v and a stack variable α,*

– $p = a * \pi$ *for some stack* π,
– $k > 0$ *and* $p = \delta(v, w) * \pi$ *for some values* v *and* w *and stack* π, *and in this case* $v[a := t] \not\equiv_j w[a := t]$ *for some* $j < k$.

Proof. Let σ be the substitution $[a := t]$. If s is non-terminating, Lemma 2 tells us that $s\sigma$ is also non-terminating, which contradicts $s\sigma \Downarrow_k$. Consequently, there is a blocked process p such that $s \succ^* p$ since $(\succ) \subseteq (\twoheadrightarrow_k)$. Using Lemma 1 we get $s\sigma \succ^* p\sigma$ from which we obtain $p\sigma \Downarrow_k$. The process p cannot be stuck, otherwise $p\sigma$ would also be stuck by Lemma 2, which would contradict $p\sigma \Downarrow_k$. Let us now suppose that $p = \delta_{v,w} * \pi$ for some values v and w and some stack π. Since $\delta_{v\sigma,w\sigma} * \pi \Downarrow_k$ there must be $i < k$ such that $v\sigma \not\equiv_j w\sigma$, otherwise this would contradict $\delta_{v\sigma,w\sigma} * \pi \Downarrow_k$. In this case we necessarily have $k > 0$, otherwise there would be no possible candidate for i. According to Lemma 4 we need to rule out four more forms of therms: $x.l * \pi$, $x * v.\pi$, $case_x\ B * \pi$ and $b * \pi$ in the case where $b \neq a$. If p was of one of these forms the substitution σ would not be able to unblock the reduction of p, which would contradict again $p\sigma \Downarrow_k$.

Lemma 6. *Let* t_1, t_2 *and* E *be terms and* a *be a term variable. For every* $k \in \mathbb{N}$, *if* $t_1 \equiv_k t_2$ *then* $E[a{:=}t_1] \equiv_k E[a{:=}t_2]$.

Proof. Let us take $k \in \mathbb{N}$, suppose that $t_1 \equiv_k t_2$ and show that $E[a := t_1] \equiv_k E[a := t_1]$. By symmetry we can assume that we have $i \leq k$, $\pi \in \Pi$ and a substitution σ such that $(E[a{:=}t_1])\sigma * \pi \Downarrow_i$ and show that $(E[a{:=}t_2])\sigma * \pi \Downarrow_i$. As we are free to rename a, we can suppose that it does not appear in $dom(\sigma)$, $TV(\pi)$, $TV(t_1)$ or $TV(t_2)$. In order to lighten the notations we define $E' = E\sigma$, $\sigma_1 = [a{:=}t_1\sigma]$ and $\sigma_2 = [a{:=}t_2\sigma]$. We are hence assuming $E'\sigma_1 * \pi \Downarrow_i$ and trying to show $E'\sigma_2 * \pi \Downarrow_i$.

We will now build a sequence $(E_i, \pi_i, l_i)_{i \in I}$ in such a way that $E'\sigma_1 * \pi \twoheadrightarrow_k^* E_i\sigma_1 * \pi_i\sigma_1$ in l_i steps for every $i \in I$. Furthermore, we require that $(l_i)_{i \in I}$ is increasing and that it has a strictly increasing subsequence. Under this condition our sequence will necessarily be finite. If it was infinite the number of reduction steps that could be taken from the state $E'\sigma_1 * \pi$ would not be bounded, which would contradict $E'\sigma_1 * \pi \Downarrow_i$. We now denote our finite sequence $(E_i, \pi_i, l_i)_{i \leq n}$ with $n \in \mathbb{N}$. In order to show that $(l_i)_{i \leq n}$ has a strictly increasing subsequence, we will ensure that it does not have three equal consecutive values. More formally, we will require that if $0 < i < n$ and $l_{i-1} = l_i$ then $l_{i+1} > l_i$.

To define (E_0, π_0, l_0) we consider the reduction of $E' * \pi$. Since we know that $(E' * \pi)\sigma_1 = E'\sigma_1 * \pi \Downarrow_i$ we use Lemma 5 to obtain a blocked state p such that $E' * \pi \succ^j p$. We can now take $E_0 * \pi_0 = p$ and $l_0 = j$. By Lemma 1 we have $(E' * \pi)\sigma_1 \succ^j E_0\sigma_1 * \pi_0\sigma_1$ from which we can deduce that $(E' * \pi)\sigma_1 \twoheadrightarrow_k^* E_0\sigma_1 * \pi_0\sigma_1$ in $l_0 = j$ steps.

To define $(E_{i+1}, \pi_{i+1}, l_{i+1})$ we consider the reduction of the process $E_i\sigma_1 * \pi_i$. By construction we know that $E'\sigma_1 * \pi \twoheadrightarrow_k^* E_i\sigma_1 * \pi_i\sigma_1 = (E_i\sigma_1 * \pi_i)\sigma_1$ in l_i steps. Using Lemma 5 we know that $E_i * \pi_i$ might be of three shapes.

– If $E_i * \pi_i = v * \alpha$ for some value v and stack variable α then the end of the sequence was reached with $n = i$.

- If $E_i = a$ then we consider the reduction of $E_i\sigma_1 * \pi_i$. Since $(E_i\sigma_1 * \pi_i)\sigma_1 \Downarrow_k$ we know from Lemma 5 that there is a blocked process p such that $E_i\sigma_1 * \pi_i \succ^j p$. Using Lemma 1 we obtain that $E_i\sigma_1 * \pi_i\sigma_1 \succ^j p\sigma_1$ from which we can deduce that $E_i\sigma_1 * \pi_i\sigma_1 \twoheadrightarrow_k p\sigma_1$ in j steps. We then take $E_{i+1} * \pi_{i+1} = p$ and $l_{i+1} = l_i + j$.
  Is it possible to have $j = 0$? This can only happen when $E_i\sigma_1 * \pi_i$ is of one of the three forms of Lemma 5. It cannot be of the form $a * \pi$ as we assumed that a does not appear in t_1 or σ. If it is of the form $v * \alpha$, then we reached the end of the sequence with $i + 1 = n$ so there is no trouble. The process $E_i\sigma_1 * \pi_i$ may be of the form $\delta(v, w) * \pi$, but we will have $l_{i+2} > l_{i+1}$.
- If $E_i = \delta(v, w)$ for some values v and w we have $m < k$ such that $v\sigma_1 \not\equiv_m w\sigma_1$. Hence $E_i\sigma_1 * \pi_i = \delta(v\sigma_1, w\sigma_1) * \pi_i \twoheadrightarrow_k v\sigma_1 * \pi_i$ by definition. Moreover $E_i\sigma_1 * \pi_i\sigma_1 \twoheadrightarrow_k v\sigma_1 * \pi_i\sigma_1$ by Lemma 1. Since $E'\sigma_1 * \pi \twoheadrightarrow_k^* E_i\sigma_1 * \pi_i\sigma_1$ in l_i steps we obtain that $E'\sigma_1 * \pi \twoheadrightarrow_k^* v\sigma_1 * \pi_i\sigma_1$ in $l_i + 1$ steps. This also gives us $(v\sigma_1 * \pi_i)\sigma_1 = v\sigma_1 * \pi_i\sigma_1 \Downarrow_k$.
  We now consider the reduction of the process $v\sigma_1 * \pi_i$. By Lemma 5 there is a blocked process p such that $v\sigma_1 * \pi_i \succ^j p$. Using Lemma 1 we obtain $v\sigma_1 * \pi_i\sigma_1 \succ^j p\sigma_1$ from which we deduce that $v\sigma_1 * \pi_i\sigma_1 \twoheadrightarrow_k^* p\sigma_1$ in j steps. We then take $E_{i+1} * \pi_{i+1} = p$ and $l_{i+1} = l_i + j + 1$. Note that in this case we have $l_{i+1} > l_i$.

Intuitively $(E_i, \pi_i, l_i)_{i \leq n}$ mimics the reduction of $E'\sigma_1 * \pi$ while making explicit every substitution of a and every reduction of a δ-like state.

To end the proof we show that for every $i \leq n$ we have $E_i\sigma_2 * \pi_i\sigma_2 \Downarrow_k$. For $i = 0$ this will give us $E'\sigma_2 * \pi \Downarrow_k$ which is the expected result. Since $E_n * \pi_n = v * \alpha$ we have $E_n\sigma_2 * \pi_n\sigma_2 = v\sigma_2 * \alpha$ from which we trivially obtain $E_n\sigma_2 * \pi_n\sigma_2 \Downarrow_k$. We now suppose that $E_{i+1}\sigma_2 * \pi_i\sigma_2 \Downarrow_k$ for $0 \leq i < n$ and show that $E_i\sigma_2 * \pi_i\sigma_2 \Downarrow_k$. By construction $E_i * \pi_i$ can be of two shapes[4]:

- If $E_i = a$ then $t_1\sigma * \pi_i \twoheadrightarrow_k^* E_{i+1} * \pi_{i+1}$. Using Lemma 1 we obtain $t_1\sigma * \pi_i\sigma_2 \twoheadrightarrow_k E_{i+1}\sigma_2 * \pi_i\sigma_2$ from which we deduce $t_1\sigma * \pi_i\sigma_2 \Downarrow_k$ by induction hypothesis. Since $t_1 \equiv_k t_2$ we obtain $t_2\sigma * \pi_i\sigma_2 = (E_i * \pi_i)\sigma_2 \Downarrow_k$.
- If $E_i = \delta(v, w)$ then $v * \pi_i \twoheadrightarrow_k E_{i+1} * \pi_{i+1}$ and hence $v\sigma_2 * \pi_i\sigma_2 \twoheadrightarrow_k E_{i+1}\sigma_2 * \pi_{i+1}\sigma_2$ by Lemma 1. Using the induction hypothesis we obtain $v\sigma_2 * \pi_i\sigma_2 \Downarrow_k$. It remains to show that $\delta(v\sigma_2, w\sigma_2) * \pi_i\sigma_2 \twoheadrightarrow_k^* v\sigma_2 * \pi_i\sigma_2$. We need to find $j < k$ such that $v\sigma_2 \not\equiv_j w\sigma_2$. By construction there is $m < k$ such that $v\sigma_1 \not\equiv_m w\sigma_1$. We are going to show that $v\sigma_2 \not\equiv_m w\sigma_2$. By using the global induction hypothesis twice we obtain $v\sigma_1 \equiv_m v\sigma_2$ and $w\sigma_1 \equiv_m v\sigma_2$. Now if $v\sigma_2 \equiv_m w\sigma_2$ then $v\sigma_1 \equiv_m v\sigma_2 \equiv_m w\sigma_2 \equiv_m w\sigma_1$ contradicts $v\sigma_1 \not\equiv w\sigma_1$. Hence we must have $v\sigma_2 \not\equiv_m w\sigma_2$.

Theorem 3. *Let t_1, t_2 and E be three terms and a be a term variable. If $t_1 \equiv t_2$ then $E[a{:=}t_1] \equiv E[a{:=}t_2]$.*

Proof. We suppose that $t_1 \equiv t_2$ which means that $t_1 \equiv_i t_2$ for every $i \in \mathbb{N}$. We need to show that $E[a := t_1] \equiv E[a := t_2]$ so we take $i_0 \in \mathbb{N}$ and show

[4] Only $E_n * \pi_n$ can be of the form $v * \alpha$.

$E[a := t_1] \equiv_{i_0} E[a := t_2]$. By hypothesis we have $t_1 \equiv_{i_0} t_2$ and hence we can conclude using Lemma 6.

6 Formulas and Semantics

The syntax presented in the previous section is part of a realizability machinery that will be built upon here. We aim at obtaining a semantical interpretation of the second-order type system that will be defined shortly. Our abstract machine slightly differs from the mainstream presentation of *Krivine's classical realizability* which is usually call-by-name. Although call-by-value presentations have rarely been published, such developments are well-known among classical realizability experts. The addition of the δ instruction and the related modifications are however due to the author.

6.1 Pole and Orthogonality

As always in classical realizability, the model is parametrized by a pole, which serves as an exchange point between the world of programs and the world of execution contexts (i.e. stacks).

Definition 8. *A* pole *is a set of processes* $\perp\!\!\!\perp \subseteq \Lambda \times \Pi$ *which is* saturated *(i.e. closed under backward reduction). More formally, if we have* $q \in \perp\!\!\!\perp$ *and* $p \twoheadrightarrow q$ *then* $p \in \perp\!\!\!\perp$.

Here, for the sake of simplicity and brevity, we are only going to use the pole

$$\perp\!\!\!\perp = \{p \in \Lambda \times \Pi \mid p \Downarrow_{\twoheadrightarrow}\}$$

which is clearly saturated. Note that this particular pole is also closed under the reduction relation ($\twoheadrightarrow$), even though this is not a general property. In particular $\perp\!\!\!\perp$ contains all final processes.

The notion of *orthogonality* is central in Krivine's classical realizability. In this framework a type is interpreted (or realized) by programs computing corresponding values. This interpretation is spread in a three-layered construction, even though it is fully determined by the first layer (and the choice of the pole). The first layer consists of a set of values that we will call the *raw semantics*. It gathers all the syntactic values that should be considered as having the corresponding type. As an example, if we were to consider the type of natural numbers, its raw semantics would be the set $\{\bar{n} \mid n \in \mathbb{N}\}$ where $\bar{n}$ is some encoding of n. The second layer, called *falsity value* is a set containing every stack that is a candidate for building a valid process using any value from the raw semantics. The notion of validity depends on the choice of the pole. Here for instance, a valid process is a normalizing one (i.e. one that reduces to a final state). The third layer, called *truth value* is a set of terms that is built by iterating the process once more. The formalism for the two levels of orthogonality is given in the following definition.

Definition 9. *For every set $\phi \subseteq \Lambda_v$ we define a set $\phi^{\perp} \subseteq \Pi$ and a set $\phi^{\perp\perp} \subseteq \Lambda$ as follows.*

$$\phi^{\perp} = \{\pi \in \Pi \mid \forall v \in \phi, v * \pi \in \perp\!\!\!\perp\}$$
$$\phi^{\perp\perp} = \{t \in \Lambda \mid \forall \pi \in \phi^{\perp}, t * \pi \in \perp\!\!\!\perp\}$$

We now give two general properties of orthogonality that are true in every classical realizability model. They will be useful when proving the soundness of our type system.

Lemma 7. *If $\phi \subseteq \Lambda_v$ is a set of values, then $\phi \subseteq \phi^{\perp\perp}$.*

Proof. Immediate following the definition of $\phi^{\perp\perp}$.

Lemma 8. *Let $\phi \subseteq \Lambda_v$ and $\psi \subseteq \Lambda_v$ be two sets of values. If $\phi \subseteq \psi$ then $\phi^{\perp\perp} \subseteq \psi^{\perp\perp}$.*

Proof. Immediate by definition of orthogonality.

The construction involving the terms of the form $\delta_{v,x}$ and $(\equiv)$ in the previous section is now going to gain meaning. The following theorem, which is our central result, does not hold in every classical realizability model. Obtaining a proof required us to internalize observational equivalence, which introduces a non-computable reduction rule.

Theorem 4. *If $\Phi \subseteq \Lambda_v$ is a set of values closed under $(\equiv)$, then $\Phi^{\perp\perp} \cap \Lambda_v = \Phi$.*

Proof. The direction $\Phi \subseteq \Phi^{\perp\perp} \cap \Lambda_v$ is straight-forward using Lemma 7. We are going to show that $\Phi^{\perp\perp} \cap \Lambda_v \subseteq \Phi$, which amounts to showing that for every value $v \in \Phi^{\perp\perp}$ we have $v \in \Phi$. We are going to show the contrapositive, so let us assume $v \notin \Phi$ and show $v \notin \Phi^{\perp\perp}$. We need to find a stack π_0 such that $v * \pi_0 \notin \perp\!\!\!\perp$ and for every value $w \in \Phi$, $w * \pi_0 \in \perp\!\!\!\perp$. We take $\pi_0 = [\lambda x\ \delta_{x,v}]\ \alpha$ and show that is is suitable. By definition of the reduction relation $v * \pi_0$ reduces to $\delta_{v,v} * \alpha$ which is not in $\perp\!\!\!\perp$ (it is stuck as $v \equiv v$ by reflexivity). Let us now take $w \in \Phi$. Again by definition, $w * \pi_0$ reduces to $\delta_{w,v} * \alpha$, but this time we have $w \not\equiv v$ since Φ was supposed to be closed under $(\equiv)$ and $v \notin \Phi$. Hence $w * \pi_0$ reduces to $w * \alpha \in \perp\!\!\!\perp$.

It is important to check that the pole we chose does not yield a degenerate model. In particular we check that no term is able to face every stacks. If it were the case, such a term could be use as a proof of $\perp$.

Theorem 5. *The pole $\perp\!\!\!\perp$ is consistent, which means that for every closed term t there is a stack π such that $t * \pi \notin \perp\!\!\!\perp$.*

Proof. Let t be a closed term and α be a stack constant. If we do not have $t*\alpha \Downarrow_{\twoheadrightarrow}$ then we can directly take $\pi = \alpha$. Otherwise we know that $t * \alpha \twoheadrightarrow^* v * \alpha$ for some value v. Since t is closed α is the only available stack variable. We now show that $\pi = [\lambda x\ \{\}]\{\}.\beta$ is suitable. We denote σ the substitution $[\alpha := \pi]$. Using a trivial extension of Lemma 1 to the $(\twoheadrightarrow)$ relation we obtain $t * \pi = (t * \alpha)\sigma \twoheadrightarrow^* (v * \alpha)\sigma = v\sigma * \pi$. We hence have $t * \pi \twoheadrightarrow^* v\sigma * [\lambda x\ \{\}]\{\}.\beta \twoheadrightarrow^2 \{\} * \{\}.\beta \notin \perp\!\!\!\perp$.

6.2 Formulas and Their Semantics

In this paper we limit ourselves to second-order logic, even though the system can easily be extended to higher-order. For every natural number n we require a countable set $\mathcal{V}_n = \{X_n, Y_n, Z_n...\}$ of n-ary predicate variables.

Definition 10. *The syntax of formulas is given by the following grammar.*

$$\begin{aligned} A, B \ ::= \ & X_n(t_1, ..., t_n) \mid A \Rightarrow B \mid \forall a\ A \mid \exists a\ A \mid \forall X_n\ A \mid \exists X_n\ A \\ & \mid \{l_i : A_i\}_{i \in I} \mid [C_i : A_i]_{i \in I} \mid t \in A \mid A \upharpoonright t \equiv u \end{aligned}$$

Terms appear in several places in formulas, in particular, they form the individuals of the logic. They can be quantified over and are used as arguments for predicate variables. Besides the ML-like formers for sums and products (i.e. records and variants) we add a membership predicate and a restriction operation. The membership predicate $t \in A$ is used to express the fact that the term t has type A. It provides a way to encode the dependent product type using universal quantification and the arrow type. In this sense, it is inspired and related to Krivine's relativization of quantifiers.

$$\Pi_{a:A}\ B \quad := \quad \forall a(a \in A \Rightarrow B)$$

The restriction operator can be thought of as a kind of conjunction with no algorithmic content. The formula $A \upharpoonright t \equiv u$ is to be interpreted in the same way as A if the equivalence $t \equiv u$ holds, and as $\bot$ otherwise[5]. In particular, we will define the following types:

$$A \upharpoonright t \not\equiv u := A \upharpoonright t \equiv u \Rightarrow \bot \qquad t \equiv u := \top \upharpoonright t \equiv u \qquad t \not\equiv u := \top \upharpoonright t \not\equiv u$$

To handle free variables in formulas we will need to generalize the notion of substitution to allow the substitution of predicate variables.

Definition 11. *A substitution is a finite map σ ranging over λ-variables, μ-variables, term and predicate variables such that:*

- *if $x \in dom(\sigma)$ then $\sigma(x) \in \Lambda_v$,*
- *if $\alpha \in dom(\sigma)$ then $\sigma(\alpha) \in \Pi$,*
- *if $a \in dom(\sigma)$ then $\sigma(a) \in \Lambda$,*
- *if $X_n \in dom(\sigma)$ then $\sigma(X_n) \in \Lambda^n \to \mathcal{P}(\Lambda_v/\equiv)$.*

Remark 6. A predicate variable of arity n will be substituted by a n-ary predicate. Semantically, such predicate will correspond to some total (set-theoretic) function building a subset of $\Lambda_v/\equiv$ from n terms. In the syntax, the binding of the arguments of a predicate variables will happen implicitly during its substitution.

Definition 12. *Given a formula A we denote $FV(A)$ the set of its free variables. Given a substitution σ such that $FV(A) \subseteq dom(\sigma)$ we write $A[\sigma]$ the closed formula built by applying σ to A.*

[5] We use the standard second-order encoding: $\bot = \forall X_0\ X_0$ and $\top = \exists X_0\ X_0$.

In the semantics we will interpret closed formulas by sets of values closed under the equivalence relation ($\equiv$).

Definition 13. *Given a formula A and a substitution σ such that $A[\sigma]$ is closed, we define the* raw semantics $[\![A]\!]_\sigma \subseteq \Lambda_v/\equiv$ *of A under the substitution σ as follows.*

$$
\begin{aligned}
[\![X_n(t_1,...,t_n)]\!]_\sigma &= \sigma(X_n)(t_1\sigma,...,t_n\sigma)\\
[\![A \Rightarrow B]\!]_\sigma &= \{\lambda x\, t \mid \forall v \in [\![A]\!]_\sigma, t[x := v] \in [\![B]\!]_\sigma^{\perp\perp}\}\\
[\![\forall a\, A]\!]_\sigma &= \cap_{t\in\Lambda^*} [\![A]\!]_{\sigma[a:=t]}\\
[\![\exists a\, A]\!]_\sigma &= \cup_{t\in\Lambda^*} [\![A]\!]_{\sigma[a:=t]}\\
[\![\forall X_n\, A]\!]_\sigma &= \cap_{P\in\Lambda^n\to\mathcal{P}(\Lambda_v/\equiv)} [\![A]\!]_{\sigma[X_n:=P]}\\
[\![\exists X_n\, A]\!]_\sigma &= \cup_{P\in\Lambda^n\to\mathcal{P}(\Lambda_v/\equiv)} [\![A]\!]_{\sigma[X_n:=P]}\\
[\![\{l_i : A_i\}_{i\in I}]\!]_\sigma &= \{\{l_i = v_i\}_{i\in I} \mid \forall i \in I\ \ v_i \in [\![A_i]\!]_\sigma\}\\
[\![[C_i : A_i]_{i\in I}]\!]_\sigma &= \cup_{i\in I}\{C_i[v] \mid v \in [\![A_i]\!]_\sigma\}\\
[\![t \in A]\!]_\sigma &= \{v \in [\![A]\!]_\sigma \mid t\sigma \equiv v\}\\
[\![A \upharpoonright t \equiv u]\!]_\sigma &= \begin{cases} [\![A]\!]_\sigma & \textit{if } t\sigma \equiv u\sigma\\ \emptyset & \textit{otherwise}\end{cases}
\end{aligned}
$$

In the model, programs will realize closed formulas in two different ways according to their syntactic class. The interpretation of values will be given in terms of raw semantics, and the interpretation of terms in general will be given in terms of truth values.

Definition 14. *Let A be a formula and σ a substitution such that $A[\sigma]$ is closed. We say that:*

- *$v \in \Lambda_v$ realizes $A[\sigma]$ if $v \in [\![A]\!]_\sigma$,*
- *$t \in \Lambda$ realizes $A[\sigma]$ if $t \in [\![A]\!]_\sigma^{\perp\perp}$.*

6.3 Contexts and Typing Rules

Before giving the typing rules of our system we need to define contexts and judgements. As explained in the introduction, several typing rules require a value restriction in our context. This is reflected in typing rule by the presence of two forms of judgements.

Definition 15. *A context is an ordered list of hypotheses. In particular, it contains type declarations for λ-variables and μ-variables, and declaration of term variables and predicate variables. In our case, a context also contains term equivalences and inequivalences. A context is built using the following grammar.*

$$
\begin{aligned}
\Gamma, \Delta ::= \bullet &\mid \Gamma, x : A \mid \Gamma, \alpha : \neg A \mid \Gamma, a : Term\\
&\mid \Gamma, X_n : Pred_n \mid \Gamma, t \equiv u \mid \Gamma, t \not\equiv u
\end{aligned}
$$

A context Γ is said to be valid if it is possible to derive Γ Valid using the rules of Fig. 1. In the following, every context will be considered valid implicitly.

$$\frac{\Gamma \text{ Valid} \qquad x \notin dom(\Gamma) \qquad FV(A) \subseteq dom(\Gamma) \cup \{x\}}{\Gamma, x : A \text{ Valid}}$$

$$\frac{\Gamma \text{ Valid} \qquad \alpha \notin dom(\Gamma) \qquad FV(A) \subseteq dom(\Gamma)}{\Gamma, \alpha : \neg A \text{ Valid}}$$

$$\frac{\Gamma \text{ Valid} \qquad a \notin dom(\Gamma)}{\Gamma, a : Term \text{ Valid}} \qquad \frac{\Gamma \text{ Valid} \qquad X_n \notin dom(\Gamma)}{\Gamma, X_n : Pred_n \text{ Valid}}$$

$$\frac{\Gamma \text{ Valid} \qquad FV(t) \cup FV(u) \subseteq dom(\Gamma)}{\Gamma, t \equiv u \text{ Valid}}$$

$$\frac{\Gamma \text{ Valid} \qquad FV(t) \cup FV(u) \subseteq dom(\Gamma)}{\Gamma, t \not\equiv u \text{ Valid}} \qquad \frac{}{\bullet \text{ Valid}}$$

Fig. 1. Rules allowing the construction of a valid context.

Definition 16. *There are two forms of typing judgements:*

- $\Gamma \vdash_{val} v : A$ *meaning that the value* v *has type* A *in context* Γ,
- $\Gamma \vdash t : A$ *meaning that the term* t *has type* A *in context* Γ.

The typing rules of the system are given in Fig. 2. Although most of them are fairly usual, our type system differs in several ways. For instance the last four rules are related to the extensionality of the calculus. One can note the value restriction in several places: both universal quantification introduction rules and the introduction of the membership predicate. In fact, some value restriction is also hidden in the rules for the elimination of the existential quantifiers and the elimination rule for the restriction connective. These rules are presented in their left-hand side variation, and only values can appear on the left of the sequent. It is not surprising that elimination of an existential quantifier requires value restriction as it is the dual of the introduction rule of a universal quantifier.

An important and interesting difference with existing type systems is the presence of $\uparrow$ and $\downarrow$. These two rules allow one to go from one kind of sequent to the other when working on values. Going from $\Gamma \vdash_{\text{val}} v : A$ to $\Gamma \vdash v : A$ is straight-forward. Going the other direction is the main motivation for our model. This allows us to lift the value restriction expressed in the syntax to a restriction expressed in terms of equivalence. For example, the two rules

$$\frac{\Gamma, t \equiv v \vdash t : A \qquad a \notin FV(\Gamma)}{\Gamma, t \equiv v \vdash t : \forall a\, A} \forall_{i,\equiv}$$

$$\frac{\Gamma, u \equiv v \vdash t : \Pi_{a:A} B \qquad \Gamma, u \equiv v \vdash u : A}{\Gamma, u \equiv v \vdash t\, u : B[a := u]} \Pi_{e,\equiv}$$

$$\frac{}{\Gamma, x : A \vdash_{\text{val}} x : A}\ \text{ax} \qquad \frac{\Gamma \vdash_{\text{val}} v : A}{\Gamma \vdash v : A}\ \uparrow \qquad \frac{\Gamma \vdash v : A}{\Gamma \vdash_{\text{val}} v : A}\ \downarrow$$

$$\frac{\Gamma \vdash t : A \Rightarrow B \qquad \Gamma \vdash u : A}{\Gamma \vdash t\, u : B}\ \Rightarrow_e \qquad \frac{\Gamma, x : A \vdash t : B}{\Gamma \vdash_{\text{val}} \lambda x\, t : A \Rightarrow B}\ \Rightarrow_i$$

$$\frac{\Gamma, \alpha : \neg A \vdash t : A}{\Gamma \vdash \mu\alpha\, t : A}\ \mu \qquad \frac{\Gamma, \alpha : \neg A \vdash t : A}{\Gamma, \alpha : \neg A \vdash t * \alpha : B}\ *$$

$$\frac{\Gamma \vdash_{\text{val}} v : A}{\Gamma \vdash_{\text{val}} v : v \in A}\ \in_i \qquad \frac{\Gamma, x : A, x \equiv u \vdash t : A}{\Gamma, x : u \in A \vdash t : A}\ \in_e$$

$$\frac{\Gamma, u_1 \equiv u_2 \vdash t : A}{\Gamma, u_1 \equiv u_2 \vdash t : A \upharpoonright u_1 \equiv u_2}\ \upharpoonright_i \qquad \frac{\Gamma, x : A, u_1 \equiv u_2 \vdash t : B}{\Gamma, x : A \upharpoonright u_1 \equiv u_2 \vdash t : B}\ \upharpoonright_e$$

$$\frac{\Gamma \vdash_{\text{val}} v : A \qquad a \notin FV(\Gamma)}{\Gamma \vdash_{\text{val}} v : \forall a\, A}\ \forall_i \qquad \frac{\Gamma \vdash t : \forall a\, A}{\Gamma \vdash t : A[a := u]}\ \forall_e$$

$$\frac{\Gamma, y : A \vdash t : B \qquad a \notin FV(\Gamma, B) \cup TV(t)}{\Gamma, y : \exists a\, A \vdash t : B}\ \exists_e \qquad \frac{\Gamma \vdash t : A[a := u]}{\Gamma \vdash t : \exists a\, A}\ \exists_i$$

$$\frac{\Gamma \vdash_{\text{val}} v : A \qquad X_n \notin FV(\Gamma)}{\Gamma \vdash_{\text{val}} v : \forall X_n\, A}\ \forall_I \qquad \frac{\Gamma \vdash t : \forall X_n\, A}{\Gamma \vdash t : A[X_n := P]}\ \forall_E$$

$$\frac{\Gamma, x : A \vdash t : B \qquad X_n \notin FV(\Gamma, B)}{\Gamma, x : \exists X_n\, A \vdash t : B}\ \exists_E \qquad \frac{\Gamma \vdash t : A[X_n := P]}{\Gamma \vdash t : \exists X_n\, A}\ \exists_I$$

$$\frac{[\Gamma \vdash_{\text{val}} v_i : A_i]_{1 \le i \le n}}{\Gamma \vdash_{\text{val}} \{l_i = v_i\}_{i=1}^{n} : \{l_i : A_i\}_{1 \le i \le n}}\ \times_i \qquad \frac{\Gamma \vdash_{\text{val}} v : \{l_i : A_i\}_{1 \le i \le n}}{\Gamma \vdash v.l_i : A_i}\ \times_e$$

$$\frac{\Gamma \vdash_{\text{val}} v : A_i}{\Gamma \vdash_{\text{val}} C_i[v] : [C_i : A_i]_{1 \le i \le n}}\ +_i$$

$$\frac{\Gamma \vdash_{\text{val}} v : [C_i : A_i]_{1 \le i \le n} \qquad [\Gamma, x : A_i, C_i[x] \equiv v \vdash t_i : B]_{1 \le i \le n}}{\Gamma \vdash case_v\ [C_i[x] \to t_i]_{1 \le i \le n} : B}\ +_e$$

$$\frac{\Gamma, w_1 \equiv w_2 \vdash t[x := w_1] : A}{\Gamma, w_1 \equiv w_2 \vdash t[x := w_2] : A}\ \equiv_{v,l} \qquad \frac{\Gamma, t_1 \equiv t_2 \vdash t[a := t_1] : A}{\Gamma, t_1 \equiv t_2 \vdash t[a := t_2] : A}\ \equiv_{t,l}$$

$$\frac{\Gamma, w_1 \equiv w_2 \vdash t : A[x := w_1]}{\Gamma, w_1 \equiv w_2 \vdash t : A[x := w_2]}\ \equiv_{v,r} \qquad \frac{\Gamma, t_1 \equiv t_2 \vdash t : A[a := t_1]}{\Gamma, t_1 \equiv t_2 \vdash t : A[a := t_2]}\ \equiv_{t,r}$$

Fig. 2. Second-order type system.

$$\dfrac{\dfrac{\dfrac{\dfrac{\dfrac{\Gamma, t \equiv v \vdash t : A}{\Gamma, t \equiv v \vdash v : A}\equiv_{t,l}}{\Gamma, t \equiv v \vdash_{\text{val}} v : A}\downarrow \qquad a \notin FV(\Gamma)}{\Gamma, t \equiv v \vdash_{\text{val}} v : \forall a\, A}\forall_i}{\Gamma, t \equiv v \vdash v : \forall a\, A}\uparrow}{\Gamma, t \equiv v \vdash t : \forall a\, A}\equiv_{t,l}$$

$$\dfrac{\dfrac{\dfrac{\Gamma, u \equiv v \vdash t : \Pi_{a:A} B}{\Gamma, u \equiv v \vdash t : \forall a (a \in A \Rightarrow B)}}{\Gamma, u \equiv v \vdash t : u \in A \Rightarrow B[a := u]}\forall_e \qquad \dfrac{\dfrac{\dfrac{\dfrac{\dfrac{\dfrac{\dfrac{\Gamma, u \equiv v \vdash u : A}{\Gamma, u \equiv v \vdash v : A}\equiv_{t,l}}{\Gamma, u \equiv v \vdash_{\text{val}} v : A}\downarrow}{\Gamma, u \equiv v \vdash_{\text{val}} v : v \in A}\in_i}{\Gamma, u \equiv v \vdash v : v \in A}\uparrow}{\Gamma, u \equiv v \vdash u : v \in A}\equiv_{t,l}}{\Gamma, u \equiv v \vdash u : u \in A}\equiv_{t,r}}{}}{\Gamma, u \equiv v \vdash t\, u : B[a := u]}\Rightarrow_e$$

Fig. 3. Derivation of the rules $\forall_{i,\equiv}$ and $\Pi_{e,\equiv}$.

can be derived in the system (see Fig. 3). The value restriction can be removed similarly on every other rule. Thus, judgements on values can be completely ignored by the user of the system. Transition to value judgements will only happen internally.

6.4 Adequacy

We are now going to prove the soundness of our type system by showing that it is compatible with our realizability model. This property is specified by the following theorem which is traditionally called the adequacy lemma.

Definition 17. *Let Γ be a (valid) context. We say that the substitution σ realizes Γ if:*

- *for every $x : A$ in Γ we have $\sigma(x) \in [\![A]\!]_\sigma$,*
- *for every $\alpha : \neg A$ in Γ we have $\sigma(\alpha) \in [\![A]\!]_\sigma^\perp$,*
- *for every $a : Term$ in Γ we have $\sigma(a) \in \Lambda$,*
- *for every $X_n : Pred_n$ in Γ we have $\sigma(X_n) \in \Lambda^n \to \Lambda_v/\equiv$,*
- *for every $t \equiv u$ in Γ we have $t\sigma \equiv u\sigma$ and*
- *for every $t \not\equiv u$ in Γ we have $t\sigma \not\equiv u\sigma$.*

Theorem 6 (Adequacy). *Let Γ be a (valid) context, A be a formula such that $FV(A) \subseteq dom(\Gamma)$ and σ be a substitution realizing Γ.*

- *If $\Gamma \vdash_{val} v : A$ then $v\sigma \in [\![A]\!]_\sigma$,*
- *if $\Gamma \vdash t : A$ then $t\sigma \in [\![A]\!]_\sigma^{\perp\perp}$.*

Proof. We proceed by induction on the derivation of the judgement $\Gamma \vdash_{\text{val}} v : A$ (resp. $\Gamma \vdash t : A$) and we reason by case on the last rule used.

(ax) By hypothesis σ realizes $\Gamma, x : A$ from which we directly obtain $x\sigma \in [\![A]\!]_\sigma$.

($\uparrow$) and ($\downarrow$) are direct consequences of Lemma 7 and Theorem 4 respectively.

($\Rightarrow_e$) We need to prove that $t\sigma\ u\sigma \in [\![B]\!]_\sigma^{\bot\bot}$, hence we take $\pi \in [\![B]\!]_\sigma^{\bot}$ and show $t\sigma\ u\sigma * \pi \in \bot\!\!\!\bot$. Since $\bot\!\!\!\bot$ is saturated, we can take a reduction step and show $u\sigma * [t\sigma]\pi \in \bot\!\!\!\bot$. By induction hypothesis $u\sigma \in [\![A]\!]_\sigma^{\bot\bot}$ so we only have to show $[t\sigma]\pi \in [\![A]\!]_\sigma^{\bot}$. To do so we take $v \in [\![A]\!]_\sigma$ and show $v * [t\sigma]\pi \in \bot\!\!\!\bot$. Here we can again take a reduction step and show $t\sigma * v.\pi \in \bot\!\!\!\bot$. By induction hypothesis we have $t\sigma \in [\![A \Rightarrow B]\!]_\sigma^{\bot\bot}$, hence it is enough to show $v.\pi \in [\![A \Rightarrow B]\!]_\sigma^{\bot}$. We now take a value $\lambda x\ t_x \in [\![A \Rightarrow B]\!]_\sigma$ and show that $\lambda x\ t_x * v.\pi \in \bot\!\!\!\bot$. We then apply again a reduction step and show $t_x[x := v] * \pi \in \bot\!\!\!\bot$. Since $\pi \in [\![B]\!]_\sigma^{\bot}$ we only need to show $t_x[x := v] \in [\![B]\!]_\sigma^{\bot\bot}$ which is true by definition of $[\![A \Rightarrow B]\!]_\sigma$.

($\Rightarrow_i$) We need to show $\lambda x\ t\sigma \in [\![A \Rightarrow B]\!]_\sigma$ so we take $v \in [\![A]\!]_\sigma$ and show $t\sigma[x := v] \in [\![B]\!]_\sigma^{\bot\bot}$. Since $\sigma[x := v]$ realizes $\Gamma, x : A$ we can conclude using the induction hypothesis.

(μ) We need to show that $\mu\alpha\ t\sigma \in [\![A]\!]_\sigma^{\bot\bot}$ hence we take $\pi \in [\![A]\!]_\sigma^{\bot}$ and show $\mu\alpha\ t\sigma * \pi \in \bot\!\!\!\bot$. Since $\bot\!\!\!\bot$ is saturated, it is enough to show $t\sigma[\alpha := \pi] * \pi \in \bot\!\!\!\bot$. As $\sigma[\alpha := \pi]$ realizes $\Gamma, \alpha : \neg A$ we conclude by induction hypothesis.

($*$) We need to show $t\sigma * \alpha\sigma \in [\![B]\!]_\sigma^{\bot\bot}$, hence we take $\pi \in [\![B]\!]_\sigma^{\bot}$ and show that $(t\sigma * \alpha\sigma) * \pi \in \bot\!\!\!\bot$. Since $\bot\!\!\!\bot$ is saturated, we can take a reduction step and show $t\sigma * \alpha\sigma \in \bot\!\!\!\bot$. By induction hypothesis $t\sigma \in [\![A]\!]_\sigma^{\bot\bot}$ hence it is enough to show $\alpha\sigma \in [\![A]\!]_\sigma^{\bot}$ which is true by hypothesis.

($\in_i$) We need to show $v\sigma \in [\![v \in A]\!]_\sigma$. We have $v\sigma \in [\![A]\!]_\sigma$ by induction hypothesis, and $v\sigma \equiv v\sigma$ by reflexivity of ($\equiv$).

($\in_e$) By hypothesis we know that σ realizes $\Gamma, x : u \in A$. To be able to conclude using the induction hypothesis, we need to show that σ realizes $\Gamma, x : A, x \equiv u$. Since we have $\sigma(x) \in [\![u \in A]\!]_\sigma$, we obtain that $x\sigma \in [\![A]\!]_\sigma$ and $x\sigma \equiv u\sigma$ by definition of $[\![u \in A]\!]_\sigma$.

($\restriction_i$) We need to show $t\sigma \in [\![A \restriction u_1 \equiv u_2]\!]_\sigma^{\bot\bot}$. By hypothesis $u_1\sigma \equiv u_2\sigma$, hence $[\![A \restriction u_1 \equiv u_2]\!]_\sigma = [\![A]\!]_\sigma$. Consequently, it is enough to show that $t\sigma \in [\![A]\!]_\sigma^{\bot\bot}$, which is exactly the induction hypothesis.

($\restriction_e$) By hypothesis we know that σ realizes $\Gamma, x : A \restriction u_1 \equiv u_2$. To be able to use the induction hypothesis, we need to show that σ realizes $\Gamma, x : A, u_1 \equiv u_2$. Since we have $\sigma(x) \in [\![A \restriction u_1 \equiv u_2]\!]_\sigma$, we obtain that $x\sigma \in [\![A]\!]_\sigma$ and that $u_1\sigma \equiv u_2\sigma$ by definition of $[\![A \restriction u_1 \equiv u_2]\!]_\sigma$.

($\forall_i$) We need to show that $v\sigma \in [\![\forall a\ A]\!]_\sigma = \bigcap_{t \in \Lambda} [\![A]\!]_{\sigma[a:=t]}$ so we take $t \in \Lambda$ and show $v\sigma \in [\![A]\!]_{\sigma[a:=t]}$. This is true by induction hypothesis since $a \notin FV(\Gamma)$ and hence $\sigma[a := t]$ realizes Γ.

($\forall_e$) We need to show $t\sigma \in [\![A[a := u]]\!]_\sigma^{\bot\bot} = [\![A]\!]_{\sigma[a:=u\sigma]}^{\bot\bot}$ for some $u \in \Lambda$. By induction hypothesis we know $t\sigma \in [\![\forall a\ A]\!]_\sigma^{\bot\bot}$, hence we only need to show that $[\![\forall a\ A]\!]_\sigma^{\bot\bot} \subseteq [\![A]\!]_{\sigma[a:=u\sigma]}^{\bot\bot}$. By definition we have $[\![\forall a\ A]\!]_\sigma \subseteq [\![A]\!]_{\sigma[a:=u\sigma]}$ so we can conclude using Lemma 8.

($\exists_e$) By hypothesis we know that σ realizes $\Gamma, x : \exists a\ A$. In particular, we know that $\sigma(x) \in [\![\exists a\ A]\!]_\sigma$, which means that there is a term $u \in \Lambda^*$ such that

$\sigma(x) \in [\![A]\!]_{\sigma[a:=u]}$. Since $a \notin FV(\Gamma)$, we obtain that the substitution $\sigma[a := u]$ realizes the context $\Gamma, x : A$. Using the induction hypothesis, we finally get $t\sigma = t\sigma[a := u] \in [\![B]\!]^{\perp\perp}_{\sigma[a:=u]} = [\![B]\!]^{\perp\perp}_{\sigma}$ since $a \notin TV(t)$ and $a \notin FV(B)$.

($\exists_i$) The proof for this rule is similar to the one for *($\forall_e$)*. We need to show that $[\![A[a := u]]\!]^{\perp\perp}_{\sigma} = [\![A]\!]^{\perp\perp}_{\sigma[a:=u\sigma]} \subseteq [\![\exists a\ A]\!]^{\perp\perp}_{\sigma}$. This follows from Lemma 8 since $[\![A]\!]_{\sigma[a:=u\sigma]} \subseteq [\![\exists a\ A]\!]_{\sigma}$ by definition.

($\forall_I$), ($\forall_E$), ($\exists_E$) and ($\exists_I$) are similar to similar to ($\forall_i$), ($\forall_e$), ($\exists_e$) and ($\exists_i$).

($\times_i$) We need to show that $\{l_i = v_i\sigma\}_{i\in I} \in [\![\{l_i : A_i\}_{i\in I}]\!]_{\sigma}$. By definition we need to show that for all $i \in I$ we have $v_i\sigma \in [\![A_i]\!]_{\sigma}$. This is immediate by induction hypothesis.

($\times_e$) We need to show that $v\sigma.l_i \in [\![A_i]\!]^{\perp\perp}_{\sigma}$ for some $i \in I$. By induction hypothesis we have $v\sigma \in [\![\{l_i : A_i\}_{i\in I}]\!]_{\sigma}$ and hence v has the form $\{l_i = v_i\}_{i\in I}$ with $v_i\sigma \in [\![A_i]\!]_{\sigma}$. Let us now take $\pi \in [\![A_i]\!]^{\perp}_{\sigma}$ and show that $\{l_i = v_i\sigma\}_{i\in I}.l_i * \pi \in \perp\!\!\!\perp$. Since $\perp\!\!\!\perp$ is saturated, it is enough to show $v_i\sigma * \pi \in \perp\!\!\!\perp$. This is true since $v_i\sigma \in [\![A_i]\!]_{\sigma}$ and $\pi \in [\![A_i]\!]^{\perp}_{\sigma}$.

($+_i$) We need to show $C_i[v\sigma] \in [\![[C_i : A_i]_{i\in I}]\!]_{\sigma}$ for some $i \in I$. By induction hypothesis $v\sigma \in [\![A_i]\!]_{\sigma}$ and hence we can conclude by definition of $[\![[C_i : A_i]_{i\in I}]\!]_{\sigma}$.

($+_e$) We need to show $case_{v\sigma}\ [C_i[x] \to t_i\sigma]_{i\in I} \in [\![B]\!]^{\perp\perp}_{\sigma}$. By induction hypothesis $v\sigma \in [\![[C_i of A_i]_{i\in I}]\!]_{\sigma}$ which means that there is $i \in I$ and $w \in [\![A_i]\!]_{\sigma}$ such that $v\sigma = C_i[w]$. We take $\pi \in [\![B]\!]^{\perp}_{\sigma}$ and show $\text{case}_{C_i[w]}\ [C_i[x] \to t_i\sigma]_{i\in I} * \pi \in \perp\!\!\!\perp$. Since $\perp\!\!\!\perp$ is saturated, it is enough to show $t_i\sigma[x := w] * \pi \in \perp\!\!\!\perp$. It remains to show that $t_i\sigma[x := w] \in [\![B]\!]^{\perp\perp}_{\sigma}$. To be able to conclude using the induction hypothesis we need to show that $\sigma[x := w]$ realizes $\Gamma, x : A_i, C_i[x] \equiv v$. This is true since σ realizes Γ, $w \in [\![A_i]\!]_{\sigma}$ and $C_i[w] \equiv v\sigma$ by reflexivity.

($\equiv_{v,l}$) We need to show $t[x := w_1]\sigma = t\sigma[x := w_1\sigma] \in [\![A]\!]_{\sigma}$. By hypothesis we know that $w_1\sigma \equiv w_2\sigma$ from which we can deduce $t\sigma[x := w_1\sigma] \equiv t\sigma[x := w_2\sigma]$ by extensionality (Theorem 2). Since $[\![A]\!]_{\sigma}$ is closed under ($\equiv$) we can conclude using the induction hypothesis.

($\equiv_{t,l}$), ($\equiv_{v,r}$) and ($\equiv_{t,r}$) are similar to ($\equiv_{v,l}$), using extensionality (Theorems 2 and 3).

Remark 7. For the sake of simplicity we fixed a pole $\perp\!\!\!\perp$ at the beginning of the current section. However, many of the properties presented here (including the adequacy lemma) remain valid with similar poles. We will make use of this fact in the proof of the following theorem.

Theorem 7 (Safety). *Let Γ be a context, A be a formula such that $FV(A) \subseteq dom(\Gamma)$ and σ be a substitution realizing Γ. If t is a term such that $\Gamma \vdash t : A$ and if $A[\sigma]$ is pure (i.e. it does not contain any $\_ \Rightarrow \_$), then for every stack $\pi \in [\![A]\!]^{\perp}_{\sigma}$ there is a value $v \in [\![A]\!]_{\sigma}$ and $\alpha \in \mathcal{V}_{\mu}$ such that $t\sigma * \pi \twoheadrightarrow^* v * \alpha$.*

Proof. We do a proof by realizability using the following pole.

$$\perp\!\!\!\perp_A = \{p \in \Lambda \times \Pi \mid p \twoheadrightarrow^* v * \alpha \ \wedge\ v \in [\![A]\!]_{\sigma}\}$$

It is well-defined as A is pure and hence $[\![A]\!]_{\sigma}$ does not depend on the pole. Using the adequacy lemma (Theorem 6) with $\perp\!\!\!\perp_A$ we obtain $t\sigma \in [\![A]\!]^{\perp\perp}_{\sigma}$. Hence for every stack $\pi \in [\![A]\!]_\sigma^\perp$ we have $t\sigma * \pi \in \perp\!\!\!\perp_A$. We can then conclude using the definition of the pole $\perp\!\!\!\perp_A$.

Remark 8. It is easy to see that if $A[\sigma]$ is closed and pure then $v \in [\![A]\!]_\sigma$ implies that $\bullet \vdash v : A$.

Theorem 8 (Consistency). *There is no t such that $\bullet \vdash t : \bot$.*

Proof. Let us suppose that $\bullet \vdash t : \bot$. Using adequacy (Theorem 6) we obtain that $t \in [\![\bot]\!]_\sigma^{\perp\perp}$. Since $[\![\bot]\!]_\sigma = \emptyset$ we know that $[\![\bot]\!]_\sigma^\perp = \Pi$ by definition. Now using Theorem 5 we obtain $[\![\bot]\!]_\sigma^{\perp\perp} = \emptyset$. This is a contradiction.

7 Deciding Program Equivalence

The type system given in Fig. 2 does not provide any way of discharging an equivalence from the context. As a consequence the truth of an equivalence cannot be used. Furthermore, an equational contradiction in the context cannot be used to derive falsehood. To address these two problems, we will rely on a partial decision procedure for the equivalence of terms. Such a procedure can be easily implemented using an algorithm similar to Knuth-Bendix, provided that we are able to extract a set of equational axioms from the definition of $(\equiv)$. In particular, we will use the following lemma to show that several reduction rules are contained in $(\equiv)$.

Lemma 9. *Let t and u be terms. If for every stack $\pi \in \Pi$ there is $p \in \Lambda \times \Pi$ such that $t * \pi \succ^* p$ and $u * \pi \succ^* p$ then $t \equiv u$.*

Proof. Since $(\succ) \subseteq (\twoheadrightarrow_i)$ for every $i \in \mathbb{N}$, we can deduce that $t * \pi \twoheadrightarrow_i^* p$ and $u * \pi \twoheadrightarrow_i^* p$ for every $i \in \mathbb{N}$. Using Lemma 1 we can deduce that for every substitution σ we have $t\sigma * \pi \twoheadrightarrow_i^* p\sigma$ and $u\sigma * \pi \twoheadrightarrow_i^* p\sigma$ for all $i \in \mathbb{N}$. Consequently we obtain $t \equiv u$.

The equivalence relation contains call-by-value β-reduction, projection on records and case analysis on variants.

Theorem 9. *For every $x \in \mathcal{V}_\lambda$, $t \in \Lambda$ and $v \in \Lambda_v$ we have $(\lambda x\ t)v \equiv t[x := v]$.*

Proof. Immediate using Lemma 9.

Theorem 10. *For all k such that $1 \leq k \leq n$ we have the following equivalences.*

$$(\lambda x\ t)v \equiv t[x := v] \qquad\qquad case_{C_k[v]}\ [C_i[x_i] \to t_i]_{1 \leq i \leq n} \equiv t_k[x_k := v]$$

Proof. Immediate using Lemma 9.

To observe contradictions, we also need to derive some inequivalences on values. For instance, we would like to deduce a contradiction if two values with a different head constructor are assumed to be equivalent.

Theorem 11. *Let $C, D \in \mathcal{C}$ be constructors, and $v, w \in \Lambda_v$ be values. If $C \neq D$ then $C[v] \not\equiv D[w]$.*

Proof. We take $\pi = [\lambda x \text{ case}_x [C[y] \to y \mid D[y] \to \Omega]]\alpha$ where Ω is an arbitrary diverging term. We then obtain $C[v] * \pi \Downarrow_0$ and $D[w] * \pi \Uparrow_0$.

Theorem 12. *Let $\{l_i = v_i\}_{i \in I}$ and $\{l_j = v_j\}_{j \in J}$ be two records. If k is a index such that $k \in I$ and $k \notin J$ then we have $\{l_i = v_i\}_{i \in I} \not\equiv \{l_j = v_j\}_{j \in J}$.*

Proof. Immediate using the stack $\pi = [\lambda x\ x.l_k]\alpha$.

Theorem 13. *For every $x \in \mathcal{V}_\lambda$, $v \in \Lambda_v$, $t \in \Lambda$, $C \in \mathcal{C}$ and for every record $\{l_i = v_i\}_{i \in I}$ we have the following inequivalences.*

$$\lambda x\ t \not\equiv C[v] \qquad \lambda x\ t \not\equiv \{l_i = v_i\}_{i \in I} \qquad C[v] \not\equiv \{l_i = v_i\}_{i \in I}$$

Proof. The proof is mostly similar to the proofs of the previous two theorems. However, there is a subtlety with the second inequivalence. If for every value v the term $t[x := v]$ diverges, then we do not have $\lambda x\ t \not\equiv \{\}$. Indeed, there is no evaluation context (or stack) that is able to distinguish the empty record $\{\}$ and a diverging function. To solve this problem, we can extend the language with a new kind of term unit_v and extend the relation $(\succ)$ with the following rule.

$$\text{unit}_{\{\}} * \pi \quad \succ \quad \{\} * \pi$$

The process $\text{unit}_v * \pi$ is stuck for every value $v \neq \{\}$. The proof can the be completed using the stack $\pi = [\lambda x\ \text{unit}_x]\alpha$.

The previous five theorems together with the extensionality of $(\equiv)$ and its properties as an equivalence relation can be used to implement a partial decision procedure for equivalence. We will incorporate this procedure into the typing rules by introducing a new form of judgment.

Definition 18. *An equational context $\mathcal{E}$ is a list of hypothetical equivalences and inequivalences. Equational contexts are built using the following grammar.*

$$\mathcal{E} \ := \ \bullet \ \mid \ \mathcal{E}, t \equiv u \ \mid \ \mathcal{E}, t \not\equiv u$$

Given a context Γ, we denote $\mathcal{E}_\Gamma$ its restriction to an equational context.

Definition 19. *Let $\mathcal{E}$ be an equational context. The judgement $\mathcal{E} \vdash \bot$ is valid if and only if the partial decision procedure is able to derive a contradiction in $\mathcal{E}$. We will write $\mathcal{E} \vdash t \equiv u$ for $\mathcal{E}, t \not\equiv u \vdash \bot$ and $\mathcal{E} \vdash t \not\equiv u$ for $\mathcal{E}, t \equiv u \vdash \bot$*

To discharge equations from the context, the following two typing rules are added to the system.

$$\frac{\Gamma, u_1 \equiv u_2 \vdash t : A \qquad \mathcal{E}_\Gamma \vdash u_1 \equiv u_2}{\Gamma \vdash t : A} \equiv$$

$$\frac{\Gamma, u_1 \not\equiv u_2 \vdash t : A \qquad \mathcal{E}_\Gamma \vdash u_1 \not\equiv u_2}{\Gamma \vdash t : A} \not\equiv$$

The soundness of these new rules follows easily since the decision procedure agrees with the semantical notion of equivalence. The axioms that were given at the beginning of this section are only used to partially reflect the semantical equivalence relation in the syntax. This is required if we are to implement the decision procedure.

Another way to use an equational context is to derive a contradiction directly. For instance, if we have a context Γ such that $\mathcal{E}_\Gamma$ yields a contradiction, one should be able to finish the corresponding proof. This is particularly useful when working with variants and case analysis. For instance, some branches of the case analysis might not be reachable due to constraints on the matched term. For instance, we know that in the term

$$\text{case}_{C[v]}\ [C[x] \rightarrow x \mid D[x] \rightarrow t]$$

the branch corresponding to the D constructor will never be reached. Consequently, we can replace t by any term and the computation will still behave correctly. For this purpose we introduce a special value 8< on which the abstract machine fails. It can be introduced with the following typing rule.

$$\frac{\mathcal{E}_\Gamma \vdash \bot}{\Gamma \vdash_{\text{val}} \texttt{8<} : \bot} \texttt{8<}$$

The soundness of this rule is again immediate.

8 Further Work

The model presented in the previous sections is intended to be used as the basis for the design of a proof assistant based on a call-by-value ML language with control operators. A first prototype (with a different theoretical foundation) was implemented by Christophe Raffalli [27]. Based on this experience, the design of a new version of the language with a clean theoretical basis can now be undertaken. The core of the system will consist of three independent components: a type-checker, a termination checker and a decision procedure for equivalence.

Working with a Curry style language has the disadvantage of making type-checking undecidable. While most proof systems avoid this problem by switching to Church style, it is possible to use heuristics making most Curry style programs that arise in practice directly typable. Christophe Raffalli implemented such a system [26] and from his experience it would seem that very little help from the user is required in general. In particular, if a term is typable then it is possible for the user to provide hints (e.g. the type of a variable) so that type-checking may succeed. This can be seen as a kind of completeness.

Proof assistants like Coq [18] or Agda [22] both have decidable type-checking algorithms. However, these systems provide mechanisms for handling implicit arguments or meta-variables which introduce some incompleteness. This does not make these systems any less usable in practice. We conjecture that going even further (i.e. full Curry style) provides a similar user experience.

To obtain a practical programming language we will need support for recursive programs. For this purpose we plan on adapting Pierre Hyvernat's termination checker [9]. It is based on size change termination and has already been used in the first prototype implementation. We will also need to extend our type system with inductive (and coinductive) types [19,25]. They can be introduced in the system using fixpoints $\mu X\, A$ (and $\nu X\, A$).

Acknowledgments. I would like to particularly thank my research advisor, Christophe Raffalli, for his guidance and input. I would also like to thank Alexandre Miquel for suggesting the encoding of dependent products. Thank you also to Pierre Hyvernat, Tom Hirschowitz, Robert Harper and the anonymous reviewers for their very helpful comments.

References

1. Casinghino, C., Sjberg, V., Weirich, S.: Combining proofs and programs in a dependently typed language. In: Jagannathan, S., Sewell, P. (eds.) 41st Annual ACM SIGPLAN-SIGACT Symposium on Principles of Programming Languages, POPL 2014, pp. 33–46. ACM, San Diego (2014)
2. Constable, R.L., Allen, S.F., Bromley, M., Cleaveland, R., Cremer, J.F., Harper, R.W., Howe, D.J., Knoblock, T.B., Mendler, N.P., Panangaden, P., Sasaki, J.T., Smith, S.F.: Implementing mathematics with the Nuprl proof development system. Prentice Hall, Upper Saddle River (1986)
3. Coquand, T., Huet, G.: The calculus of constructions. Inf. Comput. **76**(2–3), 95–120 (1988)
4. Damas, L., Milner, R.: Principal type-schemes for functional programs. In: Proceedings of the 9th ACM SIGPLAN-SIGACT Symposium on Principles of Programming Languages, POPL 1982, pp. 207–212. ACM, New York (1982)
5. Garrigue, J.: Relaxing the value restriction. In: Kameyama, Y., Stuckey, P.J. (eds.) FLOPS 2004. LNCS, vol. 2998, pp. 196–213. Springer, Heidelberg (2004)
6. Griffin, T.G.: A formulæ-as-types notion of control. In: Conference Record of the Seventeenth Annual ACM Symposium on Principles of Programming Languages, pp. 47–58. ACM Press (1990)
7. Harper, R., Lillibridge, M.: ML with callcc is unsound (1991). http://www.seas.upenn.edu/~sweirich/types/archive/1991/msg00034.html
8. Howe, D.J.: Equality in lazy computation systems. In: Proceedings of the Fourth Annual Symposium on Logic in Computer Science (LICS 1989), 5–8 June 1989, Pacific Grove, California, USA, pp. 198–203 (1989)
9. Hyvernat, P.: The size-change termination principle for constructor based languages. Logical Methods Comput. Sci. **10**(1) (2014). http://www.lmcs-online.org/ojs/viewarticle.php?id=1409&layout=abstract
10. Jia, L., Vaughan, J.A., Mazurak, K., Zhao, J., Zarko, L., Schorr, J., Zdancewic, S.: AURA: a programming language for authorization and audit. In: Hook, J., Thiemann, P. (eds.) Proceeding of the 13th ACM SIGPLAN International Conference on Functional Programming, ICFP 2008, 20–28 September 2008, Victoria, BC, Canada, pp. 27–38. ACM (2008)

11. Krivine, J.: A call-by-name lambda-calculus machine. Higher-Order Symb. Comput. **20**(3), 199–207 (2007)
12. Krivine, J.: Realizability in classical logic. In: Interactive Models of Computation and Program Behaviour, Panoramas et synthèses, vol. 27, pp. 197–229. Société Mathématique de France (2009)
13. Lepigre, R.: A realizability model for a semantical value restriction (2015). https://lama.univ-savoie.fr/~lepigre/files/docs/semvalrest2015.pdf
14. Leroy, X.: Polymorphism by name for references and continuations. In: 20th Symposium Principles of Programming Languages, pp. 220–231. ACM Press (1993)
15. Leroy, X., Weis, P.: Polymorphic type inference and assignment. In: Proceedings of the 18th ACM SIGPLAN-SIGACT Symposium on Principles of Programming Language, POPL 1991, pp. 291–302. ACM, New York (1991)
16. Licata, D.R., Harper, R.: Positively dependent types. In: Altenkirch, T., Millstein, T.D. (eds.) Proceedings of the 3rd ACM Workshop Programming Languages meets Program Verification, PLpPV 2009, 20 January 2009, Savannah, GA, USA, pp. 3–14. ACM (2009)
17. Martin-Löf, P.: Constructive mathematics and computer programming. In: Cohen, L.J., Pfeiffer, H., Podewski, K.P. (eds.) Logic, Methodology and Philosophy of Science VI, Studies in Logic and the Foundations of Mathematics, vol. 104, pp. 153–175. North-Holland (1982)
18. The Coq development team: The Coq proof assistant reference manual. LogiCal Project (2004). http://coq.inria.fr
19. Mendler, N.P.: Recursive types and type constraints in second-order lambda calculus. In: Proceedings of the Symposium on Logic in Computer Science (LICS 1987), pp. 30–36 (1987)
20. Miquel, A.: Le Calcul des constructions implicites: syntaxe et Sémantique. Ph.D. thesis, Université Paris VII (2001)
21. Munch-Maccagnoni, G.: Focalisation and classical realisability. In: Grädel, E., Kahle, R. (eds.) CSL 2009. LNCS, vol. 5771, pp. 409–423. Springer, Heidelberg (2009)
22. Norell, U.: Dependently typed programming in Agda. In: Koopman, P., Plasmeijer, R., Swierstra, D. (eds.) AFP 2008. LNCS, vol. 5832, pp. 230–266. Springer, Heidelberg (2009)
23. Owre, S., Rajan, S., Rushby, J., Shankar, N., Srivas, M.: PVS: Combining specification, proof checking, and model checking. In: Alur, R., Henzinger, T.A. (eds.) CAV 1996. LNCS, vol. 1102, pp. 411–414. Springer, Heidelberg (1996)
24. Parigot, M.: $\lambda\mu$-calculus: an algorithmic interpretation of classical. In: Voronkov, A. (ed.) LPAR 1992. LNCS, vol. 624, pp. 190–201. Springer, Heidelberg (1992)
25. Raffalli, C.: L'Arithmétiques Fonctionnelle du Second Ordre avec Points Fixes. Ph.D. thesis, Université Paris VII (1994)
26. Raffalli, C.: A normaliser for pure and typed λ-calculus (1996). http://lama.univ-savoie.fr/~raffalli/normaliser.html
27. Raffalli, C.: The PML programming language. LAMA - Université Savoie Mont-Blanc (2012). http://lama.univ-savoie.fr/tracpml/
28. Swamy, N., Chen, J., Fournet, C., Strub, P., Bhargavan, K., Yang, J.: Secure distributed programming with value-dependent types. In: Chakravarty, M.M.T., Hu, Z., Danvy, O. (eds.) Proceeding of the 16th ACM SIGPLAN international conference on Functional Programming, ICFP 2011, 19–21 September 2011, Tokyo, Japan, pp. 266–278. ACM (2011)
29. Tofte, M.: Type inference for polymorphic references. Inf. Comput. **89**(1), 1–34 (1990)

30. Wright, A.K.: Simple imperative polymorphism. LISP Symb. Comput. **8**, 343–356 (1995)
31. Wright, A.K., Felleisen, M.: A syntactic approach to type soundness. Inf. Comput. **115**(1), 38–94 (1994)
32. Xi, H.: Applied type system. In: Berardi, S., Coppo, M., Damiani, F. (eds.) TYPES 2003. LNCS, vol. 3085, pp. 394–408. Springer, Heidelberg (2004)
33. Xi, H., Pfenning, F.: Dependent types in practical programming. In: Proceedings of the 26th ACM SIGPLAN Symposium on Principles of Programming Languages, pp. 214–227, San Antonio, January 1999

Probabilistic Functions and Cryptographic Oracles in Higher Order Logic

Andreas Lochbihler(✉)

Institute of Information Securiy, Department of Computer Science, ETH Zurich, Zurich, Switzerland
andreas.lochbihler@inf.ethz.ch

Abstract. This paper presents a shallow embedding of a probabilistic functional programming language in higher order logic. The language features monadic sequencing, recursion, random sampling, failures and failure handling, and black-box access to oracles. Oracles are probabilistic functions which maintain hidden state between different invocations. To that end, we propose generative probabilistic systems as the semantic domain in which the operators of the language are defined. We prove that these operators are parametric and derive a relational program logic for reasoning about programs from parametricity. Several examples demonstrate that our language is suitable for conducting cryptographic proofs.

1 Introduction

As cryptographic algorithms and protocols are becoming increasingly complicated, flaws in their security proofs are more likely to be overlooked. So, security vulnerabilities can remain undiscovered. The game playing technique [16,29,48] helps in structuring such proofs and can thus increase the level of confidence in their correctness. In this view, security notions are expressed as programs (called games) in the same language as the cryptographic algorithms and protocols. The proof then consists of transforming the program in several small steps until the desired properties obviously hold. To achieve high assurance, several frameworks [8,14,42] and a proof assistant [13] offer machine support in formalising algorithms and security notions and in checking such sequences of game transformations. This way, many cryptographic constructions have been mechanically proven secure, e.g., [6,7,43].

For security protocols such as TLS, Kerberos, and IPSec, only few mechanised security proofs in the computational model are available, e.g., [18,21]. Instead, symbolic analysis tools [4,19,39,47] dominate. They model protocol messages as terms in an algebra rather than bitstrings and assume that cryptography is perfect. Computational soundness (CS) results [1,9,25] bridge the gap between symbolic and computational models, but to our knowledge, they have never been mechanically checked. Yet, mechanising them is desirable for three reasons. First, the proofs are extremely technical with many case distinctions. A proof assistant can check that all cases are covered and no assumption is forgotten (as has happened in early CS works), and it provides automation for dealing with the easy

P. Thiemann (Ed.): ESOP 2016, LNCS 9632, pp. 503–531, 2016.
DOI: 10.1007/978-3-662-49498-1_20

cases. Second, computational soundness results need to be formalised only once per set of cryptographic primitives, not for every protocol to which the symbolic analyser is applied. That is, one mechanised proof yields trustworthy proofs for a whole class of protocols. Third, mechanisation supports the evolution of models and proofs. If a primitive is added or an assumption weakened as in [10], the proof assistant checks the proofs again and pinpoints where adaptations are needed.

Unfortunately, the existing frameworks are not suitable for formalising CS proofs. CertiCrypt [14] and Verypto [8] formalise stateful languages in the proof assistants Coq and Isabelle, respectively. Due to the deep embedding, program transformations always require a proof about the semantics and programs cannot easily reuse the existing libraries of the proof assistants. Therefore, formalising cryptographic arguments requires a very substantial effort. CertiCrypt's successor EasyCrypt [13] provides much better automation using SMT solvers. Its logical foundation is higher order logic (HOL), but the reasoning infrastructure focuses on proofs in relational Hoare logic. However, substantial parts of CS proofs reason about the term algebra of the symbolic model for which EasyCrypt provides no support at all. The foundational cryptography framework (FCF) [42] alleviates CertiCrypt's formalisation burden by taking a semi-shallow approach in Coq. For pure deterministic functions, the framework reuses the language of the logic; only probabilistic effects and interaction with oracles are modelled syntactically as monads. This saves considerable effort in comparison to CertiCrypt. Yet, the monadic language lacks features such as recursion and exceptions, which are desirable for CS, e.g., to implement probabilistic serialisers and parsers.

Contributions. We present a framework for cryptographic proofs formalised in higher order logic. It consists of a probabilistic functional programming language and a logic for reasoning about programs and probabilities. The language features monadic sequencing, recursion, random sampling, failures and their handling, and black-box access to oracles. Oracles are probabilistic functions that maintain hidden state between different invocations. We model the language shallowly, i.e., we define the operators directly in the semantic domain. Programs which need no access to oracles are interpreted in the monad of discrete subprobabilities (Sect. 2.2); recursive functions are defined in terms of a least fixpoint operator (Sect. 2.3). For programs with oracle access, we propose *generative probabilistic systems* as semantic domain, which supports corecursive definitions (Sect. 3.2). In particular, we define operators for composing programs with oracles and other programs. We have implemented the framework in the proof assistant Isabelle/HOL [41], but it could be formalised in any other HOL-based prover, too.

The shallow embedding offers three benefits. First, we can reuse all the existing infrastructure of the proof assistant, such as name binding, higher-order unification and the module system, but also definitional packages and existing libraries. Second, we obtain a rich equational theory directly on programs, i.e., without any intervening interpretation function. Equality is important as we can replace terms by equal terms in any context (by HOL's substitution rule), i.e., there is no need for congruences. Consequently, proof automation can use the (conditional) equations directly for rewriting. Although no syntax is formalised in the logic, programs are still written as HOL terms. This suffices to guide syntax-directed proof tactics. Third, the language is not restricted to a fixed set of primitives. New operators can be defined in the semantic domain at any time.

Beyond equality, we provide a relational logic for reasoning about programs (Sects. 2.4 and 3.3). Relational parametricity [44,50] has been our guide in that most rules follow from the fact that the operators are parametric. In particular, we demonstrate that several common reasoning principles in cryptographic proofs follow from parametricity. This approach ensures soundness of the logic by construction and can also guide the discovery of proof rules for new operators. Our logic is similar to those of the other tools. The novelty is that we follow a principled way in finding the rules and establishing soundness.

Three examples demonstrate that our framework is suitable for cryptographic proofs. We proved indistinguishability under chosen plaintext attacks (IND-CPA) for (i) Elgamal public-key encryption [27] in the standard model (Sects. 2.1 and 2.5), (ii) Hashed Elgamal encryption in the random oracle model (Sects. 3.1 and 3.4), and (iii) an encryption scheme based on pseudo-random functions [42]. The examples have been chosen to enable comparisons with the existing frameworks (see Sect. 4). They show that our framework leads to concise proofs with the level of proof automation being comparable to EasyCrypt's, the current state of the art. This indicates that the framework scales to computational soundness results, although our examples are much simpler. Indeed, we have just started formalising a CS result, so this is only a first step. The framework and all examples and proofs have been formalised in Isabelle/HOL and are available online [37].

Preliminaries: HOL Notation. The meta-language HOL mostly uses everyday mathematical notation. Here, we present basic non-standard notation and a few types with their operations; further concepts will be introduced when needed.

HOL terms are simply typed lambda terms with let-polymorphism (we use Greek letters $\alpha, \beta, \ldots$ for type variables). Types include in particular the type of truth values bool and the singleton type unit with its only element $()$ and the space of total functions $\alpha \Rightarrow \beta$. Type constructors are normally written postfix, e.g., $\mathsf{bool\ list}$ denotes the type of finite lists of booleans, i.e., bitstrings. The notation $t :: \tau$ means that the HOL term t has type τ.

Pairs (type $\alpha \times \beta$) come with two projection functions π_1 and π_2, and the map function $\mathsf{map}_\times\ f\ g\ (a, b) = (f\ a, g\ b)$. Tuples are identified with pairs nested to the right, i.e., (a, b, c) is identical to $(a, (b, c))$ and $\alpha \times \beta \times \gamma$ to $\alpha \times (\beta \times \gamma)$. Dually, $\alpha + \beta$ denotes the disjoint sum of α and β; the injections are $\mathsf{Inl} :: \alpha \Rightarrow \alpha + \beta$ and $\mathsf{Inr} :: \beta \Rightarrow \alpha + \beta$. Case distinctions on freely generated types use guard-like syntax. The map function map_+ for disjoint sums, e.g., pattern matches on x to apply the appropriate function: $\mathsf{map}_+\ f\ g\ x = \mathsf{case}\ x\ \mathsf{of}\ \mathsf{Inl}\ y \Rightarrow \mathsf{Inl}\ (f\ y) \mid \mathsf{Inr}\ z \Rightarrow \mathsf{Inr}\ (g\ z)$.

Sets (type $\alpha\ \mathsf{set}$) are isomorphic to predicates (type $\alpha \Rightarrow \mathsf{bool}$) via the bijections membership $\in$ and set comprehension $\{x.\ \_\}$; the empty set is $\{\}$. Binary relations are sets of pairs and written infix, i.e., $x\ R\ y$ denotes $(x, y) \in R$. The relators $\mathsf{rel}_\times$ and rel_+ lift relations component-wise to pairs and sums.

The datatype α option = None | Some α corresponds to the Haskell type Maybe. It adjoins a new element None to α, all existing values in α are prefixed by Some. Maps (partial functions) are modelled as functions of type $\alpha \Rightarrow \beta$ option, where None represents undefinedness and $f\ x =$ Some y means that f maps x to y. The empty map $\varnothing = (\lambda\_.$ None) is undefined everywhere. Map update is defined as follows: $f(a \mapsto b) = (\lambda x.$ if $x = a$ then Some b else $f\ x)$.

2 A Shallow Probabilistic Functional Language

Security notions in the computation model are expressed as games parametrised by an adversary. In formalising such games, we want to leverage as much of the prover's infrastructure as possible. Therefore, we only model explicitly what cannot be expressed in the prover's term language, namely probabilities and access to oracles. In this section, we focus on probabilities and show the framework in action on the example of Elgamal encryption (Sects. 2.1 and 2.5).

We model games as functions which return a discrete (sub)probability distribution over outcomes. Discrete subprobabilities strike a balance between expressiveness and ease of use. They provide a monadic structure for sequencing and failure (Sect. 2.2). Thus, games can be formulated naturally and control may be transferred non-locally in error cases such as invalid data produced by the adversary. They also host a fixpoint operator for defining recursive functions (Sect. 2.3). In contrast, measure-theoretic (sub)probability distributions clutter proofs with measurability requirements. For computational soundness, discrete subprobability distributions suffice. In Sect. 2.4, we prove that the operators are relationally parametric and derive a programming logic and common cryptographic reasoning principles from parametricity.

2.1 Example: Elgamal Encryption

In this section, we formalise Elgamal's encryption scheme [27] to motivate the features of our language. In Sect. 2.5, we prove the scheme IND-CPA secure under the decisional Diffie-Hellman (DDH) assumption. We formally introduce the language only in Sect. 2.2. For now, an intuitive understanding sufficFes: monadic sequencing is written in Haskell-style do notation and $x \leftarrow$ uniform A samples x as a random element from the finite set A.

For the following, consider a fixed finite cyclic group $\mathcal{G}$ over the type α with generator g. We write $\otimes$ for group multiplication and ^ for exponentiation with natural numbers; $|\mathcal{G}|$ denotes the order of $\mathcal{G}$. In Elgamal, the public key is an arbitrary group element g ^ x and the private key is the exponent x. The security of this scheme relies on the hardness of computing the discrete logarithm. The key generation algorithm key-gen generates a new key pair by randomly sampling the exponent (Fig. 1b). Messages are group elements, too. To encrypt a message m under the public key α, the algorithm multiplies m with α raised to a random power between 0 and the order of the group (Fig. 1a).

```
aenc α m = do {
  y ← uniform {0 ..< |G|};
  return_spmf (g ^ y, (α ^ y) ⊗ m) }
```

(a) Elgamal encryption algorithm

```
key-gen = do {
  x ← uniform {0 ..< |G|};
  return_spmf (g ^ x, x) }
```

(b) Elgamal key generation

```
ind-cpa (A1, A2) = try do {
    (pk, sk) ← key-gen;
    b ← coin;
    ((m0, m1), σ) ← A1 pk;
    assert (valid-plain m0 ∧ valid-plain m1);
    c* ← aenc pk (if b then m0 else m1);
    b' ← A2 c* σ;
    return_spmf (b = b')
  } else coin
```

(c) IND-CPA security game without oracles

Fig. 1. Examples of cryptographic algorithms and games without oracle access

Elgamal's encryption scheme produces ciphertexts that are indistinguishable under chosen plaintext attacks. Chosen plaintext attacks are formalised as the game ind-cpa shown in Fig. 1c. An IND-CPA adversary $\mathcal{A}$ consists of two probabilistic functions $\mathcal{A}_1$ and $\mathcal{A}_2$. Given a public key *pk*, $\mathcal{A}_1$ chooses two plaintexts m_0 and m_1. The game then encrypts one of them as determined by the random bit b (a coin flip) and gives the challenge ciphertext c^* to $\mathcal{A}_2$ and any arbitrary state information σ produced by $\mathcal{A}_1$. Then, $\mathcal{A}_2$ produces a guess which of the two messages c^* decrypts to. Indistinguishability requires that the adversary cannot do significantly better than flipping a coin. This is measured by the IND-CPA advantage given by adv-ind-cpa $\mathcal{A} = |\text{ind-cpa } \mathcal{A} \,!\, \text{True} - 1/2|$. A concrete security theorem bounds the advantage by a quantity which is known or assumed to be small.

If any step in the game fails, ind-cpa behaves like a fair coin flip, i.e., the advantage is 0 in that case. This happens, e.g., if the plaintexts are invalid, i.e., not elements of the group, or the adversary does not produce plaintexts or a guess at all. (In an implementation, the latter could be detected using timeouts.)

The DDH assumption states that given two random group elements $\mathsf{g} \,\hat{}\, x$ and $\mathsf{g} \,\hat{}\, y$, it is hard to distinguish $\mathsf{g} \,\hat{}\, (x \cdot y)$ from another random group element $\mathsf{g} \,\hat{}\, z$. Formally, a DDH adversary $\mathcal{A}$ is a probabilistic function that takes three group elements and outputs a Boolean. We model the two settings as two games ddh_0 and ddh_1 parametrised by the adversary.

```
ddh0 A = do {                           ddh1 A = do {
    x ← uniform {0 ..< |G|};               x ← uniform {0 ..< |G|};
    y ← uniform {0 ..< |G|};               y ← uniform {0 ..< |G|};
                                           z ← uniform {0 ..< |G|};
    A (g ^ x) (g ^ y) (g ^ (x · y)) }      A (g ^ x) (g ^ y) (g ^ z) }
```

The DDH advantage captures the difficulty of $\mathcal{A}$ distinguishing the two settings. It is defined as adv-ddh $\mathcal{A} = |\text{ddh}_0\ \mathcal{A} \,!\, \text{True} - \text{ddh}_1\ \mathcal{A} \,!\, \text{True}|$. The DDH assumption states that the advantage is small, and in Sect. 2.5, we show that the IND-CPA advantage for Elgamal is bounded by the DDH advantage.

2.2 The Monad of Discrete Subprobability Distributions

A discrete subprobability distribution is given by its subprobability mass function (spmf), i.e., a non-negative real-valued function which sums up to *at most* 1. We define the type α spmf of all spmfs[1] over elementary events of type α and use variables p, q for spmfs. We make applications of spmfs explicit using the operator !. So, $p\,!\,x$ denotes the subprobability mass that the spmf p assigns to the elementary event x. An event A is a set of elementary events; its subprobability measure $p\ A$ is given by $\sum_{y \in A} p\,!\,y$. Moreover, the weight $\|p\|$ of p is the total probability mass assigned by p, i.e., $\|p\| = \sum_y p\,!\,y$. If p is a probability distribution, i.e., $\|p\| = 1$, then we call p lossless following [14] (notation lossless p). The support $\mathsf{set}_{\mathsf{spmf}}\ p = \{\, x.\ p\,!\,x > 0 \,\}$ is countable by construction.

The type α spmf hosts the polymorphic monad operations $\mathsf{return}_{\mathsf{spmf}} :: \alpha \Rightarrow \alpha\ \mathsf{spmf}$ and $\mathsf{bind}_{\mathsf{spmf}} :: \alpha\ \mathsf{spmf} \Rightarrow (\alpha \Rightarrow \beta\ \mathsf{spmf}) \Rightarrow \beta\ \mathsf{spmf}$ given by

$$\mathsf{return}_{\mathsf{spmf}}\ y\,!\,x = \begin{cases} 1 & \text{if } x = y \\ 0 & \text{otherwise} \end{cases} \qquad \mathsf{bind}_{\mathsf{spmf}}\ p\ f\,!\,x = \sum_{y \in \mathsf{set}_{\mathsf{spmf}}\ p} (p\,!\,y) \cdot (f\ y\,!\,x)$$

In this paper and in our formalisation, we use Haskell-style do notation where **do** $\{\ x \leftarrow p;\ f\ \}$ desugars to $\mathsf{bind}_{\mathsf{spmf}}\ p\ (\lambda x.\ \mathbf{do}\ f)$. The monad operations satisfy the usual monad laws: (i) $\mathsf{bind}_{\mathsf{spmf}}$ is associative and (ii) $\mathsf{return}_{\mathsf{spmf}}$ is neutral for $\mathsf{bind}_{\mathsf{spmf}}$. In addition, $\mathsf{bind}_{\mathsf{spmf}}$ is commutative and constant elements cancel.

$$\mathsf{bind}_{\mathsf{spmf}}\ p\ (\lambda x.\ \mathsf{bind}_{\mathsf{spmf}}\ q\ (f\ x)) = \mathsf{bind}_{\mathsf{spmf}}\ q\ (\lambda y.\ \mathsf{bind}_{\mathsf{spmf}}\ p\ (\lambda x.\ f\ x\ y)) \tag{1}$$

$$\mathsf{bind}_{\mathsf{spmf}}\ p\ (\lambda\_.\ q) = \mathsf{scale}\ \|p\|\ q \tag{2}$$

Here, scale $r\ p$ scales the subprobability masses of p by r, i.e., $\mathsf{scale}\ r\ p!x = r \cdot (p!x)$ for $0 \le r \le 1/\|p\|$. In particular, if p is lossless, then $\mathsf{bind}_{\mathsf{spmf}}\ p\ (\lambda\_.\ q) = q$. The monad operations give rise to the functorial action $\mathsf{map}_{\mathsf{spmf}} :: (\alpha \Rightarrow \beta) \Rightarrow \alpha\ \mathsf{spmf} \Rightarrow \beta\ \mathsf{spmf}$ given by $\mathsf{map}_{\mathsf{spmf}}\ f\ p\ = \mathsf{bind}_{\mathsf{spmf}}\ p\ (\lambda x.\ \mathsf{return}_{\mathsf{spmf}}\ (f\ x))$.

For sampling, the monad provides an operation uniform which returns the uniform distribution over a finite set. There are three special cases worth mentioning. First, for a singleton set, we have $\mathsf{uniform}\ \{\, x \,\} = \mathsf{return}_{\mathsf{spmf}}\ x$. Second, as fair coin flips are particularly prominent in cryptographic games, we abbreviate uniform $\{\, \mathsf{True}, \mathsf{False} \,\}$ with coin. Third, in case of an empty set, we let uniform $\{\}$ denote the empty subprobability distribution $\bot$ which assigns no probability to any event at all, i.e., $\bot\,!\,x = 0$ for all x. In combination with sequencing and recursion, uniform is fairly expressive.

[1] In the formalisation, we construct the type α spmf by combining the existing monad for probability mass functions [30] with an exception monad. This way, most of our primitive operations can be defined in terms of the primitive operations of the two monads. Hence, we can derive many of their properties, in particular parametricity (Sect. 2.4), from the latter's.

For example, the Bernoulli distribution bernoulli r, which returns True with probability r for any $0 \le r \le 1$, can be sampled from fair coin flips as shown on the right [32]. It can be used to define probabilistic choice.

$$
\begin{aligned}
&\mathsf{bernoulli}\ r = \mathbf{do}\ \{\\
&\quad b \leftarrow \mathsf{coin};\\
&\quad \mathsf{if}\ b\ \mathsf{then}\ \mathsf{return_{spmf}}\ (r \ge 1/2)\\
&\quad \mathsf{else\ if}\ r < 1/2\ \mathsf{then}\ \mathsf{bernoulli}\ (2 \cdot r)\\
&\quad \mathsf{else}\ \mathsf{bernoulli}\ (2 \cdot r - 1)\ \}
\end{aligned}
$$

Fig. 2. The Bernoulli distribution

Moreover, the subprobability monad contains a failure element, namely $\bot$. Failure aborts the current part of the program, as $\bot$ propagates: $\mathsf{bind_{spmf}}\ \bot\ f = \bot$. However, we hardly use $\bot$ in programs directly. It is more natural to define an assertion statement $\mathsf{assert}\ b = \mathsf{if}\ b\ \mathsf{then}\ \mathsf{return_{spmf}}\ ()\ \mathsf{else}\ \bot$. Assertions are useful in validating the inputs received from the adversary. For example, the assertion in the IND-CPA security game in Fig. 1c checks that the adversary $\mathcal{A}_1$ produced valid plaintexts.

Failures are handled using the statement $\mathsf{try}\ p\ \mathsf{else}\ q$, which distributes the probability mass not assigned by p according to q. Formally, it satisfies $(\mathsf{try}\ p\ \mathsf{else}\ q)\ !\ x = p\ !\ x + (1 - \|p\|) \cdot q\ !\ x$ for all x. Clearly, we have the equalities $\mathsf{try}\ \bot\ \mathsf{else}\ q = q$ and $\mathsf{try}\ p\ \mathsf{else}\ q = p$ if p is lossless. Moreover, try commutes with $\mathsf{bind_{spmf}}$ for lossless spmfs, i.e., we can enlarge or shrink the scope of the handler.

$$\mathsf{lossless}\ p \longrightarrow \mathsf{try}\ \mathbf{do}\ \{\ x \leftarrow p;\ f\ x\ \}\ \mathsf{else}\ q = \mathbf{do}\ \{\ x \leftarrow p;\ \mathsf{try}\ f\ x\ \mathsf{else}\ q\ \}$$

$$
\begin{aligned}
\mathsf{lossless}\ q \longrightarrow\ &\mathsf{try}\ \mathbf{do}\ \{\ x \leftarrow p;\ f\ x\ \}\ \mathsf{else}\ q =\\
&\mathsf{try}\ \mathbf{do}\ \{\ x \leftarrow p;\ \mathsf{try}\ f\ x\ \mathsf{else}\ q\ \}\ \mathsf{else}\ q
\end{aligned}
$$

The IND-CPA game in Fig. 1c treats failures as fair coin flips. This is sound as the advantage is the probability of the outcome True less $1/2$.

This completes the exposition of the language primitives except for the fixpoint combinator (see Sect. 2.3). They suffice for all examples in this paper, but note that we are not restricted to this set of operations. If necessary, users can define their own discrete subprobability distribution on the spot thanks to the shallow embedding. Also remember that all the equation in this section are equalities *inside* the logic. Hence, we can use them for rewriting in any context, not just under a semantics interpretation as with a deep embedding.

2.3 Recursive Functions in the SPMF Monad

In this section, we consider the denotation of recursive functions in the spmf monad. As usual in programming languages, we interpret a recursive specification as the least fixpoint of the associated functional. In the case of spmf, the approximation order $\sqsubseteq$ is given by $p \sqsubseteq q \leftrightarrow (\forall x.\ p\ !\ x \le q\ !\ x)$ [5]. In this order, every chain Y has a least upper bound (lub) $\bigsqcup Y$ which is taken pointwise: $\bigsqcup Y\ !\ x = \mathsf{SUP}\ \{p\ !\ x.\ p \in Y\}$ where $\mathsf{SUP}\ A$ denotes the supremum of a bounded set A of real numbers. Thus, the approximation order is a chain-complete partial order (ccpo) with least element $\bot$ (see Proposition 1 below).

By Tarski's fixpoint theorem, every monotone function f on a ccpo has a least fixpoint $\mathsf{fix}\ f$, which is obtained by the least upper bound of the transfinite iteration of f starting at the least element. Therefore, we can define recursive functions as the least fixpoint of the associated (monotone) functional.

Using Isabelle's package for recursive monadic function definitions [34], we hide the internal construction via fixpoints from the user and automate the monotonicity proof. For example, the function $\mathsf{bernoulli}$ can be specified exactly as shown in Fig. 2. The monotonicity proof succeeds as $\mathsf{bind}_{\mathsf{spmf}}$ is monotone in both arguments. Namely, if $p \sqsubseteq q$ and $f\ x \sqsubseteq g\ x$ for all x, then $\mathsf{bind}_{\mathsf{spmf}}\ p\ f \sqsubseteq \mathsf{bind}_{\mathsf{spmf}}\ q\ g$. In contrast, $\mathsf{try}\ \_\ \mathsf{else}\ \_$ is monotone only in the second argument, but not in the first. For example, $\bot \sqsubseteq \mathsf{return}_{\mathsf{spmf}}\ 0$, but $\mathsf{try}\ \bot\ \mathsf{else}\ \mathsf{return}_{\mathsf{spmf}}\ 1 = \mathsf{return}_{\mathsf{spmf}}\ 1 \not\sqsubseteq \mathsf{return}_{\mathsf{spmf}}\ 0 = \mathsf{try}\ \mathsf{return}_{\mathsf{spmf}}\ 0\ \mathsf{else}\ \mathsf{return}_{\mathsf{spmf}}\ 1$. Therefore, recursion is always possible through $\mathsf{bind}_{\mathsf{spmf}}$ and else, but not in general through try.

Proposition 1. *The approximation order $\sqsubseteq$ is a chain-complete partial order.*

Proof. We have to show that $\sqsubseteq$ is a partial order and that $\bigsqcup Y$ is well-defined and the least upper bound for every chain Y, i.e., every set of spmfs all of whose elements are comparable in $\sqsubseteq$. The difficult part is to show that $\bigsqcup Y$ is well-defined. In particular, we must show that the support of $\bigsqcup Y$ is countable even if Y is uncountable. Then, it is not hard to see that $\bigsqcup Y$ sums up to at most 1.

Clearly, we have $\mathsf{set}_{\mathsf{spmf}}\ (\bigsqcup Y) = \bigcup_{p \in Y} \mathsf{set}_{\mathsf{spmf}}\ p$. Yet, the union of an uncountable sequence of increasing countable sets need not be countable in general. In the following, we show that even for uncountable chains Y of spmfs, the union of the supports remains countable. To that end, we identify a countable sub-sequence of Y whose lub has the same support. The key idea is that for $\sqsubseteq$-comparable spmfs p and q, the order can be decided by looking only at the assigned probability masses, namely, $p \sqsubseteq q$ iff $\|p\| \le \|q\|$. So suppose without loss of generality that Y does not contain a maximal element (otherwise, the lub is the maximal element and we are done). The set of assigned probability masses $A = \{\, \|p\|.\ p \in Y \,\}$ has a supemum $r \le 1$, as 1 bounds the set from above. The closure of A contains the supremum r, so A must contain a countable increasing sequence which converges to r. This sequence gives rise to a countable sub-sequence Z of Y, for which we show $(\bigcup_{p \in Y} \mathsf{set}_{\mathsf{spmf}}\ p) \subseteq (\bigcup_{q \in Z} \mathsf{set}_{\mathsf{spmf}}\ q)$. For any $p \in Y$, there is a $q \in Z$ such that $\|p\| \le \|q\|$, as the assigned probability masses in Z converge to r from below and p is not maximal. Hence, $p \sqsubseteq q$ as p and q are related in $\sqsubseteq$, and therefore $\mathsf{set}_{\mathsf{spmf}}\ p \subseteq \mathsf{set}_{\mathsf{spmf}}\ q$ as $\mathsf{set}_{\mathsf{spmf}}$ is monotone.

The attentive reader might wonder why we need transfinite iteration for the fixpoint despite having shown that uncountable chains can be reduced to countable ones for the purpose of lubs. Countable fixpoint iteration, which defines the least fixpoint as $\bigsqcup\{\, f^i\ \bot.\ i \in \mathbb{N} \,\}$, does not suffice. (Here, function iteration is defined by $f^0 = \mathsf{id}$ and $f^{n+1} = f \circ f^n$.) The reason is that the chain $\{\, f^i\ \bot.\ i \in \mathbb{N} \,\}$ might stop before the least fixpoint is reached. Consider, e.g., the monotone spmf transformer $f :: \mathsf{unit\ spmf} \Rightarrow \mathsf{unit\ spmf}$ given below.

$$f\ p\,!\,x = \mathsf{if}\ p\,!\,x < \tfrac{1}{2}\ \mathsf{then}\ \tfrac{2 \cdot p!x + 1}{4}\ \mathsf{else}\ 1$$

The countable iteration of f starting at $\bot$ yields a sequence of spmfs which assign to () the masses 0, 1/4, 3/8, 7/16, 15/32, ... The least upper bound of this sequence assigns 1/2 to (). That is, the iteration has not yet reached f's fixed point, which assigns the mass 1 to (). This is because f is not (chain) continuous, i.e., it does not preserve lubs.

Overall, arbitrary chains and transfinite iteration are superior to ordinary fixpoint iteration in two ways. First, our fixpoint combinator can handle more functions, i.e., we can accept more recursive specifications. Second, the proof obligations that recursive specifications incur are simpler: monotonicity is usually easier to show than continuity.

2.4 Lifting and Parametricity

Game playing proofs transform games step by step. In each step, we have to bound the probability that the adversary can distinguish the original game from the transformed one. For some transformations, the equational theory suffices to prove the games equal—then, the probability is 0. Other transformations are justified by cryptographic assumptions. To bound the probability in such cases, our framework provides a relational logic for programs.

To that end, we first define an operation to lift relations over elementary events to relations over spmfs. With this lifting operator, our primitive operations are parametric. Then, we can derive the logic from parametricity.

Lifting. The lifting operation $\mathsf{rel}_{\mathsf{spmf}}$ transforms a binary relation R over elementary events into a relation over spmfs over these events. For lossless distributions, a number of definitions have appeared in the literature. We generalise the one from [30] as the relator associated with the natural transformation $\mathsf{set}_{\mathsf{spmf}}$ [45]. Formally, $\mathsf{rel}_{\mathsf{spmf}}\ R$ relates the spmfs $p :: \alpha\ \mathsf{spmf}$ and $q :: \beta\ \mathsf{spmf}$ iff there is an spmf $w :: (\alpha \times \beta)\ \mathsf{spmf}$ such that (i) $\mathsf{set}_{\mathsf{spmf}}\ w \subseteq R$, (ii) $\mathsf{map}_{\mathsf{spmf}}\ \pi_1\ w = p$, and (iii) $\mathsf{map}_{\mathsf{spmf}}\ \pi_2\ w = q$, We call w a R-joint spmf of p and q.

This definition reformulates the one by Larsen and Skou [36] for lossless spmfs. They consider w as a non-negative weight function on the relation such that the marginals are the original distribution., i.e., w must satisfy (i) $x\ R\ y$ whenever $w\ !\ (x, y) > 0$, (ii) $\sum_y w\ !\ (x, y) = p\ !\ x$ for all x, and (iii) $\sum_x w\ !\ (x, y) = q\ !\ y$ for all y, Using the functorial structure of spmfs, our definition expresses the same conditions more abstractly without summations. In previous work [30], this led to considerably shorter proofs.

Recently, Sack and Zhang [46] showed that if p and q are lossless, then

$$p\ (\mathsf{rel}_{\mathsf{spmf}}\ R)\ q \quad \text{iff} \quad \forall A.\ \mathsf{measure}\ p\ A \leq \mathsf{measure}\ q\ \{y.\ \exists x \in A.\ x\ R\ y,\}$$

generalising Desharnais' proof for the finite case [26]. In our formalisation, we assume the "if" direction of the equivalence. We have not yet proved it formally, as it relies on the max-flow min-cut theorem for countable networks [3], which itself requires a substantial formalisation effort. Still, we formally derive the following characterisation of $\mathsf{rel}_{\mathsf{spmf}}\ R$ for arbitrary spmfs from this assumption.

Lemma 1 (Characterisation of $\mathsf{rel_{spmf}}$).
The following are equivalent for all R, p, and q.

(a) $p\ (\mathsf{rel_{spmf}}\ R)\ q$
(b) $\mathsf{set_{spmf}}\ w \subseteq R$ and $\mathsf{map_{spmf}}\ \pi_1\ w = p$ and $\mathsf{map_{spmf}}\ \pi_2\ w = q$ for some w
(c) $\mathsf{measure}\ p\ A \leq \mathsf{measure}\ q\ \{y.\ \exists x \in A.\ x\ R\ y\}$ for all A and $\|p\| \geq \|q\|$

The relator enjoys a number of useful properties. For example, (i) it generalises equality, namely $\mathsf{rel_{spmf}}\ (=) = (=)$, (ii) it distributes over relation composition, and (iii) it is monotone: $p\ (\mathsf{rel_{spmf}}\ R)\ q$ implies $p\ (\mathsf{rel_{spmf}}\ R')\ q$ if $x\ R'\ y$ whenever $x\ R\ y$ and $x \in \mathsf{set_{spmf}}\ p$ and $y \in \mathsf{set_{spmf}}\ q$.

Parametricity. The program logic describes the interaction between the spmf operations and the relator. As it turns out, relational parametricity [44,50] helps us to find the rules and prove them sound.[2]

Parametricity expresses that a polymorphic function does not inspect the values of type variables, but works uniformly for all instances. Relational parametricity formalises this as follows. Types are interpreted as relations and type constructors as relation transformers. A polymorphic function is (relationally) parametric iff it is related to itself in its type's relation where type variables are interpreted as arbitrary relations. For spmfs, the relator $\mathsf{rel_{spmf}}$ is the appropriate relation transformers. For example, parametricity for $\mathsf{return_{spmf}} :: \alpha \Rightarrow \alpha\ \mathsf{spmf}$ is expressed as $\mathsf{return_{spmf}}\ (R \Mapsto \mathsf{rel_{spmf}}\ R)\ \mathsf{return_{spmf}}$ for all $R :: (\alpha \times \beta)\ \mathsf{set}$. Here, the relator $R \Mapsto S$ for the function space relates two functions f and g iff they transform relatedness in R into relatedness in S, i.e., $x\ R\ y$ implies $(f\ x)\ S\ (g\ y)$ for all x and y.

Wadler [50] proved that all functions of the polymorphic lambda calculus are parametric. He also demonstrated that adding polymorphic equality destroys this property. Higher order logic has polymorphic equality $(=)$ and description operators, so not all HOL functions are parametric. Thus, parametricity is not a free theorem in our setting; we have to prove it. For $\mathsf{return_{spmf}}$, parametricity follows directly from unfolding the definitions and taking $\mathsf{return_{spmf}}\ (x, y)$ as the joint spmf for $\mathsf{return_{spmf}}\ x$ and $\mathsf{return_{spmf}}\ y$ for all $x\ A\ y$. For $\mathsf{bind_{spmf}}$, the parametricity statement is

$$\forall R\ R'.\ \mathsf{bind_{spmf}}\ (\mathsf{rel_{spmf}}\ R \Mapsto (R \Mapsto \mathsf{rel_{spmf}}\ R') \Mapsto \mathsf{rel_{spmf}}\ R')\ \mathsf{bind_{spmf}}$$

The proof is similar to the one for $\mathsf{return_{spmf}}$: after having unfolded the definitions, we take $\mathsf{bind_{spmf}}\ w\ h$ as the joint spmf for $\mathsf{bind_{spmf}}\ p\ f$ and $\mathsf{bind_{spmf}}\ q\ g$ where w is the R-joint spmf for p and q and $h\ (x, y)$ denotes the R'-joint spmf for $f\ x$ and $g\ y$ for all $x\ R\ y$.

As function application preserves parametricity, any combination of parametric functions is parametric, too. For example, parametricity of $\mathsf{map_{spmf}}$ and assert

[2] As our embedding is shallow, we cannot define a deduction system in the logic. Rather, we derive the rules directly from the semantics, i.e., show soundness. Completeness is therefore achieved dynamically: new rules can be derived if necessary, in particular when a new operation is introduced.

follows. Similarly, try _ else _ is parametric, too. Thus, this extends to whole probabilistic programs, which we will exploit in Sect. 3.4. Such parametricity proofs are highly automated in Isabelle [31,35].

For reasoning about probabilistic programs, we derive more conventional rules by supplying some arguments. For example, we get the following rules for the monad operations. Note that parametricity dictates the shape of the rules.

$$\frac{x\ R\ y}{\mathsf{return_{spmf}}\ x\ (\mathsf{rel_{spmf}}\ R)\ \mathsf{return_{spmf}}\ y}$$

$$\frac{p\ (\mathsf{rel_{spmf}}\ R)\ q \qquad \forall (x,y) \in R.\ f\ x\ (\mathsf{rel_{spmf}}\ R')\ g\ y}{\mathsf{bind_{spmf}}\ p\ f\ (\mathsf{rel_{spmf}}\ R')\ \mathsf{bind_{spmf}}\ q\ g}$$

However, not all functions are parametric. The function uniform A, e.g., is not, because it relies on polymorphic equality: the cardinality of a set depends on the equality of elements. In detail, the relator for $\mathsf{rel_{set}}\ R$ relates two sets A and B iff R relates each element of A with one in B and vice versa; formally, $\forall x \in A.\ \exists y \in B.\ x\ R\ y$ and $\forall y \in B.\ \exists x \in A.\ x\ R\ y$. Now,

$$\mathsf{uniform}\ (\mathsf{rel_{set}}\ R \Mapsto \mathsf{rel_{spmf}}\ R)\ \mathsf{uniform} \tag{3}$$

holds if (and only if) the relation R respects equality, i.e., $(=)\ (R \Mapsto R \Mapsto \mathsf{rel_{bool}})\ (=)$ holds, where $\mathsf{rel_{bool}}$ is the identity relation on Booleans (type bool). Interestingly, this restricted parametricity property is equivalent to optimistic sampling in cryptographic proofs. Namely, if f is injective on A, then

$$\mathsf{map_{spmf}}\ f\ (\mathsf{uniform}\ A) = \mathsf{uniform}\ (f\ `\ A) \tag{4}$$

where $f\ `\ A$ denotes the image of A under f. This is one example of Wadler's free theorems [50] in our context. If we specialise A to bitstrings of a given length and f to the bitwise exclusive or (xor) with a fixed bitstring, we obtain the well-known one-time-pad lemma: $\mathsf{map_{spmf}}\ (\mathsf{xor}\ s)\ (\mathsf{uniform}\ \{0,1\}^n) = \mathsf{uniform}\ \{0,1\}^n$ where s is a bitstring of length n and $\{0,1\}^n$ denotes the set of all bitstrings of length n.

Parametricity also connects the relator with probabilities of events. Recall that measure p A denotes the probability of event A under the spmf p. The rule

$$\frac{p\ (\mathsf{rel_{spmf}}\ R)\ q \qquad A\ (\mathsf{rel_{pred}}\ R)\ B}{\mathsf{measure}\ p\ A = \mathsf{measure}\ q\ B}$$

follows directly from parametricity of measure, namely

$$\mathsf{measure}\ (\mathsf{rel_{spmf}}\ R \Mapsto \mathsf{rel_{pred}}\ R \Mapsto \mathsf{rel_{real}})\ \mathsf{measure}$$

Here, the relator $\mathsf{rel_{pred}}$ treats sets as predicates, i.e., $\mathsf{rel_{pred}}\ R\ A\ B$ iff $x \in A \leftrightarrow y \in B$ for all $x\ R\ y$, and $\mathsf{rel_{real}}$ is the identity relation on real numbers.

For example, this rule plays an important role in Bellare's and Rogaway's fundamental lemma [16]. Lacking syntax, we cannot express their syntactic condition in HOL. Borrowing ideas from EasyCrypt [13], we instead rephrase the condition in terms of the relator.

Lemma 2 (Fundamental lemma [13,16]). *Let A, F_1 and B, F_2 be events of two spmfs p and q, respectively, such that*

$$p\ (\mathsf{rel}_{\mathsf{spmf}}\ \{\ (a, b).\ a \in F_1 \leftrightarrow b \in F_2 \wedge (b \notin F_2 \longrightarrow a \in A \leftrightarrow b \in B)\ \})\ q.$$

Then, the probability difference between A occurring in p and B in q is bounded by the probability of F_1 in p, which equals F_2's in q.

$$|\mathsf{measure}\ p\ A - \mathsf{measure}\ q\ B| \leq \mathsf{measure}\ p\ F_1 = \mathsf{measure}\ q\ F_2$$

Optimistic sampling and the fundamental lemma have illustrated how cryptographic arguments follow from parametricity. But parametricity offers yet another point of view. Mitchell [40] uses parametricity to express representation independence, i.e., one can change the representation of data without affecting the overall result. In Sect. 3.4, we will exploit representation independence in the bridging steps of the game transformations.

The Fixpoint Combinator We have not yet covered one important building block of our probabilistic language in our analysis: the fixpoint combinator on spmfs. It turns out that it preserves parametricity.[3]

Theorem 1 (Parametricity of spmf fixpoints).
If $f :: \alpha\ \mathsf{spmf} \Rightarrow \alpha\ \mathsf{spmf}$ and $g :: \beta\ \mathsf{spmf} \Rightarrow \beta\ \mathsf{spmf}$ are monotone w.r.t. $\sqsubseteq$ and $f\ (\mathsf{rel}_{\mathsf{spmf}}\ R \Mapsto \mathsf{rel}_{\mathsf{spmf}}\ R)\ g$, then $\mathsf{fix}\ f\ (\mathsf{rel}_{\mathsf{spmf}}\ R)\ \mathsf{fix}\ g$.

To avoid higher-kinded types, the theorem generalises parametricity to the preservation of relatedness. In the typical use case, f and g are instances of the same polymorphic function.

We prove Theorem 1 by parallel induction on the two fixpoints. Both inductive cases are trivial. The base case requires $\mathsf{rel}_{\mathsf{spmf}}\ R$ to be strict, i.e., it relates the least elements, which holds trivially. The step case is precisely the relatedness condition of f and g which the theorem assumes. The hard part consists of showing that parallel induction is a valid proof principle. To that end, we must show that $\mathsf{rel}_{\mathsf{spmf}}\ R$ is admissible. A relation $R :: (\alpha \times \beta)\ \mathsf{set}$ is admissible w.r.t. two ccpos iff for any chain $Y \subseteq R$ of pairs in the product ccpo (the ordering is component-wise), R relates the component-wise lubs of Y.

[3] Wadler showed that if all types are ω-ccpos, all functions are continuous and all relations are admissible and strict, then the fixpoint operator (defined by countable iteration) is parametric [50]. We do not consider the fixpoint operator as part of the language itself, but as a definition principle for recursive user-specified functions. That is, we assume that fix is always applied to a (monotone) function. Consequently, preservation of parametricity suffices and we do not need Wadler's restrictions of the semantic domains. Instead, monotonicity (instead of continuity, see the discussion in Sect. 2.3) is expressed as a precondition on the given functions.

Proposition 2. *$\mathsf{rel}_{\mathsf{spmf}}$ is admissible.*

Proof. We exploit the characterisation of $\mathsf{rel}_{\mathsf{spmf}}$ in terms of measure. We must show $(\bigsqcup (\pi_1 \text{`} Y))\ (\mathsf{rel}_{\mathsf{spmf}}\ R)\ (\bigsqcup (\pi_2 \text{`} Y))$ for all chains Y of pairs in $\mathsf{rel}_{\mathsf{spmf}}\ R$. By the characterisation (Lemma 1), this holds by the following reasoning. The first and last step exploit that the lub commutes with measure, and the inequality follows from monotonicity of SUP and the characterisation of $\mathsf{rel}_{\mathsf{spmf}}$ for elements of the chain.

$$\begin{aligned} \mathsf{measure}\ (\bigsqcup (\pi_1 \text{`} Y))\ A &= \mathsf{SUP}\ (p, \_) \in Y.\ \mathsf{measure}\ p\ A \\ &\le \mathsf{SUP}\ (\_, q) \in Y.\ \mathsf{measure}\ q\ \{\, y.\ \exists x \in A.\ x\ R\ y \,\} \\ &= \mathsf{measure}\ (\bigsqcup (\pi_2 \text{`} Y))\ \{\, y. \exists x \in A.\ x\ R\ y \,\} \end{aligned}$$

Note that it is not clear how to prove admissibility via the characterisation in terms of joint spmfs. The issue is that the joint spmfs for the pairs in the chain need not form a chain themselves. So we cannot construct the joint spmf for the lubs as the lub of the joint spmfs.

Admissibility of relators is preserved by the function space (ordered point-wise) and products (ordered component-wise). Thus, analogues to Theorem 1 hold for fixpoints over $\_ \Rightarrow \alpha\ \mathsf{spmf}$, $\alpha\ \mathsf{spmf} \times \beta\ \mathsf{spmf}$, etc. They are useful to show parametricity of (mutually) recursive probabilistic functions (Sect. 3.3) rather than recursively defined spmfs.

2.5 Security of Elgamal Encryption

We are now ready to prove Elgamal encryption (Sect. 2.1) IND-CPA secure under the decisional Diffie-Hellman (DDH) assumption. The security theorem bounds the IND-CPA advantage by the DDH advantage. For Elgamal, we prove

$$\mathsf{adv\text{-}ind\text{-}cpa}\ \mathcal{A} = \mathsf{adv\text{-}ddh}\ (\mathsf{elgamal}\ \mathcal{A})$$

where the reduction elgamal transforms an IND-CPA adversary into a DDH adversary as shown in Fig. 3.

$$\begin{aligned} &\mathsf{elgamal}\ (\mathcal{A}_1, \mathcal{A}_2)\ \alpha\ \beta\ \gamma\ =\ \mathsf{try\ do}\ \{ \\ &\quad b \leftarrow \mathsf{coin}; \\ &\quad ((m_0, m_1), \sigma) \leftarrow \mathcal{A}_1\ \alpha; \\ &\quad \mathsf{assert}\ (\mathsf{valid\text{-}plain}\ m_0 \wedge \mathsf{valid\text{-}plain}\ m_1); \\ &\quad \mathsf{let}\ m = \mathsf{if}\ b\ \mathsf{then}\ m_0\ \mathsf{else}\ m_1; \\ &\quad b' \leftarrow \mathcal{A}_2\ (\beta, \gamma \otimes m)\ \sigma; \\ &\quad \mathsf{return}_{\mathsf{spmf}}\ (b = b') \\ &\}\ \mathsf{else\ coin} \end{aligned}$$

Fig. 3. Reduction for Elgamal encryption

The proof consists of two steps. First, observe that $\mathsf{ddh}_0\ (\mathsf{elgamal}\ \mathcal{A}) = \mathsf{ind\text{-}cpa}\ \mathcal{A}$, because after the definitions have been unfolded, both sides are the same except for associativity and commutativity of $\mathsf{bind}_{\mathsf{spmf}}$ and the group law $(\mathsf{g}\ \hat{}\ x)\ \hat{}\ y = \mathsf{g}\ \hat{}\ (x \cdot y)$. Second, we show that $\mathsf{ddh}_1\ (\mathsf{elgamal}\ \mathcal{A}) = \mathsf{coin}$. Note that the message m is independent of γ, which is sampled uniformly. Multiplication with a fixed group element m is a bijection on the carrier. By (4), we can omit the multiplication and the guess b' becomes independent of b. Hence, the adversary has to guess a random bit, which is equivalent to flipping a coin.

Formally, the second proof is broken up into three step. First, we rewrite the game using the identities about $\text{bind}_{\text{spmf}}$, try, and map_{spmf} such that we can apply (4) on the multiplication. Second, we rewrite the resulting game such that we can apply (4) once more on the equality test. Finally, we show that the irrelevant assignments cancel out. This holds even if the adversary is not lossless thanks to the surrounding try _ else coin. Thus, our statement does not need any technical side condition like losslessness of the adversary in CertiCrypt [14] and EasyCrypt [13].

Modules. Note that the definition of IND-CPA security does not depend on the Elgamal encryption scheme. In the formalisation, we abstract over the encryption scheme using Isabelle's module system [11]. Like an ML-style functor, the IND-CPA module takes an encryption scheme and specialises the definitions of game and advantage and the proven theorems to the scheme. Similarly, the DDH assumption has its own module which takes the group as argument. This allows to reuse security definitions and cryptographic algorithms in different contexts. For Elgamal, we import the DDH module for the given group and the IND-CPA module for the Elgamal encryption scheme.

3 Adversaries with Oracle Access

In many security games, the adversary is granted black-box access to oracles. An oracle is a probabilistic function which maintains mutable state across different invocations, but the adversary must not get access to this state. In this section, we propose a new semantic domain for probabilistic functions with oracle access (Sect. 3.2). Like in Sect. 2.4, we derive reasoning rules from parametricity and explore the connection to bisimulations (Sect. 3.3). We motivate and illustrate the key features by formalising a hashed version of Elgamal encryption (HEG) in the random oracle model (ROM) [15] (Sect. 3.1) and verifying its security under the computational Diffie-Hellman (CDH) assumption (Sect. 3.4).

3.1 Example: Hashed Elgamal Encryption

Elgamal's encryption scheme from Sect. 2.1 requires messages to be group elements, but often bitstrings of a given length are more convenient. Therefore, we consider a version of Elgamal encryption where a hash function H converts group elements into bitstring [48]. We model the hash function as a random oracle, which acts like a random function. In detail, we replace the multiplication with the group element $\alpha \,\hat{}\, y$ in Fig. 1a with the xor of its hash h; Fig. 4a shows the resulting encryption algorithm. The encryption algorithm obtains the hash by calling the oracle with a random group element.

In Sect. 3.4, we prove that HEG is IND-CPA secure under the computational Diffie Hellman (CDH) assumption. For now, we explain how the formalisation changes. Figure 4c shows the new game for chosen plaintext attacks where the key generation algorithm, the encryption function and the adversary have access to an oracle. In comparison to Fig. 1c, the monad has changed: the game uses

```
aenc α m = do {
  y ← uniform {0 ..< |𝒢|};
  h ← call (α ^ y);
  return_gpv (xor h m) }
```

(a) Hashed Elgamal encryption

```
record X x = do {
  y ← call x;
  return_gpv (y, insert x X) }
```

(b) Recorder for oracle calls

```
ind-cpa (𝒜₁, 𝒜₂) = try do {
  (pk, sk) ← key-gen;
  b ← sample coin;
  ((m₀, m₁), σ) ← 𝒜₁ pk
  assert (valid-plain m₀ ∧ valid-plain m₁);
  c* ← aenc pk (if b then m₀ else m₁);
  b′ ← 𝒜₂ c* σ;
  return_gpv (b = b′)
} else sample coin
```

(c) IND-CPA security game with oracle access

Fig. 4. Example programs in the gpv monad

the new monad of generative probabilistic values (gpv) rather than spmf; see Sect. 3.2 for details. Accordingly, the coin flips coin are embedded with the monad homomorphism sample.

In one step of the security proof, we will have to keep track of the calls that the adversary has made. This is achieved by using the oracle transformation record in Fig. 4b. It forwards all calls x and records them in its local state X.

As before, all these definitions live in different modules that abstract over the encryption scheme, group, and oracle. In fact, the programs in Fig. 4 are completely independent of the concrete oracle. We compose the game with the oracle only when we define the advantage. Thus, it now depends on an oracle $\mathcal{O}$ with initial state s: adv-ind-cpa $\mathcal{O}\ s\ \mathcal{A} = |\mathsf{run}\ \mathcal{O}\ (\mathsf{ind\text{-}cpa}\ \mathcal{A})\ s\ !\ \mathsf{True} - 1/2|$. Here, run binds the oracle calls in ind-cpa $\mathcal{A}$ to the oracle $\mathcal{O}$. It thus reduces a program with oracle access to one without, i.e., a spmf.

3.2 Generative Probabilistic Values

The example from the previous section determines a wish list of features for the language of probabilistic programs with oracle access: assertions and failure handling, calls to unspecified oracles, embedding of probabilistic programs without oracle access, and composition operators. In this section, we propose a semantic domain for probabilistic computations with oracle access and show how to express the above features in this domain.

We start by discussing why spmfs do not suffice. In our probabilistic language of spmfs, we can model an oracle as a function of type $\sigma \Rightarrow \alpha \Rightarrow (\beta \times \sigma)$ spmf, which takes a state and the arguments of the call and returns a subprobability distribution over the output and the new state. Unfortunately, we cannot model the adversary as a probabilistic program parametrised over the oracle and its initial state. Suppose we do. Then, its type has the shape $(\sigma \Rightarrow \alpha \Rightarrow (\beta \times \sigma)\ \mathsf{spmf}) \Rightarrow \sigma \Rightarrow \_\ \mathsf{spmf}$. To hide the oracle state from the adversary despite passing it as an argument, we could require that the adversary be parametric in σ. This expresses that the adversary behaves uniformly for all states, so it cannot inspect the state. Yet, we must also ensure that the adversary uses the state only linearly, i.e., it does not call the oracle twice with the same state. As we are not aware of a semantic characterisation of linearity, we cannot model the adversary like this.

Instead, we explicitly model the interactions between the adversary and the oracle. To that end, we propose the following algebraic codatatype of *generative probabilistic values* (gpv):[4]

$$\textbf{codatatype}\ (\alpha,\gamma,\rho)\ \mathsf{gpv} = \mathsf{GPV}\ (\alpha + \gamma \times (\alpha,\gamma,\rho)\ \mathsf{rpv}))\ \mathsf{spmf}$$
$$\textbf{type-synonym}\ (\alpha,\gamma,\rho)\ \mathsf{rpv} = \rho \Rightarrow (\alpha,\gamma,\rho)\ \mathsf{gpv}$$

Conceptually, a gpv is a probabilistic system in which each state chooses probabilistically between failing, terminating with a result of type α, and continuing by producing an output γ and transitioning into a *reactive probabilistic value* (rpv), which waits for a non-deterministic response of the environment (e.g., the oracle) of type ρ. Upon reception, the rpv transitions to the generative successor state.

As we are interested in a shallow embedding, the type gpv only models the observations (termination with result or failure and interaction with the environment) of the system rather than the whole system with the states. This yields a richer equational theory, i.e., we can prove more properties by rewriting without resorting to bisimulation arguments. Any probabilistic system with explicit states can be transformed into a gpv by identifying bisimilar states. The coiterator $\mathsf{coiter_{gpv}} :: (\sigma \Rightarrow (\alpha + \gamma \times (\rho \Rightarrow \sigma))\ \mathsf{spmf}) \Rightarrow \sigma \Rightarrow (\alpha,\gamma,\rho)\ \mathsf{gpv}$ formalises this: given a probabilistic system and an initial state, it constructs the corresponding gpv.

Basic Operations. The basic operations for gpv are the monadic functions $\mathsf{return_{gpv}}$ and $\mathsf{bind_{gpv}}$, calling an oracle call, sampling sample, exceptional termination fail (from which we derive assertions assert) and failure handling try _ else _. They can be implemented as shown in Fig. 5, where Pure = Inl and IO $o\ r$ = Inr (o, r) and id is the identity and un-GPV the inverse of GPV. Note that $\mathsf{bind_{spmf}}$ and try _ else _ can be defined by primitive corecursion.

$$\begin{aligned}
&\mathsf{return_{gpv}}\ x = \mathsf{GPV}\ (\mathsf{return_{spmf}}\ (\mathsf{Pure}\ x)) \\
&\mathsf{call}\ o = \mathsf{GPV}\ (\mathsf{return_{spmf}}\ (\mathsf{IO}\ o\ \mathsf{return_{gpv}})) \\
&\mathsf{sample}\ p = \mathsf{GPV}\ (\mathsf{map_{spmf}}\ \mathsf{Pure}\ p) \\
&\mathsf{fail} = \mathsf{GPV}\ \bot \\
&\mathsf{assert}\ b = \mathsf{if}\ b\ \mathsf{then}\ \mathsf{return_{gpv}}\ ()\ \mathsf{else}\ \mathsf{fail} \\
&\mathsf{try}\ \mathsf{GPV}\ p\ \mathsf{else}\ v = \\
&\quad \mathsf{GPV}\ (\mathsf{try}\ \mathsf{map_{spmf}}\ (\mathsf{map_{+}}\ \mathsf{id}\ (\mathsf{map_{\times}}\ \mathsf{id}\ (\lambda r\ x.\ \mathsf{try}\ (r\ x)\ \mathsf{else}\ v)))\ p\ \mathsf{else}\ \mathsf{un\text{-}GPV}\ v)
\end{aligned}$$

$$\begin{aligned}
&\mathsf{bind_{gpv}}\ (\mathsf{GPV}\ p)\ f = \mathsf{GPV}\ (\mathbf{do}\ \{ \\
&\quad x \leftarrow p; \\
&\quad \mathsf{case}\ x\ \mathsf{of}\ \mathsf{Pure}\ y \Rightarrow \mathsf{un\text{-}GPV}\ (f\ y) \\
&\quad \mid \mathsf{IO}\ c\ r \Rightarrow \mathsf{return_{spmf}} \\
&\qquad (\mathsf{IO}\ c\ (\lambda w.\ \mathsf{bind_{gpv}}\ (r\ w)\ f))\ \})
\end{aligned}$$

Fig. 5. Primitive operations for gpvs

The operations behave as expected. In particular, $\mathsf{return_{gpv}}$ and $\mathsf{bind_{gpv}}$ satisfy the monad laws, fail propagates, and sample is a monad homomorphism.

[4] Note that gpv is not the greatest fixpoint of a polynomial functor, as the recursion goes through the non-polynomial functor spmf. Still, the type is well-defined, as spmf is a bounded natural functor [30] which Isabelle's codatatype package supports [22].

$$\mathsf{bind}_{\mathsf{gpv}}\ \mathsf{fail}\ f = \mathsf{fail} \qquad \mathsf{sample}\ (\mathsf{return}_{\mathsf{spmf}}\ x) = \mathsf{return}_{\mathsf{gpv}}\ x \qquad \mathsf{sample}\ \bot = \mathsf{fail}$$
$$\mathsf{sample}\ (\mathbf{do}\ \{x \leftarrow p;\ f\ x\ \}) = \mathbf{do}\ \{\ x \leftarrow \mathsf{sample}\ p;\ \mathsf{sample}\ (f\ x)\ \}$$
$$\mathsf{sample}\ (\mathsf{assert}\ b) = \mathsf{assert}\ b \qquad \mathsf{sample}\ (\mathsf{try}\ p\ \mathsf{else}\ q) = \mathsf{try}\ \mathsf{sample}\ p\ \mathsf{else}\ \mathsf{sample}\ q$$

The resulting equational theory is rich again, but not as rich as for spmfs. Commutativity (1) and cancellation (2), e.g., do not carry over to $\mathsf{bind}_{\mathsf{gpv}}$ in general.

Composition Operators. Two gpvs can be composed such that one (the callee) processes all the calls of the other (the caller). Thereby, the callee may issue further calls. In games, composition is mainly used to intercept and redirect the oracle calls of the adversary, i.e., the callee is an oracle transformation like record. Syntactically, composition corresponds to inlining the callee into the caller. If programs were modelled syntactically, implementing inlining would be trivial; but with a shallow approach, we cannot rely on syntax.

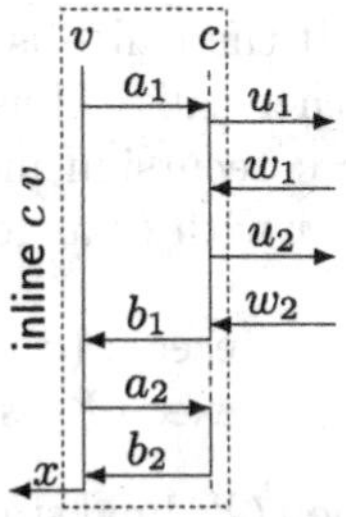

Instead, we define inlining by a combination of recursion and corecursion as shown in Fig. 6. The sequence diagram on the right illustrates what is happening in an example. The caller v issues calls of type γ which return values of type ρ. The callee c is a function from γ to a gpv which may issue further calls of type γ' which return values of type ρ'. The callee maintains its own state of type σ between invocations. Therefore, like oracles, the callee additionally takes a state as argument and the results of the gpv are the return values and the new states. The function inline first calls the auxiliary function search, which searches for the first call issued by the callee during a call by the caller. If search finds none, it returns the result x of the caller and the updated state s' of the callee. Then, inline terminates with the same outcome. Otherwise, inline issues the call u and forwards the return value w to the rpv r' of the callee, which may issue further calls (u_2 in the diagram). The result b of the callee is then fed to the rpv r of the caller and inline corecurses with the updated state s' of the callee.

```
inline :: (σ ⇒ γ ⇒ (ρ × σ, γ', ρ') gpv)          search :: (σ ⇒ γ ⇒ (ρ × σ, γ', ρ') gpv)
  ⇒ (α, γ, ρ) gpv ⇒ σ                                ⇒ (α, γ, ρ) gpv ⇒ σ
  ⇒ (α × σ, γ', ρ') gpv                              ⇒ (α × σ +
                                                         γ' × (ρ × σ, γ', ρ') rpv × (α, γ, ρ) rpv) spmf

inline c v s = GPV (do {                          search c v s = do {
  z ← search c v s                                  z ← un-GPV v;
  case z of Inl (x, s') ⇒ Pure (x, s')               case z of Pure x ⇒ return_spmf (Inl (x, s))
  | Inr (u, r', r) ⇒                                 | IO a r ⇒ do {
    IO u (λw. do {                                      y ← un-GPV (c s a);
       (b, s') ← r' w;                                  case y of Pure (b, s') ⇒ search c (r b) s'
       inline c (r b) s' } })                           | IO u r' ⇒ return_spmf (Inr (u, r', r)) } }
```

Fig. 6. Composition operator for gpvs

The function search recursively goes through the interactions between the caller and the callee. If the caller terminates with result x, there are no calls and the search terminates. Otherwise, the caller issues a call a and becomes the rpv r. In that case, search analyses the callee under the argument a. If the callee returns b without issuing a call itself, the search continues recursively on $r\ b$. Otherwise, the first call is found and the search terminates.

Note that search operates in the spmf monad. So, it can be defined using the fixpoint operator on spmf (Sect. 2.3). Conversely, inline operates in the gpv monad. So, corecursion is the appropriate definition principle. Accordingly, we prove properties about search by fixpoint induction and about inline by coinduction. For example, we show that inline is a monad homomorphism. It is also associative (we omit reassociations of tuples for clarity; $f \circ\circ g$ denotes $\lambda(x, y)\ z.\ f\ (g\ x\ z)\ y$):

$$\mathsf{inline}\ c_1\ (\mathsf{inline}\ c_2\ v\ s_2)\ s_1 = \mathsf{inline}\ (\mathsf{inline}\ c_1 \circ\circ c_2)\ v\ (s_2, s_1)$$

If the callee is an oracle $\mathcal{O}$, i.e., an spmf rather than a gpv, it cannot issue further calls. Thus, search $\mathcal{O}$ always returns a result of the form $\mathsf{Inl}\ (x, s')$, i.e., the corecursion in inline is not needed. Therefore, we define the execution of a gpv v with $\mathcal{O}$ as follows (where projl is the left inverse to Inl).

$$\mathsf{exec} :: (\sigma \Rightarrow \gamma \Rightarrow \rho \times \sigma\ \mathsf{spmf}) \Rightarrow (\alpha, \gamma, \rho)\ \mathsf{gpv} \Rightarrow \sigma \Rightarrow (\alpha \times \sigma)\ \mathsf{spmf}$$
$$\mathsf{exec}\ \mathcal{O}\ v\ s = \mathsf{map_{spmf}}\ \mathsf{projl}\ (\mathsf{search}\ (\lambda s\ x.\ \mathsf{sample}\ (\mathcal{O}\ s\ x))\ v\ s)$$

When $\mathcal{O}$'s final state does not matter, we use $\mathsf{run}\ c\ v\ s = \mathsf{map_{spmf}}\ \pi_1\ (\mathsf{exec}\ c\ v\ s)$.

Reductions are the primary use case for composition. They transform the adversary $\mathcal{A}$ for one game into an adversary for another game. In general, the oracles of the two games differ. So, the reduction emulates the original oracle $\mathcal{O}$ using an oracle transformation T, which has access to the new oracle $\mathcal{O}'$. In this view, the new adversary is built from the composition $\mathsf{inline}\ T\ \mathcal{A}$ and the cryptographic assumption executes it with access to $\mathcal{O}'$.

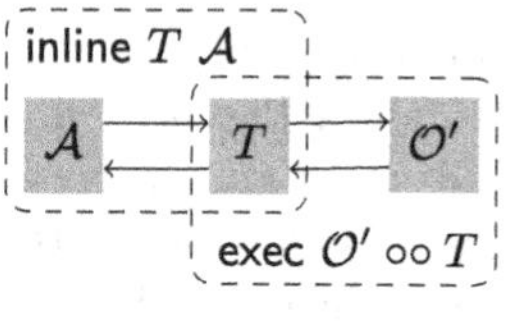

Fig. 7. Associativity of composition illustrated

By associativity of composition (see Fig. 7), this is equivalent to executing the original adversary $\mathcal{A}$ with access to the emulated oracle $\mathsf{exec}\ \mathcal{O}' \circ\circ T$. Thus, it suffices to establish that the emulation $\mathsf{exec}\ \mathcal{O}' \circ\circ T$ of $\mathcal{O}$ is good enough.

3.3 Parametricity and Bisimulation

Our framework provides a set of rules (a logic) for reasoning about the relation between games with oracles. This logic complements the equational theory derived from the shallow embedding. Like for spmf, parametricity guides us in choosing the rules and proving them sound. As the first step, we therefore define a relator $\mathsf{rel_{gpv}}$ for gpvs. As gpvs form a codatatype, the canonical definition is as a coinductive relation, namely the one specified by (5).[5]

$$\frac{\mathsf{un\text{-}GPV}\ v\ (\mathsf{rel_{spmf}}\ (\mathsf{rel_{+}}\ A\ (\mathsf{rel_{\times}}\ C\ ((=) \Rrightarrow \mathsf{rel_{gpv}}\ A\ C))))\ \mathsf{un\text{-}GPV}\ v'}{v\ (\mathsf{rel_{gpv}}\ A\ C)\ v'} \tag{5}$$

Canonicity ensures parametricity of the coiterator $\mathsf{coiter_{gpv}}$, the constructor GPV, and the selector un-GPV. For $\mathsf{coiter_{gpv}}$, e.g., we obtain that for all S, A, and C,

$$\mathsf{coiter_{gpv}}\ ((S \Rrightarrow \mathsf{rel_{spmf}}\ (\mathsf{rel_{+}}\ A\ (\mathsf{rel_{\times}}\ C\ ((=) \Rrightarrow S)))) \Rrightarrow S \Rrightarrow \mathsf{rel_{gpv}}\ A\ C)\ \mathsf{coiter_{gpv}}$$

Consequently, all the primitive operations in Fig. 5 are parametric, too. As the fixpoint operator preserves parametricity (Theorem 1), search is also parametric. And so are inline and exec and run. Thus, parametricity links $\mathsf{rel_{gpv}}$ with all the gpv operations.

Similar to spmfs (Sect. 2.4), this link leads to rules for reasoning about game transformations. We do not go into the details here. Instead, we consider the example of replacing an oracle with a bisimilar one as formalised by (6). This rule follows from the parametricity of run by unfolding the definitions.[6] The premises express that S is a bisimulation relation between the oracles $\mathcal{O}_1$ and $\mathcal{O}_2$ and relates their initial states. Bisimulation means that whenever two states s_1 and s_2 are related and the oracles are called with c, then they return the same value and the states are related again. The "then" part is expressed by the relation $\mathsf{rel_{\times}}\ (=)\ S$ which $\mathsf{rel_{spmf}}$ lifts to subprobability distributions. The second premise states that S relates the initial states. In the conclusion, we get that running a gpv v (e.g., the adversary) with two bisimilar oracles produces the same outcomes.

$$\frac{\forall s_1\ s_2\ c.\ s_1\ S\ s_2 \longrightarrow \mathcal{O}_1\ s_1\ c\ (\mathsf{rel_{spmf}}\ (\mathsf{rel_{\times}}\ (=)\ S))\ \mathcal{O}_2\ s_2\ c \qquad s_1\ S\ s_2}{\mathsf{run}\ \mathcal{O}_1\ v\ s_1 = \mathsf{run}\ \mathcal{O}_2\ v\ s_2} \tag{6}$$

In fact, the derivation may be seen as an instance of representation independence [40,44]. By design, the gpv has only black-box access to the oracle, i.e., they interface only via calls and returns. Thus, the first premise expresses exactly the requirement of representation independence: a relation S that is preserved by all operations of the interface. In Isabelle [31], so-called transfer rules express

[5] The type constructor gpv takes three type arguments, so we should expect $\mathsf{rel_{gpv}}$ to take three relations, too. However, the third argument occurs in a negative position in the codatatype definition. Therefore, the relator does not enjoy useful properties such as monotonicity and distributivity over relation composition. Consequently, Isabelle's infrastructure for parametricity treats these arguments as fixed (dead in the terminology of [22]). So, $\mathsf{rel_{gpv}}$ takes only relations for the first two arguments and fixes the third to the identity relation (=) as can be seen in (5). In practice, we have not found this specialisation to be restrictive.

[6] In fact, parametricity actually yields a rule stronger than (6), namely the gpv v need not be the same on both sides. If $v_1\ (\mathsf{rel_{gpv}}\ A\ (=))\ v_2$ and the premises of (6) hold, then $\mathsf{run}\ \mathcal{O}_1\ v_1\ s_1\ (\mathsf{rel_{spmf}}\ A)\ \mathsf{run}\ \mathcal{O}_2\ v_2\ s_2$.

$$\begin{array}{l} \mathsf{lcdh}\ \mathcal{A} = \mathbf{do}\ \{ \\ \quad x \leftarrow \mathsf{uniform}\ \{0 ..< |\mathcal{G}|\}; \\ \quad y \leftarrow \mathsf{uniform}\ \{0 ..< |\mathcal{G}|\}; \\ \quad Z \leftarrow \mathcal{A}\ (\mathsf{g}\ \hat{}\ x)\ (\mathsf{g}\ \hat{}\ y); \\ \quad \mathsf{return_{spmf}}\ (\mathsf{g}\ \hat{}\ (x \cdot y) \in Z)\ \} \end{array}$$

Fig. 8. Computational Diffie-Hellman game

$$\begin{array}{l} \mathsf{hash}\text{-}\mathcal{O}\ s_{\mathcal{O}}\ x = \\ \quad \mathsf{case}\ s_{\mathcal{O}}\ x\ \mathsf{of}\ \mathsf{None} \Rightarrow \mathbf{do}\ \{ \\ \qquad bs \leftarrow \mathsf{uniform}\ \{0,1\}^n; \\ \qquad \mathsf{return_{spmf}}\ (bs, s_{\mathcal{O}}(x \mapsto bs))\ \} \\ \quad |\ \mathsf{Some}\ bs \Rightarrow \mathsf{return_{spmf}}\ (bs, s_{\mathcal{O}}) \end{array}$$

Fig. 9. Random hash oracle

preservation in point-free style; here, $\mathcal{O}_1\ (S \Mapsto (=) \Mapsto \mathsf{rel_{spmf}}\ (\mathsf{rel}_\times\ (=)\ S))\ \mathcal{O}_2$. The HEG example exploits this idea in two game transformations (Sect. 3.4).

There are also limits to what we can derive from parametricity. For example, consider the case where only one of the oracles enters an error state, say because the adversary has guessed a secret. Then, the adversary can distinguish between the oracles and behave differently, i.e., it is not related by $\mathsf{rel_{gpv}}$ any more. Therefore, we would need a notion of bisimulation up to error, but relational parametricity cannot express this. Thus, we prove the Lemma 3 directly.

Lemma 3 (Oracle bisimulation up to error states). *Let S be a relation between the states of two oracles $\mathcal{O}_1$ and $\mathcal{O}_2$ and let F_1 and F_2 be the sets of error states. Define the relation R by $(x, s_1)\ R\ (y, s_2)$ iff $s_1 \in F_1 \leftrightarrow s_2 \in F_2$ and if $s_2 \notin F_2$ then $x = y$ and $s_1\ S\ s_2$. Then $\mathsf{exec}\ \mathcal{O}_1\ v\ s_1\ (\mathsf{rel_{spmf}}\ R)\ \mathsf{exec}\ \mathcal{O}_2\ v\ s_2$ if*

- *$\mathcal{O}_1\ (S \Mapsto (=) \Mapsto \mathsf{rel_{spmf}}\ R)\ \mathcal{O}_2$, and*
- *$s_1\ S\ s_2$ and $s_1 \in F_1 \leftrightarrow s_2 \in F_2$, and*
- *$\mathcal{O}_1$ and $\mathcal{O}_2$ are lossless in error states and error states are never left, and*
- *v issues finitely many calls and never fails, i.e., all spmfs in v are lossless.*

3.4 Security of Hashed Elgamal Encryption

Now, we illustrate how our framework supports proofs about games with oracles by reducing the IND-CPA security of Hashed Elgamal encryption to the computational Diffie-Hellman (CDH) assumption. The CDH assumption states that it is hard to compute $\mathsf{g}\ \hat{}\ (x \cdot y)$ given $\mathsf{g}\ \hat{}\ x$ and $\mathsf{g}\ \hat{}\ y$. For comparison with the existing proofs in Certicrypt [14] and EasyCrypt [13] (Sect. 4), we reduce the security to the set version LCDH of CDH, where the adversary may return a finite set of candidates for $\mathsf{g}\ \hat{}\ (x \cdot y)$. The reduction from LCDH to CDH is straightforward.

LCDH is formalised as follows. The LCDH adversary $\mathcal{A}$ is a probabilistic function from two group elements to a set of group elements. Its advantage $\mathsf{adv\text{-}lcdh}\ \mathcal{A}$ is the probability of True in the security game lcdh shown in Fig. 8.

In the random oracle model [15], hash functions are idealised as random functions. The random oracle $\mathsf{hash}\text{-}\mathcal{O}$ shown in Fig. 9 implements such a random function. Its state $s_{\mathcal{O}}$ is a map from group elements (inputs) to bitstrings (outputs), which associates previous queries with the outputs. Upon each call, the oracle looks up the input x in the map $s_{\mathcal{O}}$ and returns the corresponding output if found. If not, it returns a fresh bitstring bs of length n and updates the map $s_{\mathcal{O}}$ to associate x with bs.

The security of HEG is shown by a sequence of game transformations. They closely follow [13], so we do not present them in detail here. Instead, we focus on some steps to highlight the use of parametricity, equational reasoning, and the program logic. In the following, we assume a fixed IND-CPA adversary $\mathcal{A} = (\mathcal{A}_1, \mathcal{A}_2)$ which makes only finitely many calls and does not fail. This technical restriction is necessary to apply Lemma 3.

The first step changes the game such that it records the adversary's queries to the hash oracle using the oracle transformation record from Fig. 4b. So the first game game_1 is the same as ind-cpa from Fig. 4c except that the calls to the adversary are replaced by $(((m_0, m_1), \sigma), X) \leftarrow \mathsf{inline\ record}\ (\mathcal{A}_1\ pk)\ \{\}$ and $(b', X') \leftarrow \mathsf{inline\ record}\ (\mathcal{A}_2\ c^*\ \sigma)\ X$. The equality $\mathsf{ind\text{-}cpa}\ \mathcal{A} = \mathsf{game}_1$ follows from parametricity and bisimilarity of record and the identity oracle transformation $\mathsf{ID} = \lambda\sigma\ x.\ \mathbf{do}\ \{\ y \leftarrow \mathsf{call}\ x;\ \mathsf{return_{gpv}}\ (y, \sigma)\ \}$ due to representation independence, and the fact that ID is the identity for gpv composition. The bisimulation relation $S = \{\ (\sigma, X).\ \mathsf{True}\ \}$ identifies all states. The equality is proven automatically by Isabelle's prover for representation independence [31] using the transfer rules $()\ S\ \{\}$ and $\mathsf{ID}\ (S \Rrightarrow (=) \Rrightarrow \mathsf{rel_{spmf}}\ (\mathsf{rel_\times}\ (=)\ S))\ \mathsf{record}$ and equational rewriting. In fact, the latter rule is another instance of representation independence, as the two oracle transformations differ only in the update of the local state. The transfer rule $(\lambda\_\ s.\ s)\ ((=) \Rrightarrow S \Rrightarrow S)\ \mathsf{insert}$ formalises the connection. The parametricity prover derives the transfer rule for the oracles from this.

In the second step, we push the oracle transformation into the oracle exploiting associativity (cf. Fig. 7) and distribute the outermost run to the calls of the adversary. This changes the monad from gpv to spmf, in which $\mathsf{bind_{spmf}}$ commutes (1). Additionally, the new game game_2 returns a second boolean to flag whether the adversary caused a call to the hash oracle with the group element $\mathsf{g}\ \hat{}\ (x \cdot y)$. By equational reasoning only, we prove that $\mathsf{run\ hash\text{-}}\mathcal{O}\ \mathsf{game}_1\ \varnothing = \mathsf{map_{spmf}}\ \pi_1\ \mathsf{game}_2$ where the hash oracle starts in the initial state $\varnothing$.

$$
\begin{aligned}
&\mathsf{hElgamal}\ (\mathcal{A}_1, \mathcal{A}_2)\ \alpha\ \beta\ =\ \mathbf{do}\ \{\\
&\quad (((m_0, m_1), \sigma), s) \leftarrow \mathsf{exec\ hash\text{-}}\mathcal{O}\ (\mathcal{A}_1\ \alpha)\ \varnothing;\\
&\quad \mathsf{try}\ \mathbf{do}\ \{\\
&\qquad \mathsf{assert}\ (\mathsf{valid\text{-}plain}\ m_0 \land \mathsf{valid\text{-}plain}\ m_1);\\
&\qquad h \leftarrow\ \mathsf{uniform}\ \{0,1\}^n;\\
&\qquad (b', s') \leftarrow \mathsf{exec\ hash\text{-}}\mathcal{O}\ (\mathcal{A}_2\ (\beta, h)\ \sigma)\ s;\\
&\qquad \mathsf{return_{spmf}}\ (\mathsf{dom}\ s')\\
&\quad \}\ \mathsf{else\ return_{spmf}}\ (\mathsf{dom}\ s)\ \}
\end{aligned}
$$

Fig. 10. Reduction for Hashed Elgamal

The third transformation replaces the hash for the challenge ciphertext with a random bitstring which is not recorded in the hash oracle's map. By the fundamental lemma, the difference in the success probabilities is bounded by the error event, which is in this case the flag introduced in game_2. The assumption of the fundamental lemma is proven using the rules of the program logic. In particular, we apply Lemma 3 on the call to $\mathcal{A}_2$, as the oracles are not bisimilar if any of the remaining queries calls the hash function on $\mathsf{g}\ \hat{}\ (x \cdot y)$.

We do not go into the details of the remainder of the proof, as it applies the same techniques as before. The one time pad lemma is used to make the challenge ciphertext independent of the challenge bit b similar to optimistic sampling in Sect. 2.5. As the set of queries now is just the domain of the map of the hash oracle, we replace $\mathsf{exec}\ \mathsf{hash}\text{-}\mathcal{O} \circ\circ \mathsf{record}$ with $\mathsf{hash}\text{-}\mathcal{O}$ using representation independence. Finally, we show by equational reasoning that the first boolean of the game is just a coin flip and the second corresponds to the LCDH game for the transformed adversary $\mathsf{hElgamal}\ \mathcal{A}$ (see Fig. 10).[7] In summary, we obtain

$$\mathsf{adv\text{-}ind\text{-}cpa}\ \mathsf{hash}\text{-}\mathcal{O}\ \varnothing\ \mathcal{A} \leq \mathsf{adv\text{-}lcdh}\ (\mathsf{hElgamal}\ \mathcal{A})$$

4 Comparison with Existing Frameworks

In this section, we compare our framework with the existing tools CertiCrypt [14], EasyCrypt [13], FCF [42], and Verypto [8] in four respects: readability, expressiveness, the trusted codebase, and the formalisation effort.

Readability is important for two reasons. First, security definitions should resemble those in the cryptographic literature such that cryptographers are able to understand and evaluate them. Second, intuitive syntax supports the users during the formalisation, as they can focus on formalising the arguments rather than trying to understand hardly readable programs. All frameworks achieve good readability, but in different ways. CertiCrypt and EasyCrypt embed an imperative procedural language in their logics. They closely model Bellare's and Rogaway's idea of a stateful language with oracles as procedures [16]. Verypto deeply embeds a higher order language with mutable references based on de Bruijn indices in HOL. Readability is regained by reflecting the syntax in HOL's term language using parsing and pretty-printing tricks. In contrast, FCF and our framework shallowly embed a functional language with monadic sequencing in Coq and Isabelle/HOL, respectively. Like in Shoup's treatment [48], the state of the adversary and the oracles must be passed explicitly. This improves clarity as it makes explicit which party can access which parts of the state. Conversely, it can also be a source for errors, as it is the user who must ensure that the states be used linearly.

Expressiveness has two dimensions. First, the syntax and the semantic domain determine the expressiveness of the language. CertiCrypt and EasyCrypt support discrete subprobability distributions and a procedural while language, but no fixpoint operator, although fixpoints could be defined in CertiCrypt's semantic domain similar to our work (Sect. 2.3 and Theorem 1). Fixpoints do not increase the expressiveness over a while combinator, but lead to more natural formulations of programs. EasyCrypt additionally provides a module system to support abstraction and reuse. Verypto is the most general framework, as it

[7] The oracle transformation in this reduction is degenerate, as $\mathsf{hElgamal}$ emulates the oracle without access to further oracles. Thus, we use exec directly instead of inline.

builds on measure theory and therefore supports continuous distributions and higher order functions—at the price of incurring measurability proof obligations. FCF's semantics allows only probability distributions with finite support, so no fixpoint operator can be defined. The syntax further restricts probabilistic effects to random sampling of bitstrings and conditional probabilities. For programs with oracle access, FCF provides equivalents to our operations call, sample, and inline. Further effectful operators (such as try _ else _ cannot be added by the user, but require changes to the language formalisation itself. Conversely, FCF's deterministic pure sublanguage includes all functions and types from the library of the proof assistant thanks to the shallow embedding. Abstraction and reuse come from Coq's module system. Like FCF, our framework is integrated with the libraries and facilities of the proof assistant. It extends this advantage to probabilistic programs with oracle access, as we define also these languages directly in the semantic domain. Thus, users can define new control structures on the spot, if needed. It supports discrete subprobabilities similar to CertiCrypt and EasyCrypt and in addition features a fixpoint operator.

Second, the embedding and the logic determine what kind of security properties can be formalised. All frameworks support concrete security proofs. Thanks to the deep embedding, CertiCrypt and Verypto also support statements about efficiency and thus asymptotic security statements, which is impossible in EasyCrypt and ours, because HOL functions are extensional. FCF comes with an axiomatic cost model for efficiency, which is not formally connected to an operational model. This is possible despite the shallow embedding as long as extensionality is not assumed. In these three frameworks, asymptotic bounds are derived from concrete bounds. So no work is saved by reasoning asymptotically.

The trusted code base influences the trustworthiness of a mechanised proof and should be as small as possible. Proof assistants like Coq and Isabelle consist of a small kernel and can additionally produce proof terms or proof objects that an independent checker can certify. Consequently, CertiCrypt, FCF, and our framework achieve high ranks there. Verypto falls behind because its measure theory is only axiomatized rather than constructed definitionally. EasyCrypt does not have a small kernel, so the whole implementation in OCaml and the external SMT solvers must be trusted.

The formalisation effort determines the usability of a framework. For this comparison, we estimate the effort by the proof length measured in line counts. Clearly, proof styles affect line counts, so the numbers must be taken with a grain of salt. Nevertheless, they roughly indicate the effort required to produce such proofs. Table 1 lists the length (in lines) of the security statement for different cryptographic algorithms and frameworks. The line count includes the statement of the concrete security theorem, its proof, and all intermediate games. It does not cover the cryptographic algorithm itself nor the security definition. We obtained the numbers by inspecting the proof scripts distributed with the frameworks. Unfortunately, there are no line counts for Verypto because we could not get access to the sources.

Table 1. Framework comparison by line counts of concrete security theorems

Encryption algorithm	Framework			
	ours	CertiCrypt	EasyCrypt[a]	FCF[b]
Elgamal in the standard model (Sect. 2.1)	52	238	58	156
Hashed Elgamal in the ROM (Sect. 3.1)	236	810	210	
Pseudo-random function [42]	352			1166

[a] Version 27a6617 on github.com/EasyCrypt/easycrypt.git, 4 Jan 2016
[b] Version a445b73 on github.com/adampetcher/fcf, 13 Dec 2015

As Petcher and Morrisett have already observed [43], shallow embeddings (FCF, ours) have an advantage over deep ones (CertiCrypt, Verypto), as all the reasoning infrastructure and libraries of the proof assistant can be reused directly; a deep embedding would need to encode the libraries in the syntax of the language. Despite being more general, our framework leads to shorter proofs than FCF. We see two reasons for this gap. First, our language works directly in the semantic domain, even for effectful programs. This gives a richer equational theory and all conversions between syntax and semantics become superfluous. For example, their rule for loop fission holds only in the relational logic, but it is a HOL equality in our model. Second, Isabelle's built-in proof automation, in particularly conditional rewriting, provides a reasonable level of automation, especially for the equational proofs mentioned above. So far, we have not yet implemented any problem-specific proof tactics. Such tactics could automate the proofs even more, especially the manual reasoning with commutativity of sequencing. In comparison to EasyCrypt, the state of the art in proof automation, we achieve a similar degree of automation.

5 Further Related Work

In Sect. 4, we have already compared our framework with the existing ones for mechanising game playing proofs. In this section, we review further related work.

The tool CryptoVerif by Blanchet [20] can prove secrecy and correspondence properties such as authentication of security protocols. As it can even discover intermediate games itself, the tool achieves a much higher degree of automation than any of the frameworks including ours. The language—a process calculus inspired by the π calculus—distinguishes between a unique output process and possibly many input processes, which communicate via channels. Our gpvs also distinguish between inputs and outputs, but composition works differently. In CryptoVerif, several input processes may be able to receive an output and the semantics picks one uniformly randomly. In our setting, the callee represents all input processes and receives all calls. In principle, one could embed Blanchet's calculus in our semantic domain of gpvs using a different composition operator. Then, CryptoVerif's abstractions could be proven sound in our framework.

The functional programming language F* [17,49] has been used to verify implementations of cryptographic algorithms and protocols [12]. Security properties are formulated as type safety of an annotated, dependently-typed program and the type checker ensures type safety. While this approach scales to larger applications [18], the security properties cannot be stated concisely as the typing assertions are scattered over the whole implementation.

Affeldt et al. [2] formalise pmfs in Coq and apply this to coding theory.

Audebaud and Paulin-Mohring [5] formalised the spmf monad in Coq. They also define the approximation order $\sqsubseteq$ on spmfs and show that it forms an ω-complete partial order, i.e., *countable* chains have least upper bounds. Using Kleene's fixpoint theorem, they obtain a fixpoint operator for continuous functions. We generalise their result in that *arbitrary* spmf chains have least upper bounds. Thus, monotonicity (rather than continuity) suffices for the fixpoints.

CertiCrypt [14] uses their monad as the semantic domain for programs and adds the lifting operator $\mathsf{rel}_{\mathsf{spmf}}$. Zanella Béguelin proves a special case of Theorem 1, where the functions f and g are projections of a joint continuous function [51].

Cock [24] develops a shallow embedding of a probabilistic guarded command language in HOL. Programs are interpreted as monotone transformers of bounded expectations, which form a complete lattice. So, recursive functions can be defined using fixpoints. He focuses on proving functional correctness properties using non-relational Hoare triples and verification conditions.

Our framework reuses the existing infrastructure for relational parametricity in Isabelle/HOL, but in new ways. The Lifting package [31] exploits representation independence to transfer theorems between raw types and their quotients or subtypes. Lammich's tool AutoRef [35] uses transfer rules to refine abstract datatypes and algorithms to executable code. Blanchette et al. [23] use parametricity to express well-formedness conditions for operators under which corecursion may appear in corecursive functions. In contrast, we derive a relational logic for reasoning about shallowly embedded programs from parametricity and apply representation independence to replace oracles in games by bisimilar ones.

6 Conclusion and Future Work

In this paper, we have integrated a language for monadic probabilistic functions with black-box access to oracles in higher order logic. Several examples demonstrate that cryptographic algorithms and security definitions can be expressed in this language. A rich equational theory and a relational logic support the formalisation of cryptographic arguments. The definitions and proofs have been mechanised using the proof assistant Isabelle/HOL.

Although our logic is similar to those in FCF and EasyCrypt, our approach is different: we derive the rules in a principled way from parametricity of the operators. This approach can help in finding the appropriate rules when new operations are introduced, and in proving them sound. Petcher and Morrisett, e.g., add a monadic map operation to FCF's language and an appropriate reasoning rule to their logic [43]. They show soundness for the rule by induction, which takes 22 proof steps. In our approach, their rule is an instance of parametricity of the map operator, which Isabelle's parametricity prover can establish automatically.

This work is motivated by the goal of formalising computational soundness results. Whether our framework scales to such large applications is still an open question. In our cryptographic examples, it compares favourably to the state of the art. Indeed, our initial attempts in formalising the CoSP framework [9] are encouraging that our approach will work. Therefore, the next steps will focus on formalising these results and improving proof automation.

Our framework cannot express efficiency notions such as polynomial runtime yet. Hence, asymptotic reasoning, which dominates in CS proofs, can be used only in limited ways. This is the flipside of the shallow embedding: As HOL functions are extensional, we cannot exploit HOL syntax in the reasoning. It seems possible to adapt Petcher's and Morrisett's axiomatic cost model [42], but the benefits are not yet clear. A less axiomatic alternative is to formalise a small programming language, connect it to HOL's functions and derive the bounds in terms of the operational semantics. Verypto [8] and the higher-order complexity analysis for Coq by Jouannaud and Xu [33] might be good starting points.

Beyond cryptographic arguments and computational soundness, our semantic domain of generative probabilistic values could be applied in different contexts. In previous work [38], we used a (less abstract) precursor to model interactive programs in HOL. The domain could also serve as a basis for formalising and verifying CryptoVerif or as a backend for the new EasyCrypt, as EasyCrypt's logic and module system resemble Isabelle's.

In this direction, it would be interesting to investigate whether gpvs admit a ccpo structure in which where the basic operations are monotone. Currently, corecursion and coinduction are available. The ccpo structure would allow us to additionally define functions recursively and use induction as proof principle. The problem is that limits must preserve discreteness of the subprobability distributions. It is not easy to move to arbitrary measure-theoretic distributions, as codatatypes in HOL require a cardinality bound on the functor through which they recurse; otherwise, they cannot be defined in HOL [28].

Acknowledgements. Johannes Hölzl helped us with formalising spmfs on top of his probability formalisation and with the proof of countable support of spmf chains. Christoph Sprenger and Dmitriy Traytel and the anonymous reviewers suggested improvements of the presentation and the examples. This work was supported by SNSF grant 153217 "Formalising Computational Soundness for Protocol Implementations".

References

1. Abadi, M., Rogaway, P.: Reconciling two views of cryptography (The computational soundness of formal encryption). J. Cryptology **15**(2), 103–127 (2002)
2. Affeldt, R., Hagiwara, M., Sénizergues, J.: Formalization of Shannon's theorems. J. Automat. Reason. **53**(1), 63–103 (2014)

3. Aharoni, R., Berger, E., Georgakopoulos, A., Perlstein, A., Sprüssel, P.: The max-flow min-cut theorem for countable networks. J. Combin. Theory Ser. B **101**, 1–17 (2011)
4. Armando, A., et al.: The AVANTSSAR platform for the automated validation of trust and security of service-oriented architectures. In: Flanagan, C., König, B. (eds.) TACAS 2012. LNCS, vol. 7214, pp. 267–282. Springer, Heidelberg (2012)
5. Audebaud, P., Paulin-Mohring, C.: Proofs of randomized algorithms in Coq. Sci. Comput. Program. **74**(8), 568–589 (2009)
6. Bacelar Almeida, J., Barbosa, M., Bangerter, E., Barthe, G., Krenn, S., Zanella Béguelin, S.: Full proof cryptography: verifiable compilation of efficient zero-knowledge protocols. In: CCS 2012, pp. 488–500. ACM (2012)
7. Backes, M., Barthe, G., Berg, M., Grégoire, B., Kunz, C., Skoruppa, M., Zanella Béguelin, S.: Verified security of Merkle-Damgård. In: CSF 2012, pp. 354–368 (2012)
8. Backes, M., Berg, M., Unruh, D.: A formal language for cryptographic pseudocode. In: Cervesato, I., Veith, H., Voronkov, A. (eds.) LPAR 2008. LNCS (LNAI), vol. 5330, pp. 353–376. Springer, Heidelberg (2008)
9. Backes, M., Hofheinz, D., Unruh, D.: CoSP: a general framework for computational soundness proofs. In: CCS 2009, pp. 66–78. ACM (2009)
10. Backes, M., Malik, A., Unruh, D.: Computational soundness without protocol restrictions. In: CCS 2012, pp. 699–711. ACM (2012)
11. Ballarin, C.: Locales: A module system for mathematical theories. J. Automat. Reason. **52**(2), 123–153 (2014)
12. Barthe, G., Fournet, C., Grégoire, B., Strub, P.Y., Swamy, N., Zanella Béguelin, S.: Probabilistic relational verification for cryptographic implementations. In: POPL 2014, pp. 193–205. ACM (2014)
13. Barthe, G., Grégoire, B., Heraud, S., Béguelin, S.Z.: Computer-aided security proofs for the working cryptographer. In: Rogaway, P. (ed.) CRYPTO 2011. LNCS, vol. 6841, pp. 71–90. Springer, Heidelberg (2011)
14. Barthe, G., Grégoire, B., Zanella Béguelin, S.: Formal certification of code-based cryptographic proofs. In: POPL 2009, pp. 90–101. ACM (2009)
15. Bellare, M., Rogaway, P.: Random oracles are practical: a paradigm for designing efficient protocols. In: CCS 1993, pp. 62–73. ACM (1993)
16. Bellare, M., Rogaway, P.: The security of triple encryption and a framework for code-based game-playing proofs. In: Vaudenay, S. (ed.) EUROCRYPT 2006. LNCS, vol. 4004, pp. 409–426. Springer, Heidelberg (2006)
17. Bengtson, J., Bhargavan, K., Fournet, C., Gordon, A.D., Maffeis, S.: Refinement types for secure implementations. ACM Trans. Program. Lang. Syst. **33**(2), 8:1–8:45 (2011)
18. Bhargavan, K., Fournet, C., Kohlweiss, M., Pironti, A., Strub, P.Y.: Implementing TLS with verified cryptographic security. In: S&P 2013, pp. 445–459. IEEE (2013)
19. Blanchet, B.: An efficient cryptographic protocol verifier based on Prolog rules. In: CSFW 2001, pp. 82–96. IEEE (2001)
20. Blanchet, B.: A computationally sound mechanized prover for security protocols. IEEE Trans. Dependable Secure Comput. **5**(4), 193–207 (2008)
21. Blanchet, B., Jaggard, A.D., Rao, J., Scedrov, A., Tsay, J.K.: Refining computationally sound mechanized proofs for Kerberos. In: FCC 2009 (2009)
22. Blanchette, J.C., Hölzl, J., Lochbihler, A., Panny, L., Popescu, A., Traytel, D.: Truly modular (Co)datatypes for Isabelle/HOL. In: Klein, G., Gamboa, R. (eds.) ITP 2014. LNCS, vol. 8558, pp. 93–110. Springer, Heidelberg (2014)

23. Blanchette, J.C., Popescu, A., Traytel, D.: Foundational extensible corecursion: A proof assistant perspective. In: ICFP 2015, pp. 192–204. ACM (2015)
24. Cock, D.: Verifying probabilistic correctness in Isabelle with pGCL. In: SSV 2012. EPTCS, vol. 102, pp. 1–10 (2012)
25. Cortier, V., Kremer, S., Warinschi, B.: A survey of symbolic methods in computational analysis of cryptographic systems. J. Automat. Reason. **46**, 225–259 (2011)
26. Desharnais, J.: Labelled Markov Processes. Ph.D. thesis, McGill University (1999)
27. Elgamal, T.: A public key cryptosystem and a signature scheme based on discrete logarithms. IEEE Trans. Inf. Theory **31**(4), 469–472 (1985)
28. Gunter, E.L.: Why we can't have SML-style datatype declarations in HOL. In: Claesen, L.J.M., Gordon, M.J.C. (eds.) TPHOLs 1992, pp. 561–568. Elsevier, North-Holland (1993)
29. Halevi, S.: A plausible approach to computer-aided cryptographic proofs. Cryptology ePrint Archive, Report 2005/181 (2005)
30. Hölzl, J., Lochbihler, A., Traytel, D.: A formalized hierarchy of probabilistic system types. In: Urban, C., Zhang, X. (eds.) ITP 2015. LNCS, vol. 9236, pp. 203–220. Springer, Heidelberg (2015)
31. Huffman, B., Kunčar, O.: Lifting and Transfer: a modular design for quotients in Isabelle/HOL. In: Gonthier, G., Norrish, M. (eds.) CPP 2013. LNCS, vol. 8307, pp. 131–146. Springer, Heidelberg (2013)
32. Hurd, J.: A formal approach to probabilistic termination. In: Carreño, V.A., Muñoz, C.A., Tahar, S. (eds.) TPHOLs 2002. LNCS, vol. 2410, pp. 230–245. Springer, Heidelberg (2002)
33. Jouannaud, J.P., Xu, W.: Automatic complexity analysis for programs extracted from Coq proof. In: CLASE 2005. ENTCS, vol. 153(1), pp. 35–53 (2006)
34. Krauss, A.: Recursive definitions of monadic functions. In: PAR 2010. EPTCS, vol. 43, pp. 1–13 (2010)
35. Lammich, P.: Automatic data refinement. In: Blazy, S., Paulin-Mohring, C., Pichardie, D. (eds.) ITP 2013. LNCS, vol. 7998, pp. 84–99. Springer, Heidelberg (2013)
36. Larsen, K.G., Skou, A.: Bisimulation through probabilistic testing. Inf. Comp. **94**(1), 1–28 (1991)
37. Lochbihler, A.: Formalisation accompanying this paper. http://www.infsec.ethz.ch/research/projects/FCSPI/ESOP2016.html
38. Lochbihler, A., Züst, M.: Programming TLS in Isabelle/HOL. Isabelle Workshop 2014 (2014)
39. Meier, S., Cremers, C.J.F., Basin, D.: Efficient construction of machine-checked symbolic protocol security proofs. J. Comput. Secur. **21**(1), 41–87 (2013)
40. Mitchell, J.C.: Representation independence and data abstraction. In: POPL 1986, pp. 263–276. ACM (1986)
41. Nipkow, T., Paulson, L.C., Wenzel, M.: Isabelle/HOL – A Proof Assistant for Higher-Order Logic. LNCS, vol. 2283. Springer, Heidelberg (2002)
42. Petcher, A., Morrisett, G.: The foundational cryptography framework. In: Focardi, R., Myers, A. (eds.) POST 2015. LNCS, vol. 9036, pp. 53–72. Springer, Heidelberg (2015)
43. Petcher, A., Morrisett, G.: A mechanized proof of security for searchable symmetric encryption. In: CSF 2015, pp. 481–494. IEEE (2015)
44. Reynolds, J.C.: Types, abstraction and parametric polymorphism. In: IFIP 1983. Information Processing, vol. 83, pp. 513–523. North-Holland/IFIP (1983)
45. Rutten, J.J.M.M.: Relators and metric bisimulations. Electr. Notes Theor. Comput. Sci. **11**, 252–258 (1998)

46. Sack, J., Zhang, L.: A general framework for probabilistic characterizing formulae. In: Kuncak, V., Rybalchenko, A. (eds.) VMCAI 2012. LNCS, vol. 7148, pp. 396–411. Springer, Heidelberg (2012)
47. Schmidt, B., Meier, S., Cremers, C.J.F., Basin, D.A.: Automated analysis of Diffie-Hellman protocols and advanced security properties. In: CSF 2012, pp. 78–94. IEEE (2012)
48. Shoup, V.: Sequences of games: A tool for taming complexity in security proofs. Cryptology ePrint Archive, Report 2004/332 (2004)
49. Swamy, N., Chen, J., Fournet, C., Strub, P.Y., Bhargavan, K., Yang, J.: Secure distributed programming with value-dependent types. J. Funct. Program. **23**(4), 402–451 (2013)
50. Wadler, P.: Theorems for free! In: FPCA 1989, pp. 347–359. ACM (1989)
51. Zanella Béguelin, S.: Formal Certification of Game-Based Cryptographic Proofs. Ph.D. thesis, École Nationale Supérieure des Mines de Paris (2010)

Extensible and Efficient Automation Through Reflective Tactics

Gregory Malecha[1(✉)] and Jesper Bengtson[2]

[1] University of California, San Diego, USA
gmalecha@eng.ucsd.edu
[2] IT University of Copenhagen, Copenhagen, USA
jebe@itu.dk

Abstract. Foundational proof assistants simultaneously offer both expressive logics and strong guarantees. The price they pay for this flexibility is often the need to build and check explicit proof objects which can be expensive. In this work we develop a collection of techniques for building reflective automation, where proofs are witnessed by verified decision procedures rather than verbose proof objects. Our techniques center around a verified domain specific language for proving, $\mathcal{R}_{tac}$, written in Gallina, Coq's logic. The design of tactics makes it easy to combine them into higher-level automation that can be proved sound in a mostly automated way. Furthermore, unlike traditional uses of reflection, $\mathcal{R}_{tac}$ tactics are independent of the underlying problem domain, which allows them to be re-tasked to automate new problems with very little effort. We demonstrate the usability of $\mathcal{R}_{tac}$ through several case studies demonstrating orders of magnitude speedups for relatively little engineering work.

1 Introduction

Foundational proof assistants provide strong guarantees about properties expressed in rich logics. They have been applied to reason about operating systems [29], compilers [32], databases [35], and cyber-physical systems [18], just to name a few. In all of these contexts, users leverage the expressivity of the underlying logic to state their problem and use the automation provided by the proof assistant, often in the form of a "tactic language," to prove the properties they care about, e.g. the correctness of a compiler.

The problem with this rosy picture is that foundational proofs are large because they need to spell out the justification in complete detail. This is especially true in rich dependent type theories such as Coq [17] and Agda [1] where proofs are first-class objects with interesting structural and computational properties. Several recent projects have made the overhead of proof objects painfully clear: the Verified Software Toolchain [2], CertiKOS [41], and Bedrock [15]. All of these projects run into resource limitations, often in memory, but also in build times. Proof generating automation tends to work well when applied to small problems, but scales poorly as problems grow. To solve this problem we need a way to extend the proof checker in a trustworthy way so that it can check

P. Thiemann (Ed.): ESOP 2016, LNCS 9632, pp. 532–559, 2016.
DOI: 10.1007/978-3-662-49498-1_21

certain properties more efficiently. Doing this allows us to dramatically improve both the time and memory usage of foundational verification.

The expressivity of foundational constructive proof assistants provides a technique for "extending the proof checker": computational reflection [5,6,9,30,40]. Using computational reflection, a developer implements a custom program to check properties outright and proves that the program is sound, i.e. if it claims that a property is provable, then a proof of the property exists. With computational reflection, previously large proof objects can be replaced by calls to these custom decision procedures. Executing these procedures can be much more efficient than type checking explicit proof terms. However, the current approach to building these reflective procedures makes them difficult to construct, cumbersome to adapt to new instances, and almost impossible to compose to build higher-level automation.

In this work we show how to easily build reflective automation that is both extensible and efficient. Our approach is to separate the core reflective language from the domain-specific symbols that the automation reasons about. This enables us to build a Domain Specific Language (DSL), $\mathcal{R}_{tac}$, for reflective automation that is reusable across any base theory. We show that naïvely translating automation from $\mathcal{L}_{tac}$, Coq's built-in tactic language, to $\mathcal{R}_{tac}$ typically leads to at least an order of magnitude speedup on reasonable problem sizes.

We begin with a brief primer applying computational reflection to automate monoidal equivalence checking (Sect. 2). In Sect. 3 we highlight our techniques by reworking this example in $\mathcal{R}_{tac}$ highlighting the key pieces of our work from the client's point of view. We then proceed to our contributions:

- We develop MirrorCore, a reusable Coq library for general and extensible computational reflection built around a core λ-calculus (Sect. 4).
- We build $\mathcal{R}_{tac}$—the first foundational, feature-rich reflective tactic language (Sect. 5). By separating domain-specific meaning from generic manipulation, $\mathcal{R}_{tac}$ is able to provide high-level building blocks that are independent of the underlying domain. Additionally the user-exposed interface makes it easy to combine these general tactics into larger, domain-specific automation and derive the corresponding soundness proofs essentially for free.
- We demonstrate the extensible nature of $\mathcal{R}_{tac}$ by developing a reflective setoid rewriter as an $\mathcal{R}_{tac}$ tactic (Sect. 6). The custom implementation follows the MirrorCore recipe of separating the core syntax from the domain-specific symbols allowing the rewriter to be re-tasked to a range of problem domains. In addition, the procedure is higher-order and can invoke $\mathcal{R}_{tac}$ tactics to discharge side conditions during rewriting.
- We evaluate MirrorCore and $\mathcal{R}_{tac}$ by developing reflective procedures for different domains (Sect. 7). We show that our automation has substantially better scaling properties than traditional $\mathcal{L}_{tac}$ automation has and is quite simple to write in most cases.

Before concluding, we survey a range of related work related to automation alternatives in proof assistants (Sect. 8).

All of our results have been mechanized in the Coq proof assistant. The MirrorCore library and examples are available online:

https://github.com/gmalecha/mirror-core

2 A Computational Reflection Primer

In this section we give an overview of the core ideas in computational reflection which we build on in the remainder of the paper. We base our overview on the problem of proving equality in a commutative monoid. For example, consider proving the following problem instance where $\oplus$ is the plus operator in the monoid.

$$x \oplus 2 \oplus 3 \oplus 4 = 4 \oplus 3 \oplus 2 \oplus x$$

A naïve proof would use the transitivity of equality to witness the way to permute the elements on the left until they match those on the right. While not particularly difficult, the proof is often at least quadratic in the size of the property, which means that checking large problems quickly becomes expensive.

To use computational reflection to prove this theorem, we write a procedure that accepts the two expressions and checks the property directly. We first define a syntactic (also called "reified") representation of the problem. In this example, we use the following language.

$$\text{(expressions) } e ::= \mathsf{N}\, n \mid \mathsf{R}\, i \mid e_1 \underline{\oplus} e_2$$

The language represents constants directly (using N) but it hides quantified values such as x behind an index (using R). The syntactic representation is necessary because computations can not inspect the structure of terms, only their values. For example, pattern matching on $x \oplus y$ does not reduce since x and y are not closed values. A syntactic representation exposes the *syntax* of the goal, e.g. $\mathsf{R}\,1 \underline{\oplus} \mathsf{R}\,2$, which functions can inspect.

We formalize the meaning of the syntax through a "denotation function" ($[\![-]\!]_\rho$) parameterized by the environment of opaque symbols (ρ). For our syntax, $[\![-]\!]_\rho$ has three cases:

$$[\![\mathsf{N}\, n]\!]_\rho = n \qquad [\![\mathsf{R}\, x]\!]_\rho = \rho\, x \qquad [\![e_1 \underline{\oplus} e_2]\!]_\rho = [\![e_1]\!]_\rho \oplus [\![e_2]\!]_\rho$$

Using this syntax, the problem instance above could be represented as:

$$[\![\mathsf{R}\,0 \underline{\oplus} \mathsf{N}\,2 \underline{\oplus} \mathsf{N}\,3 \underline{\oplus} \mathsf{N}\,4]\!]_{\{0 \mapsto x\}} = x \oplus 2 \oplus 3 \oplus 4$$
$$[\![\mathsf{N}\,4 \underline{\oplus} \mathsf{N}\,3 \underline{\oplus} \mathsf{N}\,2 \underline{\oplus} \mathsf{R}\,0]\!]_{\{0 \mapsto x\}} = 4 \oplus 3 \oplus 2 \oplus x$$

With the syntax in hand, we can now write a procedure (Mcheck) that determines whether the terms are equal by flattening each expression into a list and checking whether one list is a permutation of the other. The soundness theorem of `Mcheck` states that if `Mcheck` returns true then the meaning of the two arguments are provably equal. Formally,

$$\mathsf{Mcheck\_sound} : \forall e_1\, e_2, \mathtt{Mcheck}\, e_1\, e_2 = \mathsf{true} \rightarrow \forall \rho, [\![e_1]\!]_\rho = [\![e_2]\!]_\rho$$

Using Mcheck_sound we can prove the example problem with following proof which is linear in the size of problem.

Mcheck_sound	
(R 0 $\underline{\oplus}$ N 2 $\underline{\oplus}$ N 3 $\underline{\oplus}$ N 4) (N 4 $\underline{\oplus}$ N 3 $\underline{\oplus}$ N 2 $\underline{\oplus}$ R 0)	(syntactic problem)
eq_refl	(proof `Mcheck` returned true)
$\{0 \mapsto x\}$	(environment)

3 $\mathcal{R}_{tac}$ from the Client's Perspective

Before delving into the technical machinery that underlies our framework we highlight the end result. In Fig. 1, we excerpt an $\mathcal{R}_{tac}$ implementation of the monoidal equivalence checker described in Sect. 2[1]. The automation builds directly on the Coq definitions of commutative monoids excerpted in step (0).

The first step is to build a data type that can represent the properties that we care about. In Sect. 2 we built a custom data type and spelled out all of the cases explicitly. Here, we build the syntactic representation by instantiating MirrorCore's generic language (`expr`) with domain specific types (`mon_typ`) and symbols (`mon_sym`). As we will see in Sect. 4, the `expr` language provides a variety of features that are helpful when building automation. Once we have defined the syntax, we use MirrorCore's programmable `reification` plugin to automatically construct syntactic representations of the lemmas that we will use in our automation (step (2)).

In step (3), we use these lemmas to write our reflective automation using the $\mathcal{R}_{tac}$ DSL. The entry point to the automation is the `Mcheck` tactic but the core procedures are `iter_left` and `iter_right` which permute the left- (`iter_left`) and right-hand sides (`iter_right`) of the equality until matching terms can be cancelled. Each tactic consists of a bounded recursion (`REC`) where the body tries one of several tactics (`FIRST`). For example, `iter_right` tries to apply `lem_plus_c` to remove a unit element from the right-hand-side. The double semicolon sequences two tactics together. It applies the second tactic to all (`ON_ALL`) goals produced by the first or applies a list of tactics one to each generated subgoal (`ON_EACH`).

In step (4) we prove the soundness of the automation. Soundness proofs are typically a major part of the work when developing reflective tactics; however, the compositional nature of $\mathcal{R}_{tac}$ tactics makes proving soundness almost completely automatic. The `rtac_derive_soundness_default` ($\mathcal{L}_{tac}$) tactic proves the soundness of a tactic by composing the soundness of its individual pieces.

Finally, we use `Mcheck` to verify equivalences in the monoid (step (5)). On small problems, the difference between $\mathcal{L}_{tac}$ and our technique is negligible. However, for large problem sizes, our automation performs several orders of magnitude faster. We defer a more detailed evaluation to Sect. 7.

[1] The full code can be found in the MirrorCore distribution.

```
(* (0) Develop the theory of monoids. *)
Parameter star : ℕ → ℕ → ℕ. (* ‘‘a ⊕ b’’ *)
Axiom plus_assoc_c1 : ∀ a b c d, d = a ⊕ (b ⊕ c) → d = (a ⊕ b) ⊕ c.

(* (1) Define a syntax for the problem & setup reification *)
Inductive mon_typ := tyArr (_ _ : mon_typ) | tyProp | tyNat.
Inductive mon_sym := Plus | N (_ : ℕ).
(* ...denotation functions and a few proofs about these types... *)

Let mon_term := expr mon_typ mon_sym.

Reify Declare Syntax reify_mon_term :=
  CFirst (CPatterns patterns_monoid :: ...).

(* (2) Automatically build syntactic lemmas *)
Reify BuildLemma < reify_mon_typ reify_mon_term reify_mon_term >
   lem_plus_assoc_c1 : plus_assoc_c1.
Definition lem_plus_assoc_c1_sound : lemmaD lem_plus_assoc_c1 :=
     plus_assoc_c1.
(* ...more lemmas... *)

(* (3) Build automation using tactics *)
Definition iter_right (n : ℕ) : rtac :=
  REC n (fun rec ⇒
          FIRST [ EAPPLY lem_plus_unit_c
                | EAPPLY lem_plus_assoc_c1 ;; ON_ALL rec
                | EAPPLY lem_plus_assoc_c2 ;; ON_ALL rec
                | EAPPLY lem_plus_cancel ;;
                  ON_EACH [ SOLVE solver | IDTAC ] ]) IDTAC.

Definition iter_left (k : rtac) (n : ℕ) : rtac :=
  REC n (fun rec ⇒
          FIRST [ EAPPLY lem_plus_unit_p
                | EAPPLY lem_plus_assoc_p1 ;; ON_ALL rec
                | EAPPLY lem_plus_assoc_p2 ;; ON_ALL rec
                | k ]) IDTAC.

Definition Mcheck : rtac := ...

(* (4) Prove the automation sound *)
Lemma iter_right_sound : ∀ Q, rtac_sound (iter_right Q).
Proof. unfold iter_right. intros. rtac_derive_soundness_default. Qed.

Lemma iter_left_sound : ∀ Q k, rtac_sound k → rtac_sound (iter_left k Q).
Proof. unfold iter_left. intros. rtac_derive_soundness_default. Qed.

(* (5) Use the reflective automation *)
Goal x ⊕ 2 ⊕ 3 ⊕ 4 = 4 ⊕ 3 ⊕ 2 ⊕ x.
Proof. run_tactic reify_mon_term Mcheck Mcheck_sound. Qed.
```

Fig. 1. Implementing a monoidal cancellation algorithm using $\mathcal{R}_{tac}$.

Building and Evolving Automation. While the goal of automation is a "push-button" solution, it rarely starts out that way. The automation shown in Fig. 1, like most $\mathcal{R}_{tac}$ automation, was constructed incrementally in much the same way that users build automation using $\mathcal{L}_{tac}$ [14]. The developer inspects the goal and finds the next thing to do to make progress. This same process works when developing automation in $\mathcal{R}_{tac}$. When the developer runs a tactic that does not solve the goal, a new goal is returned showing what is left to prove. By default, the process of constructing the syntactic representation is hidden from the user and new goals are returned after they have been converted back into their semantic counter-parts.

It is important to note, that while we can develop tactics incrementally, $\mathcal{R}_{tac}$ is not built to do manual proofs in the style of $\mathcal{L}_{tac}$. When run alone, the core $\mathcal{R}_{tac}$ tactics (e.g. `APPLY`) are often slower than their $\mathcal{L}_{tac}$ counter-parts. $\mathcal{R}_{tac}$'s speed comes from the ability to replace large proof terms with smaller ones, and larger proofs only arise when combining multiple reasoning steps.

4 The MirrorCore Language

A key component of reflective automation is the syntactic representation of the problem domain. We need a representation that is both expressive and easy to extend. In this section we present MirrorCore's generic `expr` language which we used in Sect. 3.

Mathematically, the `expr` language is the simply-typed λ-calculus augmented with unification variables (see Fig. 2). The `expr` language mirrors Coq's core logic, providing a rich structure that can represent higher-order functions and λ-abstractions. To provide extensibility, the language is parametric in both a type of types and a type of symbols. This parameterization allows the client to instantiate the language with domain-specific types, e.g. the monoid carrier, and symbols, e.g. monoid plus. Further, this compartmentalization makes it possible to implement and verify a variety of generic procedures for term manipulation. For example, MirrorCore includes lifting and lowering operations, beta-reduction, and a generic unification algorithm for the `expr` language.

Following the standard presentation of the λ-calculus, the language is divided into two levels: types and terms. The type language is completely user-defined but has two requirements. First, it must have a representation of function types so that λ-abstractions and applications can be typed. Second, it requires decidable equality to ensure that type checking `expr` terms is decidable. In order to use $\mathcal{R}_{tac}$ (which we discuss in Sect. 5) the type language also requires a representation of Coq's type of propositions (`Prop`).

The term language follows a mostly standard presentation of the λ-calculus using De Bruijn indices to represent bound variables. To support binders, the denotation function of terms $\left({}^{t_u}_{t_v}[\![-]\!]_t\right)$ is parameterized by two type environments (for unification variables, t_u, and regular variables, t_v) and the result type (t). These three pieces of information give us the type of the denotation. Concretely, the meaning of a term is a Coq function from the two environments (with types

Types (user specified, with restrictions)

$$\tau ::= \mathsf{tyProp} \mid \tau_1 \rightarrow \tau_2 \mid \ldots$$
$$[\![-]\!]^{\tau} \;:\; \tau \rightarrow \mathsf{Type}$$
$$\text{(Environments)} \qquad [\![-]\!]^{\vec{\tau}} \;:\; \mathsf{list}\,\tau \rightarrow \mathsf{Type}$$

$$[\![\mathsf{tyProp}]\!]^{\tau} = \mathsf{Prop} \qquad [\![t_1 \rightarrow t_2]\!]^{\tau} = [\![t_1]\!]^{\tau} \rightarrow [\![t_2]\!]^{\tau}$$

Domain-specific constants (user specified)

$$\langle - \rangle^{\tau} : b \rightarrow \tau \qquad [\![-]\!]_t : b \rightarrow \mathsf{option}\,[\![t]\!]^{\tau}$$

Terms

$$\mathcal{E} ::= e_1\, e_2 \mid \lambda\tau.e \mid x \mid ?u \mid \lceil b \rceil$$
$${}^{t_u}_{t_v}[\![-]\!]_t \;:\; \mathcal{E} \rightarrow \mathsf{option}\left([\![t_u]\!]^{\vec{\tau}} \rightarrow [\![t_v]\!]^{\vec{\tau}} \rightarrow [\![t]\!]^{\tau}\right)$$

$${}^{t_u}_{t_v}[\![e_1\; e_2]\!]_t = \lambda d_u\; d_v.\; \left({}^{t_u}_{t_v}[\![e_1]\!]_{t' \rightarrow t}\; d_u\; d_v\right)\; \left({}^{t_u}_{t_v}[\![e_2]\!]_{t'}\; d_u\; d_v\right)$$
$${}^{t_u}_{t_v}[\![\lambda t.e]\!]_{t \rightarrow t'} = \lambda d_u\; d_v\; a.\; {}^{t_u}_{t_v \cdot t}[\![e]\!]_{t'}\; d_u\; (d_v\; \cdot a)$$
$${}^{t_u}_{t_v}[\![x]\!]_t = \lambda\_\; d_v.\; d_v\; x \qquad \text{if } d_v\; x\; :\; [\![t]\!]^{\tau}$$
$${}^{t_u}_{t_v}[\![?u]\!]_t = \lambda d_u\; \_.\; d_u\; u \qquad \text{if } d_u\; u\; :\; [\![t]\!]^{\tau}$$
$${}^{t_u}_{t_v}[\![\lceil b \rceil]\!]_t = \lambda\_\;\_.\; [\![b]\!]_t$$

Fig. 2. MirrorCore's calculus for syntactic terms, typing- and denotation functions, using mathematical notation.

$[\![t_u]\!]^{\vec{\tau}}$ and $[\![t_v]\!]^{\vec{\tau}}$) to the result type ($[\![t]\!]^{\tau}$). If the term is ill-typed then it has no denotation, which we encode using Coq's `option` type. The denotation function returns `Some` with the denotation of the term if it is well-typed, or `None` if the term is ill-typed[2]. The choice to use Coq's function space for the denotation means that some of the theorems in MirrorCore rely on the axiom of functional extensionality.

The precise placement of the `option` in the type of the denotation function demarks the phase separation between type checking and computing the denotation. This phase separation is necessary to define the meaning of abstractions since the abstraction can only be introduced if the syntactic body has a denotation in the extended environment.

$${}^{t_u}_{t_v}[\![\lambda t'.e]\!]_{t' \rightarrow t} = \mathsf{Some}\,\lambda d_u\, d_v.\big(\lambda x.D\, d_u\, (x \cdot d_v)\big) \quad \text{if} \quad {}^{t_u}_{t' \cdot t_v}[\![e]\!]_t = \mathsf{Some}\, D$$

Without knowing that D is well-typed under the extended context, there is no way to construct a value of type $[\![t]\!]^{\tau}$ since not all types in Coq are inhabited.

The `expr` language also includes a representation of unification variables ($?u$), which are place-holders for arbitrary terms. The difficulty in representing unification variables comes when they are mixed with local variables. For example, suppose we represent the following proposition in `expr`

$$?u = ?u \wedge \forall x : \mathbb{N}, ?u = x$$

[2] We permit ill-typed terms in our representation to avoid indexing terms by their type. Indexed terms are larger which increases the time it takes to type-check them thus slowing down the automation.

Focusing on the right-hand conjunct, it seems that we should instantiate $?u$ with x; however, x is not in scope in the left-hand conjunct. We solve this problem in the `expr` language by preventing the instantiation of unification variables from mentioning any locally introduced variables. This choice leads to a more concise representation but requires that we are careful when dealing with unification variables that are scoped with respect to different contexts. We will return to this point in Sect. 5.

5 $\mathcal{R}_{tac}$: Verification Building Blocks

In this section we implement a fully-reflective proving language, called $\mathcal{R}_{tac}$, modeled on $\mathcal{L}_{tac}$, Coq's built-in tactic language. $\mathcal{R}_{tac}$ allows clients to build completely reflective automation easily without ever needing to write Coq functions that inspect terms. In fact, after the reification step, $\mathcal{R}_{tac}$ almost completely encapsulates the fact that we are using computational reflection at all.

$\mathcal{R}_{tac}$ packages unification variables, premises, and a conclusion, into a "goal" that programs (also called tactics) operate on. Combining these pieces into a simple interface allows $\mathcal{R}_{tac}$ to cleanly export larger granularity operations that rely on multiple pieces. For example, a common operation is to apply a lemma to the conclusion and convert its premises into new goals [36]. Doing this requires inspecting the lemma, constructing new unification variables, performing unifications, constructing new goals, and justifying it all using the lemma's proof.

Implementing $\mathcal{R}_{tac}$ requires solving two intertwined problems. In Sect. 5.1, we describe how we represent and reason about proofs embedded in arbitrary contexts which contain regular variables, unification variables, and propositions. Our reasoning principles allow us to make inferences under these contexts, and evolve the contexts by instantiating unification variables in the context without needing to re-check proofs. In Sect. 5.2, we present our compositional phrasing of tactic soundness which allows us to easily compose sound tactics to produce sound automation. We close the section (Sect. 5.3) by discussing $\mathcal{R}_{tac}$'s client-facing interface including a subset of the tactics that we have implemented and an example using them to build a small piece of automation.

5.1 Contexts and Contextualized Proofs

End-to-end, $\mathcal{R}_{tac}$ is about building proof of implications between two propositions. That is, if an $\mathcal{R}_{tac}$ tactic runs on a goal P and returns the goal Q then the soundness of the tactic proves $Q \to P$. However, in order to incrementally construct these proofs, we need to strengthen the specification. What is missing from this global specification is the ability to construct a proof in a context that contains variables, unification variables (possibly with their instantiations), and propositional facts. In $\mathcal{R}_{tac}$, this information is represented by the context datatype defined in Fig. 3. The meaning of a context is a function from propositions in the context to propositions outside of the context. That is,

$$^{t_u}_{t_v}[\![c]\!]^{\mathcal{C}} \vdash - : \left([\![t_u \cdot c_u]\!]^{\vec{\tau}} \to [\![t_v \cdot c_v]\!]^{\vec{\tau}} \to \mathsf{Prop}\right) \to \left([\![t_u]\!]^{\vec{\tau}} \to [\![t_v]\!]^{\vec{\tau}} \to \mathsf{Prop}\right)$$

$$(\text{Contexts}) \qquad \mathcal{C} ::= \epsilon \mid \mathcal{C}, \forall_\tau \mid \mathcal{C}, \exists_\tau \mid \mathcal{C}, \exists_\tau = \mathcal{E} \mid \mathcal{C}, \to \mathcal{E}$$

$$\substack{t_u \\ t_v} [\![c]\!]^{\mathcal{C}} \vdash - : \left([\![t_u \cdot c_u]\!]^{\overrightarrow{\tau}} \to [\![t_v \cdot c_v]\!]^{\overrightarrow{\tau}} \to \mathsf{Prop} \right) \to [\![t_u]\!]^{\overrightarrow{\tau}} \to [\![t_v]\!]^{\overrightarrow{\tau}} \to \mathsf{Prop}$$

$$\substack{t_u \\ t_v} [\![\epsilon]\!]^{\mathcal{C}} \vdash P \triangleq P$$

$$\substack{t_u \\ t_v} [\![c, \to e]\!]^{\mathcal{C}} \vdash P \triangleq \substack{t_u \\ t_v} [\![c]\!]^{\mathcal{C}} \vdash (\lambda d_u \, d_v. \, \substack{t_u \\ t_v} [\![e]\!]_{\mathsf{Prop}} \, d_u \, d_v \to P \, d_u \, d_v)$$

$$\substack{t_u \\ t_v} [\![c, \forall_t]\!]^{\mathcal{C}} \vdash P \triangleq \substack{t_u \\ t_v \cdot t} [\![c]\!]^{\mathcal{C}} \vdash (\lambda d_u \, d_v. \, \forall x : [\![t]\!]^\tau. \, P \, d_u \, (d_v \cdot x))$$

$$\substack{t_u \\ t_v} [\![c, \exists_t]\!]^{\mathcal{C}} \vdash P \triangleq \substack{t_u \cdot t \\ t_v} [\![c]\!]^{\mathcal{C}} \vdash (\lambda d_u \, d_v. \, \forall x : [\![t]\!]^\tau. \, P \, (d_u \cdot x) \, d_v)$$

$$\substack{t_u \\ t_v} [\![c, \exists_t = e]\!]^{\mathcal{C}} \vdash P \triangleq \substack{t_u \cdot t \\ t_v} [\![c]\!]^{\mathcal{C}} \vdash (\lambda d_u \, d_v. \, \forall x : [\![t]\!]^\tau. \, x = \substack{t_u \\ t_v} [\![e]\!]_t \, d_u \, d_v \to P \, (d_u \cdot x) \, d_v)$$

Fig. 3. The definition and denotation of contexts. The denotation of the existential quantifier as a universal quantifier captures the parametricity necessary for local proofs.

where c_u and c_v represent the unification variables and real variables introduced by the context. For exposition purposes, we will consider t_u and t_v to be empty simplifying this definition to the following:

$$[\![c]\!]^{\mathcal{C}} \vdash - : \left([\![c_u]\!]^{\overrightarrow{\tau}} \to [\![c_v]\!]^{\overrightarrow{\tau}} \to \mathsf{Prop} \right) \to \mathsf{Prop}$$

Since it is quite common to work within these contexts, we will use subscripts to mean pointwise lifting. For example,

$$P \to_c Q \triangleq \lambda d_u \, d_v. \, P \, d_u \, d_v \to Q \, d_u \, d_v$$

The intuitive interpretation of contexts, denoting unification variables as existential quantifiers, captures that property that they can be choosen in the proof, but this interpretation is not sufficient for compositional proofs. To see why, consider a proof of $[\![c]\!]^{\mathcal{C}} \vdash P$ and $[\![c]\!]^{\mathcal{C}} \vdash Q$. We would like to combine these two proofs into a proof of $[\![c]\!]^{\mathcal{C}} \vdash (P \wedge_c Q)$ but we can not because the two proofs may make contradictory choices for existentially quantified values. For example, if c is $\exists x : \mathbb{N}$, P is $x = 0$, and Q is $x = 1$ both proofs exist independently by picking the appropriate value of x but the two do not compose. To solve this problem, we use the parametric interpretation of contexts defined in Fig. 3 where unification variables are interpreted as universal quantifiers with an equation if they are instantiated. This interpretation captures the parametricity necessary to compose proofs by ensuring that proofs that do not constrain the values of unification variables hold for *any* well-typed instantiation.

The parametric interpretation provides us with several, powerful, reasoning principles for constructing and composing proofs in contexts. The first two are related to the applicative nature of the parametric interpretation of contexts.

$$\mathsf{ap} : \forall c \, P \, Q, [\![c]\!]^{\mathcal{C}} \vdash (P \to_c Q) \to [\![c]\!]^{\mathcal{C}} \vdash P \to [\![c]\!]^{\mathcal{C}} \vdash Q$$
$$\mathsf{pure} : \forall c \, P, P \to [\![c]\!]^{\mathcal{C}} \vdash P$$

Leveraging these two definitions, we can perform logical reasoning under a context. For example, we can use ap to prove modus ponens in an arbitrary context.

$$\rightarrow\text{-E} : \forall c\, P\, Q, [\![c]\!]^{\mathcal{C}} \vdash (P \rightarrow_c Q) \rightarrow [\![c]\!]^{\mathcal{C}} \vdash Q \rightarrow [\![c]\!]^{\mathcal{C}} \vdash Q$$

Similar rules hold for proving conjunctions and disjunctions under arbitrary contexts.

The final reasoning principle for contexts comes when using facts that occur in the premises. The following proof rule allows us to show that facts in the context ($p \in c$) are provable under the context.

$$\mathsf{assumption} : \forall c\, p, p \in c \rightarrow [\![c]\!]^{\mathcal{C}} \vdash [\![p]\!]$$

Context Morphisms. In addition to reasoning parametrically in a context, it is also necessary to evolve contexts by instantiating unification variables. Context morphisms capture the property that any reasoning done under the weaker context is also valid under the stronger context. The following definition captures this transport property which holds for any two contexts c and c' where c' is an evolution of c, written $c \rightsquigarrow c'$.

$$c \rightsquigarrow c' \quad \triangleq \quad \forall P,\ [\![c]\!]^{\mathcal{C}} \vdash P \rightarrow [\![c']\!]^{\mathcal{C}} \vdash P$$

The core rule for context evolution is the one for instantiating a unification variable.

$$c, \exists_\tau \rightsquigarrow c, \exists_\tau{=}e \qquad \text{if } {}^{c_u}_{c_v}[\![e]\!]_\tau \text{ is defined}$$

The proof of this rule is trivial since the context on the right simply introduces an additional equation that is not necessary when appealing to the assumption. In addition to instantiating unification variables, context evolution is both reflexive and transitive which allows us to talk about zero or multiple context updates in a uniform way. In addition, context evolution satisfies the natural structural rules allowing updates of any piece of the context. For example,

$$c \rightsquigarrow c' \quad \rightarrow \quad c, \forall_\tau \rightsquigarrow c', \forall_\tau \qquad \text{and} \qquad c \rightsquigarrow c' \quad \rightarrow \quad c, \exists_\tau \rightsquigarrow c', \exists_\tau$$

Similar rules hold for all of the context constructors and all follow straightforwardly from the definition of $\rightsquigarrow$.

5.2 Implementing $\mathcal{R}_{tac}$

The contextual reasoning principles from the previous section form the heart of the proof theory of $\mathcal{R}_{tac}$. In this section, we describe the generic language constructs and their soundness criteria.

From a language point of view, tactics operate on a single goal; however, tactics can produce multiple goals, for example when proving $P \wedge Q$, it is common to break the goal into two subgoals, one for P and one for Q. Further, while these goals may start with the same context, further reasoning may lead them to extend their contexts in different ways. In order to represent all of the goals in a meaningful way, $\mathcal{R}_{tac}$ uses goal trees defined in Fig. 4. All of the syntax maps naturally to the corresponding semantic counter-parts.

$$\text{(Goal Trees)} \quad \mathcal{G} ::= \top \mid \lceil \mathcal{E} \rceil \mid \forall \mathcal{T}.\mathcal{G} \mid \exists \mathcal{T}.\mathcal{G} \mid \exists \mathcal{T} = \mathcal{E}.\mathcal{G} \mid \mathcal{E} \rightarrow \mathcal{G} \mid \mathcal{G} \wedge \mathcal{G}$$

$$\begin{aligned}
{}^{t_u}_{t_v}[\![\top]\!]^{\mathcal{G}} &\triangleq \lambda d_u\, d_v.\, \top \\
{}^{t_u}_{t_v}[\![\lceil e \rceil]\!]^{\mathcal{G}} &\triangleq \lambda d_u\, d_v.\, {}^{t_u}_{t_v}[\![e]\!]_{\mathsf{Prop}}\, d_u\, d_v \\
{}^{t_u}_{t_v}[\![g_1 \wedge g_2]\!]^{\mathcal{G}} &\triangleq \lambda d_u\, d_v.\, {}^{t_u}_{t_v}[\![g_1]\!]^{\mathcal{G}}\, d_u\, d_v \wedge {}^{t_u}_{t_v}[\![g_2]\!]^{\mathcal{G}}\, d_u\, d_v \\
{}^{t_u}_{t_v}[\![e \rightarrow g]\!]^{\mathcal{G}} &\triangleq \lambda d_u\, d_v.\, {}^{t_u}_{t_v}[\![e]\!]_{\mathsf{Prop}}\, d_u\, d_v \rightarrow {}^{t_u}_{t_v}[\![g_2]\!]^{\mathcal{G}}\, d_u\, d_v \\
{}^{t_u}_{t_v}[\![\forall_\tau.g]\!]^{\mathcal{G}} &\triangleq \lambda d_u\, d_v.\, \forall x : \tau, {}^{t_u}_{t_v \cdot \tau}[\![g]\!]^{\mathcal{G}}\, d_u\, (d_v \cdot x) \\
{}^{t_u}_{t_v}[\![\exists_\tau.g]\!]^{\mathcal{G}} &\triangleq \lambda d_u\, d_v.\, \exists x : \tau, {}^{t_u \cdot \tau}_{t_v}[\![g]\!]^{\mathcal{G}}\, (d_u \cdot x)\, d_v \\
{}^{t_u}_{t_v}[\![\exists_\tau{=}e.g]\!]^{\mathcal{G}} &\triangleq \lambda d_u\, d_v.\, \exists x : \tau, x = {}^{t_u}_{t_v}[\![e]\!]_\tau \wedge {}^{t_u \cdot \tau}_{t_v}[\![g]\!]^{\mathcal{G}}\, (d_u \cdot x)\, d_v
\end{aligned}$$

Fig. 4. Goal trees represent the global proof structure.

On top of goal trees and the contexts from the previous section, we define the two language constructs in $\mathcal{R}_{tac}$: tactics and tactic continuations.

$$\begin{aligned}
\text{(Tactics)} \quad & \mathsf{rtac} \triangleq \mathcal{C} \rightarrow \mathcal{E} \rightarrow \mathsf{option}\,(\mathcal{C} \times \mathcal{G}) \\
\text{(Tactic continuations)} \quad & \mathsf{rtacK} \triangleq \mathcal{C} \rightarrow \mathcal{G} \rightarrow \mathsf{option}\,(\mathcal{C} \times \mathcal{G})
\end{aligned}$$

At the high level, the two constructs accept a context and a representation of the goal—a single expression in the case of tactics and a full goal tree in the case of tactic continuations—and produce a new context and a goal tree. The option in the return type allows tactics to fail, which is convenient when a particular reasoning step does not apply to the current goal. We discuss this in more detail in Sect. 5.3.

An $\mathcal{R}_{tac}$ tactic (resp. tactic continuation) is sound if, when it succeeds, the resulting goal tree is sufficient to prove the original goal (resp. goal tree) in the *resulting* context and the resulting context is a consistent extension of the original context. Mathematically[3],

$$\mathsf{rtac\_sound}\, tac \triangleq \begin{cases} \forall c\, e\, g'\, c', tac\; c\; e = \mathsf{Some}\,(c', g') \rightarrow \\ \quad c \Rightarrow c' \wedge \\ \quad [\![c']\!]^{\mathcal{C}} \vdash \left({}^{c_u}_{c_v}[\![g']\!]^{\mathcal{G}} \rightarrow_{\mathcal{C}} {}^{c_u}_{c_v}[\![e]\!]_{\mathsf{Prop}}\right) \end{cases}$$

where $c \Rightarrow c'$ states that c' is a consistent extension of the context c at all levels. For example,

$$c, \forall_\tau \Rightarrow c', \forall_\tau \quad \leftrightarrow \quad c \Rightarrow c' \wedge (c, \forall_\tau) \rightsquigarrow (c', \forall_\tau)$$

This stronger consistency definition is necessary when we need to escape from under a potentially inconsistent context. For example, when we apply a tactic under a universal quantifier, we shift the quantifier into the context and invoke the tactic with the enlarged context. Suppose that the soundness theorem of the tactic only guaranteed $c, \forall_\tau \rightsquigarrow c', \forall_\tau$, in order for our tactic to be correct,

[3] In this definition we avoid the complexities of ill-typed terms. In the code, the soundness proof gets to assume that the context and goal are both well-typed.

we must guarantee $c \rightsquigarrow c'$, but this does not follow. Informally, the consistent evolution of the smaller context should follow, but we can not argue this within Coq because we can not construct a value of type τ.

The soundness of tactics follows directly from the soundness of tactic continuations by using the denotation of goal trees rather than the denotation of terms in the conclusion. Formally,

$$\mathsf{rtacK\_sound}\, tac \triangleq \begin{cases} \forall c\, e\, g'\, c', tac\; c\; g = \mathsf{Some}\,(c', g') \rightarrow \\ \quad c \Rightarrow c' \wedge \\ \quad [\![c']\!]^{\mathcal{C}} \vdash \left({}^{c_u}_{c_v}[\![g']\!]^{\mathcal{G}} \rightarrow_{c} {}^{c_u}_{c_v}[\![g]\!]^{\mathcal{G}}\right) \end{cases}$$

Local Unification Variables. The alternation of universal and existential quantifiers in contexts leads to some complexities when manipulating unification variables. As we mentioned previously, unification variables in MIRRORCORE implicitly have a single, global scope. This choice is at odds with the potential alternation of universally quantified variables and unification variables.

In $\mathcal{R}_{tac}$ we solve the scoping problem using the context. Unification variables introduced in the context are only allowed to mention variables and unification variables that are introduced below it. For example, in '$c, \exists_\tau{=}e$', e is only allowed to mention variables and unification variables introduced by c.

This design choice comes with a deficiency when introducing multiple unification variables. For example, if we wish to introduce multiple unification variables, we need to pick an order of those unification variables and the choice is important because we can not instantiate an earlier unification variable using a later one. While there can never be cycles, the order that we pick is significant. Our solution is to introduce mutually recursive blocks of unification variables simultaneously. The reasoning principles for these blocks are quite similar to the reasoning principles that we presented in this section and the last, but there is a bit more bookkeeping involved.

Goal Minimization. Local unification variables do have a benefit for $\mathcal{R}_{tac}$. In particular, it allows us to precisely control the life-time of unification variables which allows us to substitute instantiated unification variables and entirely remove them from the goal tree. For example, the following rules state how we shift unification variables from the context into the goal.

$$[\![c, \exists_t]\!]^{\mathcal{C}} \vdash g \leftrightarrow [\![c]\!]^{\mathcal{C}} \vdash \exists_t, g \quad \text{and} \quad [\![c, \exists_t{=}\, e]\!]^{\mathcal{C}} \vdash g \leftrightarrow [\![c]\!]^{\mathcal{C}} \vdash g[e]$$

where $g[e]$ substitutes all occurrences to the top unification variable with the expression e and renumbers the remaining unification variables appropriately.

In addition to substitution of unification variables, we can also drop hypotheses and universal quantifiers on solved goals. For example,

$$[\![c, e]\!]^{\mathcal{C}} \vdash \top \;\leftrightarrow\; [\![c]\!]^{\mathcal{C}} \vdash \top \qquad \text{and} \qquad [\![c, \forall_t]\!]^{\mathcal{C}} \vdash \top \;\leftrightarrow\; [\![c]\!]^{\mathcal{C}} \vdash \top$$

and contract conjunctions of solved goals, e.g.

$$[\![c]\!]^{\mathcal{C}} \vdash \top \wedge g \;\leftrightarrow\; [\![c]\!]^{\mathcal{C}} \vdash g \qquad \text{and} \qquad [\![c]\!]^{\mathcal{C}} \vdash g \wedge \top \;\leftrightarrow\; [\![c]\!]^{\mathcal{C}} \vdash g$$

5.3 The Core Tactics

With the specification and verification strategy for tactics fleshed out, we return to the client-level. Figure 5 presents a subset of the core tactics that we implemented for $\mathcal{R}_{tac}$. While relatively small in number, the uniform interface of these tactics makes it easy to combine these tactics into higher-level automation. Further, the soundness proofs of tactics built from verified tactics is essentially free. In this section we present the soundness theorems for several representative tactics and show how they compose.

Search Tactics

IDTAC : rtac		do nothing
FAIL : rtac		fail immediately
REC : $\mathbb{N} \to (\mathsf{rtac} \to \mathsf{rtac}) \to \mathsf{rtac} \to \mathsf{rtac}$		bounded recursion
SOLVE : rtac → rtac		solve fully or fail
FIRST : list rtac → rtac		first to succeed
AT_GOAL : $(\mathcal{E} \to \mathsf{rtac}) \to \mathsf{rtac}$		
THEN : rtac → rtacK → rtac		sequencing
THENK : rtacK → rtacK → rtacK		sequencing
ON_ALL : rtac → rtacK		
ON_EACH : list rtac → rtacK		
MINIFY : rtacK		reduce the goal size

Reasoning Tactics

EAPPLY : lemma → rtac	apply a lemma
INTRO : rtac	introduce a quantifier
EEXISTS : rtac	witness an existential
SIMPL : $(\mathcal{E} \to \mathcal{E}) \to \mathsf{rtac}$	compute in the goal
EASSUMPTION : rtac	use an assumption

Fig. 5. Select $\mathcal{R}_{tac}$ tactics.

Select Soundness Theorems. The soundness theorems for individual tactics are almost completely type-directed. For example, the soundness theorem for the REC tactic is the following:

$$\begin{aligned}&\mathsf{REC\_sound} : \forall n\, f\, t,\\&\quad (\forall x, \mathsf{rtac\_sound}\, x \to \mathsf{rtac\_sound}(f\, x)) \to \mathsf{rtac\_sound}\, t \to \mathsf{rtac\_sound}(\mathtt{REC}\, n\, f\, t)\end{aligned}$$

Similarly, the FIRST tactic allows clients to try a variety of alternatives selecting the first tactic that succeeds. Its soundness simply requires that all of the given tactics are sound.

The APPLY tactic is the work-horse of $\mathcal{R}_{tac}$ and exemplifies MirrorCore's separation of manipulation and meaning. The tactic is parameterized by a syntactic representation of a lemma and attempts to apply it to the goal. Its soundness is captured by the following theorem.

```
Def tac_even : rtac := REPEAT 10
  (FIRST [ ASSUMPTION
         | APPLY even_O_syn
         | APPLY even_odd_syn
         | APPLY odd_even_syn ]).

Thm tac_even_sound : rtac_sound tac_even.
  apply REPEAT_sound.
  apply FIRST_sound; breakForall.
  - apply ASSUMPTION_sound.
  - apply APPLY_sound; exact even_O.
  - apply APPLY_sound; exact even_odd.
  - apply APPLY_sound; exact odd_even.
Qed.
```

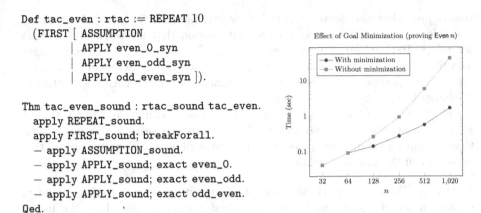

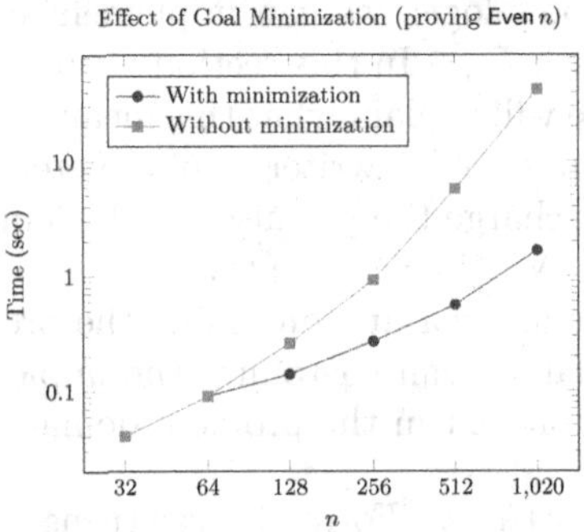

Fig. 6. Simple tactic for proving Evenness and the effect of minimization on run-time.

$$\texttt{APPLY\_sound} : \forall lem, [\![lem]\!]_{\mathsf{lemma}} \rightarrow \mathsf{rtac\_sound}\,(\texttt{APPLY}\,lem)$$

where $[\![-]\!]_{\mathsf{lemma}}$ is the denotation function for lemmas which are defined as triples containing the types of universally quantified variables, a list of premises and the conclusion. The implementation of `APPLY` is quite complex; however, all of the complexity is hidden behind the soundness of the tactic making it trivial for clients to use `APPLY`.

`AT_GOAL` allows automation to inspect the goal before choosing what to do. For example, recall the use of `REC` to iterate through the terms on each side of the equality in Fig. 1. Rather than picking an arbitrary recursion depth, we can use `AT_GOAL` to inspect the goal and compute an adequate depth for the fixpoint. The soundness rule for `AT_GOAL` simply requires that the function produces a sound tactic for *any* goal, i.e.

$$\texttt{AT\_GOAL\_sound} : \forall tac, (\forall g, \mathsf{rtac\_sound}\,(tac\,g)) \rightarrow \mathsf{rtac\_sound}\,(\texttt{AT\_GOAL}\,tac)$$

The `MINIFY` tactic continuation reduces the size of goals by substituting instantiated unification variables and removing solved branches of the proof. While we could have integrated it into all of the tactics, separating it modularizes the proof. Further, it allows the client to batch several operations before performing minimization thus amortizing the cost over more reasoning steps. A particularly extreme instance of this arises when dealing with very large terms in the substitution. Figure 6 shows a simple tactic for proving Evenness reflectively. The manual soundness proof is for presentation purposes only to demonstrate that our `rtac_derive_soundness_default` tactic truely is purely syntax directed.

6 Extending $\mathcal{R}_{tac}$: Exploiting Structure in Rewriting

$\mathcal{R}_{tac}$ allows users to develop goal-oriented automation with a tight coupling between the code we run and the justification of its soundness. In many cases, this is just what the doctor ordered; however, because $\mathcal{R}_{tac}$ is defined within Coq's logic, we can implement custom automation that inter-operates directly with $\mathcal{R}_{tac}$. In this section we present a custom $\mathcal{R}_{tac}$ tactic for setoid rewriting—we will explain what this means in a moment. In addition to being an $\mathcal{R}_{tac}$ tactic, our setoid rewriter is parameterized by lemmas to rewrite with and tactics to discharge the premises of the lemmas.

Writing custom tactics is an advanced topic that is still quite difficult, though we are working on easing the process. The benefit of writing a custom tactic is that we can customize the implementation to exploit additional structure that is present in the problem domain.

Rewriting. Formally, rewriting answers the question: "what term is equal to e using a set of equational lemmas?" *Setoid* rewriting generalizes the use of equality in this question to arbitrary relations. For example, the Fiat system for deductive synthesis [20] is built around rewriting using refinement relations.

Our rewriter is inspired by Sozeau's `rewrite_strat` tactic [42] and handles similar features, including:

- General relations, including both non-reflexive and non-transitive ones,
- Rewriting in function arguments and under binders,
- Hint databases which store the lemmas to use in rewriting, and
- Discharging side-conditions using $\mathcal{R}_{tac}$ tactics.

The reflective implementation of our rewriter allows us to avoid explicitly constructing proof terms which, as we show in Sect. 7, results in substantial performance improvements. In addition, exporting the rewriter as a tactic makes it easy to integrate into larger reflective automation.

We start the section off with an explanation of the mechanism underlying setoid rewriting using a simple example (Sect. 6.1). In Sect. 6.2 we show how we exploit this structure to make the rewriter more effective. We conclude by presenting the client-facing interface to the rewriter (Sect. 6.3).

6.1 Setoid Rewriting by Example

To demonstrate the rewriting process, consider the following example where we rewrite by an inverse entailment relation ($\dashv$), which is essentially "if":

$$\left(P \wedge \exists x : \mathbb{N}, Q(x+1)\right) \quad \dashv \quad ?_0$$

We are looking for a term to fill in $?_0$ that will make this goal provable. When we are done we will find that $?_0$ can be $\exists x : \mathbb{N}, \left(P \wedge Q(1+x)\right)$ and the entailment will be provable. We will focus on bottom-up rewriting where we rewrite in the sub-terms of an expression before attempting to rewrite the expression itself.

Proper Morphisms. Rewriting bottom-up first requires getting to the leaves. To do this we need to determine the relations to use when rewriting sub-terms to ensure that the results fit into the proof. In our example problem, we are looking for relations R_1 and R_2 such that we can combine the proofs of

$$P\,R_1\,?_1 \quad \text{and} \quad (\exists x : \mathbb{N}, Q\,(x+1))\,R_2\,?_2$$

into a proof of

$$P \wedge \exists x : \mathbb{N}, Q(x+1) \quad \dashv \quad ?_1 \wedge ?_2$$

This information is carried by *properness proofs* such as the following:

$$\mathsf{Proper\_and\_if} : \mathsf{Proper}\,(\dashv \Longrightarrow \dashv \Longrightarrow \dashv)\,\wedge$$

which means

$$\forall a\,b\,c\,d, (a \dashv b) \rightarrow (c \dashv d) \rightarrow ((a \wedge c) \dashv (b \wedge d))$$

This lemma tells us that if we use $\dashv$ for both R_1 and R_2, then we will be able to combine the sub-proofs to construct the overall proof. With concrete relations for R_1 and R_2, we can apply rewriting recursively to solve the goals and find appropriate values for $?_1$ and $?_2$.

When the rewriter recurses to solve the first obligation ($P \dashv ?_1$) it finds that there is no explicit proof about P and $\dashv$. However, the reflexivity of the $\dashv$ relation allows the rewriter to use P to instantiate $?_1$, solving the goal. While this may seem obvious, this check is necessary to support rewriting by non-reflexive relations since, for arbitrary relations, there may be no term related to P.

Rewriting on the right-hand side of the conjunction is a bit more interesting. In this case, the head symbol is an existential quantifier, which is represented using a symbol $\exists_{\mathbb{N}}$ applied to an abstraction representing the body, i.e.

$$\exists_{\mathbb{N}}(\lambda x : \mathbb{N}, Q(x+1))$$

At the highest level of syntax things are the same as above, we look up a properness proof for $\exists_{\mathbb{N}}$ and entailment and find the following:

$$\mathsf{Proper\_exists\_if} : \mathsf{Proper}\,((\mathsf{pointwise}\,\mathbb{N}\ \dashv) \Longrightarrow \dashv)\,\exists_{\mathbb{N}}$$

which means

$$\forall a\,b, (\forall x, a\,x \dashv b\,x) \rightarrow (\exists x, a\,x) \dashv (\exists x, b\,x)$$

As above, the conclusion of the lemma exactly matches our goal, so we instantiate $?_2$ with $\exists x, ?_3\,x$ and produce a new rewriting problem to solve $?_3$.

The problem gets a bit more interesting when we rewrite the body at the pointwise relation. The definition of '$\mathsf{pointwise\_relation}\,\mathbb{N}\ \dashv$' makes it clear that we can rewrite in the function body as long as the two bodies are related by $\dashv$ when applied to the same x, so we will shift a universally quantified natural number into our context and begin rewriting in the body.

Rewriting in the rest of the term is similar. The only complexity comes from determining the appropriate morphism for Q. First, if we do not find a morphism for Q, we can still rewrite $Q\,(x+1)$ into $Q\,(x+1)$ by the reflexivity of $\dashv$ but this prevents us from rewriting the addition. The solution is to derive $\mathsf{Proper}\,(= \Longrightarrow \dashv)\,Q$ by combining the fact that all Coq functions respect equality, i.e. $\mathsf{Proper}\,(= \Longrightarrow =)\,Q$, and the reflexivity of $\dashv$.

Rewriting on the Way Up. Eventually, our rewriter will hit the bottom of the term and begin coming back up. It is during this process that we make use of the actual rewriting lemmas. For example, take applying the commutativity of addition on $x + 1$. Our rewriter just solved the recursive relations stating that $x = x$ and $1 = 1$ so we have a proof of $x+1 = x+1$. However, because equality is transitive, we can perform more rewriting here. In particular, the commutativity of addition justifies rewriting $x + 1$ into $1 + x$.

The new result logically fits into our system but the justification is a bit strained. The recursive rewriting above already picked a value for the unification variable that this sub-problem was solving. Noting this issue, we realize that we should have appealed to transitivity *before* performing the recursive rewriting. Doing this requires a bit of foresight since blindly applying transitivity could yield in an unprovable goal if the relation is not also reflexive.

With the rewriting in the body completed, we continue to return upward finding no additional rewrites until we get to the top of the goal. At this point, we have proved the following:

$$P \land \exists x : \mathbb{N}, Q(x + 1) \dashv\ P \land \exists x : \mathbb{N}, Q(1 + x)$$

But we would like to continue rewriting on the left-hand side of the entailment. This rewriting is justified by the fact that $\dashv$ is a transitive relation. Again sweeping the need for foresight under the rug, we can assume that we wish to solve this rewriting goal:

$$P \land \exists x : \mathbb{N}, Q(1 + x) \dashv ?'_0$$

Here we can apply the following lemma, which justifies lifting the existential quantifier over the conjunction:

$$\forall a\, b, a \land (\exists x : \mathbb{N}, b\, x) \dashv\ (\exists x : \mathbb{N}, a \land b\, x)$$

Note that a can not mention x.

After lifting the existential quantifier to the top, our rewriting is complete. The key property to note from the example is that the only symbols that the rewriter needed to interpret where the morphisms, e.g. respectful and pointwise. All other reasoning was justified entirely by a combination of rewriting lemmas, properness lemmas, and the reflexivity and transitivity of relations. Thus, like $\mathcal{R}_{tac}$, our rewriter is parametric in the domain.

6.2 Implementing the Rewriter

There are two opportunities to make a custom rewriter more efficient than one implemented using $\mathcal{R}_{tac}$ primitives. First, rewriting tends to produce a lot of unification variables as properness rules have two unification variables for every function argument, only one of which will be solved when applying the theorem. Our small example above would introduce at least 8 unification variables where in reality none are strictly necessary. Second, rewriting needs to be clever about when it appeals to transitivity.

Expressing the rewriter as a function with a richer type allows us to solve both of these problems elegantly. Rather than representing the goal as a proposition relating a unification variable to a known term, we can explicitly carry around the known term and the relation and return the rewritten term. This insight leads us to choose the following type for the rewriter

$$\mathsf{rewriter} \triangleq \mathcal{C} \rightarrow \mathcal{E} \rightarrow \mathcal{R} \rightarrow \mathsf{option}(\mathcal{C} \times \mathcal{E})$$

where $\mathcal{R}$ is the type of relations. The attentive reader will notice the similarity to the type of tactics, which is even more apparent in the soundness criterion:

$$\mathsf{rewrite\_sound}\, rw \triangleq \begin{cases} \forall c\, e\, e'\, c', rw\; c\; e\; r = \mathsf{Some}\,(c', e') \rightarrow \\ \quad c \Rightarrow c' \wedge \\ \quad {}^{t_u}_{t_v}[\![c']\!]^{\mathcal{C}} \vdash (\lambda d_u\, d_v.\, {}^{t_u \cdot c_u}_{t_v \cdot c_v}[\![e]\!]_t\, d_u\, d_v \;\; [\![r]\!]^{\mathcal{R}} \;\; {}^{t_u \cdot c_u}_{t_v \cdot c_v}[\![e']\!]_t\, d_u\, d_v) \end{cases}$$

where $[\![-]\!]^{\mathcal{R}}$ is the denotation of relations. As one would expect, the same reasoning principles for contexts apply when verifying the rewriter. By using this representation, we are clearly reducing the number of unification variables since invoking the rewriter no longer requires a unification variable at all.

This encoding also allows us to perform additional processing after our recursive rewrites return. If we use unification variables to return results, we need to ensure that we do not instantiate that unification variable until we are certain that we have our final result. Therefore, when we make recursive calls, we would need to generate fresh unification variables and track them. Communicating the result directly solves this problem elegantly because the rewriter can inspect the results of recursive calls before it constructs its result. The key to justifying this manipulation is that, unlike $\mathcal{R}_{tac}$, the soundness proof of the rewriter gets a global view of the computation *before* it needs to provide a proof term. This gives it the flexibility to apply, or not apply, transitivity based on the entire execution of the function. That is, if multiple rewrites succeed, and the relation is transitive, then the soundness proof uses transitivity to glue the results together. If only one succeeds, there is no need to use transitivity and the proof from the recursive call is used. And if none succeed, and the relation is not reflexive then rewriting fails. It is important to note that this global view is purely a verification-time artifact. It incurs no runtime overhead.

Another benefit of accepting the term directly is that the rewriter can perform recursion on it directly. The core of the bottom-up rewriter handles the cases for the five syntactic constructs of the `expr` language, of which only application and abstraction are interesting. In the application case the rewriter accumulate the list of arguments delaying all of its decisions until it reaches the head symbol. In order to ensure that the rewriter can perform recursive calls on these sub-terms, the rewriter pairs the terms with closures representing the recursive calls on these sub-terms. This technique is reminiscent of hereditary substitutions and makes it quite easy to satisfy Coq's termination checker. Abstractions are the only construct that is treated specially within the core rewriter. For abstractions, we determine whether the relation is a pointwise relation and if so, we shift the variable into the context and make a recursive call. Otherwise, we treat the abstraction as an opaque symbol.

6.3 Instantiating the Rewriter

Figure 7 presents the types and helper functions exported by the rewriter. The interface to the rewriter defines four types of functions: `refl_dec`, `trans_dec`, `properness`, and `rewriter`. `refl_dec` (resp. `trans_dec`) returns true if the given relation is reflexive (resp. transitive). `properness` encodes properness facts and is keyed on an expression, e.g. $\lceil \wedge \rceil$, and a relation, e.g. $\dashv$, and returns suitable relations for each of the arguments, e.g. the list $[\dashv, \dashv]$. $\mathcal{L}_{tac}$'s setoid rewriter implements these three features using Coq's typeclass mechanism and these functions are essentially reified typeclass resolution functions. The `rewriter` type, which we discussed in detail in Sect. 6.2, is what actually performs rewriting. Each one of these types has a corresponding soundness property similar to `rewrite_sound`.

$$\begin{aligned}
\mathsf{refl_dec_sound}\, f &\triangleq \forall r, f\, r = \mathtt{true} \rightarrow \mathtt{Reflexive}\, [\![R]\!]^{\mathcal{R}} \\
\mathsf{trans_dec_sound}\, f &\triangleq \forall r, f\, r = \mathtt{true} \rightarrow \mathtt{Transitive}\, [\![R]\!]^{\mathcal{R}} \\
\mathsf{properness_sound}\, f &\triangleq \forall e\, r\, rs, f\, e\, r = \mathtt{Some}\, rs \rightarrow \mathtt{Proper}\, [\![rs \Longrightarrow r]\!]^{\mathcal{R}}\, {}^{\epsilon}_{\epsilon}[\![e]\!]_t
\end{aligned}$$

where $rs \Longrightarrow r$ builds a respectful morphism from rs. For example, $[r_1, r_2] \Longrightarrow r$ equals $r_1 \Longrightarrow r_2 \Longrightarrow r$.

Types

$\mathtt{refl\_dec} \triangleq R \rightarrow \mathtt{bool}$		is relation reflexive?
$\mathtt{trans\_dec} \triangleq R \rightarrow \mathtt{bool}$		is relation transitive?
$\mathtt{properness} \triangleq \mathcal{E} \rightarrow \mathcal{R} \rightarrow \mathtt{list}\, \mathcal{R}$		get relation for $\mathcal{E}$ ending in R
$\mathtt{rewriter} \triangleq \mathcal{C} \rightarrow \mathcal{E} \rightarrow \mathcal{R} \rightarrow \mathtt{option}\, (\mathcal{C} \times \mathcal{E})$		perform rewrites

Builders

$$\begin{aligned}
\mathtt{do_proper} &: \mathtt{list}\, (\mathcal{E} \times \mathcal{R}) \rightarrow \mathtt{properness} \\
\mathtt{rewrite_db} &: \mathtt{list}\, (\mathtt{rw_lemma} \times \mathtt{rtacK}) \rightarrow \mathtt{rewriter} \\
\mathtt{rw_repeat} &: \mathtt{refl_dec} \rightarrow \mathtt{trans_dec} \rightarrow \mathbb{N} \rightarrow \mathtt{rewriter} \rightarrow \mathtt{rewriter} \\
\mathtt{rw_pre_simplify} &: (\mathcal{E} \rightarrow \mathcal{E}) \rightarrow \mathtt{rewriter} \rightarrow \mathtt{rewriter} \\
\mathtt{rw_post_simplify} &: (\mathcal{E} \rightarrow \mathcal{E}) \rightarrow \mathtt{rewriter} \rightarrow \mathtt{rewriter} \\
\mathtt{bottom_up} &: \mathtt{refl_dec} \rightarrow \mathtt{trans_dec} \rightarrow \mathtt{properness} \rightarrow \mathtt{rewriter} \rightarrow \mathtt{rewriter} \\
\mathtt{setoid_rewrite} &: \mathcal{R} \rightarrow \mathtt{rewriter} \rightarrow \mathtt{rtac}
\end{aligned}$$

Fig. 7. The interface to the rewriter.

The helper functions provide simple ways to construct sound values of these types from simpler pieces. As with the $\mathcal{R}_{tac}$ tactics, their soundness theorems are essentially all type-directed. For example, `do_proper` constructs a `properness` from a list of expressions and relations where each expression is proper with respect to the relation. Formally,

$$\begin{aligned}
&\mathsf{do_proper_sound} : \forall er, \\
&\quad \mathtt{Forall}(\lambda(e, r).\mathsf{Proper}\, [\![r]\!]^{\mathcal{R}}\, {}^{\epsilon}_{\epsilon}[\![e]\!]_{e_t})\, er \rightarrow \mathsf{properness_sound}\, (\mathsf{do_proper}\, er)
\end{aligned}$$

where e_t represents the type of e. The current implementation looks up the expression and relation in the list and returns a list of the relations that the arguments must respect; however, more sophisticated implementations could use discrimination trees keyed on either the expression or the relation.

`rewrite_db` is similar in many regards to `APPLY` in $\mathcal{R}_{tac}$. It takes a list of rewriting lemmas (`rw_lemma`), which are specialized lemmas that have conclusions of the type $\mathcal{E} \times \mathcal{R} \times \mathcal{E}$, and tactic continuations used to solve the premises and builds a rewriter that tries to rewrite with each lemma sequentially. The soundness theorem is similar to the soundness of `do_proper`.

$$\texttt{rewrite\_db\_sound} : \forall r,\\ \texttt{Forall}(\lambda(l,t).[\![l]\!]_{\mathsf{rw\_lemma}} \wedge \mathsf{rtacK\_sound}\, t)\, r \rightarrow \mathsf{rewrite\_sound}\,(\texttt{rewrite\_db}\, r)$$

The `rw_pre_simplify` and `rw_post_simplify` combinators require that the function argument produces a term that is equal to the input term and are useful when we need to reduce terms to put them back into a normal form. Finally, the `setoid_rewrite` tactic converts a rewriter into an $\mathcal{R}_{tac}$ tactic. Due to the nature of rewriting in the goal, the relation to rewrite by must be a sub-relation of reverse implication. Formally,

$$\texttt{setoid\_rewrite\_sound} : \forall r\, w,\\ ([\![r]\!]^{\mathcal{R}} \subseteq \rightarrow) \rightarrow \mathsf{rewrite\_sound}\, w \rightarrow \mathsf{rtac\_sound}\,(\texttt{setoid\_rewrite}\, r\, w)$$

7 Case Studies

Using $\mathcal{R}_{tac}$, we have built several pieces of automation that perform interesting reasoning and have completely automatic proofs. Beyond these small case studies, $\mathcal{R}_{tac}$ has also been used for automating a larger program logic [22] and we are currently using it to verify Java programs with Charge! [7].

We performed our evaluation on a 2.7Ghz Core i7 running Linux and Coq 8.5rc1. Our benchmarks compare our reflective automation to similar $\mathcal{L}_{tac}$ automation. Unless otherwise noted, both implementations use the same algorithms and the $\mathcal{R}_{tac}$ implementations use only the generic tactics. We benchmark two phases: proof generation and proof checking (notated by -Qed). In the $\mathcal{L}_{tac}$ implementations, proof generation is the time it takes to interpret the tactics and construct the proof object, and the *Qed* time is the time it takes Coq to check the final proof. Note that when using $\mathcal{L}_{tac}$, the proof checking does *not* include the search necessary to find the proof. In the $\mathcal{R}_{tac}$ implementation, proof generation counts the cost to construct the syntactic representation of the goal and perform the computation on Coq's byte-code virtual machine [27]. During Qed time the syntactic representation is type-checked, its denotation is computed and checked to be equal to the proposition that needs to be checked, and the tactic is re-executed to ensure that the computation is correct.

Monoidal Equivalence. Our first case study is the monoidal equivalence checker from Sect. 3. The graph in Fig. 8 shows how the $\mathcal{R}_{tac}$ implementation scales

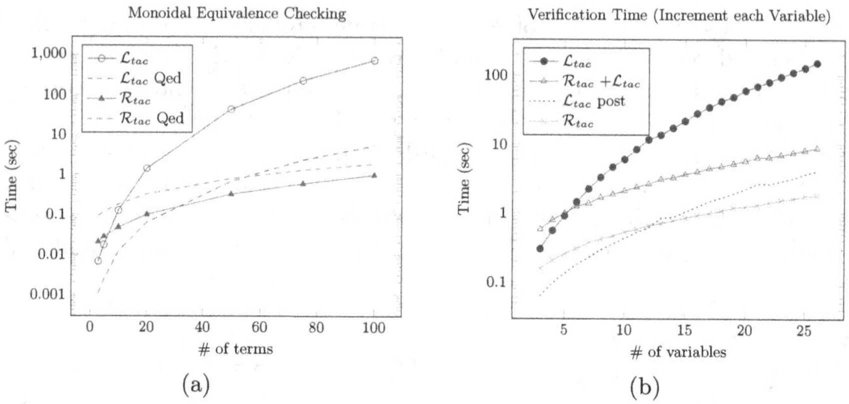

Fig. 8. Performance of (a) monoidal equivalence checking, and (b) a simple imperative program verifier.

compared to the $\mathcal{L}_{tac}$ implementation. Despite the fact that both the $\mathcal{R}_{tac}$ and the $\mathcal{L}_{tac}$ automation perform exactly the same search, the $\mathcal{R}_{tac}$ implementation scales significantly better than the $\mathcal{L}_{tac}$ implementation. The break-even point–where $\mathcal{R}_{tac}$ and $\mathcal{L}_{tac}$ are equally fast—is at roughly 8 terms where the proof size begins to increase dramatically compared to the problem size.

Even the `Qed` for $\mathcal{R}_{tac}$ becomes faster than the `Qed` for $\mathcal{L}_{tac}$, though this happens only for much larger problems. The intersection point for the `Qed` lines corresponds to the size of the problem where re-performing the entire search and type checking the syntactic problem becomes faster than checking just the final proof term. Memoizing the correct choices made during execution of the tactic in the style of Cybele [16] could further decrease `Qed` time. However, doing this would require embedding the simulation into the final proof.

Post-condition Verification. We developed a simple program verifier in $\mathcal{R}_{tac}$ for a trivial imperative programming language, which includes assignments, addition, and sequencing. All of the automation is based heavily on a simple $\mathcal{L}_{tac}$ implementation. For example, the lemmas that we reify are the same lemmas that are applied by the $\mathcal{L}_{tac}$ implementation. We built the automation incrementally, first automating only sequencing and copies and later integrating handling of simple reasoning about addition.

The graph in Fig. 8 compares the performance between pure $\mathcal{L}_{tac}$ ($\mathcal{L}_{tac}$), pure $\mathcal{R}_{tac}$ ($\mathcal{R}_{tac}$), and a hybrid of $\mathcal{L}_{tac}$ and $\mathcal{R}_{tac}$ ($\mathcal{L}_{tac}$+$\mathcal{R}_{tac}$) implementation. The problem instances increment each of n variables with the post-condition stating that each variable has been incremented. The x axis shows the number of variables (which is directly related to both the size of the program and the pre- and post-conditions) and the y axis is the verification time in seconds. There are two sub-problems in the verifier: first, the post-condition needs to be computed, and second, the entailment between the computed post-condition and the stated post-condition is checked. The blue ($\mathcal{L}_{tac}$) line automates both sub-problems in $\mathcal{L}_{tac}$. Converting the post-condition calculation tactic to $\mathcal{R}_{tac}$ and leaving the entailment checking to $\mathcal{L}_{tac}$ already gets us a substantial performance improvement for larger problems, e.g. a 31x reduction in verification time for 26 variables. The red dotted line ($\mathcal{L}_{tac}$ post) shows the amount of that time that is spent checking the final entailment in $\mathcal{L}_{tac}$. Converting the entailment checker into a reflective procedure results in another 2.6x speedup bringing the tactic to the green line at the bottom of the graph. Overall, the translation from pure $\mathcal{L}_{tac}$ to pure $\mathcal{R}_{tac}$ leads to an almost 84x reduction in the total verification time from 151 seconds to less than 2. In addition to the performance improvement on the sub-problems, solving the entire verification with a single reflective tactic avoids the need to leave the syntactic representation which is often accounts for a large portion of the time in reflective automation [34].

For this simple language, the entire translation from $\mathcal{L}_{tac}$ to $\mathcal{R}_{tac}$ took a little over a day. We encountered three main stumbling blocks in our development. First, the meta-theory for our language is built on the Charge! library [8] which relies heavily on type-classes which are not automatically handled by MirrorCore and $\mathcal{R}_{tac}$. Second, solving the entailment requires reasoning about arithmetic. In $\mathcal{L}_{tac}$, we can use Coq's built-in `omega` tactic which discharges obligations in Presburger arithmetic. Since we are building our automation reflectively, we lose access to generate-and-check-style automation. We solve this problem by writing custom $\mathcal{R}_{tac}$ to discharge the regular form of the goals that we need for this example, but more robust automation is clearly preferable and would likely benefit many clients. Finally, reasoning steps in $\mathcal{L}_{tac}$ rely on Coq's reduction mechanism. Since computational reflection treats symbols opaquely by default we needed to write reflective unfolders which replace symbols with their implementations. This is currently a quite manual task, though we believe that it could be simplified with some additional development.

For exposition purposes we have purposefully kept the automation simple. Adding support for additional language constructs is quite simple assuming they have good reasoning principles. In general, we reify the lemma and add new arms to the `FIRST` tactic to apply them. To extend the automation to a more realistic language we need to adapt the language and the automation to support heap operations and a rich separation logic. Our initial work on this suggests that this extension crucially relies on a good separation logic entailment checker. We believe that our monoidal equivalence checker is a first step in this direction, but more work is necessary to handle abstract representation predicates and more clever solving of unification variables that represent frame conditions.

Quantifier Pulling with Rewriting. To demonstrate the rewriter, we use it to lift existential quantifiers over conjunctions as we did in Sect. 6.1. Lifting of this sort is a common operation when verifying interesting programs since existential quantifiers are often buried inside representation predicates.

To perform lifting, we instantiate the rewriter using the definitions in Fig. 9. The core traversal is `quant_pull` which uses the bottom-up traversal. When the head symbol is a conjunction the recursive rewrites pull quantifiers to the top, which produces a formula similar to: $(\exists x : \mathbb{N}, P x) \wedge (\exists y : \mathbb{N}, \exists z : \mathbb{N}, Q\, y\, z)$.

```
Def the_rewrites : rewriter :=
  rw_post_simplify simple_reduce
    (rw_pre_simplify beta (rewrite_db the_lemmas)).

Def pull_all_quant : rewriter :=
  rw_repeat is_refl is_trans 300
    (bottom_up is_refl is_trans
        get_proper_only_all_ex
     the_rewrites).

Def quant_pull : rewriter :=
  bottom_up is_refl is_trans
    get_proper pull_all_quant.

Def qp_tac : rtac :=
  setoid_rewrite quant_pull.
```

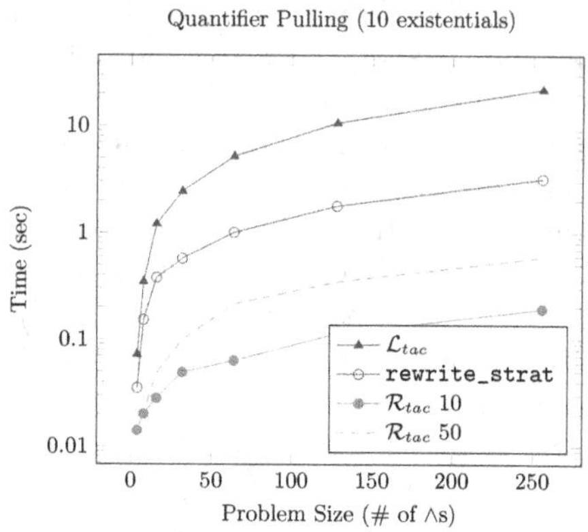

Fig. 9. Tasking the rewriter to lift quantifiers; and its scaling properties.

To lift *all* of the quantifiers from *both* sides of the conjunct, `pull_all_quant` repeatedly performs rewriting to lift the existentials over the conjunct. This rewriting also uses the bottom-up rewriter, but only uses the properness lemmas that allow the rewriter to descend into the body of existential quantifiers (`get_proper_only_all_ex`) to avoid descending into terms that we know do not contain quantifiers.

Figure 9 compares our reflective rewriter with two non-reflective strategies on a problem where 10 existential quantifiers are lifted from the leaves of a tree of conjuncts. The $\mathcal{L}_{tac}$ rewriter uses `repeat setoid_rewrite` since Coq's built-in `autorewrite` tactic does not rewrite under binders which is necessary to complete the problem. `rewrite_strat` uses Sozeau's new rewriter [42] which is more customizable and produces better proof terms. Even on small instances, the reflective rewriter is faster than both $\mathcal{L}_{tac}$ and `rewrite_strat`, e.g. at 16 conjuncts the reflective implementation is 13x faster than the strategy rewriter and 42x faster than the $\mathcal{L}_{tac}$ implementation. The performance improvement is due to the large proof terms that setoid rewriting requires.

8 Related and Future Work

The idea of computational reflection has been around since Nuprl [5,30] and also arose later in LEGO [40]. Besson [9] first demonstrated the ideas in Coq reasoning about Peano arithmetic. Since then there have been a variety of procedures that use computational reflection. Braibant's AAC tactics [12] perform reflective reasoning on associative and commutative structures such as rings. Lescuyer [33] developed a simple, reflective, SMT solver in Coq. There has also been work on reflectively checking proof traces produced by external tools in Coq [3,10]. The development of powerful reflective tactics has been facilitated by fast reduction mechanisms in Coq [11,27]. Our work tackles the problem of making computational reflection more accessible to ordinary users of Coq by making it easier to write and prove reflective automation sound, which is the main bottleneck in using computational reflection in practice.

Our work builds on the ideas for computational reflection developed by Malecha et al [34]. We extend that work by supporting a richer term and type language that is capable of representing higher-order problems and problems with local quantification[4] using a formalized version of Garillot's representation of simple types in type theory [24]. Our work differs from Garillot's by applying the representation to build reusable reflective automation. Some of the technical content in this paper is expanded in Malecha's dissertation [37].

Work by Keller describes an embedding of HOL lite in Coq [28] in order to transfer HOL proofs to Coq. Our representation in MirrorCore is very close to their work since, like MirrorCore, HOL lite does not support dependent types. Their work even discusses some of the challenges in compressing the terms that they import. For us, computational reflection solves the problem of large proof terms, though we did have to tune our representation to shrink proof terms. Separately, Fallenstein and Kumar [23] have applied reflection in HOL focusing on building self-evolving systems using logics based on large cardinals.

Recent work [21,44] has built reflective tactics in the Agda proof assistant. Unlike our work, this work axiomatizes the denotation function for syntax and relies on these axioms to prove the soundness of tactics. They argue that this axiomatization is reasonable by restricting it to only reduce on values in some cases which is sufficient for computational reflection. The reason for axiomatizing the denotation function is to avoid the overwhelming complexity of embedding a language as rich as dependent type theory within itself [4,13,19,38,39,45].

Kokke and Swierstra [31] have developed an implementation of `auto` in Agda using Agda's support for computational reflection. Their work also includes a reflective implementation of unification similar to our own. Their implementation abstracts over the search strategy allowing them to support heuristic search strategies, e.g. breadth- and depth-first search. Developing their procedure using only $\mathcal{R}_{tac}$ would be difficult because $\mathcal{R}_{tac}$'s design follows $\mathcal{L}_{tac}$'s model and only supports depth-first search. However, we can still implement a custom tactic similar to our rewriting tactic that interfaces with $\mathcal{R}_{tac}$.

Beyond computational reflection, there has been a growing body of work on proof engineering both in Coq and other proof assistants. Ziliani developed $\mathcal{M}_{tac}$ [46], a proof-generating tactic language that manipulates proofs explicitly. While it does generate proofs and thus is not truly reflective, it does provide a cleaner way to develop proofs. Prior to $\mathcal{M}_{tac}$, Gonthier [26] demonstrated how to use Coq's canonical structures to approximate disciplined proof search. Canonical structures are the workhorse of automation in the Ssreflect tactic library [25] which uses them as "small scale reflection." Our approach is based

[4] Malecha's work supports local quantification only in separation logic formulae and relies crucially on the type of separation logic formulae to be inhabited.

on large-scale computational reflection, seeking to integrate reflective automation to build automation capable of combining many steps of reasoning.

Escaping some of the complexity of dependent type theories, Stampoulis's VeriML [43] provides a way to write verified tactics within a simpler type theory. Like $\mathcal{R}_{tac}$, VeriML tactics are verified once meaning that their results do not need to be checked each time. VeriML is an entirely new proof assistant with accompanying meta-theory. Our implementation of $\mathcal{R}_{tac}$ is built directly within Coq and is being used alongside Coq's rich dependent type theory.

Future Work. The primary limitation in MirrorCore is the fact that the term representation supports only simple types. For the time being we have been able to get around this limitation by using meta-level parameterization to represent, and reason about, type constructors, polymorphism, and dependent types. Enriching MirrorCore to support these features in a first-class way would make it easier to write generic automation that can reason about these features, for example applying polymorphic lemmas. The primary limitation to doing this comes from the need to have decidable type checking for the term language. With simple types, decidable equality is simply syntactic equality, but when the type language contains functions type checking requires reduction.

Currently, the main cost of switching to reflective tactics is the loss of powerful tactics such as `omega` and `psatz`. While pieces of these tactics are reflective, integrating them into larger developments requires that they use extensible representations. Porting these tactics to work on MirrorCore would be a step towards making them usable within $\mathcal{R}_{tac}$. Unfortunately, many of these plugins rely on interesting OCaml programs to do the proof search and then emit witnesses that are checked reflectively. Accommodating this kind of computation within $\mathcal{R}_{tac}$ would require native support for invoking external procedures and reconstructing the results in Coq *a la* Claret's work [16].

9 Conclusion

We built a framework for easily building efficient automation in Coq using computational reflection. Our framework consists of MirrorCore, an extensible embedding of the simply-typed λ-calculus inside of Coq, which we use as our core syntactic representation. On top of MirrorCore, we built the reflective tactic language $\mathcal{R}_{tac}$. $\mathcal{R}_{tac}$ is modeled on $\mathcal{L}_{tac}$ which makes it easy to port simple $\mathcal{L}_{tac}$ tactics directly to $\mathcal{R}_{tac}$. Our case studies show that even naïve $\mathcal{R}_{tac}$ implementations can be nearly 2 orders of magnitude faster than their corresponding $\mathcal{L}_{tac}$ tactics. To demonstrate the extensible nature of $\mathcal{R}_{tac}$, we built a bottom-up setoid rewriter capable of inter-operating with $\mathcal{R}_{tac}$ tactics while retaining the ability to use custom data types and a global view of computation for efficiency.

The combination of MirrorCore and $\mathcal{R}_{tac}$ opens the doors to larger formalisms within dependent type theories that need to construct proof objects. $\mathcal{R}_{tac}$ allows us to combine individual reflective tactics into higher-level automation which allows us to further amortize the reification overhead across more reasoning steps. We believe that fully reflective automation will enable more and larger applications of the rich program logics currently being developed.

References

1. Agda Development Team. The Agda proof assistant reference manual, version 2.4.2. Accessed 2014 (2014)
2. Appel, A.W.: Program logics for certified compilers. Cambridge University Press, Cambridge (2014)
3. Armand, M., Faure, G., Grégoire, B., Keller, C., Théry, L., Werner, B.: A modular integration of SAT/SMT solvers to Coq through proof witnesses. In: Jouannaud, J.-P., Shao, Z. (eds.) CPP 2011. LNCS, vol. 7086, pp. 135–150. Springer, Heidelberg (2011)
4. Barras, B., Werner, B.: Coq in Coq. Technical report, INRIA-Rocquencourt (1997)
5. Barzilay, E.: Implementing reflection in Nuprl. Ph.D. thesis, Cornell University, AAI3195788 (2005)
6. Barzilay, E., Allen, S., Constable, R.: Practical reflection in NuPRL. In: Short Paper Presented at LICS 2003, pp. 22–25, June 2003
7. Bengtson, J., Jensen, J.B., Sieczkowski, F., Birkedal, L.: Verifying object-oriented programs with higher-order separation logic in Coq. In: Eekelen, M., Geuvers, H., Schmaltz, J., Wiedijk, F. (eds.) ITP 2011. LNCS, vol. 6898, pp. 22–38. Springer, Heidelberg (2011)
8. Bengtson, J., Jensen, J.B., Birkedal, L.: Charge! a framework for higher-order separation logic in Coq. In: Beringer, L., Felty, A. (eds.) ITP 2012. LNCS, vol. 7406, pp. 315–331. Springer, Heidelberg (2012)
9. Besson, F.: Fast reflexive arithmetic tactics the linear case and beyond. In: Altenkirch, T., McBride, C. (eds.) TYPES 2006. LNCS, vol. 4502, pp. 48–62. Springer, Heidelberg (2007)
10. Besson, F., Cornilleau, P.-E., Pichardie, D.: Modular SMT proofs for fast reflexive checking inside Coq. In: Jouannaud, J.-P., Shao, Z. (eds.) CPP 2011. LNCS, vol. 7086, pp. 151–166. Springer, Heidelberg (2011)
11. Boespflug, M., Dénès, M., Grégoire, B.: Full reduction at full throttle. In: Jouannaud, J.-P., Shao, Z. (eds.) CPP 2011. LNCS, vol. 7086, pp. 362–377. Springer, Heidelberg (2011)
12. Braibant, T., Pous, D.: Tactics for reasoning modulo AC in Coq. In: Jouannaud, J.-P., Shao, Z. (eds.) CPP 2011. LNCS, vol. 7086, pp. 167–182. Springer, Heidelberg (2011)
13. Chapman, J.: Type theory should eat itself. Electron. Notes Theoret. Comput. Sci. **228**, 21–36 (2009)
14. Chlipala, A.: Certified Programming with Dependent Types. MIT Press, Cambridge (2008)
15. Chlipala, A.: From network interface to multithreaded web applications: a cases-tudy in modular program verification. In: Proceedings of POPL 2015, pp. 609–622. ACM (2015)
16. Claret, G., del Carmen González Huesca, L., Régis-Gianas, Y., Ziliani, B.: Lightweight proof by reflection using a posteriori simulation of effectful computation. In: Blazy, S., Paulin-Mohring, C., Pichardie, D. (eds.) ITP 2013. LNCS, vol. 7998, pp. 67–83. Springer, Heidelberg (2013)
17. Coq Development Team. The Coq proof assistant reference manual, version 8.4. Accessed 2012 (2015)
18. Ricketts, D., Malecha, G., Alvarez, M.M., Gowda, V., Lerner, S.: Towards verification of hybrid systems in a foundational proof assistant. In: MEMOCODE 2015 (2015)

19. Danielsson, N.A.: A formalisation of a dependently typed language as an inductive-recursive family. In: Altenkirch, T., McBride, C. (eds.) TYPES 2006. LNCS, vol. 4502, pp. 93–109. Springer, Heidelberg (2007)
20. Delaware, B., Pit-Claudel, C., Gross, J., Chlipala, A.: Fiat: deductive synthesis of abstract data types in a proof assistant. In: Proceedings of POPL 2015, pp. 689–700. ACM (2015)
21. Devriese, D., Piessens, F.: Typed syntactic meta-programming. In: Proceedings of ICFP 2013, pp. 73–86. ACM (2013)
22. Dodds, J., Cao, Q., Bengtson, J., Appel, A.W.: Computational symbolic execution in interactive Hoare-logic proofs (Under submission)
23. Fallenstein, B., Kumar, R.: Proof-Producing Reflection for HOL. In: Urban, C., Zhang, X. (eds.) ITP 2015. LNCS, vol. 9236, pp. 170–186. Springer International Publishing, Switzerland (2015)
24. Garillot, F., Werner, B.: Simple types in type theory: deep and shallow encodings. In: Schneider, K., Brandt, J. (eds.) TPHOLs 2007. LNCS, vol. 4732, pp. 368–382. Springer, Heidelberg (2007)
25. Gonthier, G., Mahboubi, A., Tassi, E.: A small scale reflection extension for the Coq system. Rapport de recherche RR-6455, INRIA (2008)
26. Gonthier, G., Ziliani, B., Nanevski, A., Dreyer, D.: How to make Ad Hoc proof automation less Ad Hoc. In: Proceedings of ICFP 2011, pp. 163–175. ACM (2011)
27. Grégoire, B., Leroy, X.: A compiled implementation of strong reduction. In: Proceedings of ICFP 2002, pp. 235–246. ACM (2002)
28. Keller, C., Werner, B.: Importing HOL light into Coq. In: Kaufmann, M., Paulson, L.C. (eds.) ITP 2010. LNCS, vol. 6172, pp. 307–322. Springer, Heidelberg (2010)
29. Klein, G., Elphinstone, K., Heiser, G., Andronick, J., Cock, D., Derrin, P., Elkaduwe, D., Engelhardt, K., Kolanski, R., Norrish, M., Sewell, T., Tuch, H., Winwood, S.: seL4: formal verification of an OS kernel. In: Proceedings of SOSP, pp. 207–220. ACM (2009)
30. Knoblock, T.B., Constable, R.L.: Formalized metareasoning in type theory. Technical report, Cornell University (1986)
31. Kokke, P., Swierstra, W.: Auto in Agda. In: Hinze, R., Voigtländer, J. (eds.) MPC 2015. LNCS, vol. 9129, pp. 276–301. Springer, Heidelberg (2015)
32. Leroy, X.: Formal certification of a compiler back-end, or: programming a compiler with a proof assistant. In: 33rd ACM symposium on Principles of Programming Languages, pp. 42–54. ACM Press (2006)
33. Lescuyer, S.: Formalisation et développement d'une tactique réflexive pourla démonstration automatique en Coq. Thèse de doctorat, Université Paris-Sud, January 2011
34. Malecha, G., Chlipala, A., Braibant, T.: Compositional computational reflection. In: Klein, G., Gamboa, R. (eds.) ITP 2014. LNCS, vol. 8558, pp. 374–389. Springer, Heidelberg (2014)
35. Malecha, G., Morrisett, G., Shinnar, A., Wisnesky, R.: Toward a verified relational database management system. In: Proceedings of POPL 2010, pp. 237–248. ACM (2010)
36. Malecha, G., Wisnesky, R.: Using dependent types and tactics to enable semantic optimization of language-integrated queries. In: Proceedings of DBPL 2015, pp. 49–58. ACM (2015)
37. Malecha, G.M.: Extensible proof engineering in intensional type theory. Ph.D. thesis, Harvard University, November 2014
38. McBride, C.: Outrageous but meaningful coincidences: dependent type-safe syntax and evaluation. In: Proceedings of WGP 2010, pp. 1–12. ACM (2010)

39. Mike, S.: Homotopy type theory should eat itself (but so far, it's too big to swallow), March 2014
40. Pollack, R.: On extensibility of proof checkers. In: Smith, J., Dybjer, P., Nordström, B. (eds.) TYPES 1994. LNCS, vol. 996, pp. 140–161. Springer, Heidelberg (1995)
41. Shao, Z.: Clean-slate development of certified OS kernels. In: Proceedings of CPP 2015, pp. 95–96. ACM (2015)
42. Sozeau, M.: Proof-relevant rewriting strategies in Coq. In: At Coq Workshop, July 2014
43. Stampoulis, A., Shao, Z.: VeriML: typed computation of logical terms inside a language with effects. In: Proceedings of ICFP, pp. 333–344. ACM (2010)
44. van der Walt, P., Swierstra, W.: Engineering proof by reflection in Agda. In: Hinze, R. (ed.) IFL 2012. LNCS, vol. 8241, pp. 157–173. Springer, Heidelberg (2013)
45. Werner, B.: Sets in types, types in sets. In: Ito, T., Abadi, M. (eds.) TACS 1997. LNCS, vol. 1281, pp. 530–546. Springer, Heidelberg (1997)
46. Ziliani, B., Dreyer, D., Krishnaswami, N.R., Nanevski, A., Vafeiadis, V.: Mtac: a monad for typed tactic programming in Coq. In: Proceedings of ICFP 2013, pp. 87–100. ACM (2013)

An Algorithm Inspired by Constraint Solvers to Infer Inductive Invariants in Numeric Programs

Antoine Miné[1(✉)], Jason Breck[2], and Thomas Reps[2,3]

[1] Sorbonne Universités, UPMC Univ Paris 06, CNRS, LIP6, Paris, France
antoine.mine@lip6.fr

[2] University of Wisconsin, Madison, WI, USA

[3] GrammaTech, Inc., Ithaca, NY, USA

Abstract. This paper addresses the problem of proving a given invariance property φ of a loop in a numeric program, by inferring automatically a stronger inductive invariant ψ. The algorithm we present is based on both *abstract interpretation* and *constraint solving.* As in abstract interpretation, it computes the effect of a loop using a numeric abstract domain. As in constraint satisfaction, it works from "above"—interactively splitting and tightening a collection of abstract elements until an inductive invariant is found. Our experiments show that the algorithm can find non-linear inductive invariants that cannot normally be obtained using intervals (or octagons), even when classic techniques for increasing abstract-interpretation precision are employed—such as increasing and decreasing iterations with extrapolation, partitioning, and disjunctive completion. The advantage of our work is that because the algorithm uses standard abstract domains, it sidesteps the need to develop complex, non-standard domains specialized for solving a particular problem.

1 Introduction

A key concept in formal verification of programs is that of invariants, i.e., properties true of all executions of a program. For instance, safety properties, such as the fact that program variables stay within their expected bounds, are invariance properties, while more complex properties, such as termination, often depend

The authors wish to thank Sriram Sankaranarayanan and Charlotte Truchet for the very useful discussions that inspired this work. The work was supported, in part, by the project ANR-15-CE25-0002 Coverif from the French Agence Nationale de la Recherche; by a gift from Rajiv and Ritu Batra; by DARPA under cooperative agreement HR0011-12-2-0012; by AFRL under DARPA MUSE award FA8750-14-2-0270 and DARPA STAC award FA8750-15-C-0082; and by the UW-Madison Office of the Vice Chancellor for Research and Graduate Education with funding from the Wisconsin Alumni Research Foundation. Any opinions, findings, and conclusions or recommendations expressed in this publication are those of the authors, and do not necessarily reflect the views of the sponsoring agencies.

P. Thiemann (Ed.): ESOP 2016, LNCS 9632, pp. 560–588, 2016.
DOI: 10.1007/978-3-662-49498-1_22

entry:
  $x, y \in [-1, 1]$
body:
  $x' = 0.68 * (x - y);$
  $y' = 0.68 * (x + y);$
  $x = x'; y = y';$
invariant:
  $x, y \in [-2, 2]$

(a)

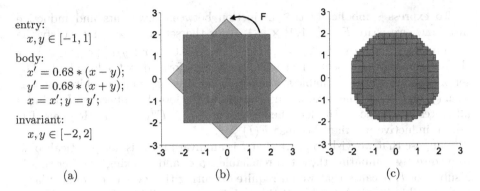

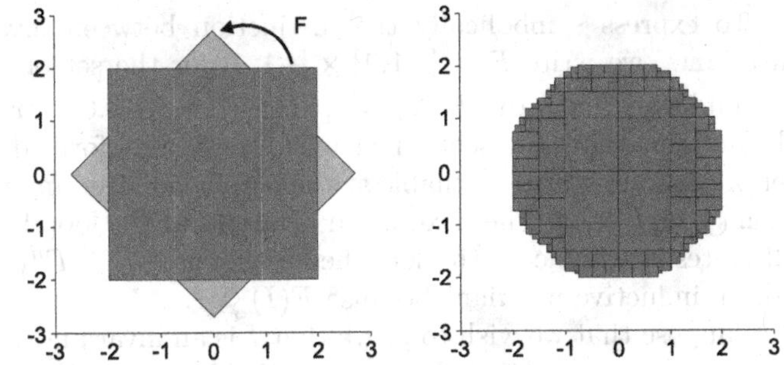

(b) (c)

Fig. 1. (a) A loop that performs a 45-degree rotation with a slight inward scaling; (b) no box is an inductive invariant; (c) inductive invariant obtained by our algorithm.

crucially on invariants. Hence, a large part of program-verification research concerns methods for checking or inferring suitable invariants. Invariants are particularly important for loops: an invariant for a loop provides a single property that holds on every loop iteration, and relieves one from having to prove the safety of each loop iteration individually (which might not be possible for infinite-state systems when the number of loop iterations is unbounded, and not practical when it is finite but large). The main principle for proving that a property is an invariant for a loop is to find a stronger property that is an *inductive invariant*, i.e., it holds when entering the loop for the first time, and is stable across a single loop iteration.

While an invariant associated with a safety property of interest can be relatively simple (e.g., a variable's value is bounded by such-and-such a quantity), it may not always be inductive. In general, it is a much more complex task to find an inductive invariant: inductive invariants can have much more complex shapes, as shown by the following example.

Consider the program in Fig. 1. It has two variables, x and y, and its loop body performs a 45-degree rotation of the point (x, y) about the origin, with a slight inward scaling. Additionally, we are given a precondition telling us that, upon entry to the loop, $x \in [-1, 1]$ and $y \in [-1, 1]$. Intuitively, no matter how many times we go around this loop, the point (x, y) will not move far away from the origin. To make this statement precise, we choose a bounding box that is aligned with the axes, such as $I \stackrel{\text{def}}{=} [-2, 2] \times [-2, 2]$, and observe that the program state, considered as a point (x, y), is guaranteed to lie inside I every time that execution reaches the head of the loop. Consequently, I is an invariant at the head of the loop.

Even though I is an invariant at the head of the loop, *it is not an inductive invariant*, because there are some points in I, such as its corners, that do not remain inside I after a 45-degree rotation. Actually, the corner points are not reachable states; however, there is no way to express that fact using an axis-aligned box. In fact, no box is an inductive invariant for this program.

To express symbolically the distinction between invariants and inductive invariants, we write $E = [-1,1] \times [-1,1]$ for the set of states that satisfy the precondition, and write $F(X) \stackrel{\text{def}}{=} \{(0.68*(x-y), 0.68*(x+y)) \mid (x,y) \in X\}$ for the function that represents the transformation performed by the loop body. The set of program states reachable at the loop head after any number of iterations is then $\bigcup_{n\in\mathbb{N}} F^n(E)$. The box I is an invariant at the loop head because I includes all states reachable at the loop head; that is, $\bigcup_{n\in\mathbb{N}} F^n(E) \subseteq I$. However, I is not an inductive invariant because $F(I) \not\subseteq I$.

Suppose that we wish to prove that I is an invariant. It is not practical to do so by directly computing the set of reachable states and checking whether that is a subset of I, because that would require executing the loop an extremely large (and possibly infinite) number of times. Instead, we will look for a set of boxes like J, shown in Fig. 1(c). One iteration of the loop maps this set of boxes into a subset of itself: the inward scaling, along with the rotation, maps the entire shape, including the jagged edges, into its own interior. Thus, even though no single box is an inductive invariant, a set of boxes, such as J, can be an inductive invariant. Note that this property can be verified by analyzing the effect of just one iteration of the loop applied to J. However, as this example illustrates, an inductive invariant like J may be significantly more complicated, and therefore more difficult to find, than an invariant such as I.

This paper is concerned with automatically strengthening a given invariant into an inductive invariant for numeric programs that manipulate reals or floats. In contrast to classical fixpoint-finding methods that start from the bottom of a lattice of abstract values and iteratively work upwards (towards an overapproximation of the infinite union mentioned above), the algorithm described in Sect. 4 starts with the invariant that the user wishes to prove and incrementally strengthens it until an inductive invariant is found.

The contributions of our work include the following:

- We demonstrate that ideas and techniques from constraint programming, such as an abstract domain consisting of disjunctions of boxes, and operators for splitting and tightening boxes, can be used to find inductive invariants.
- We present an algorithm based on those techniques and demonstrate that it is able to find inductive invariants for numerical, single-loop programs that manipulate reals or floats.
- We demonstrate the generality of our approach by extending the algorithm to optionally use an abstract domain based on octagons instead of boxes.
- We further extend our algorithm to optionally run in a "relatively-complete mode", which guarantees that an inductive invariant will be found if one exists in the appropriate abstract domain and can be proven inductive using boxes.

Organization. Section 2 presents an overview of our method and its connections to abstract interpretation and constraint programming. Section 3 recalls key facts about invariants, abstract interpretation, and constraint programming. Section 4 presents a basic version of our algorithm, using boxes to simplify the presentation. Section 5 discusses extensions, including the use of other numeric domains, methods to tighten invariants, and a modified version of the algorithm that has

entry:
  $s_0, s_1 \in [-0.1, 0.1]$
body:
  $r = 1.5 \times s_0 - 0.7 \times s_1 + [-0.1, 0.1]$;
  $s_1 = s_0$;
  $s_0 = r$;
invariant:
  $s_0, s_1 \in [-4, 4]$

(a)

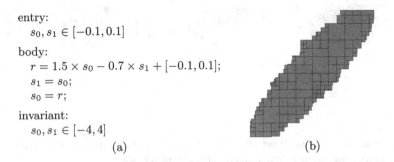

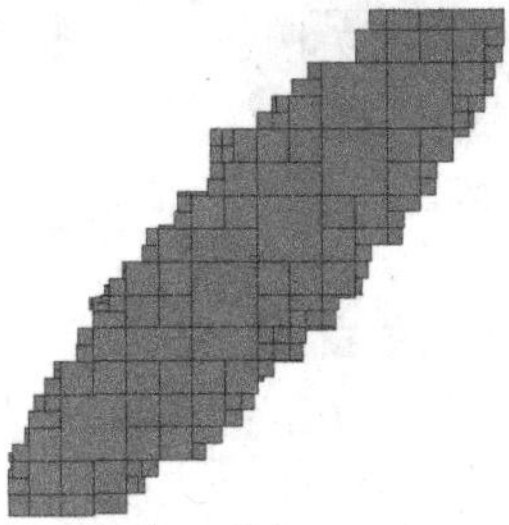

(b)

Fig. 2. (a) Second-order digital-filter program, and (b) the inductive invariant found by our method, composed of 181 boxes.

a relative-completeness property. Section 6 discusses our prototype implementation and preliminary experiments. Section 7 surveys related work. Section 8 concludes.

2 Overview

Consider Fig. 2(a), which presents a model of a loop that implements a second-order digital filter. Its state is composed of two variables, s_0 and s_1, which are initially set to values in $[-0.1, 0.1]$. On each loop iteration, the value of s_0 is shifted into s_1, while s_0 is assigned $1.5 \times s_0 - 0.7 \times s_1 + [-0.1, 0.1]$ (using a temporary variable r). The evaluation of the interval $[-0.1, 0.1]$ is understood as choosing a fresh value between -0.1 and 0.1 on each loop iteration. The evaluation occurs in the real field, and the use of an interval allows modeling rounding errors that can occur in a floating-point implementation of the filter. Note that the program is nondeterministic due to the indeterminacy in the initial state and in the evaluation of the interval, with infinitely many executions and an infinite state space.

We wish to prove that, on each iteration, the property $s_0, s_1 \in [-4, 4]$ holds. This property is indeed invariant; however, it is not inductive—and no box is inductive—for reasons similar to those explained in Sect. 1. More generally, interval arithmetic [23] is ineffective at proving that box invariants hold. Control theory teaches us that there exist quadratic properties—ellipsoids—that can be inductive. Verification techniques that exploit this knowledge *a priori* can be developed, such as [12]. However, that approach constitutes a program-specific method. Figure 2(b) shows an inductive invariant found by our method in 76 ms. While the shape of an ellipsoid is roughly recognizable, the inductive invariant found is actually the set union of 181 non-overlapping boxes. Our method employs only sets of boxes and does not use any knowledge from control theory.

Abstract Interpretation. Abstract interpretation [8] provides tools to infer inductive invariants. It starts from the observation that the most-precise loop

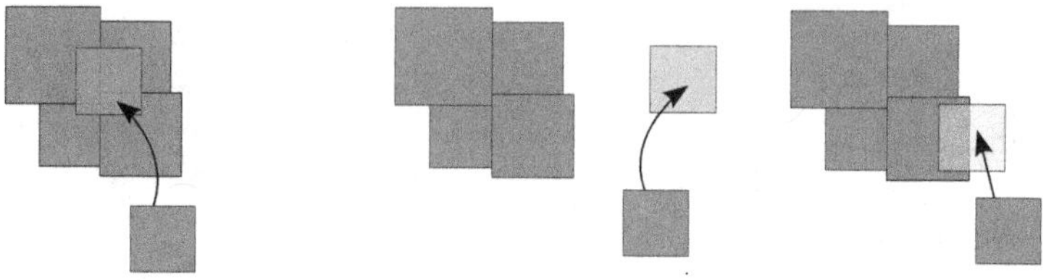

(a) (b) (c)

Fig. 3. Examples of boxes that should be (a) kept, (b) discarded, or (c) split, based on the intersection of each box's image with the other boxes.

invariant is inductive and can be expressed mathematically as a least fixpoint or, constructively, as the limit of an iteration sequence. In general, the most-precise loop invariant is not computable because the iterates live in infinite-state spaces, and the iteration sequences can require a transfinite number of iterations to reach the least fixpoint. Abstract interpretation solves the first issue by reasoning in an abstract domain of simpler, computable properties (such as intervals [8] or octagons [20]), and the second issue by using extrapolation operators (widenings and narrowings). Its effectiveness relies on the choice of an appropriate abstract domain, which must be able to represent inductive invariants, and also to support sufficiently precise operators—both to model program instructions and to perform extrapolation.

The Astrée analyzer [4] makes use of a large number of abstract domains, some of which are specific to particular application domains. In particular, the use of digital filters similar to Fig. 2(a) in aerospace software, and the inability of the interval domain to find any inductive invariant for them, motivated the design of the digital-filter domain [12] and its inclusion in Astrée. Note that Fig. 2(b) shows that an inductive invariant can, in fact, be expressed using a disjunction of boxes. However, applying classical disjunctive-domain constructions, such as disjunctive completion, or state- or trace-partitioning over the interval domain does not help in finding an inductive invariant. Indeed, these methods rely on program features, such as tests, control-flow joins, or user-provided hints, none of which occur in Fig. 2(a).

Constraint Programming. Constraint programming [22] is a declarative programming paradigm in which problems are first expressed as conjunctions of first-order logic formulas, called constraints, and then solved by generic methods. Different families of constraints come with specific operators—such as choice operators and propagators—used by the solver to explore the search space of the problem and to reduce its size, respectively.

Algorithm Synopsis. The algorithm presented in Sect. 4 was inspired by one class of constraint-solving algorithms—namely, continuous constraint solving—but applies those ideas to solve fixpoint equations. The algorithm works by

$$
\begin{array}{l}
\mathit{prog} ::= \textbf{assume } \mathit{entry} : \mathit{bexpr};\\
\qquad\quad \textbf{while true do}\\
\qquad\qquad\quad \textbf{assert } \mathit{inv} : \mathit{bexpr};\\
\qquad\qquad\quad \mathit{body} : \mathit{stat}\\
\qquad\quad \textbf{done}
\end{array}
\qquad
\begin{array}{lll}
\mathit{expr} ::= & V & V \in \mathcal{V}\\
\mid & [a, b] & a, b \in \mathbb{R}\\
\mid & -\mathit{expr} & \\
\mid & \mathit{expr} \circ \mathit{expr} & \circ \in \{+, -, \times, /\}
\end{array}
$$

$$
\begin{array}{lll}
\mathit{stat} ::= & V \leftarrow \mathit{expr} & V \in \mathcal{V}\\
\mid & \textbf{if } \mathit{bexpr} \textbf{ then } \mathit{stat} \textbf{ else } \mathit{stat} & \\
\mid & \mathit{stat}; \mathit{stat} &
\end{array}
\qquad
\begin{array}{lll}
\mathit{bexpr} ::= & \mathit{expr} \bowtie \mathit{expr} & \bowtie \in \{<, \leq, =\}\\
\mid & \neg \mathit{bexpr} & \\
\mid & \mathit{bexpr} \circ \mathit{bexpr} & \circ \in \{\wedge, \vee\}
\end{array}
$$

Fig. 4. Simple programming language.

iteratively refining a set of boxes until it becomes an inductive invariant. Figure 3 illustrates the main rules used to refine the set of boxes. When the boxes form an inductive invariant, one iteration of the loop maps each box into the areas covered by other boxes (Fig. 3(a)). To refine a set of boxes that is not yet an inductive invariant, two refinement rules are applied:

- Boxes that map to areas outside of all other boxes are discarded (Fig. 3(b)).
- If a box maps to an area partially inside and partially outside the set, then we split it into two boxes (Fig. 3(c)).

These rules, along with a few others, are applied until either the set of boxes is inductive or failure is detected.

Even when an inductive invariant can be represented in a given abstract domain, approximation due to widening can prevent an abstract interpreter from finding any inductive invariant—let alone the best one. The version of our algorithm presented in Sect. 4 shares this deficiency (although not because widening is involved); however, we modify our method to overcome this problem in Sect. 5.3.

The algorithm presented in this paper exploits simple, generic abstract domains (such as intervals) to compute effectively and efficiently the effect of a loop iteration, but (i) replaces extrapolation with a novel search algorithm inspired from constraint programming, and (ii) proposes a novel method to introduce disjunctions. Because of these features of the algorithm, it can sidestep the need to invent specialized abstract domains for specialized settings. For instance, a special digital-filter abstract domain (like the one created for Astrée [12]) is not needed to handle a digital-filter program; the interval domain suffices.

3 Terminology and Notation

3.1 Language and Semantics

The language we consider is defined in Figs. 4 and 5. It is a simple numeric language, featuring real-valued variables $V \in \mathcal{V}$; numeric expressions *expr*, including the usual operators and non-deterministic random choice ($[a, b]$); Boolean expressions *bexpr*; and various statements *stat*—assignments ($V \leftarrow \mathit{expr}$), conditionals (**if** *bexpr* **then** *stat* **else** *stat*) and sequences (*stat*; *stat*). A program

$$
\begin{aligned}
&\mathbb{E}[\![\, expr \,]\!] : \mathcal{E} \to \mathcal{P}(\mathbb{R})\\
&\mathbb{E}[\![\, V \,]\!]\rho \stackrel{\text{def}}{=} \{\, \rho(V) \,\}\\
&\mathbb{E}[\![\, e_1 \circ e_2 \,]\!]\rho \stackrel{\text{def}}{=} \{\, v_1 \circ v_2 \mid v_1 \in \mathbb{E}[\![\, e_1 \,]\!]\rho, v_2 \in \mathbb{E}[\![\, e_2 \,]\!]\rho \,\}\\
&\mathbb{E}[\![\, -e \,]\!]\rho \stackrel{\text{def}}{=} \{\, -v \mid v \in \mathbb{E}[\![\, e \,]\!]\rho \,\}\\
&\mathbb{E}[\![\, [a,b] \,]\!]\rho \stackrel{\text{def}}{=} \{\, x \in \mathbb{R} \mid a \le x \le b \,\}
\end{aligned}
$$

$$
\begin{aligned}
&\mathbb{B}[\![\, bexpr \,]\!] : \mathcal{P}(\mathcal{E}) \to \mathcal{P}(\mathcal{E})\\
&\mathbb{B}[\![\, e_1 \bowtie e_2 \,]\!]S \stackrel{\text{def}}{=} \{\, \rho \in S \mid \exists v_1 \in \mathbb{E}[\![\, e_1 \,]\!]\rho,\ v_2 \in \mathbb{E}[\![\, e_2 \,]\!]\rho,\ v_1 \bowtie v_2 \,\}\\
&\mathbb{B}[\![\, b_1 \vee b_2 \,]\!]S \stackrel{\text{def}}{=} \mathbb{B}[\![\, b_1 \,]\!]\, S \cup \mathbb{B}[\![\, b_2 \,]\!]S\\
&\mathbb{B}[\![\, b_1 \wedge b_2 \,]\!]S \stackrel{\text{def}}{=} \mathbb{B}[\![\, b_1 \,]\!]\, S \cap \mathbb{B}[\![\, b_2 \,]\!]S
\end{aligned}
$$

$$
\begin{aligned}
&\mathbb{S}[\![\, stat \,]\!] : \mathcal{P}(\mathcal{E}) \to \mathcal{P}(\mathcal{E})\\
&\mathbb{S}[\![\, V \leftarrow e \,]\!]S \stackrel{\text{def}}{=} \{\, \rho[V \mapsto v] \mid \rho \in S,\ v \in \mathbb{E}[\![\, e \,]\!]\rho \,\}\\
&\mathbb{S}[\![\, \textbf{if } b \textbf{ then } s_1 \textbf{ else } s_2 \,]\!]S \stackrel{\text{def}}{=} \mathbb{S}[\![\, s_1 \,]\!]\, (\mathbb{B}[\![\, b \,]\!]S) \cup \mathbb{S}[\![\, s_2 \,]\!](\mathbb{B}[\![\, \neg b \,]\!]S)\\
&\mathbb{S}[\![\, s_1; s_2 \,]\!]S \stackrel{\text{def}}{=} \mathbb{S}[\![\, s_2 \,]\!]\, (\mathbb{S}[\![\, s_1 \,]\!]S)
\end{aligned}
$$

Fig. 5. Language semantics.

$$
\begin{aligned}
&\mathbb{S}^\sharp[\![\, stat \,]\!] : \mathcal{D}^\sharp \to \mathcal{D}^\sharp\\
&\mathbb{S}^\sharp[\![\, V \leftarrow e \,]\!]S^\sharp \stackrel{\text{def}}{=} \mathfrak{assign}^\sharp(V, e, S^\sharp)\\
&\mathbb{S}^\sharp[\![\, \textbf{if } b \textbf{ then } s_1 \textbf{ else } s_2 \,]\!]S^\sharp \stackrel{\text{def}}{=} \mathbb{S}^\sharp[\![\, s_1 \,]\!]\, (\mathfrak{guard}^\sharp(b, S^\sharp)) \cup^\sharp \mathbb{S}^\sharp[\![\, s_2 \,]\!](\mathfrak{guard}^\sharp(\neg b, S^\sharp))\\
&\mathbb{S}^\sharp[\![\, s_1; s_2 \,]\!]S^\sharp \stackrel{\text{def}}{=} \mathbb{S}^\sharp[\![\, s_2 \,]\!]\, (\mathbb{S}^\sharp[\![\, s_1 \,]\!]S^\sharp)\\
&\mathbb{B}^\sharp[\![\, bexpr \,]\!](S^\sharp) \stackrel{\text{def}}{=} \mathfrak{guard}^\sharp(bexpr, S^\sharp)\\
&\mathbb{P}^\sharp(S^\sharp) \stackrel{\text{def}}{=} \mathbb{B}^\sharp[\![\, entry \,]\!]\, \top^\sharp \cup^\sharp \mathbb{S}^\sharp[\![\, body \,]\!]S^\sharp
\end{aligned}
$$

Fig. 6. Abstract semantics.

prog consists of a single loop that starts in an entry state *entry* specified by a Boolean expression; a program is non-terminating, and executes a *body* statement. The loop invariant to prove (a Boolean expression) is explicitly present in the loop. Furthermore, the semantics is in terms of real numbers; if a floating-point semantics is desired instead, any rounding error has to be made explicit, using for instance the technique described in [19].

The concrete semantics of the language is presented in Fig. 5. It is a simple numeric, big-step, non-deterministic semantics, where expressions evaluate to a set of values $\mathbb{E}[\![\, e \,]\!]\rho \in \mathcal{P}(\mathbb{R})$ given an environment $\rho \in \mathcal{E} \stackrel{\text{def}}{=} \mathcal{V} \to \mathbb{R}$; Boolean expressions act as environment filters $\mathbb{B}[\![\, b \,]\!] : \mathcal{P}(\mathcal{E}) \to \mathcal{P}(\mathcal{E})$; and statements as environment transformers $\mathbb{S}[\![\, s \,]\!] : \mathcal{P}(\mathcal{E}) \to \mathcal{P}(\mathcal{E})$. Given a program whose entry states are given by $entry \in bexpr$, a formula for a candidate invariant for the loop $inv \in bexpr$, and loop body $body \in stat$, the goal is to prove that inv is indeed an invariant for the loop. This problem can be expressed as the following fixpoint problem:

```
solutions ← ∅
toExplore ← ∅
push S into toExplore
while toExplore≠ ∅ do
    b ← pop(toExplore)
    b ← Hull-Consistency(b)
    if b = ∅ then nothing
    else if b contains only solutions then solutions ← solutions ∪ {b}
    else if b is small enough then solutions ← solutions ∪ {b}
    else
        split b in half along the largest dimension into b1 and b2
        push b1 and b2 into toExplore
done
```

Fig. 7. Continuous solver, from [24].

$$\text{lfp}\,\mathbb{P} \subseteq \mathbb{B}[\![\, inv \,]\!]\mathcal{E} \text{ where } \mathbb{P}(X) \stackrel{\text{def}}{=} \mathbb{B}[\![\, entry \,]\!]\,\mathcal{E} \cup \mathbb{S}[\![\, body \,]\!]X. \tag{1}$$

We will abbreviate the problem statement as $\text{lfp}\,\mathbb{P} \subseteq I$.

We can now formalize the notion of invariant and inductive invariant.

1. An *invariant* is any set I such that $\text{lfp}\,\mathbb{P} \subseteq I$.
2. An *inductive invariant* is any set I such that $\mathbb{P}(I) \subseteq I$.

By Tarski's Theorem [29], $\mathbb{P}(I) \subseteq I$ implies $\text{lfp}\,\mathbb{P} \subseteq I$. Moreover, $\text{lfp}\,\mathbb{P}$ is the smallest invariant, and it is also an inductive invariant. Because computing or approximating $\mathbb{P}(I)$ is generally much easier than $\mathbb{P}$, it is much easier to check that a property is an inductive invariant than to check that it is an invariant.

3.2 Abstract Interpretation

The key idea underlying abstract interpretation is to replace each operation in $\mathcal{P}(\mathcal{E})$ with an operation that works in an abstract domain $\mathcal{D}^\sharp$ of properties. Each abstract element $S^\sharp \in \mathcal{D}^\sharp$ represents a set of points $\gamma(S^\sharp)$ through a concretization function $\gamma : \mathcal{D}^\sharp \to \mathcal{P}(\mathcal{E})$. Additionally, we assume that there exist abstract primitives $\mathfrak{assign}^\sharp(V, expr, S^\sharp)$, $\mathfrak{guard}^\sharp(bexpr, S^\sharp)$, $\cup^\sharp$, $\cap^\sharp$, $\bot^\sharp$, $\top^\sharp \in \mathcal{D}^\sharp$ that model, respectively, the effect of $\mathbb{S}[\![\, V \leftarrow expr \,]\!]$, $\mathbb{B}[\![\, bexpr \,]\!]$, $\cup$, $\cap$, $\emptyset$, $\cup$, $\cap$, $\emptyset$, and $\mathcal{E}$. Then, the semantics of Fig. 5 can be abstracted as shown in Fig. 6.

Once an inductive invariant is found by abstract interpretation, it is a simple matter to check whether the abstract inductive invariant entails the candidate invariant I. Note that abstract interpretation does not require any knowledge of the invariant of interest to infer an inductive invariant, which is not a property enjoyed by our algorithm (or, at least, its first incarnation in Sect. 4; Sect. 5.2 will propose solutions to alleviate this limitation).

3.3 Continuous Constraint Solving

A constraint-satisfaction problem is defined by (i) a set of variables $V_1, \ldots, V_n$; (ii) a search space S given by a domain $D_1, \ldots, D_n$ for each variable; and (iii) a set of constraints $\phi_1, \ldots, \phi_p$. Because we are interested in a real-valued program semantics, we focus on continuous constraints: each constraint ϕ_i is a Boolean expression in our language (*bexpr* in Fig. 4). Moreover, each domain D_i is an interval of reals, so that the search space S is a box. The problem to be solved is to enumerate all variable valuations in the search space that satisfy every ϕ_i, i.e., to compute $\mathbb{B}[\![\wedge_i \ \phi_i]\!]S$. Because the solution set cannot generally be enumerated exactly, continuous solvers compute a collection of boxes with floating-point bounds that contain all solutions and tightly fit the solution set (i.e., contains as few non-solutions as possible). Such a solver alternates two kinds of steps:

1. *Propagation steps.* These exploit constraints to reduce the domains of variables by removing values that cannot participate in a solution. Ultimately, the goal is to achieve *consistency*, when no more values can be removed. Several notions of consistency exist. We use here so-called *hull consistency*, where domains are intervals and they are consistent when their bounds cannot be tightened anymore without possibly losing a solution.
2. *Splitting steps.* When domains cannot be reduced anymore, the solver performs an assumption: it splits a domain and continues searching in that reduced search space. The search proceeds, alternating propagation and splits, until the search space contains no solution, only solutions, or shrinks below a user-specified size. Backtracking is then used to explore other assumptions.

This algorithm is sketched in Fig. 7. It maintains a collection of search spaces yet to explore and a set of solution boxes. The algorithm always terminates, at which point every box either contains only solutions or meets the user-specified size limit, and every solution is accounted for (i.e., belongs to a box).

There are strong connections with abstract interpretation. We observed in [24] that the classic propagator for hull consistency for a constraint ϕ_i, so-called HC4 [3], is very similar to the classic algorithm for $\mathfrak{guard}^\sharp(\phi_i, S)$ in the interval abstract domain. When there are several constraints, the propagators for each constraint are applied in turn, until a fixpoint is reached; this approach is similar to Granger's method of local iterations [15] used in abstract interpretation. We went further in [24] and showed that the algorithm of Fig. 7 is an instance of a general algorithm that is parameterized by an arbitrary numeric abstract domain. While standard continuous constraint programming corresponds to the interval domain, we established that there are benefits from using relational domains instead, such as octagons [20]. In abstract-interpretation terminology, this algorithm computes decreasing iterations in the disjunctive completion of the abstract domain. These iterations can be interpreted as an iterative over-approximation of a fixpoint: gfp $\mathbb{C}$ where $\mathbb{C}(X) \stackrel{\text{def}}{=} \mathbb{B}[\![\wedge_i \ \phi_i]\!] \, (X \cap S)$, and we can check easily that this concrete fixpoint gfp $\mathbb{C}$ indeed equals $\mathbb{B}[\![\wedge_i \ \phi_i]\!]S$.

In the following, we will adapt this algorithm to over-approximate a program's semantic fixpoint, lfp $\mathbb{P}$, instead (Eq. (1)). There are two main differences between these fixpoints. First, constraint programming approximates a greatest fixpoint instead of a least fixpoint. Second, and less obvious, is that constraint programming is limited to approximating gfp $\mathbb{C}$, where $\mathbb{C}$ is reductive, i.e., $\forall S : \mathbb{C}(S) \subseteq S$. It relies on the fact that, at every solving step, the join of all the boxes (whether solutions or yet to be explored) already covers all of the solutions. In a sense, it starts with a trivial covering of the solution, the entire search space, and refines it to provide a better (tighter) covering of the solution. In contrast, when we approximate lfp $\mathbb{P}$, $\mathbb{P}$ is a join morphism, but is often neither extensive nor reductive. Moreover, the search will start with an invariant that may not be an inductive invariant.

4 Inductive-Invariant Inference

We now present our algorithm for inductive-invariant inference. We assume that we have the following abstract elements and computable abstract functions in the interval domain $\mathcal{D}^\sharp$ (cf. Sect. 3.2 and Fig. 6):

- $E^\sharp \stackrel{\text{def}}{=} \mathbb{B}^\sharp[\![\, \textit{entry} \,]\!]\, \top^\sharp \in \mathcal{D}^\sharp$: the abstraction of the entry states
- $F^\sharp \stackrel{\text{def}}{=} \mathbb{S}^\sharp[\![\, \textit{body} \,]\!] : \mathcal{D}^\sharp \to \mathcal{D}^\sharp$: the abstraction of the loop body
- $I^\sharp \in \mathcal{D}^\sharp$: an abstract *under*-approximation of the invariant I we seek, i.e., $\gamma(I^\sharp) \subseteq I$ (in general the equality holds). We assume that $\gamma(E^\sharp) \subseteq \gamma(I^\sharp)$; otherwise, no subset of $\gamma(I^\sharp)$ can contain $\gamma(E^\sharp)$ and be an inductive invariant.

We will manipulate a set of boxes, $\mathfrak{S}^\sharp \in \mathcal{P}(\mathcal{D}^\sharp)$. Similar to disjunctive completion, we define the concretization $\gamma(\mathfrak{S}^\sharp)$ of a set of boxes $\mathfrak{S}^\sharp$ as the (concrete) union of their individual concretizations:

$$\gamma(\mathfrak{S}^\sharp) \stackrel{\text{def}}{=} \cup \{ \gamma(S^\sharp) \mid S^\sharp \in \mathfrak{S}^\sharp \}. \tag{2}$$

We use $\gamma F^\sharp(\mathfrak{S}^\sharp)$ to denote the (concrete) union of the box-wise application of the abstract operator $F^\sharp$ on $\mathfrak{S}^\sharp$:

$$\gamma F^\sharp(\mathfrak{S}^\sharp) \stackrel{\text{def}}{=} \cup \{ \gamma(F^\sharp(S^\sharp)) \mid S^\sharp \in \mathfrak{S}^\sharp \}. \tag{3}$$

Our goal is to find a set of boxes $\mathfrak{S}^\sharp$ that satisfies the following properties:

Property 1

1. $\gamma(E^\sharp) \subseteq \gamma(\mathfrak{S}^\sharp)$ *($\mathfrak{S}^\sharp$ contains the entry)*
2. $\gamma(\mathfrak{S}^\sharp) \subseteq \gamma(I^\sharp)$ *($\mathfrak{S}^\sharp$ entails the invariant)*
3. $\gamma F^\sharp(\mathfrak{S}^\sharp) \subseteq \gamma(\mathfrak{S}^\sharp)$ *($\mathfrak{S}^\sharp$ is inductive)*

Property 1 is indeed sufficient to ensure we have found our inductive invariant.

Theorem 1
$\gamma(\mathfrak{S}^\sharp)$ satisfying Properties 1.1–1.3 is an inductive invariant that implies I.

Proof. See the appendix of the technical report version of this paper [21]. □

In addition to Property 1, we will ensure that the boxes in $\mathfrak{S}^\sharp$ do not overlap. Because we use the interval abstract domain, which allows non-strict inequality constraints only, we do not enforce that $\mathfrak{S}^\sharp$ forms a partition. That is, we may have $\gamma(S_1^\sharp) \cap \gamma(S_2^\sharp) \neq \emptyset$ for $S_1^\sharp \neq S_2^\sharp \in \mathfrak{S}^\sharp$; however, intersecting boxes have an intersection of null volume, $\mathrm{vol}(\gamma(S_1^\sharp) \cap \gamma(S_2^\sharp)) = 0$, where $\mathrm{vol}(S^\sharp)$ is the volume of a box $S^\sharp$.

In a manner similar to a constraint-solving algorithm, our algorithm starts with a single box $\mathfrak{S}^\sharp \stackrel{\text{def}}{=} \{I^\sharp\}$, here containing the invariant to prove, and iteratively selects a box to shrink, split, or discard, until Properties 1.1–1.3 are satisfied. Property 1.1 (entry containment) holds when the algorithm starts, and we take care never to remove box parts that intersect $E^\sharp$ from $\mathfrak{S}^\sharp$. Property 1.2 (invariant entailment) also holds when the algorithm starts, and naturally holds at every step of the algorithm because we never add any point to $\gamma(\mathfrak{S}^\sharp)$. Property 1.3 (inductiveness) does *not* hold when the algorithm begins, and it is the main property to establish. We will start by presenting a few useful operations on individual boxes, before presenting our algorithm in Sect. 4.2.

4.1 Box Operations

Box Classification. To select a box to handle in $\mathfrak{S}^\sharp$, we must first classify the boxes. We say that $S^\sharp \in \mathfrak{S}^\sharp$ is:

- *necessary* if $\gamma(S^\sharp) \cap \gamma(E^\sharp) \neq \emptyset$;
- *benign* if $\gamma(F^\sharp(S^\sharp)) \subseteq \gamma(\mathfrak{S}^\sharp)$;
- *doomed*[1] if $\gamma(F^\sharp(S^\sharp)) \cap \gamma(\mathfrak{S}^\sharp) = \emptyset$;
- *useful* if $\gamma(S^\sharp) \cap \gamma F^\sharp(\mathfrak{S}^\sharp) \neq \emptyset$.

A necessary box contains some point from the entry $E^\sharp$, and thus cannot be completely discarded. A benign box has its image under $F^\sharp$ completely covered by $\gamma(\mathfrak{S}^\sharp)$, and so does not impede inductiveness. Our goal is to make all boxes benign. In contrast, a doomed box prevents inductiveness, and no shrinking or splitting operation on this or another box will make it benign. A useful box $S^\sharp$ intersects the image of a box $S_0^\sharp$ in $\mathfrak{S}^\sharp$, i.e., $S^\sharp$ helps make $S_0^\sharp$ benign and therefore $S^\sharp$ is worth keeping.

Coverage. In addition to these qualitative criteria, we define a quantitative measure of coverage:

$$\mathrm{coverage}(S^\sharp, \mathfrak{S}^\sharp) \stackrel{\text{def}}{=} \frac{\sum \{ \mathrm{vol}(\gamma(F^\sharp(S^\sharp)) \cap \gamma(T^\sharp)) \mid T^\sharp \in \mathfrak{S}^\sharp \}}{\mathrm{vol}(\gamma(F^\sharp(S^\sharp)))}. \quad (4)$$

The coverage is a measure, in $[0, 1]$, of how benign a box is. A value of 1 indicates that the box is benign, while a value of 0 indicates that the box is doomed. Because our goal is to make all boxes benign, the algorithm will

[1] If $F^\sharp(S^\sharp)$ is empty, then $S^\sharp$ satisfies our definition of benign and our definition of doomed; in this case we consider $S^\sharp$ benign, not doomed.

consider first the boxes with the least coverage, i.e., which require the most work to become benign. If a box is doomed, there is no hope for it to become benign, and it should be discarded. Similarly, if a box's coverage is too small, there is little hope it might contain a benign sub-box, and—as a heuristic—the algorithm could consider discarding it. For this reason, the algorithm is parameterized by a coverage cut-off value ϵ_c.

Tightening. Given a box $S^\sharp \in \mathfrak{S}^\sharp$, not all parts of $\gamma(S^\sharp)$ are equally useful. Using reasoning similar to the notion of consistency in constraint solvers, we can tighten the box. In our case, we remove the parts that do not make it necessary (intersecting $E^\sharp$) nor useful (intersecting $\gamma F^\sharp(\mathfrak{S}^\sharp)$). The box $S^\sharp$ is replaced with:

$$\text{tighten}(S^\sharp, \mathfrak{S}^\sharp) \stackrel{\text{def}}{=} (S^\sharp \cap^\sharp E^\sharp) \cup^\sharp (\cup^\sharp \{ S^\sharp \cap^\sharp F^\sharp(T^\sharp) \mid T^\sharp \in \mathfrak{S}^\sharp \}), \tag{5}$$

which first gathers all the useful and necessary parts from $S^\sharp$, and then joins them in the abstract domain to obtain a box that contains all those parts. Because the $\cup^\sharp$ operator of the interval domain is optimal, tighten$(S^\sharp)$ is the smallest box containing those parts. Replacing $S^\sharp$ with tighten$(S^\sharp, \mathfrak{S}^\sharp)$ in $\mathfrak{S}^\sharp$ has precision benefits. Because we keep useful parts, $\forall T^\sharp \neq S^\sharp$: coverage$(T^\sharp, \mathfrak{S}^\sharp)$ remains unchanged while $F^\sharp(S^\sharp)$ decreases—assuming that when $S^\sharp$ shrinks so does $F^\sharp(S^\sharp)$.[2]

Splitting. As in constraint solvers, we define the *size* size$(S^\sharp)$ of a box $S^\sharp \stackrel{\text{def}}{=} [a_1, b_1] \times \cdots \times [a_n, b_n]$ as the maximum width among all variables, i.e.:

$$\text{size}(S^\sharp) = \max \{ b_i - a_i \mid i \in [1, n] \}. \tag{6}$$

Box splitting consists of replacing a box $S^\sharp \stackrel{\text{def}}{=} [a_1, b_1] \times \cdots \times [a_n, b_n] \in \mathfrak{S}^\sharp$ with two boxes: $L^\sharp \stackrel{\text{def}}{=} [a_1, b_1] \times \cdots \times [a_i, c] \times \cdots \times [a_n, b_n]$ and $U^\sharp \stackrel{\text{def}}{=} [a_1, b_1] \times \cdots \times [c, b_i] \times \cdots \times [a_n, b_n]$, where $c = (a_i + b_i)/2$ is the middle of the interval $[a_i, b_i]$, and i is such that $b_i - a_i = \text{size}(S^\sharp)$, i.e., it is an interval whose size equals the size of the box. That way, a sequence of splits will reduce a box's size. We will refrain from splitting boxes below a certain size-parameter cut-off ϵ_s, and we are guaranteed to reach a size less than ϵ_s after finitely many splits.

Splitting a box also carries precision benefits. In general, abstract functions $F^\sharp$ are sub-join morphisms: $\gamma(F^\sharp(L^\sharp)) \cup \gamma(F^\sharp(U^\sharp)) \subseteq \gamma(F^\sharp(L^\sharp \cup^\sharp U^\sharp)) = \gamma(F^\sharp(S^\sharp))$. Splitting $S^\sharp$ corresponds to a case analysis, where the effect of the loop body is analyzed separately for $V_i \leq c$ and $V_i \geq c$, which is at the core of partitioning techniques used in abstract interpretation. While replacing $S^\sharp$ with $\{L^\sharp, U^\sharp\}$ in $\mathfrak{S}^\sharp$ does not change $\gamma(\mathfrak{S}^\sharp)$, it is likely to shrink $\gamma F^\sharp(\mathfrak{S}^\sharp)$, helping Property 1.3 to hold. Further improvements can be achieved by tightening $L^\sharp$ and $U^\sharp$ after the split.

---

[2] See the note about monotonicity on p. 16.

Discarding. Constraint solvers only discard boxes when they do not contain any solution. Likewise, we can discard boxes that are neither necessary (no intersection with $E^\sharp$) nor useful (no intersection with $\gamma F^\sharp(\mathfrak{S}^\sharp)$). However, we can go further, and also remove useful boxes as well. On the one hand, this may shrink $\gamma F^\sharp(\mathfrak{S}^\sharp)$, and help Property 1.3 to hold. On the other hand, given $T^\sharp$ for which $S^\sharp$ is useful, i.e., $\gamma(F^\sharp(T^\sharp)) \cap \gamma(S^\sharp) \neq \emptyset$, it will strictly reduce $T^\sharp$'s coverage, and possibly make $T^\sharp$ not benign anymore. Nevertheless, in this latter case, it is often possible to recover from this situation later, by splitting, shrinking, or discarding $T^\sharp$ itself. The possibility to remove boxes that are unlikely to be in any inductive invariant is a particularly interesting heuristic to apply after the algorithm reaches the cut-off threshold for size or coverage. Such a removal will trigger the removal of parts of boxes whose image intersects the removed box, until—one hopes—after a cascade of similar effects, the algorithm identifies a core of boxes that forms an inductive invariant.

4.2 Algorithm

Our algorithm is presented in Fig. 8. It maintains, in $\mathfrak{S}^\sharp$, a set of boxes to explore, initialized with the candidate invariant $I^\sharp$ of interest. Then, while there are boxes to explore, the box $S^\sharp$ with smallest coverage (Eq. (4)) is removed from $\mathfrak{S}^\sharp$. If $S^\sharp$ has a coverage of 1, then so have the remaining boxes in $\mathfrak{S}^\sharp$; hence all of the boxes are benign and the algorithm has found an inductive invariant: we add back $S^\sharp$ to $\mathfrak{S}^\sharp$ and return that set of boxes. Otherwise, some work is performed to help make $S^\sharp$ benign. In the general case, where $S^\sharp$ is not necessary (does not intersect $E^\sharp$), we are free to discard $S^\sharp$, which we do if it is useless, too small to be split, or its coverage makes it unlikely to become benign; otherwise, we split $S^\sharp$. When $S^\sharp$ is necessary, however, we refrain from removing it. Hence we split it, unless it is too small and we cannot split it anymore. At this point there is no way to satisfy all of Properties 1.1 and 1.3 and the user's specified minimum box size; consequently, the algorithm fails.

Normally, the **search** function always returns through either the success or failure **return** statements in the loop body. Normal loop exit corresponds to the corner case where all boxes have been discarded, which means that no box was ever necessary, i.e., $\mathbb{B}[\![\, \textit{entry} \,]\!]\mathcal{E} = \emptyset$; we return $\emptyset$ in that case, because it is indeed an inductive invariant for loops with an empty entry state set.

The splitting procedure takes care to tighten the two sub-boxes $S_1^\sharp$ and $S_2^\sharp$ generated from the split. **split** is always called with a box of non-zero size, and it generates boxes smaller than $S^\sharp$.

Note that, given a box $S^\sharp$, it is possible that $\gamma(F^\sharp(S^\sharp)) \cap \gamma(S^\sharp) \neq \emptyset$, i.e., a box is useful to itself. For this reason, after removing $S^\sharp$ from $\mathfrak{S}^\sharp$, we take care to compute the coverage as coverage$(S^\sharp, \mathfrak{S}^\sharp \cup \{S^\sharp\})$ and not as coverage$(S^\sharp, \mathfrak{S}^\sharp)$, and similarly after a split.

The following theorem states the correctness of the algorithm:

Theorem 2. **search** *always terminates, either with a failure, or returns a set* $\mathfrak{S}^\sharp$ *of boxes satisfying Properties 1.1–1.3.*

```
search(E♯, F♯, I♯):
    𝔖♯ ← {I♯}
    while 𝔖♯ ≠ ∅ do
        S♯ ← popMinCoverage(𝔖♯)
        if coverage(S♯, 𝔖♯ ∪ {S♯}) = 1 then return 𝔖♯ ∪ {S♯}
        else if S♯ is not necessary then
            if S♯ is not useful or size(S♯) < ϵs or coverage(S♯, 𝔖♯ ∪ {S♯}) < ϵc
            then discard(S♯)
            else split(S♯)
        else
            if size(S♯) < ϵs then return failed
            else split(S♯)
    done
    return ∅

split(S♯):
    (S♯1, S♯2) ← S♯ split in half along the largest dimension
    S♯1 ← tighten(S♯1, 𝔖♯ ∪ {S♯1, S♯2})
    S♯2 ← tighten(S♯2, 𝔖♯ ∪ {S♯1, S♯2})
    push S♯1 and S♯2 into 𝔖♯
```

Fig. 8. Inductive invariant search algorithm.

Proof. See the appendix of the technical report version of this paper [21]. □

Failure. It is important to note that, unlike constraint solvers, but similarly to iteration with widening, the algorithm may fail to find an inductive invariant, even if there exists one that can be represented with boxes whose size is greater than ϵ_s. In our case, the primary cause of failure is a bad decision to discard a useful box that actually intersects the smallest inductive invariant, a fact we cannot foresee when we decide to discard it. In Sect. 5.3, we present a modified version of the algorithm that handles this problem by changing the rules for discarding and tightening boxes, in exchange for a performance cost. Another method to avoid discarding such boxes is to lower the values of ϵ_s and ϵ_c, but this change can also make the algorithm slower, because it can now spend more time splitting boxes that cannot be part of an inductive invariant. Thus, another idea for future work is to provide more clever rules for discarding boxes, and using adaptive ϵ cut-off values. We discuss one such a technique in Sect. 5.2.

Example. Figure 9 presents the evolution of $\mathfrak{S}^\sharp$ for the program from Fig. 2 through the execution of the algorithm. The benign boxes are shown in blue (dark gray), while the non-benign ones are shown in red (lighter gray). The small dotted box at the center of each figure is the entry state $E^\sharp = [-0.1, 0.1] \times [-0.1, 0.1]$. The algorithm runs for 965 iterations in 76 ms before finding an inductive invariant included in $I^\sharp = [-4, 4] \times [-4, 4]$ and composed of 181 boxes,

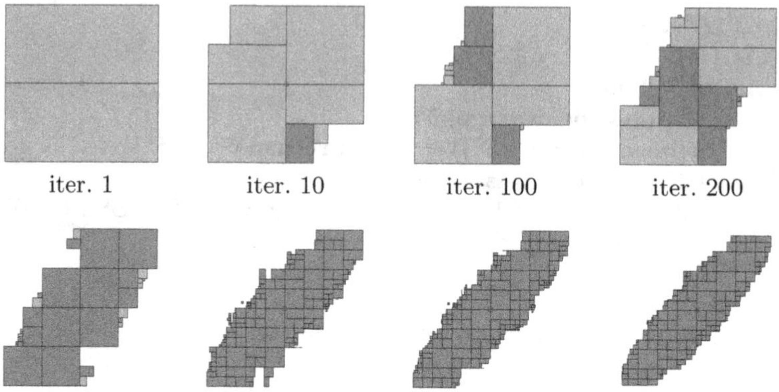

Fig. 9. Various stages of the analysis of the program from Fig. 2.

shown in Fig. 2.b. We use as cut-off values: $\epsilon_s = 0.01 \times \text{size}(I^\sharp)$ and $\epsilon_c = 0.1 \times \text{size}(I^\sharp)$. The size of the invariant box is $\text{size}(I^\sharp) = 8$ as $I^\sharp \stackrel{\text{def}}{=} [-4, 4] \times [-4, 4]$.

4.3 Implementation Details

The algorithm of Fig. 8 requires maintaining some information about boxes in $\mathfrak{S}^\sharp$, such as their coverage and whether they are benign or useful. It is important to note that modifying a single box in $\mathfrak{S}^\sharp$ may not only modify the coverage or class of the modified box, but also of other boxes in $\mathfrak{S}^\sharp$. We discuss here data structures to perform such updates efficiently, without scanning $\mathfrak{S}^\sharp$ entirely after each operation.

Partitioning. We enrich the algorithm state with a set $\mathfrak{P}^\sharp \in \mathcal{P}(\mathcal{D}^\sharp)$ of boxes that, similarly to $\mathfrak{S}^\sharp$, do not overlap, but—unlike $\mathfrak{S}^\sharp$—always covers the whole invariant space $I^\sharp$. Moreover, we ensure that every box in $\mathfrak{P}^\sharp$ contains at most one box from $\mathfrak{S}^\sharp$, hence, we maintain a *contents-of* function $\text{cnt} : \mathfrak{P}^\sharp \to (\mathfrak{S}^\sharp \cup \{\emptyset\})$ indicating which box, if any, of $\mathfrak{S}^\sharp$ is contained in each part of $\mathfrak{P}^\sharp$. Because the algorithm can discard boxes from $\mathfrak{S}^\sharp$, some parts in $P^\sharp \in \mathfrak{P}^\sharp$ may have no box at all, in which case $\text{cnt}(P^\sharp) = \emptyset$; otherwise $\gamma(\text{cnt}(P^\sharp)) \supseteq \gamma(P^\sharp)$. This property can be easily ensured by splitting boxes in $\mathfrak{P}^\sharp$ whenever a box in $\mathfrak{S}^\sharp$ is split. When a box from $\mathfrak{S}^\sharp$ is tightened or discarded, no change in $\mathfrak{P}^\sharp$ is required.

We then maintain a map $\text{post} : \mathfrak{S}^\sharp \to \mathcal{P}(\mathfrak{P}^\sharp)$ to indicate which parts of $\mathfrak{P}^\sharp$ intersect the image of a box $S^\sharp \in \mathfrak{S}^\sharp$:

$$\text{post}(S^\sharp) \stackrel{\text{def}}{=} \{\, P^\sharp \in \mathfrak{P}^\sharp \mid \gamma(F^\sharp(S^\sharp)) \cap \gamma(P^\sharp) \neq \emptyset \,\}, \tag{7}$$

which is sufficient to compute the coverage and determine if a box is benign:

$$\text{coverage}(S^\sharp) \stackrel{\text{def}}{=} \frac{\sum \{\, \text{vol}(\gamma(F^\sharp(S^\sharp)) \cap \gamma(\text{cnt}(P^\sharp))) \mid P^\sharp \in \text{post}(S^\sharp) \,\}}{\text{vol}(\gamma(F^\sharp(S^\sharp)))} \tag{8}$$

$$S^\sharp \text{ is benign } \iff \gamma(F^\sharp(S^\sharp)) \subseteq \gamma(I^\sharp) \wedge \qquad (9)$$
$$\forall P^\sharp \in \text{post}(S^\sharp) : \gamma(P^\sharp) \cap \gamma(F^\sharp(S^\sharp)) \subseteq \gamma(\text{cnt}(P^\sharp)).$$

A box $S^\sharp$ is benign if, whenever $F^\sharp(S^\sharp)$ intersects some partition $P^\sharp \in \mathfrak{P}^\sharp$, their intersection is included in $\text{cnt}(P^\sharp) \in \mathfrak{S}^\sharp$. Note, however, that this test only takes into account the part of $F^\sharp(S^\sharp)$ that is included in $\gamma(\mathfrak{P}^\sharp)$, i.e., in $\gamma(I^\sharp)$; hence, we additionally also check that $F^\sharp(S^\sharp)$ is included within $I^\sharp$.

Likewise, to compute tighten (Eq. (5)) and determine whether a box is useful, it is sufficient to know, for each box $S^\sharp \in \mathfrak{S}^\sharp$, the boxes $T^\sharp \in \mathfrak{S}^\sharp$ whose image $F^\sharp(T^\sharp)$ intersects $S^\sharp$, which we denote by:

$$\text{pre}(S^\sharp) \stackrel{\text{def}}{=} \{T^\sharp \in \mathfrak{S}^\sharp \mid \gamma(S^\sharp) \cap \gamma(F^\sharp(T^\sharp)) \neq \emptyset\}. \qquad (10)$$

The sets $\text{post}(S^\sharp)$ and $\text{pre}(S^\sharp)$ are significantly smaller than $\mathfrak{S}^\sharp$, leading to efficient ways of recomputing coverage information, usefulness, etc. They are also quite cheap to maintain through box tightening, splitting, and discarding.

We rely on the fact that, apart from the initial box $I^\sharp$, every new box considered by the algorithm comes from a parent box by splitting or tightening, and is thus smaller than a box already in $\mathfrak{S}^\sharp$. Assuming for now that, when $S^\sharp$ is shrunk into $T^\sharp$, $F^\sharp(T^\sharp)$ is also smaller than $F^\sharp(S^\sharp)$ (see the note on monotonicity below), we see that $\text{post}(T^\sharp)$ and $\text{pre}(T^\sharp)$ are subsets, respectively, of $\text{post}(S^\sharp)$ and $\text{pre}(S^\sharp)$, so that it is sufficient to iterate over these sets and filter out elements that no longer belong to them. Finally, to quickly decide for which $S^\sharp$ we must update $\text{post}(S^\sharp)$ and $\text{pre}(S^\sharp)$ whenever some element in $\mathfrak{P}^\sharp$ or $\mathfrak{S}^\sharp$ is modified or discarded, we maintain post^{-1} and pre^{-1} as well.

Float Implementation. While it is possible to use exact numbers—such as rationals with arbitrary precision—to represent interval bounds, more efficiency can be achieved using floating-point numbers. Floats suffer, however, from rounding error. It is straightforward to perform sound abstract interpretation with floating-point arithmetic. In particular, to construct a suitable $F^\sharp$ function from the program syntax, it is sufficient to round—in every computation—upper bounds towards $+\infty$ and lower bounds towards $-\infty$. In addition to the requirement that we have a sound $F^\sharp$, our algorithm requires that we can (i) compute the coverage of a box, and (ii) determine whether it is benign, necessary, or useful. Because intersection, inclusion, and emptiness checking are exact operations on float boxes, we can exactly determine whether a box is benign, necessary, or useful; it is also possible to compute a box size exactly.

In contrast, it is difficult to compute exactly the volume of a box using floating-point arithmetic, which is a necessary operation to compute coverage (Eqs. (4) and (8)). Fortunately, our algorithm does not require exact coverage information to be correct; thus, we settle for an approximate value computed naively using Eq. (8) with rounding errors. However, it is critical that we use the exact formula Eq. (9), which uses exact inclusion checking, to determine whether a box is benign; this is almost equivalent to checking whether the coverage of a box equals 1, except that the coverage calculation is subject to floating-point round-off error, so it is not safe to use here. This approach also requires changing, in Fig. 8, the test "**if** coverage(b, $\mathfrak{S}^\sharp \cup \{b\}) = 1$" into a test that all the boxes in $\mathfrak{S}^\sharp$ are benign, using Eq. (9).

Note on Monotonicity. Throughout this section, we assumed that replacing a box $S^\sharp$ with a smaller one $T^\sharp \subseteq^\sharp S^\sharp$ also results in a smaller image, i.e., $F^\sharp(T^\sharp) \subseteq^\sharp F^\sharp(S^\sharp)$. This property is obviously the case if $F^\sharp$ is monotonic, but the property does not hold in the general case (e.g., if $F^\sharp$ employs widening or reduced products). We now argue that we can handle the general case, by forcing images of boxes to decrease when the boxes decrease as follows: we remember with each box $S^\sharp$ its image img($S^\sharp$); when $S^\sharp$ is replaced with a smaller box $T^\sharp$, we set its image to:

$$\mathrm{img}(T^\sharp) := F^\sharp(T^\sharp) \cap^\sharp \mathrm{img}(S^\sharp) \tag{11}$$

instead of $F^\sharp(T^\sharp)$. We rely again on the fact that each new box comes from a larger parent box, except the initial box $I^\sharp$, for which we set $\mathrm{img}(I^\sharp) \stackrel{\text{def}}{=} F^\sharp(I^\sharp)$. We note that because the concrete semantics $\mathbb{S}[\![\, \textit{body} \,]\!]$ is monotonic, $\gamma(\mathrm{img}(T^\sharp)) \subseteq \mathbb{S}[\![\, \textit{body} \,]\!](\gamma(T^\sharp))$; that is, the use of Eq. (11) provides as sound an abstraction of $\mathbb{S}[\![\, \textit{body} \,]\!]$ as $F^\sharp$ but, in addition, it is monotonic. Hence, by replacing $F^\sharp(S^\sharp)$ with img($S^\sharp$) in the definitions from Sect. 4.1, our algorithm is correct, even if $F^\sharp$ is not monotonic.

5 Extensions

5.1 Octagonal Invariants

Following the custom from constraint solvers for continuous constraints, the algorithm presented in Sect. 4 is based on boxes: the loop body $F^\sharp$ is evaluated in the interval abstract domain. However, we showed in [24] that, in constraint solvers, boxes can be replaced with arbitrary numeric abstract domains, for instance relational domains such as polyhedra or octagons, provided that certain needed operators are provided. Similarly, the algorithm from the present paper can be generalized to use an arbitrary abstract domain $\mathcal{D}^\sharp$. Existing domains readily provide abstractions $F^\sharp$ of the loop body, together with the abstractions of $\cup$, $\cap$, and $\subseteq$ required for tightening as well as testing whether an abstract element is necessary, benign, or useful. We only need three extra operations not found in classical abstract domains for our algorithm: the volume vol (used to compute the coverage), the size operation, and a split operation. As discussed in Sect. 4.3, it is not necessary for vol to compute the exact volume, as long as it is possible to determine exactly whether an abstract element is benign, which is the case using Eq. (9). Likewise, we have a great deal of freedom in defining the size and split operations. The only requirement is that, to ensure the termination of the algorithm, after a sufficient number of splits are performed, an abstract element will be reduced below an arbitrary size.

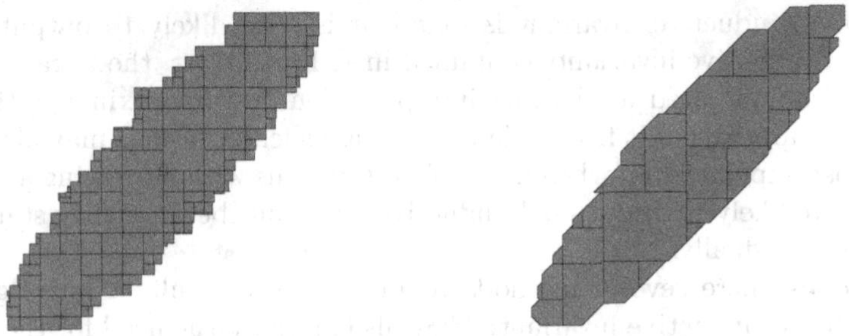

(a) 181 boxes, 965 iterations, 76 ms (b) 42 octagons, 224 iterations, 89 ms

Fig. 10. Abstract-domain choice: box solving (a) versus octagon solving (b).

Example. Consider the octagon domain [20], which is more expressive than intervals because it can represent relational information of the form $\pm X \pm Y \leq c$, with two variables and unit coefficients. We choose to approximate the volume of an octagon as the volume of its bounding box, which is far easier to compute than the actual volume of the octagon. Likewise, to create a simple and efficient implementation, we use the same split operation as for boxes, splitting only along an axis, and use the "size" of the bounding box as the "size" of an octagon. As a consequence, the elements of the partition $\mathfrak{P}^\sharp$ remain boxes. Nevertheless, the elements of $\mathfrak{S}^\sharp$ can be more complex octagons, due to tightening. We refer the reader to [24] for more advanced size and split operators for octagons.

Figure 10 compares the result of our algorithm on the program of Fig. 2 using intervals and using octagons. Inference with intervals takes 965 iterations and 76 ms and produces an inductive invariant composed of 181 parts, while, using octagons, it takes 224 iterations and 89 ms, and the inductive invariant is composed of only 42 parts. As can be seen in Fig. 10, the slant of octagons allows a much tighter fit to an ellipsoid, with far fewer elements. Octagons are also slightly slower: they require far fewer iterations and elements, but the manipulation of a single octagon is more costly than that of a single box.

Domain Choice. The choice of abstract domain $\mathcal{D}^\sharp$ may affect whether or not an inductive invariant is found, and it may also affect the cost of running the algorithm; this situation is somewhat similar to what happens in abstract interpretation. Depending on the problem, a more expressive domain, such as octagons, can result in a faster or slower analysis (see Sect. 6).

5.2 Invariant Refinement

The algorithm assumes that a candidate invariant I is provided, and by removing points only looks for an inductive invariant sufficient to prove that I holds. It over-approximates a least fixpoint from above and, as a consequence, the inductive invariant it finds may not be the smallest one. In fact, because it stops as soon as an inductive invariant is found, it is more likely to output one of the greatest inductive invariants contained in I. In contrast, the iteration-with-widening technique used in abstract interpretation over-approximates the least fixpoint, but approaches it from below. Although such iterations may also fail to find the least fixpoint, even when decreasing iterations with narrowing are used,[3] they are more likely to find a small inductive invariant, because they start small and increase gradually.

We propose here several methods to improve the result of our algorithm towards a better inductive invariant. They also mitigate the need for the user to provide a candidate invariant I, which was a drawback of our method compared to the iteration-with-widening method approaching from below. In fact, we can start the algorithm with a large box I (such as the whole range of a data type) and rely on the methods given below to discover an inductive invariant whose bounding box is much smaller than I, effectively inferring an interval invariant, alongside a more complex inductive invariant implying that invariant.

Global Tightening. The base algorithm of Fig. 8 only applies tightening (Eq. (5)) to the two boxes created after each split. This approach is not sufficient to ensure that all the boxes in $\mathfrak{S}^\sharp$ are as tight as possible. Indeed, shrinking or removing a box $S^\sharp$ also causes $\gamma F^\sharp(\mathfrak{S}^\sharp)$ to shrink. Hence, boxes in $\mathfrak{S}^\sharp$ that contained parts of $\gamma F^\sharp(\mathfrak{S}^\sharp)$ that have been removed may be tightened some more, enabling further tightening in a cascading effect. Hence, to improve our result, we may iteratively perform tightening of all the boxes in $\mathfrak{S}^\sharp$ until a fixpoint is reached. Because this operation may be costly, it is better to apply it rarely, such as after finding a first inductive invariant.

Reachability Checking. The concrete semantics has the form $\text{lfp}\,\lambda X.\,E \cup G(X)$, where $E \stackrel{\text{def}}{=} \mathbb{B}[\![\, \textit{entry} \,]\!]\,\mathcal{E}$ is the entry state and $G \stackrel{\text{def}}{=} \mathbb{S}[\![\, \textit{body} \,]\!]$ is the loop body. This fixpoint can also be seen as the limit $\cup_{i\geq 0}\, \mathbb{S}[\![\, \textit{body} \,]\!]^i$, i.e., the points reachable from the entry state after a sequence of loop iterations. To improve our result, we can thus remove parts of $\gamma(\mathfrak{S}^\sharp)$ that are definitely not reachable from the entry state. This test can be performed in the abstract domain by computing the transitive closure of $\text{cnt} \circ \text{post}$ (Eq. (7)), starting from all the necessary boxes (i.e., those intersecting $E^\sharp$). This operation may also be costly and is better performed after an inductive invariant is found.

Shell Peeling. Like iteration with narrowing, the methods given above are only effective at improving our abstraction of a *given* fixpoint, but are unable to reach an abstraction of a *smaller* fixpoint. The shell-peeling method builds on the reachability principle to discard boxes more aggressively, based on their likelihood of belonging to the most-precise inductive invariant. Intuitively, as

[3] This situation happens when the widening overshoots and settles above a fixpoint that is not the least one, because decreasing iterations can only refine up to the immediately smaller fixpoint, and not skip below a fixpoint.

imprecision accumulates by repeated applications of $F^\sharp$ from necessary boxes, boxes reachable in many steps are likely to contain the most spurious points. For each box $S^\sharp \in \mathfrak{S}^\sharp$, we compute its depth, i.e., the minimal value i such that $S^\sharp \cap^\sharp (\text{cnt} \circ \text{post})^i(T^\sharp) \neq \bot^\sharp$ for some $T^\sharp \in \mathfrak{S}^\sharp$ that intersects $E^\sharp$. Given the maximal depth $\Delta \stackrel{\text{def}}{=} \max\{\, \text{depth}(S^\sharp) \mid S^\sharp \in \mathfrak{S}^\sharp \,\}$, we merely remove all the boxes with depth greater than $\Delta - \delta$, for some user-specified δ, i.e., the boxes farthest away from the entry state in terms of applications of $F^\sharp$. Because the resulting $\mathfrak{S}^\sharp$ is not likely to be inductive, we again run the algorithm of Fig. 8 to try to recover an inductive invariant.

Resplitting. As explained in Sect. 4.1, splitting boxes in $\mathfrak{S}^\sharp$ may, by itself, improve the precision because $F^\sharp$ is generally a sub-join morphism, and so, even though it leaves $\gamma(\mathfrak{S}^\sharp)$ unchanged, $\gamma F^\sharp(\mathfrak{S}^\sharp)$ will decrease. As a consequence, some parts of $\mathfrak{S}^\sharp$ that were reachable from $E^\sharp$ through post may become unreachable. Hence, we suggest splitting boxes in $\mathfrak{S}^\sharp$ proactively, and prioritize the boxes $S^\sharp$ that are likely to reduce the size of $\text{post}(S^\sharp)$ (i.e., the number of boxes intersecting $F^\sharp(S^\sharp)$), before using other techniques such as global tightening or reachability checking. More precisely, we split all the boxes such that $|\,\text{post}(S^\sharp)|$ exceeds a user-defined threshold R.

Application. We apply all four methods on the example of Fig. 2 as follows. First, we apply the algorithm of Fig. 8, followed by global tightening and reachability checking. Then, we perform several rounds of the following steps: resplitting, shell peeling, applying the algorithm of Fig. 8, global tightening, followed by reachability checking. The result of this process is shown in Fig. 11. We set $\delta = 1$ for shell peeling, and $R = 12$ as the resplitting threshold. Moreover, each time the algorithm from Fig. 8 is run again, the ϵ values are halved, to account for the general reduction of box sizes due to resplitting and to allow finer-granularity box covering. Each refinement round results in a much tighter inductive invariant. We see a large gain in precision at the cost of higher computation time and a finer invariant decomposition (i.e., more and smaller boxes). Almost all the work goes into the four refinement methods, with just a few box-level iterations to re-establish inductiveness.

Failure Recovery. The algorithm is parameterized with ϵ values, and, as discussed in Sect. 4, a too-high value may result in too many boxes being discarded too early, and a consequent failure to find an inductive invariant. For instance, when setting ϵ_s to $0.1 \times \text{size}(I^\sharp)$ instead of $0.01 \times \text{size}(I^\sharp)$, we fail to find an inductive invariant for the program from Fig. 2. A natural, but costly, solution would be to restart the algorithm from scratch with lower ϵ values. Alternatively, we can also apply the refinement techniques above. Given the failure output $\mathfrak{S}^\sharp$ of the algorithm from Fig. 8, which satisfies Properties 1.1 and 1.2, but not Property 1.3, we iterate the following steps: global tightening, reachability checking, resplitting, and reapplying the algorithm of Fig. 8, always feeding the failure

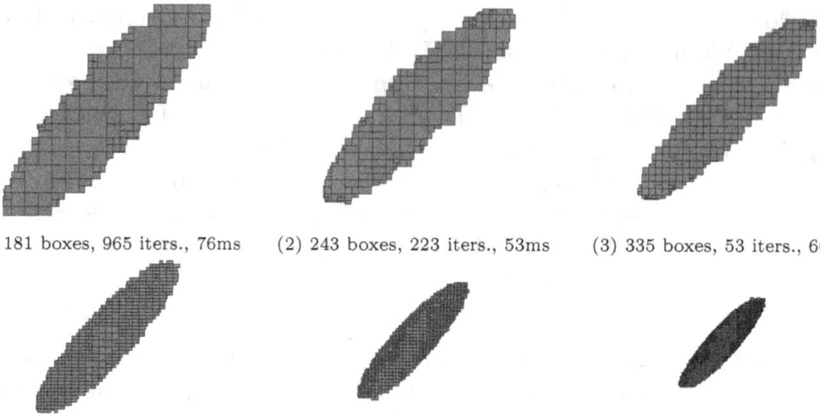

(1) 181 boxes, 965 iters., 76ms (2) 243 boxes, 223 iters., 53ms (3) 335 boxes, 53 iters., 60ms

(4) 485 boxes, 1 iters., 127ms (5) 786 boxes, 5 iter., 370ms (6) 1566 boxes, 1 iter., 1287ms

Fig. 11. Inductive-invariant refinement, using 6 rounds of tightening, reachability checking, shell peeling, resplitting, and the algorithm from Fig. 8. (Diagrams are to scale.)

output of each round to the following one without resetting $\mathfrak{S}^\sharp$ to $\{I^\sharp\}$ until an inductive invariant is found. Using the same δ and R parameters as before, and also halving the ϵ values at each round, starting from $\epsilon_s = 0.1 \times \text{size}(I^\sharp)$, we find in 5 rounds an inductive invariant, and it is as good as the one in Fig. 11.5 which was found with $\epsilon_s = 0.01 \times \text{size}(I^\sharp)$.

5.3 Relative Completeness

Our algorithm searches for loop invariants in a particular abstract domain, namely, sets of boxes with size between ϵ_s and $\epsilon_s/2$. As noted in Sect. 4.2, however, the algorithm is not guaranteed to find an inductive invariant even if one exists in this abstract domain. In this section, we define a different abstract domain and present a modified version of the algorithm that has the following *relative-completeness* property [17]: if there is an inductive invariant in the abstract domain, and its inductiveness can be proven using boxes, then the modified algorithm will find an inductive invariant. Thus, when the modified algorithm fails to find an inductive invariant, it provides a stronger guarantee than the original algorithm, because a failure of the modified algorithm can only occur when there exists no inductive invariant in the abstract domain. The modified algorithm is slower than the original, however, so we have implemented it as a variant that can be used when completeness is more important than speed.

During a run of the algorithm, if no boxes are ever discarded or tightened, the algorithm's process of box-splitting, beginning with some (abstract) candidate invariant $I^\sharp$, will eventually produce a regular grid of boxes of minimal size—i.e., having size between ϵ_s and $\epsilon_s/2$. Denote by Q the set of all boxes that can be produced in such a run. In the two-dimensional case, the boxes of Q may be conceptualized as a binary space partition; it is almost like quadtree, except that boxes are actually split along one dimension at a time, so each node in the tree has two children, not four. The width of the minimal-size boxes of Q along dimension i is $max\{2^{-k}w_i \mid k \in \mathbb{N}, 2^{-k}w_i < \epsilon_s\}$, where w_i is the width of the given invariant $I^\sharp$ along dimension i. However, Q also contains the larger boxes (unions of the minimal-size ones) that were produced at intermediate stages of the splitting process. We define the abstract domain C_Q for the modified version of the algorithm to be the set of all non-overlapping sets of boxes from Q.

There are two reasons why the original algorithm, presented in Fig. 8, lacks the relative-completeness property. First, the algorithm discards a box $S^\sharp$ if its coverage is less than ϵ_c; however, it is possible that $S^\sharp$ intersects every inductive invariant, in which case discarding $S^\sharp$ guarantees that a failure will occur. Second, the tightening operation can replace a box $S^\sharp$ that is part of Q with a box $T^\sharp$ that is not part of Q. In many cases an inductive invariant can still be found; the invariant can contain boxes that are not part of Q, and the vertices of boxes in such an invariant might not correspond to the vertices of any box from Q. However, it is also possible that $T^\sharp$, along with the other boxes of $\mathfrak{S}^\sharp$, cannot be refined into an inductive invariant.

For an example of the problem with tightening, see Fig. 12. Suppose that splitting $S^\sharp$ yields boxes $S_1^\sharp$ and $S_2^\sharp$, both having size below ϵ_s, such that $S_1^\sharp$ needs to be discarded, because it is not (and will never become) benign, and $S_2^\sharp$ needs to be kept, because it is necessary. Suppose that $T^\sharp$ is the result of applying tightening to $S^\sharp$ instead of splitting $S^\sharp$. It is possible that $T^\sharp$ has size below ϵ_s, and so cannot be split, even though it contains enough of both $S_1^\sharp$ and $S_2^\sharp$ so that it is necessary and yet it is also not benign (and will never become benign). Consequently, neither discarding nor keeping $T^\sharp$ will yield an inductive invariant. In this case, the choice to tighten $S^\sharp$ prevented the algorithm from finding an invariant that could have been found by splitting $S^\sharp$ instead.

Two simple modifications, which address the above problems, allow the algorithm to have the relative-completeness property. First, we set $\epsilon_c = 0$, and second, we never perform tightening. For each of these two modifications, we have constructed an input program for which the modified algorithm finds an invariant, but the original algorithm does not. Note that there also exist programs for which the original algorithm can find an inductive invariant, but the

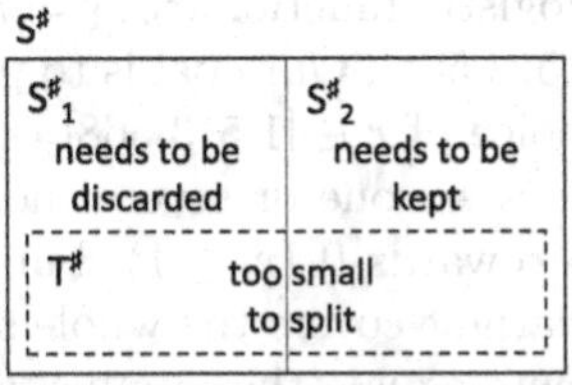

Fig. 12. If tightening is applied to a box $S^\sharp$, it may become too small to split in a case where splitting $S^\sharp$ is the only way to find an inductive invariant.

modified algorithm cannot, because there is no inductive invariant in the modified abstract domain C_Q. As an optimization to the modified algorithm, which performs no tightening, we could reintroduce the tightening operation in a modified form: instead of tightening down to an arbitrary smaller box $T^\sharp$, we could tighten down to the smallest box in Q that contains $T^\sharp$. We present a proof of the relative-completeness property of the modified algorithm in [21].

6 Experiments

We have implemented a prototype analyzer, written in OCaml. It supports a simple toy language similar to Fig. 4, with only real-valued variables, no functions, and no nested loops. It implements our main algorithm (Fig. 8) with arbitrary numeric domains (Sect. 5.1). It also implements invariant-refinement and failure-recovery methods (Sect. 5.2). It is parameterized by a numeric abstract domain, and currently supports boxes with rational bounds, boxes with float bounds, as well as octagons with float bounds (through the Apron library [18]). It exploits the data structures described in Sect. 4.3 and is sound despite floating-point round-off errors. Floating-point arithmetic is used in the implementation.

The results of our experiments are shown in Fig. 13. We show, for the floating-point interval and octagon domains, the number of iterations and time until a first inductive invariant is found, and the number of elements in each result.[4] We do not give details about the memory consumption for each example, because it always remains low (a few hundred megabytes). For most examples, we used an ϵ_s value of 0.05 or 0.01. We have analyzed a few simple loops, listed above the double line in Fig. 13:

– *Filter* is the second-order filter from Fig. 2. As discussed earlier, it performs well with intervals and octagons.

– *Linear* iterates $t = t + 1; \tau = \tau + [0.25, 0.5]$ from $t = \tau = 0$ until $t < 30$. To prove that $\tau < 30$, it is necessary to find a relation $\tau \leq 0.5 \times t$, which cannot be represented by intervals or octagons (without disjunctive completion). *Non-linear* is similar, but iterates $\tau = [1, 1.1] \times \tau$ starting from $\tau \in [0, 1]$, and also requires a non-linear inductive invariant: $\tau \leq 1.1^t$. These examples require very few iterations of our main algorithm, but rely heavily on resplitting, and hence output a large set of elements and have a relatively high run-time, on the order of a few seconds. When using octagons, the method times out after 300s.

– *Logistic map* iterates the logistic function $x_{n+1} = r \times x_n \times (1 - x_n)$, starting from $x \in [0.1, 0.9]$, for $r \in [1.5, 3.568]$. Our goal is to prove that x remains within $[0.1, 0.9]$ at all times. The choice of $r \in [1.5, 3.568]$ corresponds to various cases where the series oscillates between one or several non-zero values; it is beyond the zone where it converges towards 0 ($r \leq 1$), but before it becomes chaotic ($r \geq 3.57$). The inductive invariant covers the whole space $[0.1, 0.9] \times [1.5, 3.568]$ (hence, the number of elements equals the number of iterations), but needs to

[4] We include failure-recovery rounds from Sect. 5.2 when needed to find the first invariant, but do not perform any refinement rounds after an invariant is found.

Program	boxes			octagons		
	# elems.	# iters.	time (s)	# elems.	# iters.	time (s)
Filter	181	965	0.076	42	224	0.089
Linear	6734	10	2.08	–	–	–
Non-linear	5987	10	2.64	–	–	–
Logistic map	376	376	0.127	885	885	2.94
Newton	32	57	0.009	16	16	0.008
Sine	132	425	0.094	81	99	0.076
Square root	8	8	0.002	4	4	0.002
Lead-lag controller	44	46	0.327	30	30	65.6
Lead-lag controller (reset)	24	24	2.44	24	24	105.0
Lead-lag controller (saturate)	44	46	0.341	30	30	76.7
Harmonic oscillator	32	36	0.04	42	46	1.62
Harmonic oscillator (reset)	34	39	0.047	–	–	–
Harmonic oscillator (saturate)	4	4	0.035	3	3	0.44
Dampened oscillator	850	45400	1.49	929	45404	18.7
Dampened oscillator (reset)	925	57329	37.2	–	–	–
Dampened oscillator (saturate)	22	22	0.004	22	22	0.036
Filter2	9	160	0.01	5	5	0.003
Arrow-Hurwicz	80	1904	0.367	18	839	0.451

Fig. 13. Experimental results. For octagons, the timeout value was 300 seconds.

be partitioned so that the desired invariant can be proved in our linear abstract domains. Our algorithm performs this partitioning automatically.

– *Newton* iterates Newton's method on a polynomial taken from [11].

– The next two examples come from the conflict-driven learning method proposed in [11]: *Sine* and *Square root* compute mathematical functions through Taylor expansions. Unlike our previous examples, they do not perform an iterative computation, only a straight-line computation; nevertheless, they require partitioning of the input space to prove that the target invariant holds after the straight-line computation. These examples demonstrate that the algorithm is able to compute a strongest-postcondition of a straight-line computation, which helps to show how the algorithm could be generalized to handle programs with a mix of straight-line and looping code. In both cases, the inductive invariant matches closely the graph of the function (up to method error and rounding error), and hence provide a proof of functional correctness. As in the *Linear* and *Non-Linear* examples, these examples rely heavily on resplitting and tightening.

For more details about these examples, see the appendix of [21].

In a second batch of experiments, shown in Fig. 13 below the double line, we ran our algorithm on benchmark programs from the literature. These experiments were designed to answer the following questions:

1. Can our algorithm find invariants for programs studied in earlier work?
2. How fast is our algorithm when analyzing such programs?
3. Are we able to verify some invariants found by other algorithms?

To answer these questions, we selected three programs, in three variations each, from [26], and two programs from [1]. For each of the programs from [26], the parameter $I^\sharp$ for our algorithm (i.e., the invariant that we attempted to verify) was the bounding box of an invariant described in either the text of the publication or its additional online materials. For the programs from [1], we chose small boxes for $I^\sharp$. We analyzed the Arrow-Hurwicz loop as a two-variable program by discarding the loop condition and the two variables u and v that are not needed in the body of the loop; the algorithm was able to verify that the variables x and y remain within the box $[-2, 2] \times [-2, 2]$. For Filter2, we showed that x and y remain within $[-0.2, 1] \times [-0.2, 1]$.

Our results show that we were able to find inductive invariants for all of these programs, often in less than half a second. In the case of the dampened oscillator, we were not able to verify the bounds described in the text of [26], but we were able to verify a different bounding box described in the additional online materials.

7 Related Work

A recent line of work has identified conceptual connections between SAT-solving and abstract interpretation [10,31], and has exploited these ideas to improve SAT-solving algorithms. That idea is similar in spirit to work described in [24], except that the latter focuses on other classes of algorithms—those used in continuous constraints programming—that work on geometric entities, such as boxes, instead of formulas.

As mentioned in Sect. 2, even when an inductive invariant can be represented in the chosen domain, approximation due to widening can prevent an abstract interpreter from finding any inductive invariant—let alone the best one. A certain amount of recent work has been devoted to improved algorithms for computing fixpoints in abstract domains. In particular, methods based on policy iteration can guarantee, in certain cases, that the exact least fixpoint is computed [1]. The version of our algorithm presented in Sect. 5.3 uses a modified abstract domain and has the following *relative-completeness* property [17]: if there is an inductive invariant in the modified abstract domain, and its inductiveness can be proven using boxes, then the modified algorithm will find an inductive invariant.

Garg et al. [13] developed a framework for loop-invariant synthesis called ICE. ICE has a property that they call *robustness*, which is similar to relative completeness. They observed that many earlier algorithms consist of a teacher and a learner that communicate using a restricted protocol, and that this protocol sometimes prevents the algorithms from finding an invariant. In the restricted protocol, the teacher only communicates positive and negative examples of states, and the learner tries to find an invariant consistent with these. The authors propose an alternative protocol that also allows the teacher to communicate implication pairs (p, p'), to convey that state p can transition to state p'; this generalization allows the algorithm to postpone the decision of whether to include or exclude p and p' from the invariant, instead of arbitrarily—and perhaps incorrectly—choosing to classify p and p' as examples or counterexamples.

In our algorithm, the analogue of ICE's implication pairs, counterexamples, and examples is the set of boxes $\mathfrak{S}$ and their images. Where ICE would store a concrete implication pair to represent the fact that state p leads to state p', our algorithm would store a box containing state p along with the image of that box. As with ICE, this stored information can later lead to the box (and its image) being included in the invariant, or it can lead to the box being excluded if the image is excluded (or if part of the image is excluded and the box is too small to split). It can also happen that a box is split—an operation that has no analogue in ICE. The relative-completeness of our algorithm depends on using this information to delete a box only when necessary. Our algorithm also differs in the sense that it considers a set of boxes $\mathfrak{S}$ whose concretization only grows smaller over time; it works by iteratively strengthening an invariant until an inductive invariant is found. In contrast, an ICE-learner might successively consider larger or smaller candidate invariants.

Bradley presents an algorithm called ic3 [5], which synthesizes loop invariants in a property-directed manner by incrementally refining a sequence of formulas that overapproximate the program states reachable after different numbers of iterations of the loop. An ic3-like approach could be applied to the synthesis of loop invariants for the kind of programs that we investigated. However, the performance of this approach would depend on the precision and efficiency of the underlying SMT solver for (sometimes non-linear) floating-point arithmetic queries. Our algorithm has a performance advantage because it can test whether one area of the program's state space maps into another by using abstract interpretation, instead of calling an SMT solver.

To exclude unreachable states efficiently, an ic3 implementation needs to generalize from concrete counterexamples to some larger set of states; otherwise, it might only exclude one concrete state at a time. The generalization method determines the abstract domain of invariants that is being searched. Our "quadtree" abstract domain C_Q (see Sect. 5.3) could be used to generalize each counterexample p to the largest box from Q that (i) contains p and (ii) can be soundly excluded from the invariant.

Two recent works [14,30] search for inductive invariants using abstract interpretation, and use SMT solvers to help ease the burden of designing sound abstract transformers. Both works need to represent the program's transition relation in a logic supported by the underlying SMT solver. Both also construct their inductive invariants by iteratively weakening a formula until it is inductive. In contrast, the algorithm described in this paper constructs its inductive invariants by iterative strengthening.

The algorithm presented in this paper can be compared to the large literature on abstraction refinement [9,27]. It is similar to that work, in that splitting a box can be likened to the introduction of a new predicate that distinguishes the cases where a program variable is above or below some value. Note, however, that the algorithm described in this paper works in one continuous process; the analysis does not have to be restarted when a new split is introduced. Note also that the splitting of boxes has a useful locality property: splitting one box at some value does not automatically split other boxes at the same value; thus, the new predicates are introduced locally, and on demand. The algorithm in this paper differs from counterexample-guided abstraction refinement [6] in that it makes no direct use of concrete counterexamples.

Constraint programming is a popular paradigm, with numerous applications (scheduling, packing, layout design, etc.). It has also been applied to program analysis, and in particular invariant inference, where off-the-shelf linear and non-linear solvers [7,28], SAT solvers [32], and SMT solvers [16] have been employed. In those works, a pre-processing, or abstraction, step is necessary to transform the problem of inferring an inductive invariant, which is inherently second-order, into a first-order formula.

Our method combines abstract interpretation and constraint solving, a connection that has also been made by others. Apt observed that applying propagators can be seen as an iterative fixpoint computation [2]. Pelleau et al. expanded on this connection to describe a constraint-solving algorithm in terms of abstract interpretation; they exploited the connection to design a new class of solvers parameterized by abstract domains [24], thereby importing abstract-interpretation results and know-how into constraint programming. This paper goes the other way, and imports technology from constraint programming into abstract interpretation to help solve program-analysis problems. Several previous works, e.g., [25], combine abstract interpretation and constraint-based techniques, but generally delegate the problem of inductive-invariant inference to classic abstract-interpretation methods. Our work differs in that we devised a new algorithm for inferring inductive invariants, not a new use of an existing algorithm.

8 Conclusion

In this paper, we were inspired by one class of constraint-solving algorithms, namely, continuous constraint solving, and adapted the methods employed for such problems to devise a new algorithm for inferring inductive invariants. Instead of classical increasing iterations, as ordinarily used in abstract interpretation, our algorithm employs refinement (decreasing) iterations; it tightens and splits a collection of abstract elements until an inductive invariant is found. The algorithm is parameterized on an arbitrary numeric abstract domain, in which the semantics of the loop body is evaluated. The method is sound and can be implemented efficiently using floating-point arithmetic. We have shown the effectiveness of our method on small but intricate loop analyses. In particular, loops that do not have any linear inductive invariant, and thus would traditionally require the design of a novel, specialized abstract domain, have been successfully analyzed by our method, employing the interval domain only.

References

1. Adjé, A., Gaubert, S., Goubault, E.: Coupling policy iteration with semi-definite relaxation to compute accurate numerical invariants in static analysis. In: Gordon, A.D. (ed.) ESOP 2010. LNCS, vol. 6012, pp. 23–42. Springer, Heidelberg (2010)
2. Apt, K.R.: The essence of constraint propagation. Theor. Comput. Sci. **221**(1–2), 179–210 (1999)
3. Benhamou, F., Goualard, F., Granvilliers, L., Puget, J.-F.: Revisiting hull and box consistency. In: ICLP 1999, pp. 230–244 (1999)
4. Bertrane, J., Cousot, P., Cousot, R., Feret, J., Mauborgne, L., Miné, A., Rival, X.: Static analysis and verification of aerospace software by abstract interpretation. In: AIAA Infotech@Aerospace, number -3385 in AIAA, pp. 1–38. AIAA (2010)
5. Bradley, A.R.: SAT-based model checking without unrolling. In: Jhala, R., Schmidt, D. (eds.) VMCAI 2011. LNCS, vol. 6538, pp. 70–87. Springer, Heidelberg (2011)
6. Clarke, E.M., Grumberg, O., Jha, S., Lu, Y., Veith, H.: Counterexample-guided abstraction refinement. In: Emerson, E.A., Sistla, A.P. (eds.) CAV 2000. LNCS, vol. 1855, pp. 154–169. Springer, Heidelberg (2000)
7. Colón, M.A., Sankaranarayanan, S., Sipma, H.B.: Linear invariant generation using non-linear constraint solving. In: Hunt Jr., W.A., Somenzi, F. (eds.) CAV 2003. LNCS, vol. 2725, pp. 420–432. Springer, Heidelberg (2003)
8. Cousot, P., Cousot, R.: Abstract interpretation: a unified lattice model for static analysis of programs by construction or approximation of fixpoints. In: POPL 1977, pp. 238–252. ACM, January 1977
9. Das, S., Dill, D.L., Park, S.: Experience with predicate abstraction. In: Halbwachs, N., Peled, D.A. (eds.) CAV 1999. LNCS, vol. 1633, pp. 160–171. Springer, Heidelberg (1999)
10. D'Silva, V., Haller, L., Kroening, D.: Satisfiability solvers are static analysers. In: Miné, A., Schmidt, D. (eds.) SAS 2012. LNCS, vol. 7460, pp. 317–333. Springer, Heidelberg (2012)
11. D'Silva, V., Haller, L., Kroening, D., Tautschnig, M.: Numeric bounds analysis with conflict-driven learning. In: Flanagan, C., König, B. (eds.) TACAS 2012. LNCS, vol. 7214, pp. 48–63. Springer, Heidelberg (2012)
12. Feret, J.: Static analysis of digital filters. In: Schmidt, D. (ed.) ESOP 2004. LNCS, vol. 2986, pp. 33–48. Springer, Heidelberg (2004)
13. Garg, P., Löding, C., Madhusudan, P., Neider, D.: ICE: a robust framework for learning invariants. In: Biere, A., Bloem, R. (eds.) CAV 2014. LNCS, vol. 8559, pp. 69–87. Springer, Heidelberg (2014)
14. Garoche, P.-L., Kahsai, T., Tinelli, C.: Incremental invariant generation using logic-based automatic abstract transformers. In: Brat, G., Rungta, N., Venet, A. (eds.) NFM 2013. LNCS, vol. 7871, pp. 139–154. Springer, Heidelberg (2013)
15. Granger, P.: Improving the results of static analyses of programs by local decreasing iterations. In: Shyamasundar, R.K. (ed.) FSTTCS 1992. LNCS, vol. 652, pp. 68–79. Springer, Heidelberg (1992)
16. Gulwani, S., Srivastava, S., Venkatesan, R.: Program analysis as constraint solving. In: PLDI 2008, pp. 281–292. ACM (2008)
17. Itzhaky, S., Bjørner, N., Reps, T., Sagiv, M., Thakur, A.: Property-directed shape analysis. In: Biere, A., Bloem, R. (eds.) CAV 2014. LNCS, vol. 8559, pp. 35–51. Springer, Heidelberg (2014)

18. Jeannet, B., Miné, A.: APRON: A Library of Numerical Abstract Domains for Static Analysis. In: Bouajjani, A., Maler, O. (eds.) CAV 2009. LNCS, vol. 5643, pp. 661–667. Springer, Heidelberg (2009)
19. Miné, A.: Relational abstract domains for the detection of floating-point run-time errors. In: Schmidt, D. (ed.) ESOP 2004. LNCS, vol. 2986, pp. 3–17. Springer, Heidelberg (2004)
20. Miné, A.: The octagon abstract domain. High. Order Symbolic Comput. **19**(1), 31–100 (2006)
21. Miné, A., Breck, J., Reps, T.: An algorithm inspired by constraint solvers to infer inductive invariants in numeric programs. TR 1829, CS Dept., Univ. of Wisconsin, Madison, WI, January 2016
22. Montanari, U.: Networks of constraints: fundamental properties and applications to picture processing. Inf. Sci. **7**(2), 95–132 (1974)
23. Moore, R.E.: Interval Analysis. Prentice Hall, Englewood Cliffs (1966)
24. Pelleau, M., Miné, A., Truchet, C., Benhamou, F.: A constraint solver based on abstract domains. In: Giacobazzi, R., Berdine, J., Mastroeni, I. (eds.) VMCAI 2013. LNCS, vol. 7737, pp. 434–454. Springer, Heidelberg (2013)
25. Ponsini, O., Michel, C., Rueher, M.: Combining constraint programming and abstract interpretation for value analysis of floating-point programs. In: CSTVA 2012, pp. 775–776 (2012)
26. Roux, P., Garoche, P.-L.: Practical policy iterations - a practical use of policy iterations for static analysis: the quadratic case. FMSD **46**(2), 163–196 (2015)
27. Saïdi, H., Shankar, N.: Abstract and model check while you prove. In: Halbwachs, N., Peled, D.A. (eds.) CAV 1999. LNCS, vol. 1633, pp. 443–454. Springer, Heidelberg (1999)
28. Sankaranarayanan, S., Sipma, H.B., Manna, Z.: Constraint-based linear-relations analysis. In: Giacobazzi, R. (ed.) SAS 2004. LNCS, vol. 3148, pp. 53–68. Springer, Heidelberg (2004)
29. Tarski, A.: A lattice theoretical fixpoint theorem and its applications. Pac. J. Math. **5**, 285–310 (1955)
30. Thakur, A., Lal, A., Lim, J., Reps, T.: PostHat and all that: Automating abstract interpretation. ENTCS **311**, 15–32 (2015)
31. Thakur, A., Reps, T.: A generalization of stålmarck's method. In: Miné, A., Schmidt, D. (eds.) SAS 2012. LNCS, vol. 7460, pp. 334–351. Springer, Heidelberg (2012)
32. Xie, Y., Aiken, A.: Saturn: a SAT-based tool for bug detection. In: Etessami, K., Rajamani, S.K. (eds.) CAV 2005. LNCS, vol. 3576, pp. 139–143. Springer, Heidelberg (2005)

Functional Big-Step Semantics

Scott Owens[1(✉)], Magnus O. Myreen[2], Ramana Kumar[3], and Yong Kiam Tan[4]

[1] School of Computing, University of Kent, Canterbury, UK
S.A.Owens@kent.ac.uk
[2] CSE Department, Chalmers University of Technology, Gothenburg, Sweden
[3] NICTA, Sydney, Australia
[4] IHPC, A*STAR, Singapore, Singapore

Abstract. When doing an interactive proof about a piece of software, it is important that the underlying programming language's semantics does not make the proof unnecessarily difficult or unwieldy. Both small-step and big-step semantics are commonly used, and the latter is typically given by an inductively defined relation. In this paper, we consider an alternative: using a recursive function akin to an interpreter for the language. The advantages include a better induction theorem, less duplication, accessibility to ordinary functional programmers, and the ease of doing symbolic simulation in proofs via rewriting. We believe that this style of semantics is well suited for compiler verification, including proofs of divergence preservation. We do not claim the invention of this style of semantics: our contribution here is to clarify its value, and to explain how it supports several language features that might appear to require a relational or small-step approach. We illustrate the technique on a simple imperative language with C-like for-loops and a break statement, and compare it to a variety of other approaches. We also provide ML and lambda-calculus based examples to illustrate its generality.

1 Introduction

In the setting of mechanised proof about programming languages, it is often unclear what kind of operational semantics to use for formalising the language: common big-step and small-step approaches each have their own strengths and weaknesses. The choice depends on the size, complexity, and nature of the programming language, as well as what is being proved about it. As a rule-of-thumb, the more complex the language's features, or the more semantically intricate the desired theorem, the more likely it is that small-step semantics will be needed. This is because small-step semantics enable powerful proof techniques, including syntactic preservation/progress and step-indexed logical relations, by allowing close observation not only of the result of a program, but also how it got there. In contrast, big-step's advantages arise from following the syntactic structure of the programming language. This means that they can mesh nicely with similarly structured compilers, type systems, etc. that one is trying to verify, and reduce the overhead of mechanised proof.

For large projects, a hybrid approach can be adopted. The CompCert [16,17] verified C compiler uses big-step for some parts of its semantics and small-step for

P. Thiemann (Ed.): ESOP 2016, LNCS 9632, pp. 589–615, 2016.
DOI: 10.1007/978-3-662-49498-1_23

others. In the initial version of our own CakeML project [15], we had two different semantics for the source language: big-step for the compiler verification and small-step for the type soundness proof, with an additional proof connecting the two semantics.

In contrast, this paper advocates *functional big-step semantics*, which can support many of the proofs and languages that typically rely on a small-step approach, but with a structure that follows the language's syntax. A functional big-step semantics is essentially an interpreter written in a purely functional style and equipped with a clock to ensure that the function is total, even when run on diverging programs. Hence the interpreter can be used in a higher-order logic of total functions – the kind supported by Coq, HOL4, and Isabelle/HOL – as a formal definition of the semantics. In this way, it harkens back to Reynolds' idea of definitional interpreters [23] to give a readable account of a semantics. Additionally, by initialising the clock to a very large number, the same functional big-step semantics used for proof can also be executed on test programs for exploration and validation.

The idea of using a clock in a semantics is not new;[1] our contribution here is to analyse its advantages, especially in the context of interactive proofs, and to show how it can be used to support the kinds of proofs that push researchers to small-step semantics. We argue that:

- Functional semantics are easier to read, have a familiar feel for functional programmers, and avoid much of the duplication that occurs in big-step semantics defined with inductive relations, especially for languages with exceptions and other non-local control-flow (Sect. 2).
- Functional semantics can be used more easily in mechanised proofs based on rewriting, since functional semantics are stated in terms of equations (Sect. 3.1).
- Functional semantics also produce better induction theorems. Induction theorems for relational big-step semantics frequently force unnecessary case splits in proofs (Sect. 3.2).
- The clock used to define a functional semantics is convenient both for proofs that a compiler preserves the diverging behaviour of programs (Sects. 3.3 and 3.4), and for defining (and using) step-indexed logical relations (Sect. 6).
- Functional semantics can use an oracle in the state to support languages with I/O and non-determinism (Sect. 4).

There are a variety of advanced techniques for defining big-step semantics that solve some of these problems. For example, one can use co-induction to precisely define diverging computations [18,20], or the pretty-big-step approach to reduce duplication in the definition [10]. Notably, these techniques still define the semantics using inductive (and co-inductive) relations rather than recursive functions, and we are not aware of any relational approach with all of the advantages listed

[1] For example, CakeML initially used a clocked, but relational, semantics for its intermediate languages, and clocked recursive evaluation functions are common in Boyer-Moore-style provers such as ACL2, where inductive relations are unavailable [8,30]. Leroy and Grall [18] use a clock to define a denotational semantics in Coq. Siek has also advocated for clocks for proving type soundness [25,26].

above. However, functional semantics, as advocated in this paper, are not without their limitations. One is that the definition of a functional semantics requires introduction of a clock which must decrease on *certain* recursive calls (Sect. 2.3). Another is that languages with non-determinism require an oracle state component to factor out the non-determinism (Sect. 4). Lastly, we have not investigated languages with unstructured non-determinism, e.g. concurrency.

Our ideas about functional big-step semantics were developed in the context of the CakeML project (https://cakeml.org, [15]) where the latest version has functional big-step semantics for all of its intermediate languages (see Sect. 8); however, the bulk of this paper concentrates on a series of smaller examples, starting with a C-like language with `for` and `break` statements (Sect. 2). We use it to explain in detail how the functional approach supports the verification of a simple compiler (Sect. 3). Then, we present a series of different languages and theorems to illustrate the breadth of our approach (Sects. 4, 5, and 6). Lastly, we show how to prove the equivalence of a functional big-step and small-step semantics (Sect. 7).

All of the semantics and theorems in this paper have been formalised and proved in the HOL4 proof assistant (http://hol-theorem-prover.org). The formalisation is available in the HOL4 examples directory (https://github.com/HOL-Theorem-Prover/HOL/tree/master/examples/fun-op-sem); we encourage interested readers to consult these sources for the definitions and lemmas that we lack the space to present here.

2 Example Semantics

In this section, we motivate functional big-step semantics by defining an operational semantics for a toy language in both relational and functional styles. We call our toy language FOR, as it includes `for` loops and `break` statements that are familiar from C. We first define the big-step semantics of FOR, informally, as an interpreter in Standard ML (SML); next we explain why the semantics of FOR is difficult to capture in a conventional big-step relation, but, using a functional big-step semantics, can be defined neatly as a function in logic.

2.1 An Interpreter in SML

The FOR language has expressions `e` and statements `t`. Like C, we allow expression evaluation to have side effects (namely, assignment).

```
datatype t = Dec of string * t       datatype e = Var of string
           | Exp of e                           | Num of int
           | Break                              | Add of e * e
           | Seq of t * t                       | Assign of string * e
           | If of e * t * t         datatype r = Rval of int
           | For of e * e * t                   | Rbreak | Rfail
```

We sketch the semantics for this language by defining functions that evaluate expressions and statements, `run_e` and `run_t` respectively. Each evaluation returns an integer wrapped in Rval, signals a break Rbreak, or fails Rfail. Expression evaluation fails on an attempt to read the value of an uninitialised variable.

```
fun lookup y [] = NONE
  | lookup y ((x,v)::xs) = if y = x then SOME v else lookup y xs

fun run_e s (Var x) =
    (case lookup x s of
      NONE => (Rfail,s)
     | SOME v => (Rval v,s))
  | run_e s (Num i) = (Rval i,s)
  | run_e s (Add (e1, e2)) =
    (case run_e s e1 of
      (Rval n1, s1) =>
        (case run_e s1 e2 of
          (Rval n2, s2) => (Rval (n1+n2), s2)
         | r => r)
     | r => r)
  | run_e s (Assign (x, e)) =
    (case run_e s e of
      (Rval n1, s1) => (Rval n1, (x,n1)::s1)
     | r => r)
```

Below, evaluation of a Break statement returns Rbreak, which is propagated to the enclosing For loop. A For loop returns a normal Rval result if the body of the loop returns Rbreak.

```
fun run_t s (Exp e) = run_e s e
  | run_t s (Dec (x, t)) = run_t ((x,0)::s) t
  | run_t s Break = (Rbreak, s)
  | run_t s (Seq (t1, t2)) =
    (case run_t s t1 of
      (Rval _, s1) => run_t s1 t2
     | r => r)
  | run_t s (If (e, t1, t2)) =
    (case run_e s e of
      (Rval n1, s1) => run_t s1 (if n1 = 0 then t2 else t1)
     | r => r)
  | run_t s (For (e1, e2, t)) =
    (case run_e s e1 of
      (Rval n1, s1) =>
       if n1 = 0 then (Rval 0, s1) else
        (case run_t s1 t of
          (Rval _, s2) =>
           (case run_e s2 e2 of
             (Rval _, s3) => run_t s3 (For (e1, e2, t))
            | r => r)
         | (Rbreak, s2) => (Rval 0, s2)
         | r => r)
     | r => r)
```

These SML functions make use of catch-all patterns in case-expressions in order to conveniently propagate non-`Rval` results. We use the same approach in our functional semantics (Sect. 2.3) to keep them concise. The case expressions above are idiomatic for SML, but in a language with syntactic support for monadic computations, such as Haskell with `do`-notation, one would package the propagation of exceptional results inside a monadic bind operator.

2.2 Relational Big-Step Semantics

The definition above is a good way to describe the semantics of FOR to a programmer familiar with SML. It is, however, not directly usable as an operational semantics for interactive proofs. Next, we outline how a big-step semantics can be defined for the FOR language using conventional inductively defined relations.

Relational big-step semantics are built up from evaluation rules for an evaluation relation, typically written $\Downarrow$. Each rule states how execution of a program expression evaluates to a result. The evaluation relation for the FOR language takes as input a state and a statement; it then relates these inputs to the result pair (`r` and new state) just as the interpreter above does.

We give a flavour of the evaluation rules next. The simplest rule in the FOR language is evaluation of `Break`: evaluation always produces `Rbreak` and the state s is returned unchanged. We call this rule (B).

$$\text{(B)}\ \frac{}{(\texttt{Break},s) \Downarrow_{\texttt{t}} (\texttt{Rbreak},s)}$$

The semantics of `Seq` is defined by two evaluation rules. We need two rules because evaluation of t_2 only happens if evaluation of t_1 leads to `Rval`. The first rule for `Seq` (S1) states: if t_1 evaluates according to $(t_1\ ,s) \Downarrow_{\texttt{t}} (\texttt{Rval}\ n_1, s_1)$ and t_2 evaluates as $(t_2, s_1) \Downarrow_{\texttt{t}} r$, then $(\texttt{Seq}\ t_1\ t_2, s) \Downarrow_{\texttt{t}} r$, i.e. `Seq` $t_1\ t_2$ evaluates state s to result r. The second rule (S2) states that a non-`Rval` result in t_1 is the result for evaluation of `Seq` $t_1\ t_2$.

$$\text{(S1)}\ \frac{(t_1,s) \Downarrow_{\texttt{t}} (\texttt{Rval}\ n_1, s_1) \quad (t_2, s_1) \Downarrow_{\texttt{t}} r}{(\texttt{Seq}\ t_1\ t_2, s) \Downarrow_{\texttt{t}} r} \qquad \text{(S2)}\ \frac{(t_1,s) \Downarrow_{\texttt{t}} (r, s_1) \quad \neg\texttt{is\_Rval}\ r}{(\texttt{Seq}\ t_1\ t_2, s) \Downarrow_{\texttt{t}} (r, s_1)}$$

Defining these evaluation rules is straightforward, if the language is simple enough. We include the `For` statement in our example language in order to show how this conventional approach to big-step evaluation rules becomes awkward and repetitive. The `For` statement's semantics is defined by six rules. The first rule captures the case when the loop is not executed, i.e. when the guard expression evaluates to zero. The second rule states that errors in the evaluation of the guard are propagated.

$$\text{(F1)}\ \frac{(e_1,s) \Downarrow_{\texttt{e}} (\texttt{Rval}\ 0, s_1)}{(\texttt{For}\ e_1\ e_2\ t, s) \Downarrow_{\texttt{t}} (\texttt{Rval}\ 0, s_1)} \qquad \text{(F2)}\ \frac{(e_1,s) \Downarrow_{\texttt{e}} (r, s_1) \quad \neg\texttt{is\_Rval}\ r}{(\texttt{For}\ e_1\ e_2\ t, s) \Downarrow_{\texttt{t}} (r, s_1)}$$

Execution of the body of the For statement is described by the following four rules. The first of the following rules (F3) specifies the behaviour of an evaluation where the guard e_1, the body t, and the increment expression e_2 each return some Rval. The second rule (F4) defines the semantics for the case where evaluation of the body t signals Rbreak. The third rule (F5) states that errors in the increment expression e_2 propagate. Similarly, the fourth rule (F6) states that errors that occur in evaluation of the body propagate.

$$(\text{F3})\ \frac{\begin{array}{c}(e_1, s) \Downarrow_{\mathsf{e}} (\mathtt{Rval}\ n_1,\ s_1)\\ n_1 \neq 0\\ (t, s_1) \Downarrow_{\mathsf{t}} (\mathtt{Rval}\ n_2, s_2)\\ (e_2, s_2) \Downarrow_{\mathsf{e}} (\mathtt{Rval}\ n_3, s_3)\\ (\mathtt{For}\ e_1\ e_2\ t, s_3) \Downarrow_{\mathsf{t}} r\end{array}}{(\mathtt{For}\ e_1\ e_2\ t, s) \Downarrow_{\mathsf{t}} r} \qquad (\text{F4})\ \frac{\begin{array}{c}(e_1, s) \Downarrow_{\mathsf{e}} (\mathtt{Rval}\ n_1, s_1)\\ n_1 \neq 0\\ (t, s_1) \Downarrow_{\mathsf{t}} (\mathtt{Rbreak}, s_2)\end{array}}{(\mathtt{For}\ e_1\ e_2\ t, s) \Downarrow_{\mathsf{t}} (\mathtt{Rval}\ 0, s_2)}$$

$$(\text{F5})\ \frac{\begin{array}{c}(e_1, s) \Downarrow_{\mathsf{e}} (\mathtt{Rval}\ n_1, s_1)\\ n_1 \neq 0\\ (t, s_1) \Downarrow_{\mathsf{t}} (\mathtt{Rval}\ n_2, s_2)\\ (e_2, s_2) \Downarrow_{\mathsf{e}} (r, s_3)\\ \neg\mathtt{is\_Rval}\ r\end{array}}{(\mathtt{For}\ e_1\ e_2\ t, s) \Downarrow_{\mathsf{t}} (r,\ s_3)} \qquad (\text{F6})\ \frac{\begin{array}{c}(e_1, s) \Downarrow_{\mathsf{e}} (\mathtt{Rval}\ n_1, s_1)\\ n_1 \neq 0\\ (t, s_1) \Downarrow_{\mathsf{t}} (r, s_2)\\ \neg\mathtt{is\_Rval}\ r\\ r \neq \mathtt{Rbreak}\end{array}}{(\mathtt{For}\ e_1\ e_2\ t, s) \Downarrow_{\mathsf{t}} (r, s_2)}$$

Once one has become accustomed to this style of definition, these rules are quite easy to read. However, even an experienced semanticist may find it difficult to immediately see whether these rules cover all the cases. Maybe the last two rules above were surprising? Worse, these rules only provide semantics for terminating executions, i.e. if we want to reason about the behaviour of diverging evaluations, then these (inductive) rules are not enough as stated.

Another drawback is the duplication that rules for complex languages (even for our toy FOR language) contain. In each of the four rules above, the first three lines are almost the same. This duplication might seem innocent but it has knock-on effects on interactive proofs: the generated induction theorem also contains duplication, and from there it leaks into proof scripts. In particular, users are forced to establish the same inductive hypothesis many times (Sect. 3.4).

The rules (F2), (F5) and (F6) ensure that the Rfail value is always propagated to the top, preventing the big-step relation from doing the moral equivalent of getting 'stuck' in the small-step sense. Thus, we know that a program diverges iff it is not related to anything. We could omit these rules if we do not need or want to distinguish divergence from getting stuck, and this is often done with big-step semantics.[2] However, for the purposes of this paper, we are primarily interested in the (many) situations where the distinction is important – that is where the functional big-step approach has the largest benefit.

[2] If we had another mode of failure, e.g., from a raise expression, then these rules would still be needed to propagate that.

The above 'not related' characterisation of divergence does not yield a useful principle for reasoning about diverging programs: the relation's induction principle only applies when a program is related to something, not when we know it is not related to anything. To define divergence with a relation [18], one adds to the existing inductive evaluation relation $\Downarrow_{\mathtt{t}}$ a co-inductively defined divergence relation $\Uparrow_{\mathtt{t}}$, which provides a useful co-induction principle.

The rules for `Seq` and `For` are given below. (S1′) states that a sequence diverges if its first sub-statement does. (S2′) says that the sequence diverges if the first sub-statement returns a value, using the $\Downarrow_{\mathtt{t}}$ relation, and the second sub-statement diverges. Notice the duplication between the definitions of $\Downarrow_{\mathtt{t}}$ and $\Uparrow_{\mathtt{t}}$: both must allow the evaluation to progress normally up to a particular sub-statement, and then $\Downarrow_{\mathtt{t}}$ requires it to terminate, while $\Uparrow_{\mathtt{t}}$ requires it to diverge. This corresponds to the duplication internal to $\Downarrow_{\mathtt{t}}$ for propagating `Rbreak` and other exceptional results.

$$(\mathrm{S1'})\ \frac{(t_1,s)\ \Uparrow_{\mathtt{t}}}{(\mathtt{Seq}\ t_1\ t_2,s)\ \Uparrow_{\mathtt{t}}} \qquad (\mathrm{S2'})\ \frac{\begin{array}{c}(t_1,s)\ \Downarrow_{\mathtt{t}}\ (\mathtt{Rval}\ n_1,s_1)\\ (t_2,s_1)\ \Uparrow_{\mathtt{t}}\end{array}}{(\mathtt{Seq}\ t_1\ t_2,s)\ \Uparrow_{\mathtt{t}}}$$

$$(\mathrm{F1'})\ \frac{\begin{array}{c}(e_1,s)\ \Downarrow_{\mathtt{e}}\ (\mathtt{Rval}\ n_1,s_1)\\ n_1 \neq 0\\ (t,s_1)\ \Uparrow_{\mathtt{t}}\end{array}}{(\mathtt{For}\ e_1\ e_2\ t,s)\ \Uparrow_{\mathtt{t}}} \qquad (\mathrm{F2'})\ \frac{\begin{array}{c}(e_1,\ s)\ \Downarrow_{\mathtt{e}}\ (\mathtt{Rval}\ n_1,\ s_1)\\ n_1 \neq 0\\ (t,\ s_1)\ \Downarrow_{\mathtt{t}}\ (\mathtt{Rval}\ n_2,\ s_2)\\ (e_2,\ s_2)\ \Downarrow_{\mathtt{e}}\ (\mathtt{Rval}\ n_3,\ s_3)\\ (\mathtt{For}\ e_1\ e_2\ t,s_3)\ \Uparrow_{\mathtt{t}}\end{array}}{(\mathtt{For}\ e_1\ e_2\ t,\ s)\ \Uparrow_{\mathtt{t}}}$$

2.3 Functional Big-Step Semantics

The interpreter written in SML, given in Sect. 2.1, avoids the irritating duplication of the conventional big-step semantics. It is also arguably easier to read and clearly gives some semantics to all cases. So why can we not just take the SML code and define it as a function in logic? The answer is that the SML code does not terminate for all inputs, e.g., `run_t [] (For (Num 1, Num 1, Exp (Num 1)))`.

In order to define `run_t` as a function in logic, we need to make it total somehow. A technique for doing this is to add a clock to the function: on each recursive call for which termination is non-obvious, one adds a clock decrement. The clock is a natural number, so when it hits zero, execution is aborted with a special time-out signal.

A very simple implementation of the clocked-function solution is to add a check-and-decrement on every recursive call. The termination proof becomes trivial, but the function is cluttered with the clock mechanism.

Instead of inserting the clock on every recursive call, we suggest that the clock should only be decremented on recursive function calls for which the currently evaluated expressions does not decrease in size. For the FOR language, this means adding a clock-check-and-decrement only on the looping call in the `For` case. In the SML code, this recursive call is performed here:

```
| run_t s (For (e1, e2, t)) =
  ...
   (Rval _, s3) => run_t s3 (For (e1, e2, t))
```

In our functional big-step semantics for the FOR language, called `sem_t`, we write the line above as follows. Here `dec_clock` decrements the clock that is stored in the state.

```
sem_t s (For e1 e2 t) =
  ...
   (Rval _, s3) ⇒
    if s3.clock ≠ 0 then
     sem_t (dec_clock s3) (For e1 e2 t)
    else (Rtimeout, s3)
```

All other parts of the SML code are directly translated from SML into HOL4's logic. The complete definition of `sem_t` is given below. Because `run_e` is a pure total function, it can be translated directly into the HOL4 logic as `sem_e` without adding a clock. Here `store_var` x 0 s is state s updated to have value 0 in variable x.

```
sem_t s (Exp e) = sem_e s e
sem_t s (Dec x t) = sem_t (store_var x 0 s) t
sem_t s Break = (Rbreak, s)
sem_t s (Seq t1 t2) =
case sem_t s t1 of
  (Rval _, s1) ⇒ sem_t s1 t2
| r ⇒ r
sem_t s (If e t1 t2) =
case sem_e s e of
  (Rval n1, s1) ⇒ sem_t s1 (if n1 = 0 then t2 else t1)
| r ⇒ r
sem_t s (For e1 e2 t) =
case sem_e s e1 of
  (Rval 0, s1) ⇒ (Rval 0, s1)
| (Rval _, s1) ⇒
   (case sem_t s1 t of
     (Rval _, s2) ⇒
       (case sem_e s2 e2 of
          (Rval _, s3) ⇒
           if s3.clock ≠ 0 then
            sem_t (dec_clock s3) (For e1 e2 t)
           else (Rtimeout, s3)
        | r ⇒ r)
    | (Rbreak, s2) ⇒ (Rval 0, s2)
    | r ⇒ r)
| r ⇒ r
```

Note that, in our logic version of the semantics, we have introduced a new kind of return value called `Rtimeout`. This return value is used only to signal that the clock has aborted evaluation. It always propagates to the top, and can be used for reasoning about divergence preservation (Sect. 3.3).

Termination Proof. We prove termination of `sem_t` by providing a well-founded measure: the lexicographic ordering on the clock value and the size of the statement that is being evaluated. This measure works because the value of the clock is never increased, and, on every recursive call where the clock is not decremented, the size of the statement that is being evaluated decreases.[3]

No termination proof is required for relational big-step semantics. This requirement is, therefore, a drawback for the functional version. However, the functional representation brings some immediate benefits that are not immediate for relational definitions. The functional representation means that the semantics is total (by definition) and that the semantics is deterministic (see Sect. 4 for an account of non-deterministic languages). These are properties that can require tedious proof for relational definitions.

Semantics of Terminating and Non-terminating Evaluations. The `sem_t` function terminates for all inputs. However, at the same time, it gives semantics to both terminating and non-terminating (diverging) evaluations. We say that evaluation terminates, if there exists some initial value of the clock for which the `sem_t` returns `Rval`. An evaluation is non-terminating if `sem_t` returns `Rtimeout` for all initial values of the clock. In all other cases, the semantics fails. The top-level semantics is defined formally as follows. There are three observable outcomes: `Terminate`, `Diverge`, and `Crash`.

```
semantics t =
if ∃ c v s. sem_t (s_with_clock c) t = (Rval v,s) then Terminate
else if ∀ c. ∃ s. sem_t (s_with_clock c) t = (Rtimeout,s) then Diverge
else Crash
```

Section 3.3 verifies a compiler that preserves this semantics, and Sect. 4 extends the FOR language with input, output, and internal non-determinism.

3 Using Functional Semantics

The previous section showed how big-step semantics can be defined as functions in logic, and how they avoid the duplication that occurs in conventional big-step semantics. In this section, we highlight how the change in style of definition affects proofs that use the semantics. We compare proofs based on the functional semantics with corresponding proofs based on the relational semantics.

3.1 Rewriting with the Semantics

Since the functional semantics is defined as a function, it can be used for evaluation in the logic and used directly for proofs by rewriting. As a simple example, we can easily show that the `Dec` statement is an abbreviation for a longer program. This proof is just a simple call to the automatic rewriter in HOL4.

[3] HOL4's current definition package requires some help to prove and use the fact that the clock never increases.

$\vdash$ `sem_t` s `(Dec` v t`)` = `sem_t` s `(Seq (Exp (Assign` v `(Num 0)))` t`)`

This ability to perform symbolic evaluation within the logic is a handy tool, as any ACL2 expert will attest [19].

Sometimes rewriting with a functional semantics can get stuck in an infinite loop. This happens when the left-hand side of the definition, e.g. in our example `sem_t` s `(For` e_1 e_2 t`)`, matches a subexpression on the right-hand side of the equation, e.g. `sem_t (dec_clock` s_3`) (For` e_1 e_2 t`)`. We use a simple work-around for this: we define `STOP` x = x and prove an equation where the right-hand side is `sem_t (dec_clock` s_3`) (STOP (For` e_1 e_2 t`))`. We ensure that the automatic simplifier cannot remove `STOP` and thus cannot apply the rewrite beyond the potentially diverging recursive call.

Rewriting is possible but often more cumbersome with relational big-step semantics. In HOL4, every definition of an inductive relation produces a rewrite theorem of the following form. We only show the cases relating to `Seq`, eliding others with ellipses.

$$
\begin{array}{l}
\vdash (t, s) \Downarrow_{\mathtt{t}} res \iff \\
\quad \ldots \lor \ldots \lor \ldots \lor \\
\quad (\exists s_1\ t_1\ t_2\ n_1 . \\
\qquad (t = \mathtt{Seq}\ t_1\ t_2) \land (t_1, s) \Downarrow_{\mathtt{t}} (\mathtt{Rval}\ n_1, s_1) \land \\
\qquad (t_2, s_1) \Downarrow_{\mathtt{t}} res) \lor \\
\quad (\exists s_1\ t_1\ t_2\ r . \\
\qquad (t = \mathtt{Seq}\ t_1\ t_2) \land (res = (r, s_1)) \land (t_1, s) \Downarrow_{\mathtt{t}} (r, s_1) \land \\
\qquad \neg \mathtt{is\_Rval}\ r) \lor \ldots \lor \ldots \lor \ldots \lor \ldots \lor \ldots \lor \ldots \lor \ldots \lor \ldots \lor \ldots
\end{array}
$$

Such theorems have unrestricted left-hand sides, which easily cause HOL4's rewriter to diverge, and right-hand sides that introduce a large number of disjunctions. One can often avoid divergence by providing the rewriter with manually proved theorems with specialised left-hand sides, e.g. $(\mathtt{Seq}\ t_1\ t_2, s) \Downarrow_{\mathtt{t}} res$. Functional semantics require less work for use in proofs by rewriting.

3.2 Induction Theorem

The ability to rewrite with the functional semantics helps improve the details of interactive proofs. Surprisingly, the use of functional semantics also improves the overall structure of many proofs. The reason for this is that the induction theorems produced by functional semantics avoid the duplication that comes from the relational semantics.

The induction theorems for the FOR language are shown in Figs. 1 and 2. The induction theorem for `sem_t` only has one case for the `For` loop. In contrast, the induction theorem for the relational semantics has six cases for the `For` loop. The duplication in the relation semantics carries over to duplication in the induction theorem and, hence, to the structure of interactive proofs, making them longer and more repetitive. This difference is significant for languages with complex program constructs.

```
⊢ (∀s e. P s (Exp e)) ∧
  (∀s x t. P (store_var x 0 s) t ⇒ P s (Dec x t)) ∧
  (∀s. P s Break) ∧
  (∀s t₁ t₂.
     (∀v₂ s₁ v₅.
        (sem_t s t₁ = (v₂,s₁)) ∧ (v₂ = Rval v₅) ⇒ P s₁ t₂) ∧
     P s t₁ ⇒
     P s (Seq t₁ t₂)) ∧
  (∀s e t₁ t₂.
     (∀v₂ s₁ n₁.
        (sem_e s e = (v₂,s₁)) ∧ (v₂ = Rval n₁) ⇒
        P s₁ (if n₁ = 0 then t₂ else t₁)) ⇒
     P s (If e t₁ t₂)) ∧
  (∀s e₁ e₂ t.
     (∀v₂ s₁ n₁ v₂' s₂ n₁' v₂'' s₃ n₁''.
        (sem_e s e₁ = (v₂,s₁)) ∧ (v₂ = Rval n₁) ∧ n₁ ≠ 0 ∧
        (sem_t s₁ t = (v₂',s₂)) ∧ (v₂' = Rval n₁') ∧
        (sem_e s₂ e₂ = (v₂'',s₃)) ∧ (v₂'' = Rval n₁'') ∧
        s₃.clock ≠ 0 ⇒
        P (dec_clock s₃) (For e₁ e₂ t)) ∧
     (∀v₂ s₁ n₁.
        (sem_e s e₁ = (v₂,s₁)) ∧ (v₂ = Rval n₁) ∧ n₁ ≠ 0 ⇒
        P s₁ t) ⇒
     P s (For e₁ e₂ t)) ⇒
  ∀v v₁. P v v₁
```

Fig. 1. Induction theorem for functional big-step semantics.

Avoiding Duplication in Relations. The duplication problem can be avoided in relational big-step semantics. A trick is to define the evaluation rules such that program constructs are described by only one rule each. Below is an example of how one can package up all of the rules about For into one giant rule.

$$\frac{\begin{array}{l}(e_1,s) \Downarrow_e (r_1,s_1) \wedge \\ (\textbf{if } (r_1 = \texttt{Rval}\ n_1) \wedge n_1 \neq 0 \textbf{ then} \\ \quad (t,s_1) \Downarrow_t (r_2,s_2) \wedge \\ \quad \textbf{if } r_2 = \texttt{Rval}\ n_2 \textbf{ then} \\ \qquad (e_2,s_2) \Downarrow_e (r_3,s_3) \wedge \\ \qquad \textbf{if } r_3 = \texttt{Rval}\ n_3 \textbf{ then } (\texttt{For}\ e_1\ e_2\ t,s_3) \Downarrow_t \mathit{result} \\ \qquad \textbf{else } \mathit{result} = (r_3,s_3) \\ \quad \textbf{else } \mathit{result} = (r_2,s_2) \\ \textbf{else } (\mathit{result} = (r_1,s_1)))\end{array}}{(\texttt{For}\ e_1\ e_2\ t,s) \Downarrow_t \mathit{result}}$$

By avoiding the duplication in the rules, the induction theorem also avoids the duplication. Writing packaged rules, as shown above, is unusual and certainly not aesthetically pleasing. However, if relational definitions are to be used, packaging evaluation

$$
\begin{array}{l}
\vdash \ldots \wedge \ldots \wedge \ldots \wedge \ldots \wedge \ldots \wedge \ldots \wedge \ldots \wedge \ldots \wedge \ldots \wedge \\
\quad (\forall s\ s_1\ e_1\ e_2\ t. \\
\qquad (e_1, s) \Downarrow_{\mathsf{e}} (\texttt{Rval}\ 0, s_1) \Rightarrow P\ (\texttt{For}\ e_1\ e_2\ t, s)\ (\texttt{Rval}\ 0, s_1)) \wedge \\
\quad (\forall s\ s_1\ e_1\ e_2\ t\ r. \\
\qquad (e_1, s) \Downarrow_{\mathsf{e}} (r, s_1) \wedge \neg\texttt{is\_Rval}\ r \Rightarrow P\ (\texttt{For}\ e_1\ e_2\ t, s)\ (r, s_1)) \wedge \\
\quad (\forall s\ s_1\ s_2\ s_3\ e_1\ e_2\ t\ n_1\ n_2\ n_3\ r. \\
\qquad (e_1, s) \Downarrow_{\mathsf{e}} (\texttt{Rval}\ n_1, s_1) \wedge n_1 \neq 0 \wedge P\ (t, s_1)\ (\texttt{Rval}\ n_2, s_2) \wedge \\
\qquad (e_2, s_2) \Downarrow_{\mathsf{e}} (\texttt{Rval}\ n_3, s_3) \wedge P\ (\texttt{For}\ e_1\ e_2\ t, s_3)\ r \Rightarrow \\
\qquad P\ (\texttt{For}\ e_1\ e_2\ t, s)\ r) \wedge \\
\quad (\forall s\ s_1\ s_2\ e_1\ e_2\ t\ n_1. \\
\qquad (e_1, s) \Downarrow_{\mathsf{e}} (\texttt{Rval}\ n_1, s_1) \wedge n_1 \neq 0 \wedge P\ (t, s_1)\ (\texttt{Rbreak}, s_2) \Rightarrow \\
\qquad P\ (\texttt{For}\ e_1\ e_2\ t, s)\ (\texttt{Rval}\ 0, s_2)) \wedge \\
\quad (\forall s\ s_1\ s_2\ s_3\ e_1\ e_2\ t\ n_1\ n_2\ r. \\
\qquad (e_1, s) \Downarrow_{\mathsf{e}} (\texttt{Rval}\ n_1, s_1) \wedge n_1 \neq 0 \wedge P\ (t, s_1)\ (\texttt{Rval}\ n_2, s_2) \wedge \\
\qquad (e_2, s_2) \Downarrow_{\mathsf{e}} (r, s_3) \wedge \neg\texttt{is\_Rval}\ r \Rightarrow \\
\qquad P\ (\texttt{For}\ e_1\ e_2\ t, s)\ (r, s_3)) \wedge \\
\quad (\forall s\ s_1\ s_2\ e_1\ e_2\ t\ n_1\ r. \\
\qquad (e_1, s) \Downarrow_{\mathsf{e}} (\texttt{Rval}\ n_1, s_1) \wedge n_1 \neq 0 \wedge P\ (t, s_1)\ (r, s_2) \wedge \neg\texttt{is\_Rval}\ r \wedge \\
\qquad r \neq \texttt{Rbreak} \Rightarrow \\
\qquad P\ (\texttt{For}\ e_1\ e_2\ t, s)\ (r, s_2)) \Rightarrow \\
\quad \forall ts\ rs.\ ts \Downarrow_{\mathsf{t}} rs \Rightarrow P\ ts\ rs
\end{array}
$$

Fig. 2. Induction theorem for relational big-step semantics. Parts omitted with '. . . '.

rules as above is potentially less intrusive to proofs than use of the pretty-big-step approach, since it does not introduce new data constructors.[4]

3.3 Example Compiler Verification

Next, we outline how functional big-step semantics support compiler verification, proving that a compiler preserves the observable behaviour. Our compiler targets a simple assembly-like language, where the code is a list of instructions (`instr`).

`instr = Add reg reg reg | Int reg int | Jmp num | JmpIf reg num`

The compiler, `compile`, is a composition of three phases. The first phase, `phase1`, simplifies `For` and `Dec`; `phase2` splits assignments into simple instruction-like assignments, but stays within the source language; and `phase3` reduces the remaining subset of the source language into a list of target instructions. The first two parameters to `phase3` accumulate code location information.

`compile` t = `phase3` 0 0 (`phase2` (`phase1` t))

The first phase is a source-to-source transformation that simplifies `For` and `Dec` as follows. Here `Loop` is an abbreviation: `Loop` t = `For (Num 1) (Num 1)` t.

[4] Note that such packaged big-step rules are easy to define in HOL4. However, they do not fit well with Coq's default mechanism for defining inductive relations. Charguéraud's pretty-big-step approach was developed in the context of Coq.

$\texttt{phase1 (For}\ g\ e\ t\texttt{)} = \texttt{Loop (If}\ g\ \texttt{(Seq (phase1}\ t\texttt{) (Exp}\ e\texttt{)) Break)}$
$\texttt{phase1 (Dec}\ x\ t\texttt{)} = \texttt{Seq (Exp (Assign}\ x\ \texttt{(Num 0))) (phase1}\ t\texttt{)}$

The compilation function phase1 has a simple correctness theorem that can be proved in less than 20 lines of HOL4 script using the induction from Fig. 1.

$\vdash \forall s\ t.\ \texttt{sem\_t}\ s\ \texttt{(phase1}\ t\texttt{)} = \texttt{sem\_t}\ s\ t$

We also prove that phase1 preserves the observable semantics:

$\vdash \forall t.\ \texttt{semantics (phase1}\ t\texttt{)} = \texttt{semantics}\ t$

Subsequent phases assume that For statements have been simplified to Loop. The verification of the second phase, phase2, is almost as simple but a little longer because phase2 invents variable names to hold temporary results.

The third phase compiles the resulting subset of the FOR language into a list of instructions in the assembly-like target language. The crucial lemma, stated below, was proved by induction using the theorem shown in Fig. 1. This lemma's statement can informally be read as: if the source semantics sem_t dictates that program t successfully evaluates state s_1 to state s_2, the source program t is within the allowed syntactic subset, and the compiled code for t is installed in a store-related target state x; then the target semantics sem_a evaluates x to a new target state x' that is store-related to s_2. Below, sem_a is the functional big-step semantics for the target assembly language. The sem_a function executes one instruction at a time and is tail-recursive; its lengthy definition is omitted. phase3_subset defines the syntactic restrictions that programs must follow after phases 1 and 2. The ellipses elide several detailed parts of the conclusion that are only necessary to make the induction go through: in particular, where the program counter will point at exit based on the result *res*.

$$\begin{aligned}
&\vdash \forall s_1\ t\ res\ s_2\ x\ xs\ ys\ b.\\
&\quad (\texttt{sem_t}\ s_1\ t = (res, s_2)) \wedge \texttt{phase3_subset}\ t \wedge (x.\texttt{store} = s_1) \wedge\\
&\quad (x.\texttt{pc} = \texttt{LENGTH}\ xs) \wedge\\
&\quad (x.\texttt{instrs} = xs \mathbin{++} \texttt{phase3 (LENGTH}\ xs)\ b\ t \mathbin{++} ys) \wedge res \neq \texttt{Rfail} \wedge\\
&\quad ((res = \texttt{Rbreak}) \Rightarrow \texttt{LENGTH}\ (xs \mathbin{++} \texttt{phase3 (LENGTH}\ xs)\ b\ t) \leq b) \Rightarrow\\
&\quad \exists x'.\ (\texttt{sem_a}\ x = \texttt{sem_a}\ x') \wedge (x'.\texttt{store} = s_2) \wedge \ldots
\end{aligned}$$

From the lemma above, it is easy to prove that phase3 0 0 t preserves the observable semantics, if t is in the subset expected by the third phase and t does not Crash in the source semantics.

$$\begin{aligned}
&\vdash \forall t.\\
&\quad \texttt{semantics}\ t \neq \texttt{Crash} \wedge \texttt{phase3_subset}\ t \Rightarrow\\
&\quad (\texttt{asm_semantics (phase3 0 0}\ t\texttt{)} = \texttt{semantics}\ t)
\end{aligned}$$

Here asm_semantics is the observable semantics of the target assembly language.

$$\begin{aligned}
&\texttt{asm_semantics}\ code =\\
&\textbf{if}\ \exists c\ s.\ \texttt{sem_a (a_state}\ code\ c\texttt{)} = (\texttt{Rval}\ 0, s)\ \textbf{then}\ \texttt{Terminate}\\
&\textbf{else if}\ \forall c.\ \exists s.\ \texttt{sem_a (a_state}\ code\ c\texttt{)} = (\texttt{Rtimeout}, s)\ \textbf{then}\ \texttt{Diverge}\\
&\textbf{else}\ \texttt{Crash}
\end{aligned}$$

The following top-level compiler correctness theorem is produced by combining the semantics preservation theorems from all three phases. The assumption that the source semantics does not `Crash` is implied by a simple syntactic check `syntax_ok`, which checks that all variables been declared (`Dec`) and that all `Break` statements are contained within `For` loops.

$\vdash \forall t.\ \texttt{syntax\_ok}\ t \Rightarrow (\texttt{asm\_semantics}\ (\texttt{compile}\ t) = \texttt{semantics}\ t)$

3.4 Comparison with Proof in Relational Semantics

We provide a corresponding proof of correctness for `phase1` in the relational semantics. As a rough point of comparison, our relational proof required 43 lines while the functional big-step proof required just 18 lines. The proof is split into two parts, corresponding to the relations defining our big-step semantics:

$\vdash \forall s\ t\ res.\ (t,s) \Downarrow_t res \Rightarrow (\texttt{phase1}\ t,s) \Downarrow_t res$
$\vdash \forall s\ t.\ (t,s) \Uparrow_t \Rightarrow (\texttt{phase1}\ t,s) \Uparrow_t$

The advantage of (non-looping) functional rewriting is apparent in our proofs: we often had to manually control where rewrites were applied in the relational proof. Additionally, we had to deal with significantly more cases in the relational proofs; these extra cases came from two sources, namely, the ones arising from an additional co-inductive proof for diverging programs, and extra (similar) cases in the induction theorems.

The additional co-inductive proof is a good point of comparison, since our technique of decrementing the clock only on recursive calls in the functional big-step semantics gives us divergence preservation for free in compilation steps that do not cause additional clock ticks. The cases arising in our co-inductive proof also required a different form of reasoning from the inductive proof; this naturally arises from the difference between induction and co-induction but it meant that we could not directly adapt similar cases across both proofs.

The top-level observable semantics can be similarly defined for relational semantics:

$\texttt{rel\_semantics}\ t =$
$\textbf{if}\ \exists v\ s.\ (t,\texttt{init\_store}) \Downarrow_t (\texttt{Rval}\ v,s)\ \textbf{then}\ \texttt{Terminate}$
$\textbf{else if}\ (t,\texttt{init\_store}) \Uparrow_t\ \textbf{then}\ \texttt{Diverge}$
$\textbf{else}\ \texttt{Crash}$

So we can prove the correctness of `phase1` with respect to `rel_semantics`:

$\vdash \forall t.$
$\quad \texttt{rel\_semantics}\ t \neq \texttt{Crash} \Rightarrow$
$\quad (\texttt{rel\_semantics}\ (\texttt{phase1}\ t) = \texttt{rel\_semantics}\ t)$

This proof requires proving that the relations ($\Downarrow_t$, $\Uparrow_t$) are disjoint:

$\vdash \forall s\ t\ res.\ (t,s) \Downarrow_t res \Rightarrow \neg (t,s) \Uparrow_t$

We also attempted a proof of `phase1` with a relational pretty-big-step semantics; we found this semantics surprisingly difficult to use in HOL4. Pretty-big-step semantics requires the introduction of additional intermediate terms to factorise evaluation of sub-terms. Hence, the generated induction theorem requires reasoning over these intermediate terms. However, in our compiler proofs, we are typically concerned with the original syntactic terms – those are the only ones mentioned by the compiler – so this induction theorem cannot be applied directly, unlike in the other two semantics. There are ways around this: one can, for example, use an induction theorem that only concerns the original syntactic terms or induct on the size of derivations. Neither of these approaches are automatically supported in HOL4, and our proof of `phase1` semantics preservation using the latter approach took 81 lines. Some of Charguéraud's big-step and pretty-big-step equivalence proofs in Coq also needed to manually prove and use induction on derivation sizes. Additionally, a separate proof is still required for divergence preservation in the co-inductive interpretation of these rules; this requires the use of its co-induction theorem, which also has similar issues with intermediate terms.

To further validate the functional big-step approach, we prove the equivalence of the functional big-step semantics (`sem_t`) and the relational semantics ($\Downarrow_t$, $\Uparrow_t$). (We also prove the equivalence with a small-step semantics in Sect. 7). The equivalence is separated into two theorems: the first shows equivalence for terminating programs while the latter shows equivalence on diverging programs.

$$\vdash \forall s\ t\ r\ s'.\ (t,s) \Downarrow_t (r,s'\ \texttt{with clock} := s\texttt{.clock}) \iff \exists c'.\ (\texttt{sem\_t}\ (s\ \texttt{with clock} := c')\ t = (r,s')) \land r \neq \texttt{Rtimeout}$$

$$\vdash \forall s\ t.\ (\forall c.\ \texttt{FST}\ (\texttt{sem\_t}\ (s\ \texttt{with clock} := c)\ t) = \texttt{Rtimeout}) \iff (t,s) \Uparrow_t$$

The proofs rely on the disjointness lemma above and a determinism lemma for the relational semantics:

$$\vdash \forall s\ t\ res.\ (t,s) \Downarrow_t res \Rightarrow \forall res'.\ (t,s) \Downarrow_t res' \Rightarrow (res = res')$$

They also rely on an analogue of determinism for the functional big-step semantics: if a program does not time out for a given clock, then every increment to the clock gives the same result[5].

$$\vdash \forall s\ t\ r\ s'.\ (\texttt{sem\_t}\ s\ t = (r,s')) \land r \neq \texttt{Rtimeout} \Rightarrow \forall k.\ \texttt{sem\_t}\ (s\ \texttt{with clock} := s\texttt{.clock} + k)\ t = (r,s'\ \texttt{with clock} := s'\texttt{.clock} + k)$$

These lemmas are easy to prove compared to the main body of the equivalence proof, and our examples above demonstrate that the number of such lemmas required is comparable between the two semantics.

[5] This lemma also implies that if a program times out for a given clock, then it times out for all smaller clocks.

4 Non-determinism

We now add non-deterministic evaluation order and input/output expressions to the FOR language. The only syntactic change is the addition of two expressions: `Getchar` and `Putchar` e. However, the observable behaviours of programs have changed significantly. Instead of doing exactly one of terminating, diverging, or crashing, a program can now exhibit a set of those behaviours. Furthermore, both termination and divergence results now include the I/O stream that the program consumed/produced. For technical reasons, it also contains the choices made by the non-deterministic evaluation order (see Sect. 7). In the type of `observation`, the `llist` type is the lazy list type that contains both finite and infinite lists, and `+` is the type constructor for disjoint unions.

```
observation =
  Terminate ((io_tag + bool) list)
 | Diverge ((io_tag + bool) llist)
 | Crash
```

As a function, `sem_t` seems to be inherently deterministic: we cannot simply have it internally know what the next input character is, or choose which sub-expression to evaluate first. We are left with two options: we can factor out the input stream and all choices into the state argument of `sem_t` and then existentially quantify them in the top-level semantic function to build a set of results; or alternatively, we can change the type of `sem_t` to return sets of results (alongside partial I/O traces). Here we take the first approach which leads to only minor changes in the definition of `sem_t`.

First, the state argument of `sem_t` gets three new fields: `io_trace` to record the characters read and written; `input` to represent the (possibly infinite) input stream; and `non_det_o` which represents an infinite stream of decisions that determine the subexpression evaluation ordering. We include the inputs in the `io_trace` to accurately model the order in which the I/O operations happened.

```
io_tag = Itag int | Otag int
state =
 <| store : (string ↦ int);
    clock : num;
    io_trace : ((io_tag + bool) list);
    input : (char llist);
    non_det_o : (num -> bool) |>
```

Because all of our changes are limited to the expression language, and encapsulated in the extended state argument, which `sem_t` does not access, the definition of `sem_t` looks identical to the previous one. The changes to `sem_e` are limited to the `Add` case (where a non-deterministic choice is made), and two new cases for the new expressions.

```
sem_e s (Putchar e) =
case sem_e s e of
 (Rval n1, s1) ⇒
  (Rval n1, s1 with io_trace := s1.io_trace ++ [INL (Otag n1)])
| r ⇒ r
```

```
sem_e s Getchar =
(let (v, rest) = getchar s.input in
   (Rval v,
  s with <|input := rest; io_trace := s.io_trace ++ [INL (Itag v)] |>))

sem_e s (Add e1 e2) =
(let ((fst_e, snd_e), nd_o, switch) = permute_pair s.non_det_o (e1, e2) in
  case
   sem_e
    (s with
    <|non_det_o := nd_o; io_trace := s.io_trace ++ [INR switch] |>)
    fst_e
  of
   (Rval fst_n, s1) ⇒
    (case sem_e s1 snd_e of
      (Rval snd_n, s2) ⇒
       (let (n1, n2) = unpermute_pair (fst_n, snd_n) switch in
         (Rval (n1 + n2), s2))
     | r ⇒ r)
  | r ⇒ r)
```

The Add case is similar to before, but uses the permute_pair function to swap the sub-expressions or not, depending on the oracle. It also returns a new oracle ready to get the next choice, and whether or not it switched the sub-expressions. The latter is used to un-permute the values to apply the primitive + in the right order (which would matter for a non-commutative operator). Getchar similarly consumes one input and updates the state. Putchar adds to the I/O trace.

Critically, the above modifications are orthogonal to the clock, and do not affect the termination proof, or the usefulness of the induction theorems and rewriting equations. The changes to the semantics function are explained next.[6]

```
semantics t input (Terminate io_trace) ⟺
∃ c nd i s.
 (sem_t (init_st c nd input) t = (Rval i, s)) ∧
 (FILTER ISL s.io_trace = io_trace)
semantics t input Crash ⟺
∃ c nd r s.
 (sem_t (init_st c nd input) t = (r, s)) ∧
 ((r = Rbreak) ∨ (r = Rfail))
semantics t input (Diverge io_trace) ⟺
∃ nd.
 (∀ c. ∃ s. sem_t (init_st c nd input) t = (Rtimeout, s)) ∧
 (io_trace =
 ⋁c.
  fromList
   (FILTER ISL (SND (sem_t (init_st c nd input) t)).io_trace))
```

[6] Here FILTER is ordinary filtering over a list, and ISL is the predicate for the left injection of a sum (disjoint union), so the FILTER ISL applications get the I/O actions and discard the evaluation ordering choices.

Firstly, `semantics` is now a predicate[7] over programs, inputs, and observation. Termination and crashing are still straightforward: the non-determinism oracle and input are quantified along with the clock, and the resulting I/O trace is read out of the result state. We filter the trace so it only contains the I/O actions and not the record of the non-determinism oracle. Some choices of oracles might lead to a crash whereas others might lead to different terminating results.

Divergence is more subtle. First, note that a program can both terminate and diverge depending on evaluation order. For example, in the following `x` can be assigned either `1` or `0`, depending on which sub-expression is evaluated first.

```
Seq (Exp (Add (Assign "x" 1) (Assign "x" 0)))
    (For (Var "x") (Num 1) (Exp (Num 1)))
```

Thus, in the definition of `semantics`, we first existentially quantify the non-determinism, then check that it results in a timeout for all clock values given that particular oracle. To ensure that the resulting I/O trace is correct, we consider the set of all I/O traces for every possible clock in the complete partial order of lazy lists ordered by the prefix relation. This set forms a chain, because we prove that increasing the input clock does not alter the I/O already performed. Hence, the resulting I/O behaviour is the least upper bound, which can be either a finite or infinite lazy list. Operationally, as we increase the clock, we potentially see more I/O behaviour, and the least upper bound defines the lazy list that incorporates all of these. (Notation: the $\bigvee$ binder takes lubs in this PO.)

Adapting the Compiler Verification. Adapting the compiler verification to the I/O and non-determinism extension is an almost trivial exercise. The I/O streams were modelled in the same way in the assembly language, which we kept deterministic. The new proof engineering work stems mostly from the substantial change to the definition of the top-level semantics function `semantics`. Due to non-determinism, which the compiler removes, the correctness theorem is now stated as a subset relation: every behaviour of the generated (deterministic) assembly code is also a behaviour of the (non-deterministic) source program.

$\vdash \forall t\ inp.$ `syntax_ok` $t \Rightarrow$ `asm_semantics (compile` t`)` $inp \subseteq$ `semantics` $t\ inp$

Unclocked Relational Big-step. Non-determinism can be handled naturally with two big-step rules for `Add`, although that does introduce duplication. A big-step relation can also be used to collect I/O traces [10,17,20]. However, this requires a mixed co-inductive/inductive approach for non-terminating programs, and we can no longer choose to equate divergence with a failure to relate the program to anything.

Concurrency. The techniques described in this section can support functional big-step semantics for a large variety of practical languages, but they do share a significant limitation with other big-step approaches: concurrency. Concurrent execution would require interleaving the evaluation of multiple expressions, whereas the

[7] Note that HOL4 identifies the types α `-> bool` and α `set`.

main principle of a big-step semantics (ours included) is to evaluate an expression to a value in one step. Our non-determinism merely selects which to do first. Work-arounds, such as having `sem_t` return sets of traces of inter-thread communications, might sometimes be possible, but would significantly affect the shape of the definition of the semantics.

5 Type Soundness

Whereas big-step semantics are common in compiler verification, small-step semantics enable the standard approach to type soundness by preservation and progress lemmas [29]. A type soundness theorem says that well-typed programs do not crash; they either terminate normally or diverge. As Siek notes [25], a critical thing a semantics must provide is a good separation between divergence and crashing, and a clocked big-step semantics does this naturally. We have experimented with two type systems and found that functional big-step semantics works very well for proving type soundness.

Our first example is for the FOR language. We prove that `syntax_ok` programs do not evaluate to `Rfail`. The key is to use the induction theorem associated with the functional semantics, rather than rule induction derived from the type system.

We carry the same approach to a language with more interesting type systems: the Core ML language from Wright and Felleisen [29] equipped with a functional big-step semantics closely resembling an ML interpreter. The type system is more complex than the FOR language's, supporting references, exceptions, higher-order functions and Hindley-Milner polymorphism. However, this extra complexity in the type system factors out neatly, and does not disrupt the proof outline.

Our approach is similar to the one described by Siek [26] (followed by Rompf and Amin [24]) who uses a clocked functional big-step semantics and demonstrates the utility of the induction theorem arising from the clocked semantics. As a result, our main type soundness proof, which interacts with the big-step semantics, is easy. Siek's example type system is simpler than Core ML's: it has no references or polymorphism; but these difficult aspects can be isolated. The most difficult lemmas in our proof are about the type system, and rely on α-equivalence reasoning over type schemes. Similar lemmas, concerning the type system only, were proved by Tofte [27].

Our statement of type soundness for Core ML is: if a program is well-typed, then for all clocks, the semantics of the program is either `Rtimeout`, an exception, or a value of the correct type – never `Rfail`. The universal quantification of clocks makes this a strong statement, since it implies diverging well-typed programs also cannot fail. For contrast, we have also written un-clocked big-step semantics for Core ML and proved a similar theorem: if a program is well-typed and converges to r, then r is an exception or value of the correct type, but never `Rfail`. The proof by induction is essentially the same as for the clocked semantics, and all the type-system lemmas can be re-used exactly, but the conclusion is much weaker because diverging programs do not satisfy the assumption. The proof is also longer (330 lines vs. 200) because of the duplication in the relational semantics.

6 Logical Relations

The technique of step-indexed logical relations [2] supports reasoning about programs that have recursive types, higher-order state, or other features that introduce aspects of circularity into a language's semantics [1, 12]. The soundness of these relations is usually proved with respect to a small-step semantics, because the length of a small-step trace can be used to make the relation well-founded when following the structure of the language's cyclic constructs (e.g., when following a pointer cycle in the heap or unfolding a recursive type). Here we show that the clock in a functional big-step semantics can serve the same purpose.

Because our main purpose here is to illustrate functional big-step semantics, we first present the relation and defer its motivation to the end of this section. For now, it suffices to say that it has some significant differences from the existing literature, because it is designed to validate compiler optimisations in an untyped setting.

We start with an untyped lambda calculus with literals, variables (using de Bruijn indices), functions, and a tick expression that decrements the clock. The semantics will also use closure values, and a state with a clock.

```
exp = Lit lit | Var num | App exp exp | Fun exp | Tick exp
v = Litv lit | Clos env exp
env = v list
state = <| clock : num; store : env |>
```

We can then define the function `sem`, which implements call-by-value evaluation and decrements the clock on every function call. EL gets the nth element of a list.

```
sem env s (Lit i) = (Rval (Litv i), s)
sem env s (Var n) =
if n < LENGTH env then (Rval (EL n env), s) else (Rfail, s)
sem env s (App e1 e2) =
case sem env s e1 of
  (Rval v1, s1) ⇒
   (case sem env s1 e2 of
     (Rval v2, s2) ⇒
      if s2.clock ≠ 0 then
        case v1 of
         Litv v4 ⇒ (Rfail, s2)
        | Clos env' e ⇒ sem (v2::env') (dec_clock s2) e
      else (Rtimeout, s2)
   | r ⇒ r)
| r ⇒ r
sem env s (Fun e) = (Rval (Clos env e), s)
sem env s (Tick e) =
if s.clock ≠ 0 then sem env (dec_clock s) e else (Rtimeout, s)
```

The top-level semantic function's definition is similar to the FOR language's (Sect. 2).

We then define the relations `val_rel`, which relates two values; `exec_rel`, which relates two environment/store/expression triples (i.e., the inputs to `sem`); and `state_rel`, which relates two stores; all at a given index.

```
val_rel i (Litv l) (Litv l') ⟺ (l = l')
val_rel i (Clos env e) (Clos env' e') ⟺
 ∀i' a a' s s'.
  i' < i ⇒
  state_rel i' s s' ∧ val_rel i' a a' ⇒
  exec_rel i' (a::env,s,e) (a'::env',s',e')
val_rel i (Litv l) (Clos env e) ⟺ F
val_rel i (Clos env e) (Litv l) ⟺ F
exec_rel i (env,s,e) (env',s',e') ⟺
 ∀i'. i' ≤ i ⇒
  (let (res1,s1) = sem env (s with clock := i') e in
   let (res2,s2) = sem env' (s' with clock := i') e' in
    case (res1,res2) of
     (Rval v1,Rval v2) ⇒
      (s1.clock = s2.clock) ∧ state_rel s1.clock s1 s2 ∧
      val_rel s1.clock v1 v2
   | (Rtimeout,Rtimeout) ⇒ state_rel s1.clock s1 s2
   | (Rfail,_) ⇒ T
   | r ⇒ F)
state_rel i s s' ⟺
 LIST_REL (λ a' a. val_rel i a' a) s.store s'.store
```

The definitions of `val_rel` and `state_rel` are typical of a logical relation; `exec_rel` is where the relation interacts with the functional big-step semantics. In the small-step setting, `exec_rel` would say that the two triples are related if they remain related for i steps of the small-step semantics. With the functional big-step semantics, we instead check that the results of the `sem` function are related when we set the clock to a value less than i.

From here we prove that the relation is compatible with the language's syntax, that it is reflexive and transitive, that it is sound with respect to contextual approximation, and finally that β-value conversion is in the relation, and hence a sound optimisation for the language at any subexpression. Most of the proof is related to the semantic work at hand, rather than the details of the semantics, but we do need to rely on several easy-to-prove lemmas about the clock that capture intuitive aspects of what it means to be a clocked evaluation function. They correspond to the last lemma from Sect. 3.4.

Motivation. The language and relation are designed as a prototype of an intermediate language for CakeML that is similar to the *clambda* intermediate language in the OCaml compiler [9]. Because this is an untyped intermediate language for a typed source language, the compiler should be able to change a failing expression into anything at all. We know that we will never try to compile an expression that fails, and this design allows us to omit run-time checks that would otherwise be needed to signal failure. This is why `exec_rel` relates `Rfail` to anything, and why our relation is not an equivalence, but an approximation: the compiler must never convert a good expression into one that fails.

Furthermore, the compiler must not convert a diverging program into one that converges (or vice-versa). This is why `Rtimeout` is only related to itself, and why the clocks are both set to the same i' when running the expressions. In a typed setting, the clock for the right-hand argument is existentially quantified, thereby allowing a diverging expression to be related to a converging one, and if one wants to show equivalence, one proves the approximation both ways. Because of our treatment of failure, that is not an option here. The drawback is that we cannot support transformations that increase the number of clock ticks needed. For transformations that might reduce the number of ticks, including our β-value conversion, the transformation just needs to introduce extra `Tick` instructions.

All of the above applies in a small-step setting too. However, the functional big-step approach automatically has some flexibility for changing the amount of computation done. For example, both $1 + 2$ and 3 evaluate with the same clock, and so this type of logical relation could be used to show that constant folding is a sound optimisation without added `Tick` instructions.

7 Equivalence with Small-Step Semantics

We build a straightforward small-step semantics for the FOR language by adding a `Handle` statement to the language, to stop the propagation of `Break` statements upward, and implement `For` as follows (we write `Seq` as an infix ;):

$$\frac{}{(\texttt{For}\ e_1\ e_2\ t,\ s) \rightarrow_{\mathtt{t}} (\texttt{Handle}\ (\texttt{If}\ e_1\ (t;\texttt{Exp}\ e_2;\texttt{For}\ e_1\ e_2\ t)\ (\texttt{Exp}\ (\texttt{Num}\ 0))),s)}$$

To prove the equivalence of the functional big-step and small-step, we need two lemmas. First, that the functional semantics only gives `Rtimeout` with a clock of 0 (which is trivial to prove). Second, that any result of the functional semantics has a corresponding trace through the small-step semantics that is long enough. In the theorem below, we represent the small-step trace with a list so that we can check its length. The `check_trace` predicate checks that it is indeed a trace of $\rightarrow_{\mathtt{t}}$ steps. The length check ensures that if the functional big-step diverges, then we will be able to build a small-step trace of arbitrary length, and so it diverges too. The subtraction calculates how many clock ticks the evaluation actually used.

$$\begin{array}{l}
\vdash (\texttt{sem_t}\ s\ t = r) \Rightarrow \\
\quad \exists\, tr\,. \\
\qquad tr \neq \texttt{[]} \wedge s.\mathsf{clock} - (\texttt{SND}\ r).\mathsf{clock} \leq \texttt{LENGTH}\ tr\ \wedge \\
\qquad \texttt{check_trace}\ (\lambda\, st.\ \texttt{some}\ st'.\ st \rightarrow_{\mathtt{t}} st')\ tr\ \wedge \\
\qquad (\texttt{HD}\ tr = (s.\mathsf{store},\texttt{t_to_small_t}\ t)) \wedge \texttt{res_rel_t}\ r\ (\texttt{LAST}\ tr)
\end{array}$$

One would expect such a theorem building small-step traces from big-step executions to show up in any big-step/small-step equivalence proof. The extra length check adds very little difficulty to the proof, but ensures that we do not need to explicitly prove anything about divergence, or additionally reason going from small-step traces to big-step executions. Similar to type soundness (Sect. 5), we prove this using the induction principle of `sem_t`.

In the non-deterministic case, we extend the state of the small-step semantics with the same oracle that the functional big-step semantics uses, and we use the oracle to choose which sub-expression of an Add to start evaluating. AddL and AddR expressions are included to mark which argument is being evaluated, so that we do not consult the oracle in subsequent steps for the same decision or switch back-and-forth between subexpressions. For example, if the oracle returns false, we start evaluating the left sub-expression on the updated oracle state. The oracle_upd function puts the new oracle into s and adds F to its *io_trace*.

$$\frac{\texttt{oracle\_get}\ s.\texttt{non\_det\_o} = (\texttt{F}, o')}{(\texttt{Add}\ e_1\ e_2,\ s) \rightarrow_{e} (\texttt{AddL}\ e_1\ e_2, \texttt{oracle\_upd}\ s\ (\texttt{F}, o'))}$$

Thus, the small-step semantics remains non-deterministic, and we can use the same approach as above. There are three significant differences. One, we look at the list of all I/O actions and non-determinism oracle results stored in *io_trace* instead of the return value. This is why we need to record the oracle results there. Two, our trace-building must account for the AddL and AddR expressions. Three, we must know that the *io_trace* is monotone with respect to stepping in the small-step semantics, and with respect to the clock in the functional big-step semantics. The only difficulty in this proof, over the deterministic one, was in handling the AddL and AddR forms, not in dealing with the oracle or trace.

To get an equivalent non-deterministic labelled transition system (LTS) with I/O actions as labels, one would prove the equivalence entirely in the small-step world with a simulation between the oracle small-step and the LTS semantics.

In the above, there was nothing special about the FOR language itself, and the same connection to small-step semantics could be proved for any situation where the big-step to small-step lemma above holds, along with other basic properties of the semantics. In fact, our proof for the FOR language is based on a general theorem that distills the essence of the approach. (We omit the details, which are obscured by the need to treat the two kinds of semantics abstractly).

8 Discussion and Related Work

Logical Foundations. All of our examples are carried out in classical higher-order logic of the kind supported by HOL4, HOL Light, Isabelle/HOL, etc. However, there is nothing inherently non-constructive about our techniques, and we expect that they would carry over to Coq. We rely on the ability to make definitions by well-founded recursion (usually on the combined structure of the terms, and a natural number index), derive the corresponding induction principles, and take lubs in the CPO of lazy lists. Occasionally, we make a non-constructive definition for convenience (e.g., of the top-level `semantics` in Sect. 2, whereas Sect. 4 has a constructive definition), our proofs do not rely on classical reasoning (other than in HOL4's implementation of the features mentioned above).

Testing Semantics. To test a semantics, one must actually use it to evaluate programs. Functional big-step semantics can do this out-of-the-box, as can many small-step approaches [13, 14]. Where semantics are defined in a relational big-step style, one needs to build an interpreter that corresponds to the relation and verify that they are equivalent – essentially, building a functional big-step semantics anyway. This construction and proof has been done by hand in several projects [6,7,22], and both Coq and Isabelle have mechanisms for automatically deriving functions from inductive relations, although under certain restrictions, and not for co-inductive relations [5,28].

Interpreters and Relational Big-step Semantics. The essence of the functional big-step approach is that the semantics are just an interpreter for the language, modified with a clock to make it admissible in higher-order logic. In this sense, we are just following Reynolds' idea of definitional interpreters [23], but using higher-order logic, rather than a programming language, as the meta-language. Using a clock to handle potential non-termination keeps the mathematics unsophisticated, and fits in well with the automation available in HOL4.

Other approaches are possible, such as Danielsson's use of a co-inductive partiality monad [11] to define functional big-step semantics. He defines a compiler from a lambda calculus with non-determinism to a stack-based virtual machine, and verifies it, including divergence preservation, in Agda. The compiler that we verify here targets a language with lower abstraction. A thorough comparison is difficult to make because the necessary mixed recursion/corecursion is not available in HOL.

Nakata and Uustalu [20] give a functional big-step semantics whose co-domain is (possibly infinite) traces of all states the program has passed through, rather than final results. Although their function is recursive, it relies on co-recursive helpers for sequencing and looping: in this way it looks less like a definitional interpreter. They prove equivalence between a variety of trace-based semantics, but do not use the semantics for compiler verification or type soundness. Our FOR language with I/O also keeps traces – although not of all of the program states passed through – but they are kept in the state, rather than in the function's result. Instead of using co-recursion, we take a least upper bound to build possibly infinite traces of I/O actions.

Several improvements have been made to traditional inductive relational big-step semantics. Leroy and Grall show how to use co-inductive definitions to give a semantics to a lambda-calculus and verify type soundness, and compiler correctness (for a compiler to a VM) while properly handling divergence [18].

Charguéraud's pretty-big-step semantics keeps the co-induction and removes some of the duplication by representing partial computations with new syntax and providing rules for completing the evaluation of the partially evaluated syntax [10]. For the FOR language, he introduces new syntax, `For1`, `For2`, and `For3`, that contain semantic contexts for partial evaluations. The evaluation rule for `For` has a hypothesis about evaluation of `For1`, which represents the state of evaluation after the first expression in `For` has been evaluated. Similarly, the semantics of `For1` is given semantics in terms of `For2`, and so forth. The pretty-big-step approach leads to many rules, but there are fewer than in a conventional big-step definitions, and the duplication is removed by factoring it out into rules that introduce `For1`, `For2`, and `For3`.

Bach Poulsen and Mosses show how to derive a (co-inductive) pretty-big-step semantics from a certain kind of small-step semantics (MSOS). This allows one to get the conciseness of a small-step definition and some of the reasoning benefits of a big-step style [3]. They further show that the duplication between the inductive and co-inductive rules can be reduced by encoding in the state whether the computation is trying to diverge or converge, under certain restrictions [4]. Their approach to encoding control-flow effects in the state could be applied in the functional big-step setting. From the point of view of writing an interpreter, this would correspond to using a state monad to encode an exception monad.

Nipkow and Klein use an inductive big-step semantics for a simple imperative language, along with a small-step semantics proved equivalent, and show how to verify a compiler for it [21]. The language cannot have run-time errors, so they do not have to use co-induction. (When they add a type system and possible runtime errors, they switch to small-step). However, their compiler correctness proof and big-step/small-step equivalence proofs each rely on two lemmas. The first assumes a converging big-step execution and builds a small-step trace (their target language has a small-step semantics), just like our corresponding proofs in Sects. 3.3 and 7. Their second assumes a small-step trace and shows that the big-step semantics converges to the right thing. With functional big-step semantics, we do not need this direction because we are in a deterministic setting and we correlate the trace length with clock in the first lemma. This is significant because the second lemma has the more difficult proof: any machine state encountered when running the compiled program must be related back to some source program.

Functional Big-step in CakeML. At the time of writing, the CakeML compiler has 12 intermediate languages (ILs), totaling $\approx 5,800$ lines. There are about $\approx 40,000$ lines of proof about them. The semantics of each IL is defined in the functional big-step style, with added support for I/O using the techniques from Sect. 4. The lowest-level ILs are assembly and machine-code-like languages. Their functional big-step semantics are formulated as tail-recursive functions.

9 Conclusion

We have shown how to take an easy to understand interpreter and use it as a formal semantics suitable for use in an interactive theorem prover. To make this possible we added clocks and oracles to the interpreter. Although our example FOR language is simple, it exhibits a wide range of programming language features including divergence, I/O, exceptions (`Break`), and stores. We have also shown how the functional big-step style can support functional language semantics with Core ML and call-by-value lambda calculus examples.

Acknowledgements. We thank Arthur Charguéraud for advice on Coq and pretty-big-step. The first author was supported by the EPSRC [EP/K040561/1]. The second author was partially supported by the Swedish Research Council. NICTA is funded by the Australian Government through the Department of Communications and the Australian Research Council through the ICT Centre of Excellence Program.

References

1. Ahmed, A.: Step-indexed syntactic logical relations for recursive and quantified types. In: Sestoft, P. (ed.) ESOP 2006. LNCS, vol. 3924, pp. 69–83. Springer, Heidelberg (2006). doi:10.1007/11693024_6
2. Appel, A.W., McAllester, D.A.: An indexed model of recursive types for foundational proof-carrying code. ACM Trans. Program. Lang. Syst. **23**(5), 657–683 (2001). doi:10.1145/504709.504712
3. Bach Poulsen, C., Mosses, P.D.: Deriving pretty-big-step semantics from small-step semantics. In: Shao, Z. (ed.) ESOP 2014 (ETAPS). LNCS, vol. 8410, pp. 270–289. Springer, Heidelberg (2014). doi:10.1007/978-3-642-54833-8_15
4. Poulsen, C.B., Mosses, P.D.: Divergence as state in coinductive big-step semantics (extended abstract). In: 26th Nordic Workshop on Programming Theory, NWPT 2014 (2014). http://www.plancomps.org/nwpt2014/
5. Berghofer, S., Bulwahn, L., Haftmann, F.: Turning inductive into equational specifications. In: Berghofer, S., Nipkow, T., Urban, C., Wenzel, M. (eds.) TPHOLs 2009. LNCS, vol. 5674, pp. 131–146. Springer, Heidelberg (2009). doi:10.1007/978-3-642-03359-9_11
6. Blazy, S., Leroy, X.: Mechanized semantics for the Clight subset of the C language. J. Autom. Reasoning **43**(3), 263–288 (2009). doi:10.1007/s10817-009-9148-3
7. Bodin, M., Charguéraud, A., Filaretti, D., Gardner, P., Maffeis, S., Naudziuniene, D., Schmitt, A., Smith, G.: A trusted mechanised JavaScript specification. In: The 41st Annual ACM SIGPLAN-SIGACT Symposium on Principles of Programming Languages, POPL 2014, pp. 87–100 (2014). doi:10.1145/2535838.2535876
8. Boyer, R., Moore, J.S.: Mechanized formal reasoning about programs and computing machines. In: Automated Reasoning and Its Applications: Essays in Honor of Larry Wos. MIT Press (1996)
9. Chambart, P.: High level OCaml optimisations (2013). https://ocaml.org/meetings/ocaml/2013/slides/chambart.pdf
10. Charguéraud, A.: Pretty-big-step semantics. In: Felleisen, M., Gardner, P. (eds.) ESOP 2013. LNCS, vol. 7792, pp. 41–60. Springer, Heidelberg (2013). doi:10.1007/978-3-642-37036-6_3
11. Danielsson, N.A.: Operational semantics using the partiality monad. In: ACM SIGPLAN International Conference on Functional Programming, ICFP 2012, pp. 127–138 (2012). doi:10.1145/2364527.2364546
12. Dreyer, D., Neis, G., Birkedal, L.: The impact of higher-order state and control effects on local relational reasoning. J. Funct. Program. **22**(4–5), 477–528 (2012). doi:10.1017/S095679681200024X
13. Ellison, C., Rosu, G.: An executable formal semantics of C with applications. In: Proceedings of the 39th ACM SIGPLAN-SIGACT Symposium on Principles of Programming Languages, POpPL 2012, pp. 533–544 (2012). doi:10.1145/2103656.2103719
14. Klein, C., Clements, J., Dimoulas, C., Eastlund, C., Felleisen, M., Flatt, M., McCarthy, J.A., Rafkind, J., Tobin-Hochstadt, S., Findler, R.B.: Run your research: on the effectiveness of lightweight mechanization. In: Proceedings of the 39th ACM SIGPLAN-SIGACT Symposium on Principles of Programming Languages, POpPL 2012, pp. 285–296 (2012). doi:10.1145/2103656.2103691
15. Kumar, R., Myreen, M.O., Norrish, M., Owens, S.: CakeML: a verified implementation of ML. In: Proceedings of the 41st ACM SIGPLAN-SIGACT Symposium on Principles of Programming Languages, POPL 2014, pp. 179–191. ACM Press (2014). doi:10.1145/2535838.2535841

16. Leroy, X.: Formal certification of a compiler back-end or: programming a compiler with a proof assistant. In: Proceedings of the 33rd ACM SIGPLAN-SIGACT Symposium on Principles of Programming Languages, POpPL 2006, pp. 42–54 (2006). doi:10.1145/1111037.1111042
17. Leroy, X.: A formally verified compiler back-end. J. Autom. Reasoning **43**(4), 363–446 (2009). doi:10.1007/s10817-009-9155-4
18. Leroy, X., Grall, H.: Coinductive big-step operational semantics. Inf. Comput. **207**(2), 284–304 (2009). doi:10.1016/j.ic.2007.12.004
19. Moore, J.S.: Symbolic simulation: an ACL2 approach. In: Gopalakrishnan, G.C., Windley, P. (eds.) FMCAD 1998. LNCS, vol. 1522, pp. 334–350. Springer, Heidelberg (1998). doi:10.1007/3-540-49519-3_22
20. Nakata, K., Uustalu, T.: Trace-based coinductive operational semantics for while. In: Berghofer, S., Nipkow, T., Urban, C., Wenzel, M. (eds.) TPHOLs 2009. LNCS, vol. 5674, pp. 375–390. Springer, Heidelberg (2009). doi:10.1007/978-3-642-03359-9_26
21. Nipkow, T., Klein, G.: With Isabelle/HOL. Springer, Heidelberg (2014). doi:10.1007/978-3-319-10542-0
22. Owens, S.: A sound semantics for OCaml light. In: Drossopoulou, S. (ed.) Programming Languages and Systems. Lecture Notes in Computer Science, vol. 4960, pp. 1–15. Springer, Heidelberg (2008). doi:10.1007/978-3-540-78739-6_1
23. Reynolds, J.C.: Definitional interpreters for higher-order programming languages. Higher-order and Symbolic Comput. **11**(4), 363–397 (1998). doi:10.1023/A:1010027404223
24. Rompf, T., Amin, N.: From F to DOT: type soundness proofs with definitional interpreters (2015). CoRR abs/1510.05216
25. Siek, J.: Big-step, diverging or stuck? (2012). http://siek.blogspot.com/2012/07/big-step-diverging-or-stuck.html
26. Siek, J.: Type safety in three easy lemmas (2013). http://siek.blogspot.com/2013/05/type-safety-in-three-easy-lemmas.html
27. Tofte, M.: Type inference for polymorphic references. Inf. Comput. **89**(1), 1–34 (1990). doi:10.1016/0890-5401(90)90018-D
28. Tollitte, P.-N., Delahaye, D., Dubois, C.: Producing certified functional code from inductive specifications. In: Hawblitzel, C., Miller, D. (eds.) CPP 2012. LNCS, vol. 7679, pp. 76–91. Springer, Heidelberg (2012). doi:10.1007/978-3-642-35308-6_9
29. Wright, A.K., Felleisen, M.: A syntactic approach to type soundness. Inf. Comput. **115**(1), 38–94 (1994). doi:10.1006/inco.1994.1093
30. Young, W.D.: A mechanically verified code generator. J. Autom. Reasoning **5**(4), 493–518 (1989). doi:10.1007/BF00243134

Classical By-Need

Pierre-Marie Pédrot(✉) and Alexis Saurin

Laboratoire PPS, CNRS, UMR 7126, Univ Paris Diderot, Sorbonne Paris Cité, PiR2, INRIA Paris Rocquencourt, 75205 Paris, France
pierre-marie.pedrot@inria.fr

Abstract. Call-by-need calculi are complex to design and reason with. When adding control effects, the very notion of canonicity is irremediably lost, the resulting calculi being necessarily ad hoc. This calls for a design of call-by-need guided by logical rather than operational considerations. Ariola et al. proposed such an extension of call-by-need with control making use of Curien and Herbelin's *duality of computation* framework.

In this paper, *Classical by-need* is developed as an alternative extension of call-by-need with control, better-suited for a programming-oriented reader.This method is proof-theoretically oriented by relying on linear head reduction (LHR) – an evaluation strategy coming from linear logic – and on the $\lambda\mu$-calculus – a classical extension of the λ-calculus.

More precisely, the paper contains three main contributions:

- LHR is first reformulated by introducing closure contexts and extended to the $\lambda\mu$-calculus;
- it is then shown how to derive a call-by-need calculus from LHR. The result is compared with standard call-by-need calculi, namely those of Ariola–Felleisen and Chang–Felleisen;
- it is finally shown how to lift the previous item to classical logic, that is from the λ-calculus to the $\lambda\mu$-calculus, providing a classical by-need calculus, that is a lazy $\lambda\mu$-calculus. The result is compared with the call-by-need with control of Ariola et al.

Keywords: Call-by-need · Classical logic · Control operators · Lambda-calculus · Lambda-mu-calculus · Lazy evaluation · Linear head reduction · Linear logic · Krivine abstract machine · Sigma equivalence

1 Introduction

In his survey on the origins of continuations, Reynolds noticed that *"in the early history of continuations, basic concepts were independently discovered an extraordinary number of times"* [28]. It is actually a well-known fact of the (long) history of science that deep, structuring ideas, are re-discovered several times. Computer science and modern proof theory have much shorter history but are no

A. Saurin—This work was partially supported by ANR Project RAPIDO, ANR-14-CE25-0007.

P. Thiemann (Ed.): ESOP 2016, LNCS 9632, pp. 616–643, 2016.
DOI: 10.1007/978-3-662-49498-1_24

exception. Very much related to the question of continuations, we may think of double-negation translations or, more recently, Girard and Reynolds' discoveries of, respectively, System F [17] and of the polymorphic λ-calculus [27].

We think that this convergence of structuring ideas and independent discoveries is at play, to some extent, with call-by-need evaluation and linear head reduction: while the first is operationally motivated, the latter comes from the structure of linear logic proofs. This paper aims at demonstrating this and applying this in incorporating first-class control in call-by-need.

Computation on Demand. Executing computations which may not be used to produce a value may obviously lead to unnecessary work being done, potentially resulting in non-termination even when a value exists. An alternative is to fire a redex only when it happens to be necessary to pursue the evaluation towards a value.

For instance, it is well-known that while call-by-value may trigger computations that could be completely avoided, resulting in potential non-termination, call-by-name evaluates programs on demand. This is exemplified in:

$$t \equiv (\lambda x.\, I)\ (\Delta\ \Delta) \rightarrow_{\text{cbn}} I$$
$$t \equiv (\lambda x.\, I)\ (\Delta\ \Delta) \rightarrow_{\text{cbv}} t \rightarrow_{\text{cbv}} \ldots \rightarrow_{\text{cbv}} \ldots$$

In this example[1], call-by-value reduction will reduce $\Delta\ \Delta$ again and again when the redex is of no use for reaching a value while call-by-name simply discards the argument.

Call-by-name, and more precisely (weak) head reduction thus realizes a form of demand-driven computation: a redex is fired only if it contributes to the (weak) head normal form (usually abbreviated as (w)hnf).

On the other hand, call-by-value will happen to be more parsimonious when it comes to arguments which are actually used in the computation: they are evaluated only once, before substituting the value, while call-by-name discipline will redo the same computation several times, as in:

$$u \equiv \Delta\ (I\ I) \rightarrow_{\text{cbn}} I\ I\ (I\ I) \rightarrow_{\text{cbn}} I\ (I\ I) \rightarrow_{\text{cbn}} I\ I \rightarrow_{\text{cbn}} I$$
$$u \equiv \Delta\ (I\ I) \rightarrow_{\text{cbv}} \Delta\ I \rightarrow_{\text{cbv}} I\ I \rightarrow_{\text{cbv}} I$$

In the above example, call-by-name reduction duplicates the computation of $I\ I$ while call-by-value only duplicates value I, resulting in a shorter reduction path to value.

Interestingly, demand-driven computation resulted in two lines of work, one motivated by theoretical purposes and rooted in logic, Danos and Regnier's linear head reduction, the other being motivated by more practical concerns and resulting in the study of lazy evaluation strategies for functional languages.

---

[1] As is usual, Δ stands for $\lambda x.\, x\ x$, I for $\lambda y.\, y$ and we write $\rightarrow_{\text{cbn}}$ (resp. $\rightarrow_{\text{cbv}}$) the reductions associated with call-by-name (resp. by value). The redex which is involved in a reduction is emphasized by showing it in a grey box. We will be implicitly working up to α-conversion, and we will use Barendregt's conventions not to capture variables unwillingly.

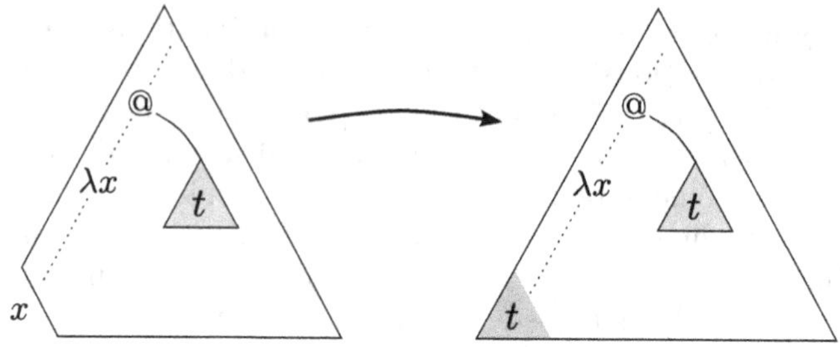

Fig. 1. Linear head reduction

Linear Head Reduction. Linear head reduction (referred as LHR) was first described by Regnier [25] in his 1992 PhD thesis, albeit under the name of *spinal reduction*. It was then studied again by Danos and Regnier [14,15] following similar observations made amongst different computational paradigms, namely the Krivine abstract machine [20], proof-nets [18,25], and game semantics [19]. The crucial remark is that the core of these systems does not implement the usual head reduction as thought commonly, but rather uses some more parsimonious reduction, which they define under the name of linear head reduction, which realizes a stronger form of computation-on-demand than call-by-name: the argument of a function cannot be said to truly contribute to the result if it never reaches head position; if it does not, the corresponding redex may only contribute to the (w)hnf in a non-essential way; for instance by blocking other redexes as in $(\lambda x\, y.\, y)\; t\; u$. Linear head reduction makes this observation formal. LHR has two main features:

- first it reduces only the β-redex binding to the leftmost variable occurrence (therefore the "head" from its name) and
- secondly it substitutes for the argument only the head occurrence of the variable (therefore the "linear" from its name) without destroying the fired redex.

A third noticeable point is that linear head reduction is not truly a reduction since it does not reduce only redexes (at least not only β-redexes), but also sorts of "hidden β-redexes" that are true β-redexes only up to an equivalence on λ-terms induced by their encoding in proof nets, namely σ-equivalence (this point shall be made clear later on) (Fig. 1).

Lazy Evaluation. Wadsworth introduced lazy evaluation [30] as a way to overcome defects of both call-by-name and call-by-value evaluation recalled in the above paragraphs. Lazy evaluation, or Call-by-need, can be viewed as a strategy conciling the best of the by-value and by-name worlds in terms of reductions: a computation is triggered only when it is needed for the evaluation to progress and, in this case, it avoids redoing computations. The price to pay is that the by-need strategy is tricky to formulate and reason about. For instance, Wadsworth had to introduce a graph reduction in order to allow sharing of subterms,

Linear head reduction	Call-by-need λ-calculus
$\Delta\ (I\ I)$	$\Delta\ (I\ I)$
$\equiv\ (\lambda x.\, x\ x)\ ((\lambda y.\, y)\ I)$	$\equiv\ (\lambda x.\, x\ x)\ ((\lambda y.\, y)\ I)$
$\to_{lh}\ (\lambda x.\, (\lambda y_0.\, y_0)\ I\ x)\ ((\lambda y.\, y)\ I)$	$\to_{\textsc{Deref}}\ (\lambda x.\, x\ x)\ ((\lambda y.\, I)\ I)$
$\to_{lh}\ (\lambda x.\, (\lambda y_0\, z_0.\, z_0)\ I\ x)\ ((\lambda y.\, y)\ I)$ $(\star)$	$\to_{\textsc{Assoc}}\ (\lambda y.\, (\lambda x.\, x\ x)\ I)\ I$
$\to_{lh}\ (\lambda x.\, (\lambda y_0\, z_0.\, x)\ I\ x)\ ((\lambda y.\, y)\ I)$	$\to_{\textsc{Deref}}\ (\lambda y.\, (\lambda x.\, (\lambda z.\, z)\ x)\ I)\ I$
$\to_{lh}\ (\lambda x.\, (\lambda y_0\, z_0.\, (\lambda y_1.\, y_1)\ I)\ I\ x)\ ((\lambda y.\, y)\ I)$	$\to_{\textsc{Deref}}\ (\lambda y.\, (\lambda x.\, (\lambda z.\, z)\ I)\ I)\ I$
$\to_{lh}\ (\lambda x.\, (\lambda y_0\, z_0.\, (\lambda y_1.\, \boxed{\lambda z_1.\, z_1})\ I)\ I\ x)\ ((\lambda y.\, y)\ I)$	$\to_{\textsc{Deref}}\ (\lambda y.\, (\lambda x.\, (\lambda z.\, \boxed{\lambda z_1.\, z_1})\ I)\ I)\ I$

Fig. 2. Example of a linear head reduction and a reduction in Ariola-Felleisen calculus.

and the following developments on lazy evaluation essentially dealt with machines. The essence of call-by-need is summarized by Danvy et al. [16]:

Demand-driven computation & memoization of intermediate results

Designing a proper calculus for call-by-need remained open for about two decades, until the mid-nineties when, in 1994, two very similar solutions to this problem were simultaneously presented by Ariola and Felleisen on the one hand, and Maraist, Odersky and Wadler on the other [8,9,22].

Ariola and Felleisen's calculus can be presented as follows:

Definition 1. *AF-calculus is defined by the following syntax:*

$$\begin{array}{lll} \textit{Term} & t, u ::= x \mid \lambda x.\, t \mid t\ u \\ \textit{Value} & v \quad ::= \lambda x.\, t \\ \textit{Answer} & A \quad ::= v \mid (\lambda x.\, A)\ t \\ \textit{Evaluationcontext} & E \quad ::= [\cdot] \mid E\ t \mid (\lambda x.\, E)\ t \mid (\lambda x.\, E[x])\ E \end{array}$$

$$\begin{array}{lll} (\textsc{Deref}) & (\lambda x.\, E[x])\ v & \to (\lambda x.\, E[v])\ v \\ (\textsc{Lift}) & (\lambda x.\, A)\ t\ u & \to (\lambda x.\, A\ u)\ t \\ (\textsc{Assoc}) & (\lambda x.\, E[x])\ ((\lambda y.\, A)\ t) & \to (\lambda y.\, (\lambda x.\, E[x])\ A)\ t \end{array}$$

Intuitively, the above calculus shall be understood as follows:

- The lazy behaviour of the calculus is coded in the structure of contexts: term $E[x]$ evidences that variable x is in needed position in term $E[x]$.
- Rule Deref then gets the argument, in case it has already been computed and it has been detected as needed. In that case, the argument is substituted for one copy of the variable x, the one in needed position. As a consequence, the application is not erased and a single occurrence of the variable has been substituted. (E is a single-hole context.)
- Rules Lift and Assoc allow for the commutation of evaluation contexts in order for deref redexes to appear despite the persisting binders.

We gave an example of a reduction sequence in Ariola-Felleisen call-by-need λ-calculus in Fig. 2. In the last line we highlighted the term that would remain after applying the garbage-collection rule considered by Maraist et al. [22]. Even though this is not part of the calculus, this convention of garbage-collecting weakening redexes is used in the rest of the paper to ease the reading of values.

Comparison Between LHR and Call-by-Need. Figure 2 shows two reductions, on the left a LHR reduction and on the right a reduction in AF-calculus. There are striking common features:

- call-by-need can be seen as an optimization of both call-by-name and call-by-value while LHR can be seen as an optimization of head reduction;
- both rely on a linear, rather than destructive, substitution (at least in Ariola-Felleisen calculus presented above);
- more importantly, both share with call-by-name the same notion of convergence and the induced observational equivalences. Being observationally indistinguishable in the pure λ-calculus, they require instead side-effects to be told apart from call-by-name.

LHR made very scarce appearances in the literature for fifteen years, seemingly falling into oblivion except for the original authors. Yet, it made a surprise comeback by the beginning of the 2010's through a research line initiated by Accattoli and Kesner [4]. Their article describes the so-called structural λ-calculus, featuring explicit substitutions and at-distance reduction, taking once again inspiration from the computational behaviour of proof-nets and revamping the σ-equivalence relation in this framework. In their system, blocks of explicits substitutions are stuck where they were created and are considered transparent for all purposes but the rule of substitution of variables, contrasting sharply with the usual treatment of explicit substitutions. In practice, this is done by splitting β-reduction in multiplicative steps (corresponding to the creation of explicit substitutions) and exponential steps (corresponding to the effective substitution of a variable by some term). LHR naturally arises from the call-by-name flavour of the at-distance rules, and indeed the connection with the historical LHR is made explicit in many articles from the subsequent trend [2,4,6] and is furthemore used to obtain results ranging from computational complexity to factorization of rewriting theories of the λ-calculus [3,5].

While it took two decades for call-by-need to be equipped with a proper calculus, the way LHR is usually defined is intricate and inconvenient to work with. We actually view this fact, together with the observational indistinguishability, as one of the reasons for the almost complete nonexistence of LHR in literature until rediscovery by Accattoli and Kesner.

Towards a Logical and Classical "By-Need" Calculus. The connections between the two formalisms are striking and actually not the least contingent. Understanding the precise relationships between the two may be useful to build call-by-need on firm, logical grounds. While comparing the merits of various call-by-need calculi in order to evidence one such calculus as being more canonical than the other may be quite dubious[2], control we make call-by-name and call-by-need observational equivalences differ. In presence of first-class continuations, one can observe intensional behavior discriminating between call-by-name and call-by-need. Consider the term

let a = callcc (**fun** k ⇒ (true, **fun** x ⇒ throw k x)) **in**
let p = fst a **in**
let q = snd a **in**
if p **then** q (false, **fun** x ⇒ 0) **else** 99

In by-name, a is immediately substituted both in p and q, duplicating the callcc so that it reduces to 0. In by-need, a must be fully evaluated before being substituted, and the callcc is fired once. This forces the term to reduce to 99 instead. The impact of control is actually deeper: we can actually distinguish between several call-by-need calculi as evidenced by the second author in joint work with Ariola and Herbelin [10] about defining call-by-need extensions of $\overline{\lambda}\mu\tilde{\mu}$ which are sequent-style $\lambda\mu$-calculus [13].

In this context, it does make sense to wonder which calculus to pick and what observational impact these choices may have. We can summarize the aim of the present paper as integrating logically call-by-need and control operators. We take a different approach from that of Ariola *et al.* [10]: instead of starting from the sequent calculus which readily integrates control [13], we show how to transform systematically LHR into call-by-need and show that this derivation can be smoothly lifted to the case of the $\lambda\mu$-calculus.

Contributions and Organization of the Paper. The contributions of the present paper are threefold.

- First, we reformulate LHR by introducing *closure contexts* and extend LHR to the $\lambda\mu$-calculus in Sect. 2.
- Then, after recalling Ariola-Felleisen's call-by-need calculus, we show in Sect. 3 how to derive a call-by-need calculus from LHR in three simple steps:
  1. restriction to a weak LHR by specializing closure contexts in Sect. 3.1,
  2. then enforcing memoization of intermediate results (by restricting to value passing) in Sect. 3.2;
  3. and finally implementing some sharing (thanks to closure contexts) in Sect. 3.3.

  We validate our constructions by comparing the resulting calculus with well-known call-by-need calculi, namely Ariola and Felleisen's or Chang and Felleisen's call-by-need. This justifies the following motto:

Lazy = Demand-driven comp	+ Memoization	+ Sharing
(weak linear head reduction)	*(by value)*	*(closure sharing)*

- Third, we finally show in Sect. 4 how to lift the previous derivation to classical logic, that is from the λ-calculus to the $\lambda\mu$-calculus, synthesizing two classical

[2] For instance Maraist, Odersky and Wadler calculus differ in their 1998 journal version from the calculus introduced by Ariola and Felleisen, but in no essential way since both calculi share the same standard reductions.

by-need calculi, that is a call-by-need $\lambda\mu$-calculus, from classical LHR. The result is compared with Ariola et al. call-by-need with control.

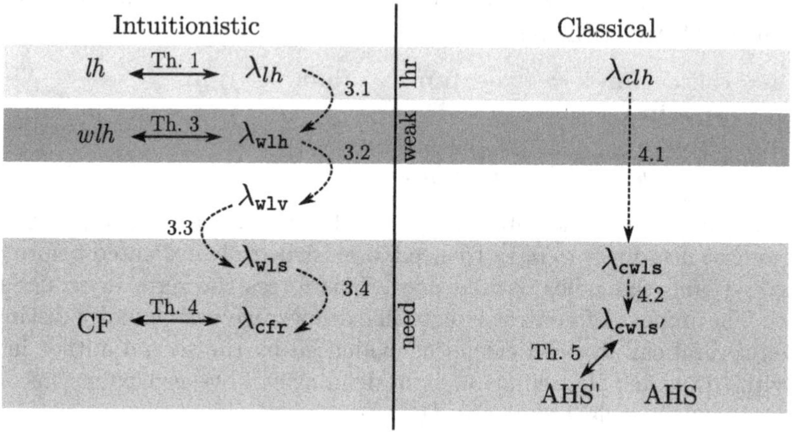

The whole picture is summarized in the above diagram. Plain arrows indicate some form of equivalence between two calculi with the corresponding theorem indicated. Dashed arrows indicate that a calculus is obtained from another by a small transformation, which is described in the section aside. Blocks indicate to which family of reduction a calculus pertains.

2 A Modern Linear Head Reduction

In the introduction, we informally introduced LHR. We now turn to the actual study of LHR, first recalling its historical presentation [15] and σ-equivalence and then giving a new formulation of the reduction based on *closure contexts*, that allows us to provide a classical variant seamlessly.

2.1 Historical Presentation of Linear Head Reduction

We first define Danos and Regnier's linear head reduction:

Definition 2. *The* **spine** *of a λ-term t is the set $\rceil\, t$ of left subterms of t, inductively defined as:*

$$\frac{}{t \in \rceil\, t} \qquad \frac{r \in \rceil\, t}{r \in \rceil\, (t)\, u} \qquad \frac{r \in \rceil\, t}{r \in \rceil\, \lambda x.\, t}$$

By construction, exactly one element of $\rceil\, t$ is a variable, written $\mathrm{hoc}\,(t)$*, for* ***head occurrence****; it is the leftmost variable of t.*

Definition 3 (Head lambdas, Prime redexes). *Let t be a λ-term. Head lambdas, $\lambda_h(t)$, and prime redexes, $p(t)$, of t are defined by induction on t:*

$$\lambda_h(x) \equiv \varepsilon \qquad\qquad p(x) \equiv \emptyset$$
$$\lambda_h(\lambda x.\, t) \equiv x{::}\lambda_h(t) \qquad\qquad p(\lambda x.\, t) \equiv p(t)$$
$$\lambda_h(t\ u) \equiv \begin{cases} \varepsilon \text{ if } \lambda_h(t) = \varepsilon \\ \ell \text{ if } \lambda_h(t) = x{::}\ell \end{cases} \qquad p(t\ u) \equiv \begin{cases} p(t) & \text{if } \lambda_h(t) = \varepsilon \\ p(t) \cup \{x \leftarrow u\} & \text{if } \lambda_h(t) = x{::}\ell \end{cases}$$

Remark 1. To understand head lambdas and prime redexes, it is convenient to consider blocks applications. We have indeed the following equalities:

$$\lambda_h((\lambda x.\, t)\, u\, \boldsymbol{r}) = \lambda_h((t)\, \boldsymbol{r}) \qquad\qquad p((\lambda x.\, t)\, u\, \boldsymbol{r}) = \{x \leftarrow u\} \cup p((t)\, \boldsymbol{r})$$

Head lambdas are precisely lambdas from the spine which will not be fed with arguments during head reduction. Now that we are equipped with the above notions, we can now formally define the linear head reduction:

Definition 4 (Linear head reduction). *Let u be a λ-term, let $x :=$ hoc$\,(u)$. We say that u linear-head reduces to r, written $u \rightarrow_{lh} r$, when:*

1. *there exists some term t s.t. $\{x \leftarrow t\} \in p(u)$;*
2. *r is u where the variable occurrence* hoc$\,(u)$ *has been substituted by t.*

Remark 2. Linear head reduction only substitutes one occurrence of a variable at a time and never destroys an application node. Likewise, it does not decrease the number of prime redexes. Thus terms keep growing, hence the name "linear" taken for linear *substitution.* An example of linear head reduction is given in Fig. 2 where prime redexes are shown in grey boxes.

2.2 Reduction Up to σ-equivalence

It is noteworthy that LHR reduces terms which are not yet redexes for β_h, i.e. lh may get the argument of a binder even if it is not directly applied to it. The third reduction ($\star$) of the example from Fig. 2 features such a cross-redex reduction. In this reduction, the λy_0 binder steps across the prime redex $\{z_0 \leftarrow x\}$ in order to recover its argument x. This kind of reduction would not have been allowed by the usual head reduction β_h. This peculiar behaviour can be made more formal thanks to a rewriting up to equivalence, also introduced by Regnier [25,26].

Definition 5 (σ-equivalence). *σ-equivalence is the reflexive, symmetric and transitive closure of the binary relation on λ-terms generated by:*

$$(\lambda x.\, t)\ u\ v \cong_\sigma (\lambda x.\, t\ v)\ u \qquad \textit{with } x \textit{ fresh for } v$$
$$(\lambda x\, y.\, t)\ u \cong_\sigma \lambda y.\, (\lambda x.\, t)\ u \qquad \textit{with } y \textit{ fresh for } u$$

Intuitively, σ-equivalence allows reduction in a term where it would have been forbidden by other essentially transparent redexes.

Proposition 1. *If $t \cong_\sigma u$, then $p(t) = p(u)$.*

Proof. By case analysis on the rules of σ-equivalence.

The following proposition highlights the strong kinship relating LHR and σ-equivalence. Let us recall that a left context L is inductively defined by the following grammar:

$$L := [\cdot] \mid Lt \mid \lambda x.\, L$$

Proposition 2. *If $t \rightarrow_{lh} r$ then there exist two left contexts L_1, L_2 such that*

$$t \cong_\sigma L_1[(\lambda x.\, L_2[x])\ u] \text{ and } r \cong_\sigma L_1[(\lambda x.\, L_2[u])\ u]$$

Proof. By induction on $p(t)$. Existence of L_1 follows from p being inductively defined over a left context, that of L_2 from the fact that the hoc is the leftmost variable.

The previous result can be slightly refined. The $\cong_\sigma$ relation is reversible, so that we can rebuild r by applying to $L_1[(\lambda x.\, L_2[u])\ u]$ the reverse σ-equivalence steps from the rewriting from t to $L_1[(\lambda x.\, L_2[x])\ u]$. We will not detail this operation here but rather move to the definition of closure contexts.

2.3 Closure Contexts and the λ_{lh}-calculus

With the aim to give a first-class status to the reduction up to σ-equivalence of Proposition 2, we introduce *closure contexts*, which will allow to reformulate linear head reduction.

Definition 6 (Closure contexts). *Closure contexts are inductively defined as:*

$$\mathcal{C} := [\cdot] \mid \mathcal{C}_1[\lambda x.\, \mathcal{C}_2]\ t$$

Closure contexts feature all the required properties that provide them with a nice algebraic behaviour, that is, composability and factorization. Composition of contexts, $E_1[E_2]$, will be written $E_1 \circ E_2$ in the following.

Proposition 3 (Composition). *Let $\mathcal{C}_1$, $\mathcal{C}_2$ be closure contexts. $\mathcal{C}_1 \circ \mathcal{C}_2$ is a closure context.*

Proposition 4 (Factorization). *Any term t can be uniquely decomposed as a maximal closure context, in the usual meaning of composition, and a subterm t_0.*

Actually, we get even more: closure contexts precisely capture the notion of prime redex as asserted by the following proposition.

Proposition 5. *Let t be a term. Then $\{x \leftarrow u\} \in p(t)$ if and only if there exist a left context L, a closure context $\mathcal{C}$ and a term t_0 such that $t = L[\mathcal{C}[\lambda x.\, t_0]\ u]$.*

Proof. By induction on $p(t)$. The proof goes same way as for Proposition 2, except that we make explicit the context $\mathcal{C}$ instead of writing it as a σ-equivalence.

Closures	$c ::= (t, \sigma)$	Push	$\langle (t\,u, \sigma) \mid \pi \rangle$	$\rightarrow \langle (t, \sigma) \mid (u, \sigma) \cdot \pi \rangle$
Environments	$\sigma ::= \emptyset \mid \sigma + (x := c)$	Pop	$\langle (\lambda x.\, t, \sigma) \mid c \cdot \pi \rangle$	$\rightarrow \langle (t, \sigma + (x := c)) \mid \pi \rangle$
Stacks	$\pi ::= \varepsilon \mid c \cdot \pi$	Grab	$\langle (x, \sigma + (x := c)) \mid \pi \rangle$	$\rightarrow \langle c \mid \pi \rangle$
Processes	$p ::= \langle c \mid \pi \rangle$	Garbage	$\langle (x, \sigma + (y := c)) \mid \pi \rangle$	$\rightarrow \langle (x, \sigma) \mid \pi \rangle$

Fig. 3. Krivine abstract machine

Owing to the fact that closure contexts capture prime redexes, we will provide an alternative and more conventional definition for the LHR. It will result in the λ_{lh}-calculus, based on contexts rather than ad-hoc variable manipulations.

Definition 7 **(λ_{lh}-calculus).** *The λ_{lh}-calculus is defined by the reduction rule:*

$$L_1[\mathcal{C}[\lambda x.\, L_2[x]]\ u] \rightarrow_{\lambda_{lh}} L_1[\mathcal{C}[\lambda x.\, L_2[u]]\ u]$$

where L_1, L_2 are left contexts, $\mathcal{C}$ is a closure context, t and u are λ-terms, with the usual freshness conditions to prevent variable capture in u.

Proposition 6 **(Stability of λ_{lh} under σ).** *Let t, u and v be terms such that $t \cong_\sigma u \rightarrow_{lh} v$, then there is w such that $t \rightarrow_{lh} w \cong_\sigma v$.*

Proof. By induction over the starting σ-equivalence, and case analysis of the possible interactions between contexts. For instance, if the λ-abstraction of the rule interacts with $\mathcal{C}$ through the second generator of the σ-equivalence, this amounts to transfer a fragment from $\mathcal{C}$ into L_2 which is transparent for the reduction rule. Similar interactions may appear at context boundaries or inside contexts.

Theorem 1. *The λ_{lh}-calculus captures the linear head reduction.*

$$t \rightarrow_{\lambda_{lh}} r \qquad \textit{iff} \qquad t \rightarrow_{lh} r.$$

Proof. Indeed, the x from the rule is precisely the hoc of the term since closure contexts are in particular left contexts, and because we are reducing up to closure contexts, Proposition 5 ensures that $\{x \leftarrow u\}$ is a prime redex.

2.4 Closure Contexts and the KAM: A Strong Relationship

Remarkably enough, closure contexts are not totally coming out of the blue. They are indeed already present in Chang-Felleisen call-by-need calculus [12], even if their intrinsic interest, their properties as well as the natural notion of LHR stemming from them were not made explicit. Maybe the main contribution of our work is to put them at work as a design principle.

Closure contexts are morally transparent for some well-behaved head reduction: one can consider that $(\mathcal{C}[\lambda x.\, [\cdot]])\, t$ is a context that only adds a binding $(x := t)$ to the environment, as well as the bindings contained in $\mathcal{C}$. This intuition can be made formal thanks to the Krivine abstract machine (KAM), recalled in Fig. 3. As stated by the following result, transitions Push and Pop of the KAM implement the computation of closure contexts.

Proposition 7. *Let t be a term, σ an environment, π a stack and $\mathcal{C}$ a closure context. We have the following reduction*

$$\langle(\mathcal{C}[t], \sigma) \mid \pi\rangle \longrightarrow^{*}_{\text{PUSH},\text{POP}} \langle(t, \sigma + [\mathcal{C}]_{\sigma}) \mid \pi\rangle$$

where $[\mathcal{C}]_{\sigma}$ is defined by induction over $\mathcal{C}$ as follows:

$$[[\cdot]]_{\sigma} \equiv \emptyset \quad [\mathcal{C}_1[\lambda x.\,\mathcal{C}_2]\ t]_{\sigma} \equiv [\mathcal{C}_1]_{\sigma} + (x := (t, \sigma)) + [\mathcal{C}_2]_{\sigma+[\mathcal{C}_1]_{\sigma}+(x:=(t,\sigma))}$$

Conversely, for all t_0 and σ_0 such that

$$\langle(t, \sigma) \mid \pi\rangle \longrightarrow^{*}_{\text{PUSH},\text{POP}} \langle(t_0, \sigma_0) \mid \pi\rangle$$

there exists $\mathcal{C}_0$ such that $t = \mathcal{C}_0[t_0]$, where $\mathcal{C}_0$ is inductively defined over σ_0.

Proof. The first property is given by a direct induction on $\mathcal{C}$, while the second is done by induction on the KAM reduction.

Actually, the KAM can even be seen as an implementation of a (weak) LHR rather than the (weak) head reduction. Indeed, the substitution is delayed in practice until a variable appears in head position, i.e. when it is the hoc of a term. Such a phenomenon was formalized by Danos and Regnier [15] who proved that the sequence of substitutions from the LHR and the sequence of closures substituted by the GRAB rule are the same.

2.5 Classical Linear Head Reduction

Thanks to the intuition provided by the closure contexts, we propose here a classical variant of the linear head calculus, presented in the $\lambda\mu$-calculus [24]. The additional binder μ quantifies over a special class of variable called *stack* variables. It allows to capture and reinstate the stack at will. Expressions of the form $[\alpha]\,t$ are called *processes* or *commands*. We recall the syntax and (call-by-name) reduction below.

$$t, u ::= x \mid \lambda x.\,t \mid t\ u \mid \mu\alpha.\,c$$

$$c ::= [\beta]\,t$$

$$\begin{array}{lcr} (\lambda x.\,t)\ u & \rightarrow & t\{x := u\} \\ (\mu\alpha.\,c)\ u & \rightarrow & \mu\alpha.\,c\{[\alpha]\,r := [\alpha]\,r\ u\} \\ [\alpha]\,\mu\beta.\,c & \rightarrow & c\{\beta := \alpha\} \end{array}$$

We will only be interested in the reduction of commands in the remainder of this section. Our calculus is a direct elaboration of the aforementioned linear head calculus, and we dedicate this section to its thorough description.

Definition 8 (Classical LHR). *We define left stack contexts K by induction, and then a classical extension of left contexts and closure contexts as follows.*

$$\begin{array}{llll} \sigma ::= \cdots \mid \sigma + (\alpha := \pi) & \textsc{Save} & \langle(\mu\alpha.c, \sigma) \mid \pi\rangle & \to \langle(c, \sigma + (\alpha := \pi)) \mid \varepsilon\rangle \\ \pi ::= \cdots \mid (\alpha, \sigma) & \textsc{Restore} & \langle([\alpha]t, \sigma) \mid \varepsilon\rangle & \to \langle(t, \sigma) \mid \sigma(\alpha)\rangle \end{array}$$

Fig. 4. μ-KAM

$$\begin{aligned} K &::= [\cdot] \mid [\alpha]\, L[\mu\beta.\, K] \\ \mathcal{C} &::= [\cdot] \mid \mathcal{C}_1[\lambda x.\, \mathcal{C}_2]\ t \mid \mathcal{C}_1[\mu\alpha.\, K[[\alpha]\, \mathcal{C}_2]] \\ L &::= [\cdot] \mid \lambda x.\, L \mid L\ t \mid \mu\beta.\, [\alpha]\, L \end{aligned}$$

The classical linear head calculus is then defined by the following reduction.

$$[\alpha]\, L_1[\mathcal{C}[\lambda x.\, L_2[x]]\ t] \to_{\lambda_{clh}} [\alpha]\, L_1[\mathcal{C}[\lambda x.\, L_2[t]]\ t]$$

We then adapt the σ-equivalence to the classical setting following Laurent [21].

Definition 9 (Classical σ-equivalence). *The σ-equivalence is extended to the $\lambda\mu$-calculus with the following generators.*

$$\begin{array}{rll} (\lambda x.\, \mu\alpha.\, [\beta]\, t)\ u \cong_\sigma \mu\alpha.\, [\beta]\, (\lambda x.\, t)\ u & & \text{with } \alpha \notin u \\ [\alpha]\, (\mu\beta.\, [\gamma]\, (\mu\delta.\, c)\ u)\ t \cong_\sigma [\gamma]\, (\mu\delta.\, [\alpha]\, (\mu\beta.\, c)\ t)\ u & & \text{with } \beta \notin u,\ \delta \notin t \\ [\alpha]\, \lambda x.\, \mu\beta.\, [\gamma]\, \lambda y.\, \mu\delta.\, c \cong_\sigma [\gamma]\, \lambda y.\, \mu\delta.\, [\alpha]\, \lambda x.\, \mu\beta.\, c & & \\ [\alpha]\, (\mu\beta.\, [\gamma]\, \lambda x.\, \mu\delta.\, c)\ t \cong_\sigma [\gamma]\, \lambda x.\, \mu\delta.\, [\alpha]\, (\mu\beta.\, c)\ t & & \text{with } x \notin t,\ \beta \notin t \end{array}$$

Proposition 8 (Stability under σ). *Let t, u and v be terms such that $t \cong_\sigma u \to_{\lambda_{clh}} v$, then there is w such that $t \to_{\lambda_{clh}} w \cong_\sigma v$.*

We now relate the classical LHR calculus with the classical extension to KAM [21,29] given in Fig. 4 where only the modifications with respect to Fig. 3 are shown.

Danos and Regnier obtain a simulation theorem relating the KAM with LHR by defining substitution sequences [15]. This can be lifted to the $\lambda\mu$-calculus: there is a simulation theorem relating the μ-KAM with the classical LHR. In order to state Theorem 2 which concludes this section, one first needs to introduce some preliminary definitions which are motivated by the following remark.

Remark 3. The λ_{clh} reduction rule is actually abusive. Recall that in its definition, t can be any term. This means that to ensure later capture-free substitution by preserving the Barendregt condition on terms, one has to rename the variables of t on the fly, so that the legitimate rule would rather be

$$[\alpha]\, L_1[\mathcal{C}[\lambda x.\, L_2[x]]\ t] \to_{\lambda_{clh}} [\alpha]\, L_1[\mathcal{C}[\lambda x.\, L_2[\#t]]\ t]$$

where $\#t$ stands for t where bound variables have been replaced by fresh variable instances.

We need to define properly the relation between the original and the substituted terms in the above rule.

Definition 10 (One-step residual). *In the above rule, we say that t is the residual of $\#t$ in the source term.*

It turns out that this definition can be extended to a reduction of arbitrary length thanks to the following lemma.

Proposition 9. *For any reduction of the form*

$$[\alpha]\, t \rightarrow_{\lambda_{clh}}{}^{*} [\alpha]\, L_1[\mathcal{C}[\lambda x.\, L_2[x]]\ r_0] \rightarrow_{\lambda_{clh}} [\alpha]\, L_1[\mathcal{C}[\lambda x.\, L_2[\#r_0]]\ r_0]$$

there exists a subterm r of t such that $r_0 \equiv \#r$, the residual *of r_0 in t.*

Proof. By induction on the reduction. The key point is that all along the reduction, all terms on the right of an application node are subterms of the original term, up to some variable renaming. The original subterm can then be traced back by jumping up into the term being substituted at each step.

Definition 11 (Substitution sequence). *Given two terms t and t_0 s.t. $t_0 \rightarrow^{*}_{\lambda_{clh}} t$, we define the substitution sequence of t w.r.t. t_0 as the (possibly infinite) sequence $\mathfrak{S}_{t_0}(t)$ of subterms of t_0 defined as follows, where α is a fresh stack variable.*

- *If $[\alpha]\, t \not\rightarrow_{\lambda_{clh}}$ then $\mathfrak{S}_{t_0}(t) ::= \emptyset$.*
- *If $[\alpha]\, t \equiv [\alpha]\, L_1[\mathcal{C}[\lambda x.\, L_2[x]]\ r] \rightarrow_{\lambda_{clh}} [\alpha]\, t'$ then $\mathfrak{S}_{t_0}(t) ::= r_0 :: \mathfrak{S}_{t_0}(t')$ where r_0 is the residual of r in t_0.*

We finally pose $\mathfrak{S}(t) ::= \mathfrak{S}_t(t)$.

The μ-KAM naturally features a similar behaviour w.r.t. residuals.

Proposition 10. *If $\langle (t, \cdot) \mid \varepsilon \rangle \rightarrow^{*} \langle (t_0, \sigma) \mid \pi \rangle$ then t_0 is a subterm of t.*

Proof. By a straightforward induction over the reduction path.

This proposition can (and actually needs to) be generalized to any source process whose stacks and closures only contain subterms of t. This leads to the definition of a similar notion of substitution sequence for the KAM.

Definition 12 (KAM substitution sequence). *For any term t, we define the KAM substitution sequence of a process p as the possibly infinite sequence of terms $\mathfrak{K}(p)$ defined as:*

- *If $p \not\rightarrow$ then $\mathfrak{K}(p) ::= \emptyset$.*
- *If $p \equiv \langle (x, \sigma) \mid \pi \rangle \rightarrow \langle (t, \tau) \mid \pi \rangle$ then $\mathfrak{K}(p) ::= t :: \mathfrak{K}(\langle (t, \tau) \mid \pi \rangle)$.*
- *Otherwise if $p \rightarrow q$ then $\mathfrak{K}(p) ::= \mathfrak{K}(q)$.*

Finally, the KAM substitution sequence of any term t is defined as $\mathfrak{K}(t) ::= \mathfrak{K}(\langle (t, \cdot) \mid \varepsilon \rangle)$.

By the previous lemma, $\mathfrak{K}(t)$ is a sequence of subterms of t. We can therefore formally relate it to $\mathfrak{S}(t)$.

Proposition 11. *Let t be a term. Then $\mathfrak{K}(t)$ is a prefix of $\mathfrak{S}(t)$.*

Proof. By coinduction, for each step of $\mathfrak{S}(t)$, it is sufficient either to construct a matching step in $\mathfrak{K}(t)$ or to stop. Let us assume that

$$[\alpha]\, t \equiv [\alpha]\, L_1[\mathcal{C}[\lambda x.\, L_2[x]]\ r_0] \to_{\lambda_{clh}} [\alpha]\, L_1[\mathcal{C}[\lambda x.\, L_2[\#\, r_0]]\ r_0] \equiv [\alpha]\, t_r$$

There are now two cases, depending on the KAM reduction of $\mathfrak{K}(\langle (t, \cdot) \mid \varepsilon \rangle)$. By a simple generalization of Lemma 7, the normal form of this process in the GRAB-free fragment of the KAM rules can be one of the two following form:

- either $\langle (x, \sigma + (x := (r_0, \tau)) \mid \pi \rangle$ for some σ, τ and π
- or a blocked state of the KAM for all rules

The second case can occur if there are too many λ-abstractions in the left contexts of the above reduction rule or if there is an free stack variable appearing in a command part of the left contexts. In this case $\mathfrak{K}(t) = \emptyset$, which is indeed a prefix of $\mathfrak{S}(t)$.

Otherwise, one has $\mathfrak{K}(t) = r_0 :: \mathfrak{K}(\langle (r_0, \tau) \mid \pi \rangle)$ and $\mathfrak{S}(t) = r_0 :: \mathfrak{S}_t(t_r)$. It it therefore sufficient to show that the property holds for the tail of those two sequences.

It is a noteworthy fact that, when we put t_r in the KAM, we obtain a reduction of the form

$$\langle (t_r, \cdot) \mid \varepsilon \rangle \to^* \langle (\#\, r_0, \sigma + (x := (r_0, \tau)) + \sigma_0) \mid \pi \rangle$$

for some σ_0, where the GRAB rule does not appear. This reduction follows indeed the very same transitions as the process made of the source term. Moreover, a careful inductive analysis of the possible transitions shows that $\sigma = \tau + \sigma_1$ for some σ_1, where the variables bound by σ_1 are not free in $\#\, r_0$. Therefore,

$$\mathfrak{K}(t_r) = \mathfrak{K}(\langle (\#\, r_0, \sigma + (x := (r_0, \tau)) + \sigma_0) \mid \pi \rangle) = \mathfrak{K}(\langle (\#\, r_0, \tau) \mid \pi \rangle)$$

because the KAM reduction is not affected by extension of closure environements with variables absent from the closure term. By applying the coinduction hypothesis, we immediatly obtain than $\mathfrak{K}(t_r)$ is a prefix of $\mathfrak{S}(t_r)$.

But now, we can conclude, because $\mathfrak{K}(\langle (\#\, r_0, \tau) \mid \pi \rangle)$ and $\mathfrak{K}(\langle (r_0, \tau) \mid \pi \rangle)$ (resp. $\mathfrak{S}(t_r)$ and $\mathfrak{S}_t(t_r)$) are the same sequence up to a renaming of the bound variables coming from $\#\, r_0$ which is common to both kinds of reduction. Thus $\mathfrak{K}(\langle (r_0, \tau) \mid \pi \rangle)$ is a prefix of $\mathfrak{S}_t(t_r)$ and we are done.

The following theorem is a direct corollary of Proposition 11.

Theorem 2. *Let $c_1 \to_{\lambda_{clh}} c_2$ where $c_1 := [\alpha]\, L_1[\mathcal{C}[\lambda x.\, L_2[x]]\ t]$, then the substitution sequence of process c_1 is either empty or of the form $t{::}\ell$ where ℓ is the substitution sequence of process c_2.*

Proposition 8 and Theorem 2 validate our calculus as a sound classical extension of LHR.

3 Towards Call-by-Need

Our journey from LHR to call-by-need will now follow three steps: first restricting LHR to a weak reduction, imposing a value-restriction and finally adding an amount of sharing.

3.1 Weak Linear Head Reduction

The LHR as given at paragraph 2.3 is a *strong* reduction: it reduces under abstractions. We now adapt λ_{lh}-calculus to the weak case. It is easy to give a weak version of the reduction in the historical LHR, which inherits the same defects as its strong counterpart.

Definition 13 *(Historical wlh-reduction). We say that t weak-linear-head reduces to r, written $t \rightarrow_{wlh} r$, iff $t \rightarrow_{lh} r$ and t does not have any head λ.*

On the other hand, the λ_{lh} reduction can be denied the possibility to reduce under abstractions by restricting the evaluation contexts inside which it can be triggered. This requires some care though. Indeed, the contexts may contain λ-abstractions, assuming they have been compensated by as many previous applications. That is, those binders must pertain to a prime redex as in $(\lambda z_1 \ldots z_n\, x.\, E^w[x])\; r_1 \ldots r_n\; u$. Plain closure contexts are not expressive enough to capture this situation.

To solve this issue, we extend the λ-calculus in a way which is inspired both by techniques used for studying reductions, residuals and developments in λ-calculus [11] and by $\lambda\mathtt{let}$-calculi [8] or explicit substitutions [1], and in particular the structural λ-calculus [4]. We are indeed going to recognize when a prime redex has been created by marking them explicitly. Yet, contrarily to standard λ-calculus rewriting theory, we will mark *lambdas* which are not necessarily actually involved in β-redexes and contrarily to $\lambda\mathtt{let}$-calculi or the structural λ-calculus, we will preserve the underlying structure of the λ-term by only marking abstractions rather than creating `let`-bindings and making them transparent for all rules. We shall discuss the significance of this design choice in Sect. 3.5.

Definition 14 (Marked λ-calculus). *The marked λ-calculus is thus inductively defined as*

$$t ::= x \mid \lambda x.\, t \mid t\; u \mid \ell x.\, t$$

where $\ell x.\, t$ is a marked version of $\lambda x.\, t$. For any marked λ-term t, we will write $[t]$ for the usual λ-term obtained from t by unmarking all abstractions. Likewise, σ-equivalence is adapted in a straightforward fashion.

We have to update the definition of closure contexts to fit into this presentation. It is actually enough to restrict all abstractions appearing inside a closure context to marked abstractions.

Definition 15 (Closure contexts). *From now on, closure contexts $\mathcal{C}$ will be defined by the inductive grammar below.*

$$\mathcal{C} ::= [\cdot] \mid \mathcal{C}_1[\ell x.\, \mathcal{C}_2]\; t$$

In general, arbitrary marked terms do not make sense, because marked abstractions may not have a matching application. This is why we define a notion of well-formed marked terms.

Definition 16 (Well-formed marked terms). *A marked term t is well-formed whenever for any decomposition $t \equiv E[\ell x.\, u]$ where E is an arbitrary context, E can be further decomposed as $E \equiv E_0[\mathcal{C}\ r]$ where E_0 is an arbitrary context, $\mathcal{C}$ a marked closure context and r a marked term.*

In the rest of the paper, we will only work with *well-formed* marked terms even when this remains implicit: all our constructions and reductions will preserve well-formedness as in the following definition:

Definition 17 ($\lambda_{\texttt{wlh}}$-calculus). *The weak linear head calculus $\lambda_{\texttt{wlh}}$ is defined by the rules:*

$$\begin{aligned} \mathcal{C}[\lambda x.\, t]\ u \quad &\rightarrow_{\lambda_{\texttt{wlh}}} \mathcal{C}[\ell x.\, t]\ u \\ \mathcal{C}[\ell x.\, E^w[x]]\ u &\rightarrow_{\lambda_{\texttt{wlh}}} \mathcal{C}[\ell x.\, E^w[u]]\ u \end{aligned}$$

together with compatibility with E^w contexts, inductively defined as follows.

$$E^w ::= [\cdot] \mid E^w\ t \mid \ell x.\, E^w.$$

Proposition 12 (Stability of λ_{wlh} by σ). *Let t, u and v be terms such that $t \cong_\sigma u \rightarrow_{\lambda_{wlh}} v$, then there is w such that $t \rightarrow_{\lambda_{wlh}} w \cong_\sigma v$.*

This property is proved similarly to Proposition 6. We can now prove that λ_{wlh} and the historical *wlh*-reduction coincide:

Theorem 3. *$t \rightarrow_{\lambda_{wlh}} r$ iff $t \rightarrow_{wlh} r$.*

Proof. They correspond since not having a head lambda is exactly equivalent to having all its subcontexts starting with an abstraction marked.

3.2 Call-by-"Value" Linear Head Reduction

In order to obtain a call-by-value LHR, we will restrict contexts that trigger substitutions to react only in front of a value. In addition, the up-to-closure paradigm used so far will also incite us to consider values up to closures defined as $W ::= \mathcal{C}[V]$ when $V ::= \lambda x.\, t$ stands for values.

Going from the usual call-by-name to the usual call-by-value is then simply a matter of adding a context forcing values. Likewise, we just add a context forcing up-to values. This construction is made in a systematic way according to the standard call-by-value encoding.

Definition 18 (Call-by-value contexts). *We define the call-by-value contexts inductively as follows.*

$$E^v ::= [\cdot] \mid E^v\ t \mid \ell x.\, E^v \mid \mathcal{C}[\ell x.\, E_1^v[x]]\ E_2^v$$

The call-by-value weak linear head reduction is obtained straightforwardly.

Definition 19 ($\lambda_{\mathtt{wlv}}$-calculus). *The $\lambda_{\mathtt{wlv}}$-calculus is the calculus defined by the E^v-compatible closure of following rules.*

$$\begin{array}{lll} \mathcal{C}[\lambda x.\,t]\ u & \rightarrow_{\lambda_{\mathtt{wlv}}} & \mathcal{C}[\ell x.\,t]\ u \\ \mathcal{C}[\ell x.\,E^v[x]]\ W & \rightarrow_{\lambda_{\mathtt{wlv}}} & \mathcal{C}[\ell x.\,E^v[W]]\ W \end{array}$$

It is easy to check that the reduction was not deeply modified, the difference lies in the clever choice of contexts. Stability by σ is proved as in Proposition 6.

Proposition 13 (Stability of $\lambda_{\mathtt{wlv}}$ by σ). *Let t, u and v be terms such that $t \cong_\sigma u \rightarrow_{\lambda_{\mathtt{wlv}}} v$, then there is w such that $t \rightarrow_{\lambda_{\mathtt{wlv}}} w \cong_\sigma v$.*

Although we branded this calculus as a call-by-value one, it already implements a call-by-need strategy since it triggers the reduction of an argument if and only if it was made necessary by the encounter of a corresponding variable in (call-by-value) hoc position. We give the reduction on our running example:

$$\begin{array}{rl} \Delta\ (I\ I) \ \equiv & (\lambda x.\,x\ x)\ ((\lambda y.\,y)\ I) \\ \rightarrow_{\mathtt{wlv}} & (\ell x.\,x\ x)\ ((\ell y.\,y)\ I) \\ \rightarrow_{\mathtt{wlv}} & (\ell x.\,x\ x)\ ((\ell y.\,y)\ I) \\ \rightarrow_{\mathtt{wlv}} & (\ell x.\,x\ x)\ ((\ell y.\,I)\ I) \\ \rightarrow_{\mathtt{wlv}} & (\ell x.\,(\ell y_1.\,\lambda z_1.\,z_1)\ I\ x)\ ((\ell y.\,I)\ I) \\ \rightarrow_{\mathtt{wlv}} & (\ell x.\,(\ell y_1\ z_1.\,z_1)\ I\ x)\ ((\ell y.\,I)\ I) \\ \rightarrow_{\mathtt{wlv}} & (\ell x.\,(\ell y_1\ z_1.\,z_1)\ I\ ((\ell y.\,I)\ I))\ ((\ell y.\,I)\ I) \\ \rightarrow_{\mathtt{wlv}} & (\ell x.\,(\ell y_1\ z_1.\,(\ell y_2.\,\boxed{I})\ I)\ I\ ((\ell y.\,I)\ I))\ ((\ell y.\,I)\ I) \end{array}$$

In the first transition, the reduction occurs in the argument required by x, returning a value (up to closure) that will then be substituted.

3.3 Closure Sharing

The $\lambda_{\mathtt{wlv}}$-calculus does not realize call-by-need reduction schemes from the literature [8]. The above example reveals a duplication of computation:

$$\mathcal{C}'[\ell x.\,E^v[x]]\ \mathcal{C}[v] \rightarrow_{\lambda_{\mathtt{wlv}}} \mathcal{C}'[\ell x.\,E^v[\mathcal{C}[v]]]\ \mathcal{C}[v]$$

In that case, $\mathcal{C}$ is copied, which will end up in recomputing its bound terms if ever they are going to be used throughout the reduction. While our running example $\Delta\ (I\ I)$ does not feature such a behaviour, this can instead be seen on $(\lambda x.\,x\ I\ x)\ (\lambda y\, z.\,y)\ (I\ I)$ because while $(\lambda y\, z.\,y)\ (I\ I)$ is already an up-to value, it also uses the argument $I\ I$ from its closure. During the substitution, this subterm is copied as-is, resulting in its recomputation at each call to x in the body of the abstraction.

It is possible to solve this issue in an elegant way akin to the Assoc rule of Ariola-Felleisen calculus. This is achieved by the extrusion of the closure of the value at the instant it is substituted. There is no need to refine contexts further, because everything is already in order. We obtain the calculus below:

$$
\begin{array}{lll}
\text{Values} & v & ::= \lambda x.\, t \\
\text{Answers} & a & ::= A[v] \\
\text{Answer contexts} & A & ::= [\cdot] \mid A_1[\lambda x.\, A_2]\, u \\
\text{Inner answer contexts} & A^{\lambda} & ::= [\cdot] \mid A[\lambda x.\, A^{\lambda}] \\
\text{Outer answer contexts} & A^{@} & ::= [\cdot] \mid A[A^{@}]\, u \\
\text{Contexts} & E & ::= [\cdot] \mid E\, u \mid A[E] \\
 & & \quad \mid A^{@}[A[\lambda x.\, A^{\lambda}[E[x]]]\, E] \\
 & & \quad \text{where } A^{@}[A^{\lambda}] \in A
\end{array}
$$

$$
A^{@}[A_1[\lambda x.\, A^{\lambda}[E[x]]]\, A_2[v]] \longrightarrow A^{@}[A_1[A_2[(A^{\lambda}[E[x]])\{x := v\}]]] \quad \text{if } A^{@}[A^{\lambda}] \in A \quad (\beta_{\mathrm{cf}})
$$

Fig. 5. Chang and Felleisen's call-by-need calculus

Definition 20. *The call-by-value LHR with sharing is defined by the rules:*

$$
\begin{array}{ll}
\mathcal{C}[\lambda x.\, t]\ u & \rightarrow_{\lambda_{\mathtt{wls}}} \mathcal{C}[\ell x.\, t]\ u \\
\mathcal{C}'[\ell x.\, E^{v}[x]]\ \mathcal{C}[v] & \rightarrow_{\lambda_{\mathtt{wls}}} \mathcal{C}[\mathcal{C}'[\ell x.\, E^{v}[v]]\ v]
\end{array}
$$

with the usual freshness conditions to prevent variable capture in $\mathcal{C}'$.

3.4 $\lambda_{\mathtt{wls}}$ is a Call-by-Need Calculus

Remarkably enough, the resulting calculus is almost exactly Chang and Felleisen's call-by-need calculus [12] (CF-calculus) which is presented in Fig. 5. The main difference lies in the fact that the latter features the usual destructive substitution, while ours is linear. One can convince oneself that their answer contexts correspond to our closure contexts, while the balancing of inner and outer contexts is transparent in our calculus thanks to the restriction to marked terms. There is a reduction mismatch though, which is that CF-calculus plugs closures in the reverse order compared to $\lambda_{\mathtt{wls}}$. The reduction β_{cfr} (see below) can be described in our formalism in a straightforward manner.

Definition 21 (CF-calculus revisited). *The marked CF-calculus is given by the E_v-compatible closure of the rules below.*

$$
\begin{array}{ll}
\mathcal{C}[\lambda x.\, t]\ u & \rightarrow_{\lambda_{\mathrm{cfr}}} \mathcal{C}[\ell x.\, t]\ u \\
\mathcal{C}'[\ell x.\, E^{v}[x]]\ \mathcal{C}[v] & \rightarrow_{\lambda_{\mathrm{cfr}}} \mathcal{C}'[\mathcal{C}[E^{v}[x]\{x := v\}]]
\end{array}
$$

Theorem 4. *For any well-formed marked terms t and r, if $t \rightarrow^{*}_{\lambda_{\mathrm{cfr}}} r$ then $[t] \rightarrow^{*}_{\beta_{cf}} [r]$ where the length of the second reduction is the number of uses of the second rule in the first reduction. Conversely, for any unmarked terms t and r s.t. $t \rightarrow_{\beta_{cf}} r$ there exist markings t' and r' of t and r where $t' \rightarrow^{*}_{\lambda_{\mathrm{cfr}}} r'$ using exactly once the second rule.*

Proof. It is sufficient to observe that well-formedness in the marked calculus is equivalent to the existence of a decomposition into inner and outer contexts that are balanced in the unmarked calculus.

The difference in the order of closure plugging may seem irrelevant in Chang and Felleisen's framework because they use non-linear destructive substitutions and both orders are possible: an ad-hoc choice was made there. On the contrary, our design – strongly guided by logic – directly led us to a plugging order compatible with linear substitution.

3.5 Comparison with Other Call-by-Need Calculi

CF-calculus is a bit peculiar in works on call-by-need. It would be better to also compare our approach to more standard calculi such as AF-calculus. Moreover, a third variant of call-by-need calculus has been defined recently by considering the linear substitution λ-calculus [2] (LS-calculus), and it turns out to be very close to our presentation. This section is devoted to the comparison of $\lambda_{\mathtt{wls}}$ with those calculi.

The major source of difference between the three calculi lies in the handling and encoding of term bindings.

- AF-calculus uses a microscopic reduction (simple, small steps) and relies on rewriting rules to build up flat binding contexts;
- LS-calculus uses a macroscopic reduction ("at distance", relying on a very-elaborated and structured context) and enforces reduction rules to be transparent w.r.t. binding contexts;
- $\lambda_{\mathtt{wls}}$ does the same thing but uses a refined version of explicit substitutions embodied by closure contexts.

We now explain to which extent these calculi are essentially the same except for the technology used for the implementation of binding contexts. Both for AF-calculus and LS-calculus, it would be natural to switch to a calculus featuring `let`-binders, or equivalently explicit substitutions [1]. Yet, we will describe them in the usual λ-calculus for uniformity with the rest of the paper and because marked λ-abstractions are not needed in this case.

Micro-Steps Linear Head Reduction. In order to compare our approach to AF-calculus, we now propose another approach to linear head reduction which starts from the rules of σ-equivalence and integrate them in the LHR calculus. It will serve to rearrange the term in order to create appropriate β-redexes: as a consequence, we will not work with redexes up to closure context (or equivalently up to σ-equivalence) but will have reductions dedicated to the creation of the linear head redex. Still, while rearranging terms, we do not want to keep the β-redexes which are not triggered by a hoc-variable yet; a restricted form of closure context will remain, which would naturally be expressed with `let`-bindings or explicit substitutions:

$$\mathcal{L} ::= [\cdot] \mid (\lambda x.\, \mathcal{L})\, t$$

Because of the slight mismatch between usual closure contexts and restricted context closures, there is a choice to be made in the microscopic reduction rule.

While the original closure contexts made prime redexes appear naturally, now we need to explicitly create β-redexes by making the potential redexes commute with the surrounding context. There are two ways to do so, each one corresponding to a generating rule of the σ-equivalence, either by pushing the application node inside closure contexts (LIFT) or by extruding applied λ-abstractions from the surrounding context (DIG):

$$((\lambda x.\, \mathcal{L}[\lambda y.\, t])\, u)\, v \to (\lambda x.\, (\mathcal{L}[\lambda y.\, t])\, v)\, u \quad (\text{LIFT})$$
$$(\mathcal{L}[(\lambda x.\, \lambda y.\, t)\, u])\, v \to (\mathcal{L}[\lambda y.\, (\lambda x.\, t)\, u])\, v \quad (\text{DIG})$$

These rules admit extensions, taking opportunity of the structure of restricted closure contexts:

$$(\mathcal{L}[\lambda y.\, t])\, v \to \mathcal{L}[(\lambda y.\, t)\, v] \quad (\text{LIFT}\star)$$
$$(\mathcal{L}[\lambda y.\, t])\, v \to (\lambda y.\, \mathcal{L}[t])\, v \quad (\text{DIG}\star)$$

Reduction (LIFT) is the most common in literature, probably because it is easier to formulate without a clear notion of closure contexts. Equipped with (LIFT), we actually obtain a calculus which precisely (up to the use of explicit `lets`) to the calculus considered by Danvy *et al.* in the preliminary section of [16], where answers A are no more than terms of the form $\mathcal{L}[\lambda x.\, t]$. Reduction (DIG) is an alternative choice. The two reductions are not only different, but also incompatible, in the sense that their left-hand sides are the same while their right-hand sides are not convertible, thus breaking confluence. Yet, the reduced terms still agree up to σ-equivalence by construction. Finally, the last rule performs the linear substitution:

$$(\lambda x.\, E[x])\, t \to (\lambda x.\, E[t])\, t$$

Here, $E[x]$ represents a left context: $E ::= [\cdot] \mid E\, t \mid \lambda x.\, E$ so that the substitution only replaces exactly one variable.

Any choice between rules (LIFT) or (DIG) will lead to call-by-need calculi. Still we consider it is more interesting to opt for (LIFT) since it allows us to recover known calculi. From the microscopic linear head calculus with (LIFT), we can apply the same three transformations as in the macroscopic case:

1. weak reduction constrain evaluation contexts to be applicative contexts up to closures: $E ::= [\cdot] \mid E\, t \mid (\lambda x.\, E)\, t$
2. restriction to value (up to closure) substitutions, which creates new call-by-value, evaluation contexts: $E ::= \cdots \mid (\lambda x.\, E[x])\, E$
3. sharing of closures, introducing the rule for commutation of closure contexts and which happens to be, with the simplified contexts, the usual (ASSOC) rule: $(\lambda x.\, E[x])\, (\lambda y.\, A)\, t \to (\lambda y.\, (\lambda x.\, E[x])\, A)\, t \quad (\text{ASSOC})$

Proposition 14. *The resulting calculus is precisely AF-calculus.*

Closure Contexts as Refined Explicit Substitutions. It turns out that LS-calculus is essentially $\lambda_{\texttt{wls}}$ where closure contexts are collapsed to a flat list of binders, i.e. $\mathcal{L}$ contexts (once again, up to the use of an explicit `let` construction). The rules can be rephrased with the previous notations as follows.

$$N ::= [\cdot] \mid \mathcal{L}[N] \mid N\ t \mid (\lambda x.\, N[x])\ N$$
$$\mathcal{L}[\lambda x.\, t]\ u \quad \rightarrow_{\lambda_{\mathtt{lsc}}} \mathcal{L}[(\lambda x.\, t)\ u]$$
$$(\lambda x.\, N[x])\ \mathcal{L}[v] \rightarrow_{\lambda_{\mathtt{lsc}}} \mathcal{L}[(\lambda x.\, N[v])\ v]$$

As one can witness, the first rule, known as the distant by-name β-rule, is just (LIFT$\star$). The second rule corresponds to the dereferencing rule of $\lambda_{\mathtt{wls}}$ without a closure context around the λ-abstraction because (LIFT$\star$) builds up explicit substitutions by putting every abstraction in front of its corresponding argument.

We can easily translate any well-formed marked term into a term with explicit substitutions: it is indeed sufficient to collapse all closure contexts $\mathcal{C}$ into flat binding contexts $\mathcal{L}(\mathcal{C})$ inductively:

$$\mathcal{L}([\cdot]) := [\cdot] \qquad \mathcal{L}(\mathcal{C}_1[\ell x.\, \mathcal{C}_2]\ t) := \mathcal{L}(\mathcal{C}_1)[(\lambda x.\, \mathcal{L}(\mathcal{C}_2))\ t]$$

Up to this translation, which is no more than taking a normal form for σ-equivalence, LS-calculus and $\lambda_{\mathtt{wls}}$ describe the same calculus. Our calculus incurs a small technical penalty because we need to restrict the set of terms w.r.t. well-formedness, while this comes for free in LS-calculus as explicit substitutions pertain to the syntax and force balancing of prime redexes.

Nonetheless, we advocate that $\lambda_{\mathtt{wls}}$ is more fine-grained and that there are cases where this may matter. Indeed, Proposition 7 shows that closure contexts are faithful reifications of KAM environments. This is not the case for flat $\mathcal{L}$ contexts which may represent several KAM environments. This mismatch can be indeed observed in presence of side-effects sensitive to the structure of environments, most notably forcing [23], but probably linear effects as well. As we precisely want to extend call-by-need with effects, we claim that closure contexts should be preferred over flat context in this setting.

4 Classical By-Need

To extend our classical LHR calculus to a fully-fledged call-by-need calculus, we follow the same three-step path that led us from LHR to call-by-need. We will not give the full details for the three steps though, and we will instead only give the final calculus.

The most delicate point is actually the introduction of weak reduction. In a classical setting, the actual applicative context of a variable may be strictly larger than it seems, because in commands of the form $[\alpha]\, t$, the α variable may be bound to a stack featuring supplementary applications. This means that we need to take into account supernumerary abstractions at the beginning of commands. Yet, the marking procedure allows us to remember which abstractions are actually paired with a corresponding application in a direct way.

We present in this section two variants of a classical by-need calculus, one effectively taking into account supernumerary arguments as described above, and a less smart variant that perfoms classical substitution upfront without caring for abstraction-application balancing on command boundaries. The advantage of the latter over the former is that it can be easily linked to a previous classical by-need calculus [10].

4.1 Classical By-Need with Classical Closure Contexts

To implement the mechanism described above, we simply need to acknowledge the requirement to go through μ binders in our contexts. This leads to the mutual definition of classical-by-value contexts E^v and closure stack fragments K^v, where closure contexts are updated as well to handle classical binders.

$$\begin{aligned}
\mathcal{C} &::= [\cdot] \mid \mathcal{C}_1[\ell x.\, \mathcal{C}_2]\; t \mid \mathcal{C}_1[\mu\alpha.\, K^v[[\alpha]\, \mathcal{C}_2]] \\
E^v &::= [\cdot] \mid E^v\; t \mid \ell x.\, E^v \mid \mathcal{C}[\ell x.\, E_1^v[x]]\; E_2^v \mid \mu\alpha.\, K^v[[\alpha]\, E^v] \\
K^v &::= [\cdot] \mid [\alpha]\, E^v[\mu\beta.\, K^v]
\end{aligned}$$

Definition 22 (Classical-by-need with classical closure contexts). *The classical-by-need calculus with classical closure contexts,* `cwls`, *is defined by the following reduction rules.*

$$\begin{aligned}
&\mathcal{C}[\lambda x.\, t]\; u &&\to_{\lambda_{\mathtt{cwls}}} \mathcal{C}[\ell x.\, t]\; u \\
&\mathcal{C}'[\ell x.\, E^v[x]]\; \mathcal{C}[v] &&\to_{\lambda_{\mathtt{cwls}}} \mathcal{C}[\mathcal{C}'[\ell x.\, E^v[v]]\; v] \\
&\mathcal{C}'[\ell x.\, E^v[x]]\; \mathcal{C}[\mu\alpha.\, c] &&\to_{\lambda_{\mathtt{cwls}}} \mathcal{C}[\mu\alpha.\, c\{\alpha := [\alpha]\, \mathcal{C}'[\ell x.\, E^v[x]]\; _\}]
\end{aligned}$$

The issue of this calculus is that the delayed classical substitution is a quite novel phenomenon that does not ressemble anything from the literature as far as we know. It is, in particular, difficult to compare with previous attempts at a call-by-need variant of the $\lambda\mu$-calculus.

4.2 Classical By-Need with Intuitionistic Closure Contexts

We describe here a modification of the above calculus whose laziness has been watered down. Instead of delaying classical substitutions, it performs them as soon as possible. The main difference with the smart calculus lies in the fact that closure contexts remain intuitionistic and do not allow to go down under μ-binders. The corresponding contexts are inductively defined as follows.

$$\begin{aligned}
\mathcal{C} &::= [\cdot] \mid \mathcal{C}_1[\ell x.\, \mathcal{C}_2]\; t \\
E^v &::= [\cdot] \mid E^v\; t \mid \ell x.\, E^v \mid \mathcal{C}[\ell x.\, E_1^v[x]]\; E_2^v \\
K^v &::= [\cdot] \mid [\alpha]\, E^v[\mu\beta.\, K^v]
\end{aligned}$$

Definition 23 (Classical-by-need with intuitionistic closure contexts). *The classical-by-need calculus with intuitionistic closure contexts,* `cwls'`, *is defined by the following reduction rules.*

$$
\begin{array}{lll}
\mathcal{C}[\lambda x.\, t]\ u & \rightarrow_{\lambda_{\mathtt{cwls}'}} & \mathcal{C}[\ell x.\, t]\ u \\
\mathcal{C}'[\ell x.\, E^v[x]]\ \mathcal{C}[v] & \rightarrow_{\lambda_{\mathtt{cwls}'}} & \mathcal{C}[\mathcal{C}'[\ell x.\, E^v[v]]\ v] \\
[\alpha]\, E^v[\mu\beta.\, K^v[[\beta]\, t]] & \rightarrow_{\lambda_{\mathtt{cwls}'}} & [\alpha]\, E^v[\mu\beta.\, K^v[[\alpha]\, E^v[t]]]
\end{array}
$$

4.3 Comparison with Existing Classical Call-by-Need Calculus

In order to better understand the calculi of the previous section, we now turn to the comparison with another classical-by-need calculus [10], referred to as AHS, which is obtained from a calculus derived from Curien and Herbelin's duality of computation. As a consequence, AHS features plain call-by-value β reduction and not a linear, non-destructive, deref rule la Ariola-Felleisen:

$$(\lambda x.\, t)\ v \ \rightarrow\ t\{x := v\} \text{ with } v\ :=\ x \mid \lambda x.\, t$$

Comparing precisely our calculi with AHS is tricky because AHS is built on destructive substitution which additionally is plain β_v. The reason for such a presentation of AHS is to be found in its sequent calculus origin [10]. As we did for the comparison with Chang-Felleisen calculus, we will consider a variant of AHS with a deref rule la Ariola-Felleisen described, in sequent style, in the last section of [7] for which we will prove that established `cwls`-reduction is sound and complete. We conjecture that the same result holds for AHS but do not yet have a proof of this fact.

AHS Modified Calculus. We now consider a slightly modified version of the previous calculus from [10]. AHS'-calculus consists in AHS-calculus where the beta reduction has been replaced by a deref rule la Ariola-Felleisen (where variables are not values) and the notion of evaluation context has been adapted accordingly. This calculus has been first described, in sequent style, in [7].

Definition 24 (Ariola-Herbelin-Saurin modified calculus). *AHS' reduction for the $\lambda\mu$-calculus is defined below.*

$$
\begin{array}{lll}
 & (\lambda x.\, t)\ u\ r & \rightarrow (\lambda x.\, t\ r)\ u \\
v\ :=\ \lambda x.\, t & (\lambda x.\, C[x])\ v & \rightarrow (\lambda x.\, C[v])\ v \\
n\ :=\ x \mid t\ u \mid \mu\alpha.\, c & (\lambda z.\, C[z])\ ((\lambda x.\, t)\ u) & \rightarrow (\lambda x.\, (\lambda z.\, C[z])\ t)\ u \\
E ::= [\cdot] \mid E\ t & (\mu\alpha.\, c)\ t & \rightarrow \mu\alpha.\, c\{[\alpha]\, r := [\alpha]\, r\ t\} \\
C ::= E \mid (\lambda z.\, C)\ t \mid & (\lambda x.\, C[x])\ (\mu\alpha.\, c) & \rightarrow \mu\alpha.\, c\{[\alpha]\, r := [\alpha]\, (\lambda x.\, C[x])\ r\} \\
\qquad (\lambda x.\, C[x])\ E & (\lambda x.\, \mu\alpha.\, [\beta]\, t)\ n & \rightarrow \mu\alpha.\, [\beta]\, (\lambda x.\, t)\ n \\
 & [\alpha]\, \mu\beta.\, c & \rightarrow c\{\beta := \alpha\}
\end{array}
$$

Theorem 5. *For any command c, there exists an infinite standard reduction in AHS'-calculus starting from c iff there exists an infinite reduction starting from c in* `cwls`$'$*-calculus.*

Proof. We show this by giving the sketch of a pair of simulation theorems. We will separate AHS' reduction rules in three groups:

- The structural rules (S) which are made of the LIFT and ASSOC rules, together with the rule $(\lambda x.\,\mu\alpha.\,[\beta]\,t)\;n \rightarrow \mu\alpha.\,[\beta]\,(\lambda x.\,t)\;n$.
- The performing rules (P) which is only the dereferencing rule.
- The classical rules (C) which are the three remaining rules.

Transforming reductions in $\mathtt{cwls}'$-calculus into AHS' is straightforward. First, assuming a closure stack fragment K_v, one can see that AHS' will normalize it into a delimited C context in the following way. For each splice of K_v of the form $[\alpha]\,E_v[\mu\beta.\,[\cdot]]$, the E_v context will be simplified by a series of applications of the (S) rules. According to the form of K_v, either the reduction stops (if there is no remaining splice) or it performs a certain number of (C) rules, until which the normalization procedure recursively applies. A dereferencing cannot occur at this point because while there are remaining splices, the current needed context cannot contain variables, as the splices all have a μ binder in needed position. Note that the resulting normalized context is still a closure stack fragment up to unmarking. By a simple size argument, this normalization procedure must terminate, so that we will consider it transparent for the simulation.

Now, assume that

$$\mathcal{C}_1[\ell x.\,E_v[x]]\;\mathcal{C}_2[v] \rightarrow \mathcal{C}_2[\mathcal{C}_1[\ell x.\,E_v[v]]\;v]$$

with the associated conditions for this rule. The (S) rules apply to $\mathcal{C}_1$ and $\mathcal{C}_2$. This effectively transforms them into answer contexts, so that a derefencing rule can occur after the E_v has been flattened as well. The important thing to observe is that the same normalization steps apply to the reduct $\mathcal{C}_2[\mathcal{C}_1[\ell x.\,E_v[v]]\;v]$ so that each step from $\mathtt{cwls}'$ is going to be matched by a growing but finite quantity of normalization steps followed by a derefencing.

The second reduction rule, corresponding to stack substitutions, is actually directly handled by the normalization procedure described just above.

We turn to the simulation of the AHS' reduction by the $\mathtt{cwls}'$-calculus. First, the standard reduction contexts are a degenerated case of K_v contexts with one splice and flattened closure contexts, which allows to easily transfer rules from the source to the target. We actually match each class of reduction (S), (P) and (C) to a given behaviour in the target calculus.

- The (S) rules are transparent for the $\mathtt{cwls}'$-calculus, because they are natively handled by closure contexts. So a (S)-reduction does not give rise to a λ_{clh}-reduction.
- A group of (C) rules can be matched by an arbitrary number of reductions, including none. This depends on the way the corresponding stack variable is used.
- The (P) rule is conversely matched by exactly one rule in the $\mathtt{cwls}'$ reduction.

The trick is to use the fact that $(C+S)$ is normalizing, as we already did in the previous case. Moreover, such reductions do not change the possibility to perform a derefencing in the corresponding $\mathtt{cwls}'$ term. So we actually consider groups of reductions $(C+S)^*, P$ in the source calculus. This is always possible to decompose a sequence of AHS' reductions as such thanks to the normalization of $(C + S)$. It it then easy to witness that the S part will have no effect, each C reduction will be matched by a finite number of context reductions in λ_{clh}, and that the final (P) will correspond to exactly one derefencing reduction in λ_{clh}.

5 Conclusion

> Nevertheless, the early history of continuations is a sharp reminder that original ideas are rarely born in full generality, and that their communication is not always a simple or straightforward task.
>
> John C. Reynolds [28]

Reaching this point of the paper, we hope to have convinced the reader, thanks to the above developments and results, that linear head reduction can be a useful tool in order to develop a classy call-by-need with control.

Contributions. After reformulating linear head reduction in a way which is somehow intermediate between traditional LHR and Accattoli *et al.*'s approach via explicit substitutions, we demonstrated the deep connections between LHR and call-by-need by showing that weak call-by-value LHR with sharing *is* a call-by-need calculus. We then strengthened this result to the case of $\lambda\mu$-calculus, that is we introduced a call-by-need calculus with control operator obtained from classical LHR, another contribution of this paper. We obtained such a calculus by a systematic derivation from LHR in three steps: (i) by restricting it to a weak reduction, (ii) by ensuring substitution of values, and (iii) by sharing closures. Closure contexts play a central role in LHR: all the structures we consider are actually closed by this construction, making them a methodological feature of our approach. While they are not novel in the intuitionistic case, it is the first time they are put in use in an explicit and articulated way, not to speak of the classical extension of closure contexts which is properly a contribution of this work. We validated our development in two ways:

- our approach to linear head reduction (using closure contexts and, to deal with weak reduction, marked terms) is validated by the fact that it transfers smoothly to $\lambda\mu$-calculus, a new result of this paper. Additionally, one can see the use of closure contexts, in particular when dealing with marked terms, as a generalization of LSC where the structure of substitutions is encoded in closure contexts, a tree-like structure, and not in substitution contexts, which are linearized: we keep closer to the original structure of the term which is important when dealing with computational effects.
- The call-by-need λ and $\lambda\mu$-calculi that we obtain in the paper are related with previously known versions of call-by-need calculi. In the case of the λ-calculus, they are related with Ariola-Felleisen's and Chang-Felleisen's calculi. In the case of $\lambda\mu$-calculi, two classical by-need calculi are actually proposed, one being related to a variant of Ariola-Herbelin-Saurin's calculus, and the other calling for further investigations.

Related Works. The most closely related works are certainly the works of Ariola *et al.* [7,10] and Accattoli *et al.* [2]. Their relations with the present work have been discussed throughout the paper. Summing up:

- we developed a different methodology from that of Ariola *et al.* in that we stayed within the framework of natural deduction and analyzed the systematic synthesis of call-by-need from LHR in a careful way resulting in the ability to lift this to the $\lambda\mu$-calculus.
- Compared with LSC, our approach can be viewed as less specified and somehow more general than that of LSC, which obviously prevents us from having results as precise as those of LSC, for instance regarding complexity analysis. On the other hand, maintaining the structure of λ-terms suggests interesting perspectives for handling various computational effects.

Future Work. We finally describe some perspectives of future work.

More Computational Effects. The robustness of our approach is encouraging for testing other computational effects where maintaining the term structure may be even more crucial than for control effects.

Classical by-Need. The comparisons with other proposals for classical variants of the call-by-need reduction [7,10] remain to be established more precisely.

We conjecture that our calculus is sound and complete not only with AHS' but also with AHS-calculus [10]. Moreover, the classical-by-need calculus with classical closure contexts remains difficult to connect to already known calculi.

Towards Full Laziness. Our design guided by σ-equivalence can do more than call-by-need and can actually already encompass a weak form of full laziness. Future work will pursue this direction.

Reduction Strategies Versus Calculi. The original motivation of our work was to relate formally LHR and call-by-need. As a result, instead of focusing on proper calculi we concentrated our attention on a specific evaluation strategy for several reasons: macroscopic and weak reductions are more naturally expressed with strategies. However, the λ_{lh}-calculus can very easily be studied as a calculus and we shall develop it as such in the future.

Acknowledgements. The authors would like to thank Beniamino Accattoli, Thibaut Balabonski, Olivier Danvy and Delia Kesner for discussions regarding this work as well as anonymous reviewers.

References

1. Abadi, M., Cardelli, L., Curien, P.-L., Lévy, J.-J.: Explicit substitutions. J. Funct. Program. **1**(4), 375–416 (1991)
2. Accattoli, B., Barenbaum, P., Mazza, D.: Distilling abstract machines. In: Jeuring, Chakravarty (eds.) ICFP 2014, pp. 363–376. ACM (2014)

3. Accattoli, B., Bonelli, E., Kesner, D., Lombardi, C.: A nonstandard standardization theorem. In: POPL 2014, San Diego, CA, USA, pp. 659–670 (2014)
4. Accattoli, B., Kesner, D.: The structural λ-calculus. In: Dawar, A., Veith, H. (eds.) CSL 2010. LNCS, vol. 6247, pp. 381–395. Springer, Heidelberg (2010)
5. Accattoli, B., Kesner, D.: The permutative λ-calculus. In: Bjørner, N., Voronkov, A. (eds.) LPAR-18 2012. LNCS, vol. 7180, pp. 23–36. Springer, Heidelberg (2012)
6. Accattoli, B., Lago, U.D.: Beta reduction is invariant, indeed. In: CSL-LICS 2014, Vienna, Austria, July 2014
7. Ariola, Z.M., Downen, P., Herbelin, H., Nakata, K., Saurin, A.: Classical call-by-need sequent calculi: the unity of semantic artifacts. In: Schrijvers, T., Thiemann, P. (eds.) FLOPS 2012. LNCS, vol. 7294, pp. 32–46. Springer, Heidelberg (2012)
8. Ariola, Z.M., Felleisen, M.: The call-by-need lambda calculus. J. Funct. Program. **7**(3), 265–301 (1997)
9. Ariola, Z.M., Felleisen, M., Maraist, J., Odersky, M., Wadler, P.: The call-by-need lambda calculus. In: POPL 1995, pp. 233–246. ACM Press (1995)
10. Ariola, Z.M., Herbelin, H., Saurin, A.: Classical call-by-need and duality. In: Ong, L. (ed.) Typed Lambda Calculi and Applications. LNCS, vol. 6690, pp. 27–44. Springer, Heidelberg (2011)
11. Barendregt, H.: The Lambda Calculus, its Syntax and Semantics. Studies in Logic and the Foundations of Mathematics. Elsevier, Amsterdam (1984)
12. Chang, S., Felleisen, M.: The call-by-need lambda calculus, revisited. In: Seidl, H. (ed.) Programming Languages and Systems. LNCS, vol. 7211, pp. 128–147. Springer, Heidelberg (2012)
13. Curien, P.-L., Herbelin, H.: The duality of computation. In: Odersky, M., Wadler, P. (eds.) ICFP 2000, pp. 233–243. ACM Press (2000)
14. Danos, V., Herbelin, H., Regnier, L.: Game semantics & abstract machines. In: LICS 1996, pp. 394–405. IEEE Press (1996)
15. Danos, V., Regnier, L.: Head linear reduction (2004) (unpublished)
16. Danvy, O., Millikin, K., Munk, J., Zerny, I.: Defunctionalized interpreters for call-by-need evaluation. In: Blume, M., Kobayashi, N., Vidal, G. (eds.) FLOPS 2010. LNCS, vol. 6009, pp. 240–256. Springer, Heidelberg (2010)
17. Girard, J.-Y.: Une extension de l'interprtation de Gdel l'analyse, et sonapplication a l'élimination des coupures dans l'analyse et la thorie destypes. In: Fenstad (ed.) Proceedings of the Second Scandinavian Logic Symposium. Studies in Logic and the Foundations of Mathematics, vol. 63, pp. 63–92. Elsevier (1971)
18. Girard, J.-Y.: Linear logic. Theoret. Comput. Sci. **50**, 1–102 (1987)
19. Hyland, M., Ong, L.: On full abstraction for PCF. Inf. Comput. **163**(2), 285–408 (2000)
20. Krivine, J.-L.: A call-by-name lambda-calculus machine. Higher-Order Symb. Comput. **20**(3), 199–207 (2007)
21. Laurent, O.: A study of polarization in logic. Ph.D. Thesis, Université de la Méditerranée - Aix-Marseille II, March 2002
22. Maraist, J., Odersky, M., Wadler, P.: The call-by-need lambda-calculus. J. Funct. Program. **8**(3), 275–317 (1998)
23. Miquel, A.: Forcing as a program transformation. In: LICS, pp. 197–206. IEEE Computer Society (2011)
24. Parigot, M.: Lambda-mu-calculus: an algorithmic interpretation of classical natural deduction. In: Voronkov, A. (ed.) LPAR 1992. LNCS, vol. 624, pp. 190–201. Springer, Heidelberg (1992)
25. Regnier, L.: Lambda-calcul et réseaux. Ph.D. Thesis, Univ. Paris VII (1992)

26. Regnier, L.: Une équivalence sur les λ-termes. Theoret. Comput. Sci. **126**, 281–292 (1994)
27. Reynolds, J.C.: Towards a theory of type structure. In: Robinet, B. (ed.) Programming Symposium. LNCS, vol. 19, pp. 408–423. Springer, Heidelberg (1974)
28. Reynolds, J.C.: The discoveries of continuations. Lisp Symb. Comput. **6**(3–4), 233–248 (1993)
29. Streicher, T., Reus, B.: Classical logic, continuation semantics and abstract machines. J. Funct. Program. **8**(6), 543–572 (1998)
30. Wadsworth, C.P.: Semantics and pragmatics of the lambda-calculus. Ph.D. Thesis, Programming Research Group, Oxford University (1971)

Macrofication: Refactoring by Reverse Macro Expansion

Christopher Schuster(✉), Tim Disney, and Cormac Flanagan

University of California, Santa Cruz, USA
{cschuste,tdisney,cormac}@ucsc.edu

Abstract. Refactoring is a code transformation performed at development time that improves the quality of code while preserving its observable behavior. Macro expansion is also a code transformation, but performed at compile time, that replaces instances of macro invocation patterns with the corresponding macro body or template. The key insight of this paper is that for each pattern-template macro, we can automatically generate a corresponding refactoring tool that finds complex code fragments matching the macro template and replaces them with the equivalent but simpler macro invocation pattern; we call this novel refactoring process *macrofication*.

Conceptually, macrofication involves running macro expansion in reverse; however, it does require a more sophisticated pattern matching algorithm and additional checks to ensure that the refactoring always preserves program behavior.

We have implemented a macrofication tool for a hygienic macro system in JavaScript, integrated it into a development environment and evaluated it by refactoring a popular open source JavaScript library. Results indicate that it is sufficiently flexible for complex refactoring and thereby enhances the development workflow while scaling well even for larger code bases.

1 Introduction

Refactoring is the process of changing code to improve its internal structure without changing its external behavior [15]. Complex restructuring of code usually requires careful design decisions by the developer but refactoring tools still provide support and automation for detecting *code smell*, selecting the right transformation and performing it in a way that preserves behavior.

As an example, consider the JavaScript code fragment in Listing 1, which employs a well-known pattern to define a constructor function `Person` that creates new objects with `sayHello` and `rename` methods.

The most recent version of JavaScript (ECMAScript 2015/ES6 [23]) adds declarative class definitions to the language which enable us to simplify the code as shown in Listing 2.

P. Thiemann (Ed.): ESOP 2016, LNCS 9632, pp. 644–671, 2016.
DOI: 10.1007/978-3-662-49498-1_25

```
function Person(name) {
  this.name = name;
}
Person.prototype.sayHello = function sayHello() {
  console.log("Hi, I'm" + this.name);
};
Person.prototype.rename = function rename(n) {
  this.name = n;
};
```

Listing 1. JavaScript example with prototype-based inheritance.

```
class Person {
  constructor(name) {
    this.name = name;
  }
  sayHello() {
    console.log("Hi, I'm" + this.name);
  }
  rename(n) {
    this.name = n;
  }
}
```

Listing 2. Declarative class definition corresponding to Listing 1.

Rewriting existing code to use class definitions instead of the object prototype pattern is a tedious and error-prone process; clearly a refactoring tool to perform this transformation automatically would be desirable.

In addition to class definitions, ES2015/ES6 also adds a more concise arrow syntax (=>) for anonymous function definitions, allowing us to rewrite the following example in a more compact way:

```
a.map(function(s) { return s.length; });      // ES5 code
a.map(s => s.length);               // equivalent ES2015 code
```

Again, an automatic refactoring tool to perform this transformation for existing code would be most helpful.

Of course, programmers should not have to wait on browser implementations to be able to use such nice syntactic extensions. In fact, many languages allow programmers to define syntactic extensions with *macro* systems. These include string-based macros as commonly used in C [24] or Assembler, and parser-level macros as supported by Lisp [50], Scheme [49], Racket [53] and more recently Rust [1] and JavaScript [10].

In the most general form, a macro is a syntax transformer, a function from syntax to syntax, which is evaluated at compile time. The kind of macros we

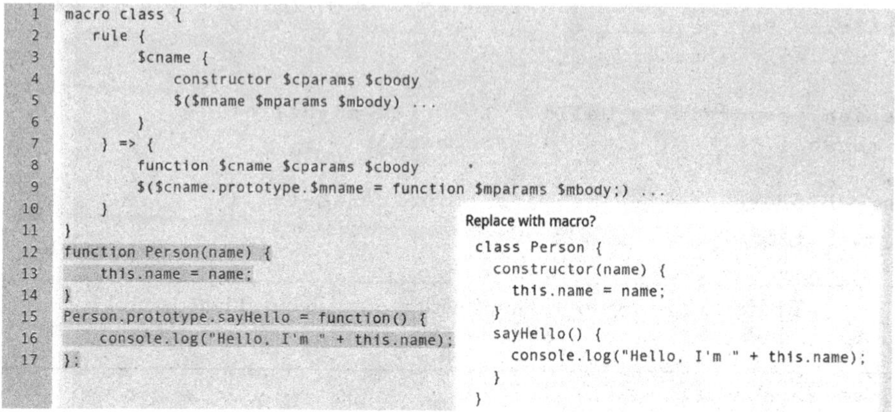
1 macro class {
2 rule {
3 $cname {
4 constructor $cparams $cbody
5 $($mname $mparams $mbody) ...
6 }
7 } => {
8 function $cname $cparams $cbody
9 $($cname.prototype.$mname = function $mparams $mbody;) ...
10 }
11 }
12 function Person(name) {
13 this.name = name;
14 }
15 Person.prototype.sayHello = function() {
16 console.log("Hello, I'm " + this.name);
17 };
Replace with macro?
class Person {
constructor(name) {
this.name = name;
}
sayHello() {
console.log("Hello, I'm " + this.name);
}
}

Fig. 1. The shown sweet.js macro named `class` adds declarative class definitions to JavaScript that expand to a object prototype pattern. Macrofication automatically detects a refactoring candidate in lines 12 to 17, so the development environment highlights the code and shows a preview of the refactored code with the class definition in an overlay.

consider are of a more restricted form called pattern-template macros (in Scheme these macros are defined with `syntax-rules` and are also known as "macro by example" [6,26]). These pattern-template macros are defined with a *pattern* that matches against syntax and a *template* that generates syntax. The template can reference syntax that was matched in the pattern via *pattern variables*. Once all macros have been expanded, the resulting program will be parsed and evaluated according to the grammar and semantics of the target language. In a hygienic macro system [21], the macro expansion also respects the scopes of variables and thereby prevents unintended name clashes between the macro and the expansion context.

Sweet.js [10], a macro system for JavaScript, enables syntactic extensions such as declarative class definitions and arrow notation for functions as described above. As an example, the `class` macro shown in Listing 3 introduces syntax for class definitions by matching a class name, a constructor and an arbitrary number of methods, and expanding to a constructor function and repeated assignments to the prototype of this constructor.

In addition to defining this macro, the programmer also has to rewrite the existing code to benefit from it and be consistent throughout the code base. This involves finding all applicable code fragments (as in Listing 1 above) and replacing them with correct macro invocation patterns (as in Listing 2) which is essentially the class refactoring mentioned above and therefore would equally benefit from automated tool support.

This paper takes of advantage of this similarity between refactoring and macro expansion to introduce *macrofication*, the idea of refactoring via reverse macro expansion. Pattern-template macros, such as the macro for class definitions, allow

```
macro class {
  rule {
    $cname {
      constructor $cparams $cbody
      $($mname $mparams $mbody)...
    }
  } => {
    function $cname $cparams $cbody
    $($cname.prototype.$mname = function $mparams $mbody;)...
  }
}
```

Listing 3. Macro for expanding class definitions to ES5 code based on prototypes.

the algorithm to automatically discover all matching occurrences of a macro template in the program that can be replaced by a corresponding macro invocation.

Figure 1 shows our development environment with the class macro and the previous code example which uses the object prototype pattern. The macrofication option automatically highlights lines 12 to 17, indicating that the code can be refactored with a macro invocation. Additionally, the environment also shows a preview of the refactored code which is a more readable class definition with the same behavior as the original code. By simply clicking on the preview, the source code will be transformed accordingly.

Conceptually, macrofication is the inverse of macro expansion; macro expansion replaces patterns with templates, whereas macrofication replaces templates with patterns. However, macrofication requires a more complicated matching algorithm than is used in current macro systems due to differences in the handling of macro variables in patterns and templates. For example, variables are often repeated in the template (e.g. `$cname` in Fig. 1) whereas current macro systems do not support repeated variables in patterns. Repetitions (denoted with ellipses '...') introduce additional complexities which we solve with a pattern matching algorithm that takes the nesting level of variables in repetitions into account to enable the correct macrofication of complex macro templates (as illustrated by `$cname` in Fig. 1 line 9 which has to be the same identifier for all methods of a class declaration).

Macrofication should preserve program behavior. Even if the syntax involved in a particular macrofication was replaced correctly, the surrounding code might lead to a different expansion and thereby a different program behavior. Furthermore, a hygienic macro system separates the scopes of variables used in the macro and in the expansion context, therefore refactoring a scoped variable potentially introduces problems if the refactoring does not account for hygienic renaming. The refactoring algorithm in this paper addresses these issues by ensuring syntactic equivalence after expansion and thereby guarantees that the resulting program behaves the same as the original program.

In addition to the expansion and macrofication algorithm, this paper also evaluates a working prototype implementation for JavaScript based on sweet.js including an integration into a development environment which highlights refactoring candidates. This implementation was successfully used to refactor the popular Backbone.js JavaScript library by changing its prototype-based code to ECMAScript 6 classes with a complex rule macro. A cursory performance analysis of refactoring both Backbone.js and the ru-lang library, which uses macros internally, indicates that this approach scales well even for large code bases.

Overall, the contributions of this paper are

- it introduces *macrofication* as a new kind of code refactoring for inferring macro invocations,
- a macrofication algorithm based on reverse expansion that takes the macro expansion order and hygiene into account,
- an advanced matching algorithm for patterns with nested pattern repetitions and repeated pattern variables,
- an implementation for sweet.js including an integration into the sweet.js development environment,
- and an evaluation of its utility and performance by refactoring Backbone.js, a popular JavaScript library.

2 Macro Expansion

In order to define macrofication, it is useful to first review how macro expansion works. Our formalism is mostly independent of the target language and only assumes that the code has been lexed into a sequence of tokens which have been further processed into a sequence of *token trees* by matching delimiters such as open and close braces. If k ranges over tokens in the language (such as identifiers, punctuation, literals or keywords), then a token tree h is either a single token k or a sequence enclosed in delimiters $\{s\}$.

$$h ::= k \mid \{s\} \qquad\qquad k : \mathit{Token}$$

The *syntax* of the program is simply a sequence s of token trees.

$$s ::= k \cdot s \mid \{s\} \cdot s \mid \epsilon$$

The actual characters used for delimiting token trees are irrelevant for the algorithm, so a sophisticated reader/lexer could support many different delimiters (e.g. { }, [ ] or ( )), including implicit delimiters for syntax trees so this approach supports both Lisp-like and JavaScript-like languages.

As an example, the JavaScript statement "`arr[i+1];`" could be represented as the following token tree sequence where the square brackets "`[`" and "`]`" become simple tokens k after delimiter matching.

```
arr   [ i + 1 ]   ;
```
$$k \cdot \{\, k \cdot k \cdot k \cdot k \cdot k \cdot \epsilon \,\} \cdot k \cdot \epsilon$$

A macro has a name n, which is a single token (usually an identifier), and a list of rules. Each rule is a pair of a pattern p and a template t, both of which might include pattern variables x. Pattern variables might be represented with a leading dollar sign `$` or question mark `?`, e.g. `$x` or `?x` in the target language but the concrete syntax for pattern variables is insignificant for the algorithm presented in this paper.

Here, we define a pattern or template as a sequence of tokens, variables and pattern/template sequences enclosed in delimiters.

$$p, t ::= k \cdot p \mid \{p\} \cdot p \mid x \cdot p \mid \epsilon \qquad\qquad x : \text{Pattern Variable}$$

In the context of the expansion and macrofication algorithm, a macro with multiple rules is equivalent to multiple macros with the same name, each having a single rule. Therefore, it is possible to represent all macro rules in the macro environment Σ as an ordered sequence of (name, pattern, template) tuples.

$$\Sigma \ : \ (n, p, t)^*$$

A pattern variable x is either unbound or bound to a token tree h. We use Θ to denote the environment of variables bindings.

$$\Theta : x \rightarrow h$$

In the simplest case, all macros are known in advance of the expansion and have global scope[1]. Given a fixed list of macros Σ, macro expansion transforms a token tree sequence s (which does not include macros definitions) into a new token tree sequence with all macros matched and expanded:

$$\text{expand}_{\Sigma} \ : \ s \rightarrow \ s$$

For every token k, expand will look up its macro environment Σ for a macro named k with a pattern p matching the following tokens. If there is no such macro, it will proceed with the remaining syntax, otherwise the first such macro is used to match the syntax, yielding new variable bindings Θ which are then used to *transcribe* the template t. The resulting token sequence might include other macro calls, so expand continues recursively until all macros have been expanded. This process is not guaranteed to terminate as rule macros are Turing-complete. For example, the following macro will result in an infinite expansion:

```
macro omega { rule {} => {omega} }
```

The algorithms for *matching* and *transcribing* generally follow the recursive structure of the provided pattern or template. *Match* uses the pattern p to enforce equivalence with the token tree sequence s while adding variables x to the pattern environment Θ. *Transcribe* uses the template t to generate new syntax s by replacing all free pattern variables x with their substitutions based on Θ.

[1] A slightly modified algorithm could also match macros and add them to the macro environment during expansion (see also Sect. 6).

```
macro unless {
  rule { $x $y } => { if (! $x) $y }
}
unless (success) fail();
```

$$
\begin{array}{lll}
 & \text{expand}_{\Sigma}\,(\underline{\texttt{unless}}\cdot\texttt{(success) fail();}) & \\
\hookrightarrow & \text{match}\,(\underline{x}\cdot y,\ \underline{\texttt{(success)}}\,\texttt{fail();}\ , & \varnothing) \\
\rightarrow & \text{match}\,(\underline{y},\ \ \underline{\texttt{fail()}}\ \texttt{;}, & [x \mapsto \texttt{(success)}]) \\
\rightarrow & \text{match}\,(\epsilon,\ \ \underline{\texttt{;}}, & [x \mapsto \texttt{(success)}, y \mapsto \texttt{fail()}]) \\
\hookrightarrow & \text{transcribe}\,(\ \texttt{if}\ (\ !\ x)\cdot y, & [x \mapsto \texttt{(success)}, y \mapsto \texttt{fail()}]) \\
\rightarrow & \texttt{if (!(success)) fail();} &
\end{array}
$$

Fig. 2. Detailed expansion process of the `unless` macro.

$$\text{match} : p \times s \times \Theta \rightarrow (\Theta, s) \qquad \text{transcribe} : t \times \Theta \rightarrow s$$

Figure 2 shows a simple example of matching and transcribing as part of macro expansion. The complete algorithm is shown in Fig. 3.

3 Macrofication

The goal of refactoring is to improve the code without changing its behavior. Analogously, macros are often used to introduce a more concise notation for equivalent, expanded code. An automatic refactoring tool in the context of macros could therefore automatically find fragments of code that can be replaced by a corresponding and simpler macro invocation. This section describes an algorithm for this *macrofication* refactoring which is based on pattern-template macros and essentially applies them in reverse, i.e. using the template of the macro for matching code and inserting the macro name and its macro invocation pattern with correct substitutions for variables. However, macro expansion and macrofication are not entirely symmetric due to non-determinism, overlapping macro rules and the way repeated variables are handled.

3.1 Basic Reverse Matching

Macro expansion uses a deterministic left-to-right recursion to process syntax until all macros have been expanded. This process takes advantage of the fact that macro invocations always start with the macro name, so if the current head of the syntax sequence does not correspond to a macro, that token will not be part of any other subsequent expansion, so the expansion recursively progresses with the rest of the syntax. During the macrofication process, however, a substitution might cause the refactored code to be part of a bigger pattern that also includes previous tokens as illustrated by the following example.

k, n Token		$h ::= k \mid \{s\}$	Token tree
		$s, r ::= k \cdot s \mid \{s\} \cdot s \mid \epsilon$	Syntax Sequence
x	Pattern Variable	$p, q, t ::= k \cdot p \mid \{p\} \cdot p \mid x \cdot p \mid \epsilon$	Pattern/Template
$\Theta : x \to h$	Bound variables	$\Sigma : (n, p, t)^*$	Macro Environment

$$
\begin{array}{lll}
\text{expand}_\Sigma & : s \to s & \\
\text{expand}_\Sigma\ (k \cdot s) & \hat{=}\ \text{let } (n,p,t) \ = \ \text{first in } \Sigma \text{ s.t. } k = n \wedge \text{ match } (p, s, \varnothing) & \\
& \quad (\Theta, r) \ = \ \text{match } (p, s, \varnothing) & \\
& \quad \text{in expand}_\Sigma(\text{transcribe}(t, \Theta) \cdot r) & \\
\text{expand}_\Sigma\ (k \cdot s) & \hat{=}\ k \ \cdot \ \text{expand}_\Sigma\ (s) & (\text{otherwise}) \\
\text{expand}_\Sigma\ (\{s\} \cdot s') & \hat{=}\ \{ \ \text{expand}_\Sigma\ (s) \ \} \ \cdot \ \text{expand}_\Sigma\ (s') & \\
\text{expand}_\Sigma\ (\epsilon) & \hat{=}\ \epsilon &
\end{array}
$$

$$
\begin{array}{ll}
\text{macrofy}_\Sigma & : s \to s^* \\
\text{macrofy}_\Sigma\ (h \cdot s) & \hat{=}\ \{h \cdot r \mid r \in \ \text{macrofy}_\Sigma\ (s)\} \\
& \cup \ \{\{r'\} \cdot s \mid h = \{s'\} \ \wedge \ r' \in \ \text{macrofy}_\Sigma\ (s')\} \\
& \cup \ \{n \ \cdot \ \text{transcribe } (p, \Theta) \cdot r' \ \mid \\
& \qquad (n, p, t) \in \Sigma \ \wedge \ \text{match } (t, h \cdot s, \varnothing)) = (\Theta, r')\} \\
\text{macrofy}_\Sigma\ (\epsilon) & \hat{=}\ \varnothing
\end{array}
$$

$$
\begin{array}{lll}
\text{match} : p \times s \times \Theta \to (\Theta, s) & & \\
\text{match } (k \cdot p, k' \cdot s, \Theta) & \hat{=}\ \text{match } (p, s, \Theta) & (k = k') \\
\text{match } (\{q\} \cdot p, \{r\} \cdot s, \Theta) & \hat{=}\ \text{match } (p, s, \Theta') & (\text{match } (q, r, \Theta) = (\Theta', \epsilon)) \\
\text{match } (x \cdot p, h \cdot s, \Theta) & \hat{=}\ \text{match } (p, s, \Theta[x \mapsto h]) & \\
\text{match } (\epsilon, s, \Theta) & \hat{=}\ (\Theta, s) &
\end{array}
$$

$$
\begin{array}{ll}
\text{transcribe} & : t \times \Theta \to s \\
\text{transcribe } (k \cdot t, \Theta) & \hat{=}\ k \ \cdot \ \text{transcribe } (t, \Theta) \\
\text{transcribe } (\{t\} \cdot t', \Theta) & \hat{=}\ \{ \ \text{transcribe } (t, \Theta) \ \} \ \cdot \ \text{transcribe } (t', \Theta) \\
\text{transcribe } (x \cdot t, \Theta) & \hat{=}\ \Theta(x) \ \cdot \ \text{transcribe } (t, \Theta) \\
\text{transcribe } (\epsilon, \Theta) & \hat{=}\ \epsilon
\end{array}
$$

Fig. 3. Basic macro expansion and macrofication algorithm without repetitions.

```
macro inc {
  rule { $x } => { $x + 1 }
}
macro inc2 {
  rule { $x } => { 1 + inc $x }
}
```

$$\begin{aligned} \text{macrofy}_{\Sigma}\ (\texttt{1 + }\underline{\texttt{2 + 1}}) &\rightarrow \texttt{1 + }\underline{\texttt{inc 2}} \\ \text{macrofy}_{\Sigma}\ (\underline{\texttt{1 + inc 2}}) &\rightarrow \underline{\texttt{inc2 2}} \end{aligned}$$

Another asymmetry between expansion and macrofication is caused by the fact that different syntax might expand to the same resulting syntax. So, while the expansion process always produces a single deterministic result for a given syntax, the macrofication process produces multiple possible candidates of refactored programs which all expand to the same result and behave identically. In the following example, two different macrofications expand to the same program.

```
macro inc {
  rule { $x } => { $x + 1 }
}
```

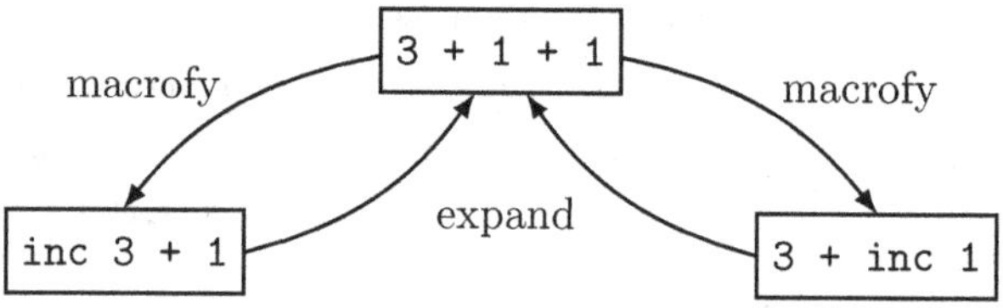

For these reasons, macrofication returns a set of programs instead of a single result (see Fig. 3). If h is the head of the syntax and s the tail, the result is the union of three sets:

1. all macrofications of s that do not involve h,
2. if h is syntax in delimiters $\{s'\}$, then also macrofications of s', and
3. the program resulting from replacing a matched template t with the macro invocation consisting of the macro name n and substituted pattern p.

It is important to note that algorithm does not recurse on macrofied token trees, so each returned result is a token tree with exactly one step of macrofication. Our development environment based on this algorithm enables the programmer to choose the best refactored program amongst these candidates according to her design decisions and then repeat this process.

3.2 Repeated Variables

The pattern matching described in Sect. 2 as part of the macrofication algorithm processes pattern variables by simply adding the matched token tree to the environment Θ. This corresponds to the common pattern matching behavior in most macro systems. However, the pattern does not enforce variables to be unique, so $x \cdot x$ is a valid pattern. Most existing macros systems including those of Racket [53], Rust [1] and JavaScript [10] do not properly handle repeated pattern variables.

This restriction of the pattern language is usually inconsequential as macro patterns are specially chosen to bind pattern variables in a concise way without unnecessary repetition. However, this repetition is actually intended when pattern variables occur more than once in the template of a macro. For example, the `twice` macro shown in Fig. 4 binds `$f` and `$x` in the pattern (`$f $x`) and then uses `$f` multiple times in the template (`$f($f($x))`). The macrofication algorithm described in Sect. 3 uses this template for pattern matching, therefore it has to handle repeated variable bindings by enforcing the tokens to exactly repeat the previously bound token tree. The following examples illustrate the desired pattern matching for repeated variables in the pattern $x\ x$.

$$\begin{array}{lllll}
\text{match}(x\ x, & a\ a, & \varnothing) & \rightarrow & [x \mapsto a] \\
\text{match}(x\ x, & a\ b, & \varnothing) & \rightarrow & \text{no match} \\
\text{match}(x\ x, & \{a\ b\}\ \{a\ b\}, & \varnothing) & \rightarrow & [x \mapsto \{a\ b\}]
\end{array}$$

To support repeated variables, it is possible to extend the match function in the simple algorithm shown in Fig. 3 with an additional case analysis. If the variable x was not assigned before, it gets bound to the corresponding token tree h in the sequence. If, on the other hand, the variable is already part of the pattern environment Θ, then the syntax h has to be identical to the previously bound syntax.

$$\begin{array}{lcll}
\text{match}(x \cdot p,\ h \cdot s,\ \Theta) & \hat{=} & \text{match}(p, s, \Theta[x \mapsto h]) & (x \notin dom(\Theta)) \\
\text{match}(x \cdot p,\ h \cdot s,\ \Theta) & \hat{=} & \text{match}(p, s, \Theta) & (\Theta(x) = h)
\end{array}$$

While this extended matching algorithm correctly handles repeated variables in simple patterns and templates, Sect. 5 outlines a more sophisticated algorithm which also supports arbitrarily nested pattern repetitions with ellipses.

In contrast to matching repeated variables in patterns, repeated variables in templates are inconsequential for the transcription process. Variables can be used zero or more times in a template without affecting other parts of the transcription process.

4 Refactoring Correctness

The macrofication algorithm presented in Sect. 3 finds all reverse macro matches that could expand again to the original program. In addition, the advanced pattern matching algorithms described in Sects. 3.2 and 5 ensure that even repeated variables are handled correctly. However, this algorithm by itself might inadvertently

```
macro twice {
  rule { $f $x } => { $f($f($x)) }
}
inc(inc(a))
```

$$\begin{aligned}&\text{macrofy}_{\Sigma}\ (\texttt{inc(inc(a))})\\ \hookrightarrow\ &\text{match}\ (f \cdot (f \cdot (x))),\ \texttt{inc}\ \ (\texttt{inc(a)}),\ \ \varnothing)\\ \rightarrow\ &([x : \texttt{a}, f : \texttt{inc}], \epsilon)\\ \hookrightarrow\ &\texttt{twice}\ \cdot\ \text{transcribe}\ (f \cdot x, [x : \texttt{a}, f : \texttt{inc}])\\ \rightarrow\ &\texttt{twice inc a}\end{aligned}$$

```
inc(dec(a))
```

$$\begin{aligned}&\text{macrofy}_{\Sigma}\ (\texttt{inc(dec(a))})\\ \hookrightarrow\ &\text{match}\ (f \cdot (f \cdot (x))),\ \texttt{inc}\ \ (\texttt{dec(a)}), \varnothing)\\ \rightarrow\ &\text{no match}\end{aligned}$$

Fig. 4. Macrofication with a macro that uses repeated variables in its template. During the matching process, the pattern variable `$f` will be bound to `inc` at its first occurrence and subsequently matched at all remaining occurrences of `$f`.

alter the behavior of the refactored code. In order to guarantee correctness, the refactoring algorithm also needs to take the order of macro expansions and variable scoping in a hygienic macro system into account.

4.1 Problem 1: Conflicts Between Macro Expansions

It is possible for multiple macros patterns to overlap. If more than one macro rule matches, the macro expansion algorithm will always expand the first such rule. Due to this behavior, the order of macro rules is significant for the expansion. A naïve refactoring algorithm might inadvertently alter the behavior by refactoring with a rule that is not used during expansion due to other rules with higher priority. As an example, the following macro declares two rules with overlapping patterns.

```
macro inc {
  rule { 1 } => { 3 }
  rule { $x } => { $x + 1 }
}
```

For the program `1 + 1`, macrofication would match the template of the second rule and use it to refactor the program to `inc 1`. However, `inc 1` would macro expand to 3 via the first rule, so macrofication would have changed the behavior of the original program.

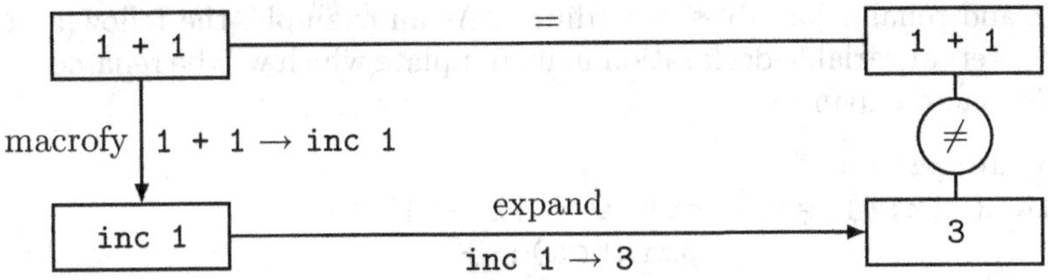

In fact, the order of macro expansion also affects refactoring correctness even if there is just one single rule:

```
macro inc {
  rule { $x } => { $x + 1 }
}
```

The program `2 + 1 + 1` can be correctly macrofied to `inc 2 + 1` but a second macrofication on the new program breaks program behavior – despite the fact that both macrofications apply the same rule on the same matched tokens.

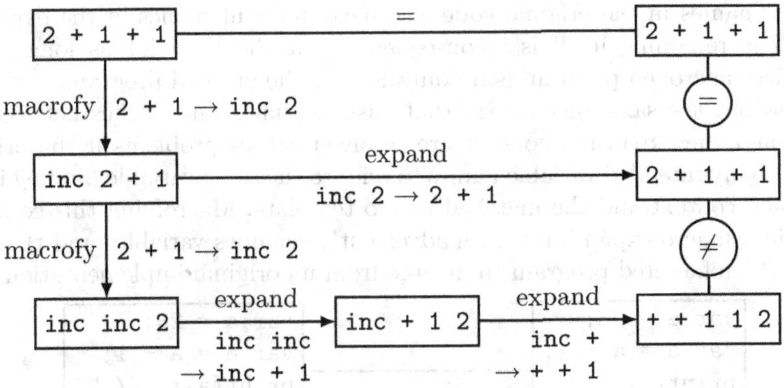

In order to prevent the incorrect second macrofication, an improved version of the macrofication algorithm would need to look back at the preceding syntax and consider all macro expansions that might affect the matched code. Unfortunately, there is no clear upper bound on the length of the prefix that has to be considered because macrofication operates on unexpanded token trees which may include additional macro invocations.

4.2 Problem 2: Hygiene

The basic premise of a hygienic macro system is that macro expansion preserves alpha equivalence, which requires that the scope of variables bound in a macro is separate from the scope in the macro expansion context [21].

So far, the expansion and macrofication algorithms presented in this paper do not address hygiene, scoped variables or the concrete grammar and semantics of the target language. However, most macro systems used in practice respect hygiene and rename variables accordingly. As an example, the following macro uses an internal variable declaration in its template which will be renamed during hygienic macro expansion.

```
macro decprint {
  rule { $x; } => { var a = $x - 1;
                     print(a); }
}
```

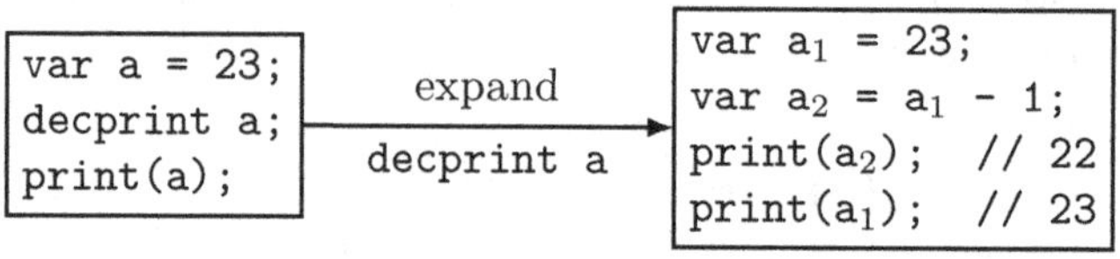

The implementation details of hygienic macro expansion are beyond the scope of this paper[2] but the symmetric relationship between expansion and macrofication suggests that renaming of scoped variables by hygienic expansion also affects macrofication.

In the general case, hygiene is compatible with macrofication as variables with different names in the original code also have different names in the expanded code. The renaming itself is inconsequential for the behavior as long as the expanded macrofied program is α-equivalent to the original program.

However, the same mechanism that ensures that name clashes between the macro and the expansion context are resolved causes problems if the original code actually intended variable names to refer to the same variable binding in the expansion context and the matched macro template. Macrofying this code will result in a macro expansion that inadvertently renames variables and therefore causes the refactored program to diverge from its original implementation.

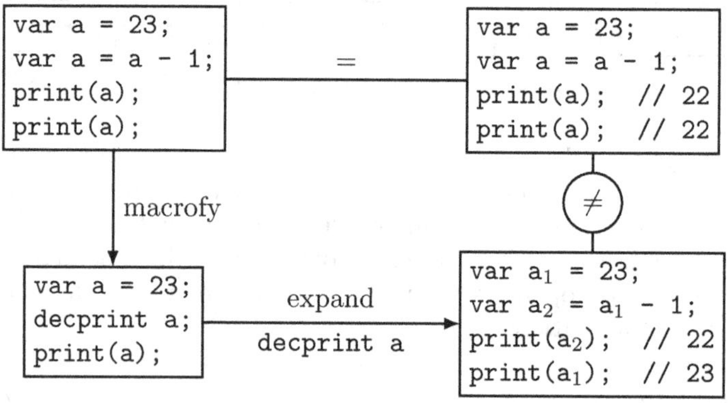

4.3 Rejecting Incorrectly Macrofied Code

The previous two sections showed macrofied code with different behavior than the original code which has to be avoided for refactoring as behavior-invariant code improvement.

[2] For a hygienic macro system for JavaScript, see sweet.js [10].

Approaches to fix these problems with an improved matching algorithm are limited by the fact that the correctness of a refactoring operation depends on the surrounding syntax including an arbitrary long prefix (see Problem 1). While this problem could be solved with a complex dynamic check during macrofication, additional difficulties arise from scoped variables that are renamed due to hygiene (see Problem 2). In contrast to the simple expansion and macrofication process, hygiene requires information about variable scopes which are usually defined in terms of parsed ASTs of the program instead of unexpanded token trees that may still include macro invocations.

We address these problems via a simple check performed after the macrofication. It rejects macrofication candidates that, when expanded, are not syntactically α-equivalent to the original program. This simple check successfully resolves these correctness concerns without complicating the macrofication algorithm[3].

$$\text{refactor}_\Sigma(s) \ \hat{=}\ \{\, r \mid r \in \text{macrofy}_\Sigma(s) \wedge \text{expand}_\Sigma(s) \underset{\alpha}{=} \text{expand}_\Sigma(r)\}$$

Here, α-equivalence $\underset{\alpha}{=}$ is used as alternative to perfect syntactic equivalence which also accommodates hygienic renaming. However, enforcing syntactic equivalence might still reject otherwise valid refactoring opportunities if there are difference that would not affect program behavior, e.g. additional or missing optional semicolons. Further relaxing this equivalence to a broader semantic equivalency might improve the robustness of macrofication but semantic equivalence itself is undecidable in the general case.

5 Repetitions in Patterns

Extending the macrofication algorithm described in the previous section with a more expressive pattern and template language does not affect the basic idea of macrofication or the correctness of the results. However, a more sophisticated pattern matching algorithm for matching arbitrarily nested *pattern repetitions* is necessary to correctly support macros like the class macro shown in Fig. 1. The details of the extended algorithm described in this section are not crucial for the remainder of the paper and could be skipped on a first reading.

Pattern repetitions in a pattern allow the use of a single pattern to model an unlimited sequence of that pattern. These pattern repetitions are supported by many macro systems and typically denoted by appending ellipses ( )... to the part of the pattern which gets repeated.

$$p, t ::= k \cdot p \mid \{p\} \cdot p \mid x^i \cdot p \mid \boldsymbol{(p)...} \cdot \boldsymbol{p} \mid \epsilon$$

Without pattern repetitions, pattern variables can only be assigned a single token tree $h = h^0$. However, if a variable is used in a pattern repetition, it

[3] Additional macro expansions performed as part of this check could potentially be further optimized to improve performance. However, performance problems due to this check did not surface during the evaluation.

can hold multiple term trees, one for each time the inner pattern was repeated. Pattern repetitions can be nested, so for the purposes of the matching algorithm, every pattern variable x^i has a *level* i which is automatically determined based on the nesting of pattern repetitions. In the simplest case, the level of a variable corresponds to the nesting of repetitions, such that x would have level 0 in the pattern $k \cdot x^0 \cdot k$ and level 1 if in a repetition group like $k \cdot (x^1 \cdot k)_{\dots}$, etc. After a successful match, a variable x^1 will hold a sequence of h^0 token trees, x^2 variables a sequence of sequences of h^0 token trees, and more generally x^i a sequence of h^{i-1} groups.

$$h ::= k \mid \{s\} \qquad\qquad h^0 ::= h \qquad\qquad h^i ::= h^{i-1} \cdot h^i \mid \epsilon$$

After successfully matching a complete pattern, the final pattern environment Θ always maps variables x^i to groups h^i of the same level. However, the environment used while matching inner patterns builds groups in the pattern environment Θ recursively, so a variable x^i might also hold a group of lower level during the matching process but the level j of its group h^j can never exceed the level i of the variable.

$$\Theta : x^i \rightarrow \bigcup_{0 \leq j \leq i} h^j$$

In order to track the current nesting level during the matching process, the match algorithm shown in Fig. 3 has to be extended with an additional parameter $j \in \mathbb{N}$ which will initially be 0 at the top level.

$$\text{match} : p \times s \times \Theta \times \mathbb{N} \rightarrow (\Theta, s)$$

For any nesting level j during the matching process, the intermediate pattern environment Θ always maps free pattern variables x^i in a (sub-)pattern p to groups of level $i - j$.

$$\forall p, s, j.\ \text{match}(p, s, \varnothing, j) = (\Theta, r) \ \Rightarrow\ \forall x^i \in FV(p).\ \Theta(x^i) \in h^{i-j}$$

5.1 Transcribing Templates with Repetitions

Transcribing a template $(t)_{\dots} \cdot t'$ with a given environment Θ, *unrolls* all groups used in t and then proceeds with t'. If there is only one group variable x^i in t with length $n = |\Theta(x^i)|$, then the template t will be transcribed n times, each time with a different assignment for x^i. The final result will then be the concatenation of all these repetitions.

$$\begin{array}{lll}
\text{transcribe}(a\ x^0, & [x^0 \mapsto b]) & \rightarrow a\ b \\
\text{transcribe}((x^1)_{\dots}, & [x^1 \mapsto [a, b, c]]) & \rightarrow a\ b\ c \\
\text{transcribe}((a\ x^1)_{\dots}, & [x^1 \mapsto [b, c]]) & \rightarrow a\ b\ a\ c \\
\text{transcribe}((x^1)_{\dots} y^0, & [x^1 \mapsto [], y^0 \mapsto a]) & \rightarrow a \\
\text{transcribe}((a\ (x^2)_{\dots})_{\dots}, & [x^2 \mapsto [[b, c], [d]]]) & \rightarrow a\ b\ c\ a\ d
\end{array}$$

If more than one group variable is used in a repetition, all variables are unrolled at the same time which is equivalent to *zipping* all the groups. The first repetition assigns each x^i the first element of each group, the second repetition assigns each x^i the second element, etc.

$$\text{transcribe}((x^1\ y^1)_{\ldots}, [x^1 \mapsto [a, b],\ y^1 \mapsto [c, d]]) \rightarrow a\ c\ b\ d$$

The inner template gets repeatedly transcribed until all the groups are empty which implies that all groups of currently repeating variables need to have the same length.

$$\forall \tilde{\Theta}.\quad \exists n \in \mathbb{N}.\quad \forall x^i \in \mathit{dom}(\tilde{\Theta}).\quad |\tilde{\Theta}(x^i)| = n$$

As mentioned in Sect. 3.2, repeated variables in a template are insignificant for the transcription process. The same is true for transcribing templates with pattern repetitions. The complete transcription algorithm is shown in Appendix A/Fig. 6.

5.2 Matching Patterns with Repetitions

Matching a pattern $(p)_{\ldots} \cdot p'$ is essentially the inverse operation to transcribing a template $(t)_{\ldots} \cdot t'$. Without repeated variables, the inner pattern p will be greedily matched as many times as possible until finally the remaining syntax s' and a new pattern environment Θ' will be returned and used to match the remaining pattern p'. Instead of destructing groups as in the transcription algorithm, each repetition constructs groups by adding the matched syntax to the corresponding group for all repeating variables.

$$\begin{array}{llr} \text{match}(a\ x^0, & a\ b, \quad\ \ \varnothing) \rightarrow & [x^0 \mapsto b] \\ \text{match}((a\ y^1)_{\ldots}, & a\ b\ a\ c, \varnothing) \rightarrow & [y^1 \mapsto [b, c]] \\ \text{match}(x^0 (y^1)_{\ldots}, & a\ b\ c, \quad \varnothing) \rightarrow & [x^0 \mapsto a, y^1 \mapsto [b, c]] \\ \text{match}((x^1\ y^1)_{\ldots}, & a\ b\ c\ d, \varnothing) \rightarrow & [x^1 \mapsto [a, c],\ y^1 \mapsto [b, d]] \end{array}$$

Unfortunately, the greedy matching of repetitions does not support patterns like $(a)_{\ldots}\ a$ as the repetition would have consumed all a tokens at the point the second a would try to match. A more sophisticated pattern matching algorithm might use either lookahead or backtracking to prevent or recover from consuming too many tokens in a repetition. However, this matching would be less efficient and macros with these kinds of pattern repetitions are unusual in practice.

5.3 Matching Repeated Variables in Patterns with Repetitions

As explained in Sect. 3.2, the pattern matching necessary for macrofication also needs to support repeated variables in patterns and templates. If a pattern variable is repeated at the same group level, the number of times the group matches as well as all matched token trees have to be identical.

$$
\begin{array}{lll}
\text{match}(x^0\ b\ x^0, & a\ b\ a) & \rightarrow [x^0 \mapsto a] \\
\text{match}(x^0\ b\ x^0, & a\ b\ c) & \rightarrow \text{no match} \\
\text{match}(\{(x^1)_{...}\}(x^1)_{...}, & \{a\ b\}\ a\ b) & \rightarrow [x^1 \mapsto [a, b]] \\
\text{match}(\{(x^1)_{...}\}(x^1)_{...}, & \{a\ b\}\ a\ c) & \rightarrow \text{no match} \\
\text{match}((a\ x^1)_{...}\ (x^1)_{...}, & a\ b\ a\ c\ b\ c) & \rightarrow [x^1 \mapsto [b, c]] \\
\text{match}((a\ x^1)_{...}\ (x^1)_{...}, & a\ b\ a\ c\ b\ d) & \rightarrow \text{no match}
\end{array}
$$

If the pattern variable is used once inside and once outside a repetition, all occurrences of that variable within the repetition have to repeat the same syntax as outside the repetition. This means that the variable assignment will be constant while repeatedly matching the pattern repetition, essentially using a lower level than the nesting would indicate.

As an example, the pattern $x^0(x^0\ y^1)_{...}$ uses two variables x^0 and y^1 where y^1 is only used once and in a repetition, so a successful match will result in a group of tokens h^1 with one assignment per repetition. In contrast, the variable x^0 is used multiple times, so every occurrence of x^0 in the pattern has to match the exact same syntax. Since x^0 is used outside of repetitions, its final assignment has to be a single token h^0 and additionally, all repetitions have to repeat this exact same syntax – instead of building up a group.

$$
\begin{array}{lll}
\text{match}(x^0(x^0\ y^1)_{...}, & a\ a\ b\ a\ c) & \rightarrow [x^0 \mapsto a, y^1 \mapsto [b, c]] \\
\text{match}(x^0(x^0\ y^1)_{...}, & a\ a\ b\ d\ c) & \rightarrow \text{no match} \\
\text{match}(x^0(x^0\ y^0)_{...}\ y^0, & a\ a\ b\ b) & \rightarrow [x^0 \mapsto a, y^0 \mapsto b] \\
\text{match}(x^0(x^0\ y^0)_{...}\ y^0, & a\ a\ b\ a\ b\ b) & \rightarrow [x^0 \mapsto a, y^0 \mapsto b] \\
\text{match}(x^0(x^0\ y^0)_{...}\ y^0, & a\ a\ b\ a\ b\ c) & \rightarrow \text{no match}
\end{array}
$$

This causes the matching processes to become more complicated as variable levels can diverge from the level of nesting. If the level of a variable is higher in the template than in the pattern, it will be matched and used as a lower level variable, i.e. as constant in a pattern repetition, in order to be compatible with the pattern. This is especially important for macrofication, as the template might use variables within a repetition that are assumed constant in the pattern. For example, the class name variable `$cname` in the template of the `class` macro in Fig. 1 appears once on the top level and once inside the repetition for every method, so the matching algorithm has to ensure that all methods use the same class name and therefore treat `$cname` as a constant at each repetition.

In order to support repeated variables in patterns with repetitions, it is necessary to extend the match algorithm. Conceptually, the first time a group variable $x^{i \geq 1}$ is encountered in a pattern, the elements are collected by greedily matching syntax and recursively constructing a group h^i. However, once a pattern variable has been assigned, all subsequent uses of that variable in a repetition will cause the pattern repetition to be unrolled following the approach of the transcribe algorithm described in Sect. 5.1.

Figure 6 in Appendix A shows the complete algorithm for matching and transcribing arbitrarily nested *pattern repetitions* with repeated variables to correctly support macros like the class macro shown in Fig. 1.

6 Implementation

Our implementation is part of sweet.js, a hygienic macro system for JavaScript which supports pattern-template macros [10]. The source code[4] as well as a live online demo[5] are both publicly available, and sweet.js is now using the extended pattern matching algorithm for macrofication and regular macro expansion.

Much of our implementation is a straightforward application of the algorithms described in the previous sections. However, there are a few JavaScript specific details. In particular, due to the complexity of JavaScript's grammar, sweet.js provides the ability for a pattern variable to match against a specific *pattern class* in addition to matching on a single or repeating token. A pattern class also allows a macro to match on multiple tokens, e.g. all tokens in an expression. To restrict a pattern variable `$x` to match an expression, the programmer can annotate the variable with the pattern class `:expr` (see Listing 4).

```
macro m {
  rule {
    ($bind:($id:ident = $val:expr) (,) ...)
  } => {
    $(var $bind;) ...
  }
}
m a = 2 + 1,   // --> var a = 2 + 1;
  b = 3        //     var b = 3;
```

Listing 4. A sweet.js macro with pattern classes `:ident`, `:expr`, a named pattern (`$bind`) and ellipses (`...`). In order to support macrofication of this macro, the pattern classes used in the pattern also have to apply to pattern variables in the template.

Considering the code fragment `arr[i + 1]`, a pattern variable `$x` matches just the single token `arr` whereas the pattern `$x:expr` matches the entire expression `arr[i + 1]`. Pattern class annotations only appear in patterns, not templates, so to support pattern classes in macrofication we move pattern class annotations from the pattern to the corresponding variables in the template prior to matching the template with the code.

[4] http://github.com/mozilla/sweet.js (see `src/reverse.js`, `src/patterns.js`).

[5] http://sweetjs.org/browser/editor.html.

Another difference between the algorithm in Fig. 3 and the implementation in sweet.js is the handling of the macro environment Σ. The algorithm assumes that the macro definitions are clearly separated from the program and globally scoped. In contrast, sweet.js macro definitions are defined in the code and cannot be used unless in scope. The current implementation of the refactoring algorithm only supports global macros but could be modified such that the macro environment Σ respects the scopes of macro definitions.

The sweet.js refactoring tool is usable from the command line as well as in the web-based sweet.js editor. Figures 1 and 5 show screen shots of this editor integration. As discussed in Sect. 3, not all refactoring options actually improve the code and could be mutually exclusive. To solve this issue, the development environment displays all options by highlighting code and opening a pop-up overlay of the refactored code on demand. This integration provides unobtrusive visual feedback about refactoring opportunities but other ways to displaying these may be preferable if there is large number of macrofication candidates.

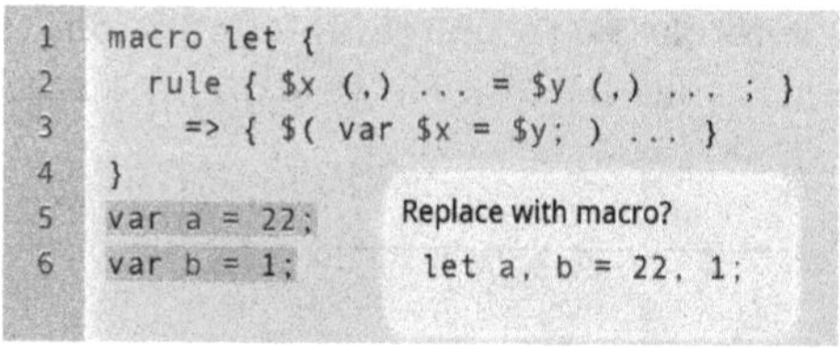

Fig. 5. A sweet.js macro which expands a parallel `let` declaration to multiple single declarations. The editor automatically detects a refactoring candidate in line 5 and 6 and shows a preview of the substituted code.

7 Evaluation

We evaluated the utility and performance of the macrofication refactoring tool by performing a complex refactoring of a JavaScript library with a specifically tailored macro and second case study on a JavaScript project with a large number of existing macros.

7.1 Experimental Results

Macros can be used to extend the language with additionally facilities that are not part of the grammar. For JavaScript, one of the most requested language features is a declarative *class* syntax, which can be desugared to code with prototypical inheritance (see Fig. 1). Indeed, the most recent version of JavaScript (ECMAScript 2015/ES6 [23]) adds class definitions to the language[6].

[6] See also the `es6-macros` project [31] which includes macros for many ES6 features.

```
macro class {
  rule {
    $name extends Events {
      constructor $cargs $cbody
      $( $mname $margs $mbody ) ...
    }
  } => {
    var $name = Backbone.$name = function $cargs $cbody;
    _.extend($name.prototype, Events.prototype, {
      $(
        $mname: function $margs $mbody
      ) (,) ...
    });
  }
}
```

Listing 5. Custom class macro for refactoring Backbone.js.

A particularly popular JavaScript framework that relies on inheritance to integrate with user-provided code is Backbone.js[7]. It is open source, widely deployed and has 1633 lines of code. The prototype objects defined by Backbone.js generally adhere to a simple class-based inheritance approach. Therefore, the code would benefit from declarative class definitions in the language.

Refactoring the Backbone.js code by automatic macrofication required a custom class macro which matches the concrete pattern used by Backbone.js to declare prototypes with the `_.extend` function. Here, '_' is a variable in the Backbone.js library with common helper functions like `extend` to add properties to objects. Since the Backbone.js code does not use any *super* calls, the simple macro shown in Listing 5 is sufficient to desugar classes to the prototype pattern used in Backbone.js. As additional manual refactoring step, non-function default properties in the Backbone.js code had to be moved into the constructor since they are not yet supported by the ES2015/ES6 class syntax[8]. After this minor change in the code, the sweet.js macrofication successfully identified all five prototypes used in Backbone.js and refactored these with class declarations without changing the program behavior.

A second case study was performed using the open source project *ru*[9] which is a collection of 66 macro rules for JavaScript inspired by Clojure. For refactoring the ru-lang library, only 27 macro rules were considered because case macros and custom operators are not currently supported by the macrofication tool. While the tool reported a large number of correct macrofication options, some of these did not improve the code quality. For example, some macrofication candidates introduce an invocation of the `cond` macro with just a single

[7] http://backbonejs.org/.

[8] It would also be possible to perform this transformation automatically with a more complex and less generic macro.

[9] http://ru-lang.org/.

default `else` branch. While this macrofication correctly expands to the original code, it essentially corresponds to replacing a JavaScript statement "`x;`" with "`if (true) x;`".

Table 1. Results of refactoring the JavaScript libraries Backbone.js and ru-lang.

Project	LOC	Time to read	Time to refactor	Macros	Macrofications
Backbone.js	1633	151 ms	984 ms	1	5
ru-lang	257	1350 ms	17921 ms	27	52

Table 1 shows the runtime of the macrofication step and the reading step as measured with the sweet.js command line running on NodeJS v0.11.13; all times reported averaged across 10 runs. The macrofication step including the expansion of the refactored code was about 6.5 to 13 times slower than the time to read/lex the input and load the macro environment. While future optimizations could improve performance, the runtime of macrofication seems generally feasible.

7.2 Discussion

Overall, the experimental results show that macrofication has major advantages over a manual refactoring approach.

1. Macrofication is guaranteed to preserve the behavior of the program and hence avoids the risks of human error.
2. The time and effort of the refactoring is dominated by the time and effort of writing the macros. Refactoring code with a given macro requires little manual effort, is fast enough for interactive use in an editor and scales well even for large code bases.

However, the experiment also showed three limitations of macrofication.

1. The macro has to be pre-existing or provided by the programmer in advance of the refactoring.
2. While small macros can be generic, larger macros may need to be specifically tailored to the code.
3. Minor differences between the macro template and the code, e.g. the order of statements or additional or missing semicolons in a language with optional semicolons, cause the macrofication algorithm to miss a potential refactoring option due to the strict syntactic equivalence check of the algorithm.

The first limitation could be overcome with an algorithm for automated macro synthesis/inference which might be a promising area for future research (see Sect. 9).

The second limitation applies to all currently used macro systems to a certain degree. Small, generic macros, e.g. new syntax for loops, may be universally applicable but larger macros are usually specific to the code. For macrofication, this applies both to the pattern as well as its template. For example, the class macro shown in Fig. 1 had to be adapted for refactoring Backbone.js.

The programmer can work around the third limitation by specifying multiple macro rules with the same pattern but in order to tolerate discrepancies between the template and the unrefactored code during the matching process, it would be helpful to remove the syntactic equivalence constraint in favor of behavioral equivalence based on the semantics of the language. This is difficult to integrate into the refactoring as semantic equivalence is generally undecidable. A conservative and decidable approximation of semantic equivalence that is more precise than syntactic equivalence might significantly help macrofication but remains a topic for future work.

8 Related Work

Our tool combines ideas from two streams of research, macro systems that give programmers additional language abstractions through syntactic extensibility and automated refactoring tools for code restructuring.

8.1 Macro Systems

Macros have been extensively used and studied in the Lisp family of languages for many years [14,37]. Scheme in particular has embraced macros, pioneering the development of declarative definitions [26] and hygiene conditions for term rewriting macros (rule macros) [6] and procedural macros (case macros) [22]. In addition there has been work to integrate procedural macros and module systems [13,19]. Racket takes this work even further by extending the Scheme macro system with deep hooks into the compilation process [12,53] and robust pattern specifications [7].

Recently work has begun on formalizing hygiene for Scheme [2]. Prior presentations of hygiene have either been operational [22] or restricted to a typed subset of Scheme that does not include `syntax-case` [21].

Languages with macro systems of varying degrees of expressiveness not based on S-expressions include Fortress [4], Dylan [5], Nemerle [48], and C++ templates [3]. Template Haskell [47] makes a tradeoff by forcing the macro call sites to always be demarcated. The means that macros are always a second class citizen; macros in Haskell cannot seamlessly build a language on top of Haskell in the same way that Scheme and Racket can.

Some systems such as SugarJ [11], and OMeta [56] provide extensible grammars but require the programmer to reason about parser details. Multi stage systems such as mython [42] and MetaML [52] can also be used to create macros systems like MacroML [16]. Some systems like Stratego [54] and Marco [28] transform syntax using their own language, separate from the host language.

As mentioned before, our tool is built on top of sweet.js [10] which enables greater levels of macro expressiveness without s-expressions as pioneered by

Honu [40,41], a JavaScript-like language. ExJS [55] is another macro system for JavaScript however their approach is based on a staged parsing architecture (rather than a more direct manipulation of syntax as in Lisp/Scheme and sweet.js) and thus they only support pattern macros.

While the goal of macrofication is to introduce new syntactic sugar, recent work on *Resugaring* aims to preserve or recover syntactic sugar during the execution to improve debugging [38,39]. In contrast to macrofication, resugaring at runtime operates on ASTs of a concrete language rather than syntax trees.

Macro systems can be generalized to term rewriting systems which have been studied extensively in the last decades. Most noteworthy, it might be possible to statically analyze properties like confluence and overlapping of macro rules (as discussed in Sect. 4.1) by adapting prior research on orthogonal term rewriting systems [25].

8.2 Refactoring

Refactoring [15,33] as an informal activity to improve the readability and maintainability of code goes back to the early days of programming. Most currently used development environments for popular languages provide built-in automated refactoring tools, e.g. Visual Studio, Eclipse or IntelliJ IDEA.

Early formal treatments look into automated means of refactoring functional and imperative [20] and object-oriented programs [34] that preserve behavior. Since then much work has been done on building tools that integrate automated refactoring directly into the development environment [43], find code smells like duplicated code [29], correctly transform code while preserving behavior [36,44–46], and improve the user experience during refactoring tasks [18].

Additionally, prior work on generic refactoring tools includes scripting and template languages for refactoring in Erlang [30], Netbeans [27] and Ekeko/X [8]. However, while these refactoring languages operate on parsed ASTs, macros describe a program transformation in terms of unexpanded token trees.

Much of the work relating refactoring and macro systems have taken place in the context of the C preprocessor (cpp), which introduces additional complexity in traditional refactoring tasks since cpp works at the lexical level rather than the syntactic level and can expand to fragments of code. Garrido [17] addresses many of the refactoring issues introduced by cpp and Overbey et al. [35] systematically address many more by defining a preprocessor dependency graph.

Kumar et al. [51] present a *demacrofying* tool that converts macros in an old C++ code base to new language features introduced by C++11. In a sense they preform the opposite work of macrofication; where demacrofying removes unnecessary macros to aid in the clarity of a code base our refactoring macros add macro invocations to a code base to similar effect.

8.3 Pattern Matching

Pattern matching in macro systems is part of a broad class of pattern matching algorithms. In particular, the handling of repeated variables in the extended pattern matching algorithm in Sect. 5 is conceptually a first-order syntactical unification which is well known in the context of logic programming languages [32].

In a broader sense, the macrofication algorithm is also related to research on optimizing compilers, e.g. reverse inlining to decrease code size [9].

9 Future Work

While the algorithm is based on refactoring macro invocations, it would also be possible to perform non-macro refactorings with this approach. For example, identifiers can be renamed with a simple, temporary, scoped macro.

As discussed in Sect. 6, the macrofication algorithm presented in this paper assumes a static macro environment. Future work could extend this algorithm such that it also refactors macro definitions, modifies macro templates, removes existing overlapping macros, or even automatically synthesizes new macros. However, the search space of possible macros is vast, so a carefully designed search which optimizes some metric for code quality would be necessary to provide only the best macro candidates to the programmer.

An additionally promising topic of future research is the extension of the presented algorithm to `syntax-case` macros. In contrast to pattern-template macros, `syntax-case` macros use a generating function instead of a template. Finding refactoring options therefore needs to find syntax that can be generated by a macro which is equivalent to finding the input of a function given its output. Despite the undecidable nature of this problem, it might still be useful to find an incomplete subset of potential macro candidates.

10 Conclusions

The algorithm presented in this paper allows automatic refactoring by macrofying code with a given set of pattern-template macros. The algorithm correctly handles repeated variables and repetitions in the pattern and template of a macro with an extended pattern matching algorithm. The order of macro expansions and hygienic renaming cause a naïve macrofication approach to produce incorrect results. To ensure that the behavior is preserved during refactoring, the algorithm checks syntactic α-equivalence of the fully expanded code before and after the macrofication. The algorithm is language-independent but was evaluated for JavaScript with an implementation based on sweet.js and used to refactor Backbone.js, a popular JavaScript library with more than one thousand lines of code. The runtime performance indicates that the approach is feasible even for large code bases. Finally, the IDE integration supports and automates the macro development process with promising extensions for future research.

Acknowledgements. This research was supported by the National Science Foundation under grants CCF-1337278 and CCF-1421016.

A Appendix

k, n Token	$h ::= k \mid \{s\}$		Token tree
	$s, r ::= k \cdot s \mid \{s\} \cdot s \mid \epsilon$		Syntax Sequence
x^i Variable	$p, q, t ::= k \cdot p \mid \{p\} \cdot p \mid x^i \cdot p \mid (p)_{\dots} \cdot p \mid \epsilon$		Pattern/Template
$i, j : \mathbb{N}$ Levels	$h^0 ::= h$	$h^i ::= h^{i-1} \cdot h^i \mid \epsilon$	Group of level i
	$\Sigma : (n, p, t)^*$		Macro Environment
	$\Theta : x^i \to \bigcup_{0 \leq j \leq i} h^j$		Pattern Environment
	$\tilde{\Theta} : x^i \to \bigcup_{1 \leq j \leq i} h^j$		Repetition Environment

$$\text{match} : p \times s \times \Theta \times \mathbb{N} \to (\Theta, s) \qquad \text{(See Fig. 3)}$$

$$\text{match}((p)_{\dots} \cdot p', s, \Theta, j) \triangleq \text{let } (\Theta', s') = \text{matchRep}(p, s, \text{groups}(p, \Theta), \Theta, j) \text{ in } \text{match}(p', s', \Theta', j)$$

$$\text{matchRep} : p \times s \times \tilde{\Theta} \times \Theta \times \mathbb{N} \to (\Theta, s)$$

$$\begin{aligned}
\text{matchRep}(p, s, \tilde{\Theta}, \Theta, j) \triangleq\ & \text{if } \forall x^i \in \mathit{dom}(\tilde{\Theta}).\ \tilde{\Theta}(x^i) \neq \epsilon \\
& \text{let } \Theta_r = \text{repeating}(\Theta, \Theta') \\
& \quad (\Theta', s') = \text{match}(p, s, \Theta \uparrow \text{head}(\tilde{\Theta}), j + 1) \\
& \quad (\Theta'', s'') = \text{matchRep}(p, s', \text{tail}(\tilde{\Theta}), \Theta' \setminus \Theta_r, j) \\
& \text{in } (\Theta'' \uparrow \text{cons}(\Theta_r, \Theta''), s'') \\
\text{matchRep}(p, s, \tilde{\Theta}, \Theta, j) \triangleq\ & \text{if } \forall x^i \in \mathit{dom}(\tilde{\Theta}).\ \tilde{\Theta}(x^i) = \epsilon \\
& (\Theta \left[x^i \mapsto \epsilon \mid x^i \in FV(p) \wedge x^i \notin \mathit{dom}(\Theta) \wedge i > j\right], s)
\end{aligned}$$

$$\text{transcribe} : t \times \Theta \to s \qquad \text{(See Fig. 3)}$$

$$\text{transcribe}((t)_{\dots} \cdot t', \Theta) \triangleq \text{transcribeRep}(t, \text{groups}(t, \Theta), \Theta) \cdot \text{transcribe}(t', \Theta)$$

$$\text{transcribeRep} : t \times \tilde{\Theta} \times \Theta \to s$$

$$\begin{aligned}
\text{transcribeRep}(t, \tilde{\Theta}, \Theta) \triangleq\ & \text{if } \forall x^i \in \mathit{dom}(\tilde{\Theta}).\ \tilde{\Theta}(x^i) \neq \epsilon \\
& \text{transcribe}(t, \Theta \uparrow \text{head}(\tilde{\Theta})) \cdot \text{transcribeRep}(t, \text{tail}(\tilde{\Theta}), \Theta) \\
\text{transcribeRep}(t, \tilde{\Theta}, \Theta) \triangleq\ & \text{if } \forall x^i \in \mathit{dom}(\tilde{\Theta}).\ \tilde{\Theta}(x^i) = \epsilon \\
& \epsilon
\end{aligned}$$

$$\begin{aligned}
\Theta \uparrow \Theta' &\triangleq \Theta \left[x^i \mapsto \Theta'(x^i) \mid x^i \in \mathit{dom}(\Theta')\right] \\
\text{cons}(\Theta, \tilde{\Theta}) &\triangleq \left[x \mapsto \Theta(x) \cdot \tilde{\Theta}(x) \mid x \in \mathit{dom}(\Theta) \ \wedge \ x \in \mathit{dom}(\tilde{\Theta})\right] \\
\text{head}(\tilde{\Theta}) &\triangleq \left[x^i \mapsto h^{j-1} \mid \tilde{\Theta}(x^i) = h^{j-1} \cdot h^j\right] \\
\text{tail}(\tilde{\Theta}) &\triangleq \left[x^i \mapsto h^j \mid \tilde{\Theta}(x^i) = h^{j-1} \cdot h^j\right] \\
\text{groups}(p, \Theta) &\triangleq \left[x^i \mapsto h^j \mid x^i \in FV(p) \ \wedge \ \Theta(x^i) = h^j \ \wedge j \geq 1\right] \\
\text{repeating}(\Theta, \Theta') &\triangleq \left[x^i \mapsto h^j \mid \Theta'(x^i) = h^j \ \wedge \ x^i \notin \mathit{dom}(\Theta) \ \wedge \ i > j\right]
\end{aligned}$$

Fig. 6. The complete algorithm for matching and transcribing patterns/templates with repeated variables and arbitrarily nested pattern repetitions as described in Sect. 5. Differences with the algorithm in Fig. 3 are shown in black.

References

1. The Rust Language. http://www.rust-lang.org/
2. Adams, M.D.: Towards the essence of hygiene. In: POPL 2015 (2015)
3. Alexandrescu, A.: Modern C++ Design: Generic Programming and Design Patterns Applied. Addison-Wesley, Reading (2001)
4. Allen, E., Culpepper, R., Nielsen, J.: Growing a syntax. In: FOOL 2009 (2009)
5. Bachrach, J., Playford, K., Street, C.: D-Expressions: Lisp Power, Dylan Style. Style DeKalb IL (1999)
6. Clinger, W.: Macros that work. In: POPL 1991 (1991)
7. Culpepper, R.: Refining syntactic sugar: tools for supporting macro development. Ph.D. thesis, Northeastern University Boston (2010)
8. De Roover, C., Inoue, K.: The Ekeko/X program transformation tool. In: SCAM 2014, pp. 53–58, September 2014
9. Debray, S.K., Evans, W., Muth, R., De Sutter, B.: Compiler techniques for code compaction. ACM Trans. Program. Lang. Syst. **22**(2), 378–415 (2000)
10. Disney, T., Faubion, N., Herman, D., Flanagan, C.: Sweeten your javascript: hygienic macros for ES5. In: Proceedings of the 10th ACM Symposium on Dynamic Languages, DLS 2014, pp. 35–44. ACM, New York (2014)
11. Erdweg, S., Rendel, T., Kästner, C., Ostermann, K.: SugarJ: library-based syntactic language extensibility. In: OOPSLA 2011 (2011)
12. Flatt, M., Culpepper, R., Darais, D., Findler, R.B.: Macros that work together. J. Funct. Prog. **22**, 181–216 (2012). doi:10.1017/S0956796812000093
13. Flatt, M.: Composable and compilable macros: you want it when? In: ICFP 2002, pp. 72–83 (2002)
14. Foderaro, J.K., Sklower, K.L., Layer, K.: The FRANZ LISP Manual. University of California, Berkeley (1983)
15. Fowler, M.: Refactoring: Improving the Design of Existing Code. Pearson Education, India (1999)
16. Ganz, S., Sabry, A., Taha, W.: Macros as multi-stage computations: type-safe, generative, binding macros in MacroML. In: ICFP 2001 (2001)
17. Garrido, A., Johnson, R.: Challenges of refactoring C programs. In: IWPSE 2002, pp. 6–14(2002)
18. Ge, X., DuBose, Q.L., Murphy-Hill, E.: Reconciling manual and automatic refactoring. In: ICSE 2012, pp. 211–221 (2012)
19. Ghuloum, A., Dybvig, R.K.: Implicit phasing for R6RS libraries. In: ICFP 2007 (2007)
20. Griswold, W.G.: Program restructuring as an aid to software maintenance. Ph.D. thesis, University of California, San Diego (1992)
21. Herman, D., Wand, M.: A theory of hygienic macros. In: Drossopoulou, S. (ed.) ESOP 2008. LNCS, vol. 4960, pp. 48–62. Springer, Heidelberg (2008)
22. Hieb, R., Dybvig, R., Bruggeman, C.: Syntactic abstraction in scheme. Lisp Symb. Comput. **5**(4), 295–326 (1992)
23. ECMA International: ECMA-262 ECMAScript Language Specification. ECMAScript, 6th edn. (2015)
24. Kernighan, B.W., Ritchie, D.M.: The C Programming Language, vol. 2. Prentice Hall, Upper Saddle River (1988)
25. Klop, J.W., Klop, J.: Term rewriting systems. Centrum voor Wiskunde en Informatica (1990)

26. Kohlbecker, E.E., Wand, M.: Macro-by-example: deriving syntactic transformations from their specifications. In: POPL 1987 (1987)
27. Lahoda, J., Bečička, J., Ruijs, R.B.: Custom declarative refactoring in NetBeans: tool demonstration. In: WRT 2012, pp. 63–64. ACM, New York (2012)
28. Lee, B., Grimm, R., Hirzel, M., McKinley, K.: Marco: safe, expressive macros for any language. In: Noble, J. (ed.) ECOOP 2012. LNCS, pp. 589–613. Springer, Heidelberg (2012)
29. Li, H., Thompson, S.: Clone detection and removal for Erlang/OTP within a refactoring environment. In: PEPM 2009. ACM (2009)
30. Li, H., Thompson, S.: Let's make refactoring tools user-extensible! In: WRT 2012, pp. 32–39. ACM, New York (2012)
31. Long, J.: The ES6-macros project. https://github.com/jlongster/es6-macros
32. Martelli, A., Montanari, U.: An efficient unification algorithm. In: TOPLAS 1982 (1982)
33. Mens, T., Tourwé, T.: A survey of software refactoring. IEEE Trans. Softw. Eng. **30**, 126–139 (2004)
34. Opdyke, W.F.: Refactoring object-oriented frameworks. Ph.D. thesis (1992)
35. Overbey, J.L., Behrang, F., Hafiz, M.: A foundation for refactoring C with macros. In: FSE 2014 (2014)
36. Overbey, J.L., Johnson, R.E.: Differential precondition checking: a lightweight, reusable analysis for refactoring tools. In: ASE (2011)
37. Pitman, K.M.: Special forms in Lisp. In: LFP 1980 (1980)
38. Pombrio, J., Krishnamurthi, S.: Resugaring: lifting evaluation sequences through syntactic sugar. In: PLDI 2014, pp. 361–371. ACM, New York (2014)
39. Pombrio, J., Krishnamurthi, S.: Hygienic resugaring of compositional desugaring. In: ICFP 2015, pp. 75–87. ACM, New York (2015)
40. Rafkind, J.: Syntactic extension for languages with implicitly delimited and infix syntax. Ph.D. thesis, The University of Utah (2013)
41. Rafkind, J., Flatt, M.: Honu: syntactic extension for algebraic notation through enforestation. In: GPCE 2012 (2012)
42. Riehl, J.: Language embedding and optimization in mython. In: DLS 2009 (2009)
43. Roberts, D., Brant, J., Johnson, R.E.: A refactoring tool for smalltalk. TAPOS **3**(4), 253–263 (1997)
44. Schäfer, M., De Moor, O.: Specifying and implementing refactorings. In: OOPSLA 2010 (2010)
45. Schäfer, M., Dolby, J., Sridharan, M., Torlak, E., Tip, F.: Correct refactoring of concurrent Java code. In: D'Hondt, T. (ed.) ECOOP 2010. LNCS, vol. 6183, pp. 225–249. Springer, Heidelberg (2010)
46. Schäfer, M., Verbaere, M., Ekman, T., de Moor, O.: Stepping stones over the refactoring rubicon. In: Drossopoulou, S. (ed.) ECOOP 2009. LNCS, vol. 5653, pp. 369–393. Springer, Heidelberg (2009)
47. Sheard, T., Jones, S.: Template meta-programming for Haskell. In: Workshop on Haskell (2002)
48. Skalski, K., Moskal, M., Olszta, P.: Meta-programming in Nemerle. In: GPCE 2004 (2004)
49. Sperber, M., Dybvig, R.K., Flatt, M., Van straaten, A., Findler, R., Matthews, J.: Revised6 report on the algorithmic language scheme. J. Funct. Prog. **19**, 1–301 (2009). doi:10.1017/S0956796809990074
50. Steele Jr., G.L.: Common LISP: The Language. Digital Press, Burlington (1990)
51. Stroustrup, B., Kumar, A., Sutton, A.: Rejuvenating C++ programs through demacrofication. In: ICSM 2012 (2012)

52. Taha, W., Sheard, T.: Multi-stage programming with explicit annotations. In: PEPM 1997 (1997)
53. Tobin-Hochstadt, S., St-Amour, V.: Languages as libraries. In: PLDI 2011 (2011)
54. Visser, E.: Program transformation with stratego/XT. In: Lengauer, C., Batory, D., Blum, A., Odersky, M. (eds.) Domain-Specific Program Generation. LNCS, vol. 3016, pp. 216–238. Springer, Heidelberg (2004)
55. Wakita, K., Homizu, K., Sasaki, A.: Hygienic macro system for JavaScript and Its light-weight implementation framework. In: ILC 2014 (2014)
56. Warth, A., Piumarta, I.: OMeta: an object-oriented language for pattern matching. In: DLS 2007 (2007)

Type Error Diagnosis for Embedded DSLs by Two-Stage Specialized Type Rules

Alejandro Serrano(✉) and Jurriaan Hage

Department of Information and Computing Sciences, Utrecht University, Utrecht, The Netherlands
{A.SerranoMena,J.Hage}@uu.nl

Abstract. In the functional programming world, it is common to embed a domain specific language (DSL) in a general purpose language. Unfortunately, the extra abstraction layer provided by the DSL is lost when a type error occurs, and internals leak to users of the DSL.

This paper presents *specialized type rules*, a way to influence which part of the program is blamed and how the particular error message is worded. These type rules match part of the programming language abstract syntax tree (AST) and guide the type checker in order to provide custom diagnostics. Our goal is to enable DSL writers to keep their high-level abstractions throughout the whole development experience. Specialized type rules have already been considered in the literature: we enhance them by providing a mechanism to allow type rules to *depend on partial type information.*

The technique presented in this paper can be readily applied to any type engine which uses constraints to perform its duty. We refine the workings of the type engine by including a *second gathering pass* in case an error is found. In that second pass, partial type information can be used to select a type rule. In particular, we have implemented our techniques in a type engine based on the OutsideIn(X) framework, which underlies the Haskell GHC compiler since version 7.

1 Introduction

Domain specific languages (DSLs) are a widely used technique, whose advantages are well-known: they solve a particular problem in an effective way with a language that is close to the domain of the experts, and are thus more likely to be used by experts, even those without prior programming experience. Examples abound, ranging from SQL for database processing to describing drawings [28] and even music harmony analysis [15].

Creating a standalone DSL involves developing a lot of tooling, including a parser, a code generator and static analyzers for the desired domain. Frameworks have been designed to help developers in this task [25]. This approach is

This work was supported by the Netherlands Organisation for Scientific Research (NWO) project on “DOMain Specific Type Error Diagnosis (DOMSTED)” (612.001.213).

P. Thiemann (Ed.): ESOP 2016, LNCS 9632, pp. 672–698, 2016.
DOI: 10.1007/978-3-662-49498-1_26

called *external*. Other authors [14] advocate instead *embedding* DSLs in a general purpose language, in order to reuse part of the machinery which is already implemented, and to allow an easy combination of DSLs. This embedded approach is common in the functional programming world.

Taha [24] describes four characteristics of a good DSL: (1) the domain is well-defined, (2) the notation is clear, (3) the informal meaning is clear, and (4) the formal meaning is clear and implemented. This overlooks one important feature of a good DSL: its implementation should communicate with the user using terms from the specific domain. Otherwise, the encoding into the host language leaks in warnings and type error messages.

Unfortunately, the converse situation is the rule when working with embedded DSLs: *error messages* are phrased in terms of the underlying general purpose language. The nice abstraction provided by the DSL is broken and the internals of the library are exposed to users of the DSL. As a concrete example, consider a DSL for extensible records in Haskell, similar to Vinyl.[1] This sort of libraries mandates fields to be declared beforehand, as follows.

$$\begin{aligned} \mathit{name} &= \mathit{Field} :: \mathit{Field}\ \texttt{"name"}\ \mathit{String} \\ \mathit{age} &= \mathit{Field} :: \mathit{Field}\ \texttt{"age"}\ \ \mathit{Integer} \end{aligned}$$

Each of the fields has the same representation in memory, but are given different types in the type annotation found after the :: symbol.

Afterwards, it becomes possible to build records with any desired combination of fields. To do so, we use *RNil* to represent a record without any field, which we populate by adding new fields and their data using *RCons*, as in:

$$\begin{aligned} \mathit{john} &= \mathit{RCons}\ \mathit{name}\ \texttt{"John"}\ \ (\mathit{RCons}\ \mathit{age}\ 30\ \mathit{RNil}) \\ \mathit{emily} &= \mathit{RCons}\ \mathit{name}\ \texttt{"Emily"}\ \mathit{RNil} \end{aligned}$$

The key point of this library is the definition of a strongly-typed *get* function, which given a field and a record, returns the value associated with such field. By strongly-typed we mean that it should reject code such as *get age emily*, where a field is requested from a record which does not contain it. This is achieved in the aforementioned library, by leveraging Haskell's type system.

$$\mathit{get} :: \mathit{Elem}\ (\mathit{Field}\ f\ t)\ \mathit{fs} \sim \mathit{True} \Rightarrow \mathit{Field}\ f\ t \rightarrow \mathit{Record}\ \mathit{fs} \rightarrow t$$

You can read this signature as ensuring that given a field named *f* with a type *t* and a record whose list of fields is *fs*, the field is an element of the list *fs*.[2] This works perfectly for type-correct programs. However, the type error message produced by GHC 7.8 for *get age emily* is far from perfect:

```
Couldn't match type 'False with 'True
```

[1] https://hackage.haskell.org/package/vinyl.

[2] *Elem* is a so called "type family", a restricted version of a type-level function, and the relation $\sim$ means "equality on types". In Haskell, Booleans are available at the type level via a technique called data type promotion.

```
Expected type: 'True
  Actual type: Elem (Field "age" Integer) '[Field "name" String]
In the expression: get age emily
```

In order to understand such a message, the user of the DSL needs to know about the internals of the library. Even more problematic, the library uses advanced type-level concepts from Haskell which the user may not know about. The direct consequence is frustration with either the language, the library, or both. In contrast, a good error message would take into account the domain knowledge and be phrased similarly to:

```
Cannot find field "age" in the record 'emily'
```

A first advantage of this message is that internals of the library are hidden from the user. The user of the DSL also profits from better guidance to fix the problem.

In order to get domain specific error messages, DSL writers need to be able to hook into the compiler and massage the messages before they are shown to the user. Several approaches are described in the literature, such as the post-processing of messages [2] and inspection of the type engine trace [20]. In our work, we build upon the concept of *specialized type rules* [11]. In short, a specialized type rule is the description of how to type a concrete piece of syntax, thereby overriding the default behaviour of the type engine for such an expression.

A specialized type rule which improves the message for *get age emily* is:

(1) **rule** *field_not_present*
(2) **case** *get* $\cdot^{\#field}$ $\cdot^{\#record}$
(3) **when** *#record* ~ *Record fs*, *Elem #field fs* ~ *False* {
(4) *#field* ~ *Field f t*,
repair { `"Cannot find field"` *f* : *ty* `"in the record"` *#record* : *expr* }
}

The rule consists of four fragments (1)–(4). Fragment (1) is merely an identifier, which is used by the system to provide information about the rule, such as failing the soundness check (Sect. 5). For example, had we mistaken writing *Recor* instead of *Record*, the system would show:

```
Rule field_not_present is not sound
```

alongside with information to help fixing the problem.

Fragment (2), headed by **case**, contains the description of which code pieces are matched by the rule. In this fragment, $\cdot$ indicates that any expression might be found in that position. Alongisde them, *#id* is used to give a name to a node of the AST, so that we can refer to it in the rest of the rule. This example matches any application of the *get* function to at least two arguments.

The fragment (4), syntactically indicated between braces, mandates the compiler to produce an error message, built from various literal strings, the type of the field and the expression which encodes the record.

Ingredients comparable to (1), (2) and (4), with a slightly different syntax, were already available in the type rules of [11]. Our *contribution* is to allow type rules to match and fire only in certain *typing contexts*. For example, fragment (3) of the previous example, indicates that this specialized type rule shall only be applied when the compiler can prove that the field is not available in the given record (at type-level, this is encoded as *Elem #field fs* being equal to *False*).

As described in Sect. 4.1, being able to apply a specialized type rule only when some typing information is known to hold has a number of interesting use cases. For example, a custom error message can be given for a specific instance of a Haskell type class. Also, common failure patterns can be detected and a fix can be suggested to the DSL user.

Being able to use typing information in specialized type rules requires changes to the type engine, as described in Sect. 4. Our approach is to perform type checking in two stages, in which a satisfiable subset of information from the first stage is used to select specialized type rules in the second stage. Furthermore, we want to ensure that the DSL writer does not render the type system unsound with a specialized type rule. Thus, we need to introduce soundness checks (Sect. 5).

A prototype implementation for a type system similar to that in the Haskell GHC compiler (including type classes, type families and higher-rank polymorphism) is available at http://cobalt.herokuapp.com.

2 Constraint-Based Type Inference

An integral part of most compilers involves performing a set of analyses on the input code, in order to detect ill behavior or prepare for optimization and transformation. Many of these analyses are described using a *type system*, which assigns types to constructs in the programming language. Statically-checked strong type systems, such as that of Haskell or ML, prevent many kinds of errors from arising at run-time. By using the type system, DSL writers can dictate how their DSL should be used.

Throughout this paper, we shall refer to the piece of software dealing with types as the *type engine*. As a first task, the type engine should be able to *check* that types match in the correct way: if the programmer has specified that an expression has an integral type, 3.5 should not be a valid value for such an expression. In many cases tagging every expression with a type is not neccessary in a program: the engine is able to reconstruct which types should be given to each expression via a process called *inference*.

There are several possible ways in which a type engine can be structured. One way is to traverse the Abstract Syntax Tree (AST) of the program, building the corresponding type at each step. This path is taken by the classical $\mathcal{W}$ and $\mathcal{M}$ implementations of the Hindley-Milner type system [3,16]. However, these syntax-directed algorithms are known to introduce some problems related to error reporting, in particular a bias coming from the fixed order in which they traverse the tree [19].

Another approach is to structure the engine around the concept of *constraints*. Instead of a single pass, the engine operates in two phases: in a first phase,

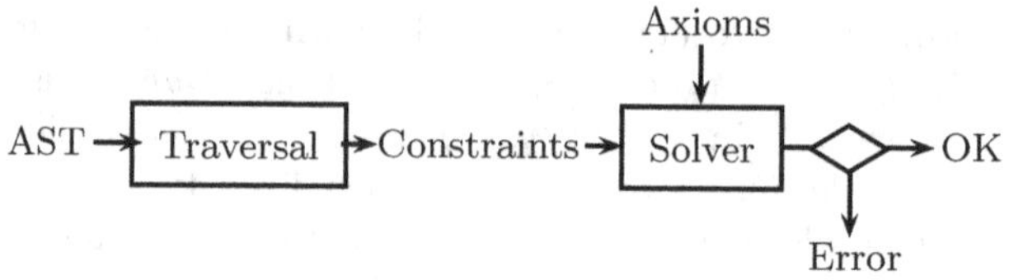

Fig. 1. Common structure of a constraint-based type engine

the AST is traversed and all the constraints that types must satisfy are gathered. Afterwards, a solution for those constraints is found. If the set of constraints happens to be inconsistent, we know that a type error exists in the program. This structure is shown in Fig. 1.

A constraint-based approach to typing is shown by Heeren *et al.* [11,13] to be a *good* choice as a basis for *domain specific error diagnosis.* The main reason is that these systems do not impose a strict order on the whole process. Furthermore, once all constraints are gathered, the solver may have a more holistic view on the structure of the program. For example, it may decide to show a different error for a given identifier based on its use sites. Other advantages of constraint-based type engines are discussed in [21] and include better modularity and a declarative description, instead of an operational one. The main disadvantage of constraint-based approaches to typing is some extra overhead.

2.1 Syntax-Directed Constraint Gathering

We assume constraint gathering to be a syntax-directed process, which traverses the code being analyzed in a top-down fashion, and builds a constraint set bottom-up. The constraint generation judgement

$$\Gamma \vdash e : \tau \rightsquigarrow C$$

represents that under an environment Γ the expression e is given a type τ subject to the constraints C. Note that Γ and e are the inputs in the process, whereas τ and C are the outputs.

Figure 2 shows the constraint generation rules for a simply-typed λ-calculus with **let**, a subset of the full Haskell language. The details on how to type full Haskell using constraints (which we implement in our prototype) are described in [26] as an instance of the general OutsideIn(X) framework.

As an example of this judgement, consider the following piece of Haskell, which returns the string representation of the successor of a given number n:

$$f = \lambda n \rightarrow \mathit{show}\ (n + 1)$$

In Fig. 3 the full derivation tree of its constraint set is given. We have omitted the $v : \tau \in \Delta$ leaves and the name of the rules applied at each step, in order to fit the entire tree on the page.

$$\frac{v : \forall \overline{a}.Q \Rightarrow \tau \in \Gamma \qquad \overline{\alpha} \text{ fresh}}{\Gamma \vdash v : [\overline{a \mapsto \alpha}]\tau \rightsquigarrow [\overline{a \mapsto \alpha}]Q}\ \text{VAR}$$

$$\frac{\alpha \text{ fresh} \qquad \Gamma, x : \alpha \vdash e : \tau \rightsquigarrow C}{\Gamma \vdash \lambda x.e : \alpha \to \tau \rightsquigarrow C}\ \text{ABS}$$

$$\frac{\alpha \text{ fresh} \qquad \Gamma \vdash e_1 : \tau_1 \rightsquigarrow C_1 \qquad \Gamma \vdash e_2 : \tau_2 \rightsquigarrow C_2}{\Gamma \vdash e_1\ e_2 : \alpha \rightsquigarrow C_1 \wedge C_2 \wedge \tau_1 \sim \tau_2 \to \alpha}\ \text{APP}$$

$$\frac{\Gamma \vdash e_1 : \tau_1 \rightsquigarrow C_1 \qquad \Gamma, x : \tau_1 \vdash e_2 : \tau_2 \rightsquigarrow C_2}{\Gamma \vdash \textbf{let } x = e_1 \textbf{ in } e_2 : \tau_2 \rightsquigarrow C_1 \wedge C_2}\ \text{LET}$$

Fig. 2. Constraint generation rules for a simply-typed λ-calculus with **let**

$$\dfrac{\dfrac{\dfrac{\vdots}{\begin{array}{l}\Delta \vdash show : \varepsilon \to String \\ \quad \rightsquigarrow Show\ \varepsilon\end{array}} \qquad \dfrac{\dfrac{\dfrac{\vdots}{\begin{array}{l}\Delta \vdash (+) : \delta \to \delta \to \delta \\ \quad \rightsquigarrow Num\ \delta\end{array}} \qquad \begin{array}{l}\Delta \vdash n : \alpha \\ \quad \rightsquigarrow \epsilon\end{array}}{\begin{array}{l}\Delta \vdash (n+) : \gamma \\ \quad \rightsquigarrow Num\ \delta \wedge \delta \to \delta \to \delta \sim \alpha \to \gamma\end{array}} \qquad \dfrac{\vdots}{\begin{array}{l}\Delta \vdash 1 : \tau \\ \quad \rightsquigarrow Num\ \tau\end{array}}}{\begin{array}{l}\Delta \vdash n + 1 : \beta \\ \quad \rightsquigarrow Num\ \delta \wedge \delta \to \delta \to \delta \sim \alpha \to \gamma \wedge Num\ \tau \wedge \gamma \sim \tau \to \beta\end{array}}}{\begin{array}{l}\Delta \vdash show\ (n+1) : \xi \\ \quad \rightsquigarrow Show\ \varepsilon \wedge Num\ \delta \wedge \delta \to \delta \to \delta \sim \alpha \to \gamma \wedge Num\ \tau \\ \qquad \wedge \gamma \sim \tau \to \beta \wedge \varepsilon \to String \sim \beta \to \xi\end{array}}}{\begin{array}{l}\Gamma \vdash \lambda n \to show\ (n+1) : \alpha \to \xi \\ \quad \rightsquigarrow Show\ \varepsilon \wedge Num\ \delta \wedge \delta \to \delta \to \delta \sim \alpha \to \gamma \wedge Num\ \tau \\ \qquad \wedge \gamma \sim \tau \to \beta \wedge \varepsilon \to String \sim \beta \to \xi\end{array}}$$

Note: in the derivation tree, we use Δ to mean $\Gamma, n : \alpha$ in order to fit the whole tree in the page.

Fig. 3. Constraint derivation tree for $\lambda n \to show\ (n+1)$

2.2 Solving Order Matters

Once the constraints are gathered, it is time for the solver to perform its magic. In full generality, a solver is represented by a judgement of the form

$$\mathcal{A} \vdash Q \twoheadrightarrow Q_r, \theta$$

which encodes that under some set of axioms $\mathcal{A}$, the set of constraints Q has a solution given by a substitution θ and a set of residual constraints Q_r. It must be the case that the conjunction of the axioms $\mathcal{A}$ and the residual constraints Q_r imply an instance of the original constraints θQ. We furthermore assume that a special constraint $\bot$ exists, which is returned when the constraint set Q is found to be inconsistent.

Continuing with the previous example, the type engine needs to solve the constraint set obtained from the gathering process:

$$\begin{aligned} Q = \quad & Show\ \varepsilon \wedge Num\ \delta \wedge \delta \to \delta \to \delta \sim \alpha \to \gamma \\ & \wedge Num\ \tau \wedge \gamma \sim \tau \to \beta \wedge \varepsilon \to String \sim \beta \to \xi \end{aligned}$$

In the Haskell Prelude, the Num type class is declared as:

$$\begin{array}{l}\textbf{class}\ Show\ a \Rightarrow Num\ a\ \textbf{where}\\ \quad (+) :: a \to a \to a\\ \quad (*)\ :: a \to a \to a\\ \quad \ldots\end{array}$$

Which means that the set of axioms $\mathcal{A}$ in which the constraints are to be solved includes, at least, $\forall a.\, Num\ a \implies Show\ a$, that is, every Num instance is guaranteed to have a corresponding $Show$ instance. Under these circumstances, the solver returns the following result:

$$\mathcal{A} \vdash Q \twoheadrightarrow Num\ \delta, [\alpha \mapsto \delta, \beta \mapsto \delta, \gamma \mapsto (\delta \to \delta), \tau \mapsto \delta, \varepsilon \mapsto \delta, \xi \mapsto String]$$

In particular, for the Haskell program this means that the inferred type is:

$$\forall d.\, Num\ d \Rightarrow d \to String$$

But what if solving a set of constraints results in $\bot$, that is, if the set is found to be inconsistent? In that case, we need to generate an error message to show to the user. This entails pointing at one or several constraints from the original set as responsible for the inconsistency: this process is called *blaming*. Note that for the same set of constraints, several ways to blame might be possible. For example, take:

$$Q = \alpha \sim Bool \wedge \alpha \sim Int \wedge \alpha \sim Char$$

It is clear that these constraints form an inconsistent set. If we decide to blame the first two constraints, the error message to show is:

```
Cannot unify Bool with Int
```

But if we choose the first and the third to blame, we get:

```
Cannot unify Bool with Char
```

Furthermore, if these constraints come from different expressions, different points in the program would also be blamed for this type violation.

The dependence of error messages on the internal workings is known in the literature as the *bias* problem. To a certain extent, this problem is unavoidable, since every solver and blamer needs to be implemented in a deterministic way in order to be executed by a computer. Our aim is to look at the reverse side of the coin: how can certain orderings in the solving of constraints help us in giving the desired error message for a given class of expressions?

2.3 Constraint Scripts

In order to be more precise about how blaming needs to be processed in the system, we need to depart from the model in which constraints form an unordered set into one in which they form a partial ordering. Formalizations of this kind have already been considered in [9]. In this paper we use a simplified version of those, consisting of three combinators:

Constraints	$C ::= \ldots$	Defined by the type system
Messages	$M ::= \ldots$	Defined by the implementation
Constraint scripts	$S ::= C \mid S^M \mid \lceil S_1, \ldots, S_n \rfloor \mid S_1 \lhd S_2$	

$\cdot^M$ The *label* combinator annotates a constraint script with information about the error message to show when the script is found to be unsatisfiable. The exact shape of the labels in implementation-defined: in this paper we use simple strings for ease of presentation.

$\lceil \ldots \rfloor$ When several scripts need to be satisfied, the *join* combinator specifies that at blaming, no preference should be given to any of the contained scripts.

$\lhd$ The *ordered* combinator introduces asymmetry in blaming. If the combination of the constraints in the two scripts gives rise to an inconsistency, then the second one should be blamed.

If we use a constraint script instead of a simple set for the problem of three different types equated to a variable α, we can be much more precise about the error message. One possibility is to have:

$$Q = (\alpha \sim Bool \lhd \alpha \sim Int) \lhd \alpha \sim Char$$

The inconsistency is found then at the stage when the constraints $\alpha \sim Bool$ and $\alpha \sim Int$ are merged, and thus the message about not being able to unify *Bool* with *Int* should be generated. If we want a custom message, we can go one step further and write a constraint script:

$$Q = (\alpha \sim Bool \lhd \alpha \sim Int)^{\texttt{"A Boolean cannot be an Int, sorry"}} \lhd \alpha \sim Char$$

One small glitch is that now we need to update the rules from Fig. 2 to produce constraint scripts instead of mere sets. The simplest approach is to change all conjunctions $\wedge$ into the join $\lceil \cdot \rfloor$ combinator. However, the implementor of the programming language may want to add some default asymmetries, e.g., giving preference to blaming constraints from e rather than from b in when using the **let** $x = e$ **in** b construct.

3 Specialized Type Rules

Specialized type rules enter the scene in the aforementioned constraint generation phase, by replacing one of the default rules with a DSL-writer-provided one. On the surface they are like any other type rule: each of them matches a syntactic form, and produces a constraints script based on those of its subcomponents.

In many cases, including Fig. 2, the gathering of constraints from an expression is syntax-directed. That is, at most one rule matches a certain set of shapes for expressions. The addition of specialized type rules breaks this property: each of them overlaps with one or more default type rules in a certain context. Thus, at each point of the AST, the type engine needs to decide whether a specialized type rule shall be used instead of the default one.

In our work, each rule defines when to be fired by two elements. The first, encoded in the **case** fragment of the specialized type rule, is a syntactic one: the expression is verified to have a specific shape. After that check, there might be a second check based on typing information, which is given in the **when** fragment of the specialized type rule. Implementation of that second check needs a two-stage type engine; we defer its explanation to Sect. 5.

The way in which a shape is conveyed to the type engine is via an *expression matcher*. Expression matchers form a subset of the term language, enlarged with *metavariables* for naming subexpressions. We need these metavariables to refer to the constraints and types of subexpressions of the expression being matched. In our prototype, expression matchers follow this grammar:[3]

$$\begin{array}{lll} m ::= & x & \text{Term variable} \\ & \mid\; m_1\, m_2 & \text{Application} \\ & \mid\; \cdot & \text{Match anything} \\ & \mid\; m^{\#id} & \text{Metavariable} \end{array}$$

The reader may notice that we do not include λ-abstractions and **let** blocks as constructs that a specialized type rule is able to match upon. We have not yet found any use case in which the DSL writer might need to alter the constraint scripts associated to those constructs. Furthermore, matching only on application alleviates us from including special syntax for changing the environment in a type rule: in applications the environment is simply inherited from the parent.

Note also that the system does *not* consider terms equated under β-reduction or **let**-inlining. For example, the code **let** $x = map\ (+1)$ **in** $x\ [1,2,3]$ is not matched by a specialized type rule with a **case** fragment $map\ \cdot^{\#fn}\ \cdot^{\#lst}$. There are two reasons which incidentally strengthen the decision of taking a completely syntactic approach instead of taking into account some rules of computation:

1. Different modes of use of the same function may correspond to different intentions on the part of the user. Thus, it makes sense to provide different specialized type rules for those different scenarios.
2. A simpler matching procedure is more predictable. If we take β-reduction or **let**-inlining into account, the DSL writer might be surprised that a rule fires (or does not) for a specific expression.

Also, one can always write an extra rule that matches on *map* with only one parameter.

Once a specialized type rule is found to match an expression, the fragment between braces is executed in order to build a constraint script. We could have used the combinators from last section to define the scripts directly, but they are

[3] In the implementation, $m^{\#id}$ is written as $\#id@(m)$, with the special case $\cdot^{\#id}$ being written simply as $\#id$.

too low-level to be easily usable by DSL writers. Instead, our prototype defines a higher-level language for constraint scripts which is then translated to the low-level one. The grammar is as follows:

Section	$\mathit{section} ::= \epsilon$	Empty script
	$\mid\ \mathit{instr}\ \mathit{section}$	Unannotated instruction
	$\mid\ \mathit{instr}\ \mathbf{error}\ \{M^*\}\ \mathit{section}$	Annotated instruction
	$\mid\ \mathbf{repair}\ \{M^*\}\ \mathit{section}$	Reparation
Instruction	$\mathit{instr} ::= C^*$	Constraint with identifiers
	$\mid\ \mathbf{constraints}\ \#\mathit{id}$	Reference
	$\mid\ \mathit{merger}\ \{\mathit{section}\}$	Nested section
Merger	$\mathit{merger} ::= \mathbf{join} \mid \mathbf{ordered}$	

The basic blocks of constraint scripts are, of course, constraints themselves. What distinguishes constraints C from the C^* mentioned in the grammar above is the ability to refer to the types of subexpressions named by a metavariable in the **case** fragment. For example, when in the introduction we wrote $\#\mathit{field} \sim \mathit{Field}\ f\ t$, the identifier $\#\mathit{field}$ refers to the type that is assigned to the first argument to the *get* function.

In most cases, a specialized type rule needs to *refer* to the constraint scripts of one or more subexpressions in order to build the script for the entire expression. The syntax for such a reference is **constraints** followed by the metavariable representing the subexpression in the matcher.[4] As an example of references, we can reformulate the rule APP for application from Fig. 2 as:

```
rule application
case .#f .#x {
  constraints #f,
  constraints #x,
  #f ~ #x → alpha
}
```

But wait a moment, we have three constraint scripts here: **constraints** $\#f$, **constraints** $\#x$, and $\#f \sim \#x \rightarrow \mathit{alpha}$; which combinator is chosen to put them together? By default, $\lhd$ is chosen; it is the most common choice when providing specialized type rules for DSLs. This choice can be reverted, though, by enclosing a section with a new *merger*: **join** switches to $\lceil\cdot\rfloor$, and **ordered** to $\lhd$ again.

Constraint scripts may also specify a custom error message tied to a combination of constraints. In the high-level syntax **error** is used. As in the case of constraint scripts, the syntax of error messages is defined by the implementation. In our case, the syntax is:

[4] Thus, metavariables introduced in the matcher can refer inside a constraint script to types or other scripts depending on the context in which they occur.

Message $M^* ::=$	$M_1^*\ M_2^*$	Concatenation
$\mid$	`"string"`	Literal string
$\mid$	$\tau : ty$	Type
$\mid$	$\#id : expr$	Expression

Sometimes, we want a specialized type rule to always generate an error message. One possibility would be to attach the message, using **error**, to an inconsistent constraint (such as $Int \sim Bool$). Given the usefulness of this scenario, we have included specialized syntax for this task: **repair**.

The translation from the high-level constraint script language to the low-level one is unsurprising. The full details of the translation can be found in [22].

3.1 Example DSLs

We have already introduced extensible records à la Vinyl as an example of a DSL which benefits from specialized type rules. In this section we introduce two examples coming from libraries which are commonly used by Haskell programmers: a database mapper called Persistent[5], and declarative vector graphics from the Diagrams[6] embedded DSL. Both libraries target a specific domain with their own terms; this makes them a perfect target for specialized type rules.

Note that in the examples we sometimes use type signatures which are simpler than their counterparts in libraries, in order to keep the irrelevant details out and obtain manageable specialized type rules.

Persistent [23]. The designers of this database mapper took a very type-safe approach: each kind of entity in the database is assigned a different Haskell type. Several advanced type-level techniques are used throughout its implementation: the result is a very flexible library, which unfortunately suffers from complicated error messages.

Apart from separating different entities via different types, Persistent imposes a strict distinction between: (1) values which are kept in the database, and which correspond to normal Haskell data types, (2) keys that identify a value in the database (like primary keys in SQL databases), which always have a *Key* type tagged with the kind of value it refers to, and (3) entities, which are a combination of key and value.

One important operation in Persistent is updating an entity in the database:

$$replace :: MonadIO\ m \Rightarrow Key\ e \rightarrow e \rightarrow m\ Result$$

Based on its intended usage, there are two scenarios which benefit from domain specific type rules. One is using a non-*Key* value as first argument; based on previous experience with other libraries, the user of the DSL may expect that something like an *Integer* is to be given at that position. We can point to information about what a *Key* in Persistent represents. Another error which benefits

[5] http://hackage.haskell.org/package/persistent.

[6] http://projects.haskell.org/diagrams/.

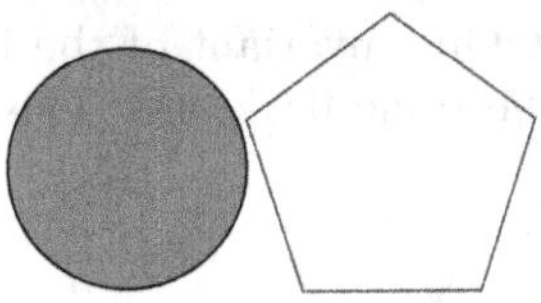

Fig. 4. Rendering of *circle* 2 # *fc green* ||| *pentagon* 3 # *lc blue*(Color figure online)

from a domain specific perspective is using a *Key a* along with a value of a different type *b*, e.g., using a key for a *Task* when you need one for a *Person*. A specialized type rule encompassing these use cases looks like:

```
rule replace_key
case ((replace#r .#key )#p .#value )#e {
  join {constraints #key, constraints #value},
  #key ~ Key v  error { #key : expr "should be a Key."
                        "Did you forget a wrapper?"},
  v      ~ #value error {"Key type" v : ty "and value type" #value : ty
                        "do not coincide"},
  join {
    constraints #r,
    #p ~ #value → m Result,
    #e ~ m Result, MonadIO m
  }
}
```

This rule brings to the table an issue which we did not have to deal with before: a specialized type rule needs to ensure that all subexpressions (i.e., all nodes in the AST) are given types. Thus, although our focus is on the first three instructions, we also need to give types to the function *replace*, to the partially applied *replace #key* and finally to the whole expression. This is mandated by the soundness check from Sect. 5, although we are currently investigating ways to add these structural constraints automatically.

Diagrams [28]. This library was originally developed by Brent Yorgey, and aims to provide a way to construct pictures in a compositional way, by combining simple pictures into more complex ones. For example, this code taken from the tutorial defines a simple picture as a LaTeX image. The result is given in Fig. 4.

```
import Diagrams.Backend.PGF
import Diagrams.Prelude
drawing :: Diagram PGF
drawing = circle 2 # fc green ||| pentagon 3 # lc blue
```

The reader may notice that the *drawing* function has in its type a tag *PGF* indicating the back-end used to render it. Other possibilities include SVG, GTK+

or the Cairo graphics library. One invariant of the library is that you can only compose drawings that use the same back-end. This is a sensible use case for a specialized type rule:[7]

rule *combine_diagrams*
case $(((|||)^{\#r} .^{\#d1})^{\#p} .^{\#d2})^{\#e}$ {
  join {
    ordered {**constraints** $\#d1$, $\#d1 \sim Diagram\ b1$}
    ordered {**constraints** $\#d2$, $\#d2 \sim Diagram\ b2$}
  },
  $b1 \sim b2$ **error** { $\#d1$: *expr* "and" $\#d2$: *expr*
          "use different back-ends"},
  join {
    $\#r \sim Diagram\ b1 \rightarrow Diagram\ b1 \rightarrow Diagram\ b1$,
    $\#p \sim Diagram\ b1 \rightarrow Diagram\ b1$,
    $\#e \sim Diagram\ b1$
  }
}

In this case, we use **join** and distinct type variables to make the type checking of each argument not influenced by the other. Then, we check that both back-ends coincide, if that fails we give a custom error message. As in the previous example, we need to incorporate types for each subexpression in the AST, something we do in the last **join** section.

4 Two-Stage Specialized Type Rules

The methodology described up to now does not include the **when** mechanism needed to make the extensible records specialized type rule, as described in the introduction, work. Before describing our solution, it is worthwhile to describe the disadvantages of the most obvious technique to reach this goal: when we need to decide whether to apply rule R or not, we look at the constraints gathered prior to that point and check whether those imply the ones in the **when** fragment. The disadvantages can be summarized as:

(1) The traversal of the tree, the process responsible for gathering the constraints for a given expression, becomes very complex: you need to move back and forth between the traversal itself and the constraint solver.
(2) It is not clear how the gathering should proceed if during the process the solver finds an inconsistency, that is, a type error.
(3) The decision of whether to apply a specialized type rule will be biased by the order in which constraints are gathered. If this is done bottom up, then we are constrained to know information only about subexpressions, whereas

[7] The actual type of $(|||)$ is more general than shown in this example. We take care of this fact in Sect. 4.1.

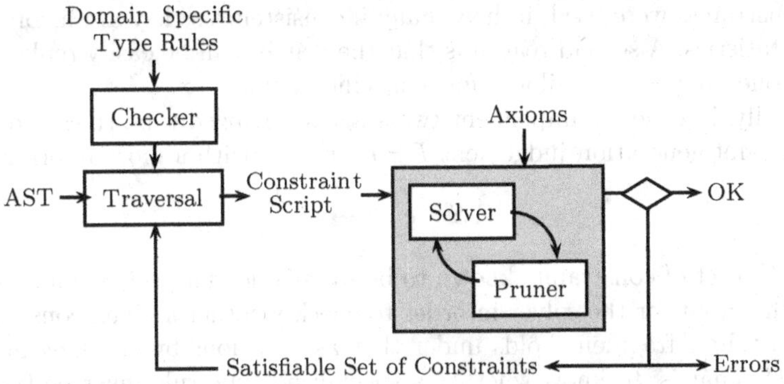

Fig. 5. Enhanced constraint-based type engine

some more information might come from later use sites. Traversing in a top down fashion only moves the bias on to the other direcion. It might be possible to sketch a bidirectional solution, but this seems both complicated and unpredictable.

Our solution is to use *two stages*, each of then comprising constraint gathering and solving, instead of a single one in which interleaving is possible. This new architecture for the type engine is depicted in Fig. 5. In the case of successful completion of the type checking and inference procedure, the type engine shall still work as in Fig. 1. However, if an error is found in the process, we prepare for a second stage by *pruning* the set of constraints C_1 obtained in the first stage until they become a satisfiable set S_1, and then use that set as input to a second gathering from which we obtain a new set of constraints C_2. The new gathering pass uses those pruned constraints to decide whether to apply or not each specialized type rule.

Note that in the second traversal of the AST we still need to call the solver in order to know whether the constraints in a given **when** fragment hold or not. The difference with the alternative described at the beginning of the section is that now the sets of constraints S_1 and C_2 coming from different stages are kept separate: solving is done over S_1, new constraints are gathered in C_2. Furthermore, we know that the constraints S_1 which we query form a satisfiable subset, since we pruned them. This relieves us from dealing with issue (2).

Our two-stage approach still suffers from bias. However, this bias is no longer structural: it is not related to the traversal of the AST, but rather to the operation of a pruner which decides which satisfiable subset of constraints to return, an easily replaceable part of the system. The pruner is now the part of the system which decides, in the presence of a type error, which constraints from the inconsistent set are kept for the second stage.

We think that this is a good choice for two reasons: first, at the stage in which the pruner is executed, it profits from a global view on the solving process, and might decide to select a different set of constraints depending on how many times those constraints were used, in how many inconsistencies they are involved, and similar statistics. A second reason is that the pruner can be easily replaced with another one, maybe one tailored for a specific domain.

Formally, in order to implement two-stage specialized type rules, we replace the constraint generation judgement $\Gamma \vdash e : \tau \rightsquigarrow C$ with a more informed one,

$$\Gamma, S \vdash e : \tau \rightsquigarrow C$$

where S is a set of constraints known to be satisfiable. This set S can be used as part of the input for the solver in order to check whether a given constraint set Q from a **when** fragment holds under that assumptions by checking $\mathcal{A} \wedge S \vdash Q \twoheadrightarrow \epsilon, \theta$.[8] That is, to know whether a specialized type rule must be triggered. The complete pipeline has now become:

- Gather constraints under an empty known satisfiable set of constraints: $\Gamma, \epsilon \vdash e : \tau_1 \rightsquigarrow C_1$. Only specialized type rules without **when** fragments play a role in this first stage.
- Try to solve the constraints $\mathcal{A} \vdash C_1 \twoheadrightarrow C_1', \theta_1$. If C_1' is empty, then solving was succesful and θ_1 is the sought-for substitution. We do not need a second stage of typing, and the compiler can proceed with the following stages.
- Otherwise, there is an error in the expression e, and we need to start the second stage. First, we prune C_1 to a satisfiable subset S_1.
- Gather constraints under this subset: $\Gamma, S_1 \vdash e : \tau_2 \rightsquigarrow C_2$. At this point, new specialized type rules, those with a **when** fragment, may be triggered.
- Solve the constraints again $\mathcal{A} \vdash C_2 \twoheadrightarrow C_2', \theta_2$. It must still be the case that $\bot \in C_2'$, but a different set of specialized type rules may now have been used, changing which constraints are blamed for the problem.
- If the part of the script being blamed contains a custom error message, this message is printed by the compiler. The compiler falls back to the default error message for a given type error when the constraint script did not generate a custom message.

We are now in a position of describing what happens exactly when *get age emily* from the introduction is type-checked. In the first pass we obtain a set of constraints which include:

$$\begin{aligned} C_1 = \quad & \#\mathit{field} \sim \mathit{Field}\ \texttt{"age"}\ \mathit{Integer} \\ \wedge\ & \#\mathit{record} \sim \mathit{Record}\ [\mathit{Field}\ \texttt{"name"}\ \mathit{String}] \\ \wedge\ & \mathit{Elem}\ \#\mathit{field}\ [\mathit{Field}\ \texttt{"name"}\ \mathit{String}] \sim \mathit{True} \end{aligned}$$

In the solving phase $\mathit{Elem}\ \#\mathit{field}\ [\mathit{Field}\ \texttt{"name"}\ \mathit{String}] \sim \mathit{True}$ is rewritten to $\mathit{Elem}\ (\mathit{Field}\ \texttt{"age"}\ \mathit{Integer})\ [\mathit{Field}\ \texttt{"name"}\ \mathit{String}] \sim \mathit{True}$ and then by the definition of the *Elem* type family, first to $\mathit{Elem}\ (\mathit{Field}\ \texttt{"age"}\ \mathit{Integer})\ [\,] \sim \mathit{True}$ and eventually to $\mathit{False} \sim \mathit{True}$. This last constraint equates two different type constructors, and is by injectivity, inconsistent.

[8] It is important that the obtained residual set of constraints is empty and not simply different from $\bot$, because in other case we would be checking only the *compatibility* of Q with S instead of its *entailment*.

As we explained above, before we perform gathering in the second stage, we need to make the set of constraints satisfiable by pruning it. How this is achieved is explained in Sect. 4.2. Here we will take as granted that such a procedure exists. If we take out the last constraint, we can reestablish satisfiability.

$$S_1 = \quad \#\mathit{field} \sim \mathit{Field}\ \texttt{"age"}\ \mathit{Integer}$$
$$\wedge\ \#\mathit{record} \sim \mathit{Record}\ [\mathit{Field}\ \texttt{"name"}\ \mathit{String}]$$

The second constraint gathering phase takes this new S_1 as extra input. At some point, we need to decide whether to apply the specialized type rule from the introduction to *get age emily*. The particular **when** fragment reads:

$$Q = \#\mathit{record} \sim \mathit{Record}\ \mathit{fs} \wedge \mathit{Elem}\ \mathit{fs} \sim \mathit{False}$$

The call to the solver returns the following result:

$$S_1 \vdash Q \twoheadrightarrow \epsilon, [\mathit{fs} \mapsto [\mathit{Field}\ \texttt{"name"}\ \mathit{String}]]$$

The fact that the residual set is ϵ means that S_1 does indeed entail the constraints in the **when** fragment. Thus, that rule will be applied instead of the default one. As a result, the constraint script generated for the expression is:

$$(\#\mathit{field} \sim \mathit{Field}\ f\ t) \lhd \bot^{\texttt{Cannot find field "age" in the record emily}}$$

It is clear that the blame for the inconsistency in this case must go to the explicit $\bot$ constraints. The message that the user of the DSL sees is the one attached to that constraint, which is the one we desired.

4.1 Improving the Example DSLs

In this section we return back to the Persistent and Diagrams DSLs, enhancing their specialized type rules with **when** fragments. Both examples showcase scenarios where our two-stage approach enables giving a more informative error message than otherwise.

Type Rules for Specific Instances. We have to admit at this point that we made quite a big simplification when explaining the Diagrams (|||) combinator. Its type is not simply

$$(|||) :: \mathit{Diagram}\ b \rightarrow \mathit{Diagram}\ b \rightarrow \mathit{Diagram}\ b$$

as we implied. Instead, the actual type (in version 1.3) is

$$(|||) :: (\mathit{InSpace}\ \mathit{V2}\ n\ a, \mathit{Num}\ n, \mathit{Juxtaposable}\ a, \mathit{Semigroup}\ a) \Rightarrow a \rightarrow a \rightarrow a$$

This generality allows the same combinator to be used with any type whose values can be put side by side (as witnessed by *Juxtaposable*) in a 2-dimensional space (as witnessed by *InSpace V2 n a*). *Diagram b* is an instance of those type classes, as are lists of diagrams, and diagrams with a modified origin.

If we use the specialized type rule given in Sect. 3.1, we get a custom error message for the *Diagram b* case. But it comes with an undesired side-effect: we can no longer use the (|||) function on other values which are not *Diagrams*.[9] Instead, we want to obtain a custom error message *when* the arguments are known to be *Diagrams*, but not for any other type. We can do so by moving some of the constraints to the **when** fragment:

rule *combine_diagrams_v2*
case $(((|||)^{\#r}\ .^{\#d1})^{\#p}\ .^{\#d2})^{\#e}$
when #*d1* ~ *Diagram b1*, #*d2* ~ *Diagram b2* {
  join {**constraints** #*d1*, **constraints** #*d2*},
  b1 ~ *b2* **error** { #*d1* : *expr* `"and"` #*d2* : *expr* `"use diff. back-ends"`},
  join {
    #*r* ~ *Diagram b1* → *Diagram b1* → *Diagram b1*,
    #*p* ~ *Diagram b1* → *Diagram b1*,
    #*e* ~ *Diagram b1*
  }
}

The (|||) function shows an important trade-off to be made in languages which support a large degree of abstraction, like Haskell. On one side, one would like to make libraries as general as possible, so they can be reused in many different scenarios. On the other hand, this usually implies a more complicated type, which results in more complicated error messages.

Haskell's libraries and language extensions provide even more compelling examples: we have *fmap*, which applies to every *Functor* and it is thereby very general, and *map*, which is the restriction of *fmap* to lists. One of the reasons why beginners are first introduced to *map* is that error messages with *fmap* can be quite scary, since they involve type classes, a concept more advanced than lists. With our system in place, a specialized type rule can be defined to regain the error messages of *map* when *fmap* is used with lists:

rule *fmap_on_lists*
case $((fmap^{\#f}\ .^{\#fn})^{\#p}\ .^{\#lst})^{\#e}$
when #*lst* ~ [*a*] {
  constraints #*fn*,
  #*fn* ~ *s* → *r* **error** { #*fn* : *expr* `"is not a function"`},
  constraints #*lst*,
  #*lst* ~ [*b*],
  s ~ *b* **error** {`"Domain type"` *s* : *ty* `"and list type"` *b* : *ty*
        `"do not coincide"`},
  join {
    #*f* ~ (*s* → *r*) → [*s*] → [*r*],
    #*p* ~ [*s*] → [*r*], #*e* ~ [*r*]
  }
}

---

[9] The type rule is *sound* but *not complete*. Sect. 5 explains how completeness is automatically checked by our system.

In the same way that we declared special type rules for *fmap*, we can do so for many other *Applicative*, *Monad*, *Foldable*, *Traversable* and *Monoid*-related functions when they apply to specific types. The functions *map* and *fmap* can now be merged without compromising the quality of type errors, and the same applies to *filter* and *mfilter*, *mapM* in its list-oriented and *Traversable*-oriented incarnations, and so on. We think that two-stage specialized type rules may have also eased the transition in the GHC base libraries to *Foldable* and *Traversable*.[10]

The same tension occurs with the reintroduction of monad comprehensions [5,27]. On the one hand, they generalize a useful construct from lists to other monads. On the other hand, error messages become less clear. As a compromise, GHC includes monad comprehensions, but they must be explicitly turned on.

Suggesting Reparations. As part of its duty as a database library, Persistent includes functionality to query a data source. One of the most common functions to perform queries is *selectList*, which returns the results of the query as a list of *Entitys* (as in our previous usage of Persistent, we assume a simpler type signature in order to focus on the aspects of our specialized type rules):

$$selectList :: MonadIO\ m \Rightarrow [Filter\ v] \rightarrow [SelectOpt\ v] \rightarrow m\ [Entity\ v]$$

Values of type *Filter v* describe those constraints that an entity must satisfy in order to be returned by the call to *selectList*. For example, one can check that a field in the row has a given value by using:

$$selectList :: MonadIO\ m \Rightarrow [Filter\ v] \rightarrow [SelectOpt\ v] \rightarrow m\ [Entity\ v]$$

Values of type *Filter v* describe those constraints that an entity must satisfy in order to be returned by the call to *selectList*. For example, one can check that a field in the row has a given value by using:

$$(\equiv.) :: PersistField\ t \Rightarrow EntityField\ v\ t \rightarrow t \rightarrow Filter\ v$$

Unfortunately, the name of $(\equiv.)$ is very close to the standard equality operator $(\equiv)$ and it is easy to confuse one for the other. This is a case where, by using our domain knowledge, we can suggest the user of the DSL how to fix the error.

The incorrect expression is of the form *field* $\equiv$ *value*, and we write a specialized type rule for this particular kind of expression. In the **when** fragment we check whether the first argument is of type *EntityField v t*. If so, it is very likely that the user intented to use $(\equiv.)$ instead. This is the specialized type rule:

```
rule wrong_eq_filter
case (≡) .#field .#value
when #field ~ EntityField #value t {
  repair {"Database field" #field : expr " is being compared."
          "Did you intend to use (==.) instead?"}
}
```

[10] Arguments for and against generalizing list functions in Haskell's Prelude have been given at https://ghc.haskell.org/trac/ghc/wiki/Prelude710.

4.2 Implementing Pruning

Up to now, we have assumed that one can prune any inconsistent set of constraints into a satisfiable subset. This is a fair assumption: many algorithms can be found in the literature to compute them [1,7]. Even better: many algorithms give us not only *any* satisfiable subset, but a *maximal* subset. That is, a subset such that adding any other of the original constraints makes it inconsistent.

The problem with these techniques is that they are non-deterministic: running them over an inconsistent set of constraints returns *a* maximal satisfiable or minimal unsatisfiable subset, but there is no direct way to influence *which*. We have discussed the importance of blaming the right constraint in order to obtain the desired diagnosis for a specific scenario, and described constraint script combinators to encode preferences. In this section we describe how to incorporate pruning into the solving phase to obey those preferences.

The solution is to replace the sequential pipeline of solving, and then pruning in case of inconsistency with an interleaving of those two processes. This combined process is defined by a judgement of the form

$$\mathcal{A} \vdash S, M \twoheadrightarrow Q_r, \theta, \mathcal{E}$$

which, compared with the judgement in Sect. 2.2, has one more input and one more output.[11] The extra input keeps track of the *current error message* to be shown in case an inconsistency is found at that point. The extra output is a set of pairs $Q \mapsto M$ which saves those error messages obtained up to that moment along with the constraints which led to them. Another important difference is that Q_r is always a satisfiable set of constraints.

The description of the process as implemented in our prototype is given in Fig. 6. For most constraint script combinators, two rules are given: the one suffixed with $_{\text{FAIL}}$ corresponds to finding an inconsistency, otherwise the corresponding $_{\text{OK}}$ rule is applied. The first two rules, SINGLE$_{\text{OK}}$ and SINGLE$_{\text{FAIL}}$, handle the base case of a single constraint. When the constraint does not lead to an inconsistency ($\bot \notin C_r$), we can return the residual constraints as satisfiable subset, with no errors attached. When the single constraint is inconsistent (like $Int \sim Bool$), the only possible pruning is an empty set of constraints. This is exactly what SINGLE$_{\text{FAIL}}$ does.

More than one inconsistency may be found in this process, coming from pruning different subsets of constraints from the script. In order to know which error message to associate with each inconsistency, the judgement uses the extra input M. This current message is updated whenever we find an annotation in a script by the MESSAGE rule. Remember that a reparation instruction such as

repair {`"my message"`}

leads to a constraint script $\bot^{\texttt{"my message"}}$. Using only these three rules, we can see that the result of combined solving and pruning is:

$$\mathcal{A} \vdash \bot^{\texttt{"my message"}}, M \twoheadrightarrow \emptyset, \epsilon, \{\bot \mapsto \texttt{"my message"}\}$$

[11] A summary of all the judgements used for gathering and solving throughout this paper is given in Fig. 7.

$$\frac{\mathcal{A} \vdash C \twoheadrightarrow C_r, \theta \quad \bot \notin C_r}{\mathcal{A} \vdash C, M \twoheadrightarrow C_r, \theta, \emptyset}\ \text{SINGLE}_{\text{OK}} \qquad \frac{\mathcal{A} \vdash C \twoheadrightarrow C_r, \theta \quad \bot \in C_r}{\mathcal{A} \vdash C, M \twoheadrightarrow \emptyset, \epsilon, \{C \mapsto M\}}\ \text{SINGLE}_{\text{FAIL}}$$

$$\frac{\mathcal{A} \vdash S, M' \twoheadrightarrow Q_r, \theta, \mathcal{E}}{\mathcal{A} \vdash S^{M'}, M \twoheadrightarrow Q_r, \theta, \mathcal{E}}\ \text{MESSAGE}$$

$$\frac{\begin{array}{c}\mathcal{A} \vdash S_i, M \twoheadrightarrow Q_{r,i}, \theta_i, \mathcal{E}_i \qquad \theta^* = \bigwedge \mathsf{intern}(\theta_i) \\ \mathcal{A} \vdash \theta^* \wedge (\bigwedge Q_{r,i}) \twoheadrightarrow Q_r, \theta' \qquad \bot \notin Q_r\end{array}}{\mathcal{A} \vdash \lceil S_1, \ldots, S_n \rfloor, M \twoheadrightarrow Q_r, \theta', \bigcup \mathcal{E}_i}\ \text{JOIN}_{\text{OK}}$$

$$\frac{\begin{array}{c}\mathcal{A} \vdash S_i, M \twoheadrightarrow Q_{r,i}, \theta_i, \mathcal{E}_i \qquad \theta^* = \bigwedge \mathsf{intern}(\theta_i) \qquad Q^* = \theta^* \wedge (\bigwedge Q_{r,i}) \\ \mathcal{A} \vdash Q^* \twoheadrightarrow Q_r, \theta' \qquad \bot \in Q_r \qquad \mathsf{prune}\,(Q^*) = \langle Q_\uparrow, \theta_\uparrow, Q_\bot \rangle\end{array}}{\mathcal{A} \vdash \lceil S_1, \ldots, S_n \rfloor, M \twoheadrightarrow Q_\uparrow, \theta_\uparrow, \{Q_\bot \mapsto M\} \cup \bigcup \mathcal{E}_i}\ \text{JOIN}_{\text{FAIL}}$$

$$\frac{\begin{array}{c}\mathcal{A} \vdash S_1, M \twoheadrightarrow Q_{r,1}, \theta_1, \mathcal{E}_1 \qquad \mathcal{A} \vdash S_2, M \twoheadrightarrow Q_{r,2}, \theta_2, \mathcal{E}_2 \\ \mathcal{A} \vdash \mathsf{intern}(\theta_1) \wedge Q_{r,1} \wedge \mathsf{intern}(\theta_2) \wedge Q_{r,2} \twoheadrightarrow Q_r, \theta' \qquad \bot \notin Q_r\end{array}}{\mathcal{A} \vdash S_1 \lhd S_2, M \twoheadrightarrow Q_r, \theta', \mathcal{E}_1 \cup \mathcal{E}_2}\ \lhd_{\text{OK}}$$

$$\frac{\begin{array}{c}\mathcal{A} \vdash S_1, M \twoheadrightarrow Q_{r,1}, \theta_1, \mathcal{E}_1 \qquad \mathcal{A} \vdash S_2, M \twoheadrightarrow Q_{r,2}, \theta_2, \mathcal{E}_2 \\ Q_1^* = \mathsf{intern}(\theta_1) \wedge Q_{r,1} \qquad Q_2^* = \mathsf{intern}(\theta_2) \wedge Q_{r,2} \\ \mathcal{A} \vdash Q_1^* \wedge Q_2^* \twoheadrightarrow Q_r, \theta' \qquad \bot \in Q_r \qquad \mathsf{aprune}\,(Q_1^*, Q_2^*) = \langle Q_\uparrow, \theta_\uparrow, Q_\bot \rangle\end{array}}{\mathcal{A} \vdash S_1 \lhd S_2, M \twoheadrightarrow Q_\uparrow, \theta_\uparrow, \{Q_\bot \mapsto M\} \cup \mathcal{E}_1 \cup \mathcal{E}_2}\ \lhd_{\text{FAIL}}$$

Fig. 6. Combined constraint script solving and pruning

The last output, the list of errors, contains the message we gave in the type rule.

The case of combining several constraint scripts, either using $\lceil\cdot\rfloor$ or $\lhd$ is a bit more involved. In both cases, we start by considering the solving and pruning of the constraint scripts being combined. Each of those executions will return a satisfiable residual subset, a substitution and a list of errors. We need to put together all those residual subsets, but we also need to ensure that substitution are compatible among themselves. In order to do so we ask the constraint system to include a intern operation which internalizes a substitution as a set of constraints (in our case, each $\alpha \mapsto \tau$ is translated into $\alpha \sim \tau$). At the end, we might end up being consistent or inconsistent. In the first case, we just pop the errors found in the children; but when an inconsistency is found, we need to first perform pruning.

Pruning is the point where the difference between $\lceil\cdot\rfloor$ and $\lhd$ needs to manifest itself. In the first case, the pruner should treat all constraints equally, without any specific preference for blaming. On the other hand, $\lhd$ imposes such a preference, which the pruner should take into account when performing its task. In the rules in Fig. 6, we encode these two modes of operation as two operations that the pruner needs to define: prune for no preference, aprune to blame constraints from its second argument preferably than from the first one.

	Original	*Enlarged*	*Changes*
Gathering	$\Gamma \vdash e : \tau \rightsquigarrow C$	$\Gamma, S \vdash e : \tau \rightsquigarrow C$	Added satisfiable constraint set S Returns a script instead of a set
Solving	$\mathcal{A} \vdash C \twoheadrightarrow C_r, \theta$	$\mathcal{A} \vdash C, M \twoheadrightarrow C_r, \theta, \mathcal{E}$	C_r and θ are pruned to satisfiability Keeps track of current message M Returns a list of errors $\mathcal{E}$

Fig. 7. Summary of judgements used in the paper

In both operations, the result is a triple $\langle Q_\uparrow, \theta_\uparrow, Q_\perp \rangle$. The first two elements are the pruned set of constraints and the pruned substitution, which are now known to be satisfiable. The last element is composed of those constraints which are blamed for the error. The set $Q_\perp$ is saved along with the current error message in order to be shown to the user once the solving is finished.

At the end of Sect. 2.3 we looked at the following constraint script:

$$(\alpha \sim Bool \lhd \alpha \sim Int)^{\texttt{"A Boolean cannot be an Int, sorry"}} \lhd \alpha \sim Char$$

Using the rules from Fig. 6, we arrive to the point of applying the $\lhd$ case:

$$\mathcal{A} \vdash \alpha \sim Bool \lhd \alpha \sim Int, \texttt{"A Boolean cannot be an Int, sorry"} \twoheadrightarrow C_r, \theta, \mathcal{E}$$

Both branches are consistent, with the residual satisfiable subset being equal to the original set. Thus, we need to check what is the result of the solver for the combined set:

$$\mathcal{A} \vdash \alpha \sim Bool \wedge \alpha \sim Int \twoheadrightarrow \perp, \theta$$

It is inconsistent, so we need to prune the set:

$$\mathsf{aprune}(\alpha \sim Bool, \alpha \sim Int) = \langle \alpha \sim Int, \epsilon, \alpha \sim Bool \rangle$$

The corresponding operator from the pruner preferred the second constraint to the first, as the semantics of $\lhd$ mandate. The blamed constraint is put into the error list along with the current message:

$$\mathcal{E} = [\alpha \sim Int \mapsto \texttt{"A Boolean cannot be an Int, sorry"}]$$

There are benefits to making the pruner a parameter of the solver. First of all, we can reuse work on maximal satisfiable subsets, improving the pruning as the state of the art advances in this respect. Furthermore, it opens the door to using heuristics for blaming [8] and even to use domain-specific pruners which understand the most common source of errors for a given domain.

5 Soundness and Completeness

Specialized type rules are intended to offer guidance to the type engine in order to provide better error diagnosis. However, a DSL writer should not be able to subvert the type system using this kind of rule, especially if this happens inadvertedly. For that reason, type rules are checked for *soundness* by the checker prior to the AST traversal, as Fig. 5 shows. A nice feature of our design is that we do not need to change the solver in order to make this soundness check.

Consider first those specialized type rules without a **when** fragment. Given such a rule, the initial step is to generate an expression which represents all the possible instances of the rule. This is achieved by building an expression e equal to the one in the **case** fragment, but where unconstrained subexpressions are replaced by fresh metavariables with fresh types assigned to them. Then, we generate two constraint scripts:

- S_{with}, by traversing e taking into account the specialized type rule we are checking at that moment,
- S_{none}, by traversing e using only the default type rules.

One small detail is needed to make this process work: we need to ensure that type variables assigned to each subexpression in the AST are stable under different traversals. This is not hard to accomplish, but deviates from the standard approach of generating completely fresh variables in every traversal.

Intuitively, we want to check whether the constraints in the set gathered using the specialized type rule, S_{with}, imply the conjunction of the constraint in the set obtained using only the default rules, S_{none}. However, our constraint solving judgement cannot use a constraint script as part of the set of assumptions (the argument at the left of the $\vdash$ symbol). Thus, we need to flatten the script back to a set, via the following auxiliary operation:

$$\begin{aligned}
\mathsf{flatten}(C) &= C \\
\mathsf{flatten}(S^M) &= \mathsf{flatten}(S) \\
\mathsf{flatten}(\lceil S_1, \ldots, S_n \rfloor) &= \bigwedge \mathsf{flatten}(S_i) \\
\mathsf{flatten}(S_1 \lhd S_2) &= \mathsf{flatten}(S_1) \wedge \mathsf{flatten}(S_2)
\end{aligned}$$

In this form, if we want to check whether S_{with} entails S_{none} given some axioms $\mathcal{A}$, we can use $\mathcal{A} \wedge \mathsf{flatten}(S_{with}) \vdash S_{none} \twoheadrightarrow S', \theta$. In particular, we must verify that S' is empty. This approach does not work in the extreme case of $\bot \in \mathsf{flatten}(S_{with})$. In that case, it is automatically the case that S_{none} is implied ("ex falso quodlibet"). This is summarized in a new judgement $\mathcal{A} \vdash S_1 \Rightarrow S_2$:

$$\frac{\bot \in \mathsf{flatten}(S_1)}{\mathcal{A} \vdash S_1 \Rightarrow S_2} \qquad \frac{\mathcal{A} \wedge \mathsf{flatten}(S_1) \vdash S_2 \twoheadrightarrow \epsilon, \theta}{\mathcal{A} \vdash S_1 \Rightarrow S_2}$$

By using $\mathcal{A} \vdash S_{with} \Rightarrow S_{none}$ we check for soundness. This means that type rules which are stricter than the defaults are allowed. One example is a type rule which restricts the type of *fmap* from $Functor\ f \Rightarrow (a \rightarrow b) \rightarrow f\ a \rightarrow f\ b$ to $(a \rightarrow b) \rightarrow [a] \rightarrow [b]$. If we want to keep the type exactly the same, the domain specific type rules must also be checked for *completeness*: this can be done easily by using the converse implication: $\mathcal{A} \vdash S_{none} \Rightarrow S_{with}$.

The definition of $\Rightarrow$ explains why we need to type every node in the AST when developing a specialized type rule. In the default gathering scheme, S_{none} contains typing information for all those nodes. Had we not included those in S_{with}, some leftover constraints remain in the residual set, which we need to be empty in order to check the implication.

The novel feature of our specialized type rules is the dependence on a typing context. When a specialized type rule includes a **when** fragment, the previous direct approach is not enough. First of all, since the soundness check has no associated context, such specialized type rules would never be applied if **when** fragments are taken into account during traversal. Thus, when gathering constraints for the soundness check we refrain from looking at **when** fragments. However, checking the implication $\mathcal{A} \vdash S_{with} \Rightarrow S_{none}$ is not correct in this scenario, since the constraints in S_{with} are only valid in a specific context. The solution is to take the constraints as additional axioms.

To illustrate, consider our running example, a specialized type rule for extensible records. This rule only fires in a specific typing context:

case *get* $^{.\#field}$ $^{.\#record}$
when *#record* $\sim$ *Record fs*, *Elem #field fs* $\sim$ *False* $\{...\}$

The expression which is generated in this case is $get\ x_1\ x_2$, where the x_i are fresh metavariables. In addition, two scripts S_{with} and S_{none} are generated by traversing the expression with and without the specialized type rule in place. But it is not correct to check whether $\mathcal{A} \vdash S_{with} \Rightarrow S_{none}$, since the type rule is only supposed to be valid when the field cannot be found in the record. The correct property to check is $\mathcal{A} \wedge \tau_2 \sim Record\ fs \wedge Elem\ \tau_1\ fs \sim False \vdash S_{with} \Rightarrow S_{none}$, where τ_1 and τ_2 are the types assigned to the *#field* and *#record* subexpressions, respectively.

More generally, let S_{with} be the script obtained from the application of the domain specific type rules, Q_{with} the checks that would have been made in order to apply those rules, and S_{none} the script obtained by the default traversal. Previously, we ensured that the following relations held between those scripts:

$$\mathcal{A} \vdash S_{with} \Rightarrow S_{none} \text{ (soundness)} \quad \mathcal{A} \vdash S_{none} \Rightarrow S_{with} \text{ (completeness)}$$

The change is to add Q_{with} to the list of axioms:

$$\mathcal{A} \wedge Q_{with} \vdash S_{with} \Rightarrow S_{none} \text{ (soundness)}$$
$$\mathcal{A} \wedge Q_{with} \vdash S_{none} \Rightarrow S_{with} \text{ (completeness)}$$

In that way, we ensure that the check is performed only for the cases in which the type rule can be applied.

6 Related Work

The system presented in this paper has a unique feature compared to other approaches to domain specific error diagnosis: using a satisfiable subset of constraints obtained from solving to trigger (more) specialized to type rules.

Helium. Our domain specific type rules were directly inspired by those found in the Helium compiler [10–13]. There are however several differences between their work and ours.

First of all, Helium focuses on the problem of providing *good* error messages. Apart from domain specific type rules, Helium uses heuristics to guide the blaming process and try to ensure that the messages shown to the user are the most helpful to fix errors. Our work focuses instead on giving DSL writers the tools to tailor error messages to the needs of the particular specific domain. For that reason, our focus is only on enhancing type rules.

Some of Helium heuristics involve reparation. A siblings heuristics is described in [13], which suggests replacing a function call with another function if the first one cannot be correctly type but it is possible in the second case. One example is replacing (++) by (:) or vice versa, a common error for beginner programmers. As seen in Sect. 4.1, our specialized type rules can handle this case using a different approach. The main disadvantage of our system is that type rule descriptions are much longer than siblings enumeration.

Another important difference lies in the source language that is addressed. Whereas Helium supports only Haskell 98 constructs, we support a wider range of Haskell features such as type families and multiparameter type classes within the same framework. This implies that the constraints involved in our type rules are more complicated than those in Helium. Furthermore, Helium heuristics are tied to a representation of the constraint solving process using type graphs. Our system, being based on OutsideIn(X) is extensible, and could be used to accomodate type system enhancements such as units of measure [6].

GHC. From version 8 on, GHC supports custom type errors for instance and type family resolution [4]. For example, you can define:

```
instance TypeError (Text "Cannot 'Show' functions." :$$:
                    Text "Perhaps there is a missing argument?")
      => Show (a -> b) where ...
```

Then, when a constraint like *Show* (*Int* → *Bool*) is found by the solver, it is rewritten to *TypeError* (*Text*...). The compiler knows that when such a constraint is in the set, it should produce an error message with the given text.

The main advantage of this approach is that it reuses type-level techniques, leveraging the abstraction facilities that Haskell provides for type programming. However, these combinators cannot influence the ordering of constraint solving, which is an important feature for precise error messages, as explained in Sect. 2.2.

Idris. The support for custom error messages in Idris [2], a dependently typed language with a syntax similar to Haskell's, is based on post-processing the errors generated by the compiler prior to showing them to the user. There is no way to influence the actual type inference and checking process. We discussed in this paper the importance of this influence: our *get age emily* example cannot be expressed using only post-processing. As future work we want to experiment with adding a post-processing stage to our own type engine, and see how it interacts with the rest of the system.

Scala. An instrumented version of the Scala compiler geared towards type feedback is described in [20]. Starting with low-level type checker events, a derivation tree is built on demand. Custom compiler plug-ins are able to inspect this tree and generate domain specific error messages. This approach is strictly more powerful than Idris', but still cannot influence the way in which the type engine performs inference.

SoundExt. Language extensions are defined in SoundExt [17] by rewriting to a core language plus specific type rules for the new construct. As in our work, the system checks for the soundness of the new type rules before they can be applied. However, the authors mention that two sound language extensions might result in an unsound combination, thus requiring extra checks when put together. In our case, the way the soundness check is performed ensures that if all specialized type rules pass the test, they can be freely combined

Racket. The programming environment offered by Racket is well-known for its focus on students [18]. Their notion of language levels, where only some constructs of the full Racket language are available, could be simulated using purposefully incomplete type rules.

7 Conclusion and Future Work

We have shown how a second stage in the type checking and inference process can be used in a constraint-based type engine to introduce custom error messages for DSLs. The way in which that information is conveyed to the compiler is via specialized type rules. The ability to depend on partial type information is provided in a dedicated fragment of the type rule.

Right now, our prototype only compiles programs for a specific subset of Haskell. We aim to implement our ideas in an actual Haskell compiler, and evaluate the power of specialized type rules for realistic libraries and programs.

In the future, we want to ease the description of specialized type rules in several ways. Right now there is no way to abstract common type rule patterns, although one may expect very similar looking rules for a big library. We aim to introduce parametrized type rules, which can be reused in different contexts by providing the missing moving parts. Another possibility is to help the DSL writer by giving a way to obtain the default type rule for a given expression. That type rule can later be refined by changing the priorities for blaming and adding custom error messages.

Another area which we aim to research is how tools can aid in the process of writing and understanding specialized type rules. For example, a graphical user interface might help when writing complicated expression matchers. Another interesting tool is a type rule debugger, which shows which rule has been applied at each point in the tree, in order to diagnose problems when a rule is applied unexpectedly more or less often than expected.

References

1. Bailey, J., Stuckey, P.J.: Discovery of minimal unsatisfiable subsets of constraints using hitting set dualization. In: Hermenegildo, M.V., Cabeza, D. (eds.) PADL 2004. LNCS, vol. 3350, pp. 174–186. Springer, Heidelberg (2005)
2. Christiansen, D.R.: Reflect on Your Mistakes!. Lightweight Domain-Specific Error Messages, Presented at TFP (2014)
3. Damas, L., Milner, R.: Principal type-schemes for functional programs. In: Proceedings of the 9th ACM SIGPLAN-SIGACT Symposium on Principles of Programming Languages, POPL 1982, NY, USA, pp. 207–212. ACM, New York (1982)
4. Diatchki, I.: Custom type errors. https://ghc.haskell.org/trac/ghc/wiki/Proposal/CustomTypeErrors
5. Giorgidze, G., Grust, T., Schweinsberg, N., Weijers, J.: Bringing back monad comprehensions. In: Proceedings of the 4th ACM Symposium on Haskell, Haskell 2011, NY, USA, pp. 13–22. ACM, New York (2011)
6. Gundry, A.: A typechecker plugin for units of measure: domain-specific constraint solving in GHC haskell. In: Proceedings of the 8th ACM SIGPLAN Symposium on Haskell, Haskell 2015, NY, USA, pp. 11–22. ACM, New York (2015)
7. Haack, C., Wells, J.B.: Type error slicing in implicitly typed higher-order languages. Sci. Comput. Program. **50**(1–3), 189–224 (2004)
8. Hage, J., Heeren, B.: Heuristics for type error discovery and recovery. In: Horváth, Z., Zsók, V., Butterfield, A. (eds.) IFL 2006. LNCS, vol. 4449, pp. 199–216. Springer, Heidelberg (2007)
9. Hage, J., Heeren, B.: Strategies for solving constraints in type and effect systems. Electron. Notes Theor. Comput. Sci. **236**, 163–183 (2009)
10. Heeren, B., Hage, J.: Type class directives. In: Hermenegildo, M.V., Cabeza, D. (eds.) PADL 2004. LNCS, vol. 3350, pp. 253–267. Springer, Heidelberg (2005)
11. Heeren, B., Hage, J., Swierstra, S.D.: Scripting the type inference process. In: Proceedings of the Eighth ACM SIGPLAN International Conference on Functional Programming, ICFP 2003, NY, USA, pp. 3–13. ACM, New York (2003)
12. Heeren, B., Leijen, D., van IJzendoorn, A.: Helium, for learning Haskell. In: Proceedings of the 2003 ACM SIGPLAN Workshop on Haskell, Haskell 2003, NY, USA, pp. 62–71. ACM, New York (2003)
13. Heeren, B.J.: Top Quality Type Error Messages. Ph.D. thesis, Universiteit Utrecht, The Netherlands, September 2005
14. Hudak, P.: Building domain-specific embedded languages. ACM Comput. Surv. **28**(4es), Article No. 196 (1996). http://dl.acm.org/citation.cfm?id=242477
15. Koops, H.V., Magalhães, J.P., De Haas, W.B.: A functional approach to automatic melody harmonisation. In: Proceedings of the First ACM SIGPLAN Workshop on Functional Art, Music, Modeling & Design, FARM 2013, pp. 47–58. ACM (2013)
16. Lee, O., Yi, K.: Proofs about a folklore let-polymorphic type inference algorithm. ACM Trans. Program. Lang. Syst. **20**(4), 707–723 (1998)
17. Lorenzen, F., Erdweg, S.: Modular and automated type-soundness verification for language extensions. In: Proceedings of the 18th ACM SIGPLAN International Conference on Functional Programming, ICFP 2013, NY, USA, pp. 331–342. ACM, New York (2013)
18. Marceau, G., Fisler, K., Krishnamurthi, S.: Mind your language: on novices' interactions with error messages. In: Proceedings of the 10th SIGPLAN Symposium on New Ideas, New Paradigms, and Reflections on Programming and Software, Onward! 2011, NY, USA, pp. 3–18. ACM, New York (2011)

19. McAdam, B.J.: On the unification of substitutions in type inference. In: Hammond, K., Davie, T., Clack, C. (eds.) IFL 1998. LNCS, vol. 1595, pp. 137–152. Springer, Heidelberg (1999)
20. Plociniczak, H., Miller, H., Odersky, M.: Improving human-compiler interaction through customizable type feedback (2014)
21. Pottier, F., Rémy, D.: The essence of ML type inference. In: Pierce, B.C. (ed.) Advanced Topics in Types and Programming Languages, chapter 10, pp. 389–489. MIT Press, Cambridge (2004). http://dl.acm.org/citation.cfm?id=1076265
22. Serrano, A., Hage, J.: Specialized type rules in Cobalt. Technical report, Department of Information and Computing Sciences, Utrecht University (2015)
23. Snoyman, M.: Developing Web Applications with Haskell and Yesod. O'Reilly Media Inc, USA (2012)
24. Taha, W.: Plenary talk III domain-specific languages. In: ICCES 2008, International Conference on Computer Engineering Systems, 2008, pp. xxiii–xxviii. November 2008
25. Voelter, M.: DSL Engineering - Designing, Implementing and Using Domain-Specific Languages. CreateSpace Independent Publishing Platform, Hamburg (2013)
26. Vytiniotis, D., Peyton Jones, S., Schrijvers, T., Sulzmann, M.: OutsideIn(X): modular type inference with local assumptions. J. Funct. Program. **21**(4–5), 333–412 (2011)
27. Wadler, P.: Comprehending monads. In: Proceedings of the 1990 ACM Conference on LISP and Functional Programming, LFP 1990, NY, USA, pp. 61–78. ACM, New York (1990)
28. Yorgey, B.A.: Monoids: Theme and variations. In: Proceedings of the 2012 Haskell Symposium, Haskell 2012, NY, USA, pp. 105–116. ACM, New York (2012)

Actor Services
Modular Verification of Message Passing Programs

Alexander J. Summers(✉) and Peter Müller

Department of Computer Science, ETH Zurich, Zurich, Switzerland
{alexander.summers,peter.mueller}@inf.ethz.ch

Abstract. We present actor services: a novel program logic for defining and verifying response and functional properties of programs which communicate via asynchronous messaging. Actor services can specify how parts of a program respond to messages, both in terms of guaranteed future messages, and relations between the program states in which messages are received and responses sent. These specifications can be composed, so that end-to-end behaviours of parts of a system can be summarised and reasoned about modularly. We provide inference rules for guaranteeing these properties about future execution states without introducing explicit traces or temporal logics.

Actor services are ultimately derived from local actor services, which express behaviours of single message handlers. We provide a proof system for verifying local services against an implementation, using a novel notion of obligations to encode the appropriate liveness requirements.

Our proof technique ensures that, under weak assumptions about the underlying system (messages may be reordered, but are never lost), as well as termination of individual message handlers, actor services will guarantee suitable liveness properties about a program, which can be augmented by rich functional properties. Our approach supports reasoning about both state kept local to an actor (as in a pure actor model), and shared state passed between actors, using a flexible combination of permissions, immutability and two-state invariants.

1 Introduction

The actor model [19] is a popular programming paradigm, which structures a program execution into independent units (actors) that communicate via asynchronous messaging. This programming style was initially adopted for distributed systems [40], but has been increasingly used to develop concurrent programs, even those intended to run on a single machine. Although some actor languages support blocking (waiting) for messages, others handle message receive implicitly via built-in event loops; programming purely in this latter style eliminates the possibility of deadlocks.

Modular specification and verification of actor programs is difficult for several reasons. (1) The intended functionality is often provided by a collaboration of several communicating actors, such that the result of a computation might not

P. Thiemann (Ed.): ESOP 2016, LNCS 9632, pp. 699–726, 2016.
DOI: 10.1007/978-3-662-49498-1_27

be sent by the same actor to which the request was sent. This makes it difficult to relate the two messages, for instance, to express the result in terms of the request's arguments. (2) The behaviour of an actor system depends on the state of the individual actors (their call stack, e.g. [40], or the heap, e.g. [27]). However, since this state is local to an actor, it cannot be directly used to specify the behaviour for clients. (3) The local state of an actor changes dynamically in reaction to the messages it receives, for instance, to set up collaborations between actors. (4) The termination of each message handler does not ensure that senders of a message eventually receive the expected result since handlers might not send any response or send messages in circles. Therefore, actor verification requires reasoning about liveness properties.

We present (to the best of our knowledge) the first technique for actor specification and verification which solves all of these problems while supporting modular reasoning. Existing works typically either rely on a notion of whole program execution or traces, or do not handle the liveness properties needed to guarantee responsiveness; we provide specific comparisons in Sect. 5. By modularity, we mean that guaranteed behaviours of parts of a program can be proved and summarised without knowledge of the whole program, and that these summaries (specifications) can be further composed in order to derive different specifications at other levels of abstraction in the software. Support for compositional reasoning of this kind is crucial for scalability and for the reuse of verified components. We make the following main contributions. Our technique:

1. allows one to prove both response and functional properties modularly. The key idea is to introduce *actor services*, a novel state-based assertion whose validity in a state expresses that in all future states each message sent to an actor will trigger a specified response. We present a program logic that can prove these assertions modularly, without resorting to trace-based or whole-program reasoning.
2. allows one to verify actor programs at the level of the source code, rather than an abstraction to e.g. message protocols. This is enabled by a Hoare logic whose assertion language includes actor services. The logic supports a notion of obligations to express which messages must eventually be sent.
3. supports the composition of actor services to summarise behaviours of collaborating actors, without exposing these actors' existence or role in the collaboration. These summarised behaviours can be further composed.
4. allows one to specify and verify code that dynamically creates and connects actors. The behaviour of the resulting actor configuration can be specified via nested actor services.
5. supports local and shared immutable state, and permits (but does not rely on) transfer of ownership of state between actors. A permission system tracks ownership and immutability. Relational (two-state) assertions allow one to express rich functional properties on state, including both response properties and invariants on the evolution of actor-local state.

We illustrate our technique on an example from the literature, which has been the subject of previous substantial verification efforts in industry [2].

2 Programming Language and Running Example

We present our work for a simple Java-like language, in which actors are instances of special classes labelled with the **actor** keyword. These *actor classes* may declare fields, but, for simplicity, neither methods nor constructors. Instead, actor classes may declare *message handlers* prefixed with the **handler** keyword).

Actors communicate via messages. A message identifies a message handler to be invoked by its name and supplies arguments. Sending a message is an asynchronous (non-blocking) operation that enters the sent message into the recipient's message queue. After its creation, an actor enters an implicit loop. In each iteration, it *receives* a message, removing one message from its message queue and executing the corresponding message handler (or blocks if there are no queued messages). We assume that a type system ensures there is a handler for each sent message with appropriately-typed arguments. We do not assume that messages arrive in order, but require that message receive is weakly fair: if an actor continues to receive messages then each message will eventually be received. We assume that messages neither get lost nor duplicated in transit.

The local state of an actor can include heap data structures. Our technique allows multiple actors to execute in the same or in different address spaces. Our techniques are formalised such that all persistent state belongs to a (single) heap. However, we can model disjoint memories by enforcing that actors own disjoint regions of this heap, and that ownership is never transferred. Note that even in a functional language such as Erlang, the response behaviours of an actor depend on actor-local state, in terms of the actor's call stack and current stack-frame values.

2.1 The Mnesia Distributed Database Query Manager

Our running example is a protocol from a distributed database query manager called Mnesia, by Ericsson [26]. Our implementation (Fig. 1) closely follows the Erlang code [2], but actor-local data is stored in the fields of an actor.

The query protocol works as follows. When a user sends a query to the database manager (via query_setup), the query is broken down into several subqueries to be processed on different physical machines. The manager creates a *worker actor* for each subquery. The manager and worker actors are set up in a ring structure: each actor points to its successor via its next field. Once the ring of workers is set up, the manager sends a ready message to the user.

When the user receives the ready message, it (or another actor) can send a req message to the manager, which specifies the number of solutions that the user requires. This message triggers query processing by sending a sols message to the first worker in the ring. Each worker performs some local computation and then sends partial results on to the next actor, which combines them with their local computation and continues. To limit the volume of data being sent over the network, the number of results in a message is bounded by a given packet size. When a worker actor computes more than this number of solutions, it caches the remainder locally. The query manager at the head of the ring also maintains a

```
actor trait User {
  handler ready(QueryManager m);
  handler response(seq<Solution> solutions);
}

actor trait class RingParticipant {
  seq<Solution> store;
  RingParticipant next;

  handler sols(seq<Solution> solutions, int packetSize);
}

actor class QueryManager extends RingParticipant {
  User user;
  int nrSolutions;

  handler query_setup(Query query, User u) {
    RingParticipant nextPid := this;
    seq<Query> subqueries := // break down query - subqueries is non-empty
    for(int i := 0; i < |subqueries|; i := i + 1) {
      nextPid := spawn QueryWorker(next := nextPid,
                          localQuery := subqueries[i], store := []);
    }
    this.next := nextPid;
    u.ready(this);
  }

  handler req(User userPid, int needed, int packetSize) {
    this.user := userPid;
    this.nrSolutions := needed;
    this.next.sols([], packetSize);
  }

  handler sols(seq<Solution> solutions, int packetSize) {
    if(this.next != null && this.user != null) { // already initialised
      seq<Solution> newStore := solutions ++ this.store;
      if(|solutions| = 0 || |newStore| >= this.nrSolutions) {
        this.user.response(newStore);
      } else {
        this.next.sols([], packetSize);
        this.store := newStore;
      }
    }
  }
}

actor class QueryWorker extends RingParticipant {
  Query localQuery;

  handler sols(seq<Solution> solutions, int packetSize) {
    if(|this.store| >= packetSize) {
      this.next.sols(take(packetSize, this.store), packetSize);
      this.store := drop(packetSize, this.store) ++
                    filter(solutions, this.localQuery);
    } else {
      seq<Solution> newStore := this.store ++
                                filter(solutions, this.localQuery);
      this.next.sols(take(packetSize, newStore), packetSize);
      this.store := drop(packetSize, newStore);
    }
  }
}
```

Fig. 1. The running example. We assume a built-in value type **seq** for sequences with the usual operations. The **spawn** statement creates a new actor and initialises its fields. The filter operation applies the worker's local subquery to the previous worker's results; we elide the details of this database computation.

store of solutions. When it receives a sols message, it adds the received solutions to the stored solutions. If it has enough solutions to satisfy the user's request or if the sols message does not contain any solutions, the manager returns its solutions to the user (via a response message). Otherwise, it requests more solutions by sending a further sols message around the ring.

Arts and Dam [2] applied a combination of custom automated techniques and substantial manual proof effort to verify the property that: when a query is made, the user will eventually receive some response. In the remainder of this paper, we will introduce our reasoning techniques for verifying such properties.

3 Reasoning with Actor Services

An *actor service* is a novel kind of assertion that describes the consequences of a message sent to a given actor, both in terms of consequent messages that will be sent, and functional properties that will be guaranteed. An actor service consists of a left-hand side message, called the *trigger message*, and a right-hand side *response pattern*, describing possible *response messages* and additional guarantees. For example, $x.m() \rightsquigarrow y.n()$ is an actor service (and therefore an assertion in our program logic), in which $x.m()$ is the trigger message, and $y.n()$ makes up the response pattern. The meaning of this actor service is that, from the current program state, all future m messages received by the actor x are guaranteed to result in an n message being sent to the actor y. An actor service expresses a stylised form of temporal property (a *response property*), without explicitly requiring temporal connectives in the assertion logic: this liveness property is formally guaranteed provided that all message handlers terminate (see Sect. 4.5). Proving termination of such code is orthogonal; actor services guarantee that a message handler cannot terminate without sending a message leading (directly or via a sequence of further messages) to a prescribed response message, and that such a sequence of messages is guaranteed to be finite.

3.1 Actor Service Instantiation and Composition

The essential building blocks for our actor service reasoning, are *local services.* These are actor services which can be proved against the implementation of a single message handler; in particular, the response message of such an actor service must be guaranteed to be sent during execution of the message handler for the trigger message. In Sect. 4 we will describe the details of our proof technique for verifying local services against the implementation of a message handler; for the moment, we will describe the justification of local services informally. Consider the query_setup message from the actor class QueryManager in Fig. 1. A simple example of a local service which can be proved against this implementation, is:

$$\underline{M}.\mathsf{query\_setup}(\underline{Q}, \underline{U}) \rightsquigarrow U.\mathsf{ready}(M) \qquad (QM1)$$

As a notational shorthand, we use underlined, capitalised variable names to implicitly indicate universal quantification across the actor service. This local service therefore represents that whenever any query_setup message is received by any QueryManager instance M (with any parameters Q and U), the code of the corresponding message handler will ensure that a ready message is sent to the User actor U. This property can be readily checked against the implementation of query_setup in Fig. 1.

All local services are quantified over the receiving actor and parameters; their meaning concerns all possible invocations of the message handler, and is independent of the program state. On the other hand, we can *instantiate* the local service (*QM1*) with respect to specific actors. Suppose, for example, that at a particular program point, program variable m is known to refer to a QueryManager actor, while u is known to refer to a User actor. We can instantiate (*QM1*) to derive the actor service $\mathsf{m.query\_setup}(\underline{Q}, \mathsf{u}) \rightsquigarrow \mathsf{u.ready(m)}$. Note that this actor service describes a property specific to these two actors, and its truth depends on the program state.

A crucial aspect of our actor service reasoning is that we can *compose* actor services to derive new ones. Suppose that the User instance u is programmed to respond to ready messages by sending *some* req message to the corresponding QueryManager. In the case of m, we can express this fact via the following actor service (we use _ to denote arguments whose values are not relevant): $\mathsf{u.ready(m)} \rightsquigarrow \mathsf{m.req}(\_,\_,\_)$ This actor service can now be combined with that above, to derive: $\mathsf{m.query\_setup}(\underline{Q}, \mathsf{u}) \rightsquigarrow \mathsf{m.req}(\_,\_,\_)$. Intuitively, this derivation "chains together" the two response properties, summarising their overall guaranteed behaviour. The derived actor service still describes a response property specific to these two actors; it might not be true when User actors other than u are passed in a query_setup message.

3.2 Heap Dependent Expressions

Actor service composition is simple in situations such as that described above, in which all relevant expressions are (program or quantified) variables. However, to allow actor services to describe properties dependent on an actor's state (and the program heap in general), we also allow actor services to include heap dependent expressions, such as field dereferences. Consider the message handler for sols in the QueryWorker actor class. In terms of guaranteed messaging behaviour, it is clear that every sols message received will result in a further sols message being passed to the **this**.next actor. Indeed, we can derive the following local service because both branches of QueryWorker's sols handler send the required response:

$$\underline{W}.\mathsf{sols}(\underline{S}, \underline{P}) \rightsquigarrow W.\mathsf{next.sols}(\_, P) \qquad (QW)$$

Heap dependent expressions in response patterns, such as W.next in this example, refer to the program heap when the response message is sent. This allows actor services to describe behaviours in terms of fields whose values might be appropriately set in response to the trigger message of the actor service (for example, when actors are initialised via messages). However, this interpretation means that actor service composition becomes more subtle to handle soundly.

For example, suppose that at some program point we have two QueryWorker instances x and y in scope, and we know that x.next = y. Instantiating the local service (QW) above for x and y, we obtain the actor services:

$$\mathsf{x.sols}(\underline{S}, \underline{P}) \rightsquigarrow \mathsf{x.next.sols}(\_, P) \quad \text{and} \quad \mathsf{y.sols}(\underline{S'}, \underline{P'}) \rightsquigarrow \mathsf{y.next.sols}(\_, P')$$

It seems that we should be able to compose these actor services, in a similar way to in the previous subsection. But we must be careful: the first actor service guarantees that, as a consequence of receiving a sols message, the actor x will send a further sols message to the actor referred to by x.next *at that time*. Based on these actor services alone, we do not have enough information to deduce whether composing the two would be sound; the equality x.next = y might not hold at the relevant future points in the program execution.

Examining the code more carefully, it becomes apparent that the fields of QueryWorker actors are not, in fact, mutable state. They are never modified by the code, and are only set when the actors are first spawned. Immutability is a commonly-used feature in such concurrent settings, and we build in native support for immutability and other invariants of actors, as described in the following subsections. Immutability ensures soundness of the above composition.

3.3 Permissions, Immutability and Future States

We organise reasoning about the program heap around the notions of *ownership* and *immutability*. We model these notions formally using a permission-based logic, in the style of *implicit dynamic frames* [35]. The resulting reasoning about ownership of heap locations is closely related to verification in separation logics [28,31], and has been used in other concurrency paradigms [24]. We employ two types of permission in our work. The standard *exclusive permission*, denoted by an assertion $\mathbf{acc}(e.f)$, represents exclusive ownership of the heap location $e.f$ and permits read and write access. We also employ a notion of *immutable permissions* $\mathbf{immut}(e.f)$, which permit read access only and guarantee that $e.f$ will *never* be modified. Immutable permissions are different from fractional permissions [5] because they guarantee that a location will remain immutable for the rest of the program execution. Since concurrent accesses to immutable state need not be restricted, immutable permissions may be freely duplicated, in contrast to exclusive permissions. Neither kind of permission subsumes the other. However, our logic permits exchanging an exclusive permission for a corresponding immutable permission, effectively *freezing* that location's value and making it safe for actors to concurrently access it in future. Note that permissions are a verification-only concept; they do not need to be represented at runtime.

Incorporating immutability into our reasoning about actor services is extremely powerful. In particular, any properties known to hold in the current program state which depend *only* on heap locations which are known to be immutable, may be automatically assumed to hold in all future states. We reflect this formally in our approach via a *future states relation*, written $\prec$, which reflects the semantics of immutable permissions: for any locations to which immutable permission is held *now*, immutable permission may be assumed to be held in the future, and the corresponding heap value may not have changed. Additionally, our semantics for actor services guarantees that once an actor service is true, it is also true in all future states. This design decision comes with restrictions (we do not handle explicit deallocation of actors in this paper), but allows for actor service composition without precise knowledge about program traces.

3.4 Actor Invariants and Message Preconditions

Exclusive permissions can be used to define the parts of the heap are owned by an actor. We represent this formally using an *actor invariant*. Similar to the classical notion of object invariant [14,25], an actor invariant is a property which must hold in between the actor's execution of each message handler. In particular, the actor's invariant may be assumed to hold at the beginning of executing the message handler, and must be shown to be re-established by the end of this execution. Both exclusive and immutable permissions may be included in an actor invariant; in the former case, this prescribes that the actor currently owns this data; in the latter, the data is immutable and may be safely shared among actors. For example, the store field of a QueryManager actor is mutated on receipt of sols messages: this can be permitted by including the exclusive permission to this field location in the actor's invariant. On the other hand, based on the observation that the next fields of QueryWorker instances are never modified, we can include **immut**(**this**.next) in the actor invariant.

Actor invariants may also include *two-state* assertions, describing constraints on the data to which permission is held. These two-state assertions can express constraints over the pairs of heaps when a message handler begins executing and when it terminates. For example, we can express in our running example that the store field of the QueryManager actor never decreases in size, using a two-state assertion **old**(|**this**.store|) $\leq$ |**this**.store|. We use the "**old**" keyword to wrap expressions which are to be evaluated in the earlier heap.

Actor invariants must be *self-framing* (written $\models_{frm} A$), meaning that they depend only on heap locations to which they also require permission. For an actor invariant to include the two-state assertion above we must also include **acc**(**this**.store) $*$ **old**(**acc**(**this**.store)). Here, the conjunction $*$ requires the permissions in both conjuncts [28]. Self-framedness guarantees that the invariants cannot be violated by other actors; all relevant heap locations are either immutable or currently owned by the actor. Actor invariants must also be *transitive* as two-state predicates: the combination of these two restrictions means that a correct actor invariant can be soundly assumed to hold across execution points spanning any number of complete message handler executions by the actor.

Our technique allows ownership of heap data to be *transferred* between actors. We prescribe that ownership of a heap location is transferred with a message, by including exclusive permission to the heap location in the precondition of the message handler. The sender may not access such a location after sending the message. As is standard, *message preconditions* (which must be self-framing) are assumed when proving properties of the message handler implementations.

3.5 Unbounded Composition: Summarising the Ring

We can now turn to the first serious step in the proof of our running example. Let us consider the code which sets up the ring of workers, in lines 20–24 of Fig. 1. In particular, we aim to prove an actor service describing the behaviour of the actor ring, using the local service (QW) as an *actor service assumption* in our proof. In the semantics of our logic, we parameterise judgements by an *actor service environment* Λ: the set of assumed actor services. For one-state assertions in our logic, our semantic judgement has the form $\Lambda, \Sigma, \sigma \models a$, in which a is a one-state assertion, Λ is an actor service environment, Σ is a *heap-state*, consisting of a heap plus sets of exclusive and immutable permissions, and σ is a mapping from variables to values. Despite representing properties about future executions, actor services are one-state assertions in our logic: whether an actor service is true or not *now* is a well-defined property regarding the behaviour of the system from now onwards[1]. The future states relation $\Sigma_1 \prec \Sigma_2$ (Sect. 3.3) holds iff for all heap locations to which Σ_1 has immutable permission, Σ_2 also has immutable permission, and the values of the heap location are the same in the two heap-states; the values of other heap locations are unconstrained.

To prove the behaviour of a loop, we require an invariant; in our technique this can include actor services. The following assertion suffices for our example:

$$\begin{aligned}&\mathsf{nextPid} \neq \mathbf{null} \wedge 0 \leq \mathsf{i} \leq |\mathsf{subqueries}| \wedge (\mathsf{i} = 0 \Rightarrow \mathsf{nextPid} = \mathbf{this}) \wedge \\ &\quad (\mathsf{i} > 0 \Rightarrow (\mathsf{nextPid.sols}(\underline{S}, \underline{P}) \rightsquigarrow (\mathbf{this}.\mathsf{sols}(\_, P)))\end{aligned}$$

This actor service expresses that the part of the ring built so far guarantees that sending a sols message to the last actor created will cause a corresponding sols message to be eventually sent to the this actor. Intuitively, this is because each actor in the ring promises—via the local service (QW)—to send such a message to the next actor in the ring, and these next fields reach **this**.

Establishing this loop invariant before the loop is uninteresting, as no actor services are required. We focus on how to justify that the loop invariant is preserved, in particular, how we derive the required actor service at the end of the loop body. Let us begin with the (simpler) case in which i is initially 0 before executing the loop body. We can instantiate the assumed actor service (QW) with nextPid as the receiver of the trigger message, to obtain the actor service $\mathsf{nextPid.sols}(\underline{S}, \underline{P}) \rightsquigarrow \mathsf{nextPid.next.sols}(\_, \underline{P})$. We now consider the rule for rewriting the response patterns of actor services; the following is a simplified version of the full rule:

$$\frac{\begin{array}{c}\Lambda, \Sigma, \sigma \models T \rightsquigarrow e.m(\overrightarrow{e_i}) \\ \forall \Sigma_1.\ \Sigma \prec \Sigma_1 \Rightarrow \Lambda, \Sigma_1, \sigma \models e = e' * (\overrightarrow{* \, e_i = e'_i})\end{array}}{\Lambda, \Sigma, \sigma \models T \rightsquigarrow e'.m(\overrightarrow{e'_i})}\ (\textit{rewrite-simple})$$

[1] Our analogous judgement for two-state assertions takes a second heap-state, and is written $\Lambda, \Sigma_1, \Sigma_2, \sigma \models A$. We also employ a judgement $\Sigma, \sigma \models_{frm} e$ (e is *framed* in the state), meaning that the expression e depends only on heap locations to which permission is held, and $\Sigma, \sigma \models_{immut} e$ to express the same restricted to immutable locations (e is *immutable* in this state).

We use the metavariable T to range over trigger messages (i.e., the left-hand-sides of actor services). The conjunction $*$ used in our formalisation is equivalent to standard logical conjunction ($\wedge$) when applied to assertions without permissions, such as these. We use the notation $(\overrightarrow{* \, e_i = e_i'})$ to represent iterated conjunction over each $e_i = e_i'$ assertion. This rule expresses that we can rewrite the expressions used in the response pattern of an actor service via equalities which can be shown to hold in *all* future states (according to the $\prec$ relation introduced in Sect. 3.3). In practice, this premise can be satisfied only if the equalities are either trivial (on identical expressions), or are known to hold in the current state, and which depend only on immutable heap locations[2].

When we create a new QueryWorker instance (on line 20), we obtain exclusive permission to the fields of the new actor. By choosing to logically *freeze* (i.e., exchange the exclusive permission for immutable permission) the location nextPid.next at the point of spawning the actor, not only are we able to establish immutable permission for the actor's invariant, but we can deduce that the equality nextPid.next $=$ **this** will indeed hold in all future states. Using the (*rewrite-simple*) rule above, we can therefore obtain the actor service required in the loop invariant.

Now let us turn to the case in which i is greater than 0 before executing the loop body. In this case, we can apply similar reasoning to obtain an actor service describing the behaviour of the newly-spawned actor; in order to establish the loop invariant we need to compose this actor service with the one from the loop invariant assumed initially. We can now present (again, a simplified form of) the rule for composing two actor services:

$$\frac{\begin{array}{c}\Lambda, \Sigma, \sigma \models T \leadsto e.m(\overrightarrow{e_i}) \\ \forall \Sigma_1.\ \Sigma \prec \Sigma_1 \ \Rightarrow \ \Lambda, \Sigma_1, \sigma \models e.m(\overrightarrow{e_i}) \leadsto R\end{array}}{\Lambda, \Sigma, \sigma \models T \leadsto R} \; (\textit{compose-simple})$$

We use the metavariable R to range over response patterns (i.e., the right-hand-sides of actor services). The second premise requires that the specified actor service will hold in any future state. Based on the technique introduced so far, there are two ways to establish this. Firstly, some actor services can be derived from the assumed actor services in Λ. Secondly, actor services known to hold in the current state can also be assumed to hold in all future states (as described by $\prec$), provided the expressions used in their trigger messages are immutable.

Returning to our example, the loop invariant provides us with the actor service nextPid$_0$.sols($\underline{S}, \underline{P}$) $\leadsto$ **this**.sols($\_, P$) at the start of the loop iteration (we write nextPid$_0$ for the value of nextPid at this point). By similar reasoning to in the i$=$ 0 case, we are able to obtain the actor service nextPid.sols($\underline{S}, \underline{P}$) $\leadsto$ nextPid$_0$.sols($\_, P$). We can then *compose* these two actor services, to obtain[3] the desired actor service nextPid.sols($\underline{S}, \underline{P}$) $\leadsto$ **this**.sols($\_, P$).

[2] The general form of this rule, however, allows for more involved cases; see Sect. 3.9.

[3] We elide the handling of the quantified variables here, but they are instantiated and generalised in a standard way, as formalised later in Fig. 2.

This simple case of composition essentially matches one response message in one actor service with the trigger message with another, and allows us to deduce a service in which this intermediate message is hidden, summarising the end-to-end behaviour of the actors. After the loop (at line 24), the loop invariant, the negation of the loop guard, and the fact that subqueries is non-empty imply $\mathsf{nextPid.sols}(\underline{S}, \underline{P}) \rightsquigarrow \textbf{this}.\mathsf{sols}(\_, P)$. After the assignment **this**.next := nextPid on line 24, which completes the ring of actors, we can deduce this actor service with **this**.next as the receiver of the trigger message instead of nextPid:

$$\textbf{this}.\mathsf{next.sols}(\underline{S}, \underline{P}) \rightsquigarrow \textbf{this}.\mathsf{sols}(\_, P) \quad (1)$$

This actor service represents a responsiveness property that is justified by the whole ring of actors created, but without revealing their number or underlying structure. In the rest of this section, we will show how our general reasoning technique allows us to further combine actor services with this one, to obtain actor services to describe the example as a whole.

3.6 General Actor Services

As well as specifying response properties in terms of guaranteed messages, it is important to specify and verify functional properties associated with these responses. For example, in the case of the req message in the QueryManager class, the **this**.user field will be set by the message handler, and never modified (we can consider the location immutable, from this point onwards). This fact is relevant for later reasoning about the response message eventually sent to this User actor.

It is also important for our response properties to be able to describe multiple *alternative* responses, as well as conditions under which they may be known to be individually guaranteed. For example, the behaviour of the sols message handler in QueryManager cannot be simply summarised by a single response message.

We achieve these goals with two complementary features: response patterns with multiple alternatives, and *where-clauses*, which describe additional properties guaranteed when response messages are sent.

Definition 1 (Actor Services). *An actor service is an assertion of the form* $\forall \overrightarrow{X_j}.(T \rightsquigarrow R)$, *where* T *is a* trigger message, *and* R *a* response pattern[4].
A trigger message T, *is a term* $e.m(\overrightarrow{e_i})$, *where* m *is a message name, and* $e, \overrightarrow{e_i}$ *are one-state expressions (i.e. do not mention* ***old****).*
Response patterns (ranged over by R*), are finite sets of* responses*; we notate response patterns in examples as* $(r_1 \mid r_2 \mid \ldots \mid r_n)$.
A response r *is a response message or empty response.*
A response message *has the form* $(e.m(\overrightarrow{e_i})$ *where* $A)$, *in which* A *is a two-state assertion (i.e., may include* ***old****), called the* where-clause.
An empty response *has the form* $(\epsilon$ *where* $\textbf{old}(a))$, *for a one-state assertion* a.
*In both cases, where-clauses may not mention exclusive (****acc****) permissions, and an omitted where-clause is the same as writing where true.*

[4] In examples, we omit the explicit quantifiers, and use (as previously) the $\underline{X}$ notation.

The meaning of an actor service with response pattern R, is that, for all trigger messages in the future, *at least one* of the cases described by the response pattern is guaranteed to eventually happen, and its where-clause will be guaranteed to hold at that point. An empty response permits that no message will be sent; this can be used to handle special cases in the actor's behaviour, or simply to weaken the meaning of an actor service. In all cases, the "**old**" heap in a where-clause refers to the heap when the trigger message was received; the two-state where-clauses can thus relate this state with the state in which response messages are sent (in the case of an empty response, there is no such state, hence the restriction to the "**old**" state). We show examples in the following subsections.

3.7 Where-Clauses and Composition

Where-clauses allow actor services to express functional properties, beyond those guaranteed by message preconditions. For example, the following local service[5] expresses the relevant behaviour of the req message handler:

$$\underline{M}.\mathsf{req}(\underline{U}, \underline{N}, \underline{P}) \rightsquigarrow M.\mathsf{next.sols}(\_, P) \textit{ where } \mathbf{immut}(M.\mathsf{user}) * M.\mathsf{user} = U \qquad (QM2)$$

As with all heap-dependent expressions in our logic, where-clauses may describe properties of heap locations only when appropriate permissions are held. In the case of a where-clause, these can either be immutable permissions included in the where-clause itself, or permissions guaranteed by the preconditions of the corresponding trigger message (in the "**old**" state of the where-clause) and response message. Such where-clauses can include additional information about the state passed around with messages, which may be true for the guaranteed response messages but not *all* messages of this kind.

Since where-clauses can only constrain state which is framed by permissions associated with the corresponding messages, their meaning is stable whether considered with respect to when those messages were sent or when they begin being handled. This allows us to extend actor service composition to "chain together" where-clauses into two-state assertions summarising their transitive guarantees:

Definition 2 (Three state composition). *We define that A_3 is a* three-state combination *of assertions A_1 and A_2 with respect to a current state, via the predicate $(\Lambda, \Sigma, \sigma)$.futureCombines$(A_1, A_2, A_3)$, which holds iff:*

$$\forall \Sigma_1, \Sigma_2, \Sigma_3.\ \Sigma \prec \Sigma_1 \prec \Sigma_2 \prec \Sigma_3 \Rightarrow$$
$$(\Lambda, \Sigma_1, \Sigma_2, \sigma \models A_1 \text{ and } \Lambda, \Sigma_2, \Sigma_3, \sigma \models A_2 \Rightarrow \Lambda, \Sigma_1, \Sigma_3, \sigma \models A_3)$$

We generalise this notion to a predicate on a single two-state assertion and two response patterns, written $(\Lambda, \Sigma, \sigma)$.futureCombines$(A, R, R')$, which holds if R' is the same response pattern as R except that each where-clause in R' is a three-state combination of A and the corresponding where-clause in R.

[5] Recall that a local actor service is one provable with respect to the code of the corresponding message handler, and which is true in all states.

$$\frac{(T \rightsquigarrow R) \in \Lambda}{\Lambda, \Sigma, \sigma \models T \rightsquigarrow R}\ (\mathit{axiom})$$

$$\frac{\begin{array}{c}\Lambda, \Sigma, \sigma \models T \rightsquigarrow ((e.m(\overrightarrow{e_i})\ \mathit{where}\ A) \cup R)\\ (\Lambda, \Sigma, \sigma).\mathit{futureEntails}(A, e.m(\overrightarrow{e_i}) \rightsquigarrow R')\\ (\Lambda, \Sigma, \sigma).\mathit{futureCombines}(A, R', R'')\end{array}}{\Lambda, \Sigma, \sigma \models T \rightsquigarrow (R'' \cup R)}\ (\mathit{compose})$$

$$\frac{\begin{array}{c}\Lambda, \Sigma, \sigma \models e.m(\overrightarrow{e_i}) \rightsquigarrow ((e'.m'(\overrightarrow{e'_j})\ \mathit{where}\ A') \cup R)\\ X, \overrightarrow{X_i} \notin \mathit{dom}(\sigma) \quad \sigma' = \sigma[X \mapsto \llbracket e \rrbracket_{\Sigma,\sigma}][\overrightarrow{X_i \mapsto \llbracket e_i \rrbracket_{\Sigma,\sigma}}]\\ A_m \ = \ \mathbf{old}(\mathit{pre}(m, X, \overrightarrow{X_i})) \quad A \ = \ A_m * \mathit{pre}(m', \overrightarrow{e', e'_j})\\ (\Lambda, \Sigma, \sigma').\mathit{futureEntails}(A * A', A * A'' * e'{=}e'' * (\circledast\, e'_j{=}e''_j))\end{array}}{\Lambda, \Sigma, \sigma \models e.m(\overrightarrow{e_i}) \rightsquigarrow ((e''.m'(\overrightarrow{e''_j})\ \mathit{where}\ A'') \cup R)}\ (\mathit{rewrite})$$

$$\frac{\Lambda, \Sigma, \sigma \models T \rightsquigarrow ((e_1.m_1(e'_1)\ \mathit{where\ false}) \cup R)}{\Lambda, \Sigma, \sigma \models T \rightsquigarrow R}\ (\mathit{elimFalse})$$

$$\frac{\begin{array}{c}\Lambda, \Sigma, \sigma \models e.m(\overrightarrow{e_i}) \rightsquigarrow ((e.m(\overrightarrow{e'_i})\ \mathit{where}\ A_1) \cup R) \quad \Sigma, \sigma \models_{\mathit{immut}} e\\ (\Lambda, \Sigma, \sigma).\mathit{futureEntails}(A_1, \mathit{localVariant}(e))\end{array}}{\Lambda, \Sigma, \sigma \models e.m(\overrightarrow{e_i}) \rightsquigarrow R}\ (\mathit{localVariant})$$

$$\frac{\Lambda, \Sigma, \sigma \models \forall x.(T \rightsquigarrow R) \quad \Sigma, \sigma \models_{\mathit{frm}} e \quad x \in FV(R) \ \Rightarrow\ \Sigma, \sigma \models_{\mathit{immut}} e}{\Lambda, \Sigma, \sigma \models (T \rightsquigarrow R)[e/x]}\ (\forall E)$$

$$\frac{X \notin \mathit{dom}(\sigma) \quad \forall v.\ (\Lambda, \Sigma, \sigma[X \mapsto v] \models (T \rightsquigarrow R)[X/x])}{\Lambda, \Sigma, \sigma \models \forall x.(T \rightsquigarrow R)}\ (\forall I)$$

Fig. 2. Semantics for actor services. *pre* denotes a message precondition instantiated with receiver and parameters. $\llbracket e \rrbracket_{\Sigma,\sigma}$ denotes evaluation of the expression e in Σ, σ.

Equipped with this definition, we can now explain the general rule for composing actor services, a simplified version of which was shown in Sect. 3.5. Figure 2 shows the full rules for deriving actor services; we consider here the rule (*compose*) (the others will be explained in the remainder of this section). Compared with the simplified version (*compose-simple*) a number of generalisations have been made. The first premise now handles the possibility of alternative response patterns R in the original actor service. The third premise prescribes that the new where-clauses in the resulting composed actor service are defined in terms of three-state combinations of A and the where-clauses in R' (the response pattern of the second actor service composed). The second premise has also been changed; the predicate $(\Lambda, \Sigma, \sigma).\mathit{futureEntails}(A_1, A_2)$ checks entailment between A_1 and A_2 in all pairs Σ_1, Σ_2 of states such that $\Sigma \prec \Sigma_1$ and $\Sigma_1 \prec \Sigma_2$. Thus, rather than requiring that the actor service in the second premise holds in *all* future states, we can use information from the where-clause A to help justify this premise.

Returning to the actor service (1), derived at line 24 in our example, if we now consider (*QM2*) an assumed actor service, we can instantiate it[6] and use the rule (*combine*) to derive the following actor service at this program point:

$$\textbf{this}.\mathsf{req}(\underline{U},\underline{N},\underline{P}) \rightsquigarrow \textbf{this}.\mathsf{sols}(\_,P)\ \textit{where}\ \textbf{immut}(\textbf{this}.\mathsf{user}) * \textbf{this}.\mathsf{user} = U \quad (2)$$

This assertion expresses the response property that a subsequent call to req on this actor will eventually cause a sols message to be received by the same actor (the first response from the ring of QueryWorker actors). We explain next how to reason about the subsequent behaviour of the ring, on receiving this message.

3.8 Local Variants: Reasoning About Callback Loops

Just as for reasoning about recursion in a sequential setting, we need extra machinery to reason about situations in which a message might result in the same message type being sent to the same actor. Assuming this behaviour is not intended to go on forever, we need a means of justifying its eventual termination. This is, however, challenging to achieve modularly, since the *reason* for termination may depend on state which is local to the actors involved.

We illustrate our solution with respect to the sols implementation in the QueryManager class, for which we require alternative responses. The most-general actor service which we prove against the implementation (i.e., it is a local service), is the following:

$$\begin{array}{ll}\underline{M}.\mathsf{sols}(\underline{S},\underline{P}) \rightsquigarrow & (M.\mathsf{user}.\mathsf{response}(\_)) \\ & \mid (M.\mathsf{next}.\mathsf{sols}(\_,P)\ \textit{where}\ \textit{localVariant}(M)) \qquad (QM3) \\ & \mid (\epsilon\ \textit{where}\ \textbf{old}(M.\mathsf{next} = \textbf{null}\ \vee\ M.\mathsf{user} = \textbf{null}))\end{array}$$

This actor service specifies that there are three possibilities: the user (as read from the actor's user field) will receive a reponse message, the next actor (i.e., the head of the ring) will receive a sols message, asking for more solutions, or, in the case where the actor was not yet properly initialised, no response message is guaranteed.

The assertion *localVariant*(M) has not yet been introduced; this is an assertion which can *only* occur in where-clauses, and we will explain its meaning and usage in this subsection. Let us consider first composing (an instantiation of) the local service (*QM3*) above (in particular, its second response message) with the actor service (1) derived at line 24. This allows us to derive the actor service:

$$\begin{array}{ll}\textbf{this}.\mathsf{sols}(\underline{S},\underline{P}) \rightsquigarrow & (\textbf{this}.\mathsf{user}.\mathsf{response}(\_)) \\ & \mid (\textbf{this}.\mathsf{sols}(\_,P)\ \textit{where}\ \textit{localVariant}(\textbf{this})) \qquad (3) \\ & \mid (\epsilon\ \textit{where}\ \textbf{old}(\textbf{this}.\mathsf{next} = \textbf{null}\ \vee\ \textbf{this}.\mathsf{user} = \textbf{null}))\end{array}$$

[6] The last premise of the ($\forall E$) rule guards against the possibility of instantiating heap-dependent expressions into contexts in which they would be interpreted with respect to other (future) heaps, *unless* they are known to be immutable (trivially true for variables such as **this** which do not depend on the heap).

Considering the second case of this response pattern, the actor service describes a looping behaviour; one possibility for the response to receiving a sols message is that the actor will eventually be sent a further sols message. This correctly describes a behaviour of the protocol, but we wish to show that this second alternative will not be taken indefinitely. By manual inspection of the code (lines 37–42), we can see that this will indeed not be the case: every time the sols message handler chooses to send a further sols message to the next actor, the number of remaining required solutions will have decreased. Note that this amount can be precisely expressed only in terms of state local to the actor: by the expression **this**.nrSolutions − |**this**.store|.

Our *localVariant* assertions solve this problem; notionally, they prescribe the *existence* of a variant expression (in the standard sense for termination checking) in terms of the actor-local state, which is guaranteed to satisfy the following property with respect to the **old** state (i.e., the state in which the handler for trigger message of the actor service began executing): for *all* subsequent message handlers executed by the actor, this expression will have a smaller value than it did in the **old** state. In the semantics of our logic, we do not define this intended meaning for *localVariant* assertions, which would depend on knowing future traces of the program. Instead, we treat *localVariant* assertions formally as *uninterpreted predicates* over the current states. The only property assumed for these assertions, is that once true they will be true for all future states, i.e.: $\Lambda, \Sigma_0, \Sigma_1, \sigma \models \mathit{localVariant}(x)$ *and* $\Sigma_1 \prec \Sigma_2 \Rightarrow \Lambda, \Sigma_0, \Sigma_2, \sigma \models \mathit{localVariant}(x)$ Note that this property was necessary for deducing actor service (3), above.

Discharging the correct proof obligations to show that a local variant indeed exists for a particular implementation is non-trivial, but we handle this problem in Sect. 4. From the perspective of our actor service semantics here, the rule (*localVariant*) of Fig. 2 allows us to make use of the *existence* of a local variant, as a justification for *removing* the corresponding response message from the alternatives. This allows us to derive a stronger actor service, reflecting that at least one of the other alternatives will happen eventually:

$$\begin{aligned}\textbf{this}.\mathsf{sols}(\underline{S}, \underline{P}) \rightsquigarrow\ & (\textbf{this}.\mathsf{user}.\mathsf{response}(\_)) \\ & \mid (\epsilon\ \mathit{where}\ \textbf{old}(\textbf{this}.\mathsf{next} = \textbf{null}\ \vee\ \textbf{this}.\mathsf{user} = \textbf{null}))\end{aligned} \quad (4)$$

3.9 Rewriting and Eliminating Alternatives

Equipped with the full rules for deriving actor services, we show now how, at the same program point in our example (line 24, after the ring has been initialised), we can derive an actor service describing the overall function of the ring. We consider first the actor service (2), and observe that the **this**.user field is guaranteed immutable and non-null, by a combination of the where-clause and the precondition of the trigger message req. We can make this explicit, by applying the general form of the (*rewrite*) rule from Fig. 2 to (2). The extra complexity in this rule allows the where-clause A' to be rewritten into a new form A'' using facts from the corresponding message preconditions: in this case, the "**old**" precondition A_m guarantees the property that the passed user parameter will be non-null. In addition, the use of *futureEntails* in this premise allows us to make use of immutable facts known at this particular program point; in particular, we can use the fact that **this**.next is non-null and immutable in the current state (after executing line 24), to rewrite the where condition further:

$$\begin{array}{l}\textbf{this}.\mathsf{req}(\underline{U},\underline{N},\underline{P}) \leadsto \textbf{this}.\mathsf{sols}(\_,P)\ \mathit{where}\ \textbf{immut}(\textbf{this}.\mathsf{user}) * \\ \textbf{this}.\mathsf{user} = U * U \neq \textbf{null} * \textbf{immut}(\textbf{this}.\mathsf{next}) * \textbf{this}.\mathsf{next} \neq \textbf{null}\end{array} \qquad (5)$$

We now compose the actor services (5) and (4); the facts about immutable data in the where condition of (5) can, where desired, be preserved in the resulting where-clause. In particular, these facts contradict the where-clause of the empty response in (4); we can derive the following actor service:

$$\begin{array}{l}\textbf{this}.\mathsf{req}(\underline{U},\underline{N},\underline{P}) \leadsto \\ \quad (\textbf{this}.\mathsf{user}.\mathsf{response}(\_)\ \mathit{where}\ \textbf{immut}(\textbf{this}.\mathsf{user}) * \textbf{this}.\mathsf{user} = U) \\ \quad \mid (\epsilon\ \mathit{where\ false})\end{array} \qquad (6)$$

Finally, we can use the rule (*rewrite*) to replace the expression **this**.user with U in the first alternative and then drop the where-clause, and the rule (*elimFalse*) to eliminate the second alternative (its where condition shows it to be an unfeasible response in this state), to derive the desired response property expressed by an actor service: $\textbf{this}.\mathsf{req}(\underline{U},\underline{N},\underline{P}) \leadsto U.\mathsf{response}(\_)$.

3.10 Nested Actor Services and Formal Semantics

With respect to our running example, we have shown how to deduce an important response property at an intermediate program point in the code of the query_setup message handler. Several of the inference steps above depended on specific properties known to hold at this program point. However, we would like to present a specification to a client of the database protocol, which will not require knowledge of this program code. We can achieve this in a natural way: we support actor services in the where-clauses of other actor services. We can then improve upon the very first actor service mentioned in this section (*QM1*), using a where-clause to describe the guaranteed functionality:

$$\underline{M}.\mathsf{query\_setup}(\underline{Q},\underline{U'}) \leadsto U'.\mathsf{ready}(M)\ \mathit{where}\ M.\mathsf{req}(\underline{U},\underline{N},\underline{P}) \leadsto U.\mathsf{response}(\_) \qquad (QM)$$

This precisely summarises the specification of the database manager from the client's perspective: *after* calling the query_setup message, the passed user is guaranteed a ready message in response, *by which time* the QueryManager will promise to respond to a subsequent req message with an eventual response message. Note that this specification exposes no details about the complexities of the implementation and messaging protocol; a simpler (but less efficient) implementation could satisfy the same specification.

The rules of Fig. 2 in fact define our formal semantics for actor service assertions. That is, we interpret a judgement $\Lambda, \Sigma, \sigma \models T \leadsto R$ according to the least fixpoint interpretation of these rules; equivalently, an actor service is true under actor service assumptions Λ in a state Σ, σ if there is a finite derivation of this fact, according to these rules[7]. Nested actor services can be simply handled with the same rules; in particular, it is possible to rewrite an actor service in a where-clause via the (*rewrite*) rule, just like any other assertion.

Throughout this section, we have required actor services as assumptions, which we have claimed to be *local services*: those which can be proved against the implementation of a particular message handler. In the next section, we will present our techniques for justifying these local services formally.

4 Proving Local Services

In this section, we define a proof system in the style of Hoare Logic, for proving properties about message handler implementations. The main goal is the proof of local services against such code; recall that a local service is an actor service whose meaning doesn't depend on a particular program state, and whose response messages must be sent *directly* by the code of the handler for the trigger message. Thus, one of the requirements on our design is that we can express proof obligations that require all executions of the message handler to *eventually* reach a point in which the requirements of a response pattern are satisfied. We achieve this with the novel notion of *obligation assertions*. These assertions are not to be used in specifications, and may not occur in actor services; they are used *only* during proofs in our Hoare Logic. They can, however, be used to encode the requirements that a (local) actor service imposes on a message handler implementation, as we will show. Judgements in our Hoare Logic (hereafter, Hoare triples) are of the form $\Lambda \vdash \{A_1\}\ s\ \{A_2\}$, where Λ is an actor service environment, A_1 is a self-framing two-state assertion, called the *precondition*, s is a statement, and A_2 is a self-framing two-state assertion, called the *postcondition*. As well as describing properties of the usual states (before/after execution of the statement), our two-state assertions can include facts about and relationships with a fixed "old" state, used in practice to denote the pre-state of execution of the entire message handler. This support for two-state assertions allows us, for example, to handle proof obligations about actor invariants: we can simply require the invariant of the actor in the postcondition of a judgement, to enforce the obligation that the invariant is re-established. The restriction to self-framing assertions in Hoare triples [37] guarantees that facts concerning heap values can only be preserved while appropriate permissions are known to be held.

We define our Hoare Logic with respect to the following language:

---

7 Nested actor services require care to ensure that this semantics is well-defined. The definition of *futureEntails* is not a simple entailment check in the case of actor service assertions. We employ a construction to guarantee that a guaranteed actor service can be added as an additional *assumption* in deriving the "entailed" formula, avoiding negative occurrences of actor services. This makes the derivation rules monotonic with respect to actor service assertions; the fixpoint is guaranteed to exist.

$$\frac{A_1 \models^{\Lambda} A'_1 \quad A'_2 \models^{\Lambda} A_2 \quad \Lambda \vdash \{A'_1\}\ s\ \{A'_2\}}{\Lambda \vdash \{A_1\}\ s\ \{A_2\}}\ (cons)$$

$$\frac{\mathit{freeze}(A_1, A'_1) \quad \mathit{freeze}(A'_2, A_2) \quad \Lambda \vdash \{A'_1\}\ s\ \{A'_2\}}{\Lambda \vdash \{A_1\}\ s\ \{A_2\}}\ (\mathit{freeze})$$

$$\frac{FV(A_3) \cap mods(s) = \emptyset \quad \models_{\mathit{frm}} A_3 \quad \Lambda \vdash \{A_1\}\ s\ \{A_2\}}{\Lambda \vdash \{A_1 * A_3\}\ s\ \{A_2 * A_3\}}\ (\mathit{frame})$$

$$\frac{}{\Lambda \vdash \{A\}\ \mathtt{skip}\ \{A\}}\ (skip) \qquad \frac{x \notin otherStateFV(A) \quad A[e/x] \models_{\mathit{frm}} e}{\Lambda \vdash \{A[e/x]\}\ x{:=}e\ \{A\}}\ (varAss)$$

$$\frac{}{\Lambda \vdash \{\mathbf{acc}(x.f)\}\ x.f{:=}y\ \{\mathbf{acc}(x.f) * x.f{=}y\}}\ (\mathit{fldAss})$$

$$\frac{\begin{array}{c} x \notin FV(A) \quad \mathit{fields}(C) = \vec{f_i} \quad \overrightarrow{A \models_{\mathit{frm}} e_i} \quad \mathit{freeze}((\ast\, \overrightarrow{\mathbf{acc}(x.f_i)}\,), A') \\ \models_{\mathit{frm}} a \quad A * A' * (\ast\, \overrightarrow{x.f_i = e_i}\,) \models^{\Lambda} A'' * a \\ \forall \Sigma_1, \sigma.\ (\Sigma_1, \sigma \models a \Rightarrow \exists \Sigma_0.\ \Sigma_0, \Sigma_1, \sigma \models \mathit{Inv}(C)[x/\mathbf{this}]) \end{array}}{\Lambda \vdash \{A\}\ x{:=}\ \mathtt{spawn}\ C(\overrightarrow{f_i{:=}e_i}\,)\ \{A''\}}\ (spawn)$$

$$\frac{a = pre(m, e, \vec{e_i}) \quad a * A' \models_{\mathit{frm}} e \quad \overrightarrow{a * A' \models_{\mathit{frm}} e_i}}{\Lambda \vdash \{a * A'\}\ e.m(\vec{e_i})\ \{A'\}}\ (messageNoObl)$$

$$\frac{\begin{array}{c} a = pre(m, e, \vec{e_i}) \quad A \models^{\Lambda} a * A' \quad (e'.m(\vec{e'_i})\ where\ A_1) \in R \\ A \models_{\mathit{frm}} e = e' \wedge (\bigwedge e_i = e'_i\,) \quad A \models^{\Lambda} e = e' \wedge (\bigwedge e_i = e'_i\,) \quad A \models_{\mathit{frm}} A_1 \\ (A_2, B_2) = \mathit{splitLocalVariant}(A_1) \quad A \models^{\Lambda} A_2 \quad A * B_2 \models^{\Lambda} A * B_3 \end{array}}{\Lambda \vdash \{A * \mathbf{obl}(R)\}\ e.m(e')\ \{A' * (B_3 \Rightarrow \mathbf{obl}(\mathit{localVariant}(\mathbf{this})))\}}\ (messageObl)$$

$$\frac{(\epsilon\ where\ \mathbf{old}(a)) \in R \quad A \models^{\Lambda} \mathbf{old}(a) \quad \Lambda \vdash \{A\}\ s\ \{A'\}}{\Lambda \vdash \{A * \mathbf{obl}(R)\}\ s\ \{A'\}}\ (emptyObl)$$

$$\frac{\begin{array}{c} C = \mathit{cls}(\mathbf{this}) \quad A * B \models^{\Lambda} a \quad \models_{immut} a \quad a * \mathit{Inv}(C) \models_{\mathit{frm}} e \leq \mathbf{old}(e) \\ a * \mathit{Inv}(C) \models^{\Lambda} e \leq \mathbf{old}(e) \quad A * B \models^{\Lambda} \mathbf{old}(e) \geq 0 \wedge e < \mathbf{old}(e) \end{array}}{\Lambda \vdash \{A * (B \Rightarrow \mathbf{obl}(\mathit{localVariant}(\mathbf{this})))\}\ \mathtt{end}\ \{A\}}\ (\mathit{localVarObl})$$

Fig. 3. Hoare Logic for Proving Message Handler Properties. $\mathit{Inv}(C)$ denotes the (two-state) actor invariant for class C.

Definition 3 (Program Syntax). Statements s *are defined by the grammar:*

$$\begin{array}{rl} s ::= & \mathtt{skip} \mid x{:=}e \mid x.f{:=}y \mid x{:=}\ \mathtt{spawn}\ C(\overrightarrow{f_i{:=}e_i}\,) \mid (s_1; s_2) \\ \mid & (\mathtt{if}\ b\ \mathtt{then}\ s_1\ \mathtt{else}\ s_2) \mid (\mathtt{while}\ b\ \mathtt{do}\ s_1) \mid e.m(\vec{e_i}) \mid \mathtt{end} \end{array}$$

Message handler bodies have the form $(s; \mathtt{end})$*, where* s *does not contain* end.

We use end as a syntactic marker for the end of a message handler body; this is useful for formalising requirements which can be checked only at this point.

4.1 Hoare Logic Derivations and Valid Programs

The rules of our Hoare Logic are given in Fig. 3. The rules for if-conditions, while loops and sequential composition are standard, and we omit them. The first premise of the (*varAss*) rule requires that x occurs neither under **old** nor in the response patterns of actor services in the assertion A; this avoids the possibility of a heap dependent e being substituted into a position in which it would be evaluated in the wrong heap.

The (*freeze*) rule is similar in nature to the rule of consequence, but allows us to rewrite assertions to replace **acc** permissions with **immut** permissions. The predicate $\mathit{freeze}(A_1, A_2)$ holds if A_2 is syntactically identical to A_1 except possibly for some $\mathbf{acc}(e.f)$ subformulas of A_1 being replaced by corresponding $\mathbf{immut}(e.f)$ formulas. The actual rule of consequence (*cons*) makes use of an entailment operator ($\models^{\Lambda}$) which is standard except that the actor service environment Λ is used when checking the entailment. This notion of entailment supports arbitrary reasoning within our overall logic: in particular, it can be used to derive new actor service assertions, according to their semantics in Fig. 2[8].

The (*spawn*) rule is relatively complex, but the various premises essentially capture the following ideas. Firstly, when an actor is spawned, exclusive permission to all of its fields (denoted by the assertion $(\overrightarrow{* \,\mathbf{acc}(x.f_i)})$) is newly made available, and we can assume that all fields have been initialised to the specified e_i expressions. The actor's invariant might require some of these exclusive permissions (in which case they must be given up in the current scope); it might also require *immutable* permission to some of these fields. To handle this possibility, the *freeze* operator can be used to obtain necessary immutable permissions in A'. The (one-state) assertion a must be strong enough to guarantee a weak form of the actor's invariant, in which all that needs to be justified about the **old** state is that its existence is not inconsistent. To satisfy this premise, the assertion a needs to include the permissions which the actor invariant requires, which forces them not to also occur in A'', unless they are immutable permissions.

Even without obligations (described in the next subsection), we can now define what it means for a message implementation to be *valid*. This judgement is independent of any actor service reasoning: it guarantees that the first four properties described in our list above are all true for a particular message implementation, and define the baseline verification condition for a given program.

Definition 4 (Valid message handler). *A handler for message m in class C is* valid, *written $C, m \vdash_{OK}$, iff (where a_{pre} is the precondition of m and s_{body} is the body of message m) there exist a one-state assertion a and expressions $\overrightarrow{e_i}$ such that:*

$$\forall \Sigma, \sigma.\ (\exists \Sigma_0.\ \Sigma_0, \Sigma, \sigma \models \mathit{Inv}(C)) \Rightarrow \Sigma, \sigma \models a) \quad \mathit{and} \quad \overrightarrow{a_{pre} * a \models_{\mathit{frm}} e_i} \quad \mathit{and}$$
$$\emptyset \vdash \{a_{pre} * a * \mathbf{old}(a_{pre} * a) * (\overrightarrow{* \, e_i = \mathbf{old}(e_i)})\}\ s_{body}\ \{\mathit{Inv}(C)\}$$

A program is valid if all of the message handlers of all actor classes are valid.

[8] Note that none of the Hoare Logic rules change this environment; the actor services included in Λ can be seen as hypotheses across the whole Hoare Logic proof.

The assertion a in the judgement above allows us information from the actor invariant which pertains to the current state. For example, permissions belonging to the actor invariant can be retained in a. Both this assertion and the message precondition are "duplicated" in the current and old states; our assertion semantics models these as independent states, but at the start of executing a message handler they should be known to be the same. The expressions e_i allow us to connect these two states with additional equalities, where relevant. The postcondition of the judgement requires that we can show that the actor invariant will hold across the entire message handler execution.

4.2 Obligation Assertions

We allow our syntax of assertions used in Hoare triple pre- and postconditions to include *obligation assertions* of the form **obl**(o); intuitively these represent the requirement that we reach *some* program point at which a condition described by o is met. Here, o is either a *non-empty* response set R or the assertion *localVariant*(**this**). In the former case, we require that the only variables mentioned in R are the parameters (including **this**) of the message handler being checked, and that *localVariant* assertions used in the where conditions of R are of the form *localVariant*(**this**) (these relate to the local state of the actor; when proving a local service, we only have access to the local state of **this**).

We must define semantics for these novel assertions, including extending the standard notion of state to reflect obligations. The essential idea of our obligation semantics can be best understood by comparing with the semantics of permission assertions such as **acc**($e.f$). In the case of permissions, such an assertion is true if it *under-approximates* the permissions actually held; we must hold *at least* the permissions required by the assertion. Obligation assertions have a dual semantics, they are true in a state if they *over-approximate* the actual obligations. This intuitively means that in a Hoare Logic proof it is allowed for permissions to be leaked but never fabricated (**acc**($e.f$) $\models^{\Lambda}$ *true* but the reverse does not hold); for obligations, the opposite is the case, and in particular, $A \models^{\Lambda}$ *true* does *not* hold in general, when A contains obligation assertions. Note that the assertion semantics does not reflect directly what the intended *meaning* of these obligations is; apart from forcing that they cannot be simply removed, they are treated as unknown assertions in the assertion semantics. Instead, their intended meaning is reflected in the Hoare Logic rules.

This design has an important outcome: obligation assertions included in the precondition of a Hoare triple cannot be removed using the rule of consequence. Instead, these can be removed only by the last three rules of Fig. 3, which specifically model the *discharge* of obligations. We can now show how to use obligation assertions to check local services against an implementation.

Definition 5 (Checking local services). *A handler for message m in class C provides the local service $\forall this, \overrightarrow{X_i}.(this.m(\overrightarrow{X_i}) \rightsquigarrow R)$ under actor service environment Λ, written $\Lambda, C, m \vdash \forall this, \overrightarrow{X_i}.(this.m(\overrightarrow{X_i}) \rightsquigarrow R)$, iff (where $a_{pre} = pre(m, this, \overrightarrow{X_i})$, and s_{body} is the body of the message handler for m in class C*

with formal parameters renamed to $\overrightarrow{X_i}$*) there exist a one-state assertion* a *and expressions* $\overrightarrow{e_i}$ *such that:*

$$\forall \Sigma, \sigma.\ (\underline{\exists \Sigma_0.\ \Sigma_0, \Sigma, \sigma \models Inv(C, this)) \ \Rightarrow\ \Sigma, \sigma \models a)} \ \ and\ \ \overrightarrow{a_{pre} * a \models_{frm} e_i}$$
$$and\ \ \Lambda \vdash \{a_{pre} * a * \mathbf{old}(a_{pre} * a) * (\ast\, e_i = \mathbf{old}(e_i)\ ) * \mathbf{obl}(R)\}\ s_{body}\ \{true\}$$

This definition is similar to Definition 4: we remove the requirement to check the actor invariant (we could keep this, but all message handlers must be checked to be valid in any case), allow for the possibility of a non-empty actor service environment, and, importantly, add the obligation assertion **obl**(R) to the precondition. The fact that *no* obligation assertions occur in the postcondition forces the message handler implementation to discharge these obligations before terminating.

4.3 Discharging Obligations

Obligation assertions of the form **obl**(R), can be discharged if *one* of the alternatives described by the response pattern R can be shown to take place. In this section, we explain the last three rules of Fig. 3, which handle discharging obligations. To illustrate the rules, we consider the proof of local service (*QM3*) against the sols message handler in the QueryManager class.

In the case that R contains an empty response as an alternative, the rule (*emptyObl*) defines the criterion for the obligation to be discharged based on this alternative. The premises require that we can show that the where condition holds (recall that where conditions for empty responses may only constrain the "**old**" state); in this case, the **obl**(R) assertion need not be included in the postcondition. For example, in the (implicit) else branch at line 35, we can apply this rule, combining the fact ¬(**this**.next = **null** ∧ **this**.user = **null**) known in this branch with **this**.next = **old**(**this**.next) ∗ (**this**.user = **old**(**this**.user)), from the precondition of the judgement (cf. Definition 5), to obtain the required where-clause.

The rule (*messageObl*) handles the similar (but more complex) case of discharging an obligation via a message send[9]. Conceptually, the first two lines of premises check that we have the message precondition, that the message send in the code matches that in the response pattern (when evaluating the receiver and parameter expressions in the current state), and that the where condition A_1 is framed by permissions in the current state. Intuitively, we would then just check that A_1 can also be shown to be true in this state. This is correct *except* in the case where A_1 includes *localVariant*(**this**) assertions. Whether a suitable local variant is established by this message handler cannot be determined at this program point; this can only be checked across the entire execution of the message handler. Our solution is to split the checking of A_1 into two parts: the requirements that the assertion makes independently of *localVariant* assertions (A_2, in the rule, which is then checked to hold), and the *condition* under which

[9] Note that rule (*messageNoObl*) can be applied instead of rule (*messageObl*), when one cannot or need not discharge an obligation via this message send statement.

A_1 requires a *localVariant*(**this**) assertion, which we use to prescribe a new obligation in the postcondition (B_2 is this condition)[10]. The last premise of the rule, which lets us potentially rewrite B_2 into a weaker condition B_3 (thus potentially requiring the resulting obligation more often) is necessary only in the case that B_2 depends on heap locations to which (exclusive) permission is given away (in a); this may force us to abstract the precise condition to one which can still be evaluated after the message send.

As an example of applying this rule, at line 40, we can use the (*messageObl*) rule; here, the corresponding A_1 assertion is simply *localVariant*(**this**), and so A_2 and B_2 are both *true*: this results in the assertion **obl**(*localVariant*(**this**)) in the postcondition. Note that at *this* program point, no suitable local variant has been established. By the end of the message handler, we will still have this obligation, but under the condition describing that we took the path through the message handler which reaches line 40.

By this point in the code (as claimed previously in Sect. 3.8), the expression **this**.nrSolutions − |**this**.store| will have been decreased since the message handler began executing. We include in the actor invariant for QueryManager that the value of the store field can never decrease in size, while the nrSolutions field is immutable (once initialised): we then know that the actor invariant guarantees that this expression will never increase in value across the execution of subsequent message handlers. These conditions make up the premises of the rule (*localVarObl*), which can be used to discharge this obligation in the proof of this message handler.

4.4 Overall Proof Strategy: Iterated Derivation of Actor Services

In order to prove local services which include actor services in their where-clauses, the rules of Fig. 3 are already sufficient. However, at the point of applying the rule (*messageObl*) explained above, it will be necessary to discharge a premise that shows that the where-clause holds at this point. When actor services occur in this where-clause, this will be possible only if the Hoare triple precondition already includes actor services, or we are able to derive them from it. In either case, it will be possible to prove any actor services *during* a Hoare Logic proof only if the actor service environment Λ is not empty. Including a non-empty actor service environment Λ makes the justification of a new local service hypothetical. We must ensure that this yields a well-founded derivation of the eventual response property; it would not be acceptable to prove a local service by first assuming it in Λ and then deriving it according to Definition 5.

We can support hierarchical derivation of actor services (new services are derived using only the results of previous proofs), as follows: firstly, some local services can be derived with an empty actor service environment. Any actor service without nested actor services in its where-clauses will (if derivable at all) not require any assumed actor services. In our running example, the three local

[10] This splitting can be achieved syntactically; we abstract its definition here with the function *splitLocalVariant*.

services (*QW*), (*QM2*) and (*QM3*) fall into this category. Then, by *assuming* these local services, we are able to derive e.g. (*QM*), whose derivation requires the arguments presented throughout Sect. 3 in order to justify the nested actor service. If local services are built up in this hierarchical fashion, the justification of the corresponding response properties is guaranteed to be well-founded.

Definition 6 (Iterative derivation of actor services). *An actor service environment Λ can be* iteratively derived *(for a given program), if there exists $n \geq 0$ and there exist actor service environments $\Lambda'_1, \Lambda_1, \Lambda'_2, \Lambda_2, \ldots, \Lambda'_n, \Lambda_n$ such that (taking $\Lambda_0 = \emptyset$), we have $\Lambda_n = \Lambda$ and for all $0 \leq i < n$:*
(1) Each $\forall\overrightarrow{X_i}.(T \rightsquigarrow R) \in \Lambda'_{i+1}$ is a local service, and $\Lambda_i, C, m \vdash \forall\overrightarrow{X_i}.T \rightsquigarrow R$ (where C, m are the class and message name of the trigger message T).
(2) For each $\forall\overrightarrow{X_i}.(T \rightsquigarrow R) \in \Lambda_{i+1}$, we have true $\models^{\Lambda'_{i+1}} \forall\overrightarrow{X_i}.T \rightsquigarrow R$.

This definition allows us to alternate between deriving new local services (Λ'_{i+1}) based on previously derived actor services, or deriving new actor services (Λ_{i+1}) from local services. The latter step can be useful for information hiding reasons: if we wish to present an actor service environment as a specification for part of the program, then presenting only local services may not be suitable: because a local service must always expose a response message which is sent directly by the message handler for its trigger message, this might expose details (of intermediate actors, messages and field names) that we do not wish to. Being able to rewrite these local services into arbitrary actor services allows us to avoid this (in our running example, this wasn't necessary, since the local service (*QM*) was derivable without exposing internal details).

4.5 Soundness

The proof technique of Definition 6 also lends itself to proving soundness of our actor service reasoning. While a formal operational semantics and soundness argument are beyond the scope of this paper, we summarise the essential points here.

Firstly, we consider only well-typed programs which are valid (Definition 4). Operationally, we consider null dereferences and data races as runtime errors. We define a notion of valid runtime state, which includes the requirement that a suitable partioning of the heap into *owned* regions and an *immutable* region must exist. As the program executes, this partitioning will change, but locations in the *immutable* region will remain so. Note that this notion of ownership is an artifact of the argument but not a feature of the operational semantics itself (which does not track permissions). Based on this idea, we can show that a valid program will never get stuck or encounter runtime errors.

To tackle the soundness of actor services, we need to relate these assertions to the intended temporal (response) property of runtime traces which they notionally represent. We can show two key results. Firstly, we can show that for any *local service* $\forall\overrightarrow{X_i}.(T \rightsquigarrow R)$ such that $\Lambda, C, m \vdash \forall\overrightarrow{X_i}.(T \rightsquigarrow R)$, any execution of the message handler for m in C will either not terminate, or will eventually reach a state in which one of the response messages is sent (or none, if an empty response pattern is included), and the corresponding where-clause will be *derivable* at this point, possibly using the actor services assumed in Λ. This result can be shown in a simplified operational semantics in which we only consider the local execution of a single actor executing the appropriate message handler. The result can be made a true liveness property if one chooses to also prove termination of each message handler, which we regard as an orthogonal problem.

Secondly, we can show tha for any actor service $\forall\overrightarrow{X_i}.(T \rightsquigarrow R)$ derivable in a program state under an actor service environment Λ, if we *assume* that all actor services in Λ describe valid response properties of the runtime traces of the program, then the actor service $\forall\overrightarrow{X_i}.(T \rightsquigarrow R)$ will also do so. This requires an induction over the derivation (according to the rules of Fig. 2) of $\forall\overrightarrow{X_i}.(T \rightsquigarrow R)$, and requires that sent messages are always eventually delivered (not necessarily in order), selection of a new message to execute is weakly fair, and all actors continue to respond (i.e., will always eventually receive another message, if any are waiting); in particular, that no actor executes a message handler forever.

As a corollary of these two results, we obtain that, in a valid program, any actor service which can be iteratively derived (Definition 6) will describe a response property true for the runtime traces of the program, under the same assumptions.

5 Related Work

With respect to the case study of Arts and Dam [2], we provide a simple proof of the same response property, using the actor services, permissions and actor invariants provided by our technique. Poetzsch-Heffter *et al.* [32] argue the need for actor reasoning techniques supporting compositionality. Kurnia and Poetzsch-Heffter [22] present such a compositional technique based on trace-based assertions. However, behaviours guaranteed by actors can only be summarised in a hierarchical fashion, according to a fixed topology [34], and callbacks in sequences of messages (such as in the ring in our example) are not permitted.

A number of other techniques base reasoning around invariants over *histories* of message-events (e.g. [1,12,13]). These approaches can express intricate properties over many successive events. The techniques involve one verification at the level of individual actors (via invariants), followed by a composition phase to derive a system-wide invariant. These safety properties cannot guarantee that certain response events will occur (after perhaps unrelated actions by the same actor). Individual actors can be verified in isolation, but it is not possible to summarise behaviour of parts of a program such that the summaries can themselves be composed later. Feng [16] makes a similar argument for hierarchical compositionality in the context of reasoning about concurrency and shared data.

Some language designs provide guarantees about actor-like programs *by design*, via reduction to model-checking [10,11], custom support in proof assistants [33], or via high-level program descriptions from which code can be safely generated [8]. These works (as well as those based on temporal logics) require reasoning in terms of the whole program and/or do not handle liveness properties.

Multiple type systems have been proposed for guaranteeing properties such as copyless messaging (ownership transfer) and immutability in actor-like programs, e.g. [6,7,17,36,41]. These type annotations could be mapped onto permissions, to combine these systems with our technique for proving response properties: Some techniques integrate protocol verification [4,15,38,39], which makes reasoning more precise and able to address other safety properties.

Extensive work has been carried out on protocol verification for message-passing programs, using (multiparty) session types [3,9,20,21]; such work typically does not address liveness or compositional reasoning. Such protocol reasoning could, however, complement our proof technique (see Sect. 6). Padovani *et al.* [29] address liveness at the protocol level; this does not guarantee that the underlying code will continue to produce messages, and does not support compositionality. Lange and Tuosto [23] show how to synthesise global descriptions of a system from local ones; this is closer in spirit to our compositional reasoning, but does not support functional specifications or liveness.

The "causal obligations" of Helm *et al.* [18] are a specification construct similar to simple local services. No proof system was defined for this construct.

6 Conclusions and Future Work

We have introduced a new modular verification technique for programs which communicate via asynchronous messaging. Our proof technique is compatible with permission-based logics; in particular, it is straightforward to adapt the assertion logic (including the where-clauses of our actor services) to incorporate standard features of these logics such as abstract predicates [30]. Our semantics for actor service assertions is largely orthogonal to the particular logic used for functional specification, provided that two-state properties can be expressed.

A natural extension is to generalise the form of actor services to express response properties with more than one response message and more than one trigger message. The former extension is straightforward, but the latter requires additional book-keeping in the reasoning, in order to represent the case that some but not all of the trigger messages have been received; we leave this extension for future work, along with a complete formalisation and soundness proof.

Our current proof technique assumes that actors must, by default, be always ready to receive any message permitted by their type. It would be interesting to combine our actor service reasoning with protocol verification techniques (such as session types and typestate reasoning), in order to make our technique more expressive and to support explicit de-allocation of actors.

Acknowledgements. We are very grateful to Sophia Drossopoulou, Sylvan Clebsch, Juliana Franco, Tim Wood, Susan Eisenbach, Malte Schwerhoff, Ernie Cohen, John Boyland, Arnd Poetzsch-Heffter, Ludovic Henrio, Pietro Ferrara and Reuben Rowe for important technical discussions and encouragement. We thank Mariangiola Dezani and Dilian Gurov for pointers to related work, and the ESOP reviewers for many helpful suggestions which have improved the paper.

References

1. Ahrendt, W., Dylla, M.: A system for compositional verification of asynchronous objects. Sci. Comput. Programm. **77**(12), 1289–1309 (2012)
2. Arts, T., Dam, M.: Verifying a distributed database lookup manager written in Erlang. In: Wing, J.M., Woodcock, J. (eds.) FM 1999. LNCS, vol. 1708, pp. 682–700. Springer, Heidelberg (1999)
3. Bocchi, L., Honda, K., Tuosto, E., Yoshida, N.: A theory of design-by-contract for distributed multiparty interactions. In: Gastin, P., Laroussinie, F. (eds.) CONCUR 2010. LNCS, vol. 6269, pp. 162–176. Springer, Heidelberg (2010)
4. Bono, V., Messa, C., Padovani, L.: Typing copyless message passing. In: Barthe, G. (ed.) ESOP 2011. LNCS, vol. 6602, pp. 57–76. Springer, Heidelberg (2011)
5. Boyland, J.: Checking interference with fractional permissions. In: Cousot, R. (ed.) SAS 2003. LNCS, vol. 2694, pp. 55–72. Springer, Heidelberg (2003)
6. Clarke, D., Wrigstad, T., Östlund, J., Johnsen, E.B.: Minimal ownership for active objects. In: Ramalingam, G. (ed.) APLAS 2008. LNCS, vol. 5356, pp. 139–154. Springer, Heidelberg (2008)
7. Clebsch, S., Drossopoulou, S., Blessing, S., McNeil, A.: Deny capabilities for safe, fast actors. In: AGERE! pp. 1–12 (2015)
8. Dalla Preda, M., Gabbrielli, M., Giallorenzo, S., Lanese, I., Mauro, J.: Dynamic choreographies. In: Holvoet, T., Viroli, M. (eds.) Coordination Models and Languages. LNCS, vol. 9037, pp. 67–82. Springer, Heidelberg (2015)
9. Deniélou, P.-M., Yoshida, N.: Dynamic multirole session types. SIGPLAN Not. **46**(1), 435–446 (2011)
10. Desai, A., Garg, P., Madhusudan, P.: Natural proofs for asynchronous programs using almost-synchronous reductions. OOPSLA **2014**, 709–725 (2014)
11. Desai, A., Gupta, V., Jackson, E., Qadeer, S., Rajamani, S., Zufferey, D.: P: safe asynchronous event-driven programming. SIGPLAN Not. **48**(6), 321–332 (2013)
12. Din, C.C., Dovland, J., Johnsen, E.B., Owe, O.: Observable behavior of distributed systems: component reasoning for concurrent objects. J. Logic Algebraic Program. **81**(3), 227–256 (2012). Proceedings of NWPT 2010
13. Dovland, J., Johnsen, E., Owe, O.: Verification of concurrent objects with asynchronous method calls. In: SwSTE, pp. 141–150 (2005)
14. Drossopoulou, S., Francalanza, A., Müller, P., Summers, A.J.: A unified framework for verification techniques for object invariants. In: Vitek, J. (ed.) ECOOP 2008. LNCS, vol. 5142, pp. 412–437. Springer, Heidelberg (2008)
15. Fähndrich, M., Aiken, M., Hawblitzel, C., Hodson, O., Hunt, G., Larus, J.R., Levi, S.: Language support for fast and reliable message-based communication in Singularity OS. In: EuroSys, pp. 177–190. ACM Press (2006)
16. Feng, X.: Local rely-guarantee reasoning. In: POPL, pp. 315–327 (2009)
17. Haller, P., Odersky, M.: Capabilities for uniqueness and borrowing. In: D'Hondt, T. (ed.) ECOOP 2010. LNCS, vol. 6183, pp. 354–378. Springer, Heidelberg (2010)

18. Helm, R., Holland, I.M., Gangopadhyay, D.: Contracts: specifying behavioral compositions in object-oriented systems. In: OOPSLA/ECOOP, pp. 169–180 (1990)
19. Hewitt, C., Bishop, P., Steiger, R.: A universal modular actor formalism for artificial intelligence. In: IJCAI, pp. 235–245 (1973)
20. Honda, K., Vasconcelos, V.T., Kubo, M.: Language primitives and type discipline for structured communication-based programming. In: Hankin, C. (ed.) ESOP 1998. LNCS, vol. 1381, p. 122. Springer, Heidelberg (1998)
21. Honda, K., Yoshida, N., Carbone, M.: Multiparty asynchronous session types. SIGPLAN Not. **43**(1), 273–284 (2008)
22. Kurnia, I.W., Poetzsch-Heffter, A.: A relational trace logic for simple hierarchical actor-based component systems. In: AGERE! 2012, pp. 47–58, October 2012
23. Lange, J., Tuosto, E.: Synthesising choreographies from local session types. In: Koutny, M., Ulidowski, I. (eds.) CONCUR 2012. LNCS, vol. 7454, pp. 225–239. Springer, Heidelberg (2012)
24. Leino, K.R.M., Müller, P.: A basis for verifying multi-threaded programs. In: Castagna, G. (ed.) ESOP 2009. LNCS, vol. 5502, pp. 378–393. Springer, Heidelberg (2009)
25. Meyer, B.: Object-Oriented Software Construction, 2nd edn. Prentice Hall, Upper Saddle River (1997)
26. Nilsson, H.: Method and apparatus for evaluating a data processing request performed by distributed processes. Patent Filed, issued on August 2003 (1998). http://patents.justia.com/patent/6604122
27. Odersky, M., Micheloud, S., Mihaylov, N., Schinz, M., Stenman, E., Zenger, M., et al.: An overview of the Scala programming language. Technical report, École Polytechnique Fédérale de Lausanne (EPFL) (2004)
28. O'Hearn, P.W., Reynolds, J.C., Yang, H.: Local reasoning about programs that alter data structures. In: Fribourg, L. (ed.) CSL 2001 and EACSL 2001. LNCS, vol. 2142, pp. 1–19. Springer, Heidelberg (2001)
29. Padovani, L., Vasconcelos, V.T., Vieira, H.T.: Typing liveness in multiparty communicating systems. In: Kühn, E., Pugliese, R. (eds.) COORDINATION 2014. LNCS, vol. 8459, pp. 147–162. Springer, Heidelberg (2014)
30. Parkinson, M., Bierman, G.: Separation logic and abstraction. In: POPL, pp. 247–258. ACM Press (2005)
31. Parkinson, M.J., Summers, A.J.: The relationship between separation logic and implicit dynamic frames. Logical Meth. Comput. Sci. **8**(3:01), 1–54 (2012)
32. Poetzsch-Heffter, A., Kurnia, I.W., Feller, C.: Verification of actor systems needs specification techniques for strong causality and hierarchical reasoning. In: FoVeOOS 2011, pp. 289–305. Technische Universität Karlsruhe, October 2011
33. Ricketts, D., Robert, V., Jang, D., Tatlock, Z., Lerner, S.: Automating formal proofs for reactive systems. SIGPLAN Not. **49**(6), 452–462 (2014)
34. Schäfer, J., Poetzsch-Heffter, A.: JCoBox: generalizing active objects to concurrent components. In: D'Hondt, T. (ed.) ECOOP 2010. LNCS, vol. 6183, pp. 275–299. Springer, Heidelberg (2010)
35. Smans, J., Jacobs, B., Piessens, F.: Implicit dynamic frames: combining dynamic frames and separation logic. In: Drossopoulou, S. (ed.) ECOOP 2009. LNCS, vol. 5653, pp. 148–172. Springer, Heidelberg (2009)
36. Srinivasan, S., Mycroft, A.: Kilim: isolation-typed actors for Java. In: Vitek, J. (ed.) ECOOP 2008. LNCS, vol. 5142, pp. 104–128. Springer, Heidelberg (2008)
37. Summers, A.J., Drossopoulou, S.: A formal semantics for isorecursive and equirecursive state abstractions. In: Castagna, G. (ed.) ECOOP 2013. LNCS, vol. 7920, pp. 129–153. Springer, Heidelberg (2013)

38. Villard, J., Lozes, É., Calcagno, C.: Proving copyless message passing. In: Hu, Z. (ed.) APLAS 2009. LNCS, vol. 5904, pp. 194–209. Springer, Heidelberg (2009)
39. Villard, J., Lozes, É., Calcagno, C.: Tracking heaps that hop with heap-hop. In: Esparza, J., Majumdar, R. (eds.) TACAS 2010. LNCS, vol. 6015, pp. 275–279. Springer, Heidelberg (2010)
40. Virding, R., Wikström, C., Williams, M.: Concurrent Programming in ERLANG, 2nd edn. Prentice Hall International (UK) Ltd., Hertfordshire (1996)
41. Zibin, Y., Potanin, A., Li, P., Ali, M., Ernst, M.D.: Ownership and immutability in generic Java. SIGPLAN Not. **45**(10), 598–617 (2010)

Transfinite Step-Indexing: Decoupling Concrete and Logical Steps

Kasper Svendsen[1(✉)], Filip Sieczkowski[2], and Lars Birkedal[3]

[1] University of Cambridge, Cambridge, UK
ks775@cl.cam.ac.uk
[2] INRIA, Paris, France
filip.sieczkowski@inria.fr
[3] Aarhus University, Aarhus, Denmark
birkedal@cs.au.dk

Abstract. Step-indexing has proven to be a powerful technique for defining logical relations for languages with advanced type systems and models of expressive program logics. In both cases, the model is stratified using natural numbers to solve a recursive equation that has no naive solutions. As a result of this stratification, current models require that each unfolding of the recursive equation – each logical step – must coincide with a concrete reduction step. This tight coupling is problematic for applications where the number of logical steps cannot be statically bounded.

In this paper we demonstrate that this tight coupling between logical and concrete steps is artificial and show how to loosen it using transfinite step-indexing. We present a logical relation that supports an arbitrary but finite number of logical steps for each concrete step.

1 Introduction

Step-indexing has proven to be a powerful technique for defining models of advanced type systems [2,5,6,10,11] and expressive higher-order program logics [4,16,18,20]. To support abstraction, such type systems and program logics often feature some notion of *impredicative invariants*. For instance, a reference type can be seen as an invariant about the type of values stored at a given location; for languages with general references this is an impredicative invariant.

Modelling impredicative invariants is difficult and a naive approach naturally leads to a circular definition with no solution. To illustrate, consider modelling a language with general references. A natural idea is to interpret types relative to a world (heap typing) that assigns semantic types to all currently allocated locations. The reference type, τ ref, can then be interpreted as the set of locations mapped to $[\![\tau]\!]$ in the current world. A world is a finite function from locations to types. Unfortunately, this idea leads to a circular definition of the semantic domain of types that has no solution in set theory:

$$\text{Type} \cong \text{World} \stackrel{mon}{\to} \mathcal{P}(\text{Val}) \qquad\qquad \text{World} = \text{Loc} \stackrel{fin}{\rightharpoonup} \text{Type}$$

P. Thiemann (Ed.): ESOP 2016, LNCS 9632, pp. 727–751, 2016.
DOI: 10.1007/978-3-662-49498-1_28

To break this circularity, step-indexed models interpret inhabitance of a type as a predicate indexed by the number of steps left "on the clock". This allows for a well-founded definition over the steps, by "going down a step" whenever an impredicative invariant is unfolded. We refer to these as *logical steps*. Since reference types require an unfolding of an impredicative invariant, the interpretation of reference types introduces a logical step: a location l is an inhabitant of type $\tau\ \mathsf{ref}$ with $n+1$ steps left on the clock, if location l contains a value that is an inhabitant of type τ with n steps left on the clock.

To use this artificially stratified model, current step-indexed models take the steps to be concrete reduction steps in the underlying operational semantics. An expression e is thus an inhabitant of type τ with n steps left on the clock, if whenever it reduces to e' in $i < n$ *concrete reduction steps*, then e' is an inhabitant of τ with $n - i$ steps left on the clock. As a consequence, each logical step must be associated with a corresponding reduction step.

This suffices to prove many interesting properties. For instance, to prove type soundness of the typing rule for dereference, we have to prove that $!l$ is an inhabitant of τ for n steps, assuming l is an inhabitant of $\tau\ \mathsf{ref}$ for n steps. Since $!l$ uses one concrete reduction step, it suffices to know that location l contains a value that is an inhabitant of τ for $n-1$ steps. Conceptually, the logical step of unfolding the invariant always happens together with the concrete step of dereferencing the location and the proof goes through. Unfortunately, this is not always the case. For instance, higher-order abstractions often introduce new logical steps without introducing corresponding concrete steps [18].

This is most easily illustrated in the setting of binary logical relations. To prove that e_1 logically approximates e_2, $\Gamma \models e_1 \leq_{log} e_2 : \tau$, current step-indexed logical relations require that each logical step must be associated with a reduction step of e_1. Let τ denote the type

$$\exists \alpha.\ (1 \to \alpha) \times (\alpha \to \mathbb{N})$$

and $f : \tau \to \tau$ denote the following function

$$\lambda x : \tau.\ \mathsf{unpack}\ x\ \mathsf{as}\ (\alpha, y)\ \mathsf{in}\ \mathsf{pack}\ (\alpha\ \mathsf{ref}, (\lambda z : 1.\ \mathsf{ref}\ (\mathsf{fst}\ y\ z), \lambda z : \alpha.\ \mathsf{snd}\ y\ (!z)))$$

The function f takes a τ ADT and returns a new one that wraps instances of the ADT in an additional reference. One might hope to be able to prove that $x : \tau \models x \cong_{log} f(x)$ and thus that the ADT returned by f is contextually equivalent to its argument. However, as far as we are aware, no current step-indexed logical relations offer a practical way of proving the left-to-right approximation, $x : \tau \models x \leq_{log} f(x)$.[1] The additional indirection through the heap forces us to introduce

[1] There are step-indexed logical relations, which are *complete* wrt. contextual approximation [15], which would seem to suggest that they should be flexible enough to prove this example, but completeness is achieved using biorthogonality (a kind of closure under evaluation contexts), which means that while the models are technically complete, they do not offer a practical way of proving this kind of example; cf. the discussion in Section 10 of [15].

an invariant for each instance of the two ADTs we create. To relate the two instances we must unfold this invariant. Unfortunately, there is no reduction step on the left to justify this unfolding.

Similar problems plague step-indexed program logics, where higher-order abstractions that introduce new logical steps without any corresponding concrete steps are more common. For instance, deriving a new simpler specification for a specific way of using a concurrent data structure from an abstract library specification often introduces a new invariant without introducing any new concrete reduction steps [18,20]. See [18, Sect. 8] for a concrete example of this problem in the context of step-indexed program logics. Existing step-indexing program logics have dealt with this issue by adding additional *skip* statements, to allow new logical steps to be related to *skip* reduction steps [14,18]. Not only is this solution semantically unsatisfying, it is also insufficient for examples where the number of logical unfoldings cannot be statically bounded.

Conceptually, the problem with earlier models is the artificial link made between unfoldings of the recursive domain equation (logical steps) and concrete reduction steps. In this paper we propose a refinement of step-indexing that relaxes this link, by allowing an arbitrary but finite number of logical steps for each concrete reduction step. To achieve this, we stratify the construction of the semantic domain using ω^2, or $\mathbb{N} \times \mathbb{N}$ ordered lexicographically, instead of ω. We then take the first step index to be concrete reduction steps in the underlying operational semantics and the second step index to be the number of logical steps possible before the next concrete reduction step. The lexicographic ordering ensures that we can pick an arbitrary but finite number of possible logical steps until the next concrete reduction step, after each concrete reduction step.

Instead of presenting a transfinitely step-indexed model of our latest and greatest program logic, we focus on a logical relation. Such a setting is simpler, thus allowing us to present our solution in greater detail and concentrate on the problem of decoupling logical and concrete steps. We develop a general theory for stratifying the construction of semantic domains using step-indexing over ω^2. This theory also applies to semantic domains used in recent step-indexed program logics and we believe our approach to decoupling logical and concrete steps also extends to these program logics.

Our main contribution is conceptual: we demonstrate how transfinite step-indexing allows us to loosen the artificial link between concrete and logical steps in step-indexed models. As a technical contribution, we extend previous results for stratifying recursive definitions using step-indexing over ω to the transfinite case of ω^2.

We have included proof sketches of the main results in the article. Full proofs can be found in the accompanying technical report, which is available at the following address: http://www.kasv.dk/transfinite-tr.pdf.

Outline. First we introduce the syntax and operational semantics of a simple higher-order language in Sect. 2. In Sect. 3 we show how to stratify the construction of semantic domains using step-indexing over ω^2 and recall some mathematical concepts for working with these domains. Next, we apply this theory

$$
\begin{aligned}
\tau, \sigma &::= 1 \mid \mathbb{N} \mid \tau \times \sigma \mid \tau \to \sigma \mid \tau \ \mathsf{ref} \mid \exists \alpha.\ \tau \mid \alpha \\
v \in \mathrm{Val} &::= * \mid \underline{n} \mid (v_1, v_2) \mid \mathsf{fix}\ f(x).\ e \mid l \mid \mathsf{pack}\ v \\
e \in \mathrm{Exp} &::= * \mid \underline{n} \mid (e_1, e_2) \mid \mathsf{fst}\ e \mid \mathsf{snd}\ e \mid \mathsf{fix}\ f(x).\ e \mid e_1\ e_2 \\
&\mid\ l \mid\ !e \mid e_1 := e_2 \mid \mathsf{ref}\ e \mid \mathsf{pack}\ e \mid \mathsf{unpack}\ e_1\ \mathsf{as}\ x\ \mathsf{in}\ e_2
\end{aligned}
$$

Fig. 1. Types, values and expressions.

to define a transfinitely step-indexed logical relation in Sect. 4. In Sect. 5 we return to the example mentioned above and prove the troublesome contextual equivalence using our transfinitely step-indexed logical relation. We defer most discussions of related work to Sect. 6. Finally, in Sect. 7 we conclude and discuss future work.

2 Syntax and Operational Semantics

In Fig. 1 we define the syntax of a higher-order functional language with general references and existential types. This set of language features and type system suffices to study the problems mentioned in the Introduction. We assume countably infinite and disjoint sets of type variables, term variables and locations, with α ranging over type variables and x over term variables and l over locations. We use a Curry-style presentation and thus do not annotate λ-abstractions or pack/unpack with types. The typing rules have the form $\Delta; \Gamma \vdash e : \tau$, where Δ is a context of type variables and Γ is a context of term variables. The well-formed type judgment, $\Delta \vdash \tau$ expresses that all free type variables in τ are bound in Δ. Figure 2 includes an excerpt of typing rules; the remaining rules are standard and have been omitted.

$$
\frac{\Delta; \Gamma \vdash e : \tau\ \mathsf{ref}}{\Delta; \Gamma \vdash\ !e : \tau}
\qquad
\frac{\Delta; \Gamma \vdash e_1 : \tau\ \mathsf{ref} \qquad \Delta; \Gamma \vdash e_2 : \tau}{\Delta; \Gamma \vdash e_1 := e_2 : 1}
\qquad
\frac{\Delta; \Gamma \vdash e : \tau}{\Delta; \Gamma \vdash \mathsf{ref}\ e : \tau\ \mathsf{ref}}
$$

$$
\frac{\Delta; \Gamma \vdash e_1 : \exists \alpha.\ \tau \qquad \Delta, \alpha; \Gamma, x : \alpha \vdash e_2 : \sigma \qquad \Delta \vdash \sigma}{\Delta; \Gamma \vdash \mathsf{unpack}\ e_1\ \mathsf{as}\ x\ \mathsf{in}\ e_2 : \sigma}
$$

Fig. 2. Excerpt of typing rules.

Note that our type system does not include store typings, assigning types to locations. Store typings are typically used to facilitate syntactic progress and preservation proofs. However, they are unnecessary for our semantic approach and we only consider source programs that do not contain location constants.

The operational semantics is defined as a small-step reduction relation between configurations consisting of an expression e and a heap h: $\langle e, h \rangle \to \langle e', h' \rangle$. A heap is a finite map from locations to values. Figure 3 includes an excerpt of the reduction rules; the rest of the rules are standard. Note that dereferencing or assigning to a location that has not already been allocated results in a stuck configuration. It will follow from our logical relation that well-typed programs never get stuck and thus never try to dereference a location that has not been allocated.

From the small-step reduction semantics we define a step-indexed reduction relation, $\langle e, h\rangle \to^n \langle e', h'\rangle$, which expresses that $\langle e, h\rangle$ reduces in n steps to $\langle e', h'\rangle$. We count every reduction step. Note that while our step-indexed logical relation will be indexed using ω^2, the operational semantics is still only indexed over ω, as is standard in step-indexed models. We use $\langle e, h\rangle \to^* \langle e', h'\rangle$ to denote the reflexive transitive closure of the small-step reduction relation.

$$
\begin{aligned}
h \in \mathrm{Heap} &\stackrel{def}{=} \mathrm{Loc} \xrightarrow{fin} \mathrm{Val}\\
K \in \mathrm{ECtx} &::= \bullet \mid (K, e) \mid (v, K) \mid \mathsf{fst}\ K \mid \mathsf{snd}\ K \mid K\ e \mid v\ K\\
&\quad\mid\ !K \mid K := e \mid v := K \mid \mathsf{ref}\ K \mid \mathsf{pack}\ K \mid \mathsf{unpack}\ K\ \mathsf{as}\ x\ \mathsf{in}\ e\\
C \in \mathrm{Ctx} &::= \bullet \mid (C, e) \mid (e, C) \mid \mathsf{fst}\ C \mid \mathsf{snd}\ C \mid C\ e \mid e\ C \mid !C \mid C := e \mid e := C \mid \mathsf{ref}\ C\\
&\quad\mid \mathsf{pack}\ C \mid \mathsf{unpack}\ C\ \mathsf{as}\ x\ \mathsf{in}\ e \mid \mathsf{unpack}\ e\ \mathsf{as}\ x\ \mathsf{in}\ C
\end{aligned}
$$

$$
\textsc{EvalRead}\ \frac{l \in \mathrm{dom}(h)}{\langle !l, h\rangle \to \langle h(l), h\rangle}
\qquad
\textsc{EvalWrite}\ \frac{l \in \mathrm{dom}(h)}{\langle l := v, h\rangle \to \langle *, h[l \mapsto v]\rangle}
\qquad
\textsc{EvalAlloc}\ \frac{l \notin \mathrm{dom}(h)}{\langle \mathsf{ref}\ v, h\rangle \to \langle l, h[l \mapsto v]\rangle}
$$

$$
\textsc{EvalUnpack}\ \frac{}{\langle \mathsf{unpack}\ (\mathsf{pack}\ v)\ \mathsf{as}\ x\ \mathsf{in}\ e, h\rangle \to \langle e[v/x], h\rangle}
\qquad
\textsc{EvalCtx}\ \frac{\langle e, h\rangle \to \langle e', h'\rangle}{\langle K[e], h\rangle \to \langle K[e'], h'\rangle}
$$

$$
\frac{}{\langle e, h\rangle \to^0 \langle e, h\rangle}
\qquad
\frac{\langle e, h\rangle \to \langle e', h'\rangle \quad \langle e', h'\rangle \to^n \langle e'', h''\rangle}{\langle e, h\rangle \to^{n+1} \langle e'', h''\rangle}
$$

Fig. 3. Excerpt of reduction rules.

Our formal definition of contextual approximation is given in Definition 1 below. We say that e_I contextually approximates e_S if for any closing context C of unit type, if $C[e_I]$ terminates with value $*$, then $C[e_S]$ terminates with value $*$. Since well-typed expressions do not contain any location constants, we can simply reduce $C[e_I]$ and $C[e_S]$ with an empty heap. The $C : (\Delta; \Gamma, \tau) \rightsquigarrow (\Delta'; \Gamma', \tau')$ relation expresses that context C takes a term e such that $\Delta; \Gamma \vdash e : \tau$ to a term $C[e]$ such that $\Delta'; \Gamma' \vdash C[e] : \tau'$. The rules for $C : (\Delta; \Gamma, \tau) \rightsquigarrow (\Delta'; \Gamma', \tau')$ are standard and have been omitted.

Definition 1 (Contextual approximation). *If $\Delta; \Gamma \vdash e_I : \tau$ and $\Delta; \Gamma \vdash e_S : \tau$, then e_I contextually approximates e_S, written $\Delta; \Gamma \vdash e_I \leq_{ctx} e_S : \tau$ iff,*

$$
\forall C : (\Delta; \Gamma, \tau) \rightsquigarrow (-; -, 1).
$$
$$
\forall h_I \in \mathrm{Heap}.\ \langle C[e_I], []\rangle \to^* \langle *, h_I\rangle \Rightarrow \exists h_S \in \mathrm{Heap}.\ \langle C[e_S], []\rangle \to^* \langle *, h_S\rangle.
$$

We refer to e_I in $\Delta; \Gamma \vdash e_I \leq e_S : \tau$ as the left expression or implementation and we refer to e_S as the right expression or specification. Contextual equivalence, $\Delta; \Gamma \vdash e_1 \cong_{ctx} e_2 : \tau$, is then defined as the conjunction of left-to-right contextual approximation and right-to-left contextual approximation.

3 Step-Indexing over ω^2

Step-indexing is often used to solve the recursive definitions of semantic domains that arise when modelling impredicative invariants. Due to a contravariant occurrence of the recursive variable, these definitions have no solution in set-theory. Instead, step-indexing is used to stratify the construction. In this section we present a general theory for stratifying the construction of semantic domains using step-indexing over ω^2.

The idea is to define the semantic domain as a fixed point of a suitably *contractive* functor over a category of step-indexed sets. For instance, recall the type-world circularity from the Introduction. Instead of solving the original equation, we wish to solve the following equation in a category of step-indexed sets:

$$\mathbf{Type} \cong \blacktriangleright((\mathrm{Loc} \stackrel{fin}{\rightharpoonup} \mathbf{Type}) \stackrel{mon}{\to} \mathbf{UPred}(\mathrm{Val}))$$

Here the *later* operator ($\blacktriangleright$) ensures that we "go down a step" when unfolding the recursive definition. Intuitively, this ensures that **Type** at step-index i is only defined in terms of **Type** at strictly smaller step-indices, $j < i$, and thus that the equation has a solution. Since the result needs to be a step-indexed set, we have also replaced predicates over values ($\mathcal{P}(\mathrm{Val})$) with its step-indexed counterpart: uniform predicates over values ($\mathbf{UPred}(\mathrm{Val})$).

For step-indexing over ω one can apply general existence theorems for fixed points of locally contractive functors on the category of ω set-indexed sets. Birkedal, Støvring and Thamsborg [12] have generalized the inverse-limit construction to show the existence of fixed points of locally contractive functors over categories where the Hom-sets can be equipped with a suitable metric structure. This existence theorem is directly applicable to the category of ω step-indexed sets. Unfortunately, the results do not apply to the category of ω^2 step-indexed sets. Intuitively, the inverse limit construction is not iterated far enough for step-indexing over ω^2.

In this section we define a category of ω^2 step-indexed sets, $\mathcal{U}$, and give a concrete construction for fixed-points of locally contractive functors on $\mathcal{U}$. While the results for step-indexing over ω^2 are novel, the structure of the development is not and follows existing work. To simplify the exposition we use Di Gianantonio and Miculan's complete ordered families of equivalences [13] to present the category of step-indexed sets and avoid the use of abstract category theory.

Complete ordered families of equivalences. Ordered families of equivalences (o.f.e.) over ω^2 are pairs consisting of a set X and a family of equivalence relations on X, indexed by ω^2. The intuition to keep in mind is that the (n, m)-th equivalence relation, $\stackrel{n,m}{=}$, expresses equality on the underlying set when there is n, m steps left "on the clock". A priori, these steps are purely artificial to break the circularity, however, in the following section we will relate the first step-index n with concrete reduction steps. We will thus think of $\stackrel{n,m}{=}$ as equality on the underlying set, with n concrete reduction steps left and m logical steps left before the next concrete reduction step. We use a lexicographic ordering on ω^2:

$$(n_1, m_1) \leq (n_2, m_2) \stackrel{\text{def}}{=} (n_1 = n_2 \wedge m_1 \leq m_2) \vee n_1 < n_2$$

Thus, every time we take one concrete reduction step, we will be able to chose an arbitrary finite number of logical steps that we may do before the next concrete reduction step.

Another intuition to keep in mind is that two elements are (n, m)-equivalent if the elements cannot distinguished with n concrete reduction steps left and m logical steps before the next concrete step. Since fewer observations are possible as the number of steps decreases, we require the equivalence to become coarser as the number of steps is decreased. With no reduction steps left no observations are possible and every element is indistinguishable. We thus require that the equivalence is the total relation at the last step index, $(0, 0)$. Lastly, we require that if two elements are indistinguishable for any number of steps, they are identical.

Definition 2 (Ordered families of equivalences over ω^2). *An ordered family of equivalence relations (o.f.e.) over ω^2 is a pair $(X, (\stackrel{a}{=})_{a\in\omega^2})$, consisting of a set X and an ω^2-indexed set of equivalence relations $\stackrel{a}{=}$, satisfying*

- $\forall x, y \in X.\ x \stackrel{0,0}{=} y$
- $\forall x, y \in X.\ \forall a, b \in \omega^2.\ a \leq b \wedge x \stackrel{b}{=} y \Rightarrow x \stackrel{a}{=} y$
- $\forall x, y \in X.\ (\forall a \in \omega^2.\ x \stackrel{a}{=} y) \Rightarrow x = y$

The function space between two ordered families of equivalences consists of non-expansive functions that map a-equivalent arguments to a-equivalent results. Intuitively, non-expansiveness of f ensures that it takes at least the same number of steps to distinguish $f(x_1)$ from $f(x_2)$ as it takes to distinguish x_1 from x_2. Similarly, a function f is contractive if it is strictly harder to distinguish $f(x_1)$ from $f(x_2)$ than it is to distinguish x_1 from x_2, i.e., if to show that the results are a-equivalent it suffices that the arguments are equivalent at all *strictly smaller* indices. Contractive functions are thus necessarily non-expansive.

Definition 3 (Non-expansive and contractive functions). *Let $\mathcal{X} = (X, (\stackrel{a}{=}_X)_{a\in\omega^2})$ and $\mathcal{Y} = (Y, (\stackrel{a}{=}_Y)_{a\in\omega^2})$ be ordered families of equivalences. A function $f : X \to Y$ is non-expansive iff*

$$\forall x_1, x_2 \in X.\ \forall a \in \omega^2.\ x_1 \stackrel{a}{=}_X x_2 \Rightarrow f(x_1) \stackrel{a}{=}_Y f(x_2)$$

and contractive iff

$$\forall x_1, x_2 \in X.\ \forall a \in \omega^2.\ (\forall b \in \omega^2.\ b < a \Rightarrow x_1 \stackrel{b}{=}_X x_2) \Rightarrow f(x_1) \stackrel{a}{=}_Y f(x_2).$$

By iterating a contractive function, we get a sequence of elements that require more and more steps to distinguish. For *complete* ordered families of equivalences, where all such sequences have limits, we can define a unique fixed point of the contractive function as a suitable limit. When step-indexing over ω it suffices to iterate a contractive function f up to ω:

$$*, f(*), f^2(*), ...$$

as the fixed point x_1 of f is simply the limit of the above sequence. For step-indexing over ω^2 we have to continue the sequence further, taking the limit of all the previous elements at each limit index $(n, 0)$ and iterating f over these intermediate limits:

$$*, f(*), f^2(*), ..., x_1, f(x_1), f^2(x_1), ..., x_2, f(x_2), f^2(x_2), ...$$

Here x_i is the limit of all the previous elements. The fixed point is then the limit of this extended "sequence".

Definition 4 (Limits). *Let $(X, (\stackrel{a}{=})_{a \in \omega^2})$ be an ordered family of equivalences and Y a subset of ω^2. A Y-indexed family $(x_y)_{y \in Y}$ is coherent iff $\forall a, b \in Y.\ a \leq b \Rightarrow x_a \stackrel{a}{=} x_b$ and x is a limit of $(x_y)_{y \in Y}$ iff $\forall a \in Y.\ x \stackrel{a}{=} x_a$.*

Note that limits of coherent families indexed by proper subsets of ω^2 are not necessarily unique. For such coherent families we thus additionally require suitably unique *chosen* limits.

Definition 5 (Chosen limits). *Let $(X, (\stackrel{a}{=})_{a \in \omega^2})$ be an ordered family of equivalences. Then $(X, (\stackrel{a}{=})_{a \in \omega^2})$ has chosen limits iff any $b \in \omega^2$ there exists a function $\lim_{a<b} x_a$ that maps a coherent family $(x_a)_{a<b}$ indexed by $\{a \in \omega^2 \mid a < b\}$ to a limit, such that for any two coherent families $(x_a)_{a<b}$ and $(y_a)_{a<b}$ indexed by $\{a \in \omega^2 \mid a < b\}$,*

$$(\forall a < b.\ x_a \stackrel{a}{=} y_a) \Rightarrow \lim_{a<b} x_a = \lim_{a<b} y_a$$

Definition 6 (Complete ordered families of equivalences). *A complete ordered family of equivalences (c.o.f.e) is an o.f.e. $\mathcal{X}$ such that all ω^2-indexed coherent families in $\mathcal{X}$ have limits and $\mathcal{X}$ has chosen limits.*

Lemma 1 (Banach's fixed point theorem). *Let $\mathcal{X} = (X, (\stackrel{a}{=})_{a \in \omega^2})$ be a complete ordered family of equivalences and $f : X \to X$ a contractive function. If $\mathcal{X}$ is inhabited (i.e., there exists an $x \in X$), then f has a unique fixed point.*

Complete ordered families of equivalences over ω^2 form a category, $\mathcal{U}$, with non-expansive functions as morphisms. We will use this category to define our semantic domains. To do so, we first introduce a few basic c.o.f.e. constructions followed by a general existence theorem for solutions of recursive domain equations in $\mathcal{U}$.

Definition 7. *Let $\mathcal{U}$ denote the category of complete ordered families of equivalences. The objects of $\mathcal{U}$ are complete ordered families of equivalences and the morphisms are non-expansive functions.*

Basic constructions. The set of non-expansive functions between two c.o.f.e.s forms a c.o.f.e., by lifting the equivalence on the co-domain and computing limits point-wise. Restricting the function space further to finite partial non-expansive functions also yields a c.o.f.e.

Lemma 2. *Let $\mathcal{X} = (X, (\stackrel{a}{=}_X)_{a\in\omega^2})$ and $\mathcal{Y} = (Y, (\stackrel{a}{=}_Y)_{a\in\omega^2})$ be complete ordered families of equivalences. Then $\mathcal{X} \to_{ne} \mathcal{Y}$ and $\mathcal{X} \stackrel{fin}{\rightharpoonup} \mathcal{Y}$ are complete ordered families of equivalences, where*

$$\mathcal{X} \to_{ne} \mathcal{Y} \stackrel{\text{def}}{=} (\{f : X \to Y \mid f \text{ is non-expansive}\}, (\stackrel{a}{=}_{\mathcal{X}\to\mathcal{Y}})_{a\in\omega^2})$$
$$\mathcal{X} \stackrel{fin}{\rightharpoonup} \mathcal{Y} \stackrel{\text{def}}{=} (\{f : X \stackrel{fin}{\rightharpoonup} Y \mid f \text{ is non-expansive}\}, (\stackrel{a}{=}_{\mathcal{X}\stackrel{fin}{\rightharpoonup}\mathcal{Y}})_{a\in\omega^2})$$

and

$$f \stackrel{a}{=}_{\mathcal{X}\to\mathcal{Y}} g \quad \text{iff} \quad \forall x \in X.\ f(x) \stackrel{a}{=}_Y g(x)$$
$$f \stackrel{a}{=}_{\mathcal{X}\stackrel{fin}{\rightharpoonup}\mathcal{Y}} g \quad \text{iff} \quad \text{dom}(f) = \text{dom}(g) \wedge \forall x \in \text{dom}(f).\ f(x) \stackrel{a}{=}_Y g(x)$$

Likewise, restricting the non-expansive function space to monotone and non-expansive functions also yields a c.o.f.e. if the partial order on the codomain respects limits in the codomain.

Lemma 3. *Let $\mathcal{X} = (X, (\stackrel{a}{=}_X)_{a\in\omega^2})$ be an ordered family of equivalences, $\mathcal{Y} = (Y, (\stackrel{a}{=}_Y)_{a\in\omega^2})$ be complete ordered families of equivalences and $\leq_X$ and $\leq_Y$ be partial orders on X and Y.*

If for any two coherent families $(x_a)_{a\in\omega^2}$ and $(y_a)_{a\in\omega^2}$

$$\forall a \in \omega^2.\ x_a \leq_Y y_a \Rightarrow \lim_a x_a \leq_Y \lim_a y_a$$

and for any $b \in \omega^2$ and any two coherent families $(x_a)_{a<b}$ and $(y_a)_{a<b}$

$$\forall a < b.\ a_a \leq_Y y_a \Rightarrow \lim_{a<b} x_a \leq_Y \lim_{a<b} y_a$$

then $\mathcal{X} \stackrel{mon}{\to} \mathcal{Y}$ is a complete ordered family of equivalences, where

$$\mathcal{X} \stackrel{mon}{\to} \mathcal{Y} \stackrel{\text{def}}{=} (\{f : X \stackrel{mon}{\to} Y \mid f \text{ is non-expansive}\}, (\stackrel{a}{=}_{\mathcal{X}\to\mathcal{Y}})_{a\in\omega^2})$$

We can model a predicate over a set X as a predicate over $\omega^2 \times X$, downwards-closed in the step index. The intuition is that $(n, m, x) \in p$ if x satisfies the step-indexed predicate p with n, m steps left on the clock. The downwards-closure captures the intuition that it takes a certain number of steps to show that x does not satisfy a given predicate. These predicates form a c.o.f.e., where we consider two predicates n, m equivalent if they agree for all step-indices strictly below n, m.

Definition 8 (Uniform predicates, UPred(X)). *Let X be a set. Then*

$$\mathbf{UPred}(X) = (\mathcal{P}^{\downarrow}(\omega^2 \times X), (\stackrel{a}{=})_{a\in\omega^2})$$

is a c.o.f.e., where

$$p \stackrel{a}{=} q \quad \textit{iff} \quad \lfloor p \rfloor_a = \lfloor q \rfloor_a, \qquad \lfloor p \rfloor_a \stackrel{\text{def}}{=} \{(b, x) \in p \mid b < a\}$$

and the ordering on $\omega^2 \times X$ *is:* $(a_1, x_1) \leq (a_2, x_2)$ *iff* $a_1 \leq a_2$ *and* $x_1 = x_2$.

Solving Recursive Domain Equations in $\mathcal{U}$. Banach's fixed point theorem (Lemma 1) allows us to show existence of recursively-defined elements of complete ordered families of equivalences. To show existence of recursively-defined complete ordered families of equivalences, we lift the fixed point theorem from contractive functions on complete ordered families of equivalences to *locally contractive* functors on the category of complete ordered families of equivalences. The fixed point theorem is stated for mixed-variance functors, $F : \mathcal{U}^{op} \times \mathcal{U} \to \mathcal{U}$, where the negative and positive occurrences of the recursive variable have been separated.

Definition 9 (Locally non-expansive and locally contractive functor). *A bi-functor* $F : \mathcal{U}^{op} \times \mathcal{U} \to \mathcal{U}$ *is locally non-expansive iff*

$$\forall \mathcal{X}, \mathcal{X}', \mathcal{Y}, \mathcal{Y}' \in obj(\mathcal{U}).\ \forall f, f' : Hom_{\mathcal{U}}(\mathcal{X}, \mathcal{X}').\ \forall g, g' : Hom_{\mathcal{U}}(\mathcal{Y}', \mathcal{Y}).$$
$$\forall a \in \omega^2.\ f \stackrel{a}{=} f' \wedge g \stackrel{a}{=} g' \Rightarrow F(f, g) \stackrel{a}{=} F(f', g')$$

and locally contractive iff

$$\forall \mathcal{X}, \mathcal{X}', \mathcal{Y}, \mathcal{Y}' \in obj(\mathcal{U}).\ \forall f, f' : Hom_{\mathcal{U}}(\mathcal{X}, \mathcal{X}').\ \forall g, g' : Hom_{\mathcal{U}}(\mathcal{Y}', \mathcal{Y}).$$
$$\forall a \in \omega^2.\ (\forall b \in \omega^2.\ b < a \Rightarrow f \stackrel{b}{=} f' \wedge g \stackrel{b}{=} g') \Rightarrow F(f, g) \stackrel{a}{=} F(f', g')$$

In both cases, the equality on the Hom-set is the point-wise lifting of the equality on the co-domain (i.e., $f \stackrel{a}{=} f'$ *iff* $\forall x \in X.\ f(x) \stackrel{a}{=} f'(x)$*).*

Theorem 1. *If* $F : \mathcal{U}^{op} \times \mathcal{U} \to \mathcal{U}$ *is a locally contractive bi-functor and* $F(1, 1)$ *is inhabited, then there exists an object* $X \in \mathcal{U}$ *such that* $F(X, X) \cong X \in \mathcal{U}$.

Proof (Sketch). The construction of the fixed point uses an inverse-limit construction. However, as for Banach's fixed point theorem, when step-indexing over ω^2 we have to iterate the construction further and repeat the inverse-limit construction.

First we show that for any $S \in \mathcal{U}$ and projection/embedding pair

$$p_S : F(S, S) \to S \qquad\qquad e_S : S \to F(S, S)$$

and step-index n such that $p_S \circ e_S = id_S$ and $e_S \circ p_S \stackrel{n,0}{=} id_{F(S,S)}$, we can define an approximate fixed point, $X \in \mathcal{U}$ with projection/embedding pair

$$p_X : F(X, X) \to X \qquad\qquad e_X : X \to F(X, X)$$

such that $p_X \circ e_X = id_X$ and $\forall m.\ e_X \circ p_X \stackrel{n,m}{=} id_{F(X,X)}$. This approximate fixed point is constructed as an inverse-limit.

Next, we iterate this construction to obtain increasingly better approximations of the fixed point. The real fixed point is then constructed as an inverse limit of these approximate fixed points. □

Returning to the recursive equation from the beginning of this Section, we can reformulate the equation as a fixed point of a bi-functor, by separating the positive and negative occurrences as follows:

$$F(X^-, X^+) \cong (\blacktriangleright \circ G)(X^-, X^+), \quad G(X^-, X^+) \stackrel{def}{=} (\mathbb{N} \stackrel{fin}{\rightharpoonup} X^-) \stackrel{mon}{\to} \mathbf{UPred}(\mathrm{Val})$$

Exponentiation using both the non-expansive monotone function space and the non-expansive finite partial function space extends to locally non-expansive bi-functors. The functor G defined above is thus locally non-expansive.

Given a locally non-expansive functor it is possible to define a locally contractive functor by shifting all the equivalence relations one step. The functor $\blacktriangleright$, defined below, takes a complete ordered family of equivalences and shifts all the equivalences one step up, such that (n, m)-equivalence becomes $(n, m+1)$-equivalence. At limits $(n+1, 0)$ the equivalence is taken to be the limit of all smaller equivalences.

Definition 10 ($\blacktriangleright$). *Let $\blacktriangleright : \mathcal{U} \to \mathcal{U}$ denote the following functor,*

$$\blacktriangleright \left(X, (\stackrel{a}{=})_{a \in \omega^2}\right) \stackrel{def}{=} \left(X, (\stackrel{a}{\equiv})_{a \in \omega^2}\right) \qquad \blacktriangleright(f) \stackrel{def}{=} f$$

where $\stackrel{0,0}{\equiv}$ is the total relation on X, $\stackrel{n,m+1}{\equiv}$ is $\stackrel{n,m}{=}$ and $\stackrel{n+1,0}{\equiv}$ is defined as follows

$$x_1 \stackrel{n+1,0}{\equiv} x_2 \quad \mathit{iff} \quad \forall m \in \mathbb{N}.\ x_1 \stackrel{n,m}{=} x_2.$$

Lemma 4. *If $F : \mathcal{U}^{op} \times \mathcal{U} \to \mathcal{U}$ is locally non-expansive then $\blacktriangleright \circ F$ is locally contractive.*

Using Lemma 4 we can obtain a locally contractive functor from a locally non-expansive functor, and thus use Theorem 1 to obtain a fixed point. However, as we will see in the following section, due to the shifting by $\blacktriangleright$, we are forced to "go down a step" if we want our definitions to remain non-expansive, whenever we unfold the isomorphism.

4 Logical Relation

In this section we define a logical relation step-indexed over ω^2 for the language introduced in Sect. 2. By only relating the first step-index with concrete reduction steps, we obtain a logical relation that allows for an arbitrary finite number of logical steps for each concrete reduction step. We prove that this logical relation is sound with respect to contextual approximation.

Semantic domains. To model dynamic allocation of references, we use a Kripke logical relation and index relations with worlds that contain general relational invariants over the heap. These invariants can themselves assert the existence of invariants and are thus also world-indexed. This leads to a recursive definition of the semantic domain of invariants with a contravariant occurrence of the recursive variable. Consequently, we use Theorem 1 to show the existence of a c.o.f.e. **Inv** satisfying the following isomorphism:

$$\xi : \mathbf{Inv} \cong \blacktriangleright((\mathbb{N} \stackrel{fin}{\rightharpoonup} \mathbf{Inv}) \stackrel{mon}{\rightarrow} \mathbf{UPred}(\text{Heap} \times \text{Heap})) \tag{1}$$

An invariant is modelled as a uniform relation on heaps, indexed by a world that is itself a finite map from invariant identifiers ($\mathbb{N}$) to invariants. The monotone function space is with respect to extension ordering on $\mathbb{N} \stackrel{fin}{\rightharpoonup} \mathbf{Inv}$ and subset inclusion on $\mathbf{UPred}(-)$. The monotonicity requirement allows us to dynamically allocate new invariants, without invaliding existing invariants. A type is modelled as a uniform relation on values indexed by a world:

$$\mathbf{World} \stackrel{def}{=} \mathbb{N} \stackrel{fin}{\rightharpoonup} \mathbf{Inv} \qquad\qquad \mathbf{Type} \stackrel{def}{=} \mathbf{World} \stackrel{mon}{\rightarrow} \mathbf{UPred}(\text{Val} \times \text{Val})$$

We use $\widehat{\mathbf{Inv}}$ as a shorthand for $\mathbf{World} \rightarrow \mathbf{UPred}(\text{Heap} \times \text{Heap})$. Note that here we index worlds by invariant identifiers ($\mathbb{N}$) rather than the physical locations (Loc) we used in the Introduction. Due to our use of general relational invariants on heaps, it is no longer necessary to index the world with physical locations. Instead, we index the world with invariant identifiers which allows us to simplify the meta-theory by allowing us to refer to individual invariants.

A reference invariant is a particular instance of these general invariants. A reference invariant, $\text{inv}(\nu, l_I, l_S) \in \widehat{\mathbf{Inv}}$, for type $\nu \in \mathbf{Type}$ and two locations l_I and l_S relates two heaps h_I and h_S if $h_I(l_I)$ and $h_S(l_S)$ are related at type ν:

$$\begin{aligned}\text{inv}(\nu, l_I, l_S) \stackrel{def}{=} \lambda W.\ \{(n, m, h_I, h_S) \mid l_I \in \text{dom}(h_I) \wedge l_S \in \text{dom}(h_S) \wedge \\ (n, m, h_I(l_I), h_S(l_S)) \in \nu(W)\}\end{aligned}$$

The more general invariants supported by our model are not necessary to define the logical relation or prove that it implies contextual approximation. However, they are very useful when relating two concrete programs directly in the model, as we will see in Sect. 5.

Heap satisfaction. To define the relational interpretation of types, we first need to define heap satisfaction, which expresses when two heaps are related at a given world. Intuitively, this is the case when the heaps satisfy all the invariants in world. However, to support local reasoning about invariant satisfaction, we borrow the idea of ownership from separation logic [19] and require each invariant to hold for a *disjoint* part of the heap. Two heaps h_I and h_S are thus related, if they can be split into disjoint parts $h_{1I}, h_{2I}, ..., h_{kI}$ and $h_{1S}, h_{2S}, ..., h_{kS}$, respectively, such that h_{jI} and h_{jS} are related by the j'th invariant. To simplify the meta-theory we indexed heap satisfaction, $\lfloor W \rfloor_{\mathcal{I}}$, with a set of invariant identifiers $\mathcal{I} \subseteq \mathbb{N}$ indicating which invariants are active (i.e., currently required to hold).

$$\begin{aligned}\lfloor W \rfloor_{\mathcal{I}} \stackrel{def}{=} \{(n, h_I, h_S) \mid (\exists r_I, r_S : \text{dom}(W) \cap \mathcal{I} \rightarrow \text{Heap}. \\ h_I = \uplus_{\iota \in \text{dom}(r_I)} r_I(\iota) \wedge h_S = \uplus_{\iota \in \text{dom}(r_S)} r_S(\iota) \wedge \\ \forall \iota \in \text{dom}(W) \cap \mathcal{I}.\ \forall m \in \mathbb{N}. \\ (n-1, m, r_I(\iota), r_S(\iota)) \in \xi(W(\iota))(W)) \vee n = 0\}\end{aligned}$$

Note that heap satisfaction is only step-indexed using one step-index, n. This is because heap satisfaction always requires that each h_{jI} and h_{jS} must be related for an arbitrary number of logical steps m, no matter how many logical steps are currently left on the clock. This pattern of universally quantifying over the number of logical steps will reappear in many definitions and is crucial in allowing us to unfold an arbitrary finite number of invariants for each concrete reduction step. Intuitively, this bakes in the assumption and proof obligation that there is always an unbounded number of possible logical steps left before the next concrete reduction step in all our definitions. Except when we are relating concrete examples we never commit to an actual number of logical steps.

Since each invariant asserts exclusive ownership of the parts of each heap that are related by the invariant, we can use $\mathcal{I}$ to reason locally about satisfaction of individual invariants. This is captured by Lemma 5. We use $\lfloor W \rfloor$ as shorthand for heap satisfaction in the case where all invariants are active, i.e., $\lfloor W \rfloor_{\mathrm{dom}(W)}$.

Lemma 5 (Invariant locality)

$$\begin{aligned}&\forall W \in \mathbf{World}.\ \forall h_I, h_S \in \mathrm{Heap}.\ \forall n \in \mathbb{N}.\ \forall \mathcal{I}_1, \mathcal{I}_2 \in \mathcal{P}(\mathbb{N}).\\ &\quad (n, h_I, h_S) \in \lfloor W \rfloor_{\mathcal{I}_1 \uplus \mathcal{I}_2} \Leftrightarrow\\ &\quad \begin{pmatrix} \exists h_{1I}, h_{2I}, h_{1S}, h_{2S} \in \mathrm{Heap}.\ h_I = h_{1I} \uplus h_{2I} \wedge h_S = h_{1S} \uplus h_{2S}\\ \wedge (n, h_{1I}, h_{1S}) \in \lfloor W \rfloor_{\mathcal{I}_1} \wedge (n, h_{2I}, h_{2S}) \in \lfloor W \rfloor_{\mathcal{I}_2}\end{pmatrix}\end{aligned}$$

As expected, two heaps satisfy the heap invariant $\mathrm{inv}(\nu, l_I, l_S)$ if and only if $h_I(l_I)$ and $h_S(l_S)$ contain ν-related values (Lemma 6). Note that Lemma 6 requires that there is at least one concrete reduction step left, even just to prove that l_I and l_S are in the domain of h_I and h_S.

Lemma 6 (Reference invariant satisfaction)

$$\begin{aligned}&\forall n \in \mathbb{N}.\ \forall \iota \in \mathbb{N}.\ \forall W \in \mathbf{World}.\ \forall \nu \in \mathbf{Type}.\ \forall h_I, h_S \in \mathrm{Heap}.\ \forall l_I, l_S \in \mathrm{Loc}.\\ &\quad n > 0 \wedge \xi(W(\iota)) \stackrel{n,0}{=} \mathrm{inv}(\nu, l_I, l_S) \Rightarrow\\ &\quad \begin{pmatrix} (n, h_I, h_S) \in \lfloor W \rfloor_{\{\iota\}} \Leftrightarrow l_I \in \mathrm{dom}(h_I) \wedge l_S \in \mathrm{dom}(h_S) \wedge \\ \qquad \forall m.\ (n-1, m, h_I(l_I), h_S(l_S)) \in \nu(W)\end{pmatrix}\end{aligned}$$

To ensure that definitions using heap satisfaction are suitably non-expansive, we require heap satisfaction to satisfy the following non-expansiveness property (Lemma 7). Intuitively, this property holds because we "go down" one step index from n to $n-1$ in the definition of heap satisfaction.

Lemma 7

$$\begin{aligned}&\forall W_1, W_2 \in \mathbf{World}.\ \forall h_I, h_S \in \mathrm{Heap}.\ \forall n, m \in \mathbb{N}.\\ &\quad W_1 \stackrel{n,m}{=}_{\mathbf{World}} W_2 \wedge (n, h_I, h_S) \in \lfloor W_1 \rfloor \Rightarrow (n, h_I, h_S) \in \lfloor W_2 \rfloor\end{aligned}$$

Proof (Sketch). Assume that two heap parts h_{1I} and h_{1S} are $n-1, m'$ related at $\xi(W_1(\iota))(W_1)$. By non-expansiveness of ξ it follows that $\xi(W_1(\iota))$ is n, m

equivalent to $\xi(W_2(\iota))$ in c.o.f.e. $\blacktriangleright\widehat{\mathbf{Inv}}$. Since $(n-1, m'+1) < (n, m)$ it follows that they are also $n-1, m'+1$ equivalent in c.o.f.e. $\widehat{\mathbf{Inv}}$. Hence, by the equivalence on uniform predicates, $\xi(W_1(\iota))(W_1)$ and $\xi(W_2(\iota))(W_2)$ agree on all step-indices strictly below $n-1, m'+1$. It follows that h_{1I} and h_{1S} are $n-1, m$ related at $\xi(W_2(\iota))(W_2)$. □

Expression closure. The expression closure, $\mathcal{E}(\nu)$, takes a semantic type $\nu \in$ **Type** and extends it to a relation on expressions. Intuitively, two expressions e_I and e_S are related by the expression closure $\mathcal{E}(\nu)$ if they reduce to ν-related values and related terminal heaps, whenever they are executed from related initial heaps. Since the expression closure is where we actually reduce the underlying expressions, this is also the definition where the steps from the step-indexed model are tied to concrete reduction steps. The idea is to tie the first step-index to concrete reduction steps and go down one step in the first step-index for every concrete reduction step of e_I. We define the expression closure, $\mathcal{E}(\nu)$, as follows, for a semantic type $\nu \in$ **Type**:

$$
\begin{aligned}
\mathcal{E}(\nu) \stackrel{def}{=} \lambda W.\ \{(n, e_I, e_S) \mid\ & \forall n' \leq n.\ \forall i < n'.\ \forall h_I, h'_I, h_S.\ \forall e'_I.\ \forall W' \geq W. \\
& (n', h_I, h_S) \in \lfloor W' \rfloor \wedge \langle e_I, h_I \rangle \to^i \langle e'_I, h'_I \rangle \not\to \ \Rightarrow \\
& e'_I \in \mathrm{Val} \wedge \exists v'_S, h'_S.\ \exists W'' \geq W'. \\
& \quad \langle e_S, h_S \rangle \to^* \langle v'_S, h'_S \rangle \wedge \\
& \quad (n'-i, h'_I, h'_S) \in \lfloor W'' \rfloor \wedge \\
& \quad \forall m.\ (n'-i, m, e'_I, v'_S) \in \nu(W'')\}
\end{aligned}
$$

The expression closure is only step-indexed using the first step-index, corresponding to the number of concrete reduction steps. If the two initial heaps are related for n' steps and $\langle e_I, h_I \rangle$ reduces in $i < n'$ steps then the terminal heaps must be related for $n'-i$ steps. Like the definition of heap satisfaction, we require the return values to be related for $n'-i$ concrete steps and an arbitrary number of logical steps, m. The reason for requiring i to be strictly smaller than n', is to ensure that we have enough concrete steps left to prove that we do not get stuck trying to dereference a location that has not been allocated. This is due to our use of general invariants, which requires that we unfold a reference invariant to prove that two τ ref related locations are currently allocated.

To ensure that the expressions remain related after more invariants have been allocated, we take initial heaps related in an arbitrary future world W'. Likewise, the terminal heaps and return value is related in some future world W'', to allow the allocation of new invariants.

The expression closure further requires that whenever $\langle e_I, h_I \rangle$ reduces to some irreducible configuration $\langle e'_I, h'_I \rangle$, then e'_I is in fact a value. This allows us to prove that well-typed expressions do not get stuck.

Just like for heap satisfaction, we need the expression closure to satisfy the following non-expansiveness property (Lemma 8), to ensure that definitions using the expression closure are suitably non-expansive.

Lemma 8

$$\forall W_1, W_2 \in \textbf{World}.\ \forall \nu \in \textbf{Type}.\ \forall n, m \in \mathbb{N}.\ \forall e_I, e_S \in \text{Exp}.$$
$$W_1 \overset{n,m}{=}_{\textbf{World}} W_2 \land (n, e_I, e_S) \in \mathcal{E}(\nu)(W_1) \Rightarrow (n, e_I, e_S) \in \mathcal{E}(\nu)(W_2)$$

Proof (Sketch). The result follows easily from non-expansiveness of ν, Lemma 7 and the following property that allows an n, m equivalence to be extended to a future world.

$$\forall W_1, W_2, W_1' \in \textbf{World}.\ \forall n, m.$$
$$W_1 \overset{n,m}{=}_{\textbf{World}} W_2 \land W_1 \leq W_1' \Rightarrow \exists W_2' \geq W_2.\ W_1' \overset{n,m}{=}_{\textbf{World}} W_2'$$

□

Interpretation. We now have all the ingredients to define the relational interpretation of types. The relational interpretation of types, $\mathcal{V}[\![\Delta \vdash \tau]\!] : \textbf{Type}^{\Delta} \rightarrow \textbf{Type}$, is defined by induction on the type well-formedness derivation, $\Delta \vdash \tau$. It is parametrized by a function $\rho \in \textbf{Type}^{\Delta}$ that assigns a semantic type to each type variable in context Δ. Intuitively, it expresses when two values are related at a given type at a particular world and step-index. The full definition is given in Fig. 4. The most interesting clauses are the interpretation of function types and reference types.

For function types, we assume that the arguments are related for an arbitrary number of logical steps m', just as we did for heap satisfaction. We also require the application to be related for one more concrete reduction step than the arguments. This is standard in step-indexed models and reflects the fact that we do at least one concrete reduction step (the beta-reduction of the application), before using the arguments.

The interpretation of reference types asserts the existence of a general invariant in the current world that is n, m equivalent to the reference invariant $\text{inv}(\mathcal{V}[\![\Delta \vdash \tau]\!]_\rho, l_I, l_S)$. Note that the equivalence is stated at the c.o.f.e., $\blacktriangleright \widehat{\textbf{Inv}}$.

In turn, the reference invariant asserts exclusive ownership of locations l_I and l_S and that these locations contain $\mathcal{V}[\![\Delta \vdash \tau]\!]_\rho$ related values.

For product types, we require that the components are pair-wise related and for existential types, we require the existence of a semantic type to interpret the abstract type.

To show that this logical relation is well-defined, we need to prove that the reference invariant, $\text{inv}(\mathcal{V}[\![\Delta \vdash \tau]\!]_\rho, l_I, l_S)$ is an element of the right c.o.f.e., $\textbf{World} \overset{mon}{\rightarrow} \textbf{UPred}(\text{Heap} \times \text{Heap})$. This reduces to proving that the reference invariant is non-expansive and monotone in the worlds, which in turn induces non-expansiveness and monotonicity requirements on $\mathcal{V}[\![\Delta \vdash \tau]\!]_\rho$.

Lemma 9. *The logical relation is well-defined. In particular,*

- $\text{inv}(\nu, l_I, l_S)$ *is non-expansive and monotone and* $\text{inv}(\nu, l_I, l_S)(W)$ *is downwards-closed for all* $\nu \in \textbf{Type}$, $l_I, l_S \in \text{Loc}$ *and* $W \in \textbf{World}$.

$$
\begin{aligned}
\mathcal{V}[\![\Delta \vdash 1]\!]_\rho(W) &\stackrel{def}{=} \{(n,m,*,*)\}\\
\mathcal{V}[\![\Delta \vdash \mathbb{N}]\!]_\rho(W) &\stackrel{def}{=} \{(n,m,\underline{k},\underline{k}) \mid k \in \mathbb{N}\}\\
\mathcal{V}[\![\Delta \vdash \tau \times \sigma]\!]_\rho(W) &\stackrel{def}{=} \{(n,m,v_I,v_S) \mid \exists v_{1I}, v_{2I}, v_{1S}, v_{2S}.\\
&\qquad v_I = (v_{1I}, v_{2I}) \wedge v_S = (v_{1S}, v_{2S}) \wedge\\
&\qquad (n,m,v_{1I},v_{1S}) \in \mathcal{V}[\![\Delta \vdash \tau]\!]_\rho(W) \wedge\\
&\qquad (n,m,v_{2I},v_{2S}) \in \mathcal{V}[\![\Delta \vdash \sigma]\!]_\rho(W)\}\\
\mathcal{V}[\![\Delta \vdash \tau \to \sigma]\!]_\rho(W) &\stackrel{def}{=} \{(n,m,v_I,v_S) \mid \forall n' < n.\ \forall W' \geq W.\ \forall u_I, u_S.\\
&\qquad (\forall m'.\ (n',m',u_I,u_S) \in \mathcal{V}[\![\Delta \vdash \tau]\!]_\rho(W'))\\
&\qquad \Rightarrow\ (n'+1, v_I\ u_I, v_S\ u_S) \in \mathcal{E}(\mathcal{V}[\![\Delta \vdash \sigma]\!]_\rho)(W')\}\\
\mathcal{V}[\![\Delta \vdash \tau\ \mathsf{ref}]\!]_\rho(W) &\stackrel{def}{=} \{(n,m,l_I,l_S) \mid \exists \iota \in \mathrm{dom}(W).\\
&\qquad \xi(W(\iota)) \stackrel{n,m}{=}_{\blacktriangleright \widehat{\mathbf{Inv}}} \mathrm{inv}(\mathcal{V}[\![\Delta \vdash \tau]\!]_\rho, l_I, l_S)\}\\
\mathcal{V}[\![\Delta, \alpha \vdash \alpha]\!]_\rho(W) &\stackrel{def}{=} \rho(\alpha)(W)\\
\mathcal{V}[\![\Delta \vdash \exists \alpha.\ \tau]\!]_\rho(W) &\stackrel{def}{=} \{(n,m,\mathsf{pack}\ v_I, \mathsf{pack}\ v_S) \mid \exists \nu \in \mathbf{Type}.\\
&\qquad (n,m,v_I,v_S) \in \mathcal{V}[\![\Delta, \alpha \vdash \tau]\!]_{\rho[\alpha \mapsto \nu]}(W)\}
\end{aligned}
$$

Fig. 4. Relational interpretation of types.

– $\mathcal{V}[\![\Delta \vdash \tau]\!]_\rho$ *is non-expansive and monotone and* $\mathcal{V}[\![\Delta \vdash \tau]\!]_\rho(W)$ *is downwards-closed for all* $\rho \in \mathbf{Type}^\Delta$ *and* $W \in \mathbf{World}$.

Proof (Sketch). We prove the second property by induction on the well-formedness derivation, $\Delta \vdash \tau$. Most of the cases are straightforward. For reference types, non-expansiveness follows from Lemma 8. □

Finally, the logical relation relates two expressions e_I and e_S at type τ if they are related for all step-indices in the expression closure of the τ-relation, after substituting related values for all free term variables.

Definition 11 (Logical relation)

$$
\begin{aligned}
\Delta; \Gamma \models e_I \leq_{log} e_S : \tau \stackrel{def}{=} & \forall n \in \mathbb{N}.\ \forall W \in \mathbf{World}.\ \forall \sigma_I, \sigma_S \in \mathrm{Val}^\Gamma.\ \forall \rho \in \mathbf{Type}^\Delta.\\
& (\forall m \in \mathbb{N}.\ \forall (x:\tau) \in \Gamma.\ (n,m,\sigma_I(x),\sigma_S(x)) \in \mathcal{V}[\![\Delta \vdash \tau]\!]_\rho(W))\\
& \Rightarrow\ (n, \sigma_I(e_I), \sigma_S(e_S)) \in \mathcal{E}(\mathcal{V}[\![\Delta \vdash \tau]\!]_\rho)(W)
\end{aligned}
$$

The logical relation is compatible with the typing rules of the language. Here we include two of the interesting cases of the compatibility proof, namely dereference and unpack. For illustrative purposes we take a more constrained versions of the lemmas where the arguments of the dereferencing and unpacking operations are values. The accompanying technical report features complete proofs of all the compatibility lemmas in their general form.

Lemma 10. *If* $\Delta; \Gamma \models v_I \leq_{log} v_S : \tau \text{ ref}$ *then* $\Delta; \Gamma \models !\, v_I \leq_{log} !\, v_S : \tau$.

Proof. We unfold the definition of the logical relation: take $n \in \mathbb{N}$, $W \in \textbf{World}$, $\sigma_I, \sigma_S \in \text{Val}^\Gamma$ and $\rho \in \textbf{Type}^\Delta$ such that

$$\forall m \in \mathbb{N}.\ \forall (x : \tau') \in \Gamma.\ (n, m, \sigma_I(x), \sigma_S(x)) \in \mathcal{V}[\![\Delta \vdash \tau']\!]_\rho(W)$$

We unfold the definition of expression closure: take $n' \leq n$, $i < n'$, $W' \geq W$ and $h_I, h'_I, h_S \in \text{Heap}$ such that

$$(n', h_I, h_S) \in \lfloor W' \rfloor \qquad\qquad \langle !\, \sigma_I(v_I), h_I\rangle \to^i \langle e'_I, h'_I\rangle \not\to$$

Since $\sigma_I(v_I)$ and $\sigma_S(v_S)$ are both values, we can use the assumption to obtain a world $W'' \geq W'$ such that $(n', h_I, h_S) \in \lfloor W'' \rfloor$ and

$$\forall m.\ (n', m, \sigma_I(v_I), \sigma_S(v_S)) \in \mathcal{V}[\![\Delta \vdash \tau \text{ ref}\,]\!]_\rho(W'').$$

By definition of the interpretation of reference types, our values must be locations, and they must be related by the reference invariant in the world. In other words, setting $m = 0$ we get two locations l_I and l_S and an invariant identifier $\iota \in \text{dom}(W'')$ such that

$$\sigma_I(v_I) = l_I \qquad \sigma_S(v_S) = l_S \qquad \xi(W''(\iota)) \overset{n',0}{=}_{\blacktriangleright \widehat{\textbf{Inv}}} \text{inv}(\mathcal{V}[\![\Delta \vdash \tau]\!]_\rho, l_I, l_S)$$

Using Lemma 5 we can obtain parts of h_I and h_S that satisfy the invariant ι: we have $h^\iota_I \subseteq h_I$ and $h^\iota_S \subseteq h_S$ such that $(n', h^\iota_I, h^\iota_S) \in \lfloor W'' \rfloor_{\{\iota\}}$. Since $0 \leq i < n'$, we can now use Lemma 6, which gives us that,

$$l_I \in \text{dom}(h^\iota_I) \qquad l_S \in \text{dom}(h^\iota_S) \qquad \forall m.\ (n' - 1, m, h^\iota_I(l_I), h^\iota_S(l_S)) \in \mathcal{V}[\![\Delta \vdash \tau]\!]_\rho(W'')$$

Now we can establish, by definition of the operational semantics, that $i = 1$, $e'_I = h_I(l_I) = h^\iota_I(l_I)$ and $h'_I = h_I$. We are now ready to pick witnesses required by the expression closure. We pick $v_S = h_S(l_S)$, $h'_S = h_S$ and use the same world, W''. Clearly, $\langle !l_S, h_S\rangle \to^* \langle h_S(l_S), h_S\rangle$ holds trivially and since the heaps did not change, we get the heap-satisfaction obligation by downwards-closure. Finally, we need to show that $(n' - 1, m, h_I(l_I), h_S(l_S)) \in \mathcal{V}[\![\Delta \vdash \tau]\!]_\rho(W'')$ for any m, which is precisely what we obtained from Lemma 6, since $h_I(l_I) = h^\iota_I(l_I)$ and $h_S(l_S) = h^\iota_S(l_S)$. □

Lemma 11. *If* $\Delta; \Gamma \models v_I \leq_{log} v_S : \exists\alpha.\ \tau$ *and* $\Delta, \alpha; \Gamma, x : \tau \models e_I \leq_{log} e_S : \sigma$ *and* $\Delta \vdash \sigma$ *then*

$$\Delta; \Gamma \models \text{unpack } v_I \text{ as } x \text{ in } e_I \leq_{log} \text{unpack } v_S \text{ as } x \text{ in } e_S : \sigma$$

Proof. We unfold the definition of the logical relation: take $n \in \mathbb{N}$, $W \in \textbf{World}$, $\sigma_I, \sigma_S \in \text{Val}^\Gamma$ and $\rho \in \textbf{Type}^\Delta$ such that

$$\forall m \in \mathbb{N}.\ \forall (x : \tau') \in \Gamma.\ (n, m, \sigma_I(x), \sigma_S(x)) \in \mathcal{V}[\![\Delta \vdash \tau']\!]_\rho(W).$$

We unfold the definition of expression closure: take $n' \leq n$, $i < n'$, $W' \geq W$ and $h_I, h'_I, h_S \in \text{Heap}$ such that

$$(n', h_I, h_S) \in \lfloor W' \rfloor \qquad \langle \mathsf{unpack}\ \sigma_I(v_I)\ \mathsf{as}\ x\ \mathsf{in}\ \sigma_I(e_I), h_I \rangle \to^i \langle e'_I, h'_I \rangle \not\to$$

Since $\sigma_I(v_I)$ and $\sigma_S(v_S)$ are both values, we can use the first assumption to obtain a world $W'' \geq W'$ such that $(n', h_I, h_S) \in \lfloor W'' \rfloor$ and

$$\forall m.\ (n', m, \sigma_I(v_I), \sigma_S(v_S)) \in \mathcal{V}[\![\Delta \vdash \exists \alpha.\ \tau]\!]_\rho(W'').$$

We pick $m = 0$, and obtain, by definition of interpretation of existential types, two values, v'_I and v'_S, and $\nu \in \mathbf{Type}$ such that

$$\sigma_I(v_I) = \mathsf{pack}\ v'_I \quad \sigma_S(v_S) = \mathsf{pack}\ v'_S \quad (n', 0, v'_I, v'_S) \in \mathcal{V}[\![\Delta, \alpha \vdash \tau]\!]_{\rho[\alpha \mapsto \nu]}(W'')$$

Looking at our reduction, we now observe that $i > 0$ and

$$\langle \mathsf{unpack}\ \sigma_I(v_I)\ \mathsf{as}\ x\ \mathsf{in}\ \sigma_I(e_I), h_I \rangle \to \langle (\sigma_I(e_I))[v'_I/x], h_I \rangle \to^{i-1} \langle e'_I, h'_I \rangle \not\to .$$

Note that $(\sigma_I(e_I))[v'_I/x] = (\sigma_I[x \mapsto v'_I])(e_I)$.

It is now time to turn to the second of our assumptions. We instantiate the definition of the logical relation with $n' - 1$, W'', $\sigma_I[x \mapsto v'_I]$, $\sigma_S[x \mapsto v'_S]$, and $\rho[\alpha \mapsto \nu]$. We need to show that the substitutions are related, i.e., that

$$(n' - 1, m, \sigma_I[x \mapsto v'_I](y), \sigma_S[x \mapsto v'_S](y)) \in \mathcal{V}[\![\Delta, \alpha \vdash \tau']\!]_{\rho[\alpha \mapsto \nu]}(W'')$$

for any $m \in \mathbb{N}$ and any $(y : \tau') \in \Gamma, x : \tau$. For all the variables other than x this holds by weakening, world monotonicity and downwards-closure; for x we obtained the necessary property relating v'_I to v'_S from the first assumption. Note that picking $n' - 1$ as the index was crucial, since we only got this final relation for 0 logical steps.[2] However, since we count unpack-pack reductions, we can safely use $n' - 1$ here.

By showing the substitutions to be related, we have learned that the expressions e_I and e_S are also related, after applying the substitutions:

$$(n' - 1, \sigma_I(e_I)[v'_I/x], \sigma_S(e_S)[v'_S/x]) \in \mathcal{E}(\mathcal{V}[\![\Delta, \alpha \vdash \tau]\!]_{\rho[\alpha \mapsto \nu]}(W'')).$$

If we unfold the definition of the expression closure, we notice that if we instantiate it with $n' - 1$, $i - 1$, h_I, h'_I, h_S and W'' we can use it to complete the proof, since $\langle \mathsf{unpack}\ \sigma_S(v_S)\ \mathsf{as}\ x\ \mathsf{in}\ \sigma_S(e_S), h_S \rangle \to \langle \sigma_S(e_S)[v'_S/x], h_S \rangle$. Thus, it suffices to show that

$$\langle (\sigma_I(e_I))[v'_I/x], h_I \rangle \to^{i-1} \langle e'_I, h'_I \rangle \not\to \qquad (n' - 1, h_I, h_S) \in \lfloor W'' \rfloor$$

However, the first of these properties we already obtained, and the second holds by downwards-closure of erasure. □

[2] This is caused by the order of quantifiers in the definition: we needed to pick a number of logical steps *before* we obtained the witnesses from the definition, including v'_I, v'_S and ν.

The fundamental theorem of logical relations (Lemma 12) and a similar property for contexts (Lemma 13) follow as corollaries of the compatibility lemmas. The proofs follow by induction on the respective typing derivations.

Lemma 12. *If* $\Delta; \Gamma \vdash e : \tau$ *then* $\Delta; \Gamma \models e \leq_{log} e : \tau$.

Lemma 13. *For any context* C *such that* $C : (\Delta_i; \Gamma_i, \tau_i) \rightsquigarrow (\Delta_o; \Gamma_o, \tau_o)$, *if* $\Delta_i; \Gamma_i \vdash e_I \leq_{log} e_S : \tau_i$ *then* $\Delta_o; \Gamma_o \vdash C[e_I] \leq_{log} C[e_S] : \tau_o$.

Theorem 2 (Soundness). *If* $\Delta; \Gamma \models e_I \leq_{log} e_S : \tau$ *then* $\Delta; \Gamma \vdash e_I \leq_{ctx} e_S : \tau$.

Proof. Let C be an arbitrary context such that $C : (\Delta; \Gamma, \tau) \rightsquigarrow (-; -, 1)$ and $\langle C[e_I], [] \rangle \to^* \langle *, h_I \rangle$. Then there exists an i such that $\langle C[e_I], [] \rangle \to^i \langle *, h_I \rangle$. By Lemma 13 it follows that $-; - \models C[e_I] \leq_{log} C[e_S] : 1$ and thus $(i+1, C[e_I], C[e_S]) \in \mathcal{E}(\mathcal{V}[\![-; - \vdash 1]\!])([])$. By definition of $\mathcal{E}$ this gives us v_S, h_S and W such that $\langle C[e_S], [] \rangle \to^* \langle v_S, h_S \rangle$ and $(1, m, *, v_S) \in \mathcal{V}[\![-; - \vdash 1]\!](W)$ for any $m \in \mathbb{N}$. From the latter we obtain $v_S = *$, which ends the proof. □

5 Example

Recall the example from the Introduction where f takes as an argument an ADT implementation of type $\exists \alpha.\, (1 \to \alpha) \times (\alpha \to \mathbb{N})$ and returns a new ADT implementation of the same type:

$$\lambda x.\ \mathsf{unpack}\ x\ \mathsf{as}\ y\ \mathsf{in}\ \mathsf{pack}\ (\lambda z.\ \mathsf{ref}\ (\pi_1(y)(z)), \lambda z.\ \pi_2(y)(!z))$$

Under the hood, f wraps instances of the new ADT implementation in an additional reference. However, since this is transparent to clients, one would expect that $f(x)$ is contextually equivalent to x:

$$-; x : \tau \vdash x \cong_{ctx} f(x) : \tau$$

where τ is the type $\exists \alpha.\, (1 \to \alpha) \times (\alpha \to \mathbb{N})$.

The left-to-right approximation, $-; x : \tau \vdash x \leq_{ctx} f(x) : \tau$, causes problems for previous step-indexed logical relations, as it requires an additional logical step without introducing a corresponding reduction step on the left. In this Section we prove the left-to-right approximation using our logical relation.

Conceptually, to prove the left-to-right approximation, we need to relate values of type α to values of type α ref, the type constructed by the right-hand-side package, given a relation ν that relates pairs of values of type α. The obvious way to proceed is to introduce an invariant that relates the value on the left, with the value stored at the given location on the right:

$$S(v_I, l_S)(W) \stackrel{def}{=} \{(n, m, h_I, h_S) \mid l_S \in \mathrm{dom}(h_S) \wedge (n, m, v_I, h_S(l_S)) \in \nu(W)\} \quad (2)$$

This definition forms a valid *invariant* for any v_I and l_S, i.e., $S(v_I, l_S) \in \widehat{\mathbf{Inv}}$. Since the objects we want to relate are existential packages, we need to pick an interpretation $\nu' \in \textbf{Type}$ for the existential type *before* any locations for the right-hand-side are actually allocated. This is why we use a Kripke logical relation: we can use the world, in much the same way as we did for the reference type in Fig. 4, and take

$$\nu'(W) \stackrel{def}{=} \{(n, m, v_I, v_S) \mid \exists \iota \in \text{dom}(W).\ \xi(W(\iota)) \stackrel{n,m}{=}_{\blacktriangleright \widehat{\textbf{Inv}}} S(v_I, v_S)\} \quad (3)$$

Thus far, we made no particular use of our transfinite step-indexing: these definitions could well be stated in a standard setup. The power of our approach comes from the following property.

Lemma 14. *For any* $k > 0$*, any pair of values* $v_I, v_S \in \text{Val}$ *such that* $(k, m + 2, v_I, v_S) \in \nu'(W)$ *and any heaps* $h_I, h_S \in \text{Heap}$ *such that* $(k+1, h_I, h_S) \in \lfloor W \rfloor$*,*

$$(k, m, v_I, h_S(v_S)) \in \nu(W).$$

The higher logical step-index in the assumption is required since, as we shall see, we need to unfold the recursive domain equation to prove it. Once we have the lemma, if we need to show that $(k, m, v_I, h_S(v_S)) \in \nu(W)$ for an *arbitrary* m, as the expression closure obliges us to do, and know that $\forall m.\ (k, m, v_I, v_S) \in \nu'(W)$, we can simply instantiate our assumption with $m + 2$ and use it. In this way, the fact that our model allows us to take arbitrary number of logical steps is crucial to allow us to prove this type of abstractions correct. We first prove the preceding lemma, and then turn to formally treating the example.

Proof (Lemma 14). By (3), we know there is an invariant identifier $\iota \in \text{dom}(W)$ such that $\xi(W(\iota)) \stackrel{k,m+2}{=}_{\blacktriangleright \widehat{\textbf{Inv}}} S(v_I, v_S)$. This last property is, by definition of $\blacktriangleright$, equivalent to

$$\xi(W(\iota)) \stackrel{k,m+1}{=}_{\widehat{\textbf{Inv}}} S(v_I, v_S).$$

Furthermore, since we know that ι defines an invariant in the world W, we can use the heap satisfaction assumption, together with Lemma 5 to obtain subheaps $h_I^\iota \subseteq h_I$ and $h_S^\iota \subseteq h_S$ such that $(k, n, h_I^\iota, h_S^\iota) \in \xi(W(\iota))(W)$ for any n. Taking $n = m$, we thus get $(k, m, h_I^\iota, h_S^\iota) \in \xi(W(\iota))(W)$, and ultimately, from the $(k, m + 1)$-equality of the invariants,

$$(k, m, h_I^\iota, h_S^\iota) \in S(v_I, v_S)(W).$$

Unfolding the definition of S, (2), we find that $(k, m, v_I, h_S^\iota(v_S)) \in \nu(W)$, which ends the proof. □

Lemma 15

$$-; x : \tau \vdash x \leq_{ctx} f(x) : \tau$$

Proof. By Theorem 2 it suffices to prove that x is logically related to $f(x)$: $-; x : \tau \models x \leq_{log} f(x) : \tau$.

Let $n \in \mathbb{N}$, $W \in \mathbf{World}$ and $\sigma_I, \sigma_S \in \mathrm{Val}^{x:\tau}$, such that

$$\forall m.\ (n, m, \sigma_I(x), \sigma_S(x)) \in \mathcal{V}[\![- \vdash \tau]\!]_{[]}(W)$$

From the interpretation of existential and product types it follows that there exists a $\nu \in \mathbf{Type}$ and $v_{1I}, v_{2I}, v_{1S}, v_{2S} \in \mathrm{Val}$ such that $\sigma_I(x) = (v_{1I}, v_{2I})$, $\sigma_S(x) = (v_{1S}, v_{2S})$ and

$$(n, 0, v_{1I}, v_{1S}) \in \mathcal{V}[\![\alpha \vdash 1 \to \alpha]\!]_{[\alpha \mapsto \nu]}(W) \tag{4}$$
$$(n, 0, v_{2I}, v_{2S}) \in \mathcal{V}[\![\alpha \vdash \alpha \to \mathbb{N}]\!]_{[\alpha \mapsto \nu]}(W) \tag{5}$$

Since $\sigma_I(x)$ is already a value and $f(\sigma_S(x))$ pure-reduces to the following value

$$v_s \stackrel{def}{=} \mathsf{pack}\ (\lambda z.\ \mathsf{ref}\ (\pi_1(v_{1S}, v_{2S})(z)), \lambda z.\ \pi_2(v_{1S}, v_{2S})(!z))$$

it suffices to prove that $\sigma_I(x)$ and v_S are related by the τ value relation:

$$\forall n' \leq n.\ \forall m \in \mathbb{N}.\ \forall W' \geq W.\ (n', m, \sigma_I(x), v_S) \in \mathcal{V}[\![- \vdash \tau]\!]_{[]}(W')$$

We thus have to pick a relational interpretation of the new abstract type. As discussed before, we relate the implementation value v_I with the specification location l_S through the type ν', defined in (3). Recall, the definition states that there exists an invariant S (2) that owns the specification location l_S and asserts that this location contains a value v_S on the specification side, such that v_I and v_S are ν-related. Next, we have to prove that the components of the pairs are related:

$$\begin{aligned}
&\forall n' \leq n.\ \forall m \in \mathbb{N}.\ \forall W' \geq W.\\
&\quad (n', m, v_{1I}, \lambda z.\ \mathsf{ref}\ (\pi_1(v_{1S}, v_{2S})(z))) \in \mathcal{V}[\![\alpha \vdash 1 \to \alpha]\!]_{[\alpha \mapsto \nu']}(W') \land\\
&\quad (n', m, v_{2I}, \lambda z.\ \pi_2(v_{1S}, v_{2S})(!z))) \in \mathcal{V}[\![\alpha \vdash \alpha \to \mathbb{N}]\!]_{[\alpha \mapsto \nu']}(W')
\end{aligned}$$

We will focus on proving the second conjunct, as this is the one that requires an unfolding of the impredicative invariant without a corresponding reduction step. From the interpretation of function types, we have to prove the functions take ν'-related arguments to $\mathbb{N}$-related expressions:

$$\begin{aligned}
&\forall n' \leq n.\ \forall W' \geq W.\ \forall n'' < n'.\ \forall u_I, u_S.\\
&\quad (\forall m \in \mathbb{N}.\ (n'', m, u_I, u_S) \in \nu'(W'))\\
&\quad\quad \Rightarrow (n'' + 1, v_{2I}\ u_I, (\lambda z.\ \pi_2(v_{1S}, v_{2S})(!z))\ u_S) \in \mathcal{E}(\mathcal{V}[\![\alpha \vdash \mathbb{N}]\!]_{[\alpha \mapsto \nu']})(W')
\end{aligned}$$

Let $n', n'' \in \mathbb{N}$, $W' \in \mathbf{World}$ and $u_I, u_S \in \mathrm{Val}$ such that

$$n'' < n' \leq n \qquad W' \geq W \qquad \forall m \in \mathbb{N}.\ (n'', m, u_I, u_S) \in \nu'(W')$$

To show that

$$(n'' + 1, m, v_{2I}\ u_I, (\lambda z.\ \pi_2(v_{1S}, v_{2S})(!z))\ u_S) \in \mathcal{E}(\mathcal{V}[\![\alpha \vdash \mathbb{N}]\!]_{[\alpha \mapsto \nu']})(W')$$

let $k, i \in \mathbb{N}$, $h_I, h_S, h'_I \in$ Heap, $W'' \in$ **World** and $e'_I \in$ Exp such that

$$i < k \leq n'' + 1 \quad W'' \geq W' \quad (k, h_I, h_S) \in \lfloor W'' \rfloor \quad \langle v_{2I}\ u_I, h_I \rangle \to^i \langle e'_I, h'_I \rangle \not\to$$

To apply our earlier hypothesis (5), $(n, 0, v_{2I}, v_{2S}) \in \mathcal{V}[\![\alpha \vdash \alpha \to \mathbb{N}]\!]_{[\alpha \mapsto \nu]}(W)$, we need to prove that u_I and $h_S(u_S)$ are $(k-1, m)$-related for an arbitrary number of logical steps m. We now revert to the earlier discussion, and use Lemma 14, which requires us to instantiate our earlier assumption about ν' relatedness of u_I and u_S with $m + 2$ logical steps (since we need two logical steps to unfold the invariant).

To show that $\forall m.\ (k - 1, m, u_I, h_S(u_S)) \in \nu(W'')$, take any $m \in \mathbb{N}$. Since $k - 1 \leq n''$ and $W'' \geq W'$ we have $(k - 1, m + 2, u_I, u_S) \in \nu'(W')$, and by Lemma 14 the property holds.

Hence, $\forall m.\ (k - 1, m, u_I, h_S(u_S)) \in \nu(W'')$. From our original assumption (5) it thus follows that $v_{2I}\ u_I$ and $v_{2S}\ (h_S(u_S))$ are k-related in the expression closure:

$$(k, v_{2I}\ u_I, v_{2S}\ h_S(u_S)) \in \mathcal{E}(\mathcal{V}[\![\alpha \vdash \mathbb{N}]\!]_{[\alpha \mapsto \nu]})(W'')$$

Since $i < k \leq k$ it thus follows that there exists h'_S, v'_S and W''' such that

$$W''' \geq W'' \qquad \langle v_{2S}\ h_S(u_S), h_S \rangle \to^* \langle v'_S, h'_S \rangle \qquad (k - i, h'_I, h'_S) \in \lfloor W''' \rfloor$$

and $\forall m.\ (k - i, m, e'_I, v'_S) \in \mathcal{V}[\![\alpha \vdash \mathbb{N}]\!]_{[\alpha \mapsto \nu]}(W''')$, as required. □

6 Related Work

Step-indexing was invented by Appel and McAllester as a way of proving type safety for a language with recursive types using only simple mathematics suitable for foundational proof-carrying code [5]. Ahmed and co-workers developed the technique to support relational reasoning and more advanced languages featuring general references and impredicative polymorphism [1–3]. These relational models have subsequently been refined with ever more powerful forms of invariants and applied to reason about local state and control effects [15], compiler correctness [7,17], type-based program transformations [11] and fine-grained concurrent data structures [22], among other things. In another concurrent line of work, step-indexing has been applied to define models of increasingly expressive capability type systems [10] and concurrent program logics [4,18,20,21]. A common thread in both of these lines of work, is increasingly powerful recursively-defined worlds to capture various forms of invariants. We believe the complexity of invariants and associated recursively-defined worlds is orthogonal to the problem of the tight coupling between concrete and logical steps. In particular, our fixed point construction for locally contractive functors (Theorem 1) allows us to define recursively-defined worlds of the same form as prior approaches.

Usually, step-indexed logical relations are indexed over ω, because the closure ordinal of the inductively-defined convergence (termination) predicate is ω. An exception is the logical relation in [8] for reasoning about must-equivalence for a pure functional language without references but with countable non-determinism. Because of the presence of countable non-determinism, the closure ordinal of the inductively defined must-convergence predicate in *loc. cit.* is not ω. However, it is bounded by ω_1, and therefore the logical relation is indexed over ω_1. Note that this use of transfinite indexing is quite different from our use of transfinite indexing in this paper. Here we use transfinite indexing even though the closure ordinal of the convergence predicate is ω, because we seek to avoid linking unfoldings of the recursive domain equation to concrete reduction steps in the operational semantics.

Various ways have been proposed for stratifying the construction of semantic domains using step-indexing. These include explicit step-indexing [3,6], Hobor et al.'s indirection theory [16], Birkedal et al.'s ultrametric approach [12] and Birkedal et al.'s guarded recursion approach [9]. Indirection theory and the ultrametric approach are both currently specific to step-indexing over ω. Birkedal et al. have shown that sheaves over any complete Heyting algebra with a well-founded base models guarded dependent type theory [9]. It would be interesting to explore the possibility of using the internal language of sheaves over $\omega^2 + 1$ to define and reason about models step-indexed over ω^2.

Di Gianantonio and Miculan [13] introduced complete ordered families of equivalences as a unifying theory for mixed-variance recursive definitions that supports transfinite fixed point constructions. They define complete ordered families of equivalences over an arbitrary well-founded order and prove a generalized fixed point theorem for contractive endofunctions over these complete ordered families of equivalences. This allows for mixed-variance recursive definitions of elements of c.o.f.e.s. We extend their theory with an explicit construction for mixed-variance recursive definitions of c.o.f.e.s, for the specific instance of c.o.f.e.s over ω^2.

7 Conclusion and Future Work

Step-indexing has proven to be a very powerful technique for modelling advanced type systems and expressive program logics. Impredicative invariants are crucial for achieving modular reasoning and they show up in many different forms in recent models of type systems and program logics. Step-indexing allows us to model impredicative invariants by stratifying the model construction using steps. Unfortunately, current step-indexed models relate these steps directly to concrete reduction steps in the underlying operational semantics and require a concrete reduction step for each logical step. This is especially problematic for higher-order abstractions that introduce new logical steps, without any corresponding reduction steps. This is a common occurrence in higher-order program logics when deriving new specifications for specific use-cases of libraries from an abstract library specification.

In this paper we have isolated the problem in the setting of logical relations and demonstrated a solution based on transfinite step-indexing. This setting is sufficiently simple that we can present all the necessary details to see how transfinite step-indexing solves the problem. To do so we have developed a general theory for solving recursive domain equations using step-indexing over ω^2. Since our theory allows us to solve the equations used in the step-indexed models of cutting-edge program logics, we believe our solution will also scale to these systems, which can hopefully lead to development of more robust reasoning principles.

A natural question to ask is whether step-indexing over ω^2 suffices or whether we might wish to index beyond ω^2. It is not clear whether indexing beyond ω^2 will allow us to prove more equivalences than with our current model. However, it seems plausible that indexing beyond ω^2 could simplify reasoning by allowing less precise counting of logical steps and in the particular case of a step-indexed program logic might help with modularity by allowing the logic to abstract over the precise number of logical steps used. We leave these questions open for future work.

Acknowledgements. This research was supported in part by the ModuRes Sapere Aude Advanced Grant from The Danish Council for Independent Research for the Natural Sciences (FNU) and Danish Council for Independent Research project DFF – 4181-00273.

References

1. Ahmed, A.: Step-indexed syntactic logical relations for recursive and quantified types. In: Sestoft, P. (ed.) ESOP 2006. LNCS, vol. 3924, pp. 69–83. Springer, Heidelberg (2006)
2. Ahmed, A., Dreyer, D., Rossberg, A.: State-dependent representation independence. In: Proceedings of POPL (2009)
3. Ahmed, A.J.: Semantics of types for mutable state. Ph.D. thesis, Princeton University (2004)
4. Appel, A.W., Dockins, R., Hobor, A., Dodds, J., Leroy, X., Blazy, S., Stewart, G., Beringer, L.: Program Logics for Certified Compilers. Cambridge University Press, Cambridge (2014)
5. Appel, A.W., McAllester, D.: An indexed model of recursive types for foundational proof-carrying code. ACM Trans. Program. Lang. Syst. **23**(5), 657–683 (2001)
6. Appel, A.W., Melliès, P.-A., Richards, C.D., Vouillon, J.: A very modal model of a modern, major, general type system. In: Proceedings of POPL (2007)
7. Benton, N., Hur, C.-K.: Biorthogonality, step-indexing and compiler correctness. In: Proceedings of ICFP (2009)
8. Birkedal, L., Bizjak, A., Schwinghammer, J.: Step-indexed relational reasoning for countable nondeterminism. Log. Methods Comput. Sci. **9**(4), 1–23 (2013)
9. Birkedal, L., Møgelberg, R.E., Schwinghammer, J., Støvring, K.: First steps in synthetic guarded domain theory: step-indexing in the topos of trees. Log. Methods Comput. Sci. **8**(4), (2012) http://www.lmcs-online.org/ojs/viewarticle.php?id=1118&layout=abstract
10. Birkedal, L., Reus, B., Schwinghammer, J., Støvring, K., Thamsborg, J., Yang, H.: Step-indexed kripke models over recursive worlds. In: Proceedings of POPL (2011)
11. Birkedal, L., Sieczkowski, F., Thamsborg, J.: A concurrent logical relation. In: Proceedings of CSL (2012)
12. Birkedal, L., Støvring, K., Thamsborg, J.: The category-theoretic solution of recursive metric-space equations. Theor. Comput. Sci. **411**, 4102–4122 (2010)

13. Di Gianantonio, P., Miculan, M.: A unifying approach to recursive and co-recursive definitions. In: Geuvers, H., Wiedijk, F. (eds.) TYPES 2002. LNCS, vol. 2646, pp. 148–161. Springer, Heidelberg (2003)
14. Dodds, M., Jagannathan, S., Parkinson, M.J., Svendsen, K., Birkedal, L.: Verifying custom synchronization constructs using higher-order separation logic. ACM Trans. Program. Lang. Syst. **38**(2), 1–72 (2016)
15. Dreyer, D., Neis, G., Birkedal, L.: The impact of higher-order state and control effects on local relational reasoning. J. Funct. Prog. **22**, 477–528 (2012)
16. Hobor, A., Dockins, R., Appel, A.W.: A theory of indirection via approximation. In: Proceedings of POPL (2010)
17. Hur, C.-K., Dreyer, D.: A kripke logical relation between ML and assembly. In: Proceedings of POPL (2011)
18. Jung, R., Swasey, D., Sieczkowski, F., Svendsen, K., Turon, A., Birkedal, L., Dreyer, D.: Iris: monoids and invariants as an orthogonal basis for concurrent reasoning. In: Proceedings of POPL (2015)
19. Reynolds, J.: Separation logic: a logic for shared mutable data structures. In: Proceedings of LICS (2002)
20. Svendsen, K., Birkedal, L.: Impredicative concurrent abstract predicates. In: Shao, Z. (ed.) ESOP 2014 (ETAPS). LNCS, vol. 8410, pp. 149–168. Springer, Heidelberg (2014)
21. Turon, A., Dreyer, D., Birkedal, L.: Unifying refinement and hoare-style reasoning in a logic for higher-order concurrency. In: Proceedings of ICFP (2013)
22. Turon, A.J., Thamsborg, J., Ahmed, A., Birkedal, L., Dreyer, D.: Logical relations for fine-grained concurrency. In: Proceedings of POPL (2013)

A Higher-Order Abstract Syntax Approach to Verified Transformations on Functional Programs

Yuting Wang and Gopalan Nadathur(✉)

University of Minnesota, Minneapolis, USA
{yuting,gopalan}@cs.umn.edu

Abstract. We describe an approach to the verified implementation of transformations on functional programs that exploits the higher-order representation of syntax. In this approach, transformations are specified using the logic of hereditary Harrop formulas. On the one hand, these specifications serve directly as implementations, being programs in the language λProlog. On the other hand, they can be used as input to the Abella system which allows us to prove properties about them and thereby about the implementations. We argue that this approach is especially effective in realizing transformations that analyze binding structure. We do this by describing concise encodings in λProlog for transformations like typed closure conversion and code hoisting that are sensitive to such structure and by showing how to prove their correctness using Abella.

1 Introduction

This paper concerns the verification of compilers for functional (programming) languages. The interest in this topic is easily explained. Functional languages support an abstract view of computation that makes it easier to construct programs and the resulting code also has a flexible structure. Moreover, these languages have a strong mathematical basis that simplifies the process of proving programs to be correct. However, there is a proviso to this observation: to derive the mentioned benefit, the reasoning must be done relative to the abstract model underlying the language, whereas programs are typically executed only in their compiled form. To close the gap, it is important also to ensure that the compiler that carries out the translation preserves the meanings of programs.

The key role that compiler verification plays in overall program correctness has been long recognized; e.g. see [22,27] for early work on this topic. With the availability of sophisticated systems such as Coq [8], Isabelle [33] and HOL [15] for mechanizing reasoning, impressive strides have been taken in recent years towards actually verifying compilers for real languages, as seen, for instance, in the CompCert project [21]. Much of this work has focused on compiling imperative languages like C. Features such as higher-order and nested functions that are present in functional languages bring an additional complexity to their

P. Thiemann (Ed.): ESOP 2016, LNCS 9632, pp. 752–779, 2016.
DOI: 10.1007/978-3-662-49498-1_29

implementation. A common approach to treating such features is to apply transformations to programs that render them into a form to which more traditional compilation methods can be applied. These transformations must manipulate binding structure in complex ways, an aspect that requires special consideration at both the implementation and the verification level [3].

Applications such as those above have motivated research towards developing good methods for representing and manipulating binding structure. Two particular approaches that have emerged from this work are those that use the nameless representation of bound variables due to De Bruijn [9] and the nominal logic framework of Pitts [35]. These approaches provide an elegant treatment of aspects such as α-convertibility but do not directly support the analysis of binding structure or the realization of binding-sensitive operations such as substitution. A third approach, commonly known as the *higher-order abstract syntax* or HOAS approach, uses the abstraction operator in a typed λ-calculus to represent binding structure in object-language syntax. When such representations are embedded within a suitable logic, they lead to a succinct and flexible treatment of many binding related operations through β-conversion and unification.

The main thesis of this paper, shared with other work such as [7,16], is that the HOAS approach is in fact well-adapted to the task of implementing and verifying compiler transformations on functional languages. Our specific objective is to demonstrate the usefulness of a particular framework in this task. This framework comprises two parts: the λProlog language [30] that is implemented, for example, in the Teyjus system [36], and the Abella proof assistant [4]. The λProlog language is a realization of the hereditary Harrop formulas or HOHH logic [25]. We show that this logic, which uses the simply typed λ-calculus as a means for representing objects, is a suitable vehicle for specifying transformations on functional programs. Moreover, HOHH specifications have a computational interpretation that makes them *implementations* of compiler transformations. The Abella system is also based on a logic that supports the HOAS approach. This logic, which is called $\mathcal{G}$, incorporates a treatment of fixed-point definitions that can also be interpreted inductively or co-inductively. The Abella system uses these definitions to embed HOHH within $\mathcal{G}$ and thereby to reason directly about the specifications written in HOHH. As we show in this paper, this yields a convenient means for verifying implementations of compiler transformations.

An important property of the framework that we consider, as also of systems like LF [17] and Beluga [34], is that it uses a weak λ-calculus for representing objects. There have been attempts to derive similar benefits from using functional languages or the language underlying systems such as Coq. Some benefits, such as the correct implementation of substitution, can be obtained even in these contexts. However, the equality relation embodied in these systems is very strong and the analysis of λ-terms in them is therefore not limited to examining just their syntactic structure. This is a significant drawback, given that such examination plays a key role in the benefits we describe in this paper. In light of this distinction, we shall use the term *λ-tree syntax* [24] for the more restricted version of HOAS whose use is the focus of our discussions.

The rest of this paper is organized as follows. In Sect. 2 we introduce the reader to the framework mentioned above. We then show in succeeding sections how this framework can be used to implement and to verify transformations on functional programs. We conclude the paper by discussing the relationship of the ideas we describe here to other existing work.[1]

2 The Framework

We describe,. in turn, the specification logic and λProlog, the reasoning logic, and the manner in which the Abella system embeds the specification logic.

2.1 The Specification Logic and λProlog

The HOHH logic is an intuitionistic and predicative fragment of Church's Simple Theory of Types [12]. Its types are formed using the function type constructor $\rightarrow$ over user defined primitive types and the distinguished type $\mathbf{o}$ for formulas. Expressions are formed from a user-defined *signature* of typed constants whose argument types do not contain $\mathbf{o}$ and the *logical constants* $\Rightarrow$ and & of type $\mathbf{o} \rightarrow \mathbf{o} \rightarrow \mathbf{o}$ and Π_τ of type $(\tau \rightarrow \mathbf{o}) \rightarrow \mathbf{o}$ for each type τ not containing $\mathbf{o}$. We write $\Rightarrow$ and &, which denote implication and conjunction respectively, in infix form. Further, we write $\Pi_\tau\ \lambda(x : \tau)M$, which represents the universal quantification of x over M, as $\Pi_\tau x\, M$.

The logic is oriented around two sets of formulas called *goal formulas* and *program clauses* that are given by the following syntax rules:

$$
\begin{array}{lll}
G & ::= & A \mid G \,\&\, G \mid D \Rightarrow G \mid \Pi_\tau x\, G \\
D & ::= & A \mid G \Rightarrow A \mid \Pi_\tau x\, D
\end{array}
$$

Here, A represents *atomic formulas* that have the form $(p\ t_1\ \ldots\ t_n)$ where p is a (user defined) *predicate constant, i.e.* a constant with target type $\mathbf{o}$. Goal formulas of the last two kinds are referred to as hypothetical and universal goals. Using the notation $\Pi_{\bar{\tau}}\bar{x}$ to denote a sequence of quantifications, we see that a program clause has the form $\Pi_{\bar{\tau}}\bar{x}\, A$ or $\Pi_{\bar{\tau}}\bar{x}\, G \Rightarrow A$. We refer to A as the head of such a clause and G as the body; in the first case the body is empty.

A collection of program clauses constitutes a *program*. A program and a signature represent a specification of all the goal formulas that can be derived from them. The derivability of a goal formula G is expressed formally by the judgment $\Sigma; \Theta; \Gamma \vdash G$ in which Σ is a signature, Θ is a collection of program clauses defined by the user and Γ is a collection of dynamically added program clauses. The validity of such a judgment—also called a sequent—is determined by provability in intuitionistic logic but can equivalently be characterized in a goal-directed fashion as follows. If G is conjunctive, it yields sequents for "solving" each of its conjuncts in the obvious way. If it is a hypothetical or a universal goal, then one of the following rules is used:

[1] The actual development of several of the proofs discussed in this paper can be found at the URL http://www-users.cs.umn.edu/~gopalan/papers/compilation/.

$$\frac{\Sigma;\Theta;\Gamma,D\vdash G}{\Sigma;\Theta;\Gamma\vdash D\Rightarrow G}\Rightarrow R \qquad \frac{(c\notin\Sigma)\quad \Sigma,c:\tau;\Theta;\Gamma\vdash G[c/x]}{\Sigma;\Theta;\Gamma\vdash \Pi_\tau x\, G}\,\Pi R$$

In the ΠR rule, c must be a constant not already in Σ; thus, these rules respectively cause the program and the signature to grow while searching for a derivation. Once G has been simplified to an atomic formula, the sequent is derived by generating an instance of a clause from Θ or Γ whose head is identical to G and by constructing a derivation of the corresponding body of the clause if it is non-empty. This operation is referred to as backchaining on a clause.

In presenting HOHH specifications in this paper we will show programs as a sequence of clauses each terminated by a period. We will leave the outermost universal quantification in these clauses implicit, indicating the variables they bind by using tokens that begin with uppercase letters. We will write program clauses of the form $G \Rightarrow A$ as A :- G. We will show goals of the form $G_1 \wedge G_2$ and $\Pi_\tau y\, G$ as G_1 ,G_2 and **pi** $y : \tau\backslash\, G$, respectively, dropping the type annotation in the latter if it can be filled in uniquely based on the context. Finally, we will write abstractions as $y\backslash M$ instead of $\lambda y\, M$.

Program clauses provide a natural means for encoding rule based specifications. Each rule translates into a clause whose head corresponds to the conclusion and whose body represents the premises of the rule. These clauses embody additional mechanisms that simplify the treatment of binding structure in object languages. They provide λ-terms as a means for representing objects, thereby allowing binding to be reflected into an explicit meta-language abstraction. Moreover, recursion over such structure, that is typically treated via side conditions on rules expressing requirements such as freshness for variables, can be captured precisely through universal and hypothetical goals. This kind of encoding is concise and has logical properties that we can use in reasoning.

We illustrate the above ideas by considering the specification of the typing relation for the simply typed λ-calculus (STLC). Let N be the only atomic type. We use the HOHH type `ty` for representations of object language types that we build using the constants `n : ty` and `arr : ty → ty → ty`. Similarly, we use the HOHH type `tm` for encodings of object language terms that we build using the constants `app : tm → tm → tm` and `abs : ty → (tm → tm) → tm`. The type of the latter constructor follows our chosen approach to encoding binding: for example, we represent the STLC expression $(\lambda(y : N \to N)\lambda(x : N)\,(y\ x))$ by the HOHH term `(abs (arr n n) (y\ (abs n (x\ (app y x)))))`. Typing for the STLC is a judgment written as $\Gamma \vdash T : \mathrm{Ty}$ that expresses a relationship between a context Γ that assigns types to variables, a term T and a type Ty. Such judgments are derived using the following rules:

$$\frac{\Gamma\vdash T_1 : Ty_1\to Ty_2 \quad \Gamma\vdash T_2 : Ty_1}{\Gamma\vdash T_1\, T_2 : Ty_2} \qquad \frac{\Gamma, y : Ty_1\vdash T : Ty_2}{\Gamma\vdash \lambda(y : Ty_1)\,T : (Ty_1\to Ty_2)}$$

The second rule has a proviso: y must be fresh to Γ. In the λ-tree syntax approach, we encode typing as a binary relation between a term and a type, treating the typing context implicitly via dynamically added clauses. Using the predicate `of` to represent this relation, we define it through the following clauses:

```
of (app T1 T2) Ty2 :- of T1 (arr Ty1 Ty2), of T2 Ty1.
of (abs Ty1 T) (arr Ty1 Ty2) :- pi y\ (of y Ty1 => of (T y) Ty2).
```

The second clause effectively says that `(abs Ty1 T)` has the type `(arr Ty1 Ty2)` if `(T y)` has type `Ty2` in an extended context that assigns `y` the type `Ty1`. Note that the universal goal ensures that `y` is new and, given our encoding of terms, `(T y)` represents the body of the object language abstraction in which the bound variable has been replaced by this new name.

The rules for deriving goal formulas give HOHH specifications a computational interpretation. We may also leave particular parts of a goal unspecified, representing them by "meta-variables," with the intention that values be found for them that make the overall goal derivable. This idea underlies the language λProlog that is implemented, for example, in the Teyjus system [36].

2.2 The Reasoning Logic and Abella

The inference rules that describe a relation are usually meant to be understood in an "if and only if" manner. Only the "if" interpretation is relevant to using rules to effect computations and their encoding in the HOHH logic captures this part adequately. To reason about the *properties* of the resulting computations, however, we must formalize the "only if" interpretation as well. This functionality is realized by the logic $\mathcal{G}$ that is implemented in the Abella system.

The logic $\mathcal{G}$ is also based on an intuitionistic and predicative version of Church's Simple Theory of Types. Its types are like those in HOHH except that the type **prop** replaces **o**. Terms are formed from user-defined constants whose argument types do not include **prop** and the following logical constants: **true** and **false** of type **prop**; $\wedge$, $\vee$ and $\rightarrow$ of type $\textbf{prop} \rightarrow \textbf{prop} \rightarrow \textbf{prop}$ for conjunction, disjunction and implication; and, for every type τ not containing **prop**, the quantifiers $\forall_\tau$ and $\exists_\tau$ of type $(\tau \rightarrow \textbf{prop}) \rightarrow \textbf{prop}$ and the equality symbol $=_\tau$ of type $\tau \rightarrow \tau \rightarrow \textbf{prop}$. The formula $B =_\tau B'$ holds if and only if B and B' are of type τ and equal under $\alpha\beta\eta$ conversion. We will omit the type τ in logical constants when its identity is clear from the context.

A novelty of $\mathcal{G}$ is that it is parameterized by *fixed-point definitions*. Such definitions consist of a collection of *definitional clauses* each of which has the form $\forall \bar{x}, A \triangleq B$ where A is an atomic formula all of whose free variables are bound by $\bar{x}$ and B is a formula whose free variables must occur in A; A is called the head of such a clause and B is called its body.[2] To illustrate definitions, let `olist` represent the type of lists of HOHH formulas and let `nil` and `::`, written in infix form, be constants for building such lists. Then the append relation at the `olist` type is defined in $\mathcal{G}$ by the following clauses:

```
append nil L L;
append (X :: L1) L2 (X :: L3) ≜ append L1 L2 L3.
```

This presentation also illustrates several conventions used in writing definitions: clauses of the form $\forall \bar{x}, A \triangleq \textbf{true}$ are abbreviated to $\forall \bar{x}, A$, the outermost

[2] To be acceptable, definitions must cumulatively satisfy certain stratification conditions [23] that we adhere to in the paper but do not explicitly discuss.

universal quantifiers in a clause are made implicit by representing the variables they bind by tokens that start with an uppercase letter, and a sequence of clauses is written using semicolon as a separator and period as a terminator.

The proof system underlying $\mathcal{G}$ interprets atomic formulas via the fixed-point definitions. Concretely, this means that definitional clauses can be used in two ways. First, they may be used in a backchaining mode to derive atomic formulas: the formula is matched with the head of a clause and the task is reduced to deriving the corresponding body. Second, they can also be used to do case analysis on an assumption. Here the reasoning structure is that if an atomic formula holds, then it must be because the body of one of the clauses defining it holds. It therefore suffices to show that the conclusion follows from each such possibility.

The clauses defining a particular predicate can further be interpreted inductively or coinductively, leading to corresponding reasoning principles relative to that predicate. As an example of how this works, consider proving

```
∀L1 L2 L3, append L1 L2 L3 → append L1 L2 L3' → L3 = L3'
```

assuming that we have designated **append** as an inductive predicate. An induction on the first occurrence of **append** then allows us to assume that the entire formula holds any time the leftmost atomic formula is replaced by a formula that is obtained by unfolding its definition and that has **append** as its predicate head.

Many arguments concerning binding require the capability of reasoning over structures with free variables where each such variable is treated as being distinct and not further analyzable. To provide this capability, $\mathcal{G}$ includes the special *generic* quantifier ∇_τ, pronounced as "nabla", for each type τ not containing **prop** [26]. In writing this quantifier, we, once again, elide the type τ. The rules for treating ∇ in an assumed formula and a formula in the conclusion are similar: a "goal" with `(∇x M)` in it reduces to one in which this formula has been replaced by `M[c/x]` where `c` is a fresh, unanalyzable constant called a *nominal constant*. Note that ∇ has a meaning that is different from that of $\forall$: for example, `(∇ x y, x = y →` **false**`)` is provable but `(∀ x y, x = y →` **false**`)` is not.

$\mathcal{G}$ allows the ∇ quantifier to be used also in the heads of definitions. The full form for a definitional clause is in fact $\forall\bar{x}\nabla\bar{z}, A \triangleq B$, where the ∇ quantifiers scope only over A. In generating an instance of such a clause, the variables in $\bar{z}$ must be replaced with nominal constants. The quantification order then means that the instantiations of the variables in $\bar{x}$ cannot contain the constants used for $\bar{z}$. This extension makes it possible to encode structural properties of terms in definitions. For example, the clause `(∇ x, name x)` defines `name` to be a recognizer of nominal constants. Similarly, the clause `(∇ x, fresh x B)` defines `fresh` such that `(fresh X B)` holds just in the case that `X` is a nominal constant and `B` is a term that does not contain `X`. As a final example, consider the following clauses in which `of` is the typing predicate from the previous subsection.

```
ctx nil;
∇x, ctx (of x T :: L) ≜ ctx L.
```

These clauses define `ctx` such that `(ctx L)` holds exactly when `L` is a list of type assignments to distinct variables.

2.3 The Two-Level Logic Approach

Our framework allows us to write specifications in HOHH and reason about them using $\mathcal{G}$. Abella supports this *two-level logic approach* by encoding HOHH derivability in a definition and providing a convenient interface to it. The user program and signature for these derivations are obtained from a λProlog program file. The state in a derivation is represented by a judgment of the form $\{\Gamma \vdash G\}$. where Γ is the list of dynamically added clauses; additions to the signature are treated implicitly via nominal constants. If Γ is empty, the judgment is abbreviated to {G}. The theorems that are to be proved mix such judgments with other ones defined directly in Abella. For example, the uniqueness of typing for the STLC based on its encoding in HOHH can be stated as follows:

```
∀L M T T', ctx L → {L ⊢ of M T} → {L ⊢ of M T'} → T = T'.
```

This formula talks about the typing of *open* terms relative to a dynamic collection of clauses that assign unique types to (potentially) free variables.

The ability to mix specifications in HOHH and definitions in Abella provides considerable expressivity to the reasoning process. This expressivity is further enhanced by the fact that both HOHH and $\mathcal{G}$ support the λ-tree syntax approach. We illustrate these observations by considering the explicit treatment of substitutions. We use the type `map` and the constant `map: tm → tm → map` to represent mappings for individual variables (encoded as nominal constants) and a list of such mappings to represent a substitution; for simplicity, we overload the constructors `nil` and `::` at this type. Then the predicate `subst` such that `subst ML M M'` holds exactly when `M'` is the result of applying the substitution `ML` to `M` can be defined by the following clauses:

```
subst nil M M;
∇x, subst ((map x V) :: ML) (R x) M ≜ subst ML (R V) M.
```

Observe how quantifier ordering is used in this definition to create a "hole" where a free variable appears in a term and application is then used to plug the hole with the substitution. This definition makes it extremely easy to prove structural properties of substitutions. For example, the fact that substitution distributes over applications and abstractions can be stated as follows:

```
∀ML M1 M2 M', subst ML (app M1 M2) M' →
   ∃M1' M2', M' = app M1' M2' ∧ subst ML M1 M1' ∧ subst ML M2 M2'.
∀ML R T M', subst ML (abs T R) M' →
   ∃R', M' = abs T R' ∧ ∇x, subst ML (R x) (R' x).
```

An easy induction over the definition of substitution proves these properties.

As another example, we may want to characterize relationships between closed terms and substitutions. For this, we can first define well-formed terms through the following HOHH clauses:

```
tm (app M N) :- tm M, tm N.
tm (abs T R) :- pi x\ tm x ⇒ tm (R x).
```

Then we characterize the context used in tm derivations in Abella as follows:

```
tm_ctx nil;
∇x, tm_ctx (tm x :: L) ≜ tm_ctx L.
```

Intuitively, if `tm_ctx L` and `{L ⊢ tm M}` hold, then `M` is a well-formed term whose free variables are given by `L`. Clearly, if `{tm M}` holds, then `M` is closed. Now we can state the fact that a closed term is unaffected by a substitution:

```
∀ML M M', {tm M} → subst ML M M' → M = M'.
```

Again, an easy induction on the definition of substitutions proves this property.

3 Implementing Transformations on Functional Programs

We now turn to the main theme of the paper, that of showing the benefits of our framework in the verified implementation of compilation-oriented program transformations for functional languages. The case we make has the following broad structure. Program transformations are often conveniently described in a syntax-directed and rule-based fashion. Such descriptions can be encoded naturally using the program clauses of the HOHH logic. In transforming functional programs, special attention must be paid to binding structure. The λ-tree syntax approach, which is supported by the HOHH logic, provides a succinct and logically precise means for treating this aspect. The executability of HOHH specifications renders them immediately into implementations. Moreover, the logical character of the specifications is useful in the process of reasoning about their correctness.

This section is devoted to substantiating our claim concerning implementation. We do this by showing how to specify transformations that are used in the compilation of functional languages. An example we consider in detail is that of closure conversion. Our interest in this transformation is twofold. First, it is an important step in the compilation of functional programs: it is, in fact, an enabler for other transformations such as code hoisting. Second, it is a transformation that involves a complex manipulation of binding structure. Thus, the consideration of this transformation helps shine a light on the special features of our framework. The observations we make in the context of closure conversion are actually applicable quite generally to the compilation process. We close the section by highlighting this fact relative to other transformations that are of interest.

3.1 The Closure Conversion Transformation

The closure conversion transformation is designed to replace (possibly nested) functions in a program by *closures* that each consist of a function and an environment. The function part is obtained from the original function by replacing its free variables by projections from a new environment parameter. Complementing this, the environment component encodes the construction of a value for the new parameter in the enclosing context. For example, when this transformation is applied to the following pseudo OCaml code segment

$$
\begin{aligned}
T &::= \mathbb{N} \mid T_1 \to T_2 \mid \textbf{unit} \mid T_1 \times T_2\\
M &::= n \mid x \mid \textbf{pred}\ M \mid M_1 + M_2\\
&\quad \mid \textbf{if}\ M_1\ \textbf{then}\ M_2\ \textbf{else}\ M_3\\
&\quad \mid () \mid (M_1, M_2) \mid \textbf{fst}\ M \mid \textbf{snd}\ M\\
&\quad \mid \textbf{let}\ x = M_1\ \textbf{in}\ M_2\\
&\quad \mid \textbf{fix}\ f\, x.M \mid (M_1\ M_2)\\
V &::= n \mid \textbf{fix}\ f\, x.M \mid () \mid (V_1, V_2)
\end{aligned}
$$

Fig. 1. Source language syntax

$$
\begin{aligned}
T &::= \mathbb{N} \mid T_1 \to T_2 \mid T_1 \Rightarrow T_2 \mid \textbf{unit} \mid T_1 \times T_2\\
M &::= n \mid x \mid \textbf{pred}\ M \mid M_1 + M_2\\
&\quad \mid \textbf{if}\ M_1\ \textbf{then}\ M_2\ \textbf{else}\ M_3\\
&\quad \mid () \mid (M_1, M_2) \mid \textbf{fst}\ M \mid \textbf{snd}\ M\\
&\quad \mid \textbf{let}\ x = M_1\ \textbf{in}\ M_2 \mid \lambda x.M \mid (M_1\ M_2)\\
&\quad \mid \langle M_1, M_2 \rangle \mid \textbf{open}\ \langle x_f, x_e \rangle = M_1\ \textbf{in}\ M_2\\
V &::= n \mid \lambda x.M \mid () \mid (V_1, V_2) \mid \langle V_1, V_2 \rangle
\end{aligned}
$$

Fig. 2. Target language syntax

```
let x = 2 in let y = 3 in (fun z. z + x + y)
```

it will yield

```
let x = 2 in let y = 3 in <fun z e. z + e.1 + e.2, (x,y)>
```

We write `<F,E>` here to represent a closure whose function part is `F` and environment part is `E`, and `e.i` to represent the i-th projection applied to an "environment parameter" `e`. This transformation makes the function part independent of the context in which it appears, thereby allowing it to be extracted out to the top-level of the program.

The Source and Target Languages. Figures 1 and 2 present the syntax of the source and target languages that we shall use in this illustration. In these figures, T, M and V stand respectively for the categories of types, terms and the terms recognized as values. $\mathbb{N}$ is the type for natural numbers and n corresponds to constants of this type. Our languages include some arithmetic operators, the conditional and the tuple constructor and destructors; note that **pred** represents the predecessor function on numbers, the behavior of the conditional is based on whether or not the "condition" is zero and **fst** and **snd** are the projection operators on pairs. The source language includes the recursion operator **fix** which abstracts simultaneously over the function and the parameter; the usual abstraction is a degenerate case in which the function parameter does not appear in the body. The target language includes the expressions $\langle M_1, M_2 \rangle$ and ($\textbf{open}\ \langle x_f, x_e \rangle = M_1\ \textbf{in}\ M_2$) representing the formation and application of closures. The target language does not have an explicit fixed point constructor. Instead, recursion is realized by parameterizing the function part of a closure with a function component; this treatment should become clear from the rules for typing closures and for evaluating the application of closures that we present below. The usual forms of abstraction and application are included in the target language to simplify the presentation of the transformation. The usual function type is reserved for closures; abstractions are given the type $T_1 \Rightarrow T_2$ in the target language. We abbreviate $(M_1, \ldots, (M_n, ()))$ by $(M_1, \ldots, M_n)$ and $\textbf{fst}\ (\textbf{snd}\ (\ldots (\textbf{snd}\ M)))$ where **snd** is applied $i - 1$ times for $i \geq 1$ by $\pi_i(M)$.

$$\frac{}{\rho \triangleright n \rightsquigarrow n}\ \text{cc-nat} \qquad \frac{(x \mapsto M) \in \rho}{\rho \triangleright x \rightsquigarrow M}\ \text{cc-var} \qquad \frac{\rho \triangleright x_1 \rightsquigarrow M_1 \quad \ldots \quad \rho \triangleright x_n \rightsquigarrow M_n}{\rho \triangleright (x_1, \ldots, x_n) \rightsquigarrow_e (M_1, \ldots, M_n)}\ \text{cc-env}$$

$$\frac{\rho \triangleright M \rightsquigarrow M'}{\rho \triangleright \mathbf{pred}\ M \rightsquigarrow \mathbf{pred}\ M'}\ \text{cc-pred} \qquad \frac{\rho \triangleright M_1 \rightsquigarrow M_1' \quad \rho \triangleright M_2 \rightsquigarrow M_2'}{\rho \triangleright M_1 + M_2 \rightsquigarrow M_1' + M_2'}\ \text{cc-plus}$$

$$\frac{\rho \triangleright M \rightsquigarrow M' \quad \rho \triangleright M_1 \rightsquigarrow M_1' \quad \rho \triangleright M_2 \rightsquigarrow M_2'}{\rho \triangleright \mathbf{if}\ M\ \mathbf{then}\ M_1\ \mathbf{else}\ M_2 \rightsquigarrow \mathbf{if}\ M'\ \mathbf{then}\ M_1'\ \mathbf{else}\ M_2'}\ \text{cc-if} \qquad \frac{}{\rho \triangleright () \rightsquigarrow ()}\ \text{cc-unit}$$

$$\frac{\rho \triangleright M_1 \rightsquigarrow M_1' \quad \rho \triangleright M_2 \rightsquigarrow M_2'}{\rho \triangleright (M_1, M_2) \rightsquigarrow (M_1', M_2')}\ \text{cc-pair} \qquad \frac{\rho \triangleright M \rightsquigarrow M'}{\rho \triangleright \mathbf{fst}\ M \rightsquigarrow \mathbf{fst}\ M'}\ \text{cc-fst} \qquad \frac{\rho \triangleright M \rightsquigarrow M'}{\rho \triangleright \mathbf{snd}\ M \rightsquigarrow \mathbf{snd}\ M'}\ \text{cc-snd}$$

$$\frac{\rho \triangleright M_1 \rightsquigarrow M_1' \quad \rho, x \mapsto y \triangleright M_2 \rightsquigarrow M_2'}{\rho \triangleright \mathbf{let}\ x = M_1\ \mathbf{in}\ M_2 \rightsquigarrow \mathbf{let}\ y = M_1'\ \mathbf{in}\ M_2'}\ \text{cc-let} \quad y \text{ must be fresh}$$

$$\frac{\rho \triangleright M_1 \rightsquigarrow M_1' \quad \rho \triangleright M_2 \rightsquigarrow M_2'}{\rho \triangleright M_1\ M_2 \rightsquigarrow \mathbf{let}\ g = M_1'\ \mathbf{in}\ \mathbf{open}\ \langle x_f, x_e \rangle = g\ \mathbf{in}\ x_f\ (g, M_2', x_e)}\ \text{cc-app} \quad g \text{ must be fresh}$$

$$\frac{(x_1, \ldots, x_n) \supseteq \mathbf{fvars}(\mathbf{fix}\ f\ x.M) \quad \rho \triangleright (x_1, \ldots, x_n) \rightsquigarrow_e M_e \quad \rho' \triangleright M \rightsquigarrow M'}{\rho \triangleright \mathbf{fix}\ f\ x.M \rightsquigarrow \langle \lambda p.\mathbf{let}\ g = \pi_1(p)\ \mathbf{in}\ \mathbf{let}\ y = \pi_2(p)\ \mathbf{in}\ \mathbf{let}\ x_e = \pi_3(p)\ \mathbf{in}\ M', M_e \rangle}\ \text{cc-fix}$$

where $\rho' = (x \mapsto y, f \mapsto g, x_1 \mapsto \pi_1(x_e), \ldots, x_n \mapsto \pi_n(x_e))$ and $p, g, y,$ and x_e are fresh variables

Fig. 3. Closure conversion rules

Typing judgments for both the source and target languages are written as $\Gamma \vdash M : T$, where Γ is a list of type assignments for variables. The rules for deriving typing judgments are routine, with the exception of those for introducing and eliminating closures in the target language that are shown below:

$$\frac{\vdash M_1 : ((T_1 \to T_2) \times T_1 \times T_e) \Rightarrow T_2 \quad \Gamma \vdash M_2 : T_e}{\Gamma \vdash \langle M_1, M_2 \rangle : T_1 \to T_2}\ \text{cof-clos}$$

$$\frac{\Gamma \vdash M_1 : T_1 \to T_2 \quad \Gamma, x_f : ((T_1 \to T_2) \times T_1 \times l) \Rightarrow T_2, x_e : l \vdash M_2 : T}{\Gamma \vdash \mathbf{open}\ \langle x_f, x_e \rangle = M_1\ \mathbf{in}\ M_2 : T}\ \text{cof-open}$$

In cof-clos, the function part of a closure must be typable in an empty context. In cof-open, x_f, x_e must be names that are new to Γ. This rule also uses a "type" l whose meaning must be explained. This symbol represents a new type constant, different from $\mathbb{N}$ and $()$ and any other type constant used in the typing derivation. This constraint in effect captures the requirement that the environment of a closure should be opaque to its user.

The operational semantics for both the source and the target language is based on a left to right, call-by-value evaluation strategy. We assume that this is given in small-step form and, overloading notation again, we write $M \hookrightarrow_1 M'$ to denote that M evaluates to M' in one step in whichever language is under consideration. The only evaluation rules that may be non-obvious are the ones for applications. For the source language, they are the following:

$$\frac{M_1 \hookrightarrow_1 M_1'}{M_1\ M_2 \hookrightarrow_1 M_1'\ M_2} \qquad \frac{M_2 \hookrightarrow_1 M_2'}{V_1\ M_2 \hookrightarrow_1 V_1\ M_2'} \qquad \frac{}{(\mathbf{fix}\ f\ x.M)\ V \hookrightarrow_1 M[\mathbf{fix}\ f\ x.M/f, V/x]}$$

For the target language, they are the following:

$$\frac{M_1 \hookrightarrow_1 M_1'}{\textbf{open}\ \langle x_f, x_e\rangle = M_1\ \textbf{in}\ M_2 \hookrightarrow_1 \textbf{open}\ \langle x_f, x_e\rangle = M_1'\ \textbf{in}\ M_2}$$

$$\frac{}{\textbf{open}\ \langle x_f, x_e\rangle = \langle V_f, V_e\rangle\ \textbf{in}\ M_2 \hookrightarrow_1 M_2[V_f/x_f, V_e/x_e]}$$

One-step evaluation generalizes in the obvious way to n-step evaluation that we denote by $M \hookrightarrow_n M'$. Finally, we write $M \hookrightarrow V$ to denote the evaluation of M to the value V through 0 or more steps.

The Transformation. In the general case, we must transform terms under mappings for their free variables: for a function term, this mapping represents the replacement of the free variables by projections from the environment variable for which a new abstraction will be introduced into the term. Accordingly, we specify the transformation as a 3-place relation written as $\rho \triangleright M \leadsto M'$, where M and M' are source and target language terms and ρ is a mapping from (distinct) source language variables to target language terms. We write $(\rho, x \mapsto M)$ to denote the extension of ρ with a mapping for x and $(x \mapsto M) \in \rho$ to mean that ρ contains a mapping of x to M. Figure 3 defines the $\rho \triangleright M \leadsto M'$ relation in a rule-based fashion; these rules use the auxiliary relation $\rho \triangleright (x_1, \ldots, x_n) \leadsto_e M_e$ that determines an environment corresponding to a tuple of variables. The cc-let and cc-fix rules have a proviso: the bound variables, x and f, x respectively, should have been renamed to avoid clashes with the domain of ρ. Most of the rules have an obvious structure. We comment only on the ones for transforming fixed point expressions and applications. The former translates into a closure. The function part of the closure is obtained by transforming the body of the abstraction, but under a new mapping for its free variables; the expression $(x_1, \ldots, x_n) \supseteq$ $\textbf{fvars}(\textbf{fix}\ f\, x.M)$ means that all the free variables of $(\textbf{fix}\ f\, x.M)$ appear in the tuple. The environment part of the closure correspondingly contains mappings for the variables in the tuple that are determined by the enclosing context. Note also that the parameter for the function part of the closure is expected to be a triple, the first item of which corresponds to the function being defined recursively in the source language expression. The transformation of a source language application makes clear how this structure is used to realize recursion: the constructed closure application has the effect of feeding the closure to its function part as the first component of its argument.

3.2 A λProlog Rendition of Closure Conversion

Our presentation of the implementation of closure conversion has two parts: we first show how to encode the source and target languages and we then present a λProlog specification of the transformation. In the first part, we discuss also the formalization of the evaluation and typing relations; these will be used in the correctness proofs that we develop later.

Encoding the Languages. We first consider the encoding of types. We will use `ty` as the λProlog type for this encoding for both languages. The constructors `tnat`, `tunit` and `prod` will encode, respectively, the natural number, unit and pair types. There are two arrow types to be treated. We will represent → by `arr` and ⇒ by `arr'`. The following signature summarizes these decisions.

```
tnat,tunit : ty          arr,prod,arr' : ty → ty → ty
```

We will use the λProlog type `tm` for encodings of source language terms. The particular constructors that we will use for representing the terms themselves are the following, assuming that `nat` is a type for representations of natural numbers:

```
nat : nat → tm                    pred,fst,snd : tm → tm           unit : tm
plus,pair,app : tm → tm → tm      ifz : tm → tm → tm → tm
let : tm → (tm → tm) → tm         fix : (tm → tm → tm) → tm
```

The only constructors that need further explanation here are `let` and `fix`. These encode binding constructs in the source language and, as expected, we use λProlog abstraction to capture their binding structure. Thus, **let** $x = n$ **in** x is encoded as `(let (nat n) (x\x))`. Similarly, the λProlog term `(fix (f\x\ app f x))` represents the source language expression (**fix** $f\,x.f\;x$).

We will use the λProlog type `tm'` for encodings of target language terms. To represent the constructs the target language shares with the source language, we will use "primed" versions of the λProlog constants seen earlier; *e.g.*, `unit'` of type `tm'` will represent the null tuple. Of course, there will be no constructor corresponding to `fix`. We will also need the following additional constructors:

```
abs' : (tm' → tm') → tm'      clos' : tm' → tm' → tm'
open' : tm' → (tm' → tm' → tm') → tm'
```

Here, `abs'` encodes λ-abstraction and `clos'` and `open'` encode closures and their application. Note again the λ-tree syntax representation for binding constructs.

Following Sect. 2, we represent typing judgments as relations between terms and types, treating contexts implicitly via dynamically added clauses that assign types to free variables. We use the predicates `of` and `of'` to encode typing in the source and target language respectively. The clauses defining these predicates are routine and we show only a few pertaining to the binding constructs. The rule for typing fixed points in the source language translates into the following.

```
of (fix R) (arr T1 T2) :-
    pi f\ pi x\ of f (arr T1 T2) => of x T1 => of (R f x) T2.
```

Note how the required freshness constraint is realized in this clause: the universal quantifiers over `f` and `x` introduce new names and the application `(R f x)` replaces the bound variables with these names to generate the new typing judgment that must be derived. For the target language, the main interesting rule is for typing the application of closures. The following clause encodes this rule.

```
of' (open' M R) T :- of' M (arr T1 T2),
  pi f\ pi e\ pi l\ of' f (arr' (prod (arr T1 T2) (prod T1 l)) T2) ⇒
                             of' e l ⇒ of' (R f e) T.
```

Here again we use universal quantifiers in goals to encode the freshness constraint. Note also how the universal quantifier over the variable `l` captures the opaqueness quality of the type of the environment of the closure involved in the construct.

We encode the one step evaluation rules for the source and target languages using the predicates `step` and `step'`. We again consider only a few interesting cases in their definition. Assuming that `val` and `val'` recognize values in the source and target languages, the clauses for evaluating the application of a fixed point and a closure are the following.

```
step (app (fix R) V) (R (fix R) V) :- val V.
step' (open' (clos' F E) R) (R F E) :- val' (clos' F E).
```

Note here how application in the meta-language realizes substitution.

We use the predicates `nstep` (which relates a natural number and two terms) and `eval` to represent the n-step and full evaluation relations for the source language, respectively. These predicates have obvious definitions. The predicates `nstep'` and `eval'` play a similar role for the target language.

Specifying Closure Conversion. To define closure conversion in λProlog, we need a representation of mappings for source language variables. We use the type `map` and the constant `map : tm → tm' → map` to represent the mapping for a single variable.[3] We use the type `map_list` for lists of such mappings, the constructors `nil` and `::` for constructing such lists and the predicate `member` for checking membership in them. We also need to represent lists of source and target language terms. We will use the types `tm_list` and `tm'_list` for these and for simplicity of discussion, we will overload the list constructors and predicates at these types. Polymorphic typing in λProlog supports such overloading but this feature has not yet been implemented in Abella; we overcome this difficulty in the actual development by using different type and constant names for each case.

The crux in formalizing the definition of closure conversion is capturing the content of the cc-fix rule. A key part of this rule is identifying the free variables in a given source language term. We realize the requirement by defining a predicate `fvars` that is such that if `(fvars M L1 L2)` holds then `L1` is a list that includes all the free variables of `M` and `L2` is another list that contains only the free variables of `M`. We show a few critical clauses in the definition of this predicate, omitting ones whose structure is easy predict.

```
fvars X _ nil :- notfree X.
fvars Y Vs (Y :: nil) :- member Y Vs.
fvars (nat _) _ nil.
```

[3] This mapping is different from the one considered in Sect. 2.3 in that it is from a *source* language variable to a *target* language term.

```
fvars (plus M1 M2) Vs FVs :-
  fvars M1 Vs FVs1, fvars M2 Vs FVs2, combine FVs1 FVs2 FVs.
...
fvars (let M R) Vs FVs :- fvars M Vs FVs1,
  (pi x\ notfree x ⇒ fvars (R x) Vs FVs2), combine FVs1 FVs2 FVs.
fvars (fix R) Vs FVs :-
  pi f\ pi x\ notfree f ⇒ notfree x ⇒ fvars (R f x) Vs FVs.
```

The predicate `combine` used in these clauses is one that holds between three lists when the last is a combination of the elements of the first two. The essence of the definition of `fvars` is in the treatment of binding constructs. Viewed operationally, the body of such a construct is descended into after instantiating the binder with a new variable marked `notfree`. Thus, the variables that are marked in this way correspond to exactly those that are explicitly bound in the term and only those that are not so marked are collected through the second clause. It is important also to note that the specification of `fvars` has a completely logical structure; this fact can be exploited during verification.

The cc-fix rule requires us to construct an environment representing the mappings for the variables found by `fvars`. The predicate `mapenv` specified by the following clauses provides this functionality.

```
mapenv nil _ unit.
mapenv (X::L) Map (pair' M ML) :- member (map X M) Map, mapenv L Map ML.
```

The cc-fix rule also requires us to create a new mapping from the variable list to projections from an environment variable. Representing the list of projection mappings as a function from the environment variable, this relation is given by the predicate `mapvar` that is defined by the following clauses.

```
mapvar nil (e\ nil).
mapvar (X::L) (e\ (map X (fst' e))::(Map (snd' e))) :- mapvar L Map.
```

We can now specify the closure conversion transformation. We provide clauses below that define the predicate `cc` such that `(cc Map Vs M M')` holds if `M'` is a transformed version of `M` under the mapping `Map` for the variables in `Vs`; we assume that `Vs` contains all the free variables of `M`.

```
cc _ _ (nat N) (nat' N).
cc Map Vs X M :- member (map X M) Map.
cc Map Vs (pred M) (pred' M') :- cc Map Vs M M'.
cc Map Vs (plus M1 M2) (plus' M1' M2') :-
   cc Map Vs M1 M1', cc Map Vs M2 M2'.
cc Map Vs (ifz M M1 M2) (ifz' M' M1' M2') :-
   cc Map Vs M M', cc Map Vs M1 M1', cc Map Vs M2 M2'.
cc Map Vs unit unit'.
cc Map Vs (pair M1 M2) (pair' M1' M2') :-
   cc Map Vs M1 M1', cc Map Vs M2 M2'.
cc Map Vs (fst M) (fst' M') :- cc Map Vs M M'.
cc Map Vs (snd M) (snd' M') :- cc Map Vs M M'.
cc Map Vs (let M R) (let' M' R') :- cc Map Vs M M',
  pi x\ pi y\ cc ((map x y) :: Map) (x :: Vs) (R x) (R' y).
```

```
cc Map Vs (fix R) (clos' (abs' (p\ let' (fst' p) (g\
                 let' (fst' (snd' p)) (y\
                 let' (snd' (snd' p)) (e\ R' g y e))))) E) :-
  fvars (fix R) Vs FVs, mapenv FVs Map E, mapvar FVs NMap,
  pi f\ pi x\ pi g\ pi y\ pi e\
   cc ((map x y)::(map f g)::(NMap e)) (x::f::FVs) (R f x) (R' g y e).
cc Map Vs (app' M1 M2)
   (let' M1' (g\ open' g (f\e\ app' f (pair' g (pair' M2' e))))) :-
  cc Map Vs M1 M1', cc Map Vs M2 M2'.
```

These clauses correspond very closely to the rules in Fig. 3. Note especially the clause for transforming an expression of the form (`fix R`) that encodes the content of the cc-fix rule. In the body of this clause, `fvars` is used to identify the free variables of the expression, and `mapenv` and `mapvar` are used to create the reified environment and the new mapping. In both this clause and in the one for transforming a `let` expression, the λ-tree representation, universal goals and (meta-language) applications are used to encode freshness and renaming requirements related to bound variables in a concise and logically precise way.

3.3 Implementing Other Transformations

We have used the ideas discussed in the preceding subsections in realizing other transformations such as code hoisting and conversion to continuation-passing style (CPS). These transformations are part of a tool-kit used by compilers for functional languages to convert programs into a form from which compilation may proceed in a manner similar to that for conventional languages like C.

Our implementation of the CPS transformation is based on the one-pass version described by Danvy and Filinski [13] that identifies and eliminates the so-called administrative redexes on-the-fly. This transformation can be encoded concisely and elegantly in λProlog by using meta-level redexes for administrative redexes. The implementation is straightforward and similar ones that use the HOAS approach have already been described in the literature; *e.g.* see [37].

Our implementation of code hoisting is more interesting: it benefits in an essential way once again from the ability to analyze binding structure. The code hoisting transformation lifts nested functions that are closed out into a flat space at the top level in the program. This transformation can be realized as a recursive procedure: given a function $(\lambda x.M)$, the procedure is applied to the subterms of M and the extracted functions are then moved out of $(\lambda x.M)$. Of course, for this movement to be possible, it must be the case that the variable x does not appear in the functions that are candidates for extraction. This "dependency checking" is easy to encode in a logical way within our framework.

To provide more insight into our implementation of code-hoisting, let us assume that it is applied after closure conversion and that its source and target languages are both the language shown in Fig. 2. Applying code hoisting to any term will result in a term of the form

$$\textbf{let } f_1 = M_1 \textbf{ in } \ldots \textbf{let } f_n = M_n \textbf{ in } M$$

where, for $1 \leq i \leq n$, M_i corresponds to an extracted function. We will write this term below as (**letf** $\vec{f} = \vec{M}$ **in** M) where $\vec{f} = (f_1, \ldots, f_n)$ and, correspondingly, $\vec{M} = (M_1, \ldots, M_n)$.

We write the judgment of code hoisting as $(\rho \triangleright M \leadsto_{ch} M')$ where ρ has the form $(x_1, \ldots, x_n)$. This judgment asserts that M' is the result of extracting all functions in M to the top level, assuming that ρ contains all the bound variables in the context in which M appears. The relation is defined by recursion on the structure of M. The main rule that deserves discussion is that for transforming functions. This rule is the following:

$$\frac{\rho, x \triangleright M \leadsto_{ch} \textbf{letf } \vec{f} = \vec{F} \textbf{ in } M'}{\rho \triangleright \lambda x.M \leadsto_{ch} \textbf{letf } (\vec{f}, g) = (\vec{F}, \lambda f.\lambda x.\textbf{letf } \vec{f} = (\pi_1(f), \ldots, \pi_n(f)) \textbf{ in } M') \textbf{ in } g\ \vec{f}}$$

We assume here that $\vec{f} = (f_1, \ldots, f_n)$ and, by an abuse of notation, we let $(g\ \vec{f})$ denote $(g\ (f_1, \ldots, f_n))$. This rule has a side condition: x must not occur in $\vec{F}$. Intuitively, the term $(\lambda x.M)$ is transformed by extracting the functions from within M and then moving them further out of the scope of x. Note that this transformation succeeds only if none of the extracted functions depend on x. The resulting function is then itself extracted. In order to do this, it must be made independent of the (previously) extracted functions, something that is achieved by a suitable abstraction; the expression itself becomes an application to a tuple of functions in an appropriate let environment.

It is convenient to use a special representation for the result of code hoisting in specifying it in λProlog. Towards this end, we introduce the following constants:

```
hbase : tm' → tm'
habs : (tm' → tm') → tm'
htm : tm'_list → tm' → tm'
```

Using these constants, the term (**letf** $(f_1, \ldots, f_n) = (M_1, \ldots, M_n)$ **in** M) that results from code hoisting will be represented by

```
htm (M1 :: ... :: Mn :: nil) (habs (f1\ ... (habs (fn\ hbase M)))).
```

We use the predicate `ch : tm' → tm' → o` to represent the code hoisting judgment. The context ρ in the judgment will be encoded implicitly through dynamically added program clauses that specify the translation of each variable `x` as `(htm nil (hbase x))`. In this context, the rule for transforming functions, the main rule of interest, is encoded in the following clause:

```
ch (abs' M) M'' :-
   (pi x\ ch x (htm nil (hbase x)) ⇒ ch (M x) (htm FE (M' x))),
   extract FE M' M''.
```

As in previous specifications, a universal and a hypothetical goal are used in this clause to realize recursion over binding structure. Note also the completely logical encoding of the requirement that the function argument must not occur in the nested functions extracted from its body: quantifier ordering ensures that `FE` cannot be instantiated by a term that contains `x` free in it. We have used the predicate `extract` to build the final result of the transformation from the transformed form of the function body and the nested functions extracted from it; the definition of this predicate is easy to construct and is not provided here.

4 Verifying Transformations on Functional Programs

We now consider the verification of λProlog implementations of transformations on functional programs. We exploit the two-level logic approach in this process, treating λProlog programs as HOHH specifications and reasoning about them using Abella. Our discussions below will show how we can use the λ-tree syntax approach and the logical nature of our specifications to benefit in the reasoning process. Another aspect that they will bring out is the virtues of the close correspondence between rule based presentations and HOHH specifications: this correspondence allows the structure of informal proofs over inference rule style descriptions to be mimicked in a formalization within our framework.

We use the closure conversion transformation as our main example in this exposition. The first two subsections below present, respectively, an informal proof of its correctness and its rendition in Abella. We then discuss the application of these ideas to other transformations. Our proofs are based on logical relation style definitions of program equivalence. Other forms of semantics preservation have also been considered in the literature. Our framework can be used to advantage in formalizing these approaches as well, an aspect we discuss in the last subsection.

4.1 Informal Verification of Closure Conversion

To prove the correctness of closure conversion, we need a notion of equivalence between the source and target programs. Following [28], we use a logical relation style definition for this purpose. A complication is that our source language includes recursion. To overcome this problem, we use the idea of step indexing [1,2]. Specifically, we define the following mutually recursive simulation relation $\sim$ between closed source and target terms and equivalence relation $\approx$ between closed source and target values, each indexed by a type and a step measure.

$$
\begin{aligned}
&M \sim_{T;k} M' \iff \forall j \leq k. \forall V. M \hookrightarrow_j V \supset \exists V'. M' \hookrightarrow V' \wedge V \approx_{T;k-j} V';\\
&n \approx_{\mathbb{N};k} n; \qquad () \approx_{\mathbf{unit};k} ();\\
&(V_1, V_2) \approx_{(T_1 \times T_2);k} (V_1', V_2') \iff V_1 \approx_{T_1;k} V_1' \wedge V_2 \approx_{T_2;k} V_2';\\
&(\mathbf{fix}\ f\, x.M) \approx_{T_1 \to T_2;k} \langle V', V_e \rangle \iff \forall j < k. \forall V_1, V_1', V_2, V_2'.\\
&\quad V_1 \approx_{T_1;j} V_1' \supset V_2 \approx_{T_1 \to T_2;j} V_2' \supset M[V_2/f, V_1/x] \sim_{T_2;j} V'\ (V_2', V_1', V_e).
\end{aligned}
$$

Note that the definition of $\approx$ in the fixed point/closure case uses $\approx$ negatively at the same type. However, it is still a well-defined notion because the index decreases. The cumulative notion of equivalence, written $M \sim_T M'$, corresponds to two expressions being equivalent under *any* index.

Analyzing the simulation relation and using the evaluation rules, we can show the following "compatibility" lemma for various constructs in the source language.

Lemma 1. *1. If $M \sim_{\mathbb{N};k} M'$ then* **pred** $M \sim_{\mathbb{N};k}$ **pred** M'. *If also $N \sim_{\mathbb{N};k} N'$ then $M + N \sim_{\mathbb{N};k} M' + N'$.*

2. If $M \sim_{T_1 \times T_2;k} M'$ then **fst** $M \sim_{T_1;k}$ **fst** M' *and* **snd** $M \sim_{T_2;k}$ **snd** M'.

3. If $M \sim_{T_1;k} M'$ and $N \sim_{T_2;k} N'$ then $(M, N) \sim_{T_1 \times T_2;k} (M', N')$.

4. If $M \sim_{\mathbb{N};k} M'$, $M_1 \sim_{T;k} M_1'$ and $M_2 \sim_{T;k} M_2'$, then **if** M **then** M_1 **else** $M_2 \sim_{T;k}$ **if** M' **then** M_1' **else** M_2'.

5. If $M_1 \sim_{T_1 \to T_2;k} M_1'$ and $M_2 \sim_{T_1;k} M_2'$ then $M_1\ M_2 \sim_{T_2;k}$ **let** $g = M_1'$ **in open** $\langle x_f, x_e \rangle = g$ **in** $x_f\ (g, M_2', x_e)$.

The proof of the last of these properties requires us to consider the evaluation of the application of a fixed point expression which involves "feeding" the expression to its own body. In working out the details, we use the easily observed property that the simulation and equivalence relations are closed under decreasing indices.

Our notion of equivalence only relates closed terms. However, our transformation typically operates on open terms, albeit under mappings for the free variables. To handle this situation, we consider semantics preservation for possibly open terms under closed substitutions. We will take substitutions in both the source and target settings to be simultaneous mappings of closed values for a finite collection of variables, written as $(V_1/x_1, \ldots, V_n/x_n)$. In defining a correspondence between source and target language substitutions, we need to consider the possibility that a collection of free variables in the first may be reified into an environment variable in the second. This motivates the following definition in which γ represents a source language substitution:

$$\gamma \approx_{x_m:T_m,\ldots,x_1:T_1;k} (V_1, \ldots, V_m) \iff \forall 1 \le i \le m.\gamma(x_i) \approx_{T_i;k} V_i.$$

Writing $\gamma_1; \gamma_2$ for the concatenation of two substitutions viewed as lists, equivalence between substitutions is then defined as follows:

$$(V_1/x_1, \ldots, V_n/x_n); \gamma \approx_{\Gamma, x_n:T_n,\ldots,x_1:T_1;k} (V_1'/y_1, \ldots, V_n'/y_n, V_e/x_e)$$
$$\iff (\forall 1 \le i \le n.V_i \approx_{T_i;k} V_i') \wedge \gamma \approx_{\Gamma;k} V_e.$$

Note that both relations are indexed by a source language typing context and a step measure. The second relation allows the substitutions to be for different variables in the source and target languages. A relevant mapping will determine a correspondence between these variables when we use the relation.

We write the application of a substitution γ to a term M as $M[\gamma]$. The first part of the following lemma, proved by an easy use of the definitions of $\approx$ and evaluation, provides the basis for justifying the treatment of free variables via their transformation into projections over environment variables introduced at function boundaries in the closure conversion transformation. The second part of the lemma is a corollary of the first part that relates a source substitution and an environment computed during the closure conversion of fixed points.

Lemma 2. *Let* $\delta = (V_1/x_1, \ldots, V_n/x_n); \gamma$ *and* $\delta' = (V_1'/y_1, \ldots, V_n'/y_n, V_e/x_e)$ *be source and target language substitutions and let* $\Gamma = (x_m' : T_m', \ldots, x_1' : T_1', x_n : T_n, \ldots, x_1 : T_1)$ *be a source language typing context such that* $\delta \approx_{\Gamma;k} \delta'$. *Further, let* $\rho = (x_1 \mapsto y_1, \ldots, x_n \mapsto y_n, x_1' \mapsto \pi_1(x_e), \ldots, x_m' \mapsto \pi_m(x_e))$.

1. *If* $x : T \in \Gamma$ *then there exists a value* V' *such that* $(\rho(x))[\delta'] \hookrightarrow V'$ *and* $\delta(x) \approx_{T;k} V'$.
2. *If* $\Gamma' = (z_1 : T_{z_1}, \ldots, z_j : T_{z_j})$ *for* $\Gamma' \subseteq \Gamma$ *and* $\rho \triangleright (z_1, \ldots, z_j) \leadsto_e M$, *then there exists* V_e' *such that* $M[\delta'] \hookrightarrow V_e'$ *and* $\delta \approx_{\Gamma';k} V_e'$.

The proof of semantics preservation also requires a result about the preservation of typing. It takes a little effort to ensure that this property holds at the point in the transformation where we cross a function boundary. That effort is encapsulated in the following strengthening lemma in the present setting.

Lemma 3. *If* $\Gamma \vdash M : T$, $\{x_1, \ldots, x_n\} \supseteq \mathbf{fvars}(M)$ *and* $x_i : T_i \in \Gamma$ *for* $1 \leq i \leq n$, *then* $x_n : T_n, \ldots, x_1 : T_1 \vdash M : T$.

The correctness theorem can now be stated as follows:

Theorem 4. *Let* $\delta = (V_1/x_1, \ldots, V_n/x_n); \gamma$ *and* $\delta' = (V_1'/y_1, \ldots, V_n'/y_n, V_e/x_e)$ *be source and target language substitutions and let* $\Gamma = (x_m' : T_m', \ldots, x_1' : T_1', x_n : T_n, \ldots, x_1 : T_1)$ *be a source language typing context such that* $\delta \approx_{\Gamma;k} \delta'$. *Further, let* $\rho = (x_1 \mapsto y_1, \ldots, x_n \mapsto y_n, x_1' \mapsto \pi_1(x_e), \ldots, x_m' \mapsto \pi_m(x_e))$. *If* $\Gamma \vdash M : T$ *and* $\rho \triangleright M \leadsto M'$, *then* $M[\delta] \sim_{T;k} M'[\delta']$.

We outline the main steps in the argument for this theorem: these will guide the development of a formal proof in Sect. 4.2. We proceed by induction on the derivation of $\rho \triangleright M \leadsto M'$, analyzing the last step in it. This obviously depends on the structure of M. The case for a number is obvious and for a variable we use Lemma 2.1. In the remaining cases, other than when M is of the form ($\mathbf{let}\ x = M_1\ \mathbf{in}\ M_2$) or ($\mathbf{fix}\ f\,x.M_1$), the argument follows a set pattern: we observe that substitutions distribute to the sub-components of expressions, we invoke the induction hypothesis over the sub-components and then we use Lemma 1 to conclude. If M is of the form ($\mathbf{let}\ x = M_1\ \mathbf{in}\ M_2$), then M' must be of the form ($\mathbf{let}\ y = M_1'\ \mathbf{in}\ M_2'$). Here again the substitutions distribute to M_1 and M_2 and to M_1' and M_2', respectively. We then apply the induction hypothesis first to M_1 and M_1' and then to M_2 and M_2'; in the latter case, we need to consider extended substitutions but these obviously remain equivalent. Finally, if M is of the form ($\mathbf{fix}\ f\,x.M_1$), then M' must have the form $\langle M_1', M_2' \rangle$. We can prove that the abstraction M_1' is closed and therefore that $M'[\sigma'] = \langle M_1', M_2'[\sigma'] \rangle$. We then apply the induction hypothesis. In order to do so, we generate the appropriate typing judgment using Lemma 3 and a new pair of equivalent substitutions (under a suitable step index) using Lemma 2.2.

4.2 Formal Verification of the Closure Conversion Implementation

In the subsections below, we present a sequence of preparatory steps, leading eventually to a formal version of the correctness theorem.

Auxiliary Predicates Used in the Formalization. We use the techniques of Sect. 2 to define some predicates related to the encodings of source and target language types and terms that are needed in the main development; unless explicitly mentioned, these definitions are in $\mathcal{G}$. First, we define the predicates `ctx` and `ctx'` to identify typing contexts for the source and target languages. Next, we define in HOHH the recognizers `tm` and `tm'` of well-formed source and target language terms. A source (target) term `M` is closed if {`tm M`} ({`tm' M`}) is derivable. The predicate `is_sty` recognizes source types. Finally, `vars_of_ctx` is a predicate such that `(vars_of_ctx L Vs)` holds if `L` is a source language typing context and `Vs` is the list of variables it pertains to.

Step indexing uses ordering on natural numbers. We represent natural numbers using `z` for 0 and `s` for the successor constructor. The predicate `is_nat` recognizes natural numbers. The predicates `lt` and `le`, whose definitions are routine, represent the "less than" and the "less than or equal to" relations.

The Simulation and Equivalence Relations. The following clauses define the simulation and equivalence relations.

```
sim T K M M' ≜ ∀J V, le J K → {nstep J M V} → {val V} →
  ∃V' N, {eval' M' V'} ∧ {add J N K} ∧ equiv T N V V';
equiv tnat K (nat N) (nat' N);
equiv tunit K unit unit';
equiv (prod T1 T2) K (pair V1 V2) (pair' V1' V2') ≜
  equiv T1 K V1 V1' ∧ equiv T2 K V2 V2' ∧
  {tm V1} ∧ {tm V2} ∧ {tm' V1'} ∧ {tm' V2'};
equiv (arr T1 T2) z (fix R) (clos' (abs' R') VE) ≜
  {val' VE} ∧ {tm (fix R)} ∧ {tm' (clos' (abs' R') VE)};
equiv (arr T1 T2) (s K) (fix R) (clos' (abs' R') VE) ≜
  equiv (arr T1 T2) K (fix R) (clos' (abs' R') VE) ∧
  ∀V1 V1' V2 V2', equiv T1 K V1 V1' → equiv (arr T1 T2) K V2 V2' →
     sim T2 K (R V2 V1) (R' (pair' V2' (pair' V1' VE))).
```

The formula `(sim T K M M')` is intended to mean that `M` simulates `M'` at type `T` in `K` steps; `(equiv T K V V')` has a similar interpretation. Note the exploitation of λ-tree syntax, specifically the use of application, to realize substitution in the definition of `equiv`. It is easily shown that `sim` holds only between closed source and target terms and similarly `equiv` holds only between closed source and target values.[4]

Compatibility lemmas in the style of Lemma 1 are easily stated for `sim`. For example, the one for pairs is the following.

```
∀T1 T2 K M1 M2 M1' M2', {is_nat K} → {is_sty T1} → {is_sty T2} →
```

[4] The definition of `equiv` uses itself negatively in the last clause and thereby violates the original stratification condition of $\mathcal{G}$. However, Abella permits this definition under a weaker stratification condition that ensures consistency provided the definition is used in restricted ways [5,38], a requirement that is adhered to in this paper.

```
sim T1 K M1 M1' → sim T2 K M2 M2' →
sim (prod T1 T2) K (pair M1 M2) (pair' M1' M2').
```

These lemmas have straightforward proofs.

Representing Substitutions. We treat substitutions as discussed in Sect. 2. For example, source substitutions satisfy the following definition.

```
subst nil;
subst ((map X V)::ML) ≜ subst ML ∧ name X ∧ {val V} ∧ {tm V} ∧
  ∀V', member (map X V') ML → V' = V.
```

By definition, these substitutions map variables to closed values. To accord with the way closure conversion is formalized, we allow multiple mappings for a given variable, but we require all of them to be to the same value. The application of a source substitution is also defined as discussed in Sect. 2.

```
app_subst nil M M;
∇x,app_subst ((map x V)::(ML x)) (R x) M ≜ ∇x,app_subst (ML x) (R V) M.
```

As before, we can easily prove properties about substitution application based on this definition such as that such an application distributes over term structure and that closed terms are not affected by substitution.

The predicates `subst'` and `app_subst'` encode target substitutions and their application. Their formalization is similar to that above.

The Equivalence Relation on Substitutions. We first define the relation `subst_env_equiv` between source substitutions and target environments:

```
subst_env_equiv nil K ML unit';
subst_env_equiv ((of X T)::L) K ML (pair' V' VE) ≜
  ∃V,subst_env_equiv L K ML VE ∧ member (map X V) ML ∧ equiv T K V V'.
```

Using `subst_env_equiv`, the needed relation between source and target substitutions is defined as follows.

```
∇e, subst_equiv L K ML ((map e VE)::nil) ≜ subst_env_equiv L K ML VE;
∇x y, subst_equiv ((of x T)::L) K ((map x V)::ML) ((map y V')::ML') ≜
  equiv T K V V' ∧ subst_equiv L K ML ML'.
```

Lemmas about `fvars`, `mapvar` and `mapenv`. Lemma 3 translates into a lemma about `fvars` in the implementation. To state it, we define a strengthening relation between source typing contexts:

```
prune_ctx nil L nil;
prune_ctx (X::Vs) L ((of X T)::L') ≜ member (of X T) L ∧ prune_ctx Vs L L'.
```

`(prune_ctx Vs L L')` holds if `L'` is a typing context that "strengthens" `L` to contain type assignments only for the variables in `Vs`. The lemma about `fvars` is then the following.

```
∀L Vs M T FVs, ctx L → vars_of_ctx L Vs → {L ⊢ of M T} →
  {fvars M Vs FVs} → ∃L', prune_ctx FVs L L' ∧ {L' ⊢ of M T}.
```

To prove this theorem, we generalize it so that the HOHH derivation of (fvars M Vs FVs) is relativized to a context that marks some variables as not free. The resulting generalization is proved by induction on the fvars derivation.

A formalization of Lemma 2 is also needed for the main theorem. We start with a lemma about mapvar.

```
∀L Vs Map ML K VE X T M' V, ∇e, {is_nat K} → ctx L → subst ML →
  subst_env_equiv L K ML VE → vars_of_ctx L Vs → {mapvar Vs Map} →
  member (of X T) L → app_subst ML X V → {member (map X (M' e)) (Map e)}
  → ∃V', {eval' (M' VE) V'} ∧ equiv T K V V'.
```

In words, this lemma states the following. If L is a source typing context for the variables $(x_1, \ldots, x_n)$, ML is a source substitution and VE is an environment equivalent to ML at L, then mapvar determines a mapping for $(x_1, \ldots, x_n)$ that are projections over an environment with the following character: if the environment is taken to be VE, then, for $1 \leq i \leq n$, x_i is mapped to a projection that must evaluate to a value equivalent to the substitution for x_i in ML. The lemma is proved by induction on the derivation of {mapvar Vs Map}.

Lemma 2 is now formalized as follows.

```
∀L ML ML' K Vs Vs' Map, {is_nat K} → ctx L → subst ML →
  subst' ML' → subst_equiv L K ML ML' → vars_of_ctx L Vs →
  vars_of_subst' ML' Vs' → to_mapping Vs Vs' Map →
  (∀ X T V M' M'', member (of X T) L → {member (map X M') Map} →
    app_subst ML X V → app_subst' ML' M' M'' →
      ∃V', {eval' M'' V'} ∧ equiv T K V V') ∧
  (∀ L' NFVs E E', prune_ctx NFVs L L' →
    {mapenv NFVs Map E} → app_subst' ML' E E' →
      ∃VE', {eval' E' VE'} ∧ subst_env_equiv L' K ML VE').
```

Two new predicates are used here. The judgment (vars_of_subst' ML' Vs') "collects" the variables in the target substitution ML' into Vs'. Given source variables Vs = $(x_1, \ldots, x_n, x'_1, \ldots, x'_m)$ and target variables Vs' = $(y_1, \ldots, y_n, x_e)$, the predicate to_mapping creates in Map the mapping

$$(x_1 \mapsto y_1, \ldots, x_n \mapsto y_n, x'_1 \mapsto \pi_1(x_e), \ldots, x'_m \mapsto \pi_m(x_e)).$$

The conclusion of the lemma is a conjunction representing the two parts of Lemma 2. The first part is proved by induction on {member (map X M') Map}, using the lemma for mapvar when X is some $x'_i (1 \leq i \leq m)$. The second part is proved by induction on {mapenv NFVs Map E} using the first part.

The Main Theorem. The semantics preservation theorem is stated as follows:

```
∀L ML ML' K Vs Vs' Map T P P' M M', {is_nat K} → ctx L → subst ML →
  subst' ML' → subst_equiv L K ML ML' → vars_of_ctx L Vs →
  vars_of_subst' ML' Vs' → to_mapping Vs Vs' Map → {L ⊢ of M T} →
  {cc Map Vs M M'} → app_subst ML M P → app_subst' ML' M' P' → sim T K P P'.
```

We use an induction on {`cc Map Vs M M'`}, the closure conversion derivation, to prove this theorem. As should be evident from the preceding development, the proof in fact closely follows the structure we outlined in Sect. 4.1.

4.3 Verifying the Implementations of Other Transformations

We have used the ideas presented in this section to develop semantics preservation proofs for other transformations such as code hoisting and the CPS transformation. We discuss the case for code hoisting below.

The first step is to define the step-indexed logical relations $\sim'$ and $\approx'$ that respectively represent the simulation and equivalence relation between the input and output terms and values for code hoisting:

$$M \sim'_{T;k} M' \iff \forall j \leq k.\forall V.M \hookrightarrow_j V \supset \exists V'.M' \hookrightarrow V' \wedge V \approx'_{T;k-j} V';$$

$$n \approx'_{\mathbb{N};k} n;$$
$$() \approx'_{\mathbf{unit};k} ();$$
$$(V_1, V_2) \approx'_{(T_1 \times T_2);k} (V'_1, V'_2) \iff V_1 \approx'_{T_1;k} V'_1 \wedge V_2 \approx'_{T_2;k} V'_2;$$
$$(\lambda x.M) \approx'_{T_1 \Rightarrow T_2;k} (\lambda x.M') \iff \forall j < k.\forall V, V'.V \approx'_{T_1;j} V' \supset M[V/x] \sim'_{T_2;j} M'[V'/x];$$
$$\langle \lambda p.M, V_e \rangle \approx'_{T_1 \to T_2;k} \langle \lambda p.M', V'_e \rangle \iff \forall j < k.\forall V_1, V'_1, V_2, V'_2.$$
$$V_1 \approx'_{T_1;j} V'_1 \supset V_2 \approx'_{T_1 \to T_2;j} V'_2 \supset M[(V_2, V_1, V_e)/p] \sim'_{T_2;j} M'[(V'_2, V'_1, V'_e)/p].$$

We can show that $\sim'$ satisfies a set of compatibility properties similar to Lemma 1.

We next define a step-indexed relation of equivalence between two substitutions $\delta = (V_1/x_1, \ldots, V_m/x_m)$ and $\delta' = (V'_1/x_1, \ldots, V'_m/x_m)$ relative to a typing context $\Gamma = (x_m : T_m, \ldots, x_1 : T_1)$:

$$\delta \approx'_{\Gamma;k} \delta' \iff \forall 1 \leq i \leq m.V_i \approx'_{T_i;k} V'_i.$$

The semantics preservation theorem for code hoisting is stated as follows:

Theorem 5. *Let $\delta = (V_1/x_1, \ldots, V_m/x_m)$ and $\delta' = (V'_1/x_1, \ldots, V'_m/x_m)$ be substitutions for the language described in Fig. 2. Let $\Gamma = (x_m : T_m, \ldots, x_1 : T_1)$ be a typing context such that $\delta \approx'_{\Gamma;k} \delta'$. Further, let $\rho = (x_1, \ldots, x_m)$. If $\Gamma \vdash M : T$ and $\rho \triangleright M \rightsquigarrow_{ch} M'$ hold, then $M[\delta] \sim'_{T;k} M'[\delta']$ holds.*

The theorem is proved by induction on the derivation for $\rho \triangleright M \rightsquigarrow_{ch} M'$. The base cases follow easily, possibly using the fact that $\delta \approx'_{\Gamma;k} \delta'$. For the inductive cases, we observe that substitutions distribute to the sub-components of expressions, we invoke the induction hypothesis over the sub-components and we use the compatibility property of $\sim'$. In the case of an abstraction, δ and δ' must be extended to include a substitution for the bound variable. For this case to work out, we must show that the additional substitution for the bound variable has no impact on the functions extracted by code hoisting. From the side condition for the rule deriving $\rho \triangleright M \rightsquigarrow_{ch} M'$ in this case, the extracted functions cannot depend on the bound variable and hence the desired observation follows.

In the formalization of this proof, we use the predicate constants `sim'` and `equiv'` to respectively represent $\sim'$ and $\approx'$. The Abella definitions of these predicates have by now a familiar structure. We also define a constant `subst_equiv'` to represent the equivalence of substitutions as follows:

```
subst_equiv' nil K nil nil;
∇x, subst_equiv' ((of' x T)::L) K ((map' x V)::ML) ((map' x V')::ML')
  ≜ equiv' T K V V' ∧ subst_equiv' L K ML ML'.
```

The representation of contexts in the code hoisting judgment in the HOHH specification is captured by the predicate `ch_ctx` that is defined as follows:

```
ch_ctx nil;
∇x, ch_ctx (ch x (htm nil (hbase x)) :: L) ≜ ch_ctx L.
```

The semantics preservation theorem is stated as follows, where `vars_of_ctx'` is a predicate for collecting variables in the typing contexts for the target language, `vars_of_ch_ctx` is a predicate such that `(vars_of_ch_ctx L Vs)` holds if `L` is a context for code hoisting and `Vs` is the list of variables it pertains to:

```
∀L K CL ML ML' M M' T FE FE' P P' Vs, {is_nat K} → ctx' L →
  ch_ctx CL → vars_of_ctx' L Vs → vars_of_ch_ctx CL Vs →
  subst' ML → subst' ML' → subst_equiv' L K ML ML' →
  {L ⊢ of' M T} → {CL ⊢ ch M (htm FE M')} → app_subst' ML M P →
  app_subst' ML' (htm FE M') (htm FE' P') → sim' T K P (htm FE' P').
```

The proof is by induction on `{CL ⊢ ch M (htm FE M')}` and its structure follows that of the informal one very closely. The fact that the extracted functions do not depend on the bound variable of an abstraction is actually explicit in the logical formulation and this leads to an exceedingly simple argument for this case.

4.4 Relevance to Other Styles of Correctness Proofs

Many compiler verification projects, such as CompCert [21] and CakeML [20], have focused primarily on verifying whole programs that produce values of atomic types. In this setting, the main requirement is to show that the source and target programs evaluate to the same atomic values. Structuring a proof around program equivalence base on a logical relation is one way to do this. Another, sometimes simpler, approach is to show that the compiler transformations permute over evaluation; this method works because transformations typically preserve values at atomic types. Although we do not present this here, we have examined proofs of this kind and have observed many of the same kinds of benefits to the λ-tree syntax approach in their context as well.

Programs are often built by composing separately compiled modules of code. In this context it is desirable that the composition of correctly compiled modules preserve correctness; this property applied to compiler verification has been called modularity. Logical relations pay attention to equivalence at function types and hence proofs based on them possess the modularity property. Another property that is desirable for correctness proofs is transitivity: we should be able to infer the correctness of a multi-stage compiler from the correctness of each of its stages. This property holds when we use logical relations if we restrict attention to programs that produce atomic values but cannot be guaranteed if equivalence at function types is also important; it is not always possible to decompose the natural logical relation between a source and target language into ones between several intermediate languages. Recent work has attempted to generalize the logical relations based approach to obtain the benefits of both transitivity and modularity [32]. Many of the same issues relating to the treatment of binding and substitution appear in this context as well and the work in this paper therefore seems to be relevant also to the formalization of proofs that use these ideas.

Finally, we note that the above comments relate only to the formalization of proofs. The underlying transformations remain unchanged and so does the significance of our framework to their implementation.

5 Related Work and Conclusion

Compiler verification has been an active area for investigation. We focus here on the work in this area that has been devoted to compiling functional languages. There have been several projects with ambitious scope even in this setting. To take some examples, the CakeML project has implemented a compiler from a subset of ML to the X86 assembly language and verified it using HOL4 [20]; Dargaye has used Coq to verify a compiler from a subset of ML into the intermediate language used by CompCert [14]; Hur and Dreyer have used Coq to develop a verified single-pass compiler from a subset of ML to assembly code based on a logical relations style definition of program equivalence [19]; and Neis *et al.* have used Coq to develop a verified multi-pass compiler called Pilsner, basing their proof on a notion of semantics preservation called Parametric Inter-Languages Simulation (PILS) [32]. All these projects have used essentially first-order treatments of binding, such as those based on a De Bruijn style representation.

A direct comparison of our work with the projects mentioned above is neither feasible nor sensible because of differences in scope and focus. Some comparison is possible with a part of the Lambda Tamer project of Chlipala in which he describes the verified implementation in Coq of a compiler for the STLC using a logical relation based definition of program equivalence [11]. This work uses a higher-order representation of syntax that does not derive all the benefits of λ-tree syntax. Chlipala's implementation of closure conversion comprises about 400 lines of Coq code, in contrast to about 70 lines of λProlog code that are needed in our implementation. Chlipala's proof of correctness comprises about 270 lines but it benefits significantly from the automation framework that was the focus of the Lambda Tamer project; that framework is built on top of the already existing Coq libraries and consists of about 1900 lines of code. The Abella proof script runs about 1600 lines. We note that Abella has virtually no automation and the current absence of polymorphism leads to some redundancy in the proof. We also note that, in contrast to Chlipala's work, our development treats a version of the STLC that includes recursion. This necessitates the use of a step-indexed logical relation which makes the overall proof more complex.

Other frameworks have been proposed in the literature that facilitate the use of HOAS in implementing and verifying compiler transformations. Hickey and Nogin describe a framework for effecting compiler transformations via rewrite rules that operate on a higher-order representation of programs [18]. However, their framework is embedded within a functional language. As a result, they are not able to support an analysis of binding structure, an ability that brings considerable benefit as we have highlighted in this paper. Moreover, this framework offers no capabilities for verification. Hannan and Pfenning have discussed using a system called Twelf that is based on LF in specifying and verifying compilers; see, for example, [16] and [29] for some applications of this framework. The way in which logical properties can be expressed in Twelf is restricted; in particular, it is not easy to encode a logical relation-style definition within it. The Beluga system [34], which implements a functional programming language based on contextual modal type theory [31], overcomes some of the shortcomings of Twelf. Rich properties of programs can be embedded in types in Beluga, and Belanger *et al.* show how this feature can be exploited to ensure type preservation for closure conversion [7]. Properties based on logical relations can also be described in Beluga [10]. It remains to be seen if semantics preservation proofs of the kind discussed in this paper can be carried out in the Beluga system.

While the framework comprising λProlog and Abella has significant benefits in the verified implementation of compiler transformations for functional languages, its current realization has some practical limitations that lead to a larger proof development effort than seems necessary. One such limitation is the absence of polymorphism in the Abella implementation. A consequence of this is that the same proofs have sometimes to be repeated at different types. This situation appears to be one that can be alleviated by allowing the user to parameterize proofs by types and we are currently investigating this matter. A second limitation arises from the emphasis on explicit proofs in the theorem-proving setup. The effect of this requirement is especially felt with respect to lemmas about contexts that arise routinely in the λ-tree syntax approach: such lemmas have fairly obvious proofs but, currently, the user must provide them to complete the overall verification task. In the Twelf and Beluga systems, such lemmas are obviated by absorbing them into the meta-theoretic framework. There are reasons related to the validation of verification that lead us to prefer explicit proofs. However, as shown in [6], it is often possible to generate these proofs automatically, thereby allowing the user to focus on the less obvious aspects. In ongoing work, we are exploring the impact of using such ideas on reducing the overall proof effort.

Acknowledgements. We are grateful to David Baelde for his help in phrasing the definition of the logical relation in Sect. 4.2. The paper has benefited from many suggestions from its reviewers. This work has been supported by the National Science Foundation grant CCF-0917140 and by the University of Minnesota through a Doctoral Dissertation Fellowship and a Grant-in-Aid of Research. Opinions, findings and conclusions or recommendations that are manifest in this material are those of the participants and do not necessarily reflect the views of the NSF.

References

1. Ahmed, A.: Step-indexed syntactic logical relations for recursive and quantified types. In: Sestoft, P. (ed.) ESOP 2006. LNCS, vol. 3924, pp. 69–83. Springer, Heidelberg (2006)
2. Appel, A.W., McAllester, D.: An indexed model of recursive types for foundational proof-carrying code. ACM Trans. Program. Lang. Syst. **23**(5), 657–683 (2001)
3. Aydemir, B.E., et al.: Mechanized metatheory for the masses: the PoplMark challenge. In: Hurd, J., Melham, T. (eds.) TPHOLs 2005. LNCS, vol. 3603, pp. 50–65. Springer, Heidelberg (2005)
4. Baelde, D., Chaudhuri, K., Gacek, A., Miller, D., Nadathur, G., Tiu, A., Wang, Y.: Abella: a system for reasoning about relational specifications. J. Formalized Reasoning **7**(2), 1–89 (2014)
5. Baelde, D., Nadathur, G.: Combining deduction modulo and logics of fixed-point definitions. In: Proceedings of the 2012 27th Annual IEEE/ACM Symposium on Logic in Computer Science, pp. 105–114. IEEE Computer Society (2012)
6. Bélanger, O.S., Chaudhuri, K.: Automatically deriving schematic theorems for dynamic contexts. In: Proceedings of the 2014 International Workshop on Logical Frameworks and Meta-languages: Theory and Practice. ACM Press (2014)
7. Savary-Belanger, O., Monnier, S., Pientka, B.: Programming type-safe transformations using higher-order abstract syntax. In: Gonthier, G., Norrish, M. (eds.) CPP 2013. LNCS, vol. 8307, pp. 243–258. Springer, Heidelberg (2013)
8. Bertot, Y., Castéran, P.: Interactive Theorem Proving and Program Development: Coq'Art: The Calculus of Inductive Constructions. Texts in Theoretical Computer Science. Springer, Heidelberg (2004)
9. de Bruijn, N.G.: Lambda calculus notation with nameless dummies, a tool for automatic formula manipulation, with application to the Church-Rosser Theorem. Indagationes Mathematicae **34**(5), 381–392 (1972)
10. Cave, A., Pientka, B.: A case study on logical relations using contextual types. In: Proceedings of the Tenth International Workshop on Logical Frameworks and Meta Languages: Theory and Practice, EPTCS, vol. 185, pp. 33–45 (2015)
11. Chlipala, A.: A certified type-preserving compiler from lambda calculus to assembly language. In: Proceedings of the 2007 ACM SIGPLAN Conference on Programming Language Design and Implementation, pp. 54–65. ACM Press (2007)
12. Church, A.: A formulation of the simple theory of types. J. Symb. Logic **5**, 56–68 (1940)
13. Danvy, O., Filinski, A.: Representing control: a study of the CPS transformation. Math. Struct. Comput. Sci. **2**, 361–391 (1992)
14. Dargaye, Z.: Vérification formelle d'un compilateur optimisant pour langages fonctionnels. Ph.D. thesis, l'Université Paris 7-Denis Diderot, France (2009)
15. Gordon, M.J.C.: Introduction to the HOL system. In: Archer, M., Joyce, J.J., Levitt, K.N., Windley, P.J. (eds.) Proceedings of the International Workshop on the HOL Theorem Proving System and its Applications, pp. 2–3. IEEE Computer Society (1991)
16. Hannan, J., Pfenning, F.: Compiler verification in LF. In: 7th Symposium on Logic in Computer Science. IEEE Computer Society Press (1992)
17. Harper, R., Honsell, F., Plotkin, G.: A framework for defining logics. J. ACM **40**(1), 143–184 (1993)
18. Hickey, J., Nogin, A.: Formal compiler construction in a logical framework. Higher-Order Symb. Comput. **19**(2–3), 197–230 (2006)

19. Hur, C.K., Dreyer, D.: A Kripke logical relation between ML and assembly. In: Proceedings of the 38th Annual ACM SIGPLAN-SIGACT Symposium on Principles of Programming Languages, pp. 133–146. ACM Press (2011)
20. Kumar, R., Myreen, M.O., Norrish, M., Owens, S.: CakeML: a verified implementation of ML. In: Proceedings of the 41st ACM SIGPLAN-SIGACT Symposium on Principles of Programming Languages, pp. 179–191. ACM Press (2014)
21. Leroy, X.: Formal certification of a compiler back-end or: programming a compiler with a proof assistant. In: Conference Record of the 33rd ACM SIGPLAN-SIGACT Symposium on Principles of Programming Languages, pp. 42–54. ACM Press (2006)
22. McCarthy, J., Painter, J.: Correctness of a compiler for arithmetic expressions. In: Proceedings of Symposia in Applied Mathematics. Mathematical Aspects of Computer Science, vol. 19, pp. 33–41. American Mathematical Society (1967)
23. McDowell, R., Miller, D.: Cut-elimination for a logic with definitions and induction. Theoret. Comput. Sci. **232**, 91–119 (2000)
24. Miller, D.: Abstract syntax for variable binders: an overview. In: Palamidessi, C., Moniz Pereira, L., Lloyd, J.W., Dahl, V., Furbach, U., Kerber, M., Lau, K.-K., Sagiv, Y., Stuckey, P.J. (eds.) CL 2000. LNCS (LNAI), vol. 1861, pp. 239–253. Springer, Heidelberg (2000)
25. Miller, D., Nadathur, G.: Programming with Higher-Order Logic. Cambridge University Press, Cambridge (2012)
26. Miller, D., Tiu, A.: A proof theory for generic judgments. ACM Trans. Comput. Logic **6**(4), 749–783 (2005)
27. Milner, R., Weyrauch, R.: Proving compiler correctness in a mechanized logic. In: Meltzer, B., Michie, D. (eds.) Machine Intelligence, vol. 7, pp. 51–72. Edinburgh University Press, Edinburgh (1972)
28. Minamide, Y., Morrisett, G., Harper, R.: Typed closure conversion. Technical report CMU-CS-95-171, School of Computer Science, Carnegie Mellon University (1995)
29. Murphy VII, T.: Modal types for mobile code. Ph.D. thesis, Carnegie Mellon University (2008)
30. Nadathur, G., Miller, D.: An overview of λProlog. In: Fifth International Logic Programming Conference, pp. 810–827. MIT Press (1988)
31. Nanevski, A., Pfenning, F., Pientka, B.: Contextual model type theory. ACM Trans. Comput. Logic **9**(3), 1–49 (2008)
32. Neis, G., Hur, C.K., Kaiser, J.O., McLaughlin, C., Dreyer, D., Vafeiadis, V.: Pilsner: a compositionally verified compiler for a higher-order imperative language. In: Proceedings of the 20th ACM SIGPLAN International Conference on Functional Programming, pp. 166–178. ACM Press (2015)
33. Nipkow, T., Paulson, L.C., Wenzel, M.: Isabelle/HOL: A Proof Assistant for Higher-Order Logic. Springer, Heidelberg (2002)
34. Pientka, B., Dunfield, J.: Beluga: a framework for programming and reasoning with deductive systems (system description). In: Giesl, J., Hähnle, R. (eds.) IJCAR 2010. LNCS, vol. 6173, pp. 15–21. Springer, Heidelberg (2010)
35. Pitts, A.M.: Nominal logic, a first order theory of names and binding. Inf. Comput. **186**(2), 165–193 (2003)
36. Qi, X., Gacek, A., Holte, S., Nadathur, G., Snow, Z.: The Teyjus system - Version 2. http://teyjus.cs.umn.edu/
37. Tian, Y.H.: Mechanically verifying correctness of CPS compilation. In: Twelfth Computing: The Australasian Theory Symposium. CRPIT, vol. 51, pp. 41–51. ACS (2006)
38. Tiu, A.: Stratification in logics of definitions. In: Gramlich, B., Miller, D., Sattler, U. (eds.) IJCAR 2012. LNCS, vol. 7364, pp. 544–558. Springer, Heidelberg (2012)

The Expressive Power of Monotonic Parallel Composition

Johannes Åman Pohjola(✉) and Joachim Parrow

Department of Information Technology, Uppsala University, Uppsala, Sweden
{johannes.aman-pohjola,joachim.parrow}@it.uu.se

Abstract. We show a separation result between on the one hand models of concurrency that contain solutions to the *consensus problem*, where many identical concurrent processes must reach agreement; and on the other hand models with *monotonic parallel composition*, where processes always have the possibility to act independently of other processes in their environment. Our definitions and proofs are easy to instantiate in order to obtain particular separation results. We illustrate this point by strengthening several results from the literature, and proving some new ones. Highlights include a separation between unreliable and reliable broadcast π, between the ρ-calculus and cc-pi, and between the full psi-calculi framework and its restriction to monotonic assertion logics.

1 Introduction

There is today a plethora of modelling formalisms for concurrent programs, focusing on different aspects and using different kinds of semantics. In order to compare two such formalisms it is natural to investigate their expressive power. If a certain behaviour can be expressed in one formalism but not in another we say that the behaviour *separates* the formalisms.

In this paper we present a simple method for separation results between transition systems with parallel composition, based on little more than whether parallel components may act independently or not. This allows us to strengthen several known separation results, and obtain new ones with pleasingly little effort. Our inspiration and examples come from process calculi, but we believe the arguments to be simple and general enough to be applicable to other models of concurrency also. The proof strategy is based on a simplification of the leader election problem which we call the *consensus problem*. It can be intuitively formulated as follows:

n observationally equivalent greasers walk into a bar. The greasers may, possibly after conferring with each other, non-deterministically declare that either Elvis Presley or Jerry Lee Lewis is the greatest singer of all time. Once either Elvis or Jerry has been declared, the other may not be declared; otherwise a bar fight will break out. A solution to the consensus problem is to find a process P, representing a greaser, such that no matter what n is, both Elvis and Jerry are possible outcomes and it can be guaranteed that a fight will never break out. Such a solution we call a *consensus process*.

P. Thiemann (Ed.): ESOP 2016, LNCS 9632, pp. 780–803, 2016.
DOI: 10.1007/978-3-662-49498-1_30

In this paper, we show that the consensus problem is unsolvable with *monotonic composition*. The most natural example, and a mainstay in process calculi, is a parallel operator $|$ on processes that admits independent behaviour via the rule

$$\text{PAR}\ \frac{P \longrightarrow P'}{P \mid Q \longrightarrow P' \mid Q}$$

This says that whatever P can do alone it can also do if Q sits inert at its side. There can additionally be other rules for interaction between P and Q; a parallel operator counts as monotonic if the rule PAR holds, i.e. if a parallel context cannot hinder a transition. Examples of the myriad transition systems with monotonic parallel composition operators include CCS, the π-calculus, the ρ-calculus [1], and the fusion calculus [2]. Developments that include transition priorities may use non-monotonic composition; for example a high priority transition in Q may mean that P cannot take any transition in parallel with Q.

We exhibit several examples of transition systems where parallel composition does not satisfy PAR, and where consensus processes can indeed be expressed: the broadcast π-calculus [3], CCS with priorities [4], cc-pi [5], TPL [6], and some instances of psi-calculi [7]. We also exhibit two sets of criteria on encodings that both preserve the property of being a consensus process. It then follows immediately that there can exist no encoding of these languages satisfying our criteria if we only use monotonic composition in the target language. By this approach we strengthen the separation results from [3,8,9]. We also obtain several hitherto unseen results; highlights are a separation between unreliable broadcast (where messages may be lost) and reliable broadcast (where they may not), a separation between concurrent constraint formalisms based on whether inconsistent stores are reachable, and between the full psi-calculi framework [7] and its restriction to monotonic assertion logics (where connectivity between channels cannot decrease).

In order to increase confidence in the correctness of our developments, we have mechanised the proofs of our main results in the interactive theorem prover Isabelle/HOL [10]. The proof scripts are available online [11].

Our work is in the tradition of leader election-based separation results of Bougé [12] and Palamidessi [13]. In the leader election problem, n parallel processes must reach agreement among themselves to elect one (and only one) of them to act as their leader. In particular we are inspired by Ene and Muntean's separation between the π-calculus and the broadcast π-calculus [3]. They show that if the n participants are allowed to differ only by alpha-renaming and are not allowed to know n in advance, the π-calculus cannot solve the leader election problem, but the broadcast π-calculus can. Hence there can be no encoding from broadcast π to π, if we require that the encoding translates leader election systems into leader election systems. Their proof relies on the fact that the π-calculus allows local synchronisation independently of the environment via its monotonic parallel operator; hence the election can be split into two cliques that independently reach different election results. By contrast, the global synchronisation imposed by broadcast communication precludes such behaviour and allows the leader election problem to be solved. Variations of this argument have been used to show separation results between process calculi with priorities and their unprioritised counterparts [8,9].

The consensus problem we consider is reminiscent of — yet distinct from — the well-studied binary distributed consensus problem in distributed computing (see e.g. [14]). Both problems are concerned with n parallel processes reaching agreement on some value. Our problem formulation is stronger in the sense that the participants do not a priori know the value of n, while in distributed consensus n is known. Intuitively we may think of this as our formulation allowing for additional greasers to enter the bar while the discussion is still ongoing, while distributed consensus requires that everyone is present at the start. On the other hand, our formulation is weaker in the sense that we do not insist on eventual termination, so crash failures are not a concern; we accept solutions that may crash or livelock as long as disagreement is avoided.

The main message of this paper is a method to obtain separation results, and it is presented so that it can be understood without knowledge of any particular process calculus, or indeed without any background in process calculi at all. In applications and examples, while we do give brief informal introductions to most languages under consideration, we will often use process calculi without formally defining them: divulging all details would seriously bog down the presentation with background material that is independent of our main message. The unacquainted reader is referred to the cited literature on the particular calculi for background; alternatively, she may safely skip examples pertaining to areas where she lacks background.

2 Definitions

2.1 Transition Systems and Composition

We consider the standard notion of non-labelled transition systems:

Definition 1 (Transition Systems). *A* transition system *is a tuple* $(\mathcal{P}, \longrightarrow)$ *where*

1. $\mathcal{P}$ *is a set of* processes, *ranged over by* P, Q, R, S, T, *and*
2. $\longrightarrow \subseteq \mathcal{P} \times \mathcal{P}$ *is called the* transition relation.

We write $P \longrightarrow Q$ *for* $(P, Q) \in \longrightarrow$, *and let* $\Longrightarrow$ *denote the reflexive and transitive closure of* $\longrightarrow$.

Definition 2 (Composition). *Let* $(\mathcal{P}, \longrightarrow)$ *be a transition system. A function* $\otimes : \mathcal{P} \times \mathcal{P} \rightarrow \mathcal{P}$ *is a* composition *if* $(\mathcal{P}, \otimes)$ *is a commutative semigroup, i.e. if it is associative and commutative. For* $n > 1$ *we write* $P^n_\otimes$ *to mean* $P \otimes P \otimes \cdots \otimes P$ *where* P *occurs* n *times.*

Definition 3 (Monotonic Composition). *A composition is* monotonic *if for all $P, Q, R \in \mathcal{P}$, $P \implies Q$ implies $P \otimes R \implies Q \otimes R$. A composition that is not monotonic is called* non-monotonic.

Most examples discussed in this paper are on languages with a parallel operator denoted $|$ as part of their syntax; unless otherwise specified, this is the composition that we have in mind. But formally $\otimes$ need not be part of the process syntax. This makes our results applicable in non-algebraic models of concurrency. It also strengthens our separation results since we do not insist that the parallel operator is translated homomorphically. For example, consider $\otimes$ as the disjoint union of place-transition nets. This operation is monotonic since any enabled transition will still be enabled if another net is put on its side. On the other hand, if $\otimes$ is ordinary (non disjoint) union it is non-monotonic, since a transition can become disabled by adding a precondition without a token.

2.2 Consensus Processes

We will separate transition systems based on their ability to represent *consensus processes.* The idea is that P is an f, g-consensus process, where f, g are process predicates, if arbitrarily many copies of P in parallel can reach a state where f holds or a state where g holds, but once either has been reached the other cannot be reached. This captures the intuitive notion of consensus: that the participants can never disagree about whether f or g holds.

Definition 4 (Process Predicates). *A* process predicate *of a transition system $(\mathcal{P}, \longrightarrow)$ is a function $f : \mathcal{P} \rightarrow \mathbb{B}$.*

A predicate f is

- $P, \otimes$-extensible *if $f(Q)$ implies $f(P \otimes Q)$;*
- $P, \otimes$-stable *if for all P', n such that $P^n_\otimes \implies P'$, f is $P', \otimes$-extensible.*

If the choice of $\otimes$ is clear from the context we often write P-stable to mean $P, \otimes$-stable. Intuitively it means that for all n, the composition with any derivative of $P^n_\otimes$ preserves f. Stable predicates are used to signal consensus; in this context stability means that once a clique of greasers decide to declare for either Elvis or Jerry, their decision remains firm in the presence of other greasers who did not partake in the decision.

Definition 5 (Consensus Process). *Let $(\mathcal{P}, \longrightarrow)$ be a transition system with composition $\otimes$. A process P is an* f,g-consensus process over $\otimes$ *if f, g are P-stable predicates such that for all $n > 1$:*

1. (can choose f) *there exists P' such that $P^n_\otimes \implies P'$ and $f(P')$ holds;*
2. (can choose g) *there exists P' such that $P^n_\otimes \implies P'$ and $g(P')$ holds; and*
3. (no conflict) *whenever $P^n_\otimes \implies P' \implies P''$, $f(P')$ implies $\neg g(P'')$, and $g(P')$ implies $\neg f(P'')$*

We say that a process P is a consensus process over $\otimes$ *if there are f, g such that P is an f, g-consensus process over $\otimes$.*

When the choice of $\otimes$ is clear from the context or irrelevant, we will often write *consensus process* to mean *consensus process over* $\otimes$.

To continue the informal example of place-transition nets: with disjoint union there exists no consensus process. This is a consequence of Theorem 15 in Sect. 3 since disjoint union is monotonic. With ordinary union we have a trivial consensus process: a net where a place with one token is precondition for two different transitions with postconditions f and g. Since union is idempotent $P^n_\cup = P$ (in other words, taking any number of greasers results in just the one greaser), and the three requirements above are satisfied.

Note that our requirements are weak in the sense that we allow P to diverge and to reach a deadlocked state. In this sense a consensus process is not of much practical use. We could add more requirements to make it more realistic, but using weak requirements strengthens our separation results: non-monotonic composition cannot solve consensus even if we admit "solutions" that do not always terminate with a result. Note that all examples of consensus processes that we exhibit in this paper are guaranteed to eventually reach consensus, and all save for Examples 8 and 9 are guaranteed to eventually terminate. In those two examples, there are other consensus processes that do terminate.

2.3 Examples of Consensus Processes

Example 6 (Test-and-set).

A multiset of anonymous threads run on a CPU with two shared memory cells x, y, both initially set to 0. The threads have the following two instructions, both of which are executed atomically:

test-and-set(x, n, z)	Put value n at cell x, and put the old value of x at z.
exit-if(x, n)	If the value at memory cell x is n, terminate.

Let $P(n)$ be a process that runs the following instruction sequence, where z is a private memory cell:

1 **test-and-set**$(x, 1, z)$
2 **exit-if**$(z, 1)$
3 **test-and-set**(y, n, z)

Then $\{P(1), P(2)\}$ is a consensus process over multiset union for predicates $y = 1$ and $y = 2$. What makes this possible is that the **test-and-set** instruction allows processes to detect whether or not they won the initial data race on x. The winner then writes her value of choice to y, while the losers all terminate.

Below, we show several examples of process calculi whose parallel operators are non-monotonic composition operators that can express consensus processes. Note that the requisite that composition is associative and commutative means that for applications to process calculi, we consider processes to be implicitly quotiented by structural congruence.

For predicates we will often use *barbs*, denoted $\downarrow_x$. We write $P \downarrow_x$ to mean that the process P offers a potential synchronisation on the channel x to the environment.

Example 7 (Broadcast π). In broadcast π [3], a sender process $\overline{a}\,x$ sends x on the channel a; when this happens, every listener $a(z).P$ on channel a instantly receives x and continues as $P[z := x]$. The following is a consensus process over $|$ in (asynchronous) broadcast π:

$$\overline{a}\,x \mid \overline{a}\,y \mid a(z).\overline{z}$$

where the process predicates are $\downarrow_x$ and $\downarrow_y$. The idea is that consensus is reached on whichever of x or y gets sent on a first. Further outputs on a can happen, but are immaterial since nobody listens. We use the non-labelled semantics for broadcast π given in [9].

Example 8 (CBS). In the broadcast calculus CBS as presented in [15], there are no channels; all messages are broadcast on the same unnamed ether. This example illustrates how to use predicates other than barbs in consensus processes, suggesting a way to connect our work to Gorla's criteria on correct encodings [16], where barbs are absent. CBS offers a *guarded choice* operator $x?p \ \&\ a!q$ that works as follows: if the environment broadcasts a message b, the process receives it and proceeds as $p[x := b]$. It may alternatively broadcast a to the environment and proceed as q. We can exploit this operator to define a consensus process over $|$ in CBS as follows:

$$x?0 \ \&\ a!\Omega \mid x?0 \ \&\ a!\checkmark$$

Here Ω is a divergent process, $\checkmark$ is the successful process, and 0 is a process with no outgoing transitions. The process predicates are "the process has diverged" and "the process has reached success".

Example 9 (CCS with Priorities). In CCS with priorities [4], underlined actions have high priority and no low-priority action can be taken if a high-priority action is possible. Let $P(x) = \tau.(\underline{x} \mid \textbf{fix}\ X.(\underline{\tau}.X))$. The process

$$P(x) \mid P(y)$$

is an $\downarrow_x$,$\downarrow_y$-consensus process over $|$ in CCS with priorities. The intuition is that once a choice has been made between x and y, all further choices are blocked because the process $\textbf{fix}\ X.(\underline{\tau}.X)$ takes precedence indefinitely.

Example 10 (cc-pi). cc-pi [5] is a calculus for specifying and negotiating quality of service requirements. It combines and extends elements of the name passing and concurrent constraint programming paradigms. The cc-pi agent **tell** c can take a step that consists in adding the constraint c to the constraint store; however, this step may only be performed if the resulting constraint store is consistent.

Let c, c' be two constraints such that their composition $c \times c'$ is inconsistent. Then the process

$$\textbf{tell}\ c \mid \textbf{tell}\ c'$$

is a consensus process over $\mid$ in cc-pi, with process predicates $\vdash c$ (meaning that the store implies c) and $\vdash c'$.

Example 11 (Psi-calculi). Psi-calculi [7] is a family of pi-calculus extensions that is parameterised on *assertions*. Assertions are facts about the environment in which processes execute. They may occur as part of the process syntax, and influence which transitions may be taken.

Consider a psi-calculus that has assertions Ψ, Ψ' that disable all further transitions. Further, let this psi-calculus have two distinct conditions ϕ, ϕ' such that $\Psi \vdash \phi$ and $\Psi' \vdash \phi'$. Then

$$\tau.(\!|\Psi|\!) \mid \tau.(\!|\Psi'|\!)$$

is a consensus process over $\mid$, where the predicates are $\vdash \phi$ and $\vdash \phi'$. There will only ever be one transition; this transition will also unguard assertions such that exactly one of $\vdash \phi$ and $\vdash \phi'$ holds. Note that the assertion logic for this psi-calculus is non-monotonic.

Example 12 (FAP). The calculus FAP [9] is a minimal fragment of CCS with priorities that contains only input, output, nil and parallel composition. Output does not have continuations, but can have either high or low priority; $\underline{\overline{x}}$ denotes high priority output on channel x, which preempts synchronisations involving low priority outputs $\overline{y}$ on all names y. Let $P(x) = a.b.(x \mid \underline{\overline{c}})$. Then the following is a consensus process in FAP for predicates $\downarrow_x$ and $\downarrow_y$.

$$\overline{a} \mid \underline{\overline{b}} \mid c.(b \mid \underline{\overline{c}}) \mid P(x) \mid P(y)$$

Initially, the only available transition is a synchronisation on a, in which either $P(x)$ or $P(y)$ takes a step. At this point the choice between x and y has already been made, but not yet communicated with the world. The synchronisation on b acts as a lock (which is initially unlocked) to make sure no other choice has already been communicated. Once a process has communicated its choice, it initiates a chain reaction of synchronisations on c, which closes all locks by consuming all the available outputs on b. After that, the remaining participants may still choose between taking steps from either $P(x)$ and $P(y)$, yet a conflict is avoided because the locks prevent this choice from being communicated by exposing x or y.

Example 13 (CPG). CPG [8] augments CCS with *priority guards* $U : \alpha.P$, where α is an action and U is a set of actions. The intuition is that $U : \alpha.P$ may act as $\alpha.P$ unless the environment offers an action in U. In the latter case $U : \alpha.P$ is blocked from proceeding until the environment ceases to offer actions from U. A consensus process in CPG with predicates $\downarrow_x$ and $\downarrow_y$ can be written

$$P(x) \mid P(y) \mid \overline{a}$$

where $P(x) = \{u\} : a.(\overline{u}|\overline{x})$. The intuition is that once a synchronisation on a where either $P(x)$ or $P(y)$ participates has been performed, all other processes are blocked from doing so by the offer being made on u.

Example 14 (TPL). Hennessy and Regan's *Temporal Process Language* [6] (*TPL* for short) extends CCS with a notion of discrete time. The main addition is the prefix $\sigma.P$, meaning that P will execute after one unit of time has passed. The time model of TPL assumes that time can only pass when there are no possible synchronisations; this is a common feature of timed calculi known as the *maximal progress assumption*. Formally, $P \xrightarrow{\sigma} P'$ can only happen if $P \not\xrightarrow{\tau}$. The effect of the σ-transition on P is to consume all top-level σ prefixes — this means that TPL assumes all agents to have synchronised clocks.

We define a non-labelled transition relation for TPL as $\longrightarrow \triangleq \xrightarrow{\tau} \cup \xrightarrow{\sigma}$. The following is an $\downarrow_x, \downarrow_y$-consensus process over $|$ in TPL:

$$\textbf{rec } X.(\sigma.(\tau.\overline{x} + \tau.\overline{y}) + \overline{a} + \underline{a}.X)$$

Intuitively, a synchronisation on a means that the sender waives the choice between $\downarrow_x$ and $\downarrow_y$. These synchronisations continue until all but one process have waived. At that point no further synchronisations are possible, and time passes for the one remaining process, unguarding the choice between $\overline{x}$ and $\overline{y}$.

3 A Method for Separation Results

In expressiveness it is common to distinguish *absolute expressiveness*, where languages are compared based on their ability to solve certain problems; and *relative expressiveness*, where languages are compared based on whether it is possible to define an encoding between them satisfying certain quality criteria. The following theorem yields an absolute expressiveness result:

Theorem 15. *Let $(\mathcal{P}, \longrightarrow)$ be a transition system with monotonic composition $\otimes$. Then there is no consensus process over $\otimes$.*

Proof (Mechanised in Isabelle). By contradiction. Assume that P is an f, g-consensus process over $\otimes$, and let $n > 1$. By Definition 5.1–2 there exists P', P'' such that $P^n_\otimes \Longrightarrow P'$ and $P^n_\otimes \Longrightarrow P''$, where $f(P')$ and $g(P'')$. By monotonicity of $\otimes$, we get $P^n_\otimes \otimes P^n_\otimes \Longrightarrow P' \otimes P^n_\otimes$ and $P' \otimes P^n_\otimes \Longrightarrow P' \otimes P''$. Hence $P^{2n}_\otimes \Longrightarrow P' \otimes P''$. By the definition of stability we get $f(P' \otimes P'')$ and $g(P' \otimes P'')$, contradicting Definition 5.3.

The main use of this theorem is to obtain relative separation results between a source language $\mathcal{S}$ and a target language $\mathcal{T}$, by the following method:

1. Exhibit a consensus process in $\mathcal{S}$.
2. Show that the composition under consideration in $\mathcal{T}$ is monotonic.

3. Obtain non-encodability of $\mathcal{S}$ in $\mathcal{T}$ by applying the corollaries of Theorem 15 to be introduced in Sects. 3.1 and 3.2.

The two corollaries yield non-encodability with two different kinds of encodings: *uniform* and *observation-respecting*. The rest of this section is devoted to defining them, and proving that they map consensus processes to consensus processes.

3.1 Uniform Encodings

We here consider a weakening of the criteria used by Ene and Muntean [3] to separate the π-calculus and the broadcast π-calculus.

Definition 16 (Invariant Predicates). *A process predicate f is P-*invariant *if for all Q, Q' such that $P \Longrightarrow Q \Longrightarrow Q'$ and $f(Q)$ it holds that $f(Q')$.*

Definition 17 (Uniform Encoding)
A relation $\prec$ on states is f-preserving *if $P \prec Q$ and $f(P)$ implies $f(Q)$. An encoding $[\![\cdot]\!] : \mathcal{P} \Rightarrow \mathcal{Q}$ between transition systems $(\mathcal{P}, \longrightarrow_{\mathcal{P}})$ and $(\mathcal{Q}, \longrightarrow_{\mathcal{Q}})$ is $f, g, \otimes_{\mathcal{P}}, \otimes_{\mathcal{Q}}$-*uniform *for the predicates $f, g : \mathcal{P} \Rightarrow \mathbb{B}$ and composition operators $\otimes_{\mathcal{P}}, \otimes_{\mathcal{Q}}$ if there exists $\hat{f}, \hat{g} : \mathcal{Q} \Rightarrow \mathbb{B}$ with an $\hat{f}, \hat{g}$-preserving relation $\prec$ and:*

1. *$P \longrightarrow_{\mathcal{P}} P'$ implies $[\![P]\!] \Longrightarrow_{\mathcal{Q}} Q' \succ [\![P']\!]$ for some Q'.*
2. *If $[\![P]\!] \Longrightarrow_{\mathcal{Q}} Q$ then there exists P', Q' such that $P \Longrightarrow_{\mathcal{P}} P'$ and $Q \Longrightarrow_{\mathcal{Q}} Q' \prec [\![P']\!]$.*
3. *If f is P-stable then $\hat{f}$ is $[\![P]\!]$-stable, if f is P-invariant then $\hat{f}$ is $[\![P]\!]$-invariant, and $f(P)$ iff $\hat{f}([\![P]\!])$.*
4. *If g is P-stable then $\hat{g}$ is $[\![P]\!]$-stable, if g is P-invariant then $\hat{g}$ is $[\![P]\!]$-invariant, and $g(P)$ iff $\hat{g}([\![P]\!])$.*
5. *$[\![P \otimes_{\mathcal{P}} P']\!] = [\![P]\!] \otimes_{\mathcal{Q}} [\![P']\!]$.*

Clauses 17.1 and 17.2 are called *operational correspondence*, and capture the intuition that an encoding should preserve and reflect the source language's transition behaviour. The role of the relation $\prec$ is to perform garbage collection of junk terms that the encoding may produce. In the literature on relative expressiveness a behavioural equivalence is typically used for the same purpose; we do not insist on equivalences since weaker conditions yield stronger separation results. The extra catch-up transition from Q in Clause 17.2 allows for the encoding to mimic behaviour with protocols whose intermediary states have no direct counterpart in the target language.

Clauses 17.3 and 17.4 state that the process predicates used to signal consensus in the source language must have some corresponding predicates in the target language.

Clause 17.5 states that the encoding must be strongly compositional w.r.t. the composition operators under consideration. This requisite captures the intuition that the encoding must preserve the degree of distribution of the source language.

Definition 18 (Power-invariant Predicates). *A process predicate f is* $P, \otimes$-power-invariant *if for all n, f is $P^n_\otimes$-invariant.*

Thus power-invariance means that for all derivatives of $P^n_\otimes$, if f becomes true it stays true.

Theorem 19. *If P is an f, g-consensus process over $\otimes_\mathcal{P}$, and if $[\![\cdot]\!]$ is an $f, g, \otimes_\mathcal{P}, \otimes_\mathcal{Q}$-uniform encoding, and if f, g are $P, \otimes_\mathcal{P}$-power-invariant, then $[\![P]\!]$ is an $\hat{f}, \hat{g}, \otimes_\mathcal{Q}$-consensus process.*

Proof (Mechanised in Isabelle). We discharge each clause of Definition 5 as follows:

1. By the definition of consensus process, for all $n > 1$ there exists P' such that $P^n_{\otimes_\mathcal{P}} \Longrightarrow_\mathcal{P} P'$ and $f(P')$. Since $[\![\cdot]\!]$ is uniform there exists Q such that $[\![P]\!]^n_{\otimes_\mathcal{Q}} = [\![P^n_{\otimes_\mathcal{P}}]\!] \Longrightarrow_\mathcal{Q} Q \succ [\![P']\!]$. By definition of uniform encoding we get $\hat{f}([\![P']\!])$, and since $[\![P']\!] \prec Q$, $\hat{f}(Q)$ follows.
2. The same, except substitute g for f.
3. By contradiction. Assume $[\![P]\!]^n_{\otimes_\mathcal{Q}} = [\![P^n_{\otimes_\mathcal{P}}]\!] \Longrightarrow_\mathcal{Q} Q \Longrightarrow_\mathcal{Q} Q'$ with $\hat{f}(Q)$ and $\hat{g}(Q')$. By uniformity of $[\![\cdot]\!]$ there exists P', Q'' such that $P^n_{\otimes_\mathcal{P}} \Longrightarrow_\mathcal{P} P'$ and $Q' \Longrightarrow_\mathcal{Q} Q'' \prec [\![P']\!]$. By invariance, we get $\hat{f}(Q'')$ and $\hat{g}(Q'')$; since $Q'' \prec [\![P']\!]$ we get $\hat{f}([\![P']\!])$ and $\hat{g}([\![P']\!])$. By uniformity of $[\![\cdot]\!]$ it then follows that $f(P')$ and $g(P')$, contradicting Definition 5.3.

Corollary 20. *If there exists an f, g-consensus process P over $\otimes_\mathcal{P}$, and if $\otimes_\mathcal{Q}$ is a monotonic composition, and if f, g are $P, \otimes_\mathcal{P}$-power-invariant, then there is no $f, g, \otimes_\mathcal{P}, \otimes_\mathcal{Q}$-uniform encoding from $\mathcal{P}$ to $\mathcal{Q}$.*

Remark 21. The invariance side conditions imposed on all process predicates used in this section are necessary to prevent a scenario where $\hat{f}$ or $\hat{g}$ may hold in some intermediate state of the target language, but ceases to hold once a state corresponding to a source language state is reached.

In practice this restriction is not severe. Of the consensus processes we consider in this paper, all but one satisfy it. The exception is the consensus process for broadcast π from Example 7, where the output $\overline{x}$ that signals consensus is non-blocking; hence it may take the transition $\overline{x} \longrightarrow 0$, causing the predicate $\downarrow_x$ to no longer hold. Fortunately, the example can be adjusted so that $\downarrow_x$ and $\downarrow_y$ are power-invariant by simply replicating the consensus signals:

$$\overline{a}\,x \mid \overline{a}\,y \mid a(z).!\overline{z}$$

3.2 Observation-Respecting Encodings

Definition 22 (Computations). *Given a transition system $(\mathcal{P}, \longrightarrow)$, the* computations, *ranged over by C, are finite or infinite sequences of processes such that* *for every process P in $\mathcal{C}$ that has a successor Q, it holds that $P \longrightarrow Q$. A computation is* maximal *if it cannot be extended, i.e. either the computation is infinite or there are no transitions from the tail.*

We overload process predicates so that we may also apply them to computations. Let $f(\mathcal{C})$, where $\mathcal{C} = P_0, P_1, \ldots$ mean that there exists i such that $f(P_i)$.

Definition 23 (Observation-respecting Encodings). *An encoding $[\![\cdot]\!] : \mathcal{P} \Rightarrow \mathcal{Q}$ between transition systems $(\mathcal{P}, \longrightarrow_{\mathcal{P}})$ and $(\mathcal{Q}, \longrightarrow_{\mathcal{Q}})$ is $f, g, \otimes_{\mathcal{P}}, \otimes_{\mathcal{Q}}$-*respecting *for the predicates $f, g : \mathcal{P} \Rightarrow \mathbb{B}$ and composition operators $\otimes_{\mathcal{P}}, \otimes_{\mathcal{Q}}$ if there are predicates $\hat{f}, \hat{g} : \mathcal{Q} \Rightarrow \mathbb{B}$ such that*

1. *For every maximal computation $\mathcal{C}$ starting from P, there exists a maximal computation $\mathcal{C}'$ starting from $[\![P]\!]$ such that $f(\mathcal{C})$ iff $\hat{f}(\mathcal{C}')$, and $g(\mathcal{C})$ iff $\hat{g}(\mathcal{C}')$.*
2. *For every maximal computation $\mathcal{C}$ starting from $[\![P]\!]$, there exists a maximal computation $\mathcal{C}'$ starting from P such that if $\hat{f}(\mathcal{C})$ then $f(\mathcal{C}')$, and if $\hat{g}(\mathcal{C})$ then $g(\mathcal{C}')$.*
3. *If f is P-stable then $\hat{f}$ is $[\![P]\!]$-stable.*
4. *If g is P-stable then $\hat{g}$ is $[\![P]\!]$-stable.*
5. *$[\![P \otimes_{\mathcal{P}} P']\!] = [\![P]\!] \otimes_{\mathcal{Q}} [\![P']\!]$.*

This set of criteria is a simplification of the criteria considered in [9], where the term observation-respecting is used with a similar meaning.[1] The intuition behind Clauses 23.1 and 23.2 is that a process and its encoding should have computations with the same observable behaviour. This requisite is often formulated in terms of the computations having the same barbs, but since we are only interested in observing the predicates f, g used to signal consensus we require no more. Clause 23.2 allows target language computations to mimic only a subset of its corresponding source language computation's observables; this means that we admit encodings that may introduce divergence and other failures.

The remaining criteria are similar to the criteria used for uniform encodings, with the notable exception that we do not require invariant predicates in this section.

Theorem 24. *If P is an f, g-consensus process over $\otimes_{\mathcal{P}}$, and if $[\![\cdot]\!]$ is an $f, g, \otimes_{\mathcal{P}}, \otimes_{\mathcal{Q}}$-respecting encoding, then $[\![P]\!]$ is an $\hat{f}, \hat{g}$-consensus process over $\otimes_{\mathcal{Q}}$.*

Proof (Mechanised in Isabelle). We discharge each clause of Definition 5 as follows:

1. By the definition of consensus process, for all $n > 1$ there exists P' such that $P^n_{\otimes_{\mathcal{P}}} \Longrightarrow_{\mathcal{P}} P'$ and $f(P')$. Then for all maximal computations $\mathcal{C}$ from $P^n_{\otimes_{\mathcal{P}}}$ through P' (of which there must be at least one), $f(\mathcal{C})$ holds. Since $[\![\cdot]\!]$ is f, g-respecting there exists $\mathcal{C}'$ starting from $[\![P]\!]^n_{\otimes_{\mathcal{Q}}}$ such that $\hat{f}(\mathcal{C}')$.
2. The same, except substitute g for f.

[1] Confusingly, the same criteria are referred to as "uniform" by Palamidessi [13] and Phillips [8].

3. By contradiction. Assume $[\![P]\!]^n_{\otimes_\mathcal{Q}} = [\![P^n_{\otimes_\mathcal{P}}]\!] \Longrightarrow_\mathcal{Q} Q \Longrightarrow_\mathcal{Q} Q'$ with $\hat{f}(Q)$ and $\hat{g}(Q')$. Then for all maximal computations $\mathcal{C}$ from $[\![P]\!]^n_{\otimes_\mathcal{Q}}$ through Q and Q' (of which there must be at least one), $\hat{f}(\mathcal{C})$ and $\hat{g}(\mathcal{C})$ holds. Since $[\![\cdot]\!]$ is f, g-respecting there exists $\mathcal{C}'$ starting from $P^n_{\otimes_\mathcal{P}}$ such that $f(\mathcal{C}')$ and $g(\mathcal{C}')$. Then $P^n_{\otimes_\mathcal{P}}$ cannot be a consensus process and we have a contradiction.

Corollary 25. *If there exists an f, g-consensus process over $\otimes_\mathcal{P}$, and if $\otimes_\mathcal{Q}$ is a monotonic composition, then there is no $f, g, \otimes_\mathcal{P}, \otimes_\mathcal{Q}$-respecting encoding from $\mathcal{P}$ to $\mathcal{Q}$.*

3.3 Comparing the Criteria

All separation results presented in this paper apply to both uniform and observation-respecting encodings. This may lead the reader to wonder whether the criteria are in fact equivalent; in this section we demonstrate that this is not the case by exhibiting counterexamples.

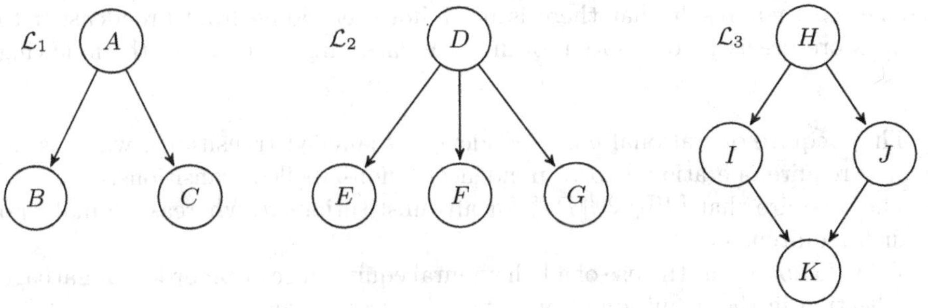

Fig. 1. The transition systems $\mathcal{L}_1, \mathcal{L}_2, \mathcal{L}_3$.

Consider the transition systems $\mathcal{L}_1, \mathcal{L}_2, \mathcal{L}_3$ whose states and transitions are shown in Fig. 1. For state predicates we will use explicit sets of states. We identify a set S with its membership function $\lambda x.x \in S$.

We assume that each of $\mathcal{L}_1, \mathcal{L}_2, \mathcal{L}_3$ additionally has an unreachable junk state $\bot$ where all predicates under consideration implicitly hold. For $\otimes$ we use the function $\lambda(x, y).\bot$ that maps every pair of states to the junk state. Note that this means that all predicates are stable, and renders all our requisites on encodings that concern composition trivially satisfied; hence we ignore composition for the remainder of this section.

There is a $\{B\}, \{C\}$-respecting encoding from $\mathcal{L}_1$ to $\mathcal{L}_3$: choose $\{I\}, \{J\}$ as target language predicates, and map A, B, C respectively to H, I, J. However, there can be no $\{B\}, \{C\}$-uniform encoding from $\mathcal{L}_1$ to $\mathcal{L}_3$ since no choice of target language predicates can simultaneously satisfy all conjuncts of Definition 17.3–4. The reason is that B and C must be mapped to different states, and since $\{B\}$ and $\{C\}$ are invariant the corresponding predicates in $\mathcal{L}_3$ must also be invariant, meaning they must both hold in K and thus cannot be disjoint.

There is an $\{E\}, \{F\}$-uniform encoding from $\mathcal{L}_2$ to $\mathcal{L}_1$: we may choose target language predicates $\{B\}$ and $\{C\}$, and let the encoding map G to A. However, there can be no $\{E\}, \{F\}$-respecting encoding because unlike $\mathcal{L}_2$, there are no maximal computations in $\mathcal{L}_1$ where neither predicate holds.

4 Applications

In this section, we demonstrate the applicability of the method described in Sect. 3 by using it to strengthen several separation results from the literature, and obtain several new separation results.

4.1 Strengthened Results from the Literature

Recall from Example 7 that broadcast π can express consensus processes. Since our requirements on encodings are weaker than Ene and Muntean's, we strengthen their result that there is no uniform encoding from broadcast π to π [3]. More precisely, our notion of uniform encoding is weaker in the following ways:

- They require operational correspondence of labelled transitions, whereas we only require operational correspondence of non-labelled transitions.
- They require that $[\![P]\!]\sigma = [\![P\sigma]\!]$ for all substitutions σ, whereas we make no such requirement.
- They do not admit the use of a behavioural equivalence or preorder for garbage collection in the definition of operational correspondence.
- They require that $[\![P \mid Q]\!] = [\![P]\!] \mid [\![Q]\!]$, whereas we require only that $[\![P \mid Q]\!] = [\![P]\!] \otimes [\![Q]\!]$ for some monotonic composition $\otimes$. For an example, our result also holds if we translate parallel composition with a context, i.e. $[\![P \mid Q]\!] = C[[\![P]\!], [\![Q]\!]]$, where the choice of C may depend on P and Q, given that the context is monotonic, associative and commutative.

From the consensus process exhibited in Example 12, we recover the result of Versari et al. [9] that there is no observation-respecting encoding of FAP in the π-calculus. Again, we achieve a strengthening by not insisting on homomorphic translation of parallel composition. A further strengthening is achieved since they require that observables used to signal the result of a leader election be exactly preserved by the translation, whereas our criteria allow the encoding to use a different signalling mechanism entirely.

From the consensus process exhibited in Example 13, we recover the result of Phillips [8] that the π-calculus has no observation-respecting encoding of CPG. We achieve a strengthening by relaxing their requirements on homomorphic translation of parallel composition, and their requisite that $[\![P]\!]\sigma = [\![P\sigma]\!]$ for all substitutions σ.

4.2 Reliable and Unreliable Broadcast

By *reliable broadcast* we mean that everyone who can listen to a broadcast must listen; this is the communication model of CBS, broadcast π and others. By contrast *unreliable broadcast* means that each potential listener may non-deterministically either hear the broadcast or not; this is the communication model used in CMN [17], broadcast psi-calculi [18] and others. It has been observed by Fehnker et al. that reliable broadcast is more practical for protocol verification, because without it we cannot prove any guarantees about eventual successful message delivery [19]. In this section, we lend additional support to their preference by showing that reliable broadcast is strictly more expressive than unreliable broadcast.

In order to obtain a separation, it suffices to observe that reliable broadcast requires non-monotonic parallel composition, but unreliable broadcast does not. For a slightly informal example, the labelled semantics of broadcast π as presented in [20] contains a rule that looks like this:

$$\frac{P \xrightarrow{\alpha} P' \qquad Q \text{ does not listen to } \alpha}{P \mid Q \xrightarrow{\alpha} P' \mid Q} \ \mathrm{bn}(\alpha) \notin \mathrm{fn}(Q)$$

An unreliable version of broadcast π is obtained by replacing this rule with the usual PAR rule:

$$\frac{P \xrightarrow{\alpha} P'}{P \mid Q \xrightarrow{\alpha} P' \mid Q} \ \mathrm{bn}(\alpha) \notin \mathrm{fn}(Q)$$

Since transitions are considered up to alpha-equivalence of bound names this rule is monotonic parallel; it follows immediately by Corollaries 20 and 25 that there is no observation-respecting or uniform encoding of (reliable) broadcast π in unreliable broadcast π.

Corollary 26. *There is no $\downarrow_x, \downarrow_y, |, |$-respecting or -uniform encoding from broadcast π to unreliable broadcast π.*

However, an encoding in the other direction is possible. It is homomorphic on all operators except input, which is encoded as

$$[\![a(z).P]\!] = (\mathbf{rec}\ X.(a(z).X + a(z).P))$$

Intuitively, the encoding mimics message loss by receiving the message, then pretending it never happened. This encoding enjoys a very tight operational correspondence:

Theorem 27. *For all processes P of unreliable broadcast π it holds that:*

1. *If α is not an input action, then*
   (a) *If $P \xrightarrow{\alpha} P'$ then $[\![P]\!] \xrightarrow{\alpha} [\![P']\!]$.*
   (b) *If $[\![P]\!] \xrightarrow{\alpha} P'$ then there exists P'' such that $P \xrightarrow{\alpha} P''$ and $[\![P'']\!] = P'$.*
2. *If $P \xrightarrow{a\,x} P'$ then $[\![P]\!] \xrightarrow{a\,x} [\![P']\!]$.*
3. *If $[\![P]\!] \xrightarrow{a\,x} P'$ then either $P' = [\![P]\!]$ or there exists P'' such that $P \xrightarrow{a\,x} P''$ and $[\![P'']\!] = P'$.*

Proof. The proof of each clause is by induction on the derivation of the transition. The clauses must be proved in reverse order: the derivation of an output or τ may have premises that depend on the derivation of inputs, but not the other way around.

Hence reliable broadcast communication is strictly more expressive than unreliable broadcast communication. Finally, note that Ene and Muntean's study of the expressiveness of point-to-point versus broadcast communication [3] applies only to reliable broadcast communication; hence the relative expressiveness of point-to-point communication and unreliable broadcast is still an open problem.

4.3 Consistency in Concurrent Constraint Formalisms

In Example 10 we exhibited a consensus process in cc-pi [5], that relies on the fact that cc-pi forbids steps that would lead to an inconsistent constraint store. The ρ-calculus [1] handles inconsistency in a different way: failure (denoted $\perp$) may be reached; once reached, it can be detected and any further computation may be aborted. Since there is no need to check the environment for potential inconsistencies when taking steps in the ρ-calculus, its parallel operator is monotonic; a separation between the ρ-calculus and cc-pi follows immediately.

Corollary 28. *There is no $\vdash c, \vdash c', |, \wedge$-respecting or -uniform encoding from cc-pi to the ρ-calculus, where c, c' are consistent but $c \times c'$ is not.*

$\wedge$ is ρ-calculus notation for the parallel operator. This result illustrates that insisting on consistent stores increases the expressive power of concurrent constraint formalisms.

4.4 Psi-Calculi with Non-monotonic and Monotonic Logics

The psi-calculi framework [7] is parameterised on an arbitrary logic, whose judgements are of the form $\Psi \vdash \varphi$. Here Ψ ranges over *assertions* and φ ranges over *conditions*, and $\vdash$ is the *entailment relation*; all three are parameters that may be chosen freely when instantiating the framework. Assertions may occur in processes, and influence the behaviour of processes in two ways. First, they influence the evaluation of *guards* in conditions. For an example, the agent $(\!|\Psi|\!) \mid$ **if** φ **then** P may take a transition to $(\!|\Psi|\!) \mid P'$ iff $P \longrightarrow P'$ and $\Psi \vdash \varphi$.

Assertions also influence which prefixes are deemed to be *channel equivalent*, i.e. which prefixes represent the same communication channel for the purposes of synchronisation. For an example, the agent $(\!|\Psi|\!) \mid \underline{a}(x).P \mid \overline{b}\,y$ may take a transition to $(\!|\Psi|\!) \mid P[x := y]$ iff $\Psi \vdash a \dot{\leftrightarrow} b$, where the condition $a \dot{\leftrightarrow} b$ is pronounced "a is channel equivalent to b".

Another parameter is the binary operator $\otimes$ on assertions, called *composition*. It determines the influence of parallel assertions upon each other. Let us return to the example above, where $(\!|\Psi|\!) \mid \mathbf{if}\ \varphi\ \mathbf{then}\ P \longrightarrow (\!|\Psi|\!) \mid P'$, and suppose $P' \equiv (\!|\Psi'|\!) \mid P''$. Only unguarded assertions influence behaviour; so now that $(\!|\Psi'|\!)$ has become unguarded, further transitions from P'' with preconditions φ will require that $\Psi \otimes \Psi' \vdash \varphi$ rather than $\Psi \vdash \varphi$.

A psi-calculus is *monotonic* if its logic is monotonic, i.e. if for all Ψ, Ψ', φ it holds that $\Psi \vdash \varphi$ implies $\Psi \otimes \Psi' \vdash \varphi$. Intuitively this means that once a condition becomes true, it will remain true forever. Hence, in a monotonic psi-calculus, adding more assertions to a process may only increase its possible behaviours, and never decrease it. By contrast, in a non-monotonic psi-calculus it may be the case that adding an assertion removes behaviour, if doing so causes the retraction of a condition that was necessary for some transition.

Previous results indicate that monotonic and non-monotonic psi-calculi are fundamentally different beasts: monotonic psi-calculi admit a far simpler treatment of weak equivalences than their non-monotonic counterparts [21], and non-monotonic psi-calculi allow priorities to be encoded [22]. Here, we lend weight to this intuition by obtaining a formal separation result.

Recall the consensus process for non-monotonic psi-calculi from Example 11. We obtain a separation between monotonic and non-monotonic psi-calculi by observing that monotonic psi-calculi have monotonic parallel composition. The rule

$$\frac{P \longrightarrow P'}{P \mid Q \longrightarrow P' \mid Q}$$

is not in general valid in a non-monotonic calculus, because it may be the case that Q contains assertions that retract the necessary conditions for the transition $P \longrightarrow P'$. However, in monotonic psi-calculi it can be derived, since if P itself already contains all necessary assertions for the derivation, then by monotonicity no assertions in Q may invalidate it. Hence

Corollary 29. *There is no $\vdash \varphi, \vdash \varphi', |, |$-respecting or -uniform encoding from the psi-calculus of Example 11 into a psi-calculus with a monotonic logic.*

4.5 Explicit Fusion with Mismatch

The π-calculus is sometimes presented with a mismatch operator $[x{\neq}y]P$, that may behave as P as long as x and y are different. Clearly the π-calculus parallel operator remains monotonic if we add mismatch, since the equality of these names depends on nothing but themselves. However, if we add a mismatch operator to the explicit fusion calculus [23] the situation is different. The explicit fusion calculus has monotonic parallel composition, but with the mismatch operator added, parallel composition becomes non-monotonic: two names that differ in P may be equivalent in $P \mid Q$ if Q fuses them. Indeed, we may then write an $\downarrow_a, \downarrow_b$-consensus process as follows:

$$\overline{x}\, y \mid [y{\neq}z]\underline{x}z.\overline{a} \mid [y{\neq}z]\underline{x}z.\overline{b}$$

In light of the thus obtained separation between explicit fusion with and without mismatch, and the separation between ρ-calculus and cc-pi obtained in Sect. 4.3, an interesting direction for future work would be to revisit Victor and Parrow's result that the ρ-calculus can be encoded in the fusion calculus [2]. As a concluding remark, the authors note that "the question whether more complex constraint systems can be handled in the same way is largely open" [2, p. 469]; the results in this paper suggest that constraint systems allowing only consistent stores are beyond the reach of the fusion calculus. It would be interesting to investigate if adding mismatch allows a good encoding of such constraint systems.

4.6 SCCS: Beyond Monotonic Composition

In this section we consider SCCS [24] as a non-trivial example of a language where the product operator $\times$ is non-monotonic, yet there is no reasonable consensus process over $\times$. To our minds, a reasonable consensus process should use predicates f, g that are *stable under strong bisimulation*, i.e. $f(P)$ and $P \sim Q$ implies $f(Q)$, and analogously for g. Using predicates that are not stable under bisimulation would mean that an observer cannot distinguish between states where f holds and where it does not, which would rather defeat the intuition that f, g signal consensus to the outside world.

SCCS is a variant of CCS where all parallel processes proceed in lockstep, rather than asynchronously as in CCS. It is parameterised on a commutative monoid $(\mathit{Act}, \cdot)$ of *actions*, ranged over by α, β. The derivation rule that can infer transitions from $P \times Q$ is the *product rule*:

$$\frac{P \xrightarrow{\alpha} P' \qquad Q \xrightarrow{\beta} Q'}{P \times Q' \xrightarrow{\alpha\cdot\beta} P' \times Q'}$$

SCCS also has a process 0, called *inaction*, with no outgoing transitions. An immediate consequence of this is that $0 \times P$ also has no outgoing transitions, since the product rule is inapplicable. Hence $0 \times P \sim 0$, where $\sim$ is strong bisimulation.

There are two reasonable ways to define a non-labelled transition relation $\longrightarrow$ from the standard LTS for SCCS: we can either let it be $\xrightarrow{1}$, where 1 is the identity of the action monoid, or $\bigcup_\alpha \xrightarrow{\alpha}$. What follows is independent of which one we choose.

We say that Q *may deadlock* if there is Q' such that $Q \Longrightarrow Q'$ and $Q' \sim 0$.

Theorem 30. *Suppose that f, g are stable under strong bisimulation. Then there is no f, g-consensus process over $\times$ in SCCS.*

Proof. By contradiction; suppose Q is an f, g-consensus process over $\times$, and fix $n > 1$. We proceed by case analysis on whether $Q^n_\times$ may deadlock.

- Suppose that $Q^n_\times$ may deadlock. By the definition of consensus processes we have that there is Q' such that $Q^n_\times \Longrightarrow Q'$ and $f(Q')$; analogously there is Q'' such that $Q^n_\times \Longrightarrow Q''$ and $g(Q'')$. Since $Q^n_\times$ may deadlock we also have that $Q^n_\times \Longrightarrow \sim 0$; by Q-stability of f, g and since f, g are stable under $\sim$, it follows that $f(Q' \times 0) = f(0)$ and $g(Q'' \times 0) = g(0)$. Hence, $Q^n_\times$ may reach a (deadlocked) state where both f and g holds, which contradicts the definition of consensus process.
- Suppose that $Q^n_\times$ may not deadlock. By definition of consensus processes there exists $R_0, \dots, R_i, S_0, \dots, S_j$ such that $Q^n_\times \longrightarrow R_0 \longrightarrow \dots \longrightarrow R_i$ and $Q^n_\times \longrightarrow S_0 \longrightarrow \dots \longrightarrow S_j$, where $f(R_i)$ and $g(S_j)$. Without loss of generality we may assume that $i \leq j$. Since $Q^n_\times$ may not deadlock there is $R_{i+1}, \dots, R_j$ such that $R_i \longrightarrow R_{i+1} \longrightarrow \dots \longrightarrow R_j$. By applying the product rule j times we get $Q^{2n}_\times \Longrightarrow R_i \times S_i \Longrightarrow R_j \times S_j$. By Q-stability we have $f(R_i \times S_i)$ and $g(R_j \times S_j)$, contradicting Definition 5.3.

Intuitively, $\times$ alone cannot express consensus processes since despite its non-monotonicity, it affords no way for one operand to constrain the behaviour of the other — unless it stops the world by unguarding 0, but in a stopped world we cannot observe what the consensus is. In SCCS the capability to constrain the behaviour of others is instead found in the interplay between the product and restriction operators. Theorem 30 does not contradict Holmer's result that there is a fully abstract encoding from CBS to SCCS [25]; what it does mean is that if we insist on encodings that satisfy $[\![P \mid Q]\!] = [\![P]\!] \times [\![Q]\!]$, Holmer's encodability result becomes a separation result.

4.7 Maximal Progress in Timed Calculi

In this section we revisit the result of Corradini et al. [26] that TPL is strictly more expressive than Moller and Toft's *loose Temporal CCS* [27] (abbreviated *lTCCS*). Our result has fewer conditions on how the encoding preserves semantics.

Recall from Exampe 14 that by using the maximal progress assumption of TPL [6] we may write a consensus process. Some calculi eschew the maximal progress assumption, and allow time to pass even if there are synchronisations that could happen; lTCCS is an example. There are two main technical differences from TPL:

- lTCCS uses an explicit time domain ranged over by s, t, and has a prefix $(t).P$, meaning that P will execute after t units of time have passed.
- A transition labelled t represents the passage of t time units. Every process may always take a t-transition.

Analogously with TPL, the non-labelled transition relation for lTCCS is the union of the τ transitions and the time elapsing steps. The parallel operator of lTCCS is non-monotonic — clocks are synchronised, as modelled by the only rule for inferring t-transitions from $P \mid Q$:

$$\frac{P \xrightarrow{t} P' \qquad P \xrightarrow{t} Q'}{P \mid Q \xrightarrow{t} P' \mid Q'}$$

Nonetheless, there is no consensus process in lTCCS:

Theorem 31. *There exists no consensus process over $\mid$ in lTCCS.*

Proof (Sketch). By contradiction. Assume P is an f, g-consensus process and fix $n > 1$. We have that $P^n \Longrightarrow P'$ and $P^n \Longrightarrow P''$ such that $f(P')$ and $g(P'')$. Then there exists R, S such that there is a transition sequence from P^{2n} that goes through both $P' \mid R$ and $S \mid P''$, where $P^n \Longrightarrow R$ and $P^n \Longrightarrow S$. By P-stability of f, g we obtain a contradiction with the definition of consensus process.

Note that the transition sequences from P^n to P' must be inferred from synchronisations interspersed with time elapsing, i.e. it performs an action sequence with labels $\widetilde{\alpha} = \widetilde{\tau} s_0 \widetilde{\tau} s_1 \ldots \widetilde{\tau} s_n \widetilde{\tau}$. The transition to P'' analogously looks like $\widetilde{\beta} = \widetilde{\tau} t_0 \widetilde{\tau} t_1 \ldots \widetilde{\tau} t_n \widetilde{\tau}$.

A transition sequence from $P^{2n} = P^n \mid P^n$ containing both $P' \mid R$ and $S \mid P''$ is then constructed via the following algorithm:

1. Perform all τ steps occurring before the first time steps of $\widetilde{\alpha}, \widetilde{\beta}$, applied respectively to the LHS and RHS of the outermost parallel operator.
2. If $s_0 \leq t_0$, perform an s_0-step. Then iterate these steps for $\widetilde{\alpha} = \widetilde{\tau} s_1 \ldots \widetilde{\tau} s_n \widetilde{\tau}$ and $\widetilde{\beta} = t_0' \widetilde{\tau} t_1 \ldots \widetilde{\tau} t_n \widetilde{\tau}$, where $t_0 = s_0 + t_0'$, until both sequences are empty. If $t_0 < s_0$ do the same except swap $\widetilde{\alpha}, \widetilde{\beta}$ and s, t.

When $\widetilde{\alpha}$ is empty, the LHS of the resulting process is exactly P'. When $\widetilde{\beta}$ is empty the RHS is exactly P''.

Corollary 32. *There is no $\downarrow_x, \downarrow_y, |, |$-respecting or -uniform encoding from TPL to lTCCS.*

Intuitively the separation holds because with maximal progress, processes can gain information about other processes through the passage of time. A process offering a synchronisation on a will know, once time passes, that no other process was willing to meet the offer. When time may pass at any time, processes learn nothing from its passage.

Corradini et al. [26] exhibit an encoding in the reverse direction that is fully abstract wrt. strong bisimulation. They then show that there can be no encoding $[\![\cdot]\!]$ from lTCCS to TPL such that $[\![P]\!] \sim [\![Q]\!]$ implies $P \sim Q$, if we additionally require that the encoding preserves labelled transitions exactly, i.e. $P \xrightarrow{\alpha} Q$ implies $[\![P]\!] \xrightarrow{\alpha} [\![Q]\!]$. For a separation result, this is a very strong semantic correspondence that rules out a priori any encoding that uses a non-trivial protocol. From Corollary 32 we obtain a separation result for encodings with a significantly weaker semantic correspondence, at the expense of requiring homomorphic translation of the parallel operator.

5 Isabelle Implementation

In order to obtain increased confidence in the correctness of our developments, we have formally proved Theorems 15, 19 and 24 and their Corollaries 20 and 25 in the interactive theorem prover Isabelle/HOL [10]. The proof scripts are available online [11]. This accounts for all the results presented in this paper that do not pertain to particular languages; mechanising those proofs would require that we first mechanise the languages under consideration, an arduous task that would justify a paper of its own.

Our mechanisation consists of 1000 lines of code and took less than a week in total to develop, meaning that the marginal cost of mechanising these results has been rather small. Perhaps surprisingly, the most challenging work was the proof of a technical lemma concerning computations: namely, that for every process P there is a maximal computation starting from P. We have chosen to mechanise computations using Lochbihler's formalisation of coinductive lists [28]. This allows us to handle finite and infinite computations in a uniform way, and grants access to the powerful proof technique of coinduction. Since we do not have a concrete transition system to work with, obtaining a witness to the existence of a maximal computation is problematic. We achieve this using iteration over the Hilbert choice function ϵ, which given a predicate A returns an arbitrary witness to the predicate if one exists (using the axiom of choice). We then prove by coinduction that the sequence $P_0, P_1, \ldots$ is a maximal computation from P, where $P_0 = P$, and $P_{n+1} = \epsilon(\lambda P'.\ P_n \longrightarrow P')$, and the candidate predicate is the set of all such iterations from P. It is unclear to us if a proof exists that avoids using the axiom of choice, at least if we insist on carrying out the proof in an abstract setting.

Isabelle's locale mechanism [29] allows us to define a local context that states what constants must be defined and what axioms they must satisfy. The proofs of our main results are carried out in this context. A locale may be *interpreted* by instantiating the constants of the locale with concrete transition systems, and showing that they satisfy the axioms; Isabelle then automatically generates concrete instances of all theorems proven in the abstract within the locale. This means that our Isabelle developments are easy to re-use and build upon.

6 Conclusion

We have defined a method for separation results between non-monotonic and monotonic composition operators, based on their ability or inability to express consensus processes. We have demonstrated the wide applicability of our method by improving on several results from the literature, and exhibiting several novel separation results. Machine-checked proofs of our main results yield high confidence in the correctness of the method.

The idea of providing methods for separation results without committing to the precise languages under comparison has been previously introduced by Gorla [16], who offers two methods. One is for separation between languages that contain inert P such that $P \mid P$ may take transitions, and those that do not; the other is for separation between languages based on their *matching degree* (the least upper bound on how many names must match to yield a transition), where greater matching degrees lead to greater expressiveness. These methods allow many well-known separation results from the literature to be proved in a simple and uniform way. However, Gorla's methods are not applicable to the separation results considered in this paper.

Palamidessi's result that mixed choice π-calculus is more expressive than separate choice π-calculus [30] was derived using leader election-based techniques; Peters and Nestmann achieved a stronger version of the same result by abstracting away from leader election and focusing instead on the problem of breaking symmetries in general [31]. Similarly to our work, Peters and Nestmann can then drop Palamidessi's requirement that the translation respects substitutions, i.e. that for all P, σ it holds that $[\![P]\!]\sigma = [\![P\theta]\!]$ for some substitution θ.

While our criteria on encodings and the languages under consideration are remarkably weak, different criteria may of course yield different results. For an example, there is an encoding of CBS into CCS due to Prasad [32], so clearly our separation results cannot hold if we weaken our criteria so that they are compatible with his. Prasad's encoding works by introducing a handler for every parallel operator that is responsible for distributing transmitted messages to the left, right and to the environment. These three activities are performed on distinct channels, so the encoding of a subterm will differ depending on whether it occurs to the left or to the right of the innermost parallel operator, meaning that it is not a composition in our sense. Further, neither $[\![P]\!]$ nor $[\![Q]\!]$ occur as subterms of $[\![P \mid Q]\!]$, so the encoding is not compositional in the sense of Gorla [16].

Traditionally, many separation results have been proven with homomorphic translation of the parallel operator as a criterion. This is usually justified by the intuition that an encoding should preserve the degree of distribution of the source language. We agree with this intuition. Our criterion that $[\![P \mid Q]\!] = [\![P]\!] \otimes [\![Q]\!]$ for some monotonic composition $\otimes$ is weaker, and can be seen as a less syntactic way to state that the degree of distribution should be preserved.

Another way to obtain a weaker criterion that still guarantees preservation of the degree of distribution has been proposed by Peters et al. [33]. Their approach is more focused on syntactic distributability, and more specifically tailored towards process calculi. It assumes that the process languages have a syntax where subprocesses can be composed with operators in an algebraic manner, and have *capabilities*, i.e. parts of a process that are removed when it transitions (such as prefixes in process calculi). Distributability is then a syntactic property of processes, where (roughly stated) a process is distributable into its set of top-level capabilities. An encoding preserves distributability if whenever a source process is distributable into some components, the target process is distributable into the same number of components, where each component of the target process is behaviourally equivalent to a corresponding component of the source process.

Hence our approach offers more flexibility in the kind of languages it can be applied to, and in designing encodings that are semantically but not syntactically distributable. For example, a *normal form* of a π-calculus process P is an equivalent process on the form $\Sigma_i\ \alpha_i.P_i$, where each P_i is also on normal form. An encoding that translates every agent of the finite fragment of the π-calculus to its normal form would satisfy our criterion that parallel must be translated by monotonic composition, but does not preserve the degree of distribution in the sense of Peters et. al. On the other hand, they do not insist on associativity and commutativity of the contexts that parallel translates into, which offers some flexibility in designing encodings that is not available with our criteria. For future work, it would be interesting to investigate if a fruitful synthesis can be achieved.

Acknowledgments. We are grateful to the anonymous reviewers for their many constructive comments.

References

1. Niehren, J., Smolka, G.: A confluent relational calculus for higher-order programming with constraints. In: Jouannaud, J.-P. (ed.) CCL 1994. LNCS, vol. 845, pp. 89–104. Springer, Heidelberg (1994)
2. Victor, B., Parrow, J.: Concurrent constraints in the fusion calculus. In: Larsen, K.G., Skyum, S., Winskel, G. (eds.) ICALP 1998. LNCS, vol. 1443, pp. 455–469. Springer, Heidelberg (1998)
3. Ene, C., Muntean, T.: Expressiveness of point-to-point versus broadcast communications. In: Ciobanu, G., Păun, G. (eds.) FCT 1999. LNCS, vol. 1684, pp. 258–268. Springer, Heidelberg (1999)
4. Cleaveland, R., Hennessy, M.: Priorities in process algebras. In: LICS, pp. 193–202. IEEE Computer Society (1988)
5. Buscemi, M.G., Montanari, U.: CC-Pi: a constraint-based language for specifying service level agreements. In: De Nicola, R. (ed.) ESOP 2007. LNCS, vol. 4421, pp. 18–32. Springer, Heidelberg (2007)
6. Hennessy, M., Regan, T.: A process algebra for timed systems. Inf. Comput. **117**, 221–239 (1995)
7. Bengtson, J., Johansson, M., Parrow, J., Victor, B.: Psi-calculi: mobile processes, nominal data, and logic. In: Proceedings of LICS 2009, pp. 39–48. IEEE (2009)

8. Phillips, I.: CCS with priority guards. In: Larsen, K.G., Nielsen, M. (eds.) CONCUR 2001. LNCS, vol. 2154, pp. 305–320. Springer, Heidelberg (2001)
9. Versari, C., Busi, N., Gorrieri, R.: On the expressive power of global and local priority in process calculi. In: Caires, L., Vasconcelos, V.T. (eds.) CONCUR 2007. LNCS, vol. 4703, pp. 241–255. Springer, Heidelberg (2007)
10. Nipkow, T., Paulson, L.C., Wenzel, M.: Isabelle/HOL: a Proof Assistant for Higher-Order Logic. Lecture Notes in Computer Science, vol. 2283. Springer, Heidelberg (2002)
11. Åman Pohjola, J.: The expressive power of monotonic parallel composition. http://www.it.uu.se/research/group/mobility/theorem/monopar.tgz. Isabelle 2014/HOL formalisation of the definitions, theorems and proofs
12. Bougé, L.: On the existence of symmetric algorithms to find leaders in networks of communicating sequential processes. Acta Inf. **25**, 179–201 (1988)
13. Palamidessi, C.: Comparing the expressive power of the synchronous and the asynchronous π-calculus. In: Proceedings of the 24th ACM SIGPLAN-SIGACT Symposium on Principles of Programming Languages. POPL 1997, 256–265. ACM, New York (1997)
14. Fischer, M.J., Lynch, N.A., Paterson, M.S.: Impossibility of distributed consensus with one faulty process. J. ACM **32**, 374–382 (1985)
15. Prasad, K.V.S.: A calculus of broadcasting systems. Science of Computer Programming **25**, 285–327 (1995)
16. Gorla, D.: Towards a Unified Approach to Encodability and Separation Results for Process Calculi. In: van Breugel, F., Chechik, M. (eds.) CONCUR 2008. LNCS, vol. 5201, pp. 492–507. Springer, Heidelberg (2008)
17. Merro, M.: An observational theory for mobile ad hoc networks (full version). J. Inf. Comput. **207**, 194–208 (2009)
18. Borgström, J., Huang, S., Johansson, M., Raabjerg, P., Victor, B., Åman Pohjola, J., Parrow, J.: Broadcast Psi-calculi with an application to wireless protocols. In: Barthe, G., Pardo, A., Schneider, G. (eds.) SEFM 2011. LNCS, vol. 7041, pp. 74–89. Springer, Heidelberg (2011)
19. Fehnker, A., van Glabbeek, R.J., Höfner, P., McIver, A., Portmann, M., Tan, W.L.: A process algebra for wireless mesh networks used for modelling, verifying and analysing AODV. CoRR abs/1312.7645 (2013)
20. Ene, C., Muntean, T.: A broadcast-based calculus for communicating systems. In: Proceedings of the 15th International Parallel & Distributed Processing Symposium, IPDPS 2001, Computer Society, p. 149. IEEE, Washington, DC (2001)
21. Johansson, M., Bengtson, J., Parrow, J., Victor, B.: Weak equivalences in Psi-calculi. In: LICS, pp. 322–331. IEEE Computer Society (2010)
22. Åman Pohjola, J., Parrow, J.: Priorities without priorities: representing preemption in Psi-calculi. In: Borgström, J., Crafa, S. (eds.) Proceedings Combined 21st International Workshop on Expressiveness in Concurrency, EXPRESS 2014, and 11th Workshop on Structural Operational Semantics, SOS 2014, Rome, Italy, 1st. vol. 160, EPTCS, 2–15 September 2014
23. Gardner, P., Wischik, L.: Explicit fusions. In: Nielsen, M., Rovan, B. (eds.) MFCS 2000. LNCS, vol. 1893, pp. 373–382. Springer, Heidelberg (2000)
24. Milner, R.: Calculi for synchrony and asynchrony. Theor. Comput. Sci. **25**, 267–310 (1983)
25. Holmer, U.: Interpreting broadcast communication in SCCS. In: Best, E. (ed.) CONCUR 1993. LNCS, vol. 715, pp. 188–201. Springer, Heidelberg (1993)
26. Corradini, F., D'Ortenzio, D., Inverardi, P.: On the relationships among four timed process algebras. Fundam. Inf. **38**, 377–395 (1999)

27. Moller, F., Tofts, C.: Relating processes with respect to speed. In: Baeten, J.C., Groote, J.F. (eds.) CONCUR '91. Lecture Notes in Computer Science, vol. 527, pp. 424–438. Springer, Berlin Heidelberg (1991)
28. Lochbihler, A.: Coinductive. Archive of Formal Proofs 2010 (2010)
29. Ballarin, C.: Locales: a module system for mathematical theories. J. Autom. Reasoning **52**, 123–153 (2014)
30. Palamidessi, C.: Comparing the expressive power of the synchronous and asynchronous pi-calculi. Math. Struct. Comput. Sci. **13**, 685–719 (2003)
31. Peters, K., Nestmann, U.: Breaking symmetries. In: Fröschle, S.B., Valencia, F.D. (eds.) Proceedings 17th International Workshop on Expressiveness in Concurrency, EXPRESS 2010, Paris, France, 30 August 2010, vol. 41, pp. 136–150. EPTCS (2010)
32. Prasad, K.V.S.: Broadcast calculus interpreted in CCS upto bisimulation. Electr. Notes Theor. Comput. Sci. **52**, 83–100 (2001)
33. Peters, K., Nestmann, U., Goltz, U.: On distributability in process calculi. In: Felleisen, M., Gardner, P. (eds.) ESOP 2013. LNCS, vol. 7792, pp. 310–329. Springer, Heidelberg (2013)

Author Index

Printed in the United States
By Bookmasters